STUDENT'S SOLUTIONS MANUAL

JUDITH A. PENNA

Indiana University Purdue University Indianapolis

ELEMENTARY AND INTERMEDIATE ALGEBRA GRAPHS AND MODELS

SECOND EDITION

Marvin L. Bittinger

Indiana University Purdue University Indianapolis

David J. Ellenbogen

Community College of Vermont

Barbara L. Johnson

Indiana University Purdue University Indianapolis

PEARSON

Addison
Wesley

Boston   San Francisco   New York
London   Toronto   Sydney   Tokyo   Singapore   Madrid
Mexico City   Munich   Paris   Cape Town   Hong Kong   Montreal

Reproduced by Pearson Addison-Wesley from electronic files supplied by the author.

Copyright © 2004 Pearson Education, Inc.
Publishing as Pearson Addison-Wesley, 75 Arlington Street, Boston, MA 02116

ISBN   0-321-16865-8

2 3 4 5 6 VHG 06 05 04

Contents

Chapter 1

Introduction to Algebraic Expressions

Exercise Set 1.1

1. Substitute 9 for a and multiply.

   $3a = 3 \cdot 9 = 27$

2. 56

3. Substitute 2 for t and add.

   $t + 6 = 2 + 6 = 8$

4. 4

5. $\dfrac{x+y}{4} = \dfrac{2+14}{4} = \dfrac{16}{4} = 4$

6. 5

7. $\dfrac{m-n}{2} = \dfrac{20-6}{2} = \dfrac{14}{2} = 7$

8. 3

9. $\dfrac{9m}{q} = \dfrac{9 \cdot 6}{18} = \dfrac{54}{18} = 3$

10. 3

11. Enter the expression in the graphing calculator, replacing a with 136 and b with 13. We see that $27a - 18b = 3438$ for $a = 136$ and $b = 13$.

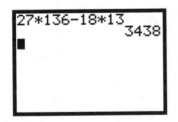

12. 47,531

13. $bh = (6 \text{ ft})(4 \text{ ft})$

    $\quad = (6)(4)(\text{ft})(\text{ft})$

    $\quad = 24 \text{ ft}^2$, or 24 square feet

14. 24 hr

15. $A = \dfrac{1}{2}bh$

    $\quad = \dfrac{1}{2}(5 \text{ cm})(6 \text{ cm})$

    $\quad = \dfrac{1}{2}(5)(6)(\text{cm})(\text{cm})$

    $\quad = \dfrac{5}{2} \cdot 6 \text{ cm}^2$

    $\quad = 15 \text{ cm}^2$, or 15 square centimeters

16. (a) 150 sec;

    (b) 450 sec;

    (c) 10 min

17. $\dfrac{h}{a} = \dfrac{10}{37}$, or about 0.270

18. 26 cm^2

19. Let j represent Jan's age. Then we have $j + 8$, or $8 + j$.

20. $4a$, or $a4$

21. $b + 6$, or $6 + b$

22. Let w represent Lou's weight; $w + 7$, or $7 + w$

23. $c - 9$

24. $d - 4$

25. $q + 6$, or $6 + q$

26. $z + 11$, or $11 + z$

27. Let s represent Phil's speed. Then we have $9s$, or $s9$.

28. $d + c$, or $c + d$

29. $y - x$

30. Let a represent Lorrie's age; $a - 2$

31. $x \div w$, or $\dfrac{x}{w}$

32. Let s and t represent the numbers; $s \div t$, or $\dfrac{s}{t}$

33. $n - m$

34. $q - p$

35. Let l and h represent the box's length and height, respectively. Then we have $l + h$, or $h + l$.

36. $d + f$, or $f + d$

37. $9 \cdot 2m$, or $2m \cdot 9$

38. Let p represent Paula's speed and w represent the wind speed; $p - 2w$

39. Let y represent "some number." Then we have $\dfrac{1}{4}y$, or $\dfrac{y}{4}$, or $y/4$, or $y \div 4$.

40. Let m and n represent the numbers; $\dfrac{1}{3}(m + n)$, or $\dfrac{m+n}{3}$

41. Let x represent the number of women attending. Then we have 64% of x, or $0.64x$.

42. Let y represent "a number;" 38% of y, or $0.38y$

43. $\$50 - x$

44. $65t$ mi

45.
$$\underline{x + 17 = 32} \quad \text{Writing the equation}$$
$$15 + 17 \ ? \ 32 \quad \text{Substituting 15 for } x$$
$$32 \ | \ 32 \quad 32 = 32 \text{ is TRUE.}$$

Since the left-hand and right-hand sides are the same, 15 is a solution.

46. No

47.
$$\underline{a - 28 = 75} \quad \text{Writing the equation}$$
$$93 - 28 \ ? \ 75 \quad \text{Substituting 93 for } a$$
$$65 \ | \ 75 \quad 65 = 75 \text{ is FALSE.}$$

Since the left-hand and right-hand sides are not the same, 93 is not a solution.

48. Yes

49.
$$\underline{\dfrac{t}{7} = 9}$$
$$\dfrac{63}{7} \ ? \ 9$$
$$9 \ | \ 9 \quad 9 = 9 \text{ is TRUE.}$$

Since the left-hand and right-hand sides are the same, 63 is a solution.

50. No

51.
$$\underline{\dfrac{108}{x} = 36}$$
$$\dfrac{108}{3} \ ? \ 36$$
$$36 \ | \ 36 \quad 36 = 36 \text{ is TRUE.}$$

Since the left-hand and right-hand sides are the same, 3 is a solution.

52. No

53. Let x represent the number.

$$\underbrace{\text{What number}}_{\downarrow \atop x} \ \underbrace{\text{added to}}_{\downarrow \atop +} \ \underset{\downarrow \downarrow \downarrow}{73 \text{ is } 201?}$$

Translating: $\quad x \quad + \quad 73 = 201$

$$x + 73 = 201$$

54. Let w represent the number; $7w = 2303$

55. Let y represent the number.

Rewording: 42 times $\underbrace{\text{what number}}$ is 2352?

Translating: 42 $\cdot$ y = 2352

$$42y = 2352$$

56. Let x represent the number; $x + 345 = 987$

57. Let s represent the number of squares your opponent controls.

Rewording:
The number of squares your opponent controls $\underbrace{\text{added to}}$ 35 is 64.

Translating: $s \quad + \quad 35 = 64$

$$s + 35 = 64$$

58. Let y represent the number of hours the carpenter worked; $\$25y = \$53,400$

59. Let x represent the total amount of waste generated, in millions of tons.

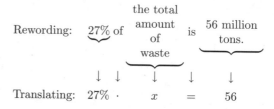

Rewording: 27% of $\underbrace{\text{the total amount of waste}}$ is $\underbrace{\text{56 million tons.}}$

Translating: 27% $\cdot$ x =   56

$$27\% \cdot x = 56, \text{ or } 0.27x = 56$$

60. Let m represent the length of the average commute in the West, in minutes; $m = 24.5 - 1.8$

61. Look for a pattern in the data. Observe that the price of unleaded premium gas at each station is 20¢ more than the price of unleaded regular gas at that station. We reword and translate.

$$\underbrace{\text{Price of premium unleaded gas}}_{\downarrow \atop p} \ \underset{\downarrow\downarrow}{\text{is 20¢}} \ \underset{\downarrow}{\text{more than}} \ \underbrace{\text{price of regular unleaded gas.}}_{\downarrow \atop r}$$

$$p \quad = 20 \quad + \quad r$$

We have $p = 20 + r$. This equation could also be written as $p = r + 20$.

62. $c = 100h$

63. Look for a pattern in the data. Observe that the daily recommended number of grams of dietary fiber for each age is 5 more than that age. We reword and translate.

$$\underbrace{\text{Grams of fiber}}_{\downarrow \atop f} \ \underset{\downarrow}{\text{is}} \ \underset{\downarrow}{5} \ \underbrace{\text{more than}}_{\downarrow \atop +} \ \underbrace{\text{the age.}}_{\downarrow \atop a}$$

$$f \quad = 5 \quad + \quad a$$

We have $f = 5 + a$. This equation could also be written as $f = a + 5$.

64. $c = p + 3$

65. Look for a pattern in the data. Observe that the number of calories burned is 300 times the number of hours spent doing calisthenics. We reword and translate.

$$\underbrace{\text{Number of calories burned}}_{} \quad \text{is 300 times} \quad \overbrace{\text{number of hours spent doing calisthenics.}}^{}$$

$$\downarrow \qquad \quad \downarrow \;\; \downarrow \qquad \downarrow \qquad\qquad \downarrow$$
$$c \qquad \quad = 300 \;\; \cdot \qquad\qquad t$$

We have $c = 300t$.

66. $w = s \div 10$

67. *Writing Exercise*

68. *Writing Exercise*

69. *Writing Exercise*

70. *Writing Exercise*

71. Area of sign: $A = \dfrac{1}{2}(3 \text{ ft})(2.5 \text{ ft}) = 3.75 \text{ ft}^2$

Cost of sign: $\$90(3.75) = \$337.50$

72. 158.75 cm^2

73. When x is twice y, then y is one-half x, so
$y = \dfrac{12}{2} = 6$.
$\dfrac{x - y}{3} = \dfrac{12 - 6}{3} = \dfrac{6}{3} = 2$

74. 9

75. When a is twice b, then b is one-half a, so $b = \dfrac{16}{2} = 8$.
$\dfrac{a + b}{4} = \dfrac{16 + 8}{4} = \dfrac{24}{4} = 6$

76. 4

77. The next whole number is one more than $w + 3$:
$w + 3 + 1 = w + 4$

78. d

79. Let a and b represent the numbers. Then we have
$\dfrac{1}{3} \cdot \dfrac{1}{2} \cdot ab$.

80. $l + w + l + w$, or $2l + 2w$

81. $s + s + s + s$, or $4s$

82. $a + 9$

83. *Writing Exercise*

Exercise Set 1.2

1. $x + 7$ Changing the order

2. $2 + a$

3. $c + ab$

4. $3y + x$

5. $3y + 9x$

6. $7b + 3a$

7. $5(1 + a)$

8. $9(5 + x)$

9. $a \cdot 2$ Changing the order

10. yx

11. ts

12. $x4$

13. $5 + ba$

14. $x + y3$

15. $(a + 1)5$

16. $(x + 5)9$

17. $a + (5 + b)$

18. $5 + (m + r)$

19. $(r + t) + 7$

20. $(x + 2) + y$

21. $ab + (c + d)$

22. $m + (np + r)$

23. $8(xy)$

24. $9(ab)$

25. $(2a)b$

26. $(9r)p$

27. $(3 \cdot 2)(a + b)$

28. $(5x)(2 + y)$

29. a) $r + (t + 6) = (t + 6) + r$ Using the commutative law
$= (6 + t) + r$ Using the commutative law again

b) $r + (t + 6) = (t + 6) + r$ Using the commutative law
$= t + (6 + r)$ Using the associative law

Answers may vary.

30. Answers may vary. $v + (w + 5); (v + 5) + w$

31. a) $(17a)b = b(17a)$ Using the commutative law
$= b(a17)$ Using the commutative law again

b) $(17a)b = (a17)b$ Using the commutative law
$= a(17b)$ Using the associative law

Answers may vary.

32. Answers may vary. $3(yx); (3x)y$

33. $(5 + x) + 2$

 $= (x + 5) + 2$ Commutative law

 $= x + (5 + 2)$ Associative law

 $= x + 7$ Simplifying

34. $(2a)4 = 4(2a)$ Commutative law

  $= (4 \cdot 2)a$ Associative law

  $= 8a$ Simplifying

35. $(m3)7 = m(3 \cdot 7)$ Associative law

   $= (3 \cdot 7)m$ Commutative law

   $= 21m$ Simplifying

36. $4 + (9 + x)$

 $= (4 + 9) + x$ Associative law

 $= x + (4 + 9)$ Commutative law

 $= x + 13$ Simplifying

37. $4(a + 3) = 4 \cdot a + 4 \cdot 3 = 4a + 12$

38. $3x + 15$

39. $6(1 + x) = 6 \cdot 1 + 6 \cdot x = 6 + 6x$

40. $6v + 24$

41. $3(x + 1) = 3 \cdot x + 3 \cdot 1 = 3x + 3$

42. $9x + 27$

43. $8(3 + y) = 8 \cdot 3 + 8 \cdot y = 24 + 8y$

44. $7s + 35$

45. $9(2x + 6) = 9 \cdot 2x + 9 \cdot 6 = 18x + 54$

46. $54m + 63$

47. $5(r + 2 + 3t) = 5 \cdot r + 5 \cdot 2 + 5 \cdot 3t = 5r + 10 + 15t$

48. $20x + 32 + 12p$

49. $(a + b)2 = a(2) + b(2) = 2a + 2b$

50. $7x + 14$

51. $(x + y + 2)5 = x(5) + y(5) + 2(5) = 5x + 5y + 10$

52. $12 + 6a + 6b$

53. $x + xyz + 19$

The terms are separated by plus signs. They are x, xyz, and 19.

54. $9, 17a, abc$

55. $2a + \dfrac{a}{b} + 5b$

The terms are separated by plus signs. They are $2a$, $\dfrac{a}{b}$, and $5b$.

56. $3xy, 20, \dfrac{4a}{b}$

57. $2a + 2b = 2(a + b)$ The common factor is 2.

Check: $2(a + b) = 2 \cdot a + 2 \cdot b = 2a + 2b$

58. $5(y + z)$

59. $7 + 7y = 7 \cdot 1 + 7 \cdot y$ The common factor is 7.

  $= 7(1 + y)$ Using the distributive law

Check: $7(1 + y) = 7 \cdot 1 + 7 \cdot y = 7 + 7y$

60. $13(1 + x)$

61. $18x + 3 = 3 \cdot 6x + 3 \cdot 1 = 3(6x + 1)$

Check: $3(6x + 1) = 3 \cdot 6x + 3 \cdot 1 = 18x + 3$

62. $5(4a + 1)$

63. $5x + 10 + 15y = 5 \cdot x + 5 \cdot 2 + 5 \cdot 3y = 5(x + 2 + 3y)$

Check: $5(x + 2 + 3y) = 5 \cdot x + 5 \cdot 2 + 5 \cdot 3y = 5x + 10 + 15y$

64. $3(1 + 9b + 2c)$

65. $12x + 9 = 3 \cdot 4x + 3 \cdot 3 = 3(4x + 3)$

Check: $3(4x + 3) = 3 \cdot 4x + 3 \cdot 3 = 12x + 9$

66. $6(x + 1)$

67. $3a + 9b = 3 \cdot a + 3 \cdot 3b = 3(a + 3b)$

Check: $3(a + 3b) = 3 \cdot a + 3 \cdot 3b = 3a + 9b$

68. $5(a + 3b)$

69. $44x + 11y + 22z = 11 \cdot 4x + 11 \cdot y + 11 \cdot 2z = 11(4x + y + 2z)$

Check: $11(4x + y + 2z) = 11 \cdot 4x + 11 \cdot y + 11 \cdot 2z = 44x + 11y + 22z$

70. $7(2a + 8b + 1)$

71. *Writing Exercise*

72. *Writing Exercise*

73. Let k represent Kara's salary. Then we have $2k$.

74. $\dfrac{1}{2} \cdot m$, or $\dfrac{m}{2}$

75. *Writing Exercise*

76. *Writing Exercise*

77. The expressions are equivalent by the distributive law.

$8 + 4(a + b) = 8 + 4a + 4b = 4(2 + a + b)$

78. The expressions are not equivalent.

Let $m = 1$. Then we have:

$7 \div 3 \cdot 1 = \dfrac{7}{3} \cdot 1 = \dfrac{7}{3}$, but

$1 \cdot 3 \div 7 = 3 \div 7 = \dfrac{3}{7}$.

79. The expressions are equivalent by the distributive law and the commutative law of multiplication.

$(rt + st)5 = 5(rt + st) = 5 \cdot t(r + s) = 5t(r + s)$

80. Yes; distributive law and commutative laws of multiplication and addition

81. The expressions are not equivalent.

Let $x = 1$ and $y = 0$. Then we have:

$$30 \cdot 0 + 1 \cdot 15 = 0 + 15 = 15, \text{ but}$$

$$5[2(1 + 3 \cdot 0)] = 5[2(1)] = 5 \cdot 2 = 10.$$

82. Yes; distributive law and commutative law of multiplication

83. *Writing Exercise*

84. *Writing Exercise*

Exercise Set 1.3

1. We write two factorizations of 50. There are other factorizations as well.

$$2 \cdot 25, 5 \cdot 10$$

List all of the factors of 50:

1, 2, 5, 10, 25, 50

2. $2 \cdot 35, 5 \cdot 14$; 1, 2, 5, 7, 10, 14, 35, 70

3. We write two factorizations of 42. There are other factorizations as well.

$$2 \cdot 21, 6 \cdot 7$$

List all of the factors of 42:

1, 2, 3, 6, 7, 14, 21, 42

4. $2 \cdot 30, 5 \cdot 12$; 1, 2, 3, 4, 5, 6, 10, 12, 15, 20, 30, 60

5. $26 = 2 \cdot 13$

6. $3 \cdot 5$

7. We begin factoring 30 in any way that we can and continue factoring until each factor is prime.

$$30 = 2 \cdot 15 = 2 \cdot 3 \cdot 5$$

8. $5 \cdot 11$

9. We begin by factoring 20 in any way that we can and continue factoring until each factor is prime.

$$20 = 4 \cdot 5 = 2 \cdot 2 \cdot 5$$

10. $2 \cdot 5 \cdot 5$

11. We begin by factoring 27 in any way that we can and continue factoring until each factor is prime.

$$27 = 3 \cdot 9 = 3 \cdot 3 \cdot 3$$

12. $2 \cdot 7 \cdot 7$

13. We begin by factoring 18 in any way that we can and continue factoring until each factor is prime.

$$18 = 2 \cdot 9 = 2 \cdot 3 \cdot 3$$

14. $2 \cdot 3 \cdot 3 \cdot 3$

15. We begin by factoring 40 in any way that we can and continue factoring until each factor is prime.

$$40 = 4 \cdot 10 = 2 \cdot 2 \cdot 2 \cdot 5$$

16. $2 \cdot 2 \cdot 2 \cdot 7$

17. 43 has exactly two different factors, 43 and 1. Thus, 43 is prime.

18. $2 \cdot 2 \cdot 2 \cdot 3 \cdot 5$

19. $210 = 2 \cdot 105 = 2 \cdot 3 \cdot 35 = 2 \cdot 3 \cdot 5 \cdot 7$

20. Prime

21. $115 = 5 \cdot 23$

22. $11 \cdot 13$

23.
$$\frac{10}{14} = \frac{2 \cdot 5}{2 \cdot 7} \qquad \text{Factoring numerator and denominator}$$

$$= \frac{2}{2} \cdot \frac{5}{7} \qquad \text{Rewriting as a product of two fractions}$$

$$= 1 \cdot \frac{5}{7} \qquad \frac{2}{2} = 1$$

$$= \frac{5}{7} \qquad \text{Using the identity property of 1}$$

24. $\dfrac{2}{3}$

25. $\dfrac{16}{56} = \dfrac{2 \cdot 8}{7 \cdot 8} = \dfrac{2}{7} \cdot \dfrac{8}{8} = \dfrac{2}{7} \cdot 1 = \dfrac{2}{7}$

26. $\dfrac{8}{3}$

27.
$$\frac{6}{48} = \frac{1 \cdot 6}{8 \cdot 6} \qquad \begin{array}{l}\text{Factoring and using the} \\ \text{identity property of 1 to} \\ \text{write 6 as } 1 \cdot 6\end{array}$$

$$= \frac{1}{8} \cdot \frac{6}{6}$$

$$= \frac{1}{8} \cdot 1 = \frac{1}{8}$$

28. $\dfrac{6}{35}$

29. $\dfrac{49}{7} = \dfrac{7 \cdot 7}{1 \cdot 7} = \dfrac{7}{1} \cdot \dfrac{7}{7} = \dfrac{7}{1} \cdot 1 = 7$

30. 12

31.
$$\frac{19}{76} = \frac{1 \cdot 19}{4 \cdot 19} \qquad \begin{array}{l}\text{Factoring and using the} \\ \text{identity property of 1 to} \\ \text{write 19 as } 1 \cdot 19\end{array}$$

$$= \frac{1 \cdot \cancel{19}}{4 \cdot \cancel{19}} \qquad \begin{array}{l}\text{Removing a factor equal} \\ \text{to 1: } \dfrac{19}{19} = 1\end{array}$$

$$= \frac{1}{4}$$

32. $\dfrac{1}{3}$

33. $\dfrac{150}{25} = \dfrac{6 \cdot 25}{1 \cdot 25}$ Factoring and using the identity property of 1 to write 25 as $1 \cdot 25$

$= \dfrac{6 \cdot \cancel{25}}{1 \cdot \cancel{25}}$ Removing a factor equal to 1: $\dfrac{25}{25} = 1$

$= \dfrac{6}{1}$

$= 6$ Simplifying

34. 5

35. $\dfrac{75}{80} = \dfrac{5 \cdot 15}{5 \cdot 16}$ Factoring the numerator and the denominator

$= \dfrac{\cancel{5} \cdot 15}{\cancel{5} \cdot 16}$ Removing a factor equal to 1: $\dfrac{5}{5} = 1$

$= \dfrac{15}{16}$

36. $\dfrac{21}{25}$

37. $\dfrac{120}{82} = \dfrac{2 \cdot 60}{2 \cdot 41}$ Factoring

$= \dfrac{\cancel{2} \cdot 60}{\cancel{2} \cdot 41}$ Removing a factor equal to 1: $\dfrac{2}{2} = 1$

$= \dfrac{60}{41}$

38. $\dfrac{5}{3}$

39. $\dfrac{210}{98} = \dfrac{2 \cdot 7 \cdot 15}{2 \cdot 7 \cdot 7}$ Factoring

$= \dfrac{\cancel{2} \cdot \cancel{7} \cdot 15}{\cancel{2} \cdot \cancel{7} \cdot 7}$ Removing a factor equal to 1: $\dfrac{2 \cdot 7}{2 \cdot 7} = 1$

$= \dfrac{15}{7}$

40. $\dfrac{2}{5}$

41. $\dfrac{1}{2} \cdot \dfrac{3}{7} = \dfrac{1 \cdot 3}{2 \cdot 7}$ Multiplying numerators and denominators

$= \dfrac{3}{14}$

42. $\dfrac{44}{25}$

43. $\dfrac{9}{2} \cdot \dfrac{3}{4} = \dfrac{9 \cdot 3}{2 \cdot 4} = \dfrac{27}{8}$

44. 1

45. $\dfrac{1}{8} + \dfrac{3}{8} = \dfrac{1 + 3}{8}$ Adding numerators; keeping the common denominator

$= \dfrac{4}{8}$

$= \dfrac{1 \cdot \cancel{4}}{2 \cdot \cancel{4}} = \dfrac{1}{2}$ Simplifying

46. $\dfrac{5}{8}$

47. $\dfrac{4}{9} + \dfrac{13}{18} = \dfrac{4}{9} \cdot \dfrac{2}{2} + \dfrac{13}{18}$ Using 18 as the common denominator

$= \dfrac{8}{18} + \dfrac{13}{18}$

$= \dfrac{21}{18}$

$= \dfrac{7 \cdot \cancel{3}}{6 \cdot \cancel{3}} = \dfrac{7}{6}$ Simplifying

48. $\dfrac{4}{3}$

49. $\dfrac{3}{a} \cdot \dfrac{b}{7} = \dfrac{3b}{7a}$ Multiplying numerators and denominators

50. $\dfrac{xy}{5z}$

51. $\dfrac{4}{a} + \dfrac{3}{a} = \dfrac{7}{a}$ Adding numerators; keeping the common denominator

52. $\dfrac{2}{a}$

53. $\dfrac{3}{10} + \dfrac{8}{15} = \dfrac{3}{10} \cdot \dfrac{3}{3} + \dfrac{8}{15} \cdot \dfrac{2}{2}$ Using 30 as the common denominator

$= \dfrac{9}{30} + \dfrac{16}{30}$

$= \dfrac{25}{30}$

$= \dfrac{5 \cdot \cancel{5}}{6 \cdot \cancel{5}} = \dfrac{5}{6}$ Simplifying

54. $\dfrac{31}{24}$

55. $\dfrac{9}{7} - \dfrac{2}{7} = \dfrac{7}{7} = 1$

56. 2

57. $\dfrac{13}{18} - \dfrac{4}{9} = \dfrac{13}{18} - \dfrac{4}{9} \cdot \dfrac{2}{2}$ Using 18 as the common denominator

$= \dfrac{13}{18} - \dfrac{8}{18}$

$= \dfrac{5}{18}$

58. $\dfrac{31}{45}$

59. Note that $\dfrac{20}{30} = \dfrac{2}{3}$. Thus, $\dfrac{20}{30} - \dfrac{2}{3} = 0$.

We can also do this exercise by finding a common denominator:

$\dfrac{20}{30} - \dfrac{2}{3} = \dfrac{20}{30} - \dfrac{2}{3} \cdot \dfrac{10}{10} = \dfrac{20}{30} - \dfrac{20}{30} = 0$

60. $\dfrac{10}{21}$

61. $\dfrac{7}{6} \div \dfrac{3}{5} = \dfrac{7}{6} \cdot \dfrac{5}{3}$ Multiplying by the reciprocal of the divisor

$$= \dfrac{35}{18}$$

62. $\dfrac{28}{15}$

63. $\dfrac{8}{9} \div \dfrac{4}{15} = \dfrac{8}{9} \cdot \dfrac{15}{4} = \dfrac{2 \cdot \cancel{4} \cdot \cancel{3} \cdot 5}{\cancel{3} \cdot 3 \cdot \cancel{4}} = \dfrac{10}{3}$

64. $\dfrac{1}{4}$

65. $12 \div \dfrac{3}{7} = \dfrac{12}{1} \cdot \dfrac{7}{3} = \dfrac{4 \cdot \cancel{3} \cdot 7}{1 \cdot \cancel{3}} = 28$

66. $\dfrac{1}{2}$

67. Note that we have a number divided by itself. Thus, the result is 1. We can also do this exercise as follows:
$$\dfrac{7}{13} \div \dfrac{7}{13} = \dfrac{7}{13} \cdot \dfrac{13}{7} = \dfrac{7 \cdot 13}{7 \cdot 13} = 1$$

68. $\dfrac{51}{20}$

69. $\dfrac{\frac{2}{7}}{\frac{5}{3}} = \dfrac{2}{7} \div \dfrac{5}{3} = \dfrac{2}{7} \cdot \dfrac{3}{5} = \dfrac{2 \cdot 3}{7 \cdot 5} = \dfrac{6}{35}$

70. $\dfrac{15}{8}$

71. $\dfrac{\frac{9}{1}}{\frac{1}{2}} = 9 \div \dfrac{1}{2} = \dfrac{9}{1} \cdot \dfrac{2}{1} = \dfrac{9 \cdot 2}{1 \cdot 1} = 18$

72. $\dfrac{7}{15}$

73. *Writing Exercise*

74. *Writing Exercise*

75. $4(x + 5) = 4 \cdot x + 4 \cdot 5 = 4x + 20$

76. $3(x + 5y + 2)$

77. *Writing Exercise*

78. *Writing Exercise*

79. We need to find the smallest number that has both 6 and 8 as factors. Starting with 6 we list some numbers with a factor of 6, and starting with 8 we also list some numbers with a factor of 8. Then we find the first number that is on both lists.

    6, 12, 18, 24, 30, 36, ...

    8, 16, 24, 32, 40, 48, ...

Since 24 is the smallest number that is on both lists, the carton should be 24 in. long.

80.

Product	56	63	36	72	140	96	168
Factor	7	7	2	36	14	8	8
Factor	8	9	18	2	10	12	21
Sum	15	16	20	38	24	20	29

81. $\dfrac{16 \cdot 9 \cdot 4}{15 \cdot 8 \cdot 12} = \dfrac{\cancel{4} \cdot \cancel{4} \cdot \cancel{3} \cdot \cancel{3} \cdot \cancel{2} \cdot 2}{\cancel{3} \cdot 5 \cdot \cancel{2} \cdot \cancel{4} \cdot \cancel{3} \cdot \cancel{4}} = \dfrac{2}{5}$

82. 1

83. $\dfrac{27pqrs}{9prst} = \dfrac{3 \cdot \cancel{9} \cdot \cancel{p} \cdot q \cdot \cancel{r} \cdot \cancel{s}}{\cancel{9} \cdot \cancel{p} \cdot \cancel{r} \cdot \cancel{s} \cdot t} = \dfrac{3q}{t}$

84. $\dfrac{8}{3}$

85. $\dfrac{15 \cdot 4xy \cdot 9}{6 \cdot 25x \cdot 15y} = \dfrac{\cancel{15} \cdot \cancel{2} \cdot 2 \cdot \cancel{x} \cdot \cancel{y} \cdot \cancel{3} \cdot 3}{\cancel{2} \cdot \cancel{3} \cdot 25 \cdot \cancel{x} \cdot \cancel{15} \cdot \cancel{y}} = \dfrac{6}{25}$

86. $\dfrac{5}{2}$

87. $\dfrac{\frac{27ab}{15mn}}{\frac{18bc}{25np}} = \dfrac{27ab}{15mn} \div \dfrac{18bc}{25np} = \dfrac{27ab}{15mn} \cdot \dfrac{25np}{18bc} =$

$\dfrac{27ab \cdot 25np}{15mn \cdot 18bc} = \dfrac{\cancel{3} \cdot \cancel{9} \cdot a \cdot \cancel{b} \cdot \cancel{5} \cdot 5 \cdot \cancel{n} \cdot p}{\cancel{3} \cdot \cancel{5} \cdot m \cdot \cancel{n} \cdot 2 \cdot \cancel{9} \cdot \cancel{b} \cdot c} = \dfrac{5ap}{2mc}$

88. $\dfrac{2yc}{b}$

89. $A = lw = \left(\dfrac{4}{5}\ \text{m}\right)\left(\dfrac{7}{9}\ \text{m}\right)$

$$= \left(\dfrac{4}{5}\right)\left(\dfrac{7}{9}\right)(\text{m})(\text{m})$$

$$= \dfrac{28}{45}\ \text{m}^2,\ \text{or}\ \dfrac{28}{45}\ \text{square meters}$$

90. $\dfrac{25}{28}\ \text{m}^2$

91. $P = 4s = 4\left(3\dfrac{5}{9}\ \text{m}\right) = 4 \cdot \dfrac{32}{9}\ \text{m} = \dfrac{128}{9}\ \text{m},\ \text{or}$

$14\dfrac{2}{9}\ \text{m}$

92. $\dfrac{142}{45}\ \text{m},\ \text{or}\ 3\dfrac{7}{45}\ \text{m}$

93. *Writing Exercise*

Exercise Set 1.4

1. The real number -19 corresponds to 19°F below zero, and the real number 59 corresponds to 59°F above zero.

2. $-2,\ 5$

3. The real number -150 corresponds to burning 150 calories, and the real number 65 corresponds to consuming 65 calories.

4. $1200,\ -800$

5. The real number -1286 corresponds to 1286 ft below sea level. The real number 29,029 corresponds to 29,029 ft above sea level.

6. Jets: -34, Strikers: 34

7. The real number 750 corresponds to a \$750 deposit, and the real number -125 corresponds to a \$125 withdrawal.

8. $24, -9$

9. The real numbers $20, -150$, and 300 correspond to the interception of the missile, the loss of the starship, and the capture of the base, respectively.

10. $-10, 235$

11. Since $\frac{10}{3} = 3\frac{1}{3}$, its graph is $\frac{1}{3}$ of a unit to the right of 3.

12.

13. The graph of -4.3 is $\frac{3}{10}$ of a unit to the left of -4.

14.

15.

16.

17. $\frac{7}{8}$ means $7 \div 8$, so we divide.

$$
\begin{array}{r}
0.8\,7\,5 \\
8\,\overline{)\,7.0\,0\,0} \\
6\,4 \\
\hline
6\,0 \\
5\,6 \\
\hline
4\,0 \\
4\,0 \\
\hline
0
\end{array}
$$

We have $\frac{7}{8} = 0.875$.

18. -0.125

19. We first find decimal notation for $\frac{3}{4}$. Since $\frac{3}{4}$ means $3 \div 4$, we divide.

$$
\begin{array}{r}
0.7\,5 \\
4\,\overline{)\,3.0\,0} \\
2\,8 \\
\hline
2\,0 \\
2\,0 \\
\hline
0
\end{array}
$$

Thus, $\frac{3}{4} = 0.75$, so $-\frac{3}{4} = -0.75$.

20. $0.8\overline{3}$

21. $\frac{7}{6}$ means $7 \div 6$, so we divide.

$$
\begin{array}{r}
1.1\,6\,6 \\
6\,\overline{)\,7.0\,0\,0} \\
6 \\
\hline
1\,0 \\
6 \\
\hline
4\,0 \\
3\,6 \\
\hline
4\,0 \\
3\,6 \\
\hline
4
\end{array}
$$

We have $\frac{7}{6} = 1.1\overline{6}$.

22. $0.41\overline{6}$

23. $\frac{2}{3}$ means $2 \div 3$, so we divide.

$$
\begin{array}{r}
0.6\,6\,6\,\ldots \\
3\,\overline{)\,2.0\,0\,0} \\
1\,8 \\
\hline
2\,0 \\
1\,8 \\
\hline
2\,0 \\
1\,8 \\
\hline
2
\end{array}
$$

We have $\frac{2}{3} = 0.\overline{6}$.

24. 0.25

25. We first find decimal notation for $\frac{1}{2}$. Since $\frac{1}{2}$ means $1 \div 2$, we divide.

$$
\begin{array}{r}
0.5 \\
2\,\overline{)\,1.0} \\
1\,0 \\
\hline
0
\end{array}
$$

Thus, $\frac{1}{2} = 0.5$, so $-\frac{1}{2} = -0.5$.

26. -0.375

27. Since the denominator is 100, we know that $\frac{13}{100} = 0.13$. We could also divide 13 by 100 to find this result.

28. -0.35

29. Since -8 is to the left of 2, we have $-8 < 2$.

30. $>$

31. Since 7 is to the right of 0, we have $7 > 0$.

32. $>$

33. Since -6 is to the left of 6, we have $-6 < 6$.

34. $>$

35. Since -8 is to the left of -5, we have $-8 < -5$.

36. $<$

37. Since -5 is to the right of -11, we have $-5 > -11$.

38. $>$

39. Since -12.5 is to the left of -9.4, we have
$-12.5 < -9.4$.

40. $>$

41. We convert to decimal notation.
$\frac{5}{12} = 0.41\overline{6}$ and $\frac{11}{25} = 0.44$. Thus, $\frac{5}{12} < \frac{11}{25}$.

42. $<$

43. $-7 > x$ has the same meaning as $x < -7$.

44. $9 < a$

45. $-10 \leq y$ has the same meaning as $y \geq -10$.

46. $t \leq 12$

47. $-3 \geq -11$ is true, since $-3 > -11$ is true.

48. False

49. $0 \geq 8$ is false, since neither $0 > 8$ nor $0 = 8$ is true.

50. True

51. $-8 \leq -8$ is true because $-8 = -8$ is true.

52. True

53. $|-23| = 23$ since -23 is 23 units from 0.

54. 47

55. $|17| = 17$ since 17 is 17 units from 0.

56. 3.1

57. $|5.6| = 5.6$ since 5.6 is 5.6 units from 0.

58. $\frac{2}{5}$

59. $|329| = 329$ since 329 is 329 units from 0.

60. 456

61. $\left| -\frac{9}{7} \right| = \frac{9}{7}$ since $-\frac{9}{7}$ is $\frac{9}{7}$ units from 0.

62. 8.02

63. $|0| = 0$ since 0 is 0 units from itself.

64. 1.07

65. $|x| = |-8| = 8$

66. 5

67. $-83, -4.7, 0, \frac{5}{9}, 8.31, 62$

68. 62

69. $-83, 0, 62$

70. $\pi, \sqrt{17}$

71. All are real numbers.

72. 0, 62

73. *Writing Exercise*

74. *Writing Exercise*

75. $3xy = 3 \cdot 2 \cdot 7 = 42$

76. $\frac{3}{5}$

77. *Writing Exercise*

78. *Writing Exercise*

79. *Writing Exercise*

80. $-17, -12, 5, 13$

81. List the numbers as they occur on the number line, from left to right: $-23, -17, 0, 4$

82. $-\frac{4}{3}, \frac{4}{9}, \frac{4}{8}, \frac{4}{6}, \frac{4}{5}, \frac{4}{3}, \frac{4}{2}$

83. $-\frac{2}{3}, \frac{1}{2}, -\frac{3}{4}, -\frac{5}{6}, \frac{3}{8}, \frac{1}{6}$ can be written in decimal notation as $-0.66\overline{6}, 0.5, -0.75, -0.83\overline{3}, 0.375, 0.16\overline{6}$, respectively. Listing from least to greatest (in fractional form), we have
$-\frac{5}{6}, -\frac{3}{4}, -\frac{2}{3}, \frac{1}{6}, \frac{3}{8}, \frac{1}{2}$.

84. $>$

85. $|4| = 4$ and $|-7| = 7$, so $|4| < |-7|$.

86. $=$

87. $|23| = 23$ and $|-23| = 23$, so $|23| = |-23|$.

88. $<$

89. $|-19| = 19$ and $|-27| = 27$, so $|-19| < |-27|$.

90. $-7, 7$

91. x represents an integer whose distance from 0 is less than 3 units. Thus, $x = -2, -1, 0, 1, 2$.

92. $-4, -3, 3, 4$

93. $0.1\overline{1} = \dfrac{0.3\overline{3}}{3} = \dfrac{\frac{1}{3}}{3} = \frac{1}{3} \cdot \frac{1}{3} = \frac{1}{9}$

94. $\frac{3}{3}$

95. $5.5\overline{5} = 50(0.1\overline{1}) = 50 \cdot \frac{1}{9} = \frac{50}{9}$
(See Exercise 93.)

96. $\frac{70}{9}$

97. *Writing Exercise*

Exercise Set 1.5

1. Start at 4. Move 7 units to the left.

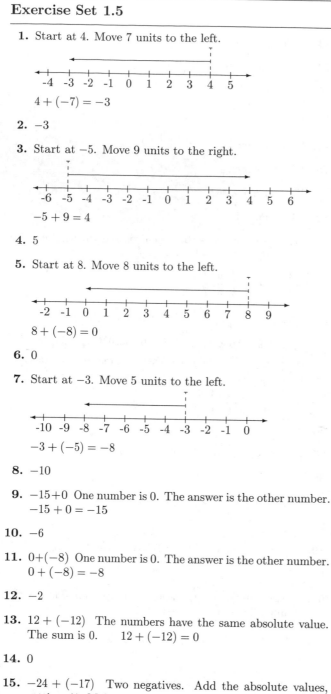

$4 + (-7) = -3$

2. -3

3. Start at -5. Move 9 units to the right.

$-5 + 9 = 4$

4. 5

5. Start at 8. Move 8 units to the left.

$8 + (-8) = 0$

6. 0

7. Start at -3. Move 5 units to the left.

$-3 + (-5) = -8$

8. -10

9. $-15 + 0$ One number is 0. The answer is the other number.
$-15 + 0 = -15$

10. -6

11. $0 + (-8)$ One number is 0. The answer is the other number.
$0 + (-8) = -8$

12. -2

13. $12 + (-12)$ The numbers have the same absolute value. The sum is 0. $12 + (-12) = 0$

14. 0

15. $-24 + (-17)$ Two negatives. Add the absolute values, getting 41. Make the answer negative.
$-24 + (-17) = -41$

16. -42

17. $-15 + 15$ The numbers have the same absolute value. The sum is 0. $-15 + 15 = 0$

18. 0

19. $18 + (-11)$ The absolute values are 18 and 11. The difference is $18 - 11$, or 7. The positive number has the larger absolute value, so the answer is positive. $18 + (-11) = 7$

20. 3

21. $10 + (-12)$ The absolute values are 10 and 12. The difference is $12 - 10$, or 2. The negative number has the larger absolute value, so the answer is negative. $10 + (-12) = -2$

22. -4

23. $-3 + 14$ The absolute values are 3 and 14. The difference is $14 - 3$, or 11. The positive number has the larger absolute value, so the answer is positive. $-3 + 14 = 11$

24. 7

25. $-14 + (-19)$ Two negatives. Add the absolute values, getting 33. Make the answer negative.
$-14 + (-19) = -33$

26. 2

27. $19 + (-19)$ The numbers has the same absolute value. The sum is 0. $19 + (-19) = 0$

28. -26

29. $23 + (-5)$ The absolute values are 23 and 5. The difference is $23 - 5$ or 18. The positive number has the larger absolute value, so the answer is positive. $23 + (-5) = 18$

30. -22

31. $-23 + (-9)$ Two negatives. Add the absolute values, getting 32. Make the answer negative.
$-23 + (-9) = -32$

32. 32

33. $40 + (-40)$ The numbers have the same absolute value. The sum is 0. $40 + (-40) = 0$

34. 0

35. $85 + (-65)$ The absolute values are 85 and 65. The difference is $85 - 65$, or 20. The positive number has the larger absolute value, so the answer is positive. $85 + (-65) = 20$

36. 45

37. $-3.6 + 1.9$ The absolute values are 3.6 and 1.9. The difference is $3.6 - 1.9$, or 1.7. The negative number has the larger absolute value, so the answer is negative.
$-3.6 + 1.9 = -1.7$

38. -1.8

39. $-5.4 + (-3.7)$ Two negatives. Add the absolute values, getting 9.1. Make the answer negative. $-5.4 + (-3.7) = -9.1$

40. -13.2

41. $\dfrac{-3}{5} + \dfrac{4}{5}$ The absolute values are $\dfrac{3}{5}$ and $\dfrac{4}{5}$. The difference is $\dfrac{4}{5} - \dfrac{3}{5}$, or $\dfrac{1}{5}$. The positive number has the larger absolute value, so the answer is positive.
$\dfrac{-3}{5} + \dfrac{4}{5} = \dfrac{1}{5}$

42. $\dfrac{1}{7}$

43. $\dfrac{-4}{7} + \dfrac{-2}{7}$ Two negatives. Add the absolute values,

getting $\dfrac{6}{7}$. Make the answer negative.

$$\dfrac{-4}{7} + \dfrac{-2}{7} = \dfrac{-6}{7}$$

44. $\dfrac{-7}{9}$

45. $-\dfrac{2}{5} + \dfrac{1}{3}$ The absolute values are $\dfrac{2}{5}$ and $\dfrac{1}{3}$. The

difference is $\dfrac{6}{15} - \dfrac{5}{15}$, or $\dfrac{1}{15}$. The negative number has the

larger absolute value, so the answer is negative.

$$-\dfrac{2}{5} + \dfrac{1}{3} = -\dfrac{1}{15}$$

46. $\dfrac{5}{26}$

47. $\dfrac{-4}{9} + \dfrac{2}{3}$ The absolute values are $\dfrac{4}{9}$ and $\dfrac{2}{3}$. The differ-

ence is $\dfrac{6}{9} - \dfrac{4}{9}$, or $\dfrac{2}{9}$. The positive number has the larger

absolute value, so the answer is positive.

$$\dfrac{-4}{9} + \dfrac{2}{3} = \dfrac{2}{9}$$

48. $\dfrac{1}{6}$

49. $\quad 35 + (-14) + (-19) + (-5)$

$= 35 + [(-14) + (-19) + (-5)]$ Using the
                                 associative law of addition

$= 35 + (-38)$ Adding the negatives

$= -3$ Adding a positive and a negative

50. -62

51. $-4.9 + 8.5 + 4.9 + (-8.5)$

Note that we have two pairs of numbers with different signs
and the same absolute value: -4.9 and 4.9, 8.5 and -8.5.
The sum of each pair is 0, so the result is $0 + 0$, or 0.

52. 37.9

53. Rewording: $\underbrace{\text{Change from withdrawals}}$ plus $\underbrace{\text{change from additions}}$

Translating: $\qquad -5 \qquad\quad + \qquad\quad 8$

plus $\underbrace{\text{change from drops}}$ is $\underbrace{\text{change in original size.}}$

$\qquad + \qquad (-6) \qquad = \qquad \text{change in original size}$

Since $-5 + 8 + (-6)$

$= 3 + (-6)$

$= -3,$

the class lost 3 students, or the class size changed by -3.

54. The new balance was $69.

55. Rewording: $\underbrace{\text{2001 loss}}$ plus $\underbrace{\text{2002 loss}}$ plus

Translating: $-26,500 \quad + \quad (-10,200) \quad +$

$\underbrace{\text{2003 profit}}$ is $\underbrace{\text{total profit or loss.}}$

$32,400 \quad = \quad \text{total profit or loss.}$

Since $-26,500 + (-10,200) + 32,400$

$= -36,700 + 32,400$

$= -4300,$

the loss was $4300, or the profit was $-$4300$.

56. The total gain was 22 yd.

57. Rewording: $\underbrace{\text{Original balance}}$ plus $\underbrace{\text{change from writing first check}}$ plus

Translating: $\qquad 350 \qquad\quad + \qquad\quad (-530) \qquad\quad +$

$\underbrace{\text{deposit}}$ plus $\underbrace{\text{change from writing second check}}$ is $\underbrace{\text{new balance.}}$

$\quad 75 \qquad + \qquad (-90) \qquad = \qquad \text{new balance}$

Since $350 + (-530) + (75) + (-90)$

$= (350 + 75) + [-530 + (-90)]$

$= 425 + (-620)$

$= -195,$

The balance is $-$195$.

58. The balance is $-$85$.

59. Rewording: $\underbrace{\text{First change}}$ plus $\underbrace{\text{second change}}$ plus

Translating: $\qquad 0.18 \qquad + \qquad (-0.50) \qquad +$

$\underbrace{\text{third change}}$ is $\underbrace{\text{total change.}}$

$\quad 0.27 \qquad = \text{total change.}$

Since $0.18 + (-0.50) + 0.27 = -0.05$, the value of the stock
fell $0.05, or the value changed $-$0.05$.

60. The elevation is 13,796 ft.

61. $7a + 5a = (7 + 5)a$ Using the distributive law
$$= 12a$$

62. $11x$

63. $-3x + 12x = (-3 + 12)x$ Using the distributive law
$$= 9x$$

64. $-5m$

65. $5t + 8t = (5 + 8)t = 13t$

66. $14a$

67. $7m + (-9m) = [7 + (-9)]m = -2m$

68. 0

69. $-5a + (-2a) = [-5 + (-2)]a = -7a$

70. $-7n$

71. $-3 + 8x + 4 + (-10x)$
$$= -3 + 4 + 8x + (-10x) \quad \text{Using the commutative law of addition}$$
$$= (-3 + 4) + [8 + (-10)]x \quad \text{Using the distributive law}$$
$$= 1 - 2x \quad \text{Adding}$$

72. $7a + 2$

73.   Perimeter $= 8 + 5x + 9 + 7x$
$$= 8 + 9 + 5x + 7x$$
$$= (8 + 9) + (5 + 7)x$$
$$= 17 + 12x$$

74. $10a + 13$

75.   Perimeter $= 9 + 6n + 7 + 8n + 4n$
$$= 9 + 7 + 6n + 8n + 4n$$
$$= (9 + 7) + (6 + 8 + 4)n$$
$$= 16 + 18n$$

76. $19n + 11$

77. *Writing Exercise*

78. *Writing Exercise*

79. Since -3 is to the left of 0, we have $-3 < 0$.

80. $<$

81. Since -2.5 is to the right of -3.8, we have $-2.5 > -3.8$.

82. $>$

83. *Writing Exercise*

84. *Writing Exercise*

85. Starting with the final value, we "undo" the rise and drop in value by adding their opposites. The result is the original value.

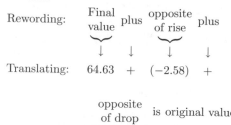

Rewording: Final value plus opposite of rise plus opposite of drop is original value.

Translating: 64.63 + (-2.58) + 3.25 = original value.

Since $64.63 + (-2.58) + 3.25 = 65.30$, the stock's original value was $\$65.30$.

86. $\$55.50$

87. $4x + \underline{} + (-9x) + (-2y)$
$$= 4x + (-9x) + \underline{} + (-2y)$$
$$= [4 + (-9)]x + \underline{} + (-2y)$$
$$= -5x + \underline{} + (-2y)$$

This expression is equivalent to $-5x - 7y$, so the missing term is the term which yields $-7y$ when added to $-2y$. Since $-5y + (-2y) = -7y$, the missing term is $-5y$.

88. $-15b$

89. $3m + 2n + \underline{} + (-2m)$
$$= 2n + \underline{} + (-2m) + 3m$$
$$= 2n + \underline{} + (-2 + 3)m$$
$$= 2n + \underline{} + m$$

This expression is equivalent to $2n + (-6m)$, so the missing term is the term which yields $-6m$ when added to m. Since $-7m + m = -6m$, the missing term is $-7m$.

90. $-3y$

91. Note that, in order for the sum to be 0, the two missing terms must be the opposites of the given terms. Thus, the missing terms are $-7t$ and -23.

92. $\dfrac{7}{2}x$

93. $-3 + (-3) + 2 + (-2) + 1 = -5$

Since the total is 5 under par after the five rounds and $-5 = -1 + (-1) + (-1) + (-1) + (-1)$, the golfer was 1 under par on average.

Exercise Set 1.6

1. The opposite of 39 is -39 because $39 + (-39) = 0$.

2. 17

3. The opposite of -9 is 9 because $-9 + 9 = 0$.

4. $-\dfrac{7}{2}$

5. The opposite of -3.14 is 3.14 because $-3.14 + 3.14 = 0$.

6. -48.2

7. If $x = 23$, then $-x = -(23) = -23$. (The opposite of 23 is -23.)

8. 26

9. If $x = -\dfrac{14}{3}$, then $-x = -\left(-\dfrac{14}{3}\right) = \dfrac{14}{3}$.

$\left(\text{The opposite of } -\dfrac{14}{3} \text{ is } \dfrac{14}{3}.\right)$

10. $-\dfrac{1}{328}$

11. If $x = 0.101$, then $-x = -(0.101) = -0.101$.
(The opposite of 0.101 is -0.101.)

12. 0

13. If $x = -72$, then $-(-x) = -(-72) = 72$
(The opposite of the opposite of 72 is 72.)

14. 29

15. If $x = -\dfrac{2}{5}$, then $-(-x) = -\left[-\left(-\dfrac{2}{5}\right)\right] = -\dfrac{2}{5}$.

$\left(\text{The opposite of the opposite of } -\dfrac{2}{5} \text{ is } -\dfrac{2}{5}.\right)$

16. -9.1

17. When we change the sign of -1 we obtain 1.

18. 7

19. When we change the sign of 7 we obtain -7.

20. -10

21. $-3 - 5$ is read "negative three minus five."
$-3 - 5 = -3 + (-5) = -8$

22. Negative four minus seven; -11

23. $2 - (-9)$ is read "two minus negative nine."
$2 - (-9) = 2 + 9 = 11$

24. Five minus negative eight; 13

25. $4 - 6$ is read "four minus six."
$4 - 6 = 4 + (-6) = -2$

26. Nine minus twelve; -3

27. $-5 - (-7)$ is read "negative five minus negative seven."
$-5 - (-7) = -5 + 7 = 2$

28. Negative two minus negative five; 3

29. $6 - 8 = 6 + (-8) = -2$

30. -9

31. $0 - 5 = 0 + (-5) = -5$

32. -8

33. $3 - 9 = 3 + (-9) = -6$

34. -10

35. $0 - 10 = 0 + (-10) = -10$

36. -7

37. $-9 - (-3) = -9 + 3 = -6$

38. -4

39. Note that we are subtracting a number from itself. The result is 0. We could also do this exercise as follows:
$$-8 - (-8) = -8 + 8 = 0$$

40. 0

41. $14 - 19 = 14 + (-19) = -5$

42. -4

43. $30 - 40 = 30 + (-40) = -10$

44. -7

45. $-7 - (-9) = -7 + 9 = 2$

46. -5

47. $-9 - (-9) = -9 + 9 = 0$
(See Exercise 39.)

48. 0

49. $5 - 5 = 5 + (-5) = 0$
(See Exercise 39.)

50. 0

51. $4 - (-4) = 4 + 4 = 8$

52. 12

53. $-7 - 4 = -7 + (-4) = -11$

54. -14

55. $6 - (-10) = 6 + 10 = 16$

56. 15

57. $-14 - 2 = -14 + (-2) = -16$

58. -19

59. $-4 - (-3) = -4 + 3 = -1$

60. -1

61. $5 - (-6) = 5 + 6 = 11$

62. 17

63. $0 - 6 = 0 + (-6) = -6$

64. -5

65. $-3 - (-1) = -3 + 1 = -2$

66. -3

67. $-9 - 16 = -9 + (-16) = -25$

68. -21

69. $0 - (-1) = 0 + 1 = 1$

70. 5

71. $-9 - 0 = -9 + 0 = -9$

72. -8

73. $12 - (-5) = 12 + 5 = 17$

74. 10

75. $18 - 63 = 18 + (-63) = -45$

76. -23

77. $-18 - 63 = -18 + (-63) = -81$

78. -68

79. $-45 - 4 = -45 + (-4) = -49$

80. -58

81. $1.5 - 9.4 = 1.5 + (-9.4) = -7.9$

82. -5.5

83. $0.825 - 1 = 0.825 + (-1) = -0.175$

84. -0.928

85. $\dfrac{3}{7} - \dfrac{5}{7} = \dfrac{3}{7} + \left(-\dfrac{5}{7}\right) = -\dfrac{2}{7}$

86. $-\dfrac{7}{11}$

87. $\dfrac{-2}{9} - \dfrac{5}{9} = \dfrac{-2}{9} + \left(\dfrac{-5}{9}\right) = \dfrac{-7}{9}$, or $-\dfrac{7}{9}$

88. $-\dfrac{4}{5}$

89. $-\dfrac{2}{13} - \left(-\dfrac{5}{13}\right) = -\dfrac{2}{13} + \dfrac{5}{13} = \dfrac{3}{13}$

90. $\dfrac{5}{17}$

91. We subtract the smaller number from the larger.

Translate: $3.8 - (-5.2)$

Simplify: $3.8 - (-5.2) = 3.8 + 5.2 = 9$

92. $-2.1 - (-5.9)$; 3.8

93. We subtract the smaller number from the larger.

Translate: $114 - (-79)$

Simplify: $114 - (-79) = 114 + 79 = 193$

94. $23 - (-17)$; 40

95. $-21 - 37 = -21 + (-37) = -58$

96. -26

97. $9 - (-25) = 9 + 25 = 34$

98. 26

99. $25 - (-12) - 7 - (-2) + 9 = 25 + 12 + (-7) + 2 + 9 = 41$

100. -22

101. $-31 + (-28) - (-14) - 17 = (-31) + (-28) + 14 + (-17) = -62$

102. 22

103. $-34 - 28 + (-33) - 44 = (-34) + (-28) + (-33) + (-44) = -139$

104. 5

105. $-93 + (-84) - (-93) - (-84)$

Note that we are subtracting -93 from -93 and -84 from -84. Thus, the result will be 0. We could also do this exercise as follows:

$-93 + (-84) - (-93) - (-84) = -93 + (-84) + 93 + 84 = 0$

106. 4

107. $-7x - 4y = -7x + (-4y)$, so the terms are $-7x$ and $-4y$.

108. $7a, -9b$

109. $9 - 5t - 3st = 9 + (-5t) + (-3st)$, so the terms are 9, $-5t$, and $-3st$.

110. $-4, -3x, 2xy$

111. $\qquad 4x - 7x$
$= 4x + (-7x) \qquad$ Adding the opposite
$= (4 + (-7))x \qquad$ Using the distributive law
$= -3x$

112. $-11a$

113. $\qquad 7a - 12a + 4$
$= 7a + (-12a) + 4 \qquad$ Adding the opposite
$= (7 + (-12))a + 4 \qquad$ Using the distributive law
$= -5a + 4$

114. $-22x + 7$

115. $\qquad -8n - 9 + n$
$= -8n + (-9) + n \qquad$ Adding the opposite
$= -8n + n + (-9) \qquad$ Using the commutative law of addition
$= -7n - 9 \qquad$ Adding like terms

116. $9n - 15$

117. $\qquad 3x + 5 - 9x$
$= 3x + 5 + (-9x)$
$= 3x + (-9x) + 5$
$= -6x + 5$

118. $3a - 5$

119.
$$2 - 6t - 9 - 2t$$
$$= 2 + (-6t) + (-9) + (-2t)$$
$$= 2 + (-9) + (-6t) + (-2t)$$
$$= -7 - 8t$$

120. $-2b - 12$

121.
$$5y + (-3x) - 9x + 1 - 2y + 8$$
$$= 5y + (-3x) + (-9x) + 1 + (-2y) + 8$$
$$= 5y + (-2y) + (-3x) + (-9x) + 1 + 8$$
$$= 3y - 12x + 9$$

122. $46 + 3x + 6z$

123.
$$13x - (-2x) + 45 - (-21) - 7x$$
$$= 13x + 2x + 45 + 21 + (-7x)$$
$$= 13x + 2x + (-7x) + 45 + 21$$
$$= 8x + 66$$

124. $6x + 39$

125. We subtract the lower temperature from the higher temperature:
$$44 - (-56) = 44 + 56 = 100$$
The temperature dropped 100°F.

126. $165

127. We subtract the lower elevation from the higher elevation:
$$29,028 - (-1312) - 30,340$$
The difference in elevation is 30,340 ft.

128. 14,494 ft

129. We subtract the lower elevation from the higher elevation:
$$-40 - (-156) = -40 + 156 = 116$$
Lake Assal is 116 m lower than the Valdes Peninsula.

130. 1767 m

131. *Writing Exercise*

132. *Writing Exercise*

133. Area $= lw = (36 \text{ ft})(12 \text{ ft}) = 432 \text{ ft}^2$

134. $2 \cdot 2 \cdot 2 \cdot 2 \cdot 2 \cdot 3 \cdot 3 \cdot 3$

135. *Writing Exercise*

136. *Writing Exercise*

137. True. For example, for $m = 5$ and $n = 3$, $5 > 3$ and $5 - 3 > 0$, or $2 > 0$. For $m = -4$ and $n = -9$, $-4 > -9$ and $-4 - (-9) > 0$, or $5 > 0$.

138. False. For example, let $m = -3$ and $n = -5$. Then $-3 > -5$, but $-3 + (-5) = -8 \not> 0$.

139. False. For example, let $m = 2$ and $n = -2$. Then 2 and -2 are opposites, but $2 - (-2) = 4 \neq 0$.

140. True. For example, for $m = 4$ and $n = -4$, $4 = -(-4)$ and $4 + (-4) = 0$; for $m = -3$ and $n = 3$, $-3 = -3$ and $-3 + 3 = 0$.

141. *Writing Exercise*

142. *Writing Exercise*

Exercise Set 1.7

1. $-4 \cdot 9 = -36$ Think: $4 \cdot 9 = 36$, make the answer negative.

2. -21

3. $-8 \cdot 7 = -56$ Think: $8 \cdot 7 = 56$, make the answer negative.

4. -18

5. $8 \cdot (-3) = -24$

6. -45

7. $-9 \cdot 8 = -72$

8. -30

9. $-6 \cdot (-7) = 42$ Multiplying absolute values; the answer is positive.

10. 10

11. $-5 \cdot (-9) = 45$ Multiplying absolute values; the answer is positive.

12. 18

13. $17 \cdot (-10) = -170$

14. 120

15. $-12 \cdot 12 = -144$

16. 195

17. $-25 \cdot (-48) = 1200$

18. -1677

19. $-3.5 \cdot (-28) = 98$

20. -203.7

21. $6 \cdot (-13) = -78$

22. -63

23. $-7 \cdot (-3.1) = 21.7$

24. 12.8

25. $\dfrac{2}{3} \cdot \left(-\dfrac{3}{5}\right) = -\left(\dfrac{2 \cdot 3}{3 \cdot 5}\right) = -\left(\dfrac{2}{5} \cdot \dfrac{3}{3}\right) = -\dfrac{2}{5}$

26. $-\dfrac{10}{21}$

27. $-\dfrac{3}{8} \cdot \left(-\dfrac{2}{9}\right) = \dfrac{\not{3} \cdot \not{2} \cdot 1}{4 \cdot \not{2} \cdot \not{3} \cdot 3} = \dfrac{1}{12}$

28. $\dfrac{1}{4}$

29. $(-5.3)(2.1) = -11.13$

30. -40.85

31. $-\dfrac{5}{9} \cdot \dfrac{3}{4} = -\dfrac{5 \cdot \cancel{3}}{\cancel{3} \cdot 3 \cdot 4} = -\dfrac{5}{12}$

32. -6

33. $\qquad 3 \cdot (-7) \cdot (-2) \cdot 6$
$\qquad = -21 \cdot (-12) \qquad$ Multiplying the first two numbers and the last two numbers
$\qquad = 252$

34. 756

35. 0, The product of 0 and any real number is 0.

36. 0

37. $-\dfrac{1}{3} \cdot \dfrac{1}{4} \cdot \left(-\dfrac{3}{7}\right) = -\dfrac{1}{12} \cdot \left(-\dfrac{3}{7}\right) = \dfrac{3}{12 \cdot 7} =$
$\dfrac{\cancel{3} \cdot 1}{\cancel{3} \cdot 4 \cdot 7} = \dfrac{1}{28}$

38. $\dfrac{3}{35}$

39. $-2 \cdot (-5) \cdot (-3) \cdot (-5) = 10 \cdot 15 = 150$

40. 30

41. 0, The product of 0 and any real number is 0.

42. 0

43. $(-8)(-9)(-10) = 72(-10) = -720$

44. 5040

45. $(-6)(-7)(-8)(-9)(-10) = 42 \cdot 72 \cdot (-10) =$
$3024 \cdot (-10) = -30,240$

46. $151,200$

47. $28 \div (-7) = -4 \qquad$ Check: $-4 \cdot (-7) = 28$

48. -8

49. $\dfrac{36}{-9} = -4 \qquad -4 \cdot (-9) = 36$

50. -2

51. $\dfrac{-16}{8} = -2 \qquad$ Check: $-2 \cdot 8 = -16$

52. 8

53. $\dfrac{-48}{-12} = 4 \qquad$ Check: $4(-12) = -48$

54. 7

55. $\dfrac{-72}{9} = -8 \qquad$ Check: $-8 \cdot 9 = -72$

56. -2

57. $-100 \div (-50) = 2 \qquad$ Check: $2(-50) = -100$

58. -25

59. $-108 \div 9 = -12 \qquad$ Check: $-12 \cdot 9 = -108$

60. $\dfrac{64}{7}$

61. $\dfrac{400}{-50} = -8 \qquad$ Check: $-8 \cdot (-50) = 400$

62. $\dfrac{300}{13}$

63. Undefined

64. 0

65. $-4.8 \div 1.2 = -4 \qquad$ Check: $-4(1.2) = -4.8$

66. -3

67. $\dfrac{0}{-9} = 0$

68. Undefined

69. $0 \div 7 = 0$

70. 0

71. $\dfrac{-8}{3} = \dfrac{8}{-3}$ and $\dfrac{-8}{3} = -\dfrac{8}{3}$

72. $\dfrac{12}{-7}, \ -\dfrac{12}{7}$

73. $\dfrac{29}{-35} = \dfrac{-29}{35}$ and $\dfrac{29}{-35} = -\dfrac{29}{35}$

74. $\dfrac{-9}{14}, \ -\dfrac{9}{14}$

75. $-\dfrac{7}{3} = \dfrac{-7}{3}$ and $-\dfrac{7}{3} = \dfrac{7}{-3}$

76. $\dfrac{-4}{15}, \ \dfrac{4}{-15}$

77. $\dfrac{-x}{2} = \dfrac{x}{-2}$ and $\dfrac{-x}{2} = -\dfrac{x}{2}$

78. $\dfrac{-9}{a}, \ -\dfrac{9}{a}$

79. The reciprocal of $\dfrac{4}{-5}$ is $\dfrac{-5}{4}$ $\left(\text{or equivalently, } -\dfrac{5}{4}\right)$ because $\dfrac{4}{-5} \cdot \dfrac{-5}{4} = 1.$

80. $-\dfrac{9}{2}$

81. The reciprocal of $-\dfrac{47}{13}$ is $-\dfrac{13}{47}$ because $-\dfrac{47}{13} \cdot \left(-\dfrac{13}{47}\right) = 1.$

82. $-\dfrac{12}{31}$

83. The reciprocal of -10 is $\dfrac{1}{-10}$ $\left(\text{or equivalently, } -\dfrac{1}{10}\right)$ because $-10\left(\dfrac{1}{-10}\right) = 1.$

84. $\dfrac{1}{13}$

85. The reciprocal of 4.3 is $\dfrac{1}{4.3}$ because $4.3\left(\dfrac{1}{4.3}\right) = 1$.

Since $\dfrac{1}{4.3} = \dfrac{1}{4.3} \cdot \dfrac{10}{10} = \dfrac{10}{43}$, the reciprocal can also be

expressed as $\dfrac{10}{43}$.

86. $-\dfrac{1}{8.5}$, or $-\dfrac{2}{17}$

87. The reciprocal of $\dfrac{-9}{4}$ is $\dfrac{4}{-9}$ $\left(\text{or equivalently, } -\dfrac{4}{9}\right)$ because

$\dfrac{-9}{4} \cdot \dfrac{4}{-9} = 1$.

88. $-\dfrac{11}{6}$

89. The reciprocal of -1 is $\dfrac{1}{-1}$, or -1 because

$(-1)(-1) = 1$.

90. $\dfrac{5}{3}$

91. $\left(\dfrac{-7}{4}\right)\left(-\dfrac{3}{5}\right)$

$= \left(-\dfrac{7}{4}\right)\left(-\dfrac{3}{5}\right)$ Rewriting $\dfrac{-7}{4}$ as $-\dfrac{7}{4}$

$= \dfrac{21}{20}$

92. $\dfrac{5}{18}$

93. $\left(\dfrac{-6}{5}\right)\left(\dfrac{2}{-11}\right)$

$= \left(\dfrac{-6}{5}\right)\left(\dfrac{-2}{11}\right)$ Rewriting $\dfrac{2}{-11}$ as $\dfrac{-2}{11}$

$= \dfrac{12}{55}$

94. $\dfrac{35}{12}$

95. $\dfrac{-3}{8} + \dfrac{-5}{8} = \dfrac{-8}{8} = -1$

96. $\dfrac{3}{5}$

97. $\left(\dfrac{-9}{5}\right)\left(\dfrac{5}{-9}\right)$

Note that this is the product of reciprocals. Thus, the result is 1.

98. $\dfrac{5}{28}$

99. $\left(-\dfrac{3}{11}\right) + \left(-\dfrac{6}{11}\right) = -\dfrac{9}{11}$

100. $-\dfrac{6}{7}$

101. $\dfrac{7}{8} \div \left(-\dfrac{1}{2}\right) = \dfrac{7}{8} \cdot \left(-\dfrac{2}{1}\right) = -\dfrac{14}{8} = -\dfrac{7 \cdot \cancel{2}}{\cancel{2} \cdot 4 \cdot 1} = -\dfrac{7}{4}$

102. $-\dfrac{9}{8}$

103. $\dfrac{9}{5} \cdot \dfrac{-20}{3} = \dfrac{9}{5}\left(-\dfrac{20}{3}\right) = -\dfrac{180}{15} = -\dfrac{\cancel{3} \cdot 3 \cdot 4 \cdot \cancel{5}}{\cancel{5} \cdot \cancel{3} \cdot 1} = -12$

104. $-\dfrac{7}{36}$

105. $\left(-\dfrac{18}{7}\right) + \left(-\dfrac{3}{7}\right) = -\dfrac{21}{7} = -3$

106. -3

107. $-\dfrac{5}{9} \div \left(-\dfrac{5}{9}\right)$

Note that we have a number divided by itself. Thus, the result is 1.

108. $\dfrac{5}{3}$

109. $-44.1 \div (-6.3) = 7$ Do the long division. The answer is positive.

110. -2

111. $\dfrac{1}{9} - \dfrac{2}{9} = -\dfrac{1}{9}$

112. $-\dfrac{4}{7}$

113. $\dfrac{-3}{10} + \dfrac{2}{5} = \dfrac{-3}{10} + \dfrac{2}{5} \cdot \dfrac{2}{2} = \dfrac{-3}{10} + \dfrac{4}{10} = \dfrac{1}{10}$

114. $\dfrac{1}{9}$

115. $\dfrac{7}{10} \div \left(\dfrac{-3}{5}\right) = \dfrac{7}{10} \div \left(-\dfrac{3}{5}\right) = \dfrac{7}{10} \cdot \left(-\dfrac{5}{3}\right) = -\dfrac{35}{30} =$

$-\dfrac{7 \cdot \cancel{5}}{2 \cdot \cancel{5} \cdot 3} = -\dfrac{7}{6}$

116. $-\dfrac{3}{2}$

117. $\dfrac{5}{7} - \dfrac{1}{-7} = \dfrac{5}{7} - \left(-\dfrac{1}{7}\right) = \dfrac{5}{7} + \dfrac{1}{7} = \dfrac{6}{7}$

118. $\dfrac{5}{9}$

119. $\dfrac{-4}{15} + \dfrac{2}{-3} = \dfrac{-4}{15} + \dfrac{-2}{3} = \dfrac{-4}{15} + \dfrac{-2}{3} \cdot \dfrac{5}{5} = \dfrac{-4}{15} + \dfrac{-10}{15} =$

$\dfrac{-14}{15}$, or $-\dfrac{14}{15}$

120. $-\dfrac{1}{2}$

121. *Writing Exercise*

122. *Writing Exercise*

123. $\dfrac{264}{468} = \dfrac{\cancel{2} \cdot \cancel{2} \cdot 2 \cdot \cancel{3} \cdot 11}{\cancel{2} \cdot \cancel{2} \cdot \cancel{3} \cdot 3 \cdot 13} = \dfrac{22}{39}$

124. No

125. *Writing Exercise*

126. *Writing Exercise*

127. Consider the sum $2 + 3$. Its reciprocal is $\dfrac{1}{2+3}$, or $\dfrac{1}{5}$, but $\dfrac{1}{2} + \dfrac{1}{3} = \dfrac{5}{6}$.

128. $-1, 1$

129. When n is negative, $-n$ is positive, so $\dfrac{m}{-n}$ is the quotient of a negative and a positive number and, thus, is negative.

130. Positive

131. When n is negative, $-n$ is positive, so $\dfrac{-n}{m}$ is the quotient of a positive and a negative number and, thus, is negative. When m is negative, $-m$ is positive, so $-m \cdot \left(\dfrac{-n}{m}\right)$ is the product of a positive and a negative number and, thus, is negative.

132. Positive

133. $m + n$ is the sum of two negative numbers, so it is negative; $\dfrac{m}{n}$ is the quotient of two negative numbers, so it is positive. Then $(m+n) \cdot \dfrac{m}{n}$ is the product of a negative and a positive number and, thus, is negative.

134. Positive

135. a) m and n have different signs;

b) either m or n is zero;

c) m and n have the same sign

136. $a(-b) + ab = a[-b + b]$ Distributive law

$= a(0)$ Law of opposites

$= 0$ Multiplicative property of 0

Therefore, $a(-b)$ is the opposite of ab by the law of opposites.

137. *Writing Exercise*

Exercise Set 1.8

1. $\underbrace{4 \cdot 4 \cdot 4}_{\text{3 factors}} = 4^3$

2. 6^4

3. $\underbrace{x \cdot x \cdot x \cdot x \cdot x \cdot x \cdot x}_{\text{7 factors}} = x^7$

4. y^6

5. $3t \cdot 3t \cdot 3t \cdot 3t \cdot 3t = (3t)^5$

6. $(5m)^5$

7. $2^4 = 2 \cdot 2 \cdot 2 \cdot 2 = 4 \cdot 4 = 16$

8. 125

9. $(-3)^2 = (-3)(-3) = 9$

10. 49

11. $-3^2 = -(3 \cdot 3) = -9$

12. -49

13. $4^3 = 4 \cdot 4 \cdot 4 = 16 \cdot 4 = 64$

14. 9

15. $(-5)^4 = (-5)(-5)(-5)(-5) = 25 \cdot 25 = 625$

16. 625

17. $7^1 = 7$ (1 factor)

18. -1

19. $(3t)^4 = (3t)(3t)(3t)(3t) = 3 \cdot 3 \cdot 3 \cdot 3 \cdot t \cdot t \cdot t \cdot t = 81t^4$

20. $25t^2$

21. $(-7x)^3 = (-7x)(-7x)(-7x) = (-7)(-7)(-7)(x)(x)(x) = -343x^3$

22. $625x^4$

23. $5 + 3 \cdot 7 = 5 + 21$ Multiplying

$= 26$ Adding

24. -5

25. $8 \cdot 7 + 6 \cdot 5 = 56 + 30$ Multiplying

$= 86$ Adding

26. 51

27. $19 - 5 \cdot 3 + 3 = 19 - 15 + 3$ Multiplying

$= 4 + 3$ Subtracting and adding from left to right

$= 7$

28. 9

29. $9 \div 3 + 16 \div 8 = 3 + 2$ Dividing

$= 5$ Adding

30. 28

31. $84 \div 28 - 84 \div 28$

Note that we are subtracting a number, $84 \div 28$, from itself. Thus, the result is 0.

32. 21

33. $4 - 8 \div 2 + 3^2$

$= 4 - 8 \div 2 + 9$ Simplifying the exponential expression

$= 4 - 4 + 9$ Dividing

$= 0 + 9$ Subtracting and

$= 9$ adding from left to right

34. 298

35. $9 - 3^2 \div 9(-1)$

$= 9 - 9 \div 9(-1)$ Simplifying the exponential expression

$= 9 - 1(-1)$ Dividing and

$= 9 + 1$ multiplying from left to right

$= 10$ Adding

36. 11

37. $(8 - 2 \cdot 3) - 9 = (8 - 6) - 9$ Multiplying inside the parentheses

$= 2 - 9$ Subtracting inside the parentheses

$= -7$

38. -36

39. $(-24) \div (-3) \cdot \left(-\dfrac{1}{2}\right) = 8 \cdot \left(-\dfrac{1}{2}\right) = -\dfrac{8}{2} = -4$

40. 32

41. $13(-10)^2 + 45 \div (-5)$

$= 13(100) + 45 \div (-5)$ Simplifying the exponential expression

$= 1300 + 45 \div (-5)$ Multiplying and

$= 1300 - 9$ dividing from left to right

$= 1291$ Subtracting

42. 13

43. $2^4 + 2^3 - 10 \div (-1)^4 = 16 + 8 - 10 \div 1 =$
$16 + 8 - 10 = 24 - 10 = 14$

44. 33

45. $5 + 3(2 - 9)^2 = 5 + 3(-7)^2 = 5 + 3 \cdot 49 = 5 + 147 = 152$

46. 13

47. $[2 \cdot (5 - 8)]^2 = [2 \cdot (-3)]^2 = (-6)^2 = 36$

48. 12

49. $\dfrac{7 + 2}{5^2 - 4^2} = \dfrac{9}{25 - 16} = \dfrac{9}{9} = 1$

50. 2

51. $8(-7) + |6(-5)| = -56 + |-30| = -56 + 30 = -26$

52. 49

53. $\dfrac{(-2)^3 + 4^2}{3 - 5^2 + 3 \cdot 6} = \dfrac{-8 + 16}{3 - 25 + 3 \cdot 6} = \dfrac{8}{3 - 25 + 18} =$
$\dfrac{8}{-22 + 18} = \dfrac{8}{-4} = -2$

54. -5

55. $\dfrac{27 - 2 \cdot 3^2}{8 \div 2^2 - (-2)^2} = \dfrac{27 - 2 \cdot 9}{8 \div 4 - 4} = \dfrac{27 - 18}{2 - 4} = \dfrac{9}{-2} = -\dfrac{9}{2}$

56. 5

57. This expression is equivalent to expression (a).

$\dfrac{5(3 - 7) + 4^3}{(-2 - 3)^2} = \dfrac{5(-4) + 4^3}{(-5)^2}$

$= \dfrac{5(-4) + 64}{25}$

$= \dfrac{-20 + 64}{25}$

$= \dfrac{44}{25}$

58. (c)

59. This expression is equivalent to expression (d).

$5(3 - 7) + 4^3 \div (-2 - 3)^2 = 5(-4) + 4^3 \div (-5)^2$

$= 5(-4) + 64 \div 25$

$= -20 + 2.56$

$= -17.44$

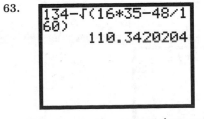

60. (b)

61.
```
(13.4-5abs(1.2+4
.6))/(9.3-5.4)²
      -1.025641026
■
```

Rounding to the nearest thousandth, we have -1.026.

62. 13,997.521

63.
```
134-√(16*35-48/1
60)
      110.3420204
```

Rounding to the nearest thousandth, we have 110.342.

64. -11.241

65. Since one factor is 0, the product $5.2(-1.7 - 3.8)^2 \cdot 0$ is 0. Thus, we have $-12.86 - 0$, or -12.86.

66. 0

67. $7 - 5x = 7 - 5 \cdot 3$ Substituting 3 for x

$\qquad = 7 - 15$ Multiplying

$\qquad = -8$ Subtracting

68. -7

69. $\qquad 24 \div t^3$

$\qquad = 24 \div (-2)^3$ Substituting -2 for t

$\qquad = 24 \div (-8)$ Simplifying the exponential expression

$\qquad = -3$ Dividing

70. 16

71. $45 \div 3 \cdot a = 45 \div 3 \cdot (-1)$ Substituting -1 for a

$\qquad = 15 \cdot (-1)$ Dividing

$\qquad = -15$ Multiplying

72. -125

73. $\qquad 5x \div 15x^2$

$\qquad = 5 \cdot 3 \div 15(3)^2$ Substituting 3 for x

$\qquad = 5 \cdot 3 \div 15 \cdot 9$ Simplifying the exponential expression

$\qquad = 15 \div 15 \cdot 9$ Multiplying and dividing

$\qquad = 1 \cdot 9$ in order from

$\qquad = 9$ left to right

74. 8

75. $(12 \cdot 17) \div (17 \cdot 12)$

Since $12 \cdot 17$ and $17 \cdot 12$ are equivalent expressions, we have a number divided by itself so the result is 1.

76. 20

77. $-x^2 - 5x = -(-3)^2 - 5(-3) = -9 - 5(-3) = -9 + 15 = 6$

78. 24

79. $\dfrac{3a - 4a^2}{a^2 - 20} = \dfrac{3 \cdot 5 - 4(5)^2}{(5)^2 - 20} = \dfrac{3 \cdot 5 - 4 \cdot 25}{25 - 20} = \dfrac{15 - 100}{5} = \dfrac{-85}{5} = -17$

80. 0

81.

```
13-(6-4)^3+10
             15
```

82. 143

83.

```
3(1.6+2*5.9)/1.6
           25.125
```

84. 283.74

85.

```
(1/2)(141+5/.2)²
          13778
```

86. 17.25

87. $-(9x + 1) = -9x - 1$ Removing parentheses and changing the sign of each term

88. $-3x - 5$

89. $-(7 - 2x) = -7 + 2x$ Removing parentheses and changing the sign of each term

90. $-6x + 7$

91. $-(4a - 3b + 7c) = -4a + 3b - 7c$

92. $-5x + 2y + 3z$

93. $-(3x^2 + 5x - 1) = -3x^2 - 5x + 1$

94. $-8x^3 + 6x - 5$

95. $\qquad 5x - (2x + 7)$

$\qquad = 5x - 2x - 7$ Removing parentheses and changing the sign of each term

$\qquad = 3x - 7$ Collecting like terms

96. $5y - 9$

97. $2a - (5a - 9) = 2a - 5a + 9 = -3a + 9$

98. $8n + 7$

99. $2x + 7x - (4x + 6) = 2x + 7x - 4x - 6 = 5x - 6$

100. $a - 7$

101. $9t - 5r - 2(3r + 6t) = 9t - 5r - 6r - 12t = -3t - 11r$

102. $-2m - 6n$

103. $\qquad 15x - y - 5(3x - 2y + 5z)$

$\qquad = 15x - y - 15x + 10y - 25z$ Multiplying each term in parentheses by -5

$\qquad = 9y - 25z$

104. $-16a + 27b - 32c$

105. $3x^2 + 7 - (2x^2 + 5) = 3x^2 + 7 - 2x^2 - 5$
$$= x^2 + 2$$

106. 0

107. $5t^3 + t - 3(t + 2t^3) = 5t^3 + t - 3t - 6t^3$
$$= -t^3 - 2t$$

108. $2n^2 - n$

109. $12a^2 - 3ab + 5b^2 - 5(-5a^2 + 4ab - 6b^2)$
$$= 12a^2 - 3ab + 5b^2 + 25a^2 - 20ab + 30b^2$$
$$= 37a^2 - 23ab + 35b^2$$

110. $-20a^2 + 29ab + 48b^2$

111. $-7t^3 - t^2 - 3(5t^3 - 3t)$
$$= -7t^3 - t^2 - 15t^3 + 9t$$
$$= -22t^3 - t^2 + 9t$$

112. $9t^4 - 45t^3 + 17t$

113. $5(2x - 7) - [4(2x - 3) + 2]$
$$= 5(2x - 7) - [8x - 12 + 2]$$
$$= 5(2x - 7) - [8x - 10]$$
$$= 10x - 35 - 8x + 10$$
$$= 2x - 25$$

114. $42x - 23$

115. *Writing Exercise*

116. *Writing Exercise*

117. Let x represent "a number." Then we have $2x + 9$.

118. Let x and y represent the numbers; $\frac{1}{2}(x + y)$.

119. *Writing Exercise*

120. *Writing Exercise*

121. $5t - \{7t - [4r - 3(t - 7)] + 6r\} - 4r$
$$= 5t - \{7t - [4r - 3t + 21] + 6r\} - 4r$$
$$= 5t - \{7t - 4r + 3t - 21 + 6r\} - 4r$$
$$= 5t - \{10t + 2r - 21\} - 4r$$
$$= 5t - 10t - 2r + 21 - 4r$$
$$= -5t - 6r + 21$$

122. $-4z$

123. $\{x - [f - (f - x)] + [x - f]\} - 3x$
$$= \{x - [f - f + x] + [x - f]\} - 3x$$
$$= \{x - [x] + [x - f]\} - 3x$$
$$= \{x - x + x - f\} - 3x$$
$$= x - f - 3x$$
$$= -2x - f$$

124. *Writing Exercise*

125. *Writing Exercise*

126. True

127. False; let $m = 1$ and $n = 2$. Then $-2 + 1 = -(2 - 1) = -1$, but $-(2 + 1) = -3$.

128. True

129. False; let $m = 2$ and $n = 3$. Then $3(-3 - 2) = 3(-5) = -15$, but $-3^2 + 3 \cdot 2 = -9 + 6 = -3$.

130. False

131. True; $-m(-n + m) = mn - m^2 = m(n - m)$

132. True

133. $[x + 3(2 - 5x) \div 7 + x](x - 3)$

When $x = 3$, the factor $x - 3$ is 0, so the product is 0.

134. 1

135. $4 \cdot 20^3 + 17 \cdot 20^2 + 10 \cdot 20 + 0 \cdot 2$
$$= 4 \cdot 8000 + 17 \cdot 400 + 10 \cdot 20 + 0 \cdot 2$$
$$= 32,000 + 6800 + 200 + 0$$
$$= 39,000$$

136. 1; 5; 0

Chapter 2

Equations, Inequalities, and Problem Solving

1. $x + 8 = 23$
$x + 8 - 8 = 23 - 8$ Subtracting 8 from both sides
$x = 15$ Simplifying

Check: $\dfrac{x + 8 = 23}{15 + 8 \ ? \ 23}$
$23 \mid 23$ TRUE

The solution is 15.

2. 3

3. $t + 9 = -4$
$t + 9 - 9 = -4 - 9$ Subtracting 9 from both sides
$t = -13$

Check: $\dfrac{t + 9 = -4}{-13 + 9 \ ? \ -4}$
$-4 \mid -4$ TRUE

The solution is -13.

4. 34

5. $y + 7 = -3$
$y + 7 - 7 = -3 - 7$
$y = -10$

Check: $\dfrac{y + 7 = -3}{-10 + 7 \ ? \ -3}$
$-3 \mid -3$ TRUE

The solution is -10.

6. -21

7. $-5 = x + 8$
$-5 - 8 = x + 8 - 8$
$-13 = x$

Check: $\dfrac{-5 = x + 8}{-5 \ ? \ -13 + 8}$
$-5 \mid -5$ TRUE

The solution is -13.

8. -31

9. $x - 9 = 6$
$x - 9 + 9 = 6 + 9$
$x = 15$

Check: $\dfrac{x - 9 = 6}{15 - 9 \ ? \ 6}$
$6 \mid 6$ TRUE

The solution is 15.

10. 13

11. $y - 6 = -14$
$y - 6 + 6 = -14 + 6$
$y = -8$

Check: $\dfrac{y - 6 = -14}{-8 - 6 \ ? \ -14}$
$-14 \mid -14$ TRUE

The solution is -8.

12. -15

13. $9 + t = 3$
$-9 + 9 + t = -9 + 3$
$t = -6$

Check: $\dfrac{9 + t = 3}{9 - 6 \ ? \ 3}$
$3 \mid 3$ TRUE

The solution is -6.

14. 18

15. $12 - -7 + y$
$7 + 12 = 7 + (-7) + y$
$19 = y$

Check: $\dfrac{12 = -7 + y}{12 \ ? \ -7 + 19}$
$12 \mid 12$ TRUE

The solution is 19.

16. 24

17. $-5 + t = -9$
$5 + (-5) + t = 5 + (-9)$
$t = -4$

Check: $\dfrac{-5 + t = -9}{-5 + (-4) \ ? \ -9}$
$-9 \mid -9$ TRUE

The solution is -4.

18. -15

19. $r + \dfrac{1}{3} = \dfrac{8}{3}$
$r + \dfrac{1}{3} - \dfrac{1}{3} = \dfrac{8}{3} - \dfrac{1}{3}$
$r = \dfrac{7}{3}$

Check: $\dfrac{r + \dfrac{1}{3} = \dfrac{8}{3}}{\dfrac{7}{3} + \dfrac{1}{3} \ ? \ \dfrac{8}{3}}$
$\dfrac{8}{3} \mid \dfrac{8}{3}$ TRUE

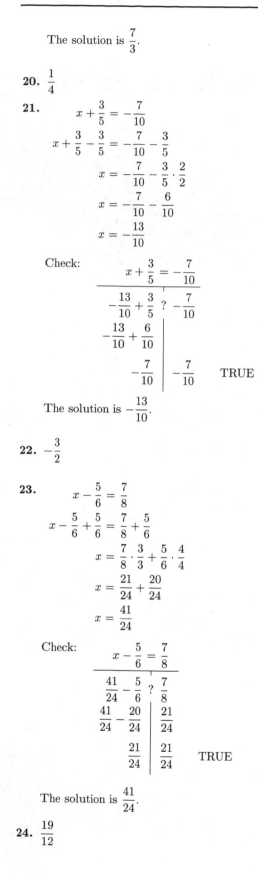

The solution is $\dfrac{7}{3}$.

20. $\dfrac{1}{4}$

21.

$$x + \frac{3}{5} = -\frac{7}{10}$$

$$x + \frac{3}{5} - \frac{3}{5} = -\frac{7}{10} - \frac{3}{5}$$

$$x = -\frac{7}{10} - \frac{3}{5} \cdot \frac{2}{2}$$

$$x = -\frac{7}{10} - \frac{6}{10}$$

$$x = -\frac{13}{10}$$

Check:

$$x + \frac{3}{5} = -\frac{7}{10}$$

$$-\frac{13}{10} + \frac{3}{5} \ ? \ -\frac{7}{10}$$

$$-\frac{13}{10} + \frac{6}{10}$$

$$-\frac{7}{10} \ \Big| \ -\frac{7}{10} \qquad \text{TRUE}$$

The solution is $-\dfrac{13}{10}$.

22. $-\dfrac{3}{2}$

23.

$$x - \frac{5}{6} = \frac{7}{8}$$

$$x - \frac{5}{6} + \frac{5}{6} = \frac{7}{8} + \frac{5}{6}$$

$$x = \frac{7}{8} \cdot \frac{3}{3} + \frac{5}{6} \cdot \frac{4}{4}$$

$$x = \frac{21}{24} + \frac{20}{24}$$

$$x = \frac{41}{24}$$

Check:

$$x - \frac{5}{6} = \frac{7}{8}$$

$$\frac{41}{24} - \frac{5}{6} \ ? \ \frac{7}{8}$$

$$\frac{41}{24} - \frac{20}{24} \ \Big| \ \frac{21}{24}$$

$$\frac{21}{24} \ \Big| \ \frac{21}{24} \qquad \text{TRUE}$$

The solution is $\dfrac{41}{24}$.

24. $\dfrac{19}{12}$

25.

$$-\frac{1}{5} + z = -\frac{1}{4}$$

$$\frac{1}{5} - \frac{1}{5} + z = \frac{1}{5} - \frac{1}{4}$$

$$z = \frac{1}{5} \cdot \frac{4}{4} - \frac{1}{4} \cdot \frac{5}{5}$$

$$z = \frac{4}{20} - \frac{5}{20}$$

$$z = -\frac{1}{20}$$

Check:

$$-\frac{1}{5} + z = -\frac{1}{4}$$

$$-\frac{1}{5} + \left(-\frac{1}{20}\right) \ ? \ -\frac{1}{4}$$

$$-\frac{4}{20} + \left(-\frac{1}{20}\right) \ \Big| \ -\frac{5}{20}$$

$$-\frac{5}{20} \ \Big| \ -\frac{5}{20} \qquad \text{TRUE}$$

The solution is $-\dfrac{1}{20}$.

26. $-\dfrac{5}{8}$

27.

$$m + 3.9 = 5.4$$

$$m + 3.9 - 3.9 = 5.4 - 3.9$$

$$m = 1.5$$

Check:

$$m + 3.9 = 5.4$$

$$1.5 + 3.9 \ ? \ 5.4$$

$$5.4 \ \Big| \ 5.4 \qquad \text{TRUE}$$

The solution is 1.5.

28. 3.4

29.

$$-9.7 = -4.7 + y$$

$$4.7 + (-9.7) = 4.7 + (-4.7) + y$$

$$-5 = y$$

Check:

$$-9.7 = -4.7 + y$$

$$-9.7 \ ? \ -4.7 + (-5)$$

$$-9.7 \ \Big| \ -9.7 \qquad \text{TRUE}$$

The solution is -5.

30. -10.6

31.

$$5x = 80$$

$$\frac{5x}{5} = \frac{80}{5} \qquad \text{Dividing both sides by 5}$$

$$1 \cdot x = 16 \qquad \text{Simplifying}$$

$$x = 16 \qquad \text{Identity property of 1}$$

Check:

$$5x = 80$$

$$5 \cdot 16 \ ? \ 80$$

$$80 \ \Big| \ 80 \qquad \text{TRUE}$$

The solution is 16.

32. 13

33. $9t = 36$

$\dfrac{9t}{9} = \dfrac{36}{9}$ Dividing both sides by 9

$1 \cdot t = 4$ Simplifying

$t = 4$ Identity property of 1

Check: $\dfrac{9t = 36}{9 \cdot 4 \ ? \ 36}$

$36 \ \big| \ 36$ TRUE

The solution is 4.

34. 12

35. $84 = 7x$

$\dfrac{84}{7} = \dfrac{7x}{7}$ Dividing both sides by 7

$12 = 1 \cdot x$

$12 = x$

Check: $\dfrac{84 = 7x}{84 \ ? \ 7 \cdot 12}$

$84 \ \big| \ 84$ TRUE

The solution is 12.

36. 8

37. $-x = 23$

$-1 \cdot x = 23$

$-1 \cdot (-1 \cdot x) = -1 \cdot 23$

$1 \cdot x = -23$

$x = -23$

Check: $\dfrac{-x = 23}{-(-23) \ ? \ 23}$

$23 \ \big| \ 23$ TRUE

The solution is -23.

38. -100

39. $-t = -8$

The equation states that the opposite of t is the opposite of 8. Thus, $t = 8$. We could also do this exercise as follows.

$-t = -8$

$-1(-t) = -1(-8)$ Multiplying both sides by -1

$t = 8$

Check: $\dfrac{-t = -8}{-(8) \ ? \ -8}$

$-8 \ \big| \ -8$ TRUE

The solution is 8.

40. 68

41. $7x = -49$

$\dfrac{7x}{7} = \dfrac{-49}{7}$

$1 \cdot x = -7$

$x = -7$

Check: $\dfrac{7x = -49}{7(-7) \ ? \ -49}$

$-49 \ \big| \ -49$ TRUE

The solution is -7.

42. -4

43. $-12x = 72$

$\dfrac{-12x}{-12} = \dfrac{72}{-12}$

$1 \cdot x = -6$

$x = -6$

Check: $\dfrac{-12x = 72}{-12(-6) \ ? \ 72}$

$72 \ \big| \ 72$ TRUE

The solution is -6.

44. -7

45. $-3.4t = -20.4$

$\dfrac{-3.4t}{-3.4} = \dfrac{-20.4}{-3.4}$

$1 \cdot t = 6$

$t = 6$

Check: $\dfrac{-3.4t = -20.4}{-3.4(6) \ ? \ -20.4}$

$-20.4 \ \big| \ -20.4$ TRUE

The solution is 6.

46. 8

47. $\dfrac{a}{4} = 13$

$\dfrac{1}{4} \cdot a = 13$

$4 \cdot \dfrac{1}{4} \cdot a = 4 \cdot 13$

$a = 52$

Check: $\dfrac{\dfrac{a}{4} = 13}{\dfrac{52}{4} \ ? \ 13}$

$\phantom{\dfrac{52}{4} \ ? \ }13 \ \big| \ 13$ TRUE

The solution is 52.

48. -88

49. $\dfrac{3}{4}x = 27$

$\dfrac{4}{3} \cdot \dfrac{3}{4}x = \dfrac{4}{3} \cdot 27$

$1 \cdot x = \dfrac{4 \cdot \cancel{3} \cdot 3 \cdot 3}{\cancel{3} \cdot 1}$

$x = 36$

Check: $\dfrac{\dfrac{3}{4}x = 27}{\dfrac{3}{4} \cdot 36 \ ? \ 27}$

$\phantom{\dfrac{3}{4} \cdot 36 \ ? \ }27 \ \big| \ 27$ TRUE

The solution is 36.

50. 20

51.
$$\frac{-t}{5} = 9$$
$$5 \cdot \frac{1}{5} \cdot (-t) = 5 \cdot 9$$
$$-t = 45$$
$$-1(-t) = -1 \cdot 45$$
$$t = -45$$

Check:
$$\frac{-t}{5} = 9$$

$$\frac{-(-45)}{5} \; ? \; 9$$

$$\frac{45}{5}$$

$$9 \;\bigg|\; 9 \quad \text{TRUE}$$

The solution is -45.

52. -54

53.
$$\frac{2}{7} = \frac{x}{3}$$
$$\frac{2}{7} = \frac{1}{3} \cdot x$$
$$3 \cdot \frac{2}{7} = 3 \cdot \frac{1}{3} \cdot x$$
$$\frac{6}{7} = x$$

Check:
$$\frac{2}{7} = \frac{x}{3}$$

$$\frac{2}{7} \; ? \; \frac{6/7}{3}$$

$$\frac{6}{7} \cdot \frac{1}{3}$$

$$\frac{6}{21}$$

$$\frac{2}{7} \;\bigg|\; \frac{2}{7} \quad \text{TRUE}$$

The solution is $\frac{6}{7}$.

54. $\frac{5}{9}$

55. $-\frac{3}{5}r = -\frac{3}{5}$

The solution of the equation is the number that is multiplied by $-\frac{3}{5}$ to get $-\frac{3}{5}$. That number is 1. We could also do this exercise as follows:
$$-\frac{3}{5}r = -\frac{3}{5}$$
$$-\frac{5}{3} \cdot \left(-\frac{3}{5}r\right) = -\frac{5}{3}\left(-\frac{3}{5}\right)$$
$$r = 1$$

Check:
$$-\frac{3}{5}r = -\frac{3}{5}$$

$$-\frac{3}{5} \cdot 1 \; ? \; -\frac{3}{5}$$

$$-\frac{3}{5} \;\bigg|\; -\frac{3}{5} \quad \text{TRUE}$$

The solution is 1.

56. $\frac{2}{3}$

57.
$$\frac{-3r}{2} = -\frac{27}{4}$$
$$-\frac{3}{2}r = -\frac{27}{4}$$
$$-\frac{2}{3} \cdot \left(-\frac{3}{2}r\right) = -\frac{2}{3} \cdot \left(-\frac{27}{4}\right)$$
$$r = \frac{\cancel{2} \cdot \cancel{3} \cdot 3 \cdot 3}{\cancel{3} \cdot \cancel{2} \cdot 2}$$
$$r = \frac{9}{2}$$

Check:
$$\frac{-3r}{2} = -\frac{27}{4}$$

$$-\frac{3}{2} \cdot \frac{9}{2} \; ? \; -\frac{27}{4}$$

$$-\frac{27}{4} \;\bigg|\; -\frac{27}{4} \quad \text{TRUE}$$

The solution is $\frac{9}{2}$.

58. -1

59.
$$4.5 + t = -3.1$$
$$4.5 + t - 4.5 = -3.1 - 4.5$$
$$t = -7.6$$

The solution is -7.6.

60. 24

61.
$$-8.2x = 20.5$$
$$\frac{-8.2x}{-8.2} = \frac{20.5}{-8.2}$$
$$x = -2.5$$

The solution is -2.5.

62. -5.5

63.
$$12 = y + 29$$
$$12 - 29 = y + 29 - 29$$
$$-17 = y$$

The solution is -17.

64. -128

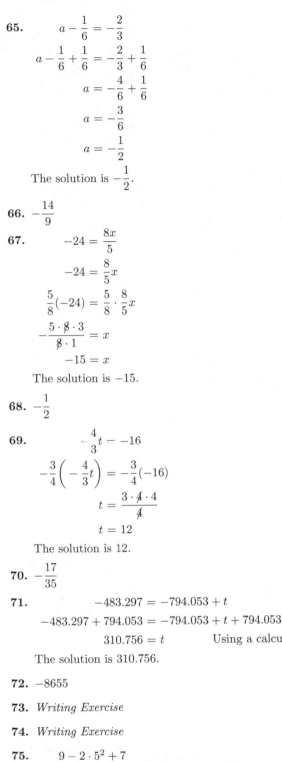

65.
$$a - \frac{1}{6} = -\frac{2}{3}$$
$$a - \frac{1}{6} + \frac{1}{6} = -\frac{2}{3} + \frac{1}{6}$$
$$a = -\frac{4}{6} + \frac{1}{6}$$
$$a = -\frac{3}{6}$$
$$a = -\frac{1}{2}$$

The solution is $-\frac{1}{2}$.

66. $-\frac{14}{9}$

67.
$$-24 = \frac{8x}{5}$$
$$-24 = \frac{8}{5}x$$
$$\frac{5}{8}(-24) = \frac{5}{8} \cdot \frac{8}{5}x$$
$$-\frac{5 \cdot \cancel{8} \cdot 3}{\cancel{8} \cdot 1} = x$$
$$-15 = x$$

The solution is -15.

68. $-\frac{1}{2}$

69.
$$-\frac{4}{3}t = -16$$
$$-\frac{3}{4}\left(-\frac{4}{3}t\right) = -\frac{3}{4}(-16)$$
$$t = \frac{3 \cdot \cancel{4} \cdot 4}{\cancel{4}}$$
$$t = 12$$

The solution is 12.

70. $-\frac{17}{35}$

71.
$$-483.297 = -794.053 + t$$
$$-483.297 + 794.053 = -794.053 + t + 794.053$$
$$310.756 = t \qquad \text{Using a calculator}$$

The solution is 310.756.

72. -8655

73. *Writing Exercise*

74. *Writing Exercise*

75.
$$9 - 2 \cdot 5^2 + 7$$
$$= 9 - 2 \cdot 25 + 7 \quad \text{Simplifying the exponential expression}$$
$$= 9 - 50 + 7 \quad \text{Multiplying}$$
$$= -41 + 7 \quad \text{Subtracting and}$$
$$= -34 \qquad \text{adding from left to right}$$

76. 41

77.
$$16 \div (2 - 3 \cdot 2) + 5$$
$$= 16 \div (2 - 6) + 5 \quad \text{Simplifying inside}$$
$$= 16 \div (-4) + 5 \quad \text{the parentheses}$$
$$= -4 + 5 \qquad \text{Dividing}$$
$$= 1 \qquad \text{Adding}$$

78. -16

79. *Writing Exercise*

80. *Writing Exercise*

81.
$$5 + x = 5 + x$$
$$5 + x - 5 = 5 + x - 5$$
$$x = x$$

$x = x$ is true for all real numbers. Thus, all real numbers are solutions.

82. No solution

83.
$$4|x| = 48$$
$$|x| = 12$$

x represents a number whose distance from 0 is 12. Thus, $x = -12$ or $x = 12$.

The solution is -12 or 12.

84. No solution

85. For all x, $0 \cdot x = 0$. Thus, all real numbers are solutions.

86. 0

87.
$$x + 4 = 5 + x$$
$$x + 4 - x = 5 + x - x$$
$$4 = 5$$

Since $4 = 5$ is false, the equation has no solution.

88. $-2, 2$

89.
$$mx = 9.4m$$
$$\frac{mx}{m} = \frac{9.4m}{m}$$
$$x = 9.4$$

The solution is 9.4.

90. 4

91.
$$\frac{7cx}{2a} = \frac{21}{a} \cdot c$$
$$\frac{7c}{2a} \cdot x = \frac{21}{a} \cdot c$$
$$\frac{2a}{7c} \cdot \frac{7c}{2a} \cdot x = \frac{2a}{7c} \cdot \frac{21}{a} \cdot \frac{c}{1}$$
$$x = \frac{2 \cdot \cancel{a} \cdot 3 \cdot \cancel{7} \cdot \cancel{c}}{\cancel{7} \cdot \cancel{c} \cdot \cancel{a} \cdot 1}$$
$$x = 6$$

The solution is 6.

92. 2

93.
$$5a = ax - 3a$$
$$5a + 3a = ax - 3a + 3a$$
$$8a = ax$$
$$\frac{8a}{a} = \frac{ax}{a}$$
$$8 = x$$

The solution is 8.

94. $-13, 13$

95.
$$x - 4720 = 1634$$
$$x - 4720 + 4720 = 1634 + 4720$$
$$x = 6354$$
$$x + 4720 = 6354 + 4720$$
$$x + 4720 = 11,074$$

96. 250

97. *Writing Exercise*

Exercise Set 2.2

1.
$$5x + 3 = 38$$
$$5x + 3 - 3 = 38 - 3 \qquad \text{Subtracting 3 from both sides}$$
$$5x = 35 \qquad \text{Simplifying}$$
$$\frac{5x}{5} = \frac{35}{5} \qquad \text{Dividing both sides by 4}$$
$$x = 7 \qquad \text{Simplifying}$$

Check:
$$\begin{array}{c|c} 5x + 3 = 38 \\ \hline 5 \cdot 7 + 3 \ ? \ 38 \\ 35 + 3 \\ 38 & 38 \quad \text{TRUE} \end{array}$$

The solution is 7.

2. 8

3.
$$8x + 4 = 68$$
$$8x + 4 - 4 = 68 - 4 \qquad \text{Subtracting 4 from both sides}$$
$$8x = 64 \qquad \text{Simplifying}$$
$$\frac{8x}{8} = \frac{64}{8} \qquad \text{Dividing both sides by 8}$$
$$x = 8 \qquad \text{Simplifying}$$

Check:
$$\begin{array}{c|c} 8x + 4 = 68 \\ \hline 8 \cdot 8 + 4 \ ? \ 68 \\ 64 + 4 \\ 68 & 68 \quad \text{TRUE} \end{array}$$

The solution is 8.

4. 9

5.
$$7t - 8 = 27$$
$$7t - 8 + 8 = 27 + 8 \qquad \text{Adding 8 to both sides}$$
$$7t = 35$$
$$\frac{7t}{7} = \frac{35}{7} \qquad \text{Dividing both sides by 7}$$
$$t = 5$$

Check:
$$\begin{array}{c|c} 7t - 8 = 27 \\ \hline 7 \cdot 5 - 8 \ ? \ 27 \\ 35 - 8 \\ 27 & 27 \quad \text{TRUE} \end{array}$$

The solution is 5.

6. 3

7.
$$3x - 9 = 33$$
$$3x - 9 + 9 = 33 + 9$$
$$3x = 42$$
$$\frac{3x}{3} = \frac{42}{3}$$
$$x = 14$$

Check:
$$\begin{array}{c|c} 3x - 9 = 33 \\ \hline 3 \cdot 14 - 9 \ ? \ 33 \\ 42 - 9 \\ 33 & 33 \quad \text{TRUE} \end{array}$$

The solution is 14.

8. 10

9.
$$8z + 2 = -54$$
$$8z + 2 - 2 = -54 - 2$$
$$8z = -56$$
$$\frac{8z}{8} = \frac{-56}{8}$$
$$z = -7$$

Check:
$$\begin{array}{c|c} 8z + 2 = -54 \\ \hline 8(-7) + 2 \ ? \ -54 \\ -56 + 2 \\ -54 & -54 \quad \text{TRUE} \end{array}$$

The solution is -7.

10. -6

11.
$$-39 = 1 + 8x$$
$$-39 - 1 = 1 + 8x - 1$$
$$-40 = 8x$$
$$\frac{-40}{8} = \frac{8x}{8}$$
$$-5 = x$$

Check:
$$\begin{array}{c|c} -39 = 1 + 8x \\ \hline -39 \ ? \ 1 + 8(-5) \\ & 1 - 40 \\ -39 & -39 \quad \text{TRUE} \end{array}$$

The solution is -5.

12. -11

13.
$$9 - 4x = 37$$
$$9 - 4x - 9 = 37 - 9$$
$$-4x = 28$$
$$\frac{-4x}{-4} = \frac{28}{-4}$$
$$x = -7$$

Check: $\dfrac{9 - 4x = 37}{}$

$9 - 4(-7) \ ? \ 37$

$9 + 28 \ \Big|$

$\qquad 37 \ \Big| \ 37 \qquad$ TRUE

The solution is -7.

14. -24

15. $\qquad -7x - 24 = -129$

$-7x - 24 + 24 = -129 + 24$

$\qquad -7x = -105$

$\qquad \dfrac{-7x}{-7} = \dfrac{-105}{-7}$

$\qquad x = 15$

Check: $\dfrac{-7x - 24 = -129}{}$

$-7 \cdot 15 - 24 \ ? \ -129$

$-105 - 24 \ \Big|$

$\qquad -129 \ \Big| \ -129 \qquad$ TRUE

The solution is 15.

16. 19

17. $\quad 48 = 5x + 7x$

$48 = 12x \qquad$ Combining like terms

$\dfrac{48}{12} = \dfrac{12x}{12} \qquad$ Dividing both sides by 12

$4 = x$

Check: $\dfrac{48 = 5x + 7x}{}$

$48 \ ? \ 5 \cdot 4 + 7 \cdot 4$

$\Big| \ 20 + 28$

$48 \ \Big| \ 48 \qquad$ TRUE

The solution is 4.

18. 5

19. $\qquad 27 - 6x = 99$

$27 - 6x - 27 = 99 - 27$

$\qquad -6x = 72$

$\qquad \dfrac{-6x}{-6} = \dfrac{72}{-6}$

$\qquad x = -12$

Check: $\dfrac{27 - 6x = 99}{}$

$27 - 6(-12) \ ? \ 99$

$27 + 72 \ \Big|$

$\qquad 99 \ \Big| \ 99 \qquad$ TRUE

The solution is -12.

20. 3

21. $4x + 3x = 42 \qquad$ Combining like terms

$\quad 7x = 42$

$\quad \dfrac{7x}{7} = \dfrac{42}{7}$

$\quad x = 6$

Check: $\dfrac{4x + 3x = 42}{}$

$4 \cdot 6 + 3 \cdot 6 \ ? \ 42$

$24 + 18 \ \Big|$

$\qquad 42 \ \Big| \ 42 \qquad$ TRUE

The solution is 6.

22. 4

23. $\quad -2a + 5a = 24$

$\qquad 3a = 24$

$\qquad \dfrac{3a}{3} = \dfrac{24}{3}$

$\qquad a = 8$

Check: $\dfrac{-2a + 5a = 24}{}$

$-2 \cdot 8 + 5 \cdot 8 \ ? \ 24$

$-16 + 40 \ \Big|$

$\qquad 24 \ \Big| \ 24 \qquad$ TRUE

The solution is 8.

24. -3

25. $\quad -7y - 8y = -15$

$\qquad -15y = -15$

$\qquad \dfrac{-15y}{-15} = \dfrac{-15}{-15}$

$\qquad y = 1$

Check: $\dfrac{-7y - 8y = -15}{}$

$-7 \cdot 1 - 8 \cdot 1 \ ? \ -15$

$-7 - 8 \ \Big|$

$\qquad -15 \ \Big| \ -15 \qquad$ TRUE

The solution is 1.

26. 4

27. $\quad 10.2y - 7.3y = -58$

$\qquad 2.9y = -58$

$\qquad \dfrac{2.9y}{2.9} = \dfrac{-58}{2.9}$

$\qquad y = -\dfrac{58}{2.9}$

$\qquad y = -20$

Check:

$\dfrac{10.2y - 7.3y = -58}{}$

$10.2(-20) - 7.3(-20) \ ? \ -58$

$-204 + 146 \ \Big|$

$\qquad -58 \ \Big| \ -58 \qquad$ TRUE

The solution is -20.

28. -20

29. $\quad x + \dfrac{1}{3}x = 8$

$\quad \left(1 + \dfrac{1}{3}\right)x = 8$

$\qquad \dfrac{4}{3}x = 8$

$\quad \dfrac{3}{4} \cdot \dfrac{4}{3}x = \dfrac{3}{4} \cdot 8$

$\qquad x = 6$

Check:
$$x + \frac{1}{3}x = 8$$

$$6 + \frac{1}{3} \cdot 6 \ ? \ 8$$

$$6 + 2$$

$$8 \ \Big| \ 8 \quad \text{TRUE}$$

The solution is 6.

30. 8

31.
$$9y - 35 = 4y$$
$$9y = 4y + 35 \qquad \text{Adding 35 and simplifying}$$
$$9y - 4y = 35 \qquad \text{Subtracting } 4y \text{ and simplifying}$$
$$5y = 35 \qquad \text{Collecting like terms}$$
$$\frac{5y}{5} = \frac{35}{5} \qquad \text{Dividing both sides by 5}$$
$$y = 7$$

Check:
$$9y - 35 = 4y$$
$$9 \cdot 7 - 35 \ ? \ 4 \cdot 7$$
$$63 - 35 \ \Big| \ 28$$
$$28 \ \Big| \ 28 \quad \text{TRUE}$$

The solution is 7.

32. −3

33.
$$6x - 5 = 7 + 2x$$
$$6x - 5 - 2x = 7 + 2x - 2x \quad \text{Subtracting } 2x \text{ on both sides}$$
$$4x - 5 = 7 \qquad \text{Simplifying}$$
$$4x - 5 + 5 = 7 + 5 \qquad \text{Adding 5 on both sides}$$
$$4x = 12 \qquad \text{Simplifying}$$
$$\frac{4x}{4} = \frac{12}{4} \qquad \text{Dividing by 4 on both sides}$$
$$x = 3$$

Check:
$$6x - 5 = 7 + 2x$$
$$6 \cdot 3 - 5 \ ? \ 7 + 2 \cdot 3$$
$$18 - 5 \ \Big| \ 7 + 6$$
$$13 \ \Big| \ 13 \quad \text{TRUE}$$

The solution is 3.

34. 5

35.
$$6x + 3 = 2x + 3$$
$$6x - 2x = 3 - 3$$
$$4x = 0$$
$$\frac{4x}{4} = \frac{0}{4}$$
$$x = 0$$

Check:
$$6x + 3 = 2x + 3$$
$$6 \cdot 0 + 3 \ ? \ 2 \cdot 0 + 3$$
$$0 + 3 \ \Big| \ 0 + 3$$
$$3 \ \Big| \ 3 \quad \text{TRUE}$$

The solution is 0.

36. 4

37.
$$5 - 2x = 3x - 7x + 25$$
$$5 - 2x = -4x + 25$$
$$4x - 2x = 25 - 5$$
$$2x = 20$$
$$\frac{2x}{2} = \frac{20}{2}$$
$$x = 10$$

Check:
$$5 - 2x = 3x - 7x + 25$$
$$5 - 2 \cdot 10 \ ? \ 3 \cdot 10 - 7 \cdot 10 + 25$$
$$5 - 20 \ \Big| \ 30 - 70 + 25$$
$$-15 \ \Big| \ -40 + 25$$
$$-15 \ \Big| \ -15 \quad \text{TRUE}$$

The solution is 10.

38. 10

39.
$$7 + 3x - 6 = 3x + 5 - x$$
$$3x + 1 = 2x + 5 \qquad \text{Combining like terms on each side}$$
$$3x - 2x = 5 - 1$$
$$x = 4$$

Check:
$$7 + 3x - 6 = 3x + 5 - x$$
$$7 + 3 \cdot 4 - 6 \ ? \ 3 \cdot 4 + 5 - 4$$
$$7 + 12 - 6 \ \Big| \ 12 + 5 - 4$$
$$19 - 6 \ \Big| \ 17 - 4$$
$$13 \ \Big| \ 13 \quad \text{TRUE}$$

The solution is 4.

40. 0

41.
$$4y - 4 + y + 24 = 6y + 20 - 4y$$
$$5y + 20 = 2y + 20$$
$$5y - 2y = 20 - 20$$
$$3y = 0$$
$$y = 0$$

Check:
$$4y - 4 + y + 24 = 6y + 20 - 4y$$
$$4 \cdot 0 - 4 + 0 + 24 \ ? \ 6 \cdot 0 + 20 - 4 \cdot 0$$
$$0 - 4 + 0 + 24 \ \Big| \ 0 + 20 - 0$$
$$20 \ \Big| \ 20 \quad \text{TRUE}$$

The solution is 0.

42. 7

43.
$$\frac{5}{4}x + \frac{1}{4}x = 2x + \frac{1}{2} + \frac{3}{4}x$$

The number 4 is the least common denominator, so we multiply by 4 on both sides.

$$4\left(\frac{5}{4}x + \frac{1}{4}x\right) = 4\left(2x + \frac{1}{2} + \frac{3}{4}x\right)$$
$$4 \cdot \frac{5}{4}x + 4 \cdot \frac{1}{4}x = 4 \cdot 2x + 4 \cdot \frac{1}{2} + 4 \cdot \frac{3}{4}x$$
$$5x + x = 8x + 2 + 3x$$
$$6x = 11x + 2$$
$$6x - 11x = 2$$
$$-5x = 2$$
$$\frac{-5x}{-5} = \frac{2}{-5}$$
$$x = -\frac{2}{5}$$

Check:

$$\frac{5}{4}x + \frac{1}{4}x = 2x + \frac{1}{2} + \frac{3}{4}x$$

$$\frac{5}{4}\left(-\frac{2}{5}\right) + \frac{1}{4}\left(-\frac{2}{5}\right) \ ? \ 2\left(-\frac{2}{5}\right) + \frac{1}{2} + \frac{3}{4}\left(-\frac{2}{5}\right)$$

$$-\frac{1}{2} - \frac{1}{10} \ \bigg| \ -\frac{4}{5} + \frac{1}{2} - \frac{3}{10}$$

$$-\frac{5}{10} - \frac{1}{10} \ \bigg| \ -\frac{8}{10} + \frac{5}{10} - \frac{3}{10}$$

$$-\frac{6}{10} \ \bigg| \ -\frac{6}{10} \qquad \text{TRUE}$$

The solution is $-\frac{2}{5}$.

44. $\frac{1}{2}$

45. $\frac{2}{3} + \frac{1}{4}t = 6$

The number 12 is the least common denominator, so we multiply by 12 on both sides.

$$12\left(\frac{2}{3} + \frac{1}{4}t\right) = 12 \cdot 6$$

$$12 \cdot \frac{2}{3} + 12 \cdot \frac{1}{4}t = 72$$

$$8 + 3t = 72$$

$$3t = 72 - 8$$

$$3t = 64$$

$$t = \frac{64}{3}$$

Check:

$$\frac{2}{3} + \frac{1}{4}t = 6$$

$$\frac{2}{3} + \frac{1}{4}\left(\frac{64}{3}\right) \ ? \ 6$$

$$\frac{2}{3} + \frac{16}{3} \ \bigg|$$

$$\frac{18}{3} \ \bigg|$$

$$6 \ \bigg| \ 6 \qquad \text{TRUE}$$

The solution is $\frac{64}{3}$.

46. $-\frac{2}{3}$

47. $\frac{2}{3} + 4t = 6t - \frac{2}{15}$

The number 15 is the least common denominator, so we multiply by 15 on both sides.

$$15\left(\frac{2}{3} + 4t\right) = 15\left(6t - \frac{2}{15}\right)$$

$$15 \cdot \frac{2}{3} + 15 \cdot 4t = 15 \cdot 6t - 15 \cdot \frac{2}{15}$$

$$10 + 60t = 90t - 2$$

$$10 + 2 = 90t - 60t$$

$$12 = 30t$$

$$\frac{12}{30} = t$$

$$\frac{2}{5} = t$$

Check:

$$\frac{2}{3} + 4t = 6t - \frac{2}{15}$$

$$\frac{2}{3} + 4 \cdot \frac{2}{5} \ ? \ 6 \cdot \frac{2}{5} - \frac{2}{15}$$

$$\frac{2}{3} + \frac{8}{5} \ \bigg| \ \frac{12}{5} - \frac{2}{15}$$

$$\frac{10}{15} + \frac{24}{15} \ \bigg| \ \frac{36}{15} - \frac{2}{15}$$

$$\frac{34}{15} \ \bigg| \ \frac{34}{15} \qquad \text{TRUE}$$

The solution is $\frac{2}{5}$.

48. -3

49. $\frac{1}{3}x + \frac{2}{5} = \frac{4}{15} + \frac{3}{5}x - \frac{2}{3}$

The number 15 is the least common denominator, so we multiply by 15 on both sides.

$$15\left(\frac{1}{3}x + \frac{2}{5}\right) = 15\left(\frac{4}{15} + \frac{3}{5}x - \frac{2}{3}\right)$$

$$15 \cdot \frac{1}{3}x + 15 \cdot \frac{2}{5} = 15 \cdot \frac{4}{15} + 15 \cdot \frac{3}{5}x - 15 \cdot \frac{2}{3}$$

$$5x + 6 = 4 + 9x - 10$$

$$5x + 6 = -6 + 9x$$

$$5x - 9x = -6 - 6$$

$$-4x = -12$$

$$\frac{-4x}{-4} = \frac{-12}{-4}$$

$$x = 3$$

Check:

$$\frac{1}{3}x + \frac{2}{5} = \frac{4}{15} + \frac{3}{5}x - \frac{2}{3}$$

$$\frac{\frac{1}{3}\cdot 3 + \frac{2}{5} \; ? \; \frac{4}{15} + \frac{3}{5}\cdot 3 - \frac{2}{3}}{}$$

$$1 + \frac{2}{5} \quad \bigg| \quad \frac{4}{15} + \frac{9}{5} - \frac{2}{3}$$

$$\frac{5}{5} + \frac{2}{5} \quad \bigg| \quad \frac{4}{15} + \frac{27}{15} - \frac{10}{15}$$

$$\frac{7}{5} \quad \bigg| \quad \frac{21}{15}$$

$$\frac{7}{5} \quad \bigg| \quad \frac{7}{5} \qquad \text{TRUE}$$

The solution is 3.

50. -3

51.

$$2.1x + 45.2 = 3.2 - 8.4x$$

Greatest number of decimal places is 1

$$10(2.1x + 45.2) = 10(3.2 - 8.4x)$$

Multiplying by 10 to clear decimals

$$10(2.1x) + 10(45.2) = 10(3.2) - 10(8.4x)$$

$$21x + 452 = 32 - 84x$$

$$21x + 84x = 32 - 452$$

$$105x = -420$$

$$x = \frac{-420}{105}$$

$$x = -4$$

Check:

$$\frac{2.1x + 45.2 = 3.2 - 8.4x}{}$$

$$\frac{2.1(-4) + 45.2 \; ? \; 3.2 - 8.4(-4)}{}$$

$$-8.4 + 45.2 \quad \bigg| \quad 3.2 + 33.6$$

$$36.8 \quad \bigg| \quad 36.8 \qquad \text{TRUE}$$

The solution is -4.

52. $\dfrac{4}{5}$, or 0.8

53.

$$0.76 + 0.21t = 0.96t - 0.49$$

Greatest number of decimal places is 2

$$100(0.76 + 0.21t) = 100(0.96t - 0.49)$$

Multiplying by 100 to clear decimals

$$100(0.76) + 100(0.21t) = 100(0.96t) - 100(0.49)$$

$$76 + 21t = 96t - 49$$

$$76 + 49 = 96t - 21t$$

$$125 = 75t$$

$$\frac{125}{75} = t$$

$$\frac{5}{3} = t, \text{ or}$$

$$1.\overline{6} = t$$

The answer checks. The solution is $\dfrac{5}{3}$, or $1.\overline{6}$.

54. 1

55.

$$\frac{2}{5}x - \frac{3}{2}x = \frac{3}{4}x + 2$$

The least common denominator is 20.

$$20\left(\frac{2}{5}x - \frac{3}{2}x\right) = 20\left(\frac{3}{4}x + 2\right)$$

$$20 \cdot \frac{2}{5}x - 20 \cdot \frac{3}{2}x = 20 \cdot \frac{3}{4}x + 20 \cdot 2$$

$$8x - 30x = 15x + 40$$

$$-22x = 15x + 40$$

$$-22x - 15x = 40$$

$$-37x = 40$$

$$\frac{-37x}{-37} = \frac{40}{-37}$$

$$x = -\frac{40}{37}$$

Check:

$$\frac{2}{5}x - \frac{3}{2}x = \frac{3}{4}x + 2$$

$$\frac{\frac{2}{5}\left(-\frac{40}{37}\right) - \frac{3}{2}\left(-\frac{40}{37}\right) \; ? \; \frac{3}{4}\left(-\frac{40}{37}\right) + 2}{}$$

$$-\frac{16}{37} + \frac{60}{37} \quad \bigg| \quad -\frac{30}{37} + \frac{74}{37}$$

$$\frac{44}{37} \quad \bigg| \quad \frac{44}{37} \qquad \text{TRUE}$$

The solution is $-\dfrac{40}{37}$.

56. $\dfrac{32}{7}$

57. $7(2a - 1) = 21$

$$14a - 7 = 21 \qquad \text{Using the distributive law}$$

$$14a = 21 + 7 \quad \text{Adding 7}$$

$$14a = 28$$

$$a = 2 \qquad \text{Dividing by 14}$$

Check:

$$\frac{7(2a - 1) = 21}{}$$

$$\frac{7(2\cdot 2 - 1) \; ? \; 21}{}$$

$$7(4 - 1) \quad \bigg|$$

$$7 \cdot 3 \quad \bigg|$$

$$21 \quad \bigg| \quad 21 \qquad \text{TRUE}$$

The solution is 2.

58. $\dfrac{9}{2}$

59. $35 = 5(3x + 1)$

$$35 = 15x + 5 \qquad \text{Using the distributive law}$$

$$35 - 5 = 15x$$

$$30 = 15x$$

$$2 = x$$

Check:

$$\frac{35 = 5(3x + 1)}{}$$

$$\frac{35 \; ? \; 5(3 \cdot 2 + 1)}{}$$

$$\bigg| \quad 5(6 + 1)$$

$$\bigg| \quad 5 \cdot 7$$

$$35 \quad \bigg| \quad 35 \qquad \text{TRUE}$$

The solution is 2.

60. 1

61. $2(3 + 4m) - 6 = 48$

$\qquad 6 + 8m - 6 = 48$

$\qquad\qquad 8m = 48 \quad$ Combining like terms

$\qquad\qquad\ m = 6$

Check: $\quad \dfrac{2(3 + 4m) - 6 = 48}{}$

$\qquad 2(3 + 4 \cdot 6) - 6 \ ? \ 48$

$\qquad\quad 2(3 + 24) - 6 \ \Big|$

$\qquad\qquad 2 \cdot 27 - 6 \ \Big|$

$\qquad\qquad\quad 54 - 6 \ \Big|$

$\qquad\qquad\qquad\quad 48 \ \Big| \ 48 \qquad$ TRUE

The solution is 6.

62. 9

63. $7r - (2r + 8) = 32$

$\qquad 7r - 2r - 8 = 32$

$\qquad\quad 5r - 8 = 32 \qquad$ Combining like terms

$\qquad\qquad 5r = 32 + 8$

$\qquad\qquad 5r = 40$

$\qquad\qquad\ r = 8$

Check: $\quad \dfrac{7r - (2r + 8) = 32}{}$

$\quad 7 \cdot 8 - (2 \cdot 8 + 8) \ ? \ 32$

$\qquad\ 56 - (16 + 8) \ \Big|$

$\qquad\qquad\quad 56 - 24 \ \Big|$

$\qquad\qquad\qquad\quad 32 \ \Big| \ 32 \qquad$ TRUE

The solution is 8.

64. 8

65. $13 - 3(2x - 1) = 4$

$\qquad 13 - 6x + 3 = 4$

$\qquad\quad 16 - 6x = 4$

$\qquad\qquad -6x = 4 - 16$

$\qquad\qquad -6x = -12$

$\qquad\qquad\quad x = 2$

Check: $\quad \dfrac{13 - 3(2x - 1) = 4}{}$

$\qquad 13 - 3(2 \cdot 2 - 1) \ ? \ 4$

$\qquad\quad 13 - 3(4 - 1) \ \Big|$

$\qquad\qquad\ 13 - 3 \cdot 3 \ \Big|$

$\qquad\qquad\qquad 13 - 9 \ \Big|$

$\qquad\qquad\qquad\qquad 4 \ \Big| \ 4 \qquad$ TRUE

The solution is 2.

66. 17

67. $3(t - 2) = 9(t + 2)$

$\qquad 3t - 6 = 9t + 18$

$\quad -6 - 18 = 9t - 3t$

$\qquad\ -24 = 6t$

$\qquad\quad -4 = t$

Check: $\quad \dfrac{3(t - 2) = 9(t + 2)}{}$

$\quad 3(-4 - 2) \ ? \ 9(-4 + 2)$

$\qquad\ 3(-6) \ \Big| \ 9(-2)$

$\qquad\quad -18 \ \Big| \ -18 \qquad$ TRUE

The solution is -4.

68. $-\dfrac{5}{3}$

69. $7(5x - 2) = 6(6x - 1)$

$\qquad 35x - 14 = 36x - 6$

$\quad -14 + 6 = 36x - 35x$

$\qquad\ -8 = x$

Check:

$\qquad \dfrac{7(5x - 2) = 6(6x - 1)}{}$

$\quad 7(5(-8) - 2) \ ? \ 6(6(-8) - 1)$

$\qquad 7(-40 - 2) \ \Big| \ 6(-48 - 1)$

$\qquad\quad 7(-42) \ \Big| \ 6(-49)$

$\qquad\qquad -294 \ \Big| \ -294 \qquad$ TRUE

The solution is -8.

70. -12

71. $19 - (2x + 3) = 2(x + 3) + x$

$\qquad 19 - 2x - 3 = 2x + 6 + x$

$\qquad\quad 16 - 2x = 3x + 6$

$\qquad 16 - 6 = 3x + 2x$

$\qquad\qquad 10 = 5x$

$\qquad\qquad\ 2 = x$

Check: $\quad \dfrac{19 - (2x + 3) = 2(x + 3) + x}{}$

$\quad 19 - (2 \cdot 2 + 3) \ ? \ 2(2 + 3) + 2$

$\qquad 19 - (4 + 3) \ \Big| \ 2 \cdot 5 + 2$

$\qquad\qquad 19 - 7 \ \Big| \ 10 + 2$

$\qquad\qquad\qquad 12 \ \Big| \ 12 \qquad$ TRUE

The solution is 2.

72. 1

73. $\quad \dfrac{1}{4}(3t - 4) = 5$

$\quad 4 \cdot \dfrac{1}{4}(3t - 4) = 4 \cdot 5$

$\qquad\quad 3t - 4 = 20$

$\qquad\qquad 3t = 24 \qquad$ Adding 4 to both sides

$\qquad\qquad\ t = 8 \qquad$ Dividing both sides by 3

Check:

$\qquad \dfrac{\dfrac{1}{4}(3t - 4) = 5}{}$

$\qquad \dfrac{1}{4}(3 \cdot 8 - 4) \ ? \ 5$

$\qquad \dfrac{1}{4}(24 - 4) \ ?$

$\qquad\qquad \dfrac{1}{4} \cdot 20 \ \Big|$

$\qquad\qquad\qquad 5 \ \Big| \ 5 \qquad$ TRUE

The solution is 8.

74. 11

75.
$$\frac{4}{3}(5x+1) = 8$$
$$\frac{3}{4}\cdot\frac{4}{3}(5x+1) = \frac{3}{4}\cdot 8$$
$$5x+1 = 6$$
$$5x = 5$$
$$x = 1$$

Check:
$$\frac{4}{3}(5x+1) = 8$$
$$\frac{4}{3}(5\cdot 1+1) \;?\; 8$$
$$\frac{4}{3}(6) \;\Big|\; 8$$
$$8 \;\Big|\; 8 \quad \text{TRUE}$$

The solution is 1.

76. 6

77.
$$\frac{3}{2}(2x+5) = -\frac{15}{2}$$
$$\frac{2}{3}\cdot\frac{3}{2}(2x+5) = \frac{2}{3}\left(-\frac{15}{2}\right)$$
$$2x+5 = -5$$
$$2x = -10$$
$$x = -5$$

Check:
$$\frac{3}{2}(2x+5) = -\frac{15}{2}$$
$$\frac{3}{2}(2(-5)+5) \;?\; -\frac{15}{2}$$
$$\frac{3}{2}(-10+5)$$
$$\frac{3}{2}(-5)$$
$$-\frac{15}{2} \;\Big|\; -\frac{15}{2} \quad \text{TRUE}$$

The solution is -5.

78. $\dfrac{16}{15}$

79.
$$\frac{3}{4}\left(3x-\frac{1}{2}\right)-\frac{2}{3} = \frac{1}{3}$$
$$\frac{9}{4}x-\frac{3}{8}-\frac{2}{3} = \frac{1}{3}$$

Multiplying by the number 24 will clear all the fractions, so we multiply by 24 on both sides.

$$24\left(\frac{9}{4}x-\frac{3}{8}-\frac{2}{3}\right) = 24\cdot\frac{1}{3}$$
$$24\cdot\frac{9}{4}x-24\cdot\frac{3}{8}-24\cdot\frac{2}{3} = 8$$
$$54x-9-16 = 8$$
$$54x-25 = 8$$
$$54x = 8+25$$
$$54x = 33$$
$$x = \frac{33}{54}$$
$$x = \frac{11}{18}$$

The check is left to the student. The solution is $\dfrac{11}{18}$.

80. $-\dfrac{5}{32}$

81.
$$0.7(3x+6) = 1.1-(x+2)$$
$$2.1x+4.2 = 1.1-x-2$$
$$10(2.1x+4.2) = 10(1.1-x-2) \quad \text{Clearing}$$
$$\hspace{9cm}\text{decimals}$$
$$21x+42 = 11-10x-20$$
$$21x+42 = -10x-9$$
$$21x+10x = -9-42$$
$$31x = -51$$
$$x = -\frac{51}{31}$$

The check is left to the student. The solution is $-\dfrac{51}{31}$.

82. $\dfrac{39}{14}$

83.
$$a+(a-3) = (a+2)-(a+1)$$
$$a+a-3 = a+2-a-1$$
$$2a-3 = 1$$
$$2a = 1+3$$
$$2a = 4$$
$$a = 2$$

Check:
$$a+(a-3) = (a+2)-(a+1)$$
$$2+(2-3) \;?\; (2+2)-(2+1)$$
$$2-1 \;\Big|\; 4-3$$
$$1 \;\Big|\; 1 \quad\quad\quad \text{TRUE}$$

The solution is 2.

84. -7.4

85. $5 + 2(x - 3) = 2[5 - 4(x + 2)]$

$5 + 2x - 6 = 2[5 - 4x - 8]$

$2x - 1 = 2[-4x - 3]$

$2x - 1 = -8x - 6$

$2x - 1 + 1 = -8x - 6 + 1$

$2x = -8x - 5$

$2x + 8x = -8x - 5 + 8x$

$10x = -5$

$\dfrac{1}{10} \cdot 10x = \dfrac{1}{10}(-5)$

$x = -\dfrac{1}{2}$

Check:

$$\frac{5 + 2(x - 3) = 2[5 - 4(x + 2)]}{}$$

$5 + 2\left(-\dfrac{1}{2} - 3\right)$? $2\left[5 - 4\left(-\dfrac{1}{2} + 2\right)\right]$

$5 + 2\left(-\dfrac{7}{2}\right)$ | $2\left[5 - 4\left(\dfrac{3}{2}\right)\right]$

$5 - 7$ | $2[5 - 6]$

-2 | $2[-1]$

-2 | -2 TRUE

The solution is $-\dfrac{1}{2}$.

86. $\dfrac{23}{8}$

87. $2x = x + x$

$2x = 2x$ Adding on the right side

The solution set is the set of all real numbers. This is an identity.

88. $\emptyset$; contradiction

89. $5x = 0$

$\dfrac{5x}{5} = \dfrac{0}{5}$

$x = 0$

The solution set is $\{0\}$. This is a conditional equation.

90. All real numbers; identity

91. $x + 8 = 3 + x + 7$

$x + 8 = 10 + x$ Adding on the right side

$x + 8 - x = 10 + x - x$

$8 = 10$

The solution set is $\emptyset$. This is a contradiction.

92. $\{0\}$; conditional

93. $5x + 7 - 3x = 2x$

$2x + 7 = 2x$

$2x + 7 - 2x = 2x - 2x$

$7 = 0$

Since the original equation is equivalent to the false equation $7 = 0$, there is no solution. The solution set is $\emptyset$. The equation is a contradiction.

94. All real numbers; identity

95. $1 + 9x = 3(4x + 1) - 2$

$1 + 9x = 12x + 3 - 2$

$1 + 9x = 12x + 1$

$1 + 9x - 1 = 12x + 1 - 1$

$9x = 12x$

$9x - 9x = 12x - 9x$

$0 = 3x$

$\dfrac{1}{3} \cdot 0 = \dfrac{1}{3} \cdot 3x$

$0 = x$

The solution set is $\{0\}$. The equation is a conditional equation.

96. $\emptyset$; contradiction

97. $-9t + 2 = -9t - 7(6 \div 2(49) + 8)$

Observe that $-7(6 \div 2(49) + 8)$ is a negative number. Then on the left side we have $-9t$ plus a positive number and on the right side we have $-9t$ plus a negative number. This is a contradiction, so the solution set is $\emptyset$.

98. $\emptyset$; contradiction

99. *Writing Exercise*

100. *Writing Exercise*

101. $3 - 5a = 3 - 5 \cdot 2 = 3 - 10 = -7$

102. 15

103. $7x - 2x = 7(-3) - 2(-3) = -21 + 6 = -15$

104. -28

105. *Writing Exercise*

106. *Writing Exercise*

107. $8.43x - 2.5(3.2 - 0.7x) = -3.455x + 9.04$

$8.43x - 8 + 1.75x = -3.455x + 9.04$

$10.18x - 8 = -3.455x + 9.04$

$10.18x + 3.455x = 9.04 + 8$

$13.635x = 17.04$

$x = 1.\overline{2497}$

The solution is $1.\overline{2497}$. If we clear fractions first, we get the answer in fraction form, $\dfrac{1136}{909}$.

108. 4.423346424

109. $-2[3(x - 2) + 4] = 4(5 - x) - 2x$

$-2[3x - 6 + 4] = 20 - 4x - 2x$

$-2[3x - 2] = 20 - 6x$

$-6x + 4 = 20 - 6x$

$4 = 20$ Adding $6x$ to both sides

This is contradiction, so the solution set is $\emptyset$.

110. $-\dfrac{7}{2}$

111.
$$3(x+4) = 3(4+x)$$
$$3x + 12 = 12 + 3x$$
$$3x + 12 - 12 = 12 + 3x - 12$$
$$3x = 3x$$

This is an identity. The solution set is the set of all real numbers.

112. $\emptyset$; contradiction

113.
$$2x(x+5) - 3(x^2 + 2x - 1) = 9 - 5x - x^2$$
$$2x^2 + 10x - 3x^2 - 6x + 3 = 9 - 5x - x^2$$
$$-x^2 + 4x + 3 = 9 - 5x - x^2$$
$$4x + 3 = 9 - 5x \quad \text{Adding } x^2$$
$$4x + 5x = 9 - 3$$
$$9x = 6$$
$$x = \frac{2}{3}$$

The solution is $\frac{2}{3}$.

114. -2

115.
$$9 - 3x = 2(5 - 2x) - (1 - 5x)$$
$$9 - 3x = 10 - 4x - 1 + 5x$$
$$9 - 3x = 9 + x$$
$$9 - 9 = x + 3x$$
$$0 = 4x$$
$$0 = x$$

The solution is 0.

116. All real numbers; identity

117. $[7 - 2(8 \div (-2))]x = 0$

Since $7 - 2(8 \div (-2)) \neq 0$ and the product on the left side of the equation is 0, then x must be 0.

118. $\frac{52}{45}$

119.
$$\frac{5x+3}{4} + \frac{25}{12} = \frac{5+2x}{3}$$
$$12\left(\frac{5x+3}{4} + \frac{25}{12}\right) = 12\left(\frac{5+2x}{3}\right)$$
$$12\left(\frac{5x+3}{4}\right) + 12 \cdot \frac{25}{12} = 4(5+2x)$$
$$3(5x+3) + 25 = 4(5+2x)$$
$$15x + 9 + 25 = 20 + 8x$$
$$15x + 34 = 20 + 8x$$
$$7x = -14$$
$$x = -2$$

The solution is -2.

120. All real numbers; identity

121.
$$3\{7 - 2[7x - 4]\} = -40x + 45$$
$$3\{7 - 14x + 8\} = -40x + 45$$
$$3\{15 - 14x\} = -40x + 45$$
$$45 - 42x = -40x + 45$$
$$0 = 2x$$
$$0 = x$$

The solution set is $\{0\}$.

122. $\emptyset$; contradiction

Exercise Set 2.3

1. We substitute 10 for t and calculate M.
$$M = \frac{1}{5} \cdot 10 = 2$$
The storm is 2 miles away.

2. 3450 watts

3. We substitute 21,345 for n and calculate f.
$$f = \frac{21,345}{15} = 1423$$
There are 1423 full-time equivalent students.

4. 54 in^2

5. We substitute 84 for c and 8 for w and calculate D.
$$D = \frac{c}{w} = \frac{84}{8} = 10.5$$
The calorie density is 10.5 calories/oz.

6. $\frac{43}{3}$ m/cycle, or $14.\overline{3}$ m/cycle

7. Enter $y = 0.5x^4 + 3.45x^3 - 96.65x^2 + 347.7x$. Then use a table set in Ask Mode to find the desired values.

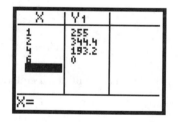

After 1 hr, 255 mg of ibuprofen remain; after 2 hr, 344.4 mg remain; after 4 hr, 193.2 mg remain; and after 6 hr, 0 mg remain.

8. 42; 90; 132; 210

9. $A = bh$
$$\frac{A}{h} = \frac{bh}{h} \quad \text{Dividing both sides by } h$$
$$\frac{A}{h} = b$$

10. $h = \frac{A}{b}$

11. $d = rt$

$\dfrac{d}{t} = \dfrac{rt}{t}$ Dividing both sides by t

$\dfrac{d}{t} = r$

12. $t = \dfrac{d}{r}$

13. $I = Prt$

$\dfrac{I}{rt} = \dfrac{Prt}{rt}$ Dividing both sides by rt

$\dfrac{I}{rt} = P$

14. $t = \dfrac{I}{Pr}$

15. $II = 65 - m$

$H + m = 65$ Adding m to both sides

$m = 65 - H$ Subtracting H from both sides

16. $h = d + 64$

17. $P = 2l + 2w$

$P - 2w = 2l + 2w - 2w$ Subtracting $2w$ from both sides

$P - 2w = 2l$

$\dfrac{P - 2w}{2} = \dfrac{2l}{2}$ Dividing both sides by 2

$\dfrac{P - 2w}{2} = l$, or

$\dfrac{P}{2} - w = l$

18. $w = \dfrac{P - 2l}{2}$, or $\dfrac{P}{2} - l$

19. $A = \pi r^2$

$\dfrac{A}{r^2} = \dfrac{\pi r^2}{r^2}$

$\dfrac{A}{r^2} = \pi$

20. $r^2 = \dfrac{A}{\pi}$

21. $A = \dfrac{1}{2}bh$

$2A = 2 \cdot \dfrac{1}{2}bh$ Multiplying both sides by 2

$2A = bh$

$\dfrac{2A}{b} = \dfrac{bh}{b}$ Dividing both sides by h

$\dfrac{2A}{b} = h$

22. $b = \dfrac{2A}{h}$

23. $E = mc^2$

$\dfrac{E}{c^2} = \dfrac{mc^2}{c^2}$ Dividing both sides by c^2

$\dfrac{E}{c^2} = m$

24. $c^2 = \dfrac{E}{m}$

25. $Q = \dfrac{c + d}{2}$

$2Q = 2 \cdot \dfrac{c + d}{2}$ Multiplying both sides by 2

$2Q = c + d$

$2Q - c = c + d - c$ Subtracting c from both sides

$2Q - c = d$

26. $p = 2Q + q$

27. $A = \dfrac{a + b + c}{3}$

$3A = 3 \cdot \dfrac{a + b + c}{3}$ Multiplying both sides by 3

$3A = a + b + c$

$3A - a - c = a + b + c - a - c$ Subtracting a and c from both sides

$3A \; a - c - b$

28. $c = 3A - a - b$

29. $M = \dfrac{A}{s}$

$s \cdot M = s \cdot \dfrac{A}{s}$ Multiplying both sides by s

$sM = A$

30. $b = \dfrac{Pc}{a}$

31. $A = at + bt$

$A = t(a + b)$ Factoring

$\dfrac{A}{a + b} = t$ Dividing both sides by $a + b$

32. $x = \dfrac{S}{r + s}$

33. $A = \dfrac{1}{2}ah + \dfrac{1}{2}bh$

$2A = 2\left(\dfrac{1}{2}ah + \dfrac{1}{2}bh\right)$

$2A = ah + bh$

$2A = h(a + b)$

$\dfrac{2A}{a + b} = h$

34. $P = \dfrac{A}{1 + rt}$

35.
$$R = r + \frac{400(W - L)}{N}$$
$$N \cdot R = N\left(r + \frac{400(W - L)}{N}\right)$$
Multiplying both sides by N
$$NR = Nr + 400(W - L)$$
$$NR = Nr + 400W - 400L$$
$$NR + 400L = Nr + 400W \quad \text{Adding } 400L \text{ to both sides}$$
$$400L = Nr + 400W - NR \quad \text{Adding } -NR \text{ to both sides}$$
$$L = \frac{Nr + 400W - NR}{400}, \text{ or}$$
$$W - \frac{N(R - r)}{400}$$

36. $r^2 = \dfrac{360A}{\pi S}$

37. *Writing Exercise*

38. *Writing Exercise*

39. $0.79(38.4)0$

One factor is 0, so the product is 0.

40. 9.18

41.
$$20 \div (-4) \cdot 2 - 3$$
$$= -5 \cdot 2 - 3 \quad \text{Dividing and}$$
$$= -10 - 3 \quad \text{multiplying from left to right}$$
$$= -13 \quad \text{Subtracting}$$

42. 65

43. *Writing Exercise*

44. *Writing Exercise*

45.
$$K = 19.18w + 7h - 9.52a + 92.4$$
$$2627 = 19.18(82) + 7(185) - 9.52a + 92.4$$
$$2627 = 1572.76 + 1295 - 9.52a + 92.4$$
$$2627 = 2960.16 - 9.52a$$
$$-333.16 = -9.52a$$
$$35 \approx a$$

The man is about 35 years old.

46. $T = t - \dfrac{h}{100}°, \ 0 \le h \le 12,000$

47.
$$c = \frac{w}{a} \cdot d$$
$$ac = a \cdot \frac{w}{a} \cdot d$$
$$ac = wd$$
$$a = \frac{wd}{c}$$

48. About 76.4 in.

49.
$$\frac{y}{z} \div \frac{z}{t} = 1$$
$$\frac{y}{z} \cdot \frac{t}{z} = 1$$
$$\frac{yt}{z^2} = 1$$
$$\frac{z^2}{t} \cdot \frac{yt}{z^2} = \frac{z^2}{t} \cdot 1$$
$$y = \frac{z^2}{t}$$

50. $c = \dfrac{d}{a - b}$

51.
$$qt = r(s + t)$$
$$qt = rs + rt$$
$$qt - rt = rs$$
$$t(q - r) = rs$$
$$t = \frac{rs}{q - r}$$

52. $a = \dfrac{c}{3 + b + d}$

53. We subtract the minimum output for a well-insulated house with a square feet from the minimum output for a poorly-insulated house with a square feet. Let S represent the number of BTU's saved.
$$S = 50a - 30a$$
$$S = 20a$$

54. $K = 917 + 13.2276w + 2.3622h - 6a$

55. $K = 19.18\left(\dfrac{w}{2.2046}\right) + 7\left(\dfrac{h}{0.3937}\right) - 9.52a + 92.4$
$$K = 8.70w + 17.78h - 9.52a + 92.4$$

Exercise Set 2.4

1. $82\% = 82 \times 0.01 \quad \text{Replacing } \% \text{ by } \times 0.01$
$$= 0.82$$

2. 0.49

3. $9\% = 9 \times 0.01 \quad \text{Replacing } \% \text{ by } \times 0.01$
$$= 0.09$$

4. 0.913

5. $43.7\% = 43.7 \times 0.01 = 0.437$

6. 0.02

7. $0.46\% = 0.46 \times 0.01 = 0.0046$

8. 0.048

9. 0.29

First move the decimal point two places to the right; then write a % symbol:

0.29.

29%

10. 78%

11. 0.998

First move the decimal point two places to the right; 0.99.8

then write a % symbol: 99.8%

12. 35.8%

13. 1.92

First move the decimal point two places to the right; 1.92.

then write a % symbol: 192%

14. 139%

15. 2.1

First move the decimal point two places to the right; 2.10.

then write a % symbol: 210%

16. 920%

17. 0.0068

First move the decimal point two places to the right; 0.00.68

then write a % symbol: 0.68%

18. 0.95%

19. $\frac{3}{8}$ $\left(\text{Note: } \frac{3}{8} = 0.375\right)$

First move the decimal point two places to the right; 0.37.5

then write a % symbol: 37.5%

20. 75%

21. $\frac{7}{25}$ $\left(\text{Note: } \frac{7}{25} = 0.28\right)$

First move the decimal point two places to the right; 0.28.

then write a % symbol: 28%

22. 80%

23. $\frac{2}{3}$ $\left(\text{Note: } \frac{2}{3} = 0.66\overline{6}\right)$

First move the decimal point two places to the right; 0.66.$\overline{6}$

then write a % symbol: 66.$\overline{6}$%

Since $0.\overline{6} = \frac{2}{3}$, this can also be expressed as $66\frac{2}{3}\%$.

24. $83\frac{1}{3}\%$

25. Translate.

What percent of 68 is 17?

$y \cdot 68 = 17$

We solve the equation and then convert to percent notation.

$$y \cdot 68 = 17$$
$$y = \frac{17}{68}$$
$$y = 0.25 = 25\%$$

The answer is 25%.

26. 26%

27. Translate.

What percent of 125 is 30?

$y \cdot 125 = 30$

We solve the equation and then convert to percent notation.

$$y \cdot 125 = 30$$
$$y = \frac{30}{125}$$
$$y = 0.24 = 24\%$$

The answer is 24%.

28. 19%

29. Translate.

14 is 30% of what number?

$14 = 30\% \cdot y$

We solve the equation.

$$14 = 0.3y \quad (30\% = 0.3)$$
$$\frac{14}{0.3} = y$$
$$46.\overline{6} = y$$

The answer is $46.\overline{6}$, or $46\frac{2}{3}$, or $\frac{140}{3}$.

30. 225

31. Translate.

0.3 is 12% of what number?

$0.3 = 12\% \cdot y$

We solve the equation.

$$0.3 = 0.12y \quad (12\% = 0.12)$$
$$\frac{0.3}{0.12} = y$$
$$2.5 = y$$

The answer is 2.5.

32. 4

33. Translate.

What number is 35% of 240?

$y = 35\% \cdot 240$

We solve the equation.

$$y = 0.35 \cdot 240 \quad (35\% = 0.35)$$
$$y = 84 \qquad \text{Multiplying}$$

The answer is 84.

34. 10,000

35. *Translate.*

$$\underbrace{\text{What percent}}_{y} \quad \text{of} \quad \underset{60}{\downarrow} \quad \underset{=}{\downarrow} \quad \underset{75}{\downarrow}$$

We solve the equation and then convert to percent notation.

$$y \cdot 60 = 75$$
$$y = \frac{75}{60}$$
$$y = 1.25 = 125\%$$

The answer is 125%.

36. 100%

37. *Translate.*

$$\underset{x}{\downarrow} \quad \underset{=}{\downarrow} \quad \underset{2\%}{\downarrow} \quad \underset{\cdot}{\downarrow} \quad \underset{40}{\downarrow}$$
What is 2% of 40?

We solve the equation.

$$x = 0.02 \cdot 40 \qquad (2\% = 0.02)$$
$$x = 0.8 \qquad \text{Multiplying}$$

The answer is 0.8.

38. 0.8

39. Observe that 25 is half of 50. Thus, the answer is 0.5, or 50%. We could also do this exercise by translating to an equation.

Translate.

$$\underset{25}{\downarrow} \quad \underset{=}{\downarrow} \quad \underbrace{\text{what percent}}_{y} \quad \text{of} \quad \underset{\cdot}{\downarrow} \quad \underset{50}{\downarrow}$$
25 is what percent of 50?

We solve the equation and convert to percent notation.

$$25 = y \cdot 50$$
$$\frac{25}{50} = y$$
$$0.5 = y, \text{ or } 50\% = y$$

The answer is 50%.

40. 400

41. Let I = the amount of interest Sarah will pay. Then we have:

$$\underset{I}{\downarrow} \quad \underset{\text{is}}{\downarrow} \quad \underset{8\%}{\downarrow} \quad \underset{\text{of}}{\downarrow} \quad \underset{\$3500}{\downarrow}$$
$$I = 0.08 \cdot \$3500$$
$$I = \$280$$

Sarah will pay $280 interest.

42. $168

43. Let p = the number of people who voted in the 2000 presidential election, in millions. Then we have:

$$\underset{48.62}{\downarrow} \quad \underset{\text{is}}{\downarrow} \quad \underset{48.36\%}{\downarrow} \quad \underset{\text{of}}{\downarrow} \underset{p}{\downarrow}$$
$$48.62 = 0.4836 \cdot p$$
$$\frac{48.62}{0.4836} = p$$
$$100.5 \approx p$$

About 100.5 million people voted in the 2000 presidential election.

44. About $11.9 billion

45. If n = the number of women who had babies in good or excellent health, we have:

$$\underset{n}{\downarrow} \underset{\text{is}}{\downarrow} \quad \underset{8\%}{\downarrow} \quad \underset{\text{of}}{\downarrow} \quad \underset{300}{\downarrow}$$
$$n = 0.08 \cdot 300$$
$$n = 24$$

24 women had babies in good or excellent health.

46. 285 women

47. Let a = the number of pounds of almonds the average American consumes each year. Then we have:

$$\underset{a}{\downarrow} \underset{\text{is}}{\downarrow} \quad \underset{25\%}{\downarrow} \quad \underset{\text{of}}{\downarrow} \quad \underset{2.25}{\downarrow}$$
$$a = 0.25 \cdot 2.25$$
$$a = 0.5625$$

The average American consumes 0.5625 lb of almonds each year.

48. 7410 brochures

49. Let b = the number of bowlers you would expect to be left-handed. Then we have:

$$\underset{b}{\downarrow} \underset{\text{is}}{\downarrow} \quad \underset{17\%}{\downarrow} \quad \underset{\text{of}}{\downarrow} \quad \underset{160}{\downarrow}$$
$$b = 0.17 \cdot 160$$
$$b \approx 27$$

You would expect 27 bowlers to be left-handed.

50. 7%

51. Let p = the percent that were correct. Then we have:

$$\underset{76}{\downarrow} \underset{\text{is}}{\downarrow} \quad \underbrace{\text{what percent}}_{p} \quad \text{of} \quad \underset{\cdot}{\downarrow} \underset{88}{\downarrow}$$
$$\frac{76}{88} = p$$
$$0.86\overline{4} = p, \text{ or }$$
$$86.\overline{4}\%, \text{ or } 86\frac{4}{11}\% = p$$

$86\frac{4}{11}\%$, or $86.\overline{4}\%$ of the items were correct.

52. 52%

53. When the sales tax is 5%, the total amount paid is 105% of the cost of the merchandise. Let c = the cost of the merchandise. Then we have:

$$\underset{37.80}{\downarrow} \quad \underset{\text{is}}{\downarrow} \quad \underset{105\%}{\downarrow} \quad \underset{\text{of}}{\downarrow} \underset{c}{\downarrow}$$
$$37.80 = 1.05 \cdot c$$
$$\frac{37.80}{1.05} = c$$
$$36 = c$$

The price of the merchandise was $36.

54. $940

55. The number of calories in a serving of Light Style Bread is 85% of the number of calories in a serving of regular bread. Let $c =$ the number of calories in a serving of regular bread. Then we have:

$$\underbrace{140 \text{ calories}}_{\downarrow} \text{ is } \underset{\downarrow}{85\%} \underset{\downarrow}{\text{ of }} \underset{\downarrow}{c}.$$

$$140 = 0.85 \cdot c$$

$$\frac{140}{0.85} = c$$

$$165 \approx c$$

There are about 165 calories in a serving of regular bread.

56. 58 calories

57. a) Self-employment income must be 20% more than non-self-employment income. That is, self-employment income must be 120% of non-self-employment income. Let $x =$ non-self-employment income and $y =$ the corresponding self-employment income. Then we have:

$$\underbrace{\text{Self-employment income}}_{\downarrow} \text{ is } \underset{\downarrow}{120\%} \underset{\downarrow}{\text{ of }} \underbrace{\text{non-self-employment income.}}_{\downarrow}$$

$$y = 1.2 \cdot x$$

Enter $y = 1.2x$ on a graphing calculator and create a table for values of x between $12 and $18.

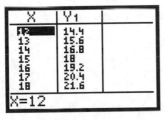

b) From the table we see that $y = 18$ when $x = 15$, so Trey would need to earn $18 per hour.

58. a)

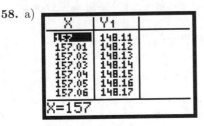

b) $148.50

59. *Writing Exercise*

60. *Writing Exercise*

61. Let n represent "some number." Then we have $n + 5$, or $5 + n$.

62. Let w represent Tino's weight; $w - 4$

63. $8 \cdot 2a$, or $2a \cdot 8$.

64. Let m and n represent the numbers; $mn + 1$, or $1 + mn$

65. *Writing Exercise*

66. *Writing Exercise*

67. Let $p =$ the population of Bardville. Then we have:

$$1332 \text{ is } 15\% \text{ of } 48\% \text{ of } \underbrace{\text{the population.}}_{\downarrow}$$

$$1332 = 0.15 \cdot 0.48 \cdot p$$

$$\frac{1332}{0.15(0.48)} = p$$

$$18,500 = p$$

The population of Bardville is 18,500.

68. Rollie's: $12.83; Sound Warp: $12.97

69. The new price is 125% of the old price. Let $p =$ the new price. Then we have:

$$p \text{ is } 125\% \text{ of } \$20,800.$$

$$p = 1.25 \cdot 20,800$$

$$p = 26,000$$

Now let $x =$ the percent of the new price represented by the old price. We have:

$$\$20,800 \text{ is } \underbrace{\text{what percent}}_{\downarrow} \text{ of } \$26,000.$$

$$20,800 = x \cdot 26,000$$

$$\frac{20,800}{26,000} = x$$

$$0.8 = x, \text{ or}$$

$$80\% = x$$

The old price is $100\% - 80\%$, or 20% lower than the new price.

70. $35\frac{5}{37}\%$

71. The number of births increased by $3.94 - 3.88$, or 0.06 million. Let $p =$ the percent of increase. Then we have:

$$\underbrace{0.06 \text{ million}}_{\downarrow} \text{ is } \underbrace{\text{what percent}}_{\downarrow} \text{ of } \underbrace{3.88 \text{ million?}}_{\downarrow}$$

$$0.06 = p \cdot 3.88$$

$$\frac{0.06}{3.88} = p$$

$$0.0155 \approx p, \text{ or}$$

$$1.55\% \approx p$$

The number of births increased by about 1.55%.

72. *Writing Exercise*

73. *Writing Exercise*

Exercise Set 2.5

1. Familiarize. Let x = the number. Then "three less than twice a number" translates to $2x - 3$.

Translate.

$$\underbrace{\text{Three less than twice a number}}_{2x - 3} \ \ \underset{=}{\text{is}} \ \ \underset{19}{\text{19.}}$$

Carry out. We solve the equation.

$$2x - 3 = 19$$
$$2x = 22 \quad \text{Adding 3}$$
$$x = 11 \quad \text{Dividing by 2}$$

Check. Twice, or two times, 11 is 22. Three less than 22 is 19. The answer checks.

State. The number is 11.

2. 8

3. Familiarize. Let a = the number. Then "five times the sum of 3 and some number" translates to $5(a + 3)$.

Translate.

$$\underbrace{\substack{\text{Five times the sum of} \\ \text{3 and some number}}}_{5(a+3)} \ \ \underset{=}{\text{is}} \ \ \underset{70}{\text{70.}}$$

Carry out. We solve the equation.

$$5(a + 3) = 70$$
$$5a + 15 = 70 \quad \text{Using the distributive law}$$
$$5a = 55 \quad \text{Subtracting 15}$$
$$a = 11 \quad \text{Dividing by 5}$$

Check. The sum of 3 and 11 is 14, and $5 \cdot 14 = 70$. The answer checks.

State. The number is 11.

4. 13

5. Familiarize. Let p = the regular price of the shoes. At 15% off, Amy paid 85% of the regular price.

Translate.

$$\underset{63.75}{\text{\$63.75}} \ \underset{=}{\text{is}} \ \underset{0.85}{\text{85\%}} \ \underset{\cdot}{\text{of}} \ \underbrace{\text{the regular price.}}_{p}$$

Carry out. We solve the equation.

$$63.75 = 0.85p$$
$$\frac{63.75}{0.08} = p \qquad \text{Dividing both sides by 0.85}$$
$$75 = p$$

Check. 85% of $75, or 0.85($75), is $63.75. The answer checks.

State. The regular price was $75.

6. $90

7. Familiarize. Let b = the price of the book itself. When the sales tax rate is 5%, the tax paid on the book is 5% of b, or $0.05b$.

Translate.

$$\underbrace{\text{Price of book}}_{b} \ \underset{+}{\text{plus}} \ \underbrace{\text{sales tax}}_{0.05b} \ \underset{=}{\text{is}} \ \underset{89.25}{\text{\$89.25.}}$$

Carry out. We solve the equation.

$$b + 0.05b = 89.25$$
$$1.05b = 89.25$$
$$b = \frac{89.25}{1.05}$$
$$b = 85$$

Check. 5% of $85, or 0.05($85), is $4.25 and $85 + $4.25 is $89.25, the total cost. The answer checks.

State. The book itself cost $85.

8. $95

9. Familiarize. Let d = Kouros' distance, in miles, from the start after 8 hr. Then the distance from the finish line is $2d$.

Translate.

$$\underbrace{\substack{\text{Distance} \\ \text{from start}}}_{d} \ \underset{+}{\text{plus}} \ \underbrace{\substack{\text{distance} \\ \text{from finish}}}_{2d} \ \underset{=}{\text{is 188 mi.}} \ \underset{188}{}$$

Carry out. We solve the equation.

$$d + 2d = 188$$
$$3d = 188$$
$$d = \frac{188}{3}, \text{ or } 62\frac{2}{3}$$

Check. If Kouros is $\frac{188}{3}$ mi from the start, then he is $2 \cdot \frac{188}{3}$, or $\frac{376}{3}$ mi from the finish. Since $\frac{188}{3} + \frac{376}{3} = \frac{564}{3} = 188$, the total distance run, the answer checks.

State. Kouros had run $62\frac{2}{3}$ mi.

10. $699\frac{1}{3}$ mi

11. Familiarize. Let x = the first page number. Then $x + 1$ = the second page number, and $x + 2$ = the third page number.

Translate.

$$\underbrace{\substack{\text{The sum of three} \\ \text{consecutive page numbers}}}_{x + (x+1) + (x+2)} \ \underset{=}{\text{is 60.}} \ \underset{60}{}$$

Carry out. We solve the equation.

$$x + (x + 1) + (x + 2) = 60$$

$$3x + 3 = 60 \quad \text{Combining like terms}$$

$$3x = 57 \quad \text{Subtracting 3 from both sides}$$

$$x = 19 \quad \text{Dividing both sides by 3}$$

If x is 19, then $x + 1$ is 20 and $x + 2 = 21$.

Check. 19, 20, and 21 are consecutive integers, and $19 + 20 + 21 = 60$. The result checks.

State. The page numbers are 19, 20, and 21.

12. 32, 33, 34

13. ***Familiarize.*** Let x = the smaller odd number. Then $x + 2$ = the next odd number.

Translate. We reword the problem.

Smaller odd number + next odd number is 60.

$$x + (x + 2) = 60$$

Carry out. We solve the equation.

$$x + (x + 2) = 60$$

$$2x + 2 = 60 \quad \text{Combining like terms}$$

$$2x = 58 \quad \text{Subtracting 2 from both sides}$$

$$x = 29 \quad \text{Dividing both sides by 2}$$

If x is 29, then $x + 2$ is 31.

Check. 29 and 31 are consecutive odd integers, and their sum is 60. The answer checks.

State. The integers are 29 and 31.

14. 53, 55

15. ***Familiarize.*** Let x = the first even integer. Then $x + 2$ = the next even integer.

Translate.

The sum of two consecutive even integers is 126.

$$x + (x + 2) = 126$$

Carry out. We solve the equation.

$$x + (x + 2) = 126$$

$$2x + 2 = 126 \quad \text{Combining like terms}$$

$$2x = 124 \quad \text{Subtracting 2 from both sides}$$

$$x = 62 \quad \text{Dividing both sides by 2}$$

If x is 62, then $x + 2$ is 64.

Check. 62 and 64 are consecutive even integers, and $62 + 64 = 126$. The result checks.

State. The numbers are 62 and 64.

16. 24, 26

17. ***Familiarize.*** Let b = the bride's age. Then $b + 19$ = the groom's age.

Translate.

Bride's age plus groom's age is 187.

$$b + b + 19 = 187$$

Carry out. We solve the equation.

$$b + (b + 19) = 187$$

$$2b + 19 = 187$$

$$2b = 168$$

$$b = 84$$

If b is 84, then $b + 19$ is 103.

Check. 103 is 19 more than 84, and $84 + 103 = 187$. The answer checks.

State. The bride was 84 yr old, and the groom was 103 yr old.

18. Man: 97 yr; woman: 91 yr

19. ***Familiarize.*** We draw a picture. We let x = the measure of the first angle. Then $3x$ = the measure of the second angle, and $x + 30$ = the measure of the third angle.

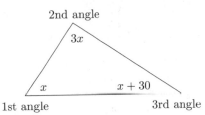

Recall that the measures of the angles of any triangle add up to $180°$.

Translate.

Measure of first angle + measure of second angle +

$$x + 3x +$$

measure of third angle is $180°$.

$$x + 30 = 180$$

Carry out. We solve the equation.

$$x + 3x + (x + 30) = 180$$

$$5x + 30 = 180$$

$$5x = 150$$

$$x = 30$$

Possible answers for the angle measures are as follows:

First angle: $x = 30°$

Second angle: $3x = 3(30)° = 90°$

Third angle: $x + 30° = 30° + 30° = 60°$

Check. Consider $30°$, $90°$, and $60°$. The second angle is three times the first, and the third is $30°$ more than the first. The sum of the measures of the angles is 180°. These numbers check.

State. The measure of the first angle is 30°, the measure of the second angle is 90°, and the measure of the third angle is 60°.

20. 22.5°, 90°, 67.5°

21. Familiarize. Let $x =$ the measure of the first angle. Then $3x =$ the measure of the second angle, and $x + 3x + 10 = 4x + 10 =$ the measure of the third angle. Recall that the sum of the measures of the angles of a triangle is 180°.

Translate.

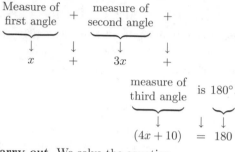

Carry out. We solve the equation.
$$x + 3x + (4x + 10) = 180$$
$$8x + 10 = 180$$
$$8x = 170$$
$$x = 21.25$$

If x is 21.25, then $3x$ is 63.75, and $4x + 10$ is 95.

Check. Consider 21.25°, 63.75°, and 95°. The second is three times the first, and the third is 10° more than the sum of the other two. The sum of the measures of the angles is 180°. These numbers check.

State. The measure of the third angle is 95°.

22. 70°

23. Familiarize. The page numbers are consecutive integers. If we let $p =$ the smaller number, then $p + 1 =$ the larger number.

Translate. We reword the problem.

$$\underbrace{\text{First integer}}_{x} + \underbrace{\text{Second integer}}_{(x+1)} = 385$$

Carry out. We solve the equation.
$$x + (x + 1) = 385$$
$$2x + 1 = 385 \quad \text{Combining like terms}$$
$$2x = 384 \quad \text{Adding } -1 \text{ on both sides}$$
$$x = 192 \quad \text{Dividing on both sides by 2}$$

Check. If $x = 192$, then $x + 1 = 193$. These are consecutive integers, and $192 + 193 = 385$. The answer checks.

State. The page numbers are 192 and 193.

24. 140, 141

25. Familiarize. Let $s =$ the length of the shortest side, in mm. Then $s + 2$ and $s + 4$ represent the lengths of the other two sides. The perimeter is the sum of the lengths of the sides.

Translate.

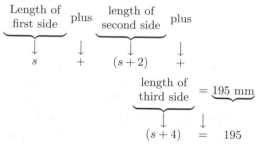

Carry out. We solve the equation.
$$s + (s + 2) + (s + 4) = 195$$
$$3s + 6 = 195$$
$$3s = 189$$
$$s = 63$$

If s is 63, then $s + 2$ is 65 and $s + 4$ is 67.

Check. The numbers 63, 65, and 67 are consecutive odd integers. Their sum is 195. These numbers check.

State. The lengths of the sides of the triangle are 63 mm, 65 mm, and 67 mm.

26. Width: 100 ft; length: 160 ft; $16,000$ ft^2

27. Familiarize. We draw a picture. Let $l =$ the length of the state, in miles. Then $l - 90 =$ the width.

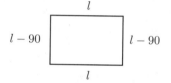

The perimeter is the sum of the lengths of the sides.

Translate. We use the definition of perimeter to write an equation.

$$\underbrace{\text{Width}}_{(l-90)} + \underbrace{\text{Width}}_{(l-90)} + \underbrace{\text{Length}}_{l} + \underbrace{\text{Length}}_{l} \text{ is } 1280.$$

Carry out. We solve the equation.
$$(l - 90) + (l - 90) + l + l = 1280$$
$$4l - 180 = 1280$$
$$4l = 1460$$
$$l = 365$$

Then $l - 90 = 275$.

Check. The width, 275 mi, is 90 mi less than the length, 365 mi. The perimeter is 275 mi + 275 mi + 365 mi + 365 mi, or 1280 mi. This checks.

State. The length is 365 mi, and the width is 275 mi.

28. Length: 27.9 cm; width: 21.6 cm

29. Familiarize. Let a = the amount Sarah invested. The investment grew by 28% of a, or $0.28a$.

Translate.

Amount invested	plus	amount of growth	is	$448.
↓	↓	↓	↓	↓
a	$+$	$0.28a$	$=$	448

Carry out. We solve the equation.

$$a + 0.28a = 448$$
$$1.28a = 448$$
$$a = 350$$

Check. 28% of $350 is 0.28($350), or $98, and $350 + $98 = $448. The answer checks.

State. Sarah invested $350.

30. $6600

31. Familiarize. Let b = the balance in the account at the beginning of the month. The balance grew by 2% of b, or $0.02b$.

Translate.

Original balance	plus	amount of growth	is	$870.
↓	↓	↓	↓	↓
b	$+$	$0.02b$	$=$	870

Carry out. We solve the equation.

$$b + 0.02b = 870$$
$$1.02b = 870$$
$$b \approx \$852.94$$

Check. 2% of $852.94 is 0.02($852.94), or $17.06, and $852.94 + $17.06 = $870. The answer checks.

State. The balance at the beginning of the month was $852.94.

32. $6540

33. Familiarize. The total cost is the initial charge plus the mileage charge. Let d = the distance, in miles, that Courtney can travel for $12. The mileage charge is the cost per mile times the number of miles traveled or $0.75d$.

Translate.

Initial charge	plus	mileage charge	is	$12.
↓	↓	↓	↓	↓
3	$+$	$0.75d$	$=$	12

Carry out. We solve the equation.

$$3 + 0.75d = 12$$
$$0.75d = 9$$
$$d = 12$$

Check. A 12-mi taxi ride from the airport would cost $3 + 12($0.75), or $3 + $9, or $12. The answer checks.

State. Courtney can travel 12 mi from the airport for $12.

34. 15 mi

35. Familiarize. The total cost is the daily charge plus the mileage charge. Let d = the distance that can be traveled, in miles, in one day for $100. The mileage charge is the cost per mile times the number of miles traveled, or $0.39d$.

Translate.

Daily rate	plus	mileage charge	is	$100.
↓	↓	↓	↓	↓
49.95	$+$	$0.39d$	$=$	100

Carry out. We solve the equation.

$$49.95 + 0.39d = 100$$
$$0.39d = 50.05$$
$$d = 128.\overline{3}, \text{ or } 128\frac{1}{3}$$

Check. For a trip of $128\frac{1}{3}$ mi, the mileage charge is $\$0.39\left(128\frac{1}{3}\right)$, or $50.05, and $49.95 + $50.05 = $100. The answer checks.

State. They can travel $128\frac{1}{3}$ mi in one day and stay within their budget.

36. 80 mi

37. Familiarize. Let x = the measure of one angle. Then $90 - x$ = the measure of its complement.

Translate.

Measure of one angle	is 15°	more than	twice the measure of its complement.
↓	↓ ↓	↓	↓
x	$= 15$	$+$	$2(90 - x)$

Carry out. We solve the equation.

$$x = 15 + 2(90 - x)$$
$$x = 15 + 180 - 2x$$
$$x = 195 - 2x$$
$$3x = 195$$
$$x = 65$$

If x is 65, then $90 - x$ is 25.

Check. The sum of the angle measures is 90°. Also, 65° is 15° more than twice its complement, 25°. The answer checks.

State. The angle measures are 65° and 25°.

38. 105°, 75°

39. Familiarize. We will use the equation

$$T = \frac{1}{4}N + 40.$$

Translate. We substitute 80 for T.

$$80 = \frac{1}{4}N + 40$$

Carry out. We solve the equation.

$$80 = \frac{1}{4}N + 40$$

$$40 = \frac{1}{4}N$$

$$160 = N \qquad \text{Multiplying by 4 on both}$$
$$\text{sides}$$

Check. When $N = 160$, we have $T = \frac{1}{4} \cdot 160 + 40 = 40 + 40 = 80$. The answer checks.

State. A cricket chirps 160 times per minute when the temperature is 80°F.

40. 2020

41. *Familiarize.* We examine the values in the table. Observe that when we divide the number of gallons by the corresponding number of inches, we get the same quotient each time:

$$100 \div 20 = 5;$$
$$120 \div 24 = 5;$$
$$200 \div 40 = 5;$$
$$250 \div 50 = 5.$$

We see that 5 gallons are required for each inch of fish. Let g = the number of gallons that would be needed for 30 inches of fish.

Translate. We reword and translate.

The size of aquarium	is 5 times	the number of inches of fish.
↓	↓ ↓ ↓	↓
g	$= 5 \cdot$	30

Carry out. We carry out the calculation.

$$g = 5 \cdot 30$$
$$g = 150$$

Check. We see that $150 \div 30 = 5$, so the answer checks.

State. A 150-gallon aquarium is needed for 30 inches of fish.

42. 2.85 days

43. *Familiarize.* We examine the values in the table. Observe that the pumpkin's weight increases by 30 pounds each day:

From August 1 to August 2: $410 - 380 = 30$ lb;

from August 2 to August 3: $440 - 410 = 30$ lb;

from August 3 to August 4: $470 - 440 = 30$ lb;

from August 4 to August 11 (11 − 4, or 7 days):

$$680 - 470 = 210 = 7 \cdot 30 \text{ lb};$$

from August 11 to August 25 (25 − 11, or 14 days):

$$1100 - 680 = 420 = 14 \cdot 30 \text{ lb}.$$

Let d = the number of days after August 1 on which the pumpkin weighed 920 pounds.

Translate. We reword and translate.

Weight on August 1	plus 30 times	number of days after August 1	is 920 pounds.
↓	↓ ↓ ↓	↓	↓ ↓
380	$+ 30 \cdot$	d	$= 920$

Carry out. We solve the equation.

$$380 + 30 \cdot d = 920$$
$$30d = 920 - 380$$
$$30d = 540$$
$$d = 18$$

Check. We use a table to check. Enter $y = 380 + 30x$ in a graphing calculator and set up a table in Ask mode. Enter the x-values as the number of days after August 1: 0, 1, 2, 3, 10, 24, and 18. We see that we get the values given in the statement of the problem for the first 6 x-values and the x-value 18 gives a weight of 920 pounds. The answer checks.

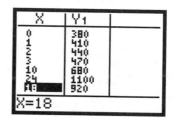

State. The pumpkin weighed 920 pounds 18 days after August 1, or on August 19.

44. 2700 ft^2

45. *Writing Exercise*

46. *Writing Exercise*

47. Since -9 is to the left of 5 on the number line, we have $-9 < 5$.

48. $<$

49. Since -4 is to the left of 7 on the number line, we have $-4 < 7$.

50. $>$

51. *Writing Exercise*

52. *Writing Exercise*

53. *Familiarize.* Let c = the amount the meal originally cost. The 15% tip is calculated on the original cost of the meal, so the tip is $0.15c$.

Translate.

Original cost	plus	tip	less	$10	is	$32.55.
↓	↓	↓	↓	↓	↓	↓
c	$+$	$0.15c$	$-$	10	$=$	32.55

Carry out. We solve the equation.

$$c + 0.15c - 10 = 32.55$$
$$1.15c - 10 = 32.55$$
$$1.15c = 42.55$$
$$c = 37$$

Check. If the meal originally cost $37, the tip was 15% of $37, or 0.15($37), or $5.55. Since $37 + $5.55 − $10 = $32.55, the answer checks.

State. The meal originally cost $37.

54. 19 questions

55. *Familiarize.* Let s = one score. Then four score = $4s$ and four score and seven = $4s + 7$.

Translate. We reword .

$$\underbrace{1776}_{\downarrow} \quad \underbrace{\text{plus}}_{\downarrow} \quad \underbrace{\text{four score and seven}}_{\downarrow} \quad \underbrace{\text{is}}_{\downarrow} \quad \underbrace{1863}_{\downarrow}$$
$$1776 \quad + \quad (4s + 7) \quad = \quad 1863$$

Carry out. We solve the equation.
$$1776 + (4s + 7) = 1863$$
$$4s + 1783 = 1863$$
$$4s = 80$$
$$s = 20$$

Check. If a score is 20 years, then four score and seven represents 87 years. Adding 87 to 1776 we get 1863. This checks.

State. A score is 20.

56. 4, 16

57. *Familiarize.* We let x = the length of the original rectangle. Then $\frac{3}{4}x$ = the width. We draw a picture of the enlarged rectangle. Each dimension is increased by 2 cm, so $x + 2$ = the length of the enlarged rectangle and $\frac{3}{4}x + 2$ = the width.

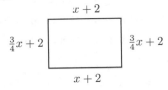

Translate. We use the perimeter of the enlarged rectangle to write an equation.

$$\underset{\downarrow}{\text{Width}} + \underset{\downarrow}{\text{Width}} + \underset{\downarrow}{\text{Length}} + \underset{\downarrow}{\text{Length is}}$$
$$\left(\frac{3}{4}x + 2\right) + \left(\frac{3}{4}x + 2\right) + (x + 2) + (x + 2) =$$

$$\underset{\downarrow}{\text{Perimeter.}}$$
$$50$$

Carry out.
$$\left(\frac{3}{4}x + 2\right) + \left(\frac{3}{4}x + 2\right) + (x + 2) + (x + 2) = 50$$
$$\frac{7}{2}x + 8 = 50$$
$$2\left(\frac{7}{2}x + 8\right) = 2 \cdot 50$$
$$7x + 16 = 100$$
$$7x = 84$$
$$x = 12$$

Then $\frac{3}{4}x = \frac{3}{4}(12) = 9$.

Check. If the dimensions of the original rectangle are 12 cm and 9 cm, then the dimensions of the enlarged rectangle are 14 cm and 11 cm. The perimeter of the enlarged rectangle is $11 + 11 + 14 + 14 = 50$ cm. Also, 9 is $\frac{3}{4}$ of 12. These values check.

State. The length is 12 cm, and the width is 9 cm.

58. 87°, 89°, 91°, 93°

59. *Familiarize.* Let x = the first even number. Then the next four even numbers are $x+2$, $x+4$, $x+6$, and $x+8$. The sum of the measures of the angles of an n-sided polygon is given by the formula $(n - 2) \cdot 180°$. Thus, the sum of the measures of the angles of a pentagon is $(5 - 2) \cdot 180°$, or $3 \cdot 180°$, or $540°$.

Translate.

$$\underbrace{\text{The sum of the measures}}_{\text{of the angles}} \qquad \underset{\downarrow \quad \downarrow}{\text{is } 540°.}$$
$$x + (x + 2) + (x + 4) + (x + 6) + (x + 8) = 540$$

Carry out. We solve the equation.
$$x + (x + 2) + (x + 4) + (x + 6) + (x + 8) = 540$$
$$5x + 20 = 540$$
$$5x = 520$$
$$x = 104$$

If x is 104, then the other numbers are 106, 108, 110, and 112.

Check. The numbers 104, 106, 108, 110, and 112 are consecutive odd numbers. Their sum is 540. The answer checks.

State. The measures of the angles are 104°, 106°, 108°, 110°, and 112°.

60. 120 apples

61. *Familiarize.* Let p = the price before the two discounts. With the first 10% discount, the price becomes 90% of p, or $0.9p$. With the second 10% discount, the final price is 90% of $0.9p$, or $0.9(0.9p)$.

Translate.
$$\underbrace{\text{The final price}}_{\downarrow} \underset{\downarrow \quad \downarrow}{\text{ is \$77.75.}}$$
$$0.9(0.9p) \quad = \quad 77.75$$

Carry out. We solve the equation.
$$0.9(0.9p) = 77.75$$
$$p = \frac{77.75}{0.9(0.9)}$$
$$p \approx 95.99$$

Check. 90% of $95.99 is $86.39 and 90% of $86.39 is $77.75. The answer checks.

State. The price before the two discounts was $95.99.

62. 30 games

63. Familiarize. Let $n =$ the number of CD's purchased. Assume that two or more CD's were purchased. Then the first CD costs \$8.49 and the total cost of the remaining $n-1$ CD's is \$3.99$(n-1)$. The shipping and handling costs are \$2.47 for the first CD, \$2.28 for the second, and a total of \$1.99$(n-2)$ for the remaining $n-2$ CD's. Then the total cost of the shipment is \$8.49 + \$3.99$(n-1)$ + \$2.47 + \$2.28 + \$1.99$(n-2)$.

Translate.

$$\underbrace{\text{Total cost of shipment}}_{8.49+3.99(n-1)+2.47+2.28+1.99(n-2)} \quad \underset{=}{\text{was}} \quad \underset{65.07}{\$65.07.}$$

Carry out. We solve the equation.

$$8.49 + 3.99(n-1) + 2.47 + 2.28 + 1.99(n-2) = 65.07$$

$$8.49 + 3.99n - 3.99 + 2.47 + 2.28 + 1.99n - 3.98 = 65.07$$

$$5.27 + 5.98n = 65.07$$

$$5.98n = 59.80$$

$$n = 10$$

Check. If 10 CD's are purchased, the total cost of the CD's is \$8.49 + \$3.99(9) = \$44.40. The total shipping and handling costs are \$2.47 + \$2.28 + \$1.99(8) = \$20.67. Then the total cost of the order is \$44.40 + \$20.67 = \$65.07.

State. There were 10 CD's in the shipment.

64. 76

65. Familiarize. At \$0.30 per $\frac{1}{5}$ mile, the mileage charge can also be given as 5(\$0.30), or \$1.50 per mile. Since it took 20 min to complete what is usually a 10-min drive, the taxi was stopped in traffic for $20 - 10$, or 10, min. Let $d =$ the distance, in miles, that Glenda traveled.

Translate.

$$\underbrace{\text{Initial charge}}_{2} \; \underset{+}{\text{plus}} \; \underbrace{\text{mileage charge}}_{1.5d} \; \underset{+}{\text{plus}} \; \underbrace{\begin{array}{c}\text{charge for}\\\text{being}\\\text{stopped}\\\text{in traffic}\end{array}}_{0.2(10)} \; \underset{=}{\text{is}} \; \underset{13}{\$13.}$$

Carry out. We solve the equation.

$$2 + 1.5d + 0.2(10) = 13$$

$$2 + 1.5d + 2 = 13$$

$$1.5d + 4 = 13$$

$$1.5d = 9$$

$$d = 6$$

Check. The mileage charge for traveling 6 mi is \$1.50(6) = \$9. The charge for being stopped in traffic is \$0.20(10) = \$2. Since \$2 + \$9 + \$2 = \$13, the answer checks.

State. Glenda traveled 6 mi.

66. *Writing Exercise*

67. *Writing Exercise*

68. Width: 23.31 cm; length: 27.56 cm

69. Familiarize. Let $s =$ the length of the first side, in cm. Then $s + 3.25 =$ the length of the second side, and $(s + 3.25) + 4.35$, or $s + 7.6 =$ the length of the third side.

Translate.

$$\underbrace{\text{The perimeter}}_{s + (s + 3.25) + (s + 7.6)} \; \underset{=}{\text{is}} \; \underbrace{\text{26.87 cm.}}_{26.87}$$

Carry out. We solve the equation.

$$s + (s + 3.25) + (s + 7.6) = 26.87$$

$$3s + 10.85 = 26.87$$

$$3s = 16.02$$

$$s = 5.34$$

If $s = 5.34$, then $s + 3.25 = 8.59$, and $s + 7.6 = 12.94$.

Check. Consider sides of 5.34 cm, 8.59 cm, and 12.94 cm. The second side is 3.25 cm longer than the first side, and the third side is 4.35 cm longer than the second side. The sum of the lengths of the sides is 26.87. The answer checks.

State. The lengths of the sides are 5.34 cm, 8.59 cm, and 12.94 cm.

Exercise Set 2.6

1. $x > -2$

a) Since $5 > -2$ is true, 5 is a solution.

b) Since $0 > -2$ is true, 0 is a solution.

c) Since $-1.9 > -2$ is true, -1.9 is a solution.

d) Since $-7.3 > -2$ is false, -7.3 is not a solution.

e) Since $1.6 > -2$ is true, 1.6 is a solution.

2. a) Yes, b) No, c) Yes, d) Yes, e) No

3. $x \geq 6$

a) Since $-6 \geq 6$ is false, -6 is not a solution.

b) Since $0 \geq 6$ is false, 0 is not a solution.

c) Since $6 \geq 6$ is true, 6 is a solution.

d) Since $6.01 \geq 6$ is true, 6.01 is a solution.

e) Since $-3\frac{1}{2} \geq 6$ is false, $-3\frac{1}{2}$ is not a solution.

4. a) Yes, b) Yes, c) Yes, d) No, e) Yes

5. The solutions of $x \leq 7$ are shown by shading the point 7 and all points to the left of 7. The closed circle at 7 indicates that 7 is part of the graph.

6.

7. The solutions of $t > -2$ are those numbers greater than -2. They are shown on the graph by shading all points to the right of -2. The open circle at -2 indicates that -2 is not part of the graph.

$$t > -2$$

8.

$$y > 4$$

9. The solutions of $1 \leq m$, or $m \geq 1$, are those numbers greater than or equal to 1. They are shown on the graph by shading the point 1 and all points to the right of 1. The closed circle at 1 indicates that 1 is part of the graph.

$$1 \leq m$$

10.

$$t \geq 0$$

11. In order to be a solution of the inequality $-3 < x \leq 5$, a number must be a solution of both $-3 < x$ and $x \leq 5$. The solution set is graphed as follows:

$$-3 < x \leq 5$$

The open circle at -3 means that -3 is not part of the graph. The closed circle at 5 means that 5 is part of the graph.

12.

$$-5 \leq x < 2$$

13. In order to be a solution of the inequality $0 < x < 3$, a number must be a solution of both $0 < x$ and $x < 3$. The solution set is graphed as follows:

$$0 < x < 3$$

The open circles at 0 and at 3 mean that 0 and 3 are not part of the graph.

14.

$$-5 \leq x \leq 0$$

15. All points to the right of -4 are shaded. The open circle at -4 indicates that -4 is not part of the graph. We have $\{x | x > -4\}$, or $(-4, \infty)$.

16. $\{x | x < 3\}$, or $(-\infty, 3)$

17. The point 2 and all points to the left of 2 are shaded. We have $\{x | x \leq 2\}$, or $(-\infty, 2]$.

18. $\{x | x \geq -2\}$, or $[-2, \infty)$

19. All points to the left of -1 are shaded. The open circle at -1 indicates that -1 is not part of the graph. We have $\{x | x < -1\}$, or $(-\infty, -1)$.

20. $\{x | x > 1\}$, or $(1, \infty)$

21. The point 0 and all points to the right of 0 are shaded. We have $\{x | x \geq 0\}$, or $[0, \infty)$.

22. $\{x | x \leq 0\}$, or $(-\infty, 0]$

23.
$$y + 2 > 9$$
$$y + 2 - 2 > 9 - 2 \quad \text{Adding } -2 \text{ to both sides}$$
$$y > 7 \quad \text{Simplifying}$$

The solution set is $\{y | y > 7\}$, or $(7, \infty)$. The graph is as follows:

24. $\{y | y > 3\}$, or $(3, \infty)$

25.
$$x + 8 \leq -10$$
$$x + 8 - 8 \leq -10 - 8 \quad \text{Subtracting 8 from both sides}$$
$$x \leq -18 \quad \text{Simplifying}$$

The solution set is $\{x | x \leq -18\}$, or $(-\infty, -18]$. The graph is as follows:

26. $\{x | x \leq -21\}$, or $(-\infty, -21]$

27.
$$x - 3 < 7$$
$$x - 3 + 3 < 7 + 3$$
$$x < 10$$

The solution set is $\{x | x < 10\}$, or $(-\infty, 10)$. The graph is as follows:

28. $\{x | x < 17\}$, or $(-\infty, 17)$

29.
$$5 \leq t + 8$$
$$5 - 8 \leq t + 8 - 8$$
$$-3 \leq t$$

The solution set is $\{t | -3 \leq t\}$, or $\{t | t \geq -3\}$, or $[-3, \infty)$. The graph is as follows:

30. $\{t | t \geq -5\}$, or $[-5, \infty)$

31.
$$y - 7 > -12$$
$$y - 7 + 7 > -12 + 7$$
$$y > -5$$

The solution set is $\{y|y > -5\}$, or $(-5, \infty)$. The graph is as follows:

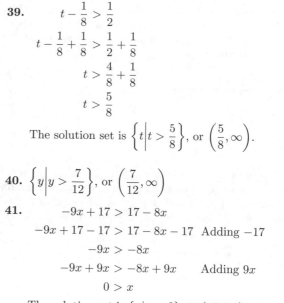

32. $\{y|y > -6\}$, or $(-6, \infty)$

33.
$$2x + 4 \le x + 9$$
$$2x + 4 - 4 \le x + 9 - 4 \quad \text{Adding } -4$$
$$2x \le x + 5 \quad \text{Simplifying}$$
$$2x - x \le x + 5 - x \quad \text{Adding } -x$$
$$x \le 5 \quad \text{Simplifying}$$

The solution set is $\{x|x \le 5\}$, or $(-\infty, 5]$. The graph is as follows:

34. $\{x|x \le -3\}$, or $(-\infty, -3]$

35.
$$5x - 6 \ge 4x - 1$$
$$5x - 6 + 6 \ge 4x - 1 + 6 \quad \text{Adding 6 to both sides}$$
$$5x \ge 4x + 5$$
$$5x - 4x \ge 4x + 5 - 4x \quad \text{Adding } -4x \text{ to both sides}$$
$$x \ge 5$$

The solution set is $\{x|x \ge 5\}$, or $[5, \infty)$.

36. $\{x|x \ge 20\}$, or $[20, \infty)$

37.
$$y + \frac{1}{3} \le \frac{5}{6}$$
$$y + \frac{1}{3} - \frac{1}{3} \le \frac{5}{6} - \frac{1}{3}$$
$$y \le \frac{5}{6} - \frac{2}{6}$$
$$y \le \frac{3}{6}$$
$$y \le \frac{1}{2}$$

The solution set is $\left\{y \middle| y \le \frac{1}{2}\right\}$, or $\left(-\infty, \frac{1}{2}\right]$.

38. $\left\{x \middle| x \le \frac{1}{4}\right\}$, or $\left(-\infty, \frac{1}{4}\right]$

39.
$$t - \frac{1}{8} > \frac{1}{2}$$
$$t - \frac{1}{8} + \frac{1}{8} > \frac{1}{2} + \frac{1}{8}$$
$$t > \frac{4}{8} + \frac{1}{8}$$
$$t > \frac{5}{8}$$

The solution set is $\left\{t \middle| t > \frac{5}{8}\right\}$, or $\left(\frac{5}{8}, \infty\right)$.

40. $\left\{y \middle| y > \frac{7}{12}\right\}$, or $\left(\frac{7}{12}, \infty\right)$

41.
$$-9x + 17 > 17 - 8x$$
$$-9x + 17 - 17 > 17 - 8x - 17 \quad \text{Adding } -17$$
$$-9x > -8x$$
$$-9x + 9x > -8x + 9x \quad \text{Adding } 9x$$
$$0 > x$$

The solution set is $\{x|x < 0\}$, or $(-\infty, 0)$.

42. $\{n|n < 0\}$, or $(-\infty, 0)$

43. $-23 < -t$

The inequality states that the opposite of 23 is less than the opposite of t. Thus, t must be less than 23, so the solution set is $\{t|t < 23\}$. To solve this inequality using the addition principle, we would proceed as follows:
$$-23 < -t$$
$$t - 23 < 0 \quad \text{Adding } t \text{ to both sides}$$
$$t < 23 \quad \text{Adding 23 to both sides}$$

The solution set is $\{t|t < 23\}$, or $(-\infty, 23)$.

44. $\{x|x < -19\}$, or $(-\infty, -19)$

45.
$$5x < 35$$
$$\frac{1}{5} \cdot 5x < \frac{1}{5} \cdot 35 \quad \text{Multiplying by } \frac{1}{5}$$
$$x < 7$$

The solution set is $\{x|x < 7\}$, or $(-\infty, 7)$. The graph is as follows:

46. $\{x|x \ge 4\}$, or $[4, \infty)$

47.
$$9y \le 81$$
$$\frac{1}{9} \cdot 9y \le \frac{1}{9} \cdot 81 \quad \text{Multiplying by } \frac{1}{9}$$
$$y \le 9$$

The solution set is $\{y|y \le 9\}$, or $(-\infty, 9]$. The graph is as follows:

48. $\{t|t < 35\}$, or $(-\infty, 35)$

49.
$$-7x < 13$$
$$-\frac{1}{7} \cdot (-7x) > -\frac{1}{7} \cdot 13 \quad \text{Multiplying by } -\frac{1}{7}$$
$$\qquad\qquad\qquad \text{The symbol has to be reversed.}$$
$$x > -\frac{13}{7} \quad \text{Simplifying}$$

The solution set is $\left\{x \middle| x > -\frac{13}{7}\right\}$, or $\left(-\frac{13}{7}, \infty\right)$.

50. $\left\{y \middle| y < \frac{17}{8}\right\}$, or $\left(-\infty, \frac{17}{8}\right)$

51.
$$-24 > 8t$$
$$-3 > t$$

The solution set is $\{t|t < -3\}$, or $(-\infty, -3)$.

52. $\{x|x > 4\}$, or $(4, \infty)$

53.
$$7y \geq -2$$
$$\frac{1}{7} \cdot 7y \geq \frac{1}{7}(-2) \quad \text{Multiplying by } \frac{1}{7}$$
$$y \geq -\frac{2}{7}$$

The solution set is $\left\{y \middle| y \geq -\frac{2}{7}\right\}$, or $\left[-\frac{2}{7}, \infty\right)$.

54. $\left\{x \middle| x > -\frac{3}{5}\right\}$, or $\left(-\frac{3}{5}, \infty\right)$

55.
$$-2y \leq \frac{1}{5}$$
$$-\frac{1}{2} \cdot (-2y) \geq -\frac{1}{2} \cdot \frac{1}{5}$$
$$\qquad\qquad\qquad \text{The symbol has to be reversed.}$$
$$y \geq -\frac{1}{10}$$

The solution set is $\left\{y \middle| y \geq -\frac{1}{10}\right\}$, or $\left[-\frac{1}{10}, \infty\right)$.

56. $\left\{x \middle| x \leq -\frac{1}{10}\right\}$, or $\left(-\infty, -\frac{1}{10}\right]$

57.
$$-\frac{8}{5} > -2x$$
$$-\frac{1}{2} \cdot \left(-\frac{8}{5}\right) < -\frac{1}{2} \cdot (-2x)$$
$$\frac{8}{10} < x$$
$$\frac{4}{5} < x, \text{ or } x > \frac{4}{5}$$

The solution set is $\left\{x \middle| \frac{4}{5} < x\right\}$, or $\left\{x \middle| x > \frac{4}{5}\right\}$, or $\left(\frac{4}{5}, \infty\right)$.

58. $\left\{y \middle| y < \frac{1}{16}\right\}$, or $\left(-\infty, \frac{1}{16}\right)$

59.
$$7 + 3x < 34$$
$$7 + 3x - 7 < 34 - 7 \quad \text{Adding } -7 \text{ to both sides}$$
$$3x < 27 \qquad\quad \text{Simplifying}$$
$$x < 9 \qquad\qquad \text{Multiplying both sides}$$
$$\qquad\qquad\qquad\qquad \text{by } \frac{1}{3}$$

The solution set is $\{x|x < 9\}$, or $(-\infty, 9)$.

60. $\{y|y < 8\}$, or $(-\infty, 8)$

61.
$$6 + 5y \geq 26$$
$$6 + 5y - 6 \geq 26 - 6 \quad \text{Adding } -6$$
$$5y \geq 20$$
$$y \geq 4 \qquad \text{Multiplying by } \frac{1}{5}$$

The solution set is $\{y|y \geq 4\}$, or $[4, \infty)$.

62. $\{x|x \geq 8\}$, or $[8, \infty)$

63.
$$4t - 5 \leq 23$$
$$4t - 5 + 5 \leq 23 + 5 \quad \text{Adding 5 to both sides}$$
$$4t \leq 28$$
$$\frac{1}{4} \cdot 4t \leq \frac{1}{4} \cdot 28 \quad \text{Multiplying both sides}$$
$$\qquad\qquad\qquad\qquad \text{by } \frac{1}{4}$$
$$x \leq 7$$

The solution set is $\{x|x \leq 7\}$, or $(-\infty, 7]$.

64. $\{y|y \leq 6\}$, or $(-\infty, 6]$

65.
$$13x - 7 < -46$$
$$13x - 7 + 7 < -46 + 7$$
$$13x < -39$$
$$\frac{1}{13} \cdot 13x < \frac{1}{13} \cdot (-39)$$
$$x < -3$$

The solution set is $\{x|x < -3\}$, or $(-\infty, -3)$.

66. $\{y|y < -6\}$, or $(-\infty, -6)$

67.
$$16 < 4 - 3y$$
$$16 - 4 < 4 - 3y - 4 \qquad \text{Adding } -4 \text{ to both sides}$$
$$12 < -3y$$
$$-\frac{1}{3} \cdot 12 > -\frac{1}{3} \cdot (-3y) \qquad \text{Multiplying by } -\frac{1}{3}$$
$$\underline{\uparrow} \text{ The symbol has to be reversed.}$$
$$-4 > y$$

The solution set is $\{y|-4 > y\}$, or $\{y|y < -4\}$, or $(-\infty, -4)$.

68. $\{x|x < -2\}$, or $(-\infty, -2)$

69.
$$39 > 3 - 9x$$
$$39 - 3 > 3 - 9x - 3 \qquad \text{Adding } -3$$
$$36 > -9x$$
$$-\frac{1}{9} \cdot 36 < -\frac{1}{9} \cdot (-9x) \qquad \text{Multiplying by } -\frac{1}{9}$$
$$\underline{\uparrow} \text{ The symbol has to be reversed.}$$
$$-4 < x$$

The solution set is $\{x|-4 < x\}$, or $\{x|x > -4\}$, or $(-4, \infty)$.

70. $\{y|y > -5\}$, or $(-5, \infty)$

71.
$$5 - 6y > 25$$
$$-5 + 5 - 6y > -5 + 25$$
$$-6y > 20$$
$$-\frac{1}{6} \cdot (-6y) < -\frac{1}{6} \cdot 20$$
$$\underline{\uparrow} \text{ The symbol has to be reversed.}$$
$$y < -\frac{20}{6}$$
$$y < -\frac{10}{3}$$

The solution set is $\left\{y\middle|y < -\frac{10}{3}\right\}$, or $\left(-\infty, -\frac{10}{3}\right)$.

72. $\{y|y < -3\}$, or $(-\infty, -3)$

73.
$$-3 < 8x + 7 - 7x$$
$$-3 < x + 7 \qquad \text{Collecting like terms}$$
$$-3 - 7 < x + 7 - 7$$
$$-10 < x$$

The solution set is $\{x|-10 < x\}$, or $\{x|x > -10\}$, or $(-10, \infty)$.

74. $\{x|x > -13\}$, or $(-13, \infty)$

75.
$$6 - 4y > 4 - 3y$$
$$6 - 4y + 4y > 4 - 3y + 4y \qquad \text{Adding } 4y$$
$$6 > 4 + y$$
$$-4 + 6 > -4 + 4 + y \qquad \text{Adding } -4$$
$$2 > y, \text{ or } y < 2$$

The solution set is $\{y|2 > y\}$, or $\{y|y < 2\}$, or $(-\infty, 2)$.

76. $\{y|y < 2\}$, or $(-\infty, 2)$

77.
$$7 - 9y \leq 4 - 8y$$
$$7 - 9y + 9y \leq 4 - 8y + 9y$$
$$7 \leq 4 + y$$
$$-4 + 7 \leq -4 + 4 + y$$
$$3 \leq y, \text{ or } y \geq 3$$

The solution set is $\{y|3 \leq y\}$, or $\{y|y \geq 3\}$, or $[3, \infty)$.

78. $\{y|y \geq 2\}$, or $[2, \infty)$

79.
$$33 - 12x < 4x + 97$$
$$33 - 12x - 97 < 4x + 97 - 97$$
$$-64 - 12x < 4x$$
$$-64 - 12x + 12x < 4x + 12x$$
$$-64 < 16x$$
$$-4 < x$$

The solution set is $\{x|-4 < x\}$, or $\{x|x > -4\}$, or $(-4, \infty)$.

80. $\left\{x\middle|x < \frac{9}{5}\right\}$, or $\left(-\infty, \frac{9}{5}\right)$

81.
$$2.1x + 43.2 > 1.2 - 8.4x$$
$$10(2.1x + 43.2) > 10(1.2 - 8.4x) \quad \text{Multiplying by}$$
$$\text{10 to clear decimals}$$
$$21x + 432 > 12 - 84x$$
$$21x + 84x > 12 - 432 \quad \text{Adding } 84x \text{ and}$$
$$-432$$
$$105x > -420$$
$$x > -4 \qquad \text{Multiplying by } \frac{1}{105}$$

The solution set is $\{x|x > -4\}$, or $(-4, \infty)$.

82. $\left\{y\middle|y \leq \frac{5}{3}\right\}$, or $\left(-\infty, \frac{5}{3}\right]$

83.
$$0.7n - 15 + n \geq 2n - 8 - 0.4n$$
$$1.7n - 15 \geq 1.6n - 8 \qquad \text{Collecting like terms}$$
$$10(1.7n - 15) \geq 10(1.6n - 8) \qquad \text{Multiplying by 10}$$
$$17n - 150 \geq 16n - 80$$
$$17n - 16n \geq -80 + 150 \quad \text{Adding } -16n \text{ and}$$
$$150$$
$$n \geq 70$$

The solution set is $\{n|n \geq 70\}$, or $[70, \infty)$.

84. $\{t|t > 1\}$, or $(1, \infty)$

85.
$$\frac{x}{3} - 4 \leq 1$$
$$3\left(\frac{x}{3} - 4\right) \leq 3 \cdot 1 \qquad \text{Multiplying by 3 to}$$
$$\text{to clear the fraction}$$
$$x - 12 \leq 3 \qquad \text{Simplifying}$$
$$x \leq 15 \qquad \text{Adding 12}$$

The solution set is $\{x|x \leq 15\}$, or $(-\infty, 15]$.

86. $\{x|x > 2\}$, or $(2, \infty)$

87.
$$3 < 5 - \frac{t}{7}$$
$$-2 < -\frac{t}{7}$$
$$-7(-2) > -7\left(-\frac{t}{7}\right)$$
$$14 > t$$

The solution set is $\{t|t < 14\}$, or $(-\infty, 14)$.

88. $\{x|x > 35\}$, or $(35, \infty)$

89. $4(2y - 3) < 36$

$8y - 12 < 36$ Removing parentheses

$8y < 48$ Adding 12

$y < 6$ Multiplying by $\frac{1}{8}$

The solution set is $\{y | y < 6\}$, or $(-\infty, 6)$.

90. $\{y | y > 5\}$, or $(5, \infty)$

91. $3(t - 2) \geq 9(t + 2)$

$3t - 6 \geq 9t + 18$

$3t - 9t > 18 + 6$

$-6t \geq 24$

$t \leq -4$ Multiplying by $-\frac{1}{6}$ and reversing the symbol

The solution set is $\{t | t \leq -4\}$, or $(-\infty, -4]$.

92. $\left\{ t \Big| t < -\frac{5}{3} \right\}$, or $\left(-\infty, -\frac{5}{3} \right)$

93. $3(r - 6) + 2 < 4(r + 2) - 21$

$3r - 18 + 2 < 4r + 8 - 21$

$3r - 16 < 4r - 13$

$-16 + 13 < 4r - 3r$

$-3 < r$, or $r > -3$

The solution set is $\{r | r > -3\}$, or $(-3, \infty)$.

94. $\{t | t > -12\}$, or $(-12, \infty)$

95. $\frac{2}{3}(2x - 1) \geq 10$

$\frac{3}{2} \cdot \frac{2}{3}(2x - 1) \geq \frac{3}{2} \cdot 10$ Multiplying by $\frac{3}{2}$

$2x - 1 \geq 15$

$2x \geq 16$

$x \geq 8$

The solution set is $\{x | x \geq 8\}$, or $[8, \infty)$.

96. $\{x | x \leq 7\}$, or $(-\infty, 7]$

97. $\frac{3}{4}\left(3x - \frac{1}{2}\right) - \frac{2}{3} < \frac{1}{3}$

$\frac{3}{4}\left(3x - \frac{1}{2}\right) < 1$ Adding $\frac{2}{3}$

$\frac{9}{4}x - \frac{3}{8} < 1$ Removing parentheses

$8 \cdot \left(\frac{9}{4}x - \frac{3}{8}\right) < 8 \cdot 1$ Clearing fractions

$18x - 3 < 8$

$18x < 11$

$x < \frac{11}{18}$

The solution set is $\left\{ x \Big| x < \frac{11}{18} \right\}$, or $\left(-\infty, \frac{11}{8} \right)$.

98. $\left\{ x \Big| x > -\frac{5}{32} \right\}$, or $\left(-\frac{5}{32}, \infty \right)$

99. *Writing Exercise*

100. *Writing Exercise*

101. Let n represent "some number." Then we have $n + 3$, or $3 + n$.

102. Let x and y represent the numbers; $2(x + y)$

103. Let x represent "a number." Then we have $2x - 3$.

104. Let y represent "a number;" $2y + 5$, or $5 + 2y$

105. *Writing Exercise*

106. *Writing Exercise*

107. $6[4 - 2(6 + 3t)] > 5[3(7 - t) - 4(8 + 2t)] - 20$

$6[4 - 12 - 6t] > 5[21 - 3t - 32 - 8t] - 20$

$6[-8 - 6t] > 5[-11 - 11t] - 20$

$-48 - 36t > -55 - 55t - 20$

$-48 - 36t > -75 - 55t$

$-36t + 55t > -75 + 48$

$19t > -27$

$t > -\frac{27}{19}$

The solution set is $\left\{ t \Big| t > -\frac{27}{19} \right\}$, or $\left(-\frac{27}{19}, \infty \right)$.

108. $\left\{ x \Big| x \leq \frac{5}{6} \right\}$, or $\left(-\infty, \frac{5}{6} \right]$

109. $-(x + 5) \geq 4a - 5$

$-x - 5 \geq 4a - 5$

$-x \geq 4a - 5 + 5$

$-x \geq 4a$

$-1(-x) \leq -1 \cdot 4a$

$x \leq -4a$

The solution set is $\{x | x \leq -4a\}$.

110. $\{x | x > 7\}$

111. $y < ax + b$ Assume $a > 0$.

$y - b < ax$

$\frac{y - b}{a} < x$ Since $a > 0$, the inequality symbol stays the same.

The solution set is $\left\{ x \Big| x > \frac{y - b}{a} \right\}$.

112. $\left\{ x \Big| x < \frac{y - b}{a} \right\}$

113. $|x| < 3$

a) Since $|3.2| = 3.2$, and $3.2 < 3$ is false, 3.2 is not a solution.

b) Since $|-2| = 2$ and $2 < 3$ is true, -2 is a solution.

c) Since $|-3| = 3$ and $3 < 3$ is false, -3 is not a solution.

d) Since $|-2.9| = 2.9$ and $2.9 < 3$ is true, -2.9 is a solution.

e) Since $|3| = 3$ and $3 < 3$ is false, 3 is not a solution.

f) Since $|1.7| = 1.7$ and $1.7 < 3$ is true, 1.7 is a solution.

114.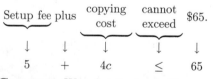

115. $|x| > -3$

Since absolute value is always nonnegative, the absolute value of any real number will be greater than -3. Thus, the solution set is $\{x | x$ is a real number$\}$, or $(-\infty, \infty)$.

116. $\emptyset$

Exercise Set 2.7

1. Let n represent the number. Then we have
$$n \geq 7.$$

2. Let n represent the number; $n \geq 5$

3. Let b represent the weight of the baby, in kilograms. Then we have
$$b > 2.$$

4. Let p represent the number of people who attended the concert; $75 < p < 100$

5. Let s represent the average speed, in mph. Then we have
$$90 < s < 110.$$

6. Let n represent the number of people who attended the Million Man March; $n \geq 400,000$

7. Let a represent the number of people who attended the Million Man March. Then we have
$$a \leq 1,200,000.$$

8. Let a represent the amount of acid, in liters; $a \leq 40$

9. Let c represent the cost, per gallon, of gasoline. Then we have
$$c \geq \$1.50.$$

10. Let t represent the temperature; $t \leq -2$

11. *Familiarize.* Let $c =$ the number of copies Myra has made. The total cost of the copies is the setup fee of \$5 plus \$4 times the number of copies, or \$4 · c.

Translate.

Setup fee	plus	copying cost	cannot exceed	\$65.
↓	↓	↓	↓	↓
5	+	4c	≤	65

Carry out. We solve the inequality.
$$5 + 4c \leq 65$$
$$4c \leq 60$$
$$c \leq 15$$

Check. As a partial check, we show that Myra can have 15 copies made and not exceed her \$65 budget.
$$\$5 + \$4 \cdot 15 = 5 + 60 = \$65$$

State. Myra can have 15 or fewer copies made and stay within her budget.

12. 25 persons

13. *Familiarize.* Let m represent the number of miles per day. Then the cost per day for those miles is \$0.46m. The total cost is the daily rate plus the daily mileage cost. The total cost cannot exceed \$200. In other words the total cost must be less than or equal to \$200, the daily budget.

Translate.

Daily rate	+	Mileage cost	≤	Budget.
↓	↓	↓	↓	↓
42.95	+	0.46m	≤	200

Carry out.
$$42.95 + 0.46m \leq 200$$
$$4295 + 46m \leq 20,000 \quad \text{Clearing decimals}$$
$$46m \leq 15,705$$
$$m \leq \frac{15,705}{46}$$
$$m \leq 341.4 \quad \begin{array}{l}\text{Rounding to the}\\\text{nearest tenth}\end{array}$$

Check. We can check to see if the solution set seems reasonable.

When $m = 342$, the total cost is
$$42.95 + 0.46(342), \text{ or } \$200.27.$$

When $m = 341.4$, the total cost is
$$42.95 + 0.46(341.4), \text{ or } \$199.99.$$

When $m = 341$, the total cost is
$$42.95 + 0.46(341), \text{ or } \$199.81.$$

From these calculations it would appear that $m \leq 341.4$ is the correct solution.

State. To stay within the budget, the number of miles the Letsons drive must not exceed 341.4.

14. 5 min or more

15. *Familiarize.* Let $t =$ the number of hours the car is parked. Then $2t =$ the number of half-hours it is parked. The total parking cost is the initial \$0.45 charge plus \$0.25 per half hour, or \$0.25 · $2t$.

Translate.

Initial charge	plus	charge for time parked	is at least	\$2.20.
↓	↓	↓	↓	↓
0.45	+	0.25 · 2t	≥	2.20

Carry out. We solve the inequality.
$$0.45 + 0.25 \cdot 2t \geq 2.20$$
$$0.45 + 0.5t \geq 2.2$$
$$0.5t \geq 1.75$$
$$t \geq 3.5$$

Check. As a partial check, we can show that the parking charge for 3.5 hr is \$2.20. Note that in 3.5 hr there are 2(3.5), or 7, half-hours.
$$\$0.45 + \$0.25(7) = \$0.45 + \$1.75 = \$2.20.$$

State. Laura's car is generally parked for 3.5 hr or more.

16. More than 2.5 hr

17. *Familiarize.* Let c = the number of courses for which Angelica registers. Her total tuition is the $35 registration fee plus $375 times the number of courses for which she registers, or $375 \cdot c$.

Translate.

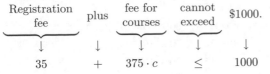

Registration fee	plus	fee for courses	cannot exceed	$1000.
↓	↓	↓	↓	↓
35	+	$375 \cdot c$	≤	1000

Carry out. We solve the inequality.

$$35 + 375c \le 1000$$
$$375c \le 965$$
$$c \le 2.57\overline{3}$$

Check. Although the solution set of the inequality is all numbers less than or equal to $2.57\overline{3}$, since c represents the number of courses for which Angelica registers, we round down to 2. If she registers for 2 courses, her tuition is $35 + \$375 \cdot 2$, or $785 which does not exceed $1000. If she registers for 3 courses, her tuition is $35 + \$375 \cdot 3$, or $1160 which exceeds $1000.

State. Angelica can register for at most 2 courses.

18. Mileages less than or equal to 525.8 mi

19. *Familiarize.* The average of the four scores is their sum divided by the number of tests, 4. We let s represent Nadia's score on the last test.

Translate. The average of the four scores is given by

$$\frac{82 + 76 + 78 + s}{4}.$$

Since this average must be at least 80, this means that it must be greater than or equal to 80. Thus, we can translate the problem to the inequality

$$\frac{82 + 76 + 78 + s}{4} \ge 80.$$

Carry out. We first multiply by 4 to clear the fraction.

$$4\left(\frac{82 + 76 + 78 + s}{4}\right) \ge 4 \cdot 80$$
$$82 + 76 + 78 + s \ge 320$$
$$236 + s \ge 320$$
$$s \ge 84$$

Check. As a partial check, we show that Nadia can get a score of 84 on the fourth test and have an average of at least 80:

$$\frac{82 + 76 + 78 + 84}{4} = \frac{320}{4} = 80.$$

State. Scores of 84 and higher will earn Nadia at least a B.

20. Scores greater than or equal to 97

21. *Familiarize.* Let s = the number of servings of fruits or vegetables Dale eats on Saturday.

Translate.

Average number of fruit or vegetable servings	is at least	5.
↓	↓	↓
$\dfrac{4 + 6 + 7 + 4 + 6 + 4 + s}{7}$	≥	5

Carry out. We first multiply by 7 to clear the fraction.

$$7\left(\frac{4 + 6 + 7 + 4 + 6 + 4 + s}{7}\right) \ge 7 \cdot 5$$
$$4 + 6 + 7 + 4 + 6 + 4 + s \ge 35$$
$$31 + s \ge 35$$
$$s \ge 4$$

Check. As a partial check, we show that Dale can eat 4 servings of fruits or vegetables on Saturday and average at least 5 servings per day for the week:

$$\frac{4 + 6 + 7 + 4 + 6 + 4 + 4}{7} = \frac{35}{7} = 5$$

State. Dale should eat at least 4 servings of fruits or vegetables on Saturday.

22. 8 credits or more

23. *Familiarize.* Let m represent the number of minutes Monroe practices on the seventh day.

Translate.

Average practice time	is at least	20 min.
↓	↓	↓
$\dfrac{15 + 28 + 30 + 0 + 15 + 25 + m}{7}$	≥	20

Carry out. We solve the inequality.

$$\frac{15 + 28 + 30 + 0 + 15 + 25 + m}{7} \ge 20$$
$$7\left(\frac{15 + 28 + 30 + 0 + 15 + 25 + m}{7}\right) \ge 7 \cdot 20$$
$$15 + 28 + 30 + 0 + 15 + 25 + m \ge 140$$
$$113 + m \ge 140$$
$$m \ge 27$$

Check. As a partial check, we show that if Monroe practices 27 min on the seventh day he meets expectations.

$$\frac{15 + 28 + 30 + 0 + 15 + 25 + 27}{7} = 20$$

State. Monroe must practice 27 min or more on the seventh day in order to meet expectations.

24. 21 calls or more

25. *Familiarize.* We first make a drawing. We let l represent the length, in feet.

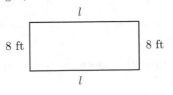

The perimeter is $P = 2l + 2w$, or $2l + 2 \cdot 8$, or $2l + 16$.

Translate. We translate to 2 inequalities.

$$\underbrace{\text{The perimeter}}_{2l + 16} \quad \underbrace{\text{is at least}}_{\geq} \quad \underbrace{200 \text{ ft.}}_{200}$$

$$\underbrace{\text{The perimeter}}_{2l + 16} \quad \underbrace{\text{is at most}}_{\leq} \quad \underbrace{200 \text{ ft.}}_{200}$$

Carry out. We solve each inequality.

$$\begin{array}{ll} 2l + 16 \geq 200 & 2l + 16 \leq 200 \\ 2l \geq 184 & 2l \leq 184 \\ l \geq 92 & l \leq 92 \end{array}$$

Check. We check to see if the solutions seem reasonable.

When $l = 91$ ft, $P = 2 \cdot 91 + 16$, or 198 ft.

When $l = 92$ ft, $P = 2 \cdot 92 + 16$, or 200 ft.

When $l = 93$ ft, $P = 2 \cdot 93 + 16$, or 202 ft.

From these calculations, it appears that the solutions are correct.

State. Lengths greater than or equal to 92 ft will make the perimeter at least 200 ft. Lengths less than or equal to 92 ft will make the perimeter at most 200 ft.

26. Lengths greater than 6 cm

27. Familiarize. We first make a drawing. Let w = the width, in feet. Then $2w$ = the length.

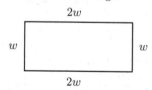

The perimeter is $P = 2l + 2w = 2 \cdot 2w + 2w = 4w + 2w = 6w$.

Translate.

$$\underbrace{\text{The perimeter}}_{6w} \quad \underbrace{\text{cannot exceed}}_{\leq} \quad \underbrace{70 \text{ ft.}}_{70}$$

Carry out. We solve the inequality.

$$6w \leq 70$$
$$w \leq \frac{35}{3}, \text{ or } 11\frac{2}{3}$$

Check. As a partial check we show that the perimeter is 70 ft when the width is $\frac{35}{3}$ ft and the length is $2 \cdot \frac{35}{3}$, or $\frac{70}{3}$ ft.

$$P = 2 \cdot \frac{70}{3} + 2 \cdot \frac{35}{3} = \frac{140}{3} + \frac{70}{3} = \frac{210}{3} = 70$$

State. Widths less than or equal to $11\frac{2}{3}$ ft will meet the given conditions.

28. George: more than 12 hr; Joan: more than 15 hr

29. Familiarize. Let t = the number of 15-min units of time for a road call. Rick's Automotive charges $\$50 + \$15 \cdot t$ for a road call, and Twin City Repair charges $\$70 + \$10 \cdot t$.

Translate.

$$\underbrace{\text{Rick's charge}}_{50 + 15t} \quad \underbrace{\text{is less than}}_{<} \quad \underbrace{\text{Twin City's charge.}}_{70 + 10t}$$

Carry out. We solve the inequality.

$$\begin{aligned} 50 + 15t &< 70 + 10t \\ 15t &< 20 + 10t \\ 5t &< 20 \\ t &< 4 \end{aligned}$$

Check. We check to see if the solution seems reasonable. When $t = 3$, Rick's charges $\$50 + \$15 \cdot 3$, or $\$95$, and Twin City charges $\$70 + \$10 \cdot 3$, or $\$100$. When $t = 4$, Rick's charges $\$50 + \$15 \cdot 4$, or $\$110$, and Twin City charges $\$70 + \$10 \cdot 4$, or $\$110$. When $t = 5$, Rick's charges $\$50 + \$15 \cdot 5$, or $\$125$, and Twin City charges $\$70 + \$10 \cdot 5$, or $\$120$. From these calculations, it appears that the solution is correct.

State. It would be more economical to call Rick's for a service call of less than 4 15-min time units, or of less than 1 hr.

30. At most $49.02

31. Familiarize. We first make a drawing. We let l represent the length.

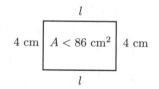

The area is the length times the width, or $4l$.

Translate.

$$\underbrace{\text{Area}}_{4l} \quad \underbrace{\text{is less than}}_{<} \quad \underbrace{86 \text{ cm}^2.}_{86}$$

Carry out.

$$\begin{aligned} 4l &< 86 \\ l &< 21.5 \end{aligned}$$

Check. We check to see if the solution seems reasonable.

When $l = 22$, the area is $22 \cdot 4$, or 88 cm^2.

When $l = 21.5$, the area is $21.5(4)$, or 86 cm^2.

When $l = 21$, the area is $21 \cdot 4$, or 84 cm^2.

From these calculations, it would appear that the solution is correct.

State. The area will be less than 86 cm^2 for lengths less than 21.5 cm.

32. Lengths greater than or equal to 16.5 yd

33. Familiarize. Let v = the blue book value of the car. Since the car was repaired, we know that $\$8500$ does not exceed $0.8v$ or, in other words, $0.8v$ is at least $\$8500$.

Translate.

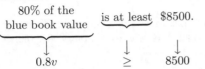

$$0.8v \qquad \geq \qquad 8500$$

Carry out.

$$0.8v \geq 8500$$
$$v \geq \frac{8500}{0.8}$$
$$v \geq 10,625$$

Check. As a partial check, we show that 80% of $10,625 is at least $8500:

$$0.8(\$10,625) = \$8500$$

State. The blue book value of the car was at least $10,625.

34. More than $16,800

35. Familiarize. We will use the formula $F = \frac{9}{5}C + 32$.

Translate.

$$\underbrace{\text{Fahrenheit temperature}}_{F} \quad \underbrace{\text{is above}}_{>} \quad \underbrace{98.6^\circ.}_{98.6}$$

Substituting $\frac{9}{5}C + 32$ for F, we have

$$\frac{9}{5}C + 32 > 98.6.$$

Carry out. We solve the inequality.

$$\frac{9}{5}C + 32 > 98.6$$
$$\frac{9}{5}C > 66.6$$
$$C > \frac{333}{9}$$
$$C > 37$$

Check. We check to see if the solution seems reasonable.

When $C = 36$, $\frac{9}{5} \cdot 36 + 32 = 96.8$.

When $C = 37$, $\frac{9}{5} \cdot 37 + 32 = 98.6$.

When $C = 38$, $\frac{9}{5} \cdot 38 + 32 = 100.4$.

It would appear that the solution is correct, considering that rounding occurred.

State. The human body is feverish for Celsius temperatures greater than 37°.

36. Temperatures less than $31.\overline{1}^\circ$C

37. Familiarize. Let $r =$ the amount of fat in a serving of the regular peanut butter, in grams. If reduced fat peanut butter has at least 25% less fat than regular peanut butter, then it has at most 75% as much fat as the regular peanut butter.

Translate.

$$\underbrace{\text{12 g of fat}}_{12} \quad \underbrace{\text{is at most}}_{\leq} \quad \underbrace{75\%}_{0.75} \quad \underbrace{\text{of}}_{\cdot} \quad \underbrace{\begin{array}{c}\text{the amount of}\\\text{fat in regular}\\\text{peanut butter.}\end{array}}_{r}$$

Carry out.

$$12 \leq 0.75r$$
$$16 \leq r$$

Check. As a partial check, we show that 12 g of fat does not exceed 75% of 16 g of fat:

$$0.75(16) = 12$$

State. Regular peanut butter contains at least 16 g of fat per serving.

38. They contain at least $6\frac{2}{3}$ g of fat per serving.

39. Familiarize. Let $d =$ the depth of the well, in feet. Then the cost on the pay-as-you-go plan is $\$500 + \$8d$. The cost of the guaranteed-water plan is $4000. We want to find the values of d for which the pay-as-you-go plan costs less than the guaranteed-water plan.

Translate.

$$\underbrace{\begin{array}{c}\text{Cost of pay-as-}\\\text{you-go plan}\end{array}}_{500 + 8d} \quad \underbrace{\text{is less than}}_{<} \quad \underbrace{\begin{array}{c}\text{cost of}\\\text{guaranteed-}\\\text{water plan}\end{array}}_{4000}$$

Carry out.

$$500 + 8d < 4000$$
$$8d < 3500$$
$$d < 437.5$$

Check. We check to see that the solution is reasonable.

When $d = 437$, $\$500 + \$8 \cdot 437 = \$3996 < \$4000$

When $d = 437.5$, $\$500 + \$8(437.5) = \$4000$

When $d = 438$, $\$500 + \$8(438) = \$4004 > \$4000$

From these calculations, it appears that the solution is correct.

State. It would save a customer money to use the pay-as-you-go plan for a well of less than 437.5 ft.

40. 8 mi or more

41. Familiarize. Let $m =$ the number of peak local minutes used. Then the charge for the minutes used is $\$0.022m$ and the total monthly charge is $\$13.55 + \$0.022m$.

Translate. We write an inequality stating that the monthly charge is at least $39.40.

$$13.55 + 0.022m \geq 39.40$$

Carry out.

$$13.55 + 0.022m \geq 39.40$$
$$0.022m \geq 25.85$$
$$m \geq 1175$$

Check. We can do a partial check by substituting a value for m less than 1175. When $m = 1174$, the monthly charge is $13.55 + \$0.022(1174) \approx \$39.38$. This is less than the maximum charge of $39.40. We cannot check all possible values for m, so we stop here.

State. A customer must speak on the phone for 1175 local peak minutes or more if the maximum charge is to apply.

42. 5170 minutes or more

43. Familiarize. We list the given information in a table.

Plan A: Monthly Income	Plan B: Monthly Income
$400 salary	$610
8% of sales	5% of sales
Total: 400 + 8% of sales	Total: 610 + 5% of sales

Suppose Toni had gross sales of $5000 one month. Then under plan A she would earn

$400 + 0.08(\$5000)$, or $800.

Under plan B she would earn

$610 + 0.05(\$5000)$, or $860.

This shows that, for gross sales of $5000, plan B is better.

If Toni had gross sales of $10,000 one month, then under plan A she would earn

$400 + 0.08(\$10,000)$, or $1200.

Under plan B she would earn

$610 + 0.05(\$10,000)$, or $1110.

This shows that, for gross sales of $10,000, plan A is better. To determine all values for which plan A is better we solve an inequality.

Translate.

Income from plan A	is greater than	income from plan B.
$400 + 0.08s$	$>$	$610 + 0.05s$

Carry out.

$$400 + 0.08s > 610 + 0.05s$$
$$400 + 0.03s > 610$$
$$0.03s > 210$$
$$s > 7000$$

Check. For $s = \$7000$, the income from plan A is

$400 + 0.08(\$7000)$, or $960

and the income from plan B is

$610 + 0.05(\$7000)$, or $960.

This shows that for sales of $7000 Toni's income is the same from each plan. In the Familiarize step we shows that, for a value less than $7000, plan B is better and, for a value greater than $7000, plan A is better. Since we cannot check all possible values, we stop here.

State. Toni should select plan A for gross sales greater than $7000.

44. Values of n greater than $85\frac{5}{7}$

45. Familiarize. Let $m =$ the amount of the medical bills. Then under plan A Giselle would pay $50 + 0.2(m - \$50)$. Under plan B she would pay $250 + 0.1(m - \$250)$.

Translate. We write an inequality stating than the cost of plan B is less than the cost of plan A.

$$250 + 0.1(m - 250) < 50 + 0.2(m - 50)$$

Carry out.

$$250 + 0.1(m - 250) < 50 + 0.2(m - 50)$$
$$250 + 0.1m - 25 < 50 + 0.2m - 10$$
$$225 + 0.1m < 40 + 0.2m$$
$$185 + 0.1m < 0.2m$$
$$185 < 0.1m$$
$$1850 < m$$

Check. We can do a partial check by substituting a value for m less than $1850 and a value for m greater than $1850. When $m = \$1840$, plan A costs $50 + 0.2(\$1840 - \$50)$, or $408, and plan B costs $250 + 0.1(\$1840 - \$250)$, or $409. When $m = \$1860$, plan A costs $50 + 0.2(\$1860 - \$50)$, or $412, and plan B costs $250 + 0.1(\$1860 - \$250)$, or $411, so plan B will save Giselle money. We cannot check all possible values for m, so we stop here.

State. Plan B will save Giselle money for medical bills greater than $1850.

46. Parties of more than 80

47. Familiarize. Let $n =$ the number of people who attend. Then the total receipts are $6 \cdot n$, and the amount of receipts over $750 is $6 \cdot n - \$750$. The band will receive $750 plus 15% of $6 \cdot n - \$750$, or $750 + 0.15(\$6 \cdot n - \$750)$.

Translate. We write an inequality stating that the amount the band receives is at least $1200.

$$750 + 0.15(6n - 750) \geq 1200$$

Carry out.

$$750 + 0.15(6n - 750) \geq 1200$$
$$750 + 0.9n - 112.5 \geq 1200$$
$$0.9n + 637.5 \geq 1200$$
$$0.9n \geq 562.5$$
$$n \geq 625$$

Check. When $n = 625$, the band receives $75 + 0.15(\$6 \cdot 625 - \$750)$, or $750 + 0.15(\$3000)$, or $750 + \$450$, or $1200. When $n = 626$, the band receives $750 + 0.15(\$6 \cdot 626 - \$750)$, or $750 + 0.15(\$3006)$, or $750 + \$450.90$, or $1200.90. Since the band receives exactly $1200 when 625 people attend and more than $1200 when 626 people attend, we have performed a partial check. We cannot check all possible solutions, so we stop here.

State. At least 625 people must attend in order for the band to receive at least $1200.

48. Dates at least 6 weeks after July 1

49. Familiarize. $R = -0.012t + 20.8$

In the formula R represents the world record in the 200-m dash and t represents the years since 1920. When $t = 0(1920)$, the record was $-0.012(0)+20.8$, or 20.8 sec. When $t = 2(1922)$, the record was $-0.012(2)+20.8$, or 20.776 sec. For what values of t will $-0.012t + 20.8$ be less than 19.8?

Translate. The record is to be less than 19.8. We have the inequality

$$R < 19.8.$$

To find the t values which satisfy this condition we substitute $-0.012t + 20.8$ for R.

$$-0.012t + 20.8 < 19.8$$

Carry out.

$$-0.012t + 20.8 < 19.8$$
$$-0.012t < -1$$
$$t > \frac{-1}{-0.012}$$
$$t > 83.\overline{3}, \text{ or } 83\frac{1}{3}$$

Check. We check to see if the solution set we obtained seems reasonable.

When $t = 83\frac{1}{4}$, $R = -0.012(83.25) + 20.8 = 19.801$.

When $t = 83\frac{1}{3}$, $R = -0.012\left(\frac{250}{3}\right) + 20.8 = 19.8$.

When $t = 83\frac{1}{2}$, $R = -0.012(83.5) + 20.8 - 19.798$.

Since $r = 19.8$ when $t = 83\frac{1}{3}$ and R decreases as t increases, R will be less than 19.8 when t is greater than $83\frac{1}{3}$.

State. The world record will be less than 19.8 seconds when t is greater than $83\frac{1}{3}$ years $\left(\text{more than } 83\frac{1}{3} \text{ years after 1920}\right)$. This occurs in years after 2003.

50. Years after 2005

51. Familiarize. Let $h =$ the height of the triangle, in ft. Recall that the formula for the area of a triangle with base b and height h is $A = \frac{1}{2}bh$.

Translate.

$$\begin{array}{ccc} \text{Area} & \underbrace{\text{is at least}} & \underbrace{3 \text{ ft}^2.} \\ \downarrow & \downarrow & \downarrow \\ \frac{1}{2}\left(1\frac{1}{2}\right)h & \geq & 3 \end{array}$$

Carry out. We solve the inequality.

$$\frac{1}{2}\left(1\frac{1}{2}\right)h \geq 3$$
$$\frac{1}{2} \cdot \frac{3}{2} \cdot h \geq 3$$
$$\frac{3}{4}h \geq 3$$
$$h \geq \frac{4}{3} \cdot 3$$
$$h \geq 3$$

Check. As a partial check, we show that the area of the triangle is 3 ft^2 when the height is 4 ft.

$$\frac{1}{2}\left(1\frac{1}{2}\right)(4) = \frac{1}{2} \cdot \frac{3}{2} \cdot \frac{4}{1} = 3$$

State. The height should be at least 4 ft.

52. Heights less than or equal to 3 ft

53. Familiarize. We will use the equation $y = 0.027x + 0.19$.

Translate.

$$\begin{array}{ccc} \underbrace{\text{The cost}} & \underbrace{\text{is at most}} & \$6. \\ \downarrow & \downarrow & \downarrow \\ 0.027x + 0.19 & \leq & 6 \end{array}$$

Carry out. We solve the inequality.

$$0.027x + 0.19 \leq 6$$
$$0.027x \leq 5.81$$
$$x \leq 215.2 \quad \text{Rounding to the nearest tenth}$$

Check. As a partial check, we show that the cost for driving 215.2 mi is \$6.

$$0.027(215.2) + 0.19 \approx \$6$$

State. The cost will be at most \$6 for mileages less than or equal to 215.2 mi.

54. Years 2001 and beyond

55. *Writing Exercise*

56. *Writing Exercise*

57. $\dfrac{9-5}{6-4} = \dfrac{4}{2} = 2$

58. $\dfrac{1}{2}$

59. $\dfrac{8-(-2)}{1-4} = \dfrac{10}{-3}, \text{ or } -\dfrac{10}{3}$

60. $-\dfrac{1}{5}$

61. *Writing Exercise*

62. *Writing Exercise*

63. Familiarize. Let $h =$ the number of hours the car has been parked. Then $h - 1 =$ the number of hours after the first hour.

Translate.

$$\begin{array}{ccccc} \underbrace{\substack{\text{Charge for} \\ \text{first hour}}} & \text{plus} & \underbrace{\substack{\text{charge for} \\ \text{additional} \\ \text{hours}}} & \text{exceeds} & \$16.50. \\ \downarrow & \downarrow & \downarrow & \downarrow & \downarrow \\ 4.00 & + & 2.50(h-1) & > & 16.50 \end{array}$$

Carry out. We solve the inequality.

$$4.00 + 2.50(h - 1) > 16.50$$

$$40 + 25(h - 1) > 165 \quad \text{Multiplying by 10}$$
$$\text{to clear decimals}$$

$$40 + 25h - 25 > 165$$

$$25h + 15 > 165$$

$$25h > 150$$

$$h > 6$$

Check. We check to see if this solution seems reasonable.

When $h = 5$, $4.00 + 2.50(5 - 1) = 14.00$.

When $h = 6$, $4.00 + 2.50(6 - 1) = 16.50$.

When $h = 7$, $4.00 + 2.50(7 - 1) = 19.00$.

It appears that the solution is correct.

State. The charge exceeds $16.50 when the car has been parked for more than 6 hr.

64. Temperatures between $-15°C$ and $-9\frac{4}{9}°C$

65. Since $8^2 = 64$, the length of a side must be less than or equal to 8 cm (and greater than 0 cm, of course). We can also use the five-step problem-solving procedure.

Familiarize. Let s represent the length of a side of the square. The area s is the square of the length of a side, or s^2.

Translate.

$$\underbrace{\text{The area}}_{\downarrow \atop s^2} \quad \underbrace{\text{is no more than}}_{\downarrow \atop \leq} \quad \underbrace{64 \text{ cm}^2.}_{\downarrow \atop 64}$$

Carry out.

$$s^2 \leq 64$$

$$s^2 - 64 \leq 0$$

$$(s + 8)(s - 8) \leq 0$$

We know that $(s + 8)(s - 8) = 0$ for $s = -8$ or $s = 8$. Now $(s + 8)(s - 8) < 0$ when the two factors have opposite signs. That is:

$s + 8 > 0$ and $s - 8 < 0$ or $s + 8 < 0$ and $s - 8 > 0$

$s > -8$ and $s < 8$ or $s < -8$ and $s > 8$

This can be expressed   This is not possible.

as $-8 < s < 8$.

Then $(s + 8)(s - 8) \leq 0$ for $-8 \leq s \leq 8$.

Check. Since the length of a side cannot be negative we only consider positive values of s, or $0 < s \leq 8$. We check to see if this solution seems reasonable.

When $s = 7$, the area is 7^2, or 49 cm^2.

When $s = 8$, the area is 8^2, or 64 cm^2.

When $s = 9$, the area is 9^2, or 81 cm^2.

From these calculations, it appears that the solution is correct.

State. Sides of length 8 cm or less will allow an area of no more than 64 cm^2. (Of course, the length of a side must be greater than 0 also.)

66. 47 and 49

67. *Familiarize.* Let $f =$ the fat content of a serving of regular tortilla chips, in grams. A product that contains 60% less fat than another product has 40% of the fat content of that product. If Reduced Fat Tortilla Pops cannot be labeled lowfat, then they contain at least 3 g of fat.

Translate.

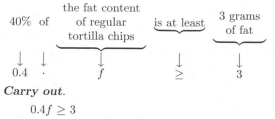

Carry out.

$$0.4f \geq 3$$

$$f \geq 7.5$$

Check. As a partial check, we show that 40% of 7.5 g is not less than 3 g.

$$0.4(7.5) = 3$$

State. A serving of regular tortilla chips contains at least 7.5 g of fat.

68. Between 5 and 9 hr

69. *Familiarize.* Let $p =$ the price of Neoma's tenth book. If the average price of each of the first 9 books is $12, then the total price of the 9 books is $9 \cdot \$12$, or $108. The average price of the first 10 books will be $\dfrac{\$108 + p}{10}$.

Translate.

$$\underbrace{\text{The average price}}_{\downarrow \atop \dfrac{108 + p}{10}} \quad \underbrace{\text{is at least}}_{\downarrow \atop \geq} \quad \underbrace{\$15.}_{\downarrow \atop 15}$$

Carry out. We solve the inequality.

$$\frac{108 + p}{10} \geq 15$$

$$108 + p \geq 150$$

$$p \geq 42$$

Check. As a partial check, we show that the average price of the 10 books is $15 when the price of the tenth book is $42.

$$\frac{\$108 + \$42}{10} = \frac{\$150}{10} = \$15$$

State. Neoma's tenth book should cost at least $42 if she wants to select a $15 book for her free book.

70. *Writing Exercise*

71. *Writing Exercise*

Chapter 3

Introduction to Graphing and Functions

Exercise Set 3.1

1. We go to the top of the bar that is above the body weight 100 lb. Then we move horizontally from the top of the bar to the vertical scale listing numbers of drinks. It appears that consuming approximately 2 drinks in one hour will give a 100 lb person a blood-alcohol level of 0.08%.

2. Approximately 3.5 drinks

3. From 4 on the vertical scale we move horizontally until we reach a bar whose top is above the horizontal line on which we are moving. The first such bar corresponds to a body weight of 220 lb. This means that for body weights represented by bars to the left of this one, consuming 4 drinks will yield a blood-alcohol level of 0.08%. The bar immediately to the left of the 220-pound bar represents 200 pounds. Thus, we can conclude an individual weighs more than 200 lb if 4 drinks are consumed in one hour without reaching a blood-alcohol level of 0.08%.

4. The person weighs more than 240 lb.

5. *Familiarize*. Since there are 272 million Americans and about one-third of them live in the South, there are about $\frac{1}{3} \cdot 272$, or $\frac{272}{3}$ million Southerners. The pie chart indicates that 3% of Americans choose brown as their favorite color. Let b = the number of Southerners, in millions, who choose brown as their favorite color.

   Translate. We reword and translate the problem.

   What is 3% of $\frac{272}{3}$ million?
   $\downarrow \quad \downarrow \quad \downarrow \quad \downarrow \qquad \downarrow$
   $b \quad = \quad 3\% \quad \cdot \qquad \dfrac{272}{3}$

   Carry out. We solve the equation.
   $$b = 0.03 \cdot \frac{272}{3} = 2.72$$

   Check. We repeat the calculations. The answer checks.

   State. About 2.72 million, or 2,720,000 Southerners choose brown as their favorite color.

6. About 5,440,000

7. *Familiarize*. Since there are 272 million Americans and about one-eighth are senior citizens, there are about $\frac{1}{8} \cdot 272$ million, or 34 million senior citizens. The pie chart indicates that 4% of Americans choose black as their favorite color. Let b = the number of senior citizens who choose black as their favorite color.

   Translate. We reword and translate the problem.

   What is 4% of 34 million?
   $\downarrow \quad \downarrow \quad \downarrow \quad \downarrow \qquad \downarrow$
   $b \quad = \quad 4\% \quad \cdot \quad 34,000,000$

   Carry out. We solve the equation.
   $$b = 0.04 \cdot 34,000,000 = 1,360,000$$

   Check. We repeat the calculations. The answer checks.

   State. About 1,360,000 senior citizens choose black as their favorite color.

8. About 1,360,000

9. *Familiarize*. From the pie chart we see that 9.9% of solid waste is plastic. We let x = the amount of plastic, in millions of tons, in the waste generated in 1998.

   Translate. We reword the problem.

   What is 9.9% of 210?
   $\downarrow \quad \downarrow \quad \downarrow \quad \downarrow \quad \downarrow$
   $x \quad = \quad 9.9\% \quad \cdot \quad 210$

   Carry out.
   $$x = 0.099 \cdot 210 = 20.79$$

   Check. We can repeat the calculation. The result checks.

   State. In 1998, about 20.79 million tons of waste was plastic.

10. About 1.7 lb

11. *Familiarize*. From the pie chart we see that 5.5% of solid waste is glass. From Exercise 9 we know that Americans generated 210 million tons of waste in 1998. Then the amount of this that is glass is

    0.055(210), or 11.55 million tons

    We let x = the amount of glass, in millions of tons, that Americans recycled in 1998.

    Translate. We reword the problem.

    What is 26% of 11.55 million tons?
    $\downarrow \quad \downarrow \quad \downarrow \quad \downarrow \qquad \downarrow$
    $x \quad = \quad 26\% \quad \cdot \qquad 11.55$

    Carry out.
    $$x = 0.26(11.55) \approx 3.0$$

    Check. We go over the calculations again. The result checks.

    State. Americans recycled about 3.0 million tons of glass in 1998.

12. About 0.02 lb

13. Locate 1997 on the horizontal scale and then move up to the line that represents CD sales. Now move to the vertical axis and read that about 70% of recordings sold in 1997 were CDs.

14. 20%

15. Locate 25% on the vertical scale, midway between 20% and 30%. Move right to the line representing cassette sales and then move down to the horizontal axis. We see that in 1995 approximately 25% of the recordings sold were cassettes.

16. 1998

17. The line slants upward most steeply from 1994 to 1995, so sales of CDs increased the most from 1994 to 1995.

18. 1996 to 1997

19. Starting at the origin:

(1,2) is 1 unit right and 2 units up;

(−2,3) is 2 units left and 3 units up;

(4,−1) is 4 units right and 1 unit down;

(−5,−3) is 5 units left and 3 units down;

(4,0) is 4 units right and 0 units up or down;

(0,−2) is 0 units right or left and 2 units down.

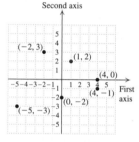

20.

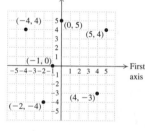

21. Starting at the origin:

(4,4) is 4 units right and 4 units up;

(−2,4) is 2 units left and 4 units up;

(5,−3) is 5 units right and 3 units down;

(−5,−5) is 5 units left and 5 units down;

(0,4) is 0 units right or left and 4 units up;

(0,−4) is 0 units right or left and 4 units down;

(3,0) is 3 units right and 0 units up or down;

(−4,0) is 4 units left and 0 units up or down.

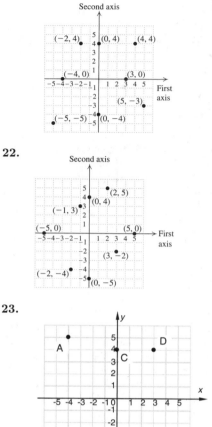

22.

23.

Point A is 4 units left and 5 units up. The coordinates of A are $(-4, 5)$.

Point B is 3 units left and 3 units down. The coordinates of B are $(-3, -3)$.

Point C is 0 units right or left and 4 units up. The coordinates of C are $(0,4)$.

Point D is 3 units right and 4 units up. The coordinates of D are $(3,4)$.

Point E is 3 units right and 4 units down. The coordinates of E are $(3, -4)$.

24. $A: (3,3), B: (0,-4), C: (-5,0), D: (-1,-1), E: (2,0)$

25.

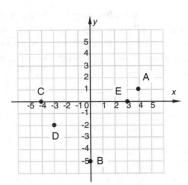

Point A is 4 units right and 1 unit up. The coordinates of A are $(4,1)$.

Point B is 0 units right or left and 5 units down. The coordinates of B are $(0,-5)$.

Point C is 4 units left and 0 units up or down. The coordinates of C are $(-4,0)$.

Point D is 3 units left and 2 units down. The coordinates of D are $(-3,-2)$.

Point E is 3 units right and 0 units up or down. The coordinates of E are $(3,0)$.

26. $A: (-5,1)$, $B: (0,5)$, $C: (5,3)$, $D: (0,-1)$, $E: (2,-4)$

27. An appropriate scale might be Xscl $= 10$, Yscl $= 10$. Answers may vary.

28. An appropriate scale might be Xscl $= 1000$, Yscl $= 100$. Answers may vary.

29. An appropriate scale might be Xscl $= 0.1$, Yscl $= 0.01$. Answers may vary.

30. An appropriate scale might be Xscl $= 5$, Yscl $= 0.1$. Answers may vary.

31. Since the first coordinate is positive and the second coordinate negative, the point $(7,-2)$ is located in quadrant IV.

32. III

33. Since both coordinates are negative, the point $(-4,-3)$ is in quadrant III.

34. IV

35. Since both coordinates are positive, the point $(2,1)$ is in quadrant I.

36. II

37. Since the first coordinate is negative and the second coordinate is positive, the point $(-4.9, 8.3)$ is in quadrant II.

38. I

39. First coordinates are positive in the quadrants that lie to the right of the origin, or in quadrants I and IV.

40. III and IV

41. Points for which both coordinates are positive lie in quadrant I, and points for which both coordinates are negative life in quadrant III. Thus, both coordinates have the same sign in quadrants I and III.

42. II and IV

43. a) First locate 1992 on the horizontal axis. From there move vertically to the line and then left to the vertical axis. We see that in 1992 there were approximately 9200 public libraries.

b) The graph is shown extended beyond 2000. Locate 2006 on the horizontal axis. From there move vertically to the line and then left to the vertical axis. We predict that in 2006 there will be approximately 9700 public libraries.

44. a) Approximately 26 million participants

b) Approximately 29 million participants

45. Draw a horizontal axis for the year and a vertical axis for the number of cigarettes smoked per capita. Number the axes with a scale that will permit us to view both the given data and the desired data. Then plot the points $(1990, 2817)$ and $(2001, 2037)$ and draw a line through them.

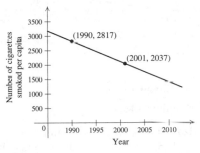

a) First locate 1995 on the horizontal axis. From there move vertically to the line and then left to the vertical axis. We see that approximately 2500 cigarettes were smoked per capita in 1995.

b) The graph is shown extended beyond 2001. Locate 2006 on the horizontal axis. From there move vertically to the line and then left to the vertical axis. We predict that approximately 1700 cigarettes will be smoked per capita in 2006.

46.

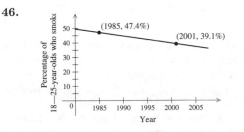

a) Approximately 45%

b) Approximately 36%

47. Draw a horizontal axis for the year and a vertical axis for U.S. college enrollment, in millions. Number the axes with a scale that will permit us to view both the given data and the desired data. Then plot the points $(1990, 13.8)$ and $(2001, 15.3)$ and draw a line segment connecting them.

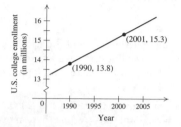

a) Locate 1996 on the horizontal axis and move up to the line. Then move horizontally to the vertical axis and estimate that U.S. college enrollment in 1996 was about 15 million students.

b) The graph is shown extended beyond 2001. Locate 2005 on the horizontal axis. From there move up to the line and across to the vertical axis. We predict that in 2005 U.S. college enrollment will be about 16 million students.

48.

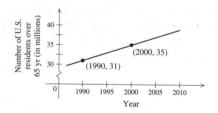

a) About 14 million students

b) About 16 million students

49. Draw a horizontal axis for the year and a vertical axis for the number of U.S. residents over the age of 65, in millions. Number the axes with a scale that will permit us to view both the given data and the desired data. Then plot the points $(1990, 31)$ and $(2000, 35)$ and draw a line segment connecting them.

a) Since 1995 is midway between 1990 and 2000, it is reasonable to estimate that in 1995 the number of U.S. residents over the age of 65 will be about midway between 31 million and 35 million or approximately 33 million.

We could also use the graph to make this estimate. Locate 1995 on the horizontal axis and move up to the line. Then move horizontally to the vertical axis and estimate that in 1995 the number of U.S. residents over the age of 65 was about 33 million.

b) The graph is shown extended beyond 2000. Locate 2010 on the horizontal axis. From there move up to the line and across to the vertical axis. We predict that in 2010 the number of U.S. residents over the age of 65 will be about 39 million.

50.

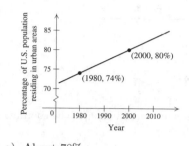

a) About 78%

b) About 82%

51. *Writing Exercise*

52. *Writing Exercise*

53. $4 \cdot 3 - 6 \cdot 5 = 12 - 30 = -18$

54. -31

55. $-\dfrac{1}{2}(-6) + 3 = 3 + 3 = 6$

56. 1

57. $3x - 2y = 6$

$\qquad -2y = -3x + 6 \quad$ Adding $-3x$ to both sides

$\qquad -\dfrac{1}{2}(-2y) = -\dfrac{1}{2}(-3x + 6)$

$\qquad\qquad y = -\dfrac{1}{2}(-3x) - \dfrac{1}{2}(6)$

$\qquad\qquad y = \dfrac{3}{2}x - 3$

58. $y = \dfrac{7}{4}x - \dfrac{7}{2}$

59. *Writing Exercise*

60. *Writing Exercise*

61. If the coordinates of a point are reciprocals of each other, they have the same sign. Thus, the point could be in quadrant I or quadrant III.

62. II or IV

63.

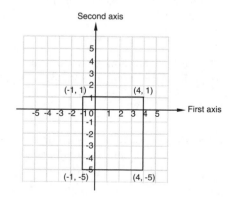

The coordinates of the fourth vertex are $(-1, -5)$.

64. $(5,2)$, $(-7,2)$, or $(3,-8)$

65. Answers may vary.

We select eight points such that the sum of the coordinates for each point is 7.

$$
\begin{array}{ll}
(0,7) & 0+7=7 \\
(1,6) & 1+6=7 \\
(2,5) & 2+5=7 \\
(3,4) & 3+4=7 \\
(4,3) & 4+3=7 \\
(5,2) & 5+2=7 \\
(6,1) & 6+1=7 \\
(7,0) & 7+0=7
\end{array}
$$

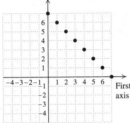

66. Answers may vary.

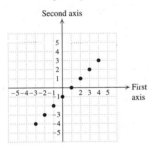

67. Plot the three given points and observe that the coordinates of the fourth vertex are $(5,3)$

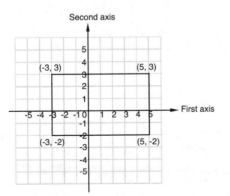

The length of the rectangle is 8 units, and the width is 5 units.

$P = 2l + 2w$

$P = 2 \cdot 8 + 2 \cdot 5 = 16 + 10 = 26$ units

68. $\dfrac{65}{2}$ sq units

69. Latitude $32.5°$ North,
Longitude $64.5°$ West

70. Latitude $27°$ North,
Longitude $81°$ West

71. *Writing Exercise*

72. *Writing Exercise*

Exercise Set 3.2

1. We substitute 0 for x and 2 for y (alphabetical order of variables).

$$
\begin{array}{c|c}
\multicolumn{2}{l}{y = 7x + 1} \\
\hline
2 \ ? \ 7 \cdot 0 + 1 & \\
0 + 1 & \\
2 \ \big| \ 1 & \text{FALSE}
\end{array}
$$

Since $2 = 1$ is false, the pair $(0,2)$ is not a solution.

2. Yes

3. We substitute 4 for x and 2 for y.

$$
\begin{array}{c|c}
\multicolumn{2}{l}{3y + 2x = 12} \\
\hline
3 \cdot 2 + 2 \cdot 4 \ ? \ 12 & \\
6 + 8 & \\
14 \ \big| \ 12 & \text{FALSE}
\end{array}
$$

Since $14 = 12$ is false, the pair $(4,2)$ is not a solution.

4. No

5. We substitute 2 for a and -1 for b.

$$
\begin{array}{c|c}
\multicolumn{2}{l}{4a - 3b = 11} \\
\hline
4 \cdot 2 - 3(-1) \ ? \ 11 & \\
8 + 3 & \\
11 \ \big| \ 11 & \text{TRUE}
\end{array}
$$

Since $11 = 11$ is true, the pair $(2,-1)$ is a solution.

6. Yes

7. To show that a pair is a solution, we substitute, replacing x with the first coordinate and y with the second coordinate in each pair.

$$
\begin{array}{c|c} \qquad\qquad
\begin{array}{c}
y = x - 2 \\
\hline
1 \ ? \ 3 - 2 \\
1 \ \big| \ 1 \quad \text{TRUE}
\end{array}
\qquad
\begin{array}{c}
y = x - 2 \\
\hline
-4 \ ? \ -2 - 2 \\
-4 \ \big| \ -4 \quad \text{TRUE}
\end{array}
\end{array}
$$

In each case the substitution results in a true equation. Thus, $(3,1)$ and $(-2,-4)$ are both solutions of $y = x - 2$. We graph these points and sketch the line passing through them.

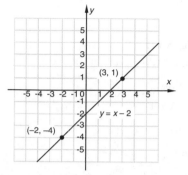

The line appears to pass through $(5,3)$ also. We check to determine if $(5,3)$ is a solution of $y = x - 2$.

$$\frac{y = x - 2}{3 \ ? \ 5 - 2}$$
$$3 \mid 3 \qquad \text{TRUE}$$

Thus, $(5,3)$ is another solution. There are other correct answers, including $(-3,-5)$, $(-1,-3)$, $(0,-2)$, $(1,-1)$, $(2,0)$, and $(4,2)$.

8. $\dfrac{y = x + 3}{2 \ ? \ -1 + 3}$ $\dfrac{y = x + 3}{7 \ ? \ 4 + 3}$

$\ \ \ 2 \mid 2 \qquad$ TRUE $\ \ \ 7 \mid 7 \qquad$ TRUE

$(2,5)$; answers may vary

9. To show that a pair is a solution, we substitute, replacing x with the first coordinate and y with the second coordinate in each pair.

$$\frac{y = \frac{1}{2}x + 3}{5 \ ? \ \frac{1}{2} \cdot 4 + 3}$$
$$\ \ \ \ \ \ \mid 2 + 3$$
$$5 \mid 5 \qquad \text{TRUE}$$

$$\frac{y = \frac{1}{2}x + 3}{2 \ ? \ \frac{1}{2}(-2) + 3}$$
$$\ \ \ \ \ \ \mid -1 + 3$$
$$2 \mid 2 \qquad \text{TRUE}$$

In each case the substitution results in a true equation. Thus, $(4,5)$ and $(-2,2)$ are both solutions of $y = \frac{1}{2}x + 3$. We graph these points and sketch the line passing through them.

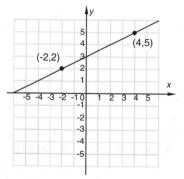

The line appears to pass through $(0,3)$ also. We check to determine if $(0,3)$ is a solution of $y = \frac{1}{2}x + 3$.

$$\frac{y = \frac{1}{2}x + 3}{3 \ ? \ \frac{1}{2} \cdot 0 + 3}$$
$$3 \mid 3 \qquad \text{TRUE}$$

Thus, $(0,3)$ is another solution. There are other correct answers, including $(-6,0)$, $(-4,1)$, $(2,4)$, and $(6,6)$.

10. $\dfrac{y = \frac{1}{2}x - 1}{2 \ ? \ \frac{1}{2} \cdot 6 - 1}$ $\dfrac{y = \frac{1}{2}x - 1}{-1 \ ? \ \frac{1}{2} \cdot 0 - 1}$

$\ \ \ \ \ \ \ \ \ \mid 3 - 1$ $\quad -1 \mid -1 \qquad$ TRUE

$\ \ 2 \mid 2 \qquad$ TRUE

$(4,1)$; answers may vary

11. To show that a pair is a solution, we substitute, replacing x with the first coordinate and y with the second coordinate in each pair.

$\dfrac{y + 3x = 7}{1 + 3 \cdot 2 \ ? \ 7}$ $\dfrac{y + 3x = 7}{-5 + 3 \cdot 4 \ ? \ 7}$

$\ \ 1 + 6 \mid$ $\quad -5 + 12 \mid$

$\qquad 7 \mid 7$ TRUE $\qquad 7 \mid 7$ TRUE

In each case the substitution results in a true equation. Thus, $(2,1)$ and $(4,-5)$ are both solutions of $y + 3x = 7$. We graph these points and sketch the line passing through them.

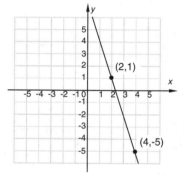

The line appears to pass through $(1,4)$ also. We check to determine if $(1,4)$ is a solution of $y + 3x = 7$.

$\dfrac{y + 3x = 7}{4 + 3 \cdot 1 \ ? \ 7}$

$\ \ 4 + 3 \mid$

$\qquad 7 \mid 7$ TRUE

Thus, $(1,4)$ is another solution. There are other correct answers, including $(3,-2)$.

12. $\dfrac{2y + x = 5}{2 \cdot 3 - 1 \ ? \ 5}$ $\dfrac{2y + x = 5}{2(-1) + 7 \ ? \ 5}$

$\ \ \ 6 - 1 \mid$ $\qquad -2 + 7 \mid$

$\qquad 5 \mid 5$ TRUE $\qquad 5 \mid 5$ TRUE

$(5,0)$; answers may vary

13. To show that a pair is a solution, we substitute, replacing x with the first coordinate and y with the second coordinate in each pair.

$$4x - 2y = 10$$
$$\frac{}{4 \cdot 0 - 2(-5) \ ? \ 10}$$
$$10 \ \Big| \ 10 \ \text{TRUE}$$

$$4x - 2y = 10$$
$$\frac{}{4 \cdot 4 - 2 \cdot 3 \ ? \ 10}$$
$$16 - 6 \ \Big|$$
$$10 \ \Big| \ 10 \ \text{TRUE}$$

In each case the substitution results in a true equation. Thus, $(0, -5)$ and $(4, 3)$ are both solutions of $4x - 2y = 10$. We graph these points and sketch the line passing through them.

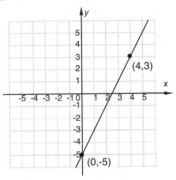

The line appears to pass through $(2, -1)$ also. We check to determine if $(2, -1)$ is a solution of $4x - 2y = 10$.

$$4x - 2y = 10$$
$$\frac{}{4 \cdot 2 - 2(-1) \ ? \ 10}$$
$$8 + 2 \ \Big|$$
$$10 \ \Big| \ 10 \ \text{TRUE}$$

Thus, $(2, -1)$ is another solution. There are other correct answers, including $(1, -3)$, $(2, -1)$, $(3, 1)$, and $(5, 5)$.

14.
$$6x - 3y = 3$$
$$\frac{}{6 \cdot 1 - 3 \cdot 1 \ ? \ 3}$$
$$6 - 3 \ \Big|$$
$$3 \ \Big| \ 3 \ \text{TRUE}$$

$$6x - 3y = 3$$
$$\frac{}{6(-1) - 3(-3) \ ? \ 3}$$
$$-6 + 9 \ \Big|$$
$$3 \ \Big| \ 3 \ \text{TRUE}$$

$(2, 3)$; answers may vary

15. $y = x - 1$

When $x = 0$, $y = 0 - 1 = -1$.

When $x = 3$, $y = 3 - 1 = 2$.

When $x = -5$, $y = -5 - 1 = -6$.

x	y
0	-1
3	2
-5	-6

Plot these points, draw the line they determine, and label the graph $y = x - 1$.

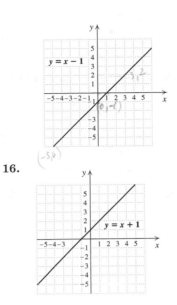

16.

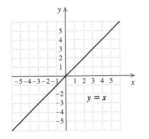

17. $y = x$

When $x = 0$, $y = 0$.

When $x = -2$, $y = -2$.

When $x = 3$, $y = 3$.

x	y
0	0
-2	-2
3	3

Plot these points, draw the line they determine, and label the graph $y = x$.

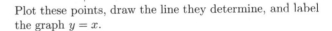

18.

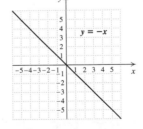

19. $y = \frac{1}{2}x$

When $x = 0$, $y = \frac{1}{2} \cdot 0 = 0$.

When $x = -4$, $y = \frac{1}{2}(-4) = -2$.

When $x = 4$, $y = \frac{1}{2} \cdot 4 = 2$.

x	y
0	0
-4	-2
4	2

Plot these points, draw the line they determine, and label the graph $y = \dfrac{1}{2}x$.

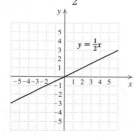

20.

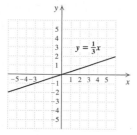

21. $y = x + 2$

When $x = 0$, $y = 0 + 2 = 2$.

When $x = -2$, $y = -2 + 2 = 0$.

When $x = 3$, $y = 3 + 2 = 5$.

x	y
0	2
-2	0
3	5

Plot these points, draw the line they determine, and label the graph $y = x + 2$.

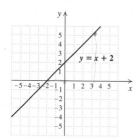

22.

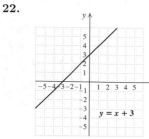

23. $y = 3x - 2$

When $x = 0$, $y = 3 \cdot 0 - 2 = 0 - 2 = -2$.

When $x = -2$, $y = 3(-2) + 2 = -6 + 2 = -4$.

When $x = 1$, $y = 3 \cdot 1 + 2 = 3 + 2 = 5$.

x	y
0	-2
-2	-4
1	5

Plot these points, draw the line they determine, and label the graph $y = 3x + 2$.

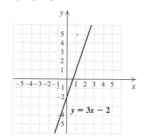

24.

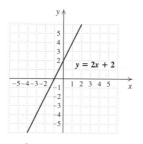

25. $y = \dfrac{1}{2}x + 1$

When $x = 0$, $y = \dfrac{1}{2} \cdot 0 + 1 = 0 + 1 = 1$.

When $x = -4$, $y = \dfrac{1}{2}(-4) + 1 = -2 + 1 = -1$.

When $x = 4$, $y = \dfrac{1}{2} \cdot 4 + 1 = 2 + 1 = 3$.

x	y
0	1
-4	-1
4	3

Plot these points, draw the line they determine, and label the graph $y = \dfrac{1}{2}x + 1$.

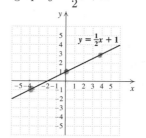

26.

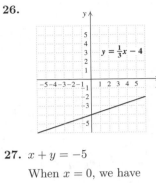

27. $x + y = -5$

When $x = 0$, we have

$$0 + y = -5$$
$$y = -5.$$

When $y = 0$, we have

$$x + 0 = -5$$
$$x = -5.$$

When $x = -1$, we have

$$-1 + y = -5$$
$$y = -4.$$

x	y
0	-5
-5	0
-1	-4

Plot these points, draw the line they determine, and label the graph $x + y = -5$.

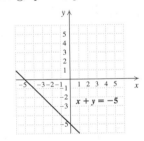

28.

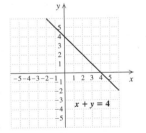

29. $y = x^2 + 1$

When $x = -2$, $y = (-2)^2 + 1 = 4 + 1 = 5$.
When $x = -1$, $y = (-1)^2 + 1 = 1 + 1 = 2$.
When $x = 0$, $y = 0^2 + 1 = 0 + 1 = 1$.
When $x = 1$, $y = 1^2 + 1 = 1 + 1 = 2$.
When $x = 2$, $y = 2^2 + 1 = 4 + 1 = 5$.

x	y
-2	5
-1	2
0	1
1	2
2	5

Plot these points, and connect them with a smooth curve, and label the graph $y = x^2 + 1$.

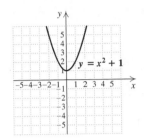

30.

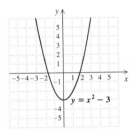

31. $x + 2y = 8$

When $x = 0$, we have

$$0 + 2y = 8$$
$$2y = 8$$
$$y = 4.$$

When $x = -2$, we have

$$-2 + 2y = 8$$
$$2y = 10$$
$$y = 5.$$

When $x = 4$, we have

$$4 + 2y = 8$$
$$2y = 4$$
$$y = 2.$$

x	y
0	4
-2	5
4	2

Plot these points, draw the line they determine, and label the graph $x + 2y = 8$.

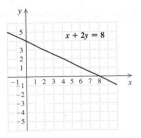

32.

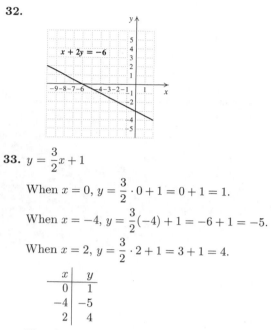

33. $y = \dfrac{3}{2}x + 1$

When $x = 0$, $y = \dfrac{3}{2} \cdot 0 + 1 = 0 + 1 = 1.$

When $x = -4$, $y = \dfrac{3}{2}(-4) + 1 = -6 + 1 = -5.$

When $x = 2$, $y = \dfrac{3}{2} \cdot 2 + 1 = 3 + 1 = 4.$

x	y
0	1
-4	-5
2	4

Plot these points, draw the line they determine, and label the graph $y = \dfrac{3}{2}x + 1$.

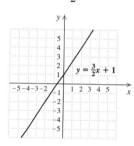

34.

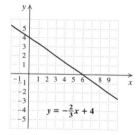

35. $6x - 3y = 9$

When $x = 0$, we have

$$6 \cdot 0 - 3y = 9$$
$$-3y = 9$$
$$y = -3.$$

When $x = -1$, we have

$$6(-1) - 3y = 9$$
$$-6 - 3y = 9$$
$$-3y = 15$$
$$y = -5.$$

When $y = 3$, we have

$$6x - 3 \cdot 3 = 9$$
$$6x - 9 = 9$$
$$6x = 18$$
$$x = 3.$$

x	y
0	-3
-1	-5
3	3

Plot these points, draw the line they determine, and label the graph $6x - 3y = 9$.

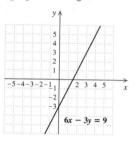

36.

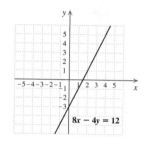

37. $8y + 2x = -4$

When $x = 0$, we have

$$8y + 2 \cdot 0 = -4$$
$$8y = -4$$
$$y = -\dfrac{1}{2}.$$

When $y = 0$, we have

$$8 \cdot 0 + 2x = -4$$
$$2x = -4$$
$$x = -2.$$

When $x = 2$, we have

$$8y + 2 \cdot 2 = -4$$
$$8y + 4 = -4$$
$$8y = -8$$
$$y = -1.$$

x	y
0	$-\dfrac{1}{2}$
-2	0
2	-1

Plot these points, draw the line they determine, and label the graph $8y + 2x = -4$.

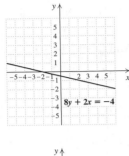

$8y + 2x = -4$

38.

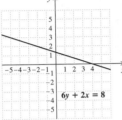

$6y + 2x = 8$

39. a) $x + 1 = 4$

$x = 4 - 1$

$x = 3$

We graph the solution of the equation, 3, on a number line.

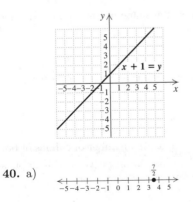

b) We graph $x + 1 = y$.

When $x = -3$, $y = -3 + 1 = -2$.

When $x = 0$, $y = 0 + 1 = 1$.

When $x = 2$, $y = 2 + 1 = 3$.

x	y
-3	-2
0	1
2	3

Plot the points, draw the line they determine, and label the graph $x + 1 = y$.

$x + 1 = y$

40. a)

$\frac{7}{2}$

b)

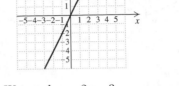

$2x = y$

41. a) We graph $y = 2x - 3$.

When $x = -1$, $y = 2(-1) - 3 = -2 - 3 = -5$.

When $x = 0$, $y = 2 \cdot 0 - 3 = 0 - 3 = -3$.

When $x = 3$, $y = 2 \cdot 3 - 3 = 6 - 3 = 3$.

x	y
-1	-5
0	-3
3	3

Plot the points, draw the line they determine, and label the graph $y = 2x - 3$.

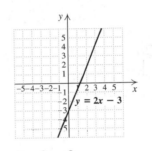

$y = 2x - 3$

b) $-7 = 2x - 3$

$-4 = 2x$

$-2 = x$

We graph the solution of the equation, -2, on a number line.

42. a)

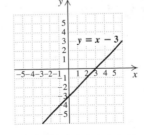

$y = x - 3$

b)

43. $y = (-3/2)\, x + 1$

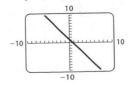

44.
$$y = (-2/3)\,x - 2$$

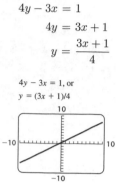

45. We solve for y first.
$$4y - 3x = 1$$
$$4y = 3x + 1$$
$$y = \frac{3x + 1}{4}$$

$4y - 3x = 1$, or
$y = (3x + 1)/4$

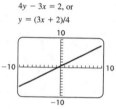

46.
$4y - 3x = 2$, or
$y = (3x + 2)/4$

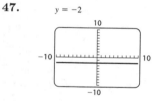

47.
$$y = -2$$

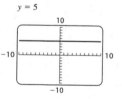

48.
$$y = 5$$

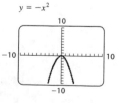

49.
$$y = -x^2$$

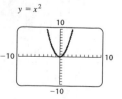

50.
$$y = x^2$$

51. We solve for y first.
$$x^2 - y = 3$$
$$-y = -x^2 + 3$$
$$y = x^2 - 3 \qquad \text{Multiplying by } -1$$

$x^2 - y = 3$, or
$y = x^2 - 3$

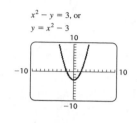

52.
$y - 2 = x^2$, or
$y = x^2 + 2$

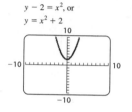

53.
$$y = x \wedge 3$$

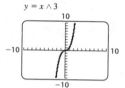

54.
$$y = x \wedge 3 - 2$$

55. Only window (b) shows where the graph crosses the x- and y-axes.

56. (b)

57. Only window (a) shows the shape of the graph and where it crosses the y-axis.

58. (a)

59. Only window (b) shows where the graph crosses the x- and y-axes.

60. (b)

61. We graph $w = \dfrac{1}{2}t + 5$. Since the number of gallons of bottled water consumed cannot be negative in this application, we select only nonnegative values for t.

If $t = 0$, $w = \dfrac{1}{2} \cdot 0 + 5 = 5$.

If $t = 4$, $w = \dfrac{1}{2} \cdot 4 + 5 = 2 + 5 = 7$.

If $t = 10$, $w = \dfrac{1}{2} \cdot 10 + 5 = 5 + 5 = 10$.

t	w
0	5
4	7
10	10

We plot the points and draw the graph.

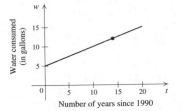

To predict the number of gallons consumed per person in 2004 we find the second coordinate associated with 14. (2004 is 14 years after 1990.) Locate the point on the line that is above 14 and then find the value on the vertical axis that corresponds to that point. That value is 12, so we predict that 12 gallons of bottled water will be consumed per person in 2004.

62.

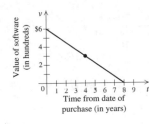

$300

63. We graph $t + w = 15$, or $w = -t + 15$. Since time cannot be negative in this application, we select only nonnegative values for t.

If $t = 0$, $w = -0 + 15 = 15$.

If $t = 2$, $w = -2 + 15 = 13$.

If $t = 5$, $w = -5 + 15 = 10$.

t	w
0	15
2	13
5	10

We plot the points and draw the graph. Since the likelihood of death cannot be negative, the graph stops at the horizontal axis.

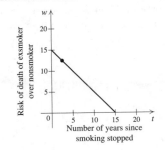

To estimate how much more likely it is for Sandy to die from lung cancer than Polly, we find the second coordinate associated with $2\frac{1}{2}$. Locate the point on the line that is above $2\frac{1}{2}$ and then find the value on the vertical axis that corresponds to that point. That value is about $12\frac{1}{2}$, so it is $12\frac{1}{2}$ times more likely for Sandy to die from lung cancer than Polly.

64.

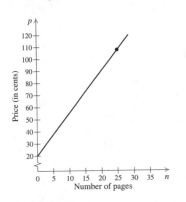

110¢, or $1.10

65. We graph $T = \frac{6}{5}c + 1$. Since the number of credits cannot be negative, we select only nonnegative values for c.

If $c = 5$, $T = \frac{6}{5} \cdot 5 + 1 = 6 + 1 = 7$.

If $c = 10$, $T = \frac{6}{5} \cdot 10 + 1 = 12 + 1 = 13$.

If $c = 15$, $T = \frac{6}{5} \cdot 15 + 1 = 18 + 1 = 19$.

c	T
5	7
10	13
15	19

We plot the points and draw the graph.

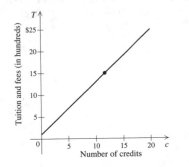

Four three-credit courses total $4 \cdot 3$, or 12, credits. To estimate the cost of tuition and fees for a student who is registered for 12 credits, we find the second coordinate associated with 12. Locate the point on the line that is above 12 and then find the value on the vertical axis that corresponds to that point. That value is about 15, so tuition and fees will cost about $1500.

66.

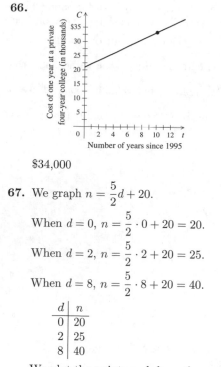

$34,000

67. We graph $n = \dfrac{5}{2}d + 20$.

When $d = 0$, $n = \dfrac{5}{2} \cdot 0 + 20 = 20$.

When $d = 2$, $n = \dfrac{5}{2} \cdot 2 + 20 = 25$.

When $d = 8$, $n = \dfrac{5}{2} \cdot 8 + 20 = 40$.

d	n
0	20
2	25
8	40

We plot the points and draw the graph.

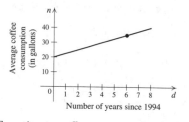

To estimate coffee consumption in 2000, we first note that 2000 is 6 years after 1994. Then we find the second coordinate associated with 6. Locate the point on the line that is above 6 and find the value on the vertical axis that corresponds to that point. That value is about 35, so 35 gal of coffee were consumed by the average U.S. consumer in 2000.

68.

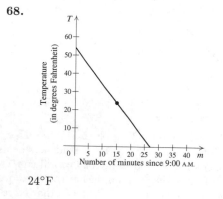

24°F

69. *Writing Exercise*

70. *Writing Exercise*

71. $5x + 3 \cdot 0 = 12$

$5x + 0 = 12$

$5x = 12$

$x = \dfrac{12}{5}$

Check: $\dfrac{5x + 3 \cdot 0 = 12}{}$

$5 \cdot \dfrac{12}{5} + 3 \cdot 0 \ ? \ 12$

$12 + 0 \ \Big|$

$12 \ \Big| \ 12 \quad$ TRUE

The solution is $\dfrac{12}{5}$.

72. $\dfrac{9}{2}$

73. $7 \cdot 0 - 4y = 10$

$0 - 4y = 10$

$y = -\dfrac{5}{2}$

Check: $\dfrac{7 \cdot 0 - 4y = 10}{}$

$7 \cdot 0 - 4\left(-\dfrac{5}{2}\right) \ ? \ 10$

$0 + 10 \ \Big|$

$10 \ \Big| \ 10 \quad$ TRUE

The solution is $-\dfrac{5}{2}$.

74. $p = \dfrac{w}{q + 1}$

75. $Ax + By = C$

$By = C - Ax \qquad$ Subtracting Ax

$y = \dfrac{C - Ax}{B} \qquad$ Dividing by B

76. $Q = 2A - T$

77. *Writing Exercise*

78. *Writing Exercise*

79. Let s represent the gear that Lauren uses on the southbound portion of her ride and n represent the gear she uses on the northbound portion. Then we have $s + n = 18$. We graph this equation, using only positive integer values for s and n.

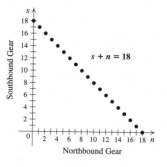

80. $x + y = 5$, or $y = -x + 5$

81. Note that the sum of the coordinates of each point on the graph is 2. Thus, we have $x + y = 2$, or $y = -x + 2$.

82. $y = x + 2$

83. Note that when $x = 0$, $y = -5$ and when $y = 0$, $x = 3$. An equation that fits this situation is $5x - 3y = 15$, or $y = \frac{5}{3}x - 5$.

84. $0.10d + 0.05n = 1.75$

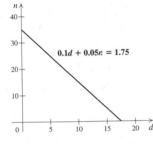

5 dimes, 25 nickels; 10 dimes, 15 nickels; 12 dimes, 11 nickels

85. The equation is $25d + 5l = 225$.

Since the number of dinners cannot be negative, we choose only nonnegative values of d when graphing the equation. The graph stops at the horizontal axis since the number of lunches cannot be negative.

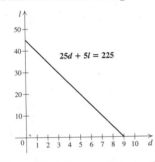

We see that three points on the graph are $(1, 40)$, $(5, 20)$, and $(8, 5)$. Thus, three combinations of dinners and lunches that total \$225 are

1 dinner, 40 lunches,

5 dinners, 20 lunches,

8 dinners, 5 lunches.

86.

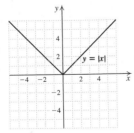

87. $y = -|x|$

x	y
-3	-3
-2	-2
-1	-1
0	0
1	-1
2	-2
3	-3

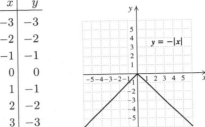

88.

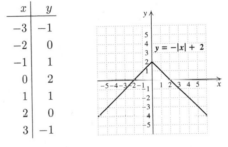

89. $y = -|x| + 2$

x	y
-3	-1
-2	0
-1	1
0	2
1	1
2	0
3	-1

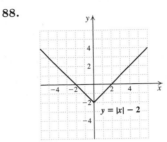

90.

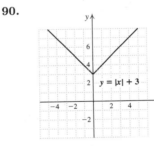

91. *Writing Exercise*

Exercise Set 3.3

1. The solution of the equation is the x-coordinate of the point of intersection of the graphs. This x-value appears to be -2.

2. 4

3. The solution of the equation is the x-coordinate of the point of intersection of the graphs. This x-value appears to be -4.

4. 1

5. The solution of the equation is the x-coordinate of the point of intersection of the graphs. This x-value appears to be 8.

6. 3

7. The solution of the equation is the first coordinate of the x-intercept of the graph. This appears to be 4.

8. 1

9. The value of x for which $y_1 = y_2$ is the x-coordinate of the point of intersection of the graphs. This x-value appears to be 0.

10. 2

11. The value of x for which $y_1 = y_2$ is the x-coordinate of the point of intersection of the graphs. This x-value appears to be 5.

12. 1

13. The value of x for which $y_1 = 0$ is the first coordinate of the x-intercept of the graph. This appears to be -3.

14. 1

15. $x - 3 = 4$

Graph $f(x) = x - 3$ and $g(x) = 4$ on the same set of axes.

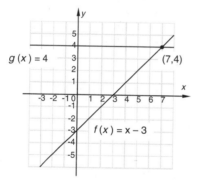

The lines appear to intersect at $(7, 4)$, so the solution is apparently 7.

Check: $\dfrac{x - 3 = 4}{}$

$\quad 7 - 3\ ?\ 4$

$\qquad\quad 4\ \big|\ 4\qquad$ TRUE

The solution is 7.

16. 2

17. $2x + 1 = 7$

Graph $f(x) = 2x + 1$ and $g(x) = 7$ on the same grid.

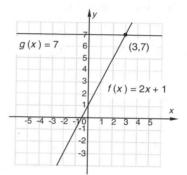

The lines appear to intersect at $(3, 7)$, so the solution is apparently 3.

Check: $\dfrac{2x + 1 = 7}{}$

$\quad 2 \cdot 3 + 1\ ?\ 7$

$\qquad 6 + 1\ \big|$

$\qquad\qquad 7\ \big|\ 7\qquad$ TRUE

The solution is 3.

18. 2

19. $\dfrac{1}{3}x - 2 = 1$

Graph $f(x) = \dfrac{1}{3}x - 2$ and $g(x) = 1$ on the same grid.

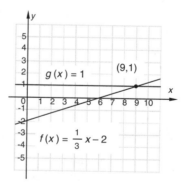

The lines appear to intersect at $(9, 1)$, so the solution is apparently 9.

Check: $\dfrac{\frac{1}{3}x - 2 = 1}{}$

$\quad \dfrac{1}{3} \cdot 9 - 2\ ?\ 1$

$\qquad 3 - 2\ \big|$

$\qquad\qquad 1\ \big|\ 1\qquad$ TRUE

The solution is 9.

20. -8

21. $x + 3 = 5 - x$

Graph $f(x) = x + 3$ and $g(x) = 5 - x$ on the same grid.

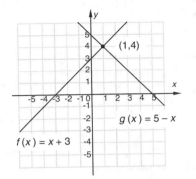

The lines appear to intersect at $(1, 4)$, so the solution is apparently 1.

Check:
$$\begin{array}{c|c} x + 3 = 5 - x \\ \hline 1 + 3 \ ? \ 5 - 1 \\ 4 \ | \ 4 \qquad \text{TRUE} \end{array}$$

The solution is 1.

22. -2

23. $5 - \dfrac{1}{2}x = x - 4$

Graph $f(x) = 5 - \dfrac{1}{2}x$ and $g(x) = x - 4$ on the same grid.

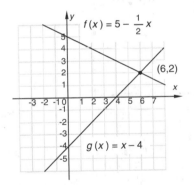

The lines appear to intersect at $(6, 2)$, so the solution is apparently 6.

Check:
$$\begin{array}{c|c} 5 - \dfrac{1}{2}x = x - 4 \\ \hline 5 - \dfrac{1}{2} \cdot 6 \ ? \ 6 - 4 \\ 5 - 3 \ \Big| \ 2 \\ 2 \ \Big| \ 2 \qquad \text{TRUE} \end{array}$$

The solution is 6.

24. 4

25. $2x - 1 = -x + 3$

Graph $f(x) = 2x - 1$ and $g(x) = -x + 3$ on the same grid.

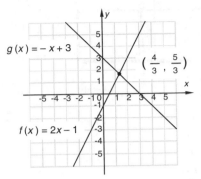

The lines appear to intersect at $\left(\dfrac{4}{3}, \dfrac{5}{3}\right)$, so the solution is apparently $\dfrac{4}{3}$.

Check:
$$\begin{array}{c|c} 2x - 1 = -x + 3 \\ \hline 2 \cdot \dfrac{4}{3} - 1 \ ? \ -\dfrac{4}{3} + 3 \\ \dfrac{8}{3} - 1 \ \Big| \ \dfrac{5}{3} \\ \dfrac{5}{3} \ \Big| \ \dfrac{5}{3} \qquad \text{TRUE} \end{array}$$

The solution is $\dfrac{4}{3}$, or $1\dfrac{1}{3}$.

26. $1\dfrac{1}{3}$

27. We will use the zero method. First we get zero on one side of the equation.

$$2(x + 6) = 8x$$
$$2(x + 6) - 8x = 0$$

Then we graph $y = 2(x + 6) - 8x$ and find the first coordinate of the point for which $y = 0$.

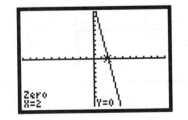

The solution is 2.

28. 3

29. We will use the zero method. First we get zero on one side of the equation.

$$80 = 10(3t + 2)$$
$$0 = 10(3t + 2) - 80$$

Then we graph $y = 10(3t + 2) - 80$ and find the first coordinate of the point for which $y = 0$.

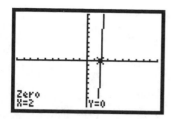

The solution is 2.

30. 1

31. We will use the zero method. First we get zero on one side of the equation.
$$-6a - 10a = -32$$
$$-6a - 10a + 32 = 0$$
Then we graph $y = -6a - 10a + 32$ and find the first coordinate of the point for which $y = 0$. (We could combine the like terms $-6a$ and $-10a$, but this is not necessary.)

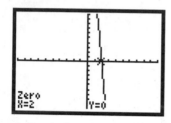

The solution is 2.

32. -2

33. We will use the zero method. First we get zero on one side of the equation.
$$0.9x - 0.7x = 4.2$$
$$0.9x - 0.7x - 4.2 = 0$$
Then we graph $y = 0.9x - 0.7x - 4.2$ and find the first coordinate of the point for which $y = 0$. (We could combine the like terms $0.9x$ and $-0.7x$, but this is not necessary.)

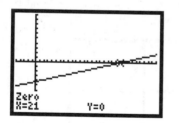

The solution is 21.

34. 130

35. $4.23x - 17.898 = -1.65x - 42.454$

Graph $y_1 = 4.23x - 17.898$ and $y_2 = -1.65x - 42.454$ and find the first coordinate of the point of intersection.

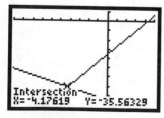

The solution is approximately -4.17619. If we convert this to fraction notation we get $-\dfrac{877}{210}$.

36. Approximately 0.21402

37. $x + 7 = 7 + x$

Since $x + 7$ and $7 + x$ are equivalent by the commutative law of addition, the equation is true regardless of the replacement for x. Thus, all real numbers are solutions and the equation is an identity.

If we graph $y_1 = x + 7$ and $y_2 = 7 + x$, we see that the graphs coincide, again showing that all real numbers are solutions of the equation and that the equation is an identity.

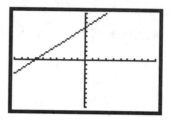

38. All real numbers; identity

39. $4x - 2x - 2 = 2x$

Graph $y_1 = 4x - 2x - 2$ and $y_2 = 2x$. If we attempt to find a point of intersection, we get an error message.

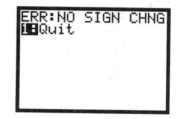

Thus there is no solution. The solution set is $\emptyset$, and the equation is contradiction.

40. All real numbers; identity

41. $x + 2 = x + 1$

Graph $y_1 = x + 2$ and $y_2 = x + 1$. If we attempt to find a point of intersection, we get an error message.

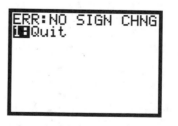

Thus there is no solution. The solution set is $\emptyset$, and the equation is contradiction.

42. $\emptyset$; contradiction

43. $\frac{1}{3}x = \frac{1}{4}x$

Graph $y_1 = \frac{1}{3}x$ and $y_2 = \frac{1}{4}x$ and find the first coordinate of the point of intersection.

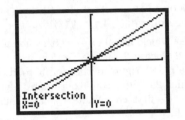

The solution is 0.

44. 0

45. *Writing Exercise*

46. *Writing Exercise*

47. $3x + 7 = 18$

$\quad\quad 3x = 11$ Subtracting 7 on both sides

$\quad\quad x = \frac{11}{3}$ Dividing by 3 on both sides

The solution is $\frac{11}{3}$.

48. $-\frac{43}{2}$

49. $3x + 7 \le 18$

$\quad\quad 3x \le 11$ Subtracting 7 on both sides

$\quad\quad x \le \frac{11}{3}$ Dividing by 3 on both sides

The solution set is $\left\{ x \middle| x \le \frac{11}{3} \right\}$, or $\left(-\infty, \frac{11}{3} \right]$.

50. $\left\{ x \middle| x < -\frac{43}{2} \right\}$, or $\left(\infty, -\frac{43}{2} \right)$

51. *Writing Exercise*

52. *Writing Exercise*

53. $2x = |x + 1|$

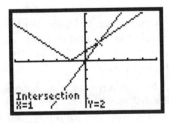

The graphs intersect at $(1, 2)$, so the solution is 1. This value checks.

54. $1\frac{2}{3}, 3$

55. $\frac{1}{2}x = 3 - |x|$

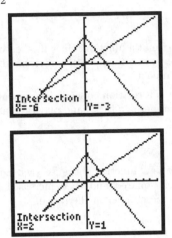

The graphs intersect at $(-6, -3)$ and at $(2, 1)$, so the solutions are -6 and 2. These values check.

56. $-\frac{1}{4}$

57. $x^2 = x + 2$

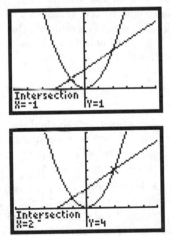

The graphs intersect at $(-1, 1)$ and at $(2, 4)$, so the solutions are -1 and 2. These values check.

58. 0, 1

Exercise Set 3.4

1. The correspondence is not a function, because a member of the domain (3) corresponds to more than one member of the range.

2. Yes

3. The correspondence is a function, because each member of the domain corresponds to just one member of the range.

4. Yes

5. The correspondence is a function, because each member of the domain corresponds to just one member of the range.

6. No

7. This correspondence is a function, because each Christmas tree has only one price.

8. Function

9. The correspondence is not a function, since it is reasonable to assume that at least one member of a rock band plays more than one instrument.

   The correspondence is a relation, since it is reasonable to assume that each member of a rock band plays at least one instrument.

10. Function

11. This correspondence is a function, because each number in the domain, when squared and then increased by 4, corresponds to only one number in the range.

12. Function

13. a) Locate 1 on the horizontal axis and then find the point on the graph for which 1 is the first coordinate. From that point, look to the vertical axis to find the corresponding y-coordinate, -2. Thus, $f(1) = -2$.

    b) To determine which member(s) of the domain are paired with 2, locate 2 on the vertical axis. From there look left and right to the graph to find any points for which 2 is the second coordinate. One such point exists. Its first coordinate is 4. Thus, the x-value for which $f(x) = 2$ is 4.

14. a) -1

    b) -3

15. a) Locate 1 on the horizontal axis and then find the point on the graph for which 1 is the first coordinate. From that point, look to the vertical axis to find the corresponding y-coordinate, 3. Thus, $f(1) = 3$.

    b) To determine which member(s) of the domain are paired with 2, locate 2 on the vertical axis. From there look left and right to the graph to find any points for which 2 is the second coordinate. One such point exists. Its first coordinate is 3. Thus, the x-value for which $f(x) = 2$ is 3.

16. a) 1

    b) -1

17. a) Locate 1 on the horizontal axis and the find the point on the graph for which 1 is the first coordinate. From that point, look to the vertical axis to find the corresponding y-coordinate. It appears to be -2. Thus, $f(1) = -2$.

    b) To determine which member(s) of the domain are paired with 2, locate 2 on the vertical axis. From there look left and right to the graph to find any points for which 2 is the second coordinate. One such point exists. Its first coordinate is -2, so the x-value for which $f(x) = 2$ is -2.

18. a) 3

    b) 0

19. a) Locate 1 on the horizontal axis and then find the point on the graph for which 1 is the first coordinate. From that point, look to the vertical axis to find the corresponding y-coordinate, 3. Thus, $f(1) = 3$.

    b) To determine which member(s) of the domain are paired with 2, locate 2 on the vertical axis. From there look left and right to the graph to find any points for which 2 is the second coordinate. One such point exists. Its first coordinate is -3. Thus, the x-value for which $f(x) = 2$ is -3.

20. a) 4

    b) -1

21. a) Locate 1 on the horizontal axis and then find the point on the graph for which 1 is the first coordinate. From that point, look to the vertical axis to find the corresponding y-coordinate, 1. Thus, $f(1) = 1$.

    b) To determine which member(s) of the domain are paired with 2, locate 2 on the vertical axis. From there look left and right to the graph to find any points for which 2 is the second coordinate. One such point exists. Its first coordinate is 3. Thus, the x-value for which $f(x) = 2$ is 3.

22. a) 3

    b) $-2, 0$

23. a) Locate 1 on the horizontal axis and then find the point on the graph for which 1 is the first coordinate. From that point, look to the vertical axis to find the corresponding y-coordinate, 4. Thus, $f(1) = 4$.

    b) To determine which member(s) of the domain are paired with 2, locate 2 on the vertical axis. From there look left and right to the graph to find any points for which 2 is the second coordinate. There are two such points, $(-1, 2)$ and $(3, 2)$. Thus, the x-values for which $f(x) = 2$ are -1 and 3.

24. a) 2

    b) $-5, 1$

25. a) Locate 1 on the horizontal axis and then find the point on the graph for which 1 is the first coordinate. From that point, look to the vertical axis to find the corresponding y-coordinate, 1. Thus, $f(1) = 1$.

    b) To determine which member(s) of the domain are paired with 2, locate 2 on the vertical axis. From there look left and right to the graph to find any points for which 2 is the second coordinate. All points in the set $\{x | 2 < x \le 5\}$ satisfy this condition. These are the x-values for which $f(x) = 2$.

26. a) 2

    b) $\{x | 0 < x \le 2\}$

27. We can use the vertical line test:

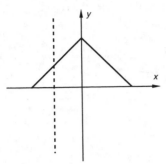

Visualize moving this vertical line across the graph. No vertical line will intersect the graph more than once. Thus, the graph is a graph of a function.

28. No

29. We can use the vertical line test:

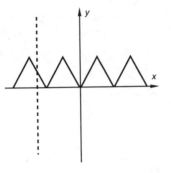

Visualize moving this vertical line across the graph. No vertical line will intersect the graph more than once. Thus, the graph is a graph of a function.

30. No

31. We can use the vertical line test.

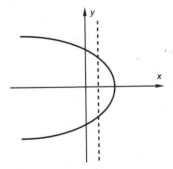

It is possible for a vertical line to intersect the graph more than once. Thus this is not the graph of a function.

32. Yes

33. We can use the vertical line test.

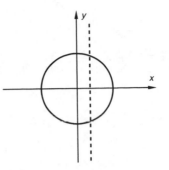

It is possible for a vertical line to intersect the graph more than once. Thus this is not a graph of a function.

34. Yes

35. $g(x) = 2x + 3$

a) $g(0) = 2 \cdot 0 + 3 = 0 + 3 = 3$

b) $g(-4) = 2(-4) + 3 = -8 + 3 = -5$

c) $g(-7) = 2(-7) + 3 = -14 + 3 = -11$

d) $g(8) = 2 \cdot 8 + 3 = 16 + 3 = 19$

e) $g(a + 2) = 2(a + 2) + 3 = 2a + 4 + 3 = 2a + 7$

f) $g(a) + 2 = (2a + 3) + 2 = 2a + 5$

36. a) 10

b) 22

c) −11

d) −14

e) $3a - 5$

f) $3a - 3$

37. $f(n) = 5n^2 + 4n$

a) $f(0) = 5 \cdot 0^2 + 4 \cdot 0 = 0 + 0 = 0$

b) $f(-1) = 5(-1)^2 + 4(-1) = 5 - 4 = 1$

c) $f(3) = 5 \cdot 3^2 + 4 \cdot 3 = 45 + 12 = 57$

d) $f(t) = 5t^2 + 4t$

e) $f(2a) = 5(2a)^2 + 4 \cdot 2a = 5 \cdot 4a^2 + 8a = 20a^2 + 8a$

f) $2 \cdot f(a) = 2(5a^2 + 4a) = 10a^2 + 8a$

38. a) 0

b) 5

c) 21

d) $3t^2 - 2t$

e) $12a^2 - 4a$

f) $6a^2 - 4a$

39. $f(x) = \dfrac{x - 3}{2x - 5}$

a) $f(0) = \dfrac{0 - 3}{2 \cdot 0 - 5} = \dfrac{-3}{0 - 5} = \dfrac{-3}{-5} = \dfrac{3}{5}$

b) $f(4) = \dfrac{4 - 3}{2 \cdot 4 - 5} = \dfrac{1}{8 - 5} = \dfrac{1}{3}$

c) $f(-1) = \dfrac{-1-3}{2(-1)-5} = \dfrac{-4}{-2-5} = \dfrac{-4}{-7} = \dfrac{4}{7}$

d) $f(3) = \dfrac{3-3}{2\cdot 3-5} = \dfrac{0}{6-5} = \dfrac{0}{1} = 0$

e) $f(x+2) = \dfrac{x+2-3}{2(x+2)-5} = \dfrac{x-1}{2x+4-5} = \dfrac{x-1}{2x-1}$

40. a) $\dfrac{26}{25}$

b) $\dfrac{2}{9}$

c) $-\dfrac{5}{12}$

d) $-\dfrac{7}{3}$

e) $\dfrac{3x+5}{2x+11}$

41. $A(s) = s^2 \dfrac{\sqrt{3}}{4}$

$A(4) = 4^2 \dfrac{\sqrt{3}}{4} = 4\sqrt{3} \approx 6.93$

The area is $4\sqrt{3}$ cm$^2 \approx 6.93$ cm^2.

42. $9\sqrt{3}$ in$^2 \approx 15.59$ in^2

43. $V(r) = 4\pi r^2$

$V(3) = 4\pi(3)^2 = 36\pi$

The area is 36π in$^2 \approx 113.10$ in^2.

44. 100π cm$^2 \approx 314.16$ cm^2

45. $F(C) = \dfrac{9}{5}C + 32$

$F(-10) = \dfrac{9}{5}(-10) + 32 = -18 + 32 = 14$

The equivalent temperature is 14°F.

46. 41°F

47. $H(x) = 2.75x + 71.48$

$H(32) = 2.75(32) + 71.48 = 159.48$

The predicted height is 159.48 cm.

48. 167.73 cm

49. Plot and connect the points, using the year as the first coordinate and the corresponding number of reported cases of AIDS as the second coordinate.

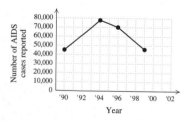

To estimate the number of cases of AIDS reported in 2002, extend the graph and extrapolate. It appears that about 24,000 cases of AIDS were reported in 2002.

50. About 61,000 cases

51. Plot and connect the points, using the year as the first coordinate and the population as the second.

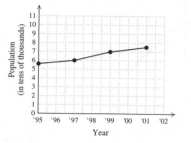

To estimate what the population was in 1998, first locate the point that is directly above 1998. Then estimate its second coordinate by moving horizontally from the point to the vertical axis. Read the approximate function value there. The population was about 65,000.

52. About 80,000

53. Plot and connect the points, using the year as the first coordinate and the sales total as the second coordinate.

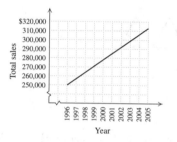

To predict the total sales for 2005, first locate the point directly above 2005. Then estimate its second coordinate by moving horizontally to the vertical axis. Read the approximate function value there. The predicted 2005 sales total is about $313,000.

54. About $271,000

55. *Writing Exercise*

56. *Writing Exercise*

57. $\dfrac{10-3^2}{9-2\cdot 3} = \dfrac{10-9}{9-6} = \dfrac{1}{3}$

58. -1

59. $S = 2lh + 2lw + 2wh$

$S - 2wh = 2lh + 2lw$

$S - 2wh = l(2h + 2w)$

$\dfrac{S - 2wh}{2h + 2w} = l$

60. $w = \dfrac{S - 2lh}{2l + 2h}$

61. $2x + 3y = 6$

$3y = 6 - 2x$

$y = \dfrac{6 - 2x}{3}$, or $2 - \dfrac{2}{3}x$, or $-\dfrac{2}{3}x + 2$

62. $y = \frac{5}{4}x - 2$

63. *Writing Exercise*

64. *Writing Exercise*

65. To find $f(g(-4))$, we first find $g(-4)$:

$g(-4) = 2(-4) + 5 = -8 + 5 = -3$.

Then $f(g(-4)) = f(-3) = 3(-3)^2 - 1 = 3 \cdot 9 - 1 = 27 - 1 = 26$.

To find $g(f(-4))$, we first find $f(-4)$:

$f(-4) = 3(-4)^2 - 1 = 3 \cdot 16 - 1 = 48 - 1 = 47$.

Then $g(f(-4)) = g(47) = 2 \cdot 47 + 5 = 94 + 5 = 99$.

66. 26; 9

67. Graph $y = (4/3)\pi x^3$ in an appropriate window such as $[0, 3, 0, 60]$, Yscl $= 10$. Then use the TRACE feature to find the value of x that corresponds to $y = 50$.

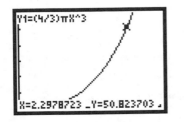

The radius is about 2.3 cm when the volume is 50 cm³.

68. About 0.659 in

69. Locate the highest point on the graph. Then move horizontally to the vertical axis and read the corresponding pressure. It is about 22 mm.

70. About 2 minutes, 50 seconds.

71. *Writing Exercise*

72. 1 every 3 minutes

73.

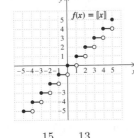

74. $g(x) = \frac{15}{4}x - \frac{13}{4}$

75. Graph the energy expenditures for walking and for bicycling on the same axes. Using the information given we plot and connect the points $\left(2\frac{1}{2}, 210\right)$ and $\left(3\frac{3}{4}, 300\right)$ for walking. We use the points $\left(5\frac{1}{2}, 210\right)$ and $(13, 660)$ for bicycling.

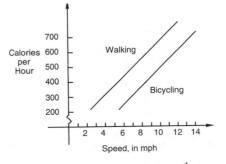

From the graph we see that walking $4\frac{1}{2}$ mph burns about 350 calories per hour and bicycling 14 mph burns about 725 calories per hour. Walking for two hours at $4\frac{1}{2}$ mph, then, would burn about $2 \cdot 350$, or 700 calories. Thus, bicycling 14 mph for one hour burns more calories than walking $4\frac{1}{2}$ mph for two hours.

Exercise Set 3.5

1. The domain is the set of all first coordinates, $\{2, 9, -2, -4\}$.

The range is the set of all second coordinates, $\{8, 3, 10, 4\}$.

2. Domain: $\{1, 2, 3, 4\}$; range: $\{2, 3, 4, 5\}$

3. The domain is the set of all first coordinates, $\{0, 4, -5, -1\}$.

The range is the set of all second coordinates, $\{0, -2\}$.

4. Domain: $\{3, 2, 1, 0\}$; range: $\{7\}$

5. The function f can be written as $\{(-4, -2), (-2, -1), (0, 0), (2, 1), (4, 2)\}$.
The domain is the set of all first coordinates, $\{-4, -2, 0, 2, 4\}$ and the range is the set of all second coordinates, $\{-2, -1, 0, 1, 2\}$.

6. Domain: $\{-4, -2, 0, 3, 5\}$; range: $\{4, 1, 3, -2, 0\}$

7. The function f can be written as $\{(-5, -1), (-3, -1), (-1, -1), (0, 1), (2, 1), (4, 1)\}$. The domain is the set of all first coordinates, $\{-5, -3, -1, 0, 2, 4\}$ and the range is the set of all second coordinates, $\{-1, 1\}$.

8. Domain: $\{-3, -2, -1, 0, 1, 2, 3\}$; range: $\{-2, -1, 1, 2\}$

9. The domain of the function is the set of all x-values that are in the graph, $\{x| -4 \leq x \leq 3\}$, or $[-4, 3]$.

The range is the set of all y-values that are in the graph, $\{y| -3 \leq y \leq 4\}$, or $[-3, 4]$.

10. Domain: $\{x| -4 \leq x \leq 3\}$, or $[-4, 3]$; range: $\{y| 0 \leq y \leq 2\}$, or $[0, 2]$

11. The domain of the function is the set of all x-values that are in the graph, $\{x| -4 \leq x \leq 5\}$, or $[-4, 5]$.

The range is the set of all y-values that are in the graph, $\{y| -2 \leq y \leq 4\}$, or $[-2, 4]$.

12. Domain: $\{x| -2 \le x \le 5\}$, or $[-2,5]$; range: $\{y| -2 \le y \le 4\}$, or $[-2,4]$

13. The domain of the function is the set of all x-values that are in the graph, $\{x| -4 \le x \le 4\}$, or $[-4,4]$.

The range is the set of all y-values that are in the graph, $\{-3, -1, 1\}$.

14. Domain: $\{x| -3 \le x \le 5\}$, or $[-3,5]$; range: $\{-2, 1, 4\}$

15. For any x-value and for any y-value there is a point on the graph. Thus,

Domain of $f = \{x|x$ is a real number$\}$ and

Range of $f = \{y|y$ is a real number$\}$.

16. Domain: $\{x|x$ is a real number$\}$;
range: $\{y|y$ is a real number$\}$

17. For any x-value there is a point on the graph. Thus,

Domain of $f = \{x|x$ is a real number$\}$.

The only y-value on the graph is 4. Thus,

Range of $f = \{4\}$.

18. Domain: $\{x|x$ is a real number$\}$; range: $\{-2\}$

19. For an x-value there is a point on the graph. Thus,

Domain of $f = \{x|x$ is a real number$\}$.

The function has no y-values less than 1 and every y-value greater than or equal to 1 corresponds to a member of the domain. Thus,

Range of $f = \{y|y \ge 1\}$, or $[1, \infty)$.

20. Domain: $\{x|x$ is a real number$\}$; range: $\{y|y \le 4\}$, or $(-\infty, 4]$

21. The hole in the graph at $(-2, -4)$ indicates that the function is not defined for $x = -2$. For any other x-value there is a point on the graph. Thus,

Domain of $f = \{x|x$ is a real number and $x \ne -2\}$.

There is no function value at $(-2, -4)$, so -4 is not in the range of the function. For any other y-value there is a point on the graph. Thus,

Range of $f = \{y|y$ is a real number and $y \ne -4\}$.

22. Domain: $\{x|x$ is a real number and $x \ne 5\}$;
range: $\{y|y$ is a real number and $y \ne 2\}$

23. The function has no x-values less than 0 and every x-value greater than or equal to 0 corresponds to a member of the domain. Thus,

Domain of $f = \{x|x \ge 0\}$, or $[0, \infty)$.

The function has no y-values less than 0 and every y-value greater than or equal to 0 corresponds to a member of the range. Thus,

Range of $f = \{y|y \ge 0\}$, or $[0, \infty)$.

24. Domain: $\{x|x \le 3\}$, or $(-\infty, 3]$; range: $\{y|y \ge 0\}$, or $[0, \infty)$

25. $f(x) = \dfrac{5}{x-3}$

Since $\dfrac{5}{x-3}$ cannot be computed when the denominator is 0, we find the x-value that causes $x - 3$ to be 0:

$$x - 3 = 0$$
$$x = 3 \quad \text{Adding 3 to both sides}$$

Thus, 3 is not in the domain of f, while all other real numbers are. The domain of f is $\{x|x$ is a real number and $x \ne 3\}$.

26. $\{x|x$ is a real number and $x \ne 6\}$

27. $f(x) = \dfrac{3}{2x-1}$

Since $\dfrac{3}{2x-1}$ cannot be computed when the denominator is 0, we find the x-value that causes $2x - 1$ to be 0:

$$2x - 1 = 0$$
$$2x = 1$$
$$x = \dfrac{1}{2}$$

Thus, $\dfrac{1}{2}$ is not in the domain of f, while all other real numbers are. The domain of f is $\left\{x|x$ is a real number and $x \ne \dfrac{1}{2}\right\}$.

28. $\left\{x\,\middle|\,x$ is a real number and $x \ne -\dfrac{3}{4}\right\}$

29. $f(x) = 2x + 1$

Since we can compute $2x + 1$ for any real number x, the domain is the set of all real numbers.

30. All real numbers

31. $g(x) = |5 - x|$

Since we can compute $|5 - x|$ for any real number x, the domain is the set of all real numbers.

32. All real numbers

33. $f(x) = \dfrac{5x}{x-9}$

Since $\dfrac{5x}{x-9}$ cannot be computed when the denominator is 0, we find the x-value that causes $x - 9$ to be 0:

$$x - 9 = 0$$
$$x = 9$$

Thus, 9 is not in the domain of f, while all other real numbers are. The domain of f is $\{x|x$ is a real number and $x \ne 9\}$.

34. $\{x|x$ is a real number and $x \ne -1\}$

35. $f(x) = x^2 - 9$

Since we can compute $x^2 - 9$ for any real number x, the domain is the set of all real numbers.

36. All real numbers

37. $f(x) = \dfrac{2x - 7}{5}$

There are no x-values that cause the denominator of $\dfrac{2x-7}{5}$ to be 0, so the domain is the set of all real numbers.

38. All real numbers

39. $R(t) = 46.8 - 0.075t$

If we assume the function is not valid for years before 1930, we must have $t \geq 0$. In addition, $R(t)$ must be positive, so we have:

$$46.8 - 0.075t > 0$$
$$-0.075t > -46.8$$
$$t < 624$$

Then the domain of the function is $\{t | 0 \leq t < 624\}$, or $[0, 624)$.

40. $\left\{ t \middle| 0 \leq t < 513\dfrac{1}{3} \right\}$, or $\left[0, 513\dfrac{1}{3}\right)$

41. $A(p) = -2.5p + 26.5$

The price must be positive, so we have $p > \$0$. In addition $A(p)$ must be nonnegative, so we have:

$$-2.5p + 26.5 \geq 0$$
$$26.5 \geq 2.5p$$
$$10.6 \geq p$$

Then the domain of the function is $\{p | \$0 < p \leq \$10.60\}$, or $(0, 10.60]$.

42. $\{p | p \geq \$5.50\}$, or $[5.50, \infty)$

43. $P(d) = 0.03d + 1$

The depth must be nonnegative, so we have $d \geq 0$. In addition, $P(d)$ must be nonnegative, so we have:

$$0.03d + 1 \geq 0$$
$$0.03d \geq -1$$
$$d \geq -33.\overline{3}$$

Then we have $d \geq 0$ *and* $d \geq -33.\overline{3}$, so the domain of the function is $\{d | d \geq 0\}$, or $[0, \infty)$.

44. $\{s | s > 0\}$, or $(0, \infty)$

45. $f(x) = \begin{cases} x, & \text{if } x < 0 \\ 2x + 1, & \text{if } x \geq 0 \end{cases}$

a) Since $-5 < 0$, we use the equation $f(x) = x$.

Thus, $f(-5) = -5$.

b) Since $0 \geq 0$, we use the equation $f(x) = 2x + 1$.

$f(0) = 2 \cdot 0 + 1 = 0 + 1 = 1$

c) Since $10 \geq 0$, we use the equation $f(x) = 2x + 1$.

$f(10) = 2 \cdot 10 + 1 = 20 + 1 = 21$

46. a) -5

b) 0

c) 18

47. $G(x) = \begin{cases} x - 5, & \text{if } x < -1 \\ x, & \text{if } -1 \leq x \leq 2 \\ x + 2, & \text{if } x > 2 \end{cases}$

a) Since $-1 \leq 0 \leq 2$, we use the equation $G(x) = x$.

$G(0) = 0$

b) Since $-1 \leq 2 \leq 2$, we use the equation $G(x) = x$.

$G(2) = 2$

c) Since $5 > 2$, we use the equation $G(x) = x + 2$.

$G(5) = 5 + 2 = 7$

48. a) -2

b) 3

c) -50

49. $f(x) = \begin{cases} x^2 - 10, & \text{if } x < -10 \\ x^2, & \text{if } -10 \leq x \leq 10 \\ x^2 + 10, & \text{if } x > 10 \end{cases}$

a) Since $-10 \leq -10 \leq 10$, we use the equation $f(x) = x^2$.

$f(-10) = (-10)^2 = 100$

b) Since $-10 \leq 10 \leq 10$, we use the equation $f(x) = x^2$.

$f(10) = 10^2 = 100$

c) Since $11 > 10$, we use the equation $f(x) = x^2 + 10$.

$f(11) = 11^2 + 10 = 121 + 10 = 131$

50. a) -3

b) 9

c) 23

51. *Writing Exercise*

52. *Writing Exercise*

53. $(x + 4) + (x^2 + x + 1) = x^2 + (x + x) + (4 + 1)$
$$= x^2 + 2x + 5$$

54. $-a + 8$

55. $(2x + y + 3) - (5y - x + 2) = 2x + y + 3 - 5y + x - 2$
$$= 3x - 4y + 1$$

56. $-2x + 21$

57. $2(11t + 4u) + 6(3 - 2u)$
$$= 22t + 8u + 18 - 12u$$
$$= 22t - 4u + 18$$

58. $10x - 4$

59. $3[x - (x + 7) + 1] - 5 = 3[x - x - 7 + 1] - 5$
$$= 3[-6] - 5$$
$$= -18 - 5$$
$$= -23$$

60. $14x + 29$

61. *Writing Exercise*

62. *Writing Exercise*

63.

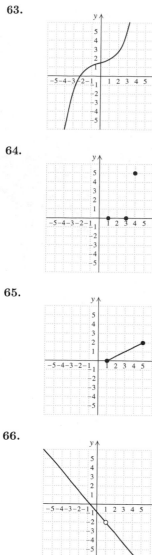

64.

65.

66.

67. The graph indicates that the function is not defined for $x = 0$. For any other x-value there is a point on the graph. Thus,

Domain of $f = \{x | x$ is a real number *and* $x \neq 0\}$.

The graph also indicates that the function is not defined for $y = 0$. For any other y-value there is a point on the graph. Thus,

Domain of $f = \{y | y$ is a real number *and* $y \neq 0\}$.

68. Domain: $\{x | x \leq -2$ *or* $x \geq 2\}$; range: $\{y | y \geq 0\}$

69. The function has no x-values for $-2 \leq x \leq 0$. For any other x-value there is a point on the graph. Thus, the domain of the function is $\{x | x < -2$ *or* $x > 0\}$.

The function has no y-values for $-2 \leq y \leq 3$. Every other y-value corresponds to a member of the range. Then the range is $\{y | y < -2$ *or* $y > 3\}$.

70. Domain: $\{x | x$ is a real number$\}$; range: $\{x | x$ is a real number$\}$

71.

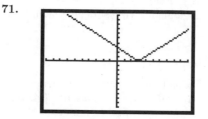

From the graph we see that the domain of f is $\{x | x$ is a real number$\}$ and the range is $\{y | y \geq 0\}$.

72. Domain: $\{x | x$ is a real number$\}$; range: $\{y | y \geq -3\}$

73.

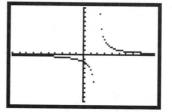

From the graph we see that the domain of f is $\{x | x$ is a real number *and* $x \neq 2\}$ and the range is $\{y | y$ is a real number *and* $y \neq 0\}$.

74. Domain: $\{x | x$ is a real number *and* $x \neq -3\}$; range: $\{y | y$ is a real number *and* $y \neq 0\}$

75. Left to the student

Exercise Set 3.6

1. Since $f(2) = -3 \cdot 2 + 1 = -5$, and $g(2) = 2^2 + 2 = 6$, we have $f(2) + g(2) = -5 + 6 = 1$.

2. 7

3. Since $f(5) = -3 \cdot 5 + 1 = -14$ and $g(5) = 5^2 + 2 = 27$, we have $f(5) - g(5) = -14 - 27 = -41$.

4. -29

5. Since $f(-1) = -3(-1) + 1 = 4$ and $g(-1) = (-1)^2 + 2 = 3$, we have $f(-1) \cdot g(-1) = 4 \cdot 3 = 12$.

6. 42

7. Since $f(-4) = -3(-4) + 1 = 13$ and $g(-4) = (-4)^2 + 2 = 18$, we have $f(-4)/g(-4) = 13/18$.

8. $-\dfrac{8}{11}$

9. Since $g(1) = 1^2 + 2 = 3$ and $f(1) = -3 \cdot 1 + 1 = -2$, we have $g(1) - f(1) = 3 - (-2) = 3 + 2 = 5$.

10. $-\dfrac{6}{5}$

11. $(f+g)(x) = f(x)+g(x) = (-3x+1)+(x^2+2) = x^2-3x+3$

12. $x^2 + 3x + 1$

13. $(F+G)(x) = F(x) + G(x)$
$$= x^2 - 2 + 5 - x$$
$$= x^2 - x + 3$$

14. $a^2 - a + 3$

15. Using our work in Exercise 13, we have
$$(F+G)(-4) = (-4)^2 - (-4) + 3$$
$$= 16 + 4 + 3$$
$$= 23.$$

16. 33

17. $(F-G)(x) = F(x) - G(x)$
$$= x^2 - 2 - (5 - x)$$
$$= x^2 - 2 - 5 + x$$
$$= x^2 + x - 7$$

Then we have
$$(F-G)(3) = 3^2 + 3 - 7$$
$$= 9 + 3 - 7$$
$$= 5.$$

18. -1

19. $(F \cdot G)(x) = F(x) \cdot G(x)$
$$= (x^2 - 2)(5 - x)$$
$$= 5x^2 - x^3 - 10 + 2x$$

Then we have
$$(F \cdot G)(-3) = 5(-3)^2 - (-3)^3 - 10 + 2(-3)$$
$$= 5 \cdot 9 - (-27) - 10 - 6$$
$$= 45 + 27 - 10 - 6$$
$$= 56.$$

20. 126

21. $(F/G)(x) = F(x)/G(x)$
$$= \frac{x^2 - 2}{5 - x}, \ x \neq 5$$

22. $-x^2 - x + 7$

23. Using our work in Exercise 21, we have
$$(F/G)(-2) = \frac{(-2)^2 - 2}{5 - (-2)} = \frac{4 - 2}{5 + 2} = \frac{2}{7}.$$

24. $-\dfrac{1}{6}$

25. $N(1980) = (R + W)(1980)$
$$= R(1980) + W(1980)$$
$$\approx 0.75 + 2.5$$
$$\approx 3.25$$

We estimate that 3.25 million U.S. women had children in 1980.

26. $1.3 + 2.6 = 3.9$

27. The number of women under 30 who gave birth dropped from 1990 to 1998.

28. Women 30 and over

29. $(n + l)(98) = n(98) + l(98)$

From the middle line of the graph, we can see that $n(98) + l(98) \approx 50$ million.

This represents the total number of passengers serviced by Newark and LaGuardia airports in 1998.

30. About 41 million; the total number of passengers serviced by Kennedy and LaGuardia airports in 1998

31. $(k - l)(94) = k(94) - l(94)$
$$\approx 29 - 21$$
$$\approx 8 \text{ million}$$

This represents how many more passengers used Kennedy airport than LaGuardia airport in 1994.

32. About 1 million; how many more passengers used Kennedy airport than Newark airport in 1994

33. $(n + l + k)(99) = n(99) + l(99) + k(99)$

From the top line of the graph, we can see that $n(99) + l(99) + k(99) \approx 89$ million.

This represents the number of passengers serviced by Newark, LaGuardia, and Kennedy airports in 1999.

34. About 69 million; the number of passengers serviced by Newark, LaGuardia, and Kennedy airports in 1998

35. The domain of f and of g is all real numbers. Thus, Domain of $f + g$ = Domain of $f - g$ = Domain of $f \cdot g$ = $\{x | x \text{ is a real number}\}$.

36. $\{x | x \text{ is a real number}\}$

37. Because division by 0 is undefined, we have

Domain of $f = \{x | x \text{ is a real number } and \ x \neq 3\}$,

and

Domain of $g = \{x | x \text{ is a real number}\}$.

Thus, Domain of $f + g$ = Domain of $f - g$ = Domain of $f \cdot g = \{x | x \text{ is a real number } and \ x \neq 3\}$.

38. $\{x | x \text{ is a real number } and \ x \neq 9\}$

39. Because division by 0 is undefined, we have

Domain of $f = \{x | x \text{ is a real number } and \ x \neq 0\}$,

and

Domain of $g = \{x | x \text{ is a real number}\}$.

Thus, Domain of $f + g$ = Domain of $f - g$ = Domain of $f \cdot g = \{x | x \text{ is a real number } and \ x \neq 0\}$.

40. $\{x | x \text{ is a real number } and \ x \neq 0\}$

41. Because division by 0 is undefined, we have

Domain of $f = \{x | x$ is a real number and $x \neq 1\}$,

and

Domain of $g = \{x | x$ is a real number$\}$.

Thus, Domain of $f + g =$ Domain of $f - g =$ Domain of $f \cdot g = \{x | x$ is a real number and $x \neq 1\}$.

42. $\{x | x$ is a real number and $x \neq 6\}$

43. Because division by 0 is undefined, we have

Domain of $f = \{x | x$ is a real number and $x \neq 2\}$,

and

Domain of $g = \{x | x$ is a real number and $x \neq 4\}$.

Thus, Domain of $f + g =$ Domain of $f - g =$ Domain of $f \cdot g = \{x | x$ is a real number and $x \neq 2$ and $x \neq 4\}$.

44. $\{x | x$ is a real number and $x \neq 3$ and $x \neq 2\}$

45. Domain of $f =$ Domain of $g =$

$\{x | x$ is a real number$\}$.

Since $g(x) = 0$ when $x - 3 = 0$, we have $g(x) = 0$ when $x = 3$. We conclude that Domain of $f/g = \{x | x$ is a real number and $x \neq 3\}$.

46. $\{x | x$ is a real number and $x \neq 5\}$

47. Domain of $f =$ Domain of $g =$

$\{x | x$ is a real number$\}$.

Since $g(x) = 0$ when $2x - 8 = 0$, we have $g(x) = 0$ when $x = 4$. We conclude that Domain of $f/g = \{x | x$ is a real number and $x \neq 4\}$.

48. $\{x | x$ is a real number and $x \neq 3\}$

49. Domain of $f = \{x | x$ is a real number and $x \neq 4\}$.

Domain of $g = \{x | x$ is a real number$\}$.

Since $g(x) = 0$ when $5 - x = 0$, we have $g(x) = 0$ when $x = 5$. We conclude that Domain of $f/g = \{x | x$ is a real number and $x \neq 4$ and $x \neq 5\}$.

50. $\{x | x$ is a real number and $x \neq 2$ and $x \neq 7\}$

51. Domain of $f = \{x | x$ is a real number and $x \neq -1\}$.

Domain of $g = \{x | x$ is a real number$\}$.

Since $g(x) = 0$ when $2x + 5 = 0$, we have $g(x) = 0$ when $x = -\dfrac{5}{2}$. We conclude that Domain of $f/g =$

$\left\{ x \left| x \text{ is a real number } and \text{ } x \neq -1 \text{ } and \text{ } x \neq -\dfrac{5}{2} \right. \right\}$.

52. $\left\{ x \left| x \text{ is a real number } and \text{ } x \neq 2 \text{ } and \text{ } x \neq -\dfrac{7}{3} \right. \right\}$

53. $(F + G)(5) = F(5) + G(5) = 1 + 3 = 4$

$(F + G)(7) = F(7) + G(7) = -1 + 4 = 3$

54. 0; 2

55. $(G - F)(7) = G(7) - F(7) = 4 - (-1) = 4 + 1 = 5$

$(G - F)(3) = G(3) - F(3) = 1 - 2 = -1$

56. $2; -\dfrac{1}{4}$

57. From the graph we see that Domain of

$F = \{x | 0 \leq x \leq 9\}$ and Domain of

$G = \{x | 3 \leq x \leq 10\}$. Then Domain of

$F + G = \{x | 3 \leq x \leq 9\}$. Since $G(x)$ is never 0, Domain of $F/G = \{x | 3 \leq x \leq 9\}$.

58. $\{x | 3 \leq x \leq 9\}$; $\{x | 3 \leq x \leq 9\}$;
$\{x | 3 \leq x \leq 9 \text{ } and \text{ } x \neq 6 \text{ } and \text{ } x \neq 8\}$

59. We use $(F + G)(x) = F(x) + G(x)$.

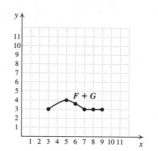

60.

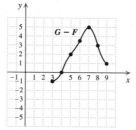

61. *Writing Exercise*

62. *Writing Exercise*

63. $3x^2 - 5y = 3(10)^2 - 5(6)$

$\qquad\quad = 3(100) - 5(6)$

$\qquad\quad = 300 - 30$

$\qquad\quad = 270$

64. 16

65. $3(x - 1) + 4(x - 2) = 3x - 3 + 4x - 8$

$\qquad\qquad\qquad\qquad = 7x - 11$

66. $-5x - 37$

67. $3(x - 1) + 4(x - 2) = 0$

$\qquad\quad 7x - 11 = 0 \qquad$ See Exercise 65.

$\qquad\qquad 7x = 11$

$\qquad\qquad\quad x = \dfrac{11}{7}$

The solution is $\dfrac{11}{7}$.

68. $-\dfrac{37}{5}$

69. Let n represent the first integer; $x + (x + 1) = 145$.

70. Let x represent the number; $x - (-x) = 20$

71. *Writing Exercise*

72. *Writing Exercise*

73. Domain of $f = \left\{ x \middle| x \text{ is a real number } and \ x \neq -\dfrac{5}{2} \right\}$; domain of $g = \{x | x \text{ is a real number } and \ x \neq -3\}$; $g(x) = 0$ when $x^4 - 1 = 0$, or when $x = 1$ or $x = -1$.

Then domain of $f/g = \left\{ x \middle| x \text{ is a real number } and \right.$

$\left. x \neq -\dfrac{5}{2} \text{ and } x \neq -3 \text{ and } x \neq 1 \text{ and } x \neq -1 \right\}.$

74. $\{x | x \text{ is a real number } and \ x \neq 4 \text{ and } x \neq 3 \text{ and } x \neq 2 \text{ and } x \neq -2\}$

75. Answers may vary.

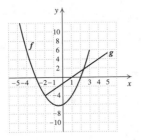

76. $\left\{ x \middle| x \text{ is a real number } and \ -1 < x < 5 \text{ and } x \neq \dfrac{3}{2} \right\}$

77. The domain of each function is the set of first coordinates for that function.

Domain of $f = \{-2, -1, 0, 1, 2\}$ and

Domain of $g = \{-4, -3, -2, -1, 0, 1\}$.

Domain of $f + g =$ Domain of $f - g =$

Domain of $f \cdot g = \{-2, -1, 0, 1\}$.

Since $g(-1) = 0$, we conclude that Domain of $f/g = \{-2, 0, 1\}$.

78. 5; 15; $\dfrac{2}{3}$

79. Answers may vary. $f(x) = \dfrac{1}{x + 2}$, $g(x) = \dfrac{1}{x - 5}$

80. Left to the student

81. Because $y_2 = 0$ when $x = 3$, the domain of $y_3 = \{x | x \text{ is a real number } and \ x \neq 3\}$. Since the graph produced using Connected mode contains the line $x = 3$, it does not represent y_3 accurately. The domain of the graph produced using Dot mode does not include 3, so it represents y_3 more accurately.

82. Left to the student

83. Think of adding, subtracting, multiplying, or dividing the y-values for various x-values.

a) IV

b) I

c) II

d) III

Chapter 4

Linear Equations, Inequalities, and Graphs

1. $5x - 3y = 15$

The equation is in the form $Ax + By = C$ with $A = 5$, $B = -3$, and $C = 15$, so it is linear.

2. Linear

3.
$$7y = x - 5$$
$$-x + 7y = -5 \quad \text{Adding } -x \text{ to both sides}$$

The equation can be written in the form $Ax + By = C$ with $A = -1$, $B = 7$, and $C = -5$, so it is linear.

4. Linear

5. $xy = 7$

We cannot write this equation in standard form. It is not linear because it has an xy-term.

6. Not linear

7.
$$16 + 4y = 0$$
$$4y = -16$$
$$0 \cdot x + 4y = -16$$

The equation can be written in the form $Ax + By = C$ with $A = 0$, $B = 4$, and $C = -16$, so it is linear.

8. Linear

9.
$$2y - \frac{3}{x} = 5$$
$$x\left(2y - \frac{3}{x}\right) = x \cdot 5$$
$$2xy - 3 = 5x$$
$$2xy = 5x + 3$$
$$-5x + 2xy = 3$$

The equation is not linear because it has an xy-term.

10. Not linear

11. (a) The graph crosses the y-axis at $(0, 5)$, so the y-intercept is $(0, 5)$.

(b) The graph crosses the x-axis at $(2, 0)$, so the x-intercept is $(2, 0)$.

12. (a) $(0, 3)$; (b) $(4, 0)$

13. (a) The graph crosses the y-axis at $(0, -4)$, so the y-intercept is $(0, -4)$.

(b) The graph crosses the x-axis at $(3, 0)$, so the x-intercept is $(3, 0)$.

14. (a) $(0, 5)$; (b) $(-3, 0)$

15. (a) The graph crosses the y-axis at $(0, -2)$, so the y-intercept is $(0, -2)$.

(b) The graph crosses the x-axis at $(-3, 0)$ and also at $(3, 0)$, so the x-intercepts are $(-3, 0)$ and $(3, 0)$.

16. (a) $(0, 1)$; (b) $(-3, 0)$

17. (a) The graph crosses the y-axis at $(0, 4)$, so the y-intercept is $(0, 4)$.

(b) The graph crosses the x-axis at $(-3, 0)$, $(3, 0)$, and $(5, 0)$. Each of these points is an x-intercept.

18. (a) $(0, -3)$; (b) $(-2, 0)$, $(2, 0)$, $(5, 0)$

19. $5x + 3y = 15$

(a) To find the y-intercept, let $x = 0$ and solve for y.
$$5 \cdot 0 + 3y = 15$$
$$3y = 15$$
$$y = 5$$

The y-intercept is $(0, 5)$.

(b) To find the x-intercept, let $y = 0$ and solve for x.
$$5x + 3 \cdot 0 = 15$$
$$5x = 15$$
$$x = 3$$

The x-intercept is $(3, 0)$.

20. (a) $(0, 10)$; (b) $(4, 0)$

21. $7x - 2y = 28$

(a) To find the y-intercept, let $x = 0$ and solve for y.
$$7 \cdot 0 - 2y = 28$$
$$-2y = 28$$
$$y = -14$$

The y-intercept is $(0, -14)$.

(b) To find the x-intercept, let $y = 0$ and solve for x.
$$7x - 2 \cdot 0 = 28$$
$$7x = 28$$
$$x = 4$$

The x-intercept is $(4, 0)$.

22. (a) $(0, -8)$; (b) $(6, 0)$

23. $-4x + 3y = 10$

   (a) To find the y-intercept, let $x = 0$ and solve for y.
$$-4 \cdot 0 + 3y = 10$$
$$3y = 10$$
$$y = \frac{10}{3}$$
   The y-intercept is $\left(0, \dfrac{10}{3}\right)$.

   (b) To find the x-intercept, let $y = 0$ and solve for x.
$$-4x + 3 \cdot 0 = 0$$
$$-4x = 10$$
$$x = -\frac{5}{2}$$
   The x-intercept is $\left(-\dfrac{5}{2}, 0\right)$.

24. (a) $\left(0, \dfrac{7}{3}\right)$; (b) $\left(-\dfrac{7}{2}, 0\right)$

25. $y = 9$

   Observe that this is the equation of a horizontal line 9 units above the x-axis. Thus, (a) the y-intercept is $(0, 9)$ and (b) there is no x-intercept.

26. (a) None; (b) $(8, 0)$

27. $x + 2y = 6$

   Find the y-intercept:
$$0 + 2y = 6$$
$$2y = 6$$
$$y = 3$$
   The y-intercept is $(0, 3)$.

   Find the x-intercept:
$$x + 2 \cdot 0 = 6$$
$$x = 6$$
   The x-intercept is $(6, 0)$.

   To find a third point we replace x with 2 and solve for y.
$$2 + 2y = 6$$
$$2y = 4$$
$$y = 2$$
   The point $(2, 2)$ appears to line up with the intercepts, so we draw the graph.

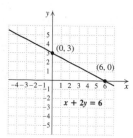

28.

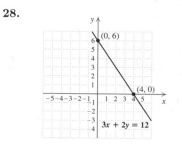

29. $6x + 9y = 36$

   Find the y-intercept:
$$6 \cdot 0 + 9y = 36$$
$$9y = 36$$
$$y = 4$$
   The y-intercept is $(0, 4)$.

   Find the x-intercept:
$$6x + 9 \cdot 0 = 36$$
$$6x = 36$$
$$x = 6$$
   The x-intercept is $(6, 0)$.

   To find a third point we replace x with -3 and solve for y.
$$6(-3) + 9y = 36$$
$$-18 + 9y = 36$$
$$9y = 54$$
$$y = 6$$
   The point $(-3, 6)$ appears to line up with the intercepts, so we draw the graph.

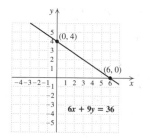

30.

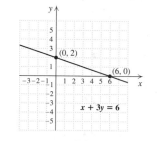

31. $-x + 3y = 9$

   Find the y-intercept:
$$-0 + 3y = 9$$
$$3y = 9$$
$$y = 3$$
   The y-intercept is $(0, 3)$.

Find the x-intercept:

$$-x + 3 \cdot 0 = 9$$
$$-x = 9$$
$$x = -9$$

The x-intercept is $(-9, 0)$.

To find a third point we replace x with 3 and solve for y.

$$-3 + 3y = 9$$
$$3y = 12$$
$$y = 4$$

The point $(3, 4)$ appears to line up with the intercepts, so we draw the graph.

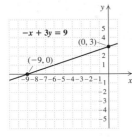

32.

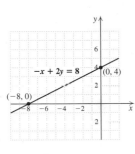

33. $2x - y = 8$

Find the y-intercept:

$$2 \cdot 0 - y = 8$$
$$-y = 8$$
$$y = -8$$

The y-intercept is $(0, -8)$.

Find the x-intercept:

$$2x - 0 = 8$$
$$2x = 8$$
$$x = 4$$

The x-intercept is $(4, 0)$.

To find a third point we replace x with 2 and solve for y.

$$2 \cdot 2 - y = 8$$
$$4 - y = 8$$
$$-y = 4$$
$$y = -4$$

The point $(2, -4)$ appears to line up with the intercepts, so we draw the graph.

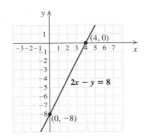

34.

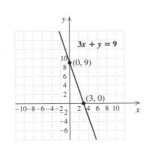

35. $y = -3x + 6$

Find the y-intercept:

$$y = -3 \cdot 0 + 6$$
$$y = 6$$

The y-intercept is $(0, 6)$.

Find the x-intercept:

$$0 = -3x + 6$$
$$3x = 6$$
$$x = 2$$

The x-intercept is $(2, 0)$.

To find a third point we replace x with 3 and find y.

$$y = -3 \cdot 3 + 6 = -9 + 6 = -3$$

The point $(3, -3)$ appears to line up with the intercepts, so we draw the graph.

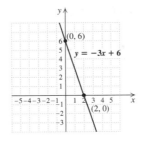

36.

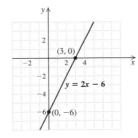

37. $5x - 10 = 5y$

We can leave the equation in the given form or rewrite it in the form $Ax + By = C$. We will use the given form.

Find the y-intercept:

$$5 \cdot 0 - 10 = 5y$$
$$-10 = 5y$$
$$-2 = y$$

The y-intercept is $(0, -2)$.

Find the x-intercept.

$$5x - 10 = 5 \cdot 0$$
$$5x - 10 = 0$$
$$5x = 10$$
$$x = 2$$

The x-intercept is $(2, 0)$.

To find a third point we replace x with 5 and solve for y.

$$5 \cdot 5 - 10 = 5y$$
$$25 - 10 = 5y$$
$$15 = 5y$$
$$3 = y$$

The point $(5, 3)$ appears to line up with the intercepts, so we draw the graph.

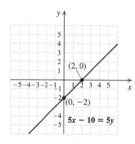

38.

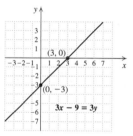

39. $2x - 5y = 10$

Find the y-intercept:

$$2 \cdot 0 - 5y = 10$$
$$-5y = 10$$
$$y = -2$$

The y-intercept is $(0, -2)$.

Find the x-intercept:

$$2x - 5 \cdot 0 = 10$$
$$2x = 10$$
$$x = 5$$

The x-intercept is $(5, 0)$.

To find a third point we replace x with -5 and solve for y.

$$2(-5) - 5y = 10$$
$$-10 - 5y = 10$$
$$-5y = 20$$
$$y = -4$$

The point $(-5, -4)$ appears to line up with the intercepts, so we draw the graph.

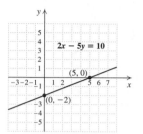

40.

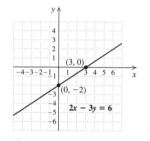

41. $6x + 2y = 12$

Find the y-intercept:

$$6 \cdot 0 + 2y = 12$$
$$2y = 12$$
$$y = 6$$

The y-intercept is $(0, 6)$.

Find the x-intercept:

$$6x + 2 \cdot 0 = 12$$
$$6x = 12$$
$$x = 2$$

The x-intercept is $(2, 0)$.

To find a third point we replace x with 3 and solve for y.

$$6 \cdot 3 + 2y = 12$$
$$18 + 2y = 12$$
$$2y = -6$$
$$y = -3$$

The point $(3, -3)$ appears to line up with the intercepts, so we draw the graph.

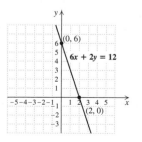

42.

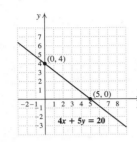

43. $x - 1 = y$

We can leave the equation in the given form or rewrite it in the form $Ax + By = C$. We will use the given form.

Find the y-intercept:

$$0 - 1 = y$$
$$-1 = y$$

The y-intercept is $(0, -1)$.

Find the x-intercept.

$$x - 1 = 0$$
$$x = 1$$

The x-intercept is $(1, 0)$.

To find a third point we replace x with -3 and solve for y.

$$-3 - 1 = y$$
$$-4 = y$$

The point $(-3, -4)$ appears to line up with the intercepts, so we draw the graph.

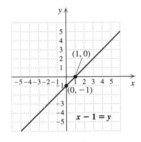

44.

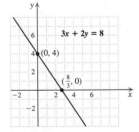

45. $2x - 6y = 18$

Find the y-intercept:

$$2 \cdot 0 - 6y = 18$$
$$-6y = 18$$
$$y = -3$$

The y-intercept is $(0, -3)$.

Find the x-intercept:

$$2x - 6 \cdot 0 = 18$$
$$2x = 18$$
$$x = 9$$

The x-intercept is $(9, 0)$.

To find a third point we replace x with 3 and solve for y.

$$2 \cdot 3 - 6y = 18$$
$$6 - 6y = 18$$
$$-6y = 12$$
$$y = -2$$

The point $(3, -2)$ appears to line up with the intercepts, so we draw the graph.

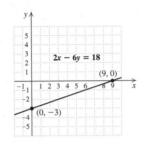

46.

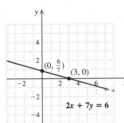

47. $4x - 3y = 12$

Find the y-intercept:

$$4 \cdot 0 - 3y = 12$$
$$-3y = 12$$
$$y = -4$$

The y-intercept is $(0, -4)$.

Find the x-intercept:

$$4x - 3 \cdot 0 = 12$$
$$4x = 12$$
$$x = 3$$

The x-intercept is $(3, 0)$.

To find a third point we replace x with 6 and solve for y.

$$4 \cdot 6 - 3y = 12$$
$$24 - 3y = 12$$
$$-3y = -12$$
$$y = 4$$

The point $(6, 4)$ appears to line up with the intercepts, so we draw the graph.

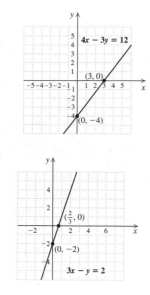

48.

50.

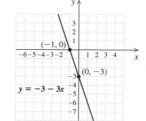

49. $-3x = 6y - 2$

We can leave the equation in the given form or rewrite it in the form $Ax + By = C$. We will use the given form.

Find the y-intercept.
$$-3 \cdot 0 = 6y - 2$$
$$0 = 6y - 2$$
$$2 = 6y$$
$$\frac{1}{3} = y$$

The y-intercept is $\left(0, \frac{1}{3}\right)$.

Find the x-intercept:
$$-3x = 6 \cdot 0 - 2$$
$$-3x = -2$$
$$x = \frac{2}{3}$$

The x-intercept is $\left(\frac{2}{3}, 0\right)$.

To find a third point we replace x with -4 and solve for y.
$$-3(-4) = 6y - 2$$
$$12 = 6y - 2$$
$$14 = 6y$$
$$\frac{7}{3} = y$$

The point $\left(-4, \frac{7}{3}\right)$ appears to line up with the intercepts, so we draw the graph.

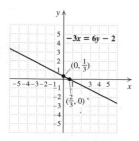

51. $3 = 2x - 5y$

Find the y-intercept:
$$3 = 2 \cdot 0 - 5y$$
$$3 = -5y$$
$$-\frac{3}{5} = y$$

The y-intercept is $\left(0, -\frac{3}{5}\right)$.

Find the x-intercept:
$$3 = 2x - 5 \cdot 0$$
$$3 = 2x$$
$$\frac{3}{2} = x$$

The x-intercept is $\left(\frac{3}{2}, 0\right)$.

To find a third point we replace x with -1 and solve for y.
$$3 = 2(-1) - 5y$$
$$3 = -2 - 5y$$
$$5 = -5y$$
$$-1 = y$$

The point $(-1, -1)$ appears to line up with the intercepts, so we draw the graph.

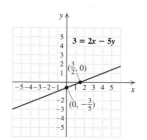

52.

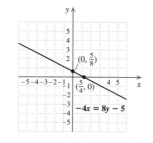

53. $x + 2y = 0$

Find the y-intercept:
$$0 + 2y = 0$$
$$2y = 0$$
$$y = 0$$

The y-intercept is $(0, 0)$. Note that this is also the x-

intercept.

In order to graph the line, we will find a second point.

When $x = 4$, $4 + 2y = 0$
$$2y = -4$$
$$y = -2.$$

Thus, a second point is $(4, -2)$.

To find a third point we replace x with -2 and solve for y.

$$-2 + 2y = 0$$
$$2y = 2$$
$$y = 1$$

The point $(-2, 1)$ appears to line up with the other two points, so we draw the graph.

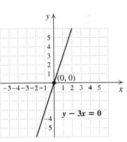

54.

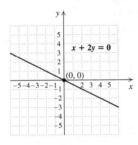

55. $y = 5$

Any ordered pair $(x, 5)$ is a solution. The variable y must be 5, but the x variable can be any number we choose. A few solutions are listed below. Plot these points and draw the line.

x	y
-3	5
0	5
2	5

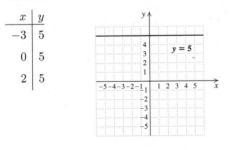

56.

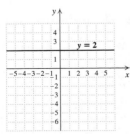

57. $x = 4$

Any ordered pair $(4, y)$ is a solution. The variable x must be 4, but the y variable can be any number we choose. A few solutions are listed below. Plot these points and draw the line.

x	y
4	-2
4	0
4	4

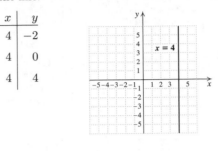

58.

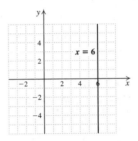

59. $y = -2$

Any ordered pair $(x, -2)$ is a solution. The variable y must be -2, but the x variable can be any number we choose. A few solutions are listed below. Plot these points and draw the line.

x	y
-3	-2
0	-2
4	-2

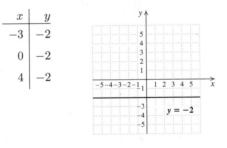

60.

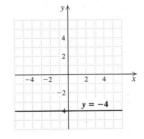

61. $x = -1$

Any ordered pair $(-1, y)$ is a solution. The variable x must be -1, but the y variable can be any number we choose. A few solutions are listed below. Plot these points and draw the line.

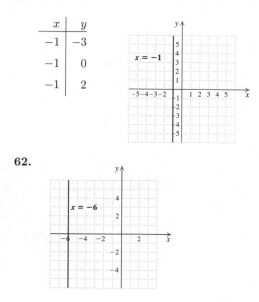

62.

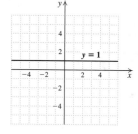

63. $y = 7$

Any ordered pair $(x, 7)$ is a solution. A few solutions are listed below. Plot these points and draw the line.

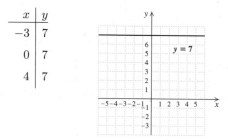

x	y
-3	7
0	7
4	7

64.

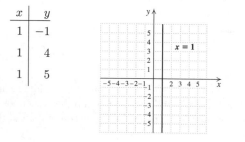

65. $x = 1$

Any ordered pair $(1, y)$ is a solution. A few solutions are listed below. Plot these points and draw the line.

x	y
1	-1
1	4
1	5

66.

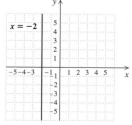

67. $y = 0$

Any ordered pair $(x, 0)$ is a solution. A few solutions are listed below. Plot these points and draw the line.

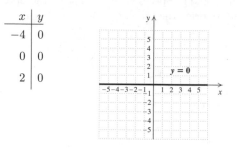

x	y
-4	0
0	0
2	0

68.

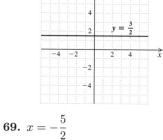

69. $x = -\dfrac{5}{2}$

Any ordered pair $\left(-\dfrac{5}{2}, y \right)$ is a solution. A few solutions are listed below. Plot these points and draw the line.

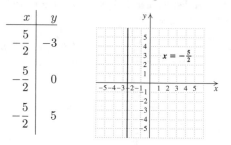

x	y
$-\dfrac{5}{2}$	-3
$-\dfrac{5}{2}$	0
$-\dfrac{5}{2}$	5

70.

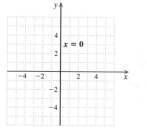

71. $-5y = 15$

Observe that $-5y = 15$ is equivalent to $y = -3$. Thus, the graph is a horizontal line 3 units below the x-axis.

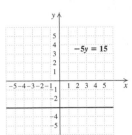

72.

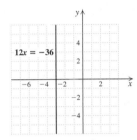

73. $35 + 7y = 0$

$$7y = -35$$
$$y = -5$$

The graph is a horizontal line 5 units below the x-axis.

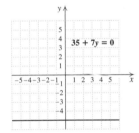

74.

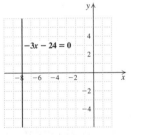

75. Note that every point on the horizontal line passing through $(0, -1)$ has -1 as the y-coordinate. Thus, the equation of the line is $y = -1$.

76. $x = -1$

77. Note that every point on the vertical line passing through $(4, 0)$ has 4 as the x-coordinate. Thus, the equation of the line is $x = 4$.

78. $y = -5$

79. Note that every point on the horizontal line passing through $(0, 0)$ has 0 as the y-coordinate. Thus, the equation of the line is $y = 0$.

80. $x = 0$

81. $f(x) = 20 - 4x$, or $f(x) = -4x + 20$

From the equation we see that the y-intercept is $(0, 20)$. Next we find the x-intercept.

$$0 = 20 - 4x$$
$$4x = 20$$
$$x = 5$$

The x-intercept is $(5, 0)$. Thus, window (c) will show both intercepts.

82. (a)

83. $p(x) = -35x + 7000$

From the equation we see that the y-intercept is $(0, 7000)$. Next we find the x-intercept.

$$0 = -35x + 7000$$
$$35x = 7000$$
$$x = 200$$

The x-intercept is $(200, 0)$. Thus, window (d) will show both intercepts.

84. (b)

85. $y = -0.72x - 15$

From the equation we see that the y-intercept is $(0, -15)$. Next we find the x-intercept.

$$0 = -0.72x - 15$$
$$15 = -0.72x$$
$$-20.8\overline{3} = x$$

The x-intercept is $(-20.8\overline{3}, 0)$. We choose a window in which both intercepts can be viewed easily. One choice is $[-30, 5, -20, 10]$, Xscl = 5, Yscl = 5.

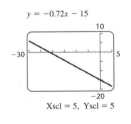

86.

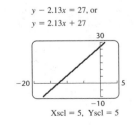

87. $5x + 6y = 84$

Find the x-intercept:

$$5x + 6 \cdot 0 = 84$$
$$5x = 84$$
$$x = 16.8$$

The x-intercept is $(16.8, 0)$. Find the y-intercept:

$$5 \cdot 0 + 6y = 84$$
$$6y = 84$$
$$y = 14$$

The y-intercept is $(0, 14)$. We choose a window in which both intercepts can be viewed easily. One choice is $[-10, 20, -10, 20]$, Xscl = 2, Yscl = 2.

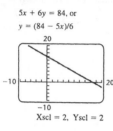

$5x + 6y = 84$, or
$y = (84 - 5x)/6$

88.

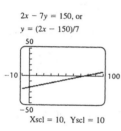

$2x - 7y = 150$, or
$y = (2x - 150)/7$

89. $19x - 17y = 200$

Find the x-intercept:

$$19x - 17 \cdot 0 = 200$$
$$19x = 200$$
$$x \approx 10.5$$

The x-intercept is approximately $(10.5, 0)$. Find the y-intercept:

$$19 \cdot 0 - 17y = 200$$
$$-17y = 200$$
$$y \approx -11.8$$

The y-intercept is approximately $(0, -11.8)$. We choose a window in which both intercepts can be viewed easily. One choice is $[-10, 20, -20, 10]$, Xscl = 2, Yscl = 2.

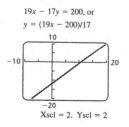

$19x - 17y = 200$, or
$y = (19x - 200)/17$

90.

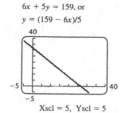

$6x + 5y = 159$, or
$y = (159 - 6x)/5$

Xscl = 5, Yscl = 5

91. *Writing Exercise*

92. *Writing Exercise*

93. $d - 7$

94. $w + 5$, or $5 + w$

95. Let x represent "a number." Then we have $2 + x$, or $x + 2$.

96. Let y represent the number; $3y$

97. Let x and y represent the numbers. Then we have $2(x + y)$.

98. Let m and n represent the numbers; $\frac{1}{2}(m + n)$.

99. *Writing Exercise*

100. *Writing Exercise*

101. The x-axis is a horizontal line, so it is of the form $y = b$. All points on the x-axis are of the form $(x, 0)$, so b must be 0 and the equation is $y = 0$.

102. $y = 5$

103. A line parallel to the y-axis has an equation of the form $x = a$. Since the x-coordinate of one point on the line is -2, then $a = -2$ and the equation is $x = -2$.

104. $(6, 6)$

105. Since the x-coordinate of the point of intersection must be -3 and y must equal x, the point of intersection is $(-3, -3)$.

106. $y = -\frac{5}{2}x + 5$, or $5x + 2y = 10$

107. The y-intercept is $(0, 5)$, so we have $y = mx + 5$. Another point on the line is $(-3, 0)$ so we have

$$0 = m(-3) + 5$$
$$-5 = -3m$$
$$\frac{5}{3} = m$$

The equation is $y = \frac{5}{3}x + 5$, or $5x - 3y = -15$, or $-5x + 3y = 15$.

108. 12

109. Substitute 0 for x and -8 for y.

$$4 \cdot 0 = C - 3(-8)$$
$$0 = C + 24$$
$$-24 = C$$

110. *Writing Exercise*

Exercise Set 4.2

1. a) We divide the number of miles traveled by the number of gallons of gas used for that amount of driving.

Rate, in miles per gallon

$$= \frac{14,014 \text{ mi} - 13,741 \text{ mi}}{13 \text{ gal}}$$

$$= \frac{273 \text{ mi}}{13 \text{ gal}}$$

$$= 21 \text{ mi/gal}$$

$$= 21 \text{ miles per gallon}$$

b) We divide the cost of the rental by the number of days. From July 1 to July 4 is $4 - 1$, or 3 days.

Average cost, in dollars per day

$$= \frac{118 \text{ dollars}}{3 \text{ days}}$$

$$\approx 39.33 \text{ dollars/day}$$

$$\approx \$39.33 \text{ per day}$$

c) We divide the number of miles traveled by the number of days. In part (a) we found that the van was driven 273 mi, and in part (b) we found that it was rented for 3 days.

Rate, in miles per day

$$= \frac{273 \text{ mi}}{3 \text{ days}}$$

$$= 91 \text{ mi/day}$$

$$= 91 \text{ mi per day}$$

d) We divide the rental rate, expressed in cents, by the number of miles driven. We are told that the rental cost $118, or 11,800¢, and in part (a) we found that the van was driven 273 mi.

Rate, in cents per mile

$$= \frac{11,800¢}{273 \text{ mi}}$$

$$\approx 43¢/\text{mi}$$

2. a) 16.5mpg

b) $46/day

c) 115.5 mi/day

d) 40¢/mi

3. a) From 2:00 to 5:00 is $5 - 2$, or 3 hr.

Average speed, in miles per hour

$$= \frac{18 \text{ mi}}{3 \text{ hr}}$$

$$= 6 \text{ mph}$$

b) From part (a) we know that the bike was rented for 3 hr.

Rate, in dollars per hour $= \dfrac{\$10.50}{3 \text{ hr}}$

$$= \$3.50 \text{ per hr}$$

c) Rate, in dollars per mile $= \dfrac{\$10.50}{18 \text{ mi}}$

$$\approx \$0.58 \text{ per mile}$$

4. a) 7 mph

b) $6/hr

c) $0.86/mi

5. a) It is 3 hr from 9:00 A.M. to noon and 5 more hours from noon to 5:00 P.M., so the typist worked $3 + 5$, or 8 hr.

Rate, in dollars per hour $= \dfrac{\$128}{8 \text{ hr}}$

$$= \$16 \text{ per hr}$$

b) The number of pages typed is $48 - 12$, or 36.

In part (a) we found that the typist worked 8 hr.

Rate, in pages per hour $= \dfrac{36 \text{ pages}}{8 \text{ hr}}$

$$= 4.5 \text{ pages per hr}$$

c) In part (b) we found that 36 pages were typed.

Rate, in dollars per page $= \dfrac{\$128}{36 \text{ pages}}$

$$\approx \$3.56 \text{ per page}$$

6. a) $15/hr

b) 5.25 pages/hr

c) $2.86/page

7. The tuition increased $1318 - \$1239$, or $79, in $1998 - 1996$ or 2 yr.

Rate of increase $= \dfrac{\text{Change in tuition}}{\text{Change in time}}$

$$= \frac{\$79}{2 \text{ yr}}$$

$$= \$39.50 \text{ per yr}$$

8. $170.67/yr

9. a) The elevator traveled $34 - 5$, or 29 floors in $2\!:\!40 - 2\!:\!38$, or 2 min.

Average rate of travel $= \dfrac{29 \text{ floors}}{2 \text{ min}}$

$$= 14.5 \text{ floors per min}$$

b) In part (a) we found that the elevator traveled 29 floors in 2 min. Note that $2 \text{ min} = 2 \times 1 \text{ min} = 2 \times 60 \text{ sec} = 120 \text{ sec}$.

Average rate of travel $= \dfrac{120 \text{ sec}}{29 \text{ floors}}$

$$\approx 4.14 \text{ sec per floor}$$

10. a) 1 driveway/hr

b) 1 hr/driveway

11. a) Krakauer ascended $29,028 \text{ ft} - 27,600 \text{ ft}$, or 1428 ft. From 7:00 A.M. to noon it is $5 \text{ hr} = 5 \times 1 \text{ hr} = 5 \times 60 \text{ min} = 300 \text{ min}$. From noon to 1:25 P.M. is another 1 hr, 25 min, or $1 \text{ hr} + 25 \text{ min} = 60 \text{ min} + 25 \text{ min} = 85 \text{ min}$. The total time of the ascent is $300 \text{ min} + 85 \text{ min}$, or 385 min.

Rate, in feet per minute $= \dfrac{1428 \text{ ft}}{385 \text{ min}}$

$$\approx 3.71 \text{ ft per min}$$

b) We use the information found in part (a).

$$\text{Rate, in minutes per foot} = \frac{385 \text{ min}}{1428 \text{ ft}}$$
$$\approx 0.27 \text{ min per ft}$$

12. a) 9.38 ft/min

b) 0.11 min/ft

13. The rate is given in millions of crimes per year, so we list number of crimes, in millions, on the vertical axis and years on the horizontal axis. If we count by 10's of millions on the vertical axis we can easily reach 37 million without needed a terribly large graph. We plot the point (1996, 37 million). Then, to display the rate of growth, we move from that point to a point that represents 2.5 million fewer crimes 1 year later. The coordinates of this point are 1996 + 1, 37 − 2.5 million), or (1997, 34.5 million). Finally, we draw a line through the two points.

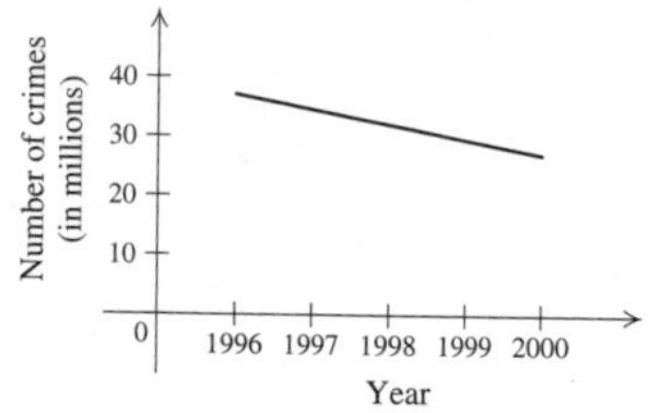

14.

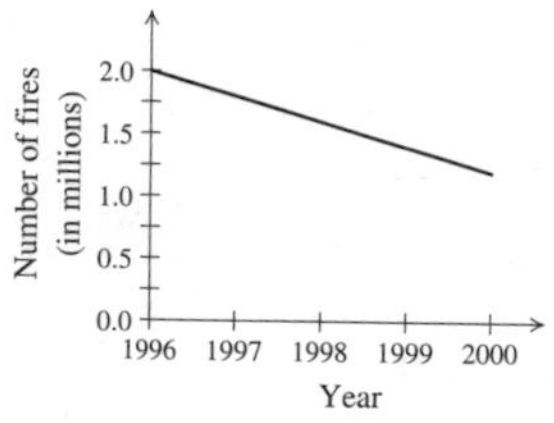

15. The rate is given in miles per hour, so we list the number of miles traveled on the vertical axis and the time of day on the horizontal axis. If we count by 100's of miles on the vertical axis we can easily reach 230 without needing a terribly large graph. We plot the point (3:00, 230). Then to display the rate of travel, we move from that point to a point that represents 90 more miles traveled 1 hour later. The coordinates of this point are (3:00 + 1 hr,230 + 90), or (4:00, 320). Finally, we draw a line through the two points.

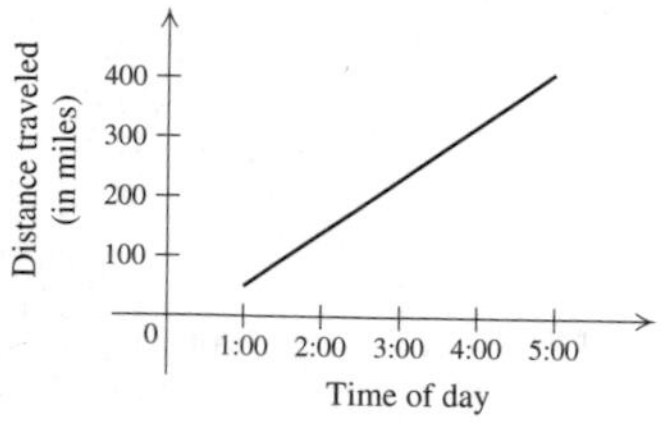

16.

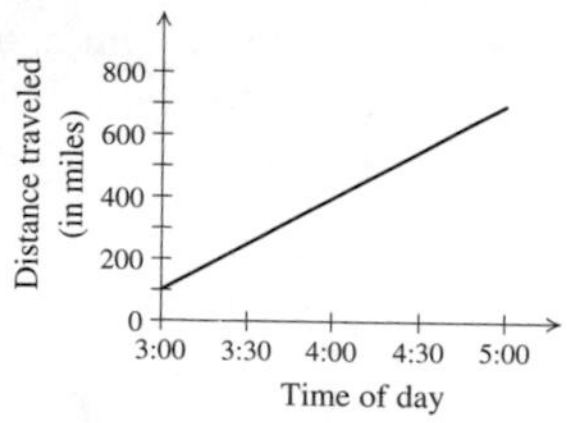

17. The rate is given in dollars per hour so we list money earned on the vertical axis and the time of day on the horizontal axis. We can count by \$20 on the vertical axis and reach \$50 without needing a terribly large graph. Next we plot the point (2:00 P.M., \$50). To display the rate we move from that point to a point that represents \$15 more 1 hour later. The coordinates of this point are (2+1, \$50+ \$15), or (3:00 P.M., \$65). Finally, we draw a line through the two points.

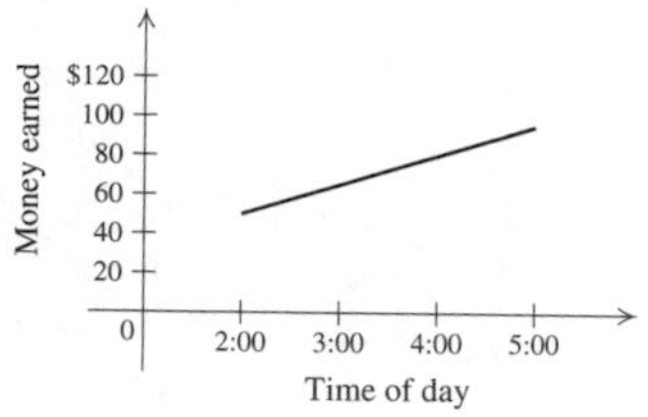

18.

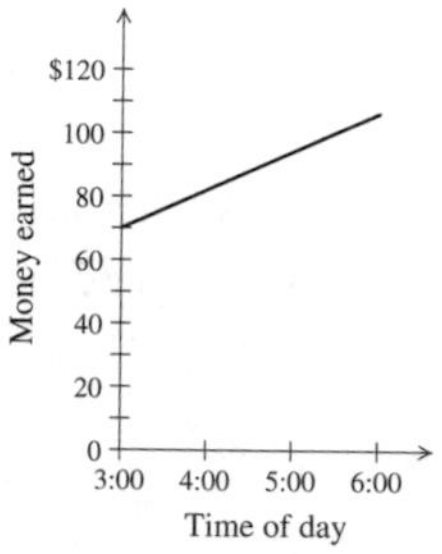

19. The rate is given in cost per minute so we list the amount of the telephone bill on the vertical axis and the number of additional minutes on the horizontal axis. We begin with \$7.50 on the vertical axis and count by \$0.50. A jagged line at the base of the axis indicates that we are not showing amounts smaller than \$7.50. We begin with 0 additional minutes on the horizontal axis and plot the point (0, \$7.50). We move from there to a point that represents \$0.10 more 1 minute later. The coordinates of this point are (0 + 1 min, \$7.50 + \$0.10), or (1 min, \$7.60). Then we draw a line through the two points.

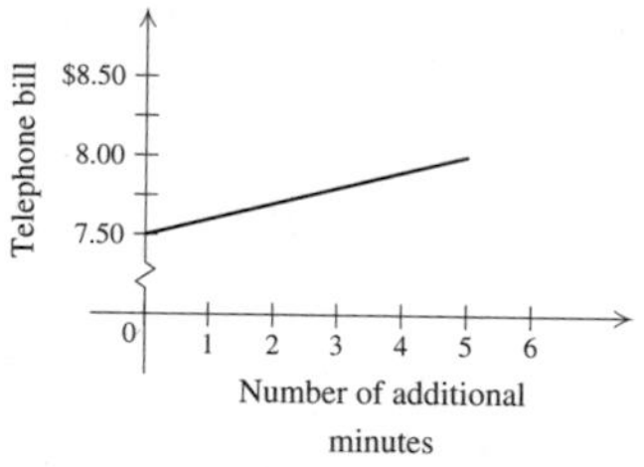

20.

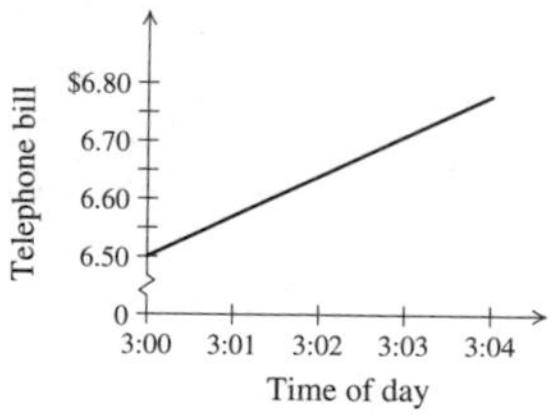

21. The points (2:00, 7 haircuts) and (5:00, 12 haircuts) are on the graph. This tells us that in the 3 hr between 2:00 and 5:00 there were 12 − 7 = 5 haircuts completed. The rate is

$$\frac{5 \text{ haircuts}}{3 \text{ hr}} = \frac{5}{3}, \text{ or } 1\frac{2}{3} \text{ haircuts per hour.}$$

22. 4 manicures/hr

23. The points (12:00, 100 mi) and (2:00, 250 mi) are on the graph. This tells us that in the 2 hr between 12:00 and 2:00 the train traveled $250 - 100 = 150$ mi. The rate is

$$\frac{150 \text{ mi}}{2 \text{hr}} = 75 \text{ mi per hr.}$$

24. 87.5 mi/hr

25. The points $(15 \text{ min}, 150\text{¢})$ and $(30 \text{ min}, 300\text{¢})$ are on the graph. This tells us that in $30 - 15 = 15$ min the cost of the call increased $300\text{¢} - 150\text{¢} = 150\text{¢}$. The rate is

$$\frac{150\text{¢}}{15 \text{ min}} = 10\text{¢} \text{ per min.}$$

26. 7¢/min

27. The points $(2 \text{ yr}, \$2000)$ and $(4 \text{ yr}, \$1000)$ are on the graph. This tells us that in $4 - 2 = 2$ yr the value of the copier changes $\$1000 - \$2000 = -\$1000$. The rate is

$$\frac{-\$1000}{2 \text{ yr}} = -\$500 \text{ per yr.}$$

This means that the value of the copier is decreasing at a rate of $500 per yr.

28. -$0.15 billion/yr

29. The points (50 mi, 2 gal) and (200 mi, 8 gal) are on the graph. This tells us that when driven $200 - 50 = 150$ mi the vehicle consumed $8 - 2 = 6$ gal of gas. The rate is

$$\frac{6 \text{ gal}}{150 \text{ mi}} = 0.04 \text{ gal per mi.}$$

30. $0.08\overline{3}$ gal/mi

31. *Writing Exercise*

32. *Writing Exercise*

33. $-2 - (-7) = -2 + 7 = 5$

34. -6

35. $\dfrac{5 - (-4)}{-2 - 7} = \dfrac{9}{-9} = -1$

36. $-\dfrac{4}{3}$

37. $\dfrac{-4 - 8}{7 - (-2)} = \dfrac{-12}{9} = -\dfrac{4}{3}$

38. $-\dfrac{4}{5}$

39. *Writing Exercise*

40. *Writing Exercise*

41. Let $t =$ flight time and $a =$ altitude. While the plane is climbing at a rate of 6500 ft/min, the equation $a = 6500t$ describes the situation. Solving $34,000 = 6500t$, we find that the cruising altitude of 34,000 ft is reached after about 5.23 min. Thus we graph $a = 6500t$ for $0 \le t \le 5.23$.

The plane cruises at 34,000 ft for 3 min, so we graph $a = 34,000$ for $5.23 < t \le 8.23$. After 8.23 min the plane descends at a rate of 3500 ft/min and lands. The equation $a = 34,000 - 3500(t - 8.23)$, or $a = -3500t + 62,805$, describes this situation. Solving $0 = -3500t + 62,805$, we find that the plane lands after about 17.94 min. Thus we graph $a = -3500t + 62,805$ for $8.23 < t \le 17.94$. The entire graph is show below.

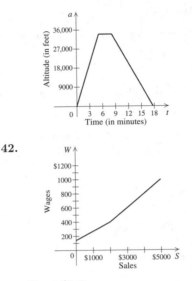

42.

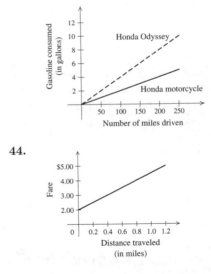

About $540

43. We begin with the graph in Exercise 29 showing the gas consumption of a Honda Odyssey. For each point (x, y) on this graph we can plot a point $(2x, y)$ on the graph that represents the gas consumption of the motorcycle.

44.

45. Penny walks forward at a rate of $\dfrac{24 \text{ ft}}{3 \text{ sec}}$, or 8 ft per sec. In addition, the boat is traveling at a rate of 5 ft per sec. Thus, with respect to land, Penny is traveling at a rate of $8 + 5$, or 13 ft per sec.

46. 0.45 min/mi

47. First we find Annette's speed in minutes per kilometer.

$$\text{Speed} = \frac{15.5 \text{ min}}{7 \text{ km} - 4 \text{ km}} = \frac{15.5}{3} \frac{\text{min}}{\text{km}}$$

Now we convert min/km to min/mi.

$$\frac{15.5}{3} \frac{\text{min}}{\text{km}} \approx \frac{15.5}{3} \frac{\text{min}}{\text{km}} \cdot \frac{1 \text{ km}}{0.621 \text{ min}} \approx \frac{15.5}{1.863} \frac{\text{min}}{\text{mi}}$$

At a rate of $\frac{15.5}{1.863} \frac{\text{min}}{\text{mi}}$, to run a 5-mi race it would take

$$\frac{15.5}{1.863} \frac{\text{min}}{\text{mi}} \cdot 5 \text{ mi} \approx 41.6 \text{ min}.$$

(Answers may vary slightly depending on the conversion factor used.)

48. 51.7 min

49. First we find Ryan's rate. Then we double it to find Marcy's rate. Note that 50 minutes $= \frac{50}{60}$ hr $= \frac{5}{6}$ hr.

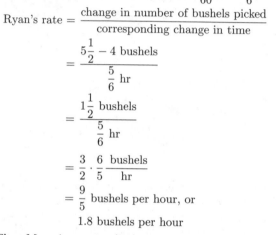

$$\text{Ryan's rate} = \frac{\text{change in number of bushels picked}}{\text{corresponding change in time}}$$

$$= \frac{5\frac{1}{2} - 4 \text{ bushels}}{\frac{5}{6} \text{ hr}}$$

$$= \frac{1\frac{1}{2} \text{ bushels}}{\frac{5}{6} \text{ hr}}$$

$$= \frac{3}{2} \cdot \frac{6}{5} \frac{\text{bushels}}{\text{hr}}$$

$$= \frac{9}{5} \text{ bushels per hour, or}$$

$$1.8 \text{ bushels per hour}$$

Then Marcy's rate is $2(1.8) = 3.6$ bushels per hour.

50. 27 candles/hr

Exercise Set 4.3

1. The rate can be found using the coordinates of any two points on the line. We use $(2, 30)$ and $(6, 90)$.

$$\text{Rate} = \frac{\text{change in number of calories burned}}{\text{corresponding change in time}}$$

$$= \frac{90 - 30 \text{ calories}}{6 - 2 \text{ min}}$$

$$= \frac{60 \text{ calories}}{4 \text{ min}}$$

$$= 15 \text{ calories per min}$$

2. 2.5 million people/yr

3. The rate can be found using the coordinates of any two points on the line. We use $(35, 490)$ and $(45, 500)$, where 35 and 45 are in \$1000's.

$$\text{Rate} = \frac{\text{change in score}}{\text{corresponding change in income}}$$

$$= \frac{500 - 490 \text{ points}}{45 - 35}$$

$$= \frac{10 \text{ points}}{10}$$

$$= 1 \text{ point per } \$1000 \text{ income}$$

4. $1\frac{1}{3}$ points/\$1000 income

5. The rate can be found using the coordinates of any two points on the line. We use $(1993, 20)$ and $(1997, 17)$.

$$\text{Rate} = \frac{\text{change in percent}}{\text{corresponding change in time}}$$

$$= \frac{17\% - 20\%}{1997 - 1993}$$

$$= \frac{-3\%}{4 \text{ yr}}$$

$$= -\frac{3}{4}\% \text{ per yr, or} -0.75\% \text{ per yr}$$

6. $0.4\%/\text{yr}$, or $-\frac{2}{5}\%/\text{yr}$

7. We can use any two points on the line, such as $(0, 1)$ and $(4, 4)$.

$$m = \frac{\text{change in } y}{\text{change in } x}$$

$$= \frac{4 - 1}{4 - 0} = \frac{3}{4}$$

8. $\frac{2}{3}$

9. We can use any two points on the line, such as $(1, 0)$ and $(3, 3)$.

$$m = \frac{\text{change in } y}{\text{change in } x}$$

$$= \frac{3 - 0}{3 - 1} = \frac{3}{2}$$

10. $\frac{1}{3}$

11. We can use any two points on the line, such as $(-3, -4)$ and $(0, -3)$.

$$m = \frac{\text{change in } y}{\text{change in } x}$$

$$= \frac{-3 - (-4)}{0 - (-3)} = \frac{1}{3}$$

12. 3 $0 + 3 =$

13. We can use any two points on the line, such as $(0, 2)$ and $(2, 0)$.

$$m = \frac{\text{change in } y}{\text{change in } x}$$

$$= \frac{2 - 0}{0 - 2} = \frac{2}{-2} = -1$$

14. $-\frac{1}{2}$

15. This is the graph of a horizontal line. Thus, the slope is 0.

16. $-\frac{3}{2}$

17. We can use any two points on the line, such as $(0, 2)$ and $(3, 1)$.

$$m = \frac{\text{change in } y}{\text{change in } x}$$
$$= \frac{1 - 2}{3 - 0} = -\frac{1}{3}$$

18. -2

19. This is the graph of a vertical line. Thus, the slope is undefined.

20. Undefined

21. We can use any two points on the line, such as $(-2, 3)$ and $(2, 2)$.

$$m = \frac{\text{change in } y}{\text{change in } x}$$
$$= \frac{2 - 3}{2 - (-2)} = -\frac{1}{4}$$

22. 0

23. We can use any two points on the line, such as $(-2, -3)$ and $(2, 3)$.

$$m = \frac{\text{change in } y}{\text{change in } x}$$
$$= \frac{3 - (-3)}{2 - (-2)} = \frac{6}{4} = \frac{3}{2}$$

24. $-\frac{2}{3}$

25. This is the graph of a horizontal line, so the slope is 0.

26. 5

27. We can use any two points on the line, such as $(-3, 5)$ and $(0, -4)$.

$$m = \frac{\text{change in } y}{\text{change in } x}$$
$$= \frac{-4 - 5}{0 - (-3)} = \frac{-9}{3} = -3$$

28. 0

29. $(1, 2)$ and $(5, 8)$

$$m = \frac{8 - 2}{5 - 1} = \frac{6}{4} = \frac{3}{2}$$

30. 2

31. $(-2, 4)$ and $(3, 0)$

$$m = \frac{4 - 0}{-2 - 3} = \frac{4}{-5} = -\frac{4}{5}$$

32. $-\frac{5}{6}$

33. $(-4, 0)$ and $(5, 7)$

$$m = \frac{7 - 0}{5 - (-4)} = \frac{7}{9}$$

34. $\frac{2}{3}$

35. $(0, 8)$ and $(-3, 10)$

$$m = \frac{8 - 10}{0 - (-3)} = \frac{8 - 10}{0 + 3} = \frac{-2}{3} = -\frac{2}{3}$$

36. $-\frac{1}{2}$

37. $(-2, 3)$ and $(-6, 5)$

$$m = \frac{5 - 3}{-6 - (-2)} = \frac{2}{-6 + 2} = \frac{2}{-4} = -\frac{1}{2}$$

38. $-\frac{11}{8}$

39. $\left(-2, \frac{1}{2}\right)$ and $\left(-5, \frac{1}{2}\right)$

Observe that the points have the same y-coordinate. Thus, they lie on a horizontal line and its slope is 0. We could also compute the slope.

$$m = \frac{\frac{1}{2} - \frac{1}{2}}{-2 - (-5)} = \frac{\frac{1}{2} - \frac{1}{2}}{-2 + 5} = \frac{0}{3} = 0$$

40. $\frac{4}{7}$

41. $(3, 4)$ and $(9, -7)$

$$m = \frac{-7 - 4}{9 - 3} = \frac{-11}{6} = -\frac{11}{6}$$

42. Undefined

43. $(6, -4)$ and $(6, 5)$

Observe that the points have the same x-coordinate. Thus, they lie on a vertical line and its slope is undefined. We could also compute the slope.

$$m = \frac{-4 - 5}{6 - 6} = \frac{-9}{0}, \text{ undefined}$$

44. 0

45. The line $x = -3$ is a vertical line. The slope is undefined.

46. Undefined

47. The line $y = 4$ is a horizontal line. A horizontal line has slope 0.

48. 0

49. The line $x = 9$ is a vertical line. The slope is undefined.

50. Undefined

51. The line $y = -9$ is a horizontal line. A horizontal line has slope 0.

52. 0

53. The grade is expressed as a percent.

$$m = \frac{106}{1325} = 0.08 = 8\%$$

54. $\frac{1}{20}$, or 0.05

55. The grade is expressed as a percent.

$$m = \frac{1}{12} = 0.08\overline{3} = 8.\overline{3}\%$$

56. 7%

57. $m = \dfrac{2.4}{8.2} = \dfrac{12}{41}$, or about 29%

58. 0.08, or 8%

59. Longs Peak rises $14,255 - 9600 = 4655$ ft.

$$m = \frac{4655}{15,840} \approx 0.29 \approx 29\%$$

60. About 64%

61. a) Graph II indicated that 200 ml of fluid was dripped in the first 3 hr, a rate of $\dfrac{200}{3}$ ml/hr. It also indicates that 400 ml of fluid was dripped in the next 3 hr, a rate of $\dfrac{400}{3}$ ml/hr, and that this rate continues until the end of the time period shown. Since the rate of $\dfrac{400}{3}$ ml/hr is double the rate of $\dfrac{200}{3}$ ml/hr, this graph is appropriate for the given situation.

b) Graph IV indicates that 300 ml of fluid was dripped in the first 2 hr, a rate of 300/2, or 150 ml/hr. In the next 2 hr, 200 ml was dripped. This is a rate of 200/2, or 100 ml/hr. Then 100 ml was dripped in the next 3 hr, a rate of 100/3, or $33\dfrac{1}{3}$ ml/hr. Finally, in the remaining 2 hr, 0 ml of fluid was dripped, a rate of 0/2, or 0 ml/hr. Since the rate at which the fluid was given decreased as time progressed and eventually became 0, this graph is appropriate for the given situation.

c) Graph I is the only graph that shows a constant rate for 5 hours, in this case from 3 PM to 8 PM. Thus, it is appropriate for the given situation.

d) Graph III indicates that 100 ml of fluid was dripped in the first 4 hr, a rate of 100/4, or 25 ml/hr. In the next 3 hr, 200 ml was dripped. This is a rate of 200/3, or $66\dfrac{2}{3}$ ml/hr. Then 100 ml was dripped in the next hour, a rate of 100 ml/hr. In the last hour 200 ml was dripped, a rate of 200 ml/hr. Since the rate at which the fluid was given gradually increased, this graph is appropriate for the given situation.

62. a) III

b) IV

c) I

d) II

63. *Writing Exercise*

64. *Writing Exercise*

65. $ax + by = c$

$by = c - ax$ Adding $-ax$ to both sides

$y = \dfrac{c - ax}{b}$ Dividing both sides by b

66. $r = \dfrac{p + mn}{x}$

67. $ax - by = c$

$-by = c - ax$ Adding $-ax$ to both sides

$y = \dfrac{c - ax}{-b}$ Dividing both sides by $-b$

We could also express this result as $y = \dfrac{ax - c}{b}$.

68. $t = \dfrac{q - rs}{n}$

69. $\dfrac{2}{3}x - 5 = \dfrac{2}{3} \cdot 12 - 5$ Substituting

$\phantom{\dfrac{2}{3}x - 5} = 8 - 5$

$\phantom{\dfrac{2}{3}x - 5} = 3$

70. 2

71. *Writing Exercise*

72. *Writing Exercise*

73. If the line passes through $(4, -7)$ and never enters the first quadrant, then it slants down from left to right or is horizontal. This means that its slope is not positive ($m \le 0$). The line will slant most steeply if it passes through $(0, 0)$. In this case, $m = \dfrac{-7 - 0}{4 - 0} = -\dfrac{7}{4}$. Thus, the numbers the line could have for its slope are $\left\{ m \middle| -\dfrac{7}{4} \le m \le 0 \right\}$.

74. $\left\{ m \middle| m \ge \dfrac{5}{2} \right\}$

75. $x + y = 18$

$y = 18 - x$

The slope is $\dfrac{y}{x}$, or $\dfrac{18 - x}{x}$.

76. $\dfrac{1}{2}$

77. Let $t =$ the number of units each tick mark on the horizontal axis represents. Note that the graph drops 1 unit for every 6 tick marks of horizontal change. Then we have:

$$\frac{-1}{6t} = -\frac{2}{3}$$

$$-1 = -4t$$

$$\frac{1}{4} = t$$

Each tick mark on the horizontal axis represents $\dfrac{1}{4}$ unit.

78. a) III

b) IV

c) I

d) II

Exercise Set 4.4

1. Slope $\frac{2}{5}$; y-intercept $(0, 1)$

We plot $(0, 1)$ and from there move up 2 units and right 5 units. This locates the point $(5, 3)$. We plot $(5, 3)$ and draw a line passing through $(0, 1)$ and $(5, 3)$.

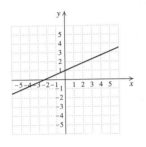

2.

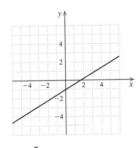

3. Slope $\frac{5}{3}$; y-intercept $(0, -2)$

We plot $(0, -2)$ and from there move up 5 units and right 3 units. This locates the point $(3, 3)$. We plot $(3, 3)$ and draw a line passing through $(0, -2)$ and $(3, 3)$.

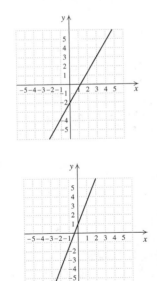

4.

5. Slope $-\frac{3}{4}$; y-intercept $(0, 5)$

We plot $(0, 5)$. We can think of the slope as $\frac{-3}{4}$, so from $(0, 5)$ we move down 3 units and right 4 units. This locates the point $(4, 2)$. We plot $(4, 2)$ and draw a line passing through $(0, 5)$ and $(4, 2)$.

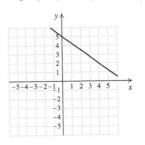

6.

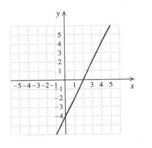

7. Slope 2; y-intercept $(0, -4)$

We plot $(0, -4)$. We can think of the slope as $\frac{2}{1}$, so from $(0, -4)$ we move up 2 units and right 1 unit. This locates the point $(1, -2)$. We plot $(1, -2)$ and draw a line passing through $(0, -4)$ and $(1, -2)$.

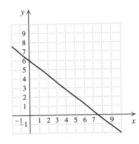

8.

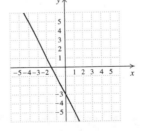

9. Slope -3; y-intercept $(0, 2)$

We plot $(0, 2)$. We can think of the slope as $\frac{-3}{1}$, so from $(0, 2)$ we move down 3 units and right 1 unit. This locates the point $(1, -1)$. We plot $(1, -1)$ and draw a line passing through $(0, 2)$ and $(1, -1)$.

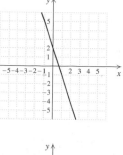

10.

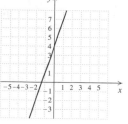

11. We read the slope and y-intercept from the equation.

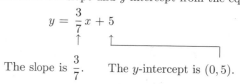

The slope is $\dfrac{3}{7}$.   The y-intercept is $(0,5)$.

12. $-\dfrac{3}{8}$, $(0,6)$

13. We read the slope and y-intercept from the equation.

$$y = -\frac{5}{6}x + 2$$

The slope is $-\dfrac{5}{6}$.   The y-intercept is $(0,2)$.

14. $\dfrac{7}{2}$, $(0,4)$

15. $y = \dfrac{9}{4}x - 7$

$$y = \frac{9}{4}x + (-7)$$

The slope is $\dfrac{9}{4}$, and the y-intercept is $(0,-7)$.

16. $\dfrac{2}{9}$, $(0,-1)$

17. $y = -\dfrac{2}{5}x$

$$y = -\frac{2}{5}x + 0$$

The slope is $-\dfrac{2}{5}$, and the y-intercept is $(0,0)$.

18. $\dfrac{4}{3}$, $(0,0)$

19. We solve for y to rewrite the equation in the form $y = mx + b$.

$$-2x + y = 4$$
$$y = 2x + 4$$

The slope is 2, and the y-intercept is $(0,4)$.

20. 5, $(0,5)$

21. $3x - 4y = 12$
$$-4y = -3x + 12$$
$$y = -\frac{1}{4}(-3x + 12)$$
$$y = \frac{3}{4}x - 3$$

The slope is $\dfrac{3}{4}$, and the y-intercept is $(0,-3)$.

22. $\dfrac{3}{2}$, $(0,-9)$

23. $x - 5y = -8$
$$-5y = -x - 8$$
$$y = -\frac{1}{5}(-x - 8)$$
$$y = \frac{1}{5}x + \frac{8}{5}$$

The slope is $\dfrac{1}{5}$, and the y-intercept is $\left(0, \dfrac{8}{5}\right)$.

24. $\dfrac{1}{6}$, $\left(0, -\dfrac{3}{2}\right)$

25. Observe that this is the equation of a horizontal line that lies 4 units above the x-axis. Thus, the slope is 0, and the y-intercept is $(0,4)$. We could also write the equation in slope-intercept form.

$$y = 4$$
$$y = 0x + 4$$

The slope is 0, and the y-intercept is $(0,4)$.

26. 0, $(0,8)$

27. a) The graph of $y = 3x - 5$ has a positive slope, 3, and the y-intercept is $(0,-5)$. Thus, graph II matches this equation.

   b) The graph of $y = 0.7x + 1$ has a positive slope, 0.7, and the y-intercept is $(0,1)$. Thus graph IV matches this equation.

   c) The graph of $y = -0.25x - 3$ has a negative slope, -0.25, and the y-intercept is $(0,-3)$. Thus graph III matches this equation.

   d) The graph of $y = -4x + 2$ has a negative slope, -4, and the y-intercept is $(0,2)$. Thus graph I matches this equation.

28. a) II

   b) IV

   c) I

   d) III

29. We use the slope-intercept form, substituting 3 for m and 7 for b:
$$f(x) = mx + b$$
$$f(x) = 3x + 7$$

30. $f(x) = -4x - 2$

31. We use the slope-intercept form, substituting $\frac{7}{8}$ for m and -1 for b:
$$f(x) = mx + b$$
$$f(x) = \frac{7}{8}x - 1$$

32. $f(x) = \frac{5}{7}x + 4$

33. We use the slope-intercept form, substituting $-\frac{5}{3}$ for m and -8 for b:
$$f(x) = mx + b$$
$$f(x) = -\frac{5}{3}x - 8$$

34. $f(x) = \frac{3}{4}x + 23$

35. Since the slope is 0, we know that the line is horizontal. Its y-intercept is $(0, 3)$, so the equation of the line must be $y = 3$.

We could also use the slope-intercept form, substituting 0 for m and 3 for b.
$$f(x) = mx + b$$
$$f(x) = 0 \cdot x + 3$$
$$f(x) = 3$$

36. $f(x) = 7x$

37. $y = \frac{3}{5}x + 2$

Slope: $\frac{3}{5}$; y-intercept: $(0, 2)$

First we plot the y-intercept $(0, 2)$. We can start at the y-intercept and use the slope, $\frac{3}{5}$, to find another point. We move up 3 units and right 5 units to get a new point $(5, 5)$. Thinking of the slope as $\frac{-3}{-5}$ we can start at $(0, 2)$ and move down 3 units and left 5 units to get another point $(-5, -1)$.

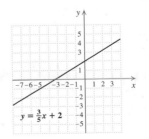

38. $-\frac{3}{5}$; $(0, -1)$

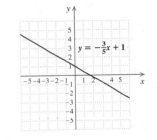

39. $y = -\frac{3}{5}x + 1$

Slope: $-\frac{3}{5}$; y-intercept: $(0, 1)$

First we plot the y-intercept $(0, 1)$. We can start at the y-intercept and, thinking of the slope as $\frac{-3}{5}$, find another point by moving down 3 units and right 5 units to the point $(5, -2)$. Thinking of the slope as $\frac{3}{-5}$ we can start at $(0, 1)$ and move up 3 units and left 5 units to get another point $(-5, 4)$.

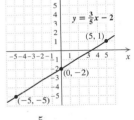

40. $\frac{3}{5}$; $(0, -2)$

41. $f(x) = \frac{5}{3}x + 3$

Slope: $\frac{5}{3}$; y-intercept: $(0, 3)$

First we plot the y-intercept $(0, 3)$. We can start at the y-intercept and use the slope, $\frac{5}{3}$, to find another point. We move up 5 units and right 3 units to get a new point $(3, 8)$. Thinking of the slope as $\frac{-5}{-3}$ we can start at $(0, 3)$ and move down 5 units and left 3 units to get another point $(-3, -2)$.

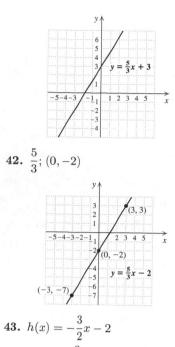

42. $\dfrac{5}{3}$; $(0, -2)$

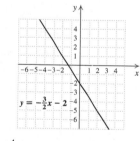

43. $h(x) = -\dfrac{3}{2}x - 2$

Slope: $-\dfrac{3}{2}$; y-intercept: $(0, -2)$

First we plot the y-intercept $(0, -2)$. We can start at the y-intercept and, thinking of the slope as $\dfrac{-3}{2}$, find another point by moving down 3 units and right 2 units to the point $(2, -5)$. Thinking of the slope as $\dfrac{3}{-2}$ we can start at $(0, -2)$ and move up 3 units and left 2 units to get another point $(-2, 1)$.

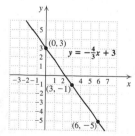

44. $-\dfrac{4}{3}$; $(0, 3)$

45. We first rewrite the equation in slope-intercept form.
$$2x + y = 1$$
$$y = -2x + 1$$
Slope: -2; y-intercept: $(0, 1)$

Plot the y-intercept $(0, 1)$. We can start at the y-intercept and, thinking of the slope as $\dfrac{-2}{1}$, find another point by moving down 2 units and right 1 unit to the point $(1, -1)$. In a similar manner, we can move from the point $(1, -1)$ to find a third point $(2, -3)$.

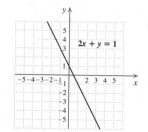

46. -3; $(0, 2)$

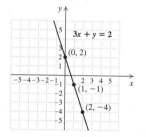

47. We first rewrite the equation in slope-intercept form.
$$3x - y = 4$$
$$-y = -3x + 4$$
$$y = 3x - 4 \quad \text{Multiplying by } -1$$
Slope: 3; y-intercept: $(0, -4)$

Plot the y-intercept $(0, -4)$. We can start at the y-intercept and, thinking of the slope as $\dfrac{3}{1}$, find another point by moving up 3 units and right 1 unit to the point $(1, -1)$. In a similar manner, we can move from the point $(1, -1)$ to find a third point $(2, 2)$.

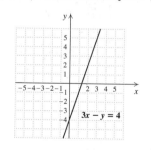

48. 2; $(0, -5)$

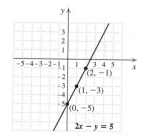

49. We first rewrite the equation in slope-intercept form.

$$2x + 3y = 9$$
$$3y = -2x + 9$$
$$y = \frac{1}{3}(-2x + 9)$$
$$y = -\frac{2}{3}x + 3$$

Slope: $-\frac{2}{3}$; y-intercept: $(0, 3)$

Plot the y-intercept $(0, 3)$. We can start at the y-intercept and, thinking of the slope as $\frac{-2}{3}$, find another point by moving down 2 units and right 3 units to the point $(3, 1)$. Thinking of the slope as $\frac{2}{-3}$ we can start at $(0, 3)$ and move up 2 units and left 3 units to get another point $(-3, 5)$.

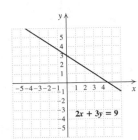

50. $-\frac{4}{5}$; $(0,3)$

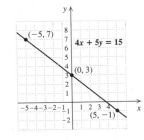

51. We first rewrite the equation in slope-intercept form.

$$x - 4y = 12$$
$$-4y = -x + 12$$
$$y = -\frac{1}{4}(-x + 12)$$
$$y = \frac{1}{4}x - 3$$

Slope: $\frac{1}{4}$; y-intercept: $(0, -3)$

Plot the y-intercept $(0, -3)$. We can start at the y-intercept and use the slope, $\frac{1}{4}$, to find another point. We move up 1 unit and right 4 units to the point $(4, -2)$. Thinking of the slope as $\frac{-1}{-4}$ we can start at $(0, -3)$ and move down 1 unit and left 4 units to get another point $(-4, -4)$.

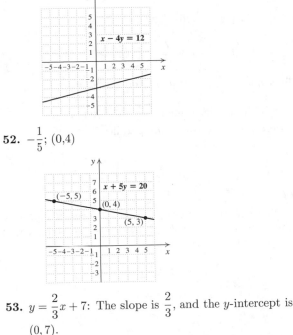

52. $-\frac{1}{5}$; $(0,4)$

53. $y = \frac{2}{3}x + 7$: The slope is $\frac{2}{3}$, and the y-intercept is $(0, 7)$.

$y = \frac{2}{3}x - 5$: The slope is $\frac{2}{3}$, and the y-intercept is $(0, -5)$.

Since both lines have slope $\frac{2}{3}$ but different y-intercepts, their graphs are parallel.

54. No

55. The equation $y = 2x - 5$ represents a line with slope 2 and y-intercept $(0, -5)$. We rewrite the second equation in slope-intercept form.

$$4x + 2y = 9$$
$$2y = -4x + 9$$
$$y = \frac{1}{2}(-4x + 9)$$
$$y = -2x + \frac{9}{2}$$

The slope is -2 and the y-intercept is $\left(0, \frac{9}{2}\right)$. Since the lines have different slopes, their graphs are not parallel.

56. Yes

57. Rewrite each equation in slope-intercept form.

$$3x + 4y = 8$$
$$4y = -3x + 8$$
$$y = \frac{1}{4}(-3x + 8)$$
$$y = -\frac{3}{4}x + 2$$

The slope is $-\frac{3}{4}$, and the y-intercept is $(0, 2)$.

$$7 - 12y = 9x$$

$$-12y = 9x - 7$$

$$y = -\frac{1}{12}(9x - 7)$$

$$y = -\frac{3}{4}x + \frac{7}{12}$$

The slope is $-\frac{3}{4}$, and the y-intercept is $\left(0, \frac{7}{12}\right)$.

Since both lines have slope $-\frac{3}{4}$ but different y-intercepts, their graphs are parallel.

58. No

59. $y = 4x - 5,$
   $4y = 8 - x$

The first equation is in slope-intercept form. It represents a line with slope 4. Now we rewrite the second equation in slope-intercept form.

$$4y = 8 - x$$

$$y = \frac{1}{4}(8 - x)$$

$$y = 2 - \frac{1}{4}x$$

$$y = -\frac{1}{4}x + 2$$

The slope of the line is $-\frac{1}{4}$.

Since $4\left(-\frac{1}{4}\right) = -1$, the equations represent perpendicular lines.

60. No

61. $y - 2y = 5,$
   $2x + 4y = 8$

We write each equation in slope-intercept form.

$$x - 2y = 5$$

$$-2y = -x + 5$$

$$y = -\frac{1}{2}(-x + 5)$$

$$y = \frac{1}{2}x - \frac{5}{2}$$

The slope is $\frac{1}{2}$.

$$2x + 4y = 8$$

$$4y = -2x + 8$$

$$y = \frac{1}{4}(-2x + 8)$$

$$y = -\frac{1}{2}x + 2$$

The slope is $-\frac{1}{2}$.

Since $\frac{1}{2}\left(-\frac{1}{2}\right) = -\frac{1}{4} \neq -1$, the equations do not represent perpendicular lines.

62. Yes

63. $2x + 3y = 1,$
   $3x - 2y = 1$

We write each equation in slope-intercept form.

$$2x + 3y = 1$$

$$3y = -2x + 1$$

$$y = \frac{1}{3}(-2x + 1)$$

$$y = -\frac{2}{3}x + \frac{1}{3}$$

The slope is $-\frac{2}{3}$.

$$3x - 2y = 1$$

$$-2y = -3x + 1$$

$$y = -\frac{1}{2}(-3x + 1)$$

$$y = \frac{3}{2}x - \frac{1}{2}$$

The slope is $\frac{3}{2}$.

Since $-\frac{2}{3}\left(\frac{3}{2}\right) = -1$, the equations represent perpendicular lines.

64. No

65. The slope of the line represented by $y = 5x - 7$ is 5. Then a line parallel to the graph of $y = 5x - 7$ has slope 5 also. Since the y-intercept is $(0, 11)$, the desired equation is $y = 5x + 11$.

66. $y = 2x - 3$

67. First find the slope of the line represented by $2x + y = 0$.

$$2x + y = 0$$

$$y = -2x$$

The slope is -2. Then the slope of a line perpendicular to the graph of $2x + y = 0$ is the negative reciprocal of -2, or $\frac{1}{2}$. Since the y-intercept is $(0, 0)$, the desired equation is $y = \frac{1}{2}x + 0$, or $y = \frac{1}{2}x$.

68. $y = -3x + 5$

69. The slope of the line represented by $y = x$ is 1. Then a line parallel to this line also has slope 1. Since the y-intercept is $(0, 3)$, the desired equation is $y = 1 \cdot x + 3$, or $y = x + 3$.

70. $y = -x$

71. First find the slope of the line represented by $x + y = 3$.

$$x + y = 3$$

$$y = -x + 3, \text{ or } y = -1 \cdot x + 3$$

The slope is -1. Then the slope of a line perpendicular to this line is the negative reciprocal is -1, or 1. Since the y-intercept is -4, the desired equation is $y = 1 \cdot x - 4$, or $y = x - 4$.

72. $y = -\dfrac{3}{2}x - 1$

73. $C(x) = 25x + 75$

25 signifies that the cost per person is \$25; 75 signifies that the setup cost for the party is \$75.

74. $\dfrac{1}{8}$ signifies that the grass grows $\dfrac{1}{8}$ in. per day; 2 signifies that the grass is 2 in. long immediately after it is cut.

75. $A(t) = \dfrac{3}{20}t + 72$ is of the form $y = mx + b$ with $m = \dfrac{3}{20}$ and $b = 72$.

$\dfrac{3}{20}$ signifies that the life expectancy of American women increases $\dfrac{3}{20}$ yr per year for years after 1950; 72 signifies that the life expectancy of American women in 1950 was 72 years.

76. $\dfrac{1}{5}$ signifies that the demand increases $\dfrac{1}{5}$ quadrillion joules per year for years after 1960; 20 signifies that the demand was 20 quadrillion joules in 1960.

77. $f(t) = 2.6t + 17.8$ is of the form $y = mx + b$ with $m = 2.6$ and $b = 17.8$.

2.6 signifies that sales increase \$2.6 billion per year, for years after 1975; 17.8 signifies that sales in 1975 were \$17.8 billion.

78. 0.1522 signifies that the price increases \$0.1522 per year, for years since 1990; 4.29 signifies that the average cost of a movie ticket in 1990 was \$4.29.

79. $C(d) = 0.75d + 2$ is of the form $y = mx + b$ with $m = 0.75$ and $b = 2$.

0.75 signifies that the cost per mile of a taxi ride is \$0.75; 2 signifies that the minimum cost of a taxi ride is \$2.

80. 0.3 signifies that the cost per mile of renting the truck is \$0.30; 20 signifies that the minimum cost is \$20.

81. $F(t) = -5000t + 90{,}000$

a) -5000 signifies that the truck's value depreciates \$5000 per year; 90,000 signifies that the original value of the truck was \$90,000.

b) We find the value of t for which $F(t) = 0$.
$$0 = -5000t + 90{,}000$$
$$5000t = 90{,}000$$
$$t = 18$$

It will take 18 yr for the truck to depreciate completely.

c) The truck's value goes from \$90,000 when $t = 0$ to \$0 when $t = 18$, so the domain of F is $\{x | 0 \le t \le 18\}$.

82. a) -2000 signifies that the color separator's value depreciates \$2000 per year; 15,000 signifies that the original value of the separator was \$15,000.

b) 7.5 yr

c) $\{t | 0 \le t \le 7.5\}$

83. $v(n) = -150n + 900$

a) -150 signifies that the snowblower's value depreciates \$150 per winter of use; 900 signifies that the original value of the snowblower was \$900.

b) We find the value of n for which $v(n) = 300$.
$$300 = -150n + 900$$
$$-600 = -150n$$
$$4 = n$$

The snowblower's trade-in value will be \$300 after 4 winters of use.

c) First we find the value of n for which $v(n) = 0$.
$$0 = -150n + 900$$
$$-900 = -150n$$
$$6 = n$$

The value of the snowblower goes from \$900 when $n = 0$ to \$0 when $n = 6$. Since the snowblower is used only in the winter we express the domain of v as $\{0, 1, 2, 3, 4, 5, 6\}$.

84. a) -300 signifies that the mower's value depreciates \$300 per summer of use; 2400 signifies that the original value of the mower was \$2400.

b) After 4 summers of use

c) $\{0, 1, 2, 3, 4, 5, 6, 7, 8\}$

85. *Writing Exercise*

86. *Writing Exercise*

87. $\quad y - k = m(x - h)$
$\qquad y = m(x - h) + k \quad$ Adding k to both sides

88. $y = -2(x + 4) + 9$

89. $-5 - (-7) = -5 + 7 = 2$

90. 16

91. $-3 - 6 = -3 + (-6) = -9$

92. -10

93. *Writing Exercise*

94. *Writing Exercise*

95. *Writing Exercise*

96. *Writing Exercise*

97. We first solve for y.
$$rx + py = s$$
$$py = -rx + s$$
$$y = -\dfrac{r}{p}x + \dfrac{s}{p}$$

The slope is $-\dfrac{r}{p}$, and the y-intercept is $\left(0, \dfrac{s}{p}\right)$.

98. Slope: $-\dfrac{r}{r+p}$; y-intercept: $\left(0, \dfrac{s}{r+p}\right)$

99. See the answer section in the text.

100. False

101. Let $c = 2$ and $d = 3$. Then $f(cd) = f(2 \cdot 3) = f(6) = m \cdot 6 + b = 6m + b$, but $f(c)f(d) = f(2)f(3) = (m \cdot 2 + b)(m \cdot 3 + b) = 6m^2 + 5mb + b^2$. Thus, the given statement is false.

102. False

103. Let $c = 5$ and $d = 2$. Then $f(c - d) = f(5 - 2) = f(3) = m \cdot 3 + b = 3m + b$, but $f(c) - f(d) = f(5) - f(2) = (m \cdot 5 + b) - (m \cdot 2 + b) = 5m + b - 2m - b = 3m$. Thus, the given statement is false.

104. $-\dfrac{31}{4}$

105. Two points on the graph are $(0, 16)$ and $(1, 16 + 1.5)$, or $(1, 17.5)$, so the y-intercept will be $(0, 16)$. Now we find the slope:
$$m = \frac{17.5 - 16}{1 - 0} = \frac{1.5}{1} = 1.5$$
Then the equation is $y = 1.5x + 16$.

106. $y = 0.07x + 4.95$

107. $C(n) = 5n + 17.5$, for $1 \le n \le 10$,
$C(n) = 6n + 17.5$, for $11 \le n \le 20$,
$C(n) = 7n + 17.5$, for $21 \le n \le 30$,
$C(n) = 8n + 17.5$ for $n \ge 31$

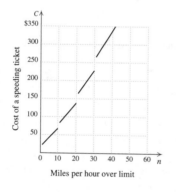

108.

$y_1 = 1.4x + 2$, $y_2 = 0.6x + 2$,
$y_3 = 1.4x + 5$, $y_4 = 0.6x + 5$

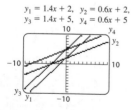

Exercise Set 4.5

1. $y - y_1 = m(x - x_1)$ Point-slope equation
$y - 3 = -2(x - 2)$ Substituting -2 for m, 2 for
$\qquad\qquad\qquad\qquad x_1$, and 3 for y_1

To graph the equation, we count off a slope of $\dfrac{-2}{1}$, starting at $(2, 3)$, and draw the line.

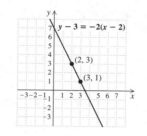

2. $y - 4 = 5(x - 7)$

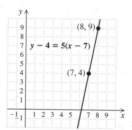

3. $y - y_1 = m(x - x_1)$ Point-slope equation
$y - 7 = 3(x - 4)$ Substituting 3 for m, 4
$\qquad\qquad\qquad\qquad$ for x_1, and 7 for y_1

To graph the equation, we count off a slope of $\dfrac{3}{1}$, starting at $(4, 7)$ and draw the line.

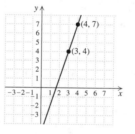

$y - 7 = 3(x - 4)$

4. $y - 3 = 2(x - 7)$

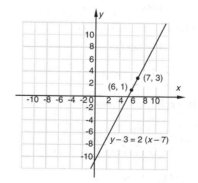

5. $y - y_1 = m(x - x_1)$ Point-slope equation
$y - (-4) = \dfrac{1}{2}[x - (-2)]$ Substituting $\dfrac{1}{2}$ for m,
$\qquad\qquad\qquad\qquad\qquad -2$ for x_1, and -4 for y_1

To graph the equation, we count off a slope of $\frac{1}{2}$, starting at $(-2,-4)$, and draw the line.

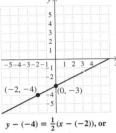

$$y - (-4) = \tfrac{1}{2}(x - (-2)), \text{ or}$$
$$y + 4 = \tfrac{1}{2}(x + 2)$$

6. $y - (-7) = 1 \cdot [x - (-5)]$, or $y - (-7) = x - (-5)$

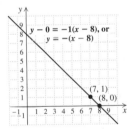

$$y - (-7) = x - (-5), \text{ or}$$
$$y + 7 = x + 5$$

7. $y - y_1 = m(x - x_1)$ Point-slope equation

$y - 0 = -1(x - 8)$ Substituting -1 for m, 8 for x_1, and 0 for y_1

To graph the equation, we count off a slope of $\frac{-1}{1}$, starting at $(8, 0)$ and draw the line.

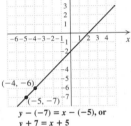

$y - 0 = -1(x - 8)$, or
$y = -(x - 8)$

8. $y - 0 = -3[x - (-2)]$

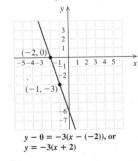

$y - 0 = -3(x - (-2))$, or
$y = -3(x + 2)$

9. $y - y_1 = m(x - x_1)$ Point-slope equation

$y - 8 = \tfrac{2}{5}[x - (-3)]$ Substituting $\frac{2}{5}$ for m, -3 for x_1, and 8 for y_1

We graph the equation by plotting $(-3, 8)$, counting off a slope of $\frac{2}{5}$, and drawing the line.

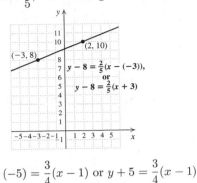

$$y - 8 = \tfrac{2}{5}(x - (-3)),$$
$$\text{or}$$
$$y - 8 = \tfrac{2}{5}(x + 3)$$

10. $y - (-5) = \dfrac{3}{4}(x - 1)$ or $y + 5 = \dfrac{3}{4}(x - 1)$

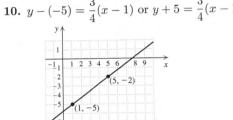

$$y - (-5) = \tfrac{3}{4}(x - 1), \text{ or}$$
$$y + 5 = \tfrac{3}{4}(x - 1)$$

11. $\quad y - 4 = \dfrac{2}{7}(x - 1)$

$y - y_1 = m(x - x_1)$

$m = \dfrac{2}{7}$, $x_1 = 1$, and $y_1 = 4$, so the slope m is $\dfrac{2}{7}$ and a point (x_1, y_1) on the graph is $(1, 4)$.

12. $9; (2, 3)$

13. $\quad y + 2 = -5(x - 7)$

$\quad y - (-2) = -5(x - 7)$

$\quad y - y_1 = m(x - x_1)$

$m = -5$, $x_1 = 7$, and $y_1 = -2$, so the slope m is -5 and a point (x_1, y_1) on the graph is $(7, -2)$.

14. $-\dfrac{2}{9}; (-5, 1)$

15. $\quad y - 1 = -\dfrac{5}{3}(x + 2)$

$\quad y - 1 = -\dfrac{5}{3}[x - (-2)]$

$\quad y - y_1 = m(x - x_1)$

$m = -\dfrac{5}{3}$, $x_1 = -2$, and $y_1 = 1$, so the slope m is $-\dfrac{5}{3}$ and a point (x_1, y_1) on the graph is $(-2, 1)$.

16. $-4; (9, -7)$

17. $y = \dfrac{4}{7}x$

The equation is of the form $y = mx$, so we know that its graph is a line through the origin with slope m. Thus, the slope is $\dfrac{4}{7}$ and a point on the graph is $(0, 0)$.

18. 3; $(0,0)$

19.

$$y - y_1 = m(x - x_1) \quad \text{Point-slope equation}$$
$$y - (-3) = 4(x - 2) \quad \text{Substituting 4 for } m, 2$$
$$\text{for } x_1, \text{ and } -3 \text{ for } y_1$$
$$y + 3 = 4x - 8 \quad \text{Simplifying}$$
$$y = 4x - 11 \quad \text{Subtracting 3 from both sides}$$
$$f(x) = 4x - 11 \quad \text{Using function notation}$$

20. $f(x) = -4x + 1$

21.

$$y - y_1 = m(x - x_1) \quad \text{Point-slope equation}$$
$$y - (-7) = -\frac{3}{5}(x - 4) \quad \text{Substituting } -\frac{3}{5} \text{ for } m, 4 \text{ for } x_1, \text{ and } -7 \text{ for } y_1$$
$$y + 7 = -\frac{3}{5}x + \frac{12}{5} \quad \text{Simplifying}$$
$$y = -\frac{3}{5}x - \frac{23}{5} \quad \text{Subtracting 7 from both sides}$$
$$f(x) = -\frac{3}{5}x - \frac{23}{5} \quad \text{Using function notation}$$

22. $f(x) = -\frac{1}{5}x + \frac{3}{5}$

23.

$$y - y_1 = m(x - x_1) \quad \text{Point-slope equation}$$
$$y - (-4) = -0.6[x - (-3)] \quad \text{Substituting } -0.6 \text{ for } m, -3 \text{ for } x_1, \text{ and } -4 \text{ for } y_1$$
$$y + 4 = -0.6(x + 3)$$
$$y + 4 = -0.6x - 1.8$$
$$y = -0.6x - 5.8$$
$$f(x) = -0.6x - 5.8 \quad \text{Using function notation}$$

24. $f(x) = 2.3x - 14.2$

25. $m = \frac{2}{7}$; $(0, -5)$

Observe that the slope is $\frac{2}{7}$ and the y-intercept is $(0, -5)$. Thus, we have $f(x) = \frac{2}{7}x - 5$.

26. $f(x) = \frac{1}{4}x + 3$

27. The slope of $y = 3x - 6$ is 3. This will also be the slope of a line parallel to $y = 3x - 6$. We find an equation in point-slope form and then find an equivalent equation in slope-intercept form.

$$y - y_1 = m(x - x_1)$$
$$y - (-5) = 3(x - 1)$$
$$y + 5 = 3x - 3$$
$$y = 3x - 8$$

28. $y = -x + 1$

29. First we find the slope of $x - 2y = 1$.

$$x - 2y = 1$$
$$-2y = -x + 1$$
$$y = \frac{1}{2}x - \frac{1}{2}$$

The slope of $y = \frac{1}{2}x - \frac{1}{2}$ is $\frac{1}{2}$. Then the slope of a line perpendicular to $x - 2y = 1$ is -2 since $\frac{1}{2}(-2) = -1$. Next we find an equation in point-slope form and then find an equivalent equation in slope-intercept form.

$$y - y_1 = m(x - x_1)$$
$$y - 0 = -2(x - 3)$$
$$y = -2x + 6$$

30. $y = -\frac{2}{3}x - \frac{1}{3}$

31. $y - 2 = \frac{1}{2}(x - 1)$ Point-slope form

The line has slope $\frac{1}{2}$ and passes through $(1, 2)$. We plot $(1, 2)$ and then find a second point by moving up 1 unit and right 2 units to $(3, 3)$. We draw the line through these points.

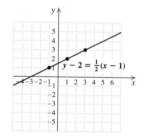

32.

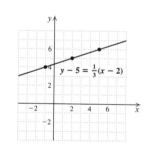

33. $y - 1 = -\frac{1}{2}(x - 3)$ Point-slope form

The line has slope $-\frac{1}{2}$, or $\frac{1}{-2}$ passes through $(3, 1)$. We plot $(3, 1)$ and then find a second point by moving up 1 unit and left 2 units to $(1, 2)$. We draw the line through these points.

$$Y - 1 = -\frac{1}{2}(x - 3)$$
$$Y - 1 = \frac{-1x}{2} + \frac{3}{1}$$

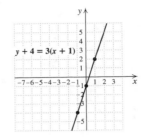

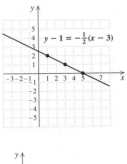

34.

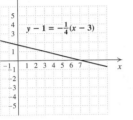

38.

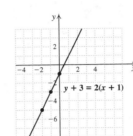

35. $y + 2 = \dfrac{1}{2}(x - 3)$, or $y - (-2) = \dfrac{1}{2}(x - 3)$

The line has slope $\dfrac{1}{2}$ and passes through $(3, -2)$. We plot $(3, -2)$ and then find a second point by moving up 1 unit and right 2 units to $(5, -1)$. We draw the line through these points.

$y + 2 = \dfrac{1}{2}(x - 3)$

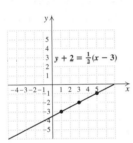

36.

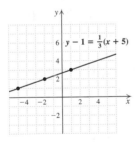

37. $y + 4 = 3(x + 1)$, or $y - (-4) = 3(x - (-1))$

The line has slope 3, or $\dfrac{3}{1}$, and passes through $(-1, -4)$. We plot $(-1, -4)$ and then find a second point by moving up 3 units and right 1 unit to $(0, -1)$. We draw the line through these points.

39. First find the slope of the line:
$$m = \frac{6 - 4}{5 - 1} = \frac{2}{4} = \frac{1}{2}$$

Use the point-slope equation with $m = \dfrac{1}{2}$ and $(1, 4) = (x_1, y_1)$. (We could let $(5, 6) = (x_1, y_1)$ instead and obtain an equivalent equation.)

$$y - 4 = \frac{1}{2}(x - 1)$$
$$y - 4 = \frac{1}{2}x - \frac{1}{2}$$
$$y = \frac{1}{2}x + \frac{7}{2}$$
$$f(x) = \frac{1}{2}x + \frac{7}{2} \quad \text{Using function notation}$$

40. $f(x) = -\dfrac{5}{2}x + 11$

41. First find the slope of the line:
$$m = \frac{3 - (-3)}{6.5 - 2.5} = \frac{3 + 3}{4} = \frac{6}{4} = 1.5$$

Use the point-slope equation with $m = 1.5$ and $(6.5, 3) = (x_1, y_1)$.

$$y - 3 = 1.5(x - 6.5)$$
$$y - 3 = 1.5x - 9.75$$
$$y = 1.5x - 6.75$$
$$f(x) = 1.5x - 6.75 \quad \text{Using function notation}$$

42. $f(x) = 0.6x - 2.5$

43. First find the slope of the line:
$$m = \frac{-2 - 3}{0 - 1} = \frac{-5}{-1} = 5$$

Observe that the y-intercept is $(0, -2)$. Then, using the slope-intercept equation we have $y = 5x - 2$.

We could also use the point-slope equation with $m = 5$ and $(1, 3) = (x_1, y_1)$.

$$y - 3 = 5(x - 1)$$
$$y - 3 = 5x - 5$$
$$y = 5x - 2$$
$$f(x) = 5x - 2$$

44. $f(x) = -\dfrac{4}{3}x - 4$

45. First find the slope of the line:
$$m = \frac{-6 - (-3)}{-4 - (-2)} = \frac{-6 + 3}{-4 + 2} = \frac{-3}{-2} = \frac{3}{2}$$

Use the point-slope equation with $m = \dfrac{3}{2}$ and $(-2, -3) = (x_1, y_1)$.
$$y - (-3) = \frac{3}{2}[x - (-2)]$$
$$y + 3 = \frac{3}{2}(x + 2)$$
$$y + 3 = \frac{3}{2}x + 3$$
$$y = \frac{3}{2}x$$
$$f(x) = \frac{3}{2}x \qquad \text{Using function notation}$$

46. $f(x) = 3x + 5$

47. a) We form pairs of the type (t, R) where t is the number of years since 1930 and R is the record. We have two pairs, $(0, 46.8)$ and $(40, 43.8)$.
These are two points on the graph of the linear function we are seeking. We use the point-slope form to write an equation relating R and t:
$$m = \frac{43.8 - 46.8}{40 - 0} = \frac{-3}{40} = -0.075$$
$$R - 46.8 = -0.075(t - 0)$$
$$R - 46.8 = -0.075t$$
$$R = -0.075t + 46.8$$
$$R(t) = -0.075t + 46.8 \qquad \text{Using function notation}$$

b) 2003 is 73 years since 1930, so to predict the record in 2003, we find $R(73)$:
$$R(73) = -0.075(73) + 46.8$$
$$= 41.325$$
The predicted record is 41.325 seconds in 2003.

2006 is 76 years since 1930, so to predict the record in 2006, we find $R(76)$:
$$R(76) = -0.075(76) + 46.8$$
$$= 41.1$$
The predicted record is 41.1 seconds in 2006.

c) Substitute 40 for $R(t)$ and solve for t:
$$40 = -0.075t + 46.8$$
$$-6.8 = -0.075t$$
$$91 \approx t$$
The record will be 40 seconds about 91 years after 1930, or in 2021.

48. a) $R(t) = -0.0075t + 3.85$

b) 3.31 min; 3.28 min

c) 2030

49. a) We form the pairs $(0, 178.6)$ and $(8, 243.1)$.

Use the point-slope form to write an equation relating A and t:
$$m = \frac{243.1 - 178.6}{8 - 0} = \frac{64.5}{8} = 8.0625$$
$$A - 178.6 = 8.0625(x - 0)$$
$$A - 178.6 = 8.0625x$$
$$A = 8.0625t + 178.6$$
$$A(t) = 8.0625t + 178.6 \qquad \text{Using function notation}$$

b) 2006 is 14 years since 1992, so we find $A(14)$:
$$A(14) = 8.0625(14) + 178.6$$
$$= 291.475$$
We predict that the amount of PAC contributions in 2006 will be $291.475 million.

50. a) $A(p) = -2.5p + 26.5$

b) 11.5 million lb

51. a) We form the pairs $(0, 43.8)$ and $(5, 62.2)$. Use the point-slope form to write an equation relating N and t:
$$m = \frac{62.2 - 43.8}{5 - 0} = \frac{18.4}{5} = 3.68$$
$$N - 43.8 = 3.68(t - 0)$$
$$N - 43.8 = 3.68t$$
$$N = 3.68t + 43.8$$
$$N(t) = 3.68t + 43.8 \qquad \text{Using function notation}$$

b) 2005 is 12 years after 1993, so we find $N(12)$:
$$N(12) = 3.68(12) + 43.8$$
$$= 87.96$$
We predict that Americans will recycle about 87.96 million tons of garbage in 2005.

52. a) $A(p) = 2p - 11$

b) 1 million lb

53. a) We form the pairs $(0, 78.8)$ and $(10, 79.8)$.

Use the point-slope form to write an equation relating E and t:
$$m = \frac{79.8 - 78.8}{10 - 0} = \frac{1}{10}, \text{ or } 0.1$$
$$E - 78.8 = 0.1(t - 0)$$
$$E - 78.8 = 0.1t$$
$$E = 0.1t + 78.8$$
$$E(t) = 0.1t + 78.8 \qquad \text{Using function notation}$$

b) 2008 is 18 years after 1990, so we find $E(18)$:

$$E(18) = 0.1(18) + 78.8$$
$$= 80.6$$

We predict that the life expectancy of females in the United States in 2008 will be 80.6 years.

54. a) $E(t) = 0.26t + 71.8$

b) 76.22 years

55. a) We form the pairs $(0, 74.9)$ and $(4, 77.7)$.

Use the point-slope form to write an equation relating A and t:

$$m = \frac{77.7 - 74.9}{4 - 0} = \frac{2.8}{4} = 0.7$$
$$A - 74.9 = 0.7(t - 0)$$
$$A - 74.9 = 0.7t$$
$$A = 0.7t + 74.9$$
$$A(t) = 0.7t + 74.9 \quad \text{Using function notation}$$

b) 2006 is 12 years after 1994, so we find $A(12)$:

$$A(12) = 0.7(12) + 74.9$$
$$= 83.3$$

We predict that there will be 83.3 million acres of land in the national park system in 2006.

56. a) $P(d) = 0.03d + 1$

b) 21.7 atm

57. The points lie approximately on a straight line, so the data appear to be linear.

58. Linear

59. The points do not lie on a straight line, so the data are not linear.

60. Not linear

61. The points lie approximately on a straight line, so the data appear to be linear.

62. Not linear

63. a) We use the point-slope form to write an equation relating S and t, where S is in thousands and t is the number of years after 1964.

$$m = \frac{33 - 13}{24 - 8} = \frac{20}{16} = 1.25$$
$$S - 13 = 1.25(t - 8)$$
$$S - 13 = 1.25t - 10$$
$$S = 1.25t + 3$$
$$S(t) = 1.25t + 3 \quad \text{Using function notation}$$

b) 2010 is 46 years after 1964, so we find $S(46)$.

$$S(46) = 1.25(46) + 3$$
$$= 60.5$$

We predict that there will be 60.5 thousand, or 60,500 shopping centers in 2010.

64. a) $G(t) = 30.8t + 1550$

b) About 2505 golf courses

65. a) Enter the data in a graphing calculator, letting x represent the number of years since 1900. Then use the linear regression feature to find the desired function. We have $W(x) = 0.183x + 62.13333333$.

b) $2008 - 1900 = 108$, so we use one of the methods discussed earlier in the text to find $W(108)$. We predict that the life expectancy in 2008 will be about 81.8 years. This estimate is higher than the one found in Exercise 53.

66. a) $M(x) = 0.1785714286x + 55.85714286$

b) 74.96 yr; this estimate is lower

67. a) Enter the data in a graphing calculator, letting x represent the number of years after 1987. Then use the linear regression feature to find the desired function. We have $C(x) = -5.027142857x + 95.21714286$.

b) $2003 - 1987 = 16$, so we use one of the methods discussed earlier in the text to find $C(16)$. We predict that the average local monthly bill for a cellular phone will be about \$14.78 in 2003.

68. a) $E(x) = 75.93023256x + 8323.372093$

b) \$9083

69. *Writing Exercise*

70. *Writing Exercise*

71. $(3x^2 + 5x) + (2x - 4) - 3x^2 + (5 + 2)x - 4 = 3x^2 + 7x - 4$

72. $5t^2 - 6t - 3$

73. $\dfrac{2t - 6}{4t + 1} = \dfrac{2 \cdot 3 - 6}{4 \cdot 3 + 1} = \dfrac{6 - 6}{12 + 1} = \dfrac{0}{13} = 0$

74. 0

75. $2x - 5y = 2 \cdot 3 - 5(-1) = 6 + 5 = 11$

76. -34

77. *Writing Exercise*

78. *Writing Exercise*

79. **Familiarize.** The value C of the computer, in dollars, after t months can be modeled by a line that contains the points $(6, 900)$ and $(8, 750)$.

Translate. We find an equation relating C and t.

$$m = \frac{750 - 900}{8 - 6} = \frac{-150}{2} = -75$$
$$C - 900 = -75(t - 6)$$
$$C - 900 = -75t + 450$$
$$C = -75t + 1350$$

Carry out. Using function notation we have $C(t) = -75t + 1350$. To find how much the computer cost we find $C(0)$:

$$C(0) = -75 \cdot 0 + 1350$$
$$= 1350$$

Check. We can repeat our calculations. We could also graph the function and determine that $(0, 1350)$ is on the graph.

State. The computer cost $1350.

80. $21.1°C$

81. Familiarize. The total cost C of the phone, in dollars, after t months, can be modeled by a line that contains the points $(5, 230)$ and $(9, 390)$.

Translate. We find an equation relating C and t.

$$m = \frac{390 - 230}{9 - 5} = \frac{160}{4} = 40$$

$$C - 230 = 40(t - 5)$$

$$C - 230 = 40t - 200$$

$$C = 40t + 30$$

Carry out. Using function notation we have $C(t) = 40t + 30$. To find the costs already incurred when the service began we find $C(0)$:

$$C(0) = 40 \cdot 0 + 30 = 30$$

Check. We can repeat the calculations. We could also graph the function and determine that $(0, 30)$ is on the graph.

State. Mel had already incurred $30 in costs when his service just began.

82. $11,000

83. Familiarize. The percentage of premiums paid out in benefits in 1993 was $103.6/124.7 \approx 83.1\%$. In 1996 the percentage was $113.8/137.1 \approx 83.0\%$. The percentage P of premiums, in dollars, paid out in benefits t years after 1993 can be modeled by a line that contains the points $(0, 83.1)$ and $(3, 83.0)$.

Translate. We find an equation relating P and t.

$$m = \frac{83.0 - 83.1}{3 - 0} = \frac{-0.1}{3} = -\frac{1}{30}$$

We know the slope and the y-intercept, so we use the slope-intercept equation.

$$P = -\frac{1}{30}t + 83.1$$

Carry out. Using function notation we have $P(t) = -\frac{1}{30}t + 83.1$. Since 2005 is 12 years after 1993, we find $P(12)$ to predict the percentage of premiums that will be paid out in benefits in 2005:

$$P(12) = -\frac{1}{30}(12) + 83.1 = 82.7$$

Check. We can repeat the calculations. We could also graph the function and determine that $(12, 82.7)$ is on the graph.

State. We estimate that 82.7% will be paid out in benefits in 2005. (Answers may vary slightly depending on when and how rounding occurred.)

84. $8.33 per pound

85. In Exercise 50(a) we found that the demand function is $A(p) = -2.5p + 26.5$, where p is the price per pound. The price must be a positive number, so we have $p > 0$. Also, $A(p)$ cannot be negative so we have

$$A(p) \geq 0$$

$$-2.5p + 26.5 \geq 0$$

$$-2.5p \geq 26.5$$

$$p \leq 10.6$$

Then the domain is $\{p | 0 < p \leq 10.6\}$.

86. $\{p | p \geq 5.5\}$

87. a) Since $g(3) = -5$ and $g(7) = -1$, we know that the points $(3, -5)$ and $(7, -1)$ are on the graph of g. We can use these points to find the function.

$$m = \frac{-1 - (-5)}{7 - 3} = \frac{-1 + 5}{4} = \frac{4}{4} = 1$$

$$y - y_1 = m(x - x_1)$$

$$y - (-5) = 1(x - 3)$$

$$y + 5 = x - 3$$

$$y = x - 8$$

$$g(x) = x - 8 \qquad \text{Using function notation}$$

b) $\quad g(x) = x - 8$

$\quad g(-2) = -2 - 8 = -10$

c) $g(a) = a - 8$

Then we have

$$g(a) = 75$$

$$a - 8 = 75$$

$$a = 83$$

Exercise Set 4.6

1. $\{7, 9, 11\} \cap \{9, 11, 13\}$

The numbers 9 and 11 are common to both sets, so the intersection is $\{9, 11\}$.

2. $\{2, 4, 8, 9, 10\}$

3. $\{1, 5, 10, 15\} \cup \{5, 15, 20\}$

The numbers in either or both sets are 1, 5, 10, 15, and 20, so the union is $\{1, 5, 10, 15, 20\}$.

4. $\{5\}$

5. $\{a, b, c, d, e, f\} \cap \{b, d, f\}$

The letters b, d, and f are common to both sets, so the intersection is $\{b, d, f\}$.

6. $\{a, b, c\}$

7. $\{r, s, t\} \cup \{r, u, t, s, v\}$

The letters in either or both sets are r, s, t, u, and v, so the union is $\{r, s, t, u, v\}$.

8. $\{m, o, p\}$

9. $\{3, 6, 9, 12\} \cap \{5, 10, 15\}$

There are no numbers common to both sets, so the solution set has no members. It is $\emptyset$.

10. $\{1, 4, 5, 6, 8, 9\}$

11. $\{3, 5, 7\} \cup \emptyset$

The numbers in either or both sets are 3, 5, and 7, so the union is $\{3, 5, 7\}$.

12. $\emptyset$

13. $3 < x < 8$

This inequality is an abbreviation for the conjunction $3 < x \ and \ x < 8$. The graph is the intersection of two separate solution sets: $\{x | 3 < x\} \cap \{x | x < 8\} = \{x | 3 < x < 8\}$.

Interval notation: $(3, 8)$

14.

$[0, 4]$

15. $-6 \le y \le -2$

This inequality is an abbreviation for the conjunction $-6 \le y \ and \ y \le -2$.

Interval notation: $[-6, -2]$

16.

$[-9, -5)$

17. $x < -2 \ or \ x > 3$

The graph of this disjunction is the union of the graphs of the individual solution sets $\{x | x < -2\}$ and $\{x | x > 3\}$.

Interval notation: $(-\infty, -2) \cup (3, \infty)$

18.

$(-\infty, -5) \cup (1, \infty)$

19. $x \le -1 \ or \ x > 5$

Interval notation: $(-\infty, -1] \cup (5, \infty)$

20.

$(-\infty, -5] \cup (2, \infty)$

21. $-4 \le -x < 2$

$\quad 4 \ge x > -2 \quad$ Multiplying by -1 and reversing
$\quad\quad\quad\quad\quad\quad$ the inequality symbols
$-2 < x \le 4 \quad$ Rewriting

Interval notation: $(-2, 4]$

22.

$(-7, -2)$

23. $x > -2 \ and \ x < 4$

This conjunction can be abbreviated as $-2 < x < 4$.

Interval notation: $(-2, 4)$

24.

$(-3, 1]$

25. $5 > a \ or \ a > 7$

Interval notation: $(-\infty, 5) \cup (7, \infty)$

26.

$(-\infty, -3) \cup [2, \infty)$

27. $x \ge 5 \ or \ -x \ge 4$

Multiplying the second inequality by -1 and reversing the inequality symbols, we get $x \ge 5 \ or \ x \le -4$.

Interval notation: $(-\infty -4] \cup [5, \infty)$

28.

$(-\infty, -6) \cup (-3, \infty)$

29. $4 > y \ and \ y \ge -6$

This conjunction can be abbreviated as $-6 \le x < 4$.

Interval notation: $[-6, 4)$

30.

$(-6, 0]$

31. $x < 7 \ and \ x \ge 3$

This conjunction can be abbreviated as $3 \le x < 7$.

Interval notation: $[3, 7)$

32.

$[-3, 3)$

33. $t < 2 \ or \ t < 5$

Observe that every number that is less than 2 is also less than 5. Then $t < 2 \ or \ t < 5$ is equivalent to $t < 5$ and the graph of this disjunction is the set $\{t | t < 5\}$.

Interval notation: $(-\infty, 5)$

34.

$(-1, \infty)$

35. $x > -1$ *or* $x \le 3$

The graph of this disjunction is the union of the graphs of the individual solution sets:

$\{x | x > -1\} \cup \{x | x \le 3\}$ = the set of all real numbers.

Interval notation: $(-\infty, \infty)$

36.

$(-\infty, \infty)$

37. $x \ge 5$ *and* $x > 7$

The graph of this conjunction is the intersection of two separate solution sets: $\{x | x \ge 5\} \cap \{x | x > 7\} = \{x | x > 7\}$.

Interval notation: $(7, \infty)$

38.

$(-\infty, -4]$

39.
$$-1 < t + 2 < 7$$
$$-1 - 2 < t < 7 - 2$$
$$-3 < t < 5$$

The solution set is $\{t | -3 < t < 5\}$, or $(-3, 5)$.

40. $\{t | -4 < t \le 4\}$, or $(-4, 4]$

41.
$$2 < x + 3 \quad and \quad x + 1 \le 5$$
$$-1 < x \quad and \quad x \le 4$$

We can abbreviate the answer as $-1 < x \le 4$. The solution set is $\{x | -1 < x \le 4\}$, or $(-1, 4]$.

42. $\{x | -3 < x < 7\}$, or $(-3, 7)$

43.
$$-7 \le 2a - 3 \quad and \quad 3a + 1 < 7$$
$$-4 \le 2a \quad and \quad 3a < 6$$
$$-2 \le a \quad and \quad a < 2$$

We can abbreviate the answer as $-2 \le a < 2$. The solution set is $\{a | -2 \le a < 2\}$, or $[-2, 2)$.

44. $\{n | -2 \le n \le 4\}$, or $[-2, 4]$

45. $x + 7 \le -2$ *or* $x + 7 \ge -3$

Observe that any real number is either less than or equal to -2 or greater than or equal to -3. Then the solution set is $\{x | x$ is a real number$\}$, or $(-\infty, \infty)$.

46. $\{x | x < -8 \text{ or } x \ge -1\}$, or $(-\infty, -8) \cup [-1, \infty)$

47.
$$2 \le 3x - 1 \le 8$$
$$3 \le 3x \le 9$$
$$1 \le x \le 3$$

The solution set is $\{x | 1 \le x \le 3\}$, or $[1, 3]$.

48. $\{x | 1 \le x \le 4\}$, or $[1, 4]$

49.
$$-21 \le -2x - 7 < 0$$
$$-14 \le -2x < 7$$
$$7 \ge x > -\frac{7}{2}, \text{ or}$$
$$-\frac{7}{2} < x \le 7$$

The solution set is $\left\{ x \middle| -\frac{7}{2} < x \le 7 \right\}$, or $\left(-\frac{7}{2}, 7 \right]$.

50. $\left\{ t \middle| -4 < t \le -\frac{10}{3} \right\}$, or $\left(-4, -\frac{10}{3} \right]$

51.
$$3x - 1 \le 2 \quad or \quad 3x - 1 \ge 8$$
$$3x \le 3 \quad or \quad 3x \ge 9$$
$$x \le 1 \quad or \quad x \ge 3$$

The solution set is $\{x | x \le 1 \text{ or } x \ge 3\}$, or $(-\infty, 1] \cup [3, \infty)$.

52. $\{x | x \le 1 \text{ or } x \ge 5\}$, or $(-\infty, 1] \cup [5, \infty)$

53.
$$2x - 7 < -1 \quad or \quad 2x - 7 > 1$$
$$2x < 6 \quad or \quad 2x > 8$$
$$x < 3 \quad or \quad x > 4$$

The solution set is $\{x | x < 3 \text{ or } x > 4\}$, or $(-\infty, 3) \cup (4, \infty)$.

54. $\left\{x \middle| x < -4 \text{ or } x > \dfrac{2}{3}\right\}$, or $(-\infty, -4) \cup \left(\dfrac{2}{3}, \infty\right)$

55. $6 > 2a - 1 \quad \text{or} \quad -4 \leq -3a + 2$

$\quad 7 > 2a \qquad \text{or} \quad -6 \leq -3a$

$\quad \dfrac{7}{2} > a \qquad \text{or} \quad 2 \geq a$

The solution set is $\left\{a \middle| \dfrac{7}{2} > a\right\} \cup \{a | 2 \geq a\} =$

$\left\{a \middle| \dfrac{7}{2} > a\right\}$, or $\left\{a \middle| a < \dfrac{7}{2}\right\}$, or $\left(-\infty, \dfrac{7}{2}\right)$.

56. All real numbers, or $(-\infty, \infty)$

57. $a + 4 < -1 \quad \text{and} \quad 3a - 5 < 7$

$\quad a < -5 \quad \text{and} \qquad 3a < 12$

$\quad a < -5 \quad \text{and} \qquad a < 4$

The solution set is $\{a | a < -5\} \cap \{a | a < 4\} =$
$\{a | a < -5\}$, or $(-\infty, -5)$.

58. $\{a | a > 4\}$, or $(4, \infty)$

59. $3x + 2 < 2 \quad \text{or} \quad 4 - 2x < 14$

$\quad 3x < 0 \quad \text{or} \qquad -2x < 10$

$\quad x < 0 \quad \text{or} \qquad x > 5$

The solution set is $\{x | x < 0\} \cup \{x | x > -5\} =$ the set of all real numbers, or $(-\infty, \infty)$.

60. $\{x | x \leq -2 \text{ or } x > 3\}$, or $(-\infty, -2] \cup (3, \infty)$

61. $2t - 7 \leq 5 \quad \text{or} \quad 5 - 2t > 3$

$\quad 2t \leq 12 \quad \text{or} \qquad -2t > -2$

$\quad t \leq 6 \quad \text{or} \qquad t < 1$

The solution set is $\{t | t \leq 6\} \cup \{t | t < 1\} = \{t | t \leq 6\}$, or $(-\infty, 6]$.

62. $\{a | a \geq -1\}$, or $[-1, \infty)$

63. From the graph we observe that the values of x for which $2x - 5 > -7$ and $2x - 5 < 7$ are $\{x | -1 < x < 6\}$, or $(-1, 6)$.

64. $(-\infty, -3) \cup (6, \infty)$

65. $f(x) = \dfrac{9}{x + 7}$

$f(x)$ cannot be computed when the denominator is 0. Since $x + 7 = 0$ is equivalent to $x = -7$, we have Domain of $f = \{x | x \text{ is a real number } and \ x \neq -7\} = (-\infty, -7) \cup (-7, \infty)$.

66. $(-\infty, -3) \cup (-3, \infty)$

67. $f(x) = \sqrt{x - 6}$

The expression $\sqrt{x - 6}$ is not a real number when $x - 6$ is negative. Thus, the domain of f is the set of all x-values for which $x - 6 \geq 0$. Since $x - 6 \geq 0$ is equivalent to $x \geq 6$, we have Domain of $f = [6, \infty)$.

68. $[2, \infty)$

69. $f(x) = \dfrac{x + 3}{2x - 5}$

$f(x)$ cannot be computed when the denominator is 0. Since $2x - 5 = 0$ is equivalent to $x = \dfrac{5}{2}$, we have

Domain of $f = \left\{x \middle| x \text{ is a real number } and \ x \neq \dfrac{5}{2}\right\}$, or

$\left(-\infty, \dfrac{5}{2}\right) \cup \left(\dfrac{5}{2}, \infty\right)$.

70. $\left(-\infty, -\dfrac{4}{3}\right) \cup \left(-\dfrac{4}{3}, \infty\right)$

71. $f(x) = \sqrt{2x + 8}$

The expression $\sqrt{2x + 8}$ is not a real number when $2x + 8$ is negative. Thus, the domain of f is the set of all x-values for which $2x + 8 \geq 0$. Since $2x + 8 \geq 0$ is equivalent to $x \geq -4$, we have Domain of $f = [-4, \infty)$.

72. $(-\infty, 2]$

73. $f(x) = \sqrt{8 - 2x}$

The expression $\sqrt{8 - 2x}$ is not a real number when $8 - 2x$ is negative. Thus, the domain of f is the set of all x-values for which $8 - 2x \geq 0$. Since $8 - 2x \geq 0$ is equivalent to $x \leq 4$, we have Domain of $f = (-\infty, 4]$.

74. $f(-\infty, 5]$

75. $f(x) = \sqrt{x + 3}, g(x) = \sqrt{4 - x}$

The domain of f is the set of all x-values for which $x + 3 \geq 0$, or $[-3, \infty)$. The domain of g is the set of all x-values for which $4 - x \geq 0$, or $(-\infty, 4]$. The intersection of the domains is $[-3, 4]$.

76. $f\left[-\dfrac{1}{2}, \dfrac{3}{5}\right]$

77. $f(x) = \sqrt{4x - 3}$, $g(x) = \sqrt{2x + 9}$

The domain of f is the set of all x-values for which $4x - 3 \geq 0$, or $\left[\frac{3}{4}, \infty\right)$. The domain of g is the set of all x-values for which $2x + 9 \geq 0$, or $\left[-\frac{9}{2}, \infty\right)$. The intersection of the domains is $\left[\frac{3}{4}, \infty\right)$.

78. $(-\infty, 1]$

79. $f(x) = \dfrac{x}{x - 5}$, $g(x) = \sqrt{3x + 2}$

The domain of f is $\{x | x$ is a real number and $x \neq 5\}$. The domain of g is $\left[-\frac{2}{3}, \infty\right)$. The intersection of the domains is $\left[-\frac{2}{3}, 5\right) \cup (5, \infty)$.

80. $f\left(-\infty, -\frac{1}{2}\right) \cup \left(-\frac{1}{2}, \frac{4}{5}\right]$

81. *Writing Exercise*

82. *Writing Exercise*

83. Graph: $y = 5$

The graph of any constant function $y = c$ is a horizontal line that crosses the vertical axis at $(0, c)$. Thus, the graph of $y = 5$ is a horizontal line that crosses the vertical axis at $(0, 5)$.

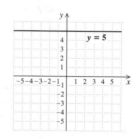

84.

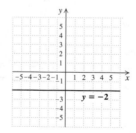

85. Graph $f(x) = |x|$

We make a table of values, plot points, and draw the graph.

x	$f(x)$
-5	5
-2	2
0	0
1	1
4	4

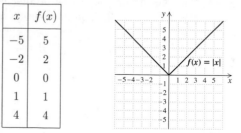

86.

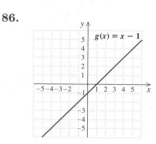

87. $2x - 5 = 3x + 1$

We will use the intersect method. Graph $y_1 = 2x - 5$ and $y_2 = 3x + 1$ and find the first coordinate of the point of intersection of the graphs.

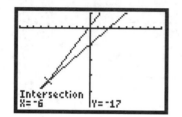

The solution is -6.

88. $1.5\overline{3}$

89. *Writing Exercise*

90. *Writing Exercise*

91. **Familiarize.** Let $c =$ the number of crossings per year. Then at the $3 per crossing rate, the total cost of c crossings is $3c$. Two six-month passes cost $2 \cdot \$15$, or $30. The additional $0.50 per crossing toll brings the total cost of c crossings to $\$30 + \$0.50c$. A one-year pass costs $150 regardless of the number of crossings.

Translate. We write an inequality that states that the cost of c crossings per year using the six-month passes is less than the cost using the $3 per crossing toll and is less than the cost using the one-year pass.

$$30 + 0.50c < 3c \ and \ 30 + 0.50c < 150$$

Carry out. We solve the inequality.

$$30 + 0.50c < 3c \quad and \quad 30 + 0.50c < 150$$
$$30 < 2.5c \ and \qquad 0.50c < 120$$
$$12 < c \qquad and \qquad\quad c < 240$$

This result can be written as $12 < c < 240$.

Check. When we substitute values of c less than 12, between 12 and 240, and greater than 240, we find that the result checks. Since we cannot check every possible value of c, we stop here.

State. For more than 12 crossings but less than 240 crossings per year the six-month passes are the most economical choice.

92. $0 \text{ ft} \leq d \leq 198 \text{ ft}$

93. Solve $32 < f(x) < 46$, or $32 < 2(x+10) < 46$.

$$32 < 2(x+10) < 46$$
$$32 < 2x + 20 < 46$$
$$12 < 2x < 26$$
$$6 < x < 13$$

For U.S. dress sizes between 6 and 13, dress sizes in Italy will be between 32 and 46.

94. From 2011 through 2036

95. a) Substitute $\frac{5}{9}(F-32)$ for C in the given inequality.

$$1063 \le \frac{5}{9}(F-32) < 2660$$
$$9 \cdot 1063 \le 9 \cdot \frac{5}{9}(F-32) < 9 \cdot 2660$$
$$9567 \le 5(F-32) < 23{,}940$$
$$9567 \le 5F - 160 < 23{,}940$$
$$9727 \le 5F < 24{,}100$$
$$1945.4 \le F < 4820$$

The inequality for Fahrenheit temperatures is $1945.4° \le F < 4820°$.

b) Substitute $\frac{5}{9}(F-32)$ for C in the given inequality.

$$960.8 \le \frac{5}{9}(F-32) < 2180$$
$$9(960.8) \le 9 \cdot \frac{5}{9}(F-32) < 9 \cdot 2180$$
$$8647.2 \le 5(F-32) < 19{,}620$$
$$8647.2 \le 5F - 160 < 19{,}620$$
$$8807.2 \le 5F < 19{,}780$$
$$1761.44 \le F < 3956$$

The inequality for Fahrenheit temperatures is $1761.44° \le F < 3956°$.

96. $1965 \le t \le 1981$

97. $4a - 2 \le a + 1 \le 3a + 4$

$$4a - 2 \le a + 1 \quad and \quad a + 1 \le 3a + 4$$
$$3a \le 3 \quad and \quad -3 \le 2a$$
$$a \le 1 \quad and \quad -\frac{3}{2} \le a$$

The solution set is $\left\{a \mid -\frac{3}{2} \le a \le 1\right\}$, or $\left[-\frac{3}{2}, 1\right]$.

98. $\left\{m \mid m < \frac{6}{5}\right\}$, or $\left(-\infty, \frac{6}{5}\right)$

99. $x - 10 < 5x + 6 \le x + 10$

$$-10 < 4x + 6 \le 10$$
$$-16 < 4x \le 4$$
$$-4 < x \le 1$$

The solution set is $\{x \mid -4 < x \le 1\}$, or $(-4, 1]$.

100. $\left\{x \mid -\frac{1}{8} < x < \frac{1}{2}\right\}$, or $\left(-\frac{1}{8}, \frac{1}{2}\right)$

101. If $-b < -a$, then $-1(-b) > -1(-a)$, or $b > a$, or $a < b$. The statement is true.

102. False

103. Let $a = 5$, $c = 12$, and $b = 2$. Then $a < c$ and $b < c$, but $a \not< b$. The given statement is false.

104. True

105. $f(x) = \dfrac{\sqrt{5 + 2x}}{x - 1}$

The expression $\sqrt{5 + 2x}$ is not a real number when $5 + 2x$ is negative. Then for $5 + 2x \ge 0$, or for $x \ge -\frac{5}{2}$, the numerator of $f(x)$ is a real number. In addition, $f(x)$ cannot be computed when the denominator is 0. Since $x - 1 = 0$ is equivalent to $x = 1$, we have Domain of $f = \left\{x \mid x \ge -\frac{5}{2} \; and \; x \ne 1\right\}$, or $\left[-\frac{5}{2}, 1\right) \cup (1, \infty)$.

106. $(-\infty, -7) \cup \left(-7, \frac{3}{4}\right]$

107. Left to the student

Exercise Set 4.7

1. The solutions of $|x + 2| = 3$ are the first coordinates of the points of intersection of $y_1 = \text{abs}(x + 2)$ and $y_2 = 3$. They are -5 and 1, so the solution set is $\{-5, 1\}$.

2. $[-5, 1]$

3. The graph of $y_1 = \text{abs}(x + 2)$ lies below the graph of $y_2 = 3$ for $\{x \mid -5 < x < 1\}$, or on $(-5, 1)$.

4. $(-\infty, -5) \cup (1, \infty)$

5. The graph of $y_1 = \text{abs}(x + 2)$ lies on or above the graph of $y_2 = 3$ for $\{x \mid x \le -5 \; or \; x \ge 1\}$, or on $(\infty, -5] \cup [1, \infty)$.

6. $\emptyset$

7. $|x| = 4$

$$x = -4 \; or \; x = 4 \quad \text{Using the absolute-value principle}$$

The solution set is $\{-4, 4\}$.

8. $\{-9, 9\}$

9. $|x| = -5$

The absolute value of a number is always nonnegative. Therefore, the solution set is $\emptyset$.

10. $\emptyset$

11. $|y| = 7.3$

$y = -7.3 \quad or \quad y = 7.3$ Using the absolute-value principle

The solution set is $\{-7.3, 7.3\}$.

12. $\{0\}$

13. $|m| = 0$

$m = 0$

$\{0\}$

The only number whose absolute value is 0 is 0. The solution set is $\{0\}$.

14. $\{-5.5, 5.5\}$

15. $|5x + 2| = 7$

$5x + 2 = -7 \quad or \quad 5x + 2 = 7$ Absolute-value principle

$5x = -9 \quad or \qquad 5x = 5$

$x = -\dfrac{9}{5} \quad or \qquad x = 1$

The solution set is $\left\{ -\dfrac{9}{5}, 1 \right\}$.

16. $\left\{ -\dfrac{1}{2}, \dfrac{7}{2} \right\}$

17. $|7x - 2| = -9$

Absolute value is always nonnegative, so the equation has no solution. The solution set is $\emptyset$.

18. $\emptyset$

19. $|x - 3| = 8$

$x - 3 = -8 \quad or \quad x - 3 = 8$ Absolute value principle

$x = -5 \quad or \qquad x = 11$

The solution set is $\{-5, 11\}$.

20. $\{-4, 8\}$

21. $|x - 6| = 1$

$x - 6 = -1 \quad or \quad x - 6 = 1$

$x = 5 \quad or \qquad x = 7$

The solution set is $\{5, 7\}$.

22. $\{2, 8\}$

23. $|x - 4| = 5$

$x - 4 = -5 \quad or \quad x - 4 = 5$

$x = -1 \quad or \qquad x = 9$

The solution set is $\{-1, 9\}$.

24. $\{-2, 16\}$

25. $|2y| - 5 = 13$

$|2y| = 18$ Adding 5

$2y = -18 \quad or \quad 2y = 18$

$y = -9 \quad or \quad y = 9$

The solution set is $\{-9, 9\}$.

26. $\{-8, 8\}$

27. $7|z| + 2 = 16$ Adding -2

$7|z| = 14$ Multiplying by $\dfrac{1}{7}$

$|z| = 2$

$z = -2 \quad or \quad z = 2$

The solution set is $\{-2, 2\}$.

28. $\left\{ -\dfrac{11}{5}, \dfrac{11}{5} \right\}$

29. $\left| \dfrac{4 - 5x}{6} \right| = 3$

$\dfrac{4 - 5x}{6} = -3 \quad or \quad \dfrac{4 - 5x}{6} = 3$

$4 - 5x = -18 \quad or \quad 4 - 5x = 18$

$-5x = -22 \quad or \qquad -5x = 14$

$x = \dfrac{22}{5} \quad or \qquad x = -\dfrac{14}{5}$

The solution set is $\left\{ -\dfrac{14}{5}, \dfrac{22}{5} \right\}$.

30. $\{-7, 8\}$

31. $|t - 7| + 1 = 4$ Adding -1

$|t - 7| = 3$

$t - 7 = -3 \quad or \quad t - 7 = 3$

$t = 4 \quad or \qquad t = 10$

The solution set is $\{4, 10\}$.

32. $\{-12, 2\}$

33. $3|2x - 5| - 7 = -1$

$3|2x - 5| = 6$

$|2x - 5| = 2$

$2x - 5 = -2 \quad or \quad 2x - 5 = 2$

$2x = 3 \quad or \qquad 2x = 7$

$x = \dfrac{3}{2} \quad or \qquad x = \dfrac{7}{2}$

The solution set is $\left\{ \dfrac{3}{2}, \dfrac{7}{2} \right\}$.

34. $\left\{ -\dfrac{1}{3}, 3 \right\}$

35. $|3x - 4| = 8$

$3x - 4 = -8 \quad or \quad 3x - 4 = 8$

$3x = -4 \quad or \qquad 3x = 12$

$x = -\dfrac{4}{3} \quad or \qquad x = 4$

The solution set is $\left\{ -\dfrac{4}{3}, 4 \right\}$.

36. $\left\{-\dfrac{3}{2}, \dfrac{17}{2}\right\}$

37. $|x| - 2 = 6.3$

$\qquad |x| = 8.3$

$\quad x = -8.3 \;\; or \;\; x = 8.3$

The solution set is $\{-8.3, 8.3\}$.

38. $\{-11, 11\}$

39. $\left|\dfrac{3x-2}{5}\right| = 2$

$\dfrac{3x-2}{5} = -2 \quad or \quad \dfrac{3x-2}{5} = 2$

$3x - 2 = -10 \;\; or \;\; 3x - 2 = 10$

$\quad 3x = -8 \;\; or \;\;\quad 3x = 12$

$\quad x = -\dfrac{8}{3} \;\; or \;\;\quad x = 4$

The solution set is $\left\{-\dfrac{8}{3}, 4\right\}$.

40. $\{-1, 2\}$

41. $|x + 4| = |2x - 7|$

$x + 4 = 2x - 7 \quad or \quad x + 4 = -(2x - 7)$

$\quad 4 = x - 7 \quad or \quad x + 4 = -2x + 7$

$\quad 11 = x \quad\quad or \;\; 3x + 4 = 7$

$\qquad\qquad\qquad\qquad 3x = 3$

$\qquad\qquad\qquad\qquad\; x = 1$

The solution set is $\{1, 11\}$.

42. $\left\{-\dfrac{11}{2}, \dfrac{1}{4}\right\}$

43. $|x - 9| = |x + 6|$

$x - 9 = x + 6 \quad or \quad x - 9 = -(x + 6)$

$\quad -9 = 6 \quad\quad or \quad x - 9 = -x - 6$

False — $\qquad\qquad\qquad 2x - 9 = -6$

yields no $\qquad\qquad\qquad 2x = 3$

solution $\qquad\qquad\qquad\quad x = \dfrac{3}{2}$

The solution set is $\left\{\dfrac{3}{2}\right\}$.

44. $\left\{-\dfrac{1}{2}\right\}$

45. $|5t + 7| = |4t + 3|$

$5t + 7 = 4t + 3 \quad or \quad 5t + 7 = -(4t + 3)$

$\quad t + 7 = 3 \quad\quad or \quad 5t + 7 = -4t - 3$

$\quad t = -4 \quad\quad or \quad 9t + 7 = -3$

$\qquad\qquad\qquad\qquad 9t = -10$

$\qquad\qquad\qquad\qquad\; t = -\dfrac{10}{9}$

The solution set is $\left\{-4, -\dfrac{10}{9}\right\}$.

46. $\left\{-\dfrac{3}{5}, 5\right\}$

47. $|n - 3| = |3 - n|$

$n - 3 = 3 - n \quad or \quad n - 3 = -(3 - n)$

$2n - 3 = 3 \qquad or \quad n - 3 = -3 + n$

$\quad 2n = 6 \qquad or \qquad -3 = -3$

$\quad n = 3 \qquad$ True for all real values of n

The solution set is the set of all real numbers.

48. All real numbers

49. $|7 - a| = |a + 5|$

$7 - a = a + 5 \quad or \quad 7 - a = -(a + 5)$

$\quad 7 = 2a + 5 \;\; or \quad 7 - a = -a - 5$

$\quad 2 = 2a \qquad or \qquad 7 = -5$

$\quad 1 = a \qquad\qquad\quad$ False

The solution set is $\{1\}$.

50. $\left\{-\dfrac{1}{2}\right\}$

51. $\left|\dfrac{1}{2}x - 5\right| = \left|\dfrac{1}{4}x + 3\right|$

$\dfrac{1}{2}x - 5 = \dfrac{1}{4}x + 3 \;\; or \;\; \dfrac{1}{2}x - 5 = -\left(\dfrac{1}{4}x + 3\right)$

$\dfrac{1}{4}x - 5 = 3 \qquad or \quad \dfrac{1}{2}x - 5 = -\dfrac{1}{4}x - 3$

$\quad \dfrac{1}{4}x = 8 \qquad or \quad \dfrac{3}{4}x - 5 = -3$

$\quad x = 32 \qquad\quad or \qquad \dfrac{3}{4}x - 2$

$\qquad\qquad\qquad\qquad\qquad x = \dfrac{8}{3}$

The solution set is $\left\{32, \dfrac{8}{3}\right\}$.

52. $\left\{-\dfrac{48}{37}, -\dfrac{144}{5}\right\}$

53. $|a| \le 7$

$-7 \le a \le 7 \qquad$ Part (b)

The solution set is $\{a| -7 \le a \le 7\}$, or $[-7, 7]$.

54. $\{x| -2 < x < 2\}$, or $(-2, 2)$

55. $|x| > 8$

$x < -8 \;\; or \;\; 8 < x \qquad$ Part (c)

The solution set is $\{x| x < -8 \;\; or \;\; x > 8\}$, or $(-\infty, -8) \cup (8, \infty)$.

56. $\{a| a \le -3 \;\; or \;\; a \ge 3\}$, or $(-\infty, -3] \cup [3, \infty)$

57. $|t| > 0$

$t < 0 \ or \ 0 < t$ Part (c)

The solution set is $\{t|t < 0 \ or \ t > 0\}$, or $\{t|t \neq 0\}$, or $(-\infty, 0) \cup (0, \infty)$.

58. $\{t|t \leq -1.7 \ or \ t \geq 1.7\}$, or $(-\infty, -1.7] \cup [1.7, \infty)$

59. $|x - 3| < 5$

$-5 < x - 3 < 5$ Part (b)

$-2 < x < 8$

The solution set is $\{x| -2 < x < 8\}$, or $(-2, 8)$.

60. $\{x| -2 < x < 4\}$, or $(-2, 4)$

61. $|x + 2| \leq 6$

$-6 \leq x + 2 \leq 6$ Part (b)

$-8 \leq x \leq 4$ Adding -2

The solution set is $\{x| -8 \leq x \leq 4\}$, or $[-8, 4]$.

62. $\{x| -5 \leq x \leq -3\}$, or $[-5, -3]$

63. $|x - 3| + 2 > 7$

$|x - 3| > 5$ Adding -2

$x - 3 < -5 \ or \ 5 < x - 3$ Part (c)

$x < -2 \ or \ 8 < x$

The solution set is $\{x|x < -2 \ or \ x > 8\}$, or $(-\infty, -2) \cup (8, \infty)$.

64. All real numbers, or $(-\infty, \infty)$

65. $|2y - 7| > -5$

Since absolute value is never negative, any value of $2y - 7$, and hence any value of y, will satisfy the inequality. The solution set is the set of all real numbers, or $(-\infty, \infty)$.

66. $\left\{y\middle|y < -\dfrac{4}{3} \ or \ y > 4\right\}$, or $\left(-\infty, -\dfrac{4}{3}\right) \cup (4, \infty)$

67. $|3a - 4| + 2 \geq 8$

$|3a - 4| \geq 6$ Adding -2

$3a - 4 \leq -6 \ or \ 6 \leq 3a - 4$ Part (c)

$3a \leq -2 \ or \ 10 \leq 3a$

$a \leq -\dfrac{2}{3} \ or \ \dfrac{10}{3} \leq a$

The solution set is $\left\{a\middle|a \leq -\dfrac{2}{3} \ or \ a \geq \dfrac{10}{3}\right\}$, or $\left(-\infty, -\dfrac{2}{3}\right] \cup \left[\dfrac{10}{3}, \infty\right)$.

68. $\left\{a\middle|a \leq -\dfrac{3}{2} \ or \ a \geq \dfrac{13}{2}\right\}$, or $\left(-\infty, -\dfrac{3}{2}\right] \cup \left[\dfrac{13}{2}, \infty\right)$

69. $|y - 3| < 12$

$-12 < y - 3 < 12$ Part (b)

$-9 < y < 15$ Adding 3

The solution set is $\{y| -9 < y < 15\}$, or $(-9, 15)$.

70. $\{p| -1 < p < 5\}$, or $(-1, 5)$

71. $9 - |x + 4| \leq 5$

$-|x + 4| \leq -4$

$|x + 4| \geq 4$ Multiplying by -1

$x + 4 \leq -4 \ or \ 4 \leq x + 4$ Part (c)

$x \leq -8 \ or \ 0 \leq x$

The solution set is $\{x|x \leq -8 \ or \ x \geq 0\}$, or $(-\infty, -8] \cup [0, \infty)$.

72. $\{x|x \leq 2 \ or \ x \geq 8\}$, or $(-\infty, 2] \cup [8, \infty)$

73. $|4 - 3y| > 8$

$4 - 3y < -8 \ or \ 8 < 4 - 3y$ Part (c)

$-3y < -12 \ or \ 4 < -3y$ Adding -4

$y > 4 \ \ or \ -\dfrac{4}{3} > y$ Multiplying by $-\dfrac{1}{3}$

The solution set is $\left\{y\middle|y < -\dfrac{4}{3} \ or \ y > 4\right\}$, or $\left(-\infty, -\dfrac{4}{3}\right) \cup (4, \infty)$.

74. $\emptyset$

75. $|3 - 4x| < -5$

Absolute value is always nonnegative, so the inequality has no solution. The solution set is $\emptyset$.

76. $\left\{a \middle| -\dfrac{7}{2} \le a \le 6\right\}$, or $\left[-\dfrac{7}{2}, 6\right]$

77. $\left|\dfrac{2 - 5x}{4}\right| \ge \dfrac{2}{3}$

$\dfrac{2 - 5x}{4} \le -\dfrac{2}{3}$ $\quad or \quad$ $\dfrac{2}{3} \le \dfrac{2 - 5x}{4}$ $\quad$ Part (c)

$2 - 5x \le -\dfrac{8}{3}$ $\quad or \quad$ $\dfrac{8}{3} \le 2 - 5x$ $\quad$ Multiplying by 4

$-5x \le -\dfrac{14}{3}$ $\quad or \quad$ $\dfrac{2}{3} \le -5x$ $\quad$ Adding -2

$x \ge \dfrac{14}{15}$ $\quad or \quad$ $-\dfrac{2}{15} \ge x$ $\quad$ Multiplying by $-\dfrac{1}{5}$

The solution set is $\left\{x \middle| x \le -\dfrac{2}{15} \ or \ x \ge \dfrac{14}{15}\right\}$, or

$\left(-\infty, -\dfrac{2}{15}\right] \cup \left[\dfrac{14}{15}, \infty\right)$.

78. $\left\{x \middle| x < -\dfrac{43}{24} \ or \ x > \dfrac{9}{8}\right\}$, or $\left(-\infty, -\dfrac{43}{24}\right) \cup \left(\dfrac{9}{8}, \infty\right)$

79. $|m + 5| + 9 \le 16$

$|m + 5| \le 7$ $\quad$ Adding -9

$-7 \le m + 5 \le 7$

$-12 \le m \le 2$

The solution set is $\{m | -12 \le m \le 2\}$, or $[-12, 2]$.

80. $\{t | t \le 6 \ or \ t \ge 8\}$, or $(-\infty, 6] \cup [8, \infty)$

81. $25 - 2|a + 3| > 19$

$-2|a + 3| > -6$

$|a + 3| < 3$ $\quad$ Multiplying by $-\dfrac{1}{2}$

$-3 < a + 3 < 3$ $\quad$ Part (b)

$-6 < a < 0$

The solution set is $\{a | -6 < a < 0\}$, or $(-6, 0)$.

82. $\left\{a \middle| -\dfrac{13}{2} < a < \dfrac{5}{2}\right\}$, or $\left(-\dfrac{13}{2}, \dfrac{5}{2}\right)$

83. $|2x - 3| \le 4$

$-4 \le 2x - 3 \le 4$ $\quad$ Part (b)

$-1 \le 2x \le 7$ $\quad$ Adding 3

$-\dfrac{1}{2} \le x \le \dfrac{7}{2}$ $\quad$ Multiplying by $\dfrac{1}{2}$

The solution set is $\left\{x \middle| -\dfrac{1}{2} \le x \le \dfrac{7}{2}\right\}$, or $\left[-\dfrac{1}{2}, \dfrac{7}{2}\right]$.

84. $\left\{x \middle| -1 \le x \le \dfrac{1}{5}\right\}$, or $\left[-1, \dfrac{1}{5}\right]$

85. $2 + |3x - 4| \ge 13$

$|3x - 4| \ge 11$

$3x - 4 \le -11$ $\quad or \quad$ $11 \le 3x - 4$ $\quad$ Part (c)

$3x \le -7$ $\quad or \quad$ $15 \le 3x$

$x \le -\dfrac{7}{3}$ $\quad or \quad$ $5 \le x$

The solution set is $\left\{x \middle| x \le -\dfrac{7}{3} \ or \ x \ge 5\right\}$, or

$\left(-\infty, -\dfrac{7}{3}\right] \cup [5, \infty)$.

86. $\left\{x \middle| x \le -\dfrac{23}{9} \ or \ x \ge 3\right\}$, or $\left(-\infty, -\dfrac{23}{9}\right] \cup [3, \infty)$

87. $7 + |2x - 1| < 16$

$|2x - 1| < 9$

$-9 < 2x - 1 < 9$ $\quad$ Part (b)

$-8 < 2x < 10$

$-4 < x < 5$

The solution set is $\{x | -4 < x < 5\}$, or $(-4, 5)$.

88. $\left\{x \middle| -\dfrac{16}{3} < x < 4\right\}$, or $\left(-\dfrac{16}{3}, 4\right)$

89. *Writing Exercise*

90. *Writing Exercise*

91. $3x - 5 = x + 7$

$2x - 5 = 7$

$2x = 12$

$x = 6$

The solution is 6.

92. $\{x \mid x > 6\}$

93. $3x - 5 = y + 7$

$3x - 12 = y$

94. 7

95. $4(t + 3) - 2t = 6t - 7(1 - t)$

$4t + 12 - 2t = 6t - 7 + 7t$

$2t + 12 = 13t - 7$

$-11t + 12 = -7$

$-11t = -19$

$t = \dfrac{19}{11}$

The solution is $\dfrac{19}{11}$.

96. $\left\{ t \mid t \geq \dfrac{19}{11} \right\}$

97. *Writing Exercise*

98. *Writing Exercise*

99. From the definition of absolute value, $|3t - 5| = 3t - 5$ only when $3t - 5 \geq 0$. Solve $3t - 5 \geq 0$.

$3t - 5 \geq 0$

$3t \geq 5$

$t \geq \dfrac{5}{3}$

The solution set is $\left\{ t \mid t \geq \dfrac{5}{3} \right\}$, or $\left[\dfrac{5}{3}, \infty \right)$.

100. All real numbers, or $(-\infty, \infty)$

101. $2 \leq |x - 1| \leq 5$

$2 \leq |x - 1|$ *and* $|x - 1| \leq 5$.

For $2 \leq |x - 1|$:

$x - 1 \leq -2$ *or* $2 \leq x - 1$

$x \leq -1$ *or* $3 \leq x$

The solution set of $2 \leq |x - 1|$ is $\{x \mid x \leq -1 \ or \ x \geq 3\}$.

For $|x - 1| \leq 5$:

$-5 \leq x - 1 \leq 5$

$-4 \leq x \leq 6$

The solution set of $|x - 1| \leq 5$ is $\{x \mid -4 \leq x \leq 6\}$.

The solution set of $2 \leq |x - 1| \leq 5$ is

$\{x \mid x \leq -1 \ or \ x \geq 3\} \cap \{x \mid -4 \leq x \leq 6\}$

$= \{x \mid -4 \leq x \leq -1 \ or \ 3 \leq x \leq 6\}$, *or*

$[-4, -1] \cup [3, 6]$.

102. $\left\{ -\dfrac{1}{7}, \dfrac{7}{3} \right\}$

103. $t - 2 \leq |t - 3|$

$t - 3 \leq -(t - 2)$ *or* $t - 2 \leq t - 3$

$t - 3 \leq -t + 2$ *or* $-2 \leq -3$

$2t - 3 \leq 2$ False

$2t \leq 5$

$t \leq \dfrac{5}{2}$

The solution set is $\left\{ t \mid t \leq \dfrac{5}{2} \right\}$, or $\left(-\infty, \dfrac{5}{2} \right]$.

104. $|x| < 3$

105. Using part (b), we find that $-5 \leq y \leq 5$ is equivalent to $|y| \leq 5$.

106. $|x| \geq 6$

107. $x < -4 \ or \ 4 < x$

$|x| > 4$ Using part (c)

108. $|x + 3| > 5$

109. $-5 < x < 1$

$-3 < x + 2 < 3$ Adding 2

$|x + 2| < 3$ Using part (b)

110. $|x - 7| < 2$, or $|7 - x| < 2$

111. The distance from x to 5 is $|x - 5|$ or $|5 - x|$, so we have $|x - 5| < 1$, or $|5 - x| < 1$.

112. $|x - 3| \leq 4$

113. The length of the segment from -4 to 8 is $|-4 - 8| = |-12| = 12$ units. The midpoint of the segment is $\dfrac{-4 + 8}{2} = \dfrac{4}{2} = 2$. Thus, the interval extends $12/2$, or 6, units on each side of 2. An inequality for which the open interval is the solution set is $|x - 2| < 6$.

114. $|x + 4| < 3$

115. The length of the segment from 2 to 12 is $|2 - 12| = |-10| = 10$ units. The midpoint of the segment is $\dfrac{2 + 12}{2} = \dfrac{14}{2} = 7$. Thus, the interval extends $10/2$, or 5, units on each side of 7. An inequality for which the closed interval is the solution set is $|x - 7| \leq 5$.

116. $\left\{ d \mid 5\dfrac{1}{2} \text{ ft} \leq d \leq 6\dfrac{1}{2} \text{ ft} \right\}$, or $\left[5\dfrac{1}{2} \text{ ft}, 6\dfrac{1}{2} \text{ ft} \right]$

Chapter 5

Polynomials

1. $r^4 \cdot r^6 = r^{4+6} = r^{10}$

2. 8^7

3. $9^5 \cdot 9^3 = 9^{5+3} = 9^8$

4. n^{23}

5. $a^6 \cdot a = a^6 \cdot a^1 = a^{6+1} = a^7$

6. y^{16}

7. $5^7 \cdot 5^8 = 5^{7+8} = 5^{15}$

8. t^{16}

9. $(3y)^4(3y)^8 = (3y)^{4+8} = (3y)^{12}$

10. $(2t)^{25}$

11. $(5t)(5t)^6 = (5t)^1(5t)^6 = (5t)^{1+6} = (5t)^7$

12. $8x$

13. $(a^2b^7)(a^3b^2) = a^2b^7a^3b^2$ Using an associative law
$= a^2a^3b^7b^2$ Using a commutative law
$= a^5b^9$ Adding exponents

14. $(m-3)^9$

15. $(x+1)^5(x+1)^7 = (x+1)^{5+7} = (x+1)^{12}$

16. $a^{12}b^4$

17. $r^3 \cdot r^7 \cdot r^0 = r^{3+7+0} = r^{10}$

18. s^{11}

19. $(xy^4)(xy)^3 = (xy^4)(x^3y^3)$
$= x \cdot x^3 \cdot y^4 \cdot y^3$
$= x^{1+3}y^{4+3}$
$= x^4y^7$

20. a^7b^5

21. $\dfrac{7^5}{7^2} = 7^{5-2} = 7^3$ Subtracting exponents

22. 4^4

23. $\dfrac{x^{15}}{x^3} = x^{15-3} = x^{12}$ Subtracting exponents

24. a^8

25. $\dfrac{t^5}{t} = \dfrac{t^5}{t^1} = t^{5-1} = t^4$

26. x^6

27. $\dfrac{(5a)^7}{(5a)^6} = (5a)^{7-6} = (5a)^1 = 5a$

28. $3m$

29. $\dfrac{(x+y)^8}{(x+y)^8}$

Observe that we have an expression divided by itself. Thus, the result is 1.

We could also do this exercise as follows:

$\dfrac{(x+y)^8}{(x+y)^8} = (x+y)^{8-8} = (x+y)^0 = 1$

30. $a-b$

31. $\dfrac{18m^5}{6m^2} = \dfrac{18}{6}m^{5-2} = 3m^3$

32. $5n^4$

33. $\dfrac{a^9b^7}{a^2b} = \dfrac{a^9}{a^2} \cdot \dfrac{b^7}{b^1} = a^{9-2}b^{7-1} = a^7b^6$

34. r^8s^6

35. $\dfrac{m^9n^8}{m^0n^4} = \dfrac{m^9}{m^0} \cdot \dfrac{n^8}{n^4} = m^{9-0}n^{8-4} = m^9n^4$

36. a^8b^{12}

37. When $x = 13$, $x^0 = 13^0 = 1$. (Any nonzero number raised to the 0 power is 1.)

38. 1

39. When $x = -4$, $5x^0 = 5(-4)^0 = 5 \cdot 1 = 5$.

40. 7

41. $8^0 + 5^0 = 1 + 1 = 2$

42. 1

43. $(-3)^1 - (-3)^0 = -3 - 1 = -4$

44. 5

45. $(x^4)^7 = x^{4 \cdot 7} = x^{28}$ Multiplying exponents

46. a^{24}

47. $(5^8)^2 = 5^{8 \cdot 2} = 5^{16}$ Multiplying exponents

48. 2^{15}, or 32,768

49. $(m^7)^5 = m^{7 \cdot 5} = m^{35}$

50. n^{18}

51. $(t^{20})^4 = t^{20 \cdot 4} = t^{80}$

52. t^{27}

53. $(7x)^2 = 7^2 \cdot x^2 = 49x^2$

54. $25a^2$

55. $(-2a)^3 = (-2)^3 a^3 = -8a^3$

56. $-27x^3$

57. $(4m^3)^2 = 4^2(m^3)^2 = 16m^6$

58. $25n^8$

59. $(a^2b)^7 = (a^2)^7(b^7) = a^{14}b^7$

60. $x^9 y^{36}$

61. $(x^3 y)^2 (x^2 y^5) = (x^3)^2 y^2 x^2 y^5 = x^6 y^2 x^2 y^5 = x^8 y^7$

62. $a^{14}b^{11}$

63. $(2x^5)^3 (3x^4) = 2^3 (x^5)^3 (3x^4) = 8x^{15} \cdot 3x^4 = 24x^{19}$

64. $50x^{13}$

65. $\left(\dfrac{a}{4}\right)^3 = \dfrac{a^3}{4^3} = \dfrac{a^3}{64}$ Raising the numerator and the denominator to the third power

66. $\dfrac{81}{x^4}$

67. $\left(\dfrac{7}{5a}\right)^2 = \dfrac{7^2}{(5a)^2} = \dfrac{49}{5^2 a^2} = \dfrac{49}{25a^2}$

68. $\dfrac{125x^3}{8}$

69. $\left(\dfrac{a^4}{b^3}\right)^5 = \dfrac{(a^4)^5}{(b^3)^5} = \dfrac{a^{20}}{b^{15}}$

70. $\dfrac{x^{35}}{y^{14}}$

71. $\left(\dfrac{y^3}{2}\right)^2 = \dfrac{(y^3)^2}{2^2} = \dfrac{y^6}{4}$

72. $\dfrac{a^{15}}{8}$

73. $\left(\dfrac{x^2 y}{z^3}\right)^4 = \dfrac{(x^2 y)^4}{(z^3)^4} = \dfrac{(x^2)^4(y^4)}{z^{12}} = \dfrac{x^8 y^4}{z^{12}}$

74. $\dfrac{x^{15}}{y^{10} z^5}$

75. $\left(\dfrac{a^3}{-2b^5}\right)^4 = \dfrac{(a^3)^4}{(-2b^5)^4} = \dfrac{a^{12}}{(-2)^4(b^5)^4} = \dfrac{a^{12}}{16b^{20}}$

76. $\dfrac{x^{20}}{81y^{12}}$

77. $\left(\dfrac{5x^7 y}{2z^4}\right)^3 = \dfrac{(5x^7 y)^3}{(2z^4)^3} = \dfrac{5^3 (x^7)^3 y^3}{2^3 (z^4)^3} = \dfrac{125x^{21} y^3}{8z^{12}}$

78. $\dfrac{64a^6 b^3}{27c^{21}}$

79. $\left(\dfrac{4x^3 y^5}{3z^7}\right)^0$

Observe that for $x \neq 0$, $y \neq 0$, and $z \neq 0$, we have a nonzero number raised to the 0 power. Thus, the result is 1.

80. 1

81. *Writing Exercise*

82. *Writing Exercise*

83. $3s - 3r + 3t = 3 \cdot s - 3 \cdot r + 3 \cdot t = 3(s - r + t)$

84. $-7(x - y + z)$

85. $9x + 2y - x - 2y = 9x - x + 2y - 2y =$
$(9 - 1)x + (2 - 2)y = 8x + 0y = 8x$

86. $-3a - 6b$

87. Graph $y = x - 5$

We can see from the equation that the y-intercept is $(0, -5)$. To find the x-intercept we replace y with 0 and solve for x.

$$0 = x - 5$$
$$5 = x$$

The x-intercept is $(5, 0)$.

To find a third point on the graph, we can replace x with 4 and solve for y.

$$y = 4 - 5$$
$$y = -1$$

The point $(4, -1)$ appears to line up with the other two points. We draw the graph.

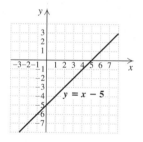

88.

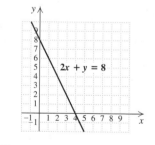

89. *Writing Exercise*

90. *Writing Exercise*

91. *Writing Exercise*

92. *Writing Exercise*

93. Choose any number except 0.

For example, let $a = 1$. Then $(a+5)^2 = (1+5)^2 = 6^2 = 36$, but $a^2 + 5^2 = 1^2 + 5^2 = 1 + 25 = 26$.

94. Choose any number except 0. For example, let $x = 1$.

$$3x^2 = 3 \cdot 1^2 = 3 \cdot 1 = 3, \text{ but}$$
$$(3x)^2 = (3 \cdot 1)^2 = 3^2 = 9.$$

95. Choose any number except $\frac{7}{6}$. For example let $a = 0$.

Then $\frac{0+7}{7} = \frac{7}{7} = 1$, but $a = 0$.

96. Choose any number except 0 or 1. For example, let $t = -1$.

Then $\frac{t^6}{t^2} = \frac{(-1)^6}{(-1)^2} = \frac{1}{1} = 1$, but $t^3 = (-1)^3 = -1$.

97. $a^{10k} \div a^{2k} = a^{10k-2k} = a^{8k}$

98. y^{6x}

99.

$$\frac{\left(\frac{1}{2}\right)^3 \left(\frac{2}{3}\right)^4}{\left(\frac{5}{6}\right)^3} = \frac{\frac{1}{8} \cdot \frac{16}{81}}{\frac{125}{216}} = \frac{1}{8} \cdot \frac{16}{81} \cdot \frac{216}{125} =$$

$$\frac{1 \cdot 2 \cdot \cancel{8} \cdot \cancel{27} \cdot 8}{\cancel{8} \cdot 3 \cdot \cancel{27} \cdot 125} = \frac{16}{375}$$

100. x^t

101.

$$\frac{t^{26}}{t^x} = t^x$$
$$t^{26-x} = t^x$$
$$26 - x = x \quad \text{Equating exponents}$$
$$26 = 2x$$
$$13 = x$$

The solution is 13.

102. $>$

103. Since the bases are the same, the expression with the larger exponent is larger. Thus, $4^2 < 4^3$.

104. $<$

105. $4^3 = 64$, $3^4 = 81$, so $4^3 < 3^4$.

106. $>$

107.

$$25^8 = (5^2)^8 = 5^{16}$$
$$125^5 = (5^3)^5 = 5^{15}$$
$$5^{16} > 5^{15}, \text{ or } 25^8 > 125^5.$$

108. 16,000; 16,384; 384

109. $2^{22} = 2^{10} \cdot 2^{10} \cdot 2^2 \approx 10^3 \cdot 10^3 \cdot 4 \approx 1000 \cdot 1000 \cdot 4 \approx 4,000,000$

Using a calculator, we find that $2^{22} = 4,194,304$. The difference between the exact value and the approximation is $4,194,304 - 4,000,000$, or 194,304.

110. 64,000,000; 67,108,864; 3,108,864

111. $2^{31} = 2^{10} \cdot 2^{10} \cdot 2^{10} \cdot 2 \approx 10^3 \cdot 10^3 \cdot 10^3 \cdot 2 \approx$
$1000 \cdot 1000 \cdot 1000 \cdot 2 = 2,000,000,000$

Using a calculator, we find that $2^{31} = 2,147,483,648$. The difference between the exact value and the approximation is $2,147,483,648 - 2,000,000,000 = 147,483,648$.

112. 57,344 bytes

113. 64 K $= 64 \times 1 \times 2^{10}$ bytes $= 65,536$ bytes

Exercise Set 5.2

1. $3x - 7$ can be written as a sum of monomials, so it is a polynomial.

2. Yes

3. $\frac{x^2 + x + 1}{x^3 - 7}$ cannot be written as a sum of monomials, so it is not a polynomial.

4. Yes

5. $\frac{1}{4}x^{10} - 8.6$ can be written as a sum of monomials, so it is a polynomial.

6. No

7. $7x^4 + x^3 - 5x + 8 = 7x^4 + x^3 + (-5x) + 8$

The terms are $7x^4$, x^3, $-5x$, and 8.

8. $5a^3$, $4a^2$, $-a$, -7

9. $-t^4 + 7t^3 - 3t^2 + 6 = -t^4 + 7t^3 + (-3t^2) + 6$

The terms are $-t^4$, $7t^3$, $-3t^2$, and 6.

10. n^5, $-4n^3$, $2n$, -8

11. $4x^5 + 7x$

Term	Coefficient	Degree
$4x^5$	4	5
$7x$	7	1

12. Coefficients: 9, -4; degrees: 3, 2

13. $9t^2 - 3t + 4$

Term	Coefficient	Degree
$9t^2$	9	2
$-3t$	-3	1
4	4	0

14. Coefficients: 7, 5, -3; degrees: 4, 1, 0

15. $x^4 - x^3 + 4x - 3$

Term	Coefficient	Degree
x^4	1	4
$-x^3$	-1	3
$4x$	4	1
-3	-3	0

16. Coefficients: 3, -1, 1, -9; degrees: 4, 3, 1, 0

17. $2a^3 + 7a^5 + a^2$

a)
Term	$2a^3$	$7a^5$	a^2
Degree	3	5	2

b) The term of highest degree is $7a^5$. This is the leading term. Then the leading coefficient is 7.

c) Since the term of highest degree is $7a^5$, the degree of the polynomial is 5.

18. a) 1, 2, 6

b) $3x^6$; 3

c) 6

19. $9x^4 + x^2 + x^7 + 4$

a)
Term	$9x^4$	x^2	x^7	4
Degree	4	2	7	0

b) The term of highest degree is x^7. This is the leading term. Then the leading coefficient is 1.

c) Since the term of highest degree is x^7, the degree of the polynomial is 7.

20. a) 0, 2, 1, 5

b) $-x^5$; -1

c) 5

21. $9a - a^4 + 3 + 2a^3$

a)
Term	$9a$	$-a^4$	3	$2a^3$
Degree	1	4	0	3

b) The term of highest degree is $-a^4$. This is the leading term. Then the leading coefficient is -1.

c) Since the term of highest degree is $-a^4$, the degree of the polynomial is 4.

22. a) 1, 5, 2, 6

b) x^6; 1

c) 6

23. $7x^2 + 8x^5 - 4x^3 + 6 - \frac{1}{2}x^4$

Term	Coefficient	Degree of Term	Degree of Polynomial
$8x^5$	8	5	
$-\frac{1}{2}x^4$	$-\frac{1}{2}$	4	
$-4x^3$	-4	3	5
$7x^2$	7	2	
6	6	0	

24.

Term	Coefficient	Degree of Term	Degree of Polynomial
$-3x^4$	-3	4	
$6x^3$	6	3	
$-2x^2$	-2	2	4
$8x$	8	1	
7	7	0	

25. Three monomials are added, so $x^2 - 23x + 17$ is a trinomial.

26. Monomial

27. The polynomial $x^3 - 7x^2 + 2x - 4$ is none of these because it is composed of four monomials.

28. Binomial

29. Two monomials are added, so $8t^2 + 5t$ is a binomial.

30. Trinomial

31. The polynomial 17 is a monomial because it is the product of a constant and a variable raised to a whole number power. (In this case the variable is raised to the power 0.)

32. None of these

33. $7x^2 + 3x + 4x^2 = (7+4)x^2 + 3x = 11x^2 + 3x$

34. $7a^2 + 8a$

35. $3a^4 - 2a + 2a + a^4 = (3+1)a^4 + (-2+2)a = 4a^4 + 0a = 4a^4$

36. $7b^5$

37. $2x^2 - 6x + 3x + 4x^2 = (2+4)x^2 + (-6+3)x = 6x^2 - 3x$

38. $4x^4 - 9x$

39. $9x^3 + 2x - 4x^3 + 5 - 3x = (9-4)x^3 + (2-3)x + 5 = 5x^3 - x + 5$

40. x^4

41. $10x^2 + 2x^3 - 3x^3 - 4x^2 - 6x^2 - x^4 = -x^4 + (2-3)x^3 + (10-4-6)x^2 = -x^4 - x^3$

42. $-x^6 + 10x^5$

43. $\frac{1}{5}x^4 + 7 - 2x^2 + 3 - \frac{2}{15}x^4 + 2x^2 =$

$\left(\frac{1}{5} - \frac{2}{15}\right)x^4 + (-2+2)x^2 + (7+3) =$

$\left(\frac{3}{15} - \frac{2}{15}\right)x^4 + 0x^2 + 10 = \frac{1}{15}x^4 + 10$

44. $-\frac{1}{6}x^3 + 4x^2 - 3$

45. $5.9x^2 - 2.1x + 6 + 3.4x - 2.5x^2 - 0.5 =$

$(5.9 - 2.5)x^2 + (-2.1 + 3.4)x + (6 - 0.5) =$

$3.4x^2 + 1.3x + 5.5$

46. $9.3x^3 - 8.4x - 1.4$

47. $6t - 9t^3 + 8t^4 + 4t + 2t^4 + 7t - 3t^3 =$
$(8+2)t^4 + (-9-3)t^3 + (6+4+7)t =$
$10t^4 - 12t^3 + 17t$

48. $6b^3 + 3b^2 + b$

49. $-7x + 5 = -7 \cdot 3 + 5$
$\qquad = -21 + 5$
$\qquad = -16$

50. -6

51. $2x^2 - 3x + 7 = 2 \cdot 3^2 - 3 \cdot 3 + 7$
$\qquad\qquad = 2 \cdot 9 - 3 \cdot 3 + 7$
$\qquad\qquad = 18 - 9 + 7$
$\qquad\qquad = 16$

52. 27

53. $5x + 7 = 5(-2) + 7$
$\qquad = -10 + 7$
$\qquad = -3$

54. 13

55. $x^2 - 3x + 1 = (-2)^2 - 3(-2) + 1$
$\qquad\qquad = 4 - 3(-2) + 1$
$\qquad\qquad = 4 + 6 + 1$
$\qquad\qquad = 11$

56. -15

57. $P(x) = 3x^2 - 2x + 7$
$P(4) = 3 \cdot 4^2 - 2 \cdot 4 + 7$
$\qquad = 48 - 8 + 7$
$\qquad = 47$
$P(0) = 3 \cdot 0^2 - 2 \cdot 0 + 7$
$\qquad = 0 - 0 + 7$
$\qquad = 7$

58. $-51; 5$

59. $P(y) = 8y^3 - 12y - 5$
$P(-2) = 8(-2)^3 - 12(-2) - 5$
$\qquad = -64 + 24 - 5$
$\qquad = -45$

$P\left(\dfrac{1}{3}\right) = 8\left(\dfrac{1}{3}\right)^3 - 12 \cdot \dfrac{1}{3} - 5$
$\qquad = 8 \cdot \dfrac{1}{27} - 4 - 5$
$\qquad = \dfrac{8}{27} - 9$
$\qquad = \dfrac{8}{27} - \dfrac{243}{27}$
$\qquad = -\dfrac{235}{27}, \text{ or } -8\dfrac{19}{27}$

60. $282; -9$

61. $f(x) = -5x^3 + 3x^2 - 4x - 3$
$f(-1) = -5(-1)^3 + 3(-1)^2 - 4(-1) - 3$
$\qquad = 5 + 3 + 4 - 3$
$\qquad = 9$

62. -6

63. $p(n) = n^3 - 3n^2 + 2n$
$p(20) = 20^3 - 3 \cdot 20^2 + 2 \cdot 20$
$\qquad = 8000 - 1200 + 40$
$\qquad = 6840$

A president, vice president, and treasurer can be elected in 6840 ways.

64. 1320

65. $s(t) = 16t^2$
$s(3) = 16 \cdot 3^2 = 16 \cdot 9 = 144$

The scaffold is 144 ft high.

66. 400 ft

67. $11.12t^2 = 11.12(10)^2 = 11.12(100) = 1112$

A skydiver has fallen approximately 1112 ft 10 seconds after jumping from a plane.

68. 3091 ft

69. Locate 10 on the horizontal axis. From there move vertically to the graph and then horizontally to the M-axis. This locates an M-value of about 9. Thus, about 9 words were memorized in 10 minutes.

70. About 17

71. Locate 8 on the horizontal axis. From there move vertically to the graph and then horizontally to the M-axis. This locates an M-value of about 6. Thus, the value of $-0.001t^3 + 0.1t^2$ for $t = 8$ is approximately 6.

72. About 13

73. Locate 2 on the horizontal axis. From there move vertically to the graph and then horizontally to the $M(t)$-axis. This locates a value of about 340. Thus, about 340 mg of ibuprofen is in the the bloodstream 2 hr after 400 mg have been swallowed.

74. About 185

75. M has a minimum value of 0 and a maximum value of about 345, so the range is $[0, 345]$.

76. $[0, 6]$

77. Substitute 1 for r and use the π key on the calculator.
$$\frac{2}{25}\pi r^3 = \frac{2}{25}\pi \cdot 1^3 \approx 0.25$$
The lifting force of a helium-filled balloon with radius 1 ft is about 0.25 lb.

78. About 251 lb

79. The function has a maximum value of 3 and no minimum is indicated, so the range is $(-\infty, 3]$.

80. $(-\infty, \infty)$

81. There is no maximum or minimum value indicated by the graph, so the range is $(-\infty, \infty)$.

82. $[-4, \infty)$

83. The function has a minimum value of -4 and no maximum is indicated, so the range is $[-4, \infty)$.

84. $(-\infty, \infty)$

85. The function has a minimum value of -65 and no maximum is indicated, so the range is $[-65, \infty)$.

86. $(-\infty, \infty)$

87. We graph $y = x^2 + 2x + 1$ in the standard viewing window.

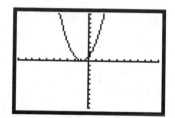

The range appears to be $[0, \infty)$.

88. $[-6.25, \infty)$

89. We graph $y = -2x^2 + 5$ in the standard viewing window.

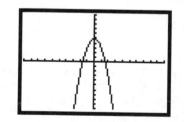

The range appears to be $(-\infty, 5]$.

90. $(-\infty, 1]$

91. We graph $y = -2x^3 + x + 5$ in the standard viewing window.

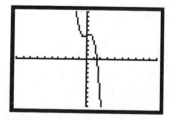

The range appears to be $(-\infty, \infty)$.

92. $(-\infty, -8.3]$

93. We graph $y = x^4 + 2x^3 - 5$ in the standard viewing window.

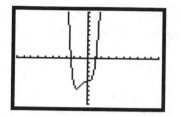

Using TRACE and ZOOM, we estimate that the range is $[-6.7, \infty)$.

94. $(-\infty, \infty)$

95. *Writing Exercise*

96. *Writing Exercise*

97. $-19 + 24$ A negative and a positive number. We subtract the absolute values: $24 - 19 = 5$. The positive number has the larger absolute value so the answer is positive.

$$-19 + 24 = 5$$

98. -9

99. $5x + 15 = 5 \cdot x + 5 \cdot 3 = 5(x + 3)$

100. $7(a - 3)$

101. **Familiarize.** Let $x =$ the cost per mile of gasoline in dollars. Then the total cost of the gasoline for the year was $14,800x$.

Translate.

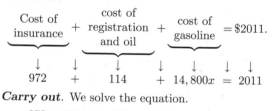

Carry out. We solve the equation.

$$972 + 114 + 14,800x = 2011$$
$$1086 + 14,800x = 2011$$
$$14,800x = 925$$
$$x = 0.0625$$

Check. If gasoline cost \$0.0625 per mile, then the total cost of the gasoline was $14,800(\$0.0625)$, or \$925. Then the total auto expense was $\$972 + \$114 + \$925$, or \$2011. The answer checks.

State. Gasoline cost \$0.0625, or 6.25¢ per mile.

102. 274 and 275

103. *Writing Exercise*

104. *Writing Exercise*

105. Answers may vary. Use an ax^5-term, where a is an integer, and 3 other terms with different degrees, each less than degree 5, and integer coefficients. Three answers are $-6x^5 + 14x^4 - x^2 + 11$, $x^5 - 8x^3 + 3x + 1$, and $23x^5 + 2x^4 - x^2 + 5x$.

106. Answers may vary. $0.2y^4 - y + \dfrac{5}{2}$

107. $(5m^5)^2 = 5^2 m^{5 \cdot 2} = 25m^{10}$

The degree is 10.

108. Answers may vary. $9y^4, -\dfrac{3}{2}y^4, 4.2y^4$

109. $\dfrac{9}{2}x^8 + \dfrac{1}{9}x^2 + \dfrac{1}{2}x^9 + \dfrac{9}{2}x + \dfrac{9}{2}x^9 + \dfrac{8}{9}x^2 +$

$\dfrac{1}{2}x - \dfrac{1}{2}x^8$

$= \left(\dfrac{1}{2} + \dfrac{9}{2}\right)x^9 + \left(\dfrac{9}{2} - \dfrac{1}{2}\right)x^8 + \left(\dfrac{1}{9} + \dfrac{8}{9}\right)x^2 +$

$\left(\dfrac{9}{2} + \dfrac{1}{2}\right)x$

$= \dfrac{10}{2}x^9 + \dfrac{8}{2}x^8 + \dfrac{9}{9}x^2 + \dfrac{10}{2}x$

$= 5x^9 + 4x^8 + x^2 + 5x$

110. $3x^6$

111. Let $c =$ the coefficient of x^3. Solve:

$c + (c - 3) + 3(c - 3) + (c + 2) = -4$
$c + c - 3 + 3c - 9 + c + 2 = -4$
$6c - 10 = -4$
$6c = 6$
$c = 1$

Coefficient of x^3, c: 1

Coefficient of x^2, $c - 3$: $1 - 3$, or -2

Coefficient of x, $3(c - 3)$: $3(1 - 3)$, or -6

Coefficient remaining (constant term), $c + 2$: $1 + 2$, or 3

The polynomial is $x^3 - 2x^2 - 6x + 3$.

112. 50

113. First we find the number of truffles in the display.

$N(x) = \dfrac{1}{6}x^3 + \dfrac{1}{2}x^2 + \dfrac{1}{3}x$

$N(5) = \dfrac{1}{6} \cdot 5^3 + \dfrac{1}{2} \cdot 5^2 + \dfrac{1}{3} \cdot 5$

$= \dfrac{1}{6} \cdot 125 + \dfrac{1}{2} \cdot 25 + \dfrac{5}{3}$

$= \dfrac{125}{6} + \dfrac{25}{2} + \dfrac{5}{3}$

$= \dfrac{125}{6} + \dfrac{75}{6} + \dfrac{10}{6}$

$= \dfrac{210}{6} = 35$

There are 35 truffles in the display. Now find the volume of one truffle. Each truffle's diameter is 3 cm, so the radius is $\dfrac{3}{2}$, or 1.5 cm.

$V(r) = \dfrac{4}{3}\pi r^3$

$V(1.5) \approx \dfrac{4}{3}(3.14)(1.5)^3 \approx 14.13 \text{ cm}^3$

Finally, multiply the number of truffles and the volume of a truffle to find the total volume of chocolate.

$35(14.13 \text{ cm}^3) = 494.55 \text{ cm}^3$

The display contains about 494.55 cm^3 of chocolate.

114. About 9.8 cm

115. The area of the base is $x \cdot x$, or x^2.
The area of each side is $x \cdot (x - 2)$.
The total area of all four sides is $4x(x - 2)$.

The surface area of this box can be expressed as a polynomial function.

$S(x) = x^2 + 4x(x - 2)$
$= x^2 + 4x^2 - 8x$
$= 5x^2 - 8x$

Exercise Set 5.3

1. $(2x + 3) + (-7x + 6) = (2 - 7)x + (3 + 6) = -5x + 9$

2. $-4x + 5$

3. $(-6x + 2) + (x^2 + x - 3) =$
$x^2 + (-6 + 1)x + (2 - 3) = x^2 - 5x - 1$

4. $x^2 + 3x - 5$

5. $(7t^2 - 3t + 6) + (2t^2 + 8t - 9) =$
$(7 + 2)t^2 + (-3 + 8)t + (6 - 9) = 9t^2 + 5t - 3$

6. $15a^2 + a - 6$

7. $(2m^3 - 4m^2 + m - 7) + (4m^3 + 7m^2 - 4m - 2) =$
$(2 + 4)m^3 + (-4 + 7)m^2 + (1 - 4)m + (-7 - 2) =$
$6m^3 + 3m^2 - 3m - 9$

8. $7n^3 - 5n^2 + 7n - 7$

9. $(3 + 6a + 7a^2 + 8a^3) + (4 + 7a - a^2 + 6a^3) =$
$(3 + 4) + (6 + 7)a + (7 - 1)a^2 + (8 + 6)a^3 =$
$7 + 13a + 6a^2 + 14a^3$

10. $9 + 5t + t^2 + 2t^3$

11. $(9x^8 - 7x^4 + 2x^2 + 5) + (8x^7 + 4x^4 - 2x) =$
$9x^8 + 8x^7 + (-7 + 4)x^4 + 2x^2 - 2x + 5 =$
$9x^8 + 8x^7 - 3x^4 + 2x^2 - 2x + 5$

12. $4x^5 + 9x^2 + 1$

13. $\left(\dfrac{1}{4}x^4 + \dfrac{2}{3}x^3 + \dfrac{5}{8}x^2 + 7\right) + \left(-\dfrac{3}{4}x^4 + \dfrac{3}{8}x^2 - 7\right) =$
$\left(\dfrac{1}{4} - \dfrac{3}{4}\right)x^4 + \dfrac{2}{3}x^3 + \left(\dfrac{5}{8} + \dfrac{3}{8}\right)x^2 + (7 - 7) =$
$-\dfrac{2}{4}x^4 + \dfrac{2}{3}x^3 + \dfrac{8}{8}x^2 + 0 =$
$-\dfrac{1}{2}x^4 + \dfrac{2}{3}x^3 + x^2$

14. $\dfrac{2}{15}x^9 - \dfrac{2}{5}x^5 + \dfrac{1}{4}x^4 - \dfrac{1}{2}x^2 + 7$

15. $(5.3t^2 - 6.4t - 9.1) + (4.2t^3 - 1.8t^2 + 7.3) =$

    $4.2t^3 + (5.3 - 1.8)t^2 - 6.4t + (-9.1 + 7.3) =$

    $4.2t^3 + 3.5t^2 - 6.4t - 1.8$

16. $4.9a^3 + 5.3a^2 - 8.8a + 4.6$

17. $\quad -3x^4 + 6x^2 + 2x - 1$

    $\underline{\qquad\quad - 3x^2 + 2x + 1}$

    $-3x^4 + 3x^2 + 4x + 0$

    $-3x^4 + 3x^2 + 4x$

18. $-4x^3 + 4x^2 + 6x$

19. Rewrite the problem so the coefficients of like terms have the same number of decimal places.

    $0.15x^4 + 0.10x^3 - 0.90x^2$

    $\qquad\quad - 0.01x^3 + 0.01x^2 + x$

    $1.25x^4 \qquad\qquad + 0.11x^2 \qquad + 0.01$

    $\qquad 0.27x^3 \qquad\qquad\qquad + 0.99$

    $\underline{-0.35x^4 \qquad\qquad + 15.00x^2 \qquad - 0.03}$

    $1.05x^4 + 0.36x^3 + 14.22x^2 + x + 0.97$

20. $1.3x^4 + 0.35x^3 + 9.53x^2 + 2x + 0.96$

21. Two forms of the opposite of $-t^3 + 4t^2 - 9$ are

    i) $-(-t^3 + 4t^2 - 9)$ and

    ii) $t^3 - 4t^2 + 9$. (Changing the sign of every term)

22. $-(-4x^3 - 5x^2 + 2x)$, $4x^3 + 5x^2 - 2x$

23. Two forms for the opposite of $12x^4 - 3x^3 + 3$ are

    i) $-(12x^4 - 3x^3 + 3)$ and

    ii) $-12x^4 + 3x^3 - 3$. (Changing the sign of every term)

24. $-(5a^3 + 2a - 17)$, $-5a^3 - 2a + 17$

25. We change the sign of every term inside parentheses.

    $-(8x - 9) = -8x + 9$

26. $6x - 5$

27. We change the sign of every term inside parentheses.

    $-(3a^4 - 5a^2 + 9) = -3a^4 + 5a^2 - 9$

28. $6a^3 - 2a^2 + 7$

29. We change the sign of every term inside parentheses.

    $-\left(-4x^4 + 6x^2 + \dfrac{3}{4}x - 8\right) = 4x^4 - 6x^2 - \dfrac{3}{4}x + 8$

30. $5x^4 - 4x^3 + x^2 - 0.9$

31. $\quad (7x + 4) - (-2x + 1)$

    $= 7x + 4 + 2x - 1$ Changing the sign of every term inside parentheses

    $= 9x + 3$

32. $7x + 2$

33. $(-5t + 4) - (t^2 + 2t - 1) = -5t + 4 - t^2 - 2t + 1 = -t^2 - 7t + 5$

34. $-2a^2 - 7a + 6$

35. $\quad (6x^4 + 3x^3 - 1) - (4x^2 - 3x + 3)$

    $= 6x^4 + 3x^3 - 1 - 4x^2 + 3x - 3$

    $= 6x^4 + 3x^3 - 4x^2 + 3x - 4$

36. $-3x^3 + x^2 + 2x - 3$

37. $\quad (1.2x^3 + 4.5x^2 - 3.8x) - (-3.4x^3 - 4.7x^2 + 23)$

    $= 1.2x^3 + 4.5x^2 - 3.8x + 3.4x^3 + 4.7x^2 - 23$

    $= 4.6x^3 + 9.2x^2 - 3.8x - 23$

38. $-1.8x^4 - 0.6x^2 - 1.8x + 4.6$

39. $(7x^3 - 2x^2 + 6) - (7x^3 - 2x^2 + 6)$

    Observe that we are subtracting the polynomial $7x^3 - 2x^2 + 6$ from itself. The result is 0.

40. x

41. $(6 + 5a + 3a^2 - a^3) - (2 + 3a - 4a^2 + 2a^3) =$

    $6 + 5a + 3a^2 - a^3 - 2 - 3a + 4a^2 - 2a^3 =$

    $4 + 2a + 7a^2 - 3a^3$

42. $6 - t - t^2 - 3t^3$

43. $\quad \dfrac{5}{8}x^3 - \dfrac{1}{4}x - \dfrac{1}{3} - \left(-\dfrac{1}{8}x^3 + \dfrac{1}{4}x - \dfrac{1}{3}\right)$

    $= \dfrac{5}{8}x^3 - \dfrac{1}{4}x - \dfrac{1}{3} + \dfrac{1}{8}x^3 - \dfrac{1}{4}x + \dfrac{1}{3}$

    $= \dfrac{6}{8}x^3 - \dfrac{2}{4}x$

    $= \dfrac{3}{4}x^3 - \dfrac{1}{2}x$

44. $\dfrac{3}{5}x^3 - \dfrac{307}{1000}$

45. $(0.07t^3 - 0.03t^2 + 0.01t) - (0.02t^3 + 0.04t^2 - 1) = 0.07t^3 - 0.03t^2 + 0.01t - 0.02t^3 - 0.04t^2 + 1 =$

    $0.05t^3 - 0.07t^2 + 0.01t + 1$

46. $-0.7a^4 + 0.9a^3 + 0.5a - 4.9$

47. $\quad x^2 + 5x + 6$

    $\underline{-(x^2 + 2x + 1)}$

    $x^2 + 5x + 6$ Changing signs and

    $\underline{-x^2 - 2x - 1}$ removing parentheses

    $\quad\;\; 3x + 5$ Adding

48. $2x^2 + 6$

49. $\quad 5x^4 + 6x^3 - 9x^2$

    $\underline{-(-6x^4 - 6x^3 + x^2)}$

    $5x^4 + 6x^3 - 9x^2$ Changing signs and

    $\underline{6x^4 + 6x^3 - x^2}$ removing parentheses

    $11x^4 + 12x^3 - 10x^2$ Adding

50. $-2x^4 - 8x^3 - x^2$

51. a)

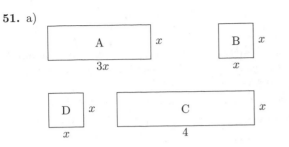

Familiarize. The area of a rectangle is the product of the length and the width.

Translate. The sum of the areas is found as follows:

$$\begin{array}{lllll} \text{Area} & & \text{Area} & & \text{Area} & & \text{Area} \\ \text{of } A & + & \text{of } B & + & \text{of } C & + & \text{of } D \\ = 3x \cdot x & + & x \cdot x & + & 4 \cdot x & + & x \cdot x \end{array}$$

Carry out. We collect like terms.

$$3x^2 + x^2 + 4x + x^2 = 5x^2 + 4x$$

Check. We can go over our calculations. We can also assign some value to x, say 2, and carry out the computation of the area in two ways.

Sum of areas: $3 \cdot 2 \cdot 2 + 2 \cdot 2 + 4 \cdot 2 + 2 \cdot 2 =$
$$12 + 4 + 8 + 4 = 28$$

Substituting in the polynomial:
$$5(2)^2 + 4 \cdot 2 = 20 + 8 = 28$$

Since the results are the same, our solution is probably correct.

State. A polynomial for the sum of the areas is $5x^2 + 4x$.

b)   For $x = 5$: $5x^2 + 4x = 5 \cdot 5^2 + 4 \cdot 5 =$
$$5 \cdot 25 + 4 \cdot 5 = 125 + 20 = 145$$

When $x = 5$, the sum of the areas is 145 square units.
For $x = 7$: $5x^2 + 4x = 5 \cdot 7^2 + 4 \cdot 7 =$
$$5 \cdot 49 + 4 \cdot 7 = 245 + 28 = 273$$

When $x = 7$, the sum of the areas is 273 square units.

52. a) $\pi r^2 + 13\pi$

b) 38π, 140.69π

53.

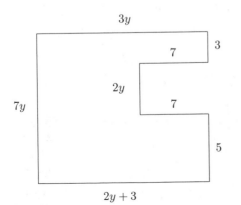

Familiarize. The perimeter is the sum of the lengths of the sides.

Translate. The sum of the lengths is found as follows:

$$3y + 7y + (2y + 3) + 5 + 7 + 2y + 7 + 3$$

Carry out. We collect like terms.

$$(3 + 7 + 2 + 2)y + (3 + 5 + 7 + 7 + 3) = 14y + 25$$

Check. We can go over our calculations. We can also assign some value to y, say 3, and carry out the computation of the perimeter in two ways.

Sum of lengths: $3 \cdot 3 + 7 \cdot 3 + (2 \cdot 3 + 3) + 5 + 7 + 2 \cdot 3 + 7 + 3 =$
$$9 + 21 + 9 + 5 + 7 + 6 + 7 + 3 = 67$$

Substituting in the polynomial:
$$14 \cdot 3 + 25 = 42 + 25 = 67$$

Since the results are the same, our solution is probably correct.

State. A polynomial for the perimeter of the figure is $14y + 25$.

54. $\dfrac{23}{2}a + 12$

55.

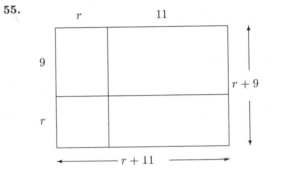

The length and width of the figure can be expressed as $r + 11$ and $r + 9$, respectively. The area of this figure (a rectangle) is the product of the length and width. An algebraic expression for the area is $(r + 11) \cdot (r + 9)$.

The algebraic expressions $9r + 99 + r^2 + 11r$ and $(r + 11) \cdot (r + 9)$ represent the same area.

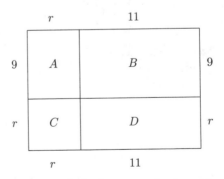

The area of the figure can be found by adding the areas of the four rectangles A, B, C, and D. The area of a rectangle is the product of the length and the width.

$$\begin{array}{lllll} \text{Area} & & \text{Area} & & \text{Area} & & \text{Area} \\ \text{of } A & + & \text{of } B & + & \text{of } C & + & \text{of } D \\ = 9 \cdot r & + & 11 \cdot 9 & + & r \cdot r & + & 11 \cdot r \\ = 9r & + & 99 & + & r^2 & + & 11r \end{array}$$

An algebraic expression for the area of the figure is $9r + 99 + r^2 + 11r$.

56. $(t+5)(t+3)$; $t^2 + 5t + 3t + 15$

57.

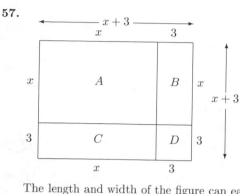

The length and width of the figure can each be expressed as $x + 3$. The area can be expressed as $(x+3) \cdot (x+3)$, or $(x+3)^2$. Another way to express the area is to find an expression for the sum of the areas of the four rectangles A, B, C, and D. The area of each rectangle is the product of its length and width.

$$
\begin{aligned}
&\text{Area} && \text{Area} && \text{Area} && \text{Area} \\
&\text{of } A &+& \text{of } B &+& \text{of } C &+& \text{of } D \\
=\; & x \cdot x &+& 3 \cdot x &+& 3 \cdot x &+& 3 \cdot 3 \\
=\; & x^2 &+& 3x &+& 3x &+& 9
\end{aligned}
$$

The algebraic expressions $(x+3)^2$ and $x^2 + 3x + 3x + 9$ represent the same area.

$$(x+3)^2 = x^2 + 3x + 3x + 9$$

58. $(x+10)(x+8)$; $8x + 80 + x^2 + 10x$

59.

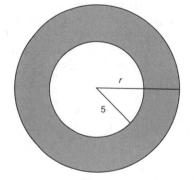

Familiarize. Recall that the area of a circle is the product of π and the square of the radius, r^2.

$$A = \pi r^2$$

Translate.

$$
\begin{array}{ccccc}
\text{Area of circle} & & \text{Area of circle} & & \text{Shaded} \\
\text{with radius } r & - & \text{with radius 5} & = & \text{area} \\
\pi \cdot r^2 & - & \pi \cdot 5^2 & & = \text{Shaded area}
\end{array}
$$

Carry out. We simplify the expression.

$$\pi \cdot r^2 - \pi \cdot 5^2 = \pi r^2 - 25\pi$$

Check. We can go over our calculations. We can also assign some value to r, say 7, and carry out the computation in two ways.

Difference of areas: $\pi \cdot 7^2 - \pi \cdot 5^2 = 49\pi - 25\pi = 24\pi$

Substituting in the polynomial: $\pi \cdot 7^2 - 25\pi = 49\pi - 25\pi = 24\pi$

Since the results are the same, our solution is probably correct.

State. A polynomial for the shaded area is $\pi r^2 - 25\pi$.

60. $m^2 - 40$

61. **Familiarize.** We label the figure with additional information.

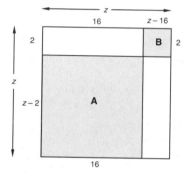

Translate.

Area of shaded sections = Area of A + Area of B

Area of shaded sections = $16(z - 2) + 2(z - 16)$

Carry out. We simplify the expression.

$16(z - 2) + 2(z - 16) = 16z - 32 + 2z - 32 = 18z - 64$

Check. We can go over the calculations. We can also assign some value to z, say 30, and carry out the computation in two ways.

Sum of areas:

$$16 \cdot 28 + 2 \cdot 14 = 448 + 28 = 476$$

Substituting in the polynomial:

$$18 \cdot 30 - 64 = 540 - 64 = 476$$

Since the results are the same, our solution is probably correct.

State. A polynomial for the shaded area is $18z - 64$.

62. $\pi r^2 - 49$

63.

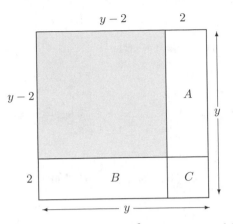

The shaded area is $(y-2)^2$. We find it as follows:

$$\text{Shaded} \atop \text{area} = \text{Area of} \atop \text{square} - \text{Area} \atop \text{of } A - \text{Area} \atop \text{of } B - \text{Area} \atop \text{of } C$$

$$(y-2)^2 = \quad y^2 \quad -2(y-2)-2(y-2)- \ 2\cdot 2$$

$$(y-2)^2 = y^2 - 2y + 4 - 2y + 4 - 4$$

$$(y-2)^2 = y^2 - 4y + 4$$

64. $100 - 40x + 4x^2$

65. Using one of the methods described on pages 347 and 348 in the text, we see that the addition is not correct.

66. Correct

67. Using one of the methods described on pages 347 and 348 in the text, we see that the subtraction is correct.

68. Not correct

69. Using one of the methods described on pages 347 and 348 in the text, we see that the calculation is not correct.

70. Not correct

71. *Writing Exercise*

72. *Writing Exercise*

73. $5(4+3) - 5\cdot 4 - 5\cdot 3$

   $= 5\cdot 7 - 5\cdot 4 - 5\cdot 3$ Adding inside the parentheses

   $= 35 - 20 - 15$ Multiplying

   $= 0$ Subtracting

74. 0

75. $2(5t+7) + 3t = 10t + 14 + 3t = 13t + 14$

76. $14t - 15$

77. $2(x+3) > 5(x-3)+7$

   $2x + 6 > 5x - 15 + 7$ Removing parentheses

   $2x + 6 > 5x - 8$ Collecting like terms

   $2x + 14 > 5x$ Adding 8 to both sides

   $14 > 3x$ Adding $-2x$ to both sides

   $\dfrac{14}{3} > x$ Dividing both sides by 3

The solution set is $\left\{x \middle| \dfrac{14}{3} > x\right\}$, or $\left\{x \middle| x < \dfrac{14}{3}\right\}$, or $\left(-\infty, \dfrac{14}{3}\right)$.

78. $\{x | x \le 12\}$, or $(-\infty, 12]$

79. *Writing Exercise*

80. *Writing Exercise*

81. $(6t^2 - 7t) + (3t^2 - 4t + 5) - (9t - 6)$

   $= 6t^2 - 7t + 3t^2 - 4t + 5 - 9t + 6$

   $= 9t^2 - 20t + 11$

82. $5x^2 - 9x - 1$

83. $(-8y^2 - 4) - (3y + 6) - (2y^2 - y)$

   $= -8y^2 - 4 - 3y - 6 - 2y^2 + y$

   $= -10y^2 - 2y - 10$

84. $4x^3 - 5x^2 + 6$

85. $(-y^4 - 7y^3 + y^2) + (-2y^4 + 5y - 2) - (-6y^3 + y^2)$

   $= -y^4 - 7y^3 + y^2 - 2y^4 + 5y - 2 + 6y^3 - y^2$

   $= -3y^4 - y^3 + 5y - 2$

86. $2 + x + 2x^2 + 4x^3$

87. $(345.099x^3 - 6.178x) - (94.508x^3 - 8.99x)$

   $= 345.099x^3 - 6.178x - 94.508x^3 + 8.99x$

   $= 250.591x^3 + 2.812x$

88. $36x + 2x^2$

89. **Familiarize**. The surface area is $2lw + 2lh + 2wh$, where l = length, w = width, and h = height of the rectangular solid. Here we have $l = 3$, $w = w$, and $h = 7$.

Translate. We substitute in the formula above.

$$2\cdot 3\cdot w + 2\cdot 3\cdot 7 + 2\cdot w\cdot 7$$

Carry out. We simplify the expression.

   $2\cdot 3\cdot w + 2\cdot 3\cdot 7 + 2\cdot w\cdot 7$

   $= 6w + 42 + 14w$

   $= 20w + 42$

Check. We can go over the calculations. We can also assign some value to w, say 6, and carry out the computation in two ways.

Using the formula: $2\cdot 3\cdot 6 + 2\cdot 3\cdot 7 + 2\cdot 6\cdot 7 = 36 + 42 + 84 = 162$

Substituting in the polynomial: $20\cdot 6 + 42 = 120 + 42 = 162$

Since the results are the same, our solution is probably correct.

State. A polynomial for the surface area is $20w + 42$.

90. $22a + 56$

91. **Familiarize**. The surface area is $2lw + 2lh + 2wh$, where l = length, w = width, and h = height of the rectangular solid. Here we have $l = x$, $w = x$, and $h = 5$.

Translate. We substitute in the formula above.

$$2\cdot x\cdot x + 2\cdot x\cdot 5 + 2\cdot x\cdot 5$$

Carry out. We simplify the expression.

$$2 \cdot x \cdot x + 2 \cdot x \cdot 5 + 2 \cdot x \cdot 5$$
$$= 2x^2 + 10x + 10x$$
$$= 2x^2 + 20x$$

Check. We can go over the calculations. We can also assign some value to x, say 3, and carry out the computation in two ways.

Using the formula: $2 \cdot 3 \cdot 3 + 2 \cdot 3 \cdot 5 + 2 \cdot 3 \cdot 5 = 18 + 30 + 30 = 78$

Substituting in the polynomial: $2 \cdot 3^2 + 20 \cdot 3 = 2 \cdot 9 + 60 = 18 + 60 = 78$

Since the results are the same, our solution is probably correct.

State. A polynomial for the surface area is $2x^2 + 20x$.

92.   a) $P(x) = -x^2 + 280x - 5000$

b) \$10,375

c) \$13,000

93.   *Writing Exercise*

Exercise Set 5.4

1. $(5x^4)6 = (5 \cdot 6)x^4 = 30x^4$

2. $28x^3$

3. $(-x^2)(-x) = (-1 \cdot x^2)(-1 \cdot x) = (-1)(-1)(x^2 \cdot x) = x^3$

4. $-x^7$

5. $(-x^5)(x^3) = (-1 \cdot x^5)(1x^3) = (-1)(1)(x^5 \cdot x^3) = -x^8$

6. x^8

7. $(7t^5)(4t^3) = (7 \cdot 4)(t^5 \cdot t^3) = 28t^8$

8. $30a^4$

9. $(-0.1x^6)(0.2x^4) = (-0.1)(0.2)(x^6 \cdot x^4) = -0.02x^{10}$

10. $-0.12x^9$

11. $\left(-\frac{1}{5}x^3\right)\left(-\frac{1}{3}x\right) = \left(-\frac{1}{5}\right)\left(-\frac{1}{3}\right)(x^3 \cdot x) = \frac{1}{15}x^4$

12. $-\frac{1}{20}x^{12}$

13. $19t^2 \cdot 0 = 0$ Any number multiplied by 0 is 0.

14. $5n^3$

15. $7x^2(-2x^3)(2x^6) = 7(-2)(2)(x^2 \cdot x^3 \cdot x^6) = -28x^{11}$

16. $72y^{10}$

17. $3x(-x + 5) = 3x(-x) + 3x(5)$
$$= -3x^2 + 15x$$

18. $8x^2 - 12x$

19. $4x(x + 1) = 4x(x) + 4x(1)$
$$= 4x^2 + 4x$$

20. $3x^2 + 6x$

21. $(a + 9)3a = a \cdot 3a + 9 \cdot 3a = 3a^2 + 27a$

22. $4a^2 - 28a$

23. $x^2(x^3 + 1) = x^2(x^3) + x^2(1)$
$$= x^5 + x^2$$

24. $-2x^5 + 2x^3$

25. $3x(2x^2 - 6x + 1) = 3x(2x^2) + 3x(-6x) + 3x(1)$
$$= 6x^3 - 18x^2 + 3x$$

26. $-8x^4 + 24x^3 + 20x^2 - 4x$

27. $5t^2(3t + 6) = 5t^2(3t) + 5t^2(6) = 15t^3 + 30t^2$

28. $14t^3 + 7t^2$

29. $-6x^2(x^2 + x) = -6x^2(x^2) - 6x^2(x)$
$$= -6x^4 - 6x^3$$

30. $-4x^4 + 4x^3$

31. $\frac{2}{3}a^4\left(6a^5 - 12a^3 - \frac{5}{8}\right)$
$$= \frac{2}{3}a^4(6a^5) - \frac{2}{3}a^4(12a^3) - \frac{2}{3}a^4\left(\frac{5}{8}\right)$$
$$= \frac{12}{3}a^9 - \frac{24}{3}a^7 - \frac{10}{24}a^4$$
$$= 4a^9 - 8a^7 - \frac{5}{12}a^4$$

32. $6t^{11} - 9t^9 + \frac{9}{7}t^5$

33. $(x + 6)(x + 3) = (x + 6)x + (x + 6)3$
$$= x \cdot x + 6 \cdot x + x \cdot 3 + 6 \cdot 3$$
$$= x^2 + 6x + 3x + 18$$
$$= x^2 + 9x + 18$$

34. $x^2 + 7x + 10$

35. $(x + 5)(x - 2) = (x + 5)x + (x + 5)(-2)$
$$= x \cdot x + 5 \cdot x + x(-2) + 5(-2)$$
$$= x^2 + 5x - 2x - 10$$
$$= x^2 + 3x - 10$$

36. $x^2 + 4x - 12$

37. $(a - 6)(a - 7) = (a - 6)a + (a - 6)(-7)$
$$= a \cdot a - 6 \cdot a + a(-7) + (-6)(-7)$$
$$= a^2 - 6a - 7a + 42$$
$$= a^2 - 13a + 42$$

38. $a^2 - 12a - 32$

39. $(x + 3)(x - 3) = (x + 3)x + (x + 3)(-3)$
$$= x \cdot x + 3 \cdot x + x(-3) + 3(-3)$$
$$= x^2 + 3x - 3x - 9$$
$$= x^2 - 9$$

40. $x^2 - 36$

41. $(5-x)(5-2x) = (5-x)5 + (5-x)(-2x)$
$$= 5\cdot 5 - x\cdot 5 + 5(-2x) - x(-2x)$$
$$= 25 - 5x - 10x + 2x^2$$
$$= 25 - 15x + 2x^2$$

42. $18 + 12x + 2x^2$

43. $\left(t+\dfrac{3}{2}\right)\left(t+\dfrac{4}{3}\right) = \left(t+\dfrac{3}{2}\right)t + \left(t+\dfrac{3}{2}\right)\left(\dfrac{4}{3}\right)$
$$= t\cdot t + \dfrac{3}{2}\cdot t + t\cdot\dfrac{4}{3} + \dfrac{3}{2}\cdot\dfrac{4}{3}$$
$$= t^2 + \dfrac{3}{2}t + \dfrac{4}{3}t + 2$$
$$= t^2 + \dfrac{9}{6}t + \dfrac{8}{6}t + 2$$
$$= t^2 + \dfrac{17}{6}t + 2$$

44. $a^2 + \dfrac{21}{10}a - 1$

45. $\left(\dfrac{1}{4}a+2\right)\left(\dfrac{3}{4}a-1\right)$
$$= \left(\dfrac{1}{4}a+2\right)\left(\dfrac{3}{4}a\right) + \left(\dfrac{1}{4}a+2\right)(-1)$$
$$= \dfrac{1}{4}a\left(\dfrac{3}{4}a\right) + 2\cdot\dfrac{3}{4}a + \dfrac{1}{4}a(-1) + 2(-1)$$
$$= \dfrac{3}{16}a^2 + \dfrac{3}{2}a - \dfrac{1}{4}a - 2$$
$$= \dfrac{3}{16}a^2 + \dfrac{6}{4}a - \dfrac{1}{4}a - 2$$
$$= \dfrac{3}{16}a^2 + \dfrac{5}{4}a - 2$$

46. $\dfrac{6}{25}t^2 - \dfrac{1}{5}t - 1$

47. Illustrate $x(x+5)$ as the area of a rectangle with width x and length $x+5$.

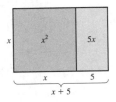

48.

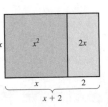

49. Illustrate $(x+1)(x+2)$ as the area of a rectangle with width $x+1$ and length $x+2$.

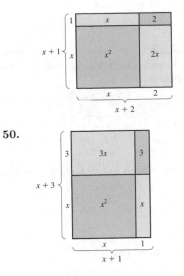

50.

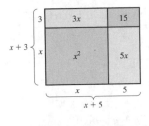

51. Illustrate $(x+5)(x+3)$ as the area of a rectangle with length $x+5$ and width $x+3$.

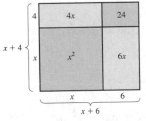

52.

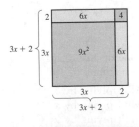

53. Illustrate $(3x+2)(3x+2)$ as the area of a square with sides of length $3x+2$.

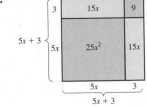

54.

55.
$$(x^2 - x + 5)(x + 1)$$
$$= (x^2 - x + 5)x + (x^2 - x + 5)1$$
$$= x^3 - x^2 + 5x + x^2 - x + 5$$
$$= x^3 + 4x + 5$$

A partial check can be made by selecting a convenient replacement for x, say 1, and comparing the values of the original expression and the result.

$$\begin{array}{ll} (1^2 - 1 + 5)(1 + 1) & 1^3 + 4 \cdot 1 + 5 \\ = (1 - 1 + 5)(1 + 1) & = 1 + 4 + 5 \\ = 5 \cdot 2 & = 10 \\ = 10 & \end{array}$$

Since the value of both expressions is 10, the multiplication is very likely correct.

56. $x^3 + 3x^2 - 5x - 14$

57.
$$(2a + 5)(a^2 - 3a + 2)$$
$$= (2a + 5)a^2 - (2a + 5)(3a) + (2a + 5)2$$
$$= 2a \cdot a^2 + 5 \cdot a^2 - 2a \cdot 3a - 5 \cdot 3a + 2a \cdot 2 + 5 \cdot 2$$
$$= 2a^3 + 5a^2 - 6a^2 - 15a + 4a + 10$$
$$= 2a^3 - a^2 - 11a + 10$$

A partial check can be made as in Exercise 55.

58. $3t^3 - 11t^2 - 17t + 4$

59.
$$(y^2 - 7)(2y^3 + y + 1)$$
$$= (y^2 - 7)(2y^3) + (y^2 - 7)y + (y^2 - 7)(1)$$
$$= y^2 \cdot 2y^3 - 7 \cdot 2y^3 + y^2 \cdot y - 7 \cdot y + y^2 \cdot 1 - 7 \cdot 1$$
$$= 2y^5 - 14y^3 + y^3 - 7y + y^2 - 7$$
$$= 2y^5 - 13y^3 + y^2 - 7y - 7$$

A partial check can be made as in Exercise 55.

60. $5a^5 + 17a^3 - a^2 - 12a - 4$

61.
$$(5x^3 - 7x^2 + 1)(x - 3x^2)$$
$$= (5x^3 - 7x^2 + 1)x - (5x^3 - 7x^2 + 1)(3x^2)$$
$$= 5x^3 \cdot x - 7x^2 \cdot x + 1 \cdot x - 5x^3 \cdot 3x^2 + 7x^2 \cdot 3x^2 - 1 \cdot 3x^2$$
$$= 5x^4 - 7x^3 + x - 15x^5 + 21x^4 - 3x^2$$
$$= -15x^5 + 26x^4 - 7x^3 - 3x^2 + x$$

A partial check can be made in Exercise 55.

62. $8x^5 - 6x^3 - 6x^2 - 5x - 3$

63.
$$\begin{array}{ll} x^2 - 3x + 2 & \text{Line up like terms} \\ x^2 + x + 1 & \text{in columns} \\ \hline x^2 - 3x + 2 & \text{Multiplying by 1} \\ x^3 - 3x^2 + 2x & \text{Multiplying by } x \\ x^4 - 3x^3 + 2x^2 & \text{Multiplying by } x^2 \\ \hline x^4 - 2x^3 \qquad - x + 2 & \end{array}$$

A partial check can be made as in Exercise 55.

64. $x^4 + 4x^3 - 3x^2 + 16x - 3$

65.
$$\begin{array}{ll} 2t^2 - 5t - 4 & \\ 3t^2 - t + 1 & \\ \hline 2t^2 - 5t - 4 & \text{Multiplying by 1} \\ -2t^3 + 5t^2 + 4t & \text{Multiplying by } -t \\ 6t^4 - 15t^3 - 12t^2 & \text{Multiplying by } 3t^2 \\ \hline 6t^4 - 17t^3 - 5t^2 - t - 4 & \end{array}$$

A partial check can be made as in Exercise 55.

66. $10t^4 + 3t^3 - 14t^2 + 4t - 3$

67. We will multiply horizontally while still aligning like terms.

$$(x + 1)(x^3 + 7x^2 + 5x + 4)$$

$$\begin{array}{ll} = x^4 + 7x^3 + 5x^2 + 4x & \text{Multiplying by } x \\ + x^3 + 7x^2 + 5x + 4 & \text{Multiplying by 1} \\ \hline = x^4 + 8x^3 + 12x^2 + 9x + 4 & \end{array}$$

A partial check can be made as in Exercise 55.

68. $x^4 + 7x^3 + 19x^2 + 21x + 6$

69. We will multiply horizontally while still aligning like terms.

$$\left(x - \frac{1}{2}\right)\left(2x^3 - 4x^2 + 3x - \frac{2}{5}\right)$$

$$= 2x^4 - 4x^3 + 3x^2 - \frac{2}{5}x$$

$$\underline{ -x^3 + 2x^2 - \frac{3}{2}x + \frac{1}{5}}$$

$$2x^4 - 5x^3 + 5x^2 - \frac{19}{10}x + \frac{1}{5}$$

A partial check can be made as in Exercise 55.

70. $6x^4 - 10x^3 - 9x^2 - \frac{7}{6}x + \frac{1}{6}$

71. *Writing Exercise*

72. *Writing Exercise*

73. $5 - 3 \cdot 2 + 7 = 5 - 6 + 7 = -1 + 7 = 6$

74. 31

75.
$$(8 - 2)(8 + 2) + 2^2 - 8^2$$
$$= 6 \cdot 10 + 2^2 - 8^2$$
$$= 6 \cdot 10 + 4 - 64$$
$$= 60 + 4 - 64$$
$$= 64 - 64$$
$$= 0$$

76. 0

77. *Writing Exercise*

78. *Writing Exercise*

79. The shaded area is the area of the large rectangle, $6y(14y - 5)$ less the area of the unshaded rectangle, $3y(3y + 5)$. We have:

$$6y(14y - 5) - 3y(3y + 5)$$
$$= 84y^2 - 30y - 9y^2 - 15y$$
$$= 75y^2 - 45y$$

80. $78t^2 + 40t$

81. Let n = the missing number. Label the figure with the known areas.

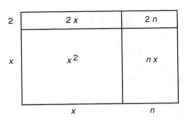

Then the area of the figure is $x^2 + 2x + nx + 2n$. This is equivalent to $x^2 + 7x + 10$, so we have $2x + nx = 7x$ and $2n = 10$. Solving either equation for n, we find that the missing number is 5.

82. 5

83.

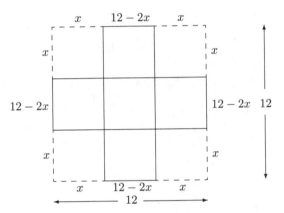

The dimensions, in inches, of the box are $12 - 2x$ by $12 - 2x$ by x. The volume is the product of the dimensions (volume = length × width × height):

$$\text{Volume} = (12 - 2x)(12 - 2x)x$$
$$= (144 - 48x + 4x^2)x$$
$$= 144x - 48x^2 + 4x^3 \text{ in}^3, \text{ or}$$
$$4x^3 - 48x^2 + 144x \text{ in}^3$$

The outside surface area is the sum of the area of the bottom and the areas of the four sides. The dimensions, in inches, of the bottom are $12 - 2x$ by $12 - 2x$, and the dimensions, in inches, of each side are x by $12 - 2x$.

$$\frac{\text{Surface}}{\text{area}} = \text{Area of bottom +}$$
$$4 \cdot \text{Area of each side}$$
$$= (12 - 2x)(12 - 2x) + 4 \cdot x(12 - 2x)$$
$$= 144 - 24x - 24x + 4x^2 + 48x - 8x^2$$
$$= 144 - 48x + 4x^2 + 48x - 8x^2$$
$$= 144 - 4x^2 \text{ in}^2, \text{ or } -4x^2 + 144 \text{ in}^2$$

84. $x^3 - 5x^2 + 8x - 4 \text{ cm}^3$

85. We have a rectangular solid with dimensions x m by x m by $x + 2$ m with a rectangular solid piece with dimensions 6 m by 5 m by 7 m cut out of it.

$$\text{Volume} = \frac{\text{Volume of}}{\text{large solid}} - \frac{\text{Volume of}}{\text{small solid}}$$
$$= (x \text{ m})(x \text{ m})(x + 2 \text{ m}) - (6 \text{ m})(5 \text{ m})(7 \text{ m})$$
$$= x^2(x + 2) \text{ m}^3 - 210 \text{ m}^3$$
$$= x^3 + 2x^2 - 210 \text{ m}^3$$

86. $x^3 + 6x^2 + 12x + 8 \text{ cm}^3$

87. Let x = the width of the garden. Then $2x$ = the length of the garden.

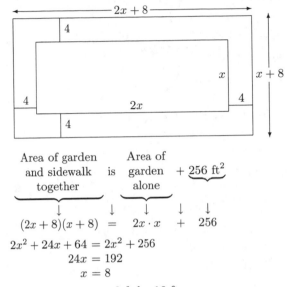

$$\underbrace{\begin{array}{c}\text{Area of garden}\\ \text{and sidewalk}\\ \text{together}\end{array}}_{} \text{ is } \underbrace{\begin{array}{c}\text{Area of}\\ \text{garden}\\ \text{alone}\end{array}}_{} + \underbrace{256 \text{ ft}^2}_{}$$

$$\downarrow \qquad \downarrow \quad \downarrow \quad \downarrow \quad \downarrow$$
$$(2x + 8)(x + 8) = 2x \cdot x + 256$$
$$2x^2 + 24x + 64 = 2x^2 + 256$$
$$24x = 192$$
$$x = 8$$

The dimensions are 8 ft by 16 ft.

88. $2x^2 + 18x + 36$

89. $(x - 2)(x - 7) - (x - 7)(x - 2)$

First observe that, by the commutative law of multiplication, $(x - 2)(x - 7)$ and $(x - 7)(x - 2)$ are equivalent expressions. Then when we subtract $(x - 7)(x - 2)$ from $(x - 2)(x - 7)$, the result is 0.

90. $16x + 16$

91. $(x - a)(x - b) \cdots (x - x)(x - y)(x - z)$
$- (x - a)(x - b) \cdots 0 \cdot (x - y)(x - z)$
$= 0$

Exercise Set 5.5

1. $(x + 4)(x^2 + 3)$
       F   O   I   L
$= x \cdot x^2 + x \cdot 3 + 4 \cdot x^2 + 4 \cdot 3$
$= x^3 + 3x + 4x^2 + 12, \text{ or } x^3 + 4x^2 + 3x + 12$

2. $x^3 - x^2 - 3x + 3$

3. $(x^3 + 6)(x + 2)$
       F   O   I   L
$= x^3 \cdot x + x^3 \cdot 2 + 6 \cdot x + 6 \cdot 2$
$= x^4 + 2x^3 + 6x + 12$

4. $x^5 + 12x^4 + 2x + 24$

5. $(y+2)(y-3)$

F$\qquad$O$\qquad$I$\qquad$L

$= y \cdot y + y \cdot (-3) + 2 \cdot y + 2 \cdot (-3)$

$= y^2 - 3y + 2y - 6$

$= y^2 - y - 6$

6. $a^2 + 4a + 4$

7. $(3x+2)(3x+5)$

F$\qquad$O$\qquad$I$\qquad$L

$= 3x \cdot 3x + 3x \cdot 5 + 2 \cdot 3x + 2 \cdot 5$

$= 9x^2 + 15x + 6x + 10$

$= 9x^2 + 21x + 10$

8. $8x^2 + 30x + 7$

9. $(5x-6)(x+2)$

F$\qquad$O$\qquad$I$\qquad$L

$= 5x \cdot x + 5x \cdot 2 + (-6) \cdot x + (-6) \cdot 2$

$= 5x^2 + 10x - 6x - 12$

$= 5x^2 + 4x - 12$

10. $t^2 - 81$

11. $(1+3t)(2-3t)$

F$\qquad$O$\qquad$I$\qquad$L

$= 1 \cdot 2 + 1(-3t) + 3t \cdot 2 + 3t(-3t)$

$= 2 - 3t + 6t - 9t^2$

$= 2 + 3t - 9t^2$

12. $14 + 19a - 3a^2$

13. $(2x-7)(x-1)$

F$\qquad$O$\qquad$I$\qquad$L

$= 2x \cdot x + 2x \cdot (-1) + (-7) \cdot x + (-7) \cdot (-1)$

$= 2x^2 - 2x - 7x + 7$

$= 2x^2 - 9x + 7$

14. $6x^2 - x - 1$

15. $\left(p - \dfrac{1}{4}\right)\left(p + \dfrac{1}{4}\right)$

F$\qquad$O$\qquad$I$\qquad$L

$= p \cdot p + p \cdot \dfrac{1}{4} + \left(-\dfrac{1}{4}\right) \cdot p + \left(-\dfrac{1}{4}\right) \cdot \dfrac{1}{4}$

$= p^2 + \dfrac{1}{4}p - \dfrac{1}{4}p - \dfrac{1}{16}$

$= p^2 - \dfrac{1}{16}$

16. $q^2 + \dfrac{3}{2}q + \dfrac{9}{16}$

17. $(x-0.1)(x+0.1)$

F$\qquad$O$\qquad$I$\qquad$L

$= x \cdot x + x \cdot (0.1) + (-0.1) \cdot x + (-0.1)(0.1)$

$= x^2 + 0.1x - 0.1x - 0.01$

$= x^2 - 0.01$

18. $x^2 - 0.1x - 0.12$

19. $(2x^2+6)(x+1)$

F$\qquad$O$\qquad$I$\qquad$L

$= 2x^3 + 2x^2 + 6x + 6$

20. $4x^3 - 2x^2 + 6x - 3$

21. $(-2x+1)(x+6)$

F$\qquad$O$\qquad$I$\qquad$L

$= -2x^2 - 12x + x + 6$

$= -2x^2 - 11x + 6$

22. $-2x^2 + 13x - 20$

23. $(a+9)(a+9)$

F$\qquad$O$\qquad$I$\qquad$L

$= a^2 + 9a + 9a + 81$

$= a^2 + 18a + 81$

24. $4y^2 + 28y + 49$

25. $(1+3t)(1-5t)$

F$\qquad$O$\qquad$I$\qquad$L

$= 1 - 5t + 3t - 15t^2$

$= 1 - 2t - 15t^2$

26. $1 - 3t^2 + 2t - 6t^3$, or $1 + 2t - 3t^2 - 6t^3$

27. $(x^2+3)(x^3-1)$

F$\qquad$O$\qquad$I$\qquad$L

$= x^5 - x^2 + 3x^3 - 3$, or $x^5 + 3x^3 - x^2 - 3$

28. $2x^5 + x^4 - 6x - 3$

29. $(3x^2-2)(x^4-2)$

F$\qquad$O$\qquad$I$\qquad$L

$= 3x^6 - 6x^2 - 2x^4 + 4$, or $3x^6 - 2x^4 - 6x^2 + 4$

30. $x^{20} - 9$

31. $(2t^3+5)(2t^3+3)$

F$\qquad$O$\qquad$I$\qquad$L

$= 4t^6 + 6t^3 + 10t^3 + 15$

$= 4t^6 + 16t^3 + 15$

32. $10t^4 + 17t^2 + 3$

33. $(8x^3+5)(x^2+2)$

F$\qquad$O$\qquad$I$\qquad$L

$= 8x^5 + 16x^3 + 5x^2 + 10$

34. $20 - 8x^2 - 10x + 4x^3$, or $20 - 10x - 8x^2 + 4x^3$

35. $(4x^2+3)(x-3)$

F$\qquad$O$\qquad$I$\qquad$L

$= 4x^3 - 12x^2 + 3x - 9$

36. $14x^2 - 53x + 14$

37. $(x+8)(x-8)$$\qquad$Product of sum and difference of the same two terms

$= x^2 - 8^2$

$= x^2 - 64$

38. $x^2 - 1$

39. $(2x + 1)(2x - 1)$ Product of sum and difference of the same two terms

$= (2x)^2 - 1^2$

$= 4x^2 - 1$

40. $x^4 - 1$

41. $(5m - 2)(5m + 2)$ Product of sum and difference of the same two terms

$= (5m)^2 - 2^2$

$= 25m^2 - 4$

42. $9x^8 - 4$

43. $(2x^2 + 3)(2x^2 - 3)$ Product of sum and difference of the same two terms

$= (2x^2)^2 - 3^2$

$= 4x^4 - 9$

44. $36x^{10} - 25$

45. $(3x^4 - 1)(3x^4 + 1)$

$= (3x^4)^2 - 1^2$

$= 9x^8 - 1$

46. $t^4 - 0.04$

47. $(x^4 + 7)(x^4 - 7)$

$= (x^4)^2 - 7^2$

$= x^8 - 49$

48. $t^6 - 16$

49. $\left(t - \dfrac{3}{4}\right)\left(t + \dfrac{3}{4}\right)$

$= t^2 - \left(\dfrac{3}{4}\right)^2$

$= t^2 - \dfrac{9}{16}$

50. $m^2 - \dfrac{4}{9}$

51. $(x + 2)^2$

$= x^2 + 2 \cdot x \cdot 2 + 2^2$ Square of a binomial

$= x^2 + 4x + 4$

52. $4x^2 - 4x + 1$

53. $(3x^5 + 1)^2$ Square of a binomial

$= (3x^5)^2 + 2 \cdot 3x^5 \cdot 1 + 1^2$

$= 9x^{10} + 6x^5 + 1$

54. $16x^6 + 8x^3 + 1$

55. $\left(a - \dfrac{2}{5}\right)^2$ Square of a binomial

$= a^2 - 2 \cdot a \cdot \dfrac{2}{5} + \left(\dfrac{2}{5}\right)^2$

$= a^2 - \dfrac{4}{5}a + \dfrac{4}{25}$

56. $t^2 - \dfrac{2}{5}t + \dfrac{1}{25}$

57. $= (t^3 + 3)^2$ Square of a binomial

$= (t^3)^2 + 2 \cdot t^3 \cdot 3 + 3^2$

$= t^6 + 6t^3 + 9$

58. $a^8 + 4a^4 + 4$

59. $(2 - 3x^4)^2 = 2^2 - 2 \cdot 2 \cdot 3x^4 + (3x^4)^2$

$= 4 - 12x^4 + 9x^8$

60. $25 - 20t^3 + 4t^6$

61. $(5 + 6t^2)^2 = 5^2 + 2 \cdot 5 \cdot 6t^2 + (6t^2)^2$

$= 25 + 60t^2 + 36t^4$

62. $9p^4 - 6p^3 + p^2$

63. $(7x - 0.3)^2 = (7x)^2 - 2(7x)(0.3) + (0.3)^2$

$= 49x^2 - 4.2x + 0.09$

64. $16a^2 - 4.8a + 0.36$

65. $5a^3(2a^2 - 1)$

$= 5a^3 \cdot 2a^2 - 5a^3 \cdot 1$ Multiplying each term of
the binomial by the monomial

$= 10a^5 - 5a^3$

66. $18x^5 - 45x^3$

67. $(a - 3)(a^2 + 2a - 4)$

$= a^3 + 2a^2 - 4a$ Multiplying horizontally

$\underline{ - 3a^2 - 6a + 12}$ and aligning like terms

$= a^3 - a^2 - 10a + 12$

68. $x^4 + x^3 - 6x^2 - 5x + 5$

69. $(3 - 2x^3)^2$

$= 3^2 - 2 \cdot 3 \cdot 2x^3 + (2x^3)^2$ Squaring a binomial

$= 9 - 12x^3 + 4x^6$

70. $x^2 - 8x^4 + 16x^6$

71. $4x(x^2 + 6x - 3)$

$= 4x \cdot x^2 + 4x \cdot 6x + 4x(-3)$ Multiplying each
term of the trinomial
by the monomial

$= 4x^3 + 24x^2 - 12x$

72. $-8x^6 + 48x^3 + 72x$

73. $(-t^3 + 1)^2$

$= (-t^3)^2 + 2(-t)^3(1) + 1^2$ Squaring a binomial

$= t^6 - 2t^3 + 1$

74. $x^4 - 2x^2 + 1$

75. $3t^2(5t^3 - t^2 + t)$

$= 3t^2 \cdot 5t^3 + 3t^2(-t^2) + 3t^2 \cdot t$ Multiplying each
term of the trinomial
by the monomial

$= 15t^5 - 3t^4 + 3t^3$

76. $-5x^5 - 40x^4 + 45x^3$

77. $(6x^4 - 3)^2$ Squaring a binomial

   $= (6x^4)^2 - 2 \cdot 6x^4 \cdot 3 + 3^2$

   $= 36x^8 - 36x^4 + 9$

78. $64a^6 + 80a^3 + 25$

79. $(3x + 2)(4x^2 + 5)$ Product of two
                                    binomials; use FOIL

   $= 3x \cdot 4x^2 + 3x \cdot 5 + 2 \cdot 4x^2 + 2 \cdot 5$

   $= 12x^3 + 15x + 8x^2 + 10$, or
      $12x^3 + 8x^2 + 15x + 10$

80. $6x^4 - 3x^2 - 63$

81. $(5 - 6x^4)^2$ Squaring a binomial

   $= 5^2 - 2 \cdot 5 \cdot 6x^4 + (6x^4)^2$

   $= 25 - 60x^4 + 36x^8$

82. $9 - 24t^5 + 16t^{10}$

83. $(a+1)(a^2 - a + 1)$

   $\begin{array}{ll} = a^3 - a^2 + a & \text{Multiplying horizontally} \\ \quad\;\; a^2 - a + 1 & \text{and aligning like terms} \\ \hline a^3 \qquad\quad + 1 \end{array}$

84. $x^3 - 125$

85.

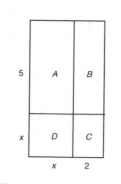

We can find the shaded area in two ways.

Method 1: The figure is a square with side $a + 1$, so the area is $(a + 1)^2 = a^2 + 2a + 1$.

Method 2: We add the areas of A, B, C, and D.

$1 \cdot a + 1 \cdot 1 + 1 \cdot a + a \cdot a = a + 1 + a + a^2 = a^2 + 2a + 1$.

Either way we find that the total shaded area is $a^2 + 2a + 1$.

86. $x^2 + 6x + 9$

87.

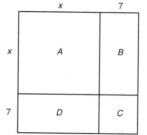

We can find the shaded area in two ways.

Method 1: The figure is a rectangle with dimensions $x + 5$ by $x + 2$, so the area is

$(x + 5)(x + 2) = x^2 + 2x + 5x + 10 = x^2 + 7x + 10$.

Method 2: We add the areas of A, B, C, and D.

$5 \cdot x + 2 \cdot 5 + 2 \cdot x + x \cdot x = 5x + 10 + 2x + x^2 = x^2 + 7x + 10$.

Either way, we find that the area is $x^2 + 7x + 10$.

88. $t^2 + 7t + 12$

89.

We can find the shaded area in two ways.

Method 1: The figure is a square with side $x + 7$, so the area is $(x + 7)^2 = x^2 + 14x + 49$.

Method 2: We add the areas of A, B, C, and D.

$x \cdot x + x \cdot 7 + 7 \cdot 7 + 7 \cdot x = x^2 + 7x + 49 + 7x = x^2 + 14x + 49$.

Either way, we find that the total shaded area is $x^2 + 14x + 49$.

90. $a^2 + 10a + 25$

91.

We can find the shaded area in two ways.

Method 1: The figure is a rectangle with dimensions $t + 6$ by $t + 4$, so the area is $(t + 6)(t + 4) = t^2 + 4t + 6t + 24 = t^2 + 10t + 24$.

Method 2: We add the areas of A, B, C, and D.

$t \cdot t + t \cdot 6 + 6 \cdot 4 + 4 \cdot t = t^2 + 6t + 24 + 4t = t^2 + 10t + 24.$

Either way, we find that the total shaded area is $t^2 + 10t + 24$.

92. $x^2 + 10x + 21$

93.

We can find the shaded area in two ways.

Method 1: The figure is a rectangle with dimensions $t + 9$ by $t + 4$, so the area is

$(t + 9)(t + 4) = t^2 + 4t + 9t + 36 = t^2 + 13t + 36$

Method 2: We add the areas of A, B, C, and D.

$9 \cdot t + t \cdot t + 4 \cdot t + 4 \cdot 9 = 9t + t^2 + 4t + 36 = t^2 + 13t + 36.$

Either way, we find that the total shaded area is $t^2 + 13t + 36$.

94. $a^2 + 8a + 7$

95.

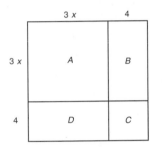

We can find the shaded area in two ways.

Method 1: The figure is a square with side $3x + 4$, so the area is $(3x + 4)^2 = 9x^2 + 24x + 16$.

Method 2: We add the areas of A, B, C, and D.

$3x \cdot 3x + 3x \cdot 4 + 4 \cdot 4 + 3x \cdot 4 = 9x^2 + 12x + 16 + 12x = 9x^2 + 24x + 16.$

Either way, we find that the total shaded area is $9x^2 + 24x + 16$.

96. $25t^2 + 20t + 4$

97. We draw a square with side $x + 5$.

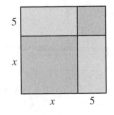

98.

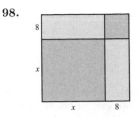

99. We draw a square with side $t + 9$.

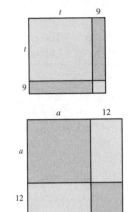

100.

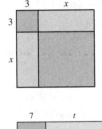

101. We draw a square with side $3 + x$.

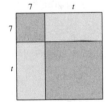

102.

103. $P(x) \cdot P(x)$

$= (4x - 1)(4x - 1)$

$= 16x^2 - 4x - 4x + 1 \qquad$ Using FOIL

$= 16x^2 - 8x + 1$

We could also consider this to be the square of a binomial:
$P(x) \cdot P(x) = (4x - 1)^2 = 16x^2 - 8x + 1.$

104. $9x^4 + 6x^2 + 1$

105. $[F(x)]^2$

$= \left(2x - \dfrac{1}{3}\right)^2 \qquad$ Squaring a binomial

$= (2x)^2 - 2 \cdot 2x \cdot \dfrac{1}{3} + \left(\dfrac{1}{3}\right)^2$

$= 4x^2 - \dfrac{4}{3}x + \dfrac{1}{9}$

106. $25x^2 - 5x + \dfrac{1}{4}$

107. *Writing Exercise*

108. *Writing Exercise*

109. Familiarize. Let $t =$ the number of watts used by the television set. Then $10t =$ the number of watts used by the lamps, and $40t =$ the number of watts used by the air conditioner.

Translate.

$$\underbrace{\text{Lamp watts}}_{\downarrow} + \underbrace{\substack{\text{Air} \\ \text{conditioner} \\ \text{watts}}}_{\downarrow} + \underbrace{\substack{\text{Television} \\ \text{watts}}}_{\downarrow} = \underbrace{\substack{\text{Total} \\ \text{watts}}}_{\downarrow}$$

$$10t \;+\; 40t \;+\; t \;=\; 2550$$

Solve. We solve the equation.

$$10t + 40t + t = 2550$$
$$51t = 2550$$
$$t = 50$$

The possible solution is:

Television, t: 50 watts

Lamps, $10t$: $10 \cdot 50$, or 500 watts

Air conditioner, $40t$: $40 \cdot 50$, or 2000 watts

Check. The number of watts used by the lamps, 500, is 10 times 50, the number used by the television. The number of watts used by the air conditioner, 2000, is 40 times 50, the number used by the television. Also, $50 + 500 + 2000 = 2550$, the total wattage used.

State. The television uses 50 watts, the lamps use 500 watts, and the air conditioner uses 2000 watts.

110. II

111. $5xy = 8$

$$y = \frac{8}{5x} \qquad \text{Dividing both sides by } 5x$$

112. $a = \dfrac{c}{3b}$

113. $ax - b = c$

$$ax = b + c \qquad \text{Adding } b \text{ to both sides}$$
$$x = \frac{b + c}{a} \qquad \text{Dividing both sides by } a$$

114. $t = \dfrac{u - r}{s}$

115. *Writing Exercise*

116. *Writing Exercise*

117. $(4x^2 + 9)(2x + 3)(2x - 3)$
$$= (4x^2 + 9)(4x^2 - 9)$$
$$= 16x^4 - 81$$

118. $81a^4 - 1$

119. $(3t - 2)^2(3t + 2)^2$
$$= [(3t - 2)(3t + 2)]^2$$
$$= (9t^2 - 4)^2$$
$$= 81t^4 - 72t^2 + 16$$

120. $625a^4 - 50a^2 + 1$

121. $(t^3 - 1)^4(t^3 + 1)^4$
$$= [(t^3 - 1)(t^3 + 1)]^4$$
$$= (t^6 - 1)^4$$
$$= [(t^6 - 1)^2]^2$$
$$= (t^{12} - 2t^6 + 1)^2$$
$$= (t^{12} - 2t^6 + 1)(t^{12} - 2t^6 + 1)$$
$$= t^{24} - 2t^{18} + t^{12} - 2t^{18} + 4t^{12} - 2t^6 + t^{12} - 2t^6 + 1$$
$$= t^{24} - 4t^{18} + 6t^{12} - 4t^6 + 1$$

122. $1050.4081x^2 + 348.0834x + 28.8369$

123. $18 \times 22 = (20 - 2)(20 + 2) = 20^2 - 2^2 = 400 - 4 = 396$

124. 9951

125. $(x + 2)(x - 5) = (x + 1)(x - 3)$
$$x^2 - 5x + 2x - 10 = x^2 - 3x + x - 3$$
$$x^2 - 3x - 10 = x^2 - 2x - 3$$
$$-3x - 10 = -2x - 3 \qquad \text{Adding} -x^2$$
$$-3x + 2x = 10 - 3 \qquad \text{Adding } 2x \text{ and } 10$$
$$-x = 7$$
$$x = -7$$

The solution is -7.

126. 0

127. If $l =$ the length, then $l + 1 =$ the height, and $l - 1 =$ the width. Recall that the volume of a rectangular solid is given by length $\times$ width $\times$ height.

Volume $= l(l - 1)(l + 1) = l(l^2 - 1) = l^3 - l$

128. $w^3 + 3w^2 + 2w$

129.

The dimensions of the shaded area, B, are $Q - 14$ by $Q - 5$, so one expression is $(Q - 14)(Q - 5)$.

To find another expression we find the area of regions B and C together and subtract the area of region C. The region consisting of B and C together has dimensions Q by $Q - 14$, so its area is $Q(Q - 14)$. Region C has dimensions 5 by $Q-14$, so its area is $5(Q-14)$. Then another expression for the shaded area, B, is $Q(Q-14) - 5(Q-14)$.

It is possible to find other equivalent expressions also.

130. $17F + 7(F - 17)$, $F^2 - (F - 17)(F - 7)$; other equivalent expressions are possible.

131.

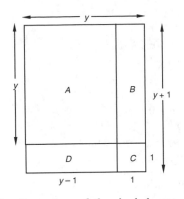

The dimensions of the shaded area, regions A and D together, are $y + 1$ by $y - 1$ so the area is $(y + 1)(y - 1)$.

To find another expression we add the areas of regions A and D. The dimensions of region A are y by $y - 1$, and the dimensions of region D are $y - 1$ by 1, so the sum of the areas is $y(y - 1) + (y - 1)(1)$, or $y(y - 1) + y - 1$.

It is possible to find other equivalent expressions also.

132. 10, 11, 12

Exercise Set 5.6

1. We replace x by 5 and y by -2.
$$x^2 - 3y^2 + 2xy = 5^2 - 3(-2)^2 + 2 \cdot 5(-2) =$$
$$25 - 12 - 20 = -7.$$

2. 85

3. We replace x by 2, y by -3, and z by -4.
$$xyz^2 - z = 2(-3)(-4)^2 - (-4) = -96 + 4 = -92$$

4. 14

5. Evaluate the polynomial for $h = 160$ and $A = 50$.
$$0.041h - 0.018A - 2.69$$
$$= 0.041(160) - 0.018(50) - 2.69$$
$$= 6.56 - 0.9 - 2.69$$
$$= 2.97$$

The woman's lung capacity is 2.97 liters.

6. 3.715 liters

7. Evaluate the polynomial for $h = 300$, $v = 40$, and $t = 2$.
$$h + vt - 4.9t^2$$
$$= 300 + 40 \cdot 2 - 4.9(2)^2$$
$$= 300 + 80 - 19.6$$
$$= 360.4$$

The rocket will be 360.4 m above the ground 2 seconds after blast off.

8. 205.9 m

9. Evaluate the polynomial for $h = 7\frac{1}{2}$, or $\frac{15}{2}$, $r = 1\frac{1}{4}$, or $\frac{5}{4}$, and $\pi \approx 3.14$.
$$2\pi rh + \pi r^2 \approx 2(3.14)\left(\frac{5}{4}\right)\left(\frac{15}{2}\right) + (3.14)\left(\frac{5}{4}\right)^2$$
$$\approx 2(3.14)\left(\frac{5}{4}\right)\left(\frac{15}{2}\right) + (3.14)\left(\frac{25}{16}\right)$$
$$\approx 58.875 + 4.90625$$
$$\approx 63.78125$$

The surface area is about 63.78125 in^2.

10. 20.60625 in^2

11. $x^3y - 2xy + 3x^2 - 5$

Term	Coefficient	Degree	
x^3y	1	4	(Think: $x^3y = x^3y^1$)
$-2xy$	-2	2	(Think: $-2xy = -2x^1y^1$)
$3x^2$	3	2	
-5	-5	0	(Think: $-5 = -5x^0$)

The degree of the polynomial is the degree of the term of highest degree. The term of highest degree is x^3y. Its degree is 4, so the degree of the polynomial is 4.

12. Coefficients: 1, -1, 9, 7

Degrees: 3, 2, 3, 0; 3

13. $17x^2y^3 - 3x^3yz - 7$

Term	Coefficient	Degree	
$17x^2y^3$	17	5	
$-3x^3yz$	-3	5	(Think: $-3x^3yz = -3x^3y^1z^1$)
-7	-7	0	(Think: $-7 = -7x^0$)

The terms of highest degree are $17x^2y^3$ and $-3x^3yz$. Each has degree 5. The degree of the polynomial is 5.

14. Coefficients: 6, -1, 8, -1

Degrees: 0, 2, 4, 5; 5

15. $7a + b - 4a - 3b = (7 - 4)a + (1 - 3)b = 3a - 2b$

16. $3r - 3s$

17. $3x^2y - 2xy^2 + x^2 + 5x$

There are <u>no</u> like terms, so none of the terms can be collected.

18. $m^3 + 2m^2n - 3m^2 + 3mn^2$

19. $2u^2v - 3uv^2 + 6u^2v - 2uv^2 + 7u^2$
$$= (2 + 6)u^2v + (-3 - 2)uv^2 + 7u^2$$
$$= 8u^2v - 5uv^2 + 7u^2$$

20. $-2x^2 - 4xy + 3y^2$

21. $5a^2c - 2ab^2 + a^2b - 3ab^2 + a^2c - 2ab^2$
$$= (5 + 1)a^2c + (-2 - 3 - 2)ab^2 + a^2b$$
$$= 6a^2c - 7ab^2 + a^2b$$

22. $2s^2t - 6r^2t - st^2$

23.
$$(4x^2 - xy + y^2) + (-x^2 - 3xy + 2y^2)$$
$$= (4 - 1)x^2 + (-1 - 3)xy + (1 + 2)y^2$$
$$= 3x^2 - 4xy + 3y^2$$

24. $-3r^3 + 2rs - 9s^2$

25.
$$(3a^4 - 5ab + 6ab^2) - (9a^4 + 3ab - ab^2)$$
$$= 3a^4 - 5ab + 6ab^2 - 9a^4 - 3ab + ab^2$$
$$\text{Adding the opposite}$$
$$= (3 - 9)a^4 + (-5 - 3)ab + (6 + 1)ab^2$$
$$= -6a^4 - 8ab + 7ab^2$$

26. $-5r^2t - 6rt + 6rt^2$

27. $(5r^2 - 4rt + t^2) + (-6r^2 - 5rt - t^2) + (-5r^2 + 4rt - t^2)$

Observe that the polynomials $5r^2 - 4rt + t^2$ and $-5r^2 + 4rt - t^2$ are opposites. Thus, their sum is 0 and the sum in the exercise is the remaining polynomial, $-6r^2 - 5rt - t^2$.

28. $2x^2 - 3xy + y^2$

29.
$$(x^3 - y^3) - (-2x^3 + x^2y - xy^2 + 2y^3)$$
$$= x^3 - y^3 + 2x^3 - x^2y + xy^2 - 2y^3$$
$$= 3x^3 - 3y^3 - x^2y + xy^2, \text{ or}$$
$$3x^3 - x^2y + xy^2 - 3y^3$$

30. $6a^3 - 2a^2b + ab^2 - 2b^3$

31.
$$(2y^4x^2 - 5y^3x) + (5y^4x^2 - y^3x) + (3y^4x^2 - 2y^3x)$$
$$= (2 + 5 + 3)y^4x^2 + (-5 - 1 - 2)y^3x$$
$$= 10y^4x^2 - 8y^3x$$

32. $15a^2b - 4ab$

33.
$$(4x + 5y) + (-5x + 6y) - (7x + 3y)$$
$$= 4x + 5y - 5x + 6y - 7x - 3y$$
$$= (4 - 5 - 7)x + (5 + 6 - 3)y$$
$$= -8x + 8y$$

34. $-5b$

35.
$$\qquad\quad \text{F} \qquad \text{O} \qquad \text{I} \qquad \text{L}$$
$$(3z - u)(2z + 3u) = 6z^2 + 9zu - 2uz - 3u^2$$
$$= 6z^2 + 7zu - 3u^2$$

36. $10x^2 - 13xy - 3y^2$

37.
$$\qquad\qquad \text{F} \qquad \text{O} \qquad \text{I} \qquad \text{L}$$
$$(xy + 7)(xy - 4) = x^2y^2 - 4xy + 7xy - 28 - 28$$
$$= x^2y^2 + 3xy - 28$$

38. $a^2b^2 - 2ab - 15$

39.
$$(2a - b)(2a + b) \quad [(A + B)(A - B) = A^2 - B^2]$$
$$= 4a^2 - b^2$$

40. $a^2 - 9b^2$

41.
$$\qquad\qquad \text{F} \qquad \text{O} \qquad \text{I} \qquad \text{L}$$
$$(5rt - 2)(3rt + 1) = 15r^2t^2 + 5rt - 6rt - 2$$
$$= 15r^2t^2 - rt - 2$$

42. $12x^2y^2 + 2xy - 2$

43.
$$(m^3n + 8)(m^3n - 6)$$
$$\qquad \text{F} \qquad \text{O} \qquad \text{I} \qquad \text{L}$$
$$= m^6n^2 - 6m^3n + 8m^3n - 48$$
$$= m^6n^2 + 2m^3n - 48$$

44. $12 - c^2d^2 - c^4d^4$

45.
$$(6x - 2y)(5x - 3y)$$
$$\qquad \text{F} \qquad \text{O} \qquad \text{I} \qquad \text{L}$$
$$= 30x^2 - 18xy - 10xy + 6y^2$$
$$= 30x^2 - 28xy + 6y^2$$

46. $35a^2 - 2ab - 24b^2$

47.
$$(pq + 0.2)(0.4pq - 0.1)$$
$$\qquad \text{F} \qquad \text{O} \qquad \text{I} \qquad \text{L}$$
$$= 0.4p^2q^2 - 0.1pq + 0.08pq - 0.02$$
$$= 0.4p^2q^2 - 0.02pq - 0.02$$

48. $0.2a^2b^2 + 0.18ab - 0.18$

49.
$$(x + h)^2$$
$$= x^2 + 2xh + h^2 \quad [(A + B)^2 = A^2 + 2AB + B^2]$$

50. $r^2 + 2rt + t^2$

51.
$$(4a + 5b)^2$$
$$= 16a^2 + 40ab + 25b^2 \quad [(A+B)^2 = A^2 + 2AB + B^2]$$

52. $9x^2 + 12xy + 4y^2$

53.
$$(c^2 - d)(c^2 + d) = (c^2)^2 - d^2$$
$$= c^4 - d^2$$

54. $p^6 - 25q^2$

55.
$$(ab + cd^2)(ab - cd^2) = (ab)^2 - (cd^2)^2$$
$$= a^2b^2 - c^2d^4$$

56. $x^2y^2 - p^2q^2$

57.
$$(a + b - c)(a + b + c)$$
$$= [(a + b) - c][(a + b) + c]$$
$$= (a + b)^2 - c^2$$
$$= a^2 + 2ab + b^2 - c^2$$

58. $x^2 + 2xy + y^2 - z^2$

59.
$$[a + b + c][a - (b + c)]$$
$$= [a + (b + c)][a - (b + c)]$$
$$= a^2 - (b + c)^2$$
$$= a^2 - (b^2 + 2bc + c^2)$$
$$= a^2 - b^2 - 2bc - c^2$$

60. $a^2 - b^2 - 2bc - c^2$

61. The figure is a rectangle with dimensions $a + b$ by $a + c$. Its area is $(a + b)(a + c) = a^2 + ac + ab + bc$.

62. $x^2 + 2xy + y^2$

63. The figure is a parallelogram with base $x + z$ and height $x - z$. Thus the area is $(x + z)(x - z) = x^2 - z^2$.

64. $\frac{1}{2}a^2b^2 - 2$

65. The figure is a square with side $x + y + z$. Thus the area is
$$(x + y + z)^2$$
$$= [(x + y) + z]^2$$
$$= (x + y)^2 + 2(x + y)(z) + z^2$$
$$= x^2 + 2xy + y^2 + 2xz + 2yz + z^2.$$

66. $a^2 + 2ac + c^2 + ad + cd + ab + bc + bd$

67. The figure is a triangle with base $x + 2y$ and height $x - y$. Thus the area is $\frac{1}{2}(x + 2y)(x - y) = \frac{1}{2}(x^2 + xy - 2y^2) = \frac{1}{2}x^2 + \frac{1}{2}xy - y^2$.

68. $m^2 - n^2$

69. We draw a rectangle with dimensions $r + s$ by $u + v$.

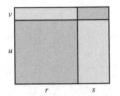

70.

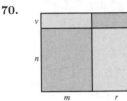

71. We draw a rectangle with dimensions $a + b + c$ by $a + d + f$.

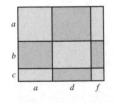

72.

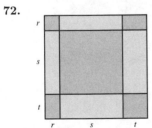

73. $A = P(1 + i)^2$
$A = P(1 + 2i + i^2)$
$A = P + 2Pi + Pi^2$

74. $A = P + Pi + \dfrac{Pi^2}{4}$

75. a) Replace x with $t - 1$.
$$f(t - 1) = (t - 1)^2 + 5$$
$$= t^2 - 2t + 1 + 5$$
$$= t^2 - 2t + 6$$

b) $f(a + h) - f(a)$
$$= [(a + h)^2 + 5] - (a^2 + 5)$$
$$= a^2 + 2ah + h^2 + 5 - a^2 - 5$$
$$= 2ah + h^2$$

c) $f(a) - f(a - h)$
$$= (a^2 + 5) - [(a - h)^2 + 5]$$
$$= a^2 + 5 - (a^2 - 2ah + h^2 + 5)$$
$$= a^2 + 5 - a^2 + 2ah - h^2 - 5$$
$$= 2ah - h^2$$

76. a) $p^2 + 2p + 8$

b) $2ah + h^2$

c) $2ah - h^2$

77. *Writing Exercise*

78. *Writing Exercise*

79.
$$5 + \frac{7 + 4 + 2 \cdot 5}{3}$$

$$= 5 + \frac{7 + 4 + 10}{3} \qquad \text{Multiplying}$$

$$= 5 + \frac{21}{3} \qquad \text{Adding in the numerator}$$

$$= 5 + 7 \qquad \text{Dividing}$$

$$= 12 \qquad \text{Adding}$$

80. 5

81.
$$(4 + 3 \cdot 5 + 8) \div 3 \cdot 3$$
$$= (4 + 15 + 8) \div 3 \cdot 3 \qquad \text{Multiplying inside the parentheses}$$
$$= 27 \div 3 \cdot 3 \qquad \text{Adding}$$
$$= 9 \cdot 3 \qquad \text{Dividing}$$
$$= 27 \qquad \text{Multiplying}$$

82. 36

83.
$$[3 \cdot 5 - 4 \cdot 2 + 7(-3)] \div (-2)$$
$$= (15 - 8 - 21) \div (-2) \qquad \text{Multiplying}$$
$$= -14 \div (-2) \qquad \text{Subtracting}$$
$$= 7 \qquad \text{Dividing}$$

84. 5

85. *Writing Exercise*

86. *Writing Exercise*

87. The unshaded region is a circle with radius $a - b$. Then the shaded area is the area of a circle with radius a less the area of a circle with radius $a - b$. Thus, we have:

Shaded area $= \pi a^2 - \pi(a-b)^2$
$$= \pi a^2 - \pi(a^2 - 2ab + b^2)$$
$$= \pi a^2 - \pi a^2 + 2\pi ab - \pi b^2$$
$$= 2\pi ab - \pi b^2$$

88. $4xy - 4y^2$

89. The shaded area is the area of a square with side a less the areas of 4 squares with side b. Thus, the shaded area is $a^2 - 4 \cdot b^2$, or $a^2 - 4b^2$.

90. $\pi x^2 + 2xy$

91. a) The figure is a square with side A, so its area is $A \cdot A$, or A^2. The unshaded square has side B, so its area is $B \cdot B$, or B^2. Then the shaded area is $A^2 - B^2$.

   b) In the upper left-hand corner we have a square with side $A - B$, so its area is $(A - B)(A - B)$, or $A^2 - 2AB + B^2$. The rectangles in the upper right-hand and lower left-hand corners have dimensions $A - B$ by B, so each has area $(A-B)(B)$, or $AB - B^2$. The sum of these three areas is $A^2 - 2AB + B^2 + AB - B^2 + AB - B^2$, or $A^2 - B^2$.

92. $2\pi nh + 2\pi mh + 2\pi n^2 - 2\pi m^2$

93. The surface area of the solid consists of the surface area of a rectangular solid with dimensions x by x by h less the areas of 2 circles with radius r plus the lateral surface area of a right circular cylinder with radius r and height h. Thus, we have

$$2x^2 + 2xh + 2xh - 2\pi r^2 + 2\pi rh, \text{ or}$$
$$2x^2 + 4xh - 2\pi r^2 + 2\pi rh.$$

94. *Writing Exercise*

95. $(x+a)(x-b)(x-a)(x+b)$
$$= [(x+a)(x-a)][(x-b)(x+b)]$$
$$= (x^2 - a^2)(x^2 - b^2)$$
$$= x^4 - b^2 x^2 - a^2 x^2 + a^2 b^2$$

96. $P + 2Pr + Pr^2$

97. Replace t with 2 and multiply.
$$P(1-r)^2$$
$$= P(1 - 2r + r^2)$$
$$= P - 2Pr + Pr^2$$

98. \$15,638.03

99. Substitute \$90,000 for P, 12.5% or 0.125 for r, and 4 for t.
$$P(1-r)^t$$
$$= \$90,000(1 - 0.125)^4$$
$$\approx \$52,756.35$$

Exercise Set 5.7

1. $\dfrac{40x^5 - 16x}{8} = \dfrac{40x^5}{8} - \dfrac{16x}{8}$
$$= \frac{40}{8}x^5 - \frac{16}{8}x \quad \text{Dividing coefficients}$$
$$= 5x^5 - 2x$$

To check, we multiply the quotient by 8:
$$(5x^5 - 2x)8 = 40x^5 - 16x$$
The answer checks.

2. $2a^4 - \dfrac{1}{2}a^2$

3. $\dfrac{u - 2u^2 + u^7}{u}$
$$= \frac{u}{u} - \frac{2u^2}{u} + \frac{u^7}{u}$$
$$= 1 - 2u + u^6$$

Check: We multiply.
$$\begin{array}{r} 1 - 2u + u^6 \\ u \\ \hline u - 2u^2 + u^7 \end{array}$$

4. $50x^4 - 7x^3 + x$

5. $(15t^3 - 24t^2 + 6t) \div (3t)$
$$= \frac{15t^3 - 24t^2 + 6t}{3t}$$
$$= \frac{15t^3}{3t} - \frac{24t^2}{3t} + \frac{6t}{3t}$$
$$= 5t^2 - 8t + 2$$

Check: We multiply.
$$\begin{array}{r} 5t^2 - 8t + 2 \\ 3t \\ \hline 15t^3 - 24t^2 + 6t \end{array}$$

6. $4t^2 - 3t + 6$

7. $\dfrac{14y^3 - 9y^2 - 8y}{2y^2}$
$$= \frac{14y^3}{2y^2} - \frac{9y^2}{2y^2} - \frac{8y}{2y^2}$$
$$= 7y - \frac{9}{2} - \frac{4}{y}$$

8. $3a^3 + \dfrac{9a}{2} - \dfrac{4}{a}$

9. $\dfrac{15x^7 - 21x^4 - 3x^2}{-3x^2}$
$$= \frac{15x^7}{-3x^2} + \frac{-21x^4}{-3x^2} + \frac{-3x^2}{-3x^2}$$
$$= -5x^5 + 7x^2 + 1$$

10. $-6y^5 + 3y^3 + 2y$

11.
$$\frac{9r^2s^2 + 3r^2s - 6rs^2}{-3rs}$$
$$= \frac{9r^2s^2}{-3rs} + \frac{3r^2s}{-3rs} - \frac{6rs^2}{-3rs}$$
$$= -3rs - r + 2s$$

Check: We multiply.
$$\begin{array}{r} -3rs - r + 2s \\ -3rs \\ \hline 9r^2s^2 + 3r^2s - 6rs^2 \end{array}$$

12. $1 - 2x^2y + 3x^4y^5$

13.
$$(a^2b - a^3b^3 - a^5b^5) \div (a^2b)$$
$$= \frac{a^2b}{a^2b} - \frac{a^3b^3}{a^2b} - \frac{a^5b^5}{a^2b}$$
$$= 1 - ab^2 - a^3b^4$$

14. $x - xy - x^2$

15.
$$(x^2 + 10x + 21) \div (x + 7)$$
$$= \frac{(x+7)(x+3)}{x+7}$$
$$= \frac{(x\!\!\!\!\diagup\!\!7)(x+3)}{x\!\!\!\!\diagup\!\!7}$$
$$= x + 3$$
The answer is $x + 3$.

16. $y - 4$

17.
$$\begin{array}{r} a - 12 \\ a+4 \overline{\smash{\big)}\,a^2 - 8a - 16} \\ \underline{a^2 + 4a} \\ -12a - 16 \quad (a^2-8a)-(a^2+4a)=-12a \\ \underline{-12a - 48} \\ 32 \quad (-12a-16)-(-12a-48)=32 \end{array}$$
The answer is $a - 12$, R 32, or $a - 12 + \dfrac{32}{a+4}$.

18. $y - 5 + \dfrac{-50}{y - 5}$

19.
$$\begin{array}{r} x - 4 \\ x-5 \overline{\smash{\big)}\,x^2 - 9x + 21} \\ \underline{x^2 - 5x} \\ -4x + 21 \\ \underline{-4x + 20} \\ 1 \end{array}$$
The answer is $x - 4$, R 1, or $x - 4 + \dfrac{1}{x - 5}$.

20. $x - 4 + \dfrac{-5}{x - 7}$

21.
$$(y^2 - 25) \div (y + 5) = \frac{y^2 - 25}{y + 5}$$
$$= \frac{(y+5)(y-5)}{y+5}$$
$$= \frac{(y\!\!\!\!\diagup\!\!5)(y-5)}{y\!\!\!\!\diagup\!\!5}$$
$$= y - 5$$

We could also find this quotient as follows.
$$\begin{array}{r} y - 5 \\ y+5 \overline{\smash{\big)}\,y^2 + 0y - 25} \quad \text{Writing in the missing} \\ \underline{y^2 + 5y} \qquad\qquad \text{term} \\ -5y - 25 \\ \underline{-5y - 25} \\ 0 \end{array}$$
The answer is $y - 5$.

22. $a + 9$

23.
$$\begin{array}{r} y^2 - 2y - 1 \\ y-2 \overline{\smash{\big)}\,y^3 - 4y^2 + 3y - 6} \\ \underline{y^3 - 2y^2} \\ -2y^2 + 3y \\ \underline{-2y^2 + 4y} \\ -y - 6 \\ \underline{-y + 2} \\ -8 \end{array}$$
The answer is $y^2 - 2y - 1$, R -8, or
$$y^2 - 2y - 1 + \frac{-8}{y - 2}.$$

24. $x^2 - 2x - 2 + \dfrac{-13}{x - 3}$

25.
$$\begin{array}{r} a^2 - 2a + 4 \\ a+2 \overline{\smash{\big)}\,a^3 + 0a^2 + 0a + 8} \quad \leftarrow \text{Writing in the missing} \\ \qquad\qquad\qquad\qquad \text{terms} \\ \underline{a^3 + 2a^2} \\ -2a^2 + 0a \quad \leftarrow a^3 - (a^3 + 2a^2) = -2a^2 \\ \underline{-2a^2 - 4a} \\ 4a + 8 \leftarrow -2a^2 - (-2a^2 - 4a) = 4a \\ \underline{4a + 8} \\ 0 \leftarrow (4a+8) - (4a+8) = 0 \end{array}$$
The answer is $a^2 - 2a + 4$.

26. $t^2 - 3t + 9$

27. $(t^3 + t - t^2 - 1) \div (t + 1)$, or $(t^3 - t^2 + t - 1) \div (t + 1)$
$$\begin{array}{r} t^2 - 2t + 3 \\ t+1 \overline{\smash{\big)}\,t^3 - t^2 + t - 1} \\ \underline{t^3 + t^2} \\ -2t^2 + t \quad \leftarrow (t^3 - t^2) - (t^3 + t^2) = -2t^2 \\ \underline{-2t^2 - 2t} \\ 3t - 1 \leftarrow (-2t^2 + t) - \\ (-2t^2 - 2t) = 3t \\ \underline{3t + 3} \\ -4 \end{array}$$
The answer is $t^2 - 2t + 3 + \dfrac{-4}{t + 1}$.

28. $x^2 + 1$

29.

$$
\begin{array}{r}
a^2 + 4a + 15 \\
a-4\overline{)\ a^3 + 0a^2 -\ a + 10} \\
\underline{a^3 - 4a^2} \\
4a^2 -\ a \\
\underline{4a^2 - 16a} \\
15a + 10 \\
\underline{15a - 60} \\
70
\end{array}
$$

The answer is $a^2 + 4a + 15$, R 70, or

$a^2 + 4a + 15 + \dfrac{70}{a-4}$.

30. $x^2 - 2x + 3$

31.

$$
\begin{array}{r}
t^2\quad -1 \\
t^2+5\overline{)\ t^4+0t^3+4t^2+3t-6} \leftarrow \text{Writing in the} \\
\underline{t^4\quad+5t^2}\qquad\qquad \text{missing term} \\
-t^2+3t-6 \leftarrow (t^4+4t^2)- \\
\underline{-t^2\qquad-5}\quad (t^4+5t^2)=-t^2 \\
3t-1 \leftarrow (-t^2+3t-6)- \\
(-t^2-5)=3t-1
\end{array}
$$

The answer is $t^2 - 1 + \dfrac{3t-1}{t^2+5}$.

32. $t^2 + 1 + \dfrac{4t-2}{t^2-3}$

33. $(4x^4-3-x-4x^2)\div(2x^2-3)$, or $(4x^4-4x^2-x-3)\div(2x^2-3)$

$$
\begin{array}{r}
2x^2\qquad +1 \\
2x^2-3\overline{)\ 4x^4+0x^3-4x^2-x-3} \leftarrow \text{Writing in the} \\
\underline{4x^4\qquad-6x^2}\qquad\qquad \text{missing term} \\
2x^2-x-3 \leftarrow (4x^4-4x^2)- \\
(4x^4-6x^2)=2x^2 \\
\underline{2x^2\qquad-3} \\
-x \leftarrow (2x^2-x-3)- \\
(2x^2-3)=-x
\end{array}
$$

The answer is $2x^2 + 1 + \dfrac{-x}{2x^2-3}$.

34. $3x^2 - 3 + \dfrac{x-1}{2x^2+1}$

35.

$$
\begin{array}{r}
4x^2 -\ 6x +\ 9 \\
2x+3\overline{)\ 8x^3\qquad\qquad +27} \\
\underline{8x^3 + 12x^2} \\
-12x^2 +\ 0x \\
\underline{-12x^2 - 18x} \\
18x + 27 \\
\underline{18x + 27} \\
0
\end{array}
$$

Since $g(x)$ is 0 for $x = -\dfrac{3}{2}$, we have

$F(x) = 4x^2 - 6x + 9$, provided $x \neq -\dfrac{3}{2}$.

36. $16x^2 + 8x + 4$, $x \neq \dfrac{1}{2}$

37. $F(x) = \dfrac{f(x)}{g(x)} = \dfrac{6x^2 - 11x - 10}{3x+2}$

$$
\begin{array}{r}
2x -\ 5 \\
3x+2\overline{)\ 6x^2 - 11x - 10} \\
\underline{6x^2 +\ 4x} \\
-15x - 10 \\
\underline{-15x - 10} \\
0
\end{array}
$$

Since $g(x)$ is 0 for $x = -\dfrac{2}{3}$, we have

$F(x) = 2x - 5$, provided $x \neq -\dfrac{2}{3}$.

38. $4x + 3$, $x \neq \dfrac{7}{2}$

39. $(x^3 - 2x^2 + 2x - 7) \div (x + 1) =$
$(x^3 - 2x^2 + 2x - 7) \div [x - (-1)]$

$$
\begin{array}{r|rrrr}
-1 & 1 & -2 & 2 & -7 \\
   &   & -1 & 3 & -5 \\
\hline
   & 1 & -3 & 5 & \!\!\!\!| -12
\end{array}
$$

The answer is $x^2 - 3x + 5$, R -12, or $x^2 - 3x + 5 + \dfrac{-12}{x+1}$.

40. $x^2 - x + 1 + \dfrac{-6}{x-1}$

41. $(a^2 + 8a + 11) \div (a + 3) =$
$(a^2 + 8a + 11) \div [a - (-3)]$

$$
\begin{array}{r|rrr}
-3 & 1 & 8 & 11 \\
   &   & -3 & -15 \\
\hline
   & 1 & 5 & \!\!\!\!| -4
\end{array}
$$

The answer is $a + 5$, R -4, or $a + 5 + \dfrac{-4}{a+3}$.

42. $a + 3 + \dfrac{-4}{a+5}$

43. $(x^3 - 7x^2 - 13x + 3) \div (x - 2)$

$$
\begin{array}{r|rrrr}
2 & 1 & -7 & -13 & 3 \\
  &   & 2 & -10 & -46 \\
\hline
  & 1 & -5 & -23 & \!\!\!\!| -43
\end{array}
$$

The answer is $x^2 - 5x - 23$, R -43, or

$x^2 - 5x - 23 + \dfrac{-43}{x-2}$.

44. $x^2 - 9x + 5 + \dfrac{-7}{x+2}$

45. $(3x^3 + 7x^2 - 4x + 3) \div (x + 3) =$
$(3x^3 + 7x^2 - 4x + 3) \div [x - (-3)]$

$$
\begin{array}{r|rrrr}
-3 & 3 & 7 & -4 & 3 \\
   &   & -9 & 6 & -6 \\
\hline
   & 3 & -2 & 2 & \!\!\!\!| -3
\end{array}
$$

The answer is $3x^2 - 2x + 2$, R -3, or

$3x^2 - 2x + 2 + \dfrac{-3}{x+3}$.

46. $3x^2 + 16x + 44 + \dfrac{135}{x-3}$

47. $(y^3 - 3y + 10) \div (y - 2) =$
$(y^3 + 0y^2 - 3y + 10) \div (y - 2)$

$$\begin{array}{r|rrrr} 2 & 1 & 0 & -3 & 10 \\ & & 2 & 4 & 2 \\ \hline & 1 & 2 & 1 & 12 \end{array}$$

The answer is $y^2 + 2y + 1$, R 12, or
$y^2 + 2y + 1 + \dfrac{12}{y-2}$.

48. $x^2 - 4x + 8 + \dfrac{-8}{x+2}$

49. $(x^5 - 32) \div (x - 2) =$
$(x^5 + 0x^4 + 0x^3 + 0x^2 + 0x - 32) \div (x - 2)$

$$\begin{array}{r|rrrrrr} 2 & 1 & 0 & 0 & 0 & 0 & -32 \\ & & 2 & 4 & 8 & 16 & 32 \\ \hline & 1 & 2 & 4 & 8 & 16 & 0 \end{array}$$

The answer is $x^4 + 2x^3 + 4x^2 + 8x + 16$.

50. $y^4 + y^3 + y^2 + y + 1$

51. $(3x^3 + 1 - x + 7x^2) \div \left(x + \dfrac{1}{3}\right) =$

$(3x^3 + 7x^2 - x + 1) \div \left[x - \left(-\dfrac{1}{3}\right)\right]$

$$\begin{array}{r|rrrr} -\frac{1}{3} & 3 & 7 & -1 & 1 \\ & & -1 & -2 & 1 \\ \hline & 3 & 6 & -3 & 2 \end{array}$$

The answer is $3x^2 + 6x - 3$ R 2, or

$3x^2 + 6x - 3 + \dfrac{2}{x + \dfrac{1}{3}}$.

52. $8x^2 - 2x + 6 + \dfrac{2}{x - \dfrac{1}{2}}$

53. *Writing Exercise*

54. *Writing Exercise*

55. $-4 + (-13)$ Two negative numbers. Add the absolute values, 4 and 13, to get 17. Make the answer negative.

$-4 + (-13) = -17$

56. -23

57. $-9 - (-7) = -9 + 7 = -2$

58. 5

59. *Familiarize.* Let $w =$ the width. Then $w + 15 =$ the length. We draw a picture.

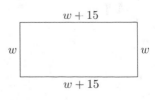

We will use the fact that the perimeter is 640 ft to find w (the width). Then we can find $w + 15$ (the length) and multiply the length and the width to find the area.

Translate.

$$\begin{array}{ccccccccc} \text{Width} & + & \text{Width} & + & \text{Length} & + & \text{Length} & = & \text{Perimeter} \\ w & + & w & + & (w+15) & + & (w+15) & = & 640 \end{array}$$

Carry out.

$$\begin{aligned} w + w + (w + 15) + (w + 15) &= 640 \\ 4w + 30 &= 640 \\ 4w &= 610 \\ w &= 152.5 \end{aligned}$$

If the width is 152.5, then the length is 152.5 + 15, or 167.5.

Check. The length, 167.5 ft, is 15 ft greater than the width, 152.5 ft. The perimeter is 152.5 + 152.5 + 167.5 + 167.5, or 640 ft. The answer checks.

State. The length is 167.5 ft.

60. 2

61. Graph: $3x - 2y = 12$.

We will graph the equation using intercepts. To find the y-intercept, we let $x = 0$ and solve for y.

$$\begin{aligned} 3 \cdot 0 - 2y &= 12 \\ -2y &= 12 \\ y &= -6 \end{aligned}$$

The y-intercept is $(0, -6)$.

To find the x-intercept, we let $y = 0$ and solve for x.

$$\begin{aligned} 3x - 2 \cdot 0 &= 12 \\ 3x &= 12 \\ x &= 4 \end{aligned}$$

The x-intercept is $(4, 0)$.

To find a third point, replace x with -2 and solve for y:

$$\begin{aligned} 3(-2) - 2y &= 12 \\ -6 - 2y &= 12 \\ -2y &= 18 \\ y &= -9 \end{aligned}$$

The point $(-2, -9)$ appears to line up with the intercepts, so we draw the graph.

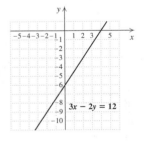

62.

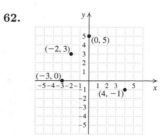

63. *Writing Exercise*

64. *Writing Exercise*

65.
$$(10x^{9k} - 32x^{6k} + 28x^{3k}) \div (2x^{3k})$$
$$= \frac{10x^{9k} - 32x^{6k} + 28x^{3k}}{2x^{3k}}$$
$$= \frac{10x^{9k}}{2x^{3k}} - \frac{32x^{6k}}{2x^{3k}} + \frac{28x^{3k}}{2x^{3k}}$$
$$= 5x^{9k-3k} - 16x^{6k-3k} + 14x^{3k-3k}$$
$$= 5x^{6k} - 16x^{3k} + 14$$

66. $15a^{6k} + 10a^{4k} - 20a^{2k}$

67.
$$\begin{array}{r} 3t^{2h} + 2t^h - 5 \\ 2t^h + 3 \overline{\smash{\big)}\ 6t^{3h} + 13t^{2h} - 4t^h - 15} \\ \underline{6t^{3h} + 9t^{2h}} \\ 4t^{2h} - 4t^h \\ \underline{4t^{2h} + 6t^h} \\ -10t^h - 15 \\ \underline{-10t^h - 15} \\ 0 \end{array}$$

The answer is $3t^{2h} + 2t^h - 5$.

68. $x^3 - ax^2 + a^2x - a^3 + \dfrac{a^2 + a^4}{x + a}$

69.
$$\begin{array}{r} a + 3 \\ 5a^2 - 7a - 2 \overline{\smash{\big)}\ 5a^3 + 8a^2 - 23a - 1} \\ \underline{5a^3 - 7a^2 - 2a} \\ 15a^2 - 21a - 1 \\ \underline{15a^2 - 21a - 6} \\ 5 \end{array}$$

The answer is $a + 3 + \dfrac{5}{5a^2 - 7a - 2}$.

70. $5y + 2 + \dfrac{-10y + 11}{3y^2 - 5y - 2}$

71.
$$(4x^5 - 14x^3 - x^2 + 3) + $$
$$(2x^5 + 3x^4 + x^3 - 3x^2 + 5x)$$
$$= 6x^5 + 3x^4 - 13x^3 - 4x^2 + 5x + 3$$

$$\begin{array}{r} 2x^2 + x - 3 \\ 3x^3 - 2x - 1 \overline{\smash{\big)}\ 6x^5 + 3x^4 - 13x^3 - 4x^2 + 5x + 3} \\ \underline{6x^5 \qquad - 4x^3 - 2x^2} \\ 3x^4 - 9x^3 - 2x^2 + 5x \\ \underline{3x^4 \qquad - 2x^2 - x} \\ -9x^3 + 6x + 3 \\ \underline{-9x^3 + 6x + 3} \\ 0 \end{array}$$

The answer is $2x^2 + x - 3$.

72. $5x^5 + 5x^4 - 8x^2 - 8x + 2$

73.
$$\begin{array}{r} x - 3 \\ x - 1 \overline{\smash{\big)}\ x^2 - 4x + c} \\ \underline{x^2 - x} \\ -3x + c \\ \underline{-3x + 3} \\ c - 3 \end{array}$$

We set the remainder equal to 0.
$$c - 3 = 0$$
$$c = 3$$

Thus, c must be 3.

74. -2

75.
$$\begin{array}{r} c^2 x + (2c + c^2) \\ x - 1 \overline{\smash{\big)}\ c^2 x^2 + 2cx + 1} \\ \underline{c^2 x^2 - c^2 x} \\ (2c + c^2)x + 1 \\ \underline{(2c + c^2)x - (2c + c^2)} \\ 1 + (2c + c^2) \end{array}$$

We set the remainder equal to 0.
$$c^2 + 2c + 1 = 0$$
$$(c + 1)^2 = 0$$
$$c + 1 = 0 \quad or \quad c + 1 = 0$$
$$c = -1 \quad or \qquad c = -1$$

Thus, c must be -1.

76. a), b)

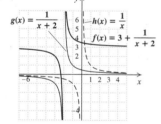

c) The graph of f looks like the graph of g, shifted up 3 units. The graph of g looks like the graph of h, shifted to the left 2 units.

77. *Writing Exercise*

Exercise Set 5.8

1. $5^{-2} = \dfrac{1}{5^2} = \dfrac{1}{25}$

2. $\dfrac{1}{2^4} = \dfrac{1}{16}$

3. $10^{-4} = \dfrac{1}{10^4} = \dfrac{1}{10,000}$

4. $\dfrac{1}{5^3} = \dfrac{1}{125}$

5. $(-2)^{-6} = \dfrac{1}{(-2)^6} = \dfrac{1}{64}$

6. $\dfrac{1}{(-3)^4} = \dfrac{1}{81}$

7. $x^{-8} = \dfrac{1}{x^8}$

8. $\dfrac{1}{t^5}$

9. $xy^{-2} = x \cdot \dfrac{1}{y^2} = \dfrac{x}{y^2}$

10. $\dfrac{b}{a^3}$

11. $r^{-5}t = \dfrac{1}{r^5} \cdot t = \dfrac{t}{r^5}$

12. $\dfrac{x}{y^9}$

13. $\dfrac{1}{t^{-7}} = t^7$

14. z^9

15. $\dfrac{1}{h^{-8}} = h^8$

16. a^{12}

17. $7^{-1} = \dfrac{1}{7^1} = \dfrac{1}{7}$

18. $\dfrac{1}{3}$

19. $\left(\dfrac{2}{5}\right)^{-2} = \left(\dfrac{5}{2}\right)^2 = \dfrac{5^2}{2^2} = \dfrac{25}{4}$

20. $\left(\dfrac{4}{3}\right)^2 = \dfrac{16}{9}$

21. $\left(\dfrac{a}{2}\right)^{-3} = \left(\dfrac{2}{a}\right)^3 = \dfrac{2^3}{a^3} = \dfrac{8}{a^3}$

22. $\left(\dfrac{3}{x}\right)^4 = \dfrac{81}{x^4}$

23. $\left(\dfrac{s}{t}\right)^{-7} = \left(\dfrac{t}{s}\right)^7 = \dfrac{t^7}{s^7}$

24. $\left(\dfrac{v}{r}\right)^5 = \dfrac{v^5}{r^5}$

25. $\dfrac{1}{7^2} = 7^{-2}$

26. 5^{-2}

27. $\dfrac{1}{t^6} = t^{-6}$

28. y^{-2}

29. $\dfrac{1}{a^4} = a^{-4}$

30. t^{-5}

31. $\dfrac{1}{p^8} = p^{-8}$

32. m^{-12}

33. $\dfrac{1}{5} = \dfrac{1}{5^1} = 5^{-1}$

34. 8^{-1}

35. $\dfrac{1}{t} = \dfrac{1}{t^1} = t^{-1}$

36. m^{-1}

37. $2^{-5} \cdot 2^8 = 2^{-5+8} = 2^3$, or 8

38. 5

39. $x^{-2} \cdot x^{-7} = x^{-2+(-7)} = x^{-9} = \dfrac{1}{x^9}$

40. $\dfrac{1}{x^{11}}$

41. $t^{-3} \cdot t = t^{-3} \cdot t^1 = t^{-3+1} = t^{-2} = \dfrac{1}{t^2}$

42. $\dfrac{1}{y^4}$

43. $(a^{-2})^9 = a^{-2\cdot 9} = a^{-18} = \dfrac{1}{a^{18}}$

44. $\dfrac{1}{x^{30}}$

45. $(t^{-3})^{-6} = t^{-3(-6)} = t^{18}$

46. a^{28}

47. $(t^4)^{-3} = t^{4(-3)} = t^{-12} = \dfrac{1}{t^{12}}$

48. $\dfrac{1}{t^{10}}$

49. $(x^{-2})^{-4} = x^{-2(-4)} = x^8$

50. t^{30}

51. $(ab)^{-3} = \dfrac{1}{(ab)^3} = \dfrac{1}{a^3 b^3}$

52. $\dfrac{1}{x^6 y^6}$

53. $(mn)^{-7} = \dfrac{1}{(mn)^7} = \dfrac{1}{m^7 n^7}$

54. $\dfrac{1}{a^9 b^9}$

55. $(3x^{-4})^2 = 3^2(x^{-4})^2 = 9x^{-8} = \dfrac{9}{x^8}$

56. $\dfrac{8}{a^{15}}$

57. $(5r^{-4}t^3)^2 = 5^2(r^{-4})^2(t^3)^2 = 25r^{-8}t^6 = \dfrac{25t^6}{r^8}$

58. $\dfrac{64x^{15}}{y^{18}}$

59. $\dfrac{t^7}{t^{-3}} = t^{7-(-3)} = t^{10}$

60. x^9

61. $\dfrac{y^{-7}}{y^{-3}} = y^{-7-(-3)} = y^{-4} = \dfrac{1}{y^4}$

62. $\dfrac{1}{z^4}$

63. $\dfrac{y^{-4}}{y^{-9}} = y^{-4-(-9)} = y^5$

64. a^4

65. $\dfrac{x^6}{x} = \dfrac{x^6}{x^1} = x^{6-1} = x^5$

66. x^2

67. $\dfrac{a^{-7}}{b^{-9}} = \dfrac{b^9}{a^7}$

68. $\dfrac{y^{10}}{x^6}$

69. $\dfrac{t^{-7}}{t^{-7}}$

Note that we have an expression divided by itself. Thus, the result is 1. We could also find this result as follows:
$$\frac{t^{-7}}{t^{-7}} = t^{-7-(-7)} = t^0 = 1.$$

70. $\dfrac{b^7}{a^5}$

71. $\dfrac{3x^{-5}}{y^{-6}z^{-2}} = \dfrac{3y^6 z^2}{x^5}$

72. $\dfrac{4b^5 c^7}{a^6}$

73. $\dfrac{3t^4}{s^{-2}u^{-4}} = 3s^2 t^4 u^4$

74. $\dfrac{5y^3}{x^8 z^2}$

75. $(x^4 y^5)^{-3} = (x^4)^{-3}(y^5)^{-3} = x^{-12}y^{-15} = \dfrac{1}{x^{12}y^{15}}$

76. $\dfrac{1}{t^{20}x^{12}}$

77. $(x^{-6}y^{-2})^{-4} = (x^{-6})^{-4}(y^{-2})^{-4} = x^{24}y^8$

78. $x^{10}y^{35}$

79. $(a^{-5}b^7 c^{-2})(a^{-3}b^{-2}c^6) = a^{-5+(-3)}b^{7+(-2)}c^{-2+6} =$ $a^{-8}b^5 c^4 = \dfrac{b^5 c^4}{a^8}$

80. $\dfrac{z^4}{xy^6}$

81. $\left(\dfrac{a^4}{3}\right)^{-2} = \left(\dfrac{3}{a^4}\right)^2 = \dfrac{3^2}{(a^4)^2} = \dfrac{9}{a^8}$

82. $\dfrac{4}{y^4}$

83. $\left(\dfrac{7}{x^{-3}}\right)^2 = (7x^3)^2 = 7^2(x^3)^2 = 49x^6$

84. $27a^6$

85. $\left(\dfrac{m^{-1}}{n^{-4}}\right)^3 = \dfrac{(m^{-1})^3}{(n^{-4})^3} = \dfrac{m^{-3}}{n^{-12}} = \dfrac{n^{12}}{m^3}$

86. $x^6 y^3 z^{15}$

87. $\left(\dfrac{2a^2}{3b^4}\right)^{-3} = \left(\dfrac{3b^4}{2a^2}\right)^3 = \dfrac{(3b^4)^3}{(2a^2)^3} = \dfrac{3^3(b^4)^3}{2^3(a^2)^3} = \dfrac{27b^{12}}{8a^6}$

88. $\dfrac{c^5 d^{15}}{a^{10}b^5}$

89. $\left(\dfrac{5x^{-2}}{3y^{-2}z}\right)^0$

Any nonzero expression raised to the 0 power is equal to 1. Thus, the answer is 1.

90. $\dfrac{4a^3 c^3}{5b^2}$

91. 7.12×10^4

Since the exponent is positive, the decimal point will move to the right.

7.1200.   The decimal point moves right 4 places.

$7.12 \times 10^4 = 71,200$

92. 892

93. 8.92×10^{-3}

Since the exponent is negative, the decimal point will move to the left.

.008.92   The decimal point moves left 3 places.

$8.92 \times 10^{-3} = 0.00892$

94. 0.000726

95. 9.04×10^8

Since the exponent is positive, the decimal point will move to the right.

9.04000000.   8 places

$9.04 \times 10^8 = 904,000,000$

96. $13,500,000$

97. 2.764×10^{-10}

Since the exponent is negative, the decimal point will move to the left.

0.0000000002.764   10 places

$2.764 \times 10^{-10} = 0.0000000002764$

98. 0.009043

99. 4.209×10^9

Since the exponent is positive, the decimal point will move to the right.

4.2090000.

$\underset{\text{7 places}}{\rule{2cm}{0.4pt}\uparrow}$

$4.209 \times 10^7 = 42,090,000$

100. $502,900,000$

101. $490,000 = 4.9 \times 10^m$

To write 4.9 as 490,000 we move the decimal point 5 places to the right. Thus, m is 5 and

$$490,000 = 4.9 \times 10^5.$$

102. 7.15×10^4

103. $0.00583 = 5.83 \times 10^m$

To write 5.83 as 0.00583 we move the decimal point 3 places to the left. Thus, m is -3 and

$$0.00583 = 5.83 \times 10^{-3}.$$

104. 8.14×10^{-2}

105. $78,000,000,000 = 7.8 \times 10^m$

To write 7.8 as 78,000,000,000 we move the decimal point 10 places to the right. Thus, m is 10 and

$$78,000,000,000 = 7.8 \times 10^{10}.$$

106. 3.7×10^{12}

107. $907,000,000,000,000,000 = 9.07 \times 10^m$

To write 9.07 as 907,000,000,000,000,000 we move the decimal point 17 places to the right. Thus, m is 17 and

$$907,000,000,000,000,000 = 9.07 \times 10^{17}.$$

108. 1.68×10^{14}

109. $0.000000527 = 5.27 \times 10^m$

To write 5.27 as 0.000000527 we move the decimal point 7 places to the left. Thus, m is -7 and

$$0.000000527 = 5.27 \times 10^{-7}.$$

110. 6.48×10^{-9}

111. $1,094,000,000,000,000 = 1.094 \times 10^m$

To write 1.094 as 1,094,000,000,000,000 we move the decimal point 15 places to the right. Thus, m is 15 and

$$1,094,000,000,000,000 = 1.094 \times 10^{15}.$$

112. 1.0302×10^{18}

113. $(4 \times 10^7)(2 \times 10^5) = (4 \cdot 2) \times (10^7 \cdot 10^5)$
$$= 8 \times 10^{7+5} \quad \text{Adding exponents}$$
$$= 8 \times 10^{12}$$

114. 6.46×10^5

115. $(3.8 \times 10^9)(6.5 \times 10^{-2}) = (3.8 \cdot 6.5) \times (10^9 \cdot 10^{-2})$
$$= 24.7 \times 10^7$$

The answer is not yet in scientific notation since 24.7 is not a number between 1 and 10. We convert to scientific notation.

$$24.7 \times 10^7 = (2.47 \times 10) \times 10^7 = 2.47 \times 10^8$$

116. 6.106×10^{-11}

117. $\dfrac{8.5 \times 10^8}{3.4 \times 10^{-5}} = \dfrac{8.5}{3.4} \times \dfrac{10^8}{10^{-5}}$
$$= 2.5 \times 10^{8-(-5)}$$
$$= 2.5 \times 10^{13}$$

118. 2.24×10^{-7}

119. $(3.0 \times 10^6) \div (6.0 \times 10^9) = \dfrac{3.0 \times 10^6}{6.0 \times 10^9}$
$$= \dfrac{3.0}{6.0} \times \dfrac{10^6}{10^9}$$
$$= 0.5 \times 10^{6-9}$$
$$= 0.5 \times 10^{-3}$$

The answer is not yet in scientific notation because 0.5 is not between 1 and 10. We convert to scientific notation.

$$0.5 \times 10^{-3} = (5.0 \times 10^{-1}) \times 10^{-3} =$$
$$5.0 \times 10^{-4}$$

120. 9.375×10^2

121. $\dfrac{7.5 \times 10^{-9}}{2.5 \times 10^{12}} = \dfrac{7.5}{2.5} \times \dfrac{10^{-9}}{10^{12}}$
$$= 3.0 \times 10^{-9-12}$$
$$= 3.0 \times 10^{-21}$$

122. 5×10^{-24}

123. $\dfrac{7.4 \times 10^{29}}{(5.4 \times 10^{-6})(2.8 \times 10^8)}$
$$= \dfrac{7.4}{(5.4 \cdot 2.8)} \times \dfrac{10^{29}}{(10^{-6} \cdot 10^8)}$$
$$\approx 0.4894179894 \times 10^{27}$$
$$\approx (4.894179894 \times 10^{-1}) \times 10^{27}$$
$$\approx 4.9 \times 10^{26}$$

124. Approximtely 6.3×10^{25}

125. $\dfrac{(7.8 \times 10^7)(8.4 \times 10^{23})}{2.1 \times 10^{-12}}$
$$= \dfrac{(7.8 \cdot 8.4)}{2.1} \times \dfrac{(10^7 \cdot 10^{23})}{10^{-12}}$$
$$= 31.2 \times 10^{42}$$
$$= (3.12 \times 10) \times 10^{42}$$
$$= 3.12 \times 10^{43}$$

126. Approximately 1.2×10^{-15}

127. *Familiarize.* The distance Venus travels in one orbit can be approximated by the circumference of a circle whose radius is the average distance from the sun to Venus, 1.08×10^8 km. Recall that the formula for the circumference of a circle is $C = 2\pi r$, where r is the radius.

Translate. Substitute 1.08×10^8 for r in the formula

$$C = 2\pi r$$
$$C = 2\pi \times 1.08 \times 10^8$$

Carry out. Do the calculation. Use a calculator with a π key.

$$C = 2\pi \times 1.08 \times 10^8$$
$$\approx 6.79 \times 10^8$$

Check. Repeat the calculation.

State. Venus travels about 6.79×10^8 km in one orbit.

128. 4.5 g

129. *Familiarize.* First we will find the number n of \$5 bills in \$4,540,000 worth of \$5 bills. Then we will find the weight w of a \$5 bill. Recall that 1 ton = 2000 lb.

Translate. To find the number of \$5 bills in \$4,540,000 worth of \$5 bills we divide:

$$n = \frac{4,540,000}{5}.$$

Then we divide again to find the weight w of a \$5 bill:

$$w = \frac{2000}{n}.$$

Carry out. We begin by finding n.

$$n = \frac{4,540,000}{5} = \frac{4.54 \times 10^6}{5} = 0.908 \times 10^6 =$$
$$(9.08 \times 10^{-1}) \times 10^6 = 9.08 \times 10^5$$

Now we find w.

$$w = \frac{2000}{n} = \frac{2000}{9.08 \times 10^5} = \frac{2 \times 10^3}{9.08 \times 10^5} \approx$$
$$0.22 \times 10^{-2} = (2.2 \times 10^{-1}) \times 10^{-2} =$$
$$2.2 \times 10^{-3}$$

Check. We recheck the translation and calculations.

State. A \$5 bill weighs about 2.2×10^{-3} lb.

130. 5.84×10^8 miles

131. *Familiarize.* From Example 3 we know that 1 light year $= 5.88 \times 10^{12}$ mi. Let $y =$ the number of light years from the earth to Sirius.

Translate. The distance from the earth to Sirius is y light years or $(5.88 \times 10^{12})y$ mi. It is also given by 4.704×10^{13} mi. We write an equation:

$$(5.88 \times 10^{12})y = 4.704 \times 10^{13}$$

Carry out. We solve the equation.

$$(5.88 \times 10^{12})y = 4.704 \times 10^{13}$$
$$y = \frac{4.704 \times 10^{13}}{5.88 \times 10^{12}}$$
$$y = \frac{4.704}{5.88} \times \frac{10^{13}}{10^{12}}$$
$$y = 0.8 \times 10$$
$$y = 8$$

Check. Since light travels 5.88×10^{12} mi in one year, in 8.00 yr it will travel $8.00 \times 5.88 \times 10^{12} = 4.704 \times 10^{13}$ mi, the distance from the earth to Sirius. The answer checks.

State. It is 8 light years from the earth to Sirius.

132. 1×10^5 light years

133. *Familiarize.* First we will find d, the number of drops in a pound. Then we will find b, the number of bacteria in a drop of U.S. mud.

Translate. To find d we convert 1 pound to drops:

$$d = 1 \text{ lb} \cdot \frac{16\text{oz}}{1 \text{ lb}} \cdot \frac{6 \text{ tsp}}{1 \text{ oz}} \cdot \frac{60 \text{ drops}}{1 \text{ tsp}}.$$

Then we divide to find b:

$$b = \frac{4.55 \times 10^{11}}{d}.$$

Carry out. We do the calculations.

$$d = 1 \text{ lb} \cdot \frac{16\text{oz}}{1 \text{ lb}} \cdot \frac{6 \text{ tsp}}{1 \text{ oz}} \cdot \frac{60 \text{ drops}}{1 \text{ tsp}}$$
$$= 5760 \text{ drops}$$

Now we find b.

$$b = \frac{4.55 \times 10^{11}}{5760} = \frac{4.55 \times 10^{11}}{5.760 \times 10^3} \approx 0.790 \times 10^8 \approx$$
$$(7.90 \times 10^{-1}) \times 10^8 = 7.90 \times 10^7$$

Check. If there are about 7.90×10^7 bacteria in a drop of U.S. mud, then in a pound there are about

$$\frac{7.90 \times 10^7}{1 \text{ drop}} \cdot \frac{60 \text{ drops}}{1 \text{ tsp}} \cdot \frac{6 \text{ tsp}}{1 \text{ oz}} \cdot \frac{16 \text{ oz}}{1 \text{ lb}} =$$
$$\frac{45,504 \times 10^7}{1 \text{ lb}} \approx 4.55 \times 10^{11} \text{ bacteria per pound. The an-}$$

swer checks.

State. About 7.90×10^7 bacteria live in a drop of U.S. mud.

134. 1.475×10^{12} mi

135. *Familiarize.* First we will find the distance C around Jupiter at the equator, in km. Then we will use the formula Speed $\times$ Time $=$ Distance to find the speed s at which Jupiter's equator is spinning.

Translate. We will use the formula for the circumference of a circle to find the distance around Jupiter at the equator:

$$C = \pi d = \pi(1.43 \times 10^5).$$

Then we find the speed s at which Jupiter's equator is spinning:

$$\underbrace{\text{Speed}}_{s} \times \underbrace{\text{Time}}_{10} = \underbrace{\text{Distance}}_{C}$$

Carry out. First we find C.

$$C = \pi(1.43 \times 10^5) \approx 4.49 \times 10^5$$

Then we find s.

$$s \times 10 = C$$
$$s \times 10 = 4.49 \times 10^5$$
$$s = \frac{4.49 \times 10^5}{10}$$
$$s = 4.49 \times 10^4$$

Check. At 4.49×10^4 km/h, in 10 hr, Jupiter's equator travels $4.49 \times 10^4 \times 10$, or 4.49×10^5 km. A circle with circumference 4.49×10^5 km has a diameter of $\dfrac{4.49 \times 10^5}{\pi} \approx 1.43 \times 10^5$ km. The answer checks.

State. Jupiter's equator spins at a speed of about 4.49×10^4 km/h.

136. $\$6.7 \times 10^4$

137. *Writing Exercise*

138. *Writing Exercise*

139.
$$(3 - 8)(9 - 12)$$
$$= (-5)(-3) \qquad \text{Subtracting}$$
$$= 15 \qquad \text{Multiplying}$$

140. 49

141.
$$7 \cdot 2 + 8^2$$
$$= 7 \cdot 2 + 64 \quad \text{Evaluating the exponential expression}$$
$$= 14 + 64 \quad \text{Multiplying}$$
$$= 78 \quad \text{Adding}$$

142. 6

143. To plot $(-3, 2)$, we start at the origin and move 3 units to the left and then 2 units up. To plot $(4, -1)$, we start at the origin and move 4 units to the right and then 1 unit down. To plot $(5, 3)$, we start at the origin and move 5 units to the right and 3 units up. To plot $(-5, -2)$, we start at the origin and move 5 units to the left and then 2 units down.

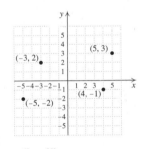

144. $t = \dfrac{r - cx}{b}$

145. *Writing Exercise*

146. *Writing Exercise*

147.
$$\frac{4.2 \times 10^8 [(2.5 \times 10^{-5}) \div (5.0 \times 10^{-9})]}{3.0 \times 10^{-12}}$$
$$= \frac{4.2 \times 10^8 [0.5 \times 10^4]}{3.0 \times 10^{-12}}$$
$$= \frac{2.1 \times 10^{12}}{3.0 \times 10^{-12}}$$
$$= 0.7 \times 10^{24}$$
$$= (7 \times 10^{-1}) \times 10^{24}$$
$$= 7 \times 10^{23}$$

148. 8×10^5

149. $\dfrac{1}{2.5 \times 10^9} = \dfrac{1}{2.5} \times \dfrac{1}{10^9} = 0.4 \times 10^{-9} = (4 \times 10^{-1}) \times 10^{-9} = 4 \times 10^{-10}$

150. 2^{-12}

151. $81^3 \cdot 27 \div 9^2 = (3^4)^3 \cdot 3^3 \div (3^2)^2 = 3^{12} \cdot 3^3 \div 3^4 = 3^{15} \div 3^4 = 3^{11}$

152. 7

153. $\dfrac{125^{-4}(25^2)^4}{125} = \dfrac{(5^3)^{-4}((5^2)^2)^4}{5^3} = \dfrac{5^{-12}(5^4)^4}{5^3} = \dfrac{5^{-12} \cdot 5^{16}}{5^3} = \dfrac{5^4}{5^3} = 5^1 = 5$

154. 9

155. a) False; let $x = 2$, $y = 3$, $m = 4$, and $n = 2$:
$$2^4 \cdot 3^2 = 16 \cdot 9 = 144, \text{ but}$$
$$(2 \cdot 3)^{4 \cdot 2} = 6^8 = 1,679,616$$

b) False; let $x = 3$, $y = 4$, and $m = 2$:
$$3^2 \cdot 4^2 = 9 \cdot 16 = 144, \text{ but}$$
$$(3 \cdot 4)^{2 \cdot 2} = 12^4 = 20,736$$

c) False; let $x = 5$, $y = 3$, and $m = 2$:
$$(5 - 3)^2 = 2^2 = 4, \text{ but}$$
$$5^2 - 3^2 = 25 - 9 = 16$$

Chapter 6

Polynomials and Factoring

1. From the graph we see that $f(x) = 0$ when $x = -3$ or $x = 5$. These are the solutions.

2. $-5, -2$

3. From the graph we see that $f(x) = 0$ when $x = -2$ or $x = 0$. These are the zeros of the function.

4. $-1, 3$

5. From the graph we see that $f(x) = 3$ when $x = -3$ or $x = 1$. These are the solutions.

6. $-2, 2$

7. From the graph we see that $f(x) = 0$ when $x = -4$ or $x = 2$. These are the solutions.

8. 1

9. We can graph $y_1 = x^2$ and $y_2 = 5x$ and use the Intersect feature to find the first coordinates of the points of intersection, or we can begin by rewriting the equation so that one side is 0:

$$x^2 = 5x$$
$$x^2 - 5x = 0 \quad \text{Subtracting } 5x \text{ on both sides}$$

Then graph $y = x^2 - 5x$ and use the Zero feature to find the roots of the equation. In either case, we find that the solutions are 0 and 5.

10. 0, 10

11. We can graph $y_1 = 4x$ and $y_2 = x^2 + 3$ and use the Intersect feature to find the first coordinates of the points of intersection, or we can begin by rewriting the equation so that one side is 0:

$$4x = x^2 + 3$$
$$0 = x^2 + 3 - 4x \quad \text{Subtracting } 4x \text{ on both sides}$$

Then graph $y = x^2 + 3 - 4x$ and use the Zero feature to find the roots of the equation. In either case, we find that the solutions are 1 and 3.

12. $-1, 1$

13. We can graph $y_1 = x^2 + 150$ and $y_2 = 25x$ and use the Intersect feature to find the first coordinates of the points of intersection, or we can begin by rewriting the equation so that one side is 0:

$$x^2 + 150 = 25x$$
$$x^2 + 150 - 25x = 0 \quad \text{Subtracting } 25 \text{ on both sides}$$

Then graph $y = x^2 + 150 - 25x$ and use the Zero feature to find the roots of the equation. In either case, we find that the solutions are 10 and 15.

14. 0.5, 25

15. Graph $y = x^3 - 3x^2 - 2x$ and use the Zero feature to find the roots of the equation. The solutions are 0, 1, and 2.

16. $-2, -1, 1$

17. Graph $y = x^3 - 3x^2 - 198x + 1080$ and use the Zero feature to find the roots of the equation. The solutions are -15, 6, and 12.

18. $-20, 1.5, 6$

19. Graph $y = 21x^2 + 2x - 3$ and use the Zero feature to find the roots of the equation. The solutions are approximately -0.42857 and 0.33333.

20. $-0.09091, 0.83333$

21. Graph $y = x^2 - 4x + 45$ and use the Zero feature to find the zeros of the function. They are -5 and 9.

22. $-5, 4$

23. Graph $y = 2x^2 - 13x - 7$ and use the Zero feature to find the zeros of the function. They are -0.5 and 7.

24. $-2.42013, -0.41320$

25. Graph $y = x^3 - 2x^2 - 3x$ and use the Zero feature to find the zeros of the function. They are -1, 0, and 3.

26. $-2, 0, 2$

27. We see that $2x - 1 = 0$ when $x = 0.5$ and $3x + 1 = 0$ when $x = -0.\overline{3}$, so graph III corresponds to the given function.

28. II

29. We see that $4 - x = 0$ when $x = 4$ and $2x - 11 = 0$ when $x = 5.5$, so graph I corresponds to the given function.

30. IV

31. $x^2 + 6x + 9$ has no equals sign, so it is an expression.

32. Equation

33. $3x^2 = 3x$ has an equals sign, so it is an equation.

34. Expression

35. $2x^3 + x^2 = 0$ has an equals sign, so it is an equation.

36. Expression

37. $2t^2 + 8t$
$$= 2t \cdot t + 2t \cdot 4$$
$$= 2t(t + 4)$$

38. $3y(y+2)$

39.
$$y^3 + 9y^2$$
$$= y \cdot y^2 + 9 \cdot y^2$$
$$= y^2(y+9)$$

40. $x^2(x+8)$

41.
$$15x^2 - 5x^4$$
$$= 5x^2 \cdot 3 - 5x^2 \cdot x^2$$
$$= 5x^2(3 - x^2)$$

42. $4y^2(2+y^2)$

43.
$$4x^2y - 12xy^2$$
$$= 4xy \cdot x - 4xy \cdot 3y$$
$$= 4xy(x - 3y)$$

44. $5x^2y^2(y+3x)$

45.
$$3y^2 - 3y - 9$$
$$= 3 \cdot y^2 - 3 \cdot y - 3 \cdot 3$$
$$= 3(y^2 - y - 3)$$

46. $5(x^2 - x + 3)$

47.
$$6ab - 4ad + 12ac$$
$$= 2a \cdot 3b - 2a \cdot 2d + 2a \cdot 6c$$
$$= 2a(3b - 2d + 6c)$$

48. $2x(4y + 5z - 7w)$

49.
$$9x^3y^6z^2 - 12x^4y^4z^4 + 15x^2y^5z^3$$
$$= 3x^2y^4z^2 \cdot 3xy^2 - 3x^2y^4z^2 \cdot 4x^2z^2 + 3x^2y^4z^2 \cdot 5yz$$
$$= 3x^2y^4z^2(3xy^2 - 4x^2z^2 + 5yz)$$

50. $7a^3b^3c^3(2ac^2 + 3b^2c - 5ab)$

51. $-5x + 35 = -5(x - 7)$

52. $-5(x + 8)$

53. $-6y - 72 = -6(y + 12)$

54. $-8(t - 9)$

55. $-2x^2 + 4x - 12 = -2(x^2 - 2x + 6)$

56. $-2(x^2 - 6x - 20)$

57. $3y - 24 = -3(-y) - 3 \cdot 8 = -3(-y + 8)$, or $-3(8 - y)$

58. $-7(-x + 8y)$, or $-7(8y - x)$

59. $7s - 14t = -7(-s) - 7 \cdot 2t = -7(-s + 2t)$, or $-7(2t - s)$

60. $-5(-r + 2s)$, or $-5(2s - r)$

61. $-x^2 + 5x - 9 = -(x^2 - 5x + 9)$

62. $-(p^3 + 4p^2 - 11)$

63. $-a^4 + 2a^3 - 13a = -a(a^3 - 2a^2 + 13)$

64. $-(m^3 + m^2 - m + 2)$

65.
$$a(b - 5) + c(b - 5)$$
$$= (b - 5)(a + c)$$

66. $(t - 3)(r - s)$

67.
$$(x + 7)(x - 1) + (x + 7)(x - 2)$$
$$= (x + 7)(x - 1 + x - 2)$$
$$= (x + 7)(2x - 3)$$

68. $(a + 5)(2a - 1)$

69.
$$a^2(x - y) + 5(y - x)$$
$$= a^2(x - y) + 5(-1)(x - y) \quad \text{Factoring out } -1$$
$$\qquad \text{to reverse the second subtraction}$$
$$= a^2(x - y) - 5(x - y) \qquad \text{Simplifying}$$
$$= (x - y)(a^2 - 5)$$

70. $(x - 6)(5x^2 - 2)$

71.
$$ac + ad + bc + bd$$
$$= a(c + d) + b(c + d)$$
$$= (c + d)(a + b)$$

72. $(y + z)(x + w)$

73.
$$b^3 - b^2 + 2b - 2$$
$$= b^2(b - 1) + 2(b - 1)$$
$$= (b - 1)(b^2 + 2)$$

74. $(y - 1)(y^2 + 3)$

75.
$$a^3 - 3a^2 + 6 - 2a$$
$$= a^2(a - 3) + 2(3 - a)$$
$$= a^2(a - 3) + 2(-1)(a - 3) \quad \text{Factoring out } -1$$
$$\qquad \text{to reverse the second subtraction}$$
$$= a^2(a - 3) - 2(a - 3)$$
$$= (a - 3)(a^2 - 2)$$

76. $(t + 6)(t^2 - 2)$

77.
$$72x^3 - 36x^2 + 24x$$
$$= 12x \cdot 6x^2 - 12x \cdot 3x + 12x \cdot 2$$
$$= 12x(6x^2 - 3x + 2)$$

78. $3a^2(4a^2 - 7a - 3)$

79.
$$x^6 - x^5 - x^3 + x^4$$
$$= x^3(x^3 - x^2 - 1 + x)$$
$$= x^3[x^2(x - 1) + x - 1] \qquad (-1 + x = x - 1)$$
$$= x^3(x - 1)(x^2 + 1)$$

80. $y(y - 1)(y^2 + 1)$

81.
$$2y^4 + 6y^2 + 5y^2 + 15$$
$$= 2y^2(y^2 + 3) + 5(y^2 + 3)$$
$$= (y^2 + 3)(2y^2 + 5)$$

82. $(2 - x)(xy - 3)$

83. a) $h(t) = -16t^2 + 72t$

$h(t) = -8t(2t - 9)$

b) Using $h(t) = -16t^2 + 72t$:

$h(1) = -16 \cdot 1^2 + 72 \cdot 1 = -16 \cdot 1 + 72$

$= -16 + 72 = 56$ ft

Using $h(t) = -8t(2t - 9)$:

$h(1) = -8(1)(2 \cdot 1 - 9) = -8(1)(-7) = 56$ ft

The expressions have the same value for $t = 1$, so the factorization is probably correct.

84. a) $h(t) = -16t(t - 6)$

b) $h(1) = 80$ ft

85. $R(n) = n^2 - n$

$R(n) = n(n - 1)$

86. $\pi r(2h + r)$

87. $P(x) = x^2 - 3x$

$P(x) = x(x - 3)$

88. $P(t) = t(t - 5)$

89. $R(x) = 280x - 0.4x^2$

$R(x) = 0.4x(700 - x)$

90. $C(x) = 0.6x(0.3 + x)$

91. $N(x) = \frac{1}{6}x^3 + \frac{1}{2}x^2 + \frac{1}{3}x$

$N(x) = \frac{1}{6}(x^3 + 3x^2 + 2x)$ Factoring out $\frac{1}{6}$

92. $f(n) = \frac{1}{2}(n^2 - n)$

93. $H(n) = \frac{1}{2}n^2 - \frac{1}{2}n$

$H(n) = \frac{1}{2}n(n - 1)$

94. $P(n) = \frac{1}{2}(n^2 - 3n)$

95. $x(x + 1) = 0$

We use the principle of zero products.

$x = 0$ or $x + 1 = 0$

$x = 0$ or $x = -1$

The solutions are 0 and -1.

96. 0, 2

97. $x^2 - 3x = 0$

$x(x - 3) = 0$ Factoring

$x = 0$ or $x - 3 = 0$ Using the principle of zero products

$x = 0$ or $x = 3$

The solutions are 0 and 3.

98. $-4, 0$

99. $-5x^2 = 15x$

$0 = 5x^2 + 15x$ Adding $5x^2$ on both sides

$0 = 5x(x + 3)$ Factoring

$5x = 0$ or $x + 3 = 0$ Using the principle of zero products

$x = 0$ or $x = -3$

The solutions are 0 and -3.

100. $0, \frac{1}{2}$

101. $12x^4 + 4x^3 = 0$

$4x^3(3x + 1) = 0$ Factoring

$4x \cdot x \cdot x(3x + 1) = 0$

$4x = 0$ or $x = 0$ or $x = 0$ or $3x + 1 = 0$

$x = 0$ or $x = 0$ or $x = 0$ or $3x = -1$

$x = 0$ or $x = 0$ or $x = 0$ or $x = -\frac{1}{3}$

The solutions are 0 and $-\frac{1}{3}$.

102. $0, \frac{1}{3}$

103. *Writing Exercise*

104. *Writing Exercise*

105. $2(-3) + 4(-5) = -6 - 20 = -26$

106. -1

107. $4(-6) - 3(2) = -24 - 6 = -30$

108. -19

109. **Familiarize.** Let $n =$ the first even number. Then $n + 2$ and $n + 4$ are the next two even numbers. Recall that the perimeter of a triangle is the sum of the lengths of the sides.

Translate.

$\underbrace{\text{The perimeter}}$ is 174.

$n + (n + 2) + (n + 4) = 174$

Carry out. We solve the equation.

$n + (n + 2) + (n + 4) = 174$

$3n + 6 = 174$

$3n = 168$

$n = 56$

When $n = 56$, then $n + 2 = 56 + 2$, or 58, and $n + 4 = 56 + 4$, or 60.

Check. The numbers 56, 58, and 60 are consecutive even integers. Also $56 + 58 + 60 = 174$. The answer checks.

State. The lengths of the sides of the triangle are 56, 58, and 60.

110. 32 oz

111. *Writing Exercise*

112. *Writing Exercise*

113. We use the principle of zero products in reverse. Since the zeros of $f(x) = x^2 + 2x - 8$ are -4 and 2, we have

$$x = -4 \quad or \quad x = 2$$
$$x + 4 = 0 \quad or \quad x - 2 = 0,$$

so $x^2 + 2x - 8 = (x+4)(x-2)$.

114. $(x-1)(x-1)$

115. $x^5y^4 + \underline{\quad} = x^3y(\underline{\quad} + xy^5)$

The term that goes in the first blank is the product of x^3y and xy^5, or x^4y^6.

The term that goes in the second blank is the expression that is multiplied with x^3y to obtain x^5y^4, or x^2y^3. Thus, we have

$$x^5y^4 + x^4y^6 = x^3y(x^2y^3 + xy^5).$$

116. $a^3b^7 - a^2b^3c^2 = a^2b^3(ab^4 - c^2)$

117.
$$rx^2 - rx + 5r + sx^2 - sx + 5s$$
$$= r(x^2 - x + 5) + s(x^2 - x + 5)$$
$$= (x^2 - x + 5)(r + s)$$

118. $(a^2 + 2a + 10)(3 + 7b)$

119.
$$a^4x^4 + a^4x^2 + 5a^4 + a^2x^4 + a^2x^2 + 5a^2 +$$
$$5x^4 + 5x^2 + 25$$
$$= a^4(x^4 + x^2 + 5) + a^2(x^4 + x^2 + 5) + 5(x^4 + x^2 + 5)$$
$$= (x^4 + x^2 + 5)(a^4 + a^2 + 5)$$

120. $x^{1/2}(1 + 5x)$

121. $x^{1/3} - 7x^{4/3} = x^{1/3} \cdot 1 - 7x \cdot x^{1/3} = x^{1/3}(1 - 7x)$

122. $x^{1/4}(x^{1/2} + x^{1/4} - 1)$

123.
$$x^{1/3} - 5x^{1/2} + 3x^{3/4}$$
$$= x^{4/12} - 5x^{6/12} + 3x^{9/12}$$
$$= x^{4/12}(1 - 5x^{2/12} + 3x^{5/12})$$
$$= x^{1/3}(1 - 5x^{1/6} + 3x^{5/12})$$

124. $2x^a(x^{2a} + 4 + 2x^a)$

125.
$$3a^{n+1} + 6a^n - 15a^{n+2}$$
$$= 3a^n \cdot a + 3a^n \cdot 2 - 3a^n(5a^2)$$
$$= 3a^n(a + 2 - 5a^2)$$

126. $x^a(4x^b + 7x^{-b})$

127.
$$7y^{2a+b} - 5y^{a+b} + 3y^{a+2b}$$
$$= y^{a+b} \cdot 7y^a - y^{a+b}(5) + y^{a+b} \cdot 3y^b$$
$$= y^{a+b}(7y^a - 5 + 3y^b)$$

Exercise Set 6.2

1. $x^2 + 8x + 12$

We look for two numbers whose product is 12 and whose sum is 8. Since 12 and 8 are both positive, we need only consider positive factors.

Pair of Factors	Sum of Factors
1, 12	13
2, 6	8

The numbers we need are 2 and 6. The factorization is $(x+2)(x+6)$.

2. $(x+1)(x+5)$

3. $t^2 + 8t + 15$

Since the constant term is positive and the coefficient of the middle term is also positive, we look for a factorization of 15 in which both factors are positive. Their sum must be 8.

Pair of Factors	Sum of Factors
1, 15	16
3, 5	8

The numbers we need are 3 and 5. The factorization is $(t+3)(t+5)$.

4. $(y+3)(y+9)$

5. $x^2 - 27 - 6x = x^2 - 6x - 27$

Since the constant term is negative, we look for a factorization of -27 in which one factor is positive and one factor is negative. Their sum must be -6, so the negative factor must have the larger absolute value. Thus we consider only pairs of factors in which the negative factor has the larger absolute value.

Pair of Factors	Sum of Factors
-27, 1	-26
-9, 3	-6

The numbers we need are -9 and 3. The factorization is $(x-9)(x+3)$.

6. $(t-5)(t+3)$

7.
$$2n^2 - 20n + 50$$
$$= 2(n^2 - 10n + 25) \quad \text{Removing the common factor}$$

We now factor $n^2 - 10n + 25$. We look for two numbers whose product is 25 and whose sum is -10. Since the constant term is positive and the coefficient of the middle term is negative, we look for factorization of 25 in which both factors are negative.

Pair of Factors	Sum of Factors
-1, -25	-26
-5, -5	-10

The numbers we need are -5 and -5.

$$n^2 - 10n + 25 = (n-5)(n-5)$$

We must not forget to include the common factor 2.

$$2n^2 - 20n + 50 = 2(n-5)(n-5), \text{ or } 2(n-5)^2$$

8. $2(a-4)^2$

9. $a^3 - a^2 - 72a$

$= a(a^2 - a - 72)$ Removing the common factor

We now factor $a^2 - a - 72$. Since the constant term is negative, we look for a factorization of -72 in which one factor is positive and one factor is negative. We consider only pairs of factors in which the negative factor has the larger absolute value, since the sum of the factors, -1, is negative.

Pair of Factors	Sum of Factors
$-72,1$	-71
$-36,2$	-34
$-18,4$	-14
$-9,8$	-1

The numbers we need are -9 and 8.

$$a^2 - a - 72 = (a-9)(a+8)$$

We must not forget to include the common factor a.

$$a^3 - a^2 - 72a = a(a-9)(a+8)$$

10. $x(x+9)(x-6)$

11. $14x + x^2 + 45 = x^2 + 14x + 45$

Since the constant term and the middle term are both positive, we look for a factorization of 45 in which both factors are positive. Their sum must be 14.

Pair of Factors	Sum of Factors
$45,1$	46
$15,3$	18
$9,5$	14

The numbers we need are 9 and 5. The factorization is $(x+9)(x+5)$.

12. $(y+8)(y+4)$

13. $3x + x^2 - 10 = x^2 + 3x - 10$

Since the constant term is negative, we look for a factorization of -10 in which one factor is positive and one factor is negative. We consider only pairs of factors in which the positive factor has the larger absolute value, since the sum of the factors, 3, is positive.

Pair of Factors	Sum of Factors
$10,-1$	9
$5,-2$	3

The numbers we need are 5 and -2. The factorization is $(x+5)(x-2)$.

14. $(x+3)(x-2)$

15. $3x^2 + 15x + 18$

$= 3(x^2 + 5x + 6)$ Removing the common factor

We now factor $x^2 + 5x + 6$. We look for two numbers whose product is 6 and whose sum is 5. Since 6 and 5 are both positive, we need consider only positive factors.

Pair of Factors	Sum of Factors
$1, 6$	7
$2, 3$	5

The numbers we need are 2 and 3.

$$x^2 + 5x + 6 = (x+2)(x+3)$$

We must not forget to include the common factor 3.

$$3x^2 + 15x + 18 = 3(x+2)(x+3)$$

16. $5(y+1)(y+7)$

17. $56 + x - x^2 = -x^2 + x + 56 = -(x^2 - x - 56)$

We now factor $x^2 - x - 56$. Since the constant term is negative, we look for a factorization of -56 in which one factor is positive and one factor is negative. We consider only pairs of factors in which the negative factor has the larger absolute value, since the sum of the factors, -1, is negative.

Pair of Factors	Sum of Factors
$-56,\ 1$	-55
$-28,\ 2$	-26
$-14,\ 4$	-10
$-8,\ 7$	-1

The numbers we need are -8 and 7. Thus, $x^2 - x - 56 = (x-8)(x+7)$. We must not forget to include the factor that was factored out earlier:

$$56 + x - x^2 = -(x-8)(x+7), \text{ or}$$
$$(-x+8)(x+7), \text{ or } (8-x)(7+x)$$

18. $(8-y)(4+y)$, or $-(y-8)(y+4)$, or $(-y+8)(y+4)$

19. $32y + 4y^2 - y^3$

There is a common factor, y. We also factor out -1 in order to make the leading coefficient positive.

$$32y + 4y^2 - y^3 = -y(-32 - 4y + y^2)$$
$$= -y(y^2 - 4y - 32)$$

Now we factor $y^2 - 4y - 32$. Since the constant term is negative, we look for a factorization of -32 in which one factor is positive and one factor is negative. We consider only pairs of factors in which the negative factor has the larger absolute value, since the sum of the factors, -4, is negative.

Pair of Factors	Sum of Factors
$-32,\ 1$	-31
$-16,\ 2$	-14
$-8,\ 4$	-4

The numbers we need are -8 and 4. Thus, $y^2 - 4y - 32 = (y-8)(y+4)$. We must not forget to include the common factor:

$$32y + 4y^2 - y^3 = -y(y-8)(y+4), \text{ or}$$
$$y(-y+8)(y+4), \text{ or } y(8-y)(4+y)$$

20. $x(8-x)(7+x)$, or $-x(x-8)(x+7)$, or $x(-x+8)(x+7)$

21. $x^4 + 11x^3 - 80x^2$

$= x^2(x^2 + 11x - 80)$ Removing the common factor

We now factor $x^2 + 11x - 80$. We look for pairs of factors of -80, one positive and one negative, such that the positive factor has the larger absolute value and the sum of the factors is 11.

Pair of Factors	Sum of Factors
80, −1	79
40, −2	38
20, −4	16
16, −5	11
10, −8	2

The numbers we need are 16 and −5. Then $x^2 + 11x - 80 = (x+16)(x-5)$. We must not forget to include the common factor:
$$x^4 + 11x^3 - 80x^2 = x^2(x+16)(x-5)$$

22. $y^2(y+12)(y-7)$

23. $x^2 + 12x + 13$

There are no factors of 13 whose sum is 12. This trinomial is not factorable into binomials with integer coefficients. The polynomial is prime.

24. Prime

25. $p^2 - 5pq - 24q^2$

We look for numbers r and s such that $p^2 - 5pq - 24q^2 = (p+rq)(p+sq)$. Our thinking is much the same as if we were factoring $p^2 - 5p - 24$. We look for factors of −24 whose sum is −5, one positive and one negative, such that the negative factor has the larger absolute value.

Pair of Factors	Sum of Factors
−24, 1	−23
−12, 2	−10
−8, 3	−5

The numbers we need are −8 and 3. The factorization is $(p-8q)(p+3q)$.

26. $(x+3y)(x+9y)$

27. $y^2 + 8yz + 16z^2$

We look for numbers p and q such that $y^2 + 8yz + 16z^2 = (y+pz)(y+qz)$. Our thinking is much the same as if we factor $y^2 + 8y + 16$. Since the constant term is positive and the coefficient of the middle term is negative, we look for a factorization of 16 in which both factors are positive. Their sum must be 8.

Pair of Factors	Sum of Factors
1, 16	17
2, 8	10
4, 4	8

The numbers we need are 4 and 4. The factorization is $(y+4z)(y+4z)$, or $(y+4z)^2$.

28. $(x-7y)(x-7y)$, or $(x-7y)^2$

29. $p^4 + 80p^3 + 79p^2$

$= p^2(p^2 + 80p + 79)$ Removing the common factor

We now factor $p^2 + 80p + 79$. We look for a pair of factors of 79 whose sum is 80. The only positive pair of factors is 1 and 79. These are the numbers we need. Then $p^2 + 80p + 79 = (p+1)(p+79)$. We must not forget to include the common factor:
$$p^4 + 80p^3 + 79p^2 = p^2(p+1)(p+79)$$

30. $x^2(x+1)(x+49)$

31. $x^2 + 8x + 12 = 0$

$(x+2)(x+6) = 0$ From Exercise 1

$x+2 = 0$ or $x+6 = 0$ Using the principle of zero products

$x = -2$ or $x = -6$

The solutions are −2 and −6.

32. −5, −1

33. $2n^2 + 50 = 20n$

$2n^2 - 20n + 50 = 0$ Subtracting 20n from both sides

$2(n-5)(n-5) = 0$ From Exercise 7

$n-5 = 0$ or $n-5 = 0$ Using the principle of zero products

$n = 5$ or $n = 5$

The solution is 5.

34. −4, 8

35. $a^3 - a^2 = 72a$

$a^3 - a^2 - 72a = 0$ Subtracting 72a on both sides

$a(a-9)(a+8) = 0$ From Exercise 9

$a = 0$ or $a-9 = 0$ or $a+8 = 0$

$a = 0$ or $a = 9$ or $a = -8$

The solutions are 0, 9, and −8.

36. −7, 0, 8

37. The x-intercepts are $(-5, 0)$ and $(1, 0)$, so the solutions are −5 and 1.

Check: For −5:

$$\begin{array}{c|c} x^2 + 4x - 5 = 0 \\ \hline (-5)^2 + 4(-5) - 5 \; ? \; 0 \\ 25 - 20 - 5 \\ 0 & 0 \quad \text{TRUE} \end{array}$$

For 1:

$$\begin{array}{c|c} x^2 + 4x - 5 = 0 \\ \hline 1^2 + 4 \cdot 1 - 5 \; ? \; 0 \\ 1 + 4 - 5 \\ 0 & 0 \quad \text{TRUE} \end{array}$$

Both numbers check, so they are the solutions.

38. −2, 3

39. The x-intercepts are $(-3, 0)$ and $(2, 0)$, so the solutions are −3 and 2.

Check: For −3:

$$\begin{array}{c|c} x^2 + x - 6 = 0 \\ \hline (-3)^2 + (-3) - 6 \; ? \; 0 \\ 9 - 3 - 6 \\ 0 & 0 \quad \text{TRUE} \end{array}$$

For 2:

$$\frac{x^2 + x - 6 = 0}{2^2 + 2 - 6 \ ? \ 0}$$
$$4 + 2 - 6 \quad \Big| $$
$$0 \ \Big| \ 0 \quad \text{TRUE}$$

Both numbers check, so they are the solutions.

40. $-5, -3$

41. The zeros of $f(x) = x^2 - 4x + 45$ are the solutions of the equation $x^2 - 4x + 45 = 0$. We factor and use the principle of zero products.

$$x^2 - 4x + 45 = 0$$
$$(x - 9)(x + 5) = 0$$
$$x - 9 = 0 \quad or \quad x + 5 = 0$$
$$x = 9 \quad or \qquad x = -5$$

The zeros are 9 and -5.

42. $-5, 4$

43. The zeros of $r(x) = x^3 - 2x^2 - 3x$ are the solutions of the equation $x^3 - 2x^2 - 3x = 0$. We factor and use the principle of zero products.

$$x^3 - 2x^2 - 3x = 0$$
$$x(x^2 - 2x - 3) = 0$$
$$x(x + 1)(x - 3) = 0$$
$$x = 0 \quad or \quad x + 1 = 0 \quad or \quad x - 3 = 0$$
$$x = 0 \quad or \qquad x = -1 \quad or \qquad x = 3$$

The zeros are 0, -1, and 3.

44. $-5, -2$

45.
$$x^2 + 4x = 45$$
$$x^2 + 4x - 45 = 0$$
$$(x + 9)(x - 5) = 0$$
$$x + 9 = 0 \quad or \quad x - 5 = 0$$
$$x = -9 \quad or \qquad x = 5$$

The solutions are -9 and 5.

46. $-4, 7$

47.
$$x^2 - 9x = 0$$
$$x(x - 9) = 0$$
$$x = 0 \quad or \quad x - 9 = 0$$
$$x = 0 \quad or \qquad x = 9$$

The solutions are 0 and 9.

48. $-18, 0$

49.
$$a^3 - 3a^2 = 40a$$
$$a^3 - 3a^2 - 40a = 0$$
$$a(a^2 - 3a - 40) = 0$$
$$a(a - 8)(a + 5) = 0$$
$$a = 0 \quad or \quad a - 8 = 0 \quad or \quad a + 5 = 0$$
$$a = 0 \quad or \qquad a = 8 \quad or \qquad a = -5$$

The solutions are 0, 8, and -5.

50. $-7, 0, 9$

51.
$$(x - 3)(x + 2) = 14$$
$$x^2 - x - 6 = 14$$
$$x^2 - x - 20 = 0$$
$$(x - 5)(x + 4) = 0$$
$$x - 5 = 0 \quad or \quad x + 4 = 0$$
$$x = 5 \quad or \qquad x = -4$$

The solutions are 5 and -4.

52. $-3, 1$

53.
$$35 - x^2 = 2x$$
$$35 - 2x - x^2 = 0$$
$$(7 + x)(5 - x) = 0$$
$$7 + x = 0 \quad or \quad 5 - x = 0$$
$$x = -7 \quad or \qquad 5 = x$$

The solutions are -7 and 5.

54. $-5, 8$

55. From the graph we see that the zeros of $f(x) = x^2 + 10x - 264$ and -22 and 12. We also know that -22 is a zero of $g(x) = x + 22$ and 12 is a zero of $h(x) = x - 12$. Using the principle of zero products in reverse, we have

$$x^2 + 10x - 264 = (x + 22)(x - 12).$$

56. $(x + 28)(x - 12)$

57. Graph $y = x^2 + 40x + 384$ and find the zeros. They are -24 and -16. We know that -24 is a zero of $y(x) = x + 24$ and -16 is a zero of $h(x) = x + 16$. Using the principle of zero products in reverse, we have

$$x^2 + 40x + 384 = (x + 24)(x + 16).$$

58. $(x + 12)(x - 25)$

59. Graph $y = x^2 + 26x - 2432$ and find the zeros. They are -64 and 38. We know that -64 is a zero of $g(x) = x + 64$ and 38 is a zero of $h(x) = x - 38$. Using the principle of zero products in reverse, we have

$$x^2 + 26x - 2432 = (x + 64)(x - 38).$$

60. $(x - 18)(x - 28)$

61. We write a linear function for each zero:

-1 is a zero of $g(x) = x + 1$;

2 is a zero of $h(x) = x - 2$.

Then $f(x) = (x + 1)(x - 2)$, or $f(x) = x^2 - x - 2$.

62. $f(x) = x^2 - 7x + 10$

63. We write a linear function for each zero:

-7 is a zero of $g(x) = x + 7$;

-10 is a zero of $h(x) = x + 10$.

Then $f(x) = (x + 7)(x + 10)$, or $f(x) = x^2 + 17x + 70$.

64. $f(x) = x^2 - 5x - 24$

65. We write a linear function for each zero:

0 is a zero of $g(x) = x$;

1 is a zero of $h(x) = x - 1$;

2 is a zero of $k(x) = x - 2$.

Then $f(x) = x(x-1)(x-2)$, or $f(x) = x^3 - 3x^2 + 2x$.

66. $f(x) = x^3 - 2x^2 - 15x$

67. *Writing Exercise*

68. *Writing Exercise*

69. $\quad (3x - 2)(5x + 1)$

$= 15x^2 + 3x - 10x - 2 \qquad$ Using FOIL

$= 15x^2 - 7x - 2$

70. $4x^2 - 12x + 9$

71. $(5a^4)^3 = 5^3(a^4)^3 = 125a^{4 \cdot 3} = 125a^{12}$

72. $-32x^{10}$

73. $\quad g(x) = -5x^2 - 7x$

$g(-3) = -5(-3)^2 - 7(-3) = -5 \cdot 9 + 21 =$

$-45 + 21 = -24$

74. 880 ft; 960 ft; 1024 ft; 624 ft; 240 ft

75. *Writing Exercise*

76. *Writing Exercise*

77. The x-coordinates of the x-intercepts are -1 and 3. Thus the solution set of $x^2 - 2x - 3 = 0$ is $\{-1, 3\}$.

From the graph we see that the x-values for which $f(x) < 5$ are in the interval $(-2, 4)$. We could also express the solution set as $\{x | -2 < x < 4\}$.

78. $\{-3, 1\}$; $[-4, 2]$, or $\{x | -4 \le x \le 2\}$

79. Answers may vary. A polynomial function of lowest degree that meets the given criteria is of the form $f(x) = ax^3 + bx^2 + cx + d$. Substituting, we have

$a \cdot 2^3 + b \cdot 2^2 + c \cdot 2 + d = 0$,

$a(-1)^3 + b(-1)^2 + c(-1) + d = 0$,

$a \cdot 3^3 + b \cdot 3^2 + c \cdot 3 + d = 0$,

$a \cdot 0^3 + b \cdot 0^2 + c \cdot 0 + d = 30$, or

$8a + 4b + 2c + d = 0$,

$-a + b - c + d = 0$,

$27a + 9b + 3c + d = 0$,

$ d = 30$.

Solving the system of equations, we get $(5, -20, 5, 30)$, so the corresponding function is $f(x) = 5x^3 - 20x^2 + 5x + 30$.

80. Answers may vary. $g(x) = 3x^3 - 9x^2 - 39x + 45$

81. Graph $y_1 = -x^2 + 13.80x$ and $y_2 = 47.61$ and use the Intersect feature to find the first coordinate of the point of intersection. The solution is 6.90.

82. $-3.33, 5.15$

83. Graph $y_1 = x^3 - 3.48x^2 + x$ and $y_2 = 3.48$ and use the Intersect feature to find the first coordinates of the points of intersection. The solution is 3.48.

84. No real-number solutions

85. $2a^4b^6 - 3a^2b^3 - 20ab^2 = ab^2(2a^3b^4 - 3ab - 20)$

The trinomial $2a^3b^4 - 3ab - 20$ cannot be factored as a product of two binomials. Thus, the complete factorization is $ab^2(2a^3b^4 - 3ab - 20)$.

86. $5(x^4y^3 + 4)(x^4y^3 + 3)$

87. $x^2 - \dfrac{4}{25} + \dfrac{3}{5}x = x^2 + \dfrac{3}{5}x - \dfrac{4}{25}$

We look for factors of $-\dfrac{4}{25}$ whose sum is $\dfrac{3}{5}$. The

factors are $\dfrac{4}{5}$ and $-\dfrac{1}{5}$. The factorization is

$\left(x + \dfrac{4}{5}\right)\left(x - \dfrac{1}{5}\right)$.

88. $\left(y + \dfrac{4}{7}\right)\left(y - \dfrac{2}{7}\right)$

89. $y^2 + 0.4y - 0.05$

We look for factors of -0.05 whose sum is 0.4. The factors are -0.1 and 0.5. The factorization is $(y - 0.1)(y + 0.5)$.

90. $(x^a + 8)(x^a - 3)$

91. $\quad x^2 + ax + bx + ab$

$= x(x + a) + b(x + a)$

$= (x + a)(x + b)$

92. $(bx + a)(dx + c)$

93. $a^2p^{2a} + a^2p^a - 2a^2 = a^2(p^{2a} + p^a - 2)$

Substitute u for p^a (and u^2 for p^{2a}). We factor $u^2 + u - 2$. Look for factors of -2 whose sum is 1. The factors are 2 and -1. We have $u^2 + u - 2 = (u + 2)(u - 1)$. Replace u by p^a: $p^{2a} + p^a - 2 = (p^a + 2)(p^a - 1)$. We must include the common factor a^2 to get a factorization of the original trinomial:

$a^2p^{2a} + a^2p^a - 2a^2 = a^2(p^a + 2)(p^a - 1)$

94. $(x - 4)(x + 8)$

95. All such m are the sums of the factors of 75.

Pair of Factors	Sum of Factors
75, 1	76
−75, −1	−76
25, 3	28
−25, −3	−28
15, 5	20
−15, −5	−20

m can be 76, -76, 28, -28, 20, or -20.

96. $31, -31, 14, -14, 4, -4$

97. $20(-365) = -7300$ and $20 + (-365) = -345$ so the other factor is $(x - 365)$.

Exercise Set 6.3

1. $6x^2 - 5x - 25$

We will use the FOIL method.

1. There is no common factor (other than 1 or -1.)

2. Factor the first term, $6x^2$. The factors are $6x$, x and $3x$, $2x$. We have these possibilities:

   $(6x+\quad)(x+\quad)$ or $(3x+\quad)(2x+\quad)$

3. Factor the last term, -25. The possibilities are $25(-1)$, $-25 \cdot 1$, and $-5 \cdot 5$.

4. We need factors for which the sum of the products (the "outer" and "inner" parts of FOIL) is the middle term, $-5x$. Try some possibilities and check by multiplying.

   $$(6x - 5)(x + 5) = 6x^2 + 25x - 25$$

   We try again.

   $$(3x + 5)(2x - 5) = 6x^2 - 5x - 25$$

   The factorization is $(3x + 5)(2x - 5)$.

2. $(3x + 2)(x - 6)$

3. $10y^3 - 12y - 7y^2 = 10y^3 - 7y^2 - 12y$

We will use the grouping method.

1. Look for a common factor. We factor out y:

   $$y(10y^2 - 7y - 12)$$

2. Factor the trinomial $10y^2 - 7y - 12$. Multiply the leading coefficient, 10, and the constant, -12.

   $$10(-12) = -120$$

3. Try to factor -120 so the sum of the factors is -7. We need only consider pairs of factors in which the negative factor has the larger absolute value, since their sum is negative.

Pair of Factors	Sum of Factors
$-120, 1$	-119
$-30, 4$	-26
$-15, 8$	-7

4. We split the middle term, $-12y$, using the results of step (3).

   $$-7y = -15y + 8y$$

5. Factor by grouping:

   $$10y^2 - 7y - 12 = 10y^2 - 15y + 8y - 12$$
   $$= 5y(2y - 3) + 4(2y - 3)$$
   $$= (2y - 3)(5y + 4)$$

We must include the common factor to get a factorization of the original trinomial:

   $$10y^3 - 12y - 7y^2 = y(2y - 3)(5y + 4)$$

4. $x(3x - 5)(2x + 3)$

5. $24a^2 - 14a + 2$

We will use the FOIL method.

1. Factor out the common factor, 2:

   $$2(12a^2 - 7a + 1)$$

2. Now we factor the trinomial $12a^2 - 7a + 1$. Factor the first term, $12a^2$. The factors are $12a$, a and $6a$, $2a$ and $4a$, $3a$. We have these possibilities:

   $(12a+\quad)(a+\quad)$, $(6a+\quad)(2a+\quad)$, $(4a+\quad)(3a+\quad)$.

3. Factor the last term, 1. The possibilities are $1 \cdot 1$ and $-1(-1)$.

4. Look for factors such that the sum of the products is the middle term, $-7a$. Trial and error leads us to the correct factorization:

   $$12a^2 - 7a + 1 = (4a - 1)(3a - 1)$$

   We must include the common factor to get a factorization of the original trinomial:

   $$24a^2 - 14a + 2 = 2(4a - 1)(3a - 1)$$

6. $(3a - 4)(a - 2)$

7. $35y^2 + 34y + 8$

We will use the grouping method.

1. There is no common factor (other than 1 or -1).

2. Multiply the leading coefficient, 35, and the constant, 8: $35(8) = 280$

3. Try to factor 280 so the sum of the factors is 34. We need only consider pairs of positive factors since 280 and 34 are both positive.

Pair of Factors	Sum of Factors
280, 1	281
140, 2	142
70, 4	74
56, 5	61
40, 7	47
28, 10	38
20, 14	34

4. Split $34y$ using the results of step (3):

   $$34y = 20y + 14y$$

5. Factor by grouping:

   $$35y^2 + 34y + 8 = 35y^2 + 20y + 14y + 8$$
   $$= 5y(7y + 4) + 2(7y + 4)$$
   $$= (7y + 4)(5y + 2)$$

8. $(3a + 2)(3a + 4)$

9. $4t + 10t^2 - 6 = 10t^2 + 4t - 6$

We will use the FOIL method.

1. Factor out the common factor, 2:
$$2(5t^2 + 2t - 3)$$

2. Now we factor the trinomial $5t^2 + 2t - 3$. Factor the first term, $5t^2$. The factors are $5t$ and t. We have this possibility: $(5t+\ )(t+\ )$

3. Factor the last term, -3. The possibilities are $(1)(-3)$ and $(-1)3$ as well as $(-3)(1)$ and $3(-1)$.

4. Look for factors such that the sum of the products is the middle term, $2t$. Trial and error leads us to the correct factorization:
$$5t^2 + 2t - 3 = (5t - 3)(t + 1)$$
We must include the common factor to get a factorization of the original trinomial:
$$4t + 10t^2 - 6 = 2(5t - 3)(t + 1)$$

10. $2(5x + 3)(3x - 1)$

11. $8x^2 - 16 - 28x = 8x^2 - 28x - 16$

We will use the grouping method.

1. Factor out the common factor, 4:
$$4(2x^2 - 7x - 4)$$

2. Now we factor the trinomial $2x^2 - 7x - 4$. Multiply the leading coefficient, 2, and the constant, -4: $2(-4) = -8$

3. Factor -8 so the sum of the factors is -7. We need only consider pairs of factors in which the negative factor has the larger absolute value, since their sum is negative.

Pair of Factors	Sum of Factors
-4, 2	-2
-8, 1	-7

4. Split $-7x$ using the results of step (3):
$$-7x = -8x + x$$

5. Factor by grouping:
$$2x^2 - 7x - 4 = 2x^2 - 8x + x - 4$$
$$= 2x(x - 4) + (x - 4)$$
$$= (x - 4)(2x + 1)$$
We must include the common factor to get a factorization of the original trinomial:
$$8x^2 - 16 - 28x = 4(x - 4)(2x + 1)$$

12. $6(3x - 4)(x + 1)$

13. $14x^4 - 19x^3 - 3x^2$

We will use the grouping method.

1. Factor out the common factor, x^2:
$$x^2(14x^2 - 19x - 3)$$

2. Now we factor the trinomial $14x^2 - 19x - 3$. Multiply the leading coefficient, 14, and the constant, -3: $14(-3) = -42$

3. Factor -42 so the sum of the factors is -19. We need only consider pairs of factors in which the negative factor has the larger absolute value, since the sum is negative.

Pair of Factors	Sum of Factors
-42, 1	-41
-21, 2	-19
-14, 3	-11
-7, 6	-1

4. Split $-19x$ using the results of step (3):
$$-19x = -21x + 2x$$

5. Factor by grouping:
$$14x^2 - 19x - 3 = 14x^2 - 21x + 2x - 3$$
$$= 7x(2x - 3) + 2x - 3$$
$$= (2x - 3)(7x + 1)$$
We must include the common factor to get a factorization of the original trinomial:
$$14x^4 - 19x^3 - 3x^2 = x^2(2x - 3)(7x + 1)$$

14. $2x^2(5x - 2)(7x - 4)$

15. $12a^2 - 4a - 16$

We will use the FOIL method.

1. Factor out the common factor, 4:
$$4(3a^2 - a - 4)$$

2. We now factor the trinomial $3a^2 - a - 4$. Factor the first term, $3a^2$. The possibility is $(3a+\ )(a+\ )$.

3. Factor the last term, -4. The possibilities are $-4 \cdot 1$, $4(-1)$, and $-2 \cdot 2$.

4. We need factors for which the sum of the products is the middle term, $-a$. Trial and error leads us to the correct factorization:
$$3a^2 - a - 4 = (3a - 4)(a + 1)$$
We must include the common factor to get a factorization of the original trinomial:
$$12a^2 - 4a - 16 = 4(3a - 4)(a + 1)$$

16. $2(6a + 5)(a - 2)$

17. $9x^2 + 15x + 4$

We will use the grouping method.

1. There is no common factor (other than 1 or -1).

2. Multiply the leading coefficient and constant: $9(4) = 36$

3. Factor 36 so the sum of the factors is 15. We need only consider pairs of positive factors since 36 and 15 are both positive.

Pair of Factors	Sum of Factors
36, 1	37
18, 2	20
12, 3	15
9, 4	13
6, 6	12

4. Split $15x$ using the results of step (3):
$$15x = 12x + 3x$$

5. Factor by grouping:
$$\begin{aligned} 9x^2 + 15x + 4 &= 9x^2 + 12x + 3x + 4 \\ &= 3x(3x+4) + 3x + 4 \\ &= (3x+4)(3x+1) \end{aligned}$$

18. $(3y - 2)(2y + 1)$

19. $4x^2 + 15x + 9$

We will use the FOIL method.

1. There is no common factor (other than 1 or -1).

2. Factor the first term, $4x^2$. The possibilities are $(4x+\quad)(x+\quad)$ and $(2x+\quad)(2x+\quad)$.

3. Factor the last term, 9. We consider only positive factors since both the middle term and the last term are positive. The possibilities are $9 \cdot 1$ and $3 \cdot 3$.

4. We need factors for which the sum of products is the middle term, $15x$. Trial and error leads us to the correct factorization:
$$(4x+3)(x+3)$$

20. $(2y + 3)(y + 2)$

21. $-8t^2 - 8t + 30$

We will use the grouping method.

1. Factor out -2: $-2(4t^2 + 4t - 15)$

2. Now we factor the trinomial $4t^2 + 4t - 15$. Multiply the leading coefficient and the constant: $4(-15) = -60$

3. Factor -60 so the sum of the factors is 4. The desired factorization is $10(-6)$.

4. Split $4t$ using the results of step (3):
$$4t = 10t - 6t$$

5. Factor by grouping:
$$\begin{aligned} 4t^2 + 4t - 15 &= 4t^2 + 10t - 6t - 15 \\ &= 2t(2t+5) - 3(2t+5) \\ &= (2t+5)(2t-3) \end{aligned}$$

We must include the common factor to get a factorization of the original trinomial:
$$-8t^2 - 8t + 30 = -2(2t+5)(2t-3)$$

22. $-3(4a - 1)(3a - 1)$

23. $8 - 6z - 9z^2$

We will use the FOIL method.

1. There is no common factor (other than 1 or -1).

2. Factor the first term, 8. The possibilities are $(8+\quad)(1+\quad)$ and $(4+\quad)(2+\quad)$.

3. Factor the last term, $-9z^2$. The possibilities are $-9z \cdot z$, $-3z \cdot 3z$, and $9z(-z)$.

4. We need factors for which the sum of products is the middle term, $-6z$. Trial and error leads us to the correct factorization:
$$(4+3z)(2-3z)$$

24. $(3 - a)(1 + 12a)$

25. $18xy^3 + 3xy^2 - 10xy$

We will use the FOIL method.

1. Factor out the common factor, xy.
$$xy(18y^2 + 3y - 10)$$

2. We now factor the trinomial $18y^2 + 3y - 10$. Factor the first term, $18y^2$. The possibilities are $(18y+\quad)(y+\quad)$, $(9y+\quad)(2y+\quad)$, and $(6y+\quad)(3y+\quad)$.

3. Factor the last term, -10. The possibilities are $-10 \cdot 1$, $-5 \cdot 2$, $10(-1)$ and $5(-2)$.

4. We need factors for which the sum of the products is the middle term, $3y$. Trial and error leads us to the correct factorization.
$$18y^2 + 3y - 10 = (6y+5)(3y-2)$$

We must include the common factor to get a factorization of the original trinomial:
$$18xy^3 + 3xy^2 - 10xy = xy(6y+5)(3y-2)$$

26. $xy^2(3x + 1)(x - 2)$

27. $24x^2 - 2 - 47x = 24x^2 - 47x - 2$

We will use the grouping method.

1. There is no common factor (other than 1 or -1).

2. Multiply the leading coefficient and the constant: $24(-2) = -48$

3. Factor -48 so the sum of the factors is -47. The desired factorization is $-48 \cdot 1$.

4. Split $-47x$ using the results of step (3):
$$-47x = -48x + x$$

5. Factor by grouping:
$$\begin{aligned} 24x^2 - 47x - 2 &= 24x^2 - 48x + x - 2 \\ &= 24x(x-2) + (x-2) \\ &= (x-2)(24x+1) \end{aligned}$$

28. $(5z + 1)(3z - 10)$

29. $63x^3 + 111x^2 + 36x$

We will use the FOIL method.

1. Factor out the common factor, $3x$.
$$3x(21x^2 + 37x + 12)$$

2. Now we will factor the trinomial $21x^2 + 37x + 12$. Factor the first term, $21x^2$. The factors are $21x$, x and $7x$, $3x$. We have these possibilities: $(21x+\quad)(x+\quad)$ and $(7x+\quad)(3x+\quad)$.

3. Factor the last term, 12. The possibilities are $12 \cdot 1$, $(-12)(-1)$, $6 \cdot 2$, $(-6)(-2)$, $4 \cdot 3$, and $(-4)(-3)$ as well as $1 \cdot 12$, $(-1)(-12)$, $2 \cdot 6$, $(-2)(-6)$, $3 \cdot 4$, and $(-3)(-4)$.

4. Look for factors such that the sum of the products is the middle term, $37x$. Trial and error leads us to the correct factorization:

$$(7x + 3)(3x + 4)$$

We must include the common factor to get a factorization of the original trinomial:

$$63x^3 + 111x^2 + 36x = 3x(7x + 3)(3x + 4)$$

30. $5t(5t + 4)(2t + 3)$

31. $48x^4 + 4x^3 - 30x^2$

We will use the grouping method.

1. We factor out the common factor, $2x^2$:

$$2x^2(24x^2 + 2x - 15)$$

2. We now factor $24x^2 + 2x - 15$. Multiply the leading coefficient and the constant:

$$24(-15) = -360$$

3. Factor -360 so the sum of the factors is 2. The desired factorization is $-18 \cdot 20$.

4. Split $2x$ using the results of step (3):

$$2x = -18x + 20x$$

5. Factor by grouping:

$$\begin{aligned} 24x^2 + 2x - 15 &= 24x^2 - 18x + 20x - 15 \\ &= 6x(4x - 3) + 5(4x - 3) \\ &= (4x - 3)(6x + 5) \end{aligned}$$

We must not forget to include the common factor:

$$48x^4 + 4x^3 - 30x^2 = 2x^2(4x - 3)(6x + 5)$$

32. $4(5y^2 + 3)(2y^2 - 1)$

33. $12a^2 - 17ab + 6b^2$

We will use the FOIL method. (Our thinking is much the same as if we were factoring $12a^2 - 17a + 6$.)

1. There is no common factor (other than 1 or -1).

2. Factor the first term, $12a^2$. The factors are $12a$, a and $6a$, $2a$ and $4a$, $3a$. We have these possibilities: $(12a+\quad)(a+\quad)$ and $(6a+\quad)(2a+\quad)$ and $(4a+\quad)(3a+\quad)$.

3. Factor the last term, $6b^2$. The possibilities are $6b \cdot b$, $(-6b)(-b)$, $3b \cdot 2b$, and $(-3b)(-2b)$ as well as $b \cdot 6b$, $(-b)(-6b)$, $2b \cdot 3b$, and $(-2b)(-3b)$.

4. Look for factors such that the sum of the products is the middle term, $-17ab$. Trial and error leads us to the correct factorization:

$$(4a - 3b)(3a - 2b)$$

34. $(4p - 3q)(5p - 2q)$

35. $2x^2 + xy - 6y^2$

We will use the grouping method.

1. There is no common factor (other than 1 or -1).

2. Multiply the coefficients of the first and last terms: $2(-6) = -12$

3. Factor -12 so the sum of the factors is 1. The desired factorization is $4(-3)$.

4. Split xy using the results of step (3):

$$xy = 4xy - 3xy$$

5. Factor by grouping:

$$\begin{aligned} 2x^2 + xy - 6y^2 &= 2x^2 + 4xy - 3xy - 6y^2 \\ &= 2x(x + 2y) - 3y(x + 2y) \\ &= (x + 2y)(2x - 3y) \end{aligned}$$

36. $(4m + 3n)(2m - 3n)$

37. $6x^2 - 29xy + 28y^2$

We will use the FOIL method.

1. There is no common factor (other than 1 or -1).

2. Factor the first term, $6x^2$. The factors are $6x$, x and $3x$, $2x$. We have these possibilities: $(6x+\quad)(x+\quad)$ and $(3x+\quad)(2x+\quad)$.

3. Factor the last term, $28y^2$. The possibilities are $28y \cdot y$, $(-28y)(-y)$, $14y \cdot 2y$, $(-14y)(-2y)$, $7y \cdot 4y$, and $(-7y)(-4y)$ as well as $y \cdot 28y$, $(-y)(-28y)$, $2y \cdot 14y$, $(-2y)(-14y)$, $4y \cdot 7y$, and $(-4y)(-7y)$.

4. Look for factors such that the sum of the products is the middle term, $-29xy$. Trial and error leads us to the correct factorization: $(3x - 4y)(2x - 7y)$

38. $(2p + 3q)(5p - 4q)$

39. $9x^2 - 30xy + 25y^2$

We will use the grouping method.

1. There is no common factor (other than 1 or -1).

2. Multiply the coefficients of the first and last terms: $9(25) = 225$

3. Factor 225 so the sum of the factors is -30. The desired factorization is $-15(-15)$.

4. Split $-30xy$ using the results of step (3):

$$-30xy = -15xy - 15xy$$

5. Factor by grouping:

$$\begin{aligned} 9x^2 - 30xy + 25y^2 &= 9x^2 - 15xy - 15xy + 25y^2 \\ &= 3x(3x - 5y) - 5y(3x - 5y) \\ &= (3x - 5y)(3x - 5y), \text{ or} \\ &\quad (3x - 5y)^2 \end{aligned}$$

40. $(2p + 3q)(2p + 3q)$, or $(2p + 3q)^2$

41. $9x^2y^2 + 5xy - 4$

Let $u = xy$ and $u^2 = x^2y^2$. Factor $9u^2 + 5u - 4$. We will use the FOIL method.

1. There is no common factor (other than 1 or -1).

2. Factor the first term, $9u^2$. The factors are $9u, u$ and $3u, 3u$. We have these possibilities: $(9u+ \ )(u+ \ )$ and $(3u+ \ )(3u+ \ )$.

3. Factor the last term, -4. The possibilities are $-4 \cdot 1$, $-2 \cdot 2$, and $-1 \cdot 4$.

4. We need factors for which the sum of the products is the middle term, $5u$. Trial and error leads us to the factorization: $(9u - 4)(u + 1)$. Replace u by xy. We have $9x^2y^2 + 5xy - 4 = (9xy - 4)(xy + 1)$.

42. $(7ab + 6)(ab + 1)$

43. $6x^2 - 5x - 25 = 0$

$(3x + 5)(2x - 5) = 0$ From Exercise 1

$3x + 5 = 0$ *or* $2x - 5 = 0$ Using the
$\qquad\qquad\qquad\qquad\qquad$ principle of zero products

$3x = -5$ *or* $2x = 5$

$x = -\dfrac{5}{3}$ *or* $x = \dfrac{5}{2}$

The solutions are $-\dfrac{5}{3}$ and $\dfrac{5}{2}$.

44. $-\dfrac{2}{3}, 6$

45. $9z^2 + 6z = 8$

$0 = 8 - 6z - 9z^2$

$0 = (4 + 3z)(2 - 3z)$ From Exercise 23

$4 + 3z = 0$ *or* $2 - 3z = 0$ Using the
$\qquad\qquad\qquad\qquad\qquad$ principle of zero products

$3z = -4$ *or* $2 = 3z$

$z = -\dfrac{4}{3}$ *or* $\dfrac{2}{3} = z$

The solutions are $-\dfrac{4}{3}$ and $\dfrac{2}{3}$.

46. $-\dfrac{1}{12}, 3$

47. $63x^3 + 111x^2 + 36x = 0$

$3x(7x + 3)(3x + 4) = 0$ From Exercise 29

$3x = 0$ *or* $7x + 3 = 0$ *or* $3x + 4 = 0$

$x = 0$ *or* $7x = -3$ *or* $3x = -4$

$x = 0$ *or* $x = -\dfrac{3}{7}$ *or* $x = -\dfrac{4}{3}$

The solutions are 0, $-\dfrac{3}{7}$, and $-\dfrac{4}{3}$.

48. $-\dfrac{3}{2}, -\dfrac{4}{5}, 0$

49. $3x^2 - 8x + 4 = 0$

$(3x - 2)(x - 2) = 0$ Factoring

$3x - 2 = 0$ *or* $x - 2 = 0$

$3x = 2$ *or* $x = 2$

$x = \dfrac{2}{3}$ *or* $x = 2$

The solutions are $\dfrac{2}{3}$ and 2.

50. $\dfrac{1}{3}, \dfrac{4}{3}$

51. $4t^3 + 11t^2 + 6t = 0$

$t(4t^2 + 11t + 6) = 0$

$t(4t + 3)(t + 2) = 0$

$t = 0$ *or* $4t + 3 = 0$ *or* $t + 2 = 0$

$t = 0$ *or* $4t = -3$ *or* $t = -2$

$t = 0$ *or* $t = -\dfrac{3}{4}$ *or* $t = -2$

The solutions are 0, $-\dfrac{3}{4}$, and -2.

52. $-\dfrac{3}{4}, -\dfrac{1}{2}, 0$

53. $6x^2 = 13x + 5$

$6x^2 - 13x - 5 = 0$

$(2x - 5)(3x + 1) = 0$

$2x - 5 = 0$ *or* $3x + 1 = 0$

$2x = 5$ *or* $3x = -1$

$x = \dfrac{5}{2}$ *or* $x = -\dfrac{1}{3}$

The solutions are $\dfrac{5}{2}$ and $-\dfrac{1}{3}$.

54. $-\dfrac{6}{5}, \dfrac{1}{8}$

55. $x(5 + 12x) = 28$

$5x + 12x^2 = 28$

$5x + 12x^2 - 28 = 0$

$12x^2 + 5x - 28 = 0$ Rearranging

$(4x + 7)(3x - 4) = 0$

$4x + 7 = 0$ *or* $3x - 4 = 0$

$4x = -7$ *or* $3x = 4$

$x = -\dfrac{7}{4}$ *or* $x = \dfrac{4}{3}$

The solutions are $-\dfrac{7}{4}$ and $\dfrac{4}{3}$.

56. $-\dfrac{5}{7}, \dfrac{2}{3}$

57. The zeros of $f(x) = 2x^2 - 13x - 7$ are the roots, or solutions, of the equation $2x^2 - 13x - 7 = 0$.

$$2x^2 - 13x - 7 = 0$$
$$(2x + 1)(x - 7) = 0$$
$$2x + 1 = 0 \quad or \quad x - 7 = 0$$
$$2x = -1 \quad or \quad \quad x = 7$$
$$x = -\frac{1}{2} \quad or \quad \quad x = 7$$

The zeros are $-\frac{1}{2}$ and 7.

58. $-\frac{3}{2}, -\frac{2}{3}$

59. We set $f(a)$ equal to 8.

$$a^2 + 12a + 40 = 8$$
$$a^2 + 12a + 32 = 0$$
$$(a + 8)(a + 4) = 0$$
$$a + 8 = 0 \quad or \quad a + 4 = 0$$
$$a = -8 \quad or \quad \quad a = -4$$

The values of a for which $f(a) = 8$ are -8 and -4.

60. $-9, -5$

61. We set $g(a)$ equal to 12.

$$2a^2 + 5a = 12$$
$$2a^2 + 5a - 12 = 0$$
$$(2a - 3)(a + 4) = 0$$
$$2a - 3 = 0 \quad or \quad a + 4 = 0$$
$$2a = 3 \quad or \quad \quad a = -4$$
$$a = \frac{3}{2} \quad or \quad \quad a = -4$$

The values of a for which $g(a) = 12$ are $\frac{3}{2}$ and -4.

62. $\frac{1}{2}, 7$

63. We set $h(a)$ equal to -27.

$$12a + a^2 = -27$$
$$12a + a^2 + 27 = 0$$
$$a^2 + 12a + 27 = 0 \quad \text{Rearranging}$$
$$(a + 3)(a + 9) = 0$$
$$a + 3 = 0 \quad or \quad a + 9 = 0$$
$$a = -3 \quad or \quad \quad a = -9$$

The values of a for which $h(a) = -27$ are -3 and -9.

64. $-4, 8$

65. $f(x) = \dfrac{3}{x^2 - 4x - 5}$

$f(x)$ cannot be calculated for any x-value for which the denominator, $x^2 - 4x - 5$, is 0. To find the excluded values, we solve:

$$x^2 - 4x - 5 = 0$$
$$(x - 5)(x + 1) = 0$$

$$x - 5 = 0 \quad or \quad x + 1 = 0$$
$$x = 5 \quad or \quad \quad x = -1$$

The domain of f is $\{x | x$ is a real number and $x \neq 5$ and $x \neq -1\}$.

66. $\{x | x$ is a real number and $x \neq 6$ and $x \neq 1\}$

67. $f(x) = \dfrac{x - 5}{9x - 18x^2}$

$f(x)$ cannot be calculated for any x-value for which the denominator, $9x - 18x^2$, is 0. To find the excluded values, we solve:

$$9x - 18x^2 = 0$$
$$9x(1 - 2x) = 0$$
$$9x = 0 \quad or \quad 1 - 2x = 0$$
$$x = 0 \quad or \quad \quad -2x = -1$$
$$x = 0 \quad or \quad \quad x = \frac{1}{2}$$

The domain of f is $\left\{ x | x \text{ is a real number } and \ x \neq 0 \ and \right.$
$\left. x \neq \frac{1}{2} \right\}$.

68. $\left\{ x | x \text{ is a real number } and \ x \neq 0 \ and \ x \neq \frac{1}{5} \right\}$

69. $f(x) = \dfrac{7}{5x^3 - 35x^2 + 50x}$

$f(x)$ cannot be calculated for any x-value for which the denominator, $5x^3 - 35x^2 + 50x$, is 0. To find the excluded values, we solve:

$$5x^3 - 35x^2 + 50x = 0$$
$$5x(x^2 - 7x + 10) = 0$$
$$5x(x - 2)(x - 5) = 0$$
$$5x = 0 \quad or \quad x - 2 = 0 \quad or \quad x - 5 = 0$$
$$x = 0 \quad or \quad \quad x = 2 \quad or \quad \quad x = 5$$

The domain of f is $\{x | x$ is a real number and $x \neq 0$ and $x \neq 2$ and $x \neq 5\}$.

70. $\{x | x$ is a real number and $x \neq 0$ and $x \neq 3$ and $x \neq -2\}$

71. *Writing Exercise*

72. *Writing Exercise*

73. $(2x + 0.1)(2x - 0.1) = (2x)^2 - (0.1)^2 = 4x^2 - 0.01$

74. -2

75. Write the equation in slope-intercept form, $y = mx + b$ where m is the slope and b is the y-intercept.

$$4x - 3y = 8$$
$$-3y = -4x + 8$$
$$y = \frac{4}{3}x - \frac{8}{3}$$

The slope is $\frac{4}{3}$, and the y-intercept is $\left(0, -\frac{8}{3}\right)$.

76. $\{27, -27\}$

77. $|5x - 6| \leq 39$

$$-39 \leq 5x - 6 \leq 39$$
$$-33 \leq 5x \leq 45$$
$$-\frac{33}{5} \leq x \leq 9$$

The solution set is $\left\{x \mid -\frac{33}{5} \leq x \leq 9\right\}$, or $\left[-\frac{33}{5}, 9\right]$.

78. $\left\{x \mid x < -\frac{33}{5} \text{ or } x > 9\right\}$, or $\left(-\infty, -\frac{33}{5}\right) \cup (9, \infty)$.

79. *Writing Exercise*

80. *Writing Exercise*

81. Graph $y = 4x^2 + 120x + 675$ and find the zeros. They are -7.5 and -22.5, or $-\frac{15}{2}$ and $-\frac{45}{2}$. We know that $-\frac{15}{2}$ is a zero of $g(x) = 2x + 15$ and $-\frac{45}{2}$ is a zero of $h(x) = 2x + 45$. We have $4x^2 + 120x + 675 = (2x + 15)(2x + 45)$.

82. $(2x + 63)(2x + 19)$

83. First factor out the largest common factor.

$$3x^3 + 150x^2 - 3672x = 3x(x^2 + 50x - 1224).$$

Now graph $y = x^2 + 50x - 1224$ and find the zeros. They are -68, and 18. We know that -68 is a zero of $g(x) = x + 68$, and 18 is a zero of $h(x) = x - 18$.

We have $x^2 + 50x - 1224 = (x + 68)(x - 18)$, so $3x^3 + 150x^2 - 3672x = 3x(x + 68)(x - 18)$.

84. $5x^2(x + 20)(x - 16)$

85.

$$(8x + 11)(12x^2 - 5x - 2) = 0$$
$$(8x + 11)(3x - 2)(4x + 1) = 0$$

$$8x + 11 = 0 \quad or \quad 3x - 2 = 0 \quad or \quad 4x + 1 = 0$$
$$8x = -11 \quad or \quad 3x = 2 \quad or \quad 4x = -1$$
$$x = -\frac{11}{8} \quad or \quad x = \frac{2}{3} \quad or \quad x = -\frac{1}{4}$$

The solutions are $-\frac{11}{8}$, $\frac{2}{3}$, and $-\frac{1}{4}$.

86. $-2, 2$

87.

$$(x - 2)^3 = x^3 - 2$$
$$x^3 - 6x^2 + 12x - 8 = x^3 - 2$$
$$0 = 6x^2 - 12x + 6$$
$$0 = 6(x^2 - 2x + 1)$$
$$0 = 6(x - 1)(x - 1)$$

$$x - 1 = 0 \quad or \quad x - 1 = 0$$
$$x = 1 \quad or \quad x = 1$$

The solution 1.

88. $(2x - 9)(3x - 22)$

89. $2a^4b^6 - 3a^2b^3 - 20$

Let $u = a^2b^3$ (and $u^2 = a^4b^6$). Factor $2u^2 - 3u - 20$. We will use the FOIL method.

1. There is no common factor (other than 1 or -1).

2. Factor the first term, $2u^2$. The factors are $2u$, u. The possibility is $(2u+\quad)(u+\quad)$.

3. Factor the last term, -20. The possibilities are $-20 \cdot 1$, $-10 \cdot 2$, $-5 \cdot 4$, $-4 \cdot 5$, $-2 \cdot 10$, and $-1 \cdot 20$.

4. We need factors for which the sum of the products is the middle term, $-3u$. Trial and error leads us to the factorization: $(2u + 5)(u - 4)$. Replace u by a^2b^3. We have $(2a^2b^3 + 5)(a^2b^3 - 4)$.

90. $5(x^4y^3 + 4)(x^4y^3 + 3)$

91. $4x^{2a} - 4x^a - 3$

Let $u = x^a$ (and $u^2 = x^{2a}$). Factor $4u^2 - 4u - 3$. We will use the grouping method. Multiply the leading coefficient and the constant: $4(-3) = -12$. Factor -12 so the sum of the factors is -4. The desired factorizations is $-6 \cdot 2$.

Split the middle term and factor by grouping.

$$4u^2 - 4u - 3 = 4u^2 - 6u + 2u - 3$$
$$= 2u(2u - 3) + (2u - 3)$$
$$= (2u - 3)(2u + 1)$$

Replace u by x^a. The factorization is $(2x^a - 3)(2x^a + 1)$.

92. $a(2r + s)(r + s)$

93. See the answer section in the text.

Exercise Set 6.4

1. $x^2 + 8x + 16 = (x + 4)^2$

Find the square terms and write the quantities that were squared with a plus sign between them.

2. $(t + 3)^2$

3. $a^2 + 16a + 64 = (a + 8)^2$

Find the square terms and write the quantities that were squared with a minus sign between them.

4. $(a - 7)^2$

5. $\quad 2a^2 + 8a + 8$

$= 2(a^2 + 4a + 4) \quad$ Factoring out the common factor

$= 2(a + 2)^2 \quad$ Factoring the perfect-square trinomial

6. $4(a - 2)^2$

7. $\quad y^2 + 36 - 12y$

$= y^2 - 12y + 36 \quad$ Changing order

$= (y - 6)^2 \quad$ Factoring the perfect-square trinomial

8. $(y+6)^2$

9. $24a^2 + a^3 + 144a$

$= a^3 + 24a^2 + 144a$ Changing order

$= a(a^2 + 24a + 144)$ Factoring out the
common factor

$= a(a+12)^2$ Factoring the perfect-square
trinomial

10. $y(y-9)^2$

11. $32x^2 + 48x + 18$

$= 2(16x^2 + 24x + 9)$ Factoring out the
common factor

$= 2(4x+3)^2$ Factoring the perfect-square
trinomial

12. $2(x-10)^2$

13. $64 + 25a^2 - 80a$

$= 25a^2 - 80a + 64$ Changing order

$= (5a-8)^2$ Factoring the perfect-square
trinomial

14. $(1-4d)^2$

15. $0.25x^2 + 0.30x + 0.09 = (0.5x + 0.3)^2$

Find the square terms and write
the quantities that were squared
with a plus sign between them.

16. $(0.2x - 0.7)^2$

17. $p^2 - 2pq + q^2 = (p-q)^2$

18. $(m+n)^2$

19. $a^3 - 10a^2 + 25a$

$= a(a^2 - 10a + 25)$

$= a(a-5)^2$

20. $y(y+4)^2$

21. $25a^2 - 30ab + 9b^2 = (5a - 3b)^2$

22. $(7p - 6q)^2$

23. $4t^2 - 8tr + 4r^2$

$= 4(t^2 - 2tr + r^2)$

$= 4(t-r)^2$

24. $5(a-b)^2$

25. $x^2 - 16 = x^2 - 4^2 = (x+4)(x-4)$

26. $(y+10)(y-10)$

27. $p^2 - 49 = p^2 - 7^2 = (p+7)(p-7)$

28. $(m+8)(m-8)$

29. $a^2b^2 - 81 = (ab)^2 - 9^2 = (ab+9)(ab-9)$

30. $(pq+5)(pq-5)$

31. $6x^2 - 6y^2$

$= 6(x^2 - y^2)$ Factoring out the common
factor

$= 6(x+y)(x-y)$ Factoring the difference
of squares

32. $8(x+y)(x-y)$

33. $7xy^4 - 7xz^4$

$= 7x(y^4 - z^4)$

$= 7x[(y^2)^2 - (z^2)^2]$

$= 7x(y^2 + z^2)(y^2 - z^2)$

$= 7x(y^2 + z^2)(y+z)(y-z)$

34. $25a(b^2 + z^2)(b+z)(b-z)$

35. $4a^3 - 49a = a(4a^2 - 49)$

$= a[(2a)^2 - 7^2]$

$= a(2a+7)(2a-7)$

36. $x^2(3x+5)(3x-5)$

37. $3x^8 - 3y^8$

$= 3(x^8 - y^8)$

$= 3[(x^4)^2 - (y^4)^2]$

$= 3(x^4 + y^4)(x^4 - y^4)$

$= 3(x^4 + y^4)[(x^2)^2 - (y^2)^2]$

$= 3(x^4 + y^4)(x^2 + y^2)(x^2 - y^2)$

$= 3(x^4 + y^4)(x^2 + y^2)(x+y)(x-y)$

38. $a^2(3a+b)(3a-b)$

39. $9a^4 - 25a^2b^4 = a^2(9a^2 - 25b^4)$

$= a^2[(3a)^2 - (5b^2)^2]$

$= a^2(3a + 5b^2)(3a - 5b^2)$

40. $x^2(4x^2 + 11y^2)(4x^2 - 11y^2)$

41. $\dfrac{1}{25} - x^2 = \left(\dfrac{1}{5}\right)^2 - x^2$

$= \left(\dfrac{1}{5} + x\right)\left(\dfrac{1}{5} - x\right)$

42. $\left(\dfrac{1}{4} + y\right)\left(\dfrac{1}{4} - y\right)$

43. $(a+b)^2 - 9 = (a+b)^2 - 3^2$

$= [(a+b) + 3][(a+b) - 3]$

$= (a+b+3)(a+b-3)$

44. $(p+q+5)(p+q-5)$

45. $x^2 - 6x + 9 - y^2$

$= (x^2 - 6x + 9) - y^2$ Grouping as a difference
of squares

$= (x-3)^2 - y^2$

$= (x-3+y)(x-3-y)$

46. $(a-4+b)(a-4-b)$

47. $m^2 - 2mn + n^2 - 25$
$= (m^2 - 2mn + n^2) - 25$ Grouping as a
$\qquad\qquad\qquad\qquad$ difference of squares
$= (m - n)^2 - 5^2$
$= (m - n + 5)(m - n - 5)$

48. $(x + y + 3)(x + y - 3)$

49. $36 - (x + y)^2 = 6^2 - (x + y)^2$
$\qquad\qquad\quad = [6 + (x + y)][6 - (x + y)]$
$\qquad\qquad\quad = (6 + x + y)(6 - x - y)$

50. $(7 + a + b)(7 - a - b)$

51. $r^2 - 2r + 1 - 4s^2$
$= (r^2 - 2r + 1) - 4s^2$ Grouping as a
$\qquad\qquad\qquad\qquad$ difference of squares
$= (r - 1)^2 - (2s)^2$
$= (r - 1 + 2s)(r - 1 - 2s)$

52. $(c + 2d + 3p)(c + 2d - 3p)$

53. $16 - a^2 - 2ab - b^2$
$= 16 - (a^2 + 2ab + b^2)$ Grouping as a
$\qquad\qquad\qquad\qquad\quad$ difference of squares
$= 4^2 - (a + b)^2$
$= [4 + (a + b)][4 - (a + b)]$
$= (4 + a + b)(4 - a - b)$

54. $(3 + x + y)(3 - x - y)$

55. $m^3 - 7m^2 - 4m + 28$
$= m^2(m - 7) - 4(m - 7)$ Factoring by
$\qquad\qquad\qquad\qquad\qquad$ grouping
$= (m - 7)(m^2 - 4)$
$= (m - 7)(m + 2)(m - 2)$ Factoring the
$\qquad\qquad\qquad\qquad\qquad\quad$ difference of squares

56. $(x + 8)(x + 1)(x - 1)$

57. $a^3 - ab^2 - 2a^2 + 2b^2$
$= a(a^2 - b^2) - 2(a^2 - b^2)$ Factoring by
$\qquad\qquad\qquad\qquad\qquad\qquad$ grouping
$= (a^2 - b^2)(a - 2)$
$= (a + b)(a - b)(a - 2)$ Factoring the
$\qquad\qquad\qquad\qquad\qquad$ difference of squares

58. $(p + 5)(p - 5)(q + 3)$

59. $x^2 + 8x + 16 = 0$
$\qquad (x + 4)^2 = 0$ From Exercise 1
$(x + 4)(x + 4) = 0$
$x + 4 = 0$ or $x + 4 = 0$
$\quad x = -4$ or $\quad x = -4$
The solution is -4.

60. 7

61. $\qquad\qquad x^2 = 16$
$\qquad x^2 - 16 = 0$
$(x + 4)(x + 4) = 0$ From Exercise 25
$x + 4 = 0$ or $x - 4 = 0$
$\quad x = -4$ or $\qquad x = 4$
The solutions are -4 and 4.

62. $-10, 10$

63. $\qquad a^2 + 1 = 2a$
$\qquad a^2 - 2a + 1 = 0$
$(a - 1)(a - 1) = 0$
$a - 1 = 0$ or $a - 1 = 0$
$\quad a = 1$ or $\qquad a = 1$
The solution is 1.

64. 4

65. $2x^2 - 24x + 72 = 0$
$2(x^2 - 12x + 36) = 0$
$2(x - 6)(x - 6) = 0$
$x - 6 = 0$ or $x - 6 = 0$
$\quad x = 6$ or $\qquad x = 6$
The solution is 6.

66. -8

67. $\qquad x^2 - 9 = 0$
$(x + 3)(x - 3) = 0$
$x + 3 = 0$ or $x - 3 = 0$
$\quad x = -3$ or $\qquad x = 3$
The solutions are -3 and 3.

68. $-8, 8$

69. $\qquad\qquad a^2 = \dfrac{1}{25}$
$\qquad a^2 - \dfrac{1}{25} = 0$
$\left(a + \dfrac{1}{5}\right)\left(a - \dfrac{1}{5}\right) = 0$
$a + \dfrac{1}{5} = 0$ or $a - \dfrac{1}{5} = 0$
$\quad a = -\dfrac{1}{5}$ or $\qquad a = \dfrac{1}{5}$
The solutions are $-\dfrac{1}{5}$ and $\dfrac{1}{5}$.

70. $-\dfrac{1}{10}, \dfrac{1}{10}$

71.
$$8x^3 + 1 = 4x^2 + 2x$$
$$8x^3 - 4x^2 - 2x + 1 = 0$$
$$4x^2(2x - 1) - (2x - 1) = 0$$
$$(2x - 1)(4x^2 - 1) = 0$$
$$(2x - 1)(2x + 1)(2x - 1) = 0$$
$$2x - 1 = 0 \quad or \quad 2x + 1 = 0 \quad or \quad 2x - 1 = 0$$
$$2x = 1 \quad or \quad 2x = -1 \quad or \quad 2x = 1$$
$$x = \frac{1}{2} \quad or \quad x = -\frac{1}{2} \quad or \quad x = \frac{1}{2}$$

The solutions are $\frac{1}{2}$ and $-\frac{1}{2}$.

72. $-\frac{2}{3}, \frac{2}{3}$

73.
$$x^3 + 3 = 3x^2 + x$$
$$x^3 - 3x^2 - x + 3 = 0$$
$$x^2(x - 3) - (x - 3) = 0$$
$$(x - 3)(x^2 - 1) = 0$$
$$(x - 3)(x + 1)(x - 1) = 0$$
$$x - 3 = 0 \; or \; x + 1 = 0 \quad or \; x - 1 = 0$$
$$x = 3 \; or \quad x = -1 \; or \quad x = 1$$

The solutions are 3, -1, and 1.

74. $-4, -1, 4$

75. The polynomial $x^2 - 3x - 7$ is prime. We solve the equation by graphing $y = x^2 - 3x - 7$ and finding the zeros. They are approximately -1.541 and 4.541. These are the solutions.

76. $0.209, 4.791$

77. The polynomial $2x^2 + 8x + 1$ is prime. We solve the equation by graphing $y = 2x^2 + 8x + 1$ and finding the zeros. They are approximately -3.871 and -0.129. These are the solutions.

78. $-0.768, 0.434$

79. The polynomial $x^3 + 3x^2 + x - 1$ is prime. We solve the equation by graphing $y = x^3 + 3x^2 + x - 1$ and finding the zeros. They are approximately -2.414, -1, and approximately 0.414. These are the solutions.

80. 0.544

81. We set $f(a)$ equal to -36.
$$a^2 - 12a = -36$$
$$a^2 - 12a + 36 = 0$$
$$(a - 6)(a - 6) = 0$$
$$a - 6 = 0 \quad or \quad a - 6 = 0$$
$$a = 6 \quad or \quad a = 6$$

The value of a for which $f(a) = -36$ is 6.

82. $-12, 12$

83. To find the zeros of $f(x) = x^2 - 16$, we find the roots of the equation $x^2 - 16 = 0$.
$$x^2 - 16 = 0$$
$$(x + 4)(x - 4) = 0$$
$$x + 4 = 0 \quad or \quad x - 4 = 0$$
$$x = -4 \; or \qquad x = 4$$

The zeros are -4 and 4.

84. 4

85. To find the zeros of $f(x) = 2x^2 + 4x + 2$, we find the roots of the equation $2x^2 + 4x + 2 = 0$.
$$2x^2 + 4x + 2 = 0$$
$$2(x^2 + 2x + 1) = 0$$
$$2(x + 1)(x + 1) = 0$$
$$x + 1 = 0 \quad or \; x + 1 = 0$$
$$x = -1 \; or \qquad x = -1$$

The zero is -1.

86. $-3, 3$

87. To find the zeros of $f(x) = x^3 - 2x^2 - x + 2$, we find the roots of the equation $x^3 - 2x^2 - x + 2 = 0$.
$$x^3 - 2x^2 - x + 2 = 0$$
$$x^2(x - 2) - (x - 2) = 0$$
$$(x - 2)(x^2 - 1) = 0$$
$$(x - 2)(x + 1)(x - 1) = 0$$
$$x - 2 = 0 \; or \; x + 1 = 0 \quad or \; x - 1 = 0$$
$$x = 2 \; or \qquad x = -1 \; or \qquad x = 1$$

The zeros are 2, -1, and 1.

88. $-2, -1, 2$

89. *Writing Exercise*

90. *Writing Exercise*

91. $(2a^4b^5)^3 = 2^3(a^4)^3(b^5)^3 = 8a^{4 \cdot 3}b^{5 \cdot 3} = 8a^{12}b^{15}$

92. $125x^6y^{12}$

93.
$$(x + y)^3$$
$$= (x + y)(x + y)^2$$
$$= (x + y)(x^2 + 2xy + y^2)$$
$$= x(x^2 + 2xy + y^2) + y(x^2 + 2xy + y^2)$$
$$= x^3 + 2x^2y + xy^2 + x^2y + 2xy^2 + y^3$$
$$= x^3 + 3x^2y + 3xy^2 + y^3$$

94. $a^3 + 3a^2 + 3a + 1$

95.
$$-2 < 5 - 7x < 9$$
$$-7 < -7x < 4 \qquad \text{Subtracting 5}$$
$$1 > x > -\frac{4}{7} \qquad \text{Dividing by } -7 \text{ and}$$
$$\qquad\qquad\qquad \text{reversing the inequality symbol}$$
$$-\frac{4}{7} < x < 1 \qquad \text{Rewriting the result}$$

The solutions set is $\left\{ x \mid -\frac{4}{7} < x < 1 \right\}$, or $\left(-\frac{4}{7}, 1 \right)$.

96. $\left\{ x \Big| x \le -\dfrac{4}{7} \ or \ x \ge 2 \right\}$, or $\left(-\infty, -\dfrac{4}{7} \right] \cup [2, \infty)$

97. $|5 - 7x| \le 9$

$$-9 \le 5 - 7x \le 9$$
$$-14 \le -7x \le 4$$
$$2 \ge x \ge -\dfrac{4}{7}$$

The solution set is $\left\{ x \Big| -\dfrac{4}{7} \le x \le 2 \right\}$, or $\left[-\dfrac{4}{7}, 2 \right]$.

98. $\left\{ x \Big| x < \dfrac{14}{19} \right\}$, or $\left(-\infty, \dfrac{14}{19} \right)$

99. *Writing Exercise*

100. *Writing Exercise*

101.
$$-\dfrac{8}{27}r^2 - \dfrac{10}{9}rs - \dfrac{1}{6}s^2 + \dfrac{2}{3}rs$$
$$= -\dfrac{8}{27}r^2 - \dfrac{4}{9}rs - \dfrac{1}{6}s^2$$
$$= -\dfrac{1}{54}(16r^2 + 24rs + 9s^2)$$
$$= -\dfrac{1}{54}(4r + 3s)^2$$

102. $\left(\dfrac{1}{6}x^4 + \dfrac{2}{3} \right)^2$, or $\dfrac{1}{36}(x^4 + 4)^2$

103. $0.09x^8 + 0.48x^4 + 0.64 = (0.3x^4 + 0.8)^2$, or $\dfrac{1}{100}(3x^4 + 8)^2$

104. $(a + b + c - 3)(a + b - c + 3)$

105.
$$r^2 - 8r - 25 - s^2 - 10s + 16$$
$$= (r^2 - 8r + 16) - (s^2 + 10s + 25)$$
$$= (r - 4)^2 - (s + 5)^2$$
$$= [(r - 4) + (s + 5)][(r - 4) - (s + 5)]$$
$$= (r - 4 + s + 5)(r - 4 - s - 5)$$
$$= (r + s + 1)(r - s - 9)$$

106. $(x^a + y)(x^a - y)$

107. $x^{4a} - y^{2b} = (x^{2a})^2 - (y^b)^2 = (x^{2a} + y^b)(x^{2a} - y^b)$

108. $4(y^{2a} + 5)^2$

109.
$$25y^{2a} - (x^{2b} - 2x^b + 1)$$
$$= (5y^a)^2 - (x^b - 1)^2$$
$$= [5y^a + (x^b - 1)][5y^a - (x^b - 1)]$$
$$= (5y^a + x^b - 1)(5y^a - x^b + 1)$$

110. $8(a - 7)^2$

111.
$$3(x + 1)^2 + 12(x + 1) + 12$$
$$= 3[(x + 1)^2 + 4(x + 1) + 4]$$
$$= 3[(x + 1) + 2]^2$$
$$= 3(x + 3)^2$$

112. $5(c^{50} + 4d^{50})(c^{25} + 2d^{25})(c^{25} - 2d^{25})$

113. $9x^{2n} - 6x^n + 1 = (3x^n)^2 - 6x^n + 1$
$$= (3x^n - 1)^2$$

114. $c(c^w + 1)^2$

115. If $P(x) = x^2$, then
$$P(a + h) - P(a)$$
$$= (a + h)^2 - a^2$$
$$= [(a + h) + a][(a + h) - a]$$
$$= (2a + h)h, \ or \ h(2a + h)$$

116. $h(2a + h)(2a^2 + 2ah + h^2)$

117. a) $\pi R^2 h - \pi r^2 h = \pi h(R^2 - r^2)$
$$= \pi h(R + r)(R - r)$$

b) Note that 4 m = 400 cm.
$$\pi R^2 h - \pi r^2 h$$
$$= \pi (50)^2(400) - \pi(10)^2(400)$$
$$= 1,000,000\pi - 40,000\pi$$
$$= 960,000\pi \ cm^3 \quad (or \ 0.96\pi \ m^3)$$
$$\approx 3,014,400 \ cm^3 \quad Using \ 3.14 \ for \ \pi$$

$$\pi h(R + r)(R - r)$$
$$= \pi(400)(50 + 10)(50 - 10)$$
$$= \pi(400)(60)(40)$$
$$= 960,000\pi \ cm^3 \quad (or \ 0.96\pi \ m^3)$$
$$\approx 3,014,400 \ cm^3 \quad Using \ 3.14 \ for \ \pi$$

118. Enter $y_1 = (x^2 - 3x + 2)^4$ and $y_2 = x^8 + 81x^4 + 16$ and look at a table of values. Observe that $y_1 \ne y_2$.

Exercise Set 6.5

1. $t^3 + 27 = t^3 + 3^3$
$$= (t + 3)(t^2 - 3t + 9)$$
$$A^3 + B^3 = (A + B)(A^2 - AB + B^2)$$

2. $(x + 4)(x^2 - 4x + 16)$

3. $x^3 - 8 = x^3 - 2^3$
$$= (x - 2)(x^2 + 2x + 4)$$
$$A^3 - B^3 = (A - B)(A^2 + AB + B^2)$$

4. $(z - 1)(z^2 + z + 1)$

5. $m^3 - 64 = m^3 - 4^3$
$$= (m - 4)(m^2 + 4m + 16)$$
$$A^3 - B^3 = (A - B)(A^2 + AB + B^2)$$

6. $(x - 3)(x^2 + 3x + 9)$

7. $8a^3 + 1 = (2a)^3 + 1^3$
$$= (2a + 1)(4a^2 - 2a + 1)$$
$$A^3 + B^3 = (A + B)(A^2 - AB + B^2)$$

8. $(3x + 1)(9x^2 - 3x + 1)$

9. $27 - 8t^3 = 3^3 - (2t)^3$
$$= (3 - 2t)(9 + 6t + 4t^2)$$

10. $(4 - 5x)(16 + 20x + 25x^2)$

11. $8x^3 + 27 = (2x)^3 + 3^3$
$$= (2x + 3)(4x^2 - 6x + 9)$$

12. $(3y + 4)(9y^2 - 12y + 16)$

13. $y^3 - z^3 = (y - z)(y^2 + yz + z^2)$

14. $(x - y)(x^2 + xy + y^2)$

15. $x^3 + \dfrac{1}{27} = x^3 + \left(\dfrac{1}{3}\right)^3$
$$= \left(x + \dfrac{1}{3}\right)\left(x^2 - \dfrac{1}{3}x + \dfrac{1}{9}\right)$$

16. $\left(a + \dfrac{1}{2}\right)\left(a^2 - \dfrac{1}{2}a + \dfrac{1}{4}\right)$

17. $2y^3 - 128 = 2(y^3 - 64)$
$$= 2(y^3 - 4^3)$$
$$= 2(y - 4)(y^2 + 4y + 16)$$

18. $8(t - 1)(t^2 + t + 1)$

19. $8a^3 + 1000 = 8(a^3 + 125)$
$$= 8(a^3 + 5^3)$$
$$= 8(a + 5)(a^2 - 5a + 25)$$

20. $2(3x + 1)(9x^2 - 3x + 1)$

21. $rs^3 + 64r = r(s^3 + 64)$
$$= r(s^3 + 4^3)$$
$$= r(s + 4)(s^2 - 4s + 16)$$

22. $a(b + 5)(b^2 - 5b + 25)$

23. $2y^3 - 54z^3 = 2(y^3 - 27z^3)$
$$= 2[y^3 - (3z)^3]$$
$$= 2(y - 3z)(y^2 + 3yz + 9z^2)$$

24. $5(x - 2z)(x^2 + 2xz + 4z^2)$

25. $y^3 + 0.125 = y^3 + (0.5)^3$
$$= (y + 0.5)(y^2 - 0.5y + 0.25)$$

26. $(x + 0.1)(x^2 - 0.1x + 0.01)$

27. $125c^6 - 8d^6 = (5c^2)^3 - (2d^2)^3$
$$= (5c^2 - 2d^2)(25c^4 + 10c^2d^2 + 4d^4)$$

28. $8(2x^2 - t^2)(4x^4 + 2x^2t^2 + t^4)$

29. $3z^5 - 3z^2 = 3z^2(z^3 - 1)$
$$= 3z^2(z^3 - 1^3)$$
$$= 3z^2(z - 1)(z^2 + z + 1)$$

30. $2y(y - 4)(y^2 + 4y + 16)$

31. $t^6 + 1 = (t^2)^3 + 1^3$
$$= (t^2 + 1)(t^4 - t^2 + 1)$$

32. $(z + 1)(z^2 - z + 1)(z - 1)(z^2 + z + 1)$

33. $p^6 - q^6$
$= (p^3)^2 - (q^3)^2$ Writing as a difference of squares
$= (p^3 + q^3)(p^3 - q^3)$ Factoring a difference of squares
$= (p + q)(p^2 - pq + q^2)(p - q)(p^2 + pq + q^2)$ Factoring a sum and a difference of cubes

34. $(t^2 + 4y^2)(t^4 - 4t^2y^2 + 16y^4)$

35. $a^9 + b^{12}c^{15}$
$= (a^3)^3 + (b^4c^5)^3$
$= (a^3 + b^4c^5)(a^6 - a^3b^4c^5 + b^8c^{10})$

36. $(x^4 - yz^4)(x^8 + x^4yz^4 + y^2z^8)$

37. $$x^3 + 1 = 0$$
$$(x + 1)(x^2 - x + 1) = 0$$
$$x + 1 = 0 \quad or \quad x^2 - x + 1 = 0$$
$$x = -1$$

We cannot factor $x^2 - x + 1$. The only real-number solution is -1.

38. 2

39. $$8x^3 = 27$$
$$8x^3 - 27 = 0$$
$$(2x - 3)(4x^2 + 6x + 9) = 0$$
$$2x - 3 = 0 \quad or \quad 4x^2 + 6x + 9 = 0$$
$$2x = 3$$
$$x = \dfrac{3}{2}$$

We cannot factor $4x^2 + 6x + 9$. The only real-number solution is $\dfrac{3}{2}$.

40. $-\dfrac{3}{4}$

41. $$2t^3 - 2000 = 0$$
$$2(t^3 - 1000) = 0$$
$$2(t - 10)(t^2 + 10t + 100) = 0$$
$$t - 10 = 0 \quad or \quad t^2 + 10t + 100 = 0$$
$$t = 10$$

We cannot factor $t^2 + 10t + 100$. The only real-number solution is 10.

42. $\dfrac{5}{2}$

43. *Writing Exercise*

44. *Writing Exercise*

45. $h(t) = -16t^2 + 80t + 224$

$h(0) = -16(0)^2 + 80(0) + 224 = 224$ ft

$h(1) = -16(1)^2 + 80(1) + 224 = 288$ ft

$h(3) = -16(3)^2 + 80(3) + 224 = 320$ ft

$h(4) = -16(4)^2 + 80(4) + 224 = 288$ ft

$h(6) = -16(6)^2 + 80(6) + 224 = 128$ ft

46. $f(x) = -\dfrac{3}{4}x - 5$

47. $\quad y - y_1 = m(x - x_1)$

$y - (-5) = 3(x - 1)$

$y + 5 = 3x - 3$

$y = 3x - 8$

$f(x) = 3x - 8 \qquad$ Using function notation

48. $f(x) = 2x - 8$

49. $\quad 3x - 5 = 0$

$3x = 5 \qquad$ Adding 5 to both sides

$x = \dfrac{5}{3} \qquad$ Dividing both sides by 3

The solution is $\dfrac{5}{3}$.

50. $-\dfrac{7}{2}$

51. *Writing Exercise*

52. *Writing Exercise*

53. $x^{6a} - y^{3b} = (x^{2a})^3 - (y^b)^3$

$= (x^{2a} - y^b)(x^{4a} + x^{2a}y^b + y^{2b})$

54. $2(x^a + 2y^b)(x^{2a} - 2x^ay^b + 4y^{2b})$

55. $\quad (x+5)^3 + (x-5)^3 \qquad$ Sum of cubes

$= [(x+5) + (x-5)][(x+5)^2 - (x+5)(x-5) + (x-5)^2]$

$= 2x[(x^2 + 10x + 25) - (x^2 - 25) + (x^2 - 10x + 25)]$

$= 2x(x^2 + 10x + 25 - x^2 + 25 + x^2 - 10x + 25)$

$= 2x(x^2 + 75)$

56. $\dfrac{1}{2}\left(\dfrac{1}{2}x^a + y^{2a}z^{3b}\right)\left(\dfrac{1}{4}x^{2a} - \dfrac{1}{2}x^ay^{2a}z^{3b} + y^{4a}z^{6b}\right)$, or

$\dfrac{1}{16}(x^a + 2y^{2a}z^{3b})(x^{2a} - 2x^ay^{2a}z^{3b} + 4y^{4a}z^{6b})$

57. $\quad 5x^3y^6 - \dfrac{5}{8}$

$= 5\left(x^3y^6 - \dfrac{1}{8}\right)$

$= 5\left(xy^2 - \dfrac{1}{2}\right)\left(x^2y^4 + \dfrac{1}{2}xy^2 + \dfrac{1}{4}\right)$

58. $-y(3x^2 + 3xy + y^2)$

59. $\quad x^{6a} - (x^{2a} + 1)^3$

$= [x^{2a} - (x^{2a} + 1)][x^{4a} + x^{2a}(x^{2a} + 1) + (x^{2a} + 1)^2]$

$= (x^{2a} - x^{2a} - 1)(x^{4a} + x^{4a} + x^{2a} + x^{4a} + 2x^{2a} + 1)$

$= -(3x^{4a} + 3x^{2a} + 1)$

60. $-(3x^{4a} - 3x^{2a} + 1)$

61. $\quad t^4 - 8t^3 - t + 8$

$= t^3(t - 8) - (t - 8)$

$= (t - 8)(t^3 - 1)$

$= (t - 8)(t - 1)(t^2 + t + 1)$

62. $h(3a^2 + 3ah + h^2)$

63. If $Q(x) = x^6$, then

$Q(a + h) - Q(a)$

$= (a + h)^6 - a^6$

$= [(a + h)^3 + a^3][(a + h)^3 - a^3]$

$= [(a + h) + a] \cdot [(a + h)^2 - (a + h)a + a^2] \cdot$

$\qquad [(a + h) - a] \cdot [(a + h)^2 + (a + h)a + a^2]$

$= (2a + h) \cdot (a^2 + 2ah + h^2 - a^2 - ah + a^2) \cdot (h) \cdot$

$\qquad (a^2 + 2ah + h^2 + a^2 + ah + a^2)$

$= h(2a + h)(a^2 + ah + h^2)(3a^2 + 3ah + h^2)$

64.

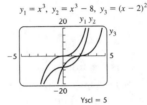

$y_1 = x^3,\ y_2 = x^3 - 8,\ y_3 = (x - 2)^2$

Yscl = 5

Exercise Set 6.6

1. $\quad 5x^2 - 45$

$= 5(x^2 - 9) \qquad$ 5 is a common factor.

$= 5(x + 3)(x - 3) \qquad$ Factoring the difference of squares

2. $10(a^2 - 64) = 10(a + 8)(a - 8)$

3. $\quad a^2 + 25 + 10a$

$= a^2 + 10a + 25 \qquad$ Perfect-square trinomial

$= (a + 5)^2$

4. $(y - 7)^2$

5. $8t^2 - 18t - 5$

There is no common factor (other than 1). This polynomial has three terms, but it is not a perfect-square trinomial. Multiply the leading coefficient and the constant, 8 and -5: $8(-5) = -40$. Try to factor -40 so that the sum of the factors is -18. The numbers we want are -20 and 2: $-20 \cdot 2 = -40$ and $-20 + 2 = -18$. Split the middle term and factor by grouping.

$8t^2 - 18t - 5 = 8t^2 - 20t + 2t - 5$

$= 4t(2t - 5) + 1(2t - 5)$

$= (2t - 5)(4t + 1)$

6. $(2t + 3)(t + 4)$

7. $x^3 - 24x^2 + 144x$

  $= x(x^2 - 24x + 144)$ x is a common factor.

  $= x(x^2 - 2 \cdot x \cdot 12 + 12^2)$ Perfect-square trinomial

  $= x(x - 12)^2$

8. $x(x - 9)^2$

9. $x^3 + 3x^2 - 4x - 12$

  $= x^2(x + 3) - 4(x + 3)$ Factoring by grouping

  $= (x + 3)(x^2 - 4)$

  $= (x + 3)(x + 2)(x - 2)$ Factoring the difference of squares

10. $(x + 5)(x - 5)^2$

11. $98t^2 - 18$

  $= 2(49t^2 - 9)$ 2 is a common factor.

  $= 2[(7t)^2 - 3^2]$ Difference of squares

  $= 2(7t + 3)(7t - 3)$

12. $3t(3t + 1)(3t - 1)$

13. $20x^3 - 4x^2 - 72x$

  $= 4x(5x^2 - x - 18)$ $4x$ is a common factor.

  $= 4x(5x + 9)(x - 2)$ Factoring the trinomial using trial and error

14. $3x(x + 3)(3x - 5)$

15. $x^2 + 4$

  The polynomial has no common factor and is not a difference of squares. It is prime.

16. Prime

17. $a^4 + 8a^2 + 8a^3 + 64a$

  $= a(a^3 + 8a + 8a^2 + 64)$ a is a common factor.

  $= a[a(a^2 + 8) + 8(a^2 + 8)]$ Factoring by grouping

  $= a(a^2 + 8)(a + 8)$

18. $t(t^2 + 7)(t - 3)$

19. $x^5 - 14x^4 + 49x^3$

  $= x^3(x^2 - 14x + 49)$ x^3 is a common factor.

  $= x^3(x^2 - 2 \cdot x \cdot 7 + 7^2)$ Trinomial square

  $= x^3(x - 7)^2$

20. $2x^4(x + 2)^2$

21. $20 - 6x - 2x^2$

  $= -2x^2 - 6x + 20$ Rewriting

  $= -2(x^2 + 3x - 10)$ -2 is a common factor.

  $= -2(x + 5)(x - 2)$ Using trial and error

  We could also express this result as $2(5 + x)(2 - x)$.

22. $3(5 - 2x)(3 + x)$

23. $t^2 - 7t - 6$

  There is no common factor (other than 1). This is not a trinomial square, because only t^2 is a square. We try factoring by trial and error. We look for two factors whose product is -6 and whose sum is -7. There are none. The polynomial cannot be factored. It is prime.

24. Prime

25. $4x^4 - 64$

  $= 4(x^4 - 16)$ 4 is a common factor.

  $= 4[(x^2)^2 - 4^2]$ Difference of squares

  $= 4(x^2 + 4)(x^2 - 4)$ Difference of squares

  $= 4(x^2 + 4)(x + 2)(x - 2)$

26. $5x(x^2 + 4)(x + 2)(x - 2)$

27. $9 + t^8$

  There is no common factor (other than 1). Although both 9 and t^8 are squares, this is not a difference of squares because the terms do not have different signs. This polynomial cannot be factored. It is prime.

28. $(t^2 + 3)(t^2 - 3)$

29. $x^5 - 4x^4 + 3x^3$

  $= x^3(x^2 - 4x + 3)$ x^3 is a common factor.

  $= x^3(x - 3)(x - 1)$ Factoring the trinomial using trial and error

30. $x^4(x^2 - 2x + 7)$

31. $x^3 - y^3$ Difference of cubes

  $= (x - y)(x^2 + xy + y^2)$

32. $(2t + 1)(4t^2 - 2t + 1)$

33. $12n^2 + 24n^3 = 12n^2(1 + 2n)$

34. $a(x^2 + y^2)$

35. $ab^2 - a^2b = ab(b - a)$

36. $9mn(4 - mn)$

37. $2\pi rh + 2\pi r^2 = 2\pi r(h + r)$

38. $2\pi r(2r + 1)$

39. $(a + b)(x - 3) + (a + b)(x + 4)$

  $= (a + b)[(x - 3) + (x + 4)]$ $(a + b)$ is a common factor.

  $= (a + b)(2x + 1)$

40. $(a^3 + b)(5c - 1)$

41. $n^2 + 2n + np + 2p$

  $= n(n + 2) + p(n + 2)$ Factoring by grouping

  $= (n + 2)(n + p)$

42. $(x + 1)(x + y)$

43. $x^2 + 2x + 1 - 81y^2 = (x+1)^2 - (9y)^2$
$$= (x+1+9y)(x+1-9y)$$

44. $(x - 5 + 3y)(x - 5 - 3y)$

45. $x^2 + y^2 + 2xy$
$= x^2 + 2xy + y^2$ Perfect-square trinomial
$= (x+y)^2$

46. $(3x - 2y)(x + 5y)$

47. $9c^2 - 6cd + d^2$
$= (3c)^2 - 2 \cdot 3c \cdot d + d^2$ Perfect-square trinomial
$= (3c - d)^2$

48. $(a - 2b)^2$

49. $7p^4 - 7q^4$
$= 7(p^4 - q^4)$ 7 is a common factor.
$= 7(p^2 + q^2)(p^2 - q^2)$ Difference of squares
$= 7(p^2 + q^2)(p + q)(p - q)$ Difference of squares

50. $(a^2b^2 + 4)(ab + 2)(ab - 2)$

51. $25z^2 + 10zy + y^2$
$= (5z)^2 + 2 \cdot 5z \cdot y + y^2$ Perfect-square trinomial
$= (5z + y)^2$

52. $(2xy + 3z)^2$

53. $m^6 - 1$
$= (m^3)^2 - 1^2$ Difference of squares
$= (m^3 + 1)(m^3 - 1)$ Sum of cubes;
                          difference of cubes
$= (m+1)(m^2 - m + 1)(m-1)(m^2 + m + 1)$

54. $(2t + 1)(4t^2 - 2t + 1)(2t - 1)(4t^2 + 2t + 1)$

55. $a^2 + ab + 2b^2$

There is no common factor (other than 1). This is not a perfect-square trinomial because only a^2 is a square. We try factoring by trial and error. We look for two factors whose product is 2 and whose sum is 1. There are none. This polynomial cannot be factored. It is prime.

56. $p(4pq - q^2 + 4p^2)$

57. $2mn - 360n^2 + m^2$
$= m^2 + 2mn - 360n^2$ Rewriting
$= (m + 20n)(m - 18n)$ Using trial and error

58. $(3b - a)(b + 6a)$

59. $m^2n^2 - 4mn - 32$
$= (mn - 8)(mn + 4)$ Using trial and error

60. $(xy + 2)(xy + 6)$

61. $p^4 - 1 + 2q - q^2 = p^4 - (1 - 2q + q^2)$
$$= (p^2)^2 - (1 - q)^2$$
$$= (p^2 + (1 - q))(p^2 - (1 - q))$$
$$= (p^2 + 1 - q)(p^2 - 1 + q)$$

This result can also be expressed as $(p^2 - q + 1)(p^2 + q - 1)$, or $(p^2 + q - 1)(p^2 - q + 1)$.

62. $(t^4 + s^5 + 6)(t^4 - s^5 - 6)$

63. $54a^4 + 16ab^3$
$= 2a(27a^3 + 8b^3)$ $2a$ is a common factor.
$= 2a[(3a)^3 + (2b)^3]$ Sum of cubes
$= 2a(3a + 2b)[(3a)^2 - 3a \cdot 2b + (2b)^2]$
$= 2a(3a + 2b)(9a^2 - 6ab + 4b^2)$

64. $2y(3x - 5y)(9x^2 + 15xy + 25y^2)$

65. $2s^6t^2 + 10s^3t^3 + 12t^4$
$= 2t^2(s^6 + 5s^3t + 6t^2)$ $2t^2$ is a common factor.
$= 2t^2(s^3 + 3t)(s^3 + 2t)$ Using trial and error

66. $x^4(x + 2y)(x - y)$

67. $a^2 + 2a^2bc + a^2b^2c^2$
$= a^2(1 + 2bc + b^2c^2)$ a^2 is a common factor.
$= a^2[1^2 + 2 \cdot 1 \cdot bc + (bc)^2]$ Perfect-square
                                   trinomial
$= a^2(1 + bc)^2$

68. $\left(6a - \dfrac{5}{4}\right)^2$

69. $\dfrac{1}{81}x^2 - \dfrac{8}{27}x + \dfrac{16}{9}$
$= \left(\dfrac{1}{9}x\right)^2 - 2 \cdot \dfrac{1}{9}x \cdot \dfrac{4}{3} + \left(\dfrac{4}{3}\right)^2$ Perfect-square
                                        trinomial
$= \left(\dfrac{1}{9}x - \dfrac{4}{3}\right)^2$

If we had factored out $\dfrac{1}{9}$ at the outset, the final result would have been $\dfrac{1}{9}\left(\dfrac{1}{3}x - 4\right)^2$.

70. $\left(\dfrac{1}{2}a + \dfrac{1}{3}b\right)^2$

71. $1 - 16x^{12}y^{12}$
$= (1 + 4x^6y^6)(1 - 4x^6y^6)$ Difference of squares
$= (1 + 4x^6y^6)(1 + 2x^3y^3)(1 - 2x^3y^3)$ Difference
                                              of squares

72. $a(b^2 + 9a^2)(b + 3a)(b - 3a)$

73. *Writing Exercise*

74. *Writing Exercise*

75.
$$\frac{y = -4x + 7}{}$$
$$11 \ ? \ -4(-1) + 7$$
$$\qquad | \ 4 + 7$$
$$11 \ | \ 11 \qquad\qquad \text{TRUE}$$
Since $11 = 11$ is true, $(-1, 11)$ is a solution.
$$\frac{y = -4x + 7}{}$$
$$7 \ ? \ -4 \cdot 0 + 7$$
$$\qquad | \ 0 + 7$$
$$7 \ | \ 7 \qquad\qquad \text{TRUE}$$
Since $7 = 7$ is true, $(0, 7)$ is a solution.
$$\frac{y = -4x + 7}{}$$
$$-5 \ ? \ -4 \cdot 3 + 7$$
$$\qquad | \ -12 + 7$$
$$-5 \ | \ -5 \qquad\qquad \text{TRUE}$$
Since $-5 = -5$ is true, $(3, -5)$ is a solution.

76. $\dfrac{4}{5}$

77. $3x + 7 = 0$
$$3x = -7 \qquad \text{Subtracting 7 from both sides}$$
$$x = -\frac{7}{3} \qquad \text{Dividing both sides by 3}$$
The solution is $-\dfrac{7}{3}$.

78. $-\dfrac{9}{2}$

79. $4x - 9 = 0$
$$4x = 9 \qquad \text{Adding 9 to both sides}$$
$$x = \frac{9}{4} \qquad \text{Dividing both sides by 4}$$
The solution is $\dfrac{9}{4}$.

80.

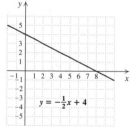

$y = -\frac{1}{2}x + 4$

81. *Writing Exercise*

82. *Writing Exercise*

83.
$$-(x^5 + 7x^3 - 18x)$$
$$= -x(x^4 + 7x^2 - 18)$$
$$= -x(x^2 + 9)(x^2 - 2)$$

84. $(a - 2)(a + 3)(a - 3)$

85.
$$3a^4 - 15a^2 + 12$$
$$= 3(a^4 - 5a^2 + 4)$$
$$= 3(a^2 - 1)(a^2 - 4)$$
$$= 3(a + 1)(a - 1)(a + 2)(a - 2)$$

86. $(x^2 + 2)(x + 3)(x - 3)$

87.
$$y^2(y + 1) - 4y(y + 1) - 21(y + 1)$$
$$= (y + 1)(y^2 - 4y - 21)$$
$$= (y + 1)(y - 7)(y + 3)$$

88. $(y - 1)^3$

89.
$$6(x - 1)^2 + 7y(x - 1) - 3y^2$$
$$= [2(x - 1) + 3y][3(x - 1) - y]$$
$$= (2x + 3y - 2)(3x - y - 3), \text{ or}$$
$$(2x - 2 + 3y)(3x - 3 - y)$$

90. $(y + 4 + x)^2$

91.
$$2(a + 3)^4 - (a + 3)^3(b - 2) - (a + 3)^2(b - 2)^2$$
$$= (a + 3)^2[2(a + 3)^2 - (a + 3)(b - 2) - (b - 2)^2]$$
$$= (a + 3)^2[2(a + 3) + (b - 2)][(a + 3) - (b - 2)]$$
$$= (a + 3)^2(2a + 6 + b - 2)(a + 3 - b + 2)$$
$$= (a + 3)^2(2a + b + 4)(a - b + 5)$$

92. $(t - 1)^3(5t - s - 4)(t - s)$

Exercise Set 6.7

1. *Familiarize*. Let x represent the number.

Translate.

Square of number plus number is 132.

$$x^2 \qquad + \qquad x \qquad = \qquad 132$$

Carry out. We solve the equation:
$$x^2 + x = 132$$
$$x^2 + x - 132 = 0$$
$$(x + 12)(x - 11) = 0$$
$$x + 12 = 0 \quad or \quad x - 11 = 0$$
$$x = -12 \quad or \qquad x = 11$$

Check. The square of -12, which is 144, plus -12 is 132. The square of 11, which is 121, plus 11 is 132. Both numbers check.

State. The number is -12 or 11.

2. -13, 12

3. *Familiarize*. We let w represent the width and $w + 5$ represent the length. We make a drawing and label it.

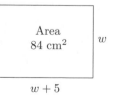

Area 84 cm²

w

$w + 5$

Recall that the formula for the area of a rectangle is $A = $ length $\times$ width.

Translate.

Area   is 84 cm^2.

$$w(w+5) = 84$$

Carry out. We solve the equation:

$$w(w+5) = 84$$
$$w^2 + 5w = 84$$
$$w^2 + 5w - 84 = 0$$
$$(w+12)(w-7) = 0$$
$$w+12 = 0 \quad or \quad w-7 = 0$$
$$w = -12 \quad or \quad w = 7$$

Check. The number -12 is not a solution, because width cannot be negative. If the width is 7 cm and the length is 5 cm more, or 12 cm, then the area is $12 \cdot 7$, or 84 cm^2. This is a solution.

State. The length is 12 cm, and the width is 7 cm.

4. Length: 12 cm; width: 8 cm

5. *Familiarize*. We make a drawing and label it. We let x represent the length of a side of the original square, in meters.

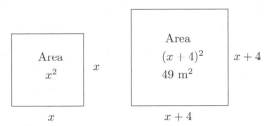

Translate.

Area of new square   is 49 m^2.

$$(x+4)^2 = 49$$

Carry out. We solve the equation:

$$(x+4)^2 = 49$$
$$x^2 + 8x + 16 = 49$$
$$x^2 + 8x - 33 = 0$$
$$(x-3)(x+11) = 0$$
$$x-3 = 0 \quad or \quad x+11 = 0$$
$$x = 3 \quad or \quad x = -11$$

Check. We check only 3 since the length of a side cannot be negative. If we increase the length by 4, the new length is $3+4$, or 7 m. Then the new area is $7 \cdot 7$, or 49 m^2. We have a solution.

State. The length of a side of the original square is 3 m.

6. 6 cm

7. *Familiarize*. We make a drawing and label it with both known and unknown information. We let x represent the width of the frame.

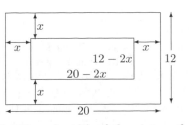

The length and width of the picture that shows are represented by $20 - 2x$ and $12 - 2x$. The area of the picture that shows is 84 cm^2.

Translate. Using the formula for the area of a rectangle, $A = l \cdot w$, we have

$$84 = (20 - 2x)(12 - 2x).$$

Carry out. We solve the equation:

$$84 = 240 - 64x + 4x^2$$
$$84 = 4(60 - 16x + x^2)$$
$$21 = 60 - 16x + x^2 \qquad \text{Dividing by 4}$$
$$0 = x^2 - 16x + 39$$
$$0 = (x-3)(x-13)$$
$$x-3 = 0 \quad or \quad x-13 = 0$$
$$x = 3 \quad or \quad x = 13$$

Check. We see that 13 is not a solution because when $x = 13$, $20 - 2x = -6$ and $12 - 2x = -14$, and the length and width of the frame cannot be negative. We check 3. When $x = 3$, $20 - 2x = 14$ and $12 - 2x = 6$ and $14 \cdot 6 = 84$. The area is 84. The value checks.

State. The width of the frame is 3 cm.

8. 2 cm

9. *Familiarize*. We let x represent the width of the walkway. We make a drawing and label it with both the known and unknown information.

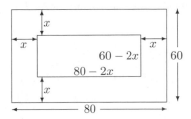

The area of the new lawn is $(80 - 2x)(60 - 2x)$.

Translate.

Area of new lawn   is 2400 ft^2.

$$(80 - 2x)(60 - 2x) = 2400$$

Carry out. We solve the equation:

$$(80 - 2x)(60 - 2x) = 2400$$
$$4800 - 280x + 4x^2 = 2400$$
$$4x^2 - 280x + 2400 = 0$$
$$x^2 - 70x + 600 = 0 \qquad \text{Dividing by 4}$$
$$(x-10)(x-60) = 0$$

$$x - 10 = 0 \quad or \quad x - 60 = 0$$
$$x = 10 \quad or \quad x = 60$$

Check. If the sidewalk is 10 ft wide, the length of the new lawn will be $80 - 2 \cdot 10$, or 60 ft, and its width will be $60 - 2 \cdot 10$, or 40 ft. Then the area of the new lawn will be $60 \cdot 40$, or 2400 ft^2. This answer checks.

If the sidewalk is 60 ft wide, the length of the new lawn will be $80 - 2 \cdot 60$, or -40 ft. Since the length cannot be negative, 60 is not a solution.

State. The sidewalk is 10 ft wide.

10. 5 ft

11. Familiarize. Let x represent the first integer, $x + 2$ the second, and $x + 4$ the third.

Translate.

$$\underbrace{\text{Square of the third}}_{(x+4)^2} \underbrace{\text{is}}_{=} \underbrace{76}_{76} \underbrace{\text{more than}}_{+} \underbrace{\text{square of the second.}}_{(x+2)^2}$$

Carry out. We solve the equation:

$$(x+4)^2 = 76 + (x+2)^2$$
$$x^2 + 8x + 16 = 76 + x^2 + 4x + 4$$
$$x^2 + 8x + 16 = x^2 + 4x + 80$$
$$4x = 64$$
$$x = 16$$

Check. We check the integers 16, 18, and 20. The square of 20, or 400, is 76 more than 324, the square of 18. The answer checks.

State. The integers are 16, 18, and 20.

12. $-10, -8, -6$ or $6, 8, 10$

13. Familiarize. Let x represent the base of the triangle and $x + 2$ represent the height. Recall that the formula for the area of the triangle with base b and height h is $\frac{1}{2}bh$.

Translate.

$$\underbrace{\text{The area}}_{\frac{1}{2}x(x+2)} \underbrace{\text{is}}_{=} \underbrace{12 \text{ ft}^2}_{12}.$$

Carry out. We solve the equation:

$$\frac{1}{2}x(x+2) = 12$$
$$x(x+2) = 24 \quad \text{Multiplying by 2}$$
$$x^2 + 2x = 24$$
$$x^2 + 2x - 24 = 0$$
$$(x+6)(x-4) = 0$$
$$x + 6 = 0 \quad or \quad x - 4 = 0$$
$$x = -6 \quad or \quad x = 4$$

Check. We check only 4 since the length of the base cannot be negative. If the base is 4 ft, then the height is $4+2$, or 6 ft, and the area is $\frac{1}{2} \cdot 4 \cdot 6$, or 12 ft^2. The answer checks.

State. The height is 6 ft, and the base is 4 ft.

14. Distance d: 12 ft; height of tower: 16 ft

15. Familiarize. Let b represent the base of the sail. Then $b+9$ represents the height. Recall that the formula for the area of a triangle is $A = \frac{1}{2} \times$ base $\times$ height.

Translate.

The area is 56 m^2.

$$\frac{1}{2}b(b+9) = 56$$

Carry out. We solve the equation:

$$\frac{1}{2}b(b+9) = 56$$
$$b(b+9) = 112 \quad \text{Multiplying by 2}$$
$$b^2 + 9b = 112$$
$$b^2 + 9b - 112 = 0$$
$$(b+16)(b-7) = 0$$
$$b + 16 = 0 \quad or \quad b - 7 = 0$$
$$b = -16 \quad or \quad b = 7$$

Check. We check only 7, since the length of the base cannot be negative. If the base is 7 m, the height is $7 + 9$, or 16 m, and the area is $\frac{1}{2} \cdot 16 \cdot 7$, or 56 m^2. We have a solution.

State. The base is 7 m, and the height is 16 m.

16. Length: 200 ft; width: 150 ft

17. Familiarize. We make a drawing. Let $h = $ the height the ladder reaches on the wall. Then the length of the ladder is $h + 1$.

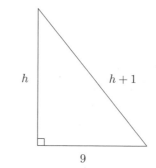

Translate. We use the Pythagorean theorem.

$$9^2 + h^2 = (h+1)^2$$

Carry out. We solve the equation:

$$81 + h^2 = h^2 + 2h + 1$$
$$80 = 2h$$
$$40 = h$$

Check. If $h = 40$, then $h + 1 = 41$; $9^2 + 40^2 = 81 + 1600 = 1681 = 41^2$, so the answer checks.

State. The ladder is 41 ft long.

18. 24 ft

19. Familiarize. Let w represent the width and $w + 25$ represent the length. Make a drawing.

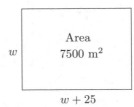

w

Area
7500 m²

$w + 25$

Recall that the formula for the area of a rectangle is $A =$ length $\times$ width.

Translate.

$$\underbrace{\text{Area}}_{} \quad \text{is} \quad \underbrace{\text{7500 m}^2}_{}.$$
$$w(w + 25) \quad = \quad 7500$$

Carry out. We solve the equation:
$$w(w + 25) = 7500$$
$$w^2 + 25w = 7500$$
$$w^2 + 25w - 7500 = 0$$
$$(w + 100)(w - 75) = 0$$
$$w + 100 = 0 \quad or \quad w - 75 = 0$$
$$w = -100 \quad or \quad w = 75$$

Check. The number -100 is not a solution because width cannot be negative. If the width is 75 m and the length is 25 m more, or 100 m, then the area will be $100 \cdot 75$, or 7500 m². This is a solution.

State. The dimensions will be 100 m by 75 m.

20. Length: 12 m; width: 9 m

21. Familiarize. The firm breaks even when the cost and the revenue are the same. We use the functions given in the text.

Translate.

$$\underbrace{\text{Cost}}_{} \quad \text{equals} \quad \underbrace{\text{revenue.}}_{}$$
$$x^2 - 2x + 10 \quad = \quad 2x^2 + x$$

Carry out. We solve the equation:
$$x^2 - 2x + 10 = 2x^2 + x$$
$$0 = x^2 + 3x - 10$$
$$0 = (x + 5)(x - 2)$$
$$x + 5 = 0 \quad or \quad x - 2 = 0$$
$$x = -5 \quad or \quad x = 2$$

Check. We check only 2 since the number of sets of cabinets cannot be negative. If 2 sets of cabinets are produced and sold, the cost is $2^2 - 2 \cdot 2 + 10 = 4 - 4 + 10 = \$10$ thousand and the revenue is $2 \cdot 2^2 + 2 = 8 + 2 = \$10$ thousand. The answer checks.

State. The company must produce and sell 2 sets of cabinets in order to break even.

22. 6 video cameras

23. Familiarize. We will use the formula in Example 5, $h(t) = -15t^2 + 75t + 10$. Note that t cannot be negative since it represents time after launch.

Translate. We need to find the value of t for which $h(t) = 100$:
$$-15t^2 + 75t + 10 = 100$$

Carry out. We solve the equation.
$$-15t^2 + 75t + 10 = 100$$
$$-15t^2 + 75t - 90 = 0$$
$$-15(t^2 - 5t + 6) = 0$$
$$-15(t - 2)(t - 3) = 0$$
$$t - 2 = 0 \quad or \quad t - 3 = 0$$
$$t = 2 \quad or \quad t = 3$$

Check. We have:
$$h(2) = -15 \cdot 2^2 + 75 \cdot 2 + 10 = -60 + 150 + 10 = 100;$$
$$h(3) = -15 \cdot 3^2 + 75 \cdot 3 + 10 = -135 + 225 + 10 = 100.$$

Both numbers check. However, the problem states that the tee shirt is caught on the way up. Thus, we reject 3 since that would indicate that the shirt is caught on the way down, after peaking.

State. The tee shirt was airborne for 2 sec before it was caught.

24. 5 sec

25. Familiarize. We will use the given formula, $h(t) = -16t^2 + 64t + 80$. Note that t cannot be negative since it represents time after launch.

Translate. We need to find the value of t for which $h(t) = 0$. We have:
$$-16t^2 + 64t + 80 = 0$$

Carry out. We solve the equation.
$$-16t^2 + 64t + 80 = 0$$
$$-16(t^2 - 4t - 5) = 0$$
$$-16(t - 5)(t + 1) = 0$$
$$t - 5 = 0 \quad or \quad t + 1 = 0$$
$$t = 5 \quad or \quad t = -1$$

Check. Since t cannot be negative, we check only 5. $h(5) = -16 \cdot 5^2 + 64 \cdot 5 + 80 = -400 + 320 + 80 = 0$ The number 5 checks.

State. The cardboard shell will reach the ground 5 sec after it is launched.

26. 7 sec

27. a) Enter the data in a graphing calculator, letting x represent the number of years after 1960. Then select item 7, quartic regression, from the STAT CALC menu to find the desired function. We have $E(x) = 0.0000256775x^4 - 0.0025507304x^3 + 0.0821803626x^2 - 0.9480449896x + 11.8202857$.

b) In 1990, $x = 30$.

$E(30) \approx 9.3$ cents per kilowatt-hour

In 2004, $x = 44$.

$E(44) \approx 8.2$ cents per kilowatt-hour

c) We solve $E(x) = 9$ graphically, looking for all the solutions between $x = 0$ and $x = 42$. Graph $y_1 = E(x)$ and $y_2 = 9$ and use the Intersect feature three times. We find that the first coordinates of the points of intersection are approximately 4, 17, and 32. Thus, the average retail cost of electricity was 9 cents per kilowatt-hour in 1964, 1977, and 1992.

28. a) $f(x) = 0.0000001957x^4 - 0.0000570879x^3 + 0.0042982745x^2 - 0.0159423087x + 1.45236808$

b) 1.986 million farms; 2.600 million farms

c) 1876, 1974

29. a) Enter the data in a graphing calculator, letting x represent the number of years after 1970. Then select item 5, quadratic regression, from the STAT CALC menu to find the desired function. We have $d(x) = -105.9592768x^2 + 3621.572598x + 42,307.79479$.

b) In 1999, $x = 29$.

$d(29) \approx 58,221$ degrees

In 2005, $x = 35$.

$d(35) \approx 39,263$ degrees

c) Graph $y_1 = d(x)$ and $y_2 = 60,000$ and use Intersect to find the first coordinates of the points of intersection of the graphs. They are approximately 6 and 28, so 60,000 engineering bachelor's degrees were earned in 1976 and in 1998.

30. a) $r(x) = -0.0085518407x^3 + 0.390736534x^2 - 4.819375298x + 69.4855836$

b) 61.3 births per 1000 women; 12.8 births per 1000 women

c) 1972, 1989, 1995

31. a) Enter the data in a graphing calculator, letting x represent the number of years after 1990. Then select item 7, quartic regression, from the STAT CALC menu to find the desired function. We have $b(x) = -1.143939394x^2 + 9.583333333x + 25.79545455$.

b) In 1992, $x = 2$.

$b(2) \approx 40\%$

In 2000, $x = 10$.

$b(10) \approx 7\%$

c) Graph $y_1 = b(x)$ and $y_2 = 30$ and use Intersect to find the first coordinates of the points of intersection of the graphs. They are approximately 0 and 8. Only 8 represents a year after 1991, so 30% of bottles were recycled in 1998.

32. a) $n(x) = 0.0113125x^4 - 0.9444166667x^3 + 24.93375x^2 - 222.4083333x + 8174$

b) 7860 newspapers; 8985 newspapers

c) 1961

33. *Writing Exercise*

34. *Writing Exercise*

35. $\dfrac{5 - 10 \cdot 3}{-4 + 11 \cdot 4} = \dfrac{5 - 30}{-4 + 44} = \dfrac{-25}{40} = -\dfrac{5}{8}$

36. 2

37.
$$-3[2(x - 5) + 3(2 - x)] - 7(x - 2)$$
$$= -3[2x - 10 + 6 - 3x] - 7x + 14$$
$$= -3[-x - 4] - 7x + 14$$
$$= 3x + 12 - 7x + 14$$
$$= -4x + 26$$

38. $3.2x - 0.3$

39.
$$2x - 14 + 9x > -8x + 16 + 10x$$

$11x - 14 > 2x + 16$	Collecting like terms
$9x - 14 > 16$	Adding $-2x$
$9x > 30$	Adding 14
$x > \dfrac{10}{3}$	Multiplying by $\dfrac{1}{9}$

The solution set is $\left\{ x \middle| x > \dfrac{10}{3} \right\}$, or $\left(\dfrac{10}{3}, \infty \right)$.

40. $\emptyset$

41. *Writing Exercise*

42. *Writing Exercise*

43. **Familiarize.** Using the labels on the drawing in the text, we let x represent the width of the piece of tin and $2x$ represent the length. Then the width and length of the base of the box are represented by $x - 4$ and $2x - 4$, respectively. Recall that the formula for the volume of a rectangular solid with length l, width w, and height h is $l \cdot w \cdot h$.

Translate.

The volume is 480 cm^3.

$$(2x - 4)(x - 4)(2) = 480$$

Carry out. We solve the equation:

$(2x - 4)(x - 4)(2) = 480$	
$(2x - 4)(x - 4) = 240$	Dividing by 2
$2x^2 - 12x + 16 = 240$	
$2x^2 - 12x - 224 = 0$	
$x^2 - 6x - 112 = 0$	Dividing by 2
$(x + 8)(x - 14) = 0$	

$$x + 8 = 0 \quad or \quad x - 14 = 0$$
$$x = -8 \quad or \quad x = 14$$

Check. We check only 14 since the width cannot be negative. If the width of the piece of tin is 14 cm, then its length is $2 \cdot 14$, or 28 cm, and the dimensions of the base of the box are $14 - 4$, or 10 cm by $28 - 4$, or 24 cm. The volume of the box is $24 \cdot 10 \cdot 2$, or 480 cm^3. The answer checks.

State. The dimensions of the piece of tin are 14 cm by 28 cm.

44. 50-year-olds

45. *Familiarize*. Let r = the speed of the tugboat and $r - 7$ = the speed of the freighter. After 4 hr they have traveled $4r$ km and $4(r - 7)$ km, respectively.

Translate. We use the Pythagorean theorem.

$$(4r)^2 + [4(r - 7)]^2 = 68^2$$

Carry out. We solve the equation.

$$(4r)^2 + [4(r - 7)]^2 = 68^2$$
$$16r^2 + 16(r^2 - 14r + 49) = 4624$$
$$16r^2 + 16r^2 - 224r + 784 = 4624$$
$$32r^2 - 224r - 3840 = 0$$
$$32(r^2 - 7r - 120) = 0$$
$$32(r - 15)(r + 8) = 0$$
$$r - 15 = 0 \quad or \quad r + 8 = 0$$
$$r = 15 \quad or \qquad r = -8$$

Check. Since the speed cannot be negative, we check only 15. If $r = 15$, then $r - 7 = 15 - 7$, or 8. At a rate of 15 km/h, in 4 hr the tugboat travels $4 \cdot 15$ or 60 km. At a rate of 8 km/h, in 4 hr the freighter travels $4 \cdot 8$, or 32 km. Since $60^2 + 32^2 = 4624 = 68^2$, the answer checks.

State. The speed of the tugboat is 15 km/h, and the speed of the freighter is 8 km/h.

46. Aabout 5.7 sec

Chapter 7

Rational Expressions, Equations, and Functions

Exercise Set 7.1

1. $H(t) = \dfrac{t^2 + 3t}{2t + 3}$

$H(5) = \dfrac{5^2 + 3 \cdot 5}{2 \cdot 5 + 3} = \dfrac{25 + 15}{10 + 3} = \dfrac{40}{13}$ hr, or $3\dfrac{1}{13}$ hr

2. $\dfrac{70}{17}$ hr, or $4\dfrac{2}{17}$ hr

3. $v(t) = \dfrac{4t^2 - 5t + 2}{t + 3}$

$v(0) = \dfrac{4 \cdot 0^2 - 5 \cdot 0 + 2}{0 + 3} = \dfrac{0 - 0 + 2}{0 + 3} = \dfrac{2}{3}$

$v(-2) = \dfrac{4(-2)^2 - 5(-2) + 2}{-2 + 3} = \dfrac{16 + 10 + 2}{-2 + 3} = 28$

$v(7) = \dfrac{4 \cdot 7^2 - 5 \cdot 7 + 2}{7 + 3} = \dfrac{196 - 35 + 2}{7 + 3} = \dfrac{163}{10}$

4. -2; $-\dfrac{11}{7}$; 15

5. $g(x) = \dfrac{2x^3 - 9}{x^2 - 4x + 4}$

$g(0) = \dfrac{2 \cdot 0^3 - 9}{0^2 - 4 \cdot 0 + 4} = \dfrac{0 - 9}{0 - 0 + 4} = -\dfrac{9}{4}$

$g(2) = \dfrac{2 \cdot 2^3 - 9}{2^2 - 4 \cdot 2 + 4} = \dfrac{16 - 9}{4 - 8 + 4} = \dfrac{7}{0}$

Since division by zero is not defined, $g(2)$ does not exist.

$g(-1) = \dfrac{2(-1)^3 - 9}{(-1)^2 - 4(-1) + 4} = \dfrac{-2 - 9}{1 + 4 + 4} = -\dfrac{11}{9}$

6. 0; $\dfrac{2}{5}$; does not exist

7. $\dfrac{25}{-7x}$

We find the real number(s) that make the denominator 0. To do so we set the denominator equal to 0 and solve for x:

$-7x = 0$
$x = 0$

The expression is undefined for $x = 0$.

8. 0

9. $\dfrac{t - 3}{t + 8}$

Set the denominator equal to 0 and solve for t:

$t + 8 = 0$
$t = -8$

The expression is undefined for $t = -8$.

10. -7

11. $\dfrac{a - 4}{3a - 12}$

Set the denominator equal to 0 and solve for a:

$3a - 12 = 0$
$3a = 12$
$a = 4$

The expression is undefined for $a = 4$.

12. 3

13. $\dfrac{x^2 - 16}{x^2 - 3x - 28}$

Set the denominator equal to 0 and solve for x:

$x^2 - 3x - 28 = 0$
$(x - 7)(x + 4) = 0$
$x - 7 = 0 \quad or \quad x + 4 = 0$
$x = 7 \quad or \qquad x = -4$

The expression is undefined for $x = 7$ and $x = -4$.

14. $2, 5$

15. $\dfrac{m^3 - 2m}{m^2 - 25}$

Set the denominator equal to 0 and solve for m:

$m^2 - 25 = 0$
$(m + 5)(m - 5) = 0$
$m + 5 = 0 \quad or \quad m - 5 = 0$
$m = -5 \quad or \qquad m = 5$

The expression is undefined for $m = -5$ and $m = 5$.

16. $-7, 7$

17. $\dfrac{15x}{5x^2}$

$= \dfrac{5x \cdot 3}{5x \cdot x}$ Factoring; the greatest common factor is $5x$.

$= \dfrac{5x}{5x} \cdot \dfrac{3}{x}$ Factoring the rational expression

$= 1 \cdot \dfrac{3}{x}$ $\dfrac{5x}{5x} = 1$

$= \dfrac{3}{x}$ Removing a factor equal to 1

18. $\dfrac{a^2}{3}$

19. $\dfrac{18t^3}{27t^7}$

$= \dfrac{9t^3 \cdot 2}{9t^3 \cdot 3t^4}$ Factoring the numerator
and the denominator

$= \dfrac{9t^3}{9t^3} \cdot \dfrac{2}{3t^4}$ Factoring the rational expression

$= \dfrac{2}{3t^4}$ Removing a factor equal to 1

20. $\dfrac{2}{y^4}$

21. $\dfrac{2a - 10}{2} = \dfrac{2(a - 5)}{2 \cdot 1} = \dfrac{2}{2} \cdot \dfrac{a - 5}{1} = a - 5$

22. $a + 4$

23. $\dfrac{3x - 12}{3x + 15} = \dfrac{3(x - 4)}{3(x + 5)} = \dfrac{3}{3} \cdot \dfrac{x - 4}{x + 5} = \dfrac{x - 4}{x + 5}$

24. $\dfrac{y - 5}{y + 3}$

25. $\dfrac{6a^2 - 3a}{7a^2 - 7a} = \dfrac{3a(2a - 1)}{7a(a - 1)}$

$= \dfrac{a}{a} \cdot \dfrac{3(2a - 1)}{7(a - 1)}$

$= 1 \cdot \dfrac{3(2a - 1)}{7(a - 1)}$

$= \dfrac{3(2a - 1)}{7(a - 1)}$

26. $\dfrac{m + 1}{2m + 3}$

27. $\dfrac{5x + 20}{x^2 + 4x} = \dfrac{5(x + 4)}{x(x + 4)} = \dfrac{5}{x} \cdot \dfrac{x + 4}{x + 4} = \dfrac{5}{x}$

28. $\dfrac{3}{x}$

29. $\dfrac{3a - 1}{2 - 6a}$

$= \dfrac{3a - 1}{2(1 - 3a)}$

$= \dfrac{-1(1 - 3a)}{2(1 - 3a)}$ Factoring out -1 in the
numerator reverses the
subtraction.

$= \dfrac{-1}{2} \cdot \dfrac{1 - 3a}{1 - 3a}$

$= -\dfrac{1}{2}$

30. $-\dfrac{1}{2}$

31. $\dfrac{8t - 16}{t^2 - 4} = \dfrac{8(t - 2)}{(t + 2)(t - 2)} = \dfrac{8}{t + 2} \cdot \dfrac{t - 2}{t - 2} = \dfrac{8}{t + 2}$

32. $\dfrac{t - 3}{5}$

33. $\dfrac{t^2 - 16}{t^2 + t - 20} = \dfrac{(t + 4)(t - 4)}{(t + 5)(t - 4)}$

$= \dfrac{t + 4}{t + 5} \cdot \dfrac{t - 4}{t - 4}$

$= \dfrac{t + 4}{t + 5} \cdot 1$

$= \dfrac{t + 4}{t + 5}$

34. $\dfrac{a - 2}{a + 3}$

35. $\dfrac{3a^2 + 9a - 12}{6a^2 - 30a + 24} = \dfrac{3(a^2 + 3a - 4)}{6(a^2 - 5a + 4)}$

$= \dfrac{3(a + 4)(a - 1)}{3 \cdot 2(a - 4)(a - 1)}$

$= \dfrac{3(a - 1)}{3(a - 1)} \cdot \dfrac{a + 4}{2(a - 4)}$

$= 1 \cdot \dfrac{a + 4}{2(a - 4)}$

$= \dfrac{a + 4}{2(a - 4)}$

36. $\dfrac{t - 2}{2(t + 4)}$

37. $\dfrac{x^2 + 8x + 16}{x^2 - 16} = \dfrac{(x + 4)(x + 4)}{(x + 4)(x - 4)}$

$= \dfrac{x + 4}{x + 4} \cdot \dfrac{x + 4}{x - 4}$

$= 1 \cdot \dfrac{x + 4}{x - 4}$

$= \dfrac{x + 4}{x - 4}$

38. $\dfrac{x + 5}{x - 5}$

39. $\dfrac{t^2 - 1}{t + 1} = \dfrac{(t + 1)(t - 1)}{t + 1}$

$= \dfrac{t + 1}{t + 1} \cdot \dfrac{t - 1}{1}$

$= 1 \cdot \dfrac{t - 1}{1}$

$= t - 1$

40. $a + 1$

41. $\dfrac{y^2 + 4}{y + 2}$ cannot be simplified.

Neither the numerator nor the denominator can be factored.

42. $\dfrac{x^2 + 1}{x + 1}$

43. $\dfrac{5x^2 - 20}{10x^2 - 40} = \dfrac{5(x^2 - 4)}{10(x^2 - 4)}$

$= \dfrac{1 \cdot \cancel{5} \cdot \cancel{(x^2 - 4)}}{2 \cdot \cancel{5} \cdot \cancel{(x^2 - 4)}}$

$= \dfrac{1}{2}$

44. $\dfrac{3}{2}$

45.
$$\begin{aligned}
\dfrac{x-8}{8-x} &= \dfrac{x-8}{-(x-8)} \\
&= \dfrac{1}{-1} \cdot \dfrac{x-8}{x-8} \\
&= \dfrac{1}{-1} \cdot 1 \\
&= -1
\end{aligned}$$

46. -1

47.
$$\begin{aligned}
& \dfrac{2t-1}{1-4t^2} \\
&= \dfrac{2t-1}{(1+2t)(1-2t)} \\
&= \dfrac{-1(1-2t)}{(1+2t)(1-2t)} \qquad \text{Factoring out } -1 \text{ in the} \\
& \qquad\qquad\qquad\qquad\qquad \text{numerator reverses the} \\
& \qquad\qquad\qquad\qquad\qquad \text{subtraction} \\
&= \dfrac{-1}{1+2t} \cdot \dfrac{1-2t}{1-2t} \\
&= -\dfrac{1}{1+2t}
\end{aligned}$$

48. $-\dfrac{1}{2+3a}$

49.
$$\begin{aligned}
& \dfrac{12-6x}{5x-10} = \dfrac{-6(-2+x)}{5(x-2)} = \dfrac{-6(x-2)}{5(x-2)} = \\
& \dfrac{-6}{5} \cdot \dfrac{x-2}{x-2} = -\dfrac{6}{5}
\end{aligned}$$

50. $-\dfrac{7}{3}$

51.
$$\begin{aligned}
& \dfrac{a^2-25}{a^2+10a+25} = \dfrac{(a+5)(a-5)}{(a+5)(a+5)} = \\
& \dfrac{a+5}{a+5} \cdot \dfrac{a-5}{a+5} = \dfrac{a-5}{a+5}
\end{aligned}$$

52. $\dfrac{a+4}{a-4}$

53. $\dfrac{7s^2-28t^2}{28t^2-7s^2}$

Note that the numerator and denominator are opposites. Thus, we have an expression divided by its opposite, so the result is -1.

54. -1

55.
$$\begin{aligned}
& \dfrac{x^2+9x+8}{x^2-3x-4} = \dfrac{(x+1)(x+8)}{(x+1)(x-4)} = \dfrac{x+1}{x+1} \cdot \dfrac{x+8}{x-4} = \\
& \dfrac{x+8}{x-4}
\end{aligned}$$

56. $\dfrac{t-9}{t+4}$

57.
$$\begin{aligned}
& \dfrac{16-t^2}{t^2-8t+16} = \dfrac{16-t^2}{16-8t+t^2} = \dfrac{(4+t)(4-t)}{(4-t)(4-t)} = \\
& \dfrac{4+t}{4-t} \cdot \dfrac{4-t}{4-t} = \dfrac{4+t}{4-t}
\end{aligned}$$

58. $\dfrac{5-p}{5+p}$

59.
$$\begin{aligned}
& \dfrac{x^3-1}{x^2-1} = \dfrac{(x-1)(x^2+x+1)}{(x+1)(x-1)} = \dfrac{x-1}{x-1} \cdot \dfrac{x^2+x+1}{x+1} = \\
& \dfrac{x^2+x+1}{x+1}
\end{aligned}$$

60. $\dfrac{a^2-2a+4}{a-2}$

61.
$$\begin{aligned}
& \dfrac{3y^3+24}{y^2-2y+4} = \dfrac{3(y^3+8)}{y^2-2y+4} = \dfrac{3(y+2)(y^2-2y+4)}{y^2-2y+4} = \\
& \dfrac{y^2-2y+4}{y^2-2y+4} \cdot \dfrac{3(y+2)}{1} = 3(y+2)
\end{aligned}$$

62. $\dfrac{x-3}{5}$

63. First we simplify the rational expression describing the function.
$$\dfrac{3x-12}{3x+15} = \dfrac{3(x-4)}{3(x+5)} = \dfrac{3}{3} \cdot \dfrac{x-4}{x+5} = \dfrac{x-4}{x+5}$$
$x+5 = 0$ when $x = -5$. Thus, the vertical asymptote is $x = -5$.

64. $x = -3$

65. First we simplify the rational expression describing the function.
$$\begin{aligned}
& \dfrac{12-6x}{5x-10} = \dfrac{-6(-2+x)}{5(x-2)} = \dfrac{-6(x-2)}{5(x-2)} = \\
& \dfrac{-6}{5} \cdot \dfrac{x-2}{x-2} = -\dfrac{6}{5}
\end{aligned}$$
The denominator of the simplified expression is not equal to 0 for any value of x, so there are no vertical asymptotes.

66. No vertical asymptotes

67. First we simplify the rational expression describing the function.
$$\begin{aligned}
& \dfrac{x^3+3x^2}{x^2+6x+9} = \dfrac{x^2(x+3)}{(x+3)(x+3)} = \dfrac{x^2}{x+3} \cdot \dfrac{x+3}{x+3} = \\
& \dfrac{x^2}{x+3}
\end{aligned}$$
$x+3 = 0$ when $x = -3$. Thus, the vertical asymptote is $x = -3$.

68. $x = \dfrac{1}{2}$

69. First we simplify the rational expression describing the function.
$$\dfrac{x^2-x-6}{x^2-6x+8} = \dfrac{(x-3)(x+2)}{(x-4)(x-2)}$$
We cannot remove a factor equal to 1. Observe that $x-4 = 0$ when $x = 4$ and $x-2 = 0$ when $x = 2$. Thus, the vertical asymptotes are $x = 4$ and $x = 2$.

70. $x = 1$

71. The vertical asymptote of $h(x) = \dfrac{1}{x}$ is $x = 0$. Observe that $h(x) > 0$ for $x > 0$ and $h(x) < 0$ for $x < 0$. Thus, graph (b) corresponds to this function.

72. (e)

73. The vertical asymptote of $f(x) = \dfrac{x}{x-3}$ is $x = 3$. Thus, graph (f) corresponds to this function.

74. (d)

75. $\dfrac{4x-2}{x^2-2x+1} = \dfrac{2(2x-1)}{(x-1)(x-1)}$

The vertical asymptote of $r(x)$ is $x = 1$. Thus, graph (a) corresponds to this function.

76. (c)

77. *Writing Exercise*

78. *Writing Exercise*

79.
$$\frac{3}{10} - \frac{8}{15} = \frac{3}{10} \cdot \frac{3}{3} - \frac{8}{15} \cdot \frac{2}{2}$$
$$= \frac{9}{30} - \frac{16}{30}$$
$$= \frac{9-16}{30} = \frac{-7}{30}$$
$$= -\frac{7}{30}$$

80. $-\dfrac{13}{40}$

81.
$$\frac{2}{3} \cdot \frac{5}{7} - \frac{5}{7} \cdot \frac{1}{6} = \frac{10}{21} - \frac{5}{42}$$
$$= \frac{10}{21} \cdot \frac{2}{2} - \frac{5}{42}$$
$$= \frac{20}{42} - \frac{5}{42}$$
$$= \frac{15}{42}$$
$$= \frac{3 \cdot 5}{3 \cdot 14} = \frac{\cancel{3} \cdot 5}{\cancel{3} \cdot 14}$$
$$= \frac{5}{14}$$

82. $\dfrac{1}{35}$

83.
$$(8x^3 - 5x^2 + 6x + 2) - (4x^3 + 2x^2 - 3x + 7)$$
$$= 8x^3 - 5x^2 + 6x + 2 - 4x^3 - 2x^2 + 3x - 7$$
$$= 4x^3 - 7x^2 + 9x - 5$$

84. $-2t^4 + 11t^3 - t^2 + 10t - 3$

85. *Writing Exercise*

86. *Writing Exercise*

87.
$$\frac{x^4 - y^4}{(y-x)^4} = \frac{(x^2+y^2)(x^2-y^2)}{[-(x-y)]^4}$$
$$= \frac{(x^2+y^2)(x+y)(\cancel{x-y})}{(-1)^4(\cancel{x-y})(x-y)^3}$$
$$= \frac{(x^2+y^2)(x+y)}{(x-y)^3}$$

88. $-(2y + x)$

89.
$$\frac{(x-1)(x^4-1)(x^2-1)}{(x^2+1)(x-1)^2(x^4-2x^2+1)} =$$
$$\frac{(x-1)(x^4-1)(x^2-1)}{(x^2+1)(x-1)^2(x^2-1)^2} =$$
$$\frac{(x-1)(x^2+1)(x^2-1)(x+1)(x-1)}{(x^2+1)(x-1)(x-1)(x^2-1)(x^2-1)} =$$
$$\frac{(\cancel{x-1})(\cancel{x^2+1})(\cancel{x^2-1})(\cancel{x+1})(\cancel{x-1}) \cdot 1}{(\cancel{x^2+1})\,(\cancel{x-1})(\cancel{x-1})(\cancel{x^2-1})(\cancel{x+1})\,(x-1)} =$$
$$\frac{1}{x-1}$$

90. $\dfrac{x^3+4}{(x^3+2)(x^2+2)}$

91.
$$\frac{x^3 + x^2 - y^3 - y^2}{x^2 - 2xy + y^2}$$
$$= \frac{(x^3 - y^3) + (x^2 - y^2)}{x^2 - 2xy + y^2}$$
$$= \frac{(x-y)(x^2+xy+y^2) + (x+y)(x-y)}{(x-y)^2}$$
$$= \frac{(x-y)[(x^2+xy+y^2) + (x+y)]}{(x-y)(x-y)}$$
$$= \frac{(\cancel{x-y})(x^2+xy+y^2+x+y)}{(\cancel{x-y})(x-y)}$$
$$= \frac{x^2+xy+y^2+x+y}{x-y}$$

92. $\dfrac{(u^2 - uv + v^2)^2}{u - v}$

93.
$$\frac{x^5 - x^3 + x^2 - 1 - (x^3 - 1)(x+1)^2}{(x^2-1)^2}$$

$$= \frac{x^5 - x^3 + (x^2 - 1) - [(x^3 - 1)(x+1)^2]}{(x^2-1)^2}$$

$$= \frac{x^3(x^2-1) + (x^2-1) - [(x-1)(x^2+x+1)(x+1)(x+1)]}{(x^2-1)^2}$$

$$= \frac{x^3(x^2-1) + (x^2-1) - [(x^2-1)(x+1)(x^2+x+1)]}{(x^2-1)^2}$$

$$= \frac{(x^2-1)[x^3 + 1 - (x+1)(x^2+x+1)]}{(x^2-1)^2}$$

$$= \frac{(x^2-1)[x^3 + 1 - (x^3 + x^2 + x + x^2 + x + 1)]}{(x^2-1)(x^2-1)}$$

$$= \frac{(x^2-1)(-2x^2-2x)}{(x^2-1)(x^2-1)}$$

$$= \frac{-2x^2-2x}{x^2-1}$$

$$= \frac{-2x(x+1)}{(x+1)(x-1)}$$

$$= \frac{-2x(x+1)}{(x+1)(x-1)}$$

$$= \frac{-2x}{x-1}, \text{ or } -\frac{2x}{x-1}$$

94. 1

95. From the graph we see that the domain consists of all real numbers except -2 and 1, so the domain is $(-\infty, -2) \cup (-2, 1) \cup (1, \infty)$. We also see that the range consists of all real numbers except 2 and 3, so the range is $(-\infty, 2) \cup (2, 3) \cup (3, \infty)$.

96. Domain: $(-\infty, -1) \cup (-1, 0) \cup (0, 1) \cup (1, \infty)$;

range: $(-\infty, -3) \cup (-3, -1) \cup (-1, 0) \cup (0, \infty)$

97. From the graph we see that the domain consists of all real numbers except -1 and 1, so the domain is $(-\infty, -1) \cup (-1, 1) \cup (1, \infty)$. We also see that the range consists of all real numbers less than or equal to -1 or greater than 0. Thus, the range is $(-\infty, -1] \cup (0, \infty)$.

98.

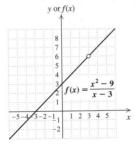

99. *Writing Exercise*

Exercise Set 7.2

1. $\dfrac{9x}{4} \cdot \dfrac{x-5}{2x+1} = \dfrac{9x(x-5)}{4(2x+1)}$

2. $\dfrac{3x(5x+2)}{4(x-1)}$

3. $\dfrac{a-4}{a+6} \cdot \dfrac{a+2}{a+6} = \dfrac{(a-4)(a+2)}{(a+6)(a+6)}, \text{ or } \dfrac{(a-4)(a+2)}{(a+6)^2}$

4. $\dfrac{(a+3)(a+3)}{(a+6)(a-1)}, \text{ or } \dfrac{(a+3)^2}{(a+6)(a-1)}$

5. $\dfrac{2x+3}{4} \cdot \dfrac{x+1}{x-5} = \dfrac{(2x+3)(x+1)}{4(x-5)}$

6. $\dfrac{4(x+2)}{(3x-4)(5x+6)}$

7. $\dfrac{5a^4}{6a} \cdot \dfrac{2}{a}$

$= \dfrac{5a^4 \cdot 2}{6a \cdot a}$ Multiplying the numerators and the denominators

$= \dfrac{5 \cdot a \cdot a \cdot a \cdot a \cdot 2}{2 \cdot 3 \cdot a \cdot a}$ Factoring the numerator and the denominator

$= \dfrac{5 \cdot a \cdot a \cdot a \cdot a \cdot 2}{2 \cdot 3 \cdot a \cdot a}$ Removing a factor equal to 1

$= \dfrac{5a^2}{3}$ Simplifying

8. $\dfrac{6}{5t^6}$

9. $\dfrac{3c}{d^2} \cdot \dfrac{8d}{6c^3}$

$= \dfrac{3c \cdot 8d}{d^2 \cdot 6c^3}$ Multiplying the numerators and the denominators

$= \dfrac{3 \cdot c \cdot 2 \cdot 4 \cdot d}{d \cdot d \cdot 3 \cdot 2 \cdot c \cdot c \cdot c}$ Factoring the numerator and the denominator

$= \dfrac{3 \cdot c \cdot 2 \cdot 4 \cdot d}{d \cdot d \cdot 3 \cdot 2 \cdot c \cdot c \cdot c}$

$= \dfrac{4}{dc^2}$

10. $\dfrac{6x}{y^2}$

11. $\dfrac{y^2-16}{4y+12} \cdot \dfrac{y+3}{y-4} = \dfrac{(y^2-16)(y+3)}{(4y+12)(y-4)}$

$= \dfrac{(y+4)(y-4)(y+3)}{4(y+3)(y-4)}$

$= \dfrac{(y+4)(y-4)(y+3)}{4(y+3)(y-4)}$

$= \dfrac{y+4}{4}$

12. $\dfrac{m+n}{4}$

13. $\dfrac{x^2-3x-10}{(x-2)^2} \cdot \dfrac{x-2}{x-5} = \dfrac{(x^2-3x-10)(x-2)}{(x-2)^2(x-5)}$

$= \dfrac{(x-5)(x+2)(x-2)}{(x-2)(x-2)(x-5)}$

$= \dfrac{(x-5)(x+2)(x-2)}{(x-2)(x-2)(x-5)}$

$= \dfrac{x+2}{x-2}$

14. $\dfrac{t-3}{t+2}$

15. $\dfrac{a^2+25}{a^2-4a+3} \cdot \dfrac{a-5}{a+5} = \dfrac{(a^2+25)(a-5)}{(a^2-4a+3)(a+5)}$

$$= \dfrac{(a^2+25)(a-5)}{(a-3)(a-1)(a+5)}$$

(No simplification is possible.)

16. $\dfrac{(x+3)(x+4)(x+1)}{(x^2+9)(x+9)}$

17. $\dfrac{a^2-9}{a^2} \cdot \dfrac{5a}{a^2+a-12} = \dfrac{(a+3)(a-3)\cdot 5\cdot a}{a\cdot a(a+4)(a-3)}$

$$= \dfrac{(a+3)\cancel{(a-3)}\cdot 5\cdot \cancel{a}}{\cancel{a}\cdot a(a+4)\cancel{(a-3)}}$$

$$= \dfrac{5(a+3)}{a(a+4)}$$

18. $\dfrac{x^2(x-1)}{5}$

19. $\dfrac{4a^2}{3a^2-12a+12} \cdot \dfrac{3a-6}{2a}$

$$= \dfrac{4a^2(3a-6)}{(3a^2-12a+12)2a}$$

$$= \dfrac{2\cdot 2\cdot a\cdot a\cdot 3\cdot (a-2)}{3\cdot (a-2)\cdot (a-2)\cdot 2\cdot a}$$

$$= \dfrac{\cancel{2}\cdot 2\cdot \cancel{a}\cdot a\cdot \cancel{3}\cdot \cancel{(a-2)}}{\cancel{3}\cdot \cancel{(a-2)}\cdot (a-2)\cdot \cancel{2}\cdot \cancel{a}}$$

$$= \dfrac{2a}{a-2}$$

20. $\dfrac{10(v-2)}{v-1}$

21. $\dfrac{t^2+2t-3}{t^2+4t-5} \cdot \dfrac{t^2-3t-10}{t^2+5t+6}$

$$= \dfrac{(t^2+2t-3)(t^2-3t-10)}{(t^2+4t-5)(t^2+5t+6)}$$

$$= \dfrac{(t+3)(t-1)(t-5)(t+2)}{(t+5)(t-1)(t+3)(t+2)}$$

$$= \dfrac{\cancel{(t+3)}\cancel{(t-1)}(t-5)\cancel{(t+2)}}{(t+5)\cancel{(t-1)}\cancel{(t+3)}\cancel{(t+2)}}$$

$$= \dfrac{t-5}{t+5}$$

22. $\dfrac{x+4}{x-4}$

23. $\dfrac{5a^2-180}{10a^2-10} \cdot \dfrac{20a+20}{2a-12}$

$$= \dfrac{(5a^2-180)(20a+20)}{(10a^2-10)(2a-12)}$$

$$= \dfrac{5(a+6)(a-6)(2)(10)(a+1)}{10(a+1)(a-1)(2)(a-6)}$$

$$= \dfrac{5(a+6)\cancel{(a-6)}\cancel{(2)}\cancel{(10)}\cancel{(a+1)}}{\cancel{10}\cancel{(a+1)}(a-1)\cancel{(2)}\cancel{(a-6)}}$$

$$= \dfrac{5(a+6)}{a-1}$$

24. $\dfrac{t+7}{4(t-1)}$

25. $\dfrac{x^2+4x+4}{(x-1)^2} \cdot \dfrac{x^2-2x+1}{(x+2)^2} = \dfrac{(x+2)^2(x-1)^2}{(x-1)^2(x+2)^2} = 1$

26. $\dfrac{1}{x+2}$

27. $\dfrac{t^2+8t+16}{(t+4)^3} \cdot \dfrac{(t+2)^3}{t^2+4t+4} = \dfrac{(t+4)^2(t+2)^3}{(t+4)^3(t+2)^2}$

$$= \dfrac{(t+4)^2(t+2)^2(t+2)}{(t+4)^2(t+4)(t+2)^2}$$

$$= \dfrac{(t+4)^2(t+2)^2}{(t+4)^2(t+2)^2} \cdot \dfrac{t+2}{t+4}$$

$$= 1\cdot \dfrac{t+2}{t+4}$$

$$= \dfrac{t+2}{t+4}$$

28. $\dfrac{y-1}{y-2}$

29. $\dfrac{7a-14}{4-a^2} \cdot \dfrac{5a^2+6a+1}{35a+7}$

$$= \dfrac{(7a-14)(5a^2+6a+1)}{(4-a^2)(35a+7)}$$

$$= \dfrac{7(a-2)(5a+1)(a+1)}{(2+a)(2-a)(7)(5a+1)}$$

$$= \dfrac{7(-1)(2-a)(5a+1)(a+1)}{(2+a)(2-a)(7)(5a+1)}$$

$$= \dfrac{\cancel{7}(-1)\cancel{(2-a)}\cancel{(5a+1)}(a+1)}{(2+a)\cancel{(2-a)}\cancel{(7)}\cancel{(5a+1)}}$$

$$= \dfrac{-1(a+1)}{2+a}$$

$$= \dfrac{-a-1}{2+a}, \text{ or } -\dfrac{a+1}{2+a}$$

30. $-\dfrac{3(a+1)}{a+6}$

31. $\dfrac{t^3-4t}{t-t^4} \cdot \dfrac{t^4-t}{4t-t^3}$

$$= \dfrac{t^3-4t}{t-t^4} \cdot \dfrac{-1(t-t^4)}{-1(t^3-4t)}$$

$$= \dfrac{(t^3-4t)(-1)(t-t^4)}{(t-t^4)(-1)(t^3-4t)}$$

$$= 1$$

32. $\dfrac{x^2(x+3)(x-3)}{-4}$

33. $\dfrac{c^3+8}{c^5-4c^3} \cdot \dfrac{c^6-4c^5+4c^4}{c^2-2c+4}$

$$= \dfrac{(c^3+8)(c^6-4c^5+4c^4)}{(c^5-4c^3)(c^2-2c+4)}$$

$$= \dfrac{(c+2)(c^2-2c+4)(c^4)(c-2)(c-2)}{c^3(c+2)(c-2)(c^2-2c+4)}$$

$$= \dfrac{c^3(c+2)(c^2-2c+4)(c-2)}{c^3(c+2)(c^2-2c+4)(c-2)} \cdot \dfrac{c(c-2)}{1}$$

$$= c(c-2)$$

34. $\dfrac{x(x-3)^2}{x+3}$

35.
$$\dfrac{a^3-b^3}{3a^2+9ab+6b^2} \cdot \dfrac{a^2+2ab+b^2}{a^2-b^2}$$
$$= \dfrac{(a^3-b^3)(a^2+2ab+b^2)}{(3a^2+9ab+6b^2)(a^2-b^2)}$$
$$= \dfrac{(a-b)(a^2+ab+b^2)(a+b)(a+b)}{3(a+b)(a+2b)(a+b)(a-b)}$$
$$= \dfrac{(a-b)(a^2+ab+b^2)(a+b)(a+b)}{3(a+b)(a+2b)(a+b)(a-b)}$$
$$= \dfrac{a^2+ab+b^2}{3(a+2b)}$$

36. $\dfrac{x^2-xy+y^2}{3(x+3y)}$

37.
$$\dfrac{4x^2-9y^2}{8x^3-27y^3} \cdot \dfrac{4x^2+6xy+9y^2}{4x^2+12xy+9y^2}$$
$$= \dfrac{(4x^2-9y^2)(4x^2+6xy+9y^2)}{(8x^3-27y^3)(4x^2+12xy+9y^2)}$$
$$= \dfrac{(2x+3y)(2x-3y)(4x^2+6xy+9y^2)\cdot 1}{(2x-3y)(4x^2+6xy+9y^2)(2x+3y)(2x+3y)}$$
$$= \dfrac{(2x+3y)(2x-3y)(4x^2+6xy+9y^2)}{(2x+3y)(2x-3y)(4x^2+6xy+9y^2)} \cdot \dfrac{1}{2x+3y}$$
$$= \dfrac{1}{2x+3y}$$

38. $\dfrac{(x-y)(2x+3y)}{2(x+y)(9x^2+6xy+4y^2)}$

39. The reciprocal of $\dfrac{3x}{7}$ is $\dfrac{7}{3x}$ because $\dfrac{3x}{7} \cdot \dfrac{7}{3x} = 1$.

40. $\dfrac{x^2+4}{3-x}$

41. The reciprocal of a^3-8a is $\dfrac{1}{a^3-8a}$ because
$$\dfrac{a^3-8a}{1} \cdot \dfrac{1}{a^3-8a} = 1.$$

42. $\dfrac{a^2-b^2}{7}$

43.
$$\dfrac{3}{8} \div \dfrac{5}{2}$$
$$= \dfrac{3}{8} \cdot \dfrac{2}{5} \quad \text{Multiplying by the reciprocal of the divisor}$$
$$= \dfrac{3\cdot 2}{8\cdot 5}$$
$$= \dfrac{3\cdot 2}{2\cdot 4\cdot 5} \quad \text{Factoring the denominator}$$
$$= \dfrac{2}{2} \cdot \dfrac{3}{4\cdot 5} \quad \text{Factoring the fractional expression}$$
$$= \dfrac{3}{20} \quad \text{Simplifying}$$

44. $\dfrac{35}{18}$

45.
$$\dfrac{x}{4} \div \dfrac{5}{x}$$
$$= \dfrac{x}{4} \cdot \dfrac{x}{5} \quad \text{Multiplying by the reciprocal of the divisor}$$
$$= \dfrac{x\cdot x}{4\cdot 5}$$
$$= \dfrac{x^2}{20}$$

46. $\dfrac{60}{x^2}$

47.
$$\dfrac{9x^5}{8y^2} \div \dfrac{3x}{16y^9}$$
$$= \dfrac{9x^5}{8y^2} \cdot \dfrac{16y^9}{3x} \quad \text{Multiplying by the reciprocal of the divisor}$$
$$= \dfrac{9x^5(16y^9)}{8y^2(3x)}$$
$$= \dfrac{3\cdot 3\cdot x\cdot x^4\cdot 2\cdot 8\cdot y^2\cdot y^7}{8\cdot y^2\cdot 3\cdot x}$$
$$= \dfrac{3\cdot 3\cdot x\cdot x^4\cdot 2\cdot 8\cdot y^2\cdot y^7}{8\cdot y^2\cdot 3\cdot x\cdot 1}$$
$$= 6x^4y^7$$

48. $\dfrac{4a^4}{b^4}$

49.
$$\dfrac{y+5}{4} \div \dfrac{y}{2} = \dfrac{y+5}{4} \cdot \dfrac{2}{y}$$
$$= \dfrac{(y+5)(2)}{4\cdot y}$$
$$= \dfrac{(y+5)(2)}{2\cdot 2y}$$
$$= \dfrac{y+5}{2y}$$

50. $\dfrac{(a+2)(a+3)}{(a-3)(a-1)}$

51.
$$\dfrac{5x+10}{x^8} \div \dfrac{x+2}{x^3} = \dfrac{5x+10}{x^8} \cdot \dfrac{x^3}{x+2}$$
$$= \dfrac{(5x+10)(x^3)}{x^8(x+2)}$$
$$= \dfrac{5(x+2)(x^3)}{x^3\cdot x^5(x+2)}$$
$$= \dfrac{5(x+2)(x^3)}{x^3\cdot x^5(x+2)}$$
$$= \dfrac{5}{x^5}$$

52. $\dfrac{3}{y^5}$

53.
$$\dfrac{4y-8}{y+2} \div \dfrac{y-2}{y^2-4} = \dfrac{4y-8}{y+2} \cdot \dfrac{y^2-4}{y-2}$$
$$= \dfrac{(4y-8)(y^2-4)}{(y+2)(y-2)}$$
$$= \dfrac{4(y-2)(y+2)(y-2)}{(y+2)(y-2)(1)}$$
$$= 4(y-2)$$

54. $\dfrac{(x-1)^2}{x}$

55. $\dfrac{a}{a-b} \div \dfrac{b}{b-a} = \dfrac{a}{a-b} \cdot \dfrac{b-a}{b}$

$\quad\quad = \dfrac{a(b-a)}{(a-b)(b)}$

$\quad\quad = \dfrac{a(-1)(a-b)}{(a-b)(b)}$

$\quad\quad = \dfrac{-a}{b} = -\dfrac{a}{b}$

56. $-\dfrac{1}{2}$

57. $\dfrac{x^2-4}{x^3} \div \dfrac{x^5-2x^4}{x+4} = \dfrac{x^2-4}{x^3} \cdot \dfrac{x+4}{x^5-2x^4}$

$\quad\quad = \dfrac{(x^2-4)(x+4)}{x^3(x^5-2x^4)}$

$\quad\quad = \dfrac{(x+2)(x-2)(x+4)}{x^3(x^4)(x-2)}$

$\quad\quad = \dfrac{(x+2)(x-2)(x+4)}{x^3(x^4)(x-2)}$

$\quad\quad = \dfrac{(x+2)(x+4)}{x^7}$

58. $\dfrac{(y-3)(y+2)}{y^6}$

59. $(y^2-9) \div \dfrac{y^2-2y-3}{y^2+1} = \dfrac{(y^2-9)}{1} \cdot \dfrac{y^2+1}{y^2-2y-3}$

$\quad\quad = \dfrac{(y^2-9)(y^2+1)}{y^2-2y-3}$

$\quad\quad = \dfrac{(y+3)(y-3)(y^2+1)}{(y-3)(y+1)}$

$\quad\quad = \dfrac{(y+3)(y-3)(y^2+1)}{(y-3)(y+1)}$

$\quad\quad = \dfrac{(y+3)(y^2+1)}{y+1}$

60. $\dfrac{(x-6)(x+6)}{x-1}$

61. $\dfrac{-6+3x}{5} \div \dfrac{4x-8}{25} = \dfrac{-6+3x}{5} \cdot \dfrac{25}{4x-8}$

$\quad\quad = \dfrac{(-6+3x) \cdot 25}{5(4x-8)}$

$\quad\quad = \dfrac{3(x-2) \cdot 5 \cdot 5}{5 \cdot 4(x-2)}$

$\quad\quad = \dfrac{3(x-2) \cdot 5 \cdot 5}{5 \cdot 4(x-2)}$

$\quad\quad = \dfrac{15}{4}$

62. 1

63. $\dfrac{a+2}{a-1} \div \dfrac{3a+6}{a-5} = \dfrac{a+2}{a-1} \cdot \dfrac{a-5}{3a+6}$

$\quad\quad = \dfrac{(a+2)(a-5)}{(a-1)(3a+6)}$

$\quad\quad = \dfrac{(a+2)(a-5)}{(a-1) \cdot 3 \cdot (a+2)}$

$\quad\quad = \dfrac{(a+2)(a-5)}{(a-1) \cdot 3 \cdot (a+2)}$

$\quad\quad = \dfrac{a-5}{3(a-1)}$

64. $\dfrac{t+1}{4(t+2)}$

65. $\dfrac{25x^2-4}{x^2-9} \div \dfrac{2-5x}{x+3} = \dfrac{25x^2-4}{x^2-9} \cdot \dfrac{x+3}{2-5x}$

$\quad\quad = \dfrac{(25x^2-4)(x+3)}{(x^2-9)(2-5x)}$

$\quad\quad = \dfrac{(5x+2)(5x-2)(x+3)}{(x+3)(x-3)(-1)(5x-2)}$

$\quad\quad = \dfrac{(5x+2)(5x-2)(x+3)}{(x+3)(x-3)(-1)(5x-2)}$

$\quad\quad = \dfrac{5x+2}{-x+3}, \text{ or } -\dfrac{5x+2}{x-3}$

66. $\dfrac{-2a-1}{a+2}$

67. $\dfrac{5y-5x}{15y^3} \div \dfrac{x^2-y^2}{3x+3y} = \dfrac{5y-5x}{15y^3} \cdot \dfrac{3x+3y}{x^2-y^2}$

$\quad\quad = \dfrac{(5y-5x)(3x+3y)}{15y^3(x^2-y^2)}$

$\quad\quad = \dfrac{5(y-x)(3)(x+y)}{5 \cdot 3 \cdot y^3(x+y)(x-y)}$

$\quad\quad = \dfrac{5(-1)(x-y)(3)(x+y)}{5 \cdot 3 \cdot y^3(x+y)(x-y)}$

$\quad\quad = \dfrac{5(-1)(x-y)(3)(x+y)}{5 \cdot 3 \cdot y^3(x+y)(x-y)}$

$\quad\quad = \dfrac{-1}{y^3}, \text{ or } -\dfrac{1}{y^3}$

68. $-x^2$

69. $(2x-1) \div \dfrac{2x^2-11x+5}{4x^2-1}$

$\quad\quad = \dfrac{2x-1}{1} \cdot \dfrac{4x^2-1}{2x^2-11x+5}$

$\quad\quad = \dfrac{(2x-1)(4x^2-1)}{1 \cdot (2x^2-11x+5)}$

$\quad\quad = \dfrac{(2x-1)(2x+1)(2x-1)}{1 \cdot (2x-1)(x-5)}$

$\quad\quad = \dfrac{(2x-1)(2x+1)(2x-1)}{1 \cdot (2x-1)(x-5)}$

$\quad\quad = \dfrac{(2x-1)(2x+1)}{x-5}$

70. $\dfrac{(a+7)(a+1)}{3a-7}$

71. $\dfrac{x^2-16}{x^2-10x+25} \div \dfrac{3x-12}{x^2-3x-10}$

$= \dfrac{x^2-16}{x^2-10x+25} \cdot \dfrac{x^2-3x-10}{3x-12}$

$= \dfrac{(x^2-16)(x^2-3x-10)}{(x^2-10x+25)(3x-12)}$

$= \dfrac{(x+4)(x-4)(x-5)(x+2)}{(x-5)(x-5)(3)(x-4)}$

$= \dfrac{(x+4)\cancel{(x-4)}\cancel{(x-5)}(x+2)}{\cancel{(x-5)}(x-5)(3)\cancel{(x-4)}}$

$= \dfrac{(x+4)(x+2)}{3(x-5)}$

72. $\dfrac{(y+6)(y+3)}{3(y-4)}$

73. $\dfrac{a^2-10a+25}{a^2+7a+12} \div \dfrac{a^2-a-20}{a^2+6a+9}$

$= \dfrac{a^2-10a+25}{a^2+7a+12} \cdot \dfrac{a^2+6a+9}{a^2-a-20}$

$= \dfrac{\cancel{(a-5)}(a-5)\cancel{(a+3)}(a+3)}{\cancel{(a+3)}(a+4)\cancel{(a-5)}(a+4)}$

$= \dfrac{(a-5)(a+3)}{(a+4)^2}$

74. $\dfrac{(a+1)^2(a-6)}{(a-1)^2(a+4)}$

75. $\dfrac{c^2+10c+21}{c^2-2c-15} \div (c^2+2c-35)$

$= \dfrac{c^2+10c+21}{c^2-2c-25} \cdot \dfrac{1}{c^2+2c-35}$

$= \dfrac{(c^2+10c+21)\cdot 1}{(c^2-2c-15)(c^2+2c-35)}$

$= \dfrac{(c+7)(c+3)}{(c-5)(c+3)(c+7)(c-5)}$

$= \dfrac{(c+7)(c+3)}{(c+7)(c+3)} \cdot \dfrac{1}{(c-5)(c-5)}$

$= \dfrac{1}{(c-5)^2}$

76. $\dfrac{1}{1+2z-z^2}$

77. $\dfrac{x^3-64}{x^3+64} \div \dfrac{x^2-16}{x^2-4x+16}$

$= \dfrac{x^3-64}{x^3+64} \cdot \dfrac{x^2-4x+16}{x^2-16}$

$= \dfrac{(x^3-64)(x^2-4x+16)}{(x^3+64)(x^2-16)}$

$= \dfrac{(x-4)(x^2+4x+16)(x^2-4x+16)}{(x+4)(x^2-4x+16)(x+4)(x-4)}$

$= \dfrac{(x-4)(x^2-4x+16)}{(x-4)(x^2-4x+16)} \cdot \dfrac{x^2+4x+16}{(x+4)(x+4)}$

$= \dfrac{x^2+4x+16}{(x+4)(x+4)}, \text{ or } \dfrac{x^2+4x+16}{(x+4)^2}$

78. $\dfrac{4y^2+6y+9}{(4y-1)(2y+3)}$

79. $\dfrac{8a^3+b^3}{2a^2+3ab+b^2} \div \dfrac{8a^2-4ab+2b^2}{4a^2+4ab+b^2}$

$= \dfrac{8a^3+b^3}{2a^2+3ab+b^2} \cdot \dfrac{4a^2+4ab+b^2}{8a^2-4ab+2b^2}$

$= \dfrac{(8a^3+b^3)(4a^2+4ab+b^2)}{(2a^2+3ab+b^2)(8a^2-4ab+2b^2)}$

$= \dfrac{(2a+b)(4a^2-2ab+b^2)(2a+b)(2a+b)}{(2a+b)(a+b)(2)(4a^2-2ab+b^2)}$

$= \dfrac{(2a+b)(4a^2-2ab+b^2)}{(2a+b)(4a^2-2ab+b^2)} \cdot \dfrac{(2a+b)(2a+b)}{(a+b)(2)}$

$= \dfrac{(2a+b)(2a+b)}{2(a+b)}, \text{ or } \dfrac{(2a+b)^2}{2(a+b)}$

80. $\dfrac{2(2x-y)}{x}$

81. *Writing Exercise*

82. *Writing Exercise*

83. $\dfrac{3}{4}+\dfrac{5}{6} = \dfrac{3}{4}\cdot\dfrac{3}{3}+\dfrac{5}{6}\cdot\dfrac{2}{2}$

$= \dfrac{9}{12}+\dfrac{10}{12}$

$= \dfrac{19}{12}$

84. $\dfrac{41}{24}$

85. $\dfrac{2}{9}-\dfrac{1}{6} = \dfrac{2}{9}\cdot\dfrac{2}{2}-\dfrac{1}{6}\cdot\dfrac{3}{3}$

$= \dfrac{4}{18}-\dfrac{3}{18}$

$= \dfrac{1}{18}$

86. $-\dfrac{1}{6}$

87. $\dfrac{2}{5}-\left(\dfrac{3}{2}\right)^2 = \dfrac{2}{5}-\dfrac{9}{4} = \dfrac{8}{20}-\dfrac{45}{20} = -\dfrac{37}{20}$

88. $\dfrac{49}{45}$

89. *Writing Exercise*

90. *Writing Exercise*

91. $\dfrac{3x-y}{2x+y} \div \dfrac{3x-y}{2x+y}$

We have the rational expression $\dfrac{3x-y}{2x+y}$ divided by itself. Thus, the result is 1.

92. $\dfrac{a}{(c-3d)(2a+5b)}$

93. $(x - 2a) \div \dfrac{a^2x^2 - 4a^4}{a^2x + 2a^3} = \dfrac{x - 2a}{1} \cdot \dfrac{a^2x + 2a^3}{a^2x^2 - 4a^4}$

$\qquad\qquad = \dfrac{(x - 2a)(a^2)(x + 2a)}{a^2(x + 2a)(x - 2a)}$

$\qquad\qquad = 1$

94. $\dfrac{1}{b^3(a - 3b)}$

95. $\dfrac{a^2 - 3b}{a^2 + 2b} \cdot \dfrac{a^2 - 2b}{a^2 + 3b} \cdot \dfrac{a^2 + 2b}{a^2 - 3b}$

Note that $\dfrac{a^2 - 3b}{a^2 + 2b} \cdot \dfrac{a^2 + 2b}{a^2 - 3b}$ is the product of reciprocals and thus is equal to 1. Then the product in the original exercise is the remaining factor, $\dfrac{a^2 - 2b}{a^2 + 3b}$.

96. $\dfrac{(z + 4)^3}{3(z - 4)^2}$

97. $\left[\dfrac{r^2 - 4s^2}{r + 2s} \div (r + 2s)\right] \cdot \dfrac{2s}{r - 2s}$

$= \left[\dfrac{r^2 - 4s^2}{r + 2s} \cdot \dfrac{1}{r + 2s}\right] \cdot \dfrac{2s}{r - 2s}$

$= \dfrac{(r^2 - 4s^2)(2s)}{(r + 2s)(r + 2s)(r - 2s)}$

$= \dfrac{(r + 2s)(r - 2s)(2s)}{(r + 2s)(r + 2s)(r - 2s)}$

$= \dfrac{(r + 2s)(r - 2s)(2s)}{(r + 2s)(r + 2s)(r - 2s)}$

$= \dfrac{2s}{r + 2s}$

98. $\dfrac{(d - 1)(d - 5)}{5d(d + 5)}$

99. $\left[\dfrac{6t^2 - 26t + 30}{8t^2 - 15t + 21} \cdot \dfrac{5t^2 - 9t - 15}{6t^2 - 14t - 20}\right] \div \dfrac{5t^2 - 9t - 15}{6t^2 - 14t - 20}$

$= \dfrac{(6t^2 - 26t + 30)(5t^2 - 9t - 15)}{(8t^2 - 15t + 21)(6t^2 - 14t - 20)} \div \dfrac{5t^2 - 9t - 15}{6t^2 - 14t - 20}$

$= \dfrac{(6t^2 - 26t + 30)(5t^2 - 9t - 15)}{(8t^2 - 15t + 21)(6t^2 - 14t - 20)} \cdot \dfrac{6t^2 - 14t - 20}{5t^2 - 9t - 15}$

$= \dfrac{(6t^2 - 26t + 30)(5t^2 - 9t - 15)(6t^2 - 14t - 20)}{(8t^2 - 15t + 21)(6t^2 - 14t - 20)(5t^2 - 9t - 15)}$

$= \dfrac{6t^2 - 26t + 30}{8t^2 - 15t + 21} \cdot \dfrac{(5t^2 - 9t - 15)(6t^2 - 14t - 20)}{(6t^2 - 14t - 20)(5t^2 - 9t - 15)}$

$= \dfrac{6t^2 - 26t + 30}{8t^2 - 15t + 21} \cdot 1$

$= \dfrac{6t^2 - 26t + 30}{8t^2 - 15t + 21},$ or $\dfrac{2(3t^2 - 13t + 15)}{8t^2 - 15t + 21}$

100. a) $\dfrac{2x + 2h + 3}{4x + 4h - 1}$

   b) $\dfrac{2x + 3}{8x - 9}$

c) $\dfrac{x + 5}{4x - 1}$

101. a) $(f \cdot g)(x) = \dfrac{4}{x^2 - 1} \cdot \dfrac{4x^2 + 8x + 4}{x^3 - 1}$

$= \dfrac{4(4x^2 + 8x + 4)}{(x^2 - 1)(x^3 - 1)}$

$= \dfrac{4 \cdot 4(x + 1)(x + 1)}{(x + 1)(x - 1)(x - 1)(x^2 + x + 1)}$

$= \dfrac{4 \cdot 4(x + 1)(x + 1)}{(x + 1)(x - 1)(x - 1)(x^2 + x + 1)}$

$= \dfrac{16(x + 1)}{(x - 1)^2(x^2 + x + 1)}$

(Note that $x \neq -1$ and $x \neq 1$ are additional restrictions since -1 is not in the domain of f and 1 is not in the domain of either f or g.)

b) $(f/g)(x) = \dfrac{4}{x^2 - 1} \div \dfrac{4x^2 + 8x + 4}{x^3 - 1}$

$= \dfrac{4}{x^2 - 1} \cdot \dfrac{x^3 - 1}{4x^2 + 8x + 4}$

$= \dfrac{4(x^3 - 1)}{(x^2 - 1)(4x^2 + 8x + 4)}$

$= \dfrac{4(x - 1)(x^2 + x + 1)}{(x + 1)(x - 1)(4)(x + 1)(x + 1)}$

$= \dfrac{4(x - 1)(x^2 + x + 1)}{(x + 1)(x - 1)(4)(x + 1)(x + 1)}$

$= \dfrac{x^2 + x + 1}{(x + 1)^3}$

(Note that $x \neq -1$ and $x \neq 1$ are additional restrictions since -1 is not in the domain of f and 1 is not in the domain of either f or g.)

c) $(g/f)(x) = \dfrac{1}{(f/g)(x)}$

$= \dfrac{(x + 1)^3}{x^2 + x + 1}$ (See part (b) above.)

(Note that $x \neq -1$ and $x \neq 1$ are restrictions, since -1 is not in the domain of f and 1 is not in the domain of either f or g.)

Exercise Set 7.3

1. $\dfrac{3}{x} + \dfrac{9}{x} = \dfrac{12}{x}$ Adding numerators

2. $\dfrac{13}{a^2}$

3. $\dfrac{x}{15} + \dfrac{2x + 5}{15} = \dfrac{3x + 5}{15}$ Adding numerators

4. $\dfrac{4a - 4}{7}$

5. $\dfrac{4}{a + 3} + \dfrac{5}{a + 3} = \dfrac{9}{a + 3}$

6. $\dfrac{13}{x + 2}$

7. $\dfrac{9}{a + 2} - \dfrac{3}{a + 2} = \dfrac{6}{a + 2}$ Subtracting numerators

8. $\dfrac{6}{x+7}$

9. $\dfrac{3y+8}{2y} - \dfrac{y+1}{2y}$

$$= \dfrac{3y+8-(y+1)}{2y}$$

$$= \dfrac{3y+8-y-1}{2y} \qquad \text{Removing parentheses}$$

$$= \dfrac{2y+7}{2y}$$

10. $\dfrac{t+4}{4t}$

11. $\dfrac{7x+8}{x+1} + \dfrac{4x+3}{x+1}$

$$= \dfrac{11x+11}{x+1} \qquad \text{Adding numerators}$$

$$= \dfrac{11(x+1)}{x+1} \qquad \text{Factoring}$$

$$= \dfrac{11(\cancel{x+1})}{\cancel{x+1}} \qquad \text{Removing a factor equal to 1}$$

$$= 11$$

12. 5

13. $\dfrac{7x+8}{x+1} - \dfrac{4x+3}{x+1} = \dfrac{7x+8-(4x+3)}{x+1}$

$$= \dfrac{7x+8-4x-3}{x+1}$$

$$= \dfrac{3x+5}{x+1}$$

14. $\dfrac{a+6}{a+4}$

15. $\dfrac{a^2}{a-4} + \dfrac{a-20}{a-4} = \dfrac{a^2+a-20}{a-4}$

$$= \dfrac{(a+5)(a-4)}{a-4}$$

$$= \dfrac{(a+5)(\cancel{a-4})}{\cancel{a-4}}$$

$$= a+5$$

16. $x+2$

17. $\dfrac{x^2}{x-2} - \dfrac{6x-8}{x-2} = \dfrac{x^2-(6x-8)}{x-2}$

$$= \dfrac{x^2-6x+8}{x-2}$$

$$= \dfrac{(x-4)(x-2)}{x-2}$$

$$= \dfrac{(x-4)(\cancel{x-2})}{\cancel{x-2}}$$

$$= x-4$$

18. $a-5$

19. $\dfrac{t^2-5t}{t-1} + \dfrac{5t-t^2}{t-1}$

Note that the numerators are opposites, so their sum is 0. Then we have $\dfrac{0}{t-1}$, or 0.

20. $y+6$

21. $\dfrac{x-4}{x^2+5x+6} + \dfrac{7}{x^2+5x+6} = \dfrac{x+3}{x^2+5x+6}$

$$= \dfrac{x+3}{(x+3)(x+2)}$$

$$= \dfrac{\cancel{x+3}}{(\cancel{x+3})(x+2)}$$

$$= \dfrac{1}{x+2}$$

22. $\dfrac{1}{x-1}$

23. $\dfrac{3a^2+14}{a^2+5a-6} - \dfrac{13a}{a^2+5a-6} = \dfrac{3a^2-13a+14}{a^2+5a-6}$

$$= \dfrac{(3a-7)(a-2)}{(a+6)(a-1)}$$

(No simplification is possible.)

24. $\dfrac{2a-5}{a-4}$

25. $\dfrac{t^2-3t}{t^2+6t+9} + \dfrac{2t-12}{t^2+6t+9} = \dfrac{t^2-t-12}{t^2+6t+9}$

$$= \dfrac{(t-4)(t+3)}{(t+3)^2}$$

$$= \dfrac{(t-4)(\cancel{t+3})}{(t+3)(\cancel{t+3})}$$

$$= \dfrac{t-4}{t+3}$$

26. $\dfrac{y-5}{y+4}$

27. $\dfrac{2x^2+x}{x^2-8x+12} - \dfrac{x^2-2x+10}{x^2-8x+12}$

$$= \dfrac{2x^2+x-(x^2-2x+10)}{x^2-8x+12}$$

$$= \dfrac{2x^2+x-x^2+2x-10}{x^2-8x+12}$$

$$= \dfrac{x^2+3x-10}{x^2-8x+12}$$

$$= \dfrac{(x+5)(x-2)}{(x-6)(x-2)}$$

$$= \dfrac{(x+5)(\cancel{x-2})}{(x-6)(\cancel{x-2})}$$

$$= \dfrac{x+5}{x-6}$$

28. 0

29. $\dfrac{3-2x}{x^2-6x+8}+\dfrac{7-3x}{x^2-6x+8}$

$=\dfrac{10-5x}{x^2-6x+8}$

$=\dfrac{5(2-x)}{(x-4)(x-2)}$

$=\dfrac{5(-1)(x-2)}{(x-4)(x-2)}$

$=\dfrac{5(-1)\cancel{(x-2)}}{(x-4)\cancel{(x-2)}}$

$=\dfrac{-5}{x-4}$, or $-\dfrac{5}{x-4}$, or $\dfrac{5}{4-x}$

30. $-\dfrac{5}{t-4}$, or $\dfrac{5}{4-t}$

31. $\dfrac{x-7}{x^2+3x-4}-\dfrac{2x-3}{x^2+3x-4}$

$=\dfrac{x-7-(2x-3)}{x^2+3x-4}$

$=\dfrac{x-7-2x+3}{x^2+3x-4}$

$=\dfrac{-x-4}{x^2+3x-4}$

$=\dfrac{-(x+4)}{(x+4)(x-1)}$

$=\dfrac{-1\cancel{(x+4)}}{\cancel{(x+4)}(x-1)}$

$=\dfrac{-1}{x-1}$, or $-\dfrac{1}{x-1}$, or $\dfrac{1}{1-x}$

32. $-\dfrac{4}{x-1}$, or $\dfrac{4}{1-x}$

33. $15=3\cdot5$

$27=3\cdot3\cdot3$

$\text{LCM}=3\cdot3\cdot3\cdot5$, or 135

34. 30

35. $8=2\cdot2\cdot2$

$9=3\cdot3$

$\text{LCM}=2\cdot2\cdot2\cdot3\cdot3$, or 72

36. 60

37. $6=2\cdot3$

$9=3\cdot3$

$21=3\cdot7$

$\text{LCM}=2\cdot3\cdot3\cdot7$, or 126

38. 360

39. $12x^2=2\cdot2\cdot3\cdot x\cdot x$

$6x^3=2\cdot3\cdot x\cdot x\cdot x$

$\text{LCM}=2\cdot2\cdot3\cdot x\cdot x\cdot x$, or $12x^3$

40. $10t^4$

41. $15a^4b^7=3\cdot5\cdot a\cdot a\cdot a\cdot a\cdot b\cdot b\cdot b\cdot b\cdot b\cdot b\cdot b$

$10a^2b^8=2\cdot5\cdot a\cdot a\cdot b\cdot b\cdot b\cdot b\cdot b\cdot b\cdot b\cdot b$

$\text{LCM}=2\cdot3\cdot5\cdot a\cdot a\cdot a\cdot a\cdot b\cdot b\cdot b\cdot b\cdot b\cdot b\cdot b\cdot b$,

$\quad$ or $30a^4b^8$

42. $18a^5b^7$

43. $2(y-3)=2\cdot(y-3)$

$6(y-3)=2\cdot3\cdot(y-3)$

$\text{LCM}=2\cdot3\cdot(y-3)$, or $6(y-3)$

44. $8(x-1)$

45. $x^2-4=(x+2)(x-2)$

$x^2+5x+6=(x+3)(x+2)$

$\text{LCM}=(x+2)(x-2)(x+3)$

46. $(x+2)(x+1)(x-2)$

47. $t^3+4t^2+4t=t(t^2+4t+4)=t(t+2)(t+2)$

$t^2-4t=t(t-4)$

$\text{LCM}=t(t+2)(t+2)(t-4)=t(t+2)^2(t-4)$

48. $y^2(y+1)(y-1)$

49. $10x^2y=2\cdot5\cdot x\cdot x\cdot y$

$6y^2z=2\cdot3\cdot y\cdot y\cdot z$

$5xz^3=5\cdot x\cdot z\cdot z\cdot z$

$\text{LCM}=2\cdot3\cdot5\cdot x\cdot x\cdot y\cdot y\cdot z\cdot z\cdot z=30x^2y^2z^3$

50. $24x^3y^5z^2$

51. $a+1=a+1$

$(a-1)^2=(a-1)(a-1)$

$a^2-1=(a+1)(a-1)$

$\text{LCM}=(a+1)(a-1)(a-1)=(a+1)(a-1)^2$

52. $(x+3)(x-3)^2$

53. $m^2-5m+6=(m-3)(m-2)$

$m^2-4m+4=(m-2)(m-2)$

$\text{LCM}=(m-3)(m-2)(m-2)=(m-3)(m-2)^2$

54. $(2x+1)(x+2)(x-1)$

55. $t-3,\ t+3,\ (t^2-9)^2$

Note that $(t^2-9)^2=[(t+3)(t-3)]^2$, so this expression is a multiple of each of the other expressions. Thus, the LCM is $(t^2-9)^2$.

56. $(a^2-10a+25)^2$

57. $6x^3-24x^2+18x=6x(x^2-4x+3)=$

$\quad 2\cdot3\cdot x(x-1)(x-3)$

$4x^5-24x^4+20x^3=4x^3(x^2-6x+5)=$

$\quad 2\cdot2\cdot x\cdot x\cdot x(x-1)(x-5)$

$\text{LCM}=2\cdot2\cdot3\cdot x\cdot x\cdot x(x-1)(x-3)(x-5)=$

$\quad 12x^3(x-1)(x-3)(x-5)$

58. $18x^3(x-2)^2(x+1)$

59. $t^3 - 1 = (t-1)(t^2 + t + 1)$

$t^2 - 1 = (t+1)(t-1)$

$\text{LCM} = (t-1)(t^2 + t + 1)(t+1)$, or

$(t+1)(t-1)(t^2 + t + 1)$

60. $5(n+1)(n^2 - n + 1)$

61. $6x^5 = 2 \cdot 3 \cdot x \cdot x \cdot x \cdot x \cdot x$

$12x^3 = 2 \cdot 2 \cdot 3 \cdot x \cdot x \cdot x$

The LCD is $2 \cdot 2 \cdot 3 \cdot x \cdot x \cdot x \cdot x \cdot x$, or $12x^5$.

The factor of the LCD that is missing from the first denominator is 2. We multiply by 1 using $2/2$:

$$\frac{5}{6x^5} \cdot \frac{2}{2} = \frac{10}{12x^5}$$

The second denominator is missing two factors of x, or x^2. We multiply by 1 using x^2/x^2:

$$\frac{y}{12x^3} \cdot \frac{x^2}{x^2} = \frac{x^2 y}{12x^5}$$

62. $\dfrac{3a^3}{10a^6}, \dfrac{2b}{10a^6}$

63. $2a^2 b = 2 \cdot a \cdot a \cdot b$

$8ab^2 = 2 \cdot 2 \cdot 2 \cdot a \cdot b \cdot b$

The LCD is $2 \cdot 2 \cdot 2 \cdot a \cdot a \cdot b \cdot b$, or $8a^2 b^2$.

We multiply the first expression by $\dfrac{4b}{4b}$ to obtain the LCD:

$$\frac{3}{2a^2 b} \cdot \frac{4b}{4b} = \frac{12b}{8a^2 b^2}$$

We multiply the second expression by a/a to obtain the LCD:

$$\frac{7}{8ab^2} \cdot \frac{a}{a} = \frac{7a}{8a^2 b^2}$$

64. $\dfrac{21y}{9x^4 y^3}, \dfrac{4x^3}{9x^4 y^3}$

65. The LCD is $(x+2)(x-2)(x+3)$. (See Exercise 45.)

$$\frac{2x}{x^2 - 4} = \frac{2x}{(x+2)(x-2)} \cdot \frac{x+3}{x+3}$$

$$= \frac{2x(x+3)}{(x+2)(x-2)(x+3)}$$

$$\frac{4x}{x^2 + 5x + 6} = \frac{4x}{(x+3)(x+2)} \cdot \frac{x-2}{x-2}$$

$$= \frac{4x(x-2)}{(x+3)(x+2)(x-2)}$$

66. $\dfrac{5x(x+8)}{(x+3)(x-3)(x+8)}, \dfrac{2x(x-3)}{(x+3)(x+8)(x-3)}$

67. *Writing Exercise*

68. *Writing Exercise*

69. $\dfrac{7}{-9} = -\dfrac{7}{9} = \dfrac{-7}{9}$

70. $\dfrac{-3}{2}, \dfrac{3}{-2}$

71. $\dfrac{5}{18} - \dfrac{7}{12} = \dfrac{5}{18} \cdot \dfrac{2}{2} - \dfrac{7}{12} \cdot \dfrac{3}{3}$

$$= \frac{10}{36} - \frac{21}{36}$$

$$= -\frac{11}{36}$$

72. $-\dfrac{7}{60}$

73. The shaded area has dimensions $x - 6$ by $x - 3$. Then the area is $(x-6)(x-3)$, or $x^2 - 9x + 18$.

74. $s^2 - \pi r^2$

75. *Writing Exercise*

76. *Writing Exercise*

77. $\dfrac{6x-1}{x-1} + \dfrac{3(2x+5)}{x-1} + \dfrac{3(2x-3)}{x-1}$

$$= \frac{6x - 1 + 6x + 15 + 6x - 9}{x-1}$$

$$= \frac{18x + 5}{x-1}$$

78. $\dfrac{30}{(x-3)(x+4)}$

79. $\dfrac{x^2}{3x^2 - 5x - 2} - \dfrac{2x}{3x+1} \cdot \dfrac{1}{x-2}$

$$= \frac{x^2}{(3x+1)(x-2)} - \frac{2x}{(3x+1)(x-2)}$$

$$= \frac{x^2 - 2x}{(3x+1)(x-2)}$$

$$= \frac{x(x-2)}{(3x+1)(x-2)}$$

$$= \frac{x}{3x+1}$$

80. 0

81. The smallest number of strands that can be used is the LCM of 10 and 3.

$10 = 2 \cdot 5$

$3 = 3$

$\text{LCM} = 2 \cdot 5 \cdot 3 = 30$

82. 24

83. If the number of strands must also be a multiple of 4, we find the smallest multiple of 30 that is also a multiple of 4.

$1 \cdot 30 = 30$, not a multiple of 4

$2 \cdot 30 = 60 = 15 \cdot 4$, a multiple of 4

The smallest number of strands that can be used is 60.

84. 1440

85. $8x^2 - 8 = 8(x^2 - 1) = 2 \cdot 2 \cdot 2(x+1)(x-1)$

$6x^2 - 12x + 6 = 6(x^2 - 2x + 1) = 2 \cdot 3(x-1)(x-1)$

$10 - 10x = 10(1-x) = 2 \cdot 5(1-x)$

Note that $x - 1$ and $1 - x$ and opposites.

$\text{LCM} = 2 \cdot 2 \cdot 2 \cdot 3 \cdot 5(x+1)(x-1)(x-1) = 120(x+1)(x-1)^2$

$\Big($We could also express the LCM as

$120(x+1)(x-1)(1-x)$. It is not necessary to include both a factor and its opposite in the LCM since $\dfrac{a}{-b} = \dfrac{-a}{b} = -\dfrac{a}{b}.\Big)$

86. $(3x+4)(3x-4)^2(2x-3)$

87. The time it takes Kim and Jed to meet again at the starting place is the LCM of the times it takes them to complete one round of the course.

$6 = 2 \cdot 3$

$8 = 2 \cdot 2 \cdot 2$

$\text{LCM} = 2 \cdot 2 \cdot 2 \cdot 3$, or 24

It takes 24 min.

88. 7:55 A.M.

89. The number of years after 2002 in which all three appliances will need to be replaced at once is the LCM of the average numbers of years each will last.

$10 = 2 \cdot 5$

$14 = 2 \cdot 7$

$20 = 2 \cdot 2 \cdot 5$

$\text{LCM} = 2 \cdot 2 \cdot 5 \cdot 7 = 140$

All three appliances will need to be replaced 140 years after 2002, or in 2142.

90. *Writing Exercise*

91. *Writing Exercise*

Exercise Set 7.4

1. $\dfrac{3}{x} + \dfrac{7}{x^2} = \dfrac{3}{x} + \dfrac{7}{x \cdot x}$ $\qquad \text{LCD} = x \cdot x$, or x^2

$\qquad = \dfrac{3}{x} \cdot \dfrac{x}{x} + \dfrac{7}{x \cdot x}$

$\qquad = \dfrac{3x + 7}{x^2}$

2. $\dfrac{5x+6}{x^2}$

3. $\left.\begin{array}{l} 6r = 2 \cdot 3 \cdot r \\ 8r = 2 \cdot 2 \cdot 2 \cdot r \end{array}\right\} \text{LCD} = 2 \cdot 2 \cdot 2 \cdot 3 \cdot r$, or $24r$

$\dfrac{1}{6r} - \dfrac{3}{8r} = \dfrac{1}{6r} \cdot \dfrac{4}{4} - \dfrac{3}{8r} \cdot \dfrac{3}{3}$

$\qquad = \dfrac{4 - 9}{24r}$

$\qquad = \dfrac{-5}{24r}$, or $-\dfrac{5}{24r}$

4. $\dfrac{13}{18t}$

5. $\left.\begin{array}{l} xy^2 = x \cdot y \cdot y \\ x^2y = x \cdot x \cdot y \end{array}\right\} \text{LCD} = x \cdot x \cdot y \cdot y$, or x^2y^2

$\dfrac{4}{xy^2} + \dfrac{2}{x^2y} = \dfrac{4}{xy^2} \cdot \dfrac{x}{x} + \dfrac{2}{x^2y} \cdot \dfrac{y}{y}$

$\qquad = \dfrac{4x + 2y}{x^2y^2}$

6. $\dfrac{2d^2 + 7c}{c^2d^3}$

7. $\left.\begin{array}{l} 9t^3 = 3 \cdot 3 \cdot t \cdot t \cdot t \\ 6t^2 = 2 \cdot 3 \cdot t \cdot t \end{array}\right\} \text{LCD} = 2 \cdot 3 \cdot 3 \cdot t \cdot t \cdot t$, or $18t^3$

$\dfrac{8}{9t^3} - \dfrac{5}{6t^2} = \dfrac{8}{9t^3} \cdot \dfrac{2}{2} - \dfrac{5}{6t^2} \cdot \dfrac{3t}{3t}$

$\qquad = \dfrac{16 - 15t}{18t^3}$

8. $\dfrac{-2xy - 18}{3x^2y^3}$

9. $\text{LCD} = 24$ (See Example 1.)

$\dfrac{x+5}{8} + \dfrac{x-3}{12} = \dfrac{x+5}{8} \cdot \dfrac{3}{3} + \dfrac{x-3}{12} \cdot \dfrac{2}{2}$

$\qquad = \dfrac{3(x+5)}{24} + \dfrac{2(x-3)}{24}$

$\qquad = \dfrac{3x+15}{24} + \dfrac{2x-6}{24}$

$\qquad = \dfrac{5x+9}{24}$ Adding numerators

10. $\dfrac{5x+7}{18}$

11. $\left.\begin{array}{l} 2 = 2 \\ 4 = 2 \cdot 2 \end{array}\right\} \text{LCD} = 4$

$\dfrac{a+2}{2} - \dfrac{a-4}{4} = \dfrac{a+2}{2} \cdot \dfrac{2}{2} - \dfrac{a-4}{4}$

$\qquad = \dfrac{2a+4}{4} - \dfrac{a-4}{4}$

$\qquad = \dfrac{2a+4 - (a-4)}{4}$

$\qquad = \dfrac{2a+4 - a+4}{4}$

$\qquad = \dfrac{a+8}{4}$

12. $\dfrac{-x-4}{6}$

13. $\left.\begin{array}{l} 3a^2 = 3 \cdot a \cdot a \\ 9a = 3 \cdot 3 \cdot a \end{array}\right\} \text{LCD} = 3 \cdot 3 \cdot a \cdot a$, or $9a^2$

$\dfrac{2a-1}{3a^2} + \dfrac{5a+1}{9a} = \dfrac{2a-1}{3a^2} \cdot \dfrac{3}{3} + \dfrac{5a+1}{9a} \cdot \dfrac{a}{a}$

$\qquad = \dfrac{6a-3}{9a^2} + \dfrac{5a^2+a}{9a^2}$

$\qquad = \dfrac{5a^2 + 7a - 3}{9a^2}$

14. $\dfrac{a^2 + 16a + 16}{16a^2}$

15. $\left.\begin{array}{l} 4x = 4 \cdot x \\ x = x \end{array}\right\}$ LCD $= 4x$

$$\dfrac{x-1}{4x} - \dfrac{2x+3}{x} = \dfrac{x-1}{4x} - \dfrac{2x+3}{x} \cdot \dfrac{4}{4}$$
$$= \dfrac{x-1}{4x} - \dfrac{8x+12}{4x}$$
$$= \dfrac{x-1-(8x+12)}{4x}$$
$$= \dfrac{x-1-8x-12}{4x}$$
$$= \dfrac{-7x-13}{4x}$$

16. $\dfrac{7z-12}{12z}$

17. $\left.\begin{array}{l} c^2 d = c \cdot c \cdot d \\ cd^2 = c \cdot d \cdot d \end{array}\right\}$ LCD $= c \cdot c \cdot d \cdot d$, or $c^2 d^2$

$$\dfrac{2c-d}{c^2 d} + \dfrac{c+d}{cd^2} = \dfrac{2c-d}{c^2 d} \cdot \dfrac{d}{d} + \dfrac{c+d}{cd^2} \cdot \dfrac{c}{c}$$
$$= \dfrac{d(2c-d) + c(c+d)}{c^2 d^2}$$
$$= \dfrac{2cd - d^2 + c^2 + cd}{c^2 d^2}$$
$$= \dfrac{c^2 + 3cd - d^2}{c^2 d^2}$$

18. $\dfrac{x^2 + 4xy + y^2}{x^2 y^2}$

19. $\left.\begin{array}{l} 2x^2 y = 2 \cdot x \cdot x \cdot y \\ xy^2 = x \cdot y \cdot y \end{array}\right\}$ LCD $= 2 \cdot x \cdot x \cdot y \cdot y$, or $2x^2 y^2$

$$\dfrac{5x+3y}{2x^2 y} - \dfrac{3x+4y}{xy^2} = \dfrac{5x+3y}{2x^2 y} \cdot \dfrac{y}{y} - \dfrac{3x+4y}{xy^2} \cdot \dfrac{2x}{2x}$$
$$= \dfrac{5xy + 3y^2}{2x^2 y^2} - \dfrac{6x^2 + 8xy}{2x^2 y^2}$$
$$= \dfrac{5xy + 3y^2 - (6x^2 + 8xy)}{2x^2 y^2}$$
$$= \dfrac{5xy + 3y^2 - 6x^2 - 8xy}{2x^2 y^2}$$
$$= \dfrac{3y^2 - 3xy - 6x^2}{2x^2 y^2}$$

(Although $3y^2 - 3xy - 6x^2$ can be factored, doing so will not enable us to simplify the result further.)

20. $\dfrac{4x^2 - 13xt + 9t^2}{3x^2 t^2}$

21. The denominators cannot be factored, so the LCD is their product, $(x-1)(x+1)$.

$$\dfrac{5}{x-1} + \dfrac{5}{x+1} = \dfrac{5}{x-1} \cdot \dfrac{x+1}{x+1} + \dfrac{5}{x+1} \cdot \dfrac{x-1}{x-1}$$
$$= \dfrac{5(x+1) + 5(x-1)}{(x-1)(x+1)}$$
$$= \dfrac{5x+5+5x-5}{(x-1)(x+1)}$$
$$= \dfrac{10x}{(x-1)(x+1)}$$

22. $\dfrac{6x}{(x-2)(x+2)}$

23. The denominators cannot be factored, so the LCD is their product, $(z-1)(z+1)$.

$$\dfrac{4}{z-1} - \dfrac{2}{z+1} = \dfrac{4}{z-1} \cdot \dfrac{z+1}{z+1} - \dfrac{2}{z+1} \cdot \dfrac{z-1}{z-1}$$
$$= \dfrac{4z+4}{(z-1)(z+1)} - \dfrac{2z-2}{(z-1)(z+1)}$$
$$= \dfrac{4z+4-(2z-2)}{(z-1)(z+1)}$$
$$= \dfrac{4z+4-2z+2}{(z-1)(z+1)}$$
$$= \dfrac{2z+6}{(z-1)(z+1)}$$

(Although $2z+6$ can be factored, doing so will not enable us to simplify the result further.)

24. $\dfrac{2x-40}{(x+5)(x-5)}$

25. $\left.\begin{array}{l} x+5 = x+5 \\ 4x = 4 \cdot x \end{array}\right\}$ LCD $= 4x(x+5)$

$$\dfrac{2}{x+5} + \dfrac{3}{4x} = \dfrac{2}{x+5} \cdot \dfrac{4x}{4x} + \dfrac{3}{4x} \cdot \dfrac{x+5}{x+5}$$
$$= \dfrac{2 \cdot 4x + 3(x+5)}{4x(x+5)}$$
$$= \dfrac{8x + 3x + 15}{4x(x+5)}$$
$$= \dfrac{11x + 15}{4x(x+5)}$$

26. $\dfrac{11x+2}{3x(x+1)}$

27. $\left.\begin{array}{l} 3t^2 - 15t = 3t(t-5) \\ 2t - 10 = 2(t-5) \end{array}\right\}$ LCD $= 6t(t-5)$

$$\dfrac{8}{3t(t-5)} - \dfrac{3}{2(t-5)}$$
$$= \dfrac{8}{3t(t-5)} \cdot \dfrac{2}{2} - \dfrac{3}{2(t-5)} \cdot \dfrac{3t}{3t}$$
$$= \dfrac{16}{6t(t-5)} - \dfrac{9t}{6t(t-5)}$$
$$= \dfrac{16 - 9t}{6t(t-5)}$$

28. $\dfrac{3-5t}{2t(t-1)}$

29. $\dfrac{4x}{x^2-25}+\dfrac{x}{x+5}$

$=\dfrac{4x}{(x+5)(x-5)}+\dfrac{x}{x+5}\quad$ LCD $=(x+5)(x-5)$

$=\dfrac{4x+x(x-5)}{(x+5)(x-5)}$

$=\dfrac{4x+x^2-5x}{(x+5)(x-5)}$

$=\dfrac{x^2-x}{(x+5)(x-5)}$

(Although x^2-x can be factored, doing so will not enable us to simplify the result further.)

30. $\dfrac{x^2+6x}{(x+4)(x-4)}$

31. $\dfrac{t}{t-3}-\dfrac{5}{4t-12}$

$=\dfrac{t}{t-3}-\dfrac{5}{4(t-3)}\quad$ LCD $=4(t-3)$

$=\dfrac{t}{t-3}\cdot\dfrac{4}{4}-\dfrac{5}{4(t-3)}$

$=\dfrac{4t-5}{4(t-3)}$

32. $\dfrac{16}{3(z+4)}$

33. $\dfrac{2}{x+3}+\dfrac{4}{(x+3)^2}\quad$ LCD $=(x+3)^2$

$=\dfrac{2}{x+3}\cdot\dfrac{x+3}{x+3}+\dfrac{4}{(x+3)^2}$

$=\dfrac{2(x+3)+4}{(x+3)^2}$

$=\dfrac{2x+6+4}{(x+3)^2}$

$=\dfrac{2x+10}{(x+3)^2}$

(Although $2x+10$ can be factored, doing so will not enable us to simplify the result further.)

34. $\dfrac{3x-1}{(x-1)^2}$

35. $\dfrac{3}{x+2}-\dfrac{8}{x^2-4}$

$=\dfrac{3}{x+2}-\dfrac{8}{(x+2)(x-2)}\quad$ LCD $=(x+2)(x-2)$

$=\dfrac{3}{x+2}\cdot\dfrac{x-2}{x-2}-\dfrac{8}{(x+2)(x-2)}$

$=\dfrac{3(x-2)-8}{(x+2)(x-2)}$

$=\dfrac{3x-6-8}{(x+2)(x-2)}$

$=\dfrac{3x-14}{(x+2)(x-2)}$

36. $\dfrac{-t-9}{(t+3)(t-3)}$

37. $\dfrac{3a}{4a-20}+\dfrac{9a}{6a-30}$

$=\dfrac{3a}{2\cdot2(a-5)}+\dfrac{9a}{2\cdot3(a-5)}$

$\qquad\qquad$ LCD $=2\cdot2\cdot3(a-5)$

$=\dfrac{3a}{2\cdot2(a-5)}\cdot\dfrac{3}{3}+\dfrac{9a}{2\cdot3(a-5)}\cdot\dfrac{2}{2}$

$=\dfrac{9a+18a}{2\cdot2\cdot3(a-5)}$

$=\dfrac{27a}{2\cdot2\cdot3(a-5)}$

$=\dfrac{\cancel{3}\cdot9\cdot a}{2\cdot3\cdot\cancel{3}(a-5)}$

$=\dfrac{9a}{4(a-5)}$

38. $\dfrac{11a}{10(a-2)}$

39. $\dfrac{x}{x-5}+\dfrac{x}{5-x}=\dfrac{x}{x-5}+\dfrac{x}{5-x}\cdot\dfrac{-1}{-1}$

$=\dfrac{x}{x-5}+\dfrac{-x}{x-5}$

$=0$

40. $\dfrac{2x^2+8x+16}{x(x+4)}$

41. $\dfrac{7}{a^2+a-2}+\dfrac{5}{a^2-4a+3}$

$=\dfrac{7}{(a+2)(a-1)}+\dfrac{5}{(a-3)(a-1)}$

$\qquad\qquad$ LCD $=(a+2)(a-1)(a-3)$

$=\dfrac{7}{(a+2)(a-1)}\cdot\dfrac{a-3}{a-3}+\dfrac{5}{(a-3)(a-1)}\cdot\dfrac{a+2}{a+2}$

$=\dfrac{7(a-3)+5(a+2)}{(a+2)(a-1)(a-3)}$

$=\dfrac{7a-21+5a+10}{(a+2)(a-1)(a-3)}$

$=\dfrac{12a-11}{(a+2)(a-1)(a-3)}$

42. $\dfrac{x^2+5x+1}{(x+1)^2(x+4)}$

43.

$$\frac{x}{x^2+9x+20}-\frac{4}{x^2+7x+12}$$

$$=\frac{x}{(x+4)(x+5)}-\frac{4}{(x+3)(x+4)}$$

$$\text{LCD}=(x+3)(x+4)(x+5)$$

$$=\frac{x}{(x+4)(x+5)}\cdot\frac{x+3}{x+3}-\frac{4}{(x+3)(x+4)}\cdot\frac{x+5}{x+5}$$

$$=\frac{x(x+3)-4(x+5)}{(x+3)(x+4)(x+5)}$$

$$=\frac{x^2+3x-4x-20}{(x+3)(x+4)(x+5)}$$

$$=\frac{x^2-x-20}{(x+3)(x+4)(x+5)}$$

$$=\frac{(x+4)(x-5)}{(x+3)(x+4)(x+5)}$$

$$=\frac{x-5}{(x+3)(x+5)}$$

44. $\dfrac{x-3}{(x+3)(x+1)}$

45.

$$\frac{2x+1}{x-y}+\frac{5x^2-5xy}{x^2-2xy+y^2}$$

$$=\frac{2x+1}{x-y}+\frac{5x(x-y)}{(x-y)(x-y)}$$

$$=\frac{2x+1}{x-y}+\frac{5x(x-y)}{(x-y)(x-y)}$$

$$=\frac{2x+1}{x-y}+\frac{5x}{x-y}$$

$$=\frac{7x+1}{x-y}$$

46. $\dfrac{2}{a-b}$

47. $\dfrac{-5}{x^2+17x+16}-\dfrac{0}{x^2+9x+8}$

Note that $\dfrac{0}{x^2+9x+8}=0$, so the difference is

$$\frac{-5}{x^2+17x+16}.$$

48. $\dfrac{x^2+5x-8}{(x+7)(x+8)(x+6)}$

49.

$$\frac{2x}{5}-\frac{x-3}{-5}=\frac{2x}{5}-\frac{x-3}{-5}\cdot\frac{-1}{-1}$$

$$=\frac{2x}{5}-\frac{3-x}{5}$$

$$=\frac{2x-(3-x)}{5}$$

$$=\frac{2x-3+x}{5}$$

$$=\frac{3x-3}{5}$$

(Although $3x-3$ can be factored, doing so will not enable us to simplify the result further.)

50. $\dfrac{4x-5}{4}$

51.

$$\frac{y^2}{y-3}+\frac{9}{3-y}=\frac{y^2}{y-3}+\frac{9}{3-y}\cdot\frac{-1}{-1}$$

$$=\frac{y^2}{y-3}+\frac{-9}{-3+y}$$

$$=\frac{y^2-9}{y-3}$$

$$=\frac{(y+3)(y-3)}{y-3}$$

$$=y+3$$

52. $t+2$

53.

$$\frac{t^2+3}{t^4-16}+\frac{7}{16-t^4}=\frac{t^2+3}{t^4-16}+\frac{-1}{-1}\cdot\frac{7}{16-t^4}$$

$$=\frac{t^2+3}{t^4-16}+\frac{-7}{t^4-16}$$

$$=\frac{t^2-4}{t^4-16}$$

$$=\frac{(t+2)(t-2)}{(t^2+4)(t+2)(t-2)}$$

$$=\frac{1\cdot(t+2)(t-2)}{(t^2+4)(t+2)(t-2)}$$

$$=\frac{1}{t^2+4}$$

54. $\dfrac{1}{y^2+9}$

55.

$$\frac{m-3n}{m^3-n^3}-\frac{2n}{n^3-m^3}-\frac{m-3n}{m^3-n^3}+\frac{1}{-1}\cdot\frac{2n}{n^3-m^3}$$

$$=\frac{m-3n}{m^3-n^3}+\frac{2n}{m^3-n^3}$$

$$=\frac{m-n}{m^3-n^3}$$

$$=\frac{m-n}{(m-n)(m^2+mn+n^2)}$$

$$=\frac{1\cdot(m-n)}{(m-n)(m^2+mn+n^2)}$$

$$=\frac{1}{m^2+mn+n^2}$$

56. $\dfrac{1}{r^2+rs+s^2}$

57.

$$\frac{y+2}{y-7}+\frac{3-y}{49-y^2}$$

$$=\frac{y+2}{y-7}+\frac{3-y}{(7+y)(7-y)}$$

$$=\frac{y+2}{y-7}+\frac{3-y}{(7+y)(7-y)}\cdot\frac{-1}{-1}$$

$$=\frac{y+2}{y-7}+\frac{y-3}{(y+7)(y-7)}\quad\text{LCD}=(y+7)(y-7)$$

$$=\frac{y+2}{y-7}\cdot\frac{y+7}{y+7}+\frac{y-3}{(y+7)(y-7)}$$

$$=\frac{y^2+9y+14+y-3}{(y+7)(y-7)}$$

$$=\frac{y^2+10y+11}{(y+7)(y-7)}$$

58. $\dfrac{p^2 + 7p + 1}{(p+5)(p-5)}$

59. $\dfrac{3x+2}{3x+6} + \dfrac{x}{4-x^2}$

$= \dfrac{3x+2}{3(x+2)} + \dfrac{x}{(2+x)(2-x)}$

$\qquad\qquad\qquad$ LCD $= 3(x+2)(2-x)$

$= \dfrac{3x+2}{3(x+2)} \cdot \dfrac{2-x}{2-x} + \dfrac{x}{(2+x)(2-x)} \cdot \dfrac{3}{3}$

$= \dfrac{(3x+2)(2-x) + x \cdot 3}{3(x+2)(2-x)}$

$= \dfrac{-3x^2 + 4x + 4 + 3x}{3(x+2)(2-x)}$

$= \dfrac{-3x^2 + 7x + 4}{3(x+2)(2-x)}$, or

$\qquad \dfrac{3x^2 - 7x - 4}{3(x+2)(x-2)}$

60. $\dfrac{a+2}{(1+a)(1-a)}$

61. $\dfrac{4-a^2}{a^2-9} - \dfrac{a-2}{3-a}$

$= \dfrac{4-a^2}{(a+3)(a-3)} - \dfrac{a-2}{3-a}$

$= \dfrac{4-a^2}{(a+3)(a-3)} - \dfrac{a-2}{3-a} \cdot \dfrac{-1}{-1}$

$= \dfrac{4-a^2}{(a+3)(a-3)} - \dfrac{2-a}{a-3}$ LCD $= (a+3)(a-3)$

$= \dfrac{4-a^2}{(a+3)(a-3)} - \dfrac{2-a}{a-3} \cdot \dfrac{a+3}{a+3}$

$= \dfrac{4-a^2 - (2a+6 - a^2 - 3a)}{(a+3)(a-3)}$

$= \dfrac{4-a^2 - 2a - 6 + a^2 + 3a}{(a+3)(a-3)}$

$= \dfrac{a-2}{(a+3)(a-3)}$

62. $\dfrac{10x+6y}{(x+y)(x-y)}$

63. $\dfrac{x-3}{2-x} - \dfrac{x+3}{x+2} + \dfrac{x+6}{4-x^2}$

$= \dfrac{x-3}{2-x} - \dfrac{x+3}{x+2} + \dfrac{x+6}{(2+x)(2-x)}$

$\qquad\qquad$ LCD $= (2+x)(2-x)$

$= \dfrac{x-3}{2-x} \cdot \dfrac{2+x}{2+x} - \dfrac{x+3}{x+2} \cdot \dfrac{2-x}{2-x} + \dfrac{x+6}{(2+x)(2-x)}$

$= \dfrac{(x-3)(2+x) - (x+3)(2-x) + (x+6)}{(2+x)(2-x)}$

$= \dfrac{x^2 - x - 6 - (-x^2 - x + 6) + x + 6}{(2+x)(2-x)}$

$= \dfrac{x^2 - x - 6 + x^2 + x - 6 + x + 6}{(2+x)(2-x)}$

$= \dfrac{2x^2 + x - 6}{(2+x)(2-x)}$

$= \dfrac{(2x-3)(x+2)}{(2+x)(2-x)}$

$= \dfrac{2x-3}{2-x}$

64. $\dfrac{-2t^2 + 2t + 11}{(t+1)(t-1)}$

65. $\dfrac{x+5}{x+3} + \dfrac{x+7}{x+2} - \dfrac{7x+19}{(x+3)(x+2)}$

$\qquad\qquad$ LCD is $(x+3)(x+2)$

$= \dfrac{x+5}{x+3} \cdot \dfrac{x+2}{x+2} + \dfrac{x+7}{x+2} \cdot \dfrac{x+3}{x+3} - \dfrac{7x+19}{(x+3)(x+2)}$

$= \dfrac{(x+5)(x+2) + (x+7)(x+3) - (7x+19)}{(x+3)(x+2)}$

$= \dfrac{x^2 + 7x + 10 + x^2 + 10x + 21 - 7x - 19}{(x+3)(x+2)}$

$= \dfrac{2x^2 + 10x + 12}{(x+3)(x+2)}$

$= \dfrac{2(x^2 + 5x + 6)}{(x+3)(x+2)}$

$= \dfrac{2(x+3)(x+2)}{(x+3)(x+2)}$

$= 2$

66. 3

67. $5 + \dfrac{t}{t+2} - \dfrac{8}{t^2-4} = \dfrac{5}{1} + \dfrac{t}{t+2} - \dfrac{8}{(t+2)(t-2)}$

$\qquad$ [LCD is $(t+2)(t-2)$.]

$= \dfrac{5}{1} \cdot \dfrac{(t+2)(t-2)}{(t+2)(t-2)} + \dfrac{t}{t+2} \cdot \dfrac{t-2}{t-2} - \dfrac{8}{(t+2)(t-2)}$

$= \dfrac{5t^2 - 20 + t^2 - 2t - 8}{(t+2)(t-2)}$

$= \dfrac{6t^2 - 2t - 28}{(t+2)(t-2)}$

$= \dfrac{2(3t-7)(t+2)}{(t+2)(t-2)}$

$= \dfrac{2(3t-7)(t+2)}{(t+2)(t-2)}$

$= \dfrac{2(3t-7)}{t-2}$

68. $\dfrac{3(t+4)}{t+3}$

69.
$$\dfrac{1}{x+y} + \dfrac{1}{x-y} - \dfrac{2x}{x^2-y^2}$$
$$\text{LCD} = (x+y)(x-y)$$
$$= \dfrac{1}{x+y} \cdot \dfrac{x-y}{x-y} + \dfrac{1}{x-y} \cdot \dfrac{x+y}{x+y} - \dfrac{2x}{(x+y)(x-y)}$$
$$= \dfrac{(x-y)+(x+y)-2x}{(x+y)(x-y)}$$
$$= 0$$

70. $\dfrac{2}{r+s}$

71.
$$\dfrac{2}{x^2-5x+6} - \dfrac{4}{x^2-2x-3} + \dfrac{2}{x^2+4x+3}$$
$$= \dfrac{2}{(x-3)(x-2)} - \dfrac{4}{(x-3)(x+1)} + \dfrac{2}{(x+3)(x+1)}$$
$$[\text{LCD is } (x-3)(x-2)(x+1)(x+3).]$$
$$= \dfrac{2}{(x-3)(x-2)} \cdot \dfrac{(x+1)(x+3)}{(x+1)(x+3)} -$$
$$\dfrac{4}{(x-3)(x+1)} \cdot \dfrac{(x-2)(x+3)}{(x-2)(x+3)} +$$
$$\dfrac{2}{(x+3)(x+1)} \cdot \dfrac{(x-3)(x-2)}{(x-3)(x-2)}$$
$$= \dfrac{2(x+1)(x+3)-4(x-2)(x+3)+2(x-3)(x-2)}{(x-3)(x-2)(x+1)(x+3)}$$
$$= \dfrac{2x^2+8x+6-4x^2-4x+24+2x^2-10x+12}{(x-3)(x-2)(x+1)(x+3)}$$
$$= \dfrac{-6x+42}{(x-3)(x-2)(x+1)(x+3)}$$

72. $\dfrac{-2}{t^2+3t+2}$

73. *Writing Exercise*

74. *Writing Exercise*

75.
$$-\dfrac{3}{7} \div \dfrac{6}{13} = -\dfrac{3}{7} \cdot \dfrac{13}{6}$$
$$= -\dfrac{\cancel{3} \cdot 13}{7 \cdot 2 \cdot \cancel{3}}$$
$$= -\dfrac{13}{14}$$

76. $-\dfrac{5}{9}$

77.
$$\dfrac{\frac{2}{9}}{\frac{5}{3}} = \dfrac{2}{9} \div \dfrac{5}{3}$$
$$= \dfrac{2}{9} \cdot \dfrac{3}{5}$$
$$= \dfrac{2 \cdot \cancel{3}}{\cancel{3} \cdot 3 \cdot 5}$$
$$= \dfrac{2}{15}$$

78. $\dfrac{7}{6}$

79. Graph: $y = -\dfrac{1}{2}x - 5$

Since the equation is in the form $y = mx + b$, we know the $y-$intercept is $(0,-5)$. We find two other solutions, substituting multiples of 2 for x to avoid fractions.

When $x = -2$, $y = -\dfrac{1}{2}(-2) - 5 = 1 - 5 = -4$.

When $x = -4$, $y = -\dfrac{1}{2}(-4) - 5 = 2 - 5 = -3$.

x	y
0	-5
-2	-4
-4	-3

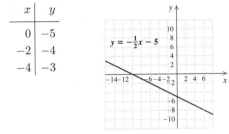

80.

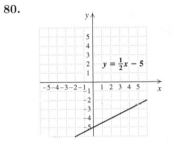

81. *Writing Exercise*

82. *Writing Exercise*

83.
$$P = 2\left(\dfrac{3}{x+4}\right) + 2\left(\dfrac{2}{x-5}\right)$$
$$= \dfrac{6}{x+4} + \dfrac{4}{x-5} \qquad \text{LCD} = (x+4)(x-5)$$
$$= \dfrac{6}{x+4} \cdot \dfrac{x-5}{x-5} + \dfrac{4}{x-5} \cdot \dfrac{x+4}{x+4}$$
$$= \dfrac{6x-30+4x+16}{(x+4)(x-5)}$$
$$= \dfrac{10x-14}{(x+4)(x-5)}, \text{ or } \dfrac{10x-14}{x^2-x-20}$$
$$A = \left(\dfrac{3}{x+4}\right)\left(\dfrac{2}{x-5}\right) = \dfrac{6}{(x+4)(x-5)}, \text{ or}$$
$$\dfrac{6}{x^2-x-20}$$

84. Perimeter: $\dfrac{4x^2+18x}{(x+4)(x+5)}$; area: $\dfrac{x^2}{(x+4)(x+5)}$

85. $\dfrac{2x+11}{x-3} \cdot \dfrac{3}{x+4} + \dfrac{2x+1}{4+x} \cdot \dfrac{3}{3-x}$

$= \dfrac{6x+33}{(x-3)(x+4)} + \dfrac{6x+3}{(4+x)(3-x)}$

$= \dfrac{6x+33}{(x-3)(x+4)} + \dfrac{6x+3}{(4+x)(3-x)} \cdot \dfrac{-1}{-1}$

$= \dfrac{6x+33}{(x-3)(x+4)} + \dfrac{-6x-3}{(x+4)(x-3)}$

$= \dfrac{6x+33-6x-3}{(x-3)(x+4)}$

$= \dfrac{30}{(x-3)(x+4)}$

86. $\dfrac{x}{3x+1}$

87. $\left(\dfrac{x}{x+7} - \dfrac{3}{x+2}\right)\left(\dfrac{x}{x+7} + \dfrac{3}{x+2}\right)$

$= \dfrac{x^2}{(x+7)^2} - \dfrac{9}{(x+2)^2} \quad \text{LCD} = (x+7)^2(x+2)^2$

$= \dfrac{x^2}{(x+7)^2} \cdot \dfrac{(x+2)^2}{(x+2)^2} - \dfrac{9}{(x+2)^2} \cdot \dfrac{(x+7)^2}{(x+7)^2}$

$= \dfrac{x^2(x+2)^2 - 9(x+7)^2}{(x+7)^2(x+2)^2}$

$= \dfrac{x^2(x^2+4x+4) - 9(x^2+14x+49)}{(x+7)^2(x+2)^2}$

$= \dfrac{x^4 + 4x^3 + 4x^2 - 9x^2 - 126x - 441}{(x+7)^2(x+2)^2}$

$= \dfrac{x^4 + 4x^3 - 5x^2 - 126x - 441}{(x+7)^2(x+2)^2}$

88. $\dfrac{-3(xy+a-2x)}{(y-3)^2(a+2x)(a-2x)}$

89. $\dfrac{2x^2+5x-3}{2x^2-9x+9} + \dfrac{x+1}{3-2x} + \dfrac{4x^2+8x+3}{x-3} \cdot \dfrac{x+3}{9-4x^2}$

$= \dfrac{2x^2+5x-3}{(2x-3)(x-3)} + \dfrac{x+1}{3-2x} +$

$\qquad\qquad \dfrac{(4x^2+8x+3)(x+3)}{(x-3)(3+2x)(3-2x)}$

$= \dfrac{2x^2+5x-3}{(2x-3)(x-3)} \cdot \dfrac{-1}{-1} + \dfrac{x+1}{3-2x} +$

$\qquad\qquad \dfrac{4x^3+20x^2+27x+9}{(x-3)(3+2x)(3-2x)}$

$= \dfrac{-2x^2-5x+3}{(3-2x)(x-3)} + \dfrac{x+1}{3-2x} + \dfrac{4x^3+20x^2+27x+9}{(x-3)(3+2x)(3-2x)}$

$\qquad\qquad \text{LCD} = (x-3)(3+2x)(3-2x)$

$= \dfrac{-2x^2-5x+3}{(3-2x)(x-3)} \cdot \dfrac{3+2x}{3+2x} + \dfrac{x+1}{3-2x} \cdot \dfrac{(x-3)(3+2x)}{(x-3)(3+2x)} +$

$\qquad\qquad \dfrac{4x^3+20x^2+27x+9}{(x-3)(3+2x)(3-2x)}$

$= [(-4x^3-16x^2-9x+9+2x^3-x^2-12x-9+$

$\qquad 4x^3+20x^2+27x+9)] /$

$\qquad [(x-3)(3+2x)(3-2x)]$

$= \dfrac{2x^3+3x^2+6x+9}{(x-3)(3+2x)(3-2x)}$

$= \dfrac{x^2(2x+3)+3(2x+3)}{(x-3)(3+2x)(3-2x)}$

$= \dfrac{(2x+3)(x^2+3)}{(x-3)(3+2x)(3-2x)}$

$= \dfrac{x^2+3}{(x-3)(3-2x)}, \text{ or } \dfrac{-x^2-3}{(x-3)(2x-3)}$

90. $\dfrac{5(a^2+2ab-b^2)}{(a-b)(3a+b)(3a-b)}$

91. $5(x-3)^{-1} + 4(x+3)^{-1} - 2(x+3)^{-2}$

$= \dfrac{5}{x-3} + \dfrac{4}{x+3} - \dfrac{2}{(x+3)^2}$

$\quad$ [LCD is $(x-3)(x+3)^2$.]

$= \dfrac{5(x+3)^2 + 4(x-3)(x+3) - 2(x-3)}{(x-3)(x+3)^2}$

$= \dfrac{5x^2+30x+45 + 4x^2-36 - 2x+6}{(x-3)(x+3)^2}$

$= \dfrac{9x^2+28x+15}{(x-3)(x+3)^2}$

92. $\dfrac{5y+23}{5-2y}$

93. Answers may vary. $\dfrac{a}{a-b} + \dfrac{3b}{b-a}$

94. Domain: $\{x | x \text{ is a real number } and \ x \neq -2 \text{ and } x \neq 1\}$; range: $\{y | y \text{ is a real number } and \ y \neq 2 \text{ and } y \neq 3\}$

95. $(f+g)(x) = \dfrac{x^3}{x^2-4} + \dfrac{x^2}{x^2+3x-10}$

$\qquad = \dfrac{x^3}{(x+2)(x-2)} + \dfrac{x^2}{(x+5)(x-2)}$

$\qquad = \dfrac{x^3(x+5) + x^2(x+2)}{(x+2)(x-2)(x+5)}$

$\qquad = \dfrac{x^4+5x^3+x^3+2x^2}{(x+2)(x-2)(x+5)}$

$\qquad = \dfrac{x^4+6x^3+2x^2}{(x+2)(x-2)(x+5)}$

96. $\dfrac{x^4+4x^3-2x^2}{(x+2)(x-2)(x+5)}$

97. $(f \cdot g)(x) = \dfrac{x^3}{x^2-4} \cdot \dfrac{x^2}{x^2+3x-10}$

$\qquad = \dfrac{x^5}{(x^2-4)(x^2+3x-10)}$

98. $\dfrac{x(x+5)}{x+2}$

(Note that $x \neq 0$, $x \neq -5$, and $x \neq 2$ are additional restrictions, since $g(0) = 0$, -5 is not in the domain of g, and 2 is not in the domain of either f or g.)

99. The denominator of $f+g$ is 0 when $x = -2$, $x = 2$, or $x = -5$. Thus the domain of $f+g$ is $\{x \mid x$ is a real number *and* $x \neq -2$ *and* $x \neq 2$ *and* $x \neq -5\}$, or $(-\infty, -5) \cup (-5, -2) \cup (-2, 2) \cup (2, \infty)$.

100. $\{x \mid x$ is a real number *and* $x \neq -2$ *and* $x \neq 0$ *and* $x \neq -5$ *and* $x \neq 2\}$

101.

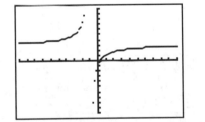

From the graph (shown in the standard window) we see that the domain of the function consists of all real numbers except -1, so the domain of f is $\{x \mid x$ is a real number *and* $x \neq -1\}$, or $(-\infty, -1) \cup (-1, \infty)$. We also see that the range consists of all real numbers except 3, so the range of f is $\{y \mid y$ is a real number *and* $y \neq 3\}$, or $(-\infty, 3) \cup (3, \infty)$.

102. Domain: $(-\infty, -1) \cup (-1, \infty)$; range: $(5, \infty)$

103.

 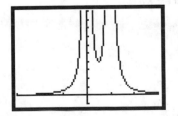

From the graph (shown in the window $[-3, 3, -2, 20]$, Yscl $= 2$), we see that the domain consists of all

real numbers except 0 and 1, so the domain of r is $\{x \mid x$ is a real number *an* $x \neq 0$ *and* $x \neq 1\}$, or $(-\infty, 0) \cup (0, 1) \cup (1, \infty)$. We also see that the range consists of all real numbers greater than 0, so the range of r is $\{y \mid y > 0\}$, or $(0, \infty)$.

Exercise Set 7.5

1. $\dfrac{7+\dfrac{1}{a}}{\dfrac{1}{a}-3} = \dfrac{7+\dfrac{1}{a}}{\dfrac{1}{a}-3} \cdot \dfrac{a}{a}$ — Multiplying by 1, using the LCD

$\qquad = \dfrac{\left(7+\dfrac{1}{a}\right)a}{\left(\dfrac{1}{a}-3\right)a}$ — Multiplying the numerators and the denominator

$\qquad = \dfrac{7 \cdot a + \dfrac{1}{a} \cdot a}{\dfrac{1}{a} \cdot a - 3 \cdot a}$

$\qquad = \dfrac{7a + \dfrac{\cancel{a}}{\cancel{a}} \cdot 1}{\dfrac{\cancel{a}}{\cancel{a}} \cdot 1 - 3a}$ — Removing factors equal to 1

$\qquad = \dfrac{7a+1}{1-3a}$ — Simplifying

2. $\dfrac{1+2y}{1-3y}$

3. $\dfrac{x-x^{-1}}{x+x^{-1}} = \dfrac{x-\dfrac{1}{x}}{x+\dfrac{1}{x}}$ — Rewriting with positive exponents

$\qquad = \dfrac{x-\dfrac{1}{x}}{x+\dfrac{1}{x}} \cdot \dfrac{x}{x}$ — Multiplying by 1, using the LCD

$\qquad = \dfrac{x \cdot x - \dfrac{1}{x} \cdot x}{x \cdot x + \dfrac{1}{x} \cdot x}$

$\qquad = \dfrac{x^2-1}{x^2+1}$

(Although the numerator can be factored, doing so does not lead to further simplification.)

4. $\dfrac{y^2+1}{y^2-1}$

5. $\dfrac{\dfrac{6}{x}+\dfrac{7}{y}}{\dfrac{7}{x}-\dfrac{6}{y}}=\dfrac{\dfrac{6}{x}+\dfrac{7}{y}}{\dfrac{7}{x}-\dfrac{6}{y}}\cdot\dfrac{xy}{xy}$ Multiplying by 1,
using the LCD

$=\dfrac{\dfrac{6}{x}\cdot xy+\dfrac{7}{y}\cdot xy}{\dfrac{7}{x}\cdot xy-\dfrac{6}{y}\cdot xy}$

$=\dfrac{6y+7x}{7y-6x}$

6. $\dfrac{5y+2z}{4y-z}$

7. $\dfrac{\dfrac{x^2-y^2}{xy}}{\dfrac{x-y}{y}}=\dfrac{x^2-y^2}{xy}\cdot\dfrac{y}{x-y}$ Multiplying by the
reciprocal of the
divisor

$=\dfrac{(x+y)(x-y)\cdot y}{xy(x-y)}$

$=\dfrac{(x+y)(x-y)\cdot y}{xy(x-y)}$

$=\dfrac{x+y}{x}$

8. $\dfrac{a+b}{a}$

9. $\dfrac{\dfrac{3x}{y}-x}{2y-\dfrac{y}{x}}=\dfrac{\dfrac{3x}{y}-x}{2y-\dfrac{y}{x}}\cdot\dfrac{xy}{xy}$ Multiplying by 1,
using the LCD

$=\dfrac{\dfrac{3x}{y}\cdot xy-x\cdot xy}{2y\cdot xy-\dfrac{y}{x}\cdot xy}$

$=\dfrac{3x^2-x^2y}{2xy^2-y^2}$

(Although both the numerator and the denominator can be
factored, doing so does not lead to further simplification.)

10. $\dfrac{3}{3x+2}$

11. $\dfrac{\dfrac{a^{-1}+b^{-1}}{a^2-b^2}}{ab}=\dfrac{\dfrac{\dfrac{1}{a}+\dfrac{1}{b}}{a^2-b^2}}{ab}$

$=\dfrac{\dfrac{1}{a}+\dfrac{1}{b}}{\dfrac{a^2-b^2}{ab}}\cdot\dfrac{ab}{ab}$ Multiplying by 1,
using the LCD

$=\dfrac{\dfrac{1}{a}\cdot ab+\dfrac{1}{b}\cdot ab}{\dfrac{a^2-b^2}{ab}\cdot ab}$

$=\dfrac{b+a}{a^2-b^2}=\dfrac{b+a}{(a+b)(a-b)}$

$=\dfrac{(a+b)\cdot(1)}{(a+b)(a-b)}$ $(b+a=a+b)$

$=\dfrac{1}{a-b}$

12. $\dfrac{1}{x-y}$

13. $\dfrac{8+\dfrac{8}{d}}{1+\dfrac{1}{d}}=\dfrac{8\left(1+\dfrac{1}{d}\right)}{1+\dfrac{1}{d}}$

$=\dfrac{8}{1}\cdot\dfrac{1+\dfrac{1}{d}}{1+\dfrac{1}{d}}$

$=8$

14. 1

15. $\dfrac{\dfrac{1}{x+h}-\dfrac{1}{x}}{h}=\dfrac{\dfrac{1}{x+h}\cdot\dfrac{x}{x}-\dfrac{1}{x}\cdot\dfrac{x+h}{x+h}}{h}$ Adding
in the numerator

$=\dfrac{\dfrac{x-x-h}{x(x+h)}}{h}=\dfrac{\dfrac{-h}{x(x+h)}}{h}$

$=\dfrac{-h}{x(x+h)}\cdot\dfrac{1}{h}$ Multiplying by
the reciprocal of the divisor

$=\dfrac{-1\cdot h\cdot 1}{x(x+h)(h)}$ $(-h=-1\cdot h)$

$=-\dfrac{1}{x(x+h)}$

16. $\dfrac{1}{a(a-h)}$

17. $\dfrac{\dfrac{x^2 - x - 12}{x^2 - 2x - 15}}{\dfrac{x^2 + 8x + 12}{x^2 - 5x - 14}}$

$= \dfrac{x^2 - x - 12}{x^2 - 2x - 15} \cdot \dfrac{x^2 - 5x - 14}{x^2 + 8x + 12}$ Multiplying by
the reciprocal of the divisor

$= \dfrac{(x-4)(x+3)}{(x-5)(x+3)} \cdot \dfrac{(x-7)(x+2)}{(x+6)(x+2)}$

$= \dfrac{(x-4)(x+3)(x-7)(x+2)}{(x-5)(x+3)(x+6)(x+2)}$

$= \dfrac{(x-4)(\cancel{x+3})(x-7)(\cancel{x+2})}{(x-5)(\cancel{x+3})(x+6)(\cancel{x+2})}$

$= \dfrac{(x-4)(x-7)}{(x-5)(x+6)}$

18. $\dfrac{(a-2)(a-7)}{(a+1)(a-6)}$

19. $\dfrac{\dfrac{1}{x-2} + \dfrac{3}{x-1}}{\dfrac{2}{x-1} + \dfrac{5}{x-2}}$

$= \dfrac{\dfrac{1}{x-2} + \dfrac{3}{x-1}}{\dfrac{2}{x-1} + \dfrac{5}{x-2}} \cdot \dfrac{(x-2)(x-1)}{(x-2)(x-1)}$

Multiplying by 1, using the LCD

$= \dfrac{\dfrac{1}{x-2} \cdot (x-2)(x-1) + \dfrac{3}{x-1} \cdot (x-2)(x-1)}{\dfrac{2}{x-1} \cdot (x-2)(x-1) + \dfrac{5}{x-2} \cdot (x-2)(x-1)}$

$= \dfrac{x - 1 + 3(x - 2)}{2(x - 2) + 5(x - 1)}$

$= \dfrac{x - 1 + 3x - 6}{2x - 4 + 5x - 5}$

$= \dfrac{4x - 7}{7x - 9}$

20. $\dfrac{3y - 1}{7y - 5}$

21. $\dfrac{a(a+3)^{-1} - 2(a-1)^{-1}}{a(a+3)^{-1} - (a-1)^{-1}}$

$= \dfrac{\dfrac{a}{a+3} - \dfrac{2}{a-1}}{\dfrac{a}{a+3} - \dfrac{1}{a-1}}$

$= \dfrac{\dfrac{a}{a+3} - \dfrac{2}{a-1}}{\dfrac{a}{a+3} - \dfrac{1}{a-1}} \cdot \dfrac{(a+3)(a-1)}{(a+3)(a-1)}$

Multiplying by 1, using the LCD

$= \dfrac{\dfrac{a}{a+3} \cdot (a+3)(a-1) - \dfrac{2}{a-1} \cdot (a+3)(a-1)}{\dfrac{a}{a+3} \cdot (a+3)(a-1) - \dfrac{1}{a-1} \cdot (a+3)(a-1)}$

$= \dfrac{a(a-1) - 2(a+3)}{a(a-1) - (a+3)}$

$= \dfrac{a^2 - a - 2a - 6}{a^2 - a - a - 3} = \dfrac{a^2 - 3a - 6}{a^2 - 2a - 3}$

(Although the denominator can be factored, doing so does not lead to further simplification.)

22. $\dfrac{a^2 - 6a - 6}{a^2 - 4a - 2}$

23. $\dfrac{\dfrac{x}{x^2 + 3x - 4} - \dfrac{1}{x^2 + 3x - 4}}{\dfrac{x}{x^2 + 6x + 8} + \dfrac{3}{x^2 + 6x + 8}}$

$= \dfrac{\dfrac{x - 1}{x^2 + 3x - 4}}{\dfrac{x + 3}{x^2 + 6x + 8}}$ Adding in the numerator
and the denominator

$= \dfrac{x - 1}{x^2 + 3x - 4} \cdot \dfrac{x^2 + 6x + 8}{x + 3}$

$= \dfrac{(x-1)(x+4)(x+2)}{(x+4)(x-1)(x+3)}$

$= \dfrac{(\cancel{x-1})(\cancel{x+4})(x+2)}{(\cancel{x+4})(\cancel{x-1})(x+3)} = \dfrac{x+2}{x+3}$

24. $\dfrac{x - 4}{x - 2}$

25.
$$\dfrac{\dfrac{2}{a^2-1}+\dfrac{1}{a+1}}{\dfrac{3}{a^2-1}+\dfrac{2}{a-1}}$$

$a+1$
$a-1$

$$\dfrac{a+1}{a-1}=\dfrac{\dfrac{2}{(a+1)(a-1)}+\dfrac{1}{a+1}}{\dfrac{3}{(a+1)(a-1)}+\dfrac{2}{a-1}}$$

$$=\dfrac{\dfrac{2}{(a+1)(a-1)}+\dfrac{1}{a+1}}{\dfrac{3}{(a+1)(a-1)}+\dfrac{2}{a-1}}\cdot\dfrac{(a+1)(a-1)}{(a+1)(a-1)}$$

Multiplying by 1, using the LCD

$$=\dfrac{\dfrac{2}{(a+1)(a-1)}\cdot(a+1)(a-1)+\dfrac{1}{a+1}\cdot(a+1)(a-1)}{\dfrac{3}{(a+1)(a-1)}\cdot(a+1)(a-1)+\dfrac{2}{a-1}\cdot(a+1)(a-1)}$$

$$=\dfrac{2+a-1}{3+2(a+1)}=\dfrac{a+1}{3+2a+2}=\dfrac{a+1}{2a+5}$$

26. $\dfrac{2a-3}{a+1}$

27.
$$\dfrac{\dfrac{5}{x^2-4}-\dfrac{3}{x-2}}{\dfrac{4}{x^2-4}-\dfrac{2}{x+2}}$$

$$=\dfrac{\dfrac{5}{(x+2)(x-2)}-\dfrac{3}{x-2}}{\dfrac{4}{(x+2)(x-2)}-\dfrac{2}{x+2}}$$

$$=\dfrac{\dfrac{5}{(x+2)(x-2)}-\dfrac{3}{x-2}}{\dfrac{4}{(x+2)(x-2)}-\dfrac{2}{x+2}}\cdot\dfrac{(x+2)(x-2)}{(x+2)(x-2)}$$

Multiplying by 1, using the LCD

$$=\dfrac{\dfrac{5}{(x+2)(x-2)}\cdot(x+2)(x-2)-\dfrac{3}{x-2}\cdot(x+2)(x-2)}{\dfrac{4}{(x+2)(x-2)}\cdot(x+2)(x-2)-\dfrac{2}{x+2}\cdot(x+2)(x-2)}$$

$$=\dfrac{5-3(x+2)}{4-2(x-2)}=\dfrac{5-3x-6}{4-2x+4}=\dfrac{-1-3x}{8-2x},\text{ or}$$

$$\dfrac{3x+1}{2x-8}$$

28. $\dfrac{7-3x}{3-2x}$, or $\dfrac{3x-7}{2x-3}$

29.
$$\dfrac{\dfrac{y}{y^2-4}+\dfrac{5}{4-y^2}}{\dfrac{y^2}{y^2-4}+\dfrac{25}{4-y^2}}$$

$$=\dfrac{\dfrac{y}{y^2-4}+\dfrac{-1}{-1}\cdot\dfrac{5}{4-y^2}}{\dfrac{y^2}{y^2-4}+\dfrac{-1}{-1}\cdot\dfrac{25}{4-y^2}}$$

$$=\dfrac{\dfrac{y}{y^2-4}-\dfrac{5}{y^2-4}}{\dfrac{y^2}{y^2-4}-\dfrac{25}{y^2-4}}$$

$$=\dfrac{\dfrac{y-5}{y^2-4}}{\dfrac{y^2-25}{y^2-4}}\quad\begin{array}{l}\text{Adding in the numerator}\\\text{and the denominator}\end{array}$$

$$=\dfrac{y-5}{y^2-4}\cdot\dfrac{y^2-4}{y^2-25}\quad\begin{array}{l}\text{Multiplying by the}\\\text{reciprocal of the divisor}\end{array}$$

$$=\dfrac{(y-5)(y^2-4)}{(y^2-4)(y+5)(y-5)}$$

$$=\dfrac{(y-5)(y^2-4)(1)}{(y^2-4)(y+5)(y-5)}$$

$$=\dfrac{1}{y+5}$$

30. $\dfrac{1}{y+3}$

31.
$$\dfrac{\dfrac{y^2}{y^2-9}-\dfrac{y}{y+3}}{\dfrac{y}{y^2-9}-\dfrac{1}{y-3}}$$

$$=\dfrac{\dfrac{y^2}{(y+3)(y-3)}-\dfrac{y}{y+3}}{\dfrac{y}{(y+3)(y-3)}-\dfrac{1}{y-3}}$$

$$=\dfrac{\dfrac{y^2}{(y+3)(y-3)}-\dfrac{y}{y+3}}{\dfrac{y}{(y+3)(y-3)}-\dfrac{1}{y-3}}\cdot\dfrac{(y+3)(y-3)}{(y+3)(y-3)}$$

Multiplying by 1, using the LCD

$$=\dfrac{\dfrac{y^2}{(y+3)(y-3)}\cdot(y+3)(y-3)-\dfrac{y}{y+3}\cdot(y+3)(y-3)}{\dfrac{y}{(y+3)(y-3)}\cdot(y+3)(y-3)-\dfrac{1}{y-3}\cdot(y+3)(y-3)}$$

$$=\dfrac{y^2-y(y-3)}{y-(y+3)}=\dfrac{y^2-y^2+3y}{y-y-3}=\dfrac{3y}{-3}$$

$$=\dfrac{3y}{-1\cdot3}=-y$$

32. $-y$

33. $\dfrac{\dfrac{a}{a+3}+\dfrac{4}{5a}}{\dfrac{a}{2a+6}+\dfrac{3}{a}}$

$=\dfrac{\dfrac{a}{a+3}+\dfrac{4}{5a}}{\dfrac{a}{2(a+3)}+\dfrac{3}{a}}$

$=\dfrac{\dfrac{a}{a+3}+\dfrac{4}{5a}}{\dfrac{a}{2(a+3)}+\dfrac{3}{a}}\cdot\dfrac{10a(a+3)}{10a(a+3)}$

           Multiplying by 1, using the LCD

$=\dfrac{\dfrac{a}{a+3}\cdot 10a(a+3)+\dfrac{4}{5a}\cdot 10a(a+3)}{\dfrac{a}{2(a+3)}\cdot 10a(a+3)+\dfrac{3}{a}\cdot 10a(a+3)}$

$=\dfrac{10a^2+8(a+3)}{5a^2+30(a+3)}=\dfrac{10a^2+8a+24}{5a^2+30a+90}$

$=\dfrac{2(5a^2+4a+12)}{5(a^2+6a+18)}$

34. $\dfrac{6a^2+30a+60}{3a^2+2a+4}$

35. $\dfrac{c+\dfrac{8}{c^2}}{1+\dfrac{2}{c}}$

$=\dfrac{c+\dfrac{8}{c^2}}{1+\dfrac{2}{c}}\cdot\dfrac{c^2}{c^2}$ Multiplying by 1, using the LCD

$=\dfrac{c\cdot c^2+\dfrac{8}{c^2}\cdot c^2}{1\cdot c^2+\dfrac{2}{c}\cdot c^2}$

$=\dfrac{c^3+8}{c^2+2c}$

$=\dfrac{(c+2)(c^2-2c+4)}{c(c+2)}$

$=\dfrac{(c\!\!\!\!\diagup+2)(c^2-2c+4)}{c(c\!\!\!\!\diagup+2)}$

$=\dfrac{c^2-2c+4}{c}$

36. $\dfrac{x^2y^2}{y^2-yx+x^2}$

37. $\dfrac{x^2+xy+y^2}{\dfrac{x^2}{y}-\dfrac{y^2}{x}}$

$=\dfrac{x^2+xy+y^2}{\dfrac{x^2}{y}-\dfrac{y^2}{x}}\cdot\dfrac{xy}{xy}$

$=\dfrac{xy(x^2+xy+y^2)}{\dfrac{x^2}{y}\cdot xy-\dfrac{y^2}{x}\cdot xy}$

$=\dfrac{xy(x^2+xy+y^2)}{x^3-y^3}$

$=\dfrac{xy(x^2+xy+y^2)}{(x-y)(x^2+xy+y^2)}$

$=\dfrac{xy}{x-y}\cdot\dfrac{x^2+xy+y^2}{x^2+xy+y^2}$

$=\dfrac{xy}{x-y}$

38. $\dfrac{a+b}{ab}$

39. $\dfrac{\dfrac{1}{x^2-3x+2}+\dfrac{1}{x^2-4}}{\dfrac{1}{x^2+4x+4}+\dfrac{1}{x^2-4}}$

$=\dfrac{\dfrac{1}{(x-1)(x-2)}+\dfrac{1}{(x+2)(x-2)}}{\dfrac{1}{(x+2)(x+2)}+\dfrac{1}{(x+2)(x-2)}}$

$=\dfrac{\dfrac{1}{(x-1)(x-2)}+\dfrac{1}{(x+2)(x-2)}}{\dfrac{1}{(x+2)(x+2)}+\dfrac{1}{(x+2)(x-2)}}\cdot$

                $\dfrac{(x-1)(x-2)(x+2)(x+2)}{(x-1)(x-2)(x+2)(x+2)}$

        Multiplying by 1, using the LCD

$=\dfrac{(x+2)(x+2)+(x-1)(x+2)}{(x-1)(x-2)+(x-1)(x+2)}$

$=\dfrac{x^2+4x+4+x^2+x-2}{x^2-3x+2+x^2+x-2}$

$=\dfrac{2x^2+5x+2}{2x^2-2x}$

(Although both the numerator and the denominator can be factored, doing so will not lead to further simplification.)

40. $\dfrac{(2x+1)(x-3)}{2(x+2)(x-1)}$

41.

$$\dfrac{\dfrac{3}{a^2-4a+3}+\dfrac{3}{a^2-5a+6}}{\dfrac{3}{a^2-3a+2}+\dfrac{3}{a^2+3a-10}}$$

$$=\dfrac{\dfrac{3}{(a-1)(a-3)}+\dfrac{3}{(a-2)(a-3)}}{\dfrac{3}{(a-1)(a-2)}+\dfrac{3}{(a+5)(a-2)}}$$

$$=\dfrac{\dfrac{3}{(a-1)(a-3)}+\dfrac{3}{(a-2)(a-3)}}{\dfrac{3}{(a-1)(a-2)}+\dfrac{3}{(a+5)(a-2)}}\cdot$$

$$\dfrac{(a-1)(a-3)(a-2)(a+5)}{(a-1)(a-3)(a-2)(a+5)}$$

Multiplying by 1, using the LCD

$$=\dfrac{3(a-2)(a+5)+3(a-1)(a+5)}{3(a-3)(a+5)+3(a-1)(a-3)}$$

$$=\dfrac{3[(a-2)(a+5)+(a-1)(a+5)]}{3[(a-3)(a+5)+(a-1)(a-3)]}$$

$$=\dfrac{\cancel{3}[(a-2)(a+5)+(a-1)(a+5)]}{\cancel{3}[(a-3)(a+5)+(a-1)(a-3)]}$$

$$=\dfrac{a^2+3a-10+a^2+4a-5}{a^2+2a-15+a^2-4a+3}$$

$$=\dfrac{2a^2+7a-15}{2a^2-2a-12}$$

(Although both the numerator and the denominator can be factored, doing so will not lead to further simplification.)

42. $\dfrac{-a^2-21a-8}{a^2+3a-34}$

43. $\dfrac{\dfrac{y}{y^2-4}-\dfrac{2y}{y^2+y-6}}{\dfrac{2y}{y^2+y-6}-\dfrac{y}{y^2-4}}$

Observe that $\dfrac{y}{y^2-4}-\dfrac{2y}{y^2+y-6}=$

$-\left(\dfrac{2y}{y^2+y-6}-\dfrac{y}{y^2-4}\right)$. Then, the numerator and denominator are opposites and thus their quotient is -1.

44. $\dfrac{-2y^2+13y-21}{2(y^2-y-20)}$, or $\dfrac{-(y-3)(2y-7)}{2(y-5)(y+4)}$

45. *Writing Exercise*

46. *Writing Exercise*

47. $2(3x-1)+5(4x-3)=3(2x+1)$

$$6x-2+20x-15=6x+3$$

$$26x-17=6x+3$$

$$20x-17=3$$

$$20x=20$$

$$x=1$$

The solution is 1.

48. $\dfrac{11}{4}$

49.

$$\dfrac{t}{s+y}=r$$

$$(s+y)\cdot\dfrac{t}{s+y}=r(s+y)$$

$$t=rs+ry$$

$$t-rs=ry$$

$$\dfrac{t-rs}{r}=y$$

50. $\{-2,5\}$

51. *Familiarize*. Let $l=$ the length of the other leg, in centimeters. Then $l+2=$ the length of the hypotenuse.

Translate. We use the Pythagorean theorem.

$$10^2+l^2=(l+2)^2$$

Carry out. We solve the equation.

$$10^2+l^2=(l+2)^2$$

$$100+l^2=l^2+4l+4$$

$$100=4l+4 \qquad \text{Subtracting } l^2$$

$$96=4l \qquad \text{Subtracting 4}$$

$$24=l \qquad \text{Dividing by 4}$$

If $l=24$, then $l+2=24+2=26$.

Check. $10^2+24^2=100+576=676=26^2$, so the answer checks.

State. The hypotenuse is 26 cm long.

52. \$34

53. *Writing Exercise*

54. *Writing Exercise*

55.

$$\dfrac{5x^{-2}+10x^{-1}y^{-1}+5y^{-2}}{3x^{-2}-3y^{-2}}$$

$$=\dfrac{\dfrac{5}{x^2}+\dfrac{10}{xy}+\dfrac{5}{y^2}}{\dfrac{3}{x^2}-\dfrac{3}{y^2}}$$

$$=\dfrac{\dfrac{5}{x^2}+\dfrac{10}{xy}+\dfrac{5}{y^2}}{\dfrac{3}{x^2}-\dfrac{3}{y^2}}\cdot\dfrac{x^2y^2}{x^2y^2}$$

$$=\dfrac{5y^2+10xy+5x^2}{3y^2-3x^2}$$

$$=\dfrac{5(y^2+2xy+x^2)}{3(y^2-x^2)}$$

$$=\dfrac{5(y+x)(y+x)}{3(y+x)(y-x)}$$

$$=\dfrac{5\cancel{(y+x)}(y+x)}{3\cancel{(y+x)}(y-x)}$$

$$=\dfrac{5(y+x)}{3(y-x)}$$

56. $\dfrac{b-a}{ab}$

57. Substitute $\dfrac{c}{4}$ for both v_1 and v_2.

$$\dfrac{\dfrac{c}{4} + \dfrac{c}{4}}{1 + \dfrac{\dfrac{c}{4} \cdot \dfrac{c}{4}}{c^2}}$$

$$= \dfrac{\dfrac{2c}{4}}{1 + \dfrac{\dfrac{c^2}{16}}{c^2}}$$

$$= \dfrac{\dfrac{c}{2}}{1 + \dfrac{c^2}{16} \cdot \dfrac{1}{c^2}}$$

$$= \dfrac{\dfrac{c}{2}}{1 + \dfrac{1}{16}}$$

$$= \dfrac{\dfrac{c}{2}}{\dfrac{17}{16}}$$

$$= \dfrac{c}{2} \cdot \dfrac{16}{17}$$

$$= \dfrac{8c}{17}$$

The observed speed is $\dfrac{8c}{17}$, or $\dfrac{8}{17}$ the speed of light.

58. 6, 7, 8

59. $\dfrac{\dfrac{x+1}{x+2}}{\dfrac{x+3}{x+4}}$

This expression is undefined for any value of x that makes a denominator 0. We see that $x + 2 = 0$ when $x = -2$, $x + 3 = 0$ when $x = -3$, and $x + 4 = 0$ when $x = -4$, so the expression is undefined for the x-values -2, -3, and -4.

60. $-\dfrac{4}{5}, \dfrac{27}{14}$

61. $\dfrac{\dfrac{3x-5}{2x-7}}{\dfrac{4x}{5} - \dfrac{5}{6}}$

This expression is undefined for any value of x that makes a denominator 0. First we find the value of x for which $2x - 7 = 0$.

$$2x - 7 = 0$$
$$2x = 7$$
$$x = \dfrac{7}{2}$$

Then we find the value of x for which $\dfrac{4x}{5} - \dfrac{5}{6} = 0$:

$$\dfrac{4x}{5} - \dfrac{5}{6} = 0$$
$$30\left(\dfrac{4x}{5} - \dfrac{5}{6}\right) = 30 \cdot 0$$
$$30 \cdot \dfrac{4x}{5} - 30 \cdot \dfrac{5}{6} = 0$$
$$24x - 25 = 0$$
$$24x = 25$$
$$x = \dfrac{25}{24}$$

The expression is undefined for the x-values $\dfrac{7}{2}$ and $\dfrac{25}{24}$.

62. $\dfrac{P(i+12)^2}{12(i+24)}$

63. $\dfrac{f(x+h) - f(x)}{h} = \dfrac{\dfrac{2}{(x+h)^2} - \dfrac{2}{x^2}}{h}$

$$= \dfrac{2x^2 - 2(x+h)^2}{x^2(x+h)^2} \cdot \dfrac{1}{h}$$

$$= \dfrac{2x^2 - 2x^2 - 4xh - 2h^2}{x^2(x+h)^2} \cdot \dfrac{1}{h}$$

$$= \dfrac{-4xh - 2h^2}{x^2(x+h)^2 h}$$

$$= \dfrac{-2h(2x + h)}{x^2(x+h)^2 h}$$

$$= \dfrac{-2\cancel{h}(2x + h)}{x^2(x+h)^2 \cancel{h}}$$

$$= \dfrac{-2(2x + h)}{x^2(x+h)^2}$$

64. $\dfrac{-3}{x(x+h)}$

65. $\dfrac{f(x+h) - f(x)}{h}$

$$= \dfrac{\dfrac{x+h}{1-x-h} - \dfrac{x}{1-x}}{h}$$

$$= \dfrac{(x+h)(1-x) - x(1-x-h)}{(1-x-h)(1-x)} \cdot \dfrac{1}{h}$$

$$= \dfrac{x - x^2 + h - xh - x + x^2 + xh}{(1-x-h)(1-x)h}$$

$$= \dfrac{h}{(1-x-h)(1-x)h}$$

$$= \dfrac{\cancel{h} \cdot 1}{(1-x-h)(1-x)\cancel{h}}$$

$$= \dfrac{1}{(1-x-h)(1-x)}$$

66. $\dfrac{2}{(1+x+h)(1+x)}$

67. To avoid division by zero in $\dfrac{1}{x}$ and $\dfrac{8}{x^2}$ we must exclude 0 from the domain of F. To avoid division by zero in the complex fraction we solve:

$$2 - \frac{8}{x^2} = 0$$

$$2x^2 - 8 = 0$$

$$2(x^2 - 4) = 0$$

$$2(x+2)(x-2) = 0$$

$$x + 2 = 0 \quad or \quad x - 2 = 0$$

$$x = -2 \quad or \qquad x = 2.$$

The domain of $F = \{x | x$ is a real number $and\ x \neq 0\ and$ $x \neq -2\ and\ x \neq 2\}$.

68. $\{x | x$ is a real number $and\ x \neq 1\ and\ x \neq -1\ and$ $x \neq 4\ and\ x \neq -4\ and\ x \neq 5\ and\ x \neq -5\}$

69. The reciprocal is $\dfrac{1}{x^2 + x + 1 + \dfrac{1}{x} + \dfrac{1}{x^2}}$.

We simplify.

$$\frac{1}{x^2 + x + 1 + \dfrac{1}{x} + \dfrac{1}{x^2}}$$

$$= \frac{1}{\dfrac{x^4 + x^3 + x^2 + x + 1}{x^2}} \quad \begin{array}{l}\text{Adding in the}\\ \text{denominator}\end{array}$$

$$= 1 \cdot \frac{x^2}{x^4 + x^3 + x^2 + x + 1}$$

$$= \frac{x^2}{x^4 + x^3 + x^2 + x + 1}$$

70. $\dfrac{2 + a}{3 + a}$

71.
$$g(x) = \frac{x + 3}{x - 1}$$

$$g(a) = \frac{a + 3}{a - 1}$$

$$g(g(a)) = \frac{\dfrac{a + 3}{a - 1} + 3}{\dfrac{a + 3}{a - 1} - 1}$$

$$= \frac{\dfrac{a + 3}{a - 1} + 3}{\dfrac{a + 3}{a - 1} - 1} \cdot \frac{a - 1}{a - 1}$$

$$= \frac{\dfrac{a + 3}{a - 1} \cdot (a - 1) + 3(a - 1)}{\dfrac{a + 3}{a - 1} \cdot (a - 1) - 1(a - 1)}$$

$$= \frac{a + 3 + 3a - 3}{a + 3 - a + 1}$$

$$= \frac{4a}{4} = a$$

72. $\dfrac{x^4}{81}$; $\{x | x$ is a real number $and\ x \neq 3\}$, or $(-\infty, 3) \cup (3, \infty)$

73.
$$\frac{30{,}000 \cdot \dfrac{0.075}{12}}{\left(1 + \dfrac{0.075}{12}\right)^{120} - 1} = \frac{30{,}000(0.00625)}{(1 + 0.00625)^{120} - 1}$$

$$= \frac{187.5}{(1.00625)^{120} - 1}$$

$$\approx \frac{187.5}{2.112064637 - 1}$$

$$\approx \frac{187.5}{1.112064637}$$

$$\approx 168.61$$

Alexis' monthly investment is \$168.61.

Exercise Set 7.6

1.
$$\frac{4}{5} + \frac{1}{3} = \frac{x}{9}, \text{ LCD is } 45$$

$$45\left(\frac{4}{5} + \frac{1}{3}\right) = 45 \cdot \frac{x}{9}$$

$$45 \cdot \frac{4}{5} + 45 \cdot \frac{1}{3} = 45 \cdot \frac{x}{9}$$

$$36 + 15 = 5x$$

$$51 = 5x$$

$$\frac{51}{5} = x$$

Check: $\dfrac{4}{5} + \dfrac{1}{3} = \dfrac{x}{9}$

$$\begin{array}{c|c} \dfrac{4}{5} + \dfrac{1}{3} \ ? & \dfrac{51/5}{9} \\[2mm] \dfrac{12}{15} + \dfrac{5}{15} & \dfrac{51}{5} \cdot \dfrac{1}{9} \\[2mm] \dfrac{17}{15} & \dfrac{17}{15} \qquad \text{TRUE} \end{array}$$

The solution is $\dfrac{51}{5}$.

2. $\dfrac{51}{2}$

3.
$$\frac{x}{3} - \frac{x}{4} = 12, \text{ LCD is } 12$$

$$12\left(\frac{x}{3} - \frac{x}{4}\right) = 12 \cdot 12$$

$$12 \cdot \frac{x}{3} - 12 \cdot \frac{x}{4} = 12 \cdot 12$$

$$4x - 3x = 144$$

$$x = 144$$

Check: $\dfrac{x}{3} - \dfrac{x}{4} = 12$

$$\begin{array}{c|c} \dfrac{144}{3} - \dfrac{144}{4} \ ? & 12 \\[2mm] 48 - 36 & \\[1mm] 12 & 12 \qquad \text{TRUE} \end{array}$$

The solution is 144.

4. $-\dfrac{225}{2}$

5. $\dfrac{1}{3} - \dfrac{1}{x} = \dfrac{5}{6}$

Because $\dfrac{1}{x}$ is undefined when x is 0, we note at the outset that $x \neq 0$. Then we multiply both sides by the LCD, $x \cdot 6$, or $6x$.

$$6x\left(\dfrac{1}{3} - \dfrac{1}{x}\right) = 6x \cdot \dfrac{5}{6}$$

$$6x \cdot \dfrac{1}{3} - 6x \cdot \dfrac{1}{x} = 6x \cdot \dfrac{5}{6}$$

$$2x - 6 = 5x$$

$$-6 = 3x$$

$$-2 = x$$

Check:
$$\dfrac{\dfrac{1}{3} - \dfrac{1}{x} = \dfrac{5}{6}}{}$$

$$\dfrac{\dfrac{1}{3} - \dfrac{1}{-2} \; ? \; \dfrac{5}{6}}{}$$

$$\dfrac{1}{3} + \dfrac{1}{2}$$

$$\dfrac{2}{6} + \dfrac{3}{6}$$

$$\dfrac{5}{6} \;\bigg|\; \dfrac{5}{6} \quad \text{TRUE}$$

The solution is -2.

6. $\dfrac{40}{9}$

7. $\dfrac{1}{2} - \dfrac{2}{7} = \dfrac{3}{2x}$

Because $\dfrac{3}{2x}$ is undefined when x is 0, we note at the outset that $x \neq 0$. Then we multiply both sides by the LCD, $2 \cdot 7 \cdot x$, or $14x$.

$$14x\left(\dfrac{1}{2} - \dfrac{2}{7}\right) = 14x \cdot \dfrac{3}{2x}$$

$$14x \cdot \dfrac{1}{2} - 14x \cdot \dfrac{2}{7} = 14x \cdot \dfrac{3}{2x}$$

$$7x - 4x = 21$$

$$3x = 21$$

$$x = 7$$

Check:
$$\dfrac{\dfrac{1}{2} - \dfrac{2}{7} = \dfrac{3}{2x}}{}$$

$$\dfrac{\dfrac{1}{2} - \dfrac{2}{7} \; ? \; \dfrac{3}{2 \cdot 7}}{}$$

$$\dfrac{7}{14} - \dfrac{4}{14} \;\bigg|\; \dfrac{3}{14}$$

$$\dfrac{3}{14} \;\bigg|\; \dfrac{3}{14} \quad \text{TRUE}$$

The solution is 7.

8. 5

9. $\dfrac{12}{15} - \dfrac{1}{3x} = \dfrac{4}{5}$

Because $\dfrac{1}{3x}$ is undefined when x is 0, we note at the outset that $x \neq 0$. Then we multiply both sides by the LCD, $3 \cdot 5 \cdot x$, or $15x$.

$$15x\left(\dfrac{12}{15} - \dfrac{1}{3x}\right) = 15x \cdot \dfrac{4}{5}$$

$$15x \cdot \dfrac{12}{15} - 15x \cdot \dfrac{1}{3x} = 15x \cdot \dfrac{4}{5}$$

$$12x - 5 = 12x$$

$$-5 = 0$$

We get a false equation. The given equation has no solution.

10. No solution

11. $\dfrac{4}{3y} - \dfrac{3}{y} = \dfrac{10}{3}$

To assure that neither denominator on the left side is 0, we note at the outset that $y \neq 0$. Then we multiply on both sides by the LCD, $3 \cdot y$, or $3y$.

$$3y\left(\dfrac{4}{3y} - \dfrac{3}{y}\right) = 3y \cdot \dfrac{10}{3}$$

$$3y \cdot \dfrac{4}{3y} - 3y \cdot \dfrac{3}{y} = 3y \cdot \dfrac{10}{3}$$

$$4 - 9 = 10y$$

$$-5 = 10y$$

$$-\dfrac{1}{2} = y$$

This value checks. The solution is $-\dfrac{1}{2}$.

12. $-4, -1$

13. $\dfrac{x-2}{x-4} = \dfrac{2}{x-4}$

To assure that neither denominator is 0, we note at the outset that $x \neq 4$. Then we multiply both sides by the LCD, $x - 4$.

$$(x-4) \cdot \dfrac{x-2}{x-4} = (x-4) \cdot \dfrac{2}{x-4}$$

$$x - 2 = 2$$

$$x = 4$$

Recall that, because of the restriction above, 4 cannot be a solution. A check confirms this.

Check:
$$\dfrac{x-2}{x-4} = \dfrac{2}{x-4}$$

$$\dfrac{4-2}{4-4} \; ? \; \dfrac{2}{4-4}$$

$$\dfrac{2}{0} \;\bigg|\; \dfrac{2}{0} \quad \text{UNDEFINED}$$

The equation has no solution.

14. No solution

15. $\dfrac{5}{4t} = \dfrac{7}{5t-2}$

To assure that neither denominator is 0, we note at the outset that $t \neq 0$ and $t \neq \dfrac{2}{5}$. Then we multiply both sides by the LCD, $4t(5t-2)$.

$$4t(5t-2) \cdot \dfrac{5}{4t} = 4t(5t-2) \cdot \dfrac{7}{5t-2}$$
$$5(5t-2) = 4t \cdot 7$$
$$25t - 10 = 28t$$
$$-10 = 3t$$
$$-\dfrac{10}{3} = t$$

This value checks. The solution is $-\dfrac{10}{3}$.

16. 11

17. $\dfrac{x^2+4}{x-1} = \dfrac{5}{x-1}$

To assure that neither denominator is 0, we note at the outset that $x \neq 1$. Then we multiply both sides by the LCD, $x-1$.

$$(x-1) \cdot \dfrac{x^2+4}{x-1} = (x-1) \cdot \dfrac{5}{x-1}$$
$$x^2 + 4 = 5$$
$$x^2 - 1 = 0$$
$$(x+1)(x-1) = 0$$
$$x + 1 = 0 \quad \text{or} \quad x - 1 = 0$$
$$x = -1 \quad \text{or} \qquad x = 1$$

Recall that, because of the restriction above, 1 cannot be a solution. The number -1 checks and is the solution.

We might also observe that since the denominators are the same, the numerators must be the same. Solving $x^2 + 4 = 5$, we get $x = -1$ or $x = 1$ as shown above. Again, because of the restriction $x \neq 1$, only -1 is a solution of the equation.

18. 2

19. $\dfrac{6}{a+1} = \dfrac{a}{a-1}$

To assure that neither denominator is 0, we note at the outset that $a \neq -1$ and $a \neq 1$. Then we multiply both sides by the LCD, $(a+1)(a-1)$.

$$(a+1)(a-1) \cdot \dfrac{6}{a+1} = (a+1)(a-1) \cdot \dfrac{a}{a-1}$$
$$6(a-1) = a(a+1)$$
$$6a - 6 = a^2 + a$$
$$0 = a^2 - 5a + 6$$
$$0 = (a-2)(a-3)$$
$$a - 2 = 0 \quad \text{or} \quad a - 3 = 0$$
$$a = 2 \quad \text{or} \qquad a = 3$$

Both values check. The solutions are 2 and 3.

20. 2, 3

21. $\dfrac{60}{t-5} - \dfrac{18}{t} = \dfrac{40}{t}$

To assure that none of the denominators is 0, we note at the outset that $t \neq 5$ and $t \neq 0$. Then we multiply on both sides by the LCD, $t(t-5)$.

$$t(t-5)\left(\dfrac{60}{t-5} - \dfrac{18}{t}\right) = t(t-5) \cdot \dfrac{40}{t}$$
$$60t - 18(t-5) = 40(t-5)$$
$$60t - 18t + 90 = 40t - 200$$
$$2t = -290$$
$$t = -145$$

This value checks. The solution is -145.

22. -23

23. $\dfrac{3}{x} + \dfrac{x}{x+2} = \dfrac{4}{x^2+2x}$

$$\dfrac{3}{x} + \dfrac{x}{x+2} = \dfrac{4}{x(x+2)}$$

To assure that none of the denominators is 0, we note at the outset that $x \neq 0$ and $x \neq -2$. Then we multiply both sides by the LCD, $x(x+2)$.

$$x(x+2)\left(\dfrac{3}{x} + \dfrac{x}{x+2}\right) = x(x+2) \cdot \dfrac{4}{x(x+2)}$$
$$3(x+2) + x \cdot x = 4$$
$$3x + 6 + x^2 = 4$$
$$x^2 + 3x + 2 = 0$$
$$(x+1)(x+2) = 0$$
$$x + 1 = 0 \quad \text{or} \quad x + 2 = 0$$
$$x = -1 \quad \text{or} \qquad x = -2$$

Recall that, because of the restrictions above, -2 cannot be a solution. The number -1 checks. The solution is -1.

24. -4

25. We find all values of a for which $2a - \dfrac{15}{a} = 7$. First note that $a \neq 0$. Then multiply on both sides by the LCD, a.

$$a\left(2a - \dfrac{15}{a}\right) = a \cdot 7$$
$$a \cdot 2a - a \cdot \dfrac{15}{a} = 7a$$
$$2a^2 - 15 = 7a$$
$$2a^2 - 7a - 15 = 0$$
$$(2a+3)(a-5) = 0$$
$$a = -\dfrac{3}{2} \text{ or } a = 5$$

Both values check. The solutions are $-\dfrac{3}{2}$ and 5.

26. $-\dfrac{3}{2}$, 2

27. We find all values of a for which $\dfrac{a-5}{a+1} = \dfrac{3}{5}$. First note that $a \neq -1$. Then multiply on both sides by the LCD, $5(a+1)$.

$$5(a+1) \cdot \frac{a-5}{a+1} = 5(a+1) \cdot \frac{3}{5}$$

$$5(a-5) = 3(a+1)$$

$$5a - 25 = 3a + 3$$

$$2a = 28$$

$$a = 14$$

This value checks. The solution is 14.

28. $\dfrac{17}{4}$

29. We find all values of a for which $\dfrac{12}{a} - \dfrac{12}{2a} = 8$. First note that $a \neq 0$. Then multiply on both sides by the LCD, $2a$.

$$2a\left(\frac{12}{a} - \frac{12}{2a}\right) = 2a \cdot 8$$

$$2a \cdot \frac{12}{a} - 2a \cdot \frac{12}{2a} = 16a$$

$$24 - 12 = 16a$$

$$12 = 16a$$

$$\frac{3}{4} = a$$

This value checks. The solution is $\dfrac{3}{4}$.

30. $\dfrac{3}{5}$

31. $$\frac{5}{x+2} - \frac{3}{x-2} = \frac{2x}{4-x^2}$$

$$\frac{5}{x+2} - \frac{3}{x-2} = \frac{2x}{(2+x)(2-x)}$$

$$\frac{5}{x+2} + \frac{3}{2-x} = \frac{2x}{(2+x)(2-x)} \quad \left(-\frac{3}{x-2} = \frac{3}{2-x}\right)$$

First note that $x \neq -2$ and $x \neq 2$. Then multiply on both sides by the LCD, $(2+x)(2-x)$.

$$(2+x)(2-x)\left(\frac{5}{x+2} + \frac{3}{2-x}\right) =$$

$$(2+x)(2-x) \cdot \frac{2x}{(2+x)(2-x)}$$

$$5(2-x) + 3(2+x) = 2x$$

$$10 - 5x + 6 + 3x = 2x$$

$$16 - 2x = 2x$$

$$16 = 4x$$

$$4 = x$$

This value checks. The solution is 4.

32. -3

33. $$\frac{2}{a+4} + \frac{2a-1}{a^2+2a-8} = \frac{1}{a-2}$$

$$\frac{2}{a+4} + \frac{2a-1}{(a+4)(a-2)} = \frac{1}{a-2}$$

First note that $a \neq -4$ and $a \neq 2$. Then multiply on both sides by the LCD, $(a+4)(a-2)$.

$$(a+4)(a-2)\left(\frac{2}{a+4} + \frac{2a-1}{(a+4)(a-2)}\right) =$$

$$(a+4)(a-2) \cdot \frac{1}{a-2}$$

$$2(a-2) + 2a - 1 = a + 4$$

$$2a - 4 + 2a - 1 = a + 4$$

$$4a - 5 = a + 4$$

$$3a = 9$$

$$a = 3$$

This value checks. The solution is 3.

34. $-6, 5$

35. $$\frac{2}{x+3} - \frac{3x+5}{x^2+4x+3} = \frac{5}{x+1}$$

$$\frac{2}{x+3} - \frac{3x+5}{(x+3)(x+1)} = \frac{5}{x+1}$$

Note that $x \neq -3$ and $x \neq -1$. Then multiply on both sides by the LCD, $(x+3)(x+1)$.

$$(x+3)(x+1)\left(\frac{2}{x+3} - \frac{3x+5}{(x+3)(x+1)}\right) =$$

$$(x+3)(x+1) \cdot \frac{5}{x+1}$$

$$2(x+1) - (3x+5) = 5(x+3)$$

$$2x + 2 - 3x - 5 = 5x + 15$$

$$-x - 3 = 5x + 15$$

$$-18 = 6x$$

$$-3 = x$$

Recall that, because of the restriction above, -3 is not a solution. Thus, the equation has no solution.

36. No solution

37. $$\frac{x-1}{x^2-2x-3} + \frac{x+2}{x^2-9} = \frac{2x+5}{x^2+4x+3}$$

$$\frac{x-1}{(x-3)(x+1)} + \frac{x+2}{(x+3)(x-3)} = \frac{2x+5}{(x+3)(x+1)}$$

Note that $x \neq 3$ and $x \neq -1$ and $x \neq -3$. Then multiply on both sides by the LCD, $(x-3)(x+1)(x+3)$.

$$(x-3)(x+1)(x+3)\left(\frac{x-1}{(x-3)(x+1)} + \frac{x+2}{(x+3)(x-3)}\right) =$$

$$(x-3)(x+1)(x+3) \cdot \frac{2x+5}{(x+3)(x+1)}$$

$$(x+3)(x-1) + (x+1)(x+2) = (x-3)(2x+5)$$

$$x^2 + 2x - 3 + x^2 + 3x + 2 = 2x^2 - x - 15$$

$$2x^2 + 5x - 1 = 2x^2 - x - 15$$

$$5x - 1 = -x - 15$$

$$6x = -14$$

$$x = -\frac{7}{3}$$

This value checks. The solution is $-\dfrac{7}{3}$.

38. $\dfrac{5}{14}$

39.
$$\frac{3}{x^2 - x - 12} + \frac{1}{x^2 + x - 6} = \frac{4}{x^2 + 3x - 10}$$

$$\frac{3}{(x-4)(x+3)} + \frac{1}{(x+3)(x-2)} = \frac{4}{(x+5)(x-2)}$$

Note that $x \neq 4$ and $x \neq -3$ and $x \neq 2$ and $x \neq -5$. Then multiply on both sides by the LCD, $(x-4)(x+3)(x-2)(x+5)$.

$$(x-4)(x+3)(x-2)(x+5)\left(\frac{3}{(x-4)(x+3)} + \frac{1}{(x+3)(x-2)}\right) =$$

$$(x-4)(x+3)(x-2)(x+5) \cdot \frac{4}{(x+5)(x-2)}$$

$$3(x-2)(x+5) + (x-4)(x+5) = 4(x-4)(x+3)$$

$$3(x^2 + 3x - 10) + x^2 + x - 20 = 4(x^2 - x - 12)$$

$$3x^2 + 9x - 30 + x^2 + x - 20 = 4x^2 - 4x - 48$$

$$4x^2 + 10x - 50 = 4x^2 - 4x - 48$$

$$10x - 50 = -4x - 48$$

$$14x = 2$$

$$x = \frac{1}{7}$$

This value checks. The solution is $\dfrac{1}{7}$.

40. $\dfrac{3}{5}$

41. *Writing Exercise*

42. *Writing Exercise*

43. To find the rate, in centimeters per day, we divide the amount of growth by the number of days. From June 9 to June 24 is $24 - 9 = 15$ days.

$$\text{Rate, in cm per day} = \frac{0.9 \text{ cm}}{15 \text{ days}}$$

$$= 0.06 \text{ cm/day}$$

$$= 0.06 \text{ cm per day}$$

44. 0.28 in. per day

45. Familiarize. Let $b =$ the base of the triangle, in cm. Then $b + 3 =$ the height. Recall that the area of a triangle is given by $\dfrac{1}{2} \times$ base $\times$ height.

Translate.

The area of the triangle is 54 cm².

$$\frac{1}{2} \cdot b \cdot (b+3) = 54$$

Carry out. We solve the equation.

$$\frac{1}{2}b(b+3) = 54$$

$$2 \cdot \frac{1}{2}b(b+3) = 2 \cdot 54$$

$$b(b+3) = 108$$

$$b^2 + 3b = 108$$

$$b^2 + 3b - 108 = 0$$

$$(b-9)(b+12) = 0$$

$$b - 9 = 0 \quad or \quad b + 12 = 0$$

$$b = 9 \quad or \quad b = -12$$

Check. The length of the base cannot be negative so we need to check only 9. If the base is 9 cm, then the height is $9+3$, or 12 cm, and the area is $\dfrac{1}{2} \cdot 9 \cdot 12$, or 54 cm². The answer checks.

State. The base measures 9 cm, and the height measures 12 cm.

46. 24,640 m²

47. Familiarize. Let $x =$ the smaller number. Then $x + 2 =$ the other number.

Translate.

The product of two consecutive positive even numbers is 288.

$$x(x+2) = 288$$

Carry out. We solve the equation.

$$x(x+2) = 288$$

$$x^2 + 2x = 288$$

$$x^2 + 2x - 288 = 0$$

$$(x+18)(x-16) = 0$$

$$x + 18 = 0 \quad or \quad x - 16 = 0$$

$$x = -18 \quad or \quad x = 16$$

Check. The exercise asks for positive even numbers, so we check only 16. If $x = 16$, then $x + 2 = 16 + 2 = 18$, and $16(18) = 288$. The answer checks.

State. The numbers are 16 and 18.

48. $\{x \mid x < -1 \ or \ x > 5\}$, or $(-\infty, -1) \cup (5, \infty)$

49. *Writing Exercise*

50. *Writing Exercise*

51.
$$f(a) = g(a)$$

$$\frac{a - \dfrac{2}{3}}{a + \dfrac{1}{2}} = \frac{a + \dfrac{2}{3}}{a - \dfrac{3}{2}}$$

$$\frac{a - \dfrac{2}{3}}{a + \dfrac{1}{2}} \cdot \frac{6}{6} = \frac{a + \dfrac{2}{3}}{a - \dfrac{3}{2}} \cdot \frac{6}{6}$$

$$\frac{6a - \dfrac{2}{3} \cdot 6}{6a + \dfrac{1}{2} \cdot 6} = \frac{6a + \dfrac{2}{3} \cdot 6}{6a - \dfrac{3}{2} \cdot 6}$$

$$\frac{6a - 4}{6a + 3} = \frac{6a + 4}{6a - 9}$$

$$\frac{6a - 4}{3(2a + 1)} = \frac{6a + 4}{3(2a - 3)}$$

To assure that neither denominator is 0, we note at the outset that $a \neq -\dfrac{1}{2}$ and $a \neq \dfrac{3}{2}$. Then we multiply both sides by the LCD, $3(2a + 1)(2a - 3)$.

$$3(2a+1)(2a-3) \cdot \frac{6a-4}{3(2a+1)} =$$
$$3(2a+1)(2a-3) \cdot \frac{6a+4}{3(2a-3)}$$
$$(2a-3)(6a-4) = (2a+1)(6a+4)$$
$$12a^2 - 26a + 12 = 12a^2 + 14a + 4$$
$$-26a + 12 = 14a + 4$$
$$-40a + 12 = 4$$
$$-40a = -8$$
$$a = \frac{1}{5}$$

This number checks. For $a = \frac{1}{5}$, $f(a) = g(a)$.

52. $-8, 8$

53. $\dfrac{a+3}{a+2} - \dfrac{a+4}{a+3} = \dfrac{a+5}{a+4} - \dfrac{a+6}{a+5}$

Note that $a \neq -2$ and $a \neq -3$ and $a \neq -4$ and $a \neq -5$.

$$(a+2)(a+3)(a+4)(a+5)\left(\frac{a+3}{a+2} - \frac{a+4}{a+3}\right) =$$
$$(a+2)(a+3)(a+4)(a+5)\left(\frac{a+5}{a+4} - \frac{a+6}{a+5}\right)$$
$$(a+3)(a+4)(a+5)(a+3) - (a+2)(a+4)(a+5)(a+4) =$$
$$(a+2)(a+3)(a+5)(a+5) - (a+2)(a+3)(a+4)(a+6)$$
$$a^4 + 15a^3 + 83a^2 + 201a + 180 -$$
$$(a^4 + 15a^3 + 82a^2 + 192a + 160) =$$
$$a^4 + 15a^3 + 81a^2 + 185a + 150 -$$
$$(a^4 + 15a^3 + 80a^2 + 180a + 144)$$
$$a^2 + 9a + 20 = a^2 + 5a + 6$$
$$4a = -14$$
$$a = -\frac{7}{2}$$

This value checks. When $a = -\dfrac{7}{2}$, $f(a) = g(a)$.

54. $\{a | a \text{ is a real number } and \ a \neq -1 \ and \ a \neq 1\}$

55. Set $f(a)$ equal to $g(a)$ and solve for a.
$$\frac{0.793}{a} + 18.15 = \frac{6.034}{a} - 43.17$$
Note that $a \neq 0$. Then multiply on both sides by the LCD, a.
$$a\left(\frac{0.793}{a} + 18.15\right) = a\left(\frac{6.034}{a} - 43.17\right)$$
$$0.793 + 18.15a = 6.034 - 43.17a$$
$$61.32a = 5.241$$
$$a \approx 0.0854697$$
This value checks. When $a \approx 0.0854697$, $f(a) = g(a)$.

56. -2.955341202

57. $\dfrac{x^2 + 6x - 16}{x - 2} = x + 8, x \neq 2$

$$\frac{(x+8)(x-2)}{x-2} = x + 8$$
$$\frac{(x+8)(x\!-\!2)}{x\!-\!2} = x + 8$$
$$x + 8 = x + 8$$
$$8 = 8$$

Since $8 = 8$ is true for all values of x, the original equation is true for any possible replacements of the variable. It is an identity.

58. Yes

Exercise Set 7.7

1. *Familiarize*. Let $x = $ the number.

Translate.

The reciprocal of 3	plus	the reciprocal of 6	is	the reciprocal of the number.
↓	↓	↓	↓	↓
$\frac{1}{3}$	$+$	$\frac{1}{6}$	$=$	$\frac{1}{x}$

Carry out. We solve the equation.
$$\frac{1}{3} + \frac{1}{6} = \frac{1}{x}, \text{ LCD is } 6x$$
$$6x\left(\frac{1}{3} + \frac{1}{6}\right) = 6x \cdot \frac{1}{x}$$
$$2x + x = 6$$
$$3x = 6$$
$$x = 2$$

Check. $\dfrac{1}{3} + \dfrac{1}{6} = \dfrac{2}{6} + \dfrac{1}{6} = \dfrac{3}{6} = \dfrac{1}{2}$. This is the reciprocal of 2, so the result checks.

State. The number is 2.

2. $\dfrac{35}{12}$

3. *Familiarize*. We let $x = $ the number.

Translate.

A number	plus	6	times	its reciprocal	is	-5.
↓	↓	↓	↓	↓	↓	↓
x	$+$	6	$\cdot$	$\frac{1}{x}$	$=$	-5

Carry out. We solve the equation.
$$x + \frac{6}{x} = -5, \text{ LCD is } x$$
$$x\left(x + \frac{6}{x}\right) = x(-5)$$
$$x^2 + 6 = -5x$$
$$x^2 + 5x + 6 = 0$$
$$(x+3)(x+2) = 0$$
$$x = -3 \ or \ x = -2$$

Check. The possible solutions are -3 and -2. We check -3 in the conditions of the problem.

Number:	-3
6 times the reciprocal of the number:	$6\left(-\dfrac{1}{3}\right) = -2$
Sum of the number and 6 times its reciprocal:	$-3 + (-2) = -5$

The number -3 checks.

Now we check -2:

Number:	-2
6 times the reciprocal of the number:	$6\left(-\dfrac{1}{2}\right) = -3$
Sum of the number and 6 times its reciprocal:	$-2 + (-3) = -5$

The number -2 also checks.

State. The number is -3 or -2.

4. $-3, -7$

5. Familiarize. We let $x =$ the first integer. Then $x + 1 =$ the second, and their product $= x(x+1)$.

Translate.

$$\underbrace{\text{Reciprocal of the product}}_{\dfrac{1}{x(x+1)}} \; \underset{=}{\overset{\text{is}}{\downarrow}} \; \underset{\dfrac{1}{42}}{\overset{\dfrac{1}{42}}{\downarrow}}.$$

Carry out. We solve the equation.

$$\frac{1}{x(x+1)} = \frac{1}{42}, \text{ LCD is } 42x(x+1)$$

$$42x(x+1) \cdot \frac{1}{x(x+1)} = 42x(x+1) \cdot \frac{1}{42}$$

$$42 = x(x+1)$$

$$42 = x^2 + x$$

$$0 = x^2 + x - 42$$

$$0 = (x+7)(x-6)$$

$$x = -7 \text{ or } x = 6$$

Check. When $x = -7$, then $x+1 = -6$ and $-7(-6) = 42$. The reciprocal of this product is $\dfrac{1}{42}$.

When $x = 6$, then $x+1 = 7$ and $6 \cdot 7 = 42$. The reciprocal of this product is also $\dfrac{1}{42}$. Both possible solutions check.

State. The integers are -7 and -6 or 6 and 7.

6. -9 and -8 or 8 and 9

7. Familiarize. The job takes Cedric 8 hours working alone and Carolyn 6 hours working alone. Then in 1 hour, Cedric does $\dfrac{1}{8}$ of the job and Carolyn does $\dfrac{1}{6}$ of the job. Working together, they can do $\dfrac{1}{8} + \dfrac{1}{6}$ of the job in 1 hour. Let t represent the number of hours required for Cedric and Carolyn, working together, to do the job.

Translate. We want to find t such that

$$t\left(\frac{1}{8}\right) + t\left(\frac{1}{6}\right) = 1, \text{ or } \frac{t}{8} + \frac{t}{6} = 1,$$

where 1 represents one entire job.

Carry out. We solve the equation.

$$\frac{t}{8} + \frac{t}{6} = 1, \text{ LCD is } 24$$

$$24\left(\frac{t}{8} + \frac{t}{6}\right) = 24 \cdot 1$$

$$3t + 4t = 24$$

$$7t = 24$$

$$t = \frac{24}{7}$$

Check. In $\dfrac{24}{7}$ hours, Cedric will do $\dfrac{1}{8} \cdot \dfrac{24}{7}$, or $\dfrac{3}{7}$ of the job and Carolyn will do $\dfrac{1}{6} \cdot \dfrac{24}{7}$, or $\dfrac{4}{7}$ of the job. Together, they do $\dfrac{3}{7} + \dfrac{4}{7}$, or 1 entire job. The answer checks.

State. It will take $\dfrac{24}{7}$ hr, or $3\dfrac{3}{7}$ hr, for Cedric and Carolyn, together, to refinish the floor.

8. $3\dfrac{3}{14}$ hr

9. Familiarize. The tank can be filled in 18 hours by only the town office well and in 22 hours with only the high school well. Then in 1 hour, the office well fills $\dfrac{1}{18}$ of the tank, and the high school well fills $\dfrac{1}{22}$ of the tank. Using both the wells, $\dfrac{1}{18} + \dfrac{1}{22}$ of the tank can be filled in 1 hour. Suppose that it takes t hours to fill the tank using both the town office well and the high school well.

Translate. We want to find t such that

$$t\left(\frac{1}{18}\right) + t\left(\frac{1}{22}\right) = 1, \text{ or } \frac{t}{18} + \frac{t}{22} = 1,$$

where 1 represents one entire job.

Carry out. We solve the equation. We multiply both sides by the LCD, 198.

$$198\left(\frac{t}{18} + \frac{t}{22}\right) = 198 \cdot 1$$

$$11t + 9t = 198$$

$$20t = 198$$

$$t = \frac{99}{10}$$

Check. The possible solution is $\dfrac{99}{10}$ hours. If the town office well is used $\dfrac{99}{10}$ hours, it fills $\dfrac{1}{18} \cdot \dfrac{99}{10}$, or $\dfrac{11}{20}$ of the tank. If the high school well is used $\dfrac{99}{10}$ hours, it fills $\dfrac{1}{22} \cdot \dfrac{99}{10}$, or $\dfrac{9}{20}$ of the tank. Using both, $\dfrac{11}{20} + \dfrac{9}{20}$ of the tank, or all of it, will be filled in $\dfrac{99}{10}$ hours.

State. Using both the town office well and the high school well, it will take $\dfrac{99}{10}$, or $9\dfrac{9}{10}$ hours, to fill the tank.

10. $8\frac{4}{7}$ hr

11. *Familiarize.* In 1 minute the HQ17 does $\frac{1}{10}$ of the job and the HQ174 does $\frac{1}{6}$ of the job. Working together, they can do $\frac{1}{10} + \frac{1}{6}$ of the job in 1 minute. Suppose it takes them t minutes, working together, to do the job.

Translate. We find t such that

$$t\left(\frac{1}{10}\right) + t\left(\frac{1}{6}\right) = 1, \text{ or } \frac{t}{10} + \frac{t}{6} = 1.$$

Carry out. We solve the equation. We multiply both sides by the LCD, 30.

$$30\left(\frac{t}{10} + \frac{t}{6}\right) = 30 \cdot 1$$
$$3t + 5t = 30$$
$$8t = 30$$
$$t = \frac{15}{4}$$

Check. In $\frac{15}{4}$ min the HQ17 will do $\frac{15}{4} \cdot \frac{1}{10}$, or $\frac{3}{8}$ of the job and the HQ174 will do $\frac{15}{4} \cdot \frac{1}{6}$, or $\frac{5}{8}$ of the job. Together they will do $\frac{3}{8} + \frac{5}{8}$, or 1 entire job. The answer checks.

State. It would take the two machines $\frac{15}{4}$ min, or $3\frac{3}{4}$ min, to clean the air working together.

12. 2.475 hr

13. *Familiarize.* Let t represent the number of hours it would take Skyler to do the job working alone. Then $t - 6$ represents the time it would take Jake to do the job alone.

In 1 hr Skyler does $\frac{1}{t}$ of the job and Jake does $\frac{1}{t-6}$ of the job.

Translate. Working together, they can do the entire job in 4 hr, so we want to find t such that

$$4\left(\frac{1}{t}\right) + 4\left(\frac{1}{t-6}\right) = 1, \text{ or } \frac{4}{t} + \frac{4}{t-6} = 1.$$

Carry out. We solve the equation.

$$\frac{4}{t} + \frac{4}{t-6} = 1, \text{ LCD is } t(t-6)$$
$$t(t-6)\left(\frac{4}{t} + \frac{4}{t-6}\right) = t(t-6) \cdot 1$$
$$4(t-6) + 4t = t^2 - 6t$$
$$4t - 24 + 4t = t^2 - 6t$$
$$8t - 24 = t^2 - 6t$$
$$0 = t^2 - 14t + 24$$
$$0 = (t-2)(t-12)$$
$$t - 2 = 0 \text{ or } t - 12 = 0$$
$$t = 2 \text{ or } t = 12$$

Check. When $t = 2$, then $t - 6 = 2 - 6 = -4$, so 2 cannot be a solution of the original problem. If Skyler does the job in 12 hr, then Jake does the job in $12 - 6$, or 6 hr. In 4 hr, Skyler does $4 \cdot \frac{1}{12}$, or $\frac{1}{3}$ of the job and Jake does $4 \cdot \frac{1}{6}$, or $\frac{2}{3}$ of the job. Together they do $\frac{1}{3} + \frac{2}{3}$, or 1 entire job in 4 hr. The number 12 checks.

State. It would take Skyler 12 hours and it would take Jake 6 hours to do the job, working alone.

14. $3\frac{9}{52}$ hr

15. *Familiarize.* Let t represent the time, in minutes, that it takes the EV25 to clean the air, working alone. Then $2t$ represents the time, in minutes, it takes the HQ17 to clean the same volume of air, working alone. In 1 minute, the EV25 does $\frac{1}{t}$ of the job and the HQ17 does $\frac{1}{2t}$ of the job.

Translate. Working together, they can do the entire job in 10 min, so we want to find t such that

$$10\left(\frac{1}{t}\right) + 10\left(\frac{1}{2t}\right) = 1, \text{ or } \frac{10}{t} + \frac{5}{t} = 1.$$

Carry out. We solve the equation.

$$\frac{10}{t} + \frac{5}{t} = 1, \text{ LCD is } t$$
$$t\left(\frac{10}{t} + \frac{5}{t}\right) = t \cdot 1$$
$$10 + 5 = t$$
$$15 = t$$

Check. If the EV25 does the job in 15 min, then in 10 min it does $10 \cdot \frac{1}{15}$, or $\frac{2}{3}$ of the job. If it takes HQ17 $2 \cdot 15$, or 30 min, to do the job, then in 10 min it does $10\left(\frac{1}{30}\right)$, or $\frac{1}{3}$ of the job. Working together they do $\frac{2}{3} + \frac{1}{3}$, or 1 entire job in 10 min. The answer checks.

State. Working alone, it takes the EV25 15 min and the HQ17 30 min to do the job.

16. Office Jet G85: $22\frac{1}{2}$ hr; Laser Jet II: 45 hr

17. *Familiarize.* Let t represent the number of hours it takes Kate to paint the floor. Then $t + 3$ represents the time it takes Sara to paint the floor. In 1 hour, Kate does $\frac{1}{t}$ of the job and Sara does $\frac{1}{t+3}$.

Translate. Working together, it takes them 2 hr to do the job, so we want to find t such that

$$2\left(\frac{1}{t}\right) + 2\left(\frac{1}{t+3}\right) = 1, \text{ or } \frac{2}{t} + \frac{2}{t+3} = 1.$$

Carry out. We solve the equation. We multiply by the LCD, $t(t+3)$.

$$t(t+3)\left(\frac{2}{t} + \frac{2}{t+3}\right) = t(t+3)(1)$$

$$2(t+3) + 2t = t^2 + 3t$$

$$2t + 6 + 2t = t^2 + 3t$$

$$4t + 6 = t^2 + 3t$$

$$0 = t^2 - t - 6$$

$$0 = (t-3)(t+2)$$

$$t = 3 \text{ or } t = -2$$

Check. We check only 3, since the time cannot be negative. If Kate does the job in 3 hr, then in 2 hr she does $2\left(\frac{1}{3}\right)$, or $\frac{2}{3}$ of the job. If Sara does the job in $3 + 3$ or 6 hr, then in 2 hr she does $2\left(\frac{1}{6}\right)$, or $\frac{1}{3}$ of the job. Together they do $\frac{2}{3} + \frac{1}{3}$, or 1 entire job in 2 hr. The result checks.

State. It would take Kate 3 hours to do the job and it would take Sara 6 hours to do the job working alone.

18. Claudia: 10 days; Jan: 40 days

19. Familiarize. Working alone, Rosita does $\frac{1}{2}$ of the job in 1 hr. Let $t =$ the time it take Helga to wax the car, working alone. Then in 1 hr she does $\frac{1}{t}$ of the job. Represent 45 min as $\frac{3}{4}$ hr.

Translate. In $\frac{3}{4}$ hr they do 1 entire job, working together, so we have

$$\frac{3}{4}\left(\frac{1}{2}\right) + \frac{3}{4}\left(\frac{1}{t}\right) = 1, \text{ or } \frac{3}{8} + \frac{3}{4t} = 1.$$

Carry out. We solve the equation.

$$8t\left(\frac{3}{8} + \frac{3}{4t}\right) = 8t \cdot 1$$

$$3t + 6 = 8t$$

$$6 = 5t$$

$$\frac{6}{5} = t$$

Check. In $\frac{3}{4}$ hr, Rosita will do $\frac{3}{4} \cdot \frac{1}{2}$, or $\frac{3}{8}$, of the job, and Helga will do $\frac{3}{4}\left(\frac{1}{6/5}\right)$, or $\frac{3}{4} \cdot \frac{5}{6} = \frac{5}{8}$, of the job. Together they do $\frac{3}{8} + \frac{5}{8} = 1$ job. The answer checks.

State. It would take Helga $\frac{6}{5}$, or $1\frac{1}{5}$ hr, working alone.

20. Zsuzanna: $\frac{4}{3}$ hr; Stan: 4 hr

21. Familiarize. We will convert hours to minutes:

$$2 \text{ hr} = 2 \cdot 60 \text{ min} = 120 \text{ min}$$

$$2 \text{ hr } 55 \text{ min} = 120 \text{ min} + 55 \text{ min} = 175 \text{ min}$$

Let $t =$ the number of minutes it takes Deb to do the job alone. Then $t + 120 =$ the number of minutes it takes John alone. In 1 hour (60 minutes) Deb does $\frac{1}{t}$ and John does $\frac{1}{t+120}$ of the job.

Translate. In 175 min John and Deb will complete one entire job, so we have

$$175\left(\frac{1}{t}\right) + 175\left(\frac{1}{t+120}\right) = 1, \text{ or}$$

$$\frac{175}{t} + \frac{175}{t+120} = 1.$$

Carry out. We solve the equation. Multiply on both sides by the LCD, $t(t+120)$.

$$t(t+120)\left(\frac{175}{t} + \frac{175}{t+120}\right) = t(t+120)(1)$$

$$175(t+120) + 175t = t^2 + 120t$$

$$175t + 21,000 + 175t = t^2 + 120t$$

$$0 = t^2 - 230t - 21,000$$

$$0 = (t-300)(t+70)$$

$$t = 300 \text{ or } t = -70$$

Check. Since negative time has no meaning in this problem, -70 is not a solution of the original problem. If the job takes Deb 300 min and it takes John $300 + 120 = 420$ min, then in 175 min they would complete

$$175\left(\frac{1}{300}\right) + 175\left(\frac{1}{420}\right) = \frac{7}{12} + \frac{5}{12} = 1 \text{ job.}$$

The result checks.

State. It would take Deb 300 min, or 5 hr, to do the job alone.

22. 8 hr

23. Familiarize. We first make a drawing. Let $r =$ the kayak's speed in still water in mph. Then $r - 3 =$ the speed upstream and $r + 3 =$ the speed downstream.

Upstream   4 miles $r - 3$ mph

10 miles $r + 3$ mph   Downstream

We organize the information in a table. The time is the same both upstream and downstream so we use t for each time.

	Distance	Speed	Time
Upstream	4	$r - 3$	t
Downstream	10	$r + 3$	t

Translate. Using the formula Time = Distance/Rate in each row of the table and the fact that the times are the same, we can write an equation.

$$\frac{4}{r-3} = \frac{10}{r+3}$$

Carry out. We solve the equation.

$$\frac{4}{r-3} = \frac{10}{r+3}, \text{ LCD is } (r-3)(r+3)$$

$$(r-3)(r+3) \cdot \frac{4}{r-3} = (r-3)(r+3) \cdot \frac{10}{r+3}$$

$$4(r+3) = 10(r-3)$$

$$4r+12 = 10r-30$$

$$42 = 6r$$

$$7 = r$$

Check. If $r = 7$ mph, then $r - 3$ is 4 mph and $r + 3$ is 10 mph. The time upstream is $\frac{4}{4}$, or 1 hour. The time downstream is $\frac{10}{10}$, or 1 hour. Since the times are the same, the answer checks.

State. The speed of the kayak in still water is 7 mph.

24. 12 mph

25. *Familiarize*. We first make a drawing. Let $r =$ Camille's speed on a nonmoving sidewalk in ft/sec. Then her speed moving forward on the moving sidewalk is $r + 1.8$, and her speed in the opposite direction is $r - 1.8$.

Forward $r + 1.8$ 105 ft
⟶

                                        Opposite
        51 ft $r - 1.8$ direction
⟵

We organize the information in a table. The time is the same both forward and in the opposite direction so we use t for each time.

	Distance	Speed	Time
Forward	105	$r + 1.8$	t
Opposite direction	51	$r - 1.8$	t

Translate. Using the formula Time = Distance/Rate in each row of the table and the fact that the times are the same, we can write an equation.

$$\frac{105}{r+1.8} = \frac{51}{r-1.8}$$

Carry out. We solve the equation.

$$\frac{105}{r+1.8} = \frac{51}{r-1.8},$$

$$\text{LCD is } (r+1.8)(r-1.8)$$

$$(r+1.8)(r-1.8) \cdot \frac{105}{r+1.8} = (r+1.8)(r-1.8) \cdot \frac{51}{r-1.8}$$

$$105(r-1.8) = 51(r+1.8)$$

$$105r - 189 = 51r + 91.8$$

$$54r = 280.8$$

$$r = 5.2$$

Check. If Camille's speed on a nonmoving sidewalk is 5.2 ft/sec, then her speed moving forward on the moving sidewalk is $5.2 + 1.8$, or 7 ft/sec, and her speed moving in the opposite direction on the sidewalk is $5.2 - 1.8$, or 3.4 ft/sec. Moving 105 ft at 7 ft/sec takes $\frac{105}{7} = 15$ sec. Moving 51 ft at 3.4 ft/sec takes 15 sec. Since the times are the same, the answer checks.

State. Camille would be walking 5.2 ft/sec on a nonmoving sidewalk.

26. 4.3 ft/sec

27. *Familiarize*. Let $r =$ the speed of the passenger train in mph. Then $r - 14 =$ the speed of the freight train in mph. We organize the information in a table. The time is the same for both trains so we use t for each time.

	Distance	Speed	Time
Passenger train	400	r	t
Freight train	330	$r - 14$	t

Translate. Using the formula Time = Distance/Rate in each row of the table and the fact that the times are the same, we can write an equation.

$$\frac{400}{r} = \frac{330}{r-14}$$

Carry out. We solve the equation.

$$\frac{400}{r} = \frac{330}{r-14}, \text{ LCD is } r(r-14)$$

$$r(r-14) \cdot \frac{400}{r} = r(r-14) \cdot \frac{330}{r-14}$$

$$400(r-14) = 330r$$

$$400r - 5600 = 330r$$

$$-5600 = -70r$$

$$80 = r$$

Check. If the passenger train's speed is 80 mph, then the freight train's speed is $80 - 14$, or 66 mph. Traveling 400 mi at 80 mph takes $\frac{400}{80} = 5$ hr. Traveling 330 mi at 66 mph takes $\frac{330}{66} = 5$ hr. Since the times are the same, the answer checks.

State. The speed of the passenger train is 80 mph; the speed of the freight train is 66 mph.

28. Rosanna: $3\frac{1}{3}$ mph; Simone: $5\frac{1}{3}$ mph

29. Note that 38 mi is 7 mi less than 45 mi and that the local bus travels 7 mph slower than the express. Then the express travels 45 mi in one hr, or 45 mph, and the local bus travels 38 mi in one hr, or 38 mph.

30. A; 46 mph; E: 58 mph

31. *Familiarize*. We let $r =$ the speed of the river, in km/h. Then $2+r =$ the paddleboat's speed downstream, in km/h, and $2 - r =$ the speed upstream, in km/h. The times are the same. Let t represent the time. We organize the information in a table.

	Distance	Speed	Time
Downstream	4	$2 + r$	t
Upstream	1	$2 - r$	t

Translate. Using the formula Time = Distance/Rate in each row of the table and the fact that the times are the same, we can write an equation.

$$\frac{4}{2+r} = \frac{1}{2-r}$$

Carry out. We solve the equation.

$$\frac{4}{2+r} = \frac{1}{2-r},$$

LCD is $(2+r)(2-r)$

$$(2+r)(2-r) \cdot \frac{4}{2+r} = (2+r)(2-r) \cdot \frac{1}{2-r}$$

$$4(2-r) = 2+r$$

$$8 - 4r = 2 + r$$

$$6 = 5r$$

$$\frac{6}{5} = r$$

Check. If $r = \frac{6}{5}$, then the speed downstream is $2 + \frac{6}{5}$, or $\frac{16}{5}$ km/h and the speed upstream is $2 - \frac{6}{5}$, or $\frac{4}{5}$ km/h. The time for the trip downstream is $\frac{4}{16/5}$, or $4 \cdot \frac{5}{16}$, or $\frac{5}{4}$ hr. The time for the trip upstream is $\frac{1}{4/5}$, or $1 \cdot \frac{5}{4}$, or $\frac{5}{4}$ hr. Since the times are the same, the answer checks.

State. The speed of the river is $\frac{6}{5}$ km/h, or $1\frac{1}{5}$ km/h.

32. 9 km/h

33. ***Familiarize***. Let $c =$ the speed of the current, in km/h. Then $7 + c =$ the speed downriver and $7 - c =$ the speed upriver. We organize the information in a table.

	Distance	Speed	Time
Downriver	45	$7+c$	t_1
Upriver	45	$7-c$	t_2

Translate. Using the formula Time = Distance/Rate we see that $t_1 = \frac{45}{7+c}$ and $t_2 = \frac{45}{7-c}$. The total time upriver and back is 14 hr, so $t_1 + t_2 = 14$, or

$$\frac{45}{7+c} + \frac{45}{7-c} = 14.$$

Carry out. We solve the equation. Multiply both sides by the LCD, $(7+c)(7-c)$.

$$(7+c)(7-c)\left(\frac{45}{7+c} + \frac{45}{7-c}\right) = (7+c)(7-c)14$$

$$45(7-c) + 45(7+c) = 14(49 - c^2)$$

$$315 - 45c + 315 + 45c = 686 - 14c^2$$

$$14c^2 - 56 = 0$$

$$14(c+2)(c-2) = 0$$

$$c + 2 = 0 \quad or \quad c - 2 = 0$$

$$c = -2 \quad or \qquad c = 2$$

Check. Since speed cannot be negative in this problem, -2 cannot be a solution of the original problem. If the speed of the current is 2 km/h, the barge travels upriver at $7 - 2$, or 5 km/h. At this rate it takes $\frac{45}{5}$, or 9 hr, to travel 45 km. The barge travels downriver at $7 + 2$, or

9 km/h. At this rate it takes $\frac{45}{9}$, or 5 hr, to travel 45 km. The total travel time is $9 + 5$, or 14 hr. The answer checks.

State. The speed of the current is 2 km/h.

34. Jaime: 23 km/h; Mara: 15 km/h

35. ***Familiarize***. Let $w =$ the wind speed, in mph. Then the speed into the wind is $350 - w$, and the speed with the wind is $350 + w$. We organize the information in a table.

	Distance	Speed	Time
Into the wind	487.5	$350 - w$	t_1
With the wind	487.5	$350 + w$	t_2

Translate. Using the formula Time = Distance/Rate we see that $t_1 = \frac{487.5}{350 - w}$ and $t_2 = \frac{487.5}{350 + w}$. The total time upstream and back is 2.8 hr, so $t_1 + t_2 = 2.8$, or

$$\frac{487.5}{350 - w} + \frac{487.5}{350 + w} = 2.8.$$

Carry out. We solve the equation. Multiply on both sides by the LCD, $(350 - w)(350 + w)$.

$$(350 - w)(350 + w)\left(\frac{487.5}{350 - w} + \frac{487.5}{350 + w}\right) =$$

$$(350 - w)(350 + w)(2.8)$$

$$487.5(350 + w) + 487.5(350 - w) =$$

$$2.8(122,500 - w^2)$$

$$170,625 + 487.5w + 170,625 - 487.5w =$$

$$343,000 - 2.8w^2$$

$$341,250 =$$

$$343,000 - 2.8w^2$$

$$2.8w^2 - 1750 = 0$$

$$2.8(w^2 - 625) = 0$$

$$2.8(w + 25)(w - 25) = 0$$

$$w = -25 \ or \ w = 25$$

Check. We check only 25 since the wind speed cannot be negative. If the wind speed is 25 mph, then the plane's speed into the wind is $350 - 25$, or 325 mph, and the speed with the wind is $350 + 25$, or 375 mph. Flying 487.5 mi into the wind takes $\frac{478.5}{325}$, or 1.5 hr. Flying 487.5 mi with the wind takes $\frac{487.5}{375}$, or 1.3 hr. The total time is $1.5 + 1.3$, or 2.8 hr. The answer checks.

State. The wind speed is 25 mph.

36. 5 m per minute

37. ***Familiarize***. Let $r =$ the speed at which the train actually traveled in mph, and let $t =$ the actual travel time in hours. We organize the information in a table.

	Distance	Speed	Time
Actual speed	120	r	t
Faster speed	120	$r + 10$	$t - 2$

Translate. From the first row of the table we have $120 = rt$, and from the second row we have $120 = (r+10)(t-2)$. Solving the first equation for t, we have $t = \dfrac{120}{r}$. Substituting for t in the second equation, we have

$$120 = (r+10)\left(\frac{120}{r} - 2\right).$$

Carry out. We solve the equation.

$$120 = (r+10)\left(\frac{120}{r} - 2\right)$$

$$120 = 120 - 2r + \frac{1200}{r} - 20$$

$$20 = -2r + \frac{1200}{r}$$

$$r \cdot 20 = r\left(-2r + \frac{1200}{r}\right)$$

$$20r = -2r^2 + 1200$$

$$2r^2 + 20r - 1200 = 0$$

$$2(r^2 + 10r - 600) = 0$$

$$2(r+30)(r-20) = 0$$

$$r = -30 \ or \ r = 20$$

Check. Since speed cannot be negative in this problem, -30 cannot be a solution of the original problem. If the speed is 20 mph, it takes $\dfrac{120}{20}$, or 6 hr, to travel 120 mi. If the speed is 10 mph faster, or 30 mph, it takes $\dfrac{120}{30}$, or 4 hr, to travel 120 mi. Since 4 hr is 2 hr less time than 6 hr, the answer checks.

State. The speed was 20 mph.

38. 12 mph

39. We write a proportion and then solve it.

$$\frac{b}{6} = \frac{7}{4}$$

$$b = \frac{7}{4} \cdot 6$$

$$b = \frac{42}{4}, \text{ or } 10.5$$

$\left(\text{Note that the proportions } \dfrac{6}{b} = \dfrac{4}{7}, \dfrac{b}{7} = \dfrac{6}{4}, \text{ or } \dfrac{7}{b} = \dfrac{4}{6} \text{ could also be used.}\right)$

40. 6.75

$\left(\text{One of the following proportions could also be used: } \dfrac{a}{9} = \dfrac{6}{8}, \dfrac{9}{8} = \dfrac{a}{6}, \dfrac{8}{9} = \dfrac{6}{a}\right)$

41. We write a proportion and then solve it.

$$\frac{4}{f} = \frac{6}{4}$$

$$4f \cdot \frac{4}{f} = 4f \cdot \frac{6}{4}$$

$$16 = 6f$$

$$\frac{8}{3} = f \qquad \text{Simplifying}$$

$\left(\text{One of the following proportions could also be used: } \dfrac{f}{4} = \dfrac{4}{6}, \dfrac{4}{f} = \dfrac{9}{6}, \dfrac{f}{4} = \dfrac{6}{9}, \dfrac{4}{9} = \dfrac{f}{6}, \dfrac{9}{4} = \dfrac{6}{f}\right)$

42. 7.5

$\left(\text{One of the following proportions could also be used: } \dfrac{10}{r} = \dfrac{8}{6}, \dfrac{r}{6} = \dfrac{10}{8}, \dfrac{6}{r} = \dfrac{8}{10}, \dfrac{r}{10} = \dfrac{12}{16}, \dfrac{10}{r} = \dfrac{16}{12}, \dfrac{r}{12} = \dfrac{10}{16}, \dfrac{12}{r} = \dfrac{16}{10}\right)$

43. We write a proportion and then solve it.

$$\frac{4}{10} = \frac{6}{l}$$

$$10l \cdot \frac{4}{10} = 10l \cdot \frac{6}{l}$$

$$4l = 60$$

$$l = 15 \text{ ft}$$

$\left(\text{One of the following proportions could also be used: } \dfrac{4}{6} = \dfrac{10}{l}, \dfrac{10}{4} = \dfrac{l}{6}, \text{ or } \dfrac{6}{4} = \dfrac{l}{10}\right)$

44. 4.5 ft

45.

$$\frac{a}{b} = \frac{c}{d}$$

$$\frac{8}{5} = \frac{6}{d}$$

$$5d \cdot \frac{8}{5} = 5d \cdot \frac{6}{d}$$

$$8d = 30$$

$$d = \frac{30}{8} = \frac{15}{4} \text{ cm, or } 3.75 \text{ cm}$$

46. $\dfrac{90}{7}$ cm

47. Let $c = b + 2$ and $d = b - 2$.

$$\frac{a}{b} = \frac{c}{d}$$

$$\frac{15}{b} = \frac{b+2}{b-2}$$

$$b(b-2) \cdot \frac{15}{b} = b(b-2) \cdot \frac{b+2}{b-2}$$

$$15(b-2) = b(b+2)$$

$$15b - 30 = b^2 + 2b$$

$$0 = b^2 - 13b + 30$$

$$0 = (b-3)(b-10)$$

$$b - 3 = 0 \ or \ b - 10 = 0$$

$$b = 3 \ or \qquad b = 10$$

If $b = 3$ m, then $c = 3 + 2$, or 5 m and $d = 3 - 2$, or 1 m.

If $b = 10$ m, then $c = 10 + 2$, or 12 m and $d = 10 - 2$, or 8 m.

48. $b = 3$ m, $c = 6$ m, $d = 1$ m; $b = 12$ m, $c = 15$ m, $d = 10$ m

49. *Familiarize.* The coffee beans from 14 trees are required to produce 7.7 kilograms of coffee, and we wish to find how many trees are required to produce 308 kilograms of coffee. We can set up ratios:

$$\frac{T}{308} \qquad \frac{14}{7.7}$$

Translate. Assuming the two ratios are the same, we can translate to a proportion.

$$\begin{array}{l}\text{Trees} \rightarrow \\ \text{Kilograms} \rightarrow\end{array} \frac{T}{308} = \frac{14}{7.7} \begin{array}{l}\leftarrow \text{Trees} \\ \leftarrow \text{Kilograms}\end{array}$$

Carry out. We solve the proportion.

$$308 \cdot \frac{T}{308} = 308 \cdot \frac{14}{7.7}$$

$$T = \frac{4312}{7.7}$$

$$T = 560$$

Check. $\dfrac{560}{308} = 1.8\overline{1} \qquad \dfrac{14}{7.7} = 1.8\overline{1}$

The ratios are the same.

State. 560 trees are required to produce 308 kg of coffee.

50. 1.92 g

51. *Familiarize.* U.S. women earn 77 cents for each dollar earned by a man. This gives us one ratio, expressed in dollars: $\dfrac{0.77}{1}$. If a male sales manager earns \$42,000, we want to find how much a female would earn for comparable work. This gives us a second ratio, also expressed in dollars: $\dfrac{F}{42,000}$.

Translate. Assuming the two ratios are the same, we can translate to a proportion.

$$\begin{array}{l}\text{Female's} \\ \text{earnings} \rightarrow \\ \text{Male's earnings} \rightarrow\end{array} \frac{0.77}{1} = \frac{F}{42,000} \begin{array}{l}\leftarrow \\ \text{earnings} \\ \leftarrow \text{Male's earnings}\end{array} \begin{array}{l}\text{Female's}\end{array}$$

Carry out. We solve the proportion.

$$42,000 \cdot \frac{0.77}{1} = 42,000 \cdot \frac{F}{42,000}$$

$$32,340 = F$$

Check.

$$\frac{0.77}{1} = 0.77 \qquad \frac{32,340}{42,000} = 0.77$$

The ratios are the same.

State. If a male sales manager earns \$42,000, a female would earn \$32,340 for comparable work.

52. $1\dfrac{11}{39}$ kg

53. *Familiarize.* The ratio of deer tagged to the total number of deer in the preserve, D, is $\dfrac{318}{D}$. Of the 168 deer caught later, 56 are tagged. The ratio of tagged deer to deer caught is $\dfrac{56}{168}$.

Translate. We translate to a proportion.

$$\begin{array}{l}\text{Deer originally} \\ \text{tagged} \\ \text{Deer} \\ \text{in preserve}\end{array} \begin{array}{l}\rightarrow \\ \rightarrow\end{array} \frac{318}{D} = \frac{56}{168} \begin{array}{l}\leftarrow \\ \leftarrow\end{array} \begin{array}{l}\text{Tagged deer} \\ \text{caught later} \\ \text{Deer} \\ \text{caught later}\end{array}$$

Carry out. We solve the proportion. We multiply by the LCD, $168D$.

$$168D \cdot \frac{318}{D} = 168D \cdot \frac{56}{168}$$

$$168 \cdot 318 = D \cdot 56$$

$$\frac{166 \cdot 318}{56} = D$$

$$954 = D$$

Check.

$$\frac{318}{954} = 0.\overline{3} \qquad \frac{56}{168} = 0.\overline{3}$$

The ratios are the same.

State. We estimate that there are 954 deer in the preserve.

54. 184 moose

55. *Familiarize.* Let $M =$ the number of miles Emmanuel will drive in 4 years if he continues to drive at the current rate. We set up two ratios:

$$\frac{16,000}{1\frac{1}{2}} \qquad \frac{M}{4}$$

Translate. We write a proportion.

$$\begin{array}{l}\text{Miles} \rightarrow \\ \text{Years} \rightarrow\end{array} \frac{16,000}{1.5} = \frac{M}{4} \begin{array}{l}\leftarrow \text{Miles} \\ \leftarrow \text{Years}\end{array}$$

Carry out. We solve the proportion.

$$1.5(4) \cdot \frac{16,000}{1.5} = 1.5(4) \cdot \frac{M}{4}$$

$$64,000 = 1.5M$$

$$42,666.\overline{6} = M$$

If this possible answer is correct, Emmanuel will not exceed the 45,000 miles allowed for four years.

Check.

$$\frac{16,000}{1.5} = 10,666.\overline{6} \qquad \frac{42,666.\overline{6}}{4} = 10,666.\overline{6}$$

The ratios are the same.

State. At this rate, Emmanuel will not exceed the mileage allowed for four years.

56. 20 duds

57. *Familiarize.* The ratio of the weight of an object on the moon to the weight of an object on Earth is 0.16 to 1.

a) We wish to find how much a 12-ton rocket would weigh on the moon.

b) We wish to find how much a 180-lb astronaut would weigh on the moon.

We can set up ratios.

$$\frac{0.16}{1} \qquad \frac{T}{12} \qquad \frac{P}{180}$$

Translate. Assuming the ratios are the same, we can translate to proportions.

a) Weight on moon → $\dfrac{0.16}{1} = \dfrac{T}{12}$ ← Weight on moon
   Weight → on Earth   ← Weight on Earth

b) Weight on moon → $\dfrac{0.16}{1} = \dfrac{P}{180}$ ← Weight on moon
   Weight → on Earth   ← Weight on Earth

Carry out. We solve each proportion.

a) $\dfrac{0.16}{1} = \dfrac{T}{12}$ b) $\dfrac{0.16}{1} = \dfrac{P}{180}$

$12(0.16) = T$ $120(0.16) = P$

$1.92 = T$ $28.8 = P$

Check. $\dfrac{0.16}{1} = 0.16$, $\dfrac{1.92}{12} = 0.16$, and $\dfrac{28.8}{180} = 0.16$. The ratios are the same.

State.

a) A 12-ton rocket would weigh 1.92 tons on the moon.

b) A 180-lb astronaut would weigh 28.8 lb on the moon.

58. a) 4.8 tons

b) 48 lb

59. *Writing Exercise*

60. *Writing Exercise*

61. Graph: $y = 2x - 6$.

We select some x-values and compute y-values.

If $x = 1$, then $y = 2 \cdot 1 - 6 = -4$.

If $x = 3$, then $y = 2 \cdot 3 - 6 = 0$.

If $x = 5$, then $y = 2 \cdot 5 - 6 = 4$.

x	y	(x, y)
1	-4	$(1, -4)$
3	0	$(3, 0)$
5	4	$(5, 4)$

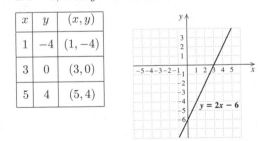

62.

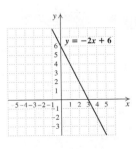

63. Graph: $3x + 2y = 12$.

We can replace either variable with a number and then calculate the other coordinate. We will find the intercepts and one other point.

If $y = 0$, we have:

$$3x + 2 \cdot 0 = 12$$
$$3x = 12$$
$$x = 4$$

The x-intercept is $(4, 0)$.

If $x = 0$, we have:

$$3 \cdot 0 + 2y = 12$$
$$2y = 12$$
$$y = 6$$

The y-intercept is $(0, 6)$.

If $y = -3$, we have:

$$3x + 2(-3) = 12$$
$$3x - 6 = 12$$
$$3x = 18$$
$$x = 6$$

The point $(6, -3)$ is on the graph.

We plot these points and draw a line through them.

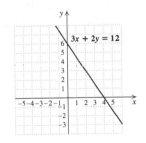

64.

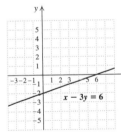

65. Graph: $y = -\dfrac{3}{4}x + 2$

We select some x-values and compute y-values. We use multiples of 4 to avoid fractions.

If $x = -4$, then $y = -\dfrac{3}{4}(-4) + 2 = 5$.

If $x = 0$, then $y = -\dfrac{3}{4} \cdot 0 + 2 = 2$.

If $x = 4$, then $y = -\dfrac{3}{4} \cdot 4 + 2 = -1$.

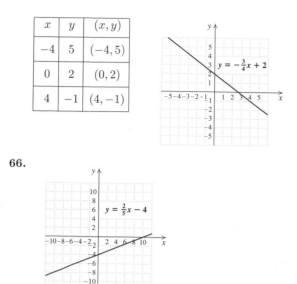

x	y	(x, y)
-4	5	$(-4, 5)$
0	2	$(0, 2)$
4	-1	$(4, -1)$

66.

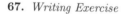

67. *Writing Exercise*

68. *Writing Exercise*

69. Familiarize. If the drainage gate is closed, $\frac{1}{9}$ of the bog is filled in 1 hr. If the bog is not being filled, $\frac{1}{11}$ of the bog is drained in 1 hr. If the bog is being filled with the drainage gate left open, $\frac{1}{9} - \frac{1}{11}$ of the bog is filled in 1 hr. Let t = the time it takes to fill the bog with the drainage gate left open.

Translate. We want to find t such that

$$t\left(\frac{1}{9} - \frac{1}{11}\right) = 1, \text{ or } \frac{t}{9} - \frac{t}{11} = 1.$$

Carry out. We solve the equation. First we multiply by the LCD, 99.

$$99\left(\frac{t}{9} - \frac{t}{11}\right) = 99 \cdot 1$$

$$11t - 9t = 99$$

$$2t = 99$$

$$t = \frac{99}{2}$$

Check. In $\frac{99}{2}$ hr, we have $\frac{99}{2}\left(\frac{1}{9} - \frac{1}{11}\right) = \frac{11}{2} - \frac{9}{2} = \frac{2}{2} =$ 1 full bog.

State. It will take $\frac{99}{2}$, or $49\frac{1}{2}$ hr, to fill the bog.

70. 40 min

71. Monica's speed downstream is $12 + 4$, or 16 mph. Using Time = Distance/Rate, we find that the time it will take Monica to motor 3 mi downstream is 3/16 hr. We can convert this time to minutes:

$$\frac{3}{16} \text{ hr} = \frac{3}{16} \times 1 \text{ hr} = \frac{3}{16} \times 60 \text{ min} = 11.25 \text{ min}$$

72. 30 min

73. Familiarize. Let p = the number of people per hour moved by the 60 cm-wide escalator. Then $2p$ = the number of people per hour moved by the 100 cm-wide escalator. We convert 1575 people per 14 minutes to people per hour:

$$\frac{1575 \text{ people}}{14 \text{ min}} \cdot \frac{60 \text{ min}}{1 \text{ hr}} = 6750 \text{ people/hr}$$

Translate. We use the information that together the escalators move 6750 people per hour to write an equation.

$$p + 2p = 6750$$

Carry out. We solve the equation.

$$p + 2p = 6750$$

$$3p = 6750$$

$$p = 2250$$

Check. If the 60 cm-wide escalator moves 2250 people per hour, then the 100 cm-wide escalator moves $2 \cdot 2250$, or 4500 people per hour. Together, they move $2250 + 4500$, or 6750 people per hour. The answer checks.

State. The 60 cm-wide escalator moves 2250 people per hour.

74. 700 mi from the airport

75. Familiarize. Let d = the distance, in miles, the paddleboat can cruise upriver before it is time to turn around. The boat's speed upriver is $12 - 5$, or 7 mph, and its speed downriver is $12 + 5$, or 17 mph. We organize the information in a table.

	Distance	Speed	Time
Upriver	d	7	t_1
Downriver	d	17	t_2

Translate. Using the formula Time = Distance/Rate we see that $t_1 = \frac{d}{7}$ and $t_2 = \frac{d}{17}$. The time upriver and back is 3 hr, so $t_1 + t_2 = 3$, or

$$\frac{d}{7} + \frac{d}{17} = 3.$$

Carry out. We solve the equation.

$$7 \cdot 17\left(\frac{d}{7} + \frac{d}{17}\right) = 7 \cdot 17 \cdot 3$$

$$17d + 7d = 357$$

$$24d = 357$$

$$d = \frac{119}{8}$$

Check. Traveling $\frac{119}{8}$ mi upriver at a speed of 7 mph takes $\frac{119/8}{7} = \frac{17}{8}$ hr. Traveling $\frac{119}{8}$ mi downriver at a speed of 17 mph takes $\frac{119/8}{17} = \frac{7}{8}$ hr. The total time is $\frac{17}{8} + \frac{7}{8} = \frac{24}{8} = 3$ hr. The answer checks.

State. The pilot can go $\frac{119}{8}$, or $14\frac{7}{8}$ mi upriver before it is time to turn around.

76. $66\frac{2}{3}$ ft

77. Familiarize. Let t = the number of minutes after 5:00 at which the hands will first be together. When the minute hand moves through t minutes, the hour hand moves through $t/12$ minutes. At 5:00 the hour hand is on the 25-minute mark, so at t minutes after 5:00 it is at $25 + t/12$.

Translate. We equate the positions of the minute hand and the hour hand.

$$t = 25 + \frac{t}{12}$$

Carry out. We solve the equation.

$$t = 25 + \frac{t}{12}$$
$$12 \cdot t = 12\left(25 + \frac{t}{12}\right)$$
$$12t = 300 + t$$
$$11t = 300$$
$$t = \frac{300}{11}, \text{ or } 27\frac{3}{11}$$

Check. When the minute hand is at $27\frac{3}{11}$ minutes after 5:00, the hour hand is at $25 + \dfrac{\frac{300}{11}}{12} =$

$$25 + \frac{300}{11} \cdot \frac{1}{12} = 25 + \frac{25}{11} = 25 + 2\frac{3}{11} = 27\frac{3}{11} \text{ minutes}$$

after 5:00 also. The answer checks.

State. After 5:00 the hands on a clock will first be together in $27\frac{3}{11}$ minutes or at $27\frac{3}{11}$ minutes after 5:00.

78. $\dfrac{D}{B} = \dfrac{C}{A}$; $\dfrac{A}{C} = \dfrac{B}{D}$; $\dfrac{D}{C} = \dfrac{B}{A}$

79. Familiarize. Let r = the speed of the current in km/h. Then $3r$ = the boat's speed in still water. Traveling up the river, the boat's speed is $3r - r$, or $2r$. Traveling down the river the boat's speed is $3r + r$, or $4r$. The total distance traveled is 100 km, so the distance each way is $\dfrac{100}{2}$, or 50 km. We organize the information in a table.

	Distance	Speed	Time
Up the river	50	$2r$	t_1
Down the river	50	$4r$	t_2

Translate. Using the formula Time = Distance/Rate in each row of the table and the fact that the total time of the trip is 10 hr, we can write an equation.

$$\frac{50}{2r} + \frac{50}{4r} = 10$$

Carry out. We solve the equation.

$$\frac{50}{2r} + \frac{50}{4r} = 10, \text{ LCD is } 4r$$
$$4r\left(\frac{50}{2r} + \frac{50}{4r}\right) = 4r \cdot 10$$
$$4r \cdot \frac{50}{2r} + 4r \cdot \frac{50}{4r} = 40r$$
$$100 + 50 = 40r$$
$$150 = 40r$$
$$\frac{15}{4} = r, \text{ or }$$
$$3\frac{3}{4} = r$$

Check. If the speed of the current is $\dfrac{15}{4}$ km/h, then the boat's speed in still water is $3 \cdot \dfrac{15}{4}$, or $\dfrac{45}{4}$ km/h, its speed up the river is $\dfrac{45}{4} - \dfrac{15}{4}$, or $\dfrac{30}{4}$, or $\dfrac{15}{2}$ km/h, and its speed down the river is $\dfrac{45}{4} + \dfrac{15}{4} = \dfrac{60}{4}$, or 15 km/h. It will take $\dfrac{50}{15/2}$, or $\dfrac{20}{3}$ hr, to travel up the river and $\dfrac{50}{15}$, or $\dfrac{10}{3}$ hr, to travel down the river. The total time of the trip is $\dfrac{20}{3} + \dfrac{10}{3}$, or $\dfrac{30}{3}$, or 10 hr. The answer checks.

State. The speed of the current is $3\frac{3}{4}$ km/h.

80. 30 mi

81. Traveling 100 km at 40 km/h takes $\dfrac{100}{40}$, or $\dfrac{5}{2}$ hr.

Traveling 100 km at 60 km/h takes $\dfrac{100}{60}$, or $\dfrac{5}{3}$ hr. The total time of the trip is $\dfrac{5}{2} + \dfrac{5}{3}$, or $\dfrac{25}{6}$ hr. We use the formula

$$\text{Average speed} = \frac{\text{Total distance}}{\text{Total time}}$$
$$= \frac{200}{25/6}$$
$$= 48$$

The average speed was 48 km/h.

82. $51\frac{3}{7}$ mph

83. *Writing Exercise*

84. *Writing Exercise*

Exercise Set 7.8

1. $\dfrac{W_1}{W_2} = \dfrac{d_1}{d_2}$

$\dfrac{d_2 W_1}{W_2} = d_1$ Multiplying by d_2

2. $W_1 = \dfrac{d_1 W_2}{d_2}$

3.
$$s = \frac{(v_1 + v_2)t}{2}$$

$$2s = (v_1 + v_2)t \quad \text{Multiplying by 2}$$

$$\frac{2s}{t} = v_1 + v_2 \quad \text{Dividing by } t$$

$$\frac{2s}{t} - v_2 = v_1$$

This result can also be expressed as $v_1 = \dfrac{2s - tv_2}{t}$.

4. $t = \dfrac{2s}{v_1 + v_2}$

5.
$$\frac{1}{f} = \frac{1}{d_i} + \frac{1}{d_o}$$

$$fd_id_o \cdot \frac{1}{f} = fd_id_o\left(\frac{1}{d_i} + \frac{1}{d_o}\right) \quad \begin{array}{l}\text{Multiplying by}\\\text{the LCD}\end{array}$$

$$d_id_o = fd_id_o \cdot \frac{1}{d_i} + fd_id_o \cdot \frac{1}{d_o}$$

$$d_id_o = fd_o + fd_i$$

$$d_id_o = f(d_o + d_i) \quad \text{Factoring out } f$$

$$\frac{d_id_o}{d_o + d_i} = f \quad \text{Multiplying by } \frac{1}{d_o + d_i}$$

6. $R = \dfrac{r_1 r_2}{r_2 + r_1}$

7.
$$I = \frac{2V}{R + 2r}$$

$$I(R + 2r) = \frac{2V}{R + 2r} \cdot (R + 2r) \quad \begin{array}{l}\text{Multiplying}\\\text{by the LCD}\end{array}$$

$$I(R + 2r) = 2V$$

$$R + 2r = \frac{2V}{I}$$

$$R = \frac{2V}{I} - 2r, \text{ or } \frac{2V - 2Ir}{I}$$

8. $r = \dfrac{2V - IR}{2I}$

9.
$$R = \frac{gs}{g + s}$$

$$(g + s) \cdot R = (g + s) \cdot \frac{gs}{g + s} \quad \begin{array}{l}\text{Multiplying}\\\text{by the LCD}\end{array}$$

$$Rg + Rs = gs$$

$$Rs = gs - Rg$$

$$Rs = g(s - R) \quad \text{Factoring out } g$$

$$\frac{Rs}{s - R} = g \quad \text{Multiplying by } \frac{1}{s - R}$$

10. $t = \dfrac{Kr}{r + K}$

11.
$$I = \frac{nE}{R + nr}$$

$$I(R + nr) = \frac{nE}{R + nr} \cdot (R + nr) \quad \begin{array}{l}\text{Multiplying}\\\text{by the LCD}\end{array}$$

$$IR + Inr = nE$$

$$IR = nE - Inr$$

$$IR = n(E - Ir)$$

$$\frac{IR}{E - Ir} = n$$

12. $r = \dfrac{nE - IR}{In}$

13.
$$\frac{1}{p} + \frac{1}{q} = \frac{1}{f}$$

$$pqf\left(\frac{1}{p} + \frac{1}{q}\right) = pqf \cdot \frac{1}{f} \quad \begin{array}{l}\text{Multiplying by}\\\text{the LCD}\end{array}$$

$$qf + pf = pq$$

$$pf = pq - qf$$

$$pf = q(p - f)$$

$$\frac{pf}{p - f} = q$$

14. $p = \dfrac{qf}{q - f}$

15.
$$S = \frac{H}{m(t_1 - t_2)}$$

$$(t_1 - t_2)S = \frac{H}{m} \quad \text{Multiplying by } t_1 - t_2$$

$$t_1 - t_2 = \frac{H}{Sm} \quad \text{Dividing by } S$$

$$t_1 = \frac{H}{Sm} + t_2, \text{ or } \frac{H + Smt_2}{Sm}$$

16. $H = m(t_1 - t_2)S$

17.
$$\frac{E}{e} = \frac{R + r}{r}$$

$$er \cdot \frac{E}{e} = er \cdot \frac{R + r}{r} \quad \text{Multiplying by the LCD}$$

$$Er = e(R + r)$$

$$Er = eR + er$$

$$Er - er = eR$$

$$r(E - e) = eR$$

$$r = \frac{eR}{E - e}$$

18. $R = \dfrac{er}{E - e}$

19.
$$S = \frac{a}{1 - r}$$

$$(1 - r)S = a \quad \text{Multiplying by the LCD, } 1 - r$$

$$1 - r = \frac{a}{S} \quad \text{Dividing by } S$$

$$1 - \frac{a}{S} = r \quad \text{Adding } r \text{ and } -\frac{a}{S}$$

This result can also be expressed as $r = \dfrac{S - a}{S}$.

20. $a = \dfrac{S - Sr}{1 - r^n}$

21.
$$c = \dfrac{f}{(a+b)c}$$
$$\dfrac{a+b}{c} \cdot c = \dfrac{a+b}{c} \cdot \dfrac{f}{(a+b)c}$$
$$a + b = \dfrac{f}{c^2}$$

22. $c + f = \dfrac{g}{d^2}$

23.
$$I_t = \dfrac{I_f}{1 - T}$$
$$(1 - T)I_t = I_f$$
$$1 - T = \dfrac{I_f}{I_t}$$
$$-T = \dfrac{I_f}{I_t} - 1$$
$$-1 \cdot (-T) = -1 \cdot \left(\dfrac{I_f}{I_t} - 1 \right)$$
$$T = -\dfrac{I_f}{I_t} + 1, \text{ or } 1 - \dfrac{I_f}{I_t}, \text{ or } \dfrac{I_t - I_f}{I_t}$$

24. $r = \dfrac{A}{P} - 1, \text{ or } \dfrac{A - P}{P}$

25.
$$\dfrac{1}{R} = \dfrac{1}{r_1} + \dfrac{1}{r_2}$$
$$Rr_1r_2 \cdot \dfrac{1}{R} = Rr_1r_2 \left(\dfrac{1}{r_1} + \dfrac{1}{r_2} \right)$$
$$r_1r_2 = Rr_1r_2 \cdot \dfrac{1}{r_1} + Rr_1r_2 \cdot \dfrac{1}{r_2}$$
$$r_1r_2 = Rr_2 + Rr_1$$
$$r_1r_2 - Rr_2 = Rr_1$$
$$r_2(r_1 - R) = Rr_1$$
$$r_2 = \dfrac{Rr_1}{r_1 - R}$$

26. $t = \dfrac{ab}{b + a}$

27.
$$a = \dfrac{v_2 - v_1}{t_2 - t_1}$$
$$(t_2 - t_1)a = v_2 - v_1$$
$$t_2 - t_1 = \dfrac{v_2 - v_1}{a}$$
$$-t_1 = \dfrac{v_2 - v_1}{a} - t_2$$
$$t_1 = t_2 - \dfrac{v_2 - v_1}{a}$$

28. $t_2 = \dfrac{d_2 - d_1}{v} + t_1, \text{ or } \dfrac{d_2 - d_1 + t_1 v}{v}$

29.
$$A = \dfrac{2Tt + Qq}{2T + Q}$$
$$(2T + Q) \cdot A = (2T + Q) \cdot \dfrac{2Tt + Qq}{2T + Q}$$
$$2AT + AQ = 2Tt + Qq$$
$$AQ - Qq = 2Tt - 2AT \quad \text{Adding } -2AT$$
$$\text{and } -Qq$$
$$Q(A - q) = 2Tt - 2AT$$
$$Q = \dfrac{2Tt - 2AT}{A - q}$$

30. $D = \dfrac{dR}{L} + d, \text{ or } \dfrac{dR + dL}{L}$

31.
$$y = kx$$
$$28 = k \cdot 4 \quad \text{Substituting}$$
$$7 = k$$
The variation constant is 7.
The equation of variation is $y = 7x$.

32. $k = \dfrac{5}{12}; \ y = \dfrac{5}{12}x$

33.
$$y = kx$$
$$3.4 = k \cdot 2 \quad \text{Substituting}$$
$$1.7 = k$$
The variation constant is 1.7.
The equation of variation is $y = 1.7x$.

34. $k = \dfrac{2}{5}; \ y = \dfrac{2}{5}x$

35.
$$y = kx$$
$$2 = k \cdot \dfrac{1}{3} \quad \text{Substituting}$$
$$6 = k \qquad \text{Multiplying by 3}$$
The variation constant is 6.

The equation of variation is $y = 6x$.

36. $k = 1.8; \ y = 1.8x$

37. *Familiarize.* Because of the phrase "$d \ldots$ varies directly as $\ldots m$," we express the distance as a function of the mass. Thus we have $d(m) = km$. We know that $d(3) = 20$.

Translate. We find the variation constant and then find the equation of variation.
$$d(m) = km$$
$$d(3) = k \cdot 3 \quad \text{Replacing } m \text{ with 3}$$
$$20 = k \cdot 3 \quad \text{Replacing } d(3) \text{ with 20}$$
$$\dfrac{20}{3} = k \qquad \text{Variation constant}$$

The equation of variation is $d(m) = \dfrac{20}{3}m$.

Carry out. We compute $d(5)$.
$$d(m) = \dfrac{20}{3}m$$
$$d(5) = \dfrac{20}{3} \cdot 5 \quad \text{Replacing } m \text{ with 5}$$
$$d(5) = \dfrac{100}{3}, \text{ or } 33\dfrac{1}{3}$$

Check. Reexamine the calculations. Note that the answer seems reasonable since $\frac{3}{20}$ and $\frac{5}{100/3}$ are equal.

State. The spring is stretched $33\frac{1}{3}$ cm by a hanging object with mass 5 kg.

38. 6 amperes

39. Familiarize. Because N varies directly as the number of people P using the cans, we write N as a function of P: $N(P) = kP$. We know that $N(250) = 60,000$.

Translate.
$$N(P) = kP$$
$$N(250) = k \cdot 250 \quad \text{Replacing } P \text{ with } 250$$
$$60,000 = k \cdot 250 \quad \text{Replacing } N(250) \text{ with } 60,000$$
$$\frac{60,000}{250} = k$$
$$240 = k \quad \text{Variation constant}$$
$$N(P) = 240P \quad \text{Equation of variation}$$

Carry out. Find $N(1,008,000)$.
$$N(P) = 240P$$
$$N(1,008,000) = 240 \cdot 1,008,000$$
$$= 241,920,000$$

Check. Reexamine the calculation.

State. 241,920,000 aluminum cans are used each year in Dallas.

40. $4.29

41. Since we have direct variation and $48 = \frac{1}{2} \cdot 96$, then the result is $\frac{1}{2} \cdot 64$ kg, or 32 kg. We could also do this problem as follows.

Familiarize. Because W varies directly as the total mass, we write $W(m) = km$. We know that $W(96) = 64$.

Translate.
$$W(m) = km$$
$$W(96) = k \cdot 96 \quad \text{Replacing } m \text{ with } 96$$
$$64 = k \cdot 96 \quad \text{Replacing } W(96) \text{ with } 64$$
$$\frac{2}{3} = k \quad \text{Variation constant}$$
$$W(m) = \frac{2}{3}m \quad \text{Equation of variation}$$

Carry out. Find $W(48)$.
$$W(m) = \frac{2}{3}m$$
$$W(48) = \frac{2}{3} \cdot 48$$
$$= 32$$

Check. Reexamine the calculations.

State. There are 32 kg of water in a 64 kg person.

42. 40 lb

43. Familiarize. Because the f-stop varies directly as F, we write $f(F) = kF$. We know that $F(150) = 6.3$.

Translate.
$$f(F) = kF$$
$$f(150) = k \cdot 150 \quad \text{Replacing } F \text{ with } 150$$
$$6.3 = k \cdot 150 \quad \text{Replacing } f(150) \text{ with } 6.3$$
$$0.042 = k \quad \text{Variation constant}$$
$$f(F) = 0.042F \quad \text{Equation of variation}$$

Carry out. Find $f(80)$.
$$f(F) = 0.042F$$
$$f(80) = 0.042(80)$$
$$= 3.36$$

Check. Reexamine the calculations.

State. An 80 mm focal length has an f-stop of 3.36.

44. 7,700,000 tons

45.
$$y = \frac{k}{x}$$
$$3 = \frac{k}{20} \quad \text{Substituting}$$
$$60 = k$$

The variation constant is 60.

The equation of variation is $y = \dfrac{60}{x}$.

46. $k = 64$; $y = \dfrac{64}{x}$

47.
$$y = \frac{k}{x}$$
$$28 = \frac{k}{4} \quad \text{Substituting}$$
$$112 = k$$

The variation constant is 112.

The equation of variation is $y = \dfrac{112}{x}$.

48. $k = 45$; $y = \dfrac{45}{x}$

49.
$$y = \frac{k}{x}$$
$$27 = \frac{k}{\frac{1}{3}} \quad \text{Substituting}$$
$$9 = k$$

The variation constant is 9.

The equation of variation is $y = \dfrac{9}{x}$.

50. $k = 9$; $y = \dfrac{9}{x}$

51. *Familiarize.* Because of the phrase "*t* varies inversely as …*u*," we write $t(u) = k/u$. We know that $t(4) = 70$.

Translate. We find the variation constant and then we find the equation of variation.

$$t(u) = \frac{k}{u}$$

$$t(4) = \frac{k}{4} \qquad \text{Replacing } u \text{ with } 4$$

$$70 = \frac{k}{4} \qquad \text{Replacing } t(4) \text{ with } 70$$

$$280 = k \qquad \text{Variation constant}$$

$$t(u) = \frac{280}{u} \qquad \text{Equation of variation}$$

Carry out. We find $t(14)$.

$$t(14) = \frac{280}{14} = 20$$

Check. Reexamine the calculations. Note that, as expected, as the UV rating increases, the time it takes to burn goes down.

State. It will take 20 min to burn when the UV rating is 14.

52. $\frac{2}{9}$ ampere

53. *Familiarize.* Because V varies inversely as P, we write $V(P) = k/P$. We know that $V(32) = 200$.

Translate.

$$V(P) = \frac{k}{P}$$

$$V(32) = \frac{k}{32} \qquad \text{Replacing } P \text{ with } 32$$

$$200 = \frac{k}{32} \qquad \text{Replacing } V(32) \text{ with } 200$$

$$6400 = k \qquad \text{Variation constant}$$

$$V(P) = \frac{6400}{P} \qquad \text{Equation of variation}$$

Carry out. Find $V(40)$.

$$V(40) = \frac{6400}{40}$$

$$= 160$$

Check. Reexamine the calculations.

State. The volume will be 160 cm³.

54. 27 min

55. *Familiarize.* Because T varies inversely as P, we write $T(p) = k/p$. We know that $T(7) = 5$.

Translate. We find the variation constant and the equation of variation.

$$T(P) = \frac{k}{p}$$

$$T(7) = \frac{k}{7} \qquad \text{Replacing } P \text{ with } 7$$

$$5 = \frac{k}{7} \qquad \text{Replacing } T(P) \text{ with } 5$$

$$35 = k \qquad \text{Variation constant}$$

$$T(P) = \frac{35}{P} \qquad \text{Equation of variation}$$

Carry out. We find $T(10)$.

$$T(10) = \frac{35}{10}$$

$$= 3.5$$

Check. Reexamine the calculations.

State. It would take 3.5 hr for 10 volunteers to complete the job.

56. 450 m

57.

$$y = kx^2$$

$$6 = k \cdot 3^2 \qquad \text{Substituting}$$

$$6 = 9k$$

$$\frac{6}{9} = k$$

$$\frac{2}{3} = k \qquad \text{Variation constant}$$

The equation of variation is $y = \frac{2}{3}x^2$.

58. $y = 15x^2$

59.

$$y = \frac{k}{x^2}$$

$$6 = \frac{k}{3^2} \qquad \text{Substituting}$$

$$6 = \frac{k}{9}$$

$$6 \cdot 9 = k$$

$$54 = k \qquad \text{Variation constant}$$

The equation of variation is $y = \frac{54}{x^2}$.

60. $y = \frac{0.0015}{x^2}$

61.

$$y = kxz^2$$

$$105 = k \cdot 14 \cdot 5^2 \qquad \text{Substituting 105 for } y,$$
$$\qquad \qquad \qquad \qquad 14 \text{ for } x, \text{ and 5 for } z$$

$$105 = 350k$$

$$\frac{105}{350} = k$$

$$0.3 = k$$

The equation of variation is $y = 0.3xz^2$.

62. $y = \frac{xz}{w}$

63.
$$y = k \cdot \frac{wx^2}{z}$$
$$49 = k \cdot \frac{3 \cdot 7^2}{12} \quad \text{Substituting}$$
$$4 = k \quad \text{Variation constant}$$

The equation of variation is $y = \dfrac{4wx^2}{z}$.

64. $y = \dfrac{6x}{wz^2}$

65. Familiarize. I varies inversely as d^2, so we write $I = k/d^2$. We know that $I = 90$ when $d = 5$.

Translate. Find k.
$$I = \frac{k}{d^2}$$
$$90 = \frac{k}{5^2}$$
$$2250 = k$$

$$I = \frac{2250}{d^2} \quad \text{Equation of variation}$$

Carry out. Substitute 7.5 for d and find for I.
$$I = \frac{2250}{(7.5)^2} = \frac{2250}{56.25} = 40$$

Check. Reexamine the calculations.

State. The intensity is 40 W/m^2 at a distance of 7.5 m from the bulb.

66. 72 ft

67. Familiarize. Because V varies directly as T and inversely as P, we write $V = kT/P$. We know that $V = 231$ when $T = 42$ and $P = 20$.

Translate. Find k and the equation of variation.
$$V = \frac{kT}{P}$$
$$231 = \frac{k \cdot 42}{20}$$
$$\frac{20}{42} \cdot 231 = k$$
$$110 = k$$
$$V = \frac{110T}{P} \quad \text{Equation of variation}$$

Carry out. Substitute 30 for T and 15 for P and find V.
$$V = \frac{110 \cdot 30}{15} = 220$$

Check. Reexamine the calculations.

State. The volume is 220 cm^3 when $T = 30°$ and $P = 15$ kg/cm^2.

68. 2.56 W/m^2

69. Familiarize. The drag W varies jointly as the surface area A and velocity v, so we write $W = kAv$. We know that $W = 222$ when $A = 37.8$ and $v = 40$.

Translate. Find k.
$$W = kAv$$
$$222 = k(37.8)(40)$$
$$\frac{222}{37.8(40)} = k$$
$$\frac{37}{252} = k$$
$$W = \frac{37}{252}Av \quad \text{Equation of variation}$$

Carry out. Substitute 51 for A and 430 for W and solve for v.
$$430 = \frac{37}{252} \cdot 51 \cdot v$$
$$57.42 \text{ mph} \approx v$$

(If we had used the rounded value 0.1468 for k, the resulting speed would have been approximately 57.43 mph.)

Check. Reexamine the calculations.

State. The car must travel about 57.42 mph.

70. About 28.3 ft^2

71. a) We graph the data, letting x represent the UV index and y represent the safe exposure time, in minutes.

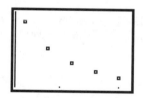

The points lie approximately on the graph of a function of the type $f(x) = \dfrac{k}{x}$, so it appears that the safe exposure time varies inversely as the UV index.

b)
$$y = \frac{k}{x}$$
$$50 = \frac{k}{6} \quad \text{Substituting 6 for } x \text{ and 50 for } y$$
$$300 = k \quad \text{Variation constant}$$

The equation of variation is $y = \dfrac{300}{x}$.

c) We substitute 3 for x in the equation of variation.
$$y = \frac{300}{x}$$
$$y = \frac{300}{3}$$
$$y = 100$$

When the UV index is 3, the safe exposure time for people with less sensitive skin is 100 min.

72. a) Inverse

b) $y = \dfrac{20}{x}$

c) 10 ft

73. a) We graph the data, letting x represent the number of persons ordering merchandise by mail, in millions, and y represent the number of persons ordering by phone, in millions.

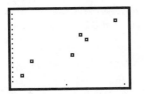

The points lie approximately on the graph of a function of the form $f(x) = kx$, so it appears that the number of people ordering by mail varies directly as the number of people ordering by phone.

b) $\quad y = kx$

$12.775 = 11.813x$ Substituting 11.813 for x and 12.775 for y

$1.08 \approx x$ Variation constant

The equation of variation is $y \approx 1.08x$.

c) Substitute 8 for x in the equation of variation.

$$y \approx 1.08x$$

$$y \approx 1.08(8)$$

$$y \approx 8.64$$

If 8 million people order by mail, then 8.64 million people will order by phone.

74. a) Directly

b) $y \approx 1.66x$

c) 0.747 million automobiles

75. *Writing Exercise*

76. *Writing Exercise*

77. $f(x) = \dfrac{2x - 1}{x^2 + 1}$

$x^2 + 1 > 0$ for all real numbers x, so the domain of f is $\{x | x \text{ is a real number}\}$.

78. All real numbers

79. $f(x) = \dfrac{1}{|2x - 1|}$ cannot be calculated when $|2x - 1| = 0$, or $2x - 1 = 0$. We find the value of x for which $2x - 1 = 0$:

$$2x - 1 = 0$$

$$2x = 1$$

$$x = \frac{1}{2}$$

The domain of f is $\left\{x \middle| x \text{ is a real number } and \ x \neq \dfrac{1}{2}\right\}$.

80. $8a^3 - 2a$

81. $t^3 + 8b^3 = t^3 + (2b)^3 = (t + 2b)(t^2 - 2tb + 4b^2)$

82. $-\dfrac{5}{3}, \dfrac{7}{2}$

83. *Writing Exercise*

84. *Writing Exercise*

85. Use the result of Example 2.

$$h = \frac{2R^2 g}{V^2} - R$$

We have $V = 6.5$ mi/sec, $R = 3960$ mi, and $g = 32.2$ ft/sec^2. We must convert 32.2 ft/sec^2 to mi/sec^2 so all units of length are the same.

$$32.2 \frac{\cancel{ft}}{sec^2} \cdot \frac{1 \text{ mi}}{5280 \cancel{ft}} \approx 0.0060984 \frac{mi}{sec^2}$$

Now we substitute and compute.

$$h = \frac{2(3960)^2(0.0060984)}{(6.5)^2} - 3960$$

$$h \approx 567$$

The satellite is about 567 mi from the surface of the earth.

86. $M = \dfrac{2ab}{b + a}$

87. $c = \dfrac{a}{a + 12} \cdot d$

$$c = \frac{2a}{2a + 12} \cdot d \quad \text{Doubling } a$$

$$= \frac{\cancel{2}a}{\cancel{2}(a + 6)} \cdot d$$

$$= \frac{a}{a + 6} \cdot d \quad \text{Simplifying}$$

The ratio of the larger dose to the smaller dose is

$$\frac{\dfrac{a}{a + 6} \cdot d}{\dfrac{a}{a + 12} \cdot d} = \frac{\dfrac{ad}{a + 6}}{\dfrac{ad}{a + 12}}$$

$$= \frac{ad}{a + 6} \cdot \frac{a + 12}{ad}$$

$$= \frac{\cancel{ad}(a + 12)}{(a + 6)\cancel{ad}}$$

$$= \frac{a + 12}{a + 6}.$$

The amount by which the dosage increases is

$$\frac{a}{a + 6} \cdot d - \frac{a}{a + 12} \cdot d$$

$$\frac{ad}{a + 6} - \frac{ad}{a + 12}$$

$$= \frac{ad}{a + 6} \cdot \frac{a + 12}{a + 12} - \frac{ad}{a + 12} \cdot \frac{a + 6}{a + 6}$$

$$= \frac{ad(a + 12) - ad(a + 6)}{(a + 6)(a + 12)}$$

$$= \frac{a^2 d + 12ad - a^2 d - 6ad}{(a + 6)(a + 12)}$$

$$= \frac{6ad}{(a + 6)(a + 12)}.$$

Then the percent by which the dosage increases is

$$\frac{\dfrac{6ad}{(a+6)(a+12)}}{\dfrac{a}{a+12}\cdot d} = \frac{\dfrac{6ad}{(a+6)(a+12)}}{\dfrac{ad}{a+12}}$$

$$= \frac{6ad}{(a+6)(a+12)}\cdot\frac{a+12}{ad}$$

$$= \frac{6\cdot a\!\!\!/d\cdot(a\!\!\!\!/+12)}{(a+6)(a\!\!\!\!/+12)\cdot a\!\!\!/d}$$

$$= \frac{6}{a+6}.$$

This is a decimal representation for the percent of increase. To give the result in percent notation we multiply by 100 and use a percent symbol. We have

$$\frac{6}{a+6}\cdot 100\%, \text{ or } \frac{600}{a+6}\%.$$

88. $x = pq$ or $x = 2pq$

89.
$$a = \frac{\dfrac{d_4-d_3}{t_4-t_3} - \dfrac{d_2-d_1}{t_2-t_1}}{t_4-t_2}$$

$$a(t_4-t_2) = \frac{d_4-d_3}{t_4-t_3} - \frac{d_2-d_1}{t_2-t_1} \quad \begin{array}{l}\text{Multiplying}\\ \text{by } t_4-t_2\end{array}$$

$$a(t_4-t_2)(t_4-t_3)(t_2-t_1) = (d_4-d_3)(t_2-t_1)-(d_2-d_1)(t_4-t_3)$$
$$\text{Multiplying by } (t_4-t_3)(t_2-t_1)$$
$$a(t_4-t_2)(t_4-t_3)(t_2-t_1)-(d_4-d_3)(t_2-t_1) =$$
$$-(d_2-d_1)(t_4-t_3)$$
$$(t_2-t_1)[a(t_4-t_2)(t_4-t_3)-(d_4-d_3)] =$$
$$-(d_2-d_1)(t_4-t_3)$$
$$t_2-t_1 = \frac{-(d_2-d_1)(t_4-t_3)}{a(t_4-t_2)(t_4-t_3)-(d_4-d_3)}$$
$$t_2 + \frac{(d_2-d_1)(t_4-t_3)}{a(t_4-t_2)(t_4-t_3)+d_3-d_4} = t_1$$

90. y is multiplied by 8.

91. $Q = \dfrac{kp^2}{q^3}$

Q varies directly as the square of p and inversely as the cube of q.

92. W varies jointly as m_1 and M_1 and inversely as the square of d.

93. **Familiarize.** We write $T = kml^2f^2$. We know that $T = 100$ when $m = 5$, $l = 2$, and $f = 80$.

Translate. Find k.
$$T = kml^2f^2$$
$$100 = k(5)(2)^2(80)^2$$
$$0.00078125 = k$$
$$T = 0.00078125ml^2f^2$$

Carry out. Substitute 72 for T, 5 for m, and 80 for f and solve for l.
$$72 = 0.00078125(5)(l^2)(80)^2$$
$$2.88 = l^2$$
$$1.697 \approx l$$

Check. Recheck the calculations.

State. The string should be about 1.697 m long.

94. $7.20

95. **Familiarize.** Because d varies inversely as s, we write $d(s) = k/s$. We know that $d(0.56) = 50$.

Translate.
$$d(s) = \frac{k}{s}$$
$$d(0.56) = \frac{k}{0.56} \quad \text{Replacing } s \text{ with } 0.56$$
$$50 = \frac{k}{0.56} \quad \text{Replacing } d(0.56) \text{ with } 50$$
$$28 = k$$
$$d(s) = \frac{28}{s} \quad \text{Equation of variation}$$

Carry out. Find $d(0.40)$.
$$d(0.40) = \frac{28}{0.40}$$
$$= 70$$

Check. Reexamine the calculations. Also observe that, as expected, when d decreases, then s increases.

State. The equation of variation is $d(s) = \dfrac{28}{s}$. The distance is 70 yd.

Chapter 8

Systems of Linear Equations and Problem Solving

Exercise Set 8.1

1. We use alphabetical order for the variables. We replace x by 1 and y by 2.

$$\begin{array}{c|c} 4x - y = 2 \\ \hline 4 \cdot 1 - 2 \ ? \ 2 \\ 4 - 2 \\ 2 \ \big| \ 2 \ \text{TRUE} \end{array} \qquad \begin{array}{c|c} 10x - 3y = 4 \\ \hline 10 \cdot 1 - 3 \cdot 2 \ ? \ 4 \\ 10 - 6 \\ 4 \ \big| \ 4 \ \text{TRUE} \end{array}$$

The pair $(1, 2)$ makes both equations true, so it is a solution of the system.

2. Yes

3. We use alphabetical order for the variables. We replace x by 2 and y by 5.

$$\begin{array}{c|c} y = 3x - 1 \\ \hline 5 \ ? \ 3 \cdot 2 - 1 \\ 6 - 1 \\ 5 \ \big| \ 5 \quad \text{TRUE} \end{array} \qquad \begin{array}{c|c} 2x + y = 4 \\ \hline 2 \cdot 2 + 5 \ ? \ 4 \\ 4 + 5 \\ 9 \ \big| \ 4 \ \text{FALSE} \end{array}$$

The pair $(2, 5)$ is not a solution of $2x + y = 4$. Therefore, it is not a solution of the system of equations.

4. No

5. We replace x by 1 and y by 5.

$$\begin{array}{c|c} x + y = 6 \\ \hline 1 + 5 \ ? \ 6 \\ 6 \ \big| \ 6 \ \text{TRUE} \end{array} \qquad \begin{array}{c|c} y = 2x + 3 \\ \hline 5 \ ? \ 2 \cdot 1 + 3 \\ 2 + 3 \\ 5 \ \big| \ 5 \quad \text{TRUE} \end{array}$$

The pair $(1, 5)$ makes both equations true, so it is a solution of the system.

6. Yes

7. Observe that if we multiply both sides of the first equation by 2, we get the second equation. Thus, if we find that the given point makes the one equation true, we will also know that it makes the other equation true. We replace x by 3 and y by 1 in the first equation.

$$\begin{array}{c|c} 3x + 4y = 13 \\ \hline 3 \cdot 3 + 4 \cdot 1 \ ? \ 13 \\ 9 + 4 \\ 13 \ \big| \ 13 \quad \text{TRUE} \end{array}$$

The pair $(3, 1)$ makes both equations true, so it is a solution of the system.

8. Yes

9. Graph both equations.

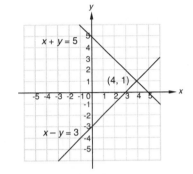

The solution (point of intersection) is apparently $(4, 1)$.

Check:

$$\begin{array}{c|c} x - y = 3 \\ \hline 4 - 1 \ ? \ 3 \\ 3 \ \big| \ 3 \quad \text{TRUE} \end{array} \qquad \begin{array}{c|c} x + y = 5 \\ \hline 4 + 1 \ ? \ 5 \\ 5 \ \big| \ 5 \quad \text{TRUE} \end{array}$$

The solution is $(4, 1)$.

10. $(3, 1)$

11. Graph the equations.

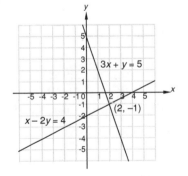

The solution (point of intersection) is apparently $(2, -1)$.

Check:

$$\begin{array}{c|c} 3x + y = 5 \\ \hline 3 \cdot 2 + (-1) \ ? \ 5 \\ 6 - 1 \\ 5 \ \big| \ 5 \ \text{TRUE} \end{array} \qquad \begin{array}{c|c} x - 2y = 4 \\ \hline 2 - 2(-1) \ ? \ 4 \\ 2 + 2 \\ 4 \ \big| \ 4 \ \text{TRUE} \end{array}$$

The solution is $(2, -1)$.

12. $(3, 2)$

13. Graph both equations.

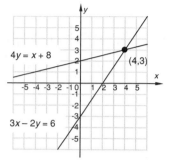

The solution (point of intersection) is apparently $(4, 3)$.
Check:

$4y = x + 8$		$3x - 2y = 6$	
$4 \cdot 3$? $4 + 8$		$3 \cdot 4 - 2 \cdot 3$? 6	
12	12 TRUE	$12 - 6$	
		6	6 TRUE

The solution is $(4, 3)$.

14. $(1, -5)$

15. Graph both equations.

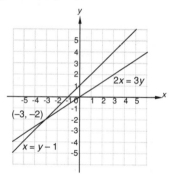

The solution (point of intersection) is apparently $(-3, -2)$.
Check:

$x = y - 1$		$2x = 3y$	
-3 ? $-2 - 1$		$2(-3)$? $3(-2)$	
-3	-3 TRUE	-6	-6 TRUE

The solution is $(-3, -2)$.

16. $(2, 1)$

17. Graph both equations.

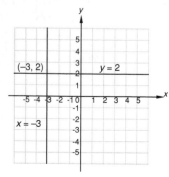

The ordered pair $(-3, 2)$ checks in both equations. It is the solution.

18. $(4, -5)$

19. Enter $y_1 = -5.43x + 10.89$ and $y_2 = 6.29x - 7.04$ on a graphing calculator and use the INTERSECT feature.

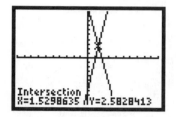

The solution is about $(1.53, 2.58)$.

20. Approximately $(-0.26, 57.06)$

21. Graph both equations.

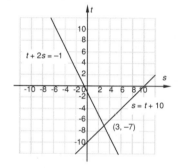

The solution (point of intersection) is apparently $(3, -7)$.
Check:

$t + 2s = -1$		$s = t + 10$	
$-7 + 2 \cdot 3$? -1		3 ? $-7 + 10$	
$-7 + 6$		3	3 TRUE
-1	-1 TRUE		

The solution is $(3, -7)$.

22. $(5, -8)$

23. Graph both equations.

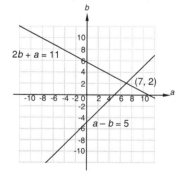

The solution (point of intersection) is apparently $(7, 2)$.

Check:

$$\frac{2b + a = 11}{2 \cdot 2 + 7 \ ? \ 11} \qquad \frac{a - b = 5}{7 - 2 \ ? \ 5}$$

$$4 + 7 \qquad\qquad 5 \ \bigm| \quad \text{TRUE}$$

$$11 \ \bigm| \ 11 \quad \text{TRUE}$$

The solution is $(7, 2)$.

24. $(3, -2)$

25. Graph both equations.

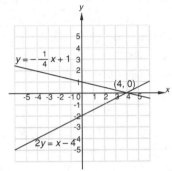

The solution (point of intersection) is apparently $(4, 0)$.

Check:

$$\frac{y = -\dfrac{1}{4}x + 1}{0 \ ? \ -\dfrac{1}{4} \cdot 4 + 1} \qquad \frac{2y = x - 4}{2 \cdot 0 \ ? \ 4 - 4}$$

$$\qquad\qquad -1 + 1 \qquad\qquad 0 \ \bigm| \ 0 \quad \text{TRUE}$$

$$0 \ \bigm| \ 0 \qquad\qquad \text{TRUE}$$

The solution is $(4, 0)$.

26. No solution

27. Solve each equation for y. We get

$$y = \frac{-2.18x + 13.78}{7.81} \text{ and } y = \frac{-5.79x + 8.94}{-3.45}. \text{ Graph these}$$

equations on a graphing calculator and use the INTER-SECT feature.

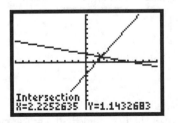

The solution is about $(2.23, 1.14)$.

28. No solution

29. Graph both equations.

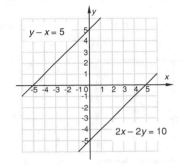

The lines are parallel. The system has no solution.

30. $(3, -4)$

31. Solve each equation for y. We get $y = \dfrac{45x + 33}{57}$ and $y = \dfrac{30x + 22}{95}$. Graph these equations on a graphing calculator and use the INTERSECT feature.

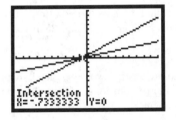

The solution is about $(-0.73, 0)$.

32. Approximately $(0.87, -0.32)$

33. Graph both equations.

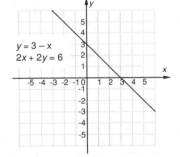

The graphs are the same. Any solution of one equation is a solution of the other. Each equation has infinitely many solutions. The solution set is the set of all pairs (x, y) for which $y = 3 - x$, or $\{(x, y) | y = 3 - x\}$. (In place of $y = 3 - x$ we could have used $2x + 2y = 6$ since the two equations are equivalent.)

34. $(-1, 2)$

35. Solve each equation for y. We get $y = \dfrac{1.9x - 1.7}{4.8}$ and $y = \dfrac{12.92x + 23.8}{32.64}$. Graph these equations on a graphing calculator and use the INTERSECT feature.

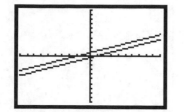

Note that the lines appear to be parallel. This is confirmed by the error message "NO SIGN CHNG" that is returned when we use the INTERSECT feature. The system of equations has no solution.

36. $\{(x, y) | 2x - 3y = 6\}$

37. A system of equations is consistent if it has at least one solution. Of the systems under consideration, only the ones in Exercises 29 and 35 have no solution. Therefore, all except the systems in Exercise 29 and 35 are consistent.

38. All except 26 and 28

39. A system of two equations in two variables is dependent if it has infinitely many solutions. Only the system in Exercise 33 is dependent.

40. 36

41. *Familiarize.* Let $x =$ the larger number and $y =$ the smaller number.

Translate.

The difference between two numbers is 11.

Rewording:

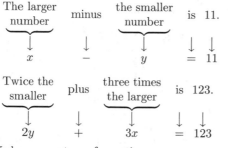

We have a system of equations:

$$x - y = 11,$$
$$3x + 2y = 123$$

42. Let $x =$ the first number and $y =$ the second number.

$$x + y = -42,$$
$$x - y = 52$$

43. *Familiarize.* Let $x =$ the number of less expensive brushes sold and $y =$ the number of more expensive brushes sold.

Translate. We organize the information in a table.

Kind of brush	Less expensive	More expensive	Total
Number sold	x	y	45
Price	\$8.50	\$9.75	
Amount taken in	8.50x	9.75y	398.75

The "Number sold" row of the table gives us one equation:

$$x + y = 45$$

The "Amount taken in" row gives us a second equation:

$$8.50x + 9.75y = 398.75$$

We have a system of equations:

$$x + y = 45,$$
$$8.50x + 9.75y = 398.75$$

We can multiply both sides of the second equation by 100 to clear the decimals:

$$x + y = 45,$$
$$850x + 975y = 39,875$$

44. Let $x =$ the number of polarfleece neckwarmers sold and $y =$ the number of wool neckwarmers sold.

$$x + y = 40,$$
$$9.9x + 12.75y = 421.65$$

45. *Familiarize.* Let $x =$ the measure of one angle and $y =$ the measure of the other angle.

Translate.

Two angles are supplementary.

Rewording: The sum of the measures is 180°.
$$x + y \qquad = \qquad 180$$

One angle is 3° less than twice the other.

Rewording: One angle is twice the other angle minus 3°.
$$x \quad = \quad 2y \quad - \quad 3$$

We have a system of equations:

$$x + y = 180,$$
$$x = 2y - 3$$

46. Let $x =$ the measure of the first angle and $y =$ the measure of the second angle.

$$x + y = 90,$$
$$x + \frac{1}{2}y = 64$$

47. *Familiarize.* Let $g =$ the number of two-point shots and $t =$ the number of free throws made.

Translate. We organize the information in a table.

Kind of shot	Two-point	Free throw	Total
Number scored	g	t	64
Points per score	2	1	
Points scored	$2g$	t	100

From the "Number scored" row of the table we get one equation:

$$g + t = 64$$

The "Points scored" row gives us another equation:

$$2g + t = 100$$

We have a system of equations:

$$g + t = 64,$$
$$2g + t = 100$$

48. Let x = the number of children's plates and y = the number of adult's plates served.

$$x + y = 250,$$
$$3.5x + 7y = 1347.5$$

49. *Familiarize*. Let h = the number of vials of Humulin Insulin sold and n = the number of vials of Novolin Insulin sold.

Translate. We organize the information in a table.

Brand	Humulin	Novolin	Total
Number sold	h	n	50
Price	$23.97	$34.39	
Amount taken in	$23.97h$	$34.39n$	1406.90

The "Number sold" row of the table gives us one equation:

$$h + n = 50$$

The "Amount taken in" row gives us a second equation:

$$23.97h + 34.39n = 1406.90$$

We have a system of equations:

$$h + n = 50,$$
$$23.97h + 34.39n = 1406.90$$

We can multiply both sides of the second equation by 100 to clear the decimals:

$$h + n = 50,$$
$$2397h + 3439n = 140,690$$

50. Let l = the length, in feet, and w = the width, in feet.

$$2l + 2w = 288,$$
$$l = w + 44$$

51. *Familiarize*. The tennis court is a rectangle with perimeter 228 ft. Let l = the length, in feet, and w = width, in feet. Recall that for a rectangle with length l and width w, the perimeter P is given by $P = 2l + 2w$.

Translate. The formula for perimeter gives us one equation:

$$2l + 2w = 228$$

The statement relating width and length gives us another equation:

The width is 42 ft less than the length.

$$w = l - 42$$

We have a system of equations:

$$2l + 2w = 228,$$
$$w = l - 42$$

52. Let x = the number of 2-pointers scored and y = the number of 3-pointers scored.

$$x + y = 40,$$
$$2x + 3y = 89$$

53. *Familiarize*. Let w = the number of wins and t = the number of ties. Then the total number of points received from wins was $2w$ and the total number of points received from ties was t.

Translate.

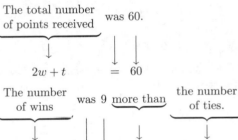

We have a system of equations:

$$2w + t = 60,$$
$$w = 9 + t$$

54. Let x = the number of 30-sec commercials and y = the number of 60-sec commercials.

$$x + y = 12,$$
$$30x + 60y = 600$$

55. *Familiarize*. Let x = the number of ounces of lemon juice and y = the number of ounces of linseed oil to be used.

Translate.

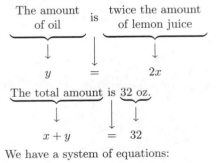

We have a system of equations:

$$y = 2x,$$
$$x + y = 32$$

56. Let $l =$ the number of pallets of lumber produced and $p =$ the number of pallets of plywood produced.

$$l + p = 42,$$
$$25l + 40p = 1245$$

57. *Familiarize*. Let $x =$ the number of general-interest films rented and $y =$ the number of children's films rented. Then $3x$ is taken in from the general-interest rentals and $1.5y$ is taken in from the children's rentals.

Translate.

$$\underbrace{\text{The number of videos rented}}_{\downarrow} \quad \underbrace{\text{is}}_{\downarrow} \quad \underbrace{77.}_{\downarrow}$$
$$x + y \qquad\qquad = \quad 77$$

$$\underbrace{\text{The amount taken in}}_{\downarrow} \quad \underbrace{\text{is}}_{\downarrow} \quad \underbrace{\$213.}_{\downarrow}$$
$$3x + 1.5y \qquad = \quad 213$$

We have a system of equations:

$$x + y = 77,$$
$$3x + 1.5y = 213$$

Clearing decimals we have

$$x + y = 77,$$
$$30x + 15y = 2130$$

58. Let $c =$ the number of coach-class seats and $f =$ the number of first-class seats.

$$c + f = 152,$$
$$c = 5 + 6f$$

59. We will let x represent the number of years after 1970. First we will use the points $(10, 51.5)$ and $(28, 59.8)$ to find a linear equation that describes the percent of women in the work force.

$$m = \frac{59.8 - 51.5}{28 - 10} = \frac{8.3}{18} = \frac{8.3}{18} \cdot \frac{10}{10} = \frac{83}{180}$$

Now we use the point-slope form.

$$y - 51.5 = \frac{83}{180}(x - 10)$$
$$y - 51.5 = \frac{83}{180}x - \frac{83}{18}$$
$$y = \frac{83}{180}x + \frac{422}{9}$$

Next we will use the points $(10, 77.4)$ and $(28, 74.9)$ to find a linear equation that describes the percent of men in the work force.

$$m = \frac{74.9 - 77.4}{28 - 10} = \frac{-2.5}{18} = -\frac{2.5}{18} \cdot \frac{10}{10} = -\frac{25}{180} = -\frac{5}{36}$$

Now we use the point-slope form.

$$y - 77.4 = -\frac{5}{36}(x - 10)$$
$$y - 77.4 = -\frac{5}{36}x + \frac{25}{18}$$
$$y = -\frac{5}{36}x + \frac{7091}{90}$$

We have a system of equations.

$$y = \frac{83}{180}x + \frac{422}{9},$$
$$y = -\frac{5}{36}x + \frac{7091}{90},$$

where y is a percent and x is the number of years after 1970.

We graph these equations on a graphing calculator and use the Intersect feature to find the coordinates of the point of intersection, approximately $(53, 71.4)$. Thus, we estimate that there will be equal percentages of men and women in the work force about 53 years after 1970, or in 2023.

60. Let y represent vehicle production, in thousands, and x the number of years since 1980.

$$y = -18.3125x + 6376,$$
$$y = 255.125x + 1634$$

About 1997

61. We will let x represent the number of years after 1990. First we will use the points $(4, 80.8)$ and $(8, 84.1)$ to find a linear function that describes the amount of paper generated, in millions of tons.

$$m = \frac{84.1 - 80.8}{8 - 4} = 0.825$$

Now we use the point-slope form.

$$y - 80.8 = 0.825(x - 4)$$
$$y - 80.8 = 0.825x - 3.3$$
$$y = 0.825x + 77.5$$

Next we will use the points $(4, 36.5)$ and $(8, 41.6)$ to find a linear equation that describes the amount of paper recycled, in millions of tons.

$$m = \frac{41.6 - 36.5}{8 - 4} = \frac{5.1}{4} = 1.275$$

Now we use the point-slope form.

$$y - 36.5 = 1.275(x - 4)$$
$$y - 36.5 = 1.275x - 5.1$$
$$y = 1.275x + 31.4$$

We have a system of equations

$$y = 0.825x + 77.5,$$
$$y = 1.275x + 31.4,$$

where y is in millions of tons and x is the number of years after 1990.

We graph these equations on a graphing calculator and use the Intersect feature to find the coordinates of the point of intersection, approximately $(102, 162)$. Thus, we estimate that the amount of paper recycled will equal the amount generated about 102 years after 1990, or in 2092.

62. Let y represent the number of meals eaten and x the number of years since 1990.

$$y = -\frac{2}{3}x + 64,$$
$$y = \frac{4}{3}x + 55$$

About 1995

63. We will let x represent the number of years after 1950. First we will use the points $(0, 38)$ and $(50, 24)$ to find a linear equation that describes the per capita consumption of milk, in gallons.

$$m = \frac{24 - 38}{50 - 0} = \frac{-14}{50} = -\frac{7}{25}$$

Using the slope-intercept equation we have

$$y = -\frac{7}{25}x + 38.$$

Next we will use the points $(0, 10)$ and $(50, 53)$ to find a linear equation that describes the per capita consumption of soft drinks, in gallons.

$$m = \frac{53 - 10}{50 - 0} = \frac{43}{50}$$

Using the slope-intercept equation we have $y = \frac{43}{50}x + 10$.

Then we have a system of equations

$$y = -\frac{7}{25}x + 38,$$

$$y = \frac{43}{50}x + 10,$$

where y is in gallons and x is in the number of years after 1950.

We graph these equations on a graphing calculator and use the Intersect feature to find the coordinates of the point of intersection, approximately $(25, 31)$. Thus, we estimate that per capita milk consumption equaled per capita soft drink consumption about 25 years after 1950, or in 1975.

64. Let y represent the per capita consumption, in pounds, and x the number of years since 1980

$$y = -\frac{1}{20}x + 17.5,$$

$$y = \frac{1}{15}x + 7.1$$

About 2069

65. Enter the number of years after 1970 in L_1, the percent of women in the work force in L_2, and the percent of men in the work force in L_3. Then use the linear regression feature to fit a line to each set of data. For women we have $y_1 = 0.5660768453x + 44.59989889$ and for men we have $y_2 = -0.1678968655x + 79.48407482$, where x represents the number of years after 1970.

We graph these equations on a graphing calculator and use the Intersect feature to find the coordinates of the point of intersection, approximately $(48, 71.5)$. Thus, we predict that there will be equal percentages of women and men in the work force about 48 years after 1970, or in 2018.

66. Passenger cars: $y_1 = -8.073170732x + 6256.121951$; trucks: $y_2 = 266.6081301x + 1423.764228$, where y_1 and y_2 are in thousands and x represents the number of years since 1980; about 1998

67. Enter the number of years after 1990 in L_1, the amount of paper waste generated in L_2, and the amount of paper recycled in L_3. Then use the linear regression feature to fit a line to each set of data. For paper waste generated we have $y_1 = 1.41x + 72.68$ and for paper recycled we have

$y_2 = 1.81x + 28.86$, where y_1 and y_2 are in millions of tons and x represents the number of years after 1990.

We graph these equations on a graphing calculator and use the Intersect feature to find the coordinates of the point of intersection, approximately $(110, 227)$. Thus, we predict that the amount of paper waste generated will equal the amount recycled about 110 years after 1990, or in 2100.

68. Regular: $y_1 = -0.0971857411x + 17.67298311$; lowfat: $y_2 = 0.0628517824x + 6.896622889$, where y_1 and y_2 are in pounds and x represents the number of years since 1980; abut 2047

69. *Writing Exercise*

70. *Writing Exercise*

71. $2(4x - 3) - 7x = 9$

$\qquad 8x - 6 - 7x = 9 \qquad$ Removing parentheses

$\qquad\qquad x - 6 = 9 \qquad$ Collecting like terms

$\qquad\qquad\qquad x = 15 \qquad$ Adding 6 to both sides

The solution is 15.

72. $\dfrac{19}{12}$

73. $4x - 5x = 8x - 9 + 11x$

$\qquad -x = 19x - 9 \qquad$ Collecting like terms

$\qquad -20x = -9 \qquad$ Adding $-19x$ to both sides

$\qquad\qquad x = \dfrac{9}{20} \qquad$ Multiplying both sides by $-\dfrac{1}{20}$

The solution is $\dfrac{9}{20}$.

74. $\dfrac{13}{3}$

75. $3x + 4y = 7$

$\qquad 4y = -3y + 7 \qquad$ Adding $-3x$ to both sides

$\qquad y = \dfrac{1}{4}(-3x + 7) \qquad$ Multiplying both sides by $\dfrac{1}{4}$

$\qquad y = -\dfrac{3}{4}x + \dfrac{7}{4}$

76. $y = \dfrac{2}{5}x - \dfrac{9}{5}$

77. *Writing Exercise*

78. *Writing Exercise*

79. The line representing the number of schools with CD-ROMs first lies above the line representing the number of schools with modems in 1994, so this is the year during which the number of schools with CD-ROMs first exceeded the number of schools with modems.

80. 1997; about 15,000 schools

81. a) There are many correct answers. One can be found by expressing the sum and difference of the two numbers:

$\qquad x + y = 6,$

$\qquad x - y = 4$

b) There are many correct answers. For example, write an equation in two variables. Then write a second equation by multiplying the left side of the first equation by one nonzero constant and multiplying the right side by another nonzero constant.

$$x + y = 1,$$
$$2x + 2y = 3$$

c) There are many correct answers. One can be found by writing an equation in two variables and then writing a nonzero constant multiple of that equation:

$$x + y = 1,$$
$$2x + 2y = 2$$

82. a) Answers may vary. $(4, -5)$

b) Infinitely many

83. Substitute 4 for x and -5 for y in the first equation:

$$A(4) - 6(-5) = 13$$
$$4A + 30 = 13$$
$$4A = -17$$
$$A = -\frac{17}{4}$$

Substitute 4 for x and -5 for y in the second equation:

$$4 - B(-5) = -8$$
$$4 + 5B = -8$$
$$5B = -12$$
$$B = -\frac{12}{5}$$

We have $A = -\frac{17}{4}$, $B = -\frac{12}{5}$.

84. Let $x =$ Burl's age now and $y =$ his son's age now.

$$x = 2y,$$
$$x - 10 = 3(y - 10)$$

85. *Familiarize.* Let $x =$ the number of years Lou has taught and $y =$ the number of years Juanita has taught. Two years ago, Lou and Juanita had taught $x - 2$ and $y - 2$ years, respectively.

Translate.

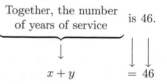

Two years ago
Lou had taught 2.5 times as many years as Juanita.

$$x - 2 = 2.5(y - 2)$$

We have a system of equations:

$$x + y = 46,$$
$$x - 2 = 2.5(y - 2)$$

86. Let $l =$ the original length, in inches, and $w =$ the original width, in inches.

$$2l + 2w = 156,$$
$$l = 4(w - 6)$$

87. *Familiarize.* Let $b =$ the number of ounces of baking soda and $v =$ the number of ounces of vinegar to be used. The amount of baking soda in the mixture will be four times the amount of vinegar.

Translate.

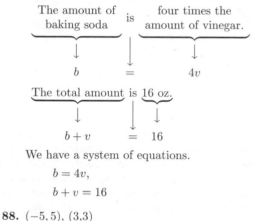

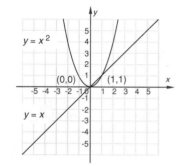

We have a system of equations.

$$b = 4v,$$
$$b + v = 16$$

88. $(-5, 5)$, $(3, 3)$

89. Graph both equations.

The solutions are apparently $(0, 0)$ and $(1, 1)$. Both pairs check.

90. (d)

91. The equations have the same slope and the same y-intercept. Thus their graphs are the same. Graph (c) matches this system.

92. (a)

93. The equations have the same slope and different y-intercepts. Thus their graphs are parallel lines. Graph (b) matches this system.

Exercise Set 8.2

1. $y = 5 - 4x,$ (1)

    $2x - 3y = 13$ (2)

We substitute $5 - 4x$ for y in the second equation and solve for x.

$$2x - 3y = 13 \quad (2)$$
$$2x - 3(5 - 4x) = 13 \quad \text{Substituting}$$
$$2x - 15 + 12x = 13$$
$$14x - 15 = 13$$
$$14x = 28$$
$$x = 2$$

Next we substitute 2 for x in either equation of the original system and solve for y.

$$y = 5 - 4x \quad (1)$$
$$y = 5 - 4 \cdot 2 \quad \text{Substituting}$$
$$y = 5 - 8$$
$$y = -3$$

We check the ordered pair $(2, -3)$.

$$\frac{y = 5 - 4x}{\begin{array}{c|c} -3 \; ? \; 5 - 4 \cdot 2 & \\ \quad\; 5 - 8 & \\ -3 & -3 \quad \text{TRUE} \end{array}}$$

$$\frac{2x - 3y = 13}{\begin{array}{c|c} 2 \cdot 2 - 3(\,3) \; ? \; 13 & \\ 4 + 9 & \\ 13 & 13 \quad \text{TRUE} \end{array}}$$

Since $(2, -3)$ checks, it is the solution.

2. $(-4, 3)$

3. $2y + x = 9,$ (1)

    $x = 3y - 3$ (2)

We substitute $3y - 3$ for x in the first equation and solve for y.

$$2y + x = 9 \quad (1)$$
$$2y + (3y - 3) = 9 \quad \text{Substituting}$$
$$5y - 3 = 9$$
$$5y = 12$$
$$y = \frac{12}{5}$$

Next we substitute $\frac{12}{5}$ for y in either equation of the original system and solve for x.

$$x = 3y - 3 \quad\quad\quad (2)$$
$$x = 3 \cdot \frac{12}{5} - 3 = \frac{36}{5} - \frac{15}{5} = \frac{21}{5}$$

We check the ordered pair $\left(\frac{21}{5}, \frac{12}{5} \right)$.

$$\frac{2y + x = 9}{\begin{array}{c|c} 2 \cdot \dfrac{12}{5} + \dfrac{21}{15} \; ? \; 9 & \\[2mm] \dfrac{24}{5} + \dfrac{21}{5} & \\[2mm] \dfrac{45}{5} & \\[2mm] 9 & 9 \quad \text{TRUE} \end{array}}$$

$$\frac{x = 3y - 3}{\begin{array}{c|c} \dfrac{21}{5} \; ? \; 3 \cdot \dfrac{12}{5} - 3 & \\[2mm] & \dfrac{36}{5} - \dfrac{15}{5} \\[2mm] \dfrac{21}{5} & \dfrac{21}{5} \quad \text{TRUE} \end{array}}$$

Since $\left(\frac{21}{5}, \frac{12}{5} \right)$ checks, it is the solution.

4. $(-3, -15)$

5. $3s - 4t = 14,$ (1)

    $5s + t = 8$ (2)

We solve the second equation for t.

$$5s + t = 8 \quad\quad\quad (2)$$
$$t = 8 - 5s \quad (3)$$

We substitute $8 - 5s$ for t in the first equation and solve for s.

$$3s - 4t = 14 \quad (1)$$
$$3s - 4(8 - 5s) = 14 \quad \text{Substituting}$$
$$3s - 32 + 20s = 14$$
$$23s - 32 = 14$$
$$23s = 46$$
$$s = 2$$

Next we substitute 2 for s in Equation (1), (2), or (3). It is easiest to use Equation (3) since it is already solved for t.

$$t = 8 - 5 \cdot 2 = 8 - 10 = -2$$

We check the ordered pair $(2, -2)$.

$$\frac{3s - 4t = 14}{\begin{array}{c|c} 3 \cdot 2 - 4(-2) \; ? \; 14 & \\ 6 + 8 & \\ 14 & 14 \quad \text{TRUE} \end{array}}$$

$$\frac{5s + t = 8}{\begin{array}{c|c} 5 \cdot 2 + (-2) \; ? \; 8 & \\ 10 - 2 & \\ 8 & 8 \quad \text{TRUE} \end{array}}$$

Since $(2, -2)$ checks, it is the solution.

6. $(2, -7)$

7. $4x - 2y = 6, \quad (1)$

$\quad 2x - 3 = y \quad (2)$

We substitute $2x - 3$ for y in the first equation and solve for x.

$$4x - 2y = 6 \quad (1)$$
$$4x - 2(2x - 3) = 6$$
$$4x - 4x + 6 = 6$$
$$6 = 6$$

We have an identity, or an equation that is always true. The equations are dependent and the solution set is infinite: $\{(x, y) | 2x - 3 = y\}$.

8. No solution

9. $-5s + t = 11, \quad (1)$

$\quad 4s + 12t = 4 \quad (2)$

We solve the first equation for t.

$$-5s + t = 11 \quad\quad (1)$$
$$t = 5s + 11 \quad (3)$$

We substitute $5s + 11$ for t in the second equation and solve for s.

$$4s + 12t = 4 \quad\quad (2)$$
$$4s + 12(5s + 11) = 4$$
$$4s + 60s + 132 = 4$$
$$64s + 132 = 4$$
$$64s = -128$$
$$s = -2$$

Next we substitute -2 for s in Equation (3).

$$t = 5s + 11 = 5(-2) + 11 = -10 + 11 = 1$$

We check the ordered pair $(-2, 1)$.

$$\frac{-5s + t = 11}{-5(-2) + 1 \ ? \ 11}$$
$$10 + 1 \ \Big|$$
$$11 \ \Big| \ 11 \quad \text{TRUE}$$

$$\frac{4s + 12t = 4}{4(-2) + 12 \cdot 1 \ ? \ 4}$$
$$-8 + 12 \ \Big|$$
$$4 \ \Big| \ 4 \quad \text{TRUE}$$

Since $(-2, 1)$ checks, it is the solution.

10. $(4, -1)$

11. $2x + 2y = 2, \quad (1)$

$\quad 3x - y = 1 \quad (2)$

We solve the second equation for y.

$$3x - y = 1 \quad\quad (2)$$
$$-y = -3x + 1$$
$$y = 3x - 1 \quad (3)$$

We substitute $3x - 1$ for y in the first equation and solve for x.

$$2x + 2y = 2 \quad (1)$$
$$2x + 2(3x - 1) = 2$$
$$2x + 6x - 2 = 2$$
$$8x - 2 = 2$$
$$8x = 4$$
$$x = \frac{1}{2}$$

Next we substitute $\frac{1}{2}$ for x in Equation (3).

$$y = 3x - 1 = 3 \cdot \frac{1}{2} - 1 = \frac{3}{2} - 1 = \frac{1}{2}$$

The ordered pair $\left(\frac{1}{2}, \frac{1}{2}\right)$ checks in both equations. It is the solution.

12. $(3, -2)$

13. $3a - b = 7, \quad (1)$

$\quad 2a + 2b = 5 \quad (2)$

We solve the first equation for b.

$$3a - b = 7 \quad\quad (1)$$
$$-b = -3a + 7$$
$$b = 3a - 7 \quad (3)$$

We substitute $3a - 7$ for b in the second equation and solve for a.

$$2a + 2b = 5 \quad\quad (2)$$
$$2a + 2(3a - 7) = 5$$
$$2a + 6a - 14 = 5$$
$$8a - 14 = 5$$
$$8a = 19$$
$$a = \frac{19}{8}$$

We substitute $\frac{19}{8}$ for a in Equation (3).

$$b = 3a - 7 = 3 \cdot \frac{19}{8} - 7 = \frac{57}{8} - \frac{56}{8} = \frac{1}{8}$$

The ordered pair $\left(\frac{19}{8}, \frac{1}{8}\right)$ checks in both equations. It is the solution.

14. $\left(\frac{25}{23}, -\frac{11}{23}\right)$

15. $2x - 3 = y \quad (1)$

$\quad y - 2x = 1, \quad (2)$

We substitute $2x - 3$ for y in the second equation and solve for x.

$$y - 2x = 1 \quad (2)$$
$$2x - 3 - 2x = 1 \quad \text{Substituting}$$
$$-3 = 1 \quad \text{Collecting like terms}$$

We have a contradiction, or an equation that is always false. Therefore, there is no solution.

16. $\{(a, b) | a - 2b = 3\}$

17.
$$x + 3y = 7 \quad (1)$$
$$\underline{-x + 4y = 7} \quad (2)$$
$$0 + 7y = 14 \quad \text{Adding}$$
$$7y = 14$$
$$y = 2$$

Substitute 2 for y in one of the original equations and solve for x.
$$x + 3y = 7 \quad (1)$$
$$x + 3 \cdot 2 = 7 \quad \text{Substituting}$$
$$x + 6 = 7$$
$$x = 1$$

Check:

$x + 3y = 7$			$-x + 4y = 7$		
$1 + 3 \cdot 2 \;?\; 7$			$-1 + 4 \cdot 2 \;?\; 7$		
$1 + 6$			$-1 + 8$		
	7	7 TRUE		7	7 TRUE

Since $(1, 2)$ checks, it is the solution.

18. $(2, 7)$

19.
$$2x + y = 6 \quad (1)$$
$$\underline{x - y = 3} \quad (2)$$
$$3x + 0 = 9 \quad \text{Adding}$$
$$3x = 9$$
$$x = 3$$

Substitute 3 for x in one of the original equations and solve for y.
$$2x + y = 6 \quad (1)$$
$$2 \cdot 3 + y = 6 \quad \text{Substituting}$$
$$6 + y = 6$$
$$y = 0$$

We obtain $(3, 0)$. This checks, so it is the solution.

20. $(10, 2)$

21.
$$9x + 3y = -3 \quad (1)$$
$$\underline{2x - 3y = -8} \quad (2)$$
$$11x + 0 = -11 \quad \text{Adding}$$
$$11x = -11$$
$$x = -1$$

Substitute -1 for x in Equation (1) and solve for y.
$$9x + 3y = -3$$
$$9(-1) + 3y = -3 \quad \text{Substituting}$$
$$-9 + 3y = -3$$
$$3y = 6$$
$$y = 2$$

We obtain $(-1, 2)$. This checks, so it is the solution.

22. $\left(\dfrac{1}{2}, -5\right)$

23.
$$5x + 3y = 19, \quad (1)$$
$$2x - 5y = 11 \quad (2)$$

We multiply twice to make two terms become opposites.

From (1): $25x + 15y = 95$ Multiplying by 5
From (2): $\underline{6x - 15y = 33}$ Multiplying by 3
$$31x + 0 = 128 \quad \text{Adding}$$
$$x = \frac{128}{31}$$

Substitute $\dfrac{128}{31}$ for x in Equation (1) and solve for y.
$$5x + 3y = 19$$
$$5 \cdot \frac{128}{31} + 3y = 19 \quad \text{Substituting}$$
$$\frac{640}{31} + 3y = \frac{589}{31}$$
$$3y = -\frac{51}{31}$$
$$\frac{1}{3} \cdot 3y = \frac{1}{3} \cdot \left(-\frac{51}{31}\right)$$
$$y = -\frac{17}{31}$$

We obtain $\left(\dfrac{128}{31}, -\dfrac{17}{31}\right)$. This checks, so it is the solution.

24. $\left(\dfrac{10}{21}, \dfrac{11}{14}\right)$

25.
$$5r - 3s = 24, \quad (1)$$
$$3r + 5s = 28 \quad (2)$$

We multiply twice to make two terms become additive inverses.

From (1): $25r - 15s = 120$ Multiplying by 5
From (2): $\underline{9r + 15s = 84}$ Multiplying by 3
$$34r + 0 = 204 \quad \text{Adding}$$
$$r = 6$$

Substitute 6 for r in Equation (2) and solve for s.
$$3r + 5s = 28$$
$$3 \cdot 6 + 5s = 28 \quad \text{Substituting}$$
$$18 + 5s = 28$$
$$5s = 10$$
$$s = 2$$

We obtain $(6, 2)$. This checks, so it is the solution.

26. $(1, 3)$

27.
$$6s + 9t = 12, \quad (1)$$
$$4s + 6t = 5 \quad (2)$$

We multiply twice to make two terms become opposites.

From (1): $12s + 18t = 24$ Multiplying by 2
From (2): $\underline{-12s - 18t = -15}$ Multiplying by -3
$$0 = 9$$

We get a contradiction, or an equation that is always false. The system has no solution.

28. No solution

29. $\dfrac{1}{2}x - \dfrac{1}{6}y = 3$ (1)

$\dfrac{2}{5}x + \dfrac{1}{2}y = 2,$ (2)

We first multiply each equation by the LCM of the denominators to clear fractions.

$3x - y = 18$ (3)   Multiplying (1) by 6

$4x + 5y = 20$ (4)   Multiplying (2) by 10

We multiply by 5 on both sides of Equation (3) and then add.

$\begin{array}{rl} 15x - 5y = & 90 \quad \text{Multiplying (3) by 5} \\ \underline{4x + 5y = } & \underline{20} \quad (4) \\ 19x + 0 = & 110 \quad \text{Adding} \end{array}$

$x = \dfrac{110}{19}$

Substitute $\dfrac{110}{19}$ for x in one of the equations in which the fractions were cleared and solve for y.

$3x - y = 18$ (3)

$3\left(\dfrac{110}{19}\right) - y = 18$ Substituting

$\dfrac{330}{19} - y = \dfrac{342}{19}$

$-y = \dfrac{12}{19}$

$y = -\dfrac{12}{19}$

We obtain $\left(\dfrac{110}{19}, -\dfrac{12}{19}\right)$. This checks, so it is the solution.

30. $(12, 15)$

31. $\dfrac{x}{2} + \dfrac{y}{3} = \dfrac{7}{6},$ (1)

$\dfrac{2x}{3} + \dfrac{3y}{4} = \dfrac{5}{4}$ (2)

We first multiply each equation by the LCM of the denominators to clear fractions.

$3x + 2y = 7$ (3)   Multiplying (1) by 6

$8x + 9y = 15$ (4)   Multiplying (2) by 12

We multiply twice to make two terms become opposites.

From (3): $27x + 18y = 63$ Multiplying by 9

From (4): $\underline{-16x - 18y = -30}$ Multiplying by -2

$ 11x = 33$ Adding

$ x = 3$

Substitute 3 for x in one of the equations in which the fractions were cleared and solve for y.

$3x + 2y = 7$ (3)

$3 \cdot 3 + 2y = 7$ Substituting

$9 + 2y = 7$

$2y = -2$

$y = -1$

We obtain $(3, -1)$. This checks, so it is the solution.

32. $(-2, 3)$

33. $12x - 6y = -15,$ (1)

$-4x + 2y = 5$ (2)

Observe that, if we multiply Equation (1) by $-\dfrac{1}{3}$, we obtain Equation (2). Thus, any pair that is a solution of Equation (1) is also a solution of Equation (2). The equations are dependent and the solution set is infinite: $\{(x, y) | -4x + 2y = 5\}$.

34. $\{(s, t) | 6s + 9t = 12\}$

35. $0.2a + 0.3b = 1,$

$0.3a - 0.2b = 4,$

We first multiply each equation by 10 to clear decimals.

$2a + 3b = 10$ (1)

$3a - 2b = 40$ (2)

We multiply so that the b-terms can be eliminated.

From (1): $4a + 6b = 20$ Multiplying by 2

From (2): $\underline{9a - 6b = 120}$ Multiplying by 3

$ 13a + 0 = 140$ Adding

$ a = \dfrac{140}{13}$

Substitute $\dfrac{140}{13}$ for a in Equation (1) and solve for b.

$2a + 3b = 10$

$2 \cdot \dfrac{140}{13} + 3b = 10$ Substituting

$\dfrac{280}{13} + 3b = \dfrac{130}{13}$

$3b = -\dfrac{150}{13}$

$b = -\dfrac{50}{13}$

We obtain $\left(\dfrac{140}{13}, -\dfrac{50}{13}\right)$. This checks, so it is the solution.

36. $(2, 3)$

37. $a - 2b = 16,$ (1)

$b + 3 = 3a$ (2)

We will use the substitution method. First solve Equation (1) for a.

$a - 2b = 16$

$a = 2b + 16$ (3)

Now substitute $2b + 16$ for a in Equation (2) and solve for b.

$b + 3 = 3a$ (2)

$b + 3 = 3(2b + 16)$ Substituting

$b + 3 = 6b + 48$

$-45 = 5b$

$-9 = b$

Substitute -9 for b in Equation (3).

$a = 2(-9) + 16 = -2$

We obtain $(-2, -9)$. This checks, so it is the solution.

38. $\left(\dfrac{1}{2}, -\dfrac{1}{2}\right)$

39. $10x + y = 306,$ (1)

$10y + x = 90$ (2)

We will use the substitution method. First solve Equation (1) for y.

$$10x + y = 306$$
$$y = -10x + 306 \quad (3)$$

Now substitute $-10x + 306$ for y in Equation (2) and solve for y.

$$10y + x = 90 \quad (2)$$
$$10(-10x + 306) + x = 90 \qquad \text{Substituting}$$
$$-100x + 3060 + x = 90$$
$$-99x + 3060 = 90$$
$$-99x = -2970$$
$$x = 30$$

Substitute 30 for x in Equation (3).

$$y = -10 \cdot 30 + 306 = 6$$

We obtain $(30, 6)$. This checks, so it is the solution.

40. $\left(-\dfrac{4}{3}, -\dfrac{19}{3}\right)$

41. $3y = x - 2,$ (1)

$x = 2 + 3y$ (2)

We will use the substitution method. Substitute $2 + 3y$ for x in the first equation and solve for y.

$$3y = x - 2 \qquad (1)$$
$$3y = 2 + 3y - 2 \qquad \text{Substituting}$$
$$3y = 3y \qquad\qquad \text{Collecting like terms}$$

We get an identity. The system is dependent and the solution set is infinite: $\{(x, y)|x = 2 + 3y\}$.

42. No solution

43. $3s - 7t = 5,$

$7t - 3s = 8$

First we rewrite the second equation with the variables in a different order. Then we use the elimination method.

$$\begin{array}{ll} 3s - 7t = 5, & (1) \\ -3s + 7t = 8 & (2) \\ \hline \quad\quad\quad 0 = 13 & \end{array}$$

We get a contradiction, so the system has no solution.

44. $\{(s, t)|2s - 13t = 120\}$

45. $0.05x + 0.25y = 22,$ (1)

$0.15x + 0.05y = 24$ (2)

We first multiply each equation by 100 to clear decimals.

$$5x + 25y = 2200$$
$$15x + 5y = 2400$$

We multiply by -5 on both sides of the second equation and add.

$$\begin{array}{ll} 5x + 25y = \quad\quad 2200 & \\ -75x - 25y = -12,000 & \text{Multiplying (2) by } -5 \\ \hline -70x \quad\quad\quad = \quad -9800 & \text{Adding} \\ x = \dfrac{-9800}{-70} & \\ x = 140 & \end{array}$$

Substitute 140 for x in one of the equations in which the decimals were cleared and solve for y.

$$5x + 25y = 2200 \quad (1)$$
$$5 \cdot 140 + 25y = 2200 \quad \text{Substituting}$$
$$700 + 25y = 2200$$
$$25y = 1500$$
$$y = 60$$

We obtain $(140, 60)$. This checks, so it is the solution.

46. $(10, 5)$

47. $13a - 7b = 9,$ (1)

$2a - 8b = 6$ (2)

We will use the elimination method. First we multiply so that the b-terms can be eliminated.

$$\begin{array}{lll} \text{From (1):} & 104a - 56b = \quad 72 & \text{Multiplying by 8} \\ \text{From (2):} & -14a + 56b = -42 & \text{Multiplying by } -7 \\ \hline & 90a \quad\quad\quad = \quad 30 & \text{Adding} \\ & a = \dfrac{1}{3} & \end{array}$$

Substitute $\dfrac{1}{3}$ for a in one of the equations and solve for b.

$$2a - 8b = 6 \qquad (2)$$
$$2 \cdot \dfrac{1}{3} - 8b = 6$$
$$\dfrac{2}{3} - 8b = 6$$
$$-8b = \dfrac{16}{3}$$
$$b = -\dfrac{2}{3}$$

We obtain $\left(\dfrac{1}{3}, -\dfrac{2}{3}\right)$. This checks, so it is the solution.

48. $\left(-\dfrac{13}{45}, -\dfrac{37}{45}\right)$

49. The point of intersection is $(140, 60)$, so window (d) is the correct answer.

50. (a)

51. The point of intersection is $(30, 6)$, so window (b) is the correct answer.

52. (c)

53. *Writing Exercise*

54. *Writing Exercise*

55. Familiarize. Let m = the number of $\frac{1}{4}$-mi units traveled after the first $\frac{1}{2}$ mi. The total distance traveled will be $\frac{1}{2}$ mi $+ m \cdot \frac{1}{4}$ mi.

Translate.

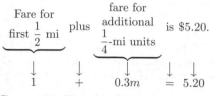

$$1 + 0.3m = 5.20$$

Carry out. We solve the equation.

$$1 + 0.3m = 5.20$$
$$0.3m = 4.20$$
$$m = 14$$

If the taxi travels the first $\frac{1}{2}$ mi plus 14 additional $\frac{1}{4}$-mi units, then it travels a total of $\frac{1}{2} + 14 \cdot \frac{1}{4}$, or $\frac{1}{2} + \frac{7}{2}$, or 4 mi.

Check. We have 4 mi $= \frac{1}{2}$ mi $+ \frac{7}{2}$ mi $= \frac{1}{2}$ mi $+ 14 \cdot \frac{1}{4}$ mi. The fare for traveling this distance is $\$1.00 + \$0.30(14) = \$1.00 + \$4.20 = \$5.20$. The answer checks.

State. It is 4 mi from Johnson Street to Elm Street.

56. 86

57. Familiarize. Let a = the amount spent to remodel bathrooms, in billions of dollars. Then $2a$ = the amount spent to remodel kitchens. The sum of these two amounts is $35 billion.

Translate.

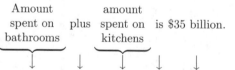

Carry out. We solve the equation.

$$a + 2a = 35$$
$$3a = 35 \qquad \text{Combining like terms}$$
$$a = \frac{35}{3}, \text{ or } 11\frac{2}{3}$$

If $a = \frac{35}{3}$, then $2a = 2 \cdot \frac{35}{3} = \frac{70}{3} = 23\frac{1}{3}$.

Check. $\frac{70}{3}$ is twice $\frac{35}{3}$, and $\frac{35}{3} + \frac{70}{3} = \frac{105}{3} = 35$. The answer checks.

State. $\$11\frac{2}{3}$ billion was spent to remodel bathrooms, and $\$23\frac{1}{3}$ billion was spent to remodel kitchens.

58. 30 m, 90 m, 360 m

59. Familiarize. The total cost is the daily charge plus the mileage charge. The mileage charge is the cost per mile times the number of miles driven. Let m = the number of miles that can be driven for $80.

Translate. We reword the problem.

Daily rate	plus	Cost per mile	times	Number of miles driven	is	Amount.
↓	↓	↓	↓	↓	↓	↓
34.95	+	0.10	·	m	=	80

Carry out. We solve the equation.

$$34.95 + 0.10m = 80$$
$$100(34.95 + 0.10m) = 100(80) \quad \text{Clearing decimals}$$
$$3495 + 10m = 8000$$
$$10m = 4505$$
$$m = 450.5$$

Check. The mileage cost is found by multiplying 450.5 by $0.10 obtaining $45.05. Then we add $45.05 to $34.95, the daily rate, and get $80.

State. The businessperson can drive 450.5 mi on the car-rental allotment.

60. 460.5 mi

61. *Writing Exercise*

62. *Writing Exercise*

63. First write $f(x) = mx + b$ as $y = mx + b$. Then substitute 1 for x and 2 for y to get one equation and also substitute -3 for x and 4 for y to get a second equation:

$$2 = m \cdot 1 + b$$
$$4 = m(-3) + b$$

Solve the resulting system of equations.

$$2 = m + b$$
$$4 = -3m + b$$

Multiply the second equation by -1 and add.

$$2 = m + b$$
$$\underline{-4 = 3m - b}$$
$$-2 = 4m$$
$$-\frac{1}{2} = m$$

Substitute $-\frac{1}{2}$ for m in the first equation and solve for b.

$$2 = -\frac{1}{2} + b$$
$$\frac{5}{2} = b$$

Thus, $m = -\frac{1}{2}$ and $b = \frac{5}{2}$.

64. $p = 2$, $q = -\frac{1}{3}$

65. Substitute -4 for x and -3 for y in both equations and solve for a and b.

$$-4a - 3b = -26, \quad (1)$$
$$-4b + 3a = 7 \quad (2)$$

$$\begin{array}{ll} -12a - 9b = -78 & \text{Multiplying (1) by 3} \\ \underline{12a - 16b = 28} & \text{Multiplying (2) by 4} \\ -25b = -50 & \\ b = 2 & \end{array}$$

Substitute 2 for b in Equation (2).

$$-4 \cdot 2 + 3a = 7$$
$$3a = 15$$
$$a = 5$$

Thus, $a = 5$ and $b = 2$.

66. $\left(\dfrac{a + 2b}{7}, \dfrac{a - 5b}{7} \right)$

67. $\dfrac{x + y}{2} - \dfrac{x - y}{5} = 1,$

$\dfrac{x - y}{2} + \dfrac{x + y}{6} = -2$

After clearing fractions we have:

$$3x + 7y = 10, \quad (1)$$
$$4x - 2y = -12 \quad (2)$$

$$\begin{array}{ll} 6x + 14y = 20 & \text{Multiplying (1) by 2} \\ \underline{28x - 14y = -84} & \text{Multiplying (2) by 7} \\ 34x = -64 & \\ x = -\dfrac{32}{17} & \end{array}$$

Substitute $-\dfrac{32}{17}$ for x in Equation (1).

$$3\left(-\dfrac{32}{17} \right) + 7y = 10$$
$$7y = \dfrac{266}{17}$$
$$y = \dfrac{38}{17}$$

The solution is $\left(-\dfrac{32}{17}, \dfrac{38}{17} \right)$.

68. Approximately $(23.118879, -12.039964)$

69. $\dfrac{2}{x} + \dfrac{1}{y} = 0, \qquad 2 \cdot \dfrac{1}{x} + \dfrac{1}{y} = 0,$

$$\text{or}$$

$\dfrac{5}{x} + \dfrac{2}{y} = -5 \qquad 5 \cdot \dfrac{1}{x} + 2 \cdot \dfrac{1}{y} = -5$

Substitute u for $\dfrac{1}{x}$ and v for $\dfrac{1}{y}$.

$$2u + v = 0, \quad (1)$$
$$5u + 2v = -5 \quad (2)$$

$$\begin{array}{ll} -4u - 2v = 0 & \text{Multiplying (1) by } -2 \\ \underline{5u + 2v = -5} & (2) \\ u = -5 & \end{array}$$

Substitute -5 for u in Equation (1).

$$2(-5) + v = 0$$
$$-10 + v = 0$$
$$v = 10$$

If $u = -5$, then $\dfrac{1}{x} = -5$. Thus $x = -\dfrac{1}{5}$.

If $v = 10$, then $\dfrac{1}{y} = 10$. Thus $y = \dfrac{1}{10}$.

The solution is $\left(-\dfrac{1}{5}, \dfrac{1}{10} \right)$.

70. $\left(-\dfrac{1}{4}, -\dfrac{1}{2} \right)$

Exercise Set 8.3

1. The Familiarize and Translate steps were done in Exercise 41 of Exercise Set 8.1

Carry out. We solve the system of equations

$$x - y = 11, \quad (1)$$
$$3x + 2y = 123 \quad (2)$$

where $x =$ the larger number and $y =$ the smaller number. We use elimination.

$$\begin{array}{ll} 2x - 2y = 22 & \text{Multiplying (1) by 2} \\ \underline{3x + 2y = 123} & \\ 5x = 145 & \\ x - 29 & \end{array}$$

Substitute 29 for x in (1) and solve for y.

$$29 - y - 11$$
$$-y = -18$$
$$y = 18$$

Check. The difference between the numbers is $29 - 18$, or 11. Also $2 \cdot 18 + 3 \cdot 29 = 36 + 87 = 123$. The numbers check.

State. The larger number is 29, and the smaller is 18.

2. $5, -47$

3. The Familiarize and Translate steps were done in Exercise 43 of Exercise Set 8.1

Carry out. We solve the system of equations

$$x + y = 45, \quad (1)$$
$$850x + 975y = 39{,}875 \quad (2)$$

where $x =$ the number of less expensive brushes sold and $y =$ the number of more expensive brushes sold. We use elimination. Begin by multiplying Equation (1) by -850.

$$\begin{array}{ll} -850x - 850y = -38{,}250 & \text{Multiplying (1)} \\ \underline{850x + 975y = 39{,}875} & \\ 125y = 1625 & \\ y = 13 & \end{array}$$

Substitute 13 for y in (1) and solve for x.

$$x + 13 = 45$$
$$x = 32$$

Check. The number of brushes sold is $32 + 13$, or 45. The amount taken in was $\$8.50(32) + \$9.75(13) = \$272 + \$126.75 = \$398.75$. The answer checks.

State. 32 of the less expensive brushes were sold, and 13 of the more expensive brushes were sold.

4. 31 polarfleece, 9 wool

5. The Familiarize and Translate steps were done in Exercise 45 of Exercise Set 8.1

Carry out. We solve the system of equations

$$x + y = 180, \quad (1)$$
$$x = 2y - 3 \quad (2)$$

where $x =$ the measure of one angle and $y =$ the measure of the other angle. We use substitution.

Substitute $2y - 3$ for x in (1) and solve for y.

$$2y - 3 + y = 180$$
$$3y - 3 = 180$$
$$3y = 183$$
$$y = 61$$

Now substitute 61 for y in (2).

$$x = 2 \cdot 61 - 3 = 122 - 3 = 119$$

Check. The sum of the angle measures is $119° + 61°$, or $180°$, so the angles are supplementary. Also $2 \cdot 61° - 3° = 122° - 3° = 119°$. The answer checks.

State. The measures of the angles are $119°$ and $61°$.

6. $38°, 52°$

7. The Familiarize and Translate steps were done in Exercise 47 of Exercise Set 8.1

Carry out. We solve the system of equations

$$g + t = 64, \quad (1)$$
$$2g + t = 100 \quad (2)$$

where $g =$ the number of two-point shots and $t =$ the number of free throws Chamberlain made. We use elimination.

$$-g - t = -64 \quad \text{Multiplying (1) by } -1$$
$$\underline{2g + t = 100}$$
$$g = 36$$

Substitute 36 for g in (1) and solve for t.

$$36 + t = 64$$
$$t = 28$$

Check. The total number of scores was $36 + 28$, or 64. The total number of points was $2 \cdot 36 + 28 = 72 + 28 = 100$. The answer checks.

State. Chamberlain made 36 two-point shots and 28 free throws.

8. 115 children's plates, 135 adult's plates

9. The Familiarize and Translate steps were done in Exercise 49 of Exercise Set 8.1

Carry out. We solve the system of equations

$$h + n = 50, \quad (1)$$
$$2397h + 3439n = 140,690 \quad (2)$$

where $h =$ the number of vials of Humulin Insulin sold and $n =$ the number of vials of Novolin Insulin sold. We use elimination.

$$-2397h - 2397n = -119,850 \quad \begin{array}{l}\text{Multiplying (1)}\\\text{by } -2397\end{array}$$
$$\underline{2397h + 3439n = 140,690}$$
$$1042n = 20,840$$
$$n = 20$$

Substitute 20 for n in (1) and solve for h.

$$h + 20 = 50$$
$$h = 30$$

Check. A total of $30 + 20$, or 50 vials, was sold. The amount collected was $\$23.97(30) + \$34.39(20) = \$719.10 + \$687.80 = \$1406.90$. The answer checks.

State. 30 vials of Humulin Insulin and 20 vials of Novolin Insulin were sold.

10. Length: 94 ft, width: 50 ft

11. The Familiarize and Translate steps were done in Exercise 51 of Exercise Set 8.1

Carry out. We solve the system of equations

$$2l + 2w = 228, \quad (1)$$
$$w = l - 42 \quad (2)$$

where $l =$ the length, in feet, and $w =$ the width, in feet, of the tennis court. We use substitution.

Substitute $l - 42$ for w in (1) and solve for l.

$$2l + 2(l - 42)w = 228$$
$$2l + 2l - 84 = 228$$
$$4l - 84 = 228$$
$$4l = 312$$
$$l = 78$$

Now substitute 78 for l in (2).

$$w = 78 - 42 = 36$$

Check. The perimeter is $2 \cdot 78 \text{ ft} + 2 \cdot 36 \text{ ft} = 156 \text{ ft} + 72 \text{ ft} = 228 \text{ ft}$. The width, 36 ft, is 42 ft less than the length, 78 ft. The answer checks.

State. The length of the tennis court is 78 ft, and the width is 36 ft.

12. 31 two-point field goals, 9 three-point field goals

13. The Familiarize and Translate steps were done in Exercise 53 of Exercise Set 8.1.

Carry out. We solve the system of equations

$$2w + t = 60, \quad (1)$$
$$w = 9 + t \quad (2)$$

where $w =$ the number of wins and $t =$ the number of ties. We use substitution.

Substitute $9 + t$ for w in (1) and solve for t.

$$2(9 + t) + t = 60$$
$$18 + 2t + t = 60$$
$$18 + 3t = 60$$
$$3t = 42$$
$$t = 14$$

Now substitute 14 for t in (2).

$$w = 9 + 14 = 23$$

Check. The total number of points is $2 \cdot 23 + 14 = 46 + 14 = 60$. The number of wins, 23, is nine more than the number of ties, 14. The answer checks.

State. The Wildcats had 23 wins and 14 ties.

14. 4 30-sec commercials, 8 60-sec commercials

15. The Familiarize and Translate steps were done in Exercise 55 of Exercise Set 8.1.

    Carry out. We solve the system of equations

$$y = 2x, \qquad (1)$$
$$x + y = 32 \quad (2)$$

where x = the number of ounces of lemon juice and y = the number of ounces of linseed oil to be used. We use substitution.

Substitute $2x$ for y in (2) and solve for x.

$$x + 2x = 32$$
$$3x = 32$$
$$x = \frac{32}{3}, \text{ or } 10\frac{2}{3}$$

Now substitute $\frac{32}{3}$ for x in (1).

$$y = 2 \cdot \frac{32}{3} = \frac{64}{3}, \text{ or } 21\frac{1}{3}$$

Check. The amount of oil, $\frac{64}{3}$ oz, is twice the amount of lemon juice, $\frac{32}{3}$ oz. The mixture contains $\frac{32}{3}$ oz $+ \frac{64}{3}$ oz $= \frac{96}{3}$ oz $= 32$ oz. The answer checks.

State. $10\frac{2}{3}$ oz of lemon juice and $21\frac{1}{3}$ oz of linseed oil are needed.

16. 29 pallets of lumber, 13 pallets of plywood

17. The Familiarize and Translate steps were done in Exercise 57 of Exercise Set 8.1.

    Carry out. We solve the system of equations

$$x + y = 77, \qquad (1)$$
$$30x + 15y = 2130 \quad (2)$$

where x = the number of general-interest films rented and y = the number of children's films rented. We use elimination.

$$-15x - 15y = -1155 \quad \text{Multiplying (1) by } -15$$
$$\underline{30x + 15y = 2130}$$
$$15x = 975$$
$$x = 65$$

Substitute 65 for x in (1) and solve for y.

$$65 + y = 77$$
$$y = 12$$

Check. The total number of films rented is $65 + 12$, or 77. The total amount taken in was $\$3(65) + \$1.50(12) = \$195 + \$18 = \$213$. The answer checks.

State. 65 general-interest videos and 12 children's videos were rented.

18. 131 coach-class seats, 21 first-class seats

19. **Familiarize**. Let f = the number of boxes of Flair pens sold and u = the number of four-packs of Uniball pens sold.

    Translate. We organize the information in a table.

	Flair boxes	Uniball four-packs	Total
Number sold	f	u	40
Price	$12	$8	
Total cost	$12f$	$8u$	372

We get one equation from the "Number sold" row of the table:

$$f + u = 40$$

The "Total cost" row yields a second equation:

$$12f + 8u = 372$$

We have translated to a system of equations:

$$f + u = 40, \qquad (1)$$
$$12f + 8u = 372 \quad (2)$$

Carry out. We solve the system of equations using the elimination method.

$$-8f - 8u = -320 \quad \text{Multiplying (1) by } -8$$
$$\underline{12f + 8u = 372}$$
$$4f = 52$$
$$f = 13$$

Now substitute 13 for f in (1) and solve for u.

$$13 + u = 40$$
$$u = 27$$

Check. The total number of boxes and four-packs sold is $13 + 27$, or 40. The total cost of these purchases is $\$12 \cdot 13 + \$8 \cdot 27 = \$156 + \$216 = \$372$. The answer checks.

State. 13 boxes of Flair pens and 27 four-packs of Uniball pens were sold.

20. 18 graph-paper, 32 college-ruled

21. **Familiarize**. Let k = the number of pounds of Kenyan French Roast coffee and s = the number of pounds of Sumatran coffee to be used in the mixture. The value of the mixture will be $\$8.40(20)$, or $\$168$.

    Translate. We organize the information in a table.

	Kenyan	Sumatran	Mixture
Number of pounds	k	s	20
Price per pound	$9	$8	$8.40
Value of coffee	$9k$	$8s$	168

The "Number of pounds" row of the table gives us one equation:

$$k + s = 20$$

The "Value of coffee" row yields a second equation:

$$9k + 8s = 168$$

We have translated to a system of equations:

$$k + s = 20, \quad (1)$$
$$9k + 8s = 168 \quad (2)$$

Carry out. We use the elimination method to solve the system of equations.

$$\begin{array}{ll} -8k - 8s = -160 & \text{Multiplying (1) by } -8 \\ \underline{9k + 8s = 168} & \\ k = 8 & \end{array}$$

Substitute 8 for k in (1) and solve for s.

$$8 + s = 20$$
$$s = 12$$

Check. The total mixture contains 8 lb + 12 lb, or 20 lb. Its value is $9 \cdot 8 + $8 \cdot 12 = $72 + $96 = 168. The answer checks.

State. 8 lb of Kenyan French Roast coffee and 12 lb of Sumatran coffee should be used.

22. 20 lb of cashews, 30 lb of Brazil nuts

23. Observe that the average of 40% and 10% is 25%:
$$\frac{40\% + 10\%}{2} = \frac{50\%}{2} = 25\%. \text{ Thus, the caterer should use}$$
equal parts of the 40% and 10% mixtures. Since a 10-lb mixture is desired, the caterer should use 5 lb each of the 40% and the 10% mixture.

24. 150 lb of soybean meal, 200 lb of corn meal

25. Familiarize. Let x = the number of liters of 25% solution and y = the number of liters of 50% solution to be used. The mixture contains 40%(10 L), or 0.4(10 L) = 4 L of acid.

Translate. We organize the information in a table.

	25% solution	50% solution	Mixture
Number of liters	x	y	10
Percent of acid	25%	50%	40%
Amount of acid	$0.25x$	$0.5y$	4 L

We get one equation from the "Number of liters" row of the table.

$$x + y = 10$$

The last row of the table yields a second equation.

$$0.25x + 0.5y = 4$$

After clearing decimals, we have the problem translated to a system of equations:

$$x + y = 10, \quad (1)$$
$$25x + 50y = 400 \quad (2)$$

Carry out. We use the elimination method to solve the system of equations.

$$\begin{array}{ll} -25x - 25y = -250 & \text{Multiplying (1) by } -25 \\ \underline{25x + 50y = 400} & \\ 25y = 150 & \\ y = 6 & \end{array}$$

Substitute 6 for y in (1) and solve for x.

$$x + 6 = 10$$
$$x = 4$$

Check. The total amount of the mixture is 4 lb + 6 lb, or 10 lb. The amount of acid in the mixture is 0.25(4 L) + 0.5(6 L) = 1 L + 3 L = 4 L. The answer checks.

State. 4 L of the 25% solution and 6 L of the 50% solution should be mixed.

26. 12 lb of Deep Thought, 8 lb of Oat Dream

27. Familiarize. Let x = the amount of the 6% loan and y = the amount of the 9% loan. Recall that the formula for simple interest is

$$\text{Interest} = \text{Principal} \cdot \text{Rate} \cdot \text{Time}.$$

Translate. We organize the information in a table.

	6% loan	9% loan	Total
Principal	x	y	$12,000
Interest Rate	6%	9%	
Time	1 yr	1 yr	
Interest	$0.06x$	$0.09y$	$855

The "Principal" row of the table gives us one equation:

$$x + y = 12,000$$

The last row of the table yields another equation:

$$0.06x + 0.09y = 855$$

After clearing decimals, we have the problem translated to a system of equations:

$$x + y = 12,000 \quad (1)$$
$$6x + 9y = 85,500 \quad (2)$$

Carry out. We use the elimination method to solve the system of equations.

$$\begin{array}{ll} -6x - 6y = -72,000 & \text{Multiplying (1) by } -6 \\ \underline{6x + 9y = 85,500} & \\ 3y = 13,500 & \\ y = 4500 & \end{array}$$

Substitute 4500 for y in (1) and solve for x.

$$x + 4500 = 12,000$$
$$x = 7500$$

Check. The loans total $7500 + $4500, or $12,000. The total interest is $0.06(\$7500) + 0.09(\$4500) = \$450 + \$405 = \$855$. The answer checks.

State. The 6% loan was for $7500, and the 9% loan was for $4500.

28. $6800 at 9%, $8200 at 10%

29. Familiarize. Let $x =$ the number of liters of Arctic Antifreeze and $y =$ the number of liters of Frost-No-More in the mixture. The amount of alcohol in the mixture is $0.15(20 \text{ L}) = 3 \text{ L}$.

Translate. We organize the information in a table.

	18% solution	10% solution	Mixture
Number of liters	x	y	20
Percent of alcohol	18%	10%	15%
Amount of alcohol	$0.18x$	$0.1y$	3

We get one equation from the "Number of liters" row of the table:

$$x + y = 20$$

The last row of the table yields a second equation:

$$0.18x + 0.1y = 3$$

After clearing decimals we have the problem translated to a system of equations:

$$x + y = 20, \quad (1)$$
$$18x + 10y = 300 \quad (2)$$

Carry out. We use the elimination method to solve the system of equations.

$$\begin{array}{rl} -10x - 10y = -200 & \text{Multiplying (1) by } -10 \\ 18x + 10y = 300 & \\ \hline 8x = 100 & \\ x = 12.5 & \end{array}$$

Substitute 12.5 for x in (1) and solve for y.

$$12.5 + y = 20$$
$$y = 7.5$$

Check. The total amount of the mixture is $12.5 \text{ L} + 7.5 \text{ L}$ or 20 L. The amount of alcohol in the mixture is $0.18(12.5 \text{ L}) + 0.1(7.5 \text{ L}) = 2.25 \text{ L} + 0.75 \text{ L} = 3 \text{ L}$. The answer checks.

State. 12.5 L of Arctic Antifreeze and 7.5 L of Frost-No-More should be used.

30. $169\frac{3}{13}$ lb of whole milk, $30\frac{10}{13}$ lb of cream

31. Familiarize. Let $l =$ the length, in meters, and $w =$ the width, in meters. Recall that the formula for the perimeter P of a rectangle with length l and width w is $P = 2l + 2w$.

Translate.

The perimeter is 190 m.

$$2l + 2w = 190$$

The width is one-fourth of the length.

$$w = \frac{1}{4} \cdot l$$

We have translated to a system of equations:

$$2l + 2w = 190, \quad (1)$$
$$w = \frac{1}{4}l$$

Carry out. We use the substitution method to solve the system of equations.

Substitute $\frac{1}{4}l$ for w in (1) and solve for l.

$$2l + 2\left(\frac{1}{4}l\right) = 190$$
$$2l + \frac{1}{2}l = 190$$
$$\frac{5}{2}l = 190$$
$$l = \frac{2}{5} \cdot 190 = 76$$

Now substitute 76 for l in (2).

$$l = \frac{1}{4} \cdot 76 = 19$$

Check. The perimeter is $2 \cdot 76 \text{ m} + 2 \cdot 19 \text{ m} = 152 \text{ m} + 38 \text{ m} = 190 \text{ m}$. The width, 19 m, is one-fourth the length, 76 m. The answer checks.

State. The length is 76 m, and the width is 19 m.

32. Length: 265 ft, width: 165 ft

33. Familiarize. The change from the $9.25 purchase is $20 - \$9.25$, or $10.75. Let $x =$ the number of quarters and $y =$ the number of fifty-cent pieces. The total value of the quarters, in dollars, is $0.25x$ and the total value of the fifty-cent pieces, in dollars, is $0.50y$.

Translate.

The total number of coins is 30.

$$x + y = 30$$

The total value of the coins is $10.75.

$$0.25x + 0.50y = 10.75$$

After clearing decimals we have the following system of equations:

$$x + y = 30, \quad (1)$$
$$25x + 50y = 1075 \quad (2)$$

Carry out. We use the elimination method to solve the system of equations.

$$\begin{array}{rl} -25x - 25y = -750 & \text{Multiplying (1) by } -25 \\ 25x + 50y = 1075 & \\ \hline 25y = 325 & \\ y = 13 & \end{array}$$

Substitute 13 for y in (1) and solve for x.

$$x + 13 = 30$$
$$x = 17$$

Check. The total number of coins is $17 + 13$, or 30. The total value of the coins is $\$0.25(17) + \$0.50(13) = \$4.25 + \$6.50 = \$10.75$. The answer checks.

State. There were 17 quarters and 13 fifty-cent pieces.

34. 7 $5 bills, 15 $1 bills

35. Familiarize. We first make a drawing.

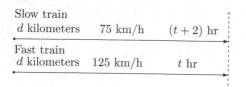

Slow train
d kilometers   75 km/h $(t + 2)$ hr

Fast train
d kilometers   125 km/h t hr

From the drawing we see that the distances are the same. Now complete the chart.

$$d = r \cdot t$$

	Distance	Rate	Time	
Slow train	d	75	$t+2$	$\to d = 75(t+2)$
Fast train	d	125	t	$\to d = 125t$

Translate. Using $d = rt$ in each row of the table, we get a system of equations:

$$d = 75(t + 2),$$
$$d = 125t$$

Carry out. We solve the system of equations.

$$125t = 75(t + 2) \quad \text{Using substitution}$$
$$125t = 75t + 150$$
$$50t = 150$$
$$t = 3$$

Then $d = 125t = 125 \cdot 3 = 375$

Check. At 125 km/h, in 3 hr the fast train will travel $125 \cdot 3 = 375$ km. At 75 km/h, in $3 + 2$, or 5 hr the slow train will travel $75 \cdot 5 = 375$ km. The numbers check.

State. The trains will meet 375 km from the station.

36. 3 hr

37. Familiarize. We first make a drawing. Let $d =$ the distance and $r =$ the speed of the canoe in still water. Then when the canoe travels downstream its speed is $r + 6$, and its speed upstream is $r - 6$. From the drawing we see that the distances are the same.

Downstream, 6 mph current

d mi, $r + 6$, 4 hr

Upstream, 6 mph current

d mi, $r - 6$, 10 hr

Organize the information in a table.

	Distance	Rate	Time
With current	d	$r+6$	4
Against current	d	$r-6$	10

Translate. Using $d = rt$ in each row of the table, we get a system of equations:

$$d = 4(r + 6), \qquad d = 4r + 24,$$
$$\text{or}$$
$$d = 10(r - 6) \qquad d = 10r - 60$$

Carry out. Solve the system of equations.

$$4r + 24 = 10r - 60 \quad \text{Using substitution}$$
$$24 = 6r - 60$$
$$84 = 6r$$
$$14 = r$$

Check. When $r = 14$, then $r + 6 = 14 + 6 = 20$, and the distance traveled in 4 hr is $4 \cdot 20 = 80$ km. Also, $r - 6 = 14 - 6 = 8$, and the distance traveled in 10 hr is $8 \cdot 10 = 80$ km. The answer checks.

State. The speed of the canoe in still water is 14 km/h.

38. 24 mph

39. Familiarize. We make a drawing. Note that the plane's speed traveling toward London is $360 + 50$, or 410 mph, and the speed traveling toward New York City is $360 - 50$, or 310 mph. Also, when the plane is d mi from New York City, it is $3458 - d$ mi from London.

New York City   London
310 mph t hours t hours   410 mph

|————————— 3458 mi —————————|

|——— d ———|——— 3458 mi $-d$ ———|

Organize the information in a table.

	Distance	Rate	Time
Toward NYC	d	310	t
Toward London	$3458 - d$	410	t

Translate. Using $d = rt$ in each row of the table, we get a system of equations:

$$d = 310t, \quad (1)$$
$$3458 - d = 410t \quad (2)$$

Carry out. We solve the system of equations.

$$3458 - 310t = 410t \quad \text{Using substitution}$$
$$3458 = 720t$$
$$4.8028 \approx t$$

Substitute 4.8028 for t in (1).

$$d \approx 310(4.8028) \approx 1489$$

Check. If the plane is 1489 mi from New York City, it can return to New York City, flying at 310 mph, in $1489/310 \approx 4.8$ hr. If the plane is $3458 - 1489$, or 1969 mi from London, it can fly to London, traveling at 410 mph, in $1969/410 \approx$ 4.8 hr. Since the times are the same, the answer checks.

State. The point of no return is about 1489 mi from New York City.

40. About 1524 mi

41. *Writing Exercise*

42. *Writing Exercise*

43. $2x - 3y + 12 = 2 \cdot 5 - 3 \cdot 2 + 12$
$$= 10 - 6 + 12$$
$$= 4 + 12$$
$$= 16$$

44. 11

45. $5a - 7b + 3c = 5(-2) - 7(3) + 3 \cdot 1$
$$= -10 - 21 + 3$$
$$= -31 + 3$$
$$= -28$$

46. -10

47. $4 - 2y + 3z = 4 - 2 \cdot \dfrac{1}{3} + 3 \cdot \dfrac{1}{4}$
$$= 4 - \frac{2}{3} + \frac{3}{4}$$
$$= \frac{48}{12} - \frac{8}{12} + \frac{9}{12}$$
$$= \frac{40}{12} + \frac{9}{12}$$
$$= \frac{49}{12}$$

48. $\dfrac{13}{10}$

49. *Writing Exercise*

50. *Writing Exercise*

51. The Familiarize and Translate steps were done in Exercise 84 of Exercise Set 8.1.

Carry out. We solve the system of equations
$$x = 2y, \quad (1)$$
$$x + 20 = 3y \quad (2)$$
where $x =$ Burl's age now and $y =$ his son's age now.
$$2y + 20 = 3y \quad \text{Substituting } 2y \text{ for } x \text{ in } (2)$$
$$20 = y$$
$$x = 2 \cdot 20 \quad \text{Substituting 20 for } y \text{ in } (1)$$
$$x = 40$$

Check. Burl's age now, 40, is twice his son's age now, 20. Ten years ago Burl was 30 and his son was 10, and $30 = 3 \cdot 10$. The numbers check.

State. Now Burl is 40 and his son is 20.

52. Lou: 32 years, Juanita: 14 years

53. The Familiarize and Translate steps were done in Exercise 86 of Exercise Set 8.1.

Carry out. We solve the system of equations
$$2l + 2w = 156, \quad (1)$$
$$l = 4(w - 6) \quad (2)$$
where $l =$ length, in inches, and $w =$ width, in inches.
$$2 \cdot 4(w - 6) + 2w = 156 \quad \text{Substituting } 4(w - 6)$$
$$\text{for } l \text{ in } (1)$$
$$8w - 48 + 2w = 156$$
$$10w - 48 = 156$$
$$10w = 204$$
$$w = \frac{204}{10}, \text{ or } \frac{102}{5}$$
$$l = 4\left(\frac{102}{5} - 6\right) \quad \text{Substituting } \frac{102}{5} \text{ for } w$$
$$\text{in } (2)$$
$$l = 4\left(\frac{102}{5} - \frac{30}{5}\right)$$
$$l = 4\left(\frac{72}{5}\right)$$
$$l = \frac{288}{5}$$

Check. The perimeter of a rectangle with width $\dfrac{102}{5}$ in. and length $\dfrac{288}{5}$ in. is
$$2\left(\frac{288}{5}\right) + 2\left(\frac{102}{5}\right) = \frac{576}{5} + \frac{204}{5} = \frac{780}{5} = 156 \text{ in.}$$
If 6 in. is cut off the width, the new width is $\dfrac{102}{5} - 6 = \dfrac{102}{5} - \dfrac{30}{5} = \dfrac{72}{5}$. The length, $\dfrac{288}{5}$, is $4\left(\dfrac{72}{5}\right)$. The numbers check.

State. The original piece of posterboard had width $\dfrac{102}{5}$ in. and length $\dfrac{288}{5}$ in.

54. $\dfrac{64}{5}$ oz of baking soda, $\dfrac{16}{5}$ oz of vinegar

55. **Familiarize.** Let $k =$ the number of pounds of Kona coffee that must be added to the Mexican coffee, and $m =$ the number of pounds of coffee in the mixture.

Translate. We organize the information in a table.

	Mexican	Kona	Mixture
Number of pounds	40	k	m
Percent of Kona	0%	100%	30%
Amount of Kona	0	k	$0.3m$

We get one equation from the "Number of pounds" row of the table:
$$40 + k = m$$
The last row of the table gives us a second equation:
$$k = 0.3m$$

After clearing the decimal we have the problem translated to a system of equations:

$$40 + k = m, \quad (1)$$
$$10k = 3m \quad (2)$$

Carry out. We use substitution to solve the system of equations. First we substitute $40 + k$ for m in (2).

$$10k = 3m \qquad (2)$$
$$10k = 3(40 + k) \quad \text{Substituting}$$
$$10k = 120 + 3k$$
$$7k = 120$$
$$k = \frac{120}{7}$$

Although the problem asks only for k, the amount of Kona coffee that should be used, we will also find m in order to check the answer.

$$40 + k = m \quad (1)$$
$$40 + \frac{120}{7} = m \quad \text{Substituting } \frac{120}{7} \text{ for } k$$
$$\frac{280}{7} + \frac{120}{7} = m$$
$$\frac{400}{7} = m$$

Check. If $\frac{400}{7}$ lb of coffee contain $\frac{120}{7}$ lb of Kona coffee, then the percent of Kona beans in the mixture is $\frac{120/7}{400/7} = \frac{120}{7} \cdot \frac{7}{400} = \frac{3}{10}$, or 30%. The answer checks.

State. $\frac{120}{7}$ lb of Kona coffee should be added to the Mexican coffee.

56. 1.8 L

57. Familiarize. Let $d =$ the distance, in km, that Natalie jogs in a trip to school, and let $t =$ the time, in hr, that she jogs. We organize the information in a table.

	Distance	Rate	Time
Jogging	d	8	t
Walking	$6 - d$	4	$1 - t$

Translate. Using $d = rt$ in each row of the table we get a system of equations:

$$d = 8t, \qquad (1)$$
$$6 - d = 4(1 - t) \quad (2)$$

Carry out. We use substitution to solve the system of equations.

$$6 - 8t = 4(1 - t) \quad \text{Substituting } 8t \text{ for } d \text{ in (2)}$$
$$6 - 8t = 4 - 4t$$
$$2 - 8t = -4t$$
$$2 = 4t$$
$$\frac{1}{2} = t$$

Substitute $\frac{1}{2}$ for t in (1).

$$d = 8 \cdot \frac{1}{2} = 4$$

Check. If Natalie jogs 4 km in $\frac{1}{2}$ hr, then she walks $6 - 4$ or 2 km, in $1 - \frac{1}{2}$, or $\frac{1}{2}$ hr. At a rate of 8 km/h, in $\frac{1}{2}$ hr she can jog $8 \cdot \frac{1}{2}$, or 4 km. At a rate of 4 km/h, in $\frac{1}{2}$ hr she can walk $4 \cdot \frac{1}{2}$, or 2 km. Then the total time is $\frac{1}{2}$ hr $+ \frac{1}{2}$ hr, or 1 hr, and the total distance is 4 km + 2 km, or 6 km. The answer checks.

State. Natalie jogs 4 km in a trip to school.

58. 180 members

59. Familiarize. Let $x =$ the ten's digit and $y =$ the unit's digit. Then the number is $10x + y$. If the digits are interchanged, the new number is $10y + x$.

Translate.

Ten's digit is 2 more than 3 times unit's digit.

$$x \quad = 2 \quad + \quad 3 \quad \cdot \quad y$$

If the digits are interchanged,

new number is half of given number minus 13.

$$10y + x \quad = \quad \frac{1}{2} \quad \cdot \quad (10x + y) \quad - \quad 13$$

The system of equations is

$$x = 2 + 3y, \qquad (1)$$
$$10y + x = \frac{1}{2}(10x + y) - 13 \quad (2)$$

Carry out. We use the substitution method. Substitute $2 + 3y$ for x in (2).

$$10y + (2 + 3y) = \frac{1}{2}[10(2 + 3y) + y] - 13$$
$$13y + 2 = \frac{1}{2}[20 + 30y + y] - 13$$
$$13y + 2 = \frac{1}{2}[20 + 31y] - 13$$
$$13y + 2 = 10 + \frac{31}{2}y - 13$$
$$13y + 2 = \frac{31}{2}y - 3$$
$$5 = \frac{5}{2}y$$
$$2 = y$$

$$x = 2 + 3 \cdot 2 \quad \text{Substituting 2 for } y \text{ in (1)}$$
$$x = 2 + 6$$
$$x = 8$$

Check. If $x = 8$ and $y = 2$, the given number is 82 and the new number is 28. In the given number the ten's digit, 8, is two more than three times the unit's digit, 2. The new number is 13 less than one-half the given number: $28 = \frac{1}{2}(82) - 13$. The values check.

State. The given integer is 82.

60. First train: 36 km/h, second train: 54 km/h

61. *Familiarize.* Let $x =$ the number of gallons of pure brown and $y =$ the number of gallons of neutral stain that should be added to the original 0.5 gal. Note that a total of 1 gal of stain needs to be added to bring the amount of stain up to 1.5 gal. The original 0.5 gal of stain contains 20%(0.5 gal), or 0.2(0.5 gal) = 0.1 gal of brown stain. The final solution contains 60%(1.5 gal), or 0.6(1.5 gal) = 0.9 gal of brown stain. This is composed of the original 0.1 gal and the x gal that are added.

Translate.

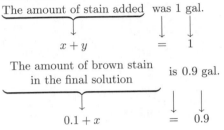

We have a system of equations.

$$x + y = 1, \quad (1)$$
$$0.1 + x = 0.9 \quad (2)$$

Carry out. First we solve (2) for x.

$$0.1 + x = 0.9$$
$$x = 0.8$$

Then substitute 0.8 for x in (1) and solve for y.

$$0.8 + y = 1$$
$$y = 0.2$$

Check. Total amount of stain: $0.5 + 0.8 + 0.2 = 1.5$ gal

Total amount of brown stain: $0.1 + 0.8 = 0.9$ gal

Total amount of neutral stain: $0.8(0.5) + 0.2 = 0.4 + 0.2 = 0.6$ gal $= 0.4(1.5$ gal$)$

The answer checks.

State. 0.8 gal of pure brown and 0.2 gal of neutral stain should be added.

62. City: 261 miles, highway: 204 miles

63. Observe that if 100% acetone is added to water to create a 10% acetone solution, then the ratio of acetone to water is 10% to 90%, or 10 to 90, or 1 to 9. Thus, for each liter of acetone, 9 liters of water are required. If 5 extra liters of acetone are added to the vat, then $9 \cdot 5$, or 45 L of additional water must be added to bring the concentration down to 10%.

64. 4 boys, 3 girls

65. The 1.5 gal mixture contains $0.1 + x$ gal of pure brown stain. (See Exercise 61.). Thus, the function $P(x) = \dfrac{0.1 + x}{1.5}$ gives the percentage of brown in the mixture as a decimal quantity. Using the Intersect feature, we confirm that when $x = 0.8$, then $P(x) = 0.6$ or 60%.

Exercise Set 8.4

1. Substitute $(2, -1, -2)$ into the three equations, using alphabetical order.

$$\frac{x + y - 2z = 5}{\underset{\begin{array}{c|c} & \\ 5 & 5 \quad \text{TRUE} \end{array}}{\begin{array}{c} 2 + (-1) - 2(-2) \ ? \ 5 \\ 2 - 1 + 4 \end{array}}}$$

$$\frac{2x - y - z = 7}{\underset{\begin{array}{c|c} & \\ 7 & 7 \quad \text{TRUE} \end{array}}{\begin{array}{c} 2 \cdot 2 - (-1) - (-2) \ ? \ 7 \\ 4 + 1 + 2 \end{array}}}$$

$$\frac{-x - 2y + 3z = 6}{\underset{\begin{array}{c|c} & \\ -6 & 6 \quad \text{FALSE} \end{array}}{\begin{array}{c} -2 - 2(-1) + 3(-2) \ ? \ 6 \\ -2 + 2 - 6 \end{array}}}$$

The triple $(2, -1, -2)$ does not make the third equation true, so it is not a solution of the system.

2. Yes

3.
$$\begin{aligned} x + y + z &= 6, \quad (1) \\ 2x - y + 3z &= 9, \quad (2) \\ -x + 2y + 2z &= 9 \quad (3) \end{aligned}$$

1., 2. The equations are already in standard form with no fractions or decimals.

3. Add Equations (1) and (2) to eliminate y:

$$\begin{array}{r} x + y + z = 6 \quad (1) \\ \underline{2x - y + 3z = 9} \quad (2) \\ 3x \qquad + 4z = 15 \quad (4) \quad \text{Adding} \end{array}$$

4. Use a different pair of equations and eliminate y:

$$\begin{array}{r} 4x - 2y + 6z = 18 \quad \text{Multiplying (2) by 2} \\ \underline{-x + 2y + 2z = 9} \quad (3) \\ 3x \qquad + 8z = 27 \quad (5) \end{array}$$

5. Now solve the system of Equations (4) and (5).

$$3x + 4z = 15 \quad (4)$$
$$3x + 8z = 27 \quad (5)$$

$$\begin{array}{r} -3x - 4z = -15 \quad \text{Multiplying (4) by } -1 \\ \underline{3x + 8z = 27} \\ 4z = 12 \\ z = 3 \end{array}$$

$$3x + 4 \cdot 3 = 15 \quad \text{Substituting 3 for } z \text{ in (4)}$$
$$3x + 12 = 15$$
$$3x = 3$$
$$x = 1$$

6. Substitute in one of the original equations to find y.

$1 + y + 3 = 6$ Substituting 1 for x and 3 for z in (1)

$y + 4 = 6$

$y = 2$

We obtain $(1, 2, 3)$. This checks, so it is the solution.

4. $(4, 0, 2)$

5. $2x - y - 3z = -1,$ (1)
   $2x - y + z = -9,$ (2)
   $x + 2y - 4z = 17$ (3)

1., 2. The equations are already in standard form with no fractions or decimals.

3., 4. We eliminate z from two different pairs of equations.

$2x - y - 3z = -1$ (1)

$\underline{6x - 3y + 3z = -27}$ Multiplying (2) by 3

$8x - 4y \qquad = -28$ (4)   Adding

$8x - 4y + 4z = -36$ Multiplying (2) by 4

$\underline{x + 2y - 4z = 17}$ (3)

$9x - 2y \qquad = -19$ (5)   Adding

5. Now solve the system of Equations (4) and (5).

$8x - 4y = -28$ (4)

$9x - 2y = -19$ (5)

$8x - 4y = -28$ (4)

$\underline{-18x + 4y = 38}$ Multiplying (5) by -2

$-10x \qquad = 10$ Adding

$x = -1$

$8(-1) - 4y = -28$ Substituting -1 for x in (4)

$-8 - 4y = -28$

$-4y = -20$

$y = 5$

6. Substitute in one of the original equations to find z.

$2(-1) - 5 + z = -9$ Substituting -1 for x and 5 for y in (2)

$-2 - 5 + z = -9$

$-7 + z = -9$

$z = -2$

We obtain $(-1, 5, -2)$. This checks, so it is the solution.

6. $(2, -2, 2)$

7. $2x - 3y + z = 5,$ (1)
   $x + 3y + 8z = 22,$ (2)
   $3x - y + 2z = 12$ (3)

1., 2. The equations are already in standard form with no fractions or decimals.

3., 4. We eliminate y from two different pairs of equations.

$2x - 3y + z = 5$ (1)

$\underline{x + 3y + 8z = 22}$ (2)

$3x \qquad + 9z = 27$ (4)   Adding

$x + 3y + 8z = 22$ (2)

$\underline{9x - 3y + 6z = 36}$ Multiplying (3) by 3

$10x \qquad + 14z = 58$ (5)   Adding

5. Solve the system of Equations (4) and (5).

$3x + 9z = 27$ (4)

$10x + 14z = 58$ (5)

$30x + 90z = 270$ Multiplying (4) by 10

$\underline{-30x - 42z = -174}$ Multiplying (5) by -3

$48z = 96$ Adding

$z = 2$

$3x + 9 \cdot 2 = 27$ Substituting 2 for z in (4)

$3x + 18 = 27$

$3x = 9$

$x = 3$

6. Substitute in one of the original equations to find y.

$2 \cdot 3 - 3y + 2 = 5$ Substituting 3 for x and 2 for z in (1)

$-3y + 8 = 5$

$-3y = -3$

$y = 1$

We obtain $(3, 1, 2)$. This checks, so it is the solution.

8. $(3, -2, 1)$

9. $3a - 2b + 7c = 13,$ (1)
   $a + 8b - 6c = -47,$ (2)
   $7a - 9b - 9c = -3$ (3)

1., 2. The equations are already in standard form with no fractions or decimals.

3., 4. We eliminate a from two different pairs of equations.

$3a - 2b + 7c = 13$ (1)

$\underline{-3a - 24b + 18c = 141}$ Multiplying (2) by -3

$-26b + 25c = 154$ (4)   Adding

$-7a - 56b + 42c = 329$ Multiplying (2) by -7

$\underline{7a - 9b - 9c = -3}$ (3)

$-65b + 33c = 326$ (5)   Adding

5. Now solve the system of Equations (4) and (5).

$-26b + 25c = 154$ (4)

$-65b + 33c = 326$ (5)

$$-130b + 125c = 770 \quad \text{Multiplying (4) by 5}$$
$$\underline{130b - 66c = -652} \quad \text{Multiplying (5) by } -2$$
$$59c = 118$$
$$c = 2$$

$$-26b + 25 \cdot 2 = 154 \quad \text{Substituting 2 for } c$$
$$\text{in (4)}$$
$$-26b + 50 = 154$$
$$-26b = 104$$
$$b = -4$$

6. Substitute in one of the original equations to find *a*.

$$a + 8(-4) - 6(2) = -47 \quad \text{Substituting } -4$$
$$\text{for } b \text{ and 2 for } c$$
$$\text{in (2)}$$
$$a - 32 - 12 = -47$$
$$a - 44 = -47$$
$$a = -3$$

We obtain $(-3, -4, 2)$. This checks, so it is the solution.

10. $(7, -3, -4)$

11. $2x + 3y + z = 17, \quad (1)$
$x - 3y + 2z = -8, \quad (2)$
$5x - 2y + 3z = 5 \quad (3)$

1., 2. The equations are already in standard form with no fractions or decimals.

3., 4. We eliminate *y* from two different pairs of equations.

$$2x + 3y + z = 17 \quad (1)$$
$$\underline{x - 3y + 2z = -8} \quad (2)$$
$$3x + 3z = 9 \quad (4) \quad \text{Adding}$$

$$4x + 6y + 2z = 34 \quad \text{Multiplying (1) by 2}$$
$$\underline{15x - 6y + 9z = 15} \quad \text{Multiplying (3) by 3}$$
$$19x + 11z = 49 \quad (5) \quad \text{Adding}$$

5. Now solve the system of Equations (4) and (5).

$$3x + 3z = 9 \quad (4)$$
$$19x + 11z = 49 \quad (5)$$

$$33x + 33z = 99 \quad \text{Multiplying (4) by 11}$$
$$\underline{-57x - 33z = -147} \quad \text{Multiplying (5) by } -3$$
$$-24x = -48$$
$$x = 2$$

$$3 \cdot 2 + 3z = 9 \quad \text{Substituting 2 for } x \text{ in (4)}$$
$$6 + 3z = 9$$
$$3z = 3$$
$$z = 1$$

6. Substitute in one of the original equations to find *y*.

$$2 \cdot 2 + 3y + 1 = 17 \quad \text{Substituting 2 for } x \text{ and}$$
$$1 \text{ for } z \text{ in (1)}$$
$$3y + 5 = 17$$
$$3y = 12$$
$$y = 4$$

We obtain $(2, 4, 1)$. This checks, so it is the solution.

12. $(2, 1, 3)$

13. $2x + y + z = -2, \quad (1)$
$2x - y + 3z = 6, \quad (2)$
$3x - 5y + 4z = 7 \quad (3)$

1., 2. The equations are already in standard form with no fractions or decimals.

3., 4. We eliminate *y* from two different pairs of equations.

$$2x + y + z = -2 \quad (1)$$
$$\underline{2x - y + 3z = 6} \quad (2)$$
$$4x + 4z = 4 \quad (4) \quad \text{Adding}$$

$$10x + 5y + 5z = -10 \quad \text{Multiplying (1) by 5}$$
$$\underline{3x - 5y + 4z = 7} \quad (3)$$
$$13x + 9z = -3 \quad (5) \quad \text{Adding}$$

5. Now solve the system of Equations (4) and (5).

$$4x + 4z = 4 \quad (4)$$
$$13x + 9z = -3 \quad (5)$$

$$36x + 36z = 36 \quad \text{Multiplying (4) by 9}$$
$$\underline{-52x - 36z = 12} \quad \text{Multiplying (5) by } -4$$
$$-16x = 48 \quad \text{Adding}$$
$$x = -3$$

$$4(-3) + 4z = 4 \quad \text{Substituting } -3 \text{ for } x \text{ in (4)}$$
$$-12 + 4z = 4$$
$$4z = 16$$
$$z = 4$$

6. Substitute in one of the original equations to find *y*.

$$2(-3) + y + 4 = -2 \quad \text{Substituting } -3 \text{ for}$$
$$x \text{ and 4 for } z \text{ in (1)}$$
$$y - 2 = -2$$
$$y = 0$$

We obtain $(-3, 0, 4)$. This checks, so it is the solution.

14. $(2, -5, 6)$

15. $x - y + z = 4, \quad (1)$
$5x + 2y - 3z = 2, \quad (2)$
$4x + 3y - 4z = -2 \quad (3)$

1., 2. The equations are already in standard form with no fractions or decimals.

3., 4. We eliminate *z* from two different pairs of equations.

$$3x - 3y + 3z = 12 \quad \text{Multiplying (1) by 3}$$
$$\underline{5x + 2y - 3z = 2 \quad (2)}$$
$$8x - y = 14 \quad (4) \quad \text{Adding}$$

$$4x - 4y + 4z = 16 \quad \text{Multiplying (1) by 4}$$
$$\underline{4x + 3y - 4z = -2 \quad (3)}$$
$$8x - y = 14 \quad (5) \quad \text{Adding}$$

5. Now solve the system of Equations (4) and (5).

$$8x - y = 14 \quad (4)$$
$$8x - y = 14 \quad (5)$$

$$8x - y = 14 \quad (4)$$
$$\underline{-8x + y = -14 \quad \text{Multiplying (5) by } -1}$$
$$0 = 0 \quad (6)$$

Equation (6) indicates Equations (1), (2), and (3) are dependent. (Note that if Equation (1) is subtracted from Equation (2), the result is Equation (3).) We could also have concluded that the equations are dependent by observing that Equations (4) and (5) are identical.

16. The equations are dependent.

17.
$$a + 2b + c = 1, \quad (1)$$
$$7a + 3b - c = -2, \quad (2)$$
$$a + 5b + 3c = 2 \quad (3)$$

1., 2. The equations are already in standard form with no fractions or decimals.

3., 4. We eliminate c from two different pairs of equations.

$$a + 2b + c = 1 \quad (1)$$
$$\underline{7a + 3b - c = -2 \quad (2)}$$
$$8a + 5b = -1 \quad (4)$$

$$21a + 9b - 3c = -6 \quad \text{Multiplying (2) by 3}$$
$$\underline{a + 5b + 3c = 2}$$
$$22a + 14b = -4 \quad (5)$$

5. Now solve the system of Equations (4) and (5).

$$8a + 5b = -1 \quad (4)$$
$$22a + 14b = -4 \quad (5)$$

$$112a + 70b = -14 \quad \text{Multiplying (4) by 14}$$
$$\underline{-110a - 70b = 20 \quad \text{Multiplying (5) by } -5}$$
$$2a = 6$$
$$a = 3$$

$$8 \cdot 3 + 5b = -1 \quad \text{Substituting in (4)}$$
$$24 + 5b = -1$$
$$5b = -25$$
$$b = -5$$

6. Substitute in one of the original equations to find c.

$$3 + 2(-5) + c = 1 \quad \text{Substituting in (1)}$$
$$-7 + c = 1$$
$$c = 8$$

We obtain $(3, -5, 8)$. This checks, so it is the solution.

18. $\left(\dfrac{1}{2}, 4, -6\right)$

19.
$$5x + 3y + \frac{1}{2}z = \frac{7}{2},$$
$$0.5x - 0.9y - 0.2z = 0.3,$$
$$3x - 2.4y + 0.4z = -1$$

1. All equations are already in standard form.

2. Multiply the first equation by 2 to clear the fractions. Also, multiply the second and third equations by 10 to clear the decimals.

$$10x + 6y + z = 7, \quad (1)$$
$$5x - 9y - 2z = 3, \quad (2)$$
$$30x - 24y + 4z = -10 \quad (3)$$

3., 4. We eliminate z from two different pairs of equations.

$$20x + 12y + 2z = 14 \quad \text{Multiplying (1) by 2}$$
$$\underline{5x - 9y - 2z = 3 \quad (2)}$$
$$25x + 3y = 17 \quad (4)$$

$$10x - 18y - 4z = 6 \quad \text{Multiplying (2) by 2}$$
$$\underline{30x - 24y + 4z = -10 \quad (3)}$$
$$40x - 42y = -4 \quad (5)$$

5. Now solve the system of Equations (4) and (5).

$$25x + 3y = 17 \quad (4)$$
$$40x - 42y = -4 \quad (5)$$

$$350x + 42y = 238 \quad \text{Multiplying (4) by 14}$$
$$\underline{40x - 42y = -4 \quad (5)}$$
$$390x = 234$$
$$x = \frac{3}{5}$$

$$25\left(\frac{3}{5}\right) + 3y = 17 \quad \text{Substituting in (4)}$$
$$15 + 3y = 17$$
$$3y = 2$$
$$y = \frac{2}{3}$$

6. Substitute in one of the original equations to find z.

$$10\left(\frac{3}{5}\right) + 6\left(\frac{2}{3}\right) + z = 7 \quad \text{Substituting in (1)}$$
$$6 + 4 + z = 7$$
$$10 + z = 7$$
$$z = -3$$

We obtain $\left(\dfrac{3}{5}, \dfrac{2}{3}, -3\right)$. This checks, so it is the solution.

20. $\left(\dfrac{1}{2}, \dfrac{1}{3}, \dfrac{1}{6}\right)$

21.
$$3p \qquad + 2r = 11, \quad (1)$$
$$q - 7r = 4, \quad (2)$$
$$p - 6q \qquad = 1 \quad (3)$$

1., 2. The equations are already in standard form with no fractions or decimals.

3., 4. Note that there is no q in Equation (1). We will use Equations (2) and (3) to obtain another equation with no q-term.

$$6q - 42r = 24 \quad \text{Multiplying (2) by 6}$$
$$\underline{p - 6q \qquad = 1 \quad (3)}$$
$$p \qquad - 42r = 25 \quad (4)$$

5. Solve the system of Equations (1) and (4).
$$3p + 2r = 11 \quad (1)$$
$$p - 42r = 25 \quad (4)$$

$$3p + 2r = 11 \quad (1)$$
$$\underline{-3p + 126r = -75 \quad \text{Multiplying (4) by } -3}$$
$$128r = -64$$
$$r = -\dfrac{1}{2}$$

$$3p + 2\left(-\dfrac{1}{2}\right) = 11 \quad \text{Substituting in (1)}$$
$$3p - 1 = 11$$
$$3p - 12$$
$$p = 4$$

6. Substitute in Equation (2) or (3) to find q.
$$q - 7\left(-\dfrac{1}{2}\right) = 4 \quad \text{Substituting in (2)}$$
$$q + \dfrac{7}{2} = 4$$
$$q = \dfrac{1}{2}$$

We obtain $\left(4, \dfrac{1}{2}, -\dfrac{1}{2}\right)$. This checks, so it is the solution.

22. $\left(\dfrac{1}{2}, \dfrac{2}{3}, -\dfrac{5}{6}\right)$

23.
$$x + y + z = 105, \quad (1)$$
$$10y - z = 11, \quad (2)$$
$$2x - 3y \qquad = 7 \quad (3)$$

1., 2. The equations are already in standard form with no fractions or decimals.

3., 4. Note that there is no z in Equation (3). We will use Equations (1) and (2) to obtain another equation with no z-term.

$$x + y + z = 105 \quad (1)$$
$$\underline{10y - z = 11 \quad (2)}$$
$$x + 11y \qquad = 116 \quad (4)$$

5. Now solve the system of Equations (3) and (4).
$$2x - 3y = 7 \quad (3)$$
$$x + 11y = 116 \quad (4)$$

$$2x - 3y = 7 \quad (3)$$
$$\underline{-2x - 22y = -232 \quad \text{Multiplying (4) by } -2}$$
$$-25y = -225$$
$$y = 9$$

$$x + 11 \cdot 9 = 116 \quad \text{Substituting in (4)}$$
$$x + 99 = 116$$
$$x = 17$$

6. Substitute in Equation (1) or (2) to find z.
$$17 + 9 + z = 105 \quad \text{Substituting in (1)}$$
$$26 + z = 105$$
$$z = 79$$

We obtain $(17, 9, 79)$. This checks, so it is the solution.

24. $(15, 33, 9)$

25.
$$2a - 3b \qquad = 2, \quad (1)$$
$$7a \qquad + 4c = \dfrac{3}{4}, \quad (2)$$
$$-3b + 2c = 1 \quad (3)$$

1. The equations are already in standard form.

2. Multiply Equation (2) by 4 to clear the fraction. The resulting system is
$$2a - 3b \qquad = 2, \quad (1)$$
$$28a \qquad + 16c = 3, \quad (4)$$
$$-3b + 2c = 1 \quad (3)$$

3. Note that there is no b in Equation (2). We will use Equations (1) and (3) to obtain another equation with no b-term.

$$2a - 3b \qquad = 2 \quad (1)$$
$$\underline{3b - 2c = -1 \quad \text{Multiplying (3) by } -1}$$
$$2a \qquad - 2c = 1 \quad (5)$$

5. Now solve the system of Equations (4) and (5).
$$28a + 16c = 3 \quad (4)$$
$$2a - 2c = 1 \quad (5)$$

$$28a + 16c = 3 \quad (4)$$
$$\underline{16a - 16c = 8 \quad \text{Multiplying (5) by 8}}$$
$$44a \qquad = 11$$
$$a = \dfrac{1}{4}$$

$2 \cdot \dfrac{1}{4} - 2c = 1$ Substituting $\dfrac{1}{4}$ for a in (5)

$\dfrac{1}{2} - 2c = 1$

$-2c = \dfrac{1}{2}$

$c = -\dfrac{1}{4}$

6. Substitute in Equation (1) or (2) to find b.

$2\left(\dfrac{1}{4}\right) - 3b = 2$ Substituting $\dfrac{1}{4}$ for a in (1)

$\dfrac{1}{2} - 3b = 2$

$-3b = \dfrac{3}{2}$

$b = -\dfrac{1}{2}$

We obtain $\left(\dfrac{1}{4}, -\dfrac{1}{2}, -\dfrac{1}{4}\right)$. This checks, so it is the solution.

26. $(3, 4, -1)$

27. $x + y + z = 182,$ (1)

$y = 2 + 3x,$ (2)

$z = 80 + x$ (3)

Observe, from Equations (2) and (3), that we can substitute $2 + 3x$ for y and $80 + x$ for z in Equation (1) and solve for x.

$x + y + x = 182$

$x + (2 + 3x) + (80 + x) = 182$

$5x + 82 = 182$

$5x = 100$

$x = 20$

Now substitute 20 for x in Equation (2).

$y = 2 + 3x = 2 + 3 \cdot 20 = 2 + 60 = 62$

Finally, substitute 20 for x in Equation (3).

$z = 80 + x = 80 + 20 = 100.$

We obtain $(20, 62, 100)$. This checks, so it is the solution.

28. $(2, 5, -3)$

29. $x + y \quad\quad = 0,$ (1)

$x \quad\quad + z = 1,$ (2)

$2x + y + z = 2$ (3)

1., 2. The equations are already in standard form with no fractions or decimals.

3., 4. Note that there is no z in Equation (1). We will use Equations (2) and (3) to obtain another equation with no z-term.

$-x \quad\quad - z = -1$ Multiplying (2) by -1

$\underline{2x + y + z = \quad 2}$ (3)

$x + y \quad\quad = \quad 1$ (4)

5. Now solve the system of Equations (1) and (4).

$x + y = 0$ (1)

$x + y = 1$ (4)

$x + y = \quad 0$ (1)

$\underline{-x - y = -1}$ Multiplying (4) by -1

$0 = -1$ Adding

We get a false equation, or contradiction. There is no solution.

30. No solution

31. $\quad\quad y + z = 1,$ (1)

$x + y + z = 1,$ (2)

$x + 2y + 2z = 2$ (3)

1., 2. The equations are already in standard form with no fractions or decimals.

3., 4. Note that there is no x in Equation (1). We will use Equations (2) and (3) to obtain another equation with no x-term.

$-x - y - z = -1$ Multiplying (2) by -1

$\underline{x + 2y + 2z = \quad 2}$ (3)

$y + z = \quad 1$ (4)

Equations (1) and (4) are identical. This means that Equations (1), (2), and (3) are dependent. (We have seen that if Equation (2) is multiplied by -1 and added to Equation (3), the result is Equation (1).)

32. The equations are dependent.

33. *Writing Exercise*

34. *Writing Exercise*

35. Let x represent the larger number and y represent the smaller number. Then we have $x = 2y$.

36. Let x represent the first number and y represent the second number; $x + y = 3x$

37. Let x, $x + 1$, and $x + 2$ represent the numbers. Then we have $x + (x + 1) + (x + 2) = 45$.

38. Let x and y represent the numbers; $x + 2y = 17$

39. Let x and y represent the first two numbers and let z represent the third number. Then we have $x + y = 5z$.

40. Let x and y represent the numbers; $xy = 2(x + y)$

41. *Writing Exercise*

42. *Writing Exercise*

43. $\dfrac{x+2}{3} - \dfrac{y+4}{2} + \dfrac{z+1}{6} = 0,$

$\dfrac{x-4}{3} + \dfrac{y+1}{4} - \dfrac{z-2}{2} = -1,$

$\dfrac{x+1}{2} + \dfrac{y}{2} + \dfrac{z-1}{4} = \dfrac{3}{4}$

1., 2. We clear fractions and write each equation in standard form.

To clear fractions, we multiply both sides of each equation by the LCM of its denominators. The LCM's are 6, 12, and 4, respectively.

$$6\left(\frac{x+2}{3} - \frac{y+4}{2} + \frac{z+1}{6}\right) = 6 \cdot 0$$
$$2(x+2) - 3(y+4) + (z+1) = 0$$
$$2x + 4 - 3y - 12 + z + 1 = 0$$
$$2x - 3y + z = 7$$

$$12\left(\frac{x-4}{3} + \frac{y+1}{4} - \frac{z-2}{2}\right) = 12 \cdot (-1)$$
$$4(x-4) + 3(y+1) - 6(z-2) = -12$$
$$4x - 16 + 3y + 3 - 6z + 12 = -12$$
$$4x + 3y - 6z = -11$$

$$4\left(\frac{x+1}{2} + \frac{y}{2} + \frac{z-1}{4}\right) = 4 \cdot \frac{3}{4}$$
$$2(x+1) + 2(y) + (z-1) = 3$$
$$2x + 2 + 2y + z - 1 = 3$$
$$2x + 2y + z = 2$$

The resulting system is
$$2x - 3y + z = 7, \quad (1)$$
$$4x + 3y - 6z = -11, \quad (2)$$
$$2x + 2y + z = 2 \quad (3)$$

3., 4. We eliminate z from two different pairs of equations.

$$12x - 18y + 6z = 42 \quad \text{Multiplying (1) by 6}$$
$$\underline{4x + 3y - 6z = -11} \quad (2)$$
$$16x - 15y = 31 \quad (4) \quad \text{Adding}$$

$$2x - 3y + z = 7 \quad (1)$$
$$\underline{-2x - 2y - z = -2} \quad \text{Multiplying (3) by } -1$$
$$-5y = 5 \quad (5) \quad \text{Adding}$$

5. Solve (5) for y: $\quad -5y = 5$
$$y = -1$$

Substitute -1 for y in (4):
$$16x - 15(-1) = 31$$
$$16x + 15 = 31$$
$$16x = 16$$
$$x = 1$$

6. Substitute 1 for x and -1 for y in (1):
$$2 \cdot 1 - 3(-1) + z = 7$$
$$5 + z = 7$$
$$z = 2$$

We obtain $(1, -1, 2)$. This checks, so it is the solution.

44. $(1, -2, 4, -1)$

45.
$$w + x - y + z = 0, \quad (1)$$
$$w - 2x - 2y - z = -5, \quad (2)$$
$$w - 3x - y + z = 4, \quad (3)$$
$$2w - x - y + 3z = 7 \quad (4)$$

The equations are already in standard form with no fractions or decimals.

Start by eliminating z from three different pairs of equations.

$$w + x - y + z = 0 \quad (1)$$
$$\underline{w - 2x - 2y - z = -5} \quad (2)$$
$$2w - x - 3y = -5 \quad (5) \quad \text{Adding}$$

$$w - 2x - 2y - z = -5 \quad (2)$$
$$\underline{w - 3x - y + z = 4} \quad (3)$$
$$2w - 5x - 3y = -1 \quad (6) \quad \text{Adding}$$

$$3w - 6x - 6y - 3z = -15 \quad \text{Multiplying (2) by 3}$$
$$\underline{2w - x - y + 3z = 7} \quad (4)$$
$$5w - 7x - 7y = -8 \quad (7) \quad \text{Adding}$$

Now solve the system of equations (5), (6), and (7).
$$2w - x - 3y = -5, \quad (5)$$
$$2w - 5x - 3y = -1, \quad (6)$$
$$5w - 7x - 7y = -8. \quad (7)$$

$$2w - x - 3y = -5 \quad (5)$$
$$\underline{-2w + 5x + 3y = 1} \quad \text{Multiplying (6) by } -1$$
$$4x = -4$$
$$x = -1$$

Substituting -1 for x in (5) and (7) and simplifying, we have
$$2w - 3y = -6, \quad (8)$$
$$5w - 7y = -15. \quad (9)$$

Now solve the system of Equations (8) and (9).
$$10w - 15y = -30 \quad \text{Multiplying (8) by 5}$$
$$\underline{-10w + 14y = 30} \quad \text{Multiplying (9) by } -2$$
$$-y = 0$$
$$y = 0$$

Substitute 0 for y in Equation (8) or (9) and solve for w.
$$2w - 3 \cdot 0 = -6 \quad \text{Substituting in (8)}$$
$$2w = -6$$
$$w = -3$$

Substitute in one of the original equations to find z.
$$-3 - 1 - 0 + z = 0 \quad \text{Substituting in (1)}$$
$$-4 + z = 0$$
$$z = 4$$

We obtain $(-3, -1, 0, 4)$. This checks, so it is the solution.

46. $\left(-1, \frac{1}{5}, -\frac{1}{2}\right)$

47. $\dfrac{2}{x} + \dfrac{2}{y} - \dfrac{3}{z} = 3,$

$\dfrac{1}{x} - \dfrac{2}{y} - \dfrac{3}{z} = 9,$

$\dfrac{7}{x} - \dfrac{2}{y} + \dfrac{9}{z} = -39$

Let u represent $\dfrac{1}{x}$, v represent $\dfrac{1}{y}$, and w represent $\dfrac{1}{z}$. Substituting, we have

$2u + 2v - 3w = 3, \quad (1)$

$u - 2v - 3w = 9, \quad (2)$

$7u - 2v + 9w = -39 \quad (3)$

1., 2. The equations in u, v, and w are in standard form with no fractions or decimals.

3., 4. We eliminate v from two different pairs of equations.

$\begin{aligned} 2u + 2v - 3w &= 3 \quad (1) \\ \underline{u - 2v - 3w} &= \underline{9} \quad (2) \\ 3u \qquad\quad - 6w &= 12 \quad (4) \text{ Adding} \end{aligned}$

$\begin{aligned} 2u + 2v - 3w &= 3 \quad (1) \\ \underline{7u - 2v + 9w} &= \underline{-39} \quad (3) \\ 9u \qquad\quad + 6w &= -36 \quad (5) \text{ Adding} \end{aligned}$

5. Now solve the system of Equations (4) and (5).

$\begin{aligned} 3u - 6w &= 12, \quad (4) \\ \underline{9u + 6w} &= \underline{-36} \quad (5) \\ 12u \qquad\quad &= -24 \\ u &= -2 \end{aligned}$

$3(-2) - 6w = 12 \quad$ Substituting in (4)

$-6 - 6w = 12$

$-6w = 18$

$w = -3$

6. Substitute in Equation (1), (2), or (3) to find v.

$2(-2) + 2v - 3(-3) = 3 \quad$ Substituting in (1)

$2v + 5 = 3$

$2v = -2$

$v = -1$

Solve for x, y, and z. We substitute -2 for u, -1 for v, and -3 for w.

$u = \dfrac{1}{x} \qquad v = \dfrac{1}{y} \qquad w = \dfrac{1}{z}$

$-2 = \dfrac{1}{x} \qquad -1 = \dfrac{1}{y} \qquad -3 = \dfrac{1}{z}$

$x = \dfrac{1}{2} \qquad\ y = -1 \qquad z = -\dfrac{1}{3}$

We obtain $\left(-\dfrac{1}{2}, -1, -\dfrac{1}{3} \right)$. This checks, so it is the solution.

48. 12

49. $5x - 6y + kz = -5, \quad (1)$

$x + 3y - 2z = 2, \quad (2)$

$2x - y + 4z = -1 \quad (3)$

Eliminate y from two different pairs of equations.

$\begin{aligned} 5x - 6y + \qquad kz &= -5 \quad (1) \\ \underline{2x + 6y - \qquad 4z} &= \underline{4} \quad \text{Multiplying (2) by 2} \\ 7x \qquad\quad + (k-4)z &= -1 \quad (4) \end{aligned}$

$\begin{aligned} x + 3y - \qquad 2z &= 2 \quad (2) \\ \underline{6x - 3y + 12z} &= \underline{-3} \quad \text{Multiplying (3) by 3} \\ 7x \qquad\quad + 10z &= -1 \quad (5) \end{aligned}$

Solve the system of Equations (4) and (5).

$7x + (k-4)z = -1 \quad (4)$

$7x + \qquad 10z = -1 \quad (5)$

$\begin{aligned} -7x - \qquad (k-4)z &= 1 \quad \text{Multiplying (4) by } -1 \\ \underline{7x + \qquad\quad 10z} &= \underline{-1} \quad (5) \\ (-k + 14)z &= 0 \quad (6) \end{aligned}$

The system is dependent for the value of k that makes Equation (6) true. This occurs when $-k + 14$ is 0. We solve for k:

$-k + 14 = 0$

$14 = k$

50. $3x + 4y + 2z = 12$

51. $z = b - mx - ny$

Three solutions are $(1, 1, 2)$, $(3, 2, -6)$, and $\left(\dfrac{3}{2}, 1, 1 \right)$. We substitute for x, y, and z and then solve for b, m, and n.

$2 = b - m - n,$

$-6 = b - 3m - 2n,$

$1 = b - \dfrac{3}{2}m - n$

1., 2. Write the equations in standard form. Also, clear the fraction in the last equation.

$b - m - n = 2, \quad (1)$

$b - 3m - 2n = -6, \quad (2)$

$2b - 3m - 2n = 2 \quad (3)$

3., 4. Eliminate b from two different pairs of equations.

$\begin{aligned} b - m - n &= 2 \quad (1) \\ \underline{-b + 3m + 2n} &= \underline{6} \quad \text{Multiplying (2) by } -1 \\ 2m + n &= 8 \quad (4) \quad \text{Adding} \end{aligned}$

$\begin{aligned} -2b + 2m + 2n &= -4 \quad \text{Multiplying (1) by } -2 \\ \underline{2b - 3m - 2n} &= \underline{2} \quad (3) \\ -m \qquad\quad &= -2 \quad (5) \quad \text{Adding} \end{aligned}$

5. We solve Equation (5) for m:

$$-m = -2$$
$$m = 2$$

Substitute in Equation (4) and solve for n.

$$2 \cdot 2 + n = 8$$
$$4 + n = 8$$
$$n = 4$$

6. Substitute in one of the original equations to find b.

$$b - 2 - 4 = 2 \quad \text{Substituting 2 for } m$$
$$\text{and 4 for } n \text{ in (1)}$$
$$b - 6 = 2$$
$$b = 8$$

The solution is $(8, 2, 4)$, so the equation is $z = 8 - 2x - 4y$.

52. Answers may vary.

$$x + y + z = 1,$$
$$2x + 2y + 2z = 2,$$
$$x + y + z = 3$$

Exercise Set 8.5

1. Familiarize. Let $x = $ the first number, $y = $ the second number, and $z = $ the third number.

Translate.

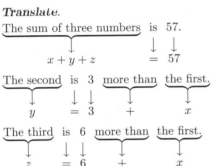

We now have a system of equations.

$$\begin{aligned} x + y + z &= 57, \quad \text{or} \quad & x + y + z &= 57, \\ y &= 3 + x \quad & -x + y &= 3, \\ z &= 6 + x \quad & -x + z &= 6 \end{aligned}$$

Carry out. Solving the system we get $(16, 19, 22)$.

Check. The sum of the three numbers is $16 + 19 + 22$, or 57. The second number, 19, is three more than the first number, 16. The third number, 22, is 6 more than the first number, 16. The numbers check.

State. The numbers are 16, 19, and 22.

2. $4, 2, -1$

3. Familiarize. Let $x = $ the first number, $y = $ the second number, and $z = $ the third number.

Translate.

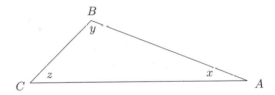

We now have a system of equations.

$$\begin{aligned} x + y + z &= 26, \quad \text{or} \quad & x + y + z &= 26, \\ 2x - y &= z - 2, \quad & 2x - y - z &= -2, \\ z &= y - 3x \quad & 3x - y + z &= 0 \end{aligned}$$

Carry out. Solving the system we get $(8, 21, -3)$.

Check. The sum of the numbers is $8 + 21 - 3$, or 26. Twice the first minus the second is $2 \cdot 8 - 21$, or -5, which is 2 less than the third. The second minus three times the first is $21 - 3 \cdot 8$, or -3, which is the third. The numbers check.

State. The numbers are 8, 21, and -3.

4. $17, 9, 79$

5. Familiarize. We first make a drawing.

```
              B
             /y\
            /   \___
           /        \___
          /  z       x \___
         C_____A
```

We let x, y, and z represent the measures of angles A, B, and C, respectively. The measures of the angles of a triangle add up to $180°$.

Translate.

The sum of the measures is $180°$.

$$x + y + z = 180$$

The measure of angle B is three times the measure of angle A.

$$y = 3x$$

The measure of angle C is $20°$ more than the measure of angle A.

$$z = x + 20$$

We now have a system of equations.

$$x + y + z = 180,$$
$$y = 3x,$$
$$z = x + 20$$

Carry out. Solving the system we get $(32, 96, 52)$.

Check. The sum of the measures is $32° + 96° + 52°$, or $180°$. Three times the measure of angle A is $3 \cdot 32°$, or $96°$, the measure of angle B. $20°$ more than the measure of angle A is $32° + 20°$, or $52°$, the measure of angle C. The numbers check.

State. The measures of angles A, B, and C are $32°$, $96°$, and $52°$, respectively.

6. $25°$, $50°$, $105°$

7. Familiarize. Let $x =$ the cost of automatic transmission, $y =$ the cost of power door locks, and $z =$ the cost of air conditioning. The prices of the options are added to the basic price of $12,685.

Translate.

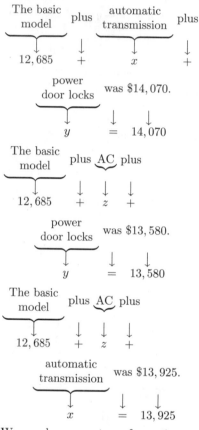

We now have a system of equations.

$$12,685 + x + y = 14,070,$$
$$12,685 + z + y = 13,580,$$
$$12,685 + z + x = 13,925$$

Carry out. Solving the system we get $(865, 520, 375)$.

Check. The basic model with automatic transmission and power door locks costs $12,685 + \$865 + \$520$, or $14,070. The basic model with AC and power door locks costs $12,685 + \$375 + \$520$, or $13,580. The basic model with AC and automatic transmission costs $12,685 + \$375 + \$865$, or $13,925. The numbers check.

State. Automatic transmission costs $865, power door locks cost $520, and AC costs $375.

8. A:1500; B: 1900; C: 2300

9. We know that Elrod, Dot, and Wendy can weld 74 linear feet per hour when working together. We also know that Elrod and Dot together can weld 44 linear feet per hour, which leads to the conclusion that Wendy can weld $74-44$, or 30 linear feet per hour alone. We also know that Elrod and Wendy together can weld 50 linear feet per hour. This, along with the earlier conclusion that Wendy can weld 30 linear feet per hour alone, leads to two conclusions: Elrod can weld $50 - 30$, or 20 linear feet per hour alone and Dot can weld $74 - 50$, or 24 linear feet per hour alone.

10. Sven: 220; Tillie: 250; Isaiah: 270

11. Familiarize. Let $x =$ the number of 10-oz cups, $y =$ the number of 14-oz cups, and $z =$ the number of 20-oz cups that Kyle filled. Note that five 96-oz pots contain $5 \cdot 96$ oz, or 480 oz of coffee. Also, x 10-oz cups contain a total of $10x$ oz of coffee and bring in \$$1.05x$, y 14-oz cups contain $14y$ oz and bring in \$$1.35y$, and z 20-oz cups contain $20z$ oz and bring in \$$1.65z$.

Translate.

The total number of coffees served   was 34.

$$x + y + z = 34$$

The total amount of coffee served   was 480 oz.

$$10x + 14y + 20z = 480$$

The total amount collected   was \$45.

$$1.05x + 1.35y + 1.65z = 45$$

Now we have a system of equations.

$$x + y + z = 34,$$
$$10x + 14y + 20z = 480,$$
$$1.05x + 1.35y + 1.65z = 45$$

Carry out. Solving the system we get $(11, 15, 8)$.

Check. The total number of coffees served was $11+15+8$, or 34, The total amount of coffee served was $10 \cdot 11 + 14 \cdot 15 + 20 \cdot 8 = 110 + 210 + 160 = 480$ oz. The total amount collected was $\$1.05(11) + \$1.35(15) + \$1.65(8) = \$11.55 + \$20.25 + \$13.20 = \$45$. The numbers check.

State. Kyle filled 11 10-oz cups, 15 14-oz cups, and 8 20-oz cups.

12. Newspaper: \$41.1 billion; television: \$36 billion; radio: \$7.7 billion

13. Familiarize. Let $x =$ the amount invested in the first fund, $y =$ the amount invested in the second fund, and $z =$ the amount invested in the third fund. Then the earnings from the investments were $0.1x$, $0.06y$, and $0.15z$.

Translate.

$$\underbrace{\text{The total amount invested}}_{x+y+z} \underset{=}{\text{was}} \underset{80,000}{\$80,000.}$$

$$\underbrace{\text{The total earnings}}_{0.1x + 0.06y + 0.15z} \underset{=}{\text{were}} \underset{8850}{\$8850.}$$

$$\underbrace{\text{The earnings from the first fund}}_{0.1x} \underset{=}{\text{were \$750}} \underset{750}{} \underbrace{\text{more than}}_{+} \underbrace{\text{the earnings from the third fund.}}_{0.15z}$$

Now we have a system of equations.

$$x + y + z = 80,000$$
$$0.1x + 0.06y + 0.15z = 8850,$$
$$0.1x = 750 + 0.15z$$

Carry out. Solving the system we get $(45,000, 10,000, 25,000)$.

Check. The total investment was $\$45,000 + \$10,000 + \$25,000$, or $\$80,000$. The total earnings were $0.1(\$45,000) + 0.06(10,000) + 0.15(25,000) = \$4500 + \$600 + \$3750 = \$8850$. The earnings from the first fund, $\$4500$, were $\$750$ more than the earnings from the second fund, $\$3750$.

State. $\$45,000$ was invested in the first fund, $\$10,000$ in the second fund, and $\$25,000$ in the third fund.

14. 10 small drinks, 25 medium drinks, 5 large drinks

15. *Familiarize.* Let $r =$ the number of servings of roast beef, $p =$ the number of baked potatoes, and $b =$ the number of servings of broccoli. Then r servings of roast beef contain $300r$ Calories, $20r$ g of protein, and no vitamin C. In p baked potatoes there are $100p$ Calories, $5p$ g of protein, and $20p$ mg of vitamin C. And b servings of broccoli contain $50b$ Calories, $5b$ g of protein, and $100b$ mg of vitamin C. The patient requires 800 Calories, 55 g of protein, and 220 mg of vitamin C.

Translate. Write equations for the total number of calories, the total amount of protein, and the total amount of vitamin C.

$$300r + 100p + 50b = 800 \quad \text{(Calories)}$$
$$20r + 5p + 5b = 55 \quad \text{(protein)}$$
$$20p + 100b = 220 \quad \text{(vitamin C)}$$

We now have a system of equations.

Carry out. Solving the system we get $(2, 1, 2)$.

Check. Two servings of roast beef provide 600 Calories, 40 g of protein, and no vitamin C. One baked potato provides 100 Calories, 5 g of protein, and 20 mg of vitamin C. And 2 servings of broccoli provide 100 Calories, 10 g of protein, and 200 mg of vitamin C. Together, then, they provide 800 Calories, 55 g of protein, and 220 mg of vitamin C. The values check.

State. The dietician should prepare 2 servings of roast beef, 1 baked potato, and 2 servings of broccoli.

16. $1\frac{1}{8}$ servings of roast beef, $2\frac{3}{4}$ baked potatoes, $3\frac{3}{4}$ servings of asparagus

17. Let x, y, and z represent the average number of times a man, a woman, and a one-year-old child cry each month, respectively.

Translate.

$$\underbrace{\text{The sum of the averages}}_{x+y+z} \underset{=}{\text{is 71.7.}} \underset{71.7}{}$$

$$\underbrace{\begin{array}{c}\text{The number}\\\text{of times a}\\\text{one-year-old}\\\text{cries}\end{array}}_{z} \underset{=}{\text{is}} \underbrace{\underset{46.4}{\begin{array}{c}46.4\\\text{times}\end{array}}}_{} \underbrace{\underset{+}{\begin{array}{c}\text{more}\\\text{than}\end{array}}}_{} \underbrace{\begin{array}{c}\text{the number}\\\text{of times}\\\text{a man cries.}\end{array}}_{x}$$

$$\underbrace{\begin{array}{c}\text{The number}\\\text{of times a}\\\text{one-year-old}\\\text{cries}\end{array}}_{z} \underset{=}{\text{is}} \underbrace{\underset{28.3}{\begin{array}{c}28.3\\\text{times}\end{array}}}_{} \underbrace{\underset{+}{\begin{array}{c}\text{more}\\\text{than}\end{array}}}_{} \underbrace{\begin{array}{c}\text{the number}\\\text{of times}\\\text{a man and a}\\\text{woman cry.}\end{array}}_{x+y}$$

Now we have a system of equations.

$$x + y + z = 71.7,$$
$$z = 46.4 + x,$$
$$z = 28.3 + x + y$$

Carry out. Solving the system, we get $(3.6, 18.1, 50)$.

Check. The sum of the average number times a man, a woman, and a one-year-old child cry each month is $3.6 + 18.1 + 50 = 71.7$. The number of times a one-year-old child cries, 50, is 46.4 more than 3.6, the average number of times a man cries each month and is 28.3 more than $3.6 + 18.1$, or 21.7, the average number of times a man and a woman cry. These numbers check.

State. In a month, a man cries an average of 3.6 times, a woman cries 18.1 times, and a one-year old child cries 50 times.

18. Asian-American: 385; African-American: 200; Caucasian: 154

19. *Familiarize.* Let x, y, and z represent the number of 2-point field goals, 3-point field goals, and 1-point foul shots made, respectively. The total number of points scored from each of these types of goals is $2x$, $3y$, and z.

Translate.

$$\underbrace{\text{The total number of points}}_{2x + 3y + z} \underset{=}{\text{was 92.}} \underset{92}{}$$

$$\underbrace{\text{The total number of baskets}}_{x + y + z} \underset{=}{\text{was 50.}} \underset{50}{}$$

The number of 2-pointers　was 19　more than　the number of foul shots.

$$x \quad = 19 \quad + \quad z$$

Now we have a system of equations.

$2x + 3y + z = 92,$

$x + y + z = 50,$

$x = 19 + z$

Carry out. Solving the system we get $(32, 5, 13)$.

Check. The total number of points was $2 \cdot 32 + 3 \cdot 5 + 13 = 64 + 15 + 13 = 92$. The number of baskets was $32 + 5 + 13$, or 50. The number of 2-pointers, 32, was 19 more than the number of foul shots, 13. The numbers check.

State. The Knicks made 32 two-point field goals, 5 three-point field goals, and 13 foul shots.

20. 1869

21. *Writing Exercise*

22. *Writing Exercise*

23. $5(-3) + 7 = -15 + 7 = -8$

24. 33

25. $-6(8) + (-7) = -48 + (-7) = -55$

26. -71

27. $\quad -7(2x - 3y + 5z) = -7 \cdot 2x - 7(-3y) - 7(5z)$
$$= -14x + 21y - 35z$$

28. $-24a - 42b + 54c$

29. $\quad -4(2a + 5b) + 3a + 20b$
$$= -8a - 20b + 3a + 20b$$
$$= -8a + 3a - 20b + 20b$$
$$= -5a$$

30. $11x$

31. *Writing Exercise*

32. *Writing Exercise*

33. Familiarize. Let $x =$ the one's digit, $y =$ the ten's digit, and $z =$ the hundred's digit. Then the number is represented by $100z + 10y + x$. When the digits are reversed, the resulting number is represented by $100x + 10y + z$.

Translate.

The sum of the digits　is　14.

$$x + y + z \quad = 14$$

The ten's digit　is 2　more than　the one's digit.

$$y \quad = 2 \quad + \quad x$$

The number　is the same as　the number with the digits reversed.

$$100z + 10y + x \quad = \quad 100x + 10y + z$$

Now we have a system of equations.

$x + y + z = 14,$

$y = 2 + x,$

$100z + 10y + x = 100x + 10y + z$

Carry out. Solving the system we get $(4, 6, 4)$.

Check. If the number is 464, then the sum of the digits is $4 + 6 + 4$, or 14. The ten's digit, 6, is 2 more than the one's digit, 4. If the digits are reversed the number is unchanged. The result checks.

State. The number is 464.

34. 20 years old

35. Familiarize. Let $x =$ the number of adults, $y =$ the number of students, and $z =$ the number of children in attendance.

Translate. The given information gives rise to two equations.

The total number in attendance　was　100.

$$x + y + z \quad = \quad 100$$

The total amount taken in　was　$100.

$$10x + 3y + 0.5z \quad = \quad 100$$

Now we have a system of equations.

$x + y + z = 100,$

$10x + 3y + 0.5z = 100$

Multiply the second equation by 2 to clear the decimal:

$x + y + z = 100, \quad (1)$

$20x + 6y + z = 200. \quad (2)$

Carry out. We use the elimination method.

$$\begin{array}{l} -x - y - z = -100 \quad \text{Multiplying (1) by } -1 \\ \underline{20x + 6y + z = 200} \quad (2) \\ 19x + 5y \quad\quad = 100 \quad (3) \end{array}$$

In (3), note that 5 is a factor of both $5y$ and 100. Therefore, 5 must also be a factor of $19x$, and hence of x, since 5 is not a factor of 19. Then for some positive integer n, $x = 5n$. (We require $n > 0$, since the number of adults clearly cannot be negative and must also be nonzero since the exercise states that the audience consists of *adults*, students, and children.) We have

$19 \cdot 5n + 5y = 100,$ or

$19n + y = 20.$ Dividing by 5 on both sides

Since n and y must both be positive, $n = 1$. Otherwise, $19n + y$ would be greater than 20. Then $x = 5 \cdot 1$, or 5.

$$19 \cdot 5 + 5y = 100 \quad \text{Substituting in (3)}$$
$$95 + 5y = 100$$
$$5y = 5$$
$$y = 1$$
$$5 + 1 + z = 100 \quad \text{Substituting in (1)}$$
$$6 + z = 100$$
$$z = 94$$

Check. The number of people in attendance was $5+1+94$, or 100. The amount of money taken in was $\$10 \cdot 5 + \$3 \cdot 1 + \$0.50(94) = \$50 + \$3 + \$47 = \$100$. The numbers check.

State. There were 5 adults, 1 student, and 94 children.

36. 35 tickets

37. Familiarize. We first make a drawing with additional labels.

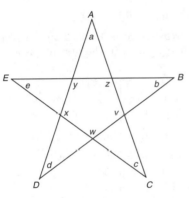

We let a, b, c, d, and e represent the angle measures at the tips of the star. We also label the interior angles of the pentagon v, w, x, y, and z. We recall the following geometric fact:

The sum of the measures of the interior angles of a polygon of n sides is given by $(n-2)180°$.

Using this fact we know:

1. The sum of the angle measures of a triangle is $(3-2)180°$, or $180°$.

2. The sum of the angle measures of a pentagon is $(5-2)180°$, or $3(180°)$.

Translate. Using fact (1) listed above we obtain a system of 5 equations.

$$a + v + d = 180$$
$$b + w + e = 180$$
$$c + x + a = 180$$
$$d + y + b = 180$$
$$e + z + c = 180$$

Carry out. Adding we obtain

$$2a + 2b + 2c + 2d + 2e + v + w + x + y + z = 5(180)$$
$$2(a + b + c + d + e) + (v + w + x + y + z) = 5(180)$$

Using fact (2) listed above we substitute $3(180)$ for $(v + w + x + y + z)$ and solve for $(a + b + c + d + e)$.

$$2(a + b + c + d + e) + 3(180) = 5(180)$$
$$2(a + b + c + d + e) = 2(180)$$
$$a + b + c + d + e = 180$$

Check. We should repeat the above calculations.

State. The sum of the angle measures at the tips of the star is $180°$.

Exercise Set 8.6

1. $9x - 2y = 5,$
$$3x - 3y = 11$$

Write a matrix using only the constants.

$$\begin{bmatrix} 9 & -2 & \vdots & 5 \\ 3 & -3 & \vdots & 11 \end{bmatrix}$$

Multiply row 2 by 3 to make the first number in row 2 a multiple of 9.

$$\begin{bmatrix} 9 & -2 & \vdots & 5 \\ 9 & -9 & \vdots & 33 \end{bmatrix} \quad \text{New Row 2} = 3(\text{Row 2})$$

Multiply row 1 by -1 and add it to row 2.

$$\begin{bmatrix} 9 & -2 & \vdots & 5 \\ 0 & -7 & \vdots & 28 \end{bmatrix} \quad \begin{array}{l} \text{New Row 2} = -1(\text{Row 1}) + \\ \text{Row 2} \end{array}$$

Reinserting the variables, we have

$$9x - 2y = 5, \quad (1)$$
$$-7y = 28. \quad (2)$$

Solve Equation (2) for y.

$$-7y = 28$$
$$y = -4$$

Substitute -4 for y in Equation (1) and solve for x.

$$9x - 2y = 5$$
$$9x - 2(-4) = 5$$
$$9x + 8 = 5$$
$$9x = -3$$
$$x = -\frac{1}{3}$$

The solution is $\left(-\dfrac{1}{3}, -4\right)$.

2. $(2, -1)$

3. $x + 4y = 8,$

$3x + 5y = 3$

We first write a matrix using only the constants.

$$\begin{bmatrix} 1 & 4 & \vdots & 8 \\ 3 & 5 & \vdots & 3 \end{bmatrix}$$

Multiply the first row by -3 and add it to the second row.

$$\begin{bmatrix} 1 & 4 & \vdots & 8 \\ 0 & -7 & \vdots & -21 \end{bmatrix} \text{New Row 2} = -3(\text{Row 1}) + \text{Row 2}$$

Reinserting the variables, we have

$x + 4y = 8,$ (1)

$\quad\quad -7y = -21.$ (2)

Solve Equation (2) for y.

$-7y = -21$

$y = 3$

Substitute 3 for y in Equation (1) and solve for x.

$x + 4 \cdot 3 = 8$

$x + 12 = 8$

$x = -4$

The solution is $(-4, 3)$.

4. $(-3, 2)$

5. $6x - 2y = 4,$

$7x + \ y = 13$

Write a matrix using only the constants.

$$\begin{bmatrix} 6 & -2 & \vdots & 4 \\ 7 & 1 & \vdots & 13 \end{bmatrix}$$

Multiply the second row by 6 to make the first number in row 2 a multiple of 6.

$$\begin{bmatrix} 6 & -2 & \vdots & 4 \\ 42 & 6 & \vdots & 78 \end{bmatrix} \text{New Row 2} = 6(\text{Row 2})$$

Now multiply the first row by -7 and add it to the second row.

$$\begin{bmatrix} 6 & -2 & \vdots & 4 \\ 0 & 20 & \vdots & 50 \end{bmatrix} \begin{array}{l} \text{New Row 2} = -7(\text{Row 1}) + \\ \text{Row 2} \end{array}$$

Reinserting the variables, we have

$6x - 2y = 4,$ (1)

$\quad\quad 20y = 50.$ (2)

Solve Equation (2) for y.

$20y = 50$

$y = \dfrac{5}{2}$

Substitute $\dfrac{5}{2}$ for y in Equation (1) and solve for x.

$6x - 2y = 4$

$6x - 2\left(\dfrac{5}{2}\right) = 4$

$6x - 5 = 4$

$6x = 9$

$x = \dfrac{3}{2}$

The solution is $\left(\dfrac{3}{2}, \dfrac{5}{2}\right)$.

6. $\left(-1, \dfrac{5}{2}\right)$

7. $3x + 2y + 2z = 3,$

$x + 2y - \ z = 5,$

$2x - 4y + \ z = 0$

We first write a matrix using only the constants.

$$\begin{bmatrix} 3 & 2 & 2 & \vdots & 3 \\ 1 & 2 & -1 & \vdots & 5 \\ 2 & -4 & 1 & \vdots & 0 \end{bmatrix}$$

First interchange rows 1 and 2 so that each number below the first number in the first row is a multiple of that number.

$$\begin{bmatrix} 1 & 2 & -1 & \vdots & 5 \\ 3 & 2 & 2 & \vdots & 3 \\ 2 & -4 & 1 & \vdots & 0 \end{bmatrix}$$

Multiply row 1 by -3 and add it to row 2.

Multiply row 1 by -2 and add it to row 3.

$$\begin{bmatrix} 1 & 2 & -1 & \vdots & 5 \\ 0 & -4 & 5 & \vdots & -12 \\ 0 & -8 & 3 & \vdots & -10 \end{bmatrix}$$

Multiply row 2 by -2 and add it to row 3.

$$\begin{bmatrix} 1 & 2 & -1 & \vdots & 5 \\ 0 & -4 & 5 & \vdots & -12 \\ 0 & 0 & -7 & \vdots & 14 \end{bmatrix}$$

Reinserting the variables, we have

$x + 2y - z = 5,$ (1)

$\quad -4y + 5z = -12,$ (2)

$\quad\quad\quad -7z = 14.$ (3)

Solve (3) for z.

$-7z = 14$

$z = -2$

Substitute -2 for z in (2) and solve for y.

$-4y + 5(-2) = -12$

$-4y - 10 = -12$

$-4y = -2$

$y = \dfrac{1}{2}$

Substitute $\frac{1}{2}$ for y and -2 for z in (1) and solve for x.

$$x + 2 \cdot \frac{1}{2} - (-2) = 5$$
$$x + 1 + 2 = 5$$
$$x + 3 = 5$$
$$x = 2$$

The solution is $\left(2, \frac{1}{2}, -2\right)$.

8. $\left(\frac{3}{2}, -4, -3\right)$

9. $p - 2q - 3r = 3,$
$2p - q - 2r = 4,$
$4p + 5q + 6r = 4$

We first write a matrix using only the constants.

$$\begin{bmatrix} 1 & -2 & -3 & | & 3 \\ 2 & -1 & -2 & | & 4 \\ 4 & 5 & 6 & | & 4 \end{bmatrix}$$

$$\begin{bmatrix} 1 & -2 & -3 & | & 3 \\ 0 & 3 & 4 & | & -2 \\ 0 & 13 & 18 & | & -8 \end{bmatrix}$$ New Row 2 = -2(Row 1) + Row 2
New Row 3 = -4(Row 1) + Row 3

$$\begin{bmatrix} 1 & -2 & -3 & | & 3 \\ 0 & 3 & 4 & | & -2 \\ 0 & 39 & 54 & | & -24 \end{bmatrix}$$ New Row 3 = 3(Row 3)

$$\begin{bmatrix} 1 & -2 & -3 & | & 3 \\ 0 & 3 & 4 & | & -2 \\ 0 & 0 & 2 & | & 2 \end{bmatrix}$$ New Row 3 = -13(Row 2)+ Row 3

Reinserting the variables, we have

$$p - 2q - 3r = 3, \quad (1)$$
$$3q + 4r = -2, \quad (2)$$
$$2r = 2 \quad (3)$$

Solve (3) for r.
$$2r = 2$$
$$r = 1$$

Substitute 1 for r in (2) and solve for q.
$$3q + 4 \cdot 1 = -2$$
$$3q + 4 = -2$$
$$3q = -6$$
$$q = -2$$

Substitute -2 for q and 1 for r in (1) and solve for p.
$$p - 2(-2) - 3 \cdot 1 = 3$$
$$p + 4 - 3 = 3$$
$$p + 1 = 3$$
$$p = 2$$

The solution is $(2, -2, 1)$.

10. $(-1, 2, -2)$

11. $3p \quad + 2r = 11,$
$q - 7r = 4,$
$p - 6q \quad = 1$

We first write a matrix using only the constants.

$$\begin{bmatrix} 3 & 0 & 2 & | & 11 \\ 0 & 1 & -7 & | & 4 \\ 1 & -6 & 0 & | & 1 \end{bmatrix}$$

$$\begin{bmatrix} 1 & -6 & 0 & | & 1 \\ 0 & 1 & -7 & | & 4 \\ 3 & 0 & 2 & | & 11 \end{bmatrix}$$ Interchange Row 1 and Row 3

$$\begin{bmatrix} 1 & -6 & 0 & | & 1 \\ 0 & 1 & -7 & | & 4 \\ 0 & 18 & 2 & | & 8 \end{bmatrix}$$ New Row 3 = -3(Row 1) + Row 3

$$\begin{bmatrix} 1 & -6 & 0 & | & 1 \\ 0 & 1 & -7 & | & 4 \\ 0 & 0 & 128 & | & -64 \end{bmatrix}$$ New Row 3 = -18(Row 2) + Row 3

Reinserting the variables, we have

$$p - 6q \quad = 1, \quad (1)$$
$$q - 7r = 4, \quad (2)$$
$$128r = -64. \quad (3)$$

Solve (3) for r.
$$128r = -64$$
$$r = -\frac{1}{2}$$

Substitute $-\frac{1}{2}$ for r in (2) and solve for q.
$$q - 7r = 4$$
$$q - 7\left(-\frac{1}{2}\right) = 4$$
$$q + \frac{7}{2} = 4$$
$$q = \frac{1}{2}$$

Substitute $\frac{1}{2}$ for q in (1) and solve for p.
$$p - 6 \cdot \frac{1}{2} = 1$$
$$p - 3 = 1$$
$$p = 4$$

The solution is $\left(4, \frac{1}{2}, -\frac{1}{2}\right)$.

12. $\left(\frac{1}{2}, \frac{2}{3}, -\frac{5}{6}\right)$

13.
$$3x + y = 8,$$
$$4x + 5y - 3z = 4,$$
$$7x + 2y - 9z = 1$$

The coefficient matrix is:

$$\begin{bmatrix} 3 & 1 & 0 & 8 \\ 4 & 5 & -3 & 4 \\ 7 & 2 & -9 & 1 \end{bmatrix}$$

We enter this on a graphing calculator and use the "rref(" command along with Frac to find the reduced row-echelon form of the matrix with the elements expressed in fractional form.

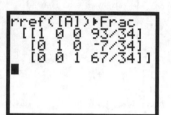

We see that $x = \dfrac{93}{34}$, $y = -\dfrac{7}{34}$, and $z = \dfrac{67}{34}$. The solution is $\left(\dfrac{93}{34}, -\dfrac{7}{34}, \dfrac{67}{34} \right)$.

14. $\left(\dfrac{23}{5}, \dfrac{5}{2}, -2 \right)$

15.
$$-0.01x + 0.7y = -0.9,$$
$$0.5x - 0.3y + 0.18z = 0.01,$$
$$50x + 6y - 75z = 12$$

The coefficient matrix is:

$$\begin{bmatrix} -0.01 & 0.7 & 0 & -0.9 \\ 0.5 & -0.3 & 0.18 & 0.01 \\ 50 & 6 & -75 & 12 \end{bmatrix}$$

We enter this on a graphing calculator and use the " rref(" command to find the row-echelon form of the matrix.

```
rref([A])
  [[1 0 0 -.53318…]
   [0 1 0 -1.2933…]
   [0 0 1 -.61892…]
■
```

We see that $x \approx -0.5332$, $y \approx -1.2933$, and $z \approx -0.6189$. The solution is $(-0.5332, -1.2933, -0.6189)$.

16. $\left(-\dfrac{167}{68}, -\dfrac{227}{68}, \dfrac{7}{2} \right)$

17. We will rewrite the equations with the variables in alphabetical order:
$$-2w + 2x + 2y - 2z = -10,$$
$$w + x + y + z = -5,$$
$$3w + x - y + 4z = -2,$$
$$w + 3x - 2y + 2z = -6$$

Write a matrix using only the constants.

$$\begin{bmatrix} -2 & 2 & 2 & -2 & | & -10 \\ 1 & 1 & 1 & 1 & | & -5 \\ 3 & 1 & -1 & 4 & | & -2 \\ 1 & 3 & -2 & 2 & | & -6 \end{bmatrix}$$

$$\begin{bmatrix} -1 & 1 & 1 & -1 & | & -5 \\ 1 & 1 & 1 & 1 & | & -5 \\ 3 & 1 & -1 & 4 & | & -2 \\ 1 & 3 & -2 & 2 & | & -6 \end{bmatrix}$$
New Row 1 = $\dfrac{1}{2}$(Row 1)

$$\begin{bmatrix} -1 & 1 & 1 & -1 & | & -5 \\ 0 & 2 & 2 & 0 & | & -10 \\ 0 & 4 & 2 & 1 & | & -17 \\ 0 & 4 & -1 & 1 & | & -11 \end{bmatrix}$$
New Row 2 = Row 1 + Row 2
New Row 3 = 3(Row 1) +Row 3
New Row 4 = Row 1 + Row 4

$$\begin{bmatrix} -1 & 1 & 1 & -1 & | & -5 \\ 0 & 2 & 2 & 0 & | & -10 \\ 0 & 0 & -2 & 1 & | & 3 \\ 0 & 0 & -5 & 1 & | & 9 \end{bmatrix}$$
New Row 3 = -2(Row 2) + Row 3
New Row 4 = -2(Row 2) + Row 4

$$\begin{bmatrix} -1 & 1 & 1 & -1 & | & -5 \\ 0 & 2 & 2 & 0 & | & -10 \\ 0 & 0 & -2 & 1 & | & 3 \\ 0 & 0 & -10 & 2 & | & 18 \end{bmatrix}$$
New Row 4 = 2(Row 4)

$$\begin{bmatrix} -1 & 1 & 1 & -1 & | & -5 \\ 0 & 2 & 2 & 0 & | & -10 \\ 0 & 0 & -2 & 1 & | & 3 \\ 0 & 0 & 0 & -3 & | & 3 \end{bmatrix}$$
New Row 4 = -5(Row 3) + Row 4

Reinserting the variables, we have
$$-w + x + y - z = -5, \quad (1)$$
$$2x + 2y = -10, \quad (2)$$
$$-2y + z = 3, \quad (3)$$
$$-3z = 3. \quad (4)$$

Solve (4) for z.
$$-3z = 3$$
$$z = -1$$

Substitute -1 for z in (3) and solve for y.
$$-2y + (-1) = 3$$
$$-2y = 4$$
$$y = -2$$

Substitute -2 for y in (2) and solve for x.

$$2x + 2(-2) = -10$$
$$2x - 4 = -10$$
$$2x = -6$$
$$x = -3$$

Substitute -3 for x, -2 for y, and -1 for z in (1) and solve for w.

$$-w + (-3) + (-2) - (-1) = -5$$
$$-w - 3 - 2 + 1 = -5$$
$$-w - 4 = -5$$
$$-w = -1$$
$$w = 1$$

The solution is $(1, -3, -2, -1)$.

18. $(7, 4, 5, 6)$

19. **Familiarize**. Let $d = $ the number of dimes and $q = $ the number of quarters. The value of d dimes is $\$0.10d$, and the value of q quarters is $\$0.25q$.

Translate.

Total number of coins is 43.

$$d + q = 43$$

Total value of coins is $7.60.

$$0.10d + 0.25q = 7.60$$

After clearing decimals, we have this system.

$$d + q = 43,$$
$$10d + 25q = 760$$

Carry out. Solve using matrices.

$$\begin{bmatrix} 1 & 1 & | & 43 \\ 10 & 25 & | & 760 \end{bmatrix}$$

$$\begin{bmatrix} 1 & 1 & | & 43 \\ 0 & 15 & | & 330 \end{bmatrix}$$ New Row 2 $= -10$(Row 1) $+$ Row 2

Reinserting the variables, we have

$$d + q = 43, \quad (1)$$
$$15q = 330. \quad (2)$$

Solve (2) for q.

$$15q = 330$$
$$q = 22$$

$$d + 22 = 43 \quad \text{Substituting in (2)}$$
$$d = 21$$

Check. The sum of the two numbers is 43. The total value is $\$0.10(21) + \$0.25(22) = \$2.10 + \$5.50 = \$7.60$. The answer checks.

State. There are 21 dimes and 22 quarters.

20. 4 dimes, 30 nickels

21. **Familiarize**. We let x represent the number of pounds of the $4.05 kind and y represent the number of pounds of the $2.70 kind of granola. We organize the information in a table.

Granola	Number of pounds	Price per pound	Value
$4.05 kind	x	$4.05	4.05x$
$2.70 kind	y	$2.70	2.70y$
Mixture	15	$3.15	$3.15 \times 15 or $47.25

Translate.

Total number of pounds is 15.

$$x + y = 15$$

Total value of mixture is $47.25.

$$4.05x + 2.70y = 47.25$$

After clearing decimals, we have this system:

$$x + y = 15,$$
$$405x + 270y = 4725$$

Carry out. Solve using matrices.

$$\begin{bmatrix} 1 & 1 & | & 15 \\ 405 & 270 & | & 4725 \end{bmatrix}$$

$$\begin{bmatrix} 1 & 1 & | & 15 \\ 0 & -135 & | & -1350 \end{bmatrix}$$ New Row 2 $=$
$$-405(\text{Row 1}) + \text{Row 2}$$

Reinserting the variables, we have

$$x + y = 15, \quad (1)$$
$$-135y = -1350 \quad (2)$$

Solve (2) for y.

$$-135y = -1350$$
$$y = 10$$

Substitute 10 for y in (1) and solve for x.

$$x + 10 = 15$$
$$x = 5$$

Check. The sum of the numbers is 15. The total value is $\$4.05(5) + \$2.70(10)$, or $\$20.25 + \$27.00$, or $\$47.25$. The numbers check.

State. 5 pounds of the $4.05 per lb granola and 10 pounds of the $2.70 per lb granola should be used.

22. 14 pounds of nuts, 6 pounds of oats

23. **Familiarize**. We let x, y, and z represent the amounts invested at 7%, 8%, and 9%, respectively. Recall the formula for simple interest:

$$\text{Interest} = \text{Principal} \times \text{Rate} \times \text{Time}$$

Translate. We organize the information in a table.

	First Invest- ment	Second Invest- ment	Third Invest- ment	Total
P	x	y	z	$2500
R	7%	8%	9%	
T	1 yr	1 yr	1 yr	
I	$0.07x$	$0.08y$	$0.09z$	$212

The first row gives us one equation:

$$x + y + z = 2500$$

The last row gives a second equation:

$$0.07x + 0.08y + 0.09z = 212$$

Amount invested at 9% is $1100 more than amount invested at 8%.

$$z = \$1100 + y$$

After clearing decimals, we have this system:

$$
\begin{aligned}
x + \; y + \; z &= \; 2500, \\
7x + 8y + 9z &= 21{,}200, \\
-y + \; z &= \; 1100
\end{aligned}
$$

Carry out. Solve using matrices.

$$
\begin{bmatrix}
1 & 1 & 1 & | & 2500 \\
7 & 8 & 9 & | & 21{,}200 \\
0 & -1 & 1 & | & 1100
\end{bmatrix}
$$

$$
\begin{bmatrix}
1 & 1 & 1 & | & 2500 \\
0 & 1 & 2 & | & 3700 \\
0 & -1 & 1 & | & 1100
\end{bmatrix}
$$

New Row 2 = -7(Row 1) + Row 2

$$
\begin{bmatrix}
1 & 1 & 1 & | & 2500 \\
0 & 1 & 2 & | & 3700 \\
0 & 0 & 3 & | & 4800
\end{bmatrix}
$$

New Row 3 = Row 2 + Row 3

Reinserting the variables, we have

$$
\begin{aligned}
x + y + z &= \; 2500, \quad (1) \\
y + 2z &= \; 3700, \quad (2) \\
3z &= 4800 \quad (3)
\end{aligned}
$$

Solve (3) for z.

$$3z = 4800$$
$$z = 1600$$

Substitute 1600 for z in (2) and solve for y.

$$y + 2 \cdot 1600 = 3700$$
$$y + 3200 = 3700$$
$$y = 500$$

Substitute 500 for y and 1600 for z in (1) and solve for x.

$$x + 500 + 1600 = 2500$$
$$x + 2100 = 2500$$
$$x = 400$$

Check. The total investment is $400 + $500 + $1600, or $2500. The total interest is 0.07($400) + 0.08($500) + 0.09($1600) = $28 + $40 + $144 = $212. The amount invested at 9%, $1600, is $1100 more than the amount invested at 8%, $500. The numbers check.

State. $400 is invested at 7%, $500 is invested at 8%, and $1600 is invested at 9%.

24. $500 at 8%, $400 at 9%, $2300 at 10%

25. *Writing Exercise*

26. *Writing Exercise*

27. $5(-3) - (-7)4 = -15 - (-28) = -15 + 28 = 13$

28. -22

29.
$$
\begin{aligned}
&-2(5 \cdot 3 - 4 \cdot 6) - 3(2 \cdot 7 - 15) + 4(3 \cdot 8 - 5 \cdot 4) \\
&= -2(15 - 24) - 3(14 - 15) + 4(24 - 20) \\
&= -2(-9) - 3(-1) + 4(4) \\
&= 18 + 3 + 16 \\
&= 21 + 16 \\
&= 37
\end{aligned}
$$

30. 422

31. *Writing Exercise*

32. *Writing Exercise*

33. *Familiarize.* Let w, x, y, and z represent the thousand's, hundred's, ten's, and one's digits, respectively.

Translate.

The sum of the digits is 10.

$$w + x + y + z = 10$$

Twice the sum of the thousand's and ten's digits is the sum of the hundred's and one's digits less one.

$$2(w + y) = x + z - 1$$

The ten's digit is twice the thousand's digit.

$$y = 2 \cdot w$$

The one's digit equals the sum of the thousand's and hundred's digits.

$$z = w + x$$

We have a system of equations which can be written as

$$
\begin{aligned}
w + x + y + z &= 10, \\
2w - x + 2y - z &= -1, \\
-2w + y &= 0, \\
w + x - z &= 0.
\end{aligned}
$$

Carry out. We can use matrices to solve the system. We get $(1, 3, 2, 4)$.

Check. The sum of the digits is 10. Twice the sum of 1 and 2 is 6. This is one less than the sum of 3 and 4. The ten's digit, 2, is twice the thousand's digit, 1. The one's digit, 4, equals $1 + 3$. The numbers check.

State. The number is 1324.

34. $x = \dfrac{ce - bf}{ae - bd}, \ y = \dfrac{af - cd}{ae - bd}$

Exercise Set 8.7

1. $\begin{vmatrix} 5 & 1 \\ 2 & 4 \end{vmatrix} = 5 \cdot 4 - 2 \cdot 1 = 20 - 2 = 18$

2. -13

3. $\begin{vmatrix} 6 & -9 \\ 2 & 3 \end{vmatrix} = 6 \cdot 3 - 2(-9) = 18 + 18 = 36$

4. 29

5.
$$\begin{vmatrix} 1 & 4 & 0 \\ 0 & -1 & 2 \\ 3 & -2 & 1 \end{vmatrix}$$
$$= 1 \begin{vmatrix} -1 & 2 \\ -2 & 1 \end{vmatrix} - 0 \begin{vmatrix} 4 & 0 \\ -2 & 1 \end{vmatrix} + 3 \begin{vmatrix} 4 & 0 \\ -1 & 2 \end{vmatrix}$$
$$= 1[-1 \cdot 1 - (-2) \cdot 2] - 0 + 3[4 \cdot 2 - (-1) \cdot 0]$$
$$= 1 \cdot 3 - 0 + 3 \cdot 8$$
$$= 3 - 0 + 24$$
$$= 27$$

6. 1

7.
$$\begin{vmatrix} -1 & -2 & -3 \\ 3 & 4 & 2 \\ 0 & 1 & 2 \end{vmatrix}$$
$$= -1 \begin{vmatrix} 4 & 2 \\ 1 & 2 \end{vmatrix} - 3 \begin{vmatrix} -2 & -3 \\ 1 & 2 \end{vmatrix} + 0 \begin{vmatrix} -2 & -3 \\ 4 & 2 \end{vmatrix}$$
$$= -1[4 \cdot 2 - 1 \cdot 2] - 3[-2 \cdot 2 - 1(-3)] + 0$$
$$= -1 \cdot 6 - 3 \cdot (-1) + 0$$
$$= -6 + 3 + 0$$
$$= -3$$

8. 3

9.
$$\begin{vmatrix} -4 & -2 & 3 \\ -3 & 1 & 2 \\ 3 & 4 & -2 \end{vmatrix}$$
$$= -4 \begin{vmatrix} 1 & 2 \\ 4 & -2 \end{vmatrix} - (-3) \begin{vmatrix} -2 & 3 \\ 4 & -2 \end{vmatrix} + 3 \begin{vmatrix} -2 & 3 \\ 1 & 2 \end{vmatrix}$$
$$= -4[1(-2) - 4 \cdot 2] + 3[-2(-2) - 4 \cdot 3] +$$
$$\qquad 3(-2 \cdot 2 - 1 \cdot 3)$$
$$= -4(-10) + 3(-8) + 3(-7)$$
$$= 40 - 24 - 21 = -5$$

10. -6

11. $5x + 8y = 1,$
$\qquad 3x + 7y = 5$

We compute D, D_x, and D_y.

$$D = \begin{vmatrix} 5 & 8 \\ 3 & 7 \end{vmatrix} = 35 - 24 = 11$$

$$D_x = \begin{vmatrix} 1 & 8 \\ 5 & 7 \end{vmatrix} = 7 - 40 = -33$$

$$D_y = \begin{vmatrix} 5 & 1 \\ 3 & 5 \end{vmatrix} = 25 - 3 = 22$$

Then,
$$x = \frac{D_x}{D} = \frac{-33}{11} = -3$$
and
$$y = \frac{D_y}{D} = \frac{22}{11} = 2.$$
The solution is $(-3, 2)$.

12. $(2, 0)$

13. $5x - 4y = -3,$
$\qquad 7x + 2y = 6$

We compute D, D_x, and D_y.

$$D = \begin{vmatrix} 5 & -4 \\ 7 & 2 \end{vmatrix} = 10 - (-28) = 38$$

$$D_x = \begin{vmatrix} -3 & -4 \\ 6 & 2 \end{vmatrix} = -6 - (-24) = 18$$

$$D_y = \begin{vmatrix} 5 & -3 \\ 7 & 6 \end{vmatrix} = 30 - (-21) = 51$$

Then,
$$x = \frac{D_x}{D} = \frac{18}{38} = \frac{9}{19}$$
and
$$y = \frac{D_y}{D} = \frac{51}{38}.$$
The solution is $\left(\dfrac{9}{19}, \dfrac{51}{38} \right)$.

14. $\left(-\dfrac{25}{2}, -\dfrac{11}{2} \right)$

15. $3x - y + 2z = 1,$
        $x - y + 2z = 3,$
    $-2x + 3y + z = 1$

We compute D, D_x, and D_y.

$$D = \begin{vmatrix} 3 & -1 & 2 \\ 1 & -1 & 2 \\ -2 & 3 & 1 \end{vmatrix}$$

$$= 3 \begin{vmatrix} -1 & 2 \\ 3 & 1 \end{vmatrix} - 1 \begin{vmatrix} -1 & 2 \\ 3 & 1 \end{vmatrix} - 2 \begin{vmatrix} -1 & 2 \\ -1 & 2 \end{vmatrix}$$

$$= 3(-7) - 1(-7) - 2(0)$$

$$= -21 + 7 - 0$$

$$= -14$$

$$D_x = \begin{vmatrix} 1 & -1 & 2 \\ 3 & -1 & 2 \\ 1 & 3 & 1 \end{vmatrix}$$

$$= 1 \begin{vmatrix} -1 & 2 \\ 3 & 1 \end{vmatrix} - 3 \begin{vmatrix} -1 & 2 \\ 3 & 1 \end{vmatrix} + 1 \begin{vmatrix} -1 & 2 \\ -1 & 2 \end{vmatrix}$$

$$= 1(-7) - 3(-7) + 1(0)$$

$$= -7 + 21 + 0$$

$$= 14$$

$$D_y = \begin{vmatrix} 3 & 1 & 2 \\ 1 & 3 & 2 \\ -2 & 1 & 1 \end{vmatrix}$$

$$= 3 \begin{vmatrix} 3 & 2 \\ 1 & 1 \end{vmatrix} - 1 \begin{vmatrix} 1 & 2 \\ 1 & 1 \end{vmatrix} - 2 \begin{vmatrix} 1 & 2 \\ 3 & 2 \end{vmatrix}$$

$$= 3 \cdot 1 - 1(-1) - 2(-4)$$

$$= 3 + 1 + 8$$

$$= 12$$

Then,

$$x = \frac{D_x}{D} = \frac{14}{-14} = -1$$

and

$$y = \frac{D_y}{D} = \frac{12}{-14} = -\frac{6}{7}.$$

Substitute in the third equation to find z.

$$-2(-1) + 3\left(-\frac{6}{7}\right) + z = 1$$

$$2 - \frac{18}{7} + z = 1$$

$$-\frac{4}{7} + z = 1$$

$$z = \frac{11}{7}$$

The solution is $\left(-1, -\frac{6}{7}, \frac{11}{7}\right)$.

16. $\left(\frac{3}{2}, \frac{13}{14}, \frac{33}{14}\right)$

17. $2x - 3y + 5z = 27,$
        $x + 2y - z = -4,$
    $5x - y + 4z = 27$

We compute D, D_x, and D_y.

$$D = \begin{vmatrix} 2 & -3 & 5 \\ 1 & 2 & -1 \\ 5 & -1 & 4 \end{vmatrix}$$

$$= 2 \begin{vmatrix} 2 & -1 \\ -1 & 4 \end{vmatrix} - 1 \begin{vmatrix} -3 & 5 \\ -1 & 4 \end{vmatrix} + 5 \begin{vmatrix} -3 & 5 \\ 2 & -1 \end{vmatrix}$$

$$= 2(7) - 1(-7) + 5(-7)$$

$$= 14 + 7 - 35$$

$$= -14$$

$$D_x = \begin{vmatrix} 27 & -3 & 5 \\ -4 & 2 & -1 \\ 27 & -1 & 4 \end{vmatrix}$$

$$= 27 \begin{vmatrix} 2 & -1 \\ -1 & 4 \end{vmatrix} - (-4) \begin{vmatrix} -3 & 5 \\ -1 & 4 \end{vmatrix} + 27 \begin{vmatrix} -3 & 5 \\ 2 & -1 \end{vmatrix}$$

$$= 27(7) + 4(-7) + 27(-7)$$

$$= 189 - 28 - 189$$

$$= -28$$

$$D_y = \begin{vmatrix} 2 & 27 & 5 \\ 1 & -4 & -1 \\ 5 & 27 & 4 \end{vmatrix}$$

$$= 2 \begin{vmatrix} -4 & -1 \\ 27 & 4 \end{vmatrix} - 1 \begin{vmatrix} 27 & 5 \\ 27 & 4 \end{vmatrix} + 5 \begin{vmatrix} 27 & 5 \\ -4 & -1 \end{vmatrix}$$

$$= 2(11) - 1(-27) + 5(-7)$$

$$= 22 + 27 - 35$$

$$= 14$$

Then,

$$x = \frac{D_x}{D} = \frac{-28}{-14} = 2,$$

and

$$y = \frac{D_y}{D} = \frac{14}{-14} = -1.$$

We substitute in the second equation to find z.

$$2 + 2(-1) - z = -4$$

$$2 - 2 - z = -4$$

$$-z = -4$$

$$z = 4$$

The solution is $(2, -1, 4)$.

18. $(-3, 2, 1)$

19.
$$r - 2s + 3t = 6,$$
$$2r - s - t = -3,$$
$$r + s + t = 6$$

We compute D, D_r, and D_s.

$$D = \begin{vmatrix} 1 & -2 & 3 \\ 2 & -1 & -1 \\ 1 & 1 & 1 \end{vmatrix}$$

$$= 1\begin{vmatrix} -1 & -1 \\ 1 & 1 \end{vmatrix} - 2\begin{vmatrix} -2 & 3 \\ 1 & 1 \end{vmatrix} + 1\begin{vmatrix} -2 & 3 \\ -1 & -1 \end{vmatrix}$$

$$= 1(0) - 2(-5) + 1(5)$$
$$= 0 + 10 + 5$$
$$= 15$$

$$D_r = \begin{vmatrix} 6 & -2 & 3 \\ -3 & -1 & -1 \\ 6 & 1 & 1 \end{vmatrix}$$

$$= 6\begin{vmatrix} -1 & -1 \\ 1 & 1 \end{vmatrix} - (-3)\begin{vmatrix} -2 & 3 \\ 1 & 1 \end{vmatrix} + 6\begin{vmatrix} -2 & 3 \\ -1 & -1 \end{vmatrix}$$

$$= 6(0) + 3(-5) + 6(5)$$
$$= 0 - 15 + 30$$
$$= 15$$

$$D_s = \begin{vmatrix} 1 & 6 & 3 \\ 2 & -3 & -1 \\ 1 & 6 & 1 \end{vmatrix}$$

$$= 1\begin{vmatrix} -3 & -1 \\ 6 & 1 \end{vmatrix} - 2\begin{vmatrix} 6 & 3 \\ 6 & 1 \end{vmatrix} + 1\begin{vmatrix} 6 & 3 \\ -3 & -1 \end{vmatrix}$$

$$= 1(3) - 2(-12) + 1(3)$$
$$= 3 + 24 + 3$$
$$= 30$$

Then,
$$r = \frac{D_r}{D} = \frac{15}{15} = 1,$$
and
$$s = \frac{D_s}{D} = \frac{30}{15} = 2.$$

Substitute in the third equation to find t.
$$1 + 2 + t = 6$$
$$3 + t = 6$$
$$t = 3$$
The solution is $(1, 2, 3)$.

20. $(3, 4, -1)$

21. *Writing Exercise*

22. *Writing Exercise*

23.
$$0.5x - 2.34 + 2.4x = 7.8x - 9$$
$$2.9x - 2.34 = 7.8x - 9$$
$$6.66 = 4.9x$$
$$\frac{6.66}{4.9} = x$$
$$\frac{666}{490} = x$$
$$\frac{333}{245} = x$$
The solution is $\frac{333}{245}$.

24. -12

25. *Familiarize*. We first make a drawing.

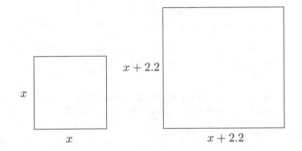

Let x represent the length of a side of the smaller square and $x + 2.2$ the length of a side of the larger square. The perimeter of the smaller square is $4x$. The perimeter of the larger square is $4(x + 2.2)$.

Translate.

The sum of the perimeters is 32.8 ft.
$$4x + 4(x + 2.2) = 32.8$$

Carry out. We solve the equation.
$$4x + 4x + 8.8 = 32.8$$
$$8x = 24$$
$$x = 3$$

Check. If $x = 3$ ft, then $x + 2.2 = 5.2$ ft. The perimeters are $4 \cdot 3$, or 12 ft, and $4(5.2)$, or 20.8 ft. The sum of the two perimeters is $12 + 20.8$, or 32.8 ft. The values check.

State. The wire should be cut into two pieces, one measuring 12 ft and the other 20.8 ft.

26. 18 scientific calculators, 27 graphing calculators

27. *Familiarize*. Let x represent the number of rolls of insulation required for the Mazzas' attic and let y represent the number of rolls required for the Kranepools' attic.

Translate.

Insulation for Mazzas' attic	is	three and a half	times	insulation for Kranepools' attic.
x	$=$	3.5	$\cdot$	y

$\underbrace{\text{Total number of rolls}}$ is 36.

$$\begin{array}{ccc} \downarrow & & \downarrow\ \downarrow \\ x+y & & =36 \end{array}$$

We have a system of equations:

$$x = 3.5y, \quad (1)$$

$$x + y = 36 \quad (2)$$

Carry out. We use the substitution method to solve the system of equations. First we substitute $3.5y$ for x in Equation (2).

$$x + y = 36 \quad (2)$$

$$3.5y + y = 36 \quad \text{Substituting}$$

$$4.5y = 36$$

$$y = 8$$

Now substitute 8 for y in Equation (1).

$$x = 3.5(8) = 28$$

Check. The number 28 is three and a half times 8. Also, the total number of rolls is $28 + 8$, or 36. The answer checks.

State. The Mazzas' attic requires 28 rolls of insulation, and the Kranepools' attic requires 8 rolls.

28. 17 buckets, 11 dinners

29. *Writing Exercise*

30. *Writing Exercise*

31. $\begin{vmatrix} y & -2 \\ 4 & 3 \end{vmatrix} = 44$

$$y \cdot 3 - 4(-2) = 44 \quad \text{Evaluating the determinant}$$

$$3y + 8 = 44$$

$$3y = 36$$

$$y = 12$$

32. 3

33. $\begin{vmatrix} m+1 & -2 \\ m-2 & 1 \end{vmatrix} = 27$

$$(m+1)(1) - (m-2)(-2) = 27 \quad \begin{array}{l}\text{Evaluating}\\ \text{the determinant}\end{array}$$

$$m + 1 + 2m - 4 = 27$$

$$3m = 30$$

$$m = 10$$

34. $\begin{vmatrix} x & y & 1 \\ x_1 & y_1 & 1 \\ x_2 & y_2 & 1 \end{vmatrix} = 0$

is equivalent to

$$x\begin{vmatrix} y_1 & 1 \\ y_2 & 1 \end{vmatrix} - x_1 \begin{vmatrix} y & 1 \\ y_2 & 1 \end{vmatrix} + x_2 \begin{vmatrix} y & 1 \\ y_1 & 1 \end{vmatrix} = 0$$

or

$$x(y_1 - y_2) - x_1(y - y_2) + x_2(y - y_1) = 0$$

or

$$xy_1 - xy_2 - x_1y + x_1y_2 + x_2y - x_2y_1 = 0. \quad (1)$$

Since the slope of the line through (x_1, y_1) and (x_2, y_2) is $\dfrac{y_2 - y_1}{x_2 - x_1}$, an equation of the line through (x_1, y_1) and (x_2, y_2) is

$$y - y_1 = \frac{y_2 - y_1}{x_2 - x_1}(x - x_1)$$

which is equivalent to

$$(x_2 - x_1)(y - y_1) = (y_2 - y_1)(x - x_1)$$

or

$$x_2y - x_2y_1 - x_1y + x_1y_1 = y_2x - y_2x_1 - y_1x + y_1x_1$$

or

$$x_2y - x_2y_1 - x_1y - xy_2 + x_1y_2 + xy_1 = 0. \quad (2)$$

Equations (1) and (2) are equivalent.

Exercise Set 8.8

1. $C(x) = 45x + 300,000 \qquad R(x) = 65x$

a) $P(x) = R(x) - C(x)$

$$= 65x - (45x + 300,000)$$

$$= 65x - 45x - 300,000$$

$$= 20x - 300,000$$

b) To find the break-even point we solve the system

$$R(x) = 65x,$$

$$C(x) = 45x + 300,000.$$

Since $R(x) = C(x)$ at the break-even point, we can rewrite the system:

$$R(x) = 65x, \qquad (1)$$

$$R(x) = 45x + 300,000 \quad (2)$$

We solve using substitution.

$$65x = 45x + 300,000 \quad \begin{array}{l}\text{Substituting } 65x \text{ for}\\ R(x) \text{ in (2)}\end{array}$$

$$20x = 300,000$$

$$x = 15,000$$

Thus, 15,000 units must be produced and sold in order to break even. This yields $R(15,000) = 65 \cdot 15,000 = \$975,000$ in revenue. The break-even point is $(15,000 \text{ units}, \$975,000)$.

2. a) $P(x) = 45x - 270,000$

b) $(6000 \text{ units}, \$420,000)$

3. $C(x) = 10x + 120,000 \qquad R(x) = 60x$

a) $P(x) = R(x) - C(x)$

$$= 60x - (10x + 120,000)$$

$$= 60x - 10x - 120,000$$

$$= 50x - 120,000$$

b) Solve the system

$$R(x) = 60x,$$

$$C(x) = 10x + 120,000.$$

Since both $R(x)$ and $C(x)$ are in dollars and they are equal at the break-even point, we can rewrite the system:

$$d = 60x, \qquad (1)$$
$$d = 10x + 120,000 \quad (2)$$

We solve using substitution.

$60x = 10x + 120,000$ Substituting $60x$ for d in (2)

$50x = 120,000$

$x = 2400$

Thus, 2400 units must be produced and sold in order to break even. This yields $R(2400) = 60 \cdot 2400 = \$144,000$ in revenue. The break-even point is (2400 units, $\$144,000$).

4. a) $P(x) == 55x - 49,500$

b) $(900 \text{ units}, \$76,500)$

5. $C(x) = 40x + 22,500 \qquad R(x) = 85x$

a) $P(x) = R(x) - C(x)$

$\qquad = 85x - (40x + 22,500)$

$\qquad = 85x - 40x - 22,500$

$\qquad = 45x - 22,500$

b) Solve the system

$\qquad R(x) = 85x,$

$\qquad C(x) = 40x + 22,500.$

Since both $R(x)$ and $C(x)$ are in dollars and they are equal at the break-even point, we can rewrite the system:

$$d = 85x, \qquad (1)$$
$$d = 40x + 22,500 \quad (2)$$

We solve using substitution.

$85x = 40x + 22,500$ Substituting $85x$ for d in (2)

$45x = 22,500$

$x = 500$

Thus, 500 units must be produced and sold in order to break even. This yields $R(500) = 85 \cdot 500 = \$42,500$ in revenue. The break-even point is (500 units, $\$42,500$).

6. a) $P(x) = 80x - 10,000$

b) $(125 \text{ units}, \$12,500)$

7. $C(x) = 22x + 16,000 \qquad R(x) = 40x$

a) $P(x) = R(x) - C(x)$

$\qquad = 40x - (22x + 16,000)$

$\qquad = 40x - 22x - 16,000$

$\qquad = 18x - 16,000$

b) Solve the system

$\qquad R(x) = 40x,$

$\qquad C(x) = 22x + 16,000.$

Since both $R(x)$ and $C(x)$ are in dollars and they are equal at the break-even point, we can rewrite the system:

$$d = 40x, \qquad (1)$$
$$d = 22x + 16,000 \quad (2)$$

We solve using substitution.

$40x = 22x + 16,000$ Substituting $40x$ for d in (2)

$18x = 16,000$

$x \approx 889$ units

Thus, 889 units must be produced and sold in order to break even. This yields $R(889) = 40 \cdot 889 = \$35,560$ in revenue. The break-even point is (889 units, $\$35,560$)

8. a) $P(x) = 40x - 75,000$

b) $(1875 \text{ units}, \$103,125)$

9. $C(x) = 75x + 100,000 \qquad R(x) = 125x$

a) $P(x) = R(x) - C(x)$

$\qquad = 125x - (75x + 100,000)$

$\qquad = 125x - 75x - 100,000$

$\qquad = 50x - 100,000$

b) Solve the system

$\qquad R(x) = 125x,$

$\qquad C(x) = 75x + 100,000.$

Since $R(x) = C(x)$ at the break-even point, we can rewrite the system:

$$R(x) = 125x, \qquad (1)$$
$$R(x) = 75x + 100,000 \quad (2)$$

We solve using substitution.

$125x = 75x + 100,000$ Substituting $125x$ for $R(x)$ in (2)

$50x = 100,000$

$x = 2000$

To break even 2000 units must be produced and sold. This yields $R(2000) = 125 \cdot 2000 = \$250,000$ in revenue. The break-even point is (2000 units, $\$250,000$)

10. a) $P(x) = 30x - 120,000$

b) $(4000 \text{ units}, \$200,000)$

11. $D(p) = 1000 - 10p,$

$\qquad S(p) = 230 + p$

Since both demand and supply are quantities, the system can be rewritten:

$$q = 1000 - 10p, \quad (1)$$
$$q = 230 + p \qquad (2)$$

Substitute $1000 - 10p$ for q in (2) and solve.

$1000 - 10p = 230 + p$

$770 = 11p$

$70 = p$

The equilibrium price is $\$70$ per unit. To find the equilibrium quantity we substitute $\$70$ into either $D(p)$ or $S(p)$.

$D(70) = 1000 - 10 \cdot 70 = 1000 - 700 = 300$

The equilibrium quantity is 300 units.

The equilibrium point is ($70, 300$).

12. ($10, 1400$)

13. $D(p) = 760 - 13p,$

$S(p) = 430 + 2p$

Rewrite the system:

$q = 760 - 13p, \quad (1)$

$q = 430 + 2p \quad \quad (2)$

Substitute $760 - 13p$ for q in (2) and solve.

$760 - 13p = 430 + 2p$

$330 = 15p$

$22 = p$

The equilibrium price is $22 per unit.

To find the equilibrium quantity we substitute $22 into either $D(p)$ or $S(p)$.

$S(22) = 430 + 2(22) = 430 + 44 = 474$

The equilibrium quantity is 474 units.

The equilibrium point is ($22, 474$).

14. ($10, 370$)

15. $D(p) = 7500 - 25p,$

$S(p) = 6000 + 5p$

Rewrite the system:

$q = 7500 - 25p, \quad (1)$

$q = 6000 + 5p \quad \quad (2)$

Substitute $7500 - 25p$ for q in (2) and solve.

$7500 - 25p = 6000 + 5p$

$1500 = 30p$

$50 = p$

The equilibrium price is $50 per unit.

To find the equilibrium quantity we substitute $50 into either $D(p)$ or $S(p)$.

$D(50) = 7500 - 25(50) = 7500 - 1250 = 6250$

The equilibrium quantity is 6250 units.

The equilibrium point is ($50, 6250$).

16. ($40, 7600$)

17. $D(p) = 1600 - 53p,$

$S(p) = 320 + 75p$

Rewrite the system:

$q = 1600 - 53p, \quad (1)$

$q = 320 + 75p \quad \quad (2)$

Substitute $1600 - 53p$ for q in (2) and solve.

$1600 - 53p = 320 + 75p$

$1280 = 128p$

$10 = p$

The equilibrium price is $10 per unit.

To find the equilibrium quantity we substitute $10 into either $D(p)$ or $S(p)$.

$S(10) = 320 + 75(10) = 320 + 750 = 1070$

The equilibrium quantity is 1070 units.

The equilibrium point is ($10, 1070$).

18. ($36, 4060$)

19. a) $C(x) = \text{Fixed costs} + \text{Variable costs}$

$C(x) = 125,300 + 450x,$

where x is the number of computers produced.

b) Each computer sells for $800. The total revenue is 800 times the number of computers sold. We assume that all computers produced are sold.

$R(x) = 800x$

c) $P(x) = R(x) - C(x)$

$P(x) = 800x - (125,300 + 450x)$

$= 800x - 125,300 - 450x$

$= 350x - 125,300$

d) $P(x) = 350x - 125,300$

$P(100) = 350(100) - 125,300$

$= 35,000 - 125,300$

$= -90,300$

The company will realize a $90,300 loss when 100 computers are produced and sold.

$P(400) = 350(400) - 125,300$

$= 140,000 - 125,300$

$= 14,700$

The company will realize a profit of $14,700 from the production and sale of 400 computers.

e) Solve the system

$R(x) = 800x,$

$C(x) = 125,300 + 450x.$

Since both $R(x)$ and $C(x)$ are in dollars and they are equal at the break-even point, we can rewrite the system:

$d = 800x, \quad \quad \quad (1)$

$d = 125,300 + 450x \quad (2)$

We solve using substitution.

$800x = 125,300 + 450x$ Substituting $800x$ for d in (2)

$350x = 125,300$

$x \approx 358$ \quad \quad \quad \quad Rounding up

The firm will break even if it produces and sells 358 computers and takes in a total of $R(358) = 800 \cdot 358 = \$286,400$ in revenue. Thus, the break-even point is (358 computers, $286,400).

20. a) $C(x) = 22,500 + 40x$

b) $R(x) = 85x$

c) $P(x) = 45x - 22,500$

d) $112,500 profit; $4500 loss

e) (500 lamps, $42,500)

21. a) $C(x) = $ Fixed costs $+$ Variable costs

$C(x) = 16,404 + 6x$,

where x is the number of caps produced, in dozens.

b) Each dozen caps sell for $18. The total revenue is 18 times the number of caps sold, in dozens. We assume that all caps produced are sold.

$R(x) = 18x$

c) $P(x) = R(x) - C(x)$

$P(x) = 18x - (16,404 + 6x)$

$\quad = 18x - 16,404 - 6x$

$\quad = 12x - 16,404$

d) $P(3000) = 12(3000) - 16,404$

$\quad\quad\quad\quad = 36,000 - 16,404$

$\quad\quad\quad\quad = 19,596$

The company will realize a profit of $19,596 when 3000 dozen caps are produced and sold.

$P(1000) = 12(1000) - 16,404$

$\quad\quad\quad\quad = 12,000 - 16,404$

$\quad\quad\quad\quad = -4404$

The company will realize a $4404 loss when 1000 dozen caps are produced and sold.

e) Solve the system

$R(x) = 18x$,

$C(x) = 16,404 + 6x$.

Since both $R(x)$ and $C(x)$ are in dollars and they are equal at the break-even point, we can rewrite the system:

$d = 18x$,   (1)

$d = 16,404 + 6x$ (2)

We solve using substitution.

$18x = 16,404 + 6x$ Substituting $18x$ for d
$\quad\quad\quad\quad\quad\quad\quad\quad\quad$ in (2)

$12x = 16,404$

$\quad x = 1367$

The firm will break even if it produces and sells 1367 dozen caps and takes in a total of $R(1367) = 18 \cdot 1367 = \$24,606$ in revenue. Thus, the break-even point is (1367 dozen caps, $24,606).

22. a) $C(x) = 10,000 + 30x$

b) $R(x) = 80x$

c) $P(x) = 50x - 10,000$

d) $90,000 profit; $7500 loss

e) (200 sport coats, $16,000)

23. a) $D(p) = -14.97p + 987.35$,

$S(p) = 98.55p - 5.13$

Rewrite the system:

$q = -14.97p + 987.35$,   (1)

$q = 98.55p - 5.13$ (2)

Substitute $-14.97p + 987.35$ for q in (2) and solve.

$-14.97p + 987.35 = 98.55p - 5.13$

$\quad\quad\quad 992.48 = 113.52p$

$\quad\quad\quad\quad 8.74 \approx p$

The equilibrium price is $8.74 per unit. A price of $8.74 per unit should be charged in order to have equilibrium between supply and demand.

b) $R(x) = 8.74x$,

$C(x) = 2.10x + 5265$

Rewrite the system:

$d = 8.74x$,   (1)

$d = 2.10x + 5265$ (2)

We solve using substitution.

$8.74x = 2.10x + 5265$ Substituting $8.74x$ for d
$\quad\quad\quad\quad\quad\quad\quad\quad\quad\quad$ in (2)

$6.64x = 5265$

$\quad x \approx 793$

Thus 793 units must be sold in order to break even.

24. a) (4526 units, $4,390,220)

b) $870

25. *Writing Exercise*

26. *Writing Exercise*

27. $3x - 9 = 27$

$\quad 3x = 36$ Adding 9 to both sides

$\quad\quad x = 12$ Dividing both sides by 3

The solution is 12.

28. 15

29. $4x - 5 = 7x - 13$

$\quad -5 = 3x - 13$ Subtracting $4x$ from both sides

$\quad\quad 8 = 3x$ Adding 13 to both sides

$\quad \dfrac{8}{3} = x$ Dividing both sides by 3

The solution is $\dfrac{8}{3}$.

30. 4

31. $7 - 2(x - 8) = 14$

$7 - 2x + 16 = 14$ Removing parentheses

$\quad -2x + 23 = 14$ Collecting like terms

$\quad\quad\quad -2x = -9$ Subtracting 23 from both sides

$\quad\quad\quad\quad x = \dfrac{9}{2}$ Dividing both sides by -2

The solution is $\dfrac{9}{2}$.

32. $\dfrac{1}{3}$

33. *Writing Exercise*

34. *Writing Exercise*

35. The supply function contains the points ($2, 100) and ($8, 500). We find its equation:

$$m = \frac{500 - 100}{8 - 2} = \frac{400}{6} = \frac{200}{3}$$

$$y - y_1 = m(x - x_1) \quad \text{Point-slope form}$$

$$y - 100 = \frac{200}{3}(x - 2)$$

$$y - 100 = \frac{200}{3}x - \frac{400}{3}$$

$$y = \frac{200}{3}x - \frac{100}{3}$$

We can equivalently express supply S as a function of price p:

$$S(p) = \frac{200}{3}p - \frac{100}{3}$$

The demand function contains the points ($1, 500) and ($9, 100). We find its equation:

$$m = \frac{100 - 500}{9 - 1} = \frac{-400}{8} = -50$$

$$y - y_1 = m(x - x_1)$$

$$y - 500 = -50(x - 1)$$

$$y - 500 = -50x + 50$$

$$y = -50x + 550$$

We can equivalently express demand D as a function of price p:

$$D(p) = -50p + 550$$

We have a system of equations

$$S(p) = \frac{200}{3}p - \frac{100}{3},$$

$$D(p) = -50p + 550.$$

Rewrite the system:

$$q = \frac{200}{3}p - \frac{100}{3}, \quad (1)$$

$$q = -50p + 550 \quad (2)$$

Substitute $\dfrac{200}{3}p - \dfrac{100}{3}$ for q in (2) and solve.

$$\frac{200}{3}p - \frac{100}{3} = -50p + 550$$

$$200p - 100 = -150p + 1650 \quad \text{Multiplying by 3}$$
$$\text{to clear fractions}$$

$$350p - 100 = 1650$$

$$350p = 1750$$

$$p = 5$$

The equilibrium price is $5 per unit.

To find the equilibrium quantity, we substitute $5 into either $S(p)$ or $D(p)$.

$$D(5) = -50(5) + 550 = -250 + 550 = 300$$

The equilibrium quantity is 300 units.

The equilibrium point is ($5, 300).

36. 308 pairs

37. a) Enter the data and use the linear regression feature to get $S(p) = 15.97p - 1.05$.

   b) Enter the data and use the linear regression feature to get $D(p) = -11.26p + 41.16$.

   c) Find the point of intersection of the graphs of the functions found in parts (a) and (b).

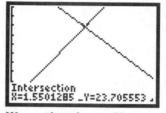

Intersection
X=1.5501285 Y=23.705553

We see that the equilibrium point is ($1.55, 23.7 million jars).

38. a) $S(p) = 3.8p - 1.82$

   b) $D(p) = -1.44p + 7.64$

   c) ($1.81, 5.0 thousand)

Exercise Set 8.9

1. We replace x with -4 and y with 2.

$$\frac{2x + 3y < -1}{2(-4) + 3 \cdot 2 \ ? \ -1}$$
$$\begin{array}{c|c} -8 + 6 & \\ -2 & -1 \quad \text{TRUE} \end{array}$$

Since $-2 < -1$ is true, $(-4, 2)$ is a solution.

2. No

3. We replace x with 8 and y with 14.

$$\frac{2y - 3x \geq 9}{2 \cdot 14 - 3 \cdot 8 \ ? \ 9}$$
$$\begin{array}{c|c} 28 - 24 & \\ 4 & 9 \quad \text{FALSE} \end{array}$$

Since $4 > 9$ is false, $(8, 14)$ is not a solution.

4. Yes

5. Graph: $y > \dfrac{1}{2}x$

We first graph the line $y = \dfrac{1}{2}x$. We draw the line dashed since the inequality symbol is $>$. To determine which half-plane to shade, test a point not on the line. We try $(0, 1)$:

$$\frac{y > \dfrac{1}{2}x}{1 \ ? \ \dfrac{1}{2} \cdot 0}$$
$$\begin{array}{c|c} 1 & 0 \quad \text{TRUE} \end{array}$$

Since $1 > 0$ is true, (0.1) is a solution as are all of the points in the half-plane containing $(0, 1)$. We shade that half-plane and obtain the graph.

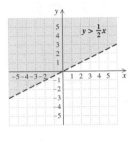

6.

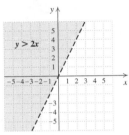

7. Graph: $y \geq x - 3$

First graph the line $y = x - 3$. Draw it solid since the inequality symbol is $\geq$. Test the point $(0, 0)$ to determine if it is a solution.

$$\frac{y \geq x - 3}{0 \; ? \; 0 - 3}$$
$$0 \; | \; -3 \qquad \text{TRUE}$$

Since $0 \geq -3$ is true, we shade the half-plane that contains $(0, 0)$ and obtain the graph.

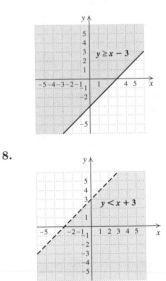

8.

9. Graph: $y \leq x + 4$

First graph the line $y = x + 4$. Draw it solid since the inequality symbol is $\leq$. Test the point $(0, 0)$ to determine if it is a solution.

$$\frac{y \leq x + 4}{0 \; ? \; 0 + 4}$$
$$0 \; | \; 4 \qquad \text{TRUE}$$

Since $0 \leq 4$ is true, we shade the half-plane that contains $(0, 0)$ and obtain the graph.

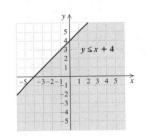

10.

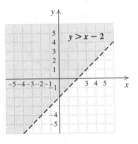

11. Graph: $x - y \leq 5$

First graph the line $x - y = 5$. Draw a solid line since the inequality symbol is $\leq$. Test the point $(0, 0)$ to determine if it is a solution.

$$\frac{x - y \leq 5}{0 - 0 \; ? \; 5}$$
$$0 \; | \; 5 \qquad \text{TRUE}$$

Since $0 \leq 5$ is true, we shade the half-plane that contains $(0, 0)$ and obtain the graph.

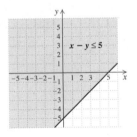

12.

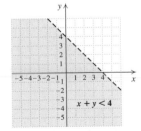

13. Graph: $2x + 3y < 6$

First graph $2x + 3y = 6$. Draw the line dashed since the inequality symbol is $<$. Test the point $(0, 0)$ to determine if it is a solution.

$$\frac{2x + 3y < 6}{2 \cdot 0 + 3 \cdot 0 \ ? \ 6}$$
$$\quad 0 \ \Big| \ 6 \qquad \text{TRUE}$$

Since $0 < 6$ is true, we shade the half-plane containing $(0, 0)$ and obtain the graph.

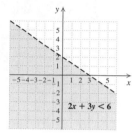

14.

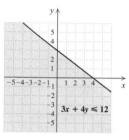

15. Graph: $2x - y \leq 4$

We first graph $2x - y = 4$. Draw the line solid since the inequality symbol is $\leq$. Test the point $(0, 0)$ to determine if it is a solution.

$$\frac{2x - y \leq 4}{2 \cdot 0 - 0 \ ? \ 4}$$
$$\quad 0 \ \Big| \ 4 \qquad \text{TRUE}$$

Since $0 \leq 4$ is true, we shade the half-plane containing $(0, 0)$ and obtain the graph.

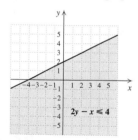

16.

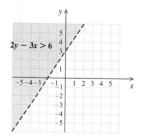

17. Graph: $2x - 2y \geq 8 + 2y$

$$2x - 4y \geq 8$$

First graph $2x - 4y = 8$. Draw the line solid since the inequality symbol is $\geq$. Test the point $(0, 0)$ to determine if it is a solution.

$$\frac{2x - 4y \geq 8}{2 \cdot 0 - 4 \cdot 0 \ ? \ 8}$$
$$\quad 0 \ \Big| \ 8 \qquad \text{FALSE}$$

Since $0 \geq 8$ is false, we shade the half-plane that does not contain $(0, 0)$ and obtain the graph.

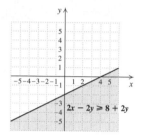

18.

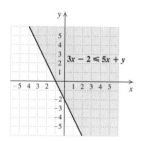

19. Graph: $y \geq 2$

We first graph $y = 2$. Draw the line solid since the inequality symbol is $\geq$. Test the point $(0, 0)$ to determine if it is a solution.

$$\frac{y \geq 2}{0 \ ? \ 2} \qquad \text{FALSE}$$

Since $0 \geq 2$ is false, we shade the half-plane that does not contain $(0, 0)$ and obtain the graph.

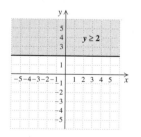

20.

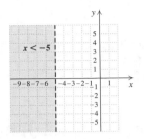

Finally, we shade the intersection of these graphs.

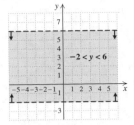

21. Graph: $x \le 7$

We first graph $x = 7$. We draw the line solid since the inequality symbol is $\le$. Test the point $(0,0)$ to determine if it is a solution.

$$\frac{x \le 7}{0 \ ? \ 7} \qquad \text{TRUE}$$

Since $0 \le 7$ is true, we shade the half-plane containing $(0,0)$ and obtain the graph.

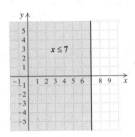

22.

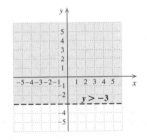

23. Graph: $-2 < y < 6$

This is a system of inequalities:

$$-2 < y,$$
$$y < 6$$

We graph the equation $-2 = y$ and see that the graph of $-2 < y$ is the half-plane above the line $-2 = y$. We also graph $y = 6$ and see that the graph of $y < 6$ is the half-plane below the line $y = 6$.

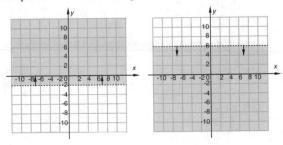

24.

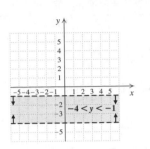

25. Graph: $-4 \le x \le 5$

This is a system of inequalities:

$$-4 \le x,$$
$$x \le 5$$

Graph $-4 \le x$ and $x \le 5$.

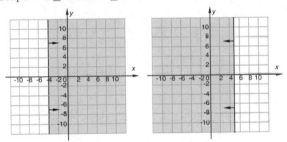

Then we shade the intersection of these graphs.

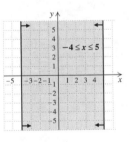

26.

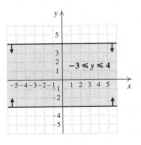

27. Graph: $0 \leq y \leq 3$

This is a system of inequalities:

$0 \leq y,$

$y \leq 3$

Graph $0 \leq y$ and $y \leq 3$.

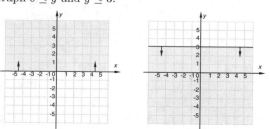

Then we shade the intersection of these graphs.

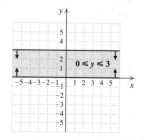

28.

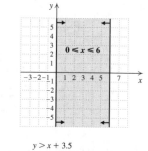

29.

 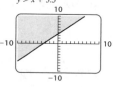

$y > x + 3.5$

30.

$7y \leq 2x + 5$

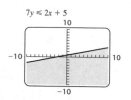

31. First get y alone on one side of the inequality.

$8x - 2y < 11$

$\qquad -2y < -8x + 11$

$\qquad\qquad y > \dfrac{-8x + 11}{-2}$

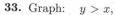

$8x - 2y < 11$

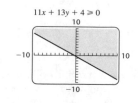

32.

$11x + 13y + 4 \geq 0$

33. Graph: $y > x,$

$\qquad\qquad y < -x + 2$

We graph the lines $y = x$ and $y = -x + 2$, using dashed lines. We indicate the region for each inequality by the arrows at the ends of the lines. Note where the regions overlap and shade the region of solutions.

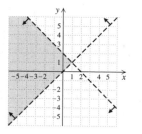

34.

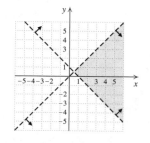

35. Graph: $y \geq x,$

$\qquad\qquad y \leq 2x - 4$

Graph $y = x$ and $y = 2x - 4$, using solid lines. Indicate the region for each inequality by arrows, and shade the region where they overlap.

 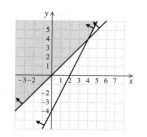

36.

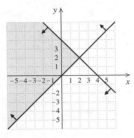

40.

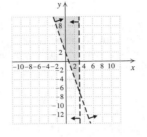

37. Graph: $y \leq -3$,

$x \geq -1$

Graph $y = -3$ and $x = -1$ using solid lines. Indicate the region for each inequality by arrows, and shade the region where they overlap.

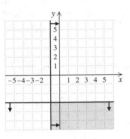

41. Graph: $y \leq 3$,

$y \geq -x + 2$

Graph the lines $y = 3$ and $y = -x + 2$, using solid lines. Indicate the region for each inequality by arrows, and shade the region where they overlap.

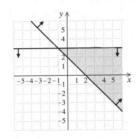

38.

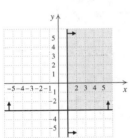

42.

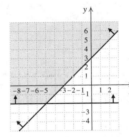

39. Graph: $x > -4$,

$y < -2x + 3$

Graph the lines $x = -4$ and $y = -2x + 3$, using dashed lines. Indicate the region for each inequality by arrows, and shade the region where they overlap.

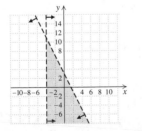

43. Graph: $x + y \leq 6$,

$x - y \leq 4$

Graph the lines $x + y = 6$ and $x - y = 4$, using solid lines. Indicate the region for each inequality by arrows, and shade the region where they overlap.

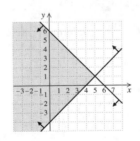

44.

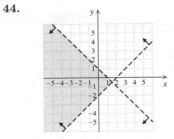

45. Graph: $y + 3x > 0,$

$y + 3x < 2$

Graph the lines $y + 3x = 0$ and $y + 3x = 2$, using dashed lines. Indicate the region for each inequality by arrows, and shade the region where they overlap.

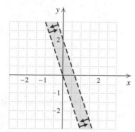

46.

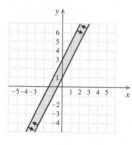

47. Graph: $y \leq 2x - 1,$ (1)

$y \geq -2x + 1,$ (2)

$x \leq 3$ (3)

Graph the lines $y = 2x - 1$, $y = -2x + 1$, and $x = 3$ using solid lines. Indicate the region for each inequality by arrows, and shade the region where they overlap.

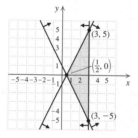

To find the vertex we solve three different systems of related equations.

From (1) and (2) we have $y = 2x - 1,$

$y = -2x + 1.$

Solving, we obtain the vertex $\left(\dfrac{1}{2}, 0\right).$

From (1) and (3) we have $y = 2x - 1,$

$x = 3.$

Solving, we obtain the vertex $(3, 5).$

From (2) and (3) we have $y = -2x + 1,$

$x = 3.$

Solving, we obtain the vertex $(3, -5).$

48.

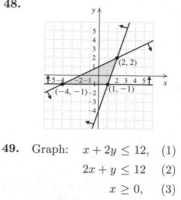

49. Graph: $x + 2y \leq 12,$ (1)

$2x + y \leq 12$ (2)

$x \geq 0,$ (3)

$y \geq 0$ (4)

Graph the lines $x + 2y = 12$, $2x + y = 12$, $x = 0$, and $y = 0$ using solid lines. Indicate the region for each inequality by arrows, and shade the region where they overlap.

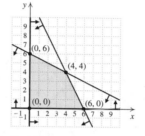

To find the vertices we solve four different systems of equations.

From (1) and (2) we have $x + 2y = 12,$

$2x + y = 12.$

Solving, we obtain the vertex $(4, 4).$

From (1) and (3) we have $x + 2y = 12,$

$x = 0.$

Solving, we obtain the vertex $(0, 6).$

From (2) and (4) we have $2x + y = 12,$

$y = 0.$

Solving, we obtain the vertex $(6, 0).$

From (3) and (4) we have $x = 0,$

$y = 0.$

Solving, we obtain the vertex $(0, 0).$

50.

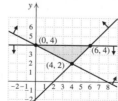

51. Graph: $8x + 5y \leq 40,$ (1)

$x + 2y \leq 8$ (2)

$x \geq 0,$ (3)

$y \geq 0$ (4)

Graph the lines $8x + 5y = 40$, $x + 2y = 8$, $x = 0$, and $y = 0$ using solid lines. Indicate the region for each inequality by arrows, and shade the region where they overlap.

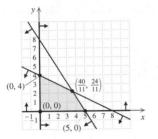

To find the vertices we solve four different systems of equations.

From (1) and (2) we have $8x + 5y = 40,$

$x + 2y = 8.$

Solving, we obtain the vertex $\left(\dfrac{40}{11}, \dfrac{24}{11}\right)$.

From (1) and (4) we have $8x + 5y = 40,$

$y = 0.$

Solving, we obtain the vertex $(5, 0)$.

From (2) and (3) we have $x + 2y = 8,$

$x = 0.$

Solving, we obtain the vertex $(0, 4)$.

From (3) and (4) we have $x = 0,$

$y = 0.$

Solving, we obtain the vertex $(0, 0)$.

52.

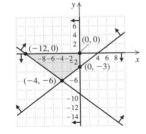

53. Graph: $y - x \geq 1,$ (1)

$y - x \leq 3,$ (2)

$2 \leq x \leq 5$ (3)

Think of (3) as two inequalities:

$2 \leq x,$ (4)

$x \leq 5$ (5)

Graph the lines $y - x = 1$, $y - x = 3$, $x = 2$, and $x = 5$, using solid lines. Indicate the region for each inequality by arrows, and shade the region where they overlap.

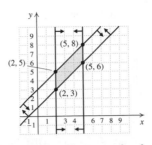

To find the vertices we solve four different systems of equations.

From (1) and (4) we have $y - x = 1,$

$x = 2.$

Solving, we obtain the vertex $(2, 3)$.

From (1) and (5) we have $y - x = 1,$

$x = 5.$

Solving, we obtain the vertex $(5, 6)$.

From (2) and (4) we have $y - x = 3,$

$x = 2.$

Solving, we obtain the vertex $(2, 5)$.

From (2) and (5) we have $y - x = 3,$

$x = 5.$

Solving, we obtain the vertex $(5, 8)$.

54.

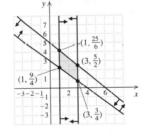

55. *Writing Exercise*

56. *Writing Exercise*

57. *Familiarize.* We let x and y represent the number of pounds of peanuts and fancy nuts in the mixture, respectively. We organize the given information in a table.

Type of nuts	Peanuts	Fancy	Mixture
Amount	x	y	10
Price per pound	$2.50	$7	
Value	$2.5x$	$7y$	40

Translate. We get a system of equations from the first and third rows of the table.

$x + y = 10,$

$2.5x + 7y = 40$

Clearing decimals we have

$x + y = 10,$ (1)

$25x + 70y = 400.$ (2)

Carry out. We use the elimination method. Multiply Equation (1) by -25 and add.

$$-25x - 25y = -250$$
$$\underline{25x + 70y = 400}$$
$$45y = 150$$
$$y = \frac{10}{3}, \text{ or } 3\frac{1}{3}$$

Substitute $\frac{10}{3}$ for y in Equation (1) and solve for x.

$$x + y = 10$$
$$x + \frac{10}{3} = 10$$
$$x = \frac{20}{3}, \text{ or } 6\frac{2}{3}$$

Check. The sum of $6\frac{2}{3}$ and $3\frac{1}{3}$ is 10. The value of the mixture is $2.5\left(\frac{20}{3}\right) + 7\left(\frac{10}{3}\right)$, or $\frac{50}{3} + \frac{70}{3}$, or \$40. These numbers check.

State. $6\frac{2}{3}$ lb of peanuts and $3\frac{1}{3}$ lb of fancy nuts should be used.

58. Hendersons: 10 bags; Savickis: 4 bags

59. *Familiarize.* Let $x =$ the number of cardholders tickets that were sold and $y =$ the number of non-cardholders tickets. We arrange the information in a table.

	Card-holders	Non-card-holders	Total
Price	\$1.25	\$2	
Number sold	x	y	203
Money taken in	1.25x	2y	\$310

Translate. The last two rows of the table give us two equations. The total number of tickets sold was 203, so we have

$$x + y = 203.$$

The total amount of money collected was \$310, so we have

$$1.25x + 2y = 310.$$

We can multiply the second equation on both sides by 100 to clear decimals. The resulting system is

$$x + y = 203, \qquad (1)$$
$$125x + 200y = 31,000. \qquad (2)$$

Carry out. We use the elimination method. We multiply on both sides of Equation (1) by -125 and then add.

$$-125x - 125y = -25,375 \quad \text{Multiplying by } -125$$
$$\underline{125x + 200y = 31,000}$$
$$75y = 5625$$
$$y = 75$$

We go back to Equation (1) and substitute 75 for y.

$$x + y = 203$$
$$x + 75 = 203$$
$$x = 128$$

Check. The number of tickets sold was $128 + 75$, or 203. The money collected was $\$1.25(128) + \$2(75)$, or $\$160 + \$150$, or \$310. These numbers check.

State. 128 cardholders tickets and 75 non-cardholders tickets were sold.

60. 70 student tickets; 130 adult tickets

61. *Familiarize.* The formula for the area of a triangle with base b and height h is $A = \frac{1}{2}bh$.

Translate. Substitute 200 for A and 16 for b in the formula.

$$A = \frac{1}{2}bh$$
$$200 = \frac{1}{2} \cdot 16 \cdot h$$

Carry out. We solve the equation.

$$200 = \frac{1}{2} \cdot 16 \cdot h$$
$$200 = 8h \qquad \text{Multiplying}$$
$$25 = h \qquad \text{Dividing by 8 on both sides}$$

Check. The area of a triangle with base 16 ft and height 25 ft is $\frac{1}{2} \cdot 16 \cdot 25$, or 200 ft^2. The answer checks.

State. The seed can fill a triangle that is 25 ft tall.

62. 11%

63. *Writing Exercise*

64. *Writing Exercise*

65. Graph: $x + y > 8,$
$$x + y \le -2$$

Graph the line $x + y = 8$ using a dashed line and graph $x + y = -2$, using a solid line. Indicate the region for each inequality by arrows. The regions do not overlap (the solution set is $\emptyset$), so we do not shade any portion of the graph.

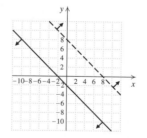

66.

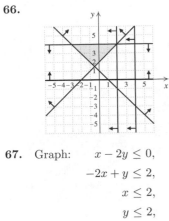

67. Graph:
$$x - 2y \le 0,$$
$$-2x + y \le 2,$$
$$x \le 2,$$
$$y \le 2,$$
$$x + y \le 4$$

Graph the five inequalities above, and shade the region where they overlap.

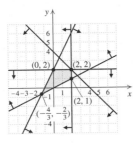

68. $x \ge -2,$
$y \le 2,$
$x \le 0,$
$y \ge 0;$ or

$x \ge 0,$
$y \le 2,$
$x \le 2,$
$y \ge 0;$ or

$x \ge 0,$
$y \le 0,$
$x \le 2,$
$y \ge -2;$ or

$x \ge -2,$
$y \le 0,$
$x \le 0,$
$y \ge -2$

69. Both the width and the height must be positive, but they must be less than 62 in. in order to be checked as luggage, so we have:
$$0 < w \le 62,$$
$$0 < h \le 62$$

The girth is represented by $2w + 2h$ and the length is 62 in. In order to meet postal regulations the sum of the girth and the length cannot exceed 108 in., so we have:

$$62 + 2w + 2h \le 108, \text{ or}$$
$$2w + 2h \le 46, \text{ or}$$
$$w + h \le 23$$

Thus, have a system of inequalities:
$$0 < w \le 62,$$
$$0 < h \le 62,$$
$$w + h \le 23$$

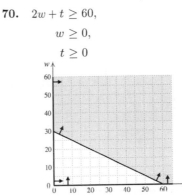

70. $2w + t \ge 60,$
$w \ge 0,$
$t \ge 0$

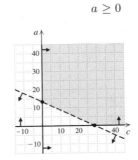

71. Graph: $35c + 75a > 1000,$
$$c \ge 0,$$
$$a \ge 0$$

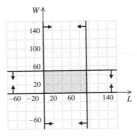

72. $0 < L \le 94,$
$0 < W \le 50$

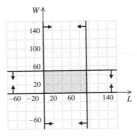

73. The shaded region lies below the graphs of $y = x$ and $y = 2$ and both lines are solid. Thus, we have

$$y \leq x,$$
$$y \leq 2.$$

74. $y \leq x + 1,$
$$x \leq 3,$$
$$y \geq -2$$

75. The shaded region lies below the graphs of $y = x + 2$ and $y = -x + 4$ and above $y = 0$, and all of the lines are solid. Thus, we have

$$y \leq x + 2,$$
$$y \leq -x + 4,$$
$$y \geq 0.$$

76. $y \leq x + 2,$
$$y \geq x - 3.$$

Chapter 9

Exponents and Radical Functions

1. The square roots of 16 are 4 and -4, because $4^2 = 16$ and $(-4)^2 = 16$.

2. $7, -7$

3. The square roots of 144 are 12 and -12, because $12^2 = 144$ and $(-12)^2 = 144$.

4. $3, -3$

5. The square roots of 81 are 9 and -9, because $9^2 = 81$ and $(-9)^2 = 81$.

6. $20, -20$

7. The square roots of 900 are 30 and -30, because $30^2 = 900$ and $(-30)^2 = 900$.

8. $15, -15$

9. Using a calculator we find that the square roots of 7 are approximately 2.6458 and -2.6458.

10. $3.8730, -3.8730$

11. Using a calculator we find that the square roots of 23.7 are approximately 4.8683 and -4.8683.

12. $0.2236, -0.2236$

13. Using a calculator we find that the square roots of $\dfrac{3}{4}$ are approximately 0.8660 and -0.8660.

14. $0.5590, -0.5590$

15. $-\sqrt{\dfrac{49}{36}} = -\dfrac{7}{6}$ Since $\sqrt{\dfrac{49}{36}} = \dfrac{7}{6}$, $-\sqrt{\dfrac{49}{36}} = -\dfrac{7}{6}$.

16. $-\dfrac{19}{3}$

17. $\sqrt{441} = 21$ Remember, $\sqrt{}$ indicates the principle square root.

18. 14

19. $-\sqrt{\dfrac{16}{81}} = -\dfrac{4}{9}$ Since $\sqrt{\dfrac{16}{81}} = \dfrac{4}{9}$, $-\sqrt{\dfrac{16}{81}} = -\dfrac{4}{9}$.

20. $-\dfrac{3}{4}$

21. $\sqrt{0.09} = 0.3$

22. 0.6

23. $-\sqrt{0.0049} = -0.07$

24. 0.12

25. $5\sqrt{p^2 + 4}$

The radicand is the expression written under the radical sign, $p^2 + 4$.

Since the index is not written, we know it is 2.

26. $y^2 - 8$; 2

27. $x^2 y^2 \sqrt[3]{\dfrac{x}{y+4}}$

The radicand is the expression written under the radical sign, $\dfrac{x}{y+4}$.

The index is 3.

28. $\dfrac{a}{a^2 - b}$; 3

29. $\begin{aligned} f(t) &= \sqrt{5t - 10} \\ f(6) &= \sqrt{5 \cdot 6 - 10} = \sqrt{20} \\ f(2) &= \sqrt{5 \cdot 2 - 10} = \sqrt{0} = 0 \\ f(1) &= \sqrt{5 \cdot 1 - 10} = \sqrt{-5} \end{aligned}$

Since negative numbers do not have real-number square roots, $f(1)$ does not exist.

$f(-1) = \sqrt{5(-1) - 10} = \sqrt{-15}$

Since negative numbers do not have real-number square roots, $f(-1)$ does not exist.

30. $\sqrt{11}$; does not exist; $\sqrt{11}$; 12

31. $\begin{aligned} t(x) &= -\sqrt{2x + 1} \\ t(4) &= -\sqrt{2 \cdot 4 + 1} = -\sqrt{9} = -3 \\ t(0) &= -\sqrt{2 \cdot 0 + 1} = -\sqrt{1} = -1 \\ t(-1) &= -\sqrt{2(-1) + 1} = -\sqrt{-1}; \end{aligned}$

$t(-1)$ does not exist.

$t\left(-\dfrac{1}{2}\right) = -\sqrt{2\left(-\dfrac{1}{2}\right) + 1} = -\sqrt{0} = 0$

32. $\sqrt{12}$; does not exist; $\sqrt{30}$; does not exist

33. $\begin{aligned} f(t) &= \sqrt{t^2 + 1} \\ f(0) &= \sqrt{0^2 + 1} = \sqrt{1} = 1 \\ f(-1) &= \sqrt{(-1)^2 + 1} = \sqrt{2} \\ f(-10) &= \sqrt{(-10)^2 + 1} = \sqrt{101} \end{aligned}$

34. $-2; -5; -4$

35. $g(x) = \sqrt{x^3 + 9}$

   $g(-2) = \sqrt{(-2)^3 + 9} = \sqrt{1} = 1$

   $g(-3) = \sqrt{(-3)^3 + 9} = \sqrt{-18}$;

   $g(-3)$ does not exist.

   $g(3) = \sqrt{3^3 + 9} = \sqrt{36} = 6$

36. Does not exist; $\sqrt{17}$; $\sqrt{54}$

37. $\sqrt{36x^2} = \sqrt{(6x)^2} = |6x| = 6|x|$

   Since x might be negative, absolute-value notation is necessary.

38. $5|t|$

39. $\sqrt{(-6b)^2} = |-6b| = |-6| \cdot |b| = 6|b|$

   Since b might be negative, absolute-value notation is necessary.

40. $7|c|$

41. $\sqrt{(7-t)^2} = |7-t|$

   Since $7 - t$ might be negative, absolute-value notation is necessary.

42. $|a + 1|$

43. $\sqrt{y^2 + 16y + 64} = \sqrt{(y+8)^2} = |y+8|$

   Since $y + 8$ might be negative, absolute-value notation is necessary.

44. $|x - 2|$

45. $\sqrt{9x^2 - 30x + 25} = \sqrt{(3x-5)^2} = |3x-5|$

   Since $3x - 5$ might be negative, absolute-value notation is necessary.

46. $|2x + 7|$

47. $-\sqrt[4]{625} = -5$ Since $5^4 = 625$

48. 4

49. $-\sqrt[5]{3^5} = -3$

50. -1

51. $\sqrt[5]{-\dfrac{1}{32}} = -\dfrac{1}{2}$ Since $\left(-\dfrac{1}{2}\right)^5 = -\dfrac{1}{32}$

52. $-\dfrac{2}{3}$

53. $\sqrt[8]{y^8} = |y|$

   The index is even. Use absolute-value notation since y could have a negative value.

54. $|x|$

55. $\sqrt[4]{(7b)^4} = |7b| = 7|b|$

   The index is even. Use absolute-value notation since b could have a negative value.

56. $5|a|$

57. $\sqrt[12]{(-10)^{12}} = |-10| = 10$

58. 6

59. $\sqrt[1976]{(2a+b)^{1976}} = |2a+b|$

   The index is even. Use absolute-value notation since $2a+b$ could have a negative value.

60. $|a + b|$

61. $\sqrt{x^{10}} = |x^5|$ Note that $(x^5)^2 = x^{10}$; x^5 could have a negative value.

62. $|a^{11}|$

63. $\sqrt{a^{14}} = |a^7|$ Note that $(a^7)^2 = a^{14}$; a^7 could have a negative value.

64. x^8

65. $\sqrt{25t^2} = \sqrt{(5t)^2} = 5t$ Assuming t is nonnegative

66. $4x$

67. $\sqrt{(7c)^2} = 7c$ Assuming c is nonnegative

68. $6b$

69. $\sqrt{(5+b)^2} = 5+b$ Assuming $5 + b$ is nonnegative

70. $a + 1$

71. $\sqrt{9x^2 + 36x + 36} = \sqrt{9(x^2 + 4x + 4)} =$

   $\sqrt{[3(x+2)]^2} = 3(x+2)$, or $3x + 6$

72. $2(x + 1)$, or $2x + 2$

73. $\sqrt{25t^2 - 20t + 4} = \sqrt{(5t-2)^2} = 5t - 2$

74. $3t - 2$

75. $-\sqrt[3]{64} = -4$ $(4^3 = 64)$

76. 3

77. $\sqrt[4]{81x^4} = \sqrt[4]{(3x)^4} = 3x$

78. $2x$

79. $-\sqrt[5]{-100,000} = -(-10) = 10$ $[(-10)^5 = -100,000]$

80. -6

81. $-\sqrt[3]{-64x^3} = -(-4x)$ $[(-4x)^3 = -64x^3]$

   $= 4x$

82. $5y$

83. $\sqrt{a^{14}} = \sqrt{(a^7)^2} = a^7$

84. a^{11}

85. $\sqrt{(x+3)^{10}} = \sqrt{[(x+3)^5]^2} = (x+3)^5$

86. $(x - 2)^4$

87. $f(x) = \sqrt[3]{x + 1}$

   $f(7) = \sqrt[3]{7 + 1} = \sqrt[3]{8} = 2$

   $f(26) = \sqrt[3]{26 + 1} = \sqrt[3]{27} = 3$

   $f(-9) = \sqrt[3]{-9 + 1} = \sqrt[3]{-8} = -2$

   $f(-65) = \sqrt[3]{-65 + 1} = \sqrt[3]{-64} = -4$

88. $1; 5; 3; -5$

89.
$$g(t) = \sqrt[4]{t - 3}$$
$$g(19) = \sqrt[4]{19 - 3} = \sqrt[4]{16} = 2$$
$$g(-13) = \sqrt[4]{-13 - 3} = \sqrt[4]{-16};$$
$$g(-13) \text{ does not exist.}$$
$$g(1) = \sqrt[4]{1 - 3} = \sqrt[4]{-2};$$
$$g(1) \text{ does not exist.}$$
$$g(84) = \sqrt[4]{84 - 3} = \sqrt[4]{81} = 3$$

90. $1;\ 2;$ does not exist; 3

91. $f(x) = \sqrt{x - 5}$

Since the index is even, the radicand, $x - 5$, must be nonnegative. We solve the inequality:
$$x - 5 \geq 0$$
$$x \geq 5$$
Domain of $f = \{x | x \geq 5\}$, or $[5, \infty)$

92. $\{x | x \geq -8\}$, or $[-8, \infty)$

93. $g(t) = \sqrt[4]{t + 3}$

Since the index is even, the radicand, $t + 3$, must be nonnegative. We solve the inequality:
$$t + 3 \geq 0$$
$$t \geq -3$$
Domain of $g = \{t | t \geq -3\}$, or $[-3, \infty)$

94. $\{x | x \geq 7\}$, or $[7, \infty)$

95. $g(x) = \sqrt[4]{5 - x}$

Since the index is even, the radicand, $5 - x$, must be nonnegative. We solve the inequality:
$$5 - x \geq 0$$
$$5 \geq x$$
Domain of $g = \{x | x \leq 5\}$, or $(-\infty, 5]$

96. $\{t | t \text{ is a real number}\}$, or $(-\infty, \infty)$

97. $f(t) = \sqrt[5]{2t + 9}$

Since the index is odd, the radicand can be any real number.

Domain of $f = \{t | t \text{ is a real number}\}$, or $(-\infty, \infty)$

98. $\left\{ t \middle| t \geq -\dfrac{5}{2} \right\}$, or $\left[-\dfrac{5}{2}, \infty \right)$

99. $h(z) = -\sqrt[6]{5z + 3}$

Since the index is even, the radicand, $5z + 3$, must be nonnegative. We solve the inequality:
$$5z + 3 \geq 0$$
$$5z \geq -3$$
$$z \geq -\frac{3}{5}$$
Domain of $h = \left\{ z \middle| z \geq -\dfrac{3}{5} \right\}$, or $\left(-\dfrac{3}{5}, \infty \right)$

100. $\left\{ x \middle| x \geq \dfrac{5}{7} \right\}$, or $\left[\dfrac{5}{7}, \infty \right)$

101. $f(t) = 7 + \sqrt[8]{t^8}$

Since we can compute $7 + \sqrt[8]{t^8}$ for any real number t, the domain is the set of real numbers, or $\{x | x \text{ is a real number}\}$, or $(-\infty, \infty)$.

102. $\{x | x \text{ is a real number}\}$, or $(-\infty, \infty)$.

103. $f(x) = \sqrt{5 - x}$

Find all values of x for which the radicand is nonnegative.
$$5 - x \geq 0$$
$$5 \geq x$$
The domain is $\{x | x \leq 5\}$, or $(-\infty, 5]$.

We graph the function in the standard window.

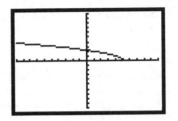

The range appears to be $\{y | y \geq 0\}$, or $[0, \infty)$.

104. Domain: $\left\{ x \middle| x \geq -\dfrac{1}{2} \right\}$, or $\left[-\dfrac{1}{2}, \infty \right)$;

range: $\{y | y \geq 0\}$, or $[0, \infty)$

105. $f(x) = 1 - \sqrt{x + 1}$

Find all values of x for which the radicand is nonnegative.
$$x + 1 \geq 0$$
$$x \geq -1$$
The domain is $\{x | x \geq -1\}$, or $[-1, \infty)$.

We graph the function in the window $[-10, 10, -5, 5]$.

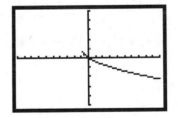

The range appears to be $\{y | y \leq 1\}$, or $(-\infty, 1]$.

106. Domain: $\left\{ x \middle| x \geq \dfrac{5}{3} \right\}$, or $\left[\dfrac{5}{3}, \infty \right)$;

range: $\{y | y \geq 2\}$, or $[2, \infty)$

107. $g(x) = 3 + \sqrt{x^2 + 4}$

Since $x^2 + 4$ is positive for all values of x, the domain is $\{x | x \text{ is a real number}\}$, or $(-\infty, \infty)$.

We graph the function in the standard window.

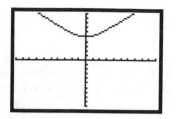

The range appears to be $\{y|y \geq 5\}$, or $[5, \infty)$.

108. Domain: $\{x|x$ is a real number$\}$, or $(-\infty, \infty)$; range: $\{y|y \leq 4\}$, or $(-\infty, 4]$

109. For $f(x) = \sqrt{x - 4}$, the domain is $[4, \infty)$ and all of the function values are nonnegative. Graph (c) corresponds to this function.

110. (a)

111. For $h(x) = \sqrt{x^2 + 4}$, the domain is $(-\infty, \infty)$. Graph (d) corresponds to this function.

112. (b)

113. A scatterplot of the data shows that it could be modeled with a radical function.

114. Yes

115. A scatterplot of the data shows that it could be modeled well with a radical function.

116. No

117. $h(x) = 10.681 + \sqrt{177.971284x - 1744.994255}$

In 1992, $x = 1992 - 1970 = 22$.

$h(22) = 10.681 + \sqrt{177.971284(22) - 1744.994255}$

≈ 57.3

In 1992, about 57.3 million households were served by cable television.

In 2001, $x = 2001 - 1970 = 31$.

$h(31) = 10.681 + \sqrt{177.971284(31) - 1744.994255}$

≈ 72.1

In 2001, about 72.1 million households were served by cable television.

118. 3.4 sec

119. *Writing Exercise*

120. *Writing Exercise*

121. $(a^3b^2c^5)^3 = a^{3\cdot3}b^{2\cdot3}c^{5\cdot3} = a^9b^6c^{15}$

122. $10a^{10}b^9$

123. $(2a^{-2}b^3c^{-4})^{-3} = 2^{-3}a^{-2(-3)}b^{3(-3)}c^{-4(-3)} =$

$\dfrac{1}{2^3}a^6b^{-9}c^{12} = \dfrac{a^6c^{12}}{8b^9}$

124. $\dfrac{x^6y^2}{25z^4}$

125. $\dfrac{8x^{-2}y^5}{4x^{-6}z^{-2}} = \dfrac{8}{4}x^{-2-(-6)}y^5z^2 = 2x^4y^5z^2$

126. $\dfrac{5c^3}{a^4b^7}$

127. First find the slope of the function.

$m = \dfrac{5419 - 3282}{16 - 0} = \dfrac{2137}{16} = 133.5625$

The y-intercept is $(0, 3282)$, so the function is $n(t) = 133.5625t + 3282$, where t is the number of years after 1980.

128. $f(x) = 134.4737456x + 3212.856476$

129. *Writing Exercise*

130. *Writing Exercise*

131. *Writing Exercise*

132. *Writing Exercise*

133. $N = 2.5\sqrt{A}$

   a) $N = 2.5\sqrt{25} = 2.5(5) = 12.5 \approx 13$

   b) $N = 2.5\sqrt{36} = 2.5(6) = 15$

   c) $N = 2.5\sqrt{49} = 2.5(7) = 17.5 \approx 18$

   d) $N = 2.5\sqrt{64} = 2.5(8) = 20$

134. $\{x| - 3 \leq x < 2\}$, or $[-3, 2)$

135. $g(x) = \dfrac{\sqrt[4]{5 - x}}{\sqrt[6]{x + 4}}$

The radical expression in the numerator has an even index, so the radicand, $5 - x$, must be nonnegative. We solve the inequality:

$5 - x \geq 0$

$5 \geq x$

The radical expression in the denominator also has an even index, so the radicand, $x + 4$, must be nonnegative in order for $\sqrt[6]{x + 4}$ to exist. In addition, the denominator cannot be zero, so the radicand must be positive. We solve the inequality:

$x + 4 > 0$

$x > -4$

We have $x \leq 5$ *and* $x > -4$ so

Domain of $g = \{x| - 4 < x \leq 5\}$, or $(-4, 5]$.

Exercise Set 9.2

1. $x^{1/4} = \sqrt[4]{x}$

2. $\sqrt[5]{y}$

3. $(16)^{1/2} = \sqrt{16} = 4$

4. 2

5. $81^{1/4} = \sqrt[4]{81} = 3$

6. 2

7. $9^{1/2} = \sqrt{9} = 3$

8. 5

9. $(xyz)^{1/3} = \sqrt[3]{xyz}$

10. $\sqrt[4]{ab}$

11. $(a^2b^2)^{1/5} = \sqrt[5]{a^2b^2}$

12. $\sqrt[4]{x^3y^3}$

13. $a^{2/3} = \sqrt[3]{a^2}$

14. $\sqrt{b^3}$

15. $16^{3/4} = \sqrt[4]{16^3} = (\sqrt[4]{16})^3 = 2^3 = 8$

16. 128

17. $49^{3/2} = \sqrt{49^3} = (\sqrt{49})^3 = 7^3 = 343$

18. 81

19. $9^{5/2} = \sqrt{9^5} = (\sqrt{9})^5 = 3^5 = 243$

20. 729

21. $(81x)^{3/4} = \sqrt[4]{(81x)^3} = \sqrt[4]{81^3x^3}$, or $\sqrt[4]{81^3} \cdot \sqrt[4]{x^3} = (\sqrt[4]{81})^3 \cdot \sqrt[4]{x^3} = 3^3\sqrt[4]{x^3} = 27\sqrt[4]{x^3}$

22. $25\sqrt[3]{a^2}$

23. $(25x^4)^{3/2} = \sqrt{(25x^4)^3} = \sqrt{25^3 \cdot x^{12}} = \sqrt{25^3} \cdot \sqrt{x^{12}} = (\sqrt{25})^3x^6 = 5^3x^6 = 125x^6$

24. $27y^9$

25. $\sqrt[3]{20} = 20^{1/3}$

26. $19^{1/3}$

27. $\sqrt{17} = 17^{1/2}$

28. $6^{1/2}$

29. $\sqrt{x^3} = x^{3/2}$

30. $a^{5/2}$

31. $\sqrt[5]{m^2} = m^{2/5}$

32. $n^{4/5}$

33. $\sqrt[4]{cd} = (cd)^{1/4}$ Parentheses are required.

34. $(xy)^{1/5}$

35. $\sqrt[5]{xy^2z} = (xy^2z)^{1/5}$

36. $(x^3y^2z^2)^{1/7}$

37. $(\sqrt{3mn})^3 = (3mn)^{3/2}$

38. $(7xy)^{4/3}$

39. $(\sqrt[7]{8x^2y})^5 = (8x^2y)^{5/7}$

40. $(2a^5b)^{7/6}$

41. $\dfrac{2x}{\sqrt[3]{z^2}} = \dfrac{2x}{z^{2/3}}$

42. $\dfrac{3a}{c^{2/5}}$

43. $x^{-1/3} = \dfrac{1}{x^{1/3}}$

44. $\dfrac{1}{y^{1/4}}$

45. $(2rs)^{-3/4} = \dfrac{1}{(2rs)^{3/4}}$

46. $\dfrac{1}{(5xy)^{5/6}}$

47. $\left(\dfrac{1}{8}\right)^{-2/3} = \left(\dfrac{8}{1}\right)^{2/3} = (2^3)^{2/3} = 2^{\frac{3}{1}\cdot\frac{2}{3}} = 2^2 = 4$

48. 8

49. $\dfrac{1}{a^{-5/7}} = a^{5/7}$

50. $a^{3/5}$

51. $2a^{3/4}b^{-1/2}c^{2/3} = 2 \cdot a^{3/4} \cdot \dfrac{1}{b^{1/2}} \cdot c^{2/3} = \dfrac{2a^{3/4}c^{2/3}}{b^{1/2}}$

52. $\dfrac{5y^{4/5}z}{x^{2/3}}$

53. $2^{-1/3}x^4y^{-2/7} = \dfrac{1}{2^{1/3}} \cdot x^4 \cdot \dfrac{1}{y^{2/7}} = \dfrac{x^4}{2^{1/3}y^{2/7}}$

54. $\dfrac{a^3}{3^{5/2}b^{7/3}}$

55. $\left(\dfrac{7x}{8yx}\right)^{-3/5} = \left(\dfrac{8yz}{7x}\right)^{3/5}$ Finding the reciprocal of the base and changing the sign of the exponent

56. $\left(\dfrac{3c}{2ab}\right)^{5/6}$

57. $\dfrac{7x}{\sqrt[3]{z}} = \dfrac{7x}{z^{1/3}}$

58. $\dfrac{6a}{b^{1/4}}$

59. $\dfrac{5a}{3c^{-1/2}} = \dfrac{5a}{3} \cdot c^{1/2} = \dfrac{5ac^{1/2}}{3}$

60. $\dfrac{2x^{1/3}z}{5}$

61. $f(x) = \sqrt[4]{x+7} = (x+7)^{1/4}$

Enter $y = (x+7)\wedge(1/4)$, or $y = (x+7)\wedge 0.25$.

Since the index is even, the domain of the function is the set of all x for which the radicand is nonnegative, or $[-7,\infty)$. One good choice of a viewing window is $[-10, 25, -1, 5]$, Xscl $= 5$.

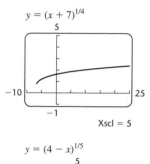
$y = (x + 7)^{1/4}$

66.

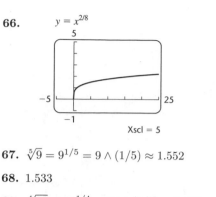
$y = x^{2/8}$

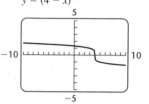
$y = (3x - 2)^{1/7}$

62.

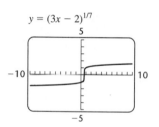
$y = (4 - x)^{1/5}$

67. $\sqrt[5]{9} = 9^{1/5} = 9 \wedge (1/5) \approx 1.552$

68. 1.533

69. $\sqrt[4]{10} = 10^{1/4} = 10 \wedge (1/4) \approx 1.778$

70. -1.998

71. $\sqrt[3]{(-3)^5} = (-3)^{5/3} = (-3) \wedge (5/3) \approx -6.240$

72. 1.275

73. $5^{3/4} \cdot 5^{1/8} = 5^{3/4+1/8} = 5^{6/8+1/8} = 5^{7/8}$

We added exponents after finding a common denominator.

74. $11^{7/6}$

75. $\dfrac{3^{5/8}}{3^{-1/8}} = 3^{5/8-(-1/8)} = 3^{5/8+1/8} = 3^{6/8} = 3^{3/4}$

We subtracted exponents and simplified.

76. $8^{9/11}$

63. $r(x) = \sqrt[7]{3x - 2} = (3x - 2)^{1/7}$

Enter $y = (3x - 2) \wedge (1/7)$. Since the index is odd the domain of the function is $(-\infty, \infty)$. One good choice of a viewing window is $[-10, 10, -5, 5]$.

77. $\dfrac{4.1^{-1/6}}{4.1^{-2/3}} = 4.1^{-1/6-(-2/3)} = 4.1^{-1/6+2/3} =$
$4.1^{-1/6+4/6} = 4.1^{3/6} = 4.1^{1/2}$

We subtracted exponents after finding a common denominator. Then we simplified.

78. $\dfrac{1}{2.3^{1/10}}$

79. $(10^{3/5})^{2/5} = 10^{3/5 \cdot 2/5} = 10^{6/25}$

We multiplied exponents.

80. $5^{15/28}$

81. $a^{2/3} \cdot a^{5/4} = a^{2/3+5/4} = a^{8/12+15/12} = a^{23/12}$

We added exponents after finding a common denominator.

82. $x^{17/12}$

64.

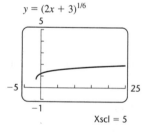
$y = (2x + 3)^{1/6}$

83. $(64^{3/4})^{4/3} = 64^{\frac{3}{4} \cdot \frac{4}{3}} = 64^1 = 64$

84. $\dfrac{1}{27}$

85. $(m^{2/3} n^{-1/4})^{1/2} = m^{2/3 \cdot 1/2} n^{-1/4 \cdot 1/2} = m^{1/3} n^{-1/8} =$
$m^{1/3} \cdot \dfrac{1}{n^{1/8}} = \dfrac{m^{1/3}}{n^{1/8}}$

65. $f(x) = \sqrt[6]{x^3} = (x^3)^{1/6} = x^{3/6}$

Enter $y = x \wedge (3/6)$. The function is defined only for nonnegative value of x, so the domain is $[0, \infty)$. One good choice of a window is $[-5, 25, -1, 5]$, Xscl $= 5$.

86. $\dfrac{y^{1/10}}{x^{1/12}}$

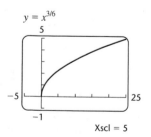
$y = x^{3/6}$

87. $\sqrt[6]{a^2} = a^{2/6}$ Converting to exponential notation

$\qquad = a^{1/3}$ Simplifying the exponent

$\qquad = \sqrt[3]{a}$ Returning to radical notation

88. $\sqrt[3]{t^2}$

89. $\sqrt[3]{x^{15}} = x^{15/3}$ Converting to exponential
notation
$= x^5$ Simplifying

90. a^3

91. $\sqrt[6]{x^{18}} = x^{18/6}$ Converting to exponential
notation
$= x^3$ Simplifying

92. a^2

93. $(\sqrt[3]{ab})^{15} = (ab)^{15/3}$ Converting to exponential
notation
$= (ab)^5$ Simplifying the exponent
$= a^5 b^5$ Using the law of exponents

94. $x^2 y^2$

95. $\sqrt[8]{(3x)^2} = (3x)^{2/8}$ Converting to exponential
notation
$= (3x)^{1/4}$ Simplifying the exponent
$= \sqrt[4]{3x}$ Returning to radical notation

96. $\sqrt{7a}$

97. $(\sqrt[10]{3a})^5 = (3a)^{5/10}$ Converting to exponential
notation
$= (3a)^{1/2}$ Simplifying the exponent
$= \sqrt{3a}$ Returning to radical
notation

98. $\sqrt[4]{8x^3}$

99. $\sqrt[4]{\sqrt{x}} = \sqrt[4]{x^{1/2}}$ Converting to
$= (x^{1/2})^{1/4}$ exponential notation
$= x^{1/8}$ Using a law of exponents
$= \sqrt[8]{x}$ Returning to radical
notation

100. $\sqrt[18]{m}$

101. $\sqrt{(ab)^6} = (ab)^{6/2}$ Converting to exponential
notation
$= (ab)^3$ Using the laws
$= a^3 b^3$ of exponents

102. $x^3 y^3$

103. $(\sqrt[3]{x^2 y^5})^{12} = (x^2 y^5)^{12/3}$ Converting to
exponential notation
$= (x^2 y^5)^4$ Simplifying the
exponent
$= x^8 y^{20}$ Using the laws
of exponents

104. $a^6 b^{12}$

105. $\sqrt[3]{\sqrt[4]{xy}} = \sqrt[3]{(xy)^{1/4}}$ Converting to
$= [(xy)^{1/4}]^{1/3}$ exponential notation
$= (xy)^{1/12}$ Using a law of exponents
$= \sqrt[12]{xy}$ Returning to radical notation

106. $\sqrt[10]{2a}$

107. *Writing Exercise*

108. *Writing Exercise*

109. $3x(x^3 - 2x^2) + 4x^2(2x^2 + 5x)$
$= 3x^4 - 6x^3 + 8x^4 + 20x^3$
$= 11x^4 + 14x^3$

110. $-3t^6 + 28t^5 - 20t^4$

111. $(3a - 4b)(5a + 3b)$
$= 3a \cdot 5a + 3a \cdot 3b - 4b \cdot 5a - 4b \cdot 3b$
$= 15a^2 + 9ab - 20ab - 12b^2$
$= 15a^2 - 11ab - 12b^2$

112. $49x^2 - 14xy + y^2$

113. **Familiarize.** Let p = the selling price of the home.
Translate.
$\underbrace{0.5\% \text{ of the selling price}}_{\downarrow}$ is \$467.50
$\qquad\qquad 0.005p \qquad\quad = \quad 467.50$
Carry out. We solve the equation.
$0.005p = 467.50$
$p = 93,500$ Dividing by 0.005
Check. 0.5% of \$93,500 is 0.005(\$93,500), or \$467.50.
The answer checks.
State. The selling price of the home was \$93,500.

114. 0, 1

115. *Writing Exercise*

116. *Writing Exercise*

117. $\sqrt[5]{x^2 y\sqrt{xy}} = \sqrt[5]{x^2 y(xy)^{1/2}} = \sqrt[5]{x^2 y x^{1/2} y^{1/2}} =$
$\sqrt[5]{x^{5/2} y^{3/2}} = (x^{5/2} y^{3/2})^{1/5} = x^{5/10} y^{3/10} =$
$(x^5 y^3)^{1/10} = \sqrt[10]{x^5 y^3}$

118. $\sqrt[6]{x^5}$

119. $\sqrt[4]{\sqrt[3]{8x^3 y^6}} = \sqrt[4]{(2^3 x^3 y^6)^{1/3}} = \sqrt[4]{2^{3/3} x^{3/3} y^{6/3}} =$
$\sqrt[4]{2xy^2}$

120. $\sqrt[6]{p+q}$

121. $f(x) = 262 \cdot 2^{x/12}$
$f(12) = 262 \cdot 2^{12/12}$
$= 262 \cdot 2^1$
$= 262 \cdot 2$
$= 524$ cycles per second

122. 1760 cycles per second

123. $2^{7/12} \approx 1.498 \approx 1.5$ so the G that is 7 half steps above middle C has a frequency that is about 1.5 times that of middle C.

124. $2^{4/12} \approx 1.2599 \approx 1.25$ which is 25% greater than 1.

125. a) $L = \dfrac{(0.000169)60^{2.27}}{1} \approx 1.8$ m

  b) $L = \dfrac{(0.000169)75^{2.27}}{0.9906} \approx 3.1$ m

  c) $L = \dfrac{(0.000169)80^{2.27}}{2.4} \approx 1.5$ m

  d) $L = \dfrac{(0.000169)100^{2.27}}{1.1} \approx 5.3$ m

126. About 7.937×10^{-13} to 1

127. $m = m_0(1 - v^2 c^{-2})^{-1/2}$

$$m = 8\left[1 - \left(\frac{9}{5} \times 10^8\right)^2 (3 \times 10^8)^{-2}\right]^{-1/2}$$

$$= 8\left[1 - \frac{\left(\frac{9}{5} \times 10^8\right)^2}{(3 \times 10^8)^2}\right]^{-1/2}$$

$$= 8\left[1 - \frac{\frac{81}{25} \times 10^{16}}{9 \times 10^6}\right]^{-1/2}$$

$$= 8\left[1 - \frac{81}{25} \cdot \frac{1}{9}\right]^{-1/2}$$

$$= 8\left[1 - \frac{9}{25}\right]^{-1/2}$$

$$= 8\left(\frac{16}{25}\right)^{-1/2}$$

$$= 8\left(\frac{25}{16}\right)^{1/2}$$

$$= 8 \cdot \frac{5}{4}$$

$$= 10$$

The particle's new mass is 10 mg.

128.

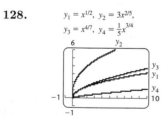

$y_1 = x^{1/2}, \; y_2 = 3x^{2/5},$
$y_3 = x^{4/7}, \; y_4 = \frac{1}{5}x^{3/4}$

Exercise Set 9.3

1. $\sqrt{10}\sqrt{7} = \sqrt{10 \cdot 7} = \sqrt{70}$

2. $\sqrt{35}$

3. $\sqrt[3]{2}\sqrt[3]{5} = \sqrt[3]{2 \cdot 5} = \sqrt[3]{10}$

4. $\sqrt[3]{14}$

5. $\sqrt[4]{8}\sqrt[4]{9} = \sqrt[4]{8 \cdot 9} = \sqrt[4]{72}$

6. $\sqrt[4]{18}$

7. $\sqrt{5a}\sqrt{6b} = \sqrt{5a \cdot 6b} = \sqrt{30ab}$

8. $\sqrt{26xy}$

9. $\sqrt[5]{9t^2}\sqrt[5]{2t} = \sqrt[5]{9t^2 \cdot 2t} = \sqrt[5]{18t^3}$

10. $\sqrt[5]{80y^4}$

11. $\sqrt{x-a}\sqrt{x+a} = \sqrt{(x-a)(x+a)} = \sqrt{x^2 - a^2}$

12. $\sqrt{y^2 - b^2}$

13. $\sqrt[3]{0.5x}\sqrt[3]{0.2x} = \sqrt[3]{0.5x \cdot 0.2x} = \sqrt[3]{0.1x^2}$

14. $\sqrt[3]{0.21y^2}$

15. $\sqrt[4]{x-1}\sqrt[4]{x^2 + x + 1} = \sqrt[4]{(x-1)(x^2 + x + 1)} = \sqrt[4]{x^3 - 1}$

16. $\sqrt[5]{(x-2)^3}$

17. $\sqrt{\dfrac{x}{6}}\sqrt{\dfrac{7}{y}} = \sqrt{\dfrac{x}{6} \cdot \dfrac{7}{y}} = \sqrt{\dfrac{7x}{6y}}$

18. $\sqrt{\dfrac{7s}{11t}}$

19. $\sqrt[7]{\dfrac{x-3}{4}}\sqrt[7]{\dfrac{5}{x+2}} = \sqrt[7]{\dfrac{x-3}{4} \cdot \dfrac{5}{x+2}} = \sqrt[7]{\dfrac{5x-15}{4x+8}}$

20. $\sqrt[6]{\dfrac{3a}{b^2 - 4}}$

21. $\sqrt{50}$

  $= \sqrt{25 \cdot 2}$ 25 is the largest perfect square factor of 50.

  $= \sqrt{25} \cdot \sqrt{2}$

  $= 5\sqrt{2}$

22. $3\sqrt{3}$

23. $\sqrt{28}$

  $= \sqrt{4 \cdot 7}$ 4 is the largest perfect square factor of 28.

  $= \sqrt{4} \cdot \sqrt{7}$

  $= 2\sqrt{7}$

24. $3\sqrt{5}$

25. $\sqrt{8} = \sqrt{4 \cdot 2} = \sqrt{4} \cdot \sqrt{2} = 2\sqrt{2}$

26. $3\sqrt{2}$

27. $\sqrt{198} = \sqrt{9 \cdot 22} = \sqrt{9} \cdot \sqrt{22} = 3\sqrt{22}$

28. $5\sqrt{13}$

29. $\sqrt{36a^4b}$

$= \sqrt{36a^4 \cdot b}$ $36a^4$ is a perfect square.

$= \sqrt{36a^4} \cdot \sqrt{b}$ Factoring into two radicals

$= 6a^2\sqrt{b}$ Taking the square root of $36a^4$

30. $5y^4\sqrt{7}$

31. $\sqrt[3]{8x^3y^2}$

$= \sqrt[3]{8x^3 \cdot y^2}$ $8x^3$ is a perfect cube.

$= \sqrt[3]{8x^3} \cdot \sqrt[3]{y^2}$ Factoring into two radicals

$= 2x\sqrt[3]{y^2}$ Taking the cube root of $8x^3$

32. $3b^2\sqrt[3]{a}$

33. $\sqrt[3]{-16x^6}$

$= \sqrt[3]{-8x^6 \cdot 2}$ $-8x^6$ is a perfect cube.

$= \sqrt[3]{-8x^6} \cdot \sqrt[3]{2}$

$= -2x^2\sqrt[3]{2}$ Taking the cube root of $-8x^6$

34. $-2a^2\sqrt[3]{4}$

35. $f(x) = \sqrt[3]{125x^5}$

$= \sqrt[3]{125x^3 \cdot x^2}$

$= \sqrt[3]{125x^3} \cdot \sqrt[3]{x^2}$

$= 5x\sqrt[3]{x^2}$

36. $2x^2\sqrt[3]{2}$

37. $f(x) = \sqrt{49(x-3)^2}$ $49(x-3)^2$ is a perfect square.

$= |7(x-3)|$, or $7|x-3|$

38. $9|x-1|$

39. $f(x) = \sqrt{5x^2 - 10x + 5}$

$= \sqrt{5(x^2 - 2x + 1)}$

$= \sqrt{5(x-1)^2}$

$= \sqrt{(x-1)^2} \cdot \sqrt{5}$

$= |x-1|\sqrt{5}$

40. $|x+2|\sqrt{2}$

41. $\sqrt{a^3b^4}$

$= \sqrt{a^2 \cdot a \cdot b^4}$ Identifying the largest even powers of a and b

$= \sqrt{a^2}\sqrt{b^4}\sqrt{a}$ Factoring into several radicals

$= ab^2\sqrt{a}$

42. $x^3y^4\sqrt{y}$

43. $\sqrt[3]{x^5y^6z^{10}}$

$= \sqrt[3]{x^3 \cdot x^2 \cdot y^6 \cdot z^9 \cdot z}$ Identifying the largest perfect-cube powers of x, y, and z

$= \sqrt[3]{x^3} \cdot \sqrt[3]{y^6} \cdot \sqrt[3]{z^9} \cdot \sqrt[3]{x^2z}$ Factoring into several radicals

$= xy^2z^3\sqrt[3]{x^2z}$

44. $a^2b^2c^4\sqrt[3]{bc}$

45. $\sqrt[5]{-32a^7b^{11}} = \sqrt[5]{-32 \cdot a^5 \cdot a^2 \cdot b^{10} \cdot b} = $
$\sqrt[5]{-32}\sqrt[5]{a^5}\sqrt[5]{b^{10}}\sqrt[5]{a^2b} = -2ab^2\sqrt[5]{a^2b}$

46. $2xy^2\sqrt[4]{xy^3}$

47. $\sqrt[5]{a^6b^8c^9} = \sqrt[5]{a^5 \cdot a \cdot b^5 \cdot b^3 \cdot c^5 \cdot c^4} = $
$\sqrt[5]{a^5}\sqrt[5]{b^5}\sqrt[5]{c^5}\sqrt[5]{ab^3c^4} = $
$abc\sqrt[5]{ab^3c^4}$

48. $x^2yz^3\sqrt[5]{x^3y^3z^2}$

49. $\sqrt[4]{810x^9} = \sqrt[4]{81 \cdot 10 \cdot x^8 \cdot x} = $
$\sqrt[4]{81} \cdot \sqrt[4]{x^8} \cdot \sqrt[4]{10x} = 3x^2\sqrt[4]{10x}$

50. $-2a^4\sqrt[3]{10a^2}$

51. $\sqrt{15}\sqrt{5} = \sqrt{15 \cdot 5} = \sqrt{75} = \sqrt{25 \cdot 3} = 5\sqrt{3}$

52. $3\sqrt{2}$

53. $\sqrt{10}\sqrt{14} = \sqrt{10 \cdot 14} = \sqrt{140} = \sqrt{4 \cdot 35} = 2\sqrt{35}$

54. $3\sqrt{35}$

55. $\sqrt[3]{2}\sqrt[3]{4} = \sqrt[3]{2 \cdot 4} = \sqrt[3]{8} = 2$

56. 3

57. $\sqrt{18a^3}\sqrt{18a^3} = \sqrt{(18a^3)^2} = 18a^3$

58. $75x^7$

59. $\sqrt[3]{5a^2}\sqrt[3]{2a} = \sqrt[3]{5a^2 \cdot 2a} = \sqrt[3]{10a^3} = \sqrt[3]{a^3 \cdot 10} = u\sqrt[3]{10}$

60. $x\sqrt[3]{21}$

61. $\sqrt{3x^5}\sqrt{15x^2} = \sqrt{45x^7} = \sqrt{9x^6 \cdot 5x} = 3x^3\sqrt{5x}$

62. $5a^5\sqrt{3}$

63. $\sqrt[3]{s^2t^4}\sqrt[3]{s^4t^6} = \sqrt[3]{s^6t^{10}} - \sqrt[3]{s^6t^9 \cdot t} = s^2t^3\sqrt[3]{t}$

64. $xy^3\sqrt[3]{xy}$

65. $\sqrt[3]{(x+5)^2}\sqrt[3]{(x+5)^4} = \sqrt[3]{(x+5)^6} = (x+5)^2$

66. $(a-b)^4$

67. $\sqrt[4]{12a^3b^7}\sqrt[4]{4a^2b^5} = \sqrt[4]{48a^5b^{12}} = \sqrt[4]{16a^4b^{12} \cdot 3a} = $
$2ab^3\sqrt[4]{3a}$

68. $3x^2y^2\sqrt[4]{xy^3}$

69. $\sqrt[5]{x^3(y+z)^4}\sqrt[5]{x^3(y+z)^6} = \sqrt[5]{x^6(y+z)^{10}} = $
$\sqrt[5]{x^5(y+z)^{10} \cdot x} = x(y+z)^2\sqrt[5]{x}$

70. $a^2(b-c)\sqrt[5]{(b-c)^3}$

71. *Writing Exercise*

72. *Writing Exercise*

73. $\dfrac{3x}{16y} + \dfrac{5y}{64x}$, LCD is $64xy$

$= \dfrac{3x}{16y} \cdot \dfrac{4x}{4x} + \dfrac{5y}{64x} \cdot \dfrac{y}{y}$

$= \dfrac{12x^2}{64xy} + \dfrac{5y^2}{64xy}$

$= \dfrac{12x^2 + 5y^2}{64xy}$

74. $\dfrac{2a + 6b^3}{a^4b^4}$

75. $\dfrac{4}{x^2 - 9} - \dfrac{7}{2x - 6}$

$= \dfrac{4}{(x+3)(x-3)} - \dfrac{7}{2(x-3)}$, LCD is $2(x+3)(x-3)$

$= \dfrac{4}{(x+3)(x-3)} \cdot \dfrac{2}{2} - \dfrac{7}{2(x-3)} \cdot \dfrac{x+3}{x+3}$

$= \dfrac{8}{2(x+3)(x-3)} - \dfrac{7(x+3)}{2(x+3)(x-3)}$

$= \dfrac{8 - 7(x+3)}{2(x+3)(x-3)}$

$= \dfrac{8 - 7x - 21}{2(x+3)(x-3)}$

$= \dfrac{-7x - 13}{2(x+3)(x-3)}$

76. $\dfrac{-3x + 1}{2(x+5)(x-5)}$

77. $\dfrac{9a^4b^7}{3a^2b^5} = \dfrac{9}{3}a^{4-2}b^{7-5} = 3a^2b^2$

78. $3ab^5$

79. *Writing Exercise*

80. *Writing Exercise*

81. $r(L) = 2\sqrt{5L}$

a) $r(L) = 2\sqrt{5 \cdot 20}$

$= 2\sqrt{100}$

$= 2 \cdot 10 = 20$ mph

b) $r(L) = 2\sqrt{5 \cdot 70}$

$= 2\sqrt{350}$

≈ 37.4 mph   Multiplying and
                        rounding

c) $r(L) = 2\sqrt{5 \cdot 90}$

$= 2\sqrt{450}$

≈ 42.4 mph   Multiplying and
                        rounding

82. a) 4.0 °F

b) -10.3°F

c) -51.1°F

d) -78.5°F

83. $(\sqrt{r^3t})^7 = \sqrt{(r^3t)^7} = \sqrt{r^{21}t^7} =$

$\sqrt{r^{20} \cdot r \cdot t^6 \cdot t} = \sqrt{r^{20}}\sqrt{t^6}\sqrt{rt} = r^{10}t^3\sqrt{rt}$

84. $25x^5\sqrt[3]{25x}$

85. $(\sqrt[3]{a^2b^4})^5 = \sqrt[3]{(a^2b^4)^5} = \sqrt[3]{a^{10}b^{20}} =$

$\sqrt[3]{a^9 \cdot a \cdot b^{18} \cdot b^2} = \sqrt[3]{a^9}\sqrt[3]{b^{18}}\sqrt[3]{ab^2} = a^3b^6\sqrt[3]{ab^2}$

86. $a^{10}b^{17}\sqrt{ab}$

87.

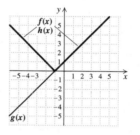

We see that $f(x) = h(x)$ and $f(x) \neq g(x)$.

88.

We see that $f(x) = h(x)$ and $f(x) \neq g(x)$.

89. $f(t) = \sqrt{t^2 - 3t - 4}$

We must have $t^2 - 3t - 4 \geq 0$, or $(t-4)(t+1) \geq 0$.

We graph $y = t^2 - 3t - 4$.

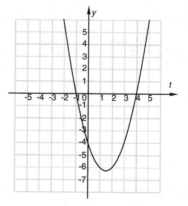

From the graph we see that $y \geq 0$ for $t \leq -1$ or $t \geq 4$, so the domain of f is $\{t | t \leq -1 \ or \ t \geq 4\}$, or $(-\infty, -1] \cup [4, \infty)$.

90. $\{x | x \leq 2 \ or \ x \geq 4\}$, or $(-\infty, 2] \cup [4, \infty)$

91. $\sqrt[3]{5x^{k+1}}\sqrt[3]{25x^k} = 5x^7$

$\qquad \sqrt[3]{5x^{k+1} \cdot 25x^k} = 5x^7$

$\qquad\qquad \sqrt[3]{125x^{2k+1}} = 5x^7$

$\qquad\qquad \sqrt[3]{125}\sqrt[3]{x^{2k+1}} = 5x^7$

$\qquad\qquad 5\sqrt[3]{x^{2k+1}} = 5x^7$

$\qquad\qquad \sqrt[3]{x^{2k+1}} = x^7$

$\qquad\qquad (x^{2k+1})^{1/3} = x^7$

$\qquad\qquad x^{\frac{2k+1}{3}} = x^7$

Since the base is the same, the exponents must be equal.
We have:

$$\frac{2k+1}{3} = 7$$

$$2k+1 = 21$$

$$2k = 20$$

$$k = 10$$

92. 6

93. *Writing Exercise*

Exercise Set 9.4

1. $\sqrt{\dfrac{25}{36}} = \dfrac{\sqrt{25}}{\sqrt{36}} = \dfrac{5}{6}$

2. $\dfrac{10}{9}$

3. $\sqrt[3]{\dfrac{64}{27}} = \dfrac{\sqrt[3]{64}}{\sqrt[3]{27}} = \dfrac{4}{3}$

4. $\dfrac{7}{10}$

5. $\sqrt{\dfrac{49}{y^2}} = \dfrac{\sqrt{49}}{\sqrt{y^2}} = \dfrac{7}{y}$

6. $\dfrac{11}{x}$

7. $\sqrt{\dfrac{25y^3}{x^4}} = \dfrac{\sqrt{25y^3}}{\sqrt{x^4}} = \dfrac{\sqrt{25y^2 \cdot y}}{\sqrt{x^4}} = \dfrac{\sqrt{25y^2}\sqrt{y}}{\sqrt{x^4}} = \dfrac{5y\sqrt{y}}{x^2}$

8. $\dfrac{6a^2\sqrt{a}}{b^3}$

9. $\sqrt[3]{\dfrac{27a^4}{8b^3}} = \dfrac{\sqrt[3]{27a^4}}{\sqrt[3]{8b^3}} = \dfrac{\sqrt[3]{27a^3 \cdot a}}{\sqrt[3]{8b^3}} = \dfrac{\sqrt[3]{27a^3}\sqrt[3]{a}}{\sqrt[3]{8b^3}} = \dfrac{3a\sqrt[3]{a}}{2b}$

10. $\dfrac{2x^2\sqrt[3]{x}}{3y^2}$

11. $\sqrt[4]{\dfrac{16a^4}{b^4c^8}} = \dfrac{\sqrt[4]{16a^4}}{\sqrt[4]{b^4c^8}} = \dfrac{2a}{bc^2}$

12. $\dfrac{3x}{y^2z}$

13. $\sqrt[4]{\dfrac{a^5b^8}{c^{10}}} = \dfrac{\sqrt[4]{a^5b^8}}{\sqrt[4]{c^{10}}} = \dfrac{\sqrt[4]{a^4b^8 \cdot a}}{\sqrt[4]{c^8 \cdot c^2}} = \dfrac{\sqrt[4]{a^4b^8}\sqrt[4]{a}}{\sqrt[4]{c^8}\sqrt[4]{c^2}} = \dfrac{ab^2\sqrt[4]{a}}{c^2\sqrt[4]{c^2}}$, or $\dfrac{ab^2}{c^2}\sqrt[4]{\dfrac{a}{c^2}}$

14. $\dfrac{x^2y^3}{z}\sqrt[4]{\dfrac{x}{z^2}}$

15. $\sqrt[5]{\dfrac{32x^6}{y^{11}}} = \dfrac{\sqrt[5]{32x^6}}{\sqrt[5]{y^{11}}} = \dfrac{\sqrt[5]{32x^5 \cdot x}}{\sqrt[5]{y^{10} \cdot y}} = \dfrac{\sqrt[5]{32x^5} \cdot \sqrt[5]{x}}{\sqrt[5]{y^{10}}\sqrt[5]{y}} = \dfrac{2x\sqrt[5]{x}}{y^2\sqrt[5]{y}}$, or $\dfrac{2x}{y^2}\sqrt[5]{\dfrac{x}{y}}$

16. $\dfrac{3a}{b^2}\sqrt[5]{\dfrac{a^4}{b^3}}$

17. $\sqrt[6]{\dfrac{x^6y^8}{z^{15}}} = \dfrac{\sqrt[6]{x^6y^8}}{\sqrt[6]{z^{15}}} = \dfrac{\sqrt[6]{x^6y^6 \cdot y^2}}{\sqrt[6]{z^{12} \cdot z^3}} = \dfrac{\sqrt[6]{x^6y^6}\sqrt[6]{y^2}}{\sqrt[6]{z^{12}}\sqrt[6]{z^3}} = \dfrac{xy\sqrt[6]{y^2}}{z^2\sqrt[6]{z^3}}$, or $\dfrac{xy}{z^2}\sqrt[6]{\dfrac{y^2}{z^3}}$

18. $\dfrac{ab^2}{c^2}\sqrt[6]{\dfrac{a^3}{c}}$

19. $\dfrac{\sqrt{35x}}{\sqrt{7x}} = \sqrt{\dfrac{35x}{7x}} = \sqrt{5}$

20. $\sqrt{7}$

21. $\dfrac{\sqrt[3]{270}}{\sqrt[3]{10}} = \sqrt[3]{\dfrac{270}{10}} = \sqrt[3]{27} = 3$

22. 2

23. $\dfrac{\sqrt{40xy^3}}{\sqrt{8x}} = \sqrt{\dfrac{40xy^3}{8x}} = \sqrt{5y^3} = \sqrt{y^2 \cdot 5y} = \sqrt{y^2}\sqrt{5y} = y\sqrt{5y}$

24. $2b\sqrt{2b}$

25. $\dfrac{\sqrt[3]{96a^4b^2}}{\sqrt[3]{12a^2b}} = \sqrt[3]{\dfrac{96a^4b^2}{12a^2b}} = \sqrt[3]{8a^2b} = \sqrt[3]{8}\sqrt[3]{a^2b} = 2\sqrt[3]{a^2b}$

26. $3xy\sqrt[3]{y^2}$

27. $\dfrac{\sqrt{100ab}}{5\sqrt{2}} = \dfrac{1}{5}\dfrac{\sqrt{100ab}}{\sqrt{2}} = \dfrac{1}{5}\sqrt{\dfrac{100ab}{2}} = \dfrac{1}{5}\sqrt{50ab} = \dfrac{1}{5}\sqrt{25 \cdot 2ab} = \dfrac{1}{5} \cdot 5\sqrt{2ab} = \sqrt{2ab}$

28. $\dfrac{5}{3}\sqrt{ab}$

29. $\dfrac{\sqrt[4]{48x^9y^{13}}}{\sqrt[4]{3xy^{-2}}} = \sqrt[4]{\dfrac{48x^9y^{13}}{3xy^{-2}}} = \sqrt[4]{16x^8y^{15}} = \sqrt[4]{16x^8y^{12}}\sqrt[4]{y^3} = 2x^2y^3\sqrt[4]{y^3}$

30. $2a^2b^6$

31. $\dfrac{\sqrt[3]{x^3-y^3}}{\sqrt[3]{x-y}} = \sqrt[3]{\dfrac{x^3-y^3}{x-y}} =$

$\sqrt[3]{\dfrac{(x-y)(x^2+xy+y^2)}{x-y}} =$

$\sqrt[3]{\dfrac{(x\!-\!y)(x^2+xy+y^2)}{x\!-\!y}} = \sqrt[3]{x^2+xy+y^2}$

32. $\sqrt[3]{r^2-rs+s^2}$

33. $\sqrt{\dfrac{5}{7}} = \sqrt{\dfrac{5}{7}\cdot\dfrac{7}{7}} = \sqrt{\dfrac{35}{49}} = \dfrac{\sqrt{35}}{\sqrt{49}} = \dfrac{\sqrt{35}}{7}$

34. $\dfrac{\sqrt{66}}{6}$

35. $\dfrac{6\sqrt{5}}{5\sqrt{3}} = \dfrac{6\sqrt{5}}{5\sqrt{3}}\cdot\dfrac{\sqrt{3}}{\sqrt{3}} = \dfrac{6\sqrt{15}}{5\cdot3} = \dfrac{2\sqrt{15}}{5}$

36. $\dfrac{2\sqrt{10}}{3}$

37. $\sqrt[3]{\dfrac{16}{9}} = \sqrt[3]{\dfrac{16}{9}\cdot\dfrac{3}{3}} = \sqrt[3]{\dfrac{48}{27}} = \dfrac{\sqrt[3]{8\cdot6}}{\sqrt[3]{27}} = \dfrac{2\sqrt[3]{6}}{3}$

38. $\dfrac{\sqrt[3]{6}}{3}$

39. $\dfrac{\sqrt[3]{3a}}{\sqrt[3]{5c}} = \dfrac{\sqrt[3]{3a}}{\sqrt[3]{5c}}\cdot\dfrac{\sqrt[3]{5^2c^2}}{\sqrt[3]{5^2c^2}} = \dfrac{\sqrt[3]{75ac^2}}{\sqrt[3]{5^3c^3}} = \dfrac{\sqrt[3]{75ac^2}}{5c}$

40. $\dfrac{\sqrt[3]{63xy^2}}{3y}$

41. $\dfrac{\sqrt[3]{5y^4}}{\sqrt[3]{6x^4}} = \dfrac{\sqrt[3]{5y^4}}{\sqrt[3]{6x^4}}\cdot\dfrac{\sqrt[3]{36x^2}}{\sqrt[3]{36x^2}} = \dfrac{\sqrt[3]{y^3\cdot180x^2y}}{\sqrt[3]{216x^6}} =$

$\dfrac{y\sqrt[3]{180x^2y}}{6x^2}$

42. $\dfrac{a\sqrt[3]{147ab}}{7b}$

43. $\sqrt[3]{\dfrac{2}{x^2y}} = \sqrt[3]{\dfrac{2}{x^2y}\cdot\dfrac{xy^2}{xy^2}} = \sqrt[3]{\dfrac{2xy^2}{x^3y^3}} = \dfrac{\sqrt[3]{2xy^2}}{\sqrt[3]{x^3y^3}} =$

$\dfrac{\sqrt[3]{2xy^2}}{xy}$

44. $\dfrac{\sqrt[3]{5a^2b}}{ab}$

45. $\sqrt{\dfrac{7a}{18}} = \sqrt{\dfrac{7a}{18}\cdot\dfrac{2}{2}} = \sqrt{\dfrac{14a}{36}} = \dfrac{\sqrt{14a}}{\sqrt{36}} = \dfrac{\sqrt{14a}}{6}$

46. $\dfrac{\sqrt{30x}}{10}$

47. $\sqrt{\dfrac{9}{20x^2y}} = \sqrt{\dfrac{9}{20x^2y}\cdot\dfrac{5y}{5y}} = \sqrt{\dfrac{9\cdot5y}{100x^2y^2}} =$

$\dfrac{\sqrt{9\cdot5y}}{\sqrt{100x^2y^2}} = \dfrac{3\sqrt{5y}}{10xy}$

48. $\dfrac{\sqrt{14b}}{8ab}$

49. $\sqrt{\dfrac{10ab^2}{72a^3b}} = \sqrt{\dfrac{5b}{36a^2}} = \dfrac{\sqrt{5b}}{6a}$

50. $\dfrac{\sqrt{7x}}{5y^2}$

51. $\dfrac{\sqrt{5}}{\sqrt{7x}} = \dfrac{\sqrt{5}}{\sqrt{7x}}\cdot\dfrac{\sqrt{5}}{\sqrt{5}} = \dfrac{\sqrt{25}}{\sqrt{35x}} = \dfrac{5}{\sqrt{35x}}$

52. $\dfrac{10}{\sqrt{30x}}$

53. $\sqrt{\dfrac{14}{21}} = \sqrt{\dfrac{2}{3}} = \sqrt{\dfrac{2}{3}\cdot\dfrac{2}{2}} = \sqrt{\dfrac{4}{6}} = \dfrac{\sqrt{4}}{\sqrt{6}} = \dfrac{2}{\sqrt{6}}$

54. $\dfrac{2}{\sqrt{5}}$

55. $\dfrac{4\sqrt{13}}{3\sqrt{7}} = \dfrac{4\sqrt{13}}{3\sqrt{7}}\cdot\dfrac{\sqrt{13}}{\sqrt{13}} = \dfrac{4\sqrt{169}}{3\sqrt{91}} = \dfrac{4\cdot13}{3\sqrt{91}} = \dfrac{52}{3\sqrt{91}}$

56. $\dfrac{105}{2\sqrt{105}}$

57. $\dfrac{\sqrt[3]{7}}{\sqrt[3]{2}} = \dfrac{\sqrt[3]{7}}{\sqrt[3]{2}}\cdot\dfrac{\sqrt[3]{7^2}}{\sqrt[3]{7^2}} = \dfrac{\sqrt[3]{7^3}}{\sqrt[3]{98}} = \dfrac{7}{\sqrt[3]{98}}$

58. $\dfrac{5}{\sqrt[3]{100}}$

59. $\sqrt{\dfrac{7x}{3y}} = \sqrt{\dfrac{7x}{3y}\cdot\dfrac{7x}{7x}} = \dfrac{\sqrt{(7x)^2}}{\sqrt{21xy}} = \dfrac{7x}{\sqrt{21xy}}$

60. $\dfrac{6a}{\sqrt{30ab}}$

61. $\sqrt[3]{\dfrac{2a^5}{5b}} = \sqrt[3]{\dfrac{2a^5}{5b}\cdot\dfrac{4a}{4a}} = \sqrt[3]{\dfrac{8a^6}{20ab}} = \dfrac{2a^2}{\sqrt[3]{20ab}}$

62. $\dfrac{2a^2}{\sqrt[3]{28a^2b}}$

63. $\sqrt{\dfrac{x^3y}{2}} = \sqrt{\dfrac{x^3y}{2}\cdot\dfrac{xy}{xy}} = \sqrt{\dfrac{x^4y^2}{2xy}} = \dfrac{\sqrt{x^4y^2}}{\sqrt{2xy}} = \dfrac{x^2y}{\sqrt{2xy}}$

64. $\dfrac{ab^3}{\sqrt{3ab}}$

65. *Writing Exercise*

66. *Writing Exercise*

67. $\dfrac{3}{x-5}\cdot\dfrac{x-1}{x+5} = \dfrac{3(x-1)}{(x-5)(x+5)}$

68. $\dfrac{7(x-2)}{(x+4)(x-4)}$

69. $\dfrac{a^2-8a+7}{a^2-49} = \dfrac{(a-1)(a-7)}{(a+7)(a-7)}$

$= \dfrac{(a-1)(a\!-\!7)}{(a+7)(a\!-\!7)}$

$= \dfrac{a-1}{a+7}$

70. $\dfrac{t+11}{t+2}$

71. $(5a^3b^4)^3 = 5^3(a^3)^3(b^4)^3 = 125a^{3\cdot3}b^{4\cdot3} = 125a^9b^{12}$

72. $225x^{10}y^6$

73. *Writing Exercise*

74. *Writing Exercise*

75. a) $T = 2\pi\sqrt{\dfrac{65}{980}} \approx 1.62$ sec

  b) $T = 2\pi\sqrt{\dfrac{98}{980}} \approx 1.99$ sec

  c) $T = 2\pi\sqrt{\dfrac{120}{980}} \approx 2.20$ sec

76. a^3bxy^2

77. $\dfrac{(\sqrt[3]{81mn^2})^2}{(\sqrt[3]{mn})^2} = \dfrac{\sqrt[3]{(81mn^2)^2}}{\sqrt[3]{(mn)^2}}$

$= \dfrac{\sqrt[3]{6561m^2n^4}}{\sqrt[3]{m^2n^2}}$

$= \sqrt[3]{\dfrac{6561m^2n^4}{m^2n^2}}$

$= \sqrt[3]{6561n^2}$

$= \sqrt[3]{729\cdot9n^2}$

$= \sqrt[3]{729}\,\sqrt[3]{9n^2}$

$= 9\sqrt[3]{9n^2}$

78. $2yz\sqrt{2z}$

79. $\sqrt{a^2-3} - \dfrac{a^2}{\sqrt{a^2-3}}$

$= \sqrt{a^2-3} - \dfrac{a^2}{\sqrt{a^2-3}}\cdot\dfrac{\sqrt{a^2-3}}{\sqrt{a^2-3}}$

$= \sqrt{a^2-3} - \dfrac{a^2\sqrt{a^2-3}}{a^2-3}$

$= \sqrt{a^2-3}\cdot\dfrac{a^2-3}{a^2-3} - \dfrac{a^2\sqrt{a^2-3}}{a^2-3}$

$= \dfrac{a^2\sqrt{a^2-3} - 3\sqrt{a^2-3} - a^2\sqrt{a^2-3}}{a^2-3}$

$= \dfrac{-3\sqrt{a^2-3}}{a^2-3}$, or $\dfrac{-3}{\sqrt{a^2-3}}$

80. $\dfrac{(5x+4y-3)\sqrt{xy}}{xy}$

81. Step 1: $\sqrt[n]{x} = x^{1/n}$, by definition;

  Step 2: $\left(\dfrac{x}{y}\right)^n = \dfrac{x^n}{y^n}$, raising a quotient to a power;

  Step 3: $x^{1/n} = \sqrt[n]{x}$, by definition

82. A number c is the nth root of a/b if $c^n = a/b$. Let $c = \sqrt[n]{a}/\sqrt[n]{b}$.

$c^n = \left(\dfrac{\sqrt[n]{a}}{\sqrt[n]{b}}\right)^n = \left(\dfrac{a^{1/n}}{b^{1/n}}\right)^n = \dfrac{(a^{1/n})^n}{(b^{1/n})^n} = \dfrac{a}{b}$

83. $f(x) = \sqrt{18x^3}$, $g(x) = \sqrt{2x}$

$(f/g)(x) = \dfrac{f(x)}{g(x)} = \dfrac{\sqrt{18x^3}}{\sqrt{2x}} = \sqrt{\dfrac{18x^3}{2x}} = \sqrt{9x^2} = 3x$

$\sqrt{2x}$ is defined for $2x \geq 0$, or $x \geq 0$. To avoid division by 0, we must exclude 0 from the domain. Thus, the domain of $f/g = \{x|x$ is a real number *and* $x > 0\}$, or $(0, \infty)$.

84. $(f/g)(t) = \dfrac{1}{5t}$;

  $\{t|t$ is a real number *and* $t > 0\}$, or $(0, \infty)$

85. $f(x) = \sqrt{x^2-9}$, $g(x) = \sqrt{x-3}$

$(f/g)(x) = \dfrac{f(x)}{g(x)} = \dfrac{\sqrt{x^2-9}}{\sqrt{x-3}} = \sqrt{\dfrac{x^2-9}{x-3}} =$

$\sqrt{\dfrac{(x+3)(x-3)}{x-3}} = \sqrt{x+3}$

$\sqrt{x-3}$ is defined for $x-3 \geq 0$, or $x \geq 3$. To avoid division by 0 we must exclude 3 from the domain. Thus, the domain of $f/g = \{x|x$ is a real number *and* $x > 3\}$, or $(3, \infty)$.

Exercise Set 9.5

1. $3\sqrt{7} + 2\sqrt{7} = (3+2)\sqrt{7} = 5\sqrt{7}$

2. $17\sqrt{5}$

3. $9\sqrt[3]{5} - 6\sqrt[3]{5} = (9-6)\sqrt[3]{5} = 3\sqrt[3]{5}$

4. $8\sqrt[5]{2}$

5. $4\sqrt[3]{y} + 9\sqrt[3]{y} = (4+9)\sqrt[3]{y} = 13\sqrt[3]{y}$

6. $6\sqrt[4]{t}$

7. $8\sqrt{2} - 6\sqrt{2} + 5\sqrt{2} = (8-6+5)\sqrt{2} = 7\sqrt{2}$

8. $7\sqrt{6}$

9. $9\sqrt[3]{7} - \sqrt{3} + 4\sqrt[3]{7} + 2\sqrt{3} =$
  $(9+4)\sqrt[3]{7} + (-1+2)\sqrt{3} = 13\sqrt[3]{7} + \sqrt{3}$

10. $6\sqrt{7} + \sqrt[4]{11}$

11. $8\sqrt{27} - 3\sqrt{3}$

  $= 8\sqrt{9\cdot3} - 3\sqrt{3}$ Factoring the

  $= 8\sqrt{9}\cdot\sqrt{3} - 3\sqrt{3}$ first radical

  $= 8\cdot3\sqrt{3} - 3\sqrt{3}$ Taking the square root of 9

  $= 24\sqrt{3} - 3\sqrt{3}$

  $= 21\sqrt{3}$ Combining like radicals

12. $41\sqrt{2}$

13. $3\sqrt{45} + 7\sqrt{20}$

$= 3\sqrt{9 \cdot 5} + 7\sqrt{4 \cdot 5}$ Factoring the

$= 3\sqrt{9} \cdot \sqrt{5} + 7\sqrt{4} \cdot \sqrt{5}$ radicals

$= 3 \cdot 3\sqrt{5} + 7 \cdot 2\sqrt{5}$ Taking the square roots

$= 9\sqrt{5} + 14\sqrt{5}$

$= 23\sqrt{5}$ Combining like radicals

14. $58\sqrt{3}$

15. $3\sqrt[3]{16} + \sqrt[3]{54} = 3\sqrt[3]{8 \cdot 2} + \sqrt[3]{27 \cdot 2} =$

$3\sqrt[3]{8} \cdot \sqrt[3]{2} + \sqrt[3]{27} \cdot \sqrt[3]{2} = 3 \cdot 2\sqrt[3]{2} + 3\sqrt[3]{2} =$

$6\sqrt[3]{2} + 3\sqrt[3]{2} = 9\sqrt[3]{2}$

16. -7

17. $\sqrt{5a} + 2\sqrt{45a^3} = \sqrt{5a} + 2\sqrt{9a^2 \cdot 5a} =$

$\sqrt{5a} + 2\sqrt{9a^2} \cdot \sqrt{5a} = \sqrt{5a} + 2 \cdot 3a\sqrt{5a} =$

$\sqrt{5a} + 6a\sqrt{5a} = (1 + 6a)\sqrt{5a}$

18. $(4x - 2)\sqrt{3x}$

19. $\sqrt[3]{6x^4} + \sqrt[3]{48x} = \sqrt[3]{x^3 \cdot 6x} + \sqrt[3]{8 \cdot 6x} =$

$\sqrt[3]{x^3} \cdot \sqrt[3]{6x} + \sqrt[3]{8} \cdot \sqrt[3]{6x} = x\sqrt[3]{6x} + 2\sqrt[3]{6x} =$

$(x + 2)\sqrt[3]{6x}$

20. $(3 - x)\sqrt[3]{2x}$

21. $\sqrt{4a - 4} + \sqrt{a - 1} = \sqrt{4(a - 4)} + \sqrt{a - 1} =$

$\sqrt{4}\sqrt{a - 1} + \sqrt{a - 1} = 2\sqrt{a - 1} + \sqrt{a - 1} = 3\sqrt{a - 1}$

22. $4\sqrt{y + 3}$

23. $\sqrt{x^3 - x^2} + \sqrt{9x - 9} = \sqrt{x^2(x - 1)} + \sqrt{9(x - 1)} =$

$\sqrt{x^2} \cdot \sqrt{x - 1} + \sqrt{9} \cdot \sqrt{x - 1} =$

$x\sqrt{x - 1} + 3\sqrt{x - 1} = (x + 3)\sqrt{x - 1}$

24. $(2 - x)\sqrt{x - 1}$

25. $\sqrt{7}(3 - \sqrt{7}) = \sqrt{7} \cdot 3 - \sqrt{7} \cdot \sqrt{7} = 3\sqrt{7} - 7$

26. $4\sqrt{3} + 3$

27. $4\sqrt{2}(\sqrt{3} - \sqrt{5}) = 4\sqrt{2} \cdot \sqrt{3} - 4\sqrt{2} \cdot \sqrt{5} = 4\sqrt{6} - 4\sqrt{10}$

28. $15 - 3\sqrt{10}$

29. $\sqrt{3}(2\sqrt{5} - 3\sqrt{4}) = \sqrt{3}(2\sqrt{5} - 3 \cdot 2) =$

$\sqrt{3} \cdot 2\sqrt{5} - \sqrt{3} \cdot 6 = 2\sqrt{15} - 6\sqrt{3}$

30. $6\sqrt{5} - 4$

31. $\sqrt[3]{2}(\sqrt[3]{4} - 2\sqrt[3]{32}) = \sqrt[3]{2} \cdot \sqrt[3]{4} - \sqrt[3]{2} \cdot 2\sqrt[3]{32} =$

$\sqrt[3]{8} - 2\sqrt[3]{64} = 2 - 2 \cdot 4 = 2 - 8 = -6$

32. $3 - 4\sqrt[3]{63}$

33. $\sqrt[3]{a}(\sqrt[3]{a^2} + \sqrt[3]{24a^2}) = \sqrt[3]{a} \cdot \sqrt[3]{a^2} + \sqrt[3]{a}\sqrt[3]{24a^2} =$

$\sqrt[3]{a^3} + \sqrt[3]{24a^3} = \sqrt[3]{a^3} + \sqrt[3]{8a^3 \cdot 3} =$

$a + 2a\sqrt[3]{3}$

34. $-2x\sqrt[3]{3}$

35. $(5 + \sqrt{6})(5 - \sqrt{6}) = 5^2 - (\sqrt{6})^2 = 25 - 6 = 19$

36. -1

37. $(3 - 2\sqrt{7})(3 + 2\sqrt{7}) = 3^2 - (2\sqrt{7})^2 = 9 - 4 \cdot 7 =$

$9 - 28 = -19$

38. -2

39. $(3 + \sqrt{5})^2 = 3^2 + 2 \cdot 3 \cdot \sqrt{5} + (\sqrt{5})^2 = 9 + 6\sqrt{5} + 5 =$

$14 + 6\sqrt{5}$

40. $52 + 14\sqrt{3}$

41. $(2\sqrt{7} - 4\sqrt{2})(3\sqrt{7} + 6\sqrt{2}) =$

$2\sqrt{7} \cdot 3\sqrt{7} + 2\sqrt{7} \cdot 6\sqrt{2} - 4\sqrt{2} \cdot 3\sqrt{7} - 4\sqrt{2} \cdot 6\sqrt{2} =$

$6 \cdot 7 + 12\sqrt{14} - 12\sqrt{14} - 24 \cdot 2 =$

$42 + 12\sqrt{14} - 12\sqrt{14} - 48 = -6$

42. $24 - 7\sqrt{15}$

43. $(2\sqrt[3]{3} - \sqrt[3]{2})(\sqrt[3]{3} + 2\sqrt[3]{2}) =$

$2\sqrt[3]{3} \cdot \sqrt[3]{3} + 2\sqrt[3]{3} \cdot 2\sqrt[3]{2} - \sqrt[3]{2} \cdot \sqrt[3]{3} - \sqrt[3]{2} \cdot 2\sqrt[3]{2} =$

$2\sqrt[3]{9} + 4\sqrt[3]{6} - \sqrt[3]{6} - 2\sqrt[3]{4} = 2\sqrt[3]{9} + 3\sqrt[3]{6} - 2\sqrt[3]{4}$

44. $6\sqrt[4]{63} - 9\sqrt[4]{42} + 2\sqrt[4]{54} - 3\sqrt[4]{36}$

45. $(\sqrt{3x} + \sqrt{y})^2$

$= (\sqrt{3x})^2 + 2 \cdot \sqrt{3x} \cdot \sqrt{y} + (\sqrt{y})^2$ Squaring a

binomial

$= 3x + 2\sqrt{3xy} + y$

46. $t - 2\sqrt{2rt} + 2r$

47. $\dfrac{2}{3 + \sqrt{5}} = \dfrac{2}{3 + \sqrt{5}} \cdot \dfrac{3 - \sqrt{5}}{3 - \sqrt{5}} =$

$\dfrac{2(3 - \sqrt{5})}{(3 + \sqrt{5})(3 - \sqrt{5})} = \dfrac{6 - 2\sqrt{5}}{3^2 - (\sqrt{5})^2} =$

$\dfrac{6 - 2\sqrt{5}}{9 - 5} = \dfrac{6 - 2\sqrt{5}}{4} = \dfrac{2(3 - \sqrt{5})}{2 \cdot 2} =$

$\dfrac{3 - \sqrt{5}}{2}$

48. $\dfrac{4 + \sqrt{7}}{3}$

49. $\dfrac{2 + \sqrt{5}}{6 - \sqrt{3}} = \dfrac{2 + \sqrt{5}}{6 - \sqrt{3}} \cdot \dfrac{6 + \sqrt{3}}{6 + \sqrt{3}} =$

$\dfrac{(2 + \sqrt{5})(6 + \sqrt{3})}{(6 - \sqrt{3})(6 + \sqrt{3})} = \dfrac{12 + 2\sqrt{3} + 6\sqrt{5} + \sqrt{15}}{36 - 3} =$

$\dfrac{12 + 2\sqrt{3} + 6\sqrt{5} + \sqrt{15}}{33}$

50. $\dfrac{3 - \sqrt{5} + 3\sqrt{2} - \sqrt{10}}{4}$

51. $\dfrac{\sqrt{a}}{\sqrt{a}+\sqrt{b}} = \dfrac{\sqrt{a}}{\sqrt{a}+\sqrt{b}} \cdot \dfrac{\sqrt{a}-\sqrt{b}}{\sqrt{a}-\sqrt{b}} =$

$\dfrac{\sqrt{a}(\sqrt{a}-\sqrt{b})}{(\sqrt{a}+\sqrt{b})(\sqrt{a}-\sqrt{b})} = \dfrac{a-\sqrt{ab}}{a-b}$

52. $\dfrac{\sqrt{xz}+z}{x-z}$

53. $\dfrac{\sqrt{7}-\sqrt{3}}{\sqrt{3}-\sqrt{7}} = \dfrac{-1(\sqrt{3}-\sqrt{7})}{\sqrt{3}-\sqrt{7}} = -1 \cdot \dfrac{\sqrt{3}-\sqrt{7}}{\sqrt{3}-\sqrt{7}} =$

$-1 \cdot 1 = -1$

54. $\dfrac{\sqrt{35}-\sqrt{14}+5-\sqrt{10}}{3}$

55. $\dfrac{3\sqrt{2}-\sqrt{7}}{4\sqrt{2}+\sqrt{5}} = \dfrac{3\sqrt{2}-\sqrt{7}}{4\sqrt{2}+\sqrt{5}} \cdot \dfrac{4\sqrt{2}-\sqrt{5}}{4\sqrt{2}-\sqrt{5}} =$

$\dfrac{(3\sqrt{2}-\sqrt{7})(4\sqrt{2}-\sqrt{5})}{(4\sqrt{2}+\sqrt{5})(4\sqrt{2}-\sqrt{5})} =$

$\dfrac{12 \cdot 2 - 3\sqrt{10} - 4\sqrt{14} + \sqrt{35}}{16 \cdot 2 - 5} =$

$\dfrac{24 - 3\sqrt{10} - 4\sqrt{14} + \sqrt{35}}{32 - 5} =$

$\dfrac{24 - 3\sqrt{10} - 4\sqrt{14} + \sqrt{35}}{27}$

56. $\dfrac{-30 - 25\sqrt{6} + 2\sqrt{33} + 5\sqrt{22}}{38}$

57. $\dfrac{5\sqrt{3}-3\sqrt{2}}{3\sqrt{2}-2\sqrt{3}} = \dfrac{5\sqrt{3}-3\sqrt{2}}{3\sqrt{2}-2\sqrt{3}} \cdot \dfrac{3\sqrt{2}+2\sqrt{3}}{3\sqrt{2}+2\sqrt{3}} =$

$\dfrac{15\sqrt{6} + 10 \cdot 3 - 9 \cdot 2 - 6\sqrt{6}}{9 \cdot 2 - 4 \cdot 3} =$

$\dfrac{15\sqrt{6} + 30 - 18 - 6\sqrt{6}}{18 - 12} = \dfrac{9\sqrt{6} + 12}{6} =$

$\dfrac{3(3\sqrt{6}+4)}{3 \cdot 2} = \dfrac{3\sqrt{6}+4}{2}$

58. $\dfrac{4\sqrt{6}+9}{3}$

59. $\dfrac{\sqrt{7}+2}{5} = \dfrac{\sqrt{7}+2}{5} \cdot \dfrac{\sqrt{7}-2}{\sqrt{7}-2} =$

$\dfrac{(\sqrt{7}+2)(\sqrt{7}-2)}{5(\sqrt{7}-2)} = \dfrac{(\sqrt{7})^2 - 2^2}{5\sqrt{7}-10} =$

$\dfrac{7-4}{5\sqrt{7}-10} = \dfrac{3}{5\sqrt{7}-10}$

60. $\dfrac{1}{2\sqrt{3}-2}$

61. $\dfrac{\sqrt{6}-2}{\sqrt{3}+7} = \dfrac{\sqrt{6}-2}{\sqrt{3}+7} \cdot \dfrac{\sqrt{6}+2}{\sqrt{6}+2} =$

$\dfrac{(\sqrt{6}-2)(\sqrt{6}+2)}{(\sqrt{3}+7)(\sqrt{6}+2)} = \dfrac{6-4}{\sqrt{18}+2\sqrt{3}+7\sqrt{6}+14} =$

$\dfrac{2}{3\sqrt{2}+2\sqrt{3}+7\sqrt{6}+14}$

62. $\dfrac{6}{-2\sqrt{5}+4\sqrt{2}+3\sqrt{10}-12}$

63. $\dfrac{\sqrt{x}-\sqrt{y}}{\sqrt{x}+\sqrt{y}} = \dfrac{\sqrt{x}-\sqrt{y}}{\sqrt{x}+\sqrt{y}} \cdot \dfrac{\sqrt{x}+\sqrt{y}}{\sqrt{x}+\sqrt{y}} =$

$\dfrac{(\sqrt{x}-\sqrt{y})(\sqrt{x}+\sqrt{y})}{(\sqrt{x}+\sqrt{y})(\sqrt{x}+\sqrt{y})} = \dfrac{x-y}{x+2\sqrt{xy}+y}$

64. $\dfrac{a-b}{a-2\sqrt{ab}+b}$

65. $\sqrt{a}\,\sqrt[4]{a^3}$

$= a^{1/2} \cdot a^{3/4}$ Converting to exponential notation

$= a^{5/4}$ Adding exponents

$= a^{1+1/4}$ Writing 5/4 as a mixed number

$= a \cdot a^{1/4}$ Factoring

$= a\sqrt[4]{a}$ Returning to radical notation

66. $x\sqrt{x}$

67. $\sqrt[5]{b^2}\sqrt{b^3}$

$= b^{2/5} \cdot b^{3/2}$ Converting to exponential notation

$= b^{19/10}$ Adding exponents

$= b^{1+9/10}$ Writing 19/10 as a mixed number

$= b \cdot b^{9/10}$ Factoring

$= b\sqrt[10]{b^9}$ Returning to radical notation

68. $a\sqrt[12]{a^5}$

69. $\sqrt{xy^3}\,\sqrt[3]{x^2y} = (xy^3)^{1/2}(x^2y)^{1/3}$

$\qquad = (xy^3)^{3/6}(x^2y)^{2/6}$

$\qquad = [(xy^3)^3(x^2y)^2]^{1/6}$

$\qquad = \sqrt[6]{x^3y^9 \cdot x^4y^2}$

$\qquad = \sqrt[6]{x^7y^{11}}$

$\qquad = \sqrt[6]{x^6y^6 \cdot xy^5}$

$\qquad = xy\sqrt[6]{xy^5}$

70. $a\sqrt[10]{ab^7}$

71. $\sqrt[4]{9ab^3}\,\sqrt{3a^4b} = (9ab^3)^{1/4}(3a^4b)^{1/2}$

$\qquad = (9ab^3)^{1/4}(3a^4b)^{2/4}$

$\qquad = [(9ab^3)(3a^4b)^2]^{1/4}$

$\qquad = \sqrt[4]{9ab^3 \cdot 9a^8b^2}$

$\qquad = \sqrt[4]{81a^9b^5}$

$\qquad = \sqrt[4]{81a^8b^4 \cdot ab}$

$\qquad = 3a^2b\sqrt[4]{ab}$

72. $2xy^2\sqrt[6]{2x^5y}$

73. $\sqrt[3]{xy^2z}\sqrt{x^3yz^2} = (xy^2z)^{1/3}(x^3yz^2)^{1/2}$

$\qquad = (xy^2z)^{2/6}(x^3yz^2)^{3/6}$

$\qquad = [(xy^2z)^2(x^3yz^2)^3]^{1/6}$

$\qquad = \sqrt[6]{x^2y^4z^2 \cdot x^9y^3z^6}$

$\qquad = \sqrt[6]{x^{11}y^7z^8}$

$\qquad = \sqrt[6]{x^6y^6z^6 \cdot x^5yz^2}$

$\qquad = xyz\sqrt[6]{x^5yz^2}$

74. $a^2b^2c^2\sqrt[6]{a^2bc^2}$

75. $\dfrac{\sqrt[3]{x^2}}{\sqrt[5]{x}}$

$\quad = \dfrac{x^{2/3}}{x^{1/5}}\qquad$ Converting to exponential notation

$\quad = x^{2/3-1/5}\quad$ Subtracting exponents

$\quad = x^{7/15}\qquad$ Converting back

$\quad = \sqrt[15]{x^7}\qquad$ to radical notation

76. $\sqrt[12]{a^5}$

77. $\dfrac{\sqrt[5]{a^4b}}{\sqrt[3]{ab}}$

$\quad = \dfrac{(a^4b)^{1/5}}{(ab)^{1/3}}\qquad$ Converting to exponential notation

$\quad = \dfrac{a^{4/5}b^{1/5}}{a^{1/3}b^{1/3}}\qquad$ Using the product and power rules

$\quad = a^{4/5-1/3}b^{1/5-1/3}\quad$ Subtracting exponents

$\quad = a^{7/15}b^{-2/15}$

$\quad = (a^7b^{-2})^{1/15}\qquad$ Converting back

$\quad = \sqrt[15]{a^7b^{-2}},\ \text{or}\qquad$ to radical notation

$\qquad \sqrt[15]{\dfrac{a^7}{b^2}}$

78. $\sqrt[12]{x^2y^5}$

79. $\dfrac{\sqrt[5]{x^3y^4}}{\sqrt{xy}}$

$\quad = \dfrac{(x^3y^4)^{1/5}}{(xy)^{1/2}}\qquad$ Converting to exponential notation

$\quad = \dfrac{x^{3/5}y^{4/5}}{x^{1/2}y^{1/2}}$

$\quad = x^{3/5-1/2}y^{4/5-1/2}\quad$ Subtracting exponents

$\quad = x^{1/10}y^{3/10}$

$\quad = (xy^3)^{1/10}\qquad$ Converting back to

$\quad = \sqrt[10]{xy^3}\qquad$ radical notation

80. $\sqrt[10]{ab^9}$

81. $\dfrac{\sqrt[3]{(2+5x)^2}}{\sqrt[4]{2+5x}}$

$\quad = \dfrac{(2+5x)^{2/3}}{(2+5x)^{1/4}}\qquad$ Converting to exponential notation

$\quad = (2+5x)^{2/3-1/4}\quad$ Subtracting exponents

$\quad = (2+5x)^{5/12}\qquad$ Converting back to

$\quad = \sqrt[12]{(2+5x)^5}\qquad$ radical notation

82. $\sqrt[20]{(3x-1)^3}$

83. $\dfrac{\sqrt[4]{(5+3x)^3}}{\sqrt[3]{(5+3x)^2}}$

$\quad = \dfrac{(5+3x)^{3/4}}{(5+3x)^{2/3}}\qquad$ Converting to exponential notation

$\quad = (5+3x)^{3/4-2/3}\quad$ Subtracting exponents

$\quad = (5+3x)^{1/12}\qquad$ Converting back

$\quad = \sqrt[12]{5+3x}\qquad$ to radical notation

84. $\sqrt[15]{(2x+1)^4}$

85. $\sqrt[3]{x^2y}\left(\sqrt{xy} - \sqrt[5]{xy^3}\right)$

$\quad = (x^2y)^{1/3}[(xy)^{1/2} - (xy^3)^{1/5}]$

$\quad = x^{2/3}y^{1/3}(x^{1/2}y^{1/2} - x^{1/5}y^{3/5})$

$\quad = x^{2/3}y^{1/3}x^{1/2}y^{1/2} - x^{2/3}y^{1/3}x^{1/5}y^{3/5}$

$\quad = x^{2/3+1/2}y^{1/3+1/2} - x^{2/3+1/5}y^{1/3+3/5}$

$\quad = x^{7/6}y^{5/6} - x^{13/15}y^{14/15}$

$\quad = x^{1\frac{1}{6}}y^{\frac{5}{6}} - x^{13/15}y^{14/15}$

$\qquad\qquad\qquad\qquad$ Writing a mixed numeral

$\quad = x\cdot x^{1/6}y^{5/6} - x^{13/15}y^{14/15}$

$\quad = x(xy^5)^{1/6} - (x^{13}y^{14})^{1/15}$

$\quad = x\sqrt[6]{xy^5} - \sqrt[15]{x^{13}y^{14}}$

86. $a\sqrt[12]{a^2b^7} - \sqrt[20]{a^{18}b^{13}}$

87. $(m + \sqrt[3]{n^2})(2m + \sqrt[4]{n})$

$\quad = (m + n^{2/3})(2m + n^{1/4})\qquad$ Converting to exponential notation

$\quad = 2m^2 + mn^{1/4} + 2mn^{2/3} + n^{2/3}n^{1/4}\quad$ Using FOIL

$\quad = 2m^2 + mn^{1/4} + 2mn^{2/3} + n^{2/3+1/4}\quad$ Adding exponents

$\quad = 2m^2 + mn^{1/4} + 2mn^{2/3} + n^{11/12}$

$\quad = 2m^2 + m\sqrt[4]{n} + 2m\sqrt[3]{n^2} + \sqrt[12]{n^{11}}\qquad$ Converting back to radical notation

88. $3r^2 - r\sqrt[5]{s} - 3r\sqrt[4]{s^3} + \sqrt[20]{s^{19}}$

89. $f(x) = \sqrt[4]{x},\ g(x) = \sqrt[4]{2x} - \sqrt[4]{x^{11}}$

$\quad (f\cdot g)(x) = \sqrt[4]{x}\left(\sqrt[4]{2x} - \sqrt[4]{x^{11}}\right)$

$\qquad\qquad = \sqrt[4]{2x^2} - \sqrt[4]{x^{12}}$

$\qquad\qquad = \sqrt[4]{2x^2} - x^3$

90. $x^2 + \sqrt[4]{3x^3}$

91. $f(x) = x + \sqrt{7}$, $g(x) = x - \sqrt{7}$

$(f \cdot g)(x) = (x + \sqrt{7})(x - \sqrt{7})$

$\qquad = x^2 - (\sqrt{7})^2$

$\qquad = x^2 - 7$

92. $x^2 + x\sqrt{6} - x\sqrt{2} - 2\sqrt{3}$

93. $f(x) = x^2$

$f(5 - \sqrt{2}) = (5 - \sqrt{2})^2 = 25 - 10\sqrt{2} + (\sqrt{2})^2 =$

$25 - 10\sqrt{2} + 2 = 27 - 10\sqrt{2}$

94. $52 + 14\sqrt{3}$

95. $f(x) = x^2$

$f(\sqrt{3} + \sqrt{5}) = (\sqrt{3} + \sqrt{5})^2 =$

$(\sqrt{3})^2 + 2 \cdot \sqrt{3} \cdot \sqrt{5} + (\sqrt{5})^2 =$

$3 + 2\sqrt{15} + 5 = 8 + 2\sqrt{15}$

96. $9 - 6\sqrt{2}$

97. *Writing Exercise*

98. *Writing Exercise*

99.
$$\frac{12x}{x - 4} - \frac{3x^2}{x + 4} = \frac{384}{x^2 - 16}$$

$$\frac{12x}{x - 4} - \frac{3x^2}{x + 4} = \frac{384}{(x + 4)(x - 4)},$$

$$\text{LCM is } (x + 4)(x - 4).$$

Note that $x \neq -4$ and $x \neq 4$.

$$(x+4)(x-4)\left[\frac{12x}{x-4} - \frac{3x^2}{x+4}\right] =$$

$$(x+4)(x-4) \cdot \frac{384}{(x+4)(x-4)}$$

$$12x(x + 4) - 3x^2(x - 4) = 384$$

$$12x^2 + 48x - 3x^3 + 12x^2 = 384$$

$$-3x^3 + 24x^2 + 48x - 384 = 0$$

$$-3(x^3 - 8x^2 - 16x + 128) = 0$$

$$-3[x^2(x - 8) - 16(x - 8)] = 0$$

$$-3(x - 8)(x^2 - 16) = 0$$

$$-3(x - 8)(x + 4)(x - 4) = 0$$

$$x - 8 = 0 \ or \ x + 4 = 0 \ \ or \ x - 4 = 0$$

$$x = 8 \ or \qquad x = -4 \ or \qquad x = 4$$

Check: For 8:

$$\frac{12x}{x - 4} - \frac{3x^2}{x + 4} = \frac{384}{x^2 - 16}$$

$\dfrac{12 \cdot 8}{8 - 4} - \dfrac{3 \cdot 8^2}{8 + 4}$	$\dfrac{384}{8^2 - 16}$
$\dfrac{96}{4} - \dfrac{192}{12}$	$\dfrac{384}{48}$
$24 - 16$	8
8	TRUE

8 is a solution.

For -4:

$$\frac{12x}{x - 4} - \frac{3x^2}{x + 4} = \frac{384}{x^2 - 16}$$

$\dfrac{12(-4)}{-4 - 4} - \dfrac{3(-4)^2}{-4 + 4}$	$\dfrac{384}{(-4)^2 - 16}$
$\dfrac{-48}{-8} - \dfrac{48}{0}$	$\dfrac{384}{16 - 16}$
	UNDEFINED

-4 is not a solution.

For 4:

$$\frac{12x}{x - 4} - \frac{3x^2}{x + 4} = \frac{384}{x^2 - 16}$$

$\dfrac{12 \cdot 4}{4 - 4} - \dfrac{3 \cdot 4^2}{4 + 4}$	$\dfrac{384}{4^2 - 16}$
$\dfrac{48}{0} - \dfrac{48}{8}$	$\dfrac{384}{16 - 16}$ UNDEFINED

4 is not a solution.

The checks confirm that -4 and 4 are not solutions. The solution is 8.

100. $\dfrac{15}{2}$

101. *Familiarize.* Let x and y represent the width and length of the rectangle, respectively.

Translate. We write two equations.

The width is one-fourth the length.

$\qquad x \quad = \quad \dfrac{1}{4} \cdot \quad y$

The area is twice the perimeter.

$\qquad xy \quad = \quad 2 \cdot \quad (2x + 2y)$

Carry out. Solving the system of equations we get (5,20).

Check. The width, 5, is one-fourth the length, 20. The area is $5 \cdot 20$, or 100. The perimeter is $2 \cdot 5 + 2 \cdot 20$, or 50. Since $100 = 2 \cdot 50$, the area is twice the perimeter. The values check.

State. The width is 5 units, and the length is 20 units.

102. $-5, 4$

103.
$$5x^2 - 6x + 1 = 0$$

$$(5x - 1)(x - 1) = 0$$

$$5x - 1 = 0 \ \ or \ \ x - 1 = 0$$

$$5x = 1 \ \ or \qquad x = 1$$

$$x = \frac{1}{5} \ \ or \qquad x = 1$$

The solutions are $\dfrac{1}{5}$ and 1.

104. $\dfrac{1}{7}, 1$

105. *Writing Exercise*

106. *Writing Exercise*

107. To add radical expressions, the <u>indices</u> and the <u>radicands</u> must be the same.

108. indices

109. To add rational expressions, the <u>denominators</u> must be the same.

110. bases

111.
$$f(x) = \sqrt{20x^2 + 4x^3} - 3x\sqrt{45 + 9x} + \sqrt{5x^2 + x^3}$$
$$= \sqrt{4x^2(5+x)} - 3x\sqrt{9(5+x)} + \sqrt{x^2(5+x)}$$
$$= \sqrt{4x^2}\sqrt{5+x} - 3x\sqrt{9}\sqrt{5+x} + \sqrt{x^2}\sqrt{5+x}$$
$$= 2x\sqrt{5+x} - 3x \cdot 3\sqrt{5+x} + x\sqrt{5+x}$$
$$= 2x\sqrt{5+x} - 9x\sqrt{5+x} + x\sqrt{5+x}$$
$$= -6x\sqrt{5+x}$$

112. $f(x) = 2x\sqrt{x-1}$

113.
$$f(x) = \sqrt[4]{x^5 - x^4} + 3\sqrt[4]{x^9 - x^8}$$
$$= \sqrt[4]{x^4(x-1)} + 3\sqrt[4]{x^8(x-1)}$$
$$= \sqrt[4]{x^4} \cdot \sqrt[4]{x-1} + 3\sqrt[4]{x^8}\sqrt[4]{x-1}$$
$$= x\sqrt[4]{x-1} + 3x^2\sqrt[4]{x-1}$$
$$= (x + 3x^2)\sqrt[4]{x-1}$$

114. $f(x) = 2x(1-x)\sqrt[4]{1+x}$

115.
$$\frac{1}{2}\sqrt{36a^5bc^4} - \frac{1}{2}\sqrt[3]{64a^4bc^6} + \frac{1}{6}\sqrt{144a^3bc^6} =$$
$$\frac{1}{2}\sqrt{36a^4c^4 \cdot ab} - \frac{1}{2}\sqrt[3]{64a^3c^6 \cdot ab} + \frac{1}{6}\sqrt{144a^2c^6 \cdot ab} =$$
$$\frac{1}{2}(6a^2c^2)\sqrt{ab} - \frac{1}{2}(4ac^2)\sqrt[3]{ab} + \frac{1}{6}(12ac^3)\sqrt{ab} =$$
$$3a^2c^2\sqrt{ab} - 2ac^2\sqrt[3]{ab} + 2ac^3\sqrt{ab}$$
$$(3a^2c^2 + 2ac^3)\sqrt{ab} - 2ac^2\sqrt[3]{ab}, \text{ or}$$
$$ac^2[(3a + 2c)\sqrt{ab} - 2\sqrt[3]{ab}]$$

116. $(7x^2 - 2y^2)\sqrt{x+y}$

117.
$$\sqrt{27a^5(b+1)}\sqrt[3]{81a(b+1)^4}$$
$$= [27a^5(b+1)]^{1/2}[81a(b+1)^4]^{1/3}$$
$$= [27a^5(b+1)]^{3/6}[81a(b+1)^4]^{2/6}$$
$$= \{[3^3a^5(b+1)]^3[3^4a(b+1)^4]^2\}^{1/6}$$
$$= \sqrt[6]{3^9a^{15}(b+1)^3 \cdot 3^8a^2(b+1)^8}$$
$$= \sqrt[6]{3^{17}a^{17}(b+1)^{11}}$$
$$= \sqrt[6]{3^{12}a^{12}(b+1)^6 \cdot 3^5a^5(b+1)^5}$$
$$= 3^2a^2(b+1)\sqrt[6]{3^5a^5(b+1)^5}, \text{ or}$$
$$9a^2(b+1)\sqrt[6]{243a^5(b+1)^5}$$

118. $4x(y+z)^3\sqrt[6]{2x(y+z)}$

119.
$$\frac{\dfrac{1}{\sqrt{w}} - \sqrt{w}}{\dfrac{\sqrt{w}+1}{\sqrt{w}}} = \frac{\dfrac{1}{\sqrt{w}} - \sqrt{w}}{\dfrac{\sqrt{w}+1}{\sqrt{w}}} \cdot \frac{\sqrt{w}}{\sqrt{w}} = \frac{1-w}{\sqrt{w}+1} =$$
$$\frac{1-w}{\sqrt{w}+1} \cdot \frac{\sqrt{w}-1}{\sqrt{w}-1} = \frac{\sqrt{w}-1-w\sqrt{w}+w}{w-1} =$$
$$\frac{(w-1) - \sqrt{w}(w-1)}{w-1} = \frac{(w-1)(1-\sqrt{w})}{w-1} =$$
$$1 - \sqrt{w}$$

120. $\dfrac{7\sqrt{3}}{39}$

121. $x - 5 = (\sqrt{x})^2 - (\sqrt{5})^2 = (\sqrt{x} + \sqrt{5})(\sqrt{x} - \sqrt{5})$

122. $(\sqrt{y} + \sqrt{7})(\sqrt{y} - \sqrt{7})$

123. $x - a = (\sqrt{x})^2 - (\sqrt{a})^2 = (\sqrt{x} + \sqrt{a})(\sqrt{x} - \sqrt{a})$

124. 6

125.
$$(\sqrt{x+2} - \sqrt{x-2})^2 =$$
$$x + 2 - 2\sqrt{(x+2)(x-2)} + x - 2 =$$
$$x + 2 - 2\sqrt{x^2 - 4} + x - 2 = 2x - 2\sqrt{x^2 - 4}$$

126. $\dfrac{ab + (a-b)\sqrt{a+b} - a - b}{a + b - b^2}$

127.
$$\frac{b + \sqrt{b}}{1 + b + \sqrt{b}} = \frac{b + \sqrt{b}}{(1+b) + \sqrt{b}} \cdot \frac{(1+b) - \sqrt{b}}{(1+b) - \sqrt{b}}$$
$$= \frac{(b + \sqrt{b})(1 + b - \sqrt{b})}{(1+b)^2 - (\sqrt{b})^2}$$
$$= \frac{b + b^2 - b\sqrt{b} + \sqrt{b} + b\sqrt{b} - b}{1 + 2b + b^2 - b}$$
$$= \frac{b^2 + \sqrt{b}}{1 + b + b^2}$$

128. $\dfrac{1}{\sqrt{y+18} + \sqrt{y}}$

129.
$$\frac{\sqrt{x+6} - 5}{\sqrt{x+6} + 5} = \frac{\sqrt{x+6} - 5}{\sqrt{x+6} + 5} \cdot \frac{\sqrt{x+6} + 5}{\sqrt{x+6} + 5}$$
$$= \frac{(x+6) - 25}{(x+6) + 10\sqrt{x+6} + 25}$$
$$= \frac{x - 19}{x + 10\sqrt{x+6} + 31}$$

Exercise Set 9.6

1.
$$\sqrt{x+3} = 5$$
$$(\sqrt{x+3})^2 = 5^2 \quad \text{Principle of powers (squaring)}$$
$$x + 3 = 25$$
$$x = 22$$

Check:
$$\sqrt{x+3} = 5$$
$$\sqrt{22+3} \ ? \ 5$$
$$\sqrt{25} \ \bigg| $$
$$5 \ \bigg| \ 5 \qquad \text{TRUE}$$

The solution is 22.

2. $\dfrac{63}{5}$

3. $\sqrt{2x} - 1 = 2$

$\qquad \sqrt{2x} = 3 \qquad$ Adding to isolate the radical

$\qquad (\sqrt{2x})^2 = 3^2 \qquad$ Principle of powers (squaring)

$\qquad 2x = 9$

$\qquad x = \dfrac{9}{2}$

Check: $\qquad \dfrac{\sqrt{2x} - 1 = 2}{}$

$\qquad \sqrt{2 \cdot \dfrac{9}{2} - 1} \ ? \ 2$

$\qquad \sqrt{9} - 1$

$\qquad 3 - 1$

$\qquad 2 \ \Big| \ 2 \qquad$ TRUE

The solution is $\dfrac{9}{2}$.

4. $\dfrac{25}{3}$

5. $\sqrt{x - 2} - 7 = -4$

$\qquad \sqrt{x - 2} = 3 \qquad$ Adding to isolate the radical

$\qquad (\sqrt{x - 2})^2 = 3^2 \qquad$ Principle of powers (squaring)

$\qquad x - 2 = 9$

$\qquad x = 11$

Check: $\qquad \dfrac{\sqrt{x - 2} - 7 = -4}{}$

$\qquad \sqrt{11 - 2} - 7 \ ? \ -4$

$\qquad \sqrt{9} - 7$

$\qquad 3 - 7$

$\qquad -4 \ \Big| \ -4 \qquad$ TRUE

The solution is 11.

6. 168

7. $\sqrt{y + 4} + 6 = 7$

$\qquad \sqrt{y + 4} = 1 \qquad$ Adding to isolate the radical

$\qquad (\sqrt{y + 4})^2 = 1^2 \qquad$ Principle of powers (squaring)

$\qquad y + 4 = 1$

$\qquad y = -3$

Check: $\qquad \dfrac{\sqrt{y + 4} + 6 = 7}{}$

$\qquad \sqrt{-3 + 4} + 6 \ ? \ 7$

$\qquad \sqrt{1} + 6$

$\qquad 1 + 6$

$\qquad 7 \ \Big| \ 7 \qquad$ TRUE

The solution is -3.

8. 56

9. $\sqrt[3]{x - 2} = 3$

$\qquad (\sqrt[3]{x - 2})^3 = 3^3$

$\qquad x - 2 = 27$

$\qquad x = 29$

Check: $\qquad \dfrac{\sqrt[3]{x - 2} = 3}{}$

$\qquad \sqrt[3]{29 - 2} \ ? \ 3$

$\qquad \sqrt[3]{27}$

$\qquad 3 \ \Big| \ 3 \qquad$ TRUE

The solution is 29.

10. 3

11. $\sqrt[4]{x + 3} = 2$

$\qquad (\sqrt[4]{x + 3})^4 = 2^4$

$\qquad x + 3 = 16$

$\qquad x = 13$

Check: $\qquad \dfrac{\sqrt[4]{x + 3} = 2}{}$

$\qquad \sqrt[4]{13 + 3} \ ? \ 2$

$\qquad \sqrt[4]{16}$

$\qquad 2 \ \Big| \ 2 \qquad$ TRUE

The solution is 13.

12. 82

13. $8\sqrt{y} = y$

$\qquad (8\sqrt{y})^2 = y^2$

$\qquad 64y = y^2$

$\qquad 0 = y^2 - 64y$

$\qquad 0 = y(y - 64)$

$\qquad y = 0 \ \ or \ \ y - 64 = 0$

$\qquad y = 0 \ \ or \ \ y = 64$

Check:

For 0: $\qquad \dfrac{8\sqrt{y} = y}{}$

$\qquad 8\sqrt{0} \ ? \ 0$

$\qquad 8 \cdot 0$

$\qquad 0 \ \Big| \ 0 \qquad$ TRUE

For 64: $\qquad \dfrac{8\sqrt{y} = y}{}$

$\qquad 8\sqrt{64} \ ? \ 64$

$\qquad 8 \cdot 8$

$\qquad 64 \ \Big| \ 64 \qquad$ TRUE

The solutions are 0 and 64.

14. 0, 9

15. $3x^{1/2} + 12 = 9$

$\qquad 3\sqrt{x} + 12 = 9$

$\qquad 3\sqrt{x} = -3$

$\qquad \sqrt{x} = -1$

Since the principal square root is never negative, this equation has no solution.

16. 64

17. $\sqrt[3]{y} = -4$

$\qquad (\sqrt[3]{y})^3 = (-4)^3$

$\qquad y = -64$

Check: $\sqrt[3]{y} = -4$

$$\frac{\sqrt[3]{-64} \ ? \ -4}{-4 \ | \ -4} \quad \text{TRUE}$$

The solution is -64.

18. -27

19. $x^{1/4} - 2 = 1$

$x^{1/4} = 3$

$(x^{1/4})^4 = 3^4$

$x = 81$

Check: $x^{1/4} - 2 = 1$

$$\frac{81^{1/4} - 2 \ ? \ 1}{3 - 2 \ |}$$
$$\frac{}{1 \ | \ 1} \quad \text{TRUE}$$

The solution is 81.

20. 125

21. $(y - 3)^{1/2} = -2$

$\sqrt{y - 3} = -2$

This equation has no solution, since the principal square root is never negative.

22. No solution

23. $\sqrt[4]{3x + 1} - 4 = -1$

$\sqrt[4]{3x + 1} = 3$

$(\sqrt[4]{3x + 1})^4 = 3^4$

$3x + 1 = 81$

$3x = 80$

$x = \dfrac{80}{3}$

Check: $\sqrt[4]{3x + 1} - 4 = -1$

$$\sqrt[4]{3 \cdot \dfrac{80}{3}} - 4 \ ? \ -1$$
$$\sqrt[4]{81} - 4 \ |$$
$$3 - 4 \ |$$
$$-1 \ | \ -1 \quad \text{TRUE}$$

The solution is $\dfrac{80}{3}$.

24. 39

25. $(x + 7)^{1/3} = 4$

$[(x + 7)^{1/3}]^3 = 4^3$

$x + 7 = 64$

$x = 57$

Check: $(x + 7)^{1/3} = 4$

$$\frac{(57 + 7)^{1/3} \ ? \ 4}{64^{1/3} \ |}$$
$$\frac{}{4 \ | \ 4} \quad \text{TRUE}$$

The solution is 57.

26. 88

27. $\sqrt[3]{3y + 6} + 2 = 3$

$\sqrt[3]{3y + 6} = 1$

$(\sqrt[3]{3y + 6})^3 = 1^3$

$3y + 6 = 1$

$3y = -5$

$y = -\dfrac{5}{3}$

Check: $\sqrt[3]{3y + 6} + 2 = 3$

$$\sqrt[3]{3\left(-\dfrac{5}{3}\right) + 6} + 2 \ ? \ 3$$
$$\sqrt[3]{1} + 2 \ |$$
$$1 + 2 \ |$$
$$3 \ | \ 3 \quad \text{TRUE}$$

The solution is $-\dfrac{5}{3}$.

28. -6

29. $\sqrt{3t + 4} = \sqrt{4t + 3}$

$(\sqrt{3t + 4})^2 = (\sqrt{4t + 3})^2$

$3t + 4 = 4t + 3$

$4 = t + 3$

$1 = t$

Check: $\sqrt{3t + 4} = \sqrt{4t + 3}$

$$\frac{\sqrt{3 \cdot 1 + 4} \ ? \ \sqrt{4 \cdot 1 + 3}}{\sqrt{7} \ | \ \sqrt{7}} \quad \text{TRUE}$$

The solution is 1.

30. 5

31. $3(4 - t)^{1/4} = 6^{1/4}$

$[3(4 - t)^{1/4}]^4 = (6^{1/4})^4$

$81(4 - t) = 6$

$324 - 81t = 6$

$-81t = -318$

$t = \dfrac{106}{27}$

The number $\dfrac{106}{27}$ checks and is the solution.

32. $\dfrac{1}{2}$

33. $3 + \sqrt{5 - x} = x$

$\sqrt{5 - x} = x - 3$

$(\sqrt{5 - x})^2 = (x - 3)^2$

$5 - x = x^2 - 6x + 9$

$0 = x^2 - 5x + 4$

$0 = (x - 1)(x - 4)$

$x - 1 = 0 \ or \ x - 4 = 0$

$x = 1 \ or \quad x = 4$

Check:

For 1:
$$3 + \sqrt{5 - x} = x$$

$$\begin{array}{c|c} 3 + \sqrt{5 - 1} \ ? \ 1 \\ 3 + \sqrt{4} \\ 3 + 2 \\ 5 & 1 \end{array} \qquad \text{FALSE}$$

For 4:
$$3 + \sqrt{5 - x} = x$$

$$\begin{array}{c|c} 3 + \sqrt{5 - 4} \ ? \ 4 \\ 3 + \sqrt{1} \\ 3 + 1 \\ 4 & 4 \end{array} \qquad \text{TRUE}$$

Since 4 checks but 1 does not, the solution is 4.

34. 5

35.
$$\sqrt{4x - 3} = 2 + \sqrt{2x - 5} \qquad \text{One radical is already isolated.}$$

$$(\sqrt{4x - 3})^2 = (2 + \sqrt{2x - 5})^2 \qquad \text{Squaring both sides}$$

$$4x - 3 = 4 + 4\sqrt{2x - 5} + 2x - 5$$

$$2x - 2 = 4\sqrt{2x - 5}$$

$$x - 1 = 2\sqrt{2x - 5}$$

$$x^2 - 2x + 1 = 8x - 20$$

$$x^2 - 10x + 21 = 0$$

$$(x - 7)(x - 3) = 0$$

$$x - 7 = 0 \quad or \quad x - 3 = 0$$

$$x = 7 \quad or \quad x = 3$$

Both numbers check. The solutions are 7 and 3.

36. 7

37.
$$\sqrt{20 - x} + 8 = \sqrt{9 - x} + 11$$

$$\sqrt{20 - x} = \sqrt{9 - x} + 3 \qquad \text{Isolating one radical}$$

$$(\sqrt{20 - x})^2 = (\sqrt{9 - x} + 3)^2 \qquad \text{Squaring both sides}$$

$$20 - x = 9 - x + 6\sqrt{9 - x} + 9$$

$$2 = 6\sqrt{9 - x} \qquad \text{Isolating the remaining radical}$$

$$1 = 3\sqrt{9 - x} \qquad \text{Multiplying by } \frac{1}{2}$$

$$1^2 = (3\sqrt{9 - x})^2 \qquad \text{Squaring both sides}$$

$$1 = 9(9 - x)$$

$$1 = 81 - 9x$$

$$-80 = -9x$$

$$\frac{80}{9} = x$$

The number $\frac{80}{9}$ checks and is the solution.

38. $\frac{15}{4}$

39.
$$\sqrt{x + 2} + \sqrt{3x + 4} = 2$$

$$\sqrt{x + 2} = 2 - \sqrt{3x + 4} \qquad \text{Isolating one radical}$$

$$(\sqrt{x + 2})^2 = (2 - \sqrt{3x + 4})^2$$

$$x + 2 = 4 - 4\sqrt{3x + 4} + 3x + 4$$

$$-2x - 6 = -4\sqrt{3x + 4} \qquad \text{Isolating the remaining radical}$$

$$x + 3 = 2\sqrt{3x + 4} \qquad \text{Multiplying by } -\frac{1}{2}$$

$$(x + 3)^2 = (2\sqrt{3x + 4})^2$$

$$x^2 + 6x + 9 = 4(3x + 4)$$

$$x^2 + 6x + 9 = 12x + 16$$

$$x^2 - 6x - 7 = 0$$

$$(x - 7)(x + 1) = 0$$

$$x - 7 = 0 \quad or \quad x + 1 = 0$$

$$x = 7 \quad or \quad x = -1$$

Check:

For 7:
$$\sqrt{x + 2} + \sqrt{3x + 4} = 2$$

$$\begin{array}{c|c} \sqrt{7 + 2} + \sqrt{3 \cdot 7 + 4} \ ? \ 2 \\ \sqrt{9} + \sqrt{25} \\ 8 & 2 \end{array} \qquad \text{FALSE}$$

For -1:
$$\sqrt{x + 2} + \sqrt{3x + 4} = 2$$

$$\begin{array}{c|c} \sqrt{-1 + 2} + \sqrt{3 \cdot (-1) + 4} \ ? \ 2 \\ \sqrt{1} + \sqrt{1} \\ 2 & 2 \end{array} \qquad \text{TRUE}$$

Since -1 checks but 7 does not, the solution is -1.

40. $-1, \frac{1}{3}$

41. We must have $f(x) = 2$, or $\sqrt{x} + \sqrt{x - 9} = 1$.

$$\sqrt{x} + \sqrt{x - 9} = 1$$

$$\sqrt{x - 9} = 1 - \sqrt{x} \qquad \text{Isolating one radical term}$$

$$(\sqrt{x - 9})^2 = (1 - \sqrt{x})^2$$

$$x - 9 = 1 - 2\sqrt{x} + x$$

$$-10 = -2\sqrt{x} \qquad \text{Isolating the remaining radical term}$$

$$5 = \sqrt{x}$$

$$25 = x$$

This value does not check. There is no solution, so there is no value of x for which $f(x) = 1$.

42. 9

43. $\sqrt{a-2} - \sqrt{4a+1} = -3$

$$\sqrt{a-2} = \sqrt{4a+1} - 3$$
$$(\sqrt{a-2})^2 = (\sqrt{4a+1} - 3)^2$$
$$a - 2 = 4a + 1 - 6\sqrt{4a+1} + 9$$
$$-3a - 12 = -6\sqrt{4a+1}$$
$$a + 4 = 2\sqrt{4a+1}$$
$$(a+4)^2 = (2\sqrt{4a+1})^2$$
$$a^2 + 8a + 16 = 4(4a+1)$$
$$a^2 + 8a + 16 = 16a + 4$$
$$a^2 - 8a + 12 = 0$$
$$(a-2)(a-6) = 0$$
$$a - 2 = 0 \quad or \quad a - 6 = 0$$
$$a = 2 \quad or \quad\quad a = 6$$

Both numbers check, so we have $f(a) = -3$ when $a = 2$ and when $a = 6$.

44. 1

45. We must have $\sqrt{2x-3} = \sqrt{x+7} - 2$.

$$\sqrt{2x-3} = \sqrt{x+7} - 2$$
$$(\sqrt{2x-3})^2 = (\sqrt{x+7} - 2)^2$$
$$2x - 3 = x + 7 - 4\sqrt{x+7} + 4$$
$$x - 14 = -4\sqrt{x+7}$$
$$(x-14)^2 = (-4\sqrt{x+7})^2$$
$$x^2 - 28x + 196 = 16(x+7)$$
$$x^2 - 28x + 196 = 16x + 112$$
$$x^2 - 44x + 84 = 0$$
$$(x-2)(x-42) = 0$$
$$x = 2 \quad or \quad x = 42$$

Since 2 checks but 42 does not, we have $f(x) = g(x)$ when $x = 2$.

46. 10

47. We must have $4 - \sqrt{a-3} = (a+5)^{1/2}$.

$$4 - \sqrt{a-3} = (a+5)^{1/2}$$
$$(4 - \sqrt{a-3})^2 = [(a+5)^{1/2}]^2$$
$$16 - 8\sqrt{a-3} + a - 3 = a + 5$$
$$-8\sqrt{a-3} = -8$$
$$\sqrt{a-3} = 1$$
$$(\sqrt{a-3})^2 = 1^2$$
$$a - 3 = 1$$
$$a = 4$$

The number 4 checks, so we have $f(a) = g(a)$ when $a = 4$.

48. 15

49. *Writing Exercise*

50. *Writing Exercise*

51. *Familiarize.* Let $h =$ the height of the triangle, in inches. Then $h + 2 =$ the base. Recall that the formula for the area of a triangle with base b and height h is $A = \frac{1}{2}bh$.

Translate. Substitute in the formula.
$$31\frac{1}{2} = \frac{1}{2}(h+2)(h)$$

Carry out. We solve the equation.
$$31\frac{1}{2} = \frac{1}{2}(h+2)(h)$$
$$\frac{63}{2} = \frac{1}{2}(h+2)(h)$$
$$63 = (h+2)(h) \quad \text{Multiplying by 2}$$
$$63 = h^2 + 2h$$
$$0 = h^2 + 2h - 63$$
$$0 = (h+9)(h-7)$$
$$h + 9 = 0 \quad or \quad h - 7 = 0$$
$$h = -9 \quad or \quad\quad h = 7$$

Check. Since the height of the triangle cannot be negative we check only 7. If the height is 7 in., then the base is $7 + 2$, or 9 in., and the area is $\frac{1}{2} \cdot 9 \cdot 7 = \frac{63}{2} = 31\frac{1}{2}$ in². The answer checks.

State. The height of the triangle is 7 in., and the base is 9 in.

52. 8 60-sec commercials

53. *Familiarize.* Let $t =$ the time, in hours, it takes Gonzalo to sew the quilt. Then $t - 6 =$ the time it takes Elaine to sew the quilt. In 4 hours Gonzalo does $\frac{4}{t}$ of the job and Elaine does $\frac{4}{t-6}$ of the job.

Translate. Together, in 4 hr one entire job is done.
$$\frac{4}{t} + \frac{4}{t-6} = 1$$

Carry out. We solve the equation. The LCD is $t(t-6)$.
$$\frac{4}{t} + \frac{4}{t-6} = 1$$
$$t(t-6)\left(\frac{4}{t} + \frac{4}{t-6}\right) = t(t-6) \cdot 1$$
$$4(t-6) + 4t = t^2 - 6t$$
$$4t - 24 + 4t = t^2 - 6t$$
$$8t - 24 = t^2 - 6t$$
$$0 = t^2 - 14t + 24$$
$$0 = (t-2)(t-12)$$
$$t - 2 = 0 \quad or \quad t - 12 = 0$$
$$t = 2 \quad or \quad\quad t = 12$$

Check. If $t = 2$, then $t - 6 = 2 - 6 = -4$. Since time cannot be negative in this application, 2 is not a solution. If Gonzalo sews the quilt in 12 hr, then Elaine sews it in $12 - 6$, or 6 hr. In 4 hr Gonzalo does 4/12, or 1/3 of the job and Elaine does 4/6, or 2/3 of the job. Together they do $1/3 + 2/3$, or 1 entire job. The answer checks.

State. It would take Elaine 6 hr and Gonzalo 12 hr to sew the quilt working alone.

54. 3.2 hr

55. Graph $y > 3x + 5$.

First graph the related equation, $y = 3x + 5$. Use a dashed line since the inequality symbol is $>$. Then test a point not on the line to determine if it is a solution of the inequality. We use $(0, 0)$.

$$\begin{array}{c|c} y > 3x + 5 \\ \hline 0 \; ? \; 3 \cdot 0 + 5 \\ \hline 0 \; | \; 5 \qquad \text{FALSE} \end{array}$$

Since $0 > 5$ is false, we shade the half-plane that does not contain $(0, 0)$.

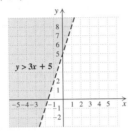

56.

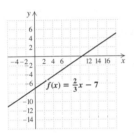

57. *Writing Exercise*

58. *Writing Exercise*

59. $S(t) = 1.087.7 \sqrt{\dfrac{9t + 2617}{2457}}$

Substitute 1502.3 for $S(t)$ and solve for t.

$$1502.3 = 1087.7 \sqrt{\dfrac{9t + 2617}{2457}}$$

$$1.3812 \approx \sqrt{\dfrac{9t + 2617}{2457}} \qquad \text{Dividing by 1087.7}$$

$$(1.3812)^2 \approx \left(\sqrt{\dfrac{9t + 2617}{2457}} \right)^2$$

$$1.9077 \approx \dfrac{9t + 2617}{2457}$$

$$4687.2189 \approx 9t + 2617$$

$$2070.2189 \approx 9t$$

$$230.0243 \approx t$$

The temperature is about $230.0°\text{C}$.

60. $524.8°\text{C}$

61.

$$S = 1087.7 \sqrt{\dfrac{9t + 2617}{2457}}$$

$$\dfrac{S}{1087.7} = \sqrt{\dfrac{9t + 2617}{2457}}$$

$$\left(\dfrac{S}{1087.7} \right)^2 = \left(\sqrt{\dfrac{9t + 2617}{2457}} \right)^2$$

$$\dfrac{S^2}{1087.7^2} = \dfrac{9t + 2617}{2457}$$

$$\dfrac{2457 S^2}{1087.7^2} = 9t + 2617$$

$$\dfrac{2457 S^2}{1087.7^2} - 2617 = 9t$$

$$\dfrac{1}{9} \left(\dfrac{2457 S^2}{1087.7^2} - 2617 \right) = t$$

62. About 4166 rpm

63. $d(n) = 0.75 \sqrt{2.8n}$

Substitute 84 for $d(n)$ and solve for n.

$$84 = 0.75 \sqrt{2.8n}$$

$$112 = \sqrt{2.8n}$$

$$(112)^2 = (\sqrt{2.8n})^2$$

$$12,544 = 2.8n$$

$$4480 = n$$

About 4480 rpm will produce peak performance.

64. $h = \dfrac{v^2 r}{2gr - v^2}$

65.

$$v = \sqrt{2gr} \sqrt{\dfrac{h}{r + h}}$$

$$v^2 = 2gr \cdot \dfrac{h}{r + h} \qquad \text{Squaring both sides}$$

$$v^2(r + h) = 2grh \qquad \text{Multiplying by } r + h$$

$$v^2 r + v^2 h = 2grh$$

$$v^2 h = 2grh - v^2 r$$

$$v^2 h = r(2gh - v^2)$$

$$\dfrac{v^2 h}{2gh - v^2} = r$$

66. 22,500 ft

67. $D(h) = 1.2 \sqrt{h}$

$$10.2 = 1.2 \sqrt{h}$$

$$8.5 = \sqrt{h}$$

$$(8.5)^2 = (\sqrt{h})^2$$

$$72.25 = h$$

The sailor must climb 72.25 ft above sea level.

68. $-\dfrac{8}{9}$

69.
$$\left(\frac{z}{4} - 5\right)^{2/3} = \frac{1}{25}$$
$$\left[\left(\frac{z}{4} - 5\right)^{2/3}\right]^3 = \left(\frac{1}{25}\right)^3$$
$$\left(\frac{z}{4} - 5\right)^2 = \frac{1}{15,625}$$
$$\frac{z^2}{16} - \frac{5}{2}z + 25 = \frac{1}{15,625}$$
$$15,625z^2 - 625,000z + 6,250,000 = 16$$
$$15,625z^2 - 625,000z + 6,249,984 = 0$$
$$(125z - 2504)(125z - 2496) = 0$$

$$125z - 2504 = 0 \quad or \quad 125z - 2496 = 0$$
$$125z = 2504 \quad or \qquad\quad 125z = 2496$$
$$z = \frac{2504}{125} \quad or \qquad\quad z = \frac{2496}{125}$$

Both numbers check. The solutions are $\dfrac{2504}{125}$ and $\dfrac{2496}{125}$.

70. $-8, 8$

71.
$$\sqrt{\sqrt{y} + 49} = 7$$
$$(\sqrt{\sqrt{y} + 49})^2 = 7^2$$
$$\sqrt{y} + 49 = 49$$
$$\sqrt{y} = 0$$
$$(\sqrt{y})^2 = 0^2$$
$$y = 0$$

This number 0 checks and is the solution.

72. $-1, 6$

73.
$$\sqrt{8 - b} = b\sqrt{8 - b}$$
$$(\sqrt{8 - b})^2 = (b\sqrt{8 - b})^2$$
$$(8 - b) = b^2(8 - b)$$
$$0 = b^2(8 - b) - (8 - b)$$
$$0 = (8 - b)(b^2 - 1)$$
$$0 = (8 - b)(b + 1)(b - 1)$$
$$8 - b = 0 \quad or \quad b + 1 = 0 \quad or \quad b - 1 = 0$$
$$8 = b \quad or \qquad b = -1 \quad or \quad b = 1$$

Since the numbers 8 and 1 check but -1 does not, 8 and 1 are the solutions.

74. $(2, 0)$

75. We find the values of x for which $g(x) = 0$.
$$6x^{1/2} + 6x^{-1/2} - 37 = 0$$
$$6\sqrt{x} + \frac{6}{\sqrt{x}} = 37$$
$$\left(6\sqrt{x} + \frac{6}{\sqrt{x}}\right)^2 = 37^2$$
$$36x + 72 + \frac{36}{x} = 1369$$
$$36x^2 + 72x + 36 = 1369x \quad \text{Multiplying by } x$$
$$36x^2 - 1297x + 36 = 0$$
$$(36x - 1)(x - 36) = 0$$

$$36x - 1 = 0 \quad or \quad x - 36 = 0$$
$$36x = 1 \quad or \qquad\quad x = 36$$
$$x = \frac{1}{36} \quad or \qquad\quad x = 36$$

Both numbers check. The x-intercepts are $\left(\dfrac{1}{36}, 0\right)$ and $(36, 0)$.

76. $(0, 0)$, $\left(\dfrac{125}{4}, 0\right)$

77. *Writing Exercise*

Exercise Set 9.7

1. $a = 5$, $b = 3$

Find c.
$$c^2 = a^2 + b^2 \quad \text{Pythagorean equation}$$
$$c^2 = 5^2 + 3^2 \quad \text{Substituting}$$
$$c^2 = 25 + 9$$
$$c^2 = 34$$
$$c = \sqrt{34} \qquad \text{Exact answer}$$
$$c \approx 5.831 \qquad \text{Approximation}$$

2. $\sqrt{164}$; 12.806

3. $a = 9$, $b = 9$

Observe that the legs have the same length, so this is an isosceles right triangle. Then we know that the length of the hypotenuse is the length of a leg times $\sqrt{2}$, or $9\sqrt{2}$, or approximately 12.728.

4. $10\sqrt{2}$; 14.142

5. $b = 12$, $c = 13$

Find a.
$$a^2 + b^2 = c^2 \quad \text{Pythagorean equation}$$
$$a^2 + 12^2 = 13^2 \quad \text{Substituting}$$
$$a^2 + 144 = 169$$
$$a^2 = 25$$
$$a = 5$$

6. $\sqrt{119}$; 10.909

7. $c = 6$, $a = \sqrt{5}$

Find b.
$$c^2 = a^2 + b^2$$
$$(\sqrt{5})^2 + b^2 = 6^2$$
$$5 + b^2 = 36$$
$$b^2 = 31$$
$$b = \sqrt{31} \qquad \text{Exact answer}$$
$$b \approx 5.568 \qquad \text{Approximation}$$

8. 4

9. $b = 2, \quad c = \sqrt{15}$

Find a.

$a^2 + b^2 = c^2$ Pythagorean equation

$a^2 + 2^2 = (\sqrt{15})^2$ Substituting

$a^2 + 4 = 15$

$a^2 = 11$

$a = \sqrt{11}$ Exact answer

$a \approx 3.317$ Approximation

10. $\sqrt{19}; 4.359$

11. $a = 1, \quad c = \sqrt{2}$

Observe that the length of the hypotenuse, $\sqrt{2}$, is $\sqrt{2}$ times the length of the given leg, 1. Thus, we have an isosceles right triangle and the length of the other leg is also 1.

12. $\sqrt{3}; 1.732$

13. We make a drawing and let $d =$ the length of the guy wire.

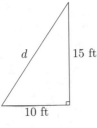

We use the Pythagorean equation to find d.

$d^2 = 10^2 + 15^2$

$d^2 = 100 + 225$

$d^2 = 325$

$d = \sqrt{325}$

$d \approx 18.028$

The wire is $\sqrt{325}$ ft, or about 18.028 ft long.

14. $\sqrt{8450}$ ft; 91.924 ft

15. We first make a drawing and let $d =$ the distance, in feet, to second base. A right triangle is formed in which the length of the leg from second base to third base is 90 ft. The length of the leg from third base to where the catcher fields the ball is $90 - 10$, or 80 ft.

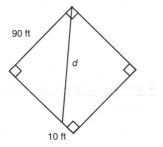

We substitute these values into the Pythagorean equation to find d.

$d^2 = 90^2 + 80^2$

$d^2 = 8100 + 6400$

$d^2 = 14,500$

$d = \sqrt{14,500}$

Exact answer: $d = \sqrt{14,500}$ ft

Approximation: $d \approx 120.416$ ft

16. 12 in.

17. We make a drawing.

25 in.   15 in.

w

We use the Pythagorean equation to find w.

$w^2 + 15^2 = 25^2$

$w^2 + 225 = 625$

$w^2 = 400$

$w = 20$

The width is 20 in.

18. $(\sqrt{340} + 8)$ ft; 26.439 ft

19.

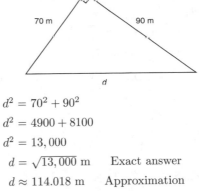

70 m   90 m

d

$d^2 = 70^2 + 90^2$

$d^2 = 4900 + 8100$

$d^2 = 13,000$

$d = \sqrt{13,000}$ m   Exact answer

$d \approx 114.018$ m   Approximation

20. 50 ft

21. Since one acute angle is $45°$, this is an isosceles right triangle with $b = 5$. Then $a = 5$ also. We substitute to find c.

$c = a\sqrt{2}$

$c = 5\sqrt{2}$

Exact answer: $a = 5, \quad c = 5\sqrt{2}$

Approximation: $c \approx 7.071$

22. $a = 14,; \quad c = 14\sqrt{2} \approx 19.799$

23. This is a 30-60-90 right triangle with $c = 14$. We substitute to find a and b.

$$c = 2a$$
$$14 = 2a$$
$$7 = a$$

$$b = a\sqrt{3}$$
$$b = 7\sqrt{3}$$

Exact answer: $a = 7,\ b = 7\sqrt{3}$

Approximation: $b \approx 12.124$

24. $a = 9; b = 9\sqrt{3} \approx 15.588$

25. This is a 30-60-90 right triangle with $b = 15$. We substitute to find a and c.

$$b = a\sqrt{3}$$
$$15 = a\sqrt{3}$$
$$\frac{15}{\sqrt{3}} = a$$
$$\frac{15\sqrt{3}}{3} = a \qquad \text{Rationalizing the denominator}$$
$$5\sqrt{3} = a \qquad \text{Simplifying}$$
$$c = 2a$$
$$c = 2 \cdot 5\sqrt{3}$$
$$c = 10\sqrt{3}$$

Exact answer: $a = 5\sqrt{3},\ c = 10\sqrt{3}$

Approximations: $a \approx 8.660,\ c \approx 17.321$

26. $a = 4\sqrt{2} \approx 5.657; b = 4\sqrt{2} \approx 5.657$

27. This is an isosceles right triangle with $c = 13$. We substitute to find a.

$$a = \frac{c\sqrt{2}}{2}$$
$$a = \frac{13\sqrt{2}}{2}$$

Since $a = b$, we have $b = \dfrac{13\sqrt{2}}{2}$ also.

Exact answer: $a = \dfrac{13\sqrt{2}}{2},\ b = \dfrac{13\sqrt{2}}{2}$

Approximations: $a \approx 9.192,\ b \approx 9.192$

28. $a = \dfrac{7\sqrt{3}}{3} \approx 4.041; c = \dfrac{14\sqrt{3}}{3} \approx 8.083$

29. This is a 30-60-90 triangle with $a = 14$. We substitute to find b and c.

$$b = a\sqrt{3} \qquad\qquad c = 2a$$
$$b = 14\sqrt{3} \qquad\qquad c = 2 \cdot 14$$
$$\qquad\qquad\qquad c = 28$$

Exact answer: $b = 14\sqrt{3},\ c = 28$

Approximation: $b \approx 24.249$

30. $b = 9\sqrt{3} \approx 15.588; c = 18$

31.

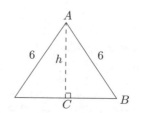

This is an equilateral triangle, so all the angles are 60°. The altitude bisects one angle and one side. Then triangle ABC is a 30-60-90 right triangle with the shorter leg of length $6/2$, or 3, and hypotenuse of length 6. We substitute to find the length of the other leg.

$$b = a\sqrt{3}$$
$$h = 3\sqrt{3} \qquad \text{Substituting } h \text{ for } b \text{ and } 3 \text{ for } a$$

Exact answer: $h = 3\sqrt{3}$

Approximation: $h \approx 5.196$

32. $5\sqrt{3} \approx 8.660$

33.

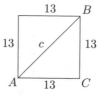

Triangle ABC is an isosceles right triangle with $a = 13$. We substitute to find c.

$$c = a\sqrt{2}$$
$$c = 13\sqrt{2}$$

Exact answer: $c = 13\sqrt{2}$

Approximation: $c \approx 18.385$

34. $7\sqrt{2} \approx 9.899$

35.

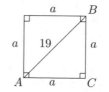

Triangle ABC is an isosceles right triangle with $c = 19$. We substitute to find a.

$$a = \frac{c\sqrt{2}}{2}$$
$$a = \frac{19\sqrt{2}}{2}$$

Exact answer: $a = \dfrac{19\sqrt{2}}{2}$

Approximation: $a \approx 13.435$

36. $\dfrac{15\sqrt{2}}{2} \approx 10.607$

37. We will express all distances in feet. Recall that 1 mi = 5280 ft.

We use the Pythagorean equation to find h.
$$h^2 + (5280)^2 = (5281)^2$$
$$h^2 + 27,878,400 = 27,888,961$$
$$h^2 = 10,561$$
$$h = \sqrt{10,561}$$
$$h \approx 102.767$$

The height of the bulge is $\sqrt{10,561}$ ft, or about 102.767 ft.

38. Neither; they have the same area.

39.

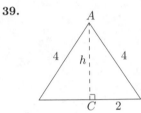

The entrance is an equilateral triangle, so all the angles are 60°. The altitude bisects one angle and one side. Then triangle ABC is a 30-60-90 right triangle with the shorter leg of length 4/2, or 2, and hypotenuse of length 4. We substitute to find h, the height of the tent.

$$b = a\sqrt{3}$$
$$h = 2\sqrt{3} \quad \text{Substituting } h \text{ for } b \text{ and 2 for } a$$

Exact answer: $h = 2\sqrt{3}$ ft

Approximation: $h \approx 3.464$ ft

40. $d = s + s\sqrt{2}$

41.

Triangle ABC is an isosceles right triangle with $c = 8\sqrt{2}$. We substitute to find a.
$$a = \frac{c\sqrt{2}}{2} = \frac{8\sqrt{2} \cdot \sqrt{2}}{2} = \frac{8 \cdot 2}{2} = 8$$

The length of a side of the square is 8 ft.

42. $\sqrt{181}$ cm ≈ 13.454 cm

43.

y

$(0, y)$

5

$|y|$

3 $(3, 0)$

x

$$|y|^2 + 3^2 = 5^2$$
$$y^2 + 9 = 25$$
$$y^2 = 16$$
$$y = \pm 4$$

The points are $(0, -4)$ and $(0, 4)$.

44. $(-3, 0), (3, 0)$

45. *Writing Exercise*

46. *Writing Exercise*

47. $47(-1)^{19} = 47(-1) = -47$

48. 5

49. $x^3 - 9x = x \cdot x^2 - 9 \cdot x = x(x^2 - 9) = x(x + 3)(x - 3)$

50. $7a(a + 2)(a - 2)$

51. $|3x - 5| = 7$

$$3x - 5 = 7 \quad or \quad 3x - 5 = -7$$
$$3x = 12 \quad or \quad 3x = -2$$
$$x = 4 \quad or \quad x = -\frac{2}{3}$$

The solution set is $\left\{4, -\frac{2}{3}\right\}$.

52. $\left\{10, -\frac{4}{3}\right\}$

53. *Writing Exercise*

54. *Writing Exercise*

55.

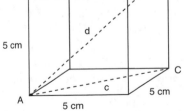

First find the length of a diagonal of the base of the cube. It is the hypotenuse of an isosceles right triangle with $a = 5$ cm. Then $c = a\sqrt{2} = 5\sqrt{2}$ cm.

Triangle ABC is a right triangle with legs of $5\sqrt{2}$ cm and 5 cm and hypotenuse d. Use the Pythagorean equation to find d, the length of the diagonal that connects two opposite corners of the cube.

$$d^2 = (5\sqrt{2})^2 + 5^2$$
$$d^2 = 25 \cdot 2 + 25$$
$$d^2 = 50 + 25$$
$$d^2 = 75$$
$$d = \sqrt{75}$$

Exact answer: $d = \sqrt{75}$ cm

56. 9 packets

57.

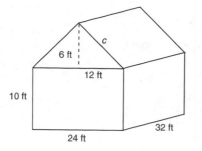

The area to be painted consists of two 10 ft by 24 ft rectangles, two 10 ft by 32 ft rectangles, and two triangles with height 6 ft and base 24 ft. The area of the two 10 ft by 24 ft rectangles is $2 \cdot 10$ ft $\cdot 24$ ft $= 480$ ft^2. The area of the two 10 ft by 32 ft rectangles is $2 \cdot 10$ ft $\cdot 32$ ft $= 640$ ft^2. The area of the two triangles is $2 \cdot \dfrac{1}{2} \cdot 24$ ft $\cdot 6$ ft $= 144$ ft^2. Thus, the total area to be painted is 480 ft^2 + 640 ft^2 + 144 ft^2 = 1264 ft^2.

One gallon of paint covers 275 ft^2, so we divide to determine how many gallons of paint are required: $\dfrac{1264}{275} \approx 4.6$. Thus, 4 gallons of paint should be bought to paint the house. This answer assumes that the total area of the doors and windows is 164 ft^2 or more. ($4 \cdot 275 = 1100$ and $1264 = 1100 + 164$)

58. 49.5 ft by 49.5 ft

59. First we find the radius of a circle with an area of 6160 ft^2.

$$A = \pi r^2$$
$$6160 = \pi r^2$$
$$\frac{6160}{\pi} = r^2$$
$$\sqrt{\frac{6160}{\pi}} = r$$
$$44.28 \approx r$$

Now we make a drawing. Let $s =$ the length of a side of the room.

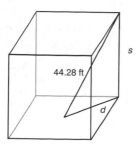

We make a drawing of the floor of the room to help us find d.

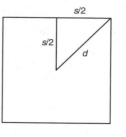

We have an isosceles right triangle, so $d = \dfrac{s}{2} \cdot \sqrt{2}$, or $\dfrac{s\sqrt{2}}{2}$.

Now we use the Pythagorean theorem to find s.

$$d^2 + s^2 = (44.28)^2$$
$$\left(\frac{s\sqrt{2}}{2}\right)^2 + s^2 = (44.28)^2 \quad \text{Substituting } \frac{s\sqrt{2}}{2} \text{ for } d.$$
$$\frac{s^2}{2} + s^2 = (44.28)^2$$
$$\frac{3s^2}{2} = (44.28)^2$$
$$s^2 = \frac{2}{3}(44.28)^2$$
$$s = 44.28\sqrt{\frac{2}{3}}$$
$$s \approx 36.15$$

The dimensions of the room are 36.15 ft by 36.15 ft by 36.15 ft.

Exercise Set 9.8

1. $\sqrt{-25} = \sqrt{-1 \cdot 25} = \sqrt{-1} \cdot \sqrt{25} = i \cdot 5 = 5i$

2. $6i$

3. $\sqrt{-13} = \sqrt{-1 \cdot 13} = \sqrt{-1} \cdot \sqrt{13} = i\sqrt{13}$, or $\sqrt{13}i$

4. $i\sqrt{19}$, or $\sqrt{19}i$

5. $\sqrt{-18} = \sqrt{-1} \cdot \sqrt{9} \cdot \sqrt{2} = i \cdot 3 \cdot \sqrt{2} = 3i\sqrt{2}$, or $3\sqrt{2}i$

6. $7i\sqrt{2}$, or $7\sqrt{2}i$

7. $\sqrt{-3} = \sqrt{-1 \cdot 3} = \sqrt{-1} \cdot \sqrt{3} = i\sqrt{3}$, or $\sqrt{3}i$

8. $2i$

9. $\sqrt{-81} = \sqrt{-1 \cdot 81} = \sqrt{-1} \cdot \sqrt{81} = i \cdot 9 = 9i$

10. $3i\sqrt{3}$, or $3\sqrt{3}i$

11. $\sqrt{-300} = \sqrt{-1} \cdot \sqrt{100} \cdot \sqrt{3} = i \cdot 10 \cdot \sqrt{3} = 10i\sqrt{3}$, or $10\sqrt{3}i$

12. $-5i\sqrt{3}$, or $-5\sqrt{3}i$

13. $-\sqrt{-49} = -\sqrt{-1 \cdot 49} = -\sqrt{-1} \cdot \sqrt{49} = -i \cdot 7 = -7i$

14. $-5i\sqrt{5}$, or $-5\sqrt{5}i$

15. $4 - \sqrt{-60} = 4 - \sqrt{-1 \cdot 60} = 4 - \sqrt{-1} \cdot \sqrt{60} =$
$4 - i \cdot 2\sqrt{15} = 4 - 2\sqrt{15}i$, or $4 - 2i\sqrt{15}$

16. $6 - 2i\sqrt{21}$, or $6 - 2\sqrt{21}i$

17. $\sqrt{-4} + \sqrt{-12} = \sqrt{-1 \cdot 4} + \sqrt{-1 \cdot 12} =$
$\sqrt{-1} \cdot \sqrt{4} + \sqrt{-1} \cdot \sqrt{12} = i \cdot 2 + i \cdot 2\sqrt{3} =$
$(2 + 2\sqrt{3})i$

18. $(-2\sqrt{19} + 5\sqrt{5})i$

19. $\sqrt{-72} - \sqrt{-25} = \sqrt{-1 \cdot 36 \cdot 2} - \sqrt{-1 \cdot 25} =$
$\sqrt{-1}\sqrt{36 \cdot 2} - \sqrt{-1}\sqrt{25} = i \cdot 6\sqrt{2} - i \cdot 5 =$
$(6\sqrt{2} - 5)i$

20. $(3\sqrt{2} - 10)i$

21. $\quad (7 + 8i) + (5 + 3i)$
$= (7 + 5) + (8 + 3)i \qquad$ Combining the real and
$\qquad\qquad\qquad\qquad$ the imaginary parts
$= 12 + 11i$

22. $7 + 4i$

23. $(9 + 8i) - (5 + 3i) = (9 - 5) + (8 - 3)i$
$= 4 + 5i$

24. $7 + 3i$

25. $(5 - 3i) - (9 + 2i) = (5 - 9) + (-3 - 2)i$
$= -4 - 5i$

26. $2 - i$

27. $(-2 + 6i) - (-7 + i) = -2 - (-7) + (6 - 1)i$
$= 5 + 5i$

28. $-12 - 5i$

29. $\quad 6i \cdot 9i = 54 \cdot i^2$
$= 54 \cdot (-1) \qquad i^2 = -1$
$= -54$

30. -42

31. $\quad 7i \cdot (-8i) = -56 \cdot i^2$
$= -56 \cdot (-1) \qquad i^2 = -1$
$= 56$

32. -24

33. $\sqrt{-49}\sqrt{-25} = \sqrt{-1} \cdot \sqrt{49} \cdot \sqrt{-1} \cdot \sqrt{25}$
$= i \cdot 7 \cdot i \cdot 5$
$= i^2 \cdot 35$
$= -1 \cdot 35$
$= -35$

34. -18

35. $\sqrt{-6}\sqrt{-7} = \sqrt{-1} \cdot \sqrt{6} \cdot \sqrt{-1} \cdot \sqrt{7}$
$= i \cdot \sqrt{6} \cdot i \cdot \sqrt{7}$
$= i^2 \cdot \sqrt{42}$
$= -1 \cdot \sqrt{42}$
$= -\sqrt{42}$

36. $-\sqrt{10}$

37. $\sqrt{-15}\sqrt{-10} = \sqrt{-1} \cdot \sqrt{15} \cdot \sqrt{-1} \cdot \sqrt{10}$
$= i \cdot \sqrt{15} \cdot i \cdot \sqrt{10}$
$= i^2 \cdot \sqrt{150}$
$= -\sqrt{25 \cdot 6}$
$= -5\sqrt{6}$

38. $-3\sqrt{14}$

39. $\quad 2i(7 + 3i)$
$= 2i \cdot 7 + 2i \cdot 3i \quad$ Using the distributive law
$= 14i + 6i^2$
$= 14i - 6 \qquad\qquad i^2 = -1$
$= -6 + 14i$

40. $-30 + 10i$

41. $\quad -4i(6 - 5i) = -4i \cdot 6 - 4i(-5i)$
$= -24i + 20i^2$
$= -24i - 20$
$= -20 - 24i$

42. $-28 - 21i$

43. $\quad (1 + 5i)(4 + 3i)$
$= 4 + 3i + 20i + 15i^2 \quad$ Using FOIL
$= 4 + 3i + 20i - 15 \qquad i^2 = -1$
$= -11 + 23i$

44. $1 + 5i$

45. $(5 - 6i)(2 + 5i) = 10 + 25i - 12i - 30i^2$
$= 10 + 25i - 12i + 30$
$= 40 + 13i$

46. $38 + 9i$

47. $(-4 + 5i)(3 - 4i) = -12 + 16i + 15i - 20i^2$
$= -12 + 16i + 15i + 20$
$= 8 + 31i$

48. $2 - 46i$

49. $(7 - 3i)(4 - 7i) = 28 - 49i - 12i + 21i^2 =$
$28 - 49i - 12i - 21 = 7 - 61i$

50. $5 - 37i$

51. $(-3 + 6i)(-3 + 4i) = 9 - 12i - 18i + 24i^2 =$
$9 - 12i - 18i - 24 = -15 - 30i$

52. $-11 - 16i$

53. $(2 + 9i)(-3 - 5i) = -6 - 10i - 27i - 45i^2 =$
$-6 - 10i - 27i + 45 = 39 - 37i$

54. $13 - 47i$

55. $(1 - 2i)^2$

$= 1^2 - 2 \cdot 1 \cdot 2i + (2i)^2$ Squaring a binomial

$= 1 - 4i + 4i^2$

$= 1 - 4i - 4$ $\qquad i^2 = -1$

$= -3 - 4i$

56. $12 - 16i$

57. $(3 + 2i)^2$

$= 3^2 + 2 \cdot 3 \cdot 2i + (2i)^2$ Squaring a binomial

$= 9 + 12i + 4i^2$

$= 9 + 12i - 4$ $\qquad i^2 = -1$

$= 5 + 12i$

58. $-5 + 12i$

59. $(-5 - 2i)^2 = 25 + 20i + 4i^2 = 25 + 20i - 4 =$
$21 + 20i$

60. $-5 - 12i$

61. $\dfrac{3}{2 - i}$

$= \dfrac{3}{2 - i} \cdot \dfrac{2 + i}{2 + i}$ Multiplying by 1, using the conjugate

$= \dfrac{6 + 3i}{4 - i^2}$ Multiplying

$= \dfrac{6 + 3i}{4 - (-1)}$ $\qquad i^2 = -1$

$= \dfrac{6 + 3i}{5}$

$= \dfrac{6}{5} + \dfrac{3}{5}i$

62. $\dfrac{6}{5} - \dfrac{2}{5}i$

63. $\dfrac{3i}{5 + 2i}$

$= \dfrac{3i}{5 + 2i} \cdot \dfrac{5 - 2i}{5 - 2i}$ Multiplying by 1, using the conjugate

$= \dfrac{15i - 6i^2}{25 - 4i^2}$ Multiplying

$= \dfrac{15i + 6}{25 + 4}$

$= \dfrac{15i + 6}{29}$

$= \dfrac{6}{29} + \dfrac{15}{29}i$

64. $-\dfrac{6}{17} + \dfrac{10}{17}i$

65. $\dfrac{7}{9i} = \dfrac{7}{9i} \cdot \dfrac{i}{i} = \dfrac{7i}{9i^2} = \dfrac{7i}{-9} = -\dfrac{7}{9}i$

66. $-\dfrac{5}{8}i$

67. $\dfrac{5 - 3i}{4i} = \dfrac{5 - 3i}{4i} \cdot \dfrac{i}{i} = \dfrac{5i - 3i^2}{4i^2} = \dfrac{5i + 3}{-4} =$
$-\dfrac{3}{4} - \dfrac{5}{4}i$

68. $\dfrac{7}{5} - \dfrac{2}{5}i$

69. $\dfrac{7i + 14}{7i} = \dfrac{7i}{7i} + \dfrac{14}{7i} = 1 + \dfrac{2}{i} = 1 + \dfrac{2}{i} \cdot \dfrac{i}{i} =$
$1 + \dfrac{2i}{i^2} = 1 + \dfrac{2i}{-1} = 1 - 2i$

70. $2 - i$

71. $\dfrac{4 + 5i}{3 - 7i} = \dfrac{4 + 5i}{3 - 7i} \cdot \dfrac{3 + 7i}{3 + 7i} = \dfrac{12 + 28i + 15i + 35i^2}{9 - 49i^2} =$
$\dfrac{12 + 28i + 15i - 35}{9 + 49} = \dfrac{-23 + 43i}{58} = -\dfrac{23}{58} + \dfrac{43}{58}i$

72. $\dfrac{23}{65} + \dfrac{41}{65}i$

73. $\dfrac{3 - 2i}{4 + 3i} = \dfrac{3 - 2i}{4 + 3i} \cdot \dfrac{4 - 3i}{4 - 3i} = \dfrac{12 - 9i - 8i + 6i^2}{16 - 9i^2} =$
$\dfrac{12 - 9i - 8i - 6}{16 + 9} = \dfrac{6 - 17i}{25} = \dfrac{6}{25} - \dfrac{17}{25}i$

74. $\dfrac{1}{15} - \dfrac{4}{5}i$

75. $i^7 = i^6 \cdot i = (i^2)^3 \cdot i = (-1)^3 \cdot i = -1 \cdot i = -i$

76. $-i$

77. $i^{24} = (i^2)^{12} = (-1)^{12} = 1$

78. $-i$

79. $i^{42} = (i^2)^{21} = (-1)^{21} = -1$

80. 1

81. $i^9 = (i^2)^4 \cdot i = (-1)^4 \cdot i = 1 \cdot i = i$

82. i

83. $i^6 = (i^2)^3 = (-1)^3 = -1$

84. 1

85. $(5i)^3 = 5^3 \cdot i^3 = 125 \cdot i^2 \cdot i = 125(-1)(i) = -125i$

86. $-243i$

87. $i^2 + i^4 = -1 + (i^2)^2 = -1 + (-1)^2 = -1 + 1 = 0$

88. i

89. *Writing Exercise*

90. *Writing Exercise*

91. $f(x) = x^2 - 3x,\ g(x) = 2x - 5$

$(f + g)(-2) = f(-2) + g(-2)$

$= (-2)^2 - 3(-2) + 2(-2) - 5$

$= 4 + 6 - 4 - 5$

$= 1$

92. 1

93. $(f \cdot g)(5) = f(5)g(5)$
$$= (5^2 - 3 \cdot 5)(2 \cdot 5 - 5)$$
$$= (25 - 15)(10 - 5)$$
$$= 10 \cdot 5$$
$$= 50$$

94. 0

95. $28 = 3x^2 - 17x$

$$0 = 3x^2 - 17x - 28$$

$$0 = (3x + 4)(x - 7)$$

$3x + 4 = 0 \quad or \quad x - 7 = 0$

$3x = -4 \quad or \qquad x = 7$

$x = -\dfrac{4}{3} \quad or \qquad x = 7$

Both values check. The solutions are $-\dfrac{4}{3}$ and 7.

96. $\left\{ x \left| -\dfrac{29}{3} < x < 5 \right. \right\}$, or $\left(-\dfrac{29}{3}, 5 \right)$

97. *Writing Exercise*

98. *Writing Exercise*

99. $g(3i) = \dfrac{(3i)^4 - (3i)^2}{3i - 1} = \dfrac{81i^4 - 9i^2}{-1 + 3i} = \dfrac{81 + 9}{-1 + 3i} =$

$\dfrac{90}{-1 + 3i} = \dfrac{90}{-1 + 3i} \cdot \dfrac{-1 - 3i}{-1 - 3i} = \dfrac{90(-1 - 3i)}{1 - 9i^2} =$

$\dfrac{90(-1 - 3i)}{1 + 9} = \dfrac{90(-1 - 3i)}{10} = \dfrac{9 \cdot \cancel{10}(-1 - 3i)}{\cancel{10}} =$

$9(-1 - 3i) = -9 - 27i$

100. $-2 + 4i$

101. First we simplify $g(z)$.

$$g(z) = \dfrac{z^4 - z^2}{z - 1} = \dfrac{z^2(z^2 - 1)}{z - 1} = \dfrac{z^2(z + 1)(z - 1)}{z - 1} =$$

$$\dfrac{z^2(z + 1)(\cancel{z - 1})}{\cancel{z - 1}} = z^2(z + 1)$$

Now we substitute.

$g(5i - 1) = (5i - 1)^2(5i - 1 + 1) =$

$(25i^2 - 10i + 1)(5i) =$

$(-25 - 10i + 1)(5i) = (-24 - 10i)(5i) =$

$-120i - 50i^2 = 50 - 120i$

102. $-51 - 21i$

103. $\dfrac{1}{\dfrac{1 - i}{10} - \left(\dfrac{1 - i}{10} \right)^2} = \dfrac{1}{\dfrac{1 - i}{10} - \left(\dfrac{-2i}{100} \right)} =$

$\dfrac{1}{\dfrac{1 - i}{10} + \dfrac{i}{50}} = \dfrac{1}{\dfrac{1 - i}{10} + \dfrac{i}{50}} \cdot \dfrac{50}{50} = \dfrac{50}{5 - 5i + i} =$

$\dfrac{50}{5 - 4i} = \dfrac{50}{5 - 4i} \cdot \dfrac{5 + 4i}{5 + 4i} = \dfrac{250 + 200i}{41} = \dfrac{250}{41} + \dfrac{200}{41}i$

104. 0

105. $(1 - i)^3(1 + i)^3 =$

$(1 - i)(1 + i) \cdot (1 - i)(1 + i) \cdot (1 - i)(1 + i) =$

$(1 - i^2)(1 - i^2)(1 - i^2) = (1 + 1)(1 + 1)(1 + 1) =$

$2 \cdot 2 \cdot 2 = 8$

106. $-1 - \sqrt{5}i$

107. $\dfrac{6}{1 + \dfrac{3}{i}} = \dfrac{6}{\dfrac{i + 3}{i}} = \dfrac{6i}{i + 3} = \dfrac{6i}{i + 3} \cdot \dfrac{-i + 3}{-i + 3} =$

$\dfrac{-6i^2 + 18i}{-i^2 + 9} = \dfrac{6 + 18i}{10} = \dfrac{6}{10} + \dfrac{18}{10}i = \dfrac{3}{5} + \dfrac{9}{5}i$

108. $-\dfrac{2}{3}i$

109. $\dfrac{i - i^{38}}{1 + i} = \dfrac{i - (i^2)^{19}}{1 + i} = \dfrac{i - (-1)^{19}}{1 + i} = \dfrac{i - (-1)}{1 + i} =$

$\dfrac{i + 1}{1 + i} = 1$

Chapter 10

Quadratic Functions and Equations

1. There are 2 x-intercepts, so there are 2 real-number solutions.

2. 0

3. There is 1 x-intercept, so there is 1 real-number solution.

4. 2

5. There are no x-intercepts, so there are no real-number solutions.

6. 1

7. $\quad 7x^2 = 21$

$\qquad x^2 = 3 \qquad$ Multiplying by $\dfrac{1}{7}$

$\quad x = \sqrt{3} \text{ or } x = -\sqrt{3} \quad$ Using the principle of square roots

The solutions are $\sqrt{3}$ and $-\sqrt{3}$, or $\pm\sqrt{3}$.

8. $\pm\sqrt{5}$

9. $\qquad 25x^2 + 4 = 0$

$\qquad x^2 = -\dfrac{4}{25} \qquad$ Isolating x^2

$\quad x = \sqrt{-\dfrac{4}{25}} \text{ or } x = -\sqrt{-\dfrac{4}{25}} \quad$ Principle of square roots

$\quad x = \sqrt{\dfrac{4}{25}}\sqrt{-1} \text{ or } x = -\sqrt{\dfrac{4}{25}}\sqrt{-1}$

$\qquad x = \dfrac{2}{5}i \text{ or } x = -\dfrac{2}{5}i$

The solutions are $\dfrac{2}{5}i$ and $-\dfrac{2}{5}i$, or $\pm\dfrac{2}{5}i$.

10. $\pm\dfrac{4}{3}i$

11. $\quad 3t^2 - 2 = 0$

$\qquad 3t^2 = 2$

$\qquad t^2 = \dfrac{2}{3}$

$\quad t = \sqrt{\dfrac{2}{3}} \quad \text{or} \quad t = -\sqrt{\dfrac{2}{3}} \quad$ Principle of square roots

$\quad t = \sqrt{\dfrac{2}{3}\cdot\dfrac{3}{3}} \quad \text{or} \quad t = -\sqrt{\dfrac{2}{3}\cdot\dfrac{3}{3}} \quad$ Rationalizing denominators

$\quad t = \dfrac{\sqrt{6}}{3} \quad \text{or} \quad t = \dfrac{-\sqrt{6}}{3}$

The solutions are $\sqrt{\dfrac{2}{3}}$ and $-\sqrt{\dfrac{2}{3}}$. This can also be written as $\pm\sqrt{\dfrac{2}{3}}$ or, if we rationalize the denominator, $\pm\dfrac{\sqrt{6}}{3}$.

12. $\pm\dfrac{\sqrt{35}}{5}$

13. $\quad (x+2)^2 = 25$

$\quad x + 2 = 5 \text{ or } x + 2 = -5 \quad$ Principle of square roots

$\qquad x = 3 \text{ or } x = -7$

The solutions are 3 and -7.

14. $-6, 8$

15. $\qquad (a+5)^2 = 8$

$\quad a + 5 = \sqrt{8} \text{ or } a + 5 = -\sqrt{8} \quad$ Principle of square roots

$\quad a + 5 = 2\sqrt{2} \text{ or } a + 5 = -2\sqrt{2} \quad (\sqrt{8} = \sqrt{4\cdot 2} = 2\sqrt{2})$

$\quad a = -5 + 2\sqrt{2} \text{ or } a = -5 - 2\sqrt{2}$

The solutions are $-5 + 2\sqrt{2}$ and $-5 - 2\sqrt{2}$, or $-5 \pm 2\sqrt{2}$.

16. $13 \pm 3\sqrt{2}$

17. $(x-1)^2 = -49$

$\quad x - 1 = \sqrt{-49} \quad \text{or} \quad x - 1 = -\sqrt{-49}$

$\quad x - 1 = 7i \qquad \text{or} \quad x - 1 = -7i$

$\qquad x = 1 + 7i \text{ or } \qquad x = 1 - 7i$

The solutions are $1 + 7i$ and $1 - 7i$, or $1 \pm 7i$.

18. $-1 \pm 3i$

19. $\left(t + \dfrac{3}{2}\right)^2 = \dfrac{7}{2}$

$\quad t + \dfrac{3}{2} = \sqrt{\dfrac{7}{2}} \text{ or } t + \dfrac{3}{2} = -\sqrt{\dfrac{7}{2}}$

$\quad t + \dfrac{3}{2} = \sqrt{\dfrac{7}{2}\cdot\dfrac{2}{2}} \text{ or } t + \dfrac{3}{2} = -\sqrt{\dfrac{7}{2}\cdot\dfrac{2}{2}}$

$\quad t + \dfrac{3}{2} = \dfrac{\sqrt{14}}{2} \text{ or } t + \dfrac{3}{2} = -\dfrac{\sqrt{14}}{2}$

$\quad t = -\dfrac{3}{2} + \dfrac{\sqrt{14}}{2} \text{ or } t = -\dfrac{3}{2} - \dfrac{\sqrt{14}}{2}$

$\quad t = \dfrac{-3 + \sqrt{14}}{2} \text{ or } t = \dfrac{-3 - \sqrt{14}}{2}$

The solutions are $\dfrac{-3 + \sqrt{14}}{2}$ and $\dfrac{-3 - \sqrt{14}}{2}$, or $\dfrac{-3 \pm \sqrt{14}}{2}$.

20. $\dfrac{-3 \pm \sqrt{17}}{4}$

21. $x^2 - 6x + 9 = 100$

$\qquad (x-3)^2 = 100$

$\qquad x - 3 = 10 \ or \ x - 3 = -10$

$\qquad\qquad x = 13 \ or \ x = -7$

The solutions are 13 and -7.

22. $-3, 13$

23. $\qquad f(x) = 16$

$\qquad (x-5)^2 = 16 \qquad$ Substituting

$\qquad x - 5 = 4 \ or \ x - 5 = -4$

$\qquad x = 9 \ \ or \ \ x = 1$

The solutions are 9 and 1.

24. $-3, 7$

25. $\qquad F(t) = 13$

$\qquad (t+4)^2 = 13 \quad$ Substituting

$\qquad t + 4 = \sqrt{13} \qquad or \ \ t + 4 = -\sqrt{13}$

$\qquad\quad t = -4 + \sqrt{13} \ or \qquad t = -4 - \sqrt{13}$

The solutions are $-4 + \sqrt{13}$ and $-4 - \sqrt{13}$, or $-4 \pm \sqrt{13}$.

26. $-6 \pm \sqrt{15}$

27. $g(x) = x^2 + 14x + 49$

Observe first that $g(0) = 49$. Also observe that when $x = -14$, then $x^2 + 14x = (-14)^2 - (14)(14) = (14)^2 - (14)^2 = 0$, so $g(-14) = 49$ as well. Thus, we have $x = 0$ or $x = 14$.

We can also do this problem as follows.

$\qquad\qquad g(x) = 49$

$\qquad x^2 + 14x + 49 = 49 \quad$ Substituting

$\qquad\qquad (x+7)^2 = 49$

$\qquad x + 7 = 7 \ \ or \ \ x + 7 = -7$

$\qquad\quad x = 0 \ \ or \qquad x = -14$

The solutions are 0 and -14.

28. $-7, -1$

29. $x^2 + 8x$

We take half the coefficient of x and square it:

Half of 8 is 4, and $4^2 = 16$. We add 16.

$x^2 + 8x + 16, \ (x+4)^2$

30. $x^2 + 16x + 64, \ (x+8)^2$

31. $x^2 - 6x$

We take half the coefficient of x and square it:

Half of -6 is -3, and $(-3)^2 = 9$. We add 9.

$x^2 - 6x + 9, \ (x-3)^2$

32. $x^2 - 10x + 25, \ (x-5)^2$

33. $x^2 - 24x$

We take half the coefficient of x and square it:

$\dfrac{1}{2}(-24) = -12$ and $(-12)^2 = 144$. We add 144.

$x^2 - 24x + 144, \ (x-12)^2$

34. $x^2 - 18x + 81, \ (x-9)^2$

35. $t^2 + 9t$

$\dfrac{1}{2} \cdot 9 = \dfrac{9}{2}$, and $\left(\dfrac{9}{2}\right)^2 = \dfrac{81}{4}$. We add $\dfrac{81}{4}$.

$t^2 + 9t + \dfrac{81}{4}, \ \left(t + \dfrac{9}{2}\right)^2$

36. $t^2 + 3t + \dfrac{9}{4}, \ \left(t + \dfrac{3}{2}\right)^2$

37. $x^2 - 3x$

We take half the coefficient of x and square it:

$\dfrac{1}{2}(-3) = -\dfrac{3}{2}$ and $\left(-\dfrac{3}{2}\right)^2 = \dfrac{9}{4}$. We add $\dfrac{9}{4}$.

$x^2 - 3x + \dfrac{9}{4}, \ \left(x - \dfrac{3}{2}\right)^2$

38. $x^2 - 7x + \dfrac{49}{4}, \ \left(x - \dfrac{7}{2}\right)^2$

39. $x^2 + \dfrac{2}{3}x$

$\dfrac{1}{2} \cdot \dfrac{2}{3} = \dfrac{1}{3}$, and $\left(\dfrac{1}{3}\right)^2 = \dfrac{1}{9}$. We add $\dfrac{1}{9}$.

$x^2 + \dfrac{2}{3}x + \dfrac{1}{9}, \ \left(x + \dfrac{1}{3}\right)^2$

40. $x^2 + \dfrac{2}{5}x + \dfrac{1}{25}, \ \left(x + \dfrac{1}{5}\right)^2$

41. $t^2 - \dfrac{5}{3}t$

$\dfrac{1}{2}\left(-\dfrac{5}{3}\right) = -\dfrac{5}{6}$, and $\left(-\dfrac{5}{6}\right)^2 = \dfrac{25}{36}$. We add $\dfrac{25}{36}$.

$t^2 - \dfrac{5}{3}t + \dfrac{25}{36}, \ \left(t - \dfrac{5}{6}\right)^2$

42. $t^2 - \dfrac{5}{6}t + \dfrac{25}{144}, \ \left(t - \dfrac{5}{12}\right)^2$

43. $x^2 + \dfrac{9}{5}x$

$\dfrac{1}{2} \cdot \dfrac{9}{5} = \dfrac{9}{10}$, and $\left(\dfrac{9}{10}\right)^2 = \dfrac{81}{100}$. We add $\dfrac{81}{100}$.

$x^2 + \dfrac{9}{5}x + \dfrac{81}{100}, \ \left(x + \dfrac{9}{10}\right)^2$

44. $x^2 + \dfrac{9}{4}x + \dfrac{81}{64}, \ \left(x + \dfrac{9}{8}\right)^2$

45. $x^2 + 6x = 7$

$x^2 + 6x + 9 = 7 + 9$ Adding 9 to both sides to complete the square

$(x+3)^2 = 16$ Factoring

$x + 3 = \pm 4$ Principle of square roots

$x = -3 \pm 4$

$x = -3 + 4$ *or* $x = -3 - 4$

$x = 1$ *or* $x = -7$

The solutions are 1 and -7.

46. $-9, 1$

47. $x^2 - 10x = 22$

$x^2 - 10x + 25 = 22 + 25$ Adding 25 to both sides to complete the square

$(x-5)^2 = 47$

$x - 5 = \pm\sqrt{47}$ Principle of square roots

$x = 5 \pm \sqrt{47}$

The solutions are $5 \pm \sqrt{47}$.

48. $2 \pm i\sqrt{5}$

49. $x^2 + 8x + 7 = 0$

$x^2 + 8x = -7$ Adding -7 to both sides

$x^2 + 8x + 16 = -7 + 16$ Completing the square

$(x+4)^2 = 9$

$x + 4 = +3$

$x = -4 \pm 3$

$x = -4 - 3$ *or* $x = -4 + 3$

$x = -7$ *or* $x = -1$

The solutions are -7 and -1.

50. $-9, -1$

51. $x^2 - 10x + 21 = 0$

$x^2 - 10x = -21$

$x^2 - 10x + 25 = -21 + 25$

$(x-5)^2 = 4$

$x - 5 = \pm 2$

$x = 5 \pm 2$

$x = 5 - 2$ *or* $x = 5 + 2$

$x = 3$ *or* $x = 7$

The solutions are 3 and 7.

52. $4, 6$

53. $t^2 + 5t + 3 = 0$

$t^2 + 5t = -3$

$t^2 + 5t + \dfrac{25}{4} = -3 + \dfrac{25}{4}$

$\left(t + \dfrac{5}{2}\right)^2 = \dfrac{13}{4}$

$t + \dfrac{5}{2} = \pm\dfrac{\sqrt{13}}{2}$

$t = -\dfrac{5}{2} \pm \dfrac{\sqrt{13}}{2}$

$t = \dfrac{-5 \pm \sqrt{13}}{2}$

The solutions are $\dfrac{-5 \pm \sqrt{13}}{2}$.

54. $-3 \pm \sqrt{2}$

55. $x^2 + 10 = 6x$

$x^2 - 6x = -10$

$x^2 - 6x + 9 = -10 + 9$

$(x-3)^2 = -1$

$x - 3 = \pm\sqrt{-1}$

$x - 3 = \pm i$

$x = 3 \pm i$

The solutions are $3 \pm i$.

56. $5 \pm \sqrt{2}$

57. $s^2 + 4s + 13 = 0$

$s^2 + 4s = -13$

$s^2 + 4s + 4 = -13 + 4$

$(s+2)^2 = -9$

$s + 2 = \pm\sqrt{-9}$

$s + 2 = \pm 3i$

$s = -2 \pm 3i$

The solutions are $-2 \pm 3i$.

58. $-6 \pm \sqrt{11}$

59. $2x^2 - 5x - 3 = 0$

$2x^2 - 5x = 3$

$x^2 - \dfrac{5}{2}x = \dfrac{3}{2}$ Dividing both sides by 2

$x^2 - \dfrac{5}{2}x + \dfrac{25}{16} = \dfrac{3}{2} + \dfrac{25}{16}$

$\left(x - \dfrac{5}{4}\right)^2 = \dfrac{49}{16}$

$x - \dfrac{5}{4} = \pm\dfrac{7}{4}$

$x = \dfrac{5}{4} \pm \dfrac{7}{4}$

$x = \dfrac{5}{4} - \dfrac{7}{4}$ *or* $x = \dfrac{5}{4} + \dfrac{7}{4}$

$x = -\dfrac{1}{2}$ *or* $x = 3$

The solutions are $-\dfrac{1}{2}$ and 3.

60. $-2, \dfrac{1}{3}$

61. $4x^2 + 8x + 3 = 0$

$$4x^2 + 8x = -3$$

$$x^2 + 2x = -\dfrac{3}{4}$$

$$x^2 + 2x + 1 = -\dfrac{3}{4} + 1$$

$$(x+1)^2 = \dfrac{1}{4}$$

$$x + 1 = \pm\dfrac{1}{2}$$

$$x = -1 \pm \dfrac{1}{2}$$

$$x = -1 - \dfrac{1}{2} \quad or \quad x = -1 + \dfrac{1}{2}$$

$$x = -\dfrac{3}{2} \quad\quad or \quad x = -\dfrac{1}{2}$$

The solutions are $-\dfrac{3}{2}$ and $-\dfrac{1}{2}$.

62. $-\dfrac{4}{3}, -\dfrac{2}{3}$

63. $6x^2 - x = 15$

$$x^2 - \dfrac{1}{6}x = \dfrac{5}{2}$$

$$x^2 - \dfrac{1}{6}x + \dfrac{1}{144} = \dfrac{5}{2} + \dfrac{1}{144}$$

$$\left(x - \dfrac{1}{12}\right)^2 = \dfrac{361}{144}$$

$$x - \dfrac{1}{12} = \pm\dfrac{19}{12}$$

$$x = \dfrac{1}{12} \pm \dfrac{19}{12}$$

$$x = \dfrac{1}{12} + \dfrac{19}{12} \quad or \quad x = \dfrac{1}{12} - \dfrac{19}{12}$$

$$x = \dfrac{20}{12} \quad\quad or \quad x = -\dfrac{18}{12}$$

$$x = \dfrac{5}{3} \quad\quad or \quad x = -\dfrac{3}{2}$$

The solutions are $\dfrac{5}{3}$ and $-\dfrac{3}{2}$.

64. $-\dfrac{1}{2}, \dfrac{2}{3}$

65. $2x^2 + 4x + 1 = 0$

$$2x^2 + 4x = -1$$

$$x^2 + 2x = -\dfrac{1}{2}$$

$$x^2 + 2x + 1 = -\dfrac{1}{2} + 1$$

$$(x+1)^2 = \dfrac{1}{2}$$

$$x + 1 = \pm\sqrt{\dfrac{1}{2}}$$

$$x + 1 = \pm\dfrac{\sqrt{2}}{2} \qquad \text{Rationalizing the}$$
$$\text{denominator}$$

$$x = -1 \pm \dfrac{\sqrt{2}}{2}$$

The solutions are $-1 \pm \dfrac{\sqrt{2}}{2}$, or $\dfrac{-2 \pm \sqrt{2}}{2}$.

66. $-2, -\dfrac{1}{2}$

67. $3x^2 - 5x - 3 = 0$

$$3x^2 - 5x = 3$$

$$x^2 - \dfrac{5}{3}x = 1$$

$$x^2 - \dfrac{5}{3}x + \dfrac{25}{36} = 1 + \dfrac{25}{36}$$

$$\left(x - \dfrac{5}{6}\right)^2 = \dfrac{61}{36}$$

$$x - \dfrac{5}{6} = \pm\dfrac{\sqrt{61}}{6}$$

$$x = \dfrac{5 \pm \sqrt{61}}{6}$$

The solutions are $\dfrac{5 \pm \sqrt{61}}{6}$.

68. $\dfrac{3 \pm \sqrt{13}}{4}$

69. Familiarize. We are already familiar with the compound-interest formula.

Translate. We substitute into the formula.
$$A = P(1+r)^t$$
$$2420 = 2000(1+r)^2$$

Carry out. We solve for r.
$$2420 = 2000(1+r)^2$$

$$\dfrac{2420}{2000} = (1+r)^2$$

$$\dfrac{121}{100} = (1+r)^2$$

$$\pm\sqrt{\dfrac{121}{100}} = 1+r$$

$$\pm\dfrac{11}{10} = 1+r$$

$$-\dfrac{10}{10} + \dfrac{11}{10} = r$$

$$\dfrac{1}{10} = r \ or \ -\dfrac{21}{10} = r$$

Check. Since the interest rate cannot be negative, we need only check $\frac{1}{10}$, or 10%. If \$2000 were invested at 10% interest, compounded annually, then in 2 years it would grow to $\$2000(1.1)^2$, or \$2420. The number 10% checks.

State. The interest rate is 10%.

70. 6.25%

71. Familiarize. We are already familiar with the compound-interest formula.

Translate. We substitute into the formula.
$$A = P(1+r)^t$$
$$1805 = 1280(1+r)^2$$

Carry out. We solve for r.
$$1805 = 1280(1+r)^2$$
$$\frac{1805}{1280} = (1+r)^2$$
$$\frac{361}{256} = (1+r)^2$$
$$\pm\frac{19}{16} = 1+r$$
$$-\frac{16}{16} \pm \frac{19}{16} = r$$
$$\frac{3}{16} = r \ or \ -\frac{35}{16} = r$$

Check. Since the interest rate cannot be negative, we need only check $\frac{3}{16}$ or 18.75%. If \$1280 were invested at 18.75% interest, compounded annually, then in 2 years it would grow to $\$1280(1.1875)^2$, or \$1805. The number 18.75% checks.

State. The interest rate is 18.75%.

72. 20%

73. Familiarize. We are already familiar with the compound-interest formula.

Translate. We substitute into the formula.
$$A = P(1+r)^t$$
$$6760 = 6250(1+r)^2$$

Carry out. We solve for r.
$$\frac{6760}{6250} = (1+r)^2$$
$$\frac{676}{625} = (1+r)^2$$
$$\pm\frac{26}{25} = 1+r$$
$$-\frac{25}{25} \pm \frac{26}{25} = r$$
$$\frac{1}{25} = r \ or \ -\frac{51}{25} = r$$

Check. Since the interest rate cannot be negative, we need only check $\frac{1}{25}$, or 4%. If \$6250 were invested at 4% interest, compounded annually, then in 2 years it would grow to $\$6250(1.04)^2$, or \$6760. The number 4% checks.

State. The interest rate is 4%.

74. 8%

75. Familiarize. We will use the formula $s = 16t^2$.

Translate. We substitute into the formula.
$$s = 16t^2$$
$$1815 = 16t^2$$

Carry out. We solve for t.
$$1815 = 16t^2$$
$$\frac{1815}{16} = t^2$$
$$\sqrt{\frac{1815}{16}} = t \quad \text{Principle of square roots;}$$
$$\qquad\qquad\qquad \text{rejecting the negative}$$
$$\qquad\qquad\qquad \text{square root}$$
$$10.7 \approx t$$

Check. Since $16(10.7)^2 = 1831.84 \approx 1815$, our answer checks.

State. It would take an object about 10.7 sec to fall freely from the top of the CN Tower.

76. About 6.8 sec

77. Familiarize. We will use the formula $s = 16t^2$.

Translate. We substitute into the formula.
$$s = 16t^2$$
$$640 = 16t^2$$

Carry out. We solve for t.
$$640 = 16t^2$$
$$40 = t^2$$
$$\sqrt{40} = t \quad \text{Principle of square roots;}$$
$$\qquad\qquad \text{rejecting the negative square}$$
$$\qquad\qquad \text{root}$$
$$6.3 \approx t$$

Check. Since $16(6.3)^2 = 635.04 \approx 640$, our answer checks.

State. It would take an object about 6.3 sec to fall freely from the top of the Gateway Arch.

78. About 9.5 sec

79. *Writing Exercise*

80. *Writing Exercise*

81. $at^2 - bt = 3 \cdot 4^2 - 5 \cdot 4$
$$= 3 \cdot 16 - 5 \cdot 4$$
$$= 48 - 20$$
$$= 28$$

82. -92

83. $\sqrt[3]{270} = \sqrt[3]{27 \cdot 10} = \sqrt[3]{27}\sqrt[3]{10} = 3\sqrt[3]{10}$

84. $4\sqrt{5}$

85. $f(x) = \sqrt{3x-5}$
$$f(10) = \sqrt{3 \cdot 10 - 5} = \sqrt{30 - 5} = \sqrt{25} = 5$$

86. 7

87. *Writing Exercise*

88. *Writing Exercise*

89. In order for $x^2 + bx + 81$ to be a square, the following must be true:

$$\left(\frac{b}{2}\right)^2 = 81$$
$$\frac{b^2}{4} = 81$$
$$b^2 = 324$$
$$b = 18 \ or \ b = -18$$

90. ± 14

91. We see that x is a factor of each term, so x is also a factor of $f(x)$. We have $f(x) = x(2x^4 - 9x^3 - 66x^2 + 45x + 280)$. Since $x^2 - 5$ is a factor of $f(x)$ it is also a factor of $2x^4 - 9x^3 - 66x^2 + 45x + 280$. We divide to find another factor.

$$
\begin{array}{r}
2x^2 - 9x - 56 \\
x^2 - 5 \overline{\big)\ 2x^4 - 9x^3 - 66x^2 + 45x + 280} \\
\underline{2x^4 \phantom{{}- 9x^3} - 10x^2 } \\
-9x^3 - 56x^2 + 45x \\
\underline{-9x^3 \phantom{{}- 56x^2} + 45x } \\
-56x^2 + 280 \\
\underline{-56x^2 + 280} \\
0
\end{array}
$$

Then we have $f(x) = x(x^2 - 5)(2x^2 - 9x - 56)$, or $f(x) = x(x^2 - 5)(2x + 7)(x - 8)$. Now we find the values of a for which $f(a) = 0$.

$$f(a) = 0$$
$$a(a^2 - 5)(2a + 7)(a - 8) = 0$$

$a=0 \ or \ a^2-5=0 \quad or \ 2a+7=0 \quad or \ a-8=0$

$a=0 \ or \quad a^2=5 \quad or \quad 2a=-7 \ or \quad a=8$

$a=0 \ or \quad a=\pm\sqrt{5} \ or \quad a=-\dfrac{7}{2} \ or \quad a=8$

The solutions are 0, $\sqrt{5}$, $-\sqrt{5}$, $-\dfrac{7}{2}$, and 8.

92. $\dfrac{1}{3}, \pm\dfrac{2\sqrt{6}}{3}i$

93. **Familiarize**. It is helpful to list information in a chart and make a drawing. Let r represent the speed of the fishing boat. Then $r - 7$ represents the speed of the barge.

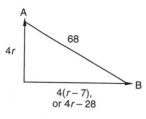

Boat	r	t	d
Fishing	r	4	$4r$
Barge	$r - 7$	4	$4(r - 7)$

Translate. We use the Pythagorean equation:

$$a^2 + b^2 = c^2$$
$$(4r - 28)^2 + (4r)^2 = 68^2$$

Carry out.

$$(4r - 28)^2 + (4r)^2 = 68^2$$
$$16r^2 - 224r + 784 + 16r^2 = 4624$$
$$32r^2 - 224r - 3840 = 0$$
$$r^2 - 7r - 120 = 0$$
$$(r + 8)(r - 15) = 0$$

$r + 8 = 0 \quad or \ r - 15 = 0$

$r = -8 \ or \qquad r = 15$

Check. We check only 15 since the speeds of the boats cannot be negative. If the speed of the fishing boat is 15 km/h, then the speed of the barge is $15 - 7$, or 8 km/h, and the distances they travel are $4 \cdot 15$ (or 60) and $4 \cdot 8$ (or 32).

$$60^2 + 32^2 = 3600 + 1024 = 4624 = 68^2$$

The values check.

State. The speed of the fishing boat is 15 km/h, and the speed of the barge is 8 km/h.

94. 5, 6, 7

Exercise Set 10.2

1. $x^2 + 7x - 3 = 0$

$a = 1, \ b = 7, \ c = -3$

$$x = \frac{-b \pm \sqrt{b^2 - 4ac}}{2a}$$

$$x = \frac{-7 \pm \sqrt{7^2 - 4 \cdot 1 \cdot (-3)}}{2 \cdot 1} = \frac{-7 \pm \sqrt{49 + 12}}{2}$$

$$x = \frac{-7 \pm \sqrt{61}}{2}$$

The solutions are $\dfrac{7 + \sqrt{61}}{2}$ and $\dfrac{7 - \sqrt{61}}{2}$.

2. $\dfrac{7 \pm \sqrt{33}}{2}$

3. $\qquad 3p^2 = 18p - 6$

$3p^2 - 18p + 6 = 0$

$p^2 - 6p + 2 = 0 \qquad$ Dividing by 3

$a = 1, \ b = -6, \ c = 2$

$$p = \frac{-b \pm \sqrt{b^2 - 4ac}}{2a}$$

$$p = \frac{-(-6) \pm \sqrt{(-6)^2 - 4 \cdot 1 \cdot 2}}{2 \cdot 1} = \frac{6 \pm \sqrt{36 - 8}}{2}$$

$$p = \frac{6 \pm \sqrt{28}}{2} = \frac{6 \pm 2\sqrt{7}}{2}$$

$$p = \frac{2(3 \pm \sqrt{7})}{2} = 3 \pm \sqrt{7}$$

The solutions are $3 + \sqrt{7}$ and $3 - \sqrt{7}$.

4. $1, \dfrac{5}{3}$

5. $x^2 - x + 2 = 0$

$a = 1, b = -1, c = 2$

$x = \dfrac{-b \pm \sqrt{b^2 - 4ac}}{2a}$

$x = \dfrac{-(-1) \pm \sqrt{(-1)^2 - 4 \cdot 1 \cdot 2}}{2 \cdot 1} = \dfrac{1 \pm \sqrt{1 - 8}}{2}$

$x = \dfrac{1 \pm \sqrt{-7}}{2} = \dfrac{1 \pm i\sqrt{7}}{2}$

The solutions are $\dfrac{1 + i\sqrt{7}}{2}$ and $\dfrac{1 - i\sqrt{7}}{2}$, or $\dfrac{1}{2} + \dfrac{\sqrt{7}}{2}i$ and $\dfrac{1}{2} - \dfrac{\sqrt{7}}{2}i$.

6. $-\dfrac{1}{2} \pm \dfrac{\sqrt{3}}{2}i$

7. $\qquad x^2 + 13 = 4x$

$x^2 - 4x + 13 = 0$

$a = 1, b = -4, c = 13$

$x = \dfrac{-b \pm \sqrt{b^2 - 4ac}}{2a}$

$x = \dfrac{-(-4) \pm \sqrt{(-4)^2 - 4 \cdot 1 \cdot 13}}{2 \cdot 1} = \dfrac{4 \pm \sqrt{16 - 52}}{2}$

$x = \dfrac{4 \pm \sqrt{-36}}{2} = \dfrac{4 \pm 6i}{2}$

$x = \dfrac{2(2 \pm 3i)}{2} = 2 \pm 3i$

The solutions are $2 + 3i$ and $2 - 3i$.

8. $3 \pm 2i$

The solutions are $3 + 2i$ and $3 - 2i$.

9. $\qquad h^2 + 4 = 6h$

$h^2 - 6h + 4 = 0$

$a = 1, b = -6, c = 4$

$x = \dfrac{-(-6) \pm \sqrt{(-6)^2 - 4 \cdot 1 \cdot 4}}{2 \cdot 1} = \dfrac{6 \pm \sqrt{36 - 16}}{2}$

$x = \dfrac{6 \pm \sqrt{20}}{2} = \dfrac{6 \pm \sqrt{4 \cdot 5}}{2} = \dfrac{6 \pm 2\sqrt{5}}{2}$

$x = 3 \pm \sqrt{5}$

The solutions are $3 + \sqrt{5}$ and $3 - \sqrt{5}$.

10. $\dfrac{-3 \pm \sqrt{41}}{2}$

11. $\qquad 3 + \dfrac{8}{x} = \dfrac{1}{x^2}$, LCD is x^2

$x^2\left(3 + \dfrac{8}{x}\right) = x^2 \cdot \dfrac{1}{x^2}$

$3x^2 + 8x = 1$

$3x^2 + 8x - 1 = 0$

$a = 3, b = 8, c = -1$

$x = \dfrac{-8 \pm \sqrt{8^2 - 4 \cdot 3 \cdot (-1)}}{2 \cdot 3} = \dfrac{-8 \pm \sqrt{64 + 12}}{6}$

$x = \dfrac{-8 \pm \sqrt{76}}{6} = \dfrac{-8 \pm \sqrt{4 \cdot 19}}{6} = \dfrac{-8 \pm 2\sqrt{19}}{6}$

$x = \dfrac{-4 \pm \sqrt{19}}{3}$

The solutions are $\dfrac{-4 + \sqrt{19}}{3}$ and $\dfrac{-4 - \sqrt{19}}{3}$.

12. $\dfrac{9 \pm \sqrt{41}}{4}$

13. $\qquad 3x + x(x - 2) = 4$

$3x + x^2 - 2x = 4$

$x^2 + x = 4$

$x^2 + x - 4 = 0$

$a = 1, b = 1, c = -4$

$x = \dfrac{-1 \pm \sqrt{1^2 - 4 \cdot 1 \cdot (-4)}}{2 \cdot 1} = \dfrac{-1 \pm \sqrt{1 + 16}}{2}$

$x = \dfrac{-1 \pm \sqrt{17}}{2}$

The solutions are $\dfrac{-1 + \sqrt{17}}{2}$ and $\dfrac{-1 - \sqrt{17}}{2}$.

14. $\dfrac{-1 \pm \sqrt{21}}{2}$

15. $\qquad 12x^2 + 9t = 1$

$12t^2 + 9t - 1 = 0$

$a = 12, b = 9, c = -1$

$t = \dfrac{-9 \pm \sqrt{9^2 - 4 \cdot 12 \cdot (-1)}}{2 \cdot 12} = \dfrac{-9 \pm \sqrt{81 + 48}}{24}$

$t = \dfrac{-9 \pm \sqrt{129}}{24}$

The solutions are $\dfrac{-9 + \sqrt{129}}{24}$ and $\dfrac{-9 - \sqrt{129}}{24}$.

16. $-\dfrac{2}{3}, \dfrac{1}{5}$

17. $\qquad 25x^2 - 20x + 4 = 0$

$(5x - 2)(5x - 2) = 0$

$5x - 2 = 0 \quad or \quad 5x - 2 = 0$

$5x = 2 \quad or \qquad 5x = 2$

$x = \dfrac{2}{5} \quad or \qquad x = \dfrac{2}{5}$

The solution is $\dfrac{2}{5}$.

18. $-\dfrac{7}{6}$

19. $7x(x+2) + 5 = 3x(x+1)$

$7x^2 + 14x + 5 = 3x^2 + 3x$

$4x^2 + 11x + 5 = 0$

$a = 4,\, b = 11,\, c = 5$

$x = \dfrac{-11 \pm \sqrt{11^2 - 4 \cdot 4 \cdot 5}}{2 \cdot 4} = \dfrac{-11 \pm \sqrt{121 - 80}}{8}$

$x = \dfrac{-11 \pm \sqrt{41}}{8}$

The solutions are $\dfrac{-11 + \sqrt{41}}{8}$ and $\dfrac{-11 - \sqrt{41}}{8}$.

20. $\dfrac{-3 \pm \sqrt{37}}{2}$

21. $14(x-4) - (x+2) = (x+2)(x-4)$

$14x - 56 - x - 2 = x^2 - 2x - 8$ Removing parentheses

$13x - 58 = x^2 - 2x - 8$

$0 = x^2 - 15x + 50$

$0 = (x - 10)(x - 5)$

$x - 10 = 0 \quad or \quad x - 5 = 0$

$x = 10 \quad or \quad\quad x = 5$

The solutions are 10 and 5.

22. 1, 15

23. $5x^2 = 13x + 17$

$5x^2 - 13x - 17 = 0$

$a = 5,\, b = -13,\, c = -17$

$x = \dfrac{-(-13) \pm \sqrt{(-13)^2 - 4(5)(-17)}}{2 \cdot 5}$

$x = \dfrac{13 \pm \sqrt{169 + 340}}{10} = \dfrac{13 \pm \sqrt{509}}{10}$

The solutions are $\dfrac{13 + \sqrt{509}}{10}$ and $\dfrac{13 - \sqrt{509}}{10}$.

24. $\dfrac{4}{3}, 7$

25. $x^2 + 9 = 4x$

$x^2 - 4x + 9 = 0$

$a = 1,\, b = -4,\, c = 9$

$x = \dfrac{-(-4) \pm \sqrt{(-4)^2 - 4 \cdot 1 \cdot 9}}{2 \cdot 1} = \dfrac{4 \pm \sqrt{16 - 36}}{2}$

$x = \dfrac{4 \pm \sqrt{-20}}{2} = \dfrac{4 \pm \sqrt{-4 \cdot 5}}{2}$

$x = \dfrac{4 \pm 2i\sqrt{5}}{2} = 2 \pm i\sqrt{5}$

The solutions are $2 + i\sqrt{5}$ and $2 - i\sqrt{5}$.

26. $\dfrac{3}{2} \pm \dfrac{\sqrt{19}}{2}i$

27. $x^3 - 8 = 0$

$x^3 - 2^3 = 0$

$(x - 2)(x^2 + 2x + 4) = 0$

$x - 2 = 0 \quad or \quad x^2 + 2x + 4 = 0$

$x = 2 \quad or \quad x = \dfrac{-2 \pm \sqrt{2^2 - 4 \cdot 1 \cdot 4}}{2 \cdot 1}$

$x = 2 \quad or \quad x = \dfrac{-2 \pm \sqrt{-12}}{2} = \dfrac{-2 \pm 2i\sqrt{3}}{2}$

$x = 2 \quad or \quad x = -1 \pm i\sqrt{3}$

The solutions are 2, $-1 + i\sqrt{3}$, and $-1 - i\sqrt{3}$.

28. $\dfrac{1}{2} \pm \dfrac{\sqrt{3}}{2}i$

29. $f(x) = 0$

$3x^2 - 5x - 1 = 0$ Substituting

$a = 3,\, b = -5,\, c = -1$

$x = \dfrac{-(-5) \pm \sqrt{(-5)^2 - 4 \cdot 3 \cdot (-1)}}{2 \cdot 3}$

$x = \dfrac{5 \pm \sqrt{25 + 12}}{6} = \dfrac{5 \pm \sqrt{37}}{6}$

The solutions are $\dfrac{5 + \sqrt{37}}{6}$ and $\dfrac{5 - \sqrt{37}}{6}$.

30. $\dfrac{1 \pm \sqrt{13}}{4}$

31. $f(x) = 1$

$\dfrac{7}{x} + \dfrac{7}{x + 4} = 1$ Substituting

$x(x+4)\left(\dfrac{7}{x} + \dfrac{7}{x+4}\right) = x(x+4) \cdot 1$

             Multiplying by the LCD

$7(x + 4) + 7x = x^2 + 4x$

$7x + 28 + 7x = x^2 + 4x$

$14x + 28 = x^2 + 4x$

$0 = x^2 - 10x - 28$

$a = 1,\, b = -10,\, c = -28$

$x = \dfrac{-(-10) \pm \sqrt{(-10)^2 - 4 \cdot 1 \cdot (-28)}}{2 \cdot 1}$

$x = \dfrac{10 \pm \sqrt{100 + 112}}{2} = \dfrac{10 \pm \sqrt{212}}{2}$

$x = \dfrac{10 \pm \sqrt{4 \cdot 53}}{2} = \dfrac{10 \pm 2\sqrt{53}}{2}$

$x = 5 \pm \sqrt{53}$

The solutions are $5 + \sqrt{53}$ and $5 - \sqrt{53}$.

32. $-2, 3$

33. $F(x) = G(x)$

$\dfrac{x + 3}{x} = \dfrac{x - 4}{3}$ Substituting

$3x\left(\dfrac{x+3}{x}\right) = 3x\left(\dfrac{x-4}{3}\right)$ Multiplying by the LCD

$3x + 9 = x^2 - 4x$

$0 = x^2 - 7x - 9$

$a = 1,\, b = -7,\, c = -9$

$$x = \frac{-(-7) \pm \sqrt{(-7)^2 - 4 \cdot 1 \cdot (-9)}}{2 \cdot 1}$$

$$x = \frac{7 \pm \sqrt{49 + 36}}{2} = \frac{7 \pm \sqrt{85}}{2}$$

The solutions are $\dfrac{7 + \sqrt{85}}{2}$ and $\dfrac{7 - \sqrt{85}}{2}$.

34. $\dfrac{3 \pm \sqrt{5}}{2}$

35.
$$f(x) = g(x)$$
$$\frac{15 - 2x}{6} = \frac{3}{x}, \text{ LCD is } 6x$$
$$6x \cdot \frac{15 - 2x}{6} = 6x \cdot \frac{3}{x}$$
$$x(15 - 2x) = 6 \cdot 3$$
$$15x - 2x^2 = 18$$
$$0 = 2x^2 - 15x + 18$$
$$0 = (2x - 3)(x - 6)$$
$$2x - 3 = 0 \quad or \quad x - 6 = 0$$
$$2x = 3 \quad or \quad x = 6$$
$$x = \frac{3}{2} \quad or \quad x = 6$$

The solutions are $\dfrac{3}{2}$ and 6.

36. $\pm 2\sqrt{7}$

37. $x^2 + 4x - 7 = 0$

$a = 1, b = 4, c = -7$

$$x = \frac{-4 \pm \sqrt{4^2 - 4 \cdot 1 \cdot (-7)}}{2 \cdot 1} = \frac{-4 \pm \sqrt{16 + 28}}{2}$$

$$x = \frac{-4 \pm \sqrt{44}}{2}$$

Using a calculator we find that $\dfrac{-4 + \sqrt{44}}{2} \approx 1.3166$ and $\dfrac{-4 - \sqrt{44}}{2} \approx -5.3166$.

The solutions are approximately 1.3166 and −5.3166.

38. −5.2361, −0.7639

39. $x^2 - 6x + 4 = 0$

$a = 1, b = -6, c = 4$

$$x = \frac{-(-6) \pm \sqrt{(-6)^2 - 4 \cdot 1 \cdot 4}}{2 \cdot 1} = \frac{6 \pm \sqrt{36 - 16}}{2}$$

$$x = \frac{6 \pm \sqrt{20}}{2}$$

Using a calculator we find that $\dfrac{6 + \sqrt{20}}{2} \approx 5.2361$ and $\dfrac{6 - \sqrt{20}}{2} \approx 0.7639$.

The solutions are approximately 5.2361 and 0.7639.

40. 0.2679, 3.7321

41. $2x^2 - 3x - 7 = 0$

$a = 2, b = -3, c = -7$

$$x = \frac{-(-3) \pm \sqrt{(-3)^2 - 4 \cdot 2 \cdot (-7)}}{2 \cdot 2}$$

$$x = \frac{3 \pm \sqrt{9 + 56}}{4} = \frac{3 \pm \sqrt{65}}{4}$$

Using a calculator we find that $\dfrac{3 + \sqrt{65}}{4} \approx 2.7656$ and $\dfrac{3 - \sqrt{65}}{4} \approx -1.2656$.

The solutions are approximately 2.7656 and −1.2656.

42. −0.4574, 1.4574

43. *Writing Exercise*

44. *Writing Exercise*

45. **Familiarize**. Let x = the number of pounds of Kenyan coffee and y = the number of pounds of Peruvian coffee in the mixture. We organize the information in a table.

Type of Coffee	Kenyan	Peruvian	Mixture
Price per pound	$6.75	$11.25	$8.55
Number of pounds	x	y	50
Total cost	$6.75x$	$11.25y$	8.55×50, or $427.50

Translate. From the last two rows of the table we get a system of equations.

$$x + y = 50,$$
$$6.75x + 11.25y = 427.50$$

Solve. Solving the system of equations, we get $(30, 20)$.

Check. The total number of pounds in the mixture is $30 + 20$, or 50. The total cost of the mixture is $6.75(30) + 11.25(20) = 427.50$. The values check.

State. The mixture should consist of 30 lb of Kenyan coffee and 20 lb of Peruvian coffee.

46. 46 cream-filled; 44 glazed

47. $\sqrt{27a^2b^5} \cdot \sqrt{6a^3b} = \sqrt{27a^2b^5 \cdot 6a^3b} =$
$\sqrt{162a^5b^6} = \sqrt{81a^4b^6 \cdot 2a} = \sqrt{81a^4b^6}\sqrt{2a} =$
$9a^2b^3\sqrt{2a}$

48. $4a^2b^3\sqrt{6}$

49.

$$\dfrac{\dfrac{3}{x-1}}{\dfrac{1}{x+1}+\dfrac{2}{x-1}}$$

$$=\dfrac{\dfrac{3}{x-1}}{\dfrac{1}{x+1}+\dfrac{2}{x-1}}\cdot\dfrac{(x-1)(x+1)}{(x-1)(x+1)}$$

$$=\dfrac{3(x+1)}{x-1+2(x+1)}$$

$$=\dfrac{3x+3}{x-1+2x+2}$$

$$=\dfrac{3x+3}{3x+1},\ \text{or}\ \dfrac{3(x+1)}{3x+1}$$

50. $\dfrac{4b}{3ab^2-4a^2}$

51. *Writing Exercise*

52. *Writing Exercise*

53. $f(x)=\dfrac{x^2}{x-2}+1$

To find the x-coordinates of the x-intercepts of the graph of f, we solve $f(x)=0$.

$$\dfrac{x^2}{x-2}+1=0$$
$$x^2+x-2=0 \quad \text{Multiplying by } x-2$$
$$(x+2)(x-1)=0$$

$x=-2\ \text{ or }\ x=1$

The x-intercepts are $(-2,0)$ and $(1,0)$.

54. $(-5-\sqrt{37},0),\ (-5+\sqrt{37},0)$

55.

$$f(x)=g(x)$$
$$\dfrac{x^2}{x-2}+1=\dfrac{4x-2}{x-2}+\dfrac{x+4}{2}$$

Substituting

$$2(x-2)\left(\dfrac{x^2}{x-2}+1\right)=2(x-2)\left(\dfrac{4x-2}{x-2}+\dfrac{x+4}{2}\right)$$

Multiplying by the LCD

$$2x^2+2(x-2)=2(4x-2)+(x-2)(x+4)$$
$$2x^2+2x-4=8x-4+x^2+2x-8$$
$$2x^2+2x-4=x^2+10x-12$$
$$x^2-8x+8=0$$

$a=1,\ b=-8,\ c=8$

$$x=\dfrac{-(-8)\pm\sqrt{(-8)^2-4\cdot1\cdot8}}{2\cdot1}=\dfrac{8\pm\sqrt{64-32}}{2}$$

$$x=\dfrac{8\pm\sqrt{32}}{2}=\dfrac{8\pm\sqrt{16\cdot2}}{2}=\dfrac{8\pm4\sqrt{2}}{2}$$

$$x=4\pm2\sqrt{2}$$

The solutions are $4+2\sqrt{2}$ and $4-2\sqrt{2}$.

56. $-0.4253905297,\ 1.17539053$

57. $z^2+0.84z-0.4=0$

$a=1,\ b=0.84,\ c=-0.4$

$$z=\dfrac{-0.84\pm\sqrt{(0.84)^2-4\cdot1\cdot(-0.4)}}{2\cdot1}$$

$$z=\dfrac{-0.84\pm\sqrt{2.3056}}{2}$$

$$z=\dfrac{-0.84+\sqrt{2.3056}}{2}\approx0.3392101158$$

$$z=\dfrac{-0.84-\sqrt{2.3056}}{2}\approx-1.179210116$$

The solutions are approximately 0.3392101158 and -1.179210116.

58. $\sqrt{3},\ \dfrac{3-\sqrt{3}}{2}$

59. $\sqrt{2}x^2+5x+\sqrt{2}=0$

$$x=\dfrac{-5\pm\sqrt{5^2-4\cdot\sqrt{2}\cdot\sqrt{2}}}{2\sqrt{2}}=\dfrac{-5\pm\sqrt{17}}{2\sqrt{2}},\ \text{or}$$

$$x=\dfrac{-5\pm\sqrt{17}}{2\sqrt{2}}\cdot\dfrac{\sqrt{2}}{\sqrt{2}}=\dfrac{-5\sqrt{2}\pm\sqrt{34}}{4}$$

The solutions are $\dfrac{-5\sqrt{2}\pm\sqrt{34}}{4}$.

60. $-i\pm i\sqrt{1-i}$

61.

$$kx^2+3x-k=0$$
$$k(-2)^2+3(-2)-k=0 \quad \text{Substituting } -2 \text{ for } x$$
$$4k-6-k=0$$
$$3k=6$$
$$k=2$$
$$2x^2+3x-2=0 \quad \text{Substituting } 2 \text{ for } k$$
$$(2x-1)(x+2)=0$$

$2x-1=0\ \text{ or }\ x+2=0$

$x=\dfrac{1}{2}\ \text{ or }\ \qquad x=-2$

The other solution is $\dfrac{1}{2}$.

62. *Writing Exercise*

Exercise Set 10.3

1. *Familiarize*. We first make a drawing, labeling it with the known and unknown information. We can also organize the information in a table. We let r represent the speed and t the time for the first part of the trip.

$$\underset{\text{60 km}}{r\text{ km/h}\quad t\text{ hr}}\quad\bullet\quad\underset{\text{24 km}}{r-4\text{ km/h}\quad 8-t\text{ hr}}$$

Canoe trip	Distance	Speed	Time
1st part	60	r	t
2nd part	24	$r-4$	$8-t$

Translate. Using $r = \dfrac{d}{t}$, we get two equations from the table, $r = \dfrac{60}{t}$ and $r - 4 = \dfrac{24}{8-t}$.

Carry out. We substitute $\dfrac{60}{t}$ for r in the second equation and solve for t.

$$\frac{60}{t} - 4 = \frac{24}{8-t}, \quad \text{LCD is } t(8-t)$$

$$t(8-t)\left(\frac{60}{t} - 4\right) = t(8-t) \cdot \frac{24}{8-t}$$

$$60(8-t) - 4t(8-t) = 24t$$

$$480 - 60t - 32t + 4t^2 = 24t$$

$$4t^2 - 116t + 480 = 0 \qquad \text{Standard form}$$

$$t^2 - 29t + 120 = 0 \qquad \text{Multiplying by } \frac{1}{4}$$

$$(t - 24)(t - 5) = 0$$

$$t = 24 \quad or \quad t = 5$$

Check. Since the time cannot be negative (If $t = 24$, $8 - t = -16$.), we check only 5 hr. If $t = 5$, then $8 - t = 3$. The speed of the first part is $\dfrac{60}{5}$, or 12 km/h. The speed of the second part is $\dfrac{24}{3}$, or 8 km/h. The speed of the second part is 4 km/h slower than the first part. The value checks.

State. The speed of the first part was 12 km/h, and the speed of the second part was 8 km/h.

2. First part: 60 mph; second part: 50 mph

3. Familiarize. We first make a drawing. We also organize the information in a table. We let $r =$ the speed and $t =$ the time of the slower trip.

280 mi	r mph	t hr
280 mi	$r + 5$ mph	$t - 1$ hr

Trip	Distance	Speed	Time
Slower	280	r	t
Faster	280	$r + 5$	$t - 1$

Translate. Using $t = \dfrac{d}{r}$, we get two equations from the table, $t = \dfrac{280}{r}$, and $t - 1 = \dfrac{280}{r+5}$.

Carry out. We substitute $\dfrac{280}{r}$ for t in the second equation and solve for r.

$$\frac{280}{r} - 1 = \frac{280}{r+5}, \quad \text{LCD is } r(r+5)$$

$$r(r+5)\left(\frac{280}{r} - 1\right) = r(r+5) \cdot \frac{280}{r+5}$$

$$280(r+5) - r(r+5) = 280r$$

$$280r + 1400 - r^2 - 5r = 280r$$

$$0 = r^2 + 5r - 1400$$

$$0 = (r - 35)(r + 40)$$

$$r = 35 \quad or \quad r = -40$$

Check. Since negative speed has no meaning in this problem, we check only 35. If $r = 35$, then the time for the slow trip is $\dfrac{280}{35}$, or 8 hours. If $r = 35$ then $r + 5 = 40$ and the time for the fast trip is $\dfrac{280}{40}$, or 7 hours. This is 1 hour less time than the slow trip took, so we have an answer to the problem.

State. The speed is 35 mph.

4. 40 mph

5. Familiarize. We make a drawing and then organize the information in a table. We let $r =$ the speed and $t =$ the time of the Cessna.

600 mi	r mph	t hr
1000 mi	$r + 50$ mph	$t + 1$ hr

Plane	Distance	Speed	Time
Cessna	600	r	t
Beechcraft	1000	$r + 50$	$t + 1$

Translate. Using $t = d/r$, we get two equations from the table:

$$t = \frac{600}{r} \quad \text{and} \quad t + 1 = \frac{1000}{r+50}$$

Carry out. We substitute $\dfrac{600}{r}$ for t in the second equation and solve for r.

$$\frac{600}{r} + 1 - \frac{1000}{r+50},$$
$$\text{LCD is } r(r+50)$$

$$r(r+50)\left(\frac{600}{r} + 1\right) = r(r+50) \cdot \frac{1000}{r+50}$$

$$600(r+50) + r(r+50) = 1000r$$

$$600r + 30,000 + r^2 + 50r = 1000r$$

$$r^2 - 350r + 30,000 = 0$$

$$(r - 150)(r - 200) = 0$$

$$r = 150 \quad or \quad r = 200$$

Check. If $r = 150$, then the Cessna's time is $\dfrac{600}{150}$, or 4 hr and the Beechcraft's time is $\dfrac{1000}{150+50}$, or $\dfrac{1000}{200}$, or 5 hr. If $r = 200$, then the Cessna's time is $\dfrac{600}{200}$, or 3 hr and the Beechcraft's time is $\dfrac{1000}{200+50}$, or $\dfrac{1000}{250}$, or 4 hr. Since the Beechcraft's time is 1 hr longer in each case, both values check. There are two solutions.

State. The speed of the Cessna is 150 mph and the speed of the Beechcraft is 200 mph; or the speed of the Cessna is 200 mph and the speed of the Beechcraft is 250 mph.

6. Super-prop: 350 mph; turbo-jet: 400 mph

7. Familiarize. We make a drawing and then organize the information in a table. We let r represent the speed and t the time of the trip to Hillsboro.

Trip	Distance	Speed	Time
To Hillsboro	40	r	t
Return	40	$r - 6$	$14 - t$

Translate. Using $t = \dfrac{d}{r}$, we get two equations from the table,

$$t = \frac{40}{r} \quad \text{and} \quad 14 - t = \frac{40}{r - 6}.$$

Carry out. We substitute $\dfrac{40}{r}$ for t in the second equation and solve for r.

$$14 - \frac{40}{r} = \frac{40}{r - 6},$$
$$\text{LCD is } r(r - 6)$$
$$r(r - 6)\left(14 - \frac{40}{r}\right) = r(r - 6) \cdot \frac{40}{r - 6}$$
$$14r(r - 6) - 40(r - 6) = 40r$$
$$14r^2 - 84r - 40r + 240 = 40r$$
$$14r^2 - 164r + 240 = 0$$
$$7r^2 - 82r + 120 = 0$$
$$(7r - 12)(r - 10) = 0$$
$$r = \frac{12}{7} \quad or \quad r = 10$$

Check. Since negative speed has no meaning in this problem (If $r = \dfrac{12}{7}$, then $r - 6 = -\dfrac{30}{7}$.), we check only 10 mph. If $r = 10$, then the time of the trip to Hillsboro is $\dfrac{40}{10}$, or 4 hr. The speed of the return trip is $10 - 6$, or 4 mph, and the time is $\dfrac{40}{4}$, or 10 hr. The total time for the round trip is 4 hr + 10 hr, or 14 hr. The value checks.

State. Naoki's speed on the trip to Hillsboro was 10 mph and it was 4 mph on the return trip.

8. Average speed to Richmond: 60 mph; average speed returning: 50 mph

9. **Familiarize.** We make a drawing and organize the information in a table. Let r represent the speed of the barge in still water, and let t represent the time of the trip upriver.

Trip	Distance	Speed	Time
Upriver	24	$r - 4$	t
Downriver	24	$r + 4$	$5 - t$

Translate. Using $t = \dfrac{d}{r}$, we get two equations from the table,

$$t = \frac{24}{r - 4} \quad \text{and} \quad 5 - t = \frac{24}{r + 4}.$$

Carry out. We substitute $\dfrac{24}{r - 4}$ for t in the second equation and solve for r.

$$5 - \frac{24}{r - 4} = \frac{24}{r + 4},$$
$$\text{LCD is } (r - 4)(r + 4)$$
$$(r - 4)(r + 4)\left(5 - \frac{24}{r - 4}\right) = (r - 4)(r + 4) \cdot \frac{24}{r + 4}$$
$$5(r - 4)(r + 4) - 24(r + 4) = 24(r - 4)$$
$$5r^2 - 80 - 24r - 96 = 24r - 96$$
$$5r^2 - 48r - 80 = 0$$

We use the quadratic formula.

$$r = \frac{-(-48) \pm \sqrt{(-48)^2 - 4 \cdot 5 \cdot (-80)}}{2 \cdot 5}$$
$$r = \frac{48 \pm \sqrt{3904}}{10}$$
$$r \approx 11 \quad or \quad r \approx -1.5$$

Check. Since negative speed has no meaning in this problem, we check only 11 mph. If $r \approx 11$, then the speed upriver is about $11 - 4$, or 7 mph, and the time is about $\dfrac{24}{7}$, or 3.4 hr. The speed downriver is about $11 + 4$, or 15 mph, and the time is about $\dfrac{24}{15}$, or 1.6 hr. The total time of the round trip is $3.4 + 1.6$, or 5 hr. The value checks.

State. The barge must be able to travel about 11 mph in still water.

10. About 14 mph

11. **Familiarize.** Let x represent the time it takes one well to fill the pool. Then $x - 6$ represents the time it takes the other well to fill the pool. It takes them 4 hr to fill the pool when both wells are working together, so they can fill $\dfrac{1}{4}$ of the pool in 1 hr. The first well will fill $\dfrac{1}{x}$ of the pool in 1 hr, and the other well will fill $\dfrac{1}{x - 6}$ of the pool in 1 hr.

Translate. We have an equation.

$$\frac{1}{x} + \frac{1}{x - 6} = \frac{1}{4}$$

Carry out. We solve the equation.

We multiply by the LCD, $4x(x - 6)$.

$$4x(x - 6)\left(\frac{1}{x} + \frac{1}{x - 6}\right) = 4x(x - 6) \cdot \frac{1}{4}$$
$$4(x - 6) + 4x = x(x - 6)$$
$$4x - 24 + 4x = x^2 - 6x$$
$$0 = x^2 - 14x + 24$$
$$0 = (x - 2)(x - 12)$$
$$x = 2 \quad or \quad x = 12$$

Check. Since negative time has no meaning in this problem, 2 is not a solution ($2 - 6 = -4$). We check only 12 hr.

This is the time it would take the first well working alone. Then the other well would take $12 - 6$, or 6 hr working alone. The second well would fill $4\left(\frac{1}{6}\right)$, or $\frac{2}{3}$, of the pool in 4 hr, and the first well would fill $4\left(\frac{1}{12}\right)$, or $\frac{1}{3}$, of the pool in 4 hr. Thus in 4 hr they would fill $\frac{2}{3} + \frac{1}{3}$ of the pool. This is all of it, so the numbers check.

State. It takes the first well, working alone, 12 hr to fill the pool.

12. 6 hr

13. We make a drawing and then organize the information in a table. We let r represent Ellen's speed in still water. Then $r - 2$ is the speed upstream and $r + 2$ is the speed downstream. Using $t = \dfrac{d}{r}$, we let $\dfrac{1}{r - 2}$ represent the time upstream and $\dfrac{1}{r + 2}$ represent the time downstream.

1 mi $r - 2$ mph
$\cdot$————————————→ Upstream

        1 mi $r + 2$ mph
Downstream ←————————————$\cdot$

Trip	Distance	Speed	Time
Upstream	1	$r - 2$	$\dfrac{1}{r-2}$
Downstream	1	$r + 2$	$\dfrac{1}{r+2}$

Translate. The time for the round trip is 1 hour. We now have an equation.
$$\frac{1}{r-2} + \frac{1}{r+2} - 1$$

Carry out. We solve the equation. We multiply by the LCD, $(r - 2)(r + 2)$.

$$(r-2)(r+2)\left(\frac{1}{r-2} + \frac{1}{r+2}\right) = (r-2)(r+2) \cdot 1$$
$$(r+2) + (r-2) = (r-2)(r+2)$$
$$2r = r^2 - 4$$
$$0 = r^2 - 2r - 4$$

$a = 1,\ b = -2,\ c = -4$

$$r = \frac{-(-2) \pm \sqrt{(-2)^2 - 4 \cdot 1(-4)}}{2 \cdot 1}$$

$$r = \frac{2 \pm \sqrt{4 + 16}}{2} = \frac{2 \pm \sqrt{20}}{2}$$

$$r = \frac{2 \pm 2\sqrt{5}}{2} = 1 \pm \sqrt{5}$$

$$1 + \sqrt{5} \approx 1 + 2.236 \approx 3.24$$
$$1 - \sqrt{5} \approx 1 - 2.236 \approx -1.24$$

Check. Since negative speed has no meaning in this problem, we check only 3.24 mph. If $r \approx 3.24$, then $r - 2 \approx 1.24$ and $r + 2 \approx 5.24$. The time it takes to travel upstream is approximately $\dfrac{1}{1.24}$, or 0.806 hr, and the time it takes

to travel downstream is approximately $\dfrac{1}{5.24}$, or 0.191 hr. The total time is 0.997 which is approximately 1 hour. The value checks.

State. Ellen's speed in still water is approximately 3.24 mph.

14. About 9.34 km/h

15.
$$A = 4\pi r^2$$

$$\frac{A}{4\pi} = r^2 \qquad \text{Dividing by } 4\pi$$

$$\frac{1}{2}\sqrt{\frac{A}{\pi}} = r \qquad \text{Taking the positive square root}$$

16. $s = \sqrt{\dfrac{A}{6}}$

17.
$$A = 2\pi r^2 + 2\pi rh$$

$$0 = 2\pi r^2 + 2\pi rh - A \qquad \text{Standard form}$$
$$a = 2\pi,\ b = 2\pi h,\ c = -A$$
$$r = \frac{-2\pi h \pm \sqrt{(2\pi h)^2 - 4 \cdot 2\pi \cdot (-A)}}{2 \cdot 2\pi} \qquad \begin{array}{l}\text{Using the}\\\text{quadratic formula}\end{array}$$
$$r = \frac{-2\pi h \pm \sqrt{4\pi^2 h^2 + 8\pi A}}{4\pi}$$
$$r = \frac{-2\pi h \pm 2\sqrt{\pi^2 h^2 + 2\pi A}}{4\pi}$$
$$r = \frac{-\pi h \pm \sqrt{\pi^2 h^2 + 2\pi A}}{2\pi}$$

Since taking the negative square root would result in a negative answer, we take the positive one.
$$r = \frac{-\pi h + \sqrt{\pi^2 h^2 + 2\pi A}}{2\pi}$$

18. $r = \sqrt{\dfrac{Gm_1 m_2}{F}}$

19.
$$N = \frac{kQ_1 Q_2}{s^2}$$

$$Ns^2 = kQ_1 Q_2 \qquad \text{Multiplying by } s^2$$

$$s^2 = \frac{kQ_1 Q_2}{N} \qquad \text{Dividing by } N$$

$$s = \sqrt{\frac{kQ_1 Q_2}{N}} \qquad \begin{array}{l}\text{Taking the positive square}\\\text{root}\end{array}$$

20. $r = \sqrt{\dfrac{A}{\pi}}$

21.
$$T = 2\pi\sqrt{\frac{l}{g}}$$

$$\frac{T}{2\pi} = \sqrt{\frac{l}{g}} \qquad \text{Multiplying by } \frac{1}{2\pi}$$

$$\frac{T^2}{4\pi^2} = \frac{l}{g} \qquad \text{Squaring}$$

$$gT^2 = 4\pi^2 l \qquad \text{Multiplying by } 4\pi^2 g$$

$$g = \frac{4\pi^2 l}{T^2} \qquad \text{Multiplying by } \frac{1}{T^2}$$

22. $b = \sqrt{c^2 - a^2}$

23. $a^2 + b^2 + c^2 = d^2$

$$c^2 = d^2 - a^2 - b^2 \quad \text{Subtracting } a^2 \text{ and } b^2$$

$$c = \sqrt{d^2 - a^2 - b^2} \quad \text{Taking the positive square root}$$

24. $k = \dfrac{3 + \sqrt{9 + 8N}}{2}$

25. $s = v_0 t + \dfrac{gt^2}{2}$

$$0 = \frac{gt^2}{2} + v_0 t - s \quad \text{Standard form}$$

$$a = \frac{g}{2},\ b = v_0,\ c = -s$$

$$t = \frac{-v_0 \pm \sqrt{v_0^2 - 4\left(\frac{g}{2}\right)(-s)}}{2\left(\frac{g}{2}\right)}$$

$$t = \frac{-v_0 \pm \sqrt{v_0^2 + 2gs}}{g}$$

Since taking the negative square root would result in a negative answer, we take the positive one.

$$t = \frac{-v_0 + \sqrt{v_0^2 + 2gs}}{g}$$

26. $r = \dfrac{-\pi s + \sqrt{\pi^2 s^2 + 4\pi A}}{2\pi}$

27. $N = \dfrac{1}{2}(n^2 - n)$

$$N = \frac{1}{2}n^2 - \frac{1}{2}n$$

$$0 = \frac{1}{2}n^2 - \frac{1}{2}n - N$$

$$a = \frac{1}{2},\ b = -\frac{1}{2},\ c = -N$$

$$n = \frac{-\left(-\frac{1}{2}\right) \pm \sqrt{\left(-\frac{1}{2}\right)^2 - 4 \cdot \frac{1}{2} \cdot (-N)}}{2\left(\frac{1}{2}\right)}$$

$$n = \frac{1}{2} \pm \sqrt{\frac{1}{4} + 2N}$$

$$n = \frac{1}{2} \pm \sqrt{\frac{1 + 8N}{4}}$$

$$n = \frac{1}{2} \pm \frac{1}{2}\sqrt{1 + 8N}$$

Since taking the negative square root would result in a negative answer, we take the positive one.

$$n = \frac{1}{2} + \frac{1}{2}\sqrt{1 + 8N}, \text{ or } \frac{1 + \sqrt{1 + 8N}}{2}$$

28. $r = 1 - \sqrt{\dfrac{A}{A_0}}$

29. $V = 3.5\sqrt{h}$

$$V = 12.25h \quad \text{Squaring}$$

$$\frac{V^2}{12.25} = h$$

30. $L = \dfrac{1}{W^2 C}$

31. $at^2 + bt + c = 0$

The quadratic formula gives the result.

$$t = \frac{-b \pm \sqrt{b^2 - 4ac}}{2a}$$

32. $r = -1 + \dfrac{-P_2 + \sqrt{P_2^2 + 4AP_1}}{2P_1}$

33. a) *Familiarize and Translate.* From Example 4, we know

$$t = \frac{-v_0 + \sqrt{v_0^2 + 19.6s}}{9.8}.$$

Carry out. Substituting 500 for s and 0 for v_0, we have

$$t = \frac{0 + \sqrt{0^2 + 19.6(500)}}{9.8}$$

$$t \approx 10.1$$

Check. Substitute 10.1 for t and 0 for v_0 in the original formula. (See Example 4.)

$$s = 4.9t^2 + v_0 t = 4.9(10.1)^2 + 0 \cdot (10.1)^2$$
$$\approx 500$$

The answer checks.

State. It takes about 10.1 sec to reach the ground.

b) *Familiarize and Translate.* From Example 4, we know

$$t = \frac{-v_0 + \sqrt{v_0^2 + 19.6s}}{9.8}.$$

Carry out. Substitute 500 for s and 30 for v_0.

$$t = \frac{-30 + \sqrt{30^2 + 19.6(500)}}{9.8}$$

$$t \approx 7.49$$

Check. Substitute 30 for v_0 and 7.49 for t in the original formula. (See Example 4.)

$$s = 4.9t^2 + v_0 t = 4.9(7.49)^2 + (30)(7.49)$$
$$\approx 500$$

The answer checks.

State. It takes about 7.49 sec to reach the ground.

c) *Familiarize and Translate.* We will use the formula in Example 4, $s = 4.9t^2 + v_0 t$.

Carry out. Substitute 5 for t and 30 for v_0.

$$s = 4.9(5)^2 + 30(5) = 272.5$$

Check. We can substitute 30 for v_0 and 272.5 for s in the form of the formula we used in part (b).

$$t = \frac{-v_0 + \sqrt{v_0^2 + 19.6s}}{9.8}$$

$$= \frac{-30 + \sqrt{(30)^2 + 19.6(272.5)}}{9.8} = 5$$

The answer checks.

State. The object will fall 272.5 m.

34. a) 3.9 sec

b) 1.9 sec

c) 79.6 m

35. *Familiarize and Translate*. From Example 4, we know

$$t = \frac{-v_0 + \sqrt{v_0^2 + 19.6s}}{9.8}.$$

Carry out. Substituting 40 for s and 0 for v_0 we have

$$t = \frac{0 + \sqrt{0^2 + 19.6(40)}}{9.8}$$

$$t \approx 2.9$$

Check. Substitute 2.9 for t and 0 for v_0 in the original formula. (See Example 4.)

$$s = 4.9t^2 + v_0t = 4.9(2.9)^2 + 0(2.9)$$

$$\approx 40$$

The answer checks.

State. He will be falling for about 2.9 sec.

36. 30.625 m

37. *Familiarize and Translate*. From Example 3, we know

$$T = \frac{\sqrt{3V}}{12}.$$

Carry out. Substituting 36 for V, we have

$$T = \frac{\sqrt{3 \cdot 36}}{12}$$

$$T \approx 0.87$$

Check. Substitute 0.87 for T in the original formula. (See Example 3.)

$$48T^2 = V$$

$$48(0.87)^2 = V$$

$$36 \approx V$$

The answer checks.

State. Vince Carter's hang time is about 0.87 sec.

38. 12

39. *Familiarize and Translate*. We will use the formula in Example 4, $s = 4.9t^2 + v_0t$.

Carry out. Solve the formula for v_0.

$$s - 4.9t^2 = v_0t$$

$$\frac{s - 4.9t^2}{t} = v_0$$

Now substitute 51.6 for s and 3 for t.

$$\frac{51.6 - 4.9(3)^2}{3} = v_0$$

$$2.5 = v_0$$

Check. Substitute 3 for t and 2.5 for v_0 in the original formula.

$$s = 4.9(3)^2 + 2.5(3) = 51.6$$

The solution checks.

State. The initial velocity is 2.5 m/sec.

40. 3.2 m/sec

41. *Familiarize and Translate*. From Exercise 32 we know that

$$r = -1 + \frac{-P_2 + \sqrt{P_2^2 + 4P_1A}}{2P_1},$$

where A is the total amount in the account after two years, P_1 is the amount of the original deposit, P_2 is deposited at the beginning of the second year, and r is the annual interest rate.

Carry out. Substitute 3000 for P_1, 1700 for P_2, and 5253.70 for A.

$$r = -1 + \frac{-1700 + \sqrt{(1700)^2 + 4(3000)(5253.70)}}{2(3000)}$$

Using a calculator, we have $r = 0.07$.

Check. Substitute in the original formula in Exercise 32.

$$P_1(1 + r)^2 + P_2(1 + r) = A$$

$$3000(1.07)^2 + 1700(1.07) = A$$

$$5253.70 = A$$

The answer checks.

State. The annual interest rate is 0.07, or 7%.

42. 8.5%

43. *Writing Exercise*

44. *Writing Exercise*

45. $b^2 - 4ac = 6^2 - 4 \cdot 5 \cdot 7$

$$= 36 - 4 \cdot 5 \cdot 7$$

$$= 36 - 140$$

$$= -104$$

46. $2i\sqrt{11}$

47. $\dfrac{x^2 + xy}{2x} = \dfrac{x(x + y)}{2x}$

$$= \frac{x(x + y)}{2 \cdot x}$$

$$= \frac{\cancel{x}(x + y)}{2 \cdot \cancel{x}}$$

$$= \frac{x + y}{2}$$

48. $\dfrac{a^2 - b^2}{b}$

49. $\dfrac{3 + \sqrt{45}}{6} = \dfrac{3 + \sqrt{9 \cdot 5}}{6} = \dfrac{3 + 3\sqrt{5}}{6} = \dfrac{\cancel{3}(1 + \sqrt{5})}{\cancel{3} \cdot 2} =$

$$\frac{1 + \sqrt{5}}{2}$$

50. $\dfrac{1 - \sqrt{7}}{5}$

51. *Writing Exercise*

52. *Writing Exercise*

53.
$$A = 6.5 - \frac{20.4t}{t^2 + 36}$$

$$(t^2 + 36)A = (t^2 + 36)\left(6.5 - \frac{20.4t}{t^2 + 36}\right)$$

$$At^2 + 36A = (t^2 + 36)(6.5) - (t^2 + 36)\left(\frac{20.4t}{t^2 + 36}\right)$$

$$At^2 + 36A = 6.5t^2 + 234 - 20.4t$$

$$At^2 - 6.5t^2 + 20.4 + 36A - 234 = 0$$

$$(A - 6.5)t^2 + 20.4t + (36A - 234) = 0$$

$$a = A - 6.5, \ b = 20.4, \ c = 36A - 234$$

$$t = \frac{-20.4 \pm \sqrt{(20.4)^2 - 4(A - 6.5)(36A - 234)}}{2(A - 6.5)}$$

$$t = \frac{-20.4 \pm \sqrt{416.16 - 144A^2 + 1872A - 6084}}{2(A - 6.5)}$$

$$t = \frac{-20.4 \pm \sqrt{-144A^2 + 1872A - 5667.84}}{2(A - 6.5)}$$

$$t = \frac{-20.4 \pm \sqrt{144(-A^2 + 13A - 39.36)}}{2(A - 6.5)}$$

$$t = \frac{-20.4 \pm 12\sqrt{-A^2 + 13A - 39.36}}{2(A - 6.5)}$$

$$t = \frac{2(-10.2 \pm 6\sqrt{-A^2 + 13A - 39.36})}{2(A - 6.5)}$$

$$t = \frac{-10.2 \pm 6\sqrt{-A^2 + 13A - 39.36}}{A - 6.5}$$

54. $c = \dfrac{mv}{\sqrt{m^2 - m_0^2}}$

55.
$$\frac{w}{l} = \frac{l}{w + l}$$

$$l(w + l) \cdot \frac{w}{l} = l(w + l) \cdot \frac{l}{w + l}$$

$$w(w + l) = l^2$$

$$w^2 + lw = l^2$$

$$0 = l^2 - lw - w^2$$

Use the quadratic formula with $a = 1$, $b = -w$, and $c = -w^2$.

$$l = \frac{-(-w) \pm \sqrt{(-w)^2 - 4 \cdot 1 (-w^2)}}{2 \cdot 1}$$

$$l = \frac{w \pm \sqrt{w^2 + 4w^2}}{2} = \frac{w \pm \sqrt{5w^2}}{2}$$

$$l = \frac{w \pm w\sqrt{5}}{2}$$

Since $\dfrac{w - w\sqrt{5}}{2}$ is negative we use the positive square root:

$$l = \frac{w + w\sqrt{5}}{2}$$

56. $L(A) = \sqrt{\dfrac{A}{2}}$

57. Familiarize. Let $a =$ the number. Then $a - 1$ is 1 less than a and the reciprocal of that number is $\dfrac{1}{a - 1}$. Also, 1 more than the number is $a + 1$.

Translate.

The reciprocal of 1 less than a number	is	1 more than the number.
$\dfrac{1}{(a - 1)}$	$=$	$a + 1$

Carry out. We solve the equation.

$$\frac{1}{a - 1} = a + 1, \ \text{LCD is } a - 1$$

$$(a - 1) \cdot \frac{1}{a - 1} = (a - 1)(a + 1)$$

$$1 = a^2 - 1$$

$$2 = a^2$$

$$\pm\sqrt{2} = a$$

Check. $\dfrac{1}{\sqrt{2} - 1} \approx 2.4142 \approx \sqrt{2} + 1$ and $\dfrac{1}{-\sqrt{2} - 1} \approx -0.4142 \approx -\sqrt{2} + 1$. The answers check.

State. The numbers are $\sqrt{2}$ and $-\sqrt{2}$, or $\pm\sqrt{2}$.

58. \$2.50

59. $mn^4 - r^2pm^3 - r^2n^2 + p = 0$

Let $u = n^2$. Substitute and rearrange.

$$mu^2 - r^2u - r^2pm^3 + p = 0$$

$$a = m, \ b = -r^2, \ c = -r^2pm^3 + p$$

$$u = \frac{-(-r^2) \pm \sqrt{(-r^2)^2 - 4 \cdot m(-r^2pm^3 + p)}}{2 \cdot m}$$

$$u = \frac{r^2 \pm \sqrt{r^4 + 4m^4r^2p - 4mp}}{2m}$$

$$n^2 = \frac{r^2 \pm \sqrt{r^4 + 4m^4r^2p - 4mp}}{2m}$$

$$n = \pm\sqrt{\frac{r^2 \pm \sqrt{r^4 + 4m^4r^2p - 4mp}}{2m}}$$

60. $d = \dfrac{-\pi h + \sqrt{\pi^2 h^2 + 2\pi A}}{\pi}$

61. Let s represent a length of a side of the cube, let S represent the surface area of the cube, and let A represent the surface area of the sphere. Then the diameter of the sphere is s, so the radius r is $s/2$. From Exercise 15, we know, $A = 4\pi r^2$, so when $r = s/2$ we have $A = 4\pi\left(\dfrac{s}{2}\right)^2 = 4\pi \cdot \dfrac{s^2}{4} = \pi s^2$. From the formula for the surface area of a cube (See Exercise 16.) we know that $S = 6s^2$, so $\dfrac{S}{6} = s^2$ and then $A = \pi \cdot \dfrac{S}{6}$, or $A(S) = \dfrac{\pi S}{6}$.

62. *Writing Exercise*

Exercise Set 10.4

1. $x^2 - 5x + 3 = 0$

$a = 1$, $b = -5$, $c = 3$

We substitute and compute the discriminant.

$b^2 - 4ac = (-5)^2 - 4 \cdot 1 \cdot 3$

$\qquad = 25 - 12$

$\qquad = 13$

Since the discriminant is a positive number that is not a perfect square, there are two irrational solutions.

2. Two irrational

3. $x^2 + 5 = 0$

$a = 1$, $b = 0$, $c = 5$

We substitute and compute the discriminant.

$b^2 - 4ac = 0^2 - 4 \cdot 1 \cdot 5$

$\qquad = -20$

Since the discriminant is negative, there are two imaginary-number solutions.

4. Two imaginary

5. $x^2 - 3 = 0$

$a = 1$, $b = 0$, $c = -3$

We substitute and compute the discriminant.

$b^2 - 4ac = 0^2 - 4 \cdot 1 \cdot (-3)$

$\qquad = 12$

Since the discriminant is a positive number that is not a perfect square, there are two irrational solutions.

6. Two irrational

7. $4x^2 - 12x + 9 = 0$

$a = 4$, $b = -12$, $c = 9$

We substitute and compute the discriminant.

$b^2 - 4ac = (-12)^2 - 4 \cdot 4 \cdot 9$

$\qquad = 144 - 144$

$\qquad = 0$

Since the discriminant is 0, there is just one solution, and it is a rational number.

8. Two rational

9. $x^2 - 2x + 4 = 0$

$a = 1$, $b = -2$, $c = 4$

We substitute and compute the discriminant.

$b^2 - 4ac = (-2)^2 - 4 \cdot 1 \cdot 4$

$\qquad = 4 - 16$

$\qquad = -12$

Since the discriminant is negative, there are two imaginary-number solutions.

10. Two imaginary

11. $6t^2 - 19t - 20 = 0$

$a = 6$, $b = -19$, $c = -20$

We substitute and compute the discriminant.

$b^2 - 4ac = (-19)^2 - 4 \cdot 6 \cdot (-20)$

$\qquad = 361 + 480$

$\qquad = 841$

Since the discriminant is a positive number and a perfect square, there are two rational solutions.

12. One rational

13. $6x^2 + 5x - 4 = 0$

$a = 6$, $b = 5$, $c = -4$

We substitute and compute the discriminant.

$b^2 - 4ac = 5^2 - 4 \cdot 6 \cdot (-4)$

$\qquad = 25 + 96 = 121$

Since the discriminant is a positive number and a perfect square, there are two rational solutions.

14. Two rational

15. $9t^2 - 3t = 0$

Observe that we can factor $9t^2 - 3t$. This tells us that there are two rational solutions. We could also do this problem as follows.

$a = 9$, $b = -3$, $c = 0$

We substitute and compute the discriminant.

$b^2 - 4ac = (-3)^2 - 4 \cdot 9 \cdot 0$

$\qquad = 9 - 0$

$\qquad = 9$

Since the discriminant is a positive number and a perfect square, there are two rational solutions.

16. Two rational

17. $x^2 + 4x = 8$

$x^2 + 4x - 8 = 0$ Standard form

$a = 1$, $b = 4$, $c = -8$

We substitute and compute the discriminant.

$b^2 - 4ac = 4^2 - 4 \cdot 1 \cdot (-8)$

$\qquad = 16 + 32 = 48$

Since the discriminant is a positive number that is not a perfect square, there are two irrational solutions.

18. Two irrational

19. $\qquad 2a^2 - 3a = -5$

$2a^2 - 3a + 5 = 0$ Standard form

$a = 2$, $b = -3$, $c = 5$

We substitute and compute the discriminant.

$b^2 - 4ac = (-3)^2 - 4 \cdot 2 \cdot 5$

$\qquad = 9 - 40$

$\qquad = -31$

Since the discriminant is negative, there are two imaginary-number solutions.

20. Two imaginary

21.
$$y^2 + \frac{9}{4} = 4y$$

$$y^2 - 4y + \frac{9}{4} = 0 \quad \text{Standard form}$$

$a = 1, \, b = -4, \, c = \dfrac{9}{4}$

We substitute and compute the discriminant.

$$b^2 - 4ac = (-4)^2 - 4 \cdot 1 \cdot \frac{9}{4}$$
$$= 16 - 9$$
$$= 7$$

The discriminant is a positive number that is not a perfect square. There are two irrational solutions.

22. Two imaginary

23. The solutions are -7 and 3.
$$x = -7 \quad or \quad x = 3$$
$$x + 7 = 0 \quad or \quad x - 3 = 0$$
$$(x + 7)(x - 3) = 0 \quad \text{Principle of zero products}$$
$$x^2 + 4x - 21 = 0 \quad \text{FOIL}$$

24. $x^2 + 2x - 24 = 0$

25. The only solution is 3. It must be a repeated solution.
$$x = 3 \quad or \quad x = 3$$
$$x - 3 = 0 \quad or \quad x - 3 = 0$$
$$(x - 3)(x - 3) = 0 \quad \text{Principle of zero products}$$
$$x^2 - 6x + 9 = 0 \quad \text{FOIL}$$

26. $x^2 + 10x + 25 = 0$

27. The solutions are -2 and -5.
$$x = -2 \quad or \quad x = -5$$
$$x + 2 = 0 \quad or \quad x + 5 = 0$$
$$(x + 2)(x + 5) = 0$$
$$x^2 + 7x + 10 = 0$$

28. $x^2 + 4x + 3 = 0$

29. The solutions are 4 and $\dfrac{2}{3}$.
$$x = 4 \quad or \quad x = \frac{2}{3}$$
$$x - 4 = 0 \quad or \quad x - \frac{2}{3} = 0$$
$$(x - 4)\left(x - \frac{2}{3}\right) = 0$$
$$x^2 - \frac{2}{3}x - 4x + \frac{8}{3} = 0$$
$$x^2 - \frac{14}{3}x + \frac{8}{3} = 0$$
$$3x^2 - 14x + 8 = 0 \quad \text{Multiplying by 3}$$

30. $4x^2 - 23x + 15 = 0$

31. The solutions are $\dfrac{1}{2}$ and $\dfrac{1}{3}$.
$$x = \frac{1}{2} \quad or \quad x = \frac{1}{3}$$
$$x - \frac{1}{2} = 0 \quad or \quad x - \frac{1}{3} = 0$$
$$\left(x - \frac{1}{2}\right)\left(x - \frac{1}{3}\right) = 0$$
$$x^2 - \frac{1}{3}x - \frac{1}{2}x + \frac{1}{6} = 0$$
$$x^2 - \frac{5}{6}x + \frac{1}{6} = 0$$
$$6x^2 - 5x + 1 = 0 \quad \text{Multiplying by 6}$$

32. $8x^2 + 6x + 1 = 0$

33. The solutions are -0.6 and 1.4.
$$x = -0.6 \quad or \quad x = 1.4$$
$$x + 0.6 = 0 \quad or \quad x - 1.4 = 0$$
$$(x + 0.6)(x - 1.4) = 0$$
$$x^2 - 1.4x + 0.6x - 0.84 = 0$$
$$x^2 - 0.8x - 0.84 = 0$$

34. $x^2 - 2x - 0.96 = 0$

35. The solutions are $-\sqrt{7}$ and $\sqrt{7}$.
$$x = -\sqrt{7} \quad or \quad x = \sqrt{7}$$
$$x + \sqrt{7} = 0 \quad or \quad x - \sqrt{7} = 0$$
$$(x + \sqrt{7})(x - \sqrt{7}) = 0$$
$$x^2 - 7 = 0$$

36. $x^2 - 3 = 0$

37. The solutions are $3\sqrt{2}$ and $-3\sqrt{2}$.
$$x = 3\sqrt{2} \quad or \quad x = -3\sqrt{2}$$
$$x - 3\sqrt{2} = 0 \quad or \quad x + 3\sqrt{2} = 0$$
$$(x - 3\sqrt{2})(x + 3\sqrt{2}) = 0$$
$$x^2 - (3\sqrt{2})^2 = 0$$
$$x^2 - 9 \cdot 2 = 0$$
$$x^2 - 18 = 0$$

38. $x^2 - 20 = 0$

39. The solutions are $3i$ and $-3i$.
$$x = 3i \quad or \quad x = -3i$$
$$x - 3i = 0 \quad or \quad x + 3i = 0$$
$$(x - 3i)(x + 3i) = 0$$
$$x^2 - (3i)^2 = 0$$
$$x^2 + 9 = 0$$

40. $x^2 + 16 = 0$

41. The solutions are $5 - 2i$ and $5 + 2i$.
$$x = 5 - 2i \quad or \quad x = 5 + 2i$$
$$x - 5 + 2i = 0 \quad or \quad x - 5 - 2i = 0$$

$$[x + (-5 + 2i)][x + (-5 - 2i)] = 0$$
$$x^2 + x(-5-2i) + x(-5+2i) + (-5+2i)(-5-2i) = 0$$
$$x^2 - 5x - 2xi - 5x + 2xi + 25 - 4i^2 = 0$$
$$x^2 - 10x + 29 = 0$$
$$(i^2 = -1)$$

42. $x^2 - 4x + 53 = 0$

43. The solutions are $2 - \sqrt{10}$ and $2 + \sqrt{10}$.
$$x = 2 - \sqrt{10} \quad or \quad x = 2 + \sqrt{10}$$
$$x - (2 - \sqrt{10}) = 0 \quad or \quad x - (2 + \sqrt{10}) = 0$$
$$[x - (2 - \sqrt{10})][x - (2 + \sqrt{10})] = 0$$
$$x^2 - x(2 + \sqrt{10}) - x(2 - \sqrt{10}) + (2 - \sqrt{10})(2 + \sqrt{10}) = 0$$
$$x^2 - 2x - x\sqrt{10} - 2x + x\sqrt{10} + 4 - 10 = 0$$
$$x^2 - 4x - 6 = 0$$

44. $x^2 - 6x - 5 = 0$

45. The solutions are -2, 1, and 5.
$$x = -2 \quad or \quad x = 1 \quad or \quad x = 5$$
$$x + 2 = 0 \quad or \quad x - 1 = 0 \quad or \quad x - 5 = 0$$
$$(x+2)(x-1)(x-5) = 0$$
$$(x^2 + x - 2)(x-5) = 0$$
$$x^3 + x^2 - 2x - 5x^2 - 5x + 10 = 0$$
$$x^3 - 4x^2 - 7x + 10 = 0$$

46. $x^3 + 3x^2 - 10x = 0$

47. The solutions are -1, 0, and 3.
$$x = -1 \quad or \quad x = 0 \quad or \quad x = 3$$
$$x + 1 = 0 \quad or \quad x = 0 \quad or \quad x - 3 = 0$$
$$(x+1)(x)(x-3) = 0$$
$$(x^2 + x)(x-3) = 0$$
$$x^3 - 3x^2 + x^2 - 3x = 0$$
$$x^3 - 2x^2 - 3x = 0$$

48. $x^3 - 3x^2 - 4x + 12 = 0$

49. *Writing Exercise*

50. *Writing Exercise*

51. $(3a^2)^4 = 3^4(a^2)^4 = 81a^{2 \cdot 4} = 81a^8$

52. $16x^6$

53. $f(x) = x^2 - 7x - 8$

We find the values of x for which $f(x) = 0$.
$$x^2 - 7x - 8 = 0$$
$$(x-8)(x+1) = 0$$
$$x - 8 = 0 \quad or \quad x + 1 = 0$$
$$x = 8 \quad or \quad x = -1$$

The x-intercepts are $(8, 0)$ and $(-1, 0)$.

54. $(2, 0)$, $(4, 0)$

55. *Familiarize*. Let x and y represent the number of 30-sec and 60-sec commercials, respectively. Then the amount of time for the 30-sec commercials was $30x$ sec, or $\dfrac{30x}{60} = \dfrac{x}{2}$ min. The amount of time for the 60-sec commercials was $60x$ sec, or $\dfrac{60x}{60} = x$ min.

Translate. Rewording, we write two equations. We will express time in minutes.

$$\underbrace{\text{Total number of commercials}}_{x+y} \underbrace{\text{is}}_{=} \underbrace{12.}_{12}$$

$$\underbrace{\begin{array}{c}\text{Time for}\\\text{30-sec}\\\text{commercials}\end{array}}_{\dfrac{x}{2}} \underbrace{\text{is}}_{=} \underbrace{\begin{array}{c}\text{total}\\\text{commercial}\\\text{time}\end{array}}_{\dfrac{x}{2}+x} \underbrace{\text{less}}_{-} \underbrace{\text{6 min.}}_{6}$$

Carry out. Solving the system of equations we get $(6, 6)$.

Check. If there are six 30-sec and six 60-sec commercials, the total number of commercials is 12. The amount of time for six 30-sec commercials is 180 sec, or 3 min, and for six 60-sec commercials is 360 sec, or 6 min. The total commercial time is 9 min, and the amount of time for 30-sec commercials is 6 min less than this. The numbers check.

State. There were six 30-sec commercials.

56.

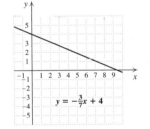

57. *Writing Exercise*

58. *Writing Exercise*

59. The graph includes the points $(-3, 0)$, $(0, -3)$, and $(1, 0)$. Substituting in $y = ax^2 + bx + c$, we have three equations.
$$0 = 9a - 3b + c,$$
$$-3 = \qquad\qquad c,$$
$$0 = a + b + c$$

The solution of this system of equations is $a = 1$, $b = 2$, $c = -3$.

60. Consider a quadratic equation in standard form, $ax^2 + bx + c = 0$. The solutions are
$$\frac{-b \pm \sqrt{b^2 - 4ac}}{2a}.$$
The product of the solutions is
$$\left(\frac{-b + \sqrt{b^2 - 4ac}}{2a}\right)\left(\frac{-b - \sqrt{b^2 - 4ac}}{2a}\right) =$$
$$\frac{(-b)^2 - (\sqrt{b^2 - 4ac})^2}{(2a)^2} = \frac{b^2 - (b^2 - 4ac)}{4a^2} = \frac{4ac}{4a^2} = \frac{c}{a}.$$

61. a) $kx^2 - 2x + k = 0$; one solution is -3

We first find k by substituting -3 for x.

$$k(-3)^2 - 2(-3) + k = 0$$
$$9k + 6 + k = 0$$
$$10k = -6$$
$$k = -\frac{6}{10}$$
$$k = -\frac{3}{5}$$

b) Now substitute $-\frac{3}{5}$ for k in the original equation.

$$-\frac{3}{5}x^2 - 2x + \left(-\frac{3}{5}\right) = 0$$
$$3x^2 + 10x + 3 = 0 \quad \text{Multiplying by } -5$$
$$(3x + 1)(x + 3) = 0$$
$$x = -\frac{1}{3} \text{ or } x = -3$$

The other solution is $-\frac{1}{3}$.

62. a) 2

b) $1 - i$

63. a) $x^2 - (6 + 3i)x + k = 0$; one solution is 3.

We first find k by substituting 3 for x.

$$3^2 - (6 + 3i)3 + k = 0$$
$$9 - 18 - 9i + k = 0$$
$$-9 - 9i + k = 0$$
$$k = 9 + 9i$$

b) Now we substitute $9 + 9i$ for k in the original equation.

$$x^2 - (6 + 3i)x + (9 + 9i) = 0$$
$$x^2 - (6 + 3i)x + 3(3 + 3i) = 0$$
$$[x - (3 + 3i)][x - 3] = 0$$
$$x = 3 + 3i \text{ or } x = 3$$

The other solution is $3 + 3i$.

64. Consider a quadratic equation in standard form, $ax^2 + bx + c = 0$. The solutions are

$$\frac{-b \pm \sqrt{b^2 - 4ac}}{2a}.$$

The sum of the solutions is

$$\frac{-b + \sqrt{b^2 - 4ac}}{2a} + \frac{-b - \sqrt{b^2 - 4ac}}{2a} = \frac{-2b}{2a} = -\frac{b}{a}.$$

65. The solutions of $ax^2 + bx + c = 0$ are $x = \dfrac{-b \pm \sqrt{b^2 - 4ac}}{2a}$.

When there is just one solution, $b^2 - 4ac = 0$, so $x = \dfrac{-b \pm 0}{2a} = -\dfrac{b}{2a}$.

66. $h = -36$, $k = 15$

67. We substitute $(-3, 0)$, $\left(\frac{1}{2}, 0\right)$, and $(0, -12)$ in $f(x) = ax^2 + bx + c$ and get three equations.

$$0 = 9a - 3b + c,$$
$$0 = \frac{1}{4}a + \frac{1}{2}b + c,$$
$$-12 = c$$

The solution of this system of equations is $a = 8$, $b = 20$, $c = -12$.

68. $x^4 - 14x^3 + 70x^2 - 126x + 29 = 0$

69. If $1 - \sqrt{5}$ and $3 + 2i$ are two solutions, then $1 + \sqrt{5}$ and $3 - 2i$ are also solutions. The equation of lowest degree that has these solutions is found as follows.

$$[x - (1 - \sqrt{5})][x - (1 + \sqrt{5})][x - (3 + 2i)][x - (3 - 2i)] = 0$$
$$(x^2 - 2x - 4)(x^2 - 6x + 13) = 0$$
$$x^4 - 8x^3 + 21x^2 - 2x - 52 = 0$$

70. *Writing Exercise*

Exercise Set 10.5

1. $x^4 - 10x^2 + 9 = 0$

Let $u = x^2$ and $u^2 = x^4$.

$$u^2 - 10u + 9 = 0 \quad \text{Substituting}$$
$$(u - 1)(u - 9) = 0$$
$$u - 1 = 0 \text{ or } u - 9 = 0$$
$$u = 1 \text{ or } \quad u = 9$$

Now replace u with x^2 and solve these equations:

$$x^2 = 1 \quad \text{or } x^2 = 9$$
$$x = \pm 1 \quad \text{or} \quad x = \pm 3$$

The numbers 1, -1, 3, and -3 check. They are the solutions.

2. $\pm 1, \pm 2$

3. $x^4 - 12x^2 + 27 = 0$

Let $u = x^2$ and $u^2 = x^4$.

$$u^2 - 12u + 27 = 0 \quad \text{Substituting } u \text{ for } x^2$$
$$(u - 9)(u - 3) = 0$$
$$u = 9 \text{ or } u = 3$$

Now replace u with x^2 and solve these equations:

$$x^2 = 9 \quad \text{or } x^2 = 3$$
$$x = \pm 3 \text{ or} \quad x = \pm\sqrt{3}$$

The numbers 3, -3, $\sqrt{3}$, and $-\sqrt{3}$ check. They are the solutions.

4. $\pm\sqrt{5}, \pm 2$

5. $9x^4 - 14x^2 + 5 = 0$

Let $u = x^2$ and $u^2 = x^4$.

$$9u^2 - 14u + 5 = 0 \quad \text{Substituting}$$
$$(9u - 5)(u - 1) = 0$$

$9u - 5 = 0$ or $u - 1 = 0$

$9u = 5$ or $u = 1$

$u = \dfrac{5}{9}$ or $u = 1$

Now replace u with x^2 and solve these equations:

$x^2 = \dfrac{5}{9}$ or $x^2 = 1$

$x = \pm\dfrac{\sqrt{5}}{3}$ or $x = \pm 1$

The numbers $\dfrac{\sqrt{5}}{3}$, $-\dfrac{\sqrt{5}}{3}$, 1, and -1 check. They are the solutions.

6. $\pm\dfrac{\sqrt{3}}{2}, \pm 2$

7. $x - 4\sqrt{x} - 1 = 0$

Let $u = \sqrt{x}$ and $u^2 = x$.

$u^2 - 4u - 1 = 0$ Substituting

$u = \dfrac{-(-4) \pm \sqrt{(-4)^2 - 4 \cdot 1 \cdot (-1)}}{2 \cdot 1}$

$u = \dfrac{4 \pm \sqrt{20}}{2} = \dfrac{2 \cdot 2 \pm 2\sqrt{5}}{2}$

$u = 2 \pm \sqrt{5}$

$u = 2 + \sqrt{5}$ or $u = 2 - \sqrt{5}$

Replace u with $\sqrt{x}$ and solve these equations.

$\sqrt{x} = 2 + \sqrt{5}$ or $\sqrt{x} = 2 - \sqrt{5}$

$(\sqrt{x})^2 = (2 + \sqrt{5})^2$ No solution:

$2 - \sqrt{5}$ is negative

$x = 4 + 4\sqrt{5} + 5$

$x = 9 + 4\sqrt{5}$

The number $9 + 4\sqrt{5}$ checks. It is the solution.

8. $8 + 2\sqrt{7}$

9. $(x^2 - 7)^2 - 3(x^2 - 7) + 2 = 0$

Let $u = x^2 - 7$ and $u^2 = (x^2 - 7)^2$.

$u^2 - 3u + 2 = 0$ Substituting

$(u - 1)(u - 2) = 0$

$u = 1$ or $u = 2$

$x^2 - 7 = 1$ or $x^2 - 7 = 2$ Replacing u
with $x^2 - 7$

$x^2 = 8$ or $x^2 = 9$

$x = \pm\sqrt{8}$ or $x = \pm 3$

$x = \pm 2\sqrt{2}$ or $x = \pm 3$

The numbers $2\sqrt{2}$, $-2\sqrt{3}$, 3, and -3 check. They are the solutions.

10. $\pm\sqrt{3}, \pm 2$

11. $(1 + \sqrt{x})^2 + 5(1 + \sqrt{x}) + 6 = 0$

Let $u = 1 + \sqrt{x}$ and $u^2 = (1 + \sqrt{x})^2$.

$u^2 + 5u + 6 = 0$ Substituting

$(u + 3)(u + 2) = 0$

$u = -3$ or $u = -2$

$1 + \sqrt{x} = -3$ or $1 + \sqrt{x} = -2$ Replacing u
with $1 + \sqrt{x}$

$\sqrt{x} = -4$ or $\sqrt{x} = -3$

Since the principal square root cannot be negative, this equation has no solution.

12. No solution

13. $x^{-2} - x^{-1} - 6 = 0$

Let $u = x^{-1}$ and $u^2 = x^{-2}$.

$u^2 - u - 6 = 0$ Substituting

$(u - 3)(u + 2) = 0$

$u = 3$ or $u = -2$

Now we replace u with x^{-1} and solve these equations:

$x^{-1} = 3$ or $x^{-1} = -2$

$\dfrac{1}{x} = 3$ or $\dfrac{1}{x} = -2$

$\dfrac{1}{3} = x$ or $-\dfrac{1}{2} = x$

Both $\dfrac{1}{3}$ and $-\dfrac{1}{2}$ check. They are the solutions.

14. $-2, 1$

15. $4x^{-2} + x^{-1} - 5 = 0$

Let $u = x^{-1}$ and $u^2 = x^{-2}$.

$4u^2 + u - 5 = 0$ Substituting

$(4u + 5)(u - 1) = 0$

$u = -\dfrac{5}{4}$ or $u = 1$

Now we replace u with x^{-1} and solve these equations:

$x^{-1} = -\dfrac{5}{4}$ or $x^{-1} = 1$

$\dfrac{1}{x} = -\dfrac{5}{4}$ or $\dfrac{1}{x} = 1$

$4 = -5x$ or $1 = x$

$-\dfrac{4}{5} = x$ or $1 = x$

The numbers $-\dfrac{4}{5}$ and 1 check. They are the solutions.

16. $-\dfrac{1}{10}, 1$

17. $t^{2/3} + t^{1/3} - 6 = 0$

Let $u = t^{1/3}$ and $u^2 = t^{2/3}$.

$u^2 + u - 6 = 0$ Substituting

$(u + 3)(u - 2) = 0$

$u = -3$ or $u = 2$

Now we replace u with $t^{1/3}$ and solve these equations:

$t^{1/3} = -3$ or $t^{1/3} = 2$

$t = (-3)^3$ or $t = 2^3$ Raising to the
third power

$t = -27$ or $t = 8$

Both -27 and 8 check. They are the solutions.

18. $-8, 64$

19. $y^{1/3} - y^{1/6} - 6 = 0$

Let $u = y^{1/6}$ and $u^2 = y^{2/3}$.

$u^2 - u - 6 = 0$ Substituting

$(u - 3)(u + 2) = 0$

$u = 3$ or $u = -2$

Now we replace u with $y^{1/6}$ and solve these equations:

$y^{1/6} = 3$ or $y^{1/6} = -2$

$\sqrt[6]{y} = 3$ or $\sqrt[6]{y} = -2$

$y = 3^6$ This equation has no

$y = 729$ solution since principal

              sixth roots are never negative.

The number 729 checks and is the solution.

20. No solution

21. $t^{1/3} + 2t^{1/6} = 3$

$t^{1/3} + 2t^{1/6} - 3 = 0$

Let $u = t^{1/6}$ and $u^2 = t^{2/6} = t^{1/3}$.

$u^2 + 2u - 3 = 0$ Substituting

$(u + 3)(u - 1) = 0$

$u = -3$ or $u = 1$

$t^{1/6} = -3$ or $t^{1/6} = 1$ Substituting $t^{1/6}$ for u

No solution $t = 1$

The number 1 checks and is the solution.

22. $16, 81$

23. $(3 - \sqrt{x})^2 - 10(3 - \sqrt{x}) + 23 = 0$

Let $u = 3 - \sqrt{x}$ and $u^2 = (3 - \sqrt{x})^2$.

$u^2 - 10u + 23 = 0$ Substituting

$u = \dfrac{-(-10) \pm \sqrt{(-10)^2 - 4 \cdot 1 \cdot 23}}{2 \cdot 1}$

$u = \dfrac{10 \pm \sqrt{8}}{2} = \dfrac{2 \cdot 5 \pm 2\sqrt{2}}{2}$

$u = 5 \pm \sqrt{2}$

$u = 5 + \sqrt{2}$ or $u = 5 - \sqrt{2}$

Now we replace u with $3 - \sqrt{x}$ and solve these equations:

$3 - \sqrt{x} = 5 + \sqrt{2}$ or $3 - \sqrt{x} = 5 - \sqrt{2}$

$-\sqrt{x} = 2 + \sqrt{2}$ or $-\sqrt{x} = 2 - \sqrt{2}$

$\sqrt{x} = -2 - \sqrt{2}$ or $\sqrt{x} = -2 + \sqrt{2}$

Since both $-2 - \sqrt{2}$ and $-2 + \sqrt{2}$ are negative and principal square roots are never negative, the equation has no solution.

24. $4 + 2\sqrt{3}$

25. $16\left(\dfrac{x-1}{x-8}\right)^2 + 8\left(\dfrac{x-1}{x-8}\right) + 1 = 0$

Let $u = \dfrac{x-1}{x-8}$ and $u^2 = \left(\dfrac{x-1}{x-8}\right)^2$.

$16u^2 + 8u + 1 = 0$ Substituting

$(4u + 1)(4u + 1) = 0$

$u = -\dfrac{1}{4}$

Now we replace u with $\dfrac{x-1}{x-8}$ and solve this equation:

$\dfrac{x-1}{x-8} = -\dfrac{1}{4}$

$4x - 4 = -x + 8$ Multiplying by $4(x - 8)$

$5x = 12$

$x = \dfrac{12}{5}$

The number $\dfrac{12}{5}$ checks and is the solution.

26. $-\dfrac{3}{2}$

27. The x-intercepts occur where $f(x) = 0$. Thus, we must have $5x + 13\sqrt{x} - 6 = 0$.

Let $u = \sqrt{x}$ and $u^2 = x$.

$5u^2 + 13u - 6 = 0$ Substituting

$(5u - 2)(u + 3) = 0$

$u = \dfrac{2}{5}$ or $u = -3$

Now replace u with $\sqrt{x}$ and solve these equations:

$\sqrt{x} = \dfrac{2}{5}$ or $\sqrt{x} = -3$

$x = \dfrac{4}{25}$ No solution

The number $\dfrac{4}{25}$ checks. Thus, the x-intercept is $\left(\dfrac{4}{25}, 0\right)$.

28. $\left(\dfrac{4}{9}, 0\right)$

29. The x-intercepts occur where $f(x) = 0$. Thus, we must have $(x^2 - 3x)^2 - 10(x^2 - 3x) + 24 = 0$.

Let $u = x^2 - 3x$ and $u^2 = (x^2 - 3x)^2$.

$u^2 - 10u + 24 = 0$ Substituting

$(u - 6)(u - 4) = 0$

$u = 6$ or $u = 4$

Now replace u with $x^2 - 3x$ and solve these equations:

$x^2 - 3x = 6$ or $x^2 - 3x = 4$

$x^2 - 3x - 6 = 0$ or $x^2 - 3x - 4 = 0$

$x = \dfrac{-(-3) \pm \sqrt{(-3)^2 - 4(1)(-6)}}{2 \cdot 1}$ or

$(x - 4)(x + 1) = 0$

$x = \dfrac{3 \pm \sqrt{33}}{2}$ or $x = 4$ or $x = -1$

All four numbers check. Thus, the x-intercepts are $\left(\dfrac{3 + \sqrt{33}}{2}, 0\right)$, $\left(\dfrac{3 - \sqrt{33}}{2}, 0\right)$, $(4, 0)$, and $(-1, 0)$.

30. $(-1, 0), (1, 0), (5, 0), (7, 0)$

31. The x-intercepts occur where $f(x) = 0$. Thus, we must have $x^{2/5} + x^{1/5} - 6 = 0$.

Let $u = x^{1/5}$ and $u^2 = x^{2/5}$.

$$u^2 + u - 6 = 0 \quad \text{Substituting}$$

$$(u + 3)(u - 2) = 0$$

$$u = -3 \quad or \quad u = 2$$

$$x^{1/5} = -3 \quad or \quad x^{1/5} = 2 \quad \begin{array}{l}\text{Replacing } u \\ \text{with } x^{1/5}\end{array}$$

$$x = -243 \, or \quad x = 32 \quad \begin{array}{l}\text{Raising to the fifth} \\ \text{power}\end{array}$$

Both -243 and 32 check. Thus, the x-intercepts are $(-243, 0)$ and $(32, 0)$.

32. $(81, 0)$

33. $f(x) = \left(\dfrac{x^2 + 2}{x}\right)^4 + 7\left(\dfrac{x^2 + 2}{x}\right)^2 + 5$

Observe that, for all real numbers x, each term is positive. Thus, there are no real-number values of x for which $f(x) = 0$ and hence no x-intercepts.

34. No x-intercepts

35. *Writing Exercise*

36. *Writing Exercise*

37. Graph $f(x) = \dfrac{3}{2}x$.

We find some ordered pairs, plot points, and draw the graph.

x	y
-4	-6
-2	-3
0	0
2	3
4	6

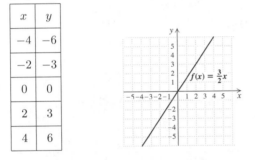

38.

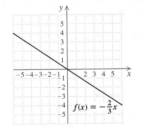

39. Graph $g(x) = \dfrac{2}{x}$.

We find some ordered pairs, plot points, and draw the graph. Note that we cannot use 0 as a first coordinate since division by 0 is undefined.

x	y
-4	$-\dfrac{1}{2}$
-2	-1
$-\dfrac{1}{2}$	-4
$\dfrac{1}{2}$	4
2	1
4	$\dfrac{1}{2}$

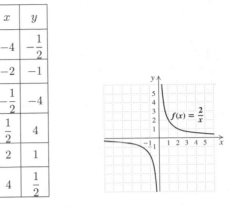

40.

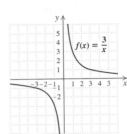

41. *Familiarize.* Let $a =$ the number of liters of solution A in the mixture and $b =$ the number of liters of solution B. We organize the information in a table.

Solution	A	B	Mixture
Number of liters	a	b	12
Percent of alcohol	18%	45%	36%
Amount of alcohol	$0.18a$	$0.45b$	0.36(12), or 4.32 L

From the first row of the table we get one equation:

$$a + b = 12$$

We get a second equation from the last row of the table:

$$0.18a + 0.45b = 4.32$$

After clearing decimals, we have the following system of equations:

$$a + \quad b = 12, \quad (1)$$

$$18a + 45b = 432 \quad (2)$$

Carry out. We use the elimination method. First we multiply equation (1) by -18 and then add.

$$-18a - 18b = -216$$

$$\underline{18a + 45b = 432}$$

$$27b = 216$$

$$b = 8$$

Now we substitute 8 for b in one of the original equations and solve for a.

$$a + b = 12 \quad (1)$$

$$a + 8 = 12$$

$$a = 4$$

Check. If 4 L of solution A and 8 L of solution B are used, the mixture has $4 + 8$, or 12 L. The amount of alcohol in 4 L of solution A is $0.18(4)$, or 0.72 L. The amount of alcohol in 8 L of solution B is $0.45(8)$, or 3.6 L. Then the amount of alcohol in the mixture is $0.72 + 3.6$, or 4.32 L. The answer checks.

State. The mixture should contain 4 L of solution A and 8 L of solution B.

42. $a^2 + a$

43. *Writing Exercise*

44. *Writing Exercise*

45. $5x^4 - 7x^2 + 1 = 0$

Let $u = x^2$ and $u^2 = x^4$.

$5u^2 - 7u + 1 = 0$ Substituting

$$u = \frac{-(-7) \pm \sqrt{(-7)^2 - 4 \cdot 5 \cdot 1}}{2 \cdot 5}$$

$$u = \frac{7 \pm \sqrt{29}}{10}$$

$$x^2 = \frac{7 \pm \sqrt{29}}{10} \qquad \text{Replacing } u \text{ with } x^2$$

$$x = \pm\sqrt{\frac{7 \pm \sqrt{29}}{10}}$$

All four numbers check and are the solutions.

46. $\pm\sqrt{\dfrac{-5 \pm \sqrt{37}}{6}}$

47. $(x^2 - 4x - 2)^2 - 13(x^2 - 4x - 2) + 30 = 0$

Let $u = x^2 - 4x - 2$ and $u^2 = (x^2 - 4x - 2)^2$.

$u^2 - 13u + 30 = 0$ Substituting

$(u - 3)(u - 10) = 0$

$u = 3$ *or* $u = 10$

$x^2 - 4x - 2 = 3$ *or* $x^2 - 4x - 2 = 10$

Replacing u with $x^2 - 4x - 2$

$x^2 - 4x - 5 = 0$ *or* $x^2 - 4x - 12 = 0$

$(x - 5)(x + 1) = 0$ *or* $(x - 6)(x + 2) = 0$

$x = 5$ *or* $x = -1$ *or* $x = 6$ *or* $x = -2$

All four numbers check and are the solutions.

48. $-2, -1, 6, 7$

49. $\dfrac{x}{x - 1} - 6\sqrt{\dfrac{x}{x - 1}} - 40 = 0$

Let $u = \sqrt{\dfrac{x}{x - 1}}$ and $u^2 = \dfrac{x}{x - 1}$.

$u^2 - 6u - 40 = 0$ Substituting

$(u - 10)(u + 4) = 0$

$u = 10$ *or* $u = -4$

$\sqrt{\dfrac{x}{x - 1}} = 10$ *or* $\sqrt{\dfrac{x}{x - 1}} = -4$

$\dfrac{x}{x - 1} = 100$ *or* No solution

$x = 100x - 100$ Multiplying by $(x - 1)$

$100 = 99x$

$\dfrac{100}{99} = x$

The number $\dfrac{100}{99}$ checks. It is the solution.

50. $\dfrac{432}{143}$

51. $a^5(a^2 - 25) + 13a^3(25 - a^2) + 36a(a^2 - 25) = 0$

$a^5(a^2 - 25) - 13a^3(a^2 - 25) + 36a(a^2 - 25) = 0$

$a(a^2 - 25)(a^4 - 13a^2 + 36) = 0$

$a(a^2 - 25)(a^2 - 4)(a^2 - 9) = 0$

$a=0$ *or* $a^2 - 25=0$ *or* $a^2 - 4=0$ *or* $a^2 - 9 = 0$

$a=0$ *or* $a^2=25$ *or* $a^2=4$ *or* $a^2 = 9$

$a=0$ *or* $a=\pm5$ *or* $a=\pm2$ *or* $a = \pm3$

All seven numbers check. The solutions are 0, 5, -5, 2, -2, 3, and -3.

52. 9

53. $x^6 - 28x^3 + 27 = 0$

Let $u = x^3$.

$u^2 - 28u + 27 = 0$

$(u - 27)(u - 1) = 0$

$u = 27$ *or* $u = 1$

$x^3 = 27$ *or* $x^3 = 1$

$x = 3$ *or* $x = 1$

Both 3 and 1 check. They are the solutions.

54. $-2, 1$

Exercise Set 10.6

1. a) The parabola opens upward, so a is positive.

b) The vertex is $(3, 1)$.

c) The axis of symmetry is $x = 3$.

d) The range is $[1, \infty)$.

2. a) Negative

b) $(-1, 2)$

c) $x = -1$

d) $(-\infty, 2]$

3. a) The parabola opens downward, so a is negative.

b) The vertex is $(-2, -3)$.

c) The axis of symmetry is $x = -2$.

d) The range is $(-\infty, -3]$.

4. a) Positive

   b) $(2, 0)$

   c) $x = 2$

   d) $[0, \infty)$

5. a) The parabola opens upward, so a is positive.

   b) The vertex is $(-3, 0)$.

   c) The axis of symmetry is $x = -3$.

   d) The range is $[0, \infty)$.

6. a) Negative

   b) $(1, -2)$

   c) $x = 1$

   d) $(-\infty, -2]$

7. $a = 3$ and $3 > 0$, so the graph opens up; the vertex is $(0, 0)$. Graph (f) matches this function.

8. (c)

9. $a = -1$ and $-1 < 0$, so the graph opens down; the vertex is $(2, 0)$. Graph (e) matches this function.

10. (b)

11. $a = \dfrac{2}{3}$ and $\dfrac{2}{3} > 0$, so the graph opens up; the vertex is $(-3, 1)$. Graph (d) matches this function.

12. (a)

13. $f(x) = x^2$

See Example 1 in the text.

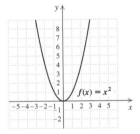

14.

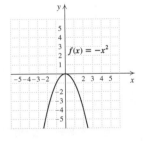

15. $f(x) = -2x^2$

We choose some numbers for x and compute $f(x)$ for each one. Then we plot the ordered pairs $(x, f(x))$ and connect them with a smooth curve.

x	$f(x) = -4x^2$
0	0
1	-2
2	-8
-1	-2
-2	-8

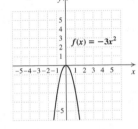

16.

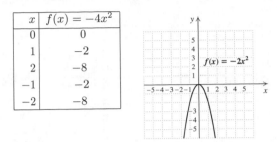

17. $g(x) = \dfrac{1}{3}x^2$

x	$g(x) = \dfrac{1}{3}x^2$
0	0
1	$\dfrac{1}{3}$
2	$\dfrac{4}{3}$
3	3
-1	$\dfrac{1}{3}$
-2	$\dfrac{4}{3}$
-3	3

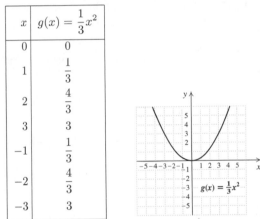

18.

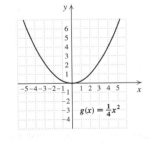

19. $h(x) = -\dfrac{1}{3}x^2$

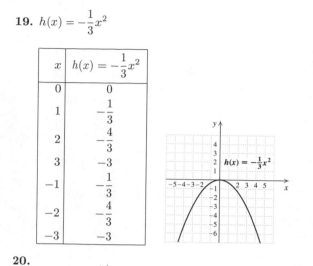

x	$h(x) = -\dfrac{1}{3}x^2$
0	0
1	$-\dfrac{1}{3}$
2	$-\dfrac{4}{3}$
3	-3
-1	$-\dfrac{1}{3}$
-2	$-\dfrac{4}{3}$
-3	-3

20.

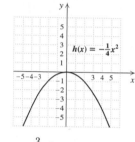

21. $f(x) = \dfrac{3}{2}x^2$

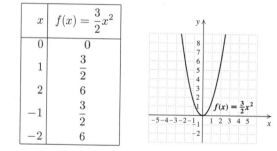

x	$f(x) = \dfrac{3}{2}x^2$
0	0
1	$\dfrac{3}{2}$
2	6
-1	$\dfrac{3}{2}$
-2	6

22.

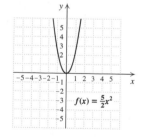

23. $g(x) = (x+1)^2 = [x - (-1)]^2$

We know that the graph of $g(x) = (x+1)^2$ looks like the graph of $f(x) = x^2$ (see Exercise 13) but moved to the left 1 unit.

Vertex: $(-1, 0)$, axis of symmetry: $x = -1$

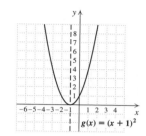

24.

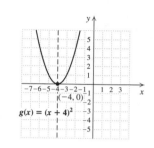

25. $f(x) = (x-2)^2$

The graph of $f(x) = (x-2)^2$ looks like the graph of $f(x) = x^2$ (see Exercise 13) but moved to the right 2 units.

Vertex: $(2, 0)$, axis of symmetry: $x = 2$

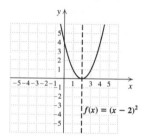

26.

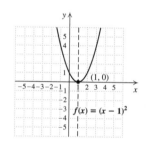

27. $f(x) = -(x+4)^2 = -[x - (-4)]^2$

The graph of $f(x) = -(x+4)^2$ looks like the graph of $f(x) = x^2$ (see Exercise 13) but moved to the left 4 units. It will also open downward because of the negative coefficient, -1.

Vertex: $(-4, 0)$, axis of symmetry: $x = -4$

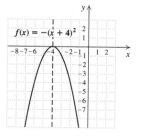

28.

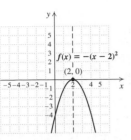

29. $f(x) = 2(x+1)^2$

The graph of $f(x) = 2(x+1)^2$ looks like the graph of $h(x) = 2x^2$ (see graph following Example 1) but moved to the left 1 unit.

Vertex: $(-1, 0)$, axis of symmetry: $x = -1$

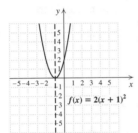

30.

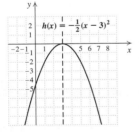

31. $h(x) = -\dfrac{1}{2}(x-3)^2$

The graph of $h(x) = -\dfrac{1}{2}(x-3)^2$ looks like the graph of $g(x) = \dfrac{1}{2}x^2$ (see graph following Example 1) but moved to the right 3 units. It will also open downward because of the negative coefficient, $-\dfrac{1}{2}$.

Vertex: $(3, 0)$, axis of symmetry: $x = 3$

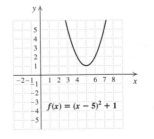

32.

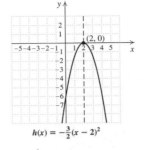

33. $f(x) = \dfrac{1}{2}(x-1)^2$

The graph of $f(x) = \dfrac{1}{2}(x-1)^2$ looks like the graph of $g(x) = \dfrac{1}{2}x^2$ (see graph following Example 1) but moved to the right 1 unit.

Vertex: $(1, 0)$, axis of symmetry: $x = 1$

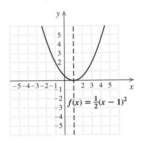

34.

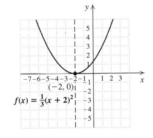

35. $f(x) = (x-5)^2 + 1$

We know that the graph looks like the graph of $f(x) = x^2$ (see Example 1) but moved to the right 5 units and up 1 unit. The vertex is $(5, 1)$, and the axis of symmetry is $x = 5$. Since the coefficient of $(x-5)^2$ is positive ($1 > 0$), there is a minimum function value, 1.

36. $f(x) = (x+3)^2 - 2$

Vertex: $(-3, -2)$, axis of symmetry: $x = -3$

Minimum: -2

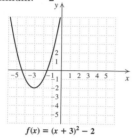

$f(x) = (x + 3)^2 - 2$

37. $f(x) = (x+1)^2 - 2$

We know that the graph looks like the graph of $f(x) = x^2$ (see Example 1) but moved to the left 1 unit and down 2 units. The vertex is $(-1, -2)$, and the axis of symmetry is $x = -1$. Since the coefficient of $(x+1)^2$ is positive $(1 > 0)$, there is a minimum function value, -2.

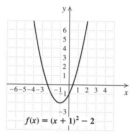

$f(x) = (x + 1)^2 - 2$

38. $g(x) = -(x-2)^2 - 4$

Vertex: $(2, -4)$, axis of symmetry: $x = 2$

Maximum: -4

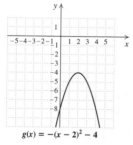

$g(x) = -(x - 2)^2 - 4$

39. $h(x) = -2(x-1)^2 - 3$

We know that the graph looks like the graph of $h(x) = x^2$ (see Example 1) but it is more narrow, moved to the right 1 unit and down 3 units, and turned upside down. The vertex is $(1, -3)$, and the axis of symmetry is $x = 1$. The maximum function value is -3.

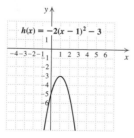

$h(x) = -2(x - 1)^2 - 3$

40. $h(x) = -2(x+1)^2 + 4$

Vertex: $(-1, 4)$, axis of symmetry: $x = -1$

Maximum: 4

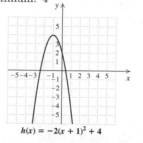

$h(x) = -2(x + 1)^2 + 4$

41. $f(x) = 2(x+4)^2 + 1$

We know that the graph looks like the graph of $f(x) = x^2$ (see Example 1) but it is more narrow and is moved to the left 4 units and up 1 unit. The vertex is $(-4, 1)$, the axis of symmetry is $x = -4$, and the minimum function value is 1.

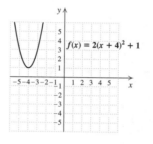

$f(x) = 2(x + 4)^2 + 1$

42. $f(x) = 2(x-5)^2 - 3$

Vertex: $(5, -3)$, axis of symmetry: $x = 5$

Minimum: -3

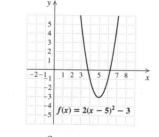

$f(x) = 2(x - 5)^2 - 3$

43. $g(x) = -\dfrac{3}{2}(x-1)^2 + 2$

We know that the graph looks like the graph of $f(x) = \dfrac{3}{2}x^2$ (see Exercise 21) but moved to the right 1 unit and up 2 units and turned upside down. The vertex is $(1, 2)$, the axis of symmetry is $x = 1$, and the maximum function value is 2.

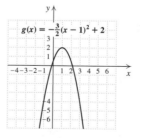

$g(x) = -\dfrac{3}{2}(x - 1)^2 + 2$

44. $g(x) = \dfrac{3}{2}(x+2)^2 - 1$

Vertex: $(-2, -1)$, axis of symmetry: $x = -2$

Minimum: -1

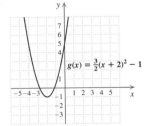

45. $f(x) = 8(x-9)^2 + 5$

This function is of the form $f(x) = a(x-h)^2 + k$ with $a = 8$, $h = 9$, and $k = 5$. The vertex is (h, k), or $(9, 5)$. The axis of symmetry is $x = h$, or $x = 9$. Since $a > 0$, then k, or 5, is the minimum function value. The range is $[5, \infty)$.

46. Vertex: $(-5, -8)$

Axis of symmetry: $x = -5$

Minimum: -8

Range: $[-8, \infty)$

47. $h(x) = -\dfrac{2}{7}(x+6)^2 + 11$

This function is of the form $f(x) = a(x-h)^2 + k$ with $a = -\dfrac{2}{7}$, $h = -6$, and $k = 11$. The vertex is (h, k), or $(-6, 11)$. The axis of symmetry is $x = h$, or $x = -6$. Since $a < 0$, then k, or 11, is the maximum function value. The range is $(-\infty, 11]$.

48. Vertex: $(7, -9)$

Axis of symmetry: $x = 7$

Maximum: -9

Range: $(-\infty, -9]$

49. $f(x) = 5\left(x + \dfrac{1}{4}\right)^2 - 13$

This function is of the form $f(x) = a(x-h)^2 + k$ with $a = 5$, $h = -\dfrac{1}{4}$, and $k = -13$. The vertex is (h, k), or $\left(-\dfrac{1}{4}, -13\right)$. The axis of symmetry is $x = h$, or $x = -\dfrac{1}{4}$. Since $a > 0$, then k, or -13, is the minimum function value. The range is $[-13, \infty)$.

50. Vertex: $\left(\dfrac{1}{4}, 19\right)$

Axis of symmetry: $x = \dfrac{1}{4}$

Minimum: 19

Range: $[19, \infty)$

51. $f(x) = \sqrt{2}(x + 4.58)^2 + 65\pi$

This function is of the form $f(x) = a(x-h)^2 + k$ with $a = \sqrt{2}$, $h = -4.58$, and $k = 65\pi$. The vertex is (h, k),

or $(-4.58, 65\pi)$. The axis of symmetry is $x = h$, or $x = -4.58$. Since $a > 0$, then k, or 65π, is the minimum function value. The range is $[65\pi, \infty)$.

52. Vertex: $(38.2, -\sqrt{34})$

Axis of symmetry: $x = 38.2$

Minimum: $-\sqrt{34}$

Range: $[-\sqrt{34}, \infty)$

53. *Writing Exercise*

54. *Writing Exercise*

55. Graph $2x - 7y = 28$.

Find the x-intercept.

$$2x - 7 \cdot 0 = 28$$
$$2x = 28$$
$$x = 14$$

The x-intercept is $(14, 0)$.

Find the y-intercept.

$$2 \cdot 0 - 7y = 28$$
$$-7y = 28$$
$$y = -4$$

The y-intercept is $(0, -4)$.

Plot the intercepts and draw a line through them. A third point can be plotted as a check.

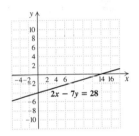

56.

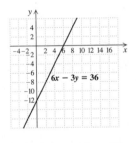

57. $3x + 4y = -19$, (1)

$7x - 6y = -29$ (2)

Multiply Equation (1) by 3 and multiply Equation (2) by 2. Then add the equations to eliminate the y-term.

$$\begin{array}{r} 9x + 12y = -57 \\ 14x - 12y = -58 \\ \hline 23x = -115 \\ x = -5 \end{array}$$

Now substitute -5 for x in one of the original equations and solve for y. We use Equation (1).

$$3(-5) + 4y = -19$$
$$-15 + 4y = -19$$
$$4y = -4$$
$$y = -1$$

The pair $(-5, -1)$ checks and it is the solution.

58. $(-1, 2)$

59. $x^2 + 5x$

We take half the coefficient of x and square it.

$$\frac{1}{2} \cdot 5 = \frac{5}{2}, \ \left(\frac{5}{2}\right)^2 = \frac{25}{4}$$

Then we have $x^2 + 5x + \dfrac{25}{4}$.

60. $x^2 - 9x + \dfrac{81}{4}$

61. *Writing Exercise*

62. *Writing Exercise*

63. The equation will be of the form $f(x) = \dfrac{3}{5}(x - h)^2 + k$ with $h = 4$ and $k = 1$:

$$f(x) = \frac{3}{5}(x - 4)^2 + 1$$

64. $f(x) = \dfrac{3}{5}(x - 2)^2 + 6$

65. The equation will be of the form $f(x) = \dfrac{3}{5}(x - h)^2 + k$ with $h = 3$ and $k = -1$:

$$f(x) = \frac{3}{5}(x - 3)^2 + (-1), \text{ or}$$
$$f(x) = \frac{3}{5}(x - 3)^2 - 1$$

66. $f(x) = \dfrac{3}{5}(x - 5)^2 - 6$

67. The equation will be of the form $f(x) = \dfrac{3}{5}(x - h)^2 + k$ with $h = -2$ and $k = -5$:

$$f(x) = \frac{3}{5}[x - (-2)]^2 + (-5), \text{ or}$$
$$f(x) = \frac{3}{5}(x + 2)^2 - 5$$

68. $f(x) = \dfrac{3}{5}(x + 4)^2 - 2$

69. Since there is a maximum at $(5, 0)$, the parabola will have the same shape as $g(x) = -2x^2$. It will be of the form $g(x) = -2(x - h)^2 + k$ with $h = 5$ and $k = 0$: $g(x) = -2(x - 5)^2$

70. $f(x) = 2(x - 2)^2$

71. Since there is a minimum at $(-4, 0)$, the parabola will have the same shape as $f(x) = 2x^2$. It will be of the form $f(x) = 2(x - h)^2 + k$ with $h = -4$ and $k = 0$: $f(x) = 2[x - (-4)]^2$, or $f(x) = 2(x + 4)^2$

72. $g(x) = -2x^2 + 3$

73. Since there is a maximum at $(3, 8)$, the parabola will have the same shape as $g(x) = -2x^2$. It will be of the form $g(x) = -2(x - h)^2 + k$ with $h = 3$ and $k = 8$: $g(x) = -2(x - 3)^2 + 8$

74. $f(x) = 2(x + 2)^2 + 3$

75. The maximum value of $g(x)$ is 1 and occurs at the point $(5, 1)$, so for $F(x)$ we have $h = 5$ and $k = 1$. $F(x)$ has the same shape as $f(x)$ and has a minimum, so $a = 3$. Thus, $F(x) = 3(x - 5)^2 + 1$.

76. $F(x) = -\dfrac{1}{3}(x + 4)^2 - 6$

77. The function is of the form $F(x) = a(x - h)^2 + k$. Substitute 2 for h, -3 for k, 1 for x, and -5 for $F(x)$ and find a.

$$F(x) = a(x - h)^2 + k$$
$$-5 = a(1 - 2)^2 + (-3)$$
$$-5 = a(-1)^2 - 3$$
$$-5 = a - 3$$
$$-2 = a$$

Keeping in mind that $h = 2$ and $k = -3$, we have $F(x) = -2(x - 2)^2 - 3$.

78. $F(x) = -\dfrac{5}{4}(x - 3)^2 - 1$

79. The graph of $y = f(x - 1)$ looks like the graph of $y = f(x)$ moved 1 unit to the right.

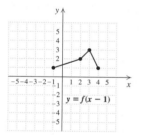

80.

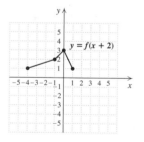

81. The graph of $y = f(x) + 2$ looks like the graph of $y = f(x)$ moved up 2 units.

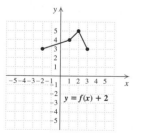

82.

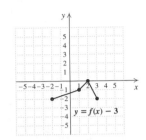

83. The graph of $y = f(x + 3) - 2$ looks like the graph of $y = f(x)$ moved 3 units to the left and also moved down 2 units.

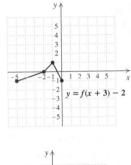

84.

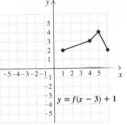

Exercise Set 10.7

1. a) $f(x) = x^2 - 4x + 5$
$$= (x^2 - 4x + 4 - 4) + 5 \quad \text{Adding } 4 - 4$$
$$= (x^2 - 4x + 4) - 4 + 5 \quad \text{Regrouping}$$
$$= (x - 2)^2 + 1$$

b) The vertex is $(2, 1)$; the axis of symmetry is $x = 2$.

2. a) $f(x) = (x + 3)^2 + 4$

b) Vertex: $(-3, 4)$; line of symmetry: $x = -3$

3. a) $f(x) = -x^2 + 3x - 10$
$$= -(x^2 - 3x) - 10$$
$$= -\left(x^2 - 3x + \frac{9}{4} - \frac{9}{4}\right) - 10$$
$$= -\left(x^2 - 3x + \frac{9}{4}\right) + \left[-\left(-\frac{9}{4}\right)\right] - 10$$
$$= -\left(x - \frac{3}{2}\right)^2 + \frac{9}{4} - 10$$
$$= -\left(x - \frac{3}{2}\right)^2 - \frac{31}{4}$$

b) The vertex is $\left(\frac{3}{2}, -\frac{31}{4}\right)$; the axis of symmetry is $x = \frac{3}{2}$.

4. a) $f(x) = \left(x + \frac{5}{2}\right)^2 - \frac{9}{4}$

b) Vertex: $\left(-\frac{5}{2}, -\frac{9}{4}\right)$; axis of symmetry: $x = -\frac{5}{2}$

5. a) $f(x) = 2x^2 - 7x + 1$
$$= 2\left(x^2 - \frac{7}{2}x\right) + 1$$
$$= 2\left(x^2 - \frac{7}{2}x + \frac{49}{16} - \frac{49}{16}\right) + 1$$
$$= 2\left(x^2 - \frac{7}{2}x + \frac{49}{16}\right) + 2\left(-\frac{49}{16}\right) + 1$$
$$= 2\left(x - \frac{7}{4}\right)^2 - \frac{49}{8} + 1$$
$$= 2\left(x - \frac{7}{4}\right)^2 - \frac{41}{8}$$

b) Vertex: $\left(\frac{7}{4}, -\frac{41}{8}\right)$; axis of symmetry: $x = \frac{7}{4}$

6. a) $f(x) = -2\left(x - \frac{5}{4}\right)^2 + \frac{17}{8}$

b) Vertex: $\left(\frac{5}{4}, \frac{17}{8}\right)$; axis of symmetry: $x = \frac{5}{4}$

7. $f(x) = x^2 + 4x + 5$
$$= (x^2 + 4x + 4 - 4) + 5 \quad \text{Adding } 4 - 4$$
$$= (x^2 + 4x + 4) - 4 + 5 \quad \text{Regrouping}$$
$$= (x + 2)^2 + 1$$

The vertex is $(-2, 1)$, the axis of symmetry is $x = -2$, and the graph opens upward since the coefficient 1 is positive. We plot a few points as a check and draw the curve.

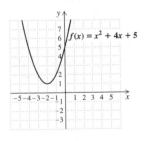

8. $f(x) = (x + 1)^2 - 6$

Vertex: $(-1, -6)$, axis of symmetry: $x = -1$

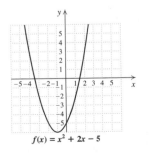
$$f(x) = x^2 + 2x - 5$$

9. $f(x) = x^2 + 8x + 20$

$\quad = (x^2 + 8x + 16 - 16) + 20 \quad$ Adding $16 - 16$

$\quad = (x^2 + 8x + 16) - 16 + 20 \quad$ Regrouping

$\quad = (x + 4)^2 + 4$

The vertex is $(-4, 4)$, the axis of symmetry is $x = -4$, and the graph opens upward since the coefficient 1 is positive.

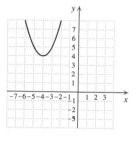

10. $f(x) = (x - 5)^2 - 4$

Vertex: $(5, -4)$, axis of symmetry: $x = 5$

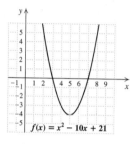

11. $h(x) = 2x^2 - 16x + 25$

$\quad = 2(x^2 - 8x) + 25 \quad$ Factoring 2 from the first two terms

$\quad = 2(x^2 - 8x + 16 - 16) + 25 \quad$ Adding $16 - 16$ inside the parentheses

$\quad = 2(x^2 - 8x + 16) + 2(-16) + 25 \quad$ Distributing to obtain a trinomial square

$\quad = 2(x - 4)^2 - 7$

The vertex is $(4, -7)$, the axis of symmetry is $x = 4$, and the graph opens upward since the coefficient 2 is positive.

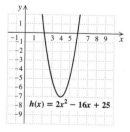

12. $h(x) = 2(x + 4)^2 - 9$

Vertex: $(-4, -9)$, axis of symmetry: $x = -4$

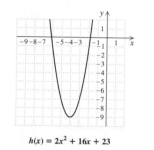

$h(x) = 2x^2 + 16x + 23$

13. $f(x) = -x^2 + 2x + 5$

$\quad = -(x^2 - 2x) + 5 \quad$ Factoring -1 from the first two terms

$\quad = -(x^2 - 2x + 1 - 1) + 5 \quad$ Adding $1 - 1$ inside the parentheses

$\quad = -(x^2 - 2x + 1) - (-1) + 5$

$\quad = -(x - 1)^2 + 6$

The vertex is $(1, 6)$, the axis of symmetry is $x = 1$, and the graph opens downward since the coefficient -1 is negative.

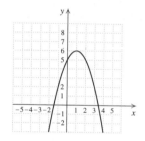

14. $f(x) = -(x + 1)^2 + 8$

Vertex: $(-1, 8)$, axis of symmetry: $x = -1$

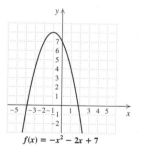

$f(x) = -x^2 - 2x + 7$

15. $g(x) = x^2 + 3x - 10$

$\quad = \left(x^2 + 3x + \dfrac{9}{4} - \dfrac{9}{4}\right) - 10$

$\quad = \left(x^2 + 3x + \dfrac{9}{4}\right) - \dfrac{9}{4} - 10$

$\quad = \left(x + \dfrac{3}{2}\right)^2 - \dfrac{49}{4}$

The vertex is $\left(-\dfrac{3}{2}, -\dfrac{49}{4}\right)$, the axis of symmetry is $x = -\dfrac{3}{2}$, and the graph opens upward since the coefficient 1 is positive.

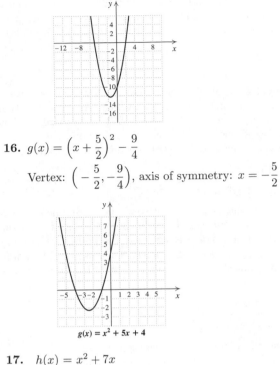

16. $g(x) = \left(x + \dfrac{5}{2}\right)^2 - \dfrac{9}{4}$

Vertex: $\left(-\dfrac{5}{2}, -\dfrac{9}{4}\right)$, axis of symmetry: $x = -\dfrac{5}{2}$

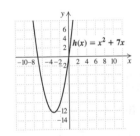

$g(x) = x^2 + 5x + 4$

17. $h(x) = x^2 + 7x$

$= \left(x^2 + 7x + \dfrac{49}{4}\right) - \dfrac{49}{4}$

$= \left(x + \dfrac{7}{2}\right)^2 - \dfrac{49}{4}$

The vertex is $\left(-\dfrac{7}{2}, -\dfrac{49}{4}\right)$, the axis of symmetry is $x = -\dfrac{7}{2}$, and the graph opens upward since the coefficient 1 is positive.

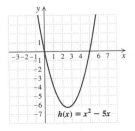

18. $h(x) = \left(x - \dfrac{5}{2}\right)^2 - \dfrac{25}{4}$

Vertex: $\left(\dfrac{5}{2}, -\dfrac{25}{4}\right)$, axis of symmetry: $x = \dfrac{5}{2}$

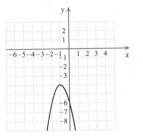

19. $f(x) = -2x^2 - 4x - 6$

$= -2(x^2 + 2x) - 6$ Factoring

$= -2(x^2 + 2x + 1 - 1) - 6$

         Adding $1 - 1$ inside
         the parentheses

$= -2(x^2 + 2x + 1) - 2(-1) - 6$

$= -2(x + 1)^2 - 4$

The vertex is $(-1, -4)$, the axis of symmetry is $x = -1$, and the graph opens downward since the coefficient -2 is negative.

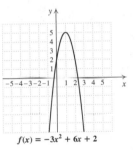

20. $f(x) = -3(x - 1)^2 + 5$

Vertex: $(1, 5)$, axis of symmetry: $x = 1$

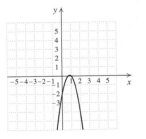

$f(x) = -3x^2 + 6x + 2$

21. $f(x) = -3x^2 + 5x - 2$

$= -3\left(x^2 - \dfrac{5}{3}x\right) - 2$ Factoring

$= -3\left(x^2 - \dfrac{5}{3}x + \dfrac{25}{36} - \dfrac{25}{36}\right) - 2$

       Adding $\dfrac{25}{36} - \dfrac{25}{36}$ inside

       the parentheses

$= -3\left(x^2 - \dfrac{5}{3}x + \dfrac{25}{36}\right) - 3\left(-\dfrac{25}{36}\right) - 2$

$= -3\left(x - \dfrac{5}{6}\right)^2 + \dfrac{1}{12}$

The vertex is $\left(\dfrac{5}{6}, \dfrac{1}{12}\right)$, the axis of symmetry is $x = \dfrac{5}{6}$, and the graph opens downward since the coefficient -3 is negative.

22. $f(x) = -3\left(x + \frac{7}{6}\right)^2 + \frac{73}{12}$

Vertex: $\left(-\frac{7}{6}, \frac{73}{12}\right)$, axis of symmetry: $x = -\frac{7}{6}$

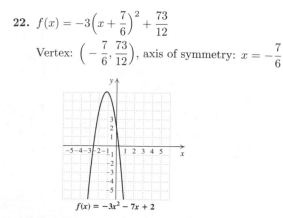

$f(x) = -3x^2 - 7x + 2$

23. $h(x) = \frac{1}{2}x^2 + 4x + \frac{19}{3}$

$= \frac{1}{2}(x^2 + 8x) + \frac{19}{3}$　　　　Factoring

$= \frac{1}{2}(x^2 + 8x + 16 - 16) + \frac{19}{3}$

$\qquad\qquad\qquad$ Adding $16 - 16$ inside
$\qquad\qquad\qquad$ the parentheses

$= \frac{1}{2}(x^2 + 8x + 16) + \frac{1}{2}(-16) + \frac{19}{3}$

$= \frac{1}{2}(x + 4)^2 - \frac{5}{3}$

The vertex is $\left(-4, -\frac{5}{3}\right)$, the axis of symmetry is $x = -4$, and the graph opens upward since the coefficient $\frac{1}{2}$ is positive.

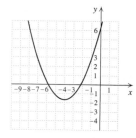

24. $h(x) = \frac{1}{2}(x - 3)^2 - \frac{5}{2}$

Vertex: $\left(3, -\frac{5}{2}\right)$, axis of symmetry: $x = 3$

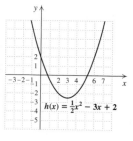

$h(x) = \frac{1}{2}x^2 - 3x + 2$

25. $f(x) = x^2 + x - 6$

The coefficient of x^2 is positive so the graph opens upward and the function has a minimum value. Graph the function in a window that shows the vertex. The standard window is one good choice. Then use the Minimum feature from the CALC menu to find that the vertex is $(-0.5, -6.25)$.

26. $(-1, -6)$

27. $f(x) = 5x^2 - x + 1$

The coefficient of x^2 is positive so the graph opens upward and the function has a minimum value. Graph the function in a window that shows the vertex. The standard window is one good choice. Then use the Minimum feature from the CALC menu to find that the vertex is $(0.1, 0.95)$.

28. $(-0.375, 7.5625)$

29. $f(x) = -0.2x^2 + 1.4x - 6.7$

The coefficient of x^2 is negative so the graph opens downward and the function has a maximum value. Graph the function in a window that shows the vertex. The standard window is one good choice. Then use the Maximum feature from the CALC menu to find that the vertex is $(3.5, -4.25)$.

30. $(-2.4, 0.32)$

31. $f(x) = x^2 - 6x + 3$

To find the x-intercepts, solve the equation $0 = x^2 - 6x + 3$. Use the quadratic formula.

$$x = \frac{-(-6) \pm \sqrt{(-6)^2 - 4 \cdot 1 \cdot 3}}{2 \cdot 1}$$

$$x = \frac{6 \pm \sqrt{24}}{2} = \frac{6 \pm 2\sqrt{6}}{2} = 3 \pm \sqrt{6}$$

The x-intercepts are $(3 - \sqrt{6}, 0)$ and $(3 + \sqrt{6}, 0)$.

The y-intercept is $(0, f(0))$, or $(0, 3)$.

32. x-intercepts: $\left(\frac{-5 - \sqrt{17}}{2}, 0\right)$, $\left(\frac{-5 + \sqrt{17}}{2}, 0\right)$;

y-intercept: $(0, 2)$

33. $g(x) = -x^2 + 2x + 3$

To find the x-intercepts, solve the equation $0 = -x^2 + 2x + 3$. We factor.

$0 = -x^2 + 2x + 3$

$0 = x^2 - 2x - 3$　　　Multiplying by -1

$0 = (x - 3)(x + 1)$

$x = 3 \ or \ x = -1$

The x-intercepts are $(-1, 0)$ and $(3, 0)$.

The y-intercept is $(0, g(0))$, or $(0, 3)$.

34. x-intercept: $(3, 0)$; y-intercept: $(0, 9)$

35. $f(x) = x^2 - 9x$

To find the x-intercepts, solve the equation $0 = x^2 - 9x$. We factor.

$0 = x^2 - 9x$

$0 = x(x - 9)$

$x = 0 \ or \ x = 9$

The x-intercepts are $(0, 0)$ and $(9, 0)$.

Since $(0, 0)$ is an x-intercept, we observe that $(0, 0)$ is also the y-intercept.

36. x-intercepts: $(0,0)$, $(7,0)$; y-intercept: $(0,0)$

37. $h(x) = -x^2 + 4x - 4$

To find the x-intercepts, solve the equation $0 = -x^2 + 4x - 4$. We factor.

$$0 = -x^2 + 4x - 4$$
$$0 = x^2 - 4x + 4 \qquad \text{Multiplying by } -1$$
$$0 = (x-2)(x-2)$$
$$x = 2 \text{ or } x = 2$$

The x-intercept is $(2, 0)$.

The y-intercept is $(0, h(0))$, or $(0, -4)$.

38. x-intercepts: $\left(\dfrac{3 - \sqrt{6}}{2}, 0\right)$, $\left(\dfrac{3 + \sqrt{6}}{2}, 0\right)$;

y-intercept: $(0, 3)$

39. $f(x) = 2x^2 - 4x + 6$

To find the x-intercepts, solve the equation $0 = 2x^2 - 4x + 6$. We use the quadratic formula.

$$x = \frac{-(-4) \pm \sqrt{(-4)^2 - 4 \cdot 2 \cdot 6}}{2 \cdot 2}$$

$$x = \frac{4 \pm \sqrt{-32}}{4} = \frac{4 \pm 4i\sqrt{2}}{2} = 2 \pm 2i\sqrt{2}$$

There are no real-number solutions, so there is no x-intercept.

The y-intercept is $(0, f(0))$, or $(0, 6)$.

40. No x-intercept; y-intercept: $(0, 2)$

41. $f(x) = 2.31x^2 - 3.135x - 5.89$

a) The coefficient of x^2 is positive so the graph opens upward and the function has a minimum value. Graph the function in a window that shows the vertex. The standard window is one good choice. Then use the Minimum feature from the CALC menu to find that the minimum value is about -6.95.

b) To find the first coordinates of the x-intercepts we use the Zero feature from the CALC menu to find the zeros of the function. They are about -1.06 and 2.41, so the x-intercepts are $(-1.06, 0)$ and $(2.41, 0)$.

The y-intercept is $(0, f(0))$, or $(0, -5.89)$.

42. a) About 7.01

b) x-intercepts: $(-0.40, 0)$, $(0.82, 0)$; y-intercept: $(0, 6.18)$

43. $g(x) = -1.25x^2 + 3.42x - 2.79$

a) The coefficient of x^2 is negative so the graph opens downward and the function has a maximum value. Graph the function in a window that shows the vertex. The standard window is one good choice. Then use the Maximum feature from the CALC menu to find that the maximum value is about -0.45.

b) The graph has no x-intercepts. The y-intercept is $(0, f(0))$, or $(0, -2.79)$.

44. a) About 11.28

b) No x-intercepts; y-intercept: $(0, 12.92)$

45. *Writing Exercise*

46. *Writing Exercise*

47. $5x - 3y = 16$, (1)

$4x + 2y = 4$ (2)

Multiply equation (1) by 2 and equation (2) by 3 and add.

$$10x - 6y = 32$$
$$\underline{12x + 6y = 12}$$
$$22x \qquad = 44$$
$$x = 2$$

Substitute 2 for x in one of the original equations and solve for y.

$$4x + 2y = 4 \qquad (1)$$
$$4 \cdot 2 + 2y = 4$$
$$8 + 2y = 4$$
$$2y = -4$$
$$y = -2$$

The solution is $(2, -2)$.

48. $(7, 1)$

49. $4a - 5b + c = 3$, (1)

$3a - 4b + 2c = 3$, (2)

$a + b - 7c = -2$ (3)

First multiply equation (1) by -2 and add it to equation (2).

$$-8a + 10b - 2c = -6$$
$$\underline{3a \quad - 4b + 2c = \quad 3}$$
$$-5a + 6b \qquad = -3 \quad (4)$$

Next multiply equation (1) by 7 and add it to equation (3).

$$28a - 35b + 7c = 21$$
$$\underline{a + \quad b - 7c = -2}$$
$$29a - 34b \qquad = 19 \quad (5)$$

Now we solve the system of equations (4) and (5). Multiply equation (4) by 29 and equation (5) by 5 and add.

$$-145a + 174b = -87$$
$$\underline{145a - 170b = \quad 95}$$
$$4b = \quad 8$$
$$b = \quad 2$$

Substitute 2 for b in equation (4) and solve for a.

$$-5a + 6 \cdot 2 = -3$$
$$-5a + 12 = -3$$
$$-5a = -15$$
$$a = 3$$

Now substitute 3 for a and 2 for b in equation (1) and solve for c.

$$4 \cdot 3 - 5 \cdot 2 + c = 3$$
$$12 - 10 + c = 3$$
$$2 + c = 3$$
$$c = 1$$

The solution is $(3, 2, 1)$.

50. $(1, -3, 2)$

51.
$$\sqrt{4x - 4} = \sqrt{x + 4} + 1$$
$$4x - 4 = x + 4 + 2\sqrt{x + 4} + 1$$
     Squaring both sides
$$3x - 9 = 2\sqrt{x + 4}$$
$$9x^2 - 54x + 81 = 4(x + 4) \quad \text{Squaring both}$$
     sides again
$$9x^2 - 54x + 81 = 4x + 16$$
$$9x^2 - 58x + 65 = 0$$
$$(9x - 13)(x - 5) = 0$$
$$x = \frac{13}{9} \quad \text{or} \quad x = 5$$

Check: For $x = \frac{13}{9}$:

$$\frac{\sqrt{4x - 4} = \sqrt{x + 4} + 1}{\sqrt{4\left(\frac{13}{9}\right) - 4} \ ? \ \sqrt{\frac{13}{9} + 4} + 1}$$

$$\sqrt{\frac{16}{9}} \ \Big| \ \sqrt{\frac{49}{9}} + 1$$

$$\frac{4}{3} \ \Big| \ \frac{7}{3} + 1$$

$$\frac{4}{3} \ \Big| \ \frac{10}{3} \qquad \text{FALSE}$$

For $x = 5$:

$$\frac{\sqrt{4x - 4} = \sqrt{x + 4} + 1}{\sqrt{4 \cdot 5 - 4} \ ? \ \sqrt{5 + 4} + 1}$$

$$\sqrt{16} \ \Big| \ \sqrt{9} + 1$$

$$4 \ \Big| \ 3 + 1$$

$$4 \ \Big| \ 4 \qquad \text{TRUE}$$

5 checks, but $\frac{13}{9}$ does not. The solution is 5.

52. 4

53. *Writing Exercise*

54. *Writing Exercise*

55. $f(x) = x^2 - x - 6$

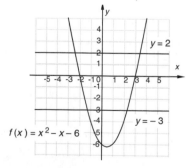

a) The solutions of $x^2 - x - 6 = 2$ are the first coordinates of the points of intersection of the graphs of $f(x) = x^2 - x - 6$ and $y = 2$. From the graph we see that the solutions are approximately -2.4 and 3.4.

b) The solutions of $x^2 - x - 6 = -3$ are the first coordinates of the points of intersection of the graphs of $f(x) = x^2 - x - 6$ and $y = -3$. From the graph we see that the solutions are approximately -1.3 and 2.3.

56. a) $-3, 1$

b) $-3.4, 1.4$

c) $-3.8, 1.8$

57. $f(x) = mx^2 - nx + p$
$$= m\left(x^2 - \frac{n}{m}x\right) + p$$
$$= m\left(x^2 - \frac{n}{m}x + \frac{n^2}{4m^2} - \frac{n^2}{4m^2}\right) + p$$
$$= m\left(x - \frac{n}{2m}\right)^2 - \frac{n^2}{4m} + p$$
$$= m\left(x - \frac{n}{2m}\right)^2 + \frac{-n^2 + 4mp}{4m}, \text{ or}$$
$$m\left(x - \frac{n}{2m}\right)^2 + \frac{4mp - n^2}{4m}$$

58. $f(x) = 3\left[x - \left(-\frac{m}{6}\right)\right]^2 + \frac{11m^2}{12}$

59. The horizontal distance from $(-1, 0)$ to $(3, -5)$ is $|3 - (-1)|$, or 4, so by symmetry the other x-intercept is $(3 + 4, 0)$, or $(7, 0)$. Substituting the three ordered pairs $(-1, 0)$, $(3, -5)$, and $(7, 0)$ in the equation $f(x) = ax^2 + bx + c$ yields a system of equations:
$$0 = a - b + c,$$
$$-5 = 9a + 3b + c,$$
$$0 = 49a + 7b + c$$
The solution of this system of equations is
$$\left(\frac{5}{16}, -\frac{15}{8}, -\frac{35}{16}\right), \text{ so } f(x) = \frac{5}{16}x^2 - \frac{15}{8}x - \frac{35}{16}.$$

60. $f(x) = -0.28x^2 - 0.56x + 6.72.$, or $f(x) = -\frac{7}{25}(x + 1)^2 + 7$

61. $f(x) = |x^2 - 1|$

We plot some points and draw the curve. Note that it will lie entirely on or above the x-axis since absolute value is never negative.

x	$f(x)$
-3	8
-2	3
-1	0
0	1
1	0
2	3
3	8

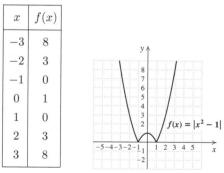

62.

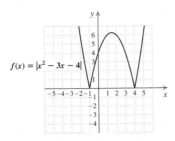

$f(x) = |x^2 - 3x - 4|$

63. $f(x) = |2(x-3)^2 - 5|$

We plot some points and draw the curve. Note that it will lie entirely on or above the x–axis since absolute value is never negative.

x	$f(x)$
-1	27
0	13
1	3
2	3
3	5
4	3
5	3
6	13

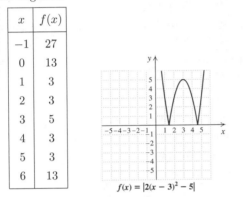

$f(x) = |2(x-3)^2 - 5|$

Exercise Set 10.8

1. *Familiarize and Translate*. We are given the function $V(x) = x^2 - 6x + 13$.

Carry out. To find the value of x for which $V(x)$ is a minimum, we first find $-\dfrac{b}{2a}$:

$$-\frac{b}{2a} = -\frac{-6}{2 \cdot 1} = 3$$

Now we find the minimum value of the function, $V(3)$:

$$V(3) = 3^2 - 6 \cdot 3 + 13 = 9 - 18 + 13 = 4$$

Check. We can go over the calculations again. We could also solve the problem again by completing the square. The answer checks.

State. The lowest value $V(x)$ will reach is \$4. This occurs 3 months after January 2001.

2. \$120/bicycle; 350 bicycles

3. *Familiarize and Translate*. We are given the function $N(x) = -0.4x^2 + 9x + 11$.

Carry out. To find the value of x for which $N(x)$ is a maximum, we first find $-\dfrac{b}{2a}$:

$$-\frac{b}{2a} = -\frac{9}{2(-0.4)} = 11.25$$

Now we find the maximum value of the function $N(11.25)$:

$$N(11.25) = -0.4(11.25)^2 + 9(11.25) + 11 = 61.625$$

Check. We can go over the calculations again. We could also solve the problem again by completing the square. The answer checks.

State. Daily ticket sales will peak 11 days after the concert was announced. About 62 tickets will be sold that day.

4. $P(x) = -x^2 + 980x - 3000$; \$237,100 at $x = 490$

5. *Familiarize*. We make a drawing and label it.

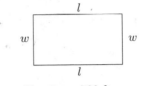

Perimeter: $2l + 2w = 720$ ft

Area: $A = l \cdot w$

Translate. We have a system of equations.

$$2l + 2w = 720,$$
$$A = lw$$

Carry out. Solving the first equation for l, we get $l = 360 - w$. Substituting for l in the second equation we get a quadratic function A:

$$A = (360 - w)w$$
$$A = -w^2 + 360w$$

Completing the square, we get

$$A = -(w - 180)^2 + 32,400.$$

The maximum function value is 32,400. It occurs when w is 180. When $w = 180$, $l = 360 - 180$, or 180.

Check. We check a function value for w less than 180 and for w greater than 180.

$$A(179) = -179^2 + 360(179) = 32,399$$
$$A(181) = -181^2 + 360(181) = 32,399$$

Since 32,400 is greater than these numbers, it looks as though we have a maximum.

State. The maximum area occurs when the dimensions are 180 ft by 180 ft.

6. 21 in. by 21 in.

7. *Familiarize*. We make a drawing and label it.

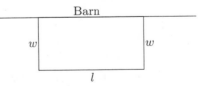

Translate. We have two equations.

$$l + 2w = 40,$$
$$A = lw$$

Carry out. Solve the first equation for l.

$$l = 40 - 2w$$

Substitute for l in the second equation.

$$A = (40 - 2w)w$$
$$A = -2w^2 + 40w$$

Completing the square, we get

$$A = -2(w - 10)^2 + 200.$$

The maximum function value of 200 occurs when $w = 10$. When $w = 10$, $l = 40 - 2 \cdot 10 = 20$.

Check. Check a function value for w less than 10 and for w greater than 10.

$$A(9) = -2 \cdot 9^2 + 40 \cdot 9 = 198$$
$$A(11) = -2 \cdot 11^2 + 40 \cdot 11 = 198$$

Since 200 is greater than these numbers, it looks as though we have a maximum.

State. The maximum area of 200 ft^2 will occur when the dimensions are 10 ft by 20 ft.

8. 450 ft^2; 15 ft by 30 ft (The house serves as the 30-ft side.)

9. Familiarize. Let x represent the height of the file and y represent the width. We make a drawing.

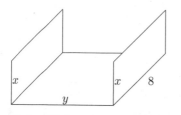

Translate. We have two equations.

$$2x + y = 14$$
$$V = 8xy$$

Carry out. Solve the first equation for y.

$$y = 14 - 2x$$

Substitute for y in the second equation.

$$V = 8x(14 - 2x)$$
$$V = -16x^2 + 112x$$

Completing the square, we get

$$V = -16\left(x - \frac{7}{2}\right)^2 + 196.$$

The maximum function value of 196 occurs when $x = \frac{7}{2}$. When $x = \frac{7}{2}$, $y = 14 - 2 \cdot \frac{7}{2} = 7$.

Check. Check a function value for x less than $\frac{7}{2}$ and for x greater than $\frac{7}{2}$.

$$V(3) = -16 \cdot 3^2 + 112 \cdot 3 = 192$$
$$V(4) = -16 \cdot 4^2 + 112 \cdot 4 = 192$$

Since 196 is greater than these numbers, it looks as though we have a maximum.

State. The file should be $\frac{7}{2}$ in., or 3.5 in., tall.

10. 4 ft by 4 ft

11. Familiarize. We let x and y represent the numbers, and we let P represent their product.

Translate. We have two equations.

$$x + y = 18,$$
$$P = xy$$

Carry out. Solving the first equation for y, we get $y = 18 - x$. Substituting for y in the second equation we get a quadratic function P:

$$P = x(18 - x)$$
$$P = -x^2 + 18x$$

Completing the square, we get

$$P = -(x - 9)^2 + 81.$$

The maximum function value is 81. It occurs when $x = 9$. When $x = 9$, $y = 18 - 9$, or 9.

Check. We can check a function value for x less than 9 and for x greater than 9.

$$P(10) = -10^2 + 18 \cdot 10 = 80$$
$$P(8) = -8^2 + 18 \cdot 8 = 80$$

Since 81 is greater than these numbers, it looks as though we have a maximum.

State. The maximum product of 81 occurs for the numbers 9 and 9.

12. 169; 13 and 13

13. Familiarize. We let x and y represent the two numbers, and we let P represent their product.

Translate. We have two equations.

$$x - y = 8,$$
$$P = xy$$

Carry out. Solve the first equation for x.

$$x = 8 + y$$

Substitute for x in the second equation.

$$P = (8 + y)y$$
$$P = y^2 + 8y$$

Completing the square, we get

$$P = (y + 4)^2 - 16.$$

The minimum function value is -16. It occurs when $y = -4$. When $y = -4$, $x = 8 + (-4)$, or 4.

Check. Check a function value for y less than -4 and for y greater than -4.

$$P(-5) = (-5)^2 + 8(-5) = -15$$
$$P(-3) = (-3)^2 + 8(-3) = -15$$

Since -16 is less than these numbers, it looks as though we have a minimum.

State. The minimum product of -16 occurs for the numbers 4 and -4.

14. $-\dfrac{49}{4}$; $\dfrac{7}{2}$ and $-\dfrac{7}{2}$

15. From the results of Exercises 11 and 12, we might observe that the numbers are -5 and -5 and that the maximum product is 25. We could also solve this problem as follows.

Familiarize. We let x and y represent the two numbers, and we let P represent their product.

Translate. We have two equations.

$$x + y = -10,$$
$$P = xy$$

Carry out. Solve the first equation for y.

$$y = -10 - x$$

Substitute for y in the second equation.

$$P = x(-10 - x)$$
$$P = -x^2 - 10x$$

Completing the square, we get

$$P = -(x + 5)^2 + 25$$

The maximum function value is 25. It occurs when $x = -5$. When $x = -5$, $y = -10 - (-5)$, or -5.

Check. Check a function value for x less than -5 and for x greater than -5.

$$P(-6) = -(-6)^2 - 10(-6) = 24$$
$$P(-4) = -(-4)^2 - 10(-4) = 24$$

Since 25 is greater than these numbers, it looks as though we have a maximum.

State. The maximum product of 25 occurs for the numbers -5 and -5.

16. 36; -6 and -6

17. The data points fall and then rise. The graph appears to represent a quadratic function because the data points approximate a parabola that opens upward.

18. Quadratic; the data approximate a parabola that opens downward.

19. The data points rise, in general. The graph does not appear to represent a quadratic function in which the data points would rise and then fall or vise versa. That is, the data points do not approximate a parabola.

20. Not quadratic; the data do not approximate a parabola.

21. The data appear nearly linear so the graph does not approximate a parabola. A linear function is a better model for this situation than a quadratic function.

22. Quadratic; the data approximate a parabola that opens upward.

23. The data points do not approximate a parabola, so the graph does not appear to represent a quadratic function.

24. Quadratic; the data approximate half a parabola opening upward.

25. The data points resemble the right half of a parabola that opens upward, so a quadratic function $f(x) = ax^2 + bx + c$, $a > 0$, $x \geq 0$, could be used to model the situation.

26. Not quadratic; the data do not approximate a parabola.

27. We look for a function of the form $f(x) = ax^2 + bx + c$. Substituting the data points, we get

$$4 = a(1)^2 + b(1) + c,$$
$$-2 = a(-1)^2 + b(-1) + c,$$
$$13 = a(2)^2 + b(2) + c,$$

or

$$4 = a + b + c,$$
$$-2 = a - b + c,$$
$$13 = 4a + 2b + c.$$

Solving this system, we get

$$a = 2, \ b = 3, \text{ and } c = -1.$$

Therefore the function we are looking for is

$$f(x) = 2x^2 + 3x - 1.$$

28. $f(x) = 3x^2 - x + 2$

29. We look for a function of the form $f(x) = ax^2 + bx + c$. Substituting the data points, we get

$$0 = a(2)^2 + b(2) + c,$$
$$3 = a(4)^2 + b(4) + c,$$
$$-5 = a(12)^2 + b(12) + c,$$

or

$$0 = 4a + 2b + c,$$
$$3 = 16a + 4b + c,$$
$$-5 = 144a + 12b + c.$$

Solving this system, we get

$$a = -\frac{1}{4}, \ b = 3, \ c = -5.$$

Therefore the function we are looking for is

$$f(x) = -\frac{1}{4}x^2 + 3x - 5.$$

30. $f(x) = -\frac{1}{3}x^2 + 5x - 12$

31. a) **Familiarize.** We look for a function of the form $A(s) = as^2 + bs + c$, where $A(s)$ represents the number of nighttime accidents (for every 200 million km) and s represents the travel speed (in km/h).

Translate. We substitute the given values of s and $A(s)$.

$$400 = a(60)^2 + b(60) + c,$$
$$250 = a(80)^2 + b(80) + c,$$
$$250 = a(100)^2 + b(100) + c,$$

or

$$400 = 3600a + 60b + c,$$
$$250 = 6400a + 80b + c,$$
$$250 = 10,000a + 100b + c.$$

Carry out. Solving the system of equations, we get

$$a = \frac{3}{16}, \ b = -\frac{135}{4}, \ c = 1750.$$

Check. Recheck the calculations.

State. The function

$$A(s) = \frac{3}{16}s^2 - \frac{135}{4}s + 1750 \text{ fits the data.}$$

b) Find $A(50)$.

$$A(50) = \frac{3}{16}(50)^2 - \frac{135}{4}(50) + 1750 = 531.25$$

About 531 accidents occur at 50 km/h.

32. a) $A(s) = 0.05x^2 - 5.5x + 250$

b) 100 accidents occur

33. *Familiarize*. Think of a coordinate system placed on the drawing in the text with the origin at the point where the arrow is released. Then three points on the arrow's parabolic path are $(0, 0)$, $(63, 27)$, and $(126, 0)$. We look for a function of the form $h(d) = ad^2 + bd + c$, where $h(d)$ represents the arrow's height and d represents the distance the arrow has traveled horizontally.

Translate. We substitute the values given above for d and $h(d)$.

$$0 = a \cdot 0^2 + b \cdot 0 + c,$$
$$27 = a \cdot 63^2 + b \cdot 63 + c,$$
$$0 = a \cdot 126^2 + b \cdot 126 + c$$

or

$$0 = c,$$
$$27 = 3969a + 63b + c,$$
$$0 = 15,876a + 126b + c$$

Carry out. Solving the system of equations, we get $a \approx -0.0068$, $b \approx 0.8571$, and $c = 0$.

Check. Recheck the calculations.

State. The function $h(d) = -0.0068d^2 + 0.8571d$ expresses the arrow's height as a function of the distance it has traveled horizontally.

34. a) $P(d) = \dfrac{1}{64}d^2 + \dfrac{5}{16}d + \dfrac{5}{2}$

     b) \$9.94

35. a) Enter the data and then use the quadratic regression feature. We have $D(x) = -0.0082833093x^2 + 0.8242996891x + 0.2121786608$.

     b) $D(70) \approx 17.325$, so we estimate that the river is about 17.325 ft deep 70 ft from the left bank.

36. a) $W(x) = 0.0111428571x^2 - 0.6637142857x + 21.42857143$, where x is the number of years after 1960.

     b) 16.1%

37. a) Enter the data and then use the quadratic regression feature. We have $c(x) = 261.875x^2 - 882.5642857x + 2134.571429$, where x is the number of years after 1992.

     b) In 2004, $x = 2004 - 1992 = 12$.

     $c(12) \approx 29,254$, so we estimate that about 29,254 cars will be fueled by electricity in 2004.

38. a) $h(x) = 1.577142857x^2 - 11.08571429x + 50.82857143$, where x is the number of years after 1960.

     b) \$3439

39. *Writing Exercise*

40. *Writing Exercise*

41.
$$\frac{x}{x^2 + 17x + 72} - \frac{8}{x^2 + 15x + 56}$$
$$= \frac{x}{(x+8)(x+9)} - \frac{8}{(x+8)(x+7)}$$
$$= \frac{x}{(x+8)(x+9)} \cdot \frac{x+7}{x+7} - \frac{8}{(x+8)(x+7)} \cdot \frac{x+9}{x+9}$$
$$= \frac{x(x+7) - 8(x+9)}{(x+8)(x+9)(x+7)}$$
$$= \frac{x^2 + 7x - 8x - 72}{(x+8)(x+9)(x+7)}$$
$$= \frac{x^2 - x - 72}{(x+8)(x+9)(x+7)} = \frac{(x-9)(x+8)}{(x+8)(x+9)(x+7)}$$
$$= \frac{x-9}{(x+9)(x+7)}$$

42. $\dfrac{(x-3)(x+1)}{(x-7)(x+3)}$

43. $5x - 9 < 31$

     $5x < 40$

     $x < 8$

The solutions set is $\{x | x < 8\}$, or $(-\infty, 8)$.

44. $\{x | x \geq 10\}$, or $[10, \infty)$

45. First find the slope.
$$m = \frac{46,782 - 23,505}{20 - 4} = \frac{23,277}{16} = 1454.8125.$$
Now use the point-slope equation. We will use the point $(4, 23,505)$.

$$y - y_1 = m(x - x_1)$$
$$y - 23,505 = 1454.8125(x - 4)$$
$$y - 23,505 = 1454.8125x - 5819.25$$
$$y = 1454.8125x + 17,685.75$$

46. $r(x) = 1514.092857x + 17,505.2381$, where x is the number of years after 1980.

47. *Writing Exercise*

48. *Writing Exercise*

49. *Familiarize*. We make a drawing and label it.

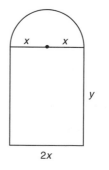

The perimeter of the semicircular portion of the window is $\dfrac{1}{2} \cdot 2\pi x$, or πx. The perimeter of the rectangular portion is $y + 2x + y$, or $2x + 2y$. The area of the semicircular portion of the window is $\frac{1}{2} \cdot \pi x^2$, or $\frac{\pi}{2} x^2$. The area of the rectangular portion is $2xy$.

Translate. We have two equations, one giving the perimeter of the window and the other giving the area.

$$\pi x + 2x + 2y = 24,$$
$$A = \frac{\pi}{2} x^2 + 2xy$$

Carry out. Solve the first equation for y.

$$\pi x + 2x + 2y = 24$$
$$2y = 24 - \pi x - 2x$$
$$y = 12 - \frac{\pi x}{2} - x$$

Substitute for y in the second equation.

$$A = \frac{\pi}{2} x^2 + 2x \left(12 - \frac{\pi x}{2} - x \right)$$
$$A = \frac{\pi}{2} x^2 + 24x - \pi x^2 - 2x^2$$
$$A = -2x^2 - \frac{\pi}{2} x^2 + 24x$$
$$A = -\left(2x + \frac{\pi}{2} \right) x^2 + 24x$$

Completing the square, we get

$$A = -\left(2 + \frac{\pi}{2} \right) \left(x^2 + \frac{24}{-\left(2 + \frac{\pi}{2} \right)} x \right)$$
$$A = -\left(2 + \frac{\pi}{2} \right) \left(x^2 - \frac{48}{4 + \pi} x \right)$$
$$A = -\left(2 + \frac{\pi}{2} \right) \left(x - \frac{24}{4 + \pi} \right)^2 + \left(\frac{24}{4 + \pi} \right)^2$$

The maximum function value occurs when $x = \frac{24}{4 + \pi}$. When $x = \frac{24}{4 + \pi}$,

$$y = 12 - \frac{\pi}{2} \left(\frac{24}{4 + \pi} \right) - \frac{24}{4 + \pi} - $$
$$\frac{48 + 12\pi}{4 + \pi} - \frac{12\pi}{4 + \pi} - \frac{24}{4 + \pi} = \frac{24}{4 + \pi}.$$

Check. Recheck the calculations.

State. The radius of the circular portion of the window and the height of the rectangular portion should each be $\frac{24}{4 + \pi}$ ft.

50. The length of the piece used to form the circle is $\frac{36\pi}{4 + \pi}$ in. and the length of the piece used to form the square is $\frac{144}{4 + \pi}$ in.

51. Familiarize. Let x represent the number of trees added to an acre. Then $20 + x$ represents the total number of trees per acre and $40 - x$ represents the corresponding yield per tree. Let T represent the total yield per acre.

Translate. Since total yield is number of trees times yield per tree we have the following function for total yield per acre.

$$T(x) = (20 + x)(40 - x)$$
$$T(x) = -x^2 + 20x + 800$$

Carry out. Completing the square, we get

$$T(x) = -(x - 10)^2 + 900.$$

The maximum function value of 900 occurs when $x = 10$. When $x = 10$, the number of trees per acre is $20 + 10$, or 30.

Check. We check a function value for x less than 10 and for x greater than 10.

$$T(9) = (20 + 9)(40 - 9) = 899$$
$$T(11) = (20 + 11)(40 - 11) = 899$$

Since 900 is greater than these numbers, it looks as though we have a maximum.

State. The grower should plant 30 trees per acre.

52. $15

53. Familiarize. We want to find the maximum value of a function of the form $h(t) = at^2 + bt + c$ that fits the following data.

Time (sec)	Height (ft)
0	0
3	0
3 + 2, or 5	−64

Translate. Substitute the given values for t and $h(t)$.

$$0 = a(0)^2 + b(0) + c,$$
$$0 = a(3)^2 + b(3) + c,$$
$$-64 = a(5)^2 + b(5) + c,$$

or

$$0 = c,$$
$$0 = 9a + 3b + c,$$
$$-64 = 25a + 5b + c.$$

Carry out. Solving the system of equations, we get $a = -6.4$, $b = 19.2$, $c = 0$. The function $h(t) = -6.4t^2 + 19.2t$ fits the data.

Completing the square, we get

$$h(t) = -6.4(t - 1.5)^2 + 14.4.$$

The maximum function value of 14.4 occurs at $t = 1.5$.

Check. Recheck the calculations. Also check a function value for t less than 1.5 and for t greater than 1.5.

$$h(1) = -6.4(1)^2 + 19.2(1) = 12.8$$
$$h(2) = -6.4(2)^2 + 19.2(2) = 12.8$$

Since 14.4 is greater than these numbers, it looks as though we have a maximum.

State. The maximum height above the cliff is 14.4 ft. The maximum height above sea level is $64 + 14.4$, or 78.4 ft.

54. 158 ft

Exercise Set 10.9

1. We see that $p(x) = 0$ when $x = -4$ or $x = \dfrac{3}{2}$, and $p(x) < 0$ between -4 and $\dfrac{3}{2}$. The solution set of the inequality is $\left[-4, \dfrac{3}{2}\right]$.

2. $\left(-4, -\dfrac{2}{3}\right)$

3.
$$x^4 + 12x > 3x^3 + 4x^2$$
$$x^4 - 3x^3 - 4x^2 + 12x > 0$$

From the graph we see that $p(x) > 0$ on $(-\infty, -2) \cup (0, 2) \cup (3, \infty)$. This is the solution set of the inequality.

4. $(-\infty, -3] \cup \{0\} \cup [2, \infty)$

5.
$$\dfrac{x-1}{x+2} < 3$$
$$\dfrac{x-1}{x+2} - 3 < 0$$

We see that $r(x) < 0$ on $\left(-\infty, -\dfrac{7}{2}\right) \cup (-2, \infty)$. This is the solution set of the inequality.

6. $(-\infty, -4] \cup (5, \infty)$

7. $(x+4)(x-3) < 0$

We solve the related equation.
$$(x+4)(x-3) = 0$$
$$x + 4 = 0 \quad or \quad x - 3 = 0$$
$$x = -4 \quad or \quad x = 3$$

The numbers -4 and 3 divide the number line into 3 intervals.

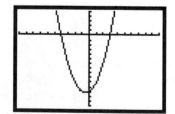

We graph $p(x) = (x+4)(x-3)$ in the window $[-10, 10, -15, 5]$ and determine the sign of the function in each interval.

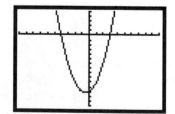

We see that $p(x) < 0$ in interval B, or in $(-4, 3)$. Thus, the solution set of the inequality is $(-4, 3)$, or $\{x | -4 < x < 3\}$.

8. $(-\infty, -2) \cup (5, \infty)$, or $\{x | x < -2 \ or \ x > 5\}$

9. $(x+7)(x-2) \geq 0$

The solutions of $(x+7)(x-2) = 0$ are -7 and 2. They divide the number line into three intervals as shown:

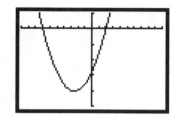

We graph $p(x) = (x+7)(x-2)$ in the window $[-10, 10, -25, 5]$, Yscl $= 5$.

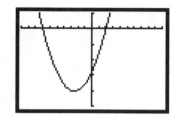

We see that $p(x) \geq 0$ in intervals A and C, or in $(-\infty, -7) \cup (2, \infty)$. We also know that $p(-7) = 0$ and $p(2) = 0$. Thus, the solution set of the inequality is $(-\infty, -7] \cup [2, \infty)$, or $\{x | x \leq -7 \ or \ x \geq 2\}$.

10. $[-4, 1]$, or $\{x | -4 \leq x \leq 1\}$

11. $x^2 - x - 2 < 0$

$(x+1)(x-2) < 0$ Factoring

The solutions of $(x+1)(x-2) = 0$ are -1 and 2. They divide the number line into three intervals as shown:

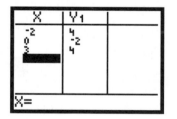

We enter $p(x) = x^2 - x - 2$ on a graphing calculator and try a test number in each interval. We choose -2 from interval A, 0 from B, and 3 from C.

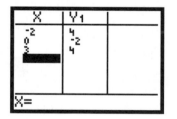

We see that $p(x) < 0$ in interval B, so the solution set is $(-1, 2)$, or $\{x | -1 < x < 2\}$.

12. $(-2, 1)$, or $\{x | -2 < x < 1\}$

13.
$$25 - x^2 \geq 0$$
$$(5 - x)(5 + x) \geq 0$$

The solutions of $(5-x)(5+x) = 0$ are 5 and -5. Graph $p(x) = 25 - x^2$ in the window $[-10, 10, -10, 30]$, Yscl $= 5$.

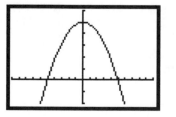

We see that $p(x) > 0$ in $(-5, 5)$; also $p(-5) = 0$ and $p(5) = 0$. The solution set is $[-5, 5]$, or $\{x| -5 \le x \le 5\}$.

14. $[-2, 2]$, or $\{x| -2 \le x \le 2\}$

15. $x^2 + 4x + 4 < 0$

$(x + 2)^2 < 0$

Observe that $(x + 2)^2 \ge 0$ for all values of z. Thus, the solution set is $\emptyset$.

The graph of $p(x) = x^2 + 4x + 4$ confirms this.

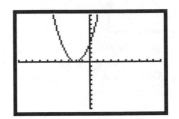

16. $\emptyset$

17. $x^2 - 4x < 12$

$x^2 - 4x - 12 < 0$

$(x - 6)(x + 2) < 0$

The solutions of $(x - 6)(x + 2) = 0$ are 6 and -2. Graph $p(x) = x^2 - 4x - 12$ in the window $[-10, 10, -20, 5]$, Yscl = 5.

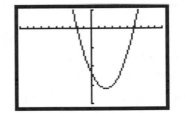

We see that $p(x) < 0$ in the interval $(-2, 6)$ or $\{x| -2 < x < 6\}$. This is the solution set of the inequality.

18. $(-\infty, -4) \cup (-2, \infty)$, or $\{x|x < -4 \text{ or } x > -2\}$

19. $3x(x + 2)(x - 2) < 0$

The solutions of $3x(x + 2)(x - 2) = 0$ are 0, -2, and 2. Graph $p(x) = 3x(x + 2)(x - 2)$ in the window $[-5, 5, -10, 10]$.

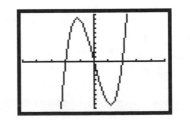

We see that $p(x) < 0$ on $(-\infty, -2) \cup (0, 2)$, or $\{x|x < -2 \text{ or } x > 2\}$. This is the solution set of the inequality.

20. $(-1, 0) \cup (1, \infty)$, or $\{x| -1 < x < 0 \text{ or } x > 1\}$

21. $(x + 3)(x - 2)(x + 1) > 0$

The solutions of $(x + 3)(x - 2)(x + 1) = 0$ are -3, 2, and -1. Graph $p(x) = (x + 3)(x - 2)(x - 1)$ in the window $[-5, 5, -10, 10]$.

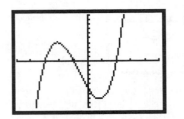

We see that $p(x) > 0$ on $(-3, -1) \cup (2, \infty)$, or $\{x| -3 < x < -1 \text{ or } x > 2\}$. This is the solution set of the inequality.

22. $(-\infty, -2) \cup (1, 4)$, or $\{x|x < -2 \text{ or } 1 < x < 4\}$

23. $(x + 3)(x + 2)(x - 1) < 0$

The solutions of $(x + 3)(x + 2)(x - 1) = 0$ are -3, -2, and 1. Graph $p(x) = (x + 3)(x + 2)(x - 1)$ in the window $[-5, 5, -10, 10]$.

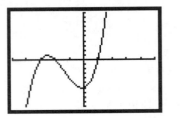

We see that $p(x) < 0$ in $(-\infty, -3) \cup (-2, 1)$, or $\{x|x < -3 \text{ or } -2 < x < 1\}$. This is the solution set of the inequality.

24. $(-\infty, -1) \cup (2, 3)$, or $\{x|x < -1 \text{ or } 2 < x < 3\}$

25. $4.32x^2 - 3.54x - 5.34 \le 0$

Graph $p(x) = 4.32x^2 - 3.54x - 5.34$ in the window $[-5, 5, -10, 10]$.

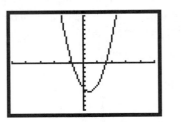

Using the Zero feature we find that $p(x) = 0$ when $x \approx -0.78$ and when $x \approx 1.59$. Also observe that $p(x) < 0$ on the interval $(-0.78, 1.59)$. Thus, the solution set of the inequality is $[-0.78, 1.59]$, or $\{x| -0.78 \le x \le 1.59\}$.

26. $(-\infty, -0.21] \cup [2.47, \infty)$, or $\{x|x \le -0.21 \text{ or } x \ge 2.47\}$

27. $x^3 - 2x^2 - 5x + 6 < 0$

Graph $p(x) = x^3 - 2x^2 - 5x + 6$ in the window $[-5, 5, -10, 10]$.

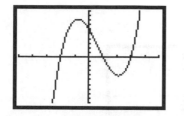

Using the Zero feature we find that $p(x) = 0$ when $x = -2$, when $x = 1$, and when $x = 3$. Then we see that $p(x) < 0$ on $(-\infty, -2) \cup (1, 3)$, or $\{x | x < -2 \text{ } or \text{ } 1 < x < 3\}$. This is the solution set of the inequality.

28. $(-2, 1) \cup (1, \infty)$, or $\{x | -2 < x < 1 \text{ } or \text{ } x > 1\}$

29. $\dfrac{1}{x+3} < 0$

We write the related equation by changing the $<$ symbol to $=$:

$$\frac{1}{x+3} = 0$$

We solve the related equation.

$$(x+3) \cdot \frac{1}{x+3} = (x+3) \cdot 0$$
$$1 = 0$$

The related equation has no solution.

Next we find the values that make the denominator 0 by setting the denominate equal to 0 and solving:

$$x + 3 = 0$$
$$x = -3$$

We use -3 to divide the number line into two intervals as shown:

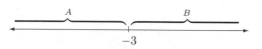

We try a test number in each interval. Enter $y = \dfrac{1}{x+3}$ on a graphing calculator and use the Table feature set in ASK mode. We try -4 in interval A and 0 in B.

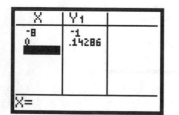

We see that $y < 0$ in interval A, so the solution set of the inequality is $(-\infty, -3)$ or $\{x | x < -3\}$.

30. $(-4, \infty)$, or $\{x | x > -4\}$

31. $\dfrac{x+1}{x-5} \geq 0$

Graph $r(x) = \dfrac{x+1}{x-5}$ using DOT mode in the window $[-5, 15, -5, 5]$.

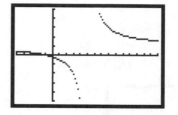

Using the Zero feature we find that $r(x) = 0$ when $x = -1$. Also observe that $r(x) > 0$ on the intervals $(-\infty, -1)$ and $(5, \infty)$. Thus, the solution set of the inequality is $(-\infty, -1] \cup (5, \infty)$, or $\{x | x \leq 1 \text{ } or \text{ } x > 5\}$.

32. $(-5, 2]$, or $\{x | -5 < x \leq 2\}$

33. $\dfrac{3x+2}{2x-4} \leq 0$

Graph $r(x) = \dfrac{3x+2}{2x-4}$ using DOT mode in the standard window.

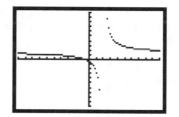

Using the Zero feature we find that $r(x) = 0$ when $x = -0.\overline{6}$, or $-\dfrac{2}{3}$. Also observe that $r(x) < 0$ on $\left(-\dfrac{2}{3}, 2\right)$.

Thus, the solution set is $\left[-\dfrac{2}{3}, 2\right)$.

34. $\left(-\infty, -\dfrac{3}{4}\right) \cup \left[\dfrac{5}{2}, \infty\right)$, or $\left\{x \middle| x < -\dfrac{3}{4} \text{ } or \text{ } x \geq \dfrac{5}{2}\right\}$

35. $\dfrac{x+1}{x+6} > 1$

$$\frac{x+1}{x+6} - 1 > 0$$

If $r(x) = \dfrac{x+1}{x+6} - 1$, the solution set of the inequality is all values of x for which $r(x) > 0$.

First we solve $r(x) = 0$.

$$\frac{x+1}{x+6} - 1 = 0$$
$$(x+6)\left(\frac{x+1}{x+6} - 1\right) = (x+6) \cdot 0$$
$$(x+6)\left(\frac{x+1}{x+6}\right) - (x+6) \cdot 1 = 0$$
$$x + 1 - x - 6 = 0$$
$$-5 = 0$$

This equation has no solution.

Find the values that make the denominator 0.

$$x + 6 = 0$$
$$x = -6$$

Use -6 to divide the number line into intervals.

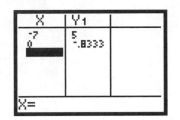

Enter $y = r(x)$ on a graphing calculator and evaluate a test number in each interval. We test -7 and 0.

X	Y₁	
-7	5	
0	-.8333	
X=		

We see that $r(x) > 0$ in interval A. The solution set is $(-\infty, -6)$, or $\{x | x < -6\}$.

36. $(-\infty, 2)$, or $\{x | x < 2\}$

37. $\dfrac{(x-2)(x+1)}{x-5} \leq 0$

Solve the related equation.

$$\frac{(x-2)(x+1)}{x-5} = 0$$
$$(x-2)(x+1) = 0$$
$$x = 2 \ or \ x = -1$$

Find the values that make the denominator 0.

$$x - 5 = 0$$
$$x = 5$$

Use the numbers 2, -1, and 5 to divide the number line into intervals as shown:

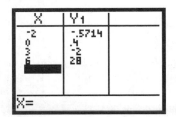

Enter $r(x) = \dfrac{(x-2)(x+1)}{x-5}$ and evaluate a test number in each interval. We test -2, 0, 3, and 6.

X	Y₁	
-2	-.5714	
0	.4	
3	-2	
6	28	
X=		

We see that $r(x) < 0$ in intervals A and C. From above we also know that $r(x) = 0$ when $x = 2$ or $x = -1$. Thus, the solution set is $(-\infty, -1] \cup [2, 5)$, or $\{x | x \leq -1 \ or \ 2 \leq x < 5\}$.

38. $[-4, -3) \cup [1, \infty)$, or $\{x | -4 \leq x < -3 \ or \ x \geq 1\}$

39. $\dfrac{x}{x+3} \geq 0$

Graph $r(x) = \dfrac{x}{x+3}$ using DOT mode in the window $[-10, 10, -5, 5]$.

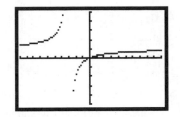

Using the Zero feature we find that $r(x) = 0$ when $x = 0$. Also observe that $r(x) > 0$ in the interval $(-\infty, -3)$ and in $(0, \infty)$. Then the solution set is $(-\infty, -3) \cup [0, \infty)$, or $\{x | x < -3 \ or \ x \geq 0\}$.

40. $(0, 2]$, or $\{x | 0 < x \leq 2\}$

41. $\dfrac{x-5}{x} < 1$

$$\frac{x-5}{x} - 1 < 0$$

Let $r(x) = \dfrac{x-5}{x} - 1$ and solve $r(x) = 0$.

$$\frac{x-5}{x} - 1 = 0$$
$$x\left(\frac{x-5}{x} - 1\right) = x \cdot 0$$
$$x\left(\frac{x-5}{x}\right) - x \cdot 1 = 0$$
$$x - 5 - x = 0$$
$$-5 = 0$$

This equation has no solution.

Find the values that make the denominator 0.

$$x = 0$$

Use the number 0 to divide the number line into two intervals as shown.

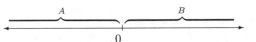

Enter $y = r(x)$ in a graphing calculator and evaluate a test number in each interval. We test -1 and 1.

X	Y₁	
-1	5	
1	-5	
X=		

We see that $r(x) < 0$ in interval B. Thus, the solution set is $(0, \infty)$, or $\{x | x > 0\}$.

42. $(1, 2)$, or $\{x | 1 < x < 2\}$

43. $\dfrac{x-1}{(x-3)(x+4)} \le 0$

Solve the related equation.

$$\dfrac{x-1}{(x-3)(x+4)} = 0$$

$$x - 1 = 0$$

$$x = 1$$

Find the values that make the denominator 0.

$$(x-3)(x+4) = 0$$

$$x = 3 \ or \ x = -4$$

Use the numbers 1, 3, and -4 to divide the number line into intervals as shown:

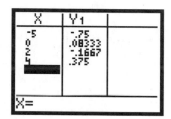

Enter $r(x) = \dfrac{x-1}{(x-3)(x+4)}$ in a graphing calculator and evaluate a test point in each interval. We test -5, 0, 2, and 4.

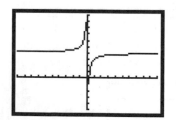

We see that $r(x) < 0$ in intervals A and C. From above we also know that $r(x) = 0$ when $x = 1$. Thus, the solution set is $(-\infty, -4) \cup [1, 3)$, or $\{x | x < -4 \ or \ 1 \le x < 3\}$.

44. $(-7, -2] \cup (2, \infty)$, or $\{x| -7 < x \le -2 \ or \ x > 2\}$

45. $4 < \dfrac{1}{x}$

$$4 - \dfrac{1}{x} < 0$$

Graph $r(x) = 4 - \dfrac{1}{x}$ in the window $[-10, 10, -5, 10]$.

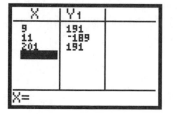

Using the Zero feature we find that $r(x) = 0$ when $x = 0.25$. Observe that $r(x) < 0$ on $(0, 0.25)$, or $\left(0, \dfrac{1}{4}\right)$, or $\left\{x \middle| 0 < x < \dfrac{1}{4}\right\}$. This is the solution set of the inequality.

46. $(-\infty, 0) \cup \left[\dfrac{1}{5}, \infty\right)$, or $\left\{x \middle| x < 0 \ or \ x \ge \dfrac{1}{5}\right\}$

47. *Writing Exercise*

48. *Writing Exercise*

49. $(2a^3 b^2 c^4)^3 = 2^3 (a^3)^3 (b^2)^3 (c^4)^3 = 8a^{3 \cdot 3} b^{2 \cdot 3} c^{4 \cdot 3} = 8a^9 b^6 c^{12}$

50. $25a^8 b^{14}$

51. $2^{-5} = \dfrac{1}{2^5} = \dfrac{1}{32}$

52. $\dfrac{1}{81}$

53. $f(x) = 3x^2$

$f(a+1) = 3(a+1)^2 = 3(a^2 + 2a + 1) = 3a^2 + 6a + 3$

54. $5a + 7$

55. *Writing Exercise*

56. *Writing Exercise*

57. $x^2 + 2x < 5$

$$x^2 + 2x - 5 < 0$$

Using the quadratic formula, we find that the solutions of the related equation are $x = -1 \pm \sqrt{6}$. Graph $p(x) = x^2 + 2x - 5$ in the standard window. Observe that $p(x) < 0$ on $(-1 - \sqrt{6}, -1 + \sqrt{6})$, or $\{x | -1 - \sqrt{6} < x < -1 + \sqrt{6}\}$. This is the solution set of the inequality. This can also be expressed as $(-3.24, 1.24)$, or $\{x | -3.24 < x < 1.24\}$.

58. $(-\infty, \infty)$, or the set of all real numbers

59. $x^4 + 3x^2 \le 0$

$$x^2(x^2 + 3) \le 0$$

$x^2 = 0$ for $x = 0$, $x^2 > 0$ for $x \ne 0$, $x^2 + 3 > 0$ for all x

The solution set is $\{0\}$.

60. $(-\infty, 0.25] \cup [2.5, \infty)$, or $\{x | x \le 0.25 \ or \ x \ge 2.5\}$

61. a) $-3x^2 + 630x - 6000 > 0$

$$x^2 - 210x + 2000 < 0 \quad \text{Multiplying by } -\dfrac{1}{3}$$

$$(x - 200)(x - 10) < 0$$

The solutions of $f(x) = (x - 200)(x - 10) = 0$ are 200 and 10. They divide the number line as shown:

Enter $p(x) = x^2 - 210x + 2000$ in a graphing calculator and evaluate a test point in each interval. We test 9, 11, and 201.

We see that $p(x) < 0$ in interval B, so the company makes a profit for values of x such that $10 < x < 200$, or for values of x in the interval $(10, 200)$, or in the set $\{x | 10 < x < 200\}$.

b) See part (a). Keep in mind that x must be nonnegative since negative numbers have no meaning in this application.

The company loses money for values of x such that $0 \leq x < 10$ or $x > 200$, or for values of x in the interval $[0, 10) \cup (200, \infty)$, or in the set $\{x | 0 \leq x < 10 \text{ or } x > 200\}$.

62. a) $\{t | 0 \text{ sec} < t < 2 \text{ sec}\}$

b) $\{t | t > 10 \text{ sec}\}$

63. We find values of n such that $N \geq 66 \text{ and } N \leq 300$.

For $N \geq 66$:

$$\frac{n(n-1)}{2} \geq 66$$
$$n(n-1) \geq 132$$
$$n^2 - n - 132 \geq 0$$
$$(n-12)(n+11) \geq 0$$

The solutions of $f(n) = (n-12)(n+11) = 0$ are 12 and -11. They divide the number line as shown:

However, only positive values of n have meaning in this exercise so we need only consider the intervals shown below:

Enter $p(x) = x^2 - x - 132$ in a graphing calculator and evaluate a test point in each interval. We test 1 and 13.

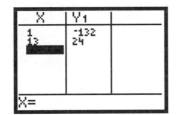

We see that $p(x) > 0$ in interval B. From above we also know that $p(12) = 0$, so the solution set for this inequality is $[12, \infty)$.

For $N \leq 300$:

$$\frac{n(n-1)}{2} \leq 300$$
$$n(n-1) \leq 600$$
$$n^2 - n - 600 \leq 0$$
$$(n-25)(n+24) \leq 0$$

The solutions of $f(n) = (n-25)(n+24) = 0$ are 25 and -24. They divide the number line as shown:

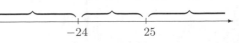

However, only positive values of n have meaning in this exercise so we need only consider the intervals shown below:

Enter $p(x) = x^2 - x - 600$ in a graphing calculator and evaluate a test point in each interval. We test 1 and 26.

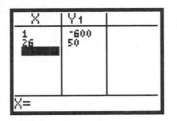

We see that $p(x) < 0$ in interval A. From above we also know that $p(25) = 0$, so the solution set for this inequality is $(0, 25]$. Then $66 \leq N \leq 300$ for $[12, \infty) \cap (0, 25]$, or on $[12, 25]$. We can express the solution set as $\{n | n \text{ is an integer and } 12 \leq n \leq 25\}$.

64. $\{n | n \text{ is an integer and } 9 \leq n \leq 23\}$

65. From the graph we determine the following:

$f(x)$ has no zeros.

The solutions $f(x) < 0$ are $(-\infty, 0)$, or $\{x | x < 0\}$.

The solutions of $f(x) > 0$ are $(0, \infty)$, or $\{x | x > 0\}$.

66. $f(x) = 0$ for $x = 0$ or $x = 1$;

$f(x) < 0$ for $(0, 1)$, or $\{x | 0 < x < 1\}$;

$f(x) > 0$ for $(1, \infty)$, or $\{x | x > 1\}$

67. From the graph we determine the following:

The solutions of $f(x) = 0$ are -2, 1, and 3.

The solution of $f(x) < 0$ is $(-\infty, -2) \cup (1, 3)$, or $\{x | x < -2 \text{ or } 1 < x < 3\}$.

The solution of $f(x) > 0$ is $(-2, 1) \cup (3, \infty)$, or $\{x | -2 < x < 1 \text{ or } x > 3\}$.

68. $f(x) = 0$ for -2, 1, 2, and 3;

$f(x) < 0$ for $(-2, 1) \cup (2, 3)$, or $\{x | -2 < x < 1 \text{ or } 2 < x < 3\}$;

$f(x) > 0$ for $(-\infty, -2) \cup (1, 2) \cup (3, \infty)$, or $\{x | x < -2 \text{ or } 1 < x < 2 \text{ or } x > 3\}$.

69. a) Enter the data and then use the quadratic regression feature. We have $w(x) = 1388.888889x^2 - 14,900x + 73,800$, where x is the number of years after 1994.

b) Graph $y_1 = w(x)$ and $y_2 = 50,000$. We choose the window $[0, 15, 0, 100, 000]$, Yscl $= 10,000$.

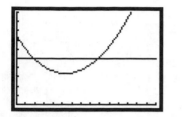

We use the Intersect feature to find that the first coordinates of the points of intersection of the graphs are approximately 2 and 9. Observe that the graph of y_1 lies above the graph of y_2 to the left of $x = 2$ and to the right of $x = 9$. Then the number of welfare cases is greater than 50,000 from 1994 to about 2 years after 1994, or from 1994 to 1996, and also after about 9 years after 1994, or after 2003.

Chapter 11

Exponential and Logarithmic Functions

1. $(f \circ g)(1) = f(g(1)) = f(2 \cdot 1 + 1)$
   $= f(3) = 3^2 + 3$
   $= 9 + 3 = 12$

   $(g \circ f)(1) = g(f(1)) = g(1^2 + 3)$
   $= g(4) = 2 \cdot 4 + 1 = 9$

   $(f \circ g)(x) = f(g(x)) = f(2x + 1)$
   $= (2x + 1)^2 + 3$
   $= 4x^2 + 4x + 1 + 3$
   $= 4x^2 + 4x + 4$

   $(g \circ f)(x) = g(f(x)) = g(x^2 + 3)$
   $= 2(x^2 + 3) + 1$
   $= 2x^2 + 6 + 1$
   $= 2x^2 + 7$

2. $-7; 4; 2x^2 - 9; 4x^2 + 4x - 4$

3. $(f \circ g)(x) = f(g(1)) = f(5 \cdot 1^2 + 2)$
   $= f(7) = 3 \cdot 7 - 1$
   $= 21 - 1 = 20$

   $(g \circ f)(1) = g(f(1)) = g(3 \cdot 1 - 1)$
   $= g(2) = 5 \cdot 2^2 + 2$
   $= 5 \cdot 4 + 2 = 20 + 2 = 22$

   $(f \circ g)(x) = f(g(x)) = f(5x^2 + 2)$
   $= 3(5x^2 + 2) - 1$
   $= 15x^2 + 6 - 1$
   $= 15x^2 + 5$

   $(g \circ f)(x) = g(f(x)) = g(3x - 1)$
   $= 5(3x - 1)^2 + 2$
   $= 5(9x^2 - 6x + 1) + 2$
   $= 45x^2 - 30x + 5 + 2$
   $= 45x^2 - 30x + 7$

4. $31; 27; 48x^2 - 24x + 7; 12x^2 + 15$

5. $(f \circ g)(1) = f(g(1)) = f\left(\dfrac{1}{1^2}\right)$
   $= f(1) = 1 + 7 = 8$

   $(g \circ f)(1) = g(f(1)) = g(1 + 7)$
   $= g(8) = \dfrac{1}{8^2} = \dfrac{1}{64}$

   $(f \circ g)(x) = f(g(x))$
   $= f\left(\dfrac{1}{x^2}\right) = \dfrac{1}{x^2} + 7$

$(g \circ f)(x) = g(f(x))$
$= g(x + 7) = \dfrac{1}{(x + 7)^2}$

6. $\dfrac{1}{9}; 3; \dfrac{1}{(x + 2)^2}; \dfrac{1}{x^2} + 2$

7. Since $(y_1 \circ y_2)(-3) = y_1(y_2(-3))$, we first find $y_2(-3)$. Locate -3 in the x-column and then move across to the y_2-column to find that $y_2(-3) = 1$. Now we have $y_1(y_2(-3)) = y_1(1)$. Locate 1 in the x-column and then move across to the y_1-column to find that $y_1(1) = 8$. Thus, $(y_1 \circ y_2)(-3) = 8$.

8. Not defined

9. Since $(y_1 \circ y_2)(-1) = y_1(y_2(-1))$, we first find $y_2(-1)$. Locate -1 in the x-column and then move across to the y_2-column to find that $y_2(-1) = -3$. Now we have $y_1(y_2(-1)) = y_1(-3)$. Locate -3 in the x-column and then move across to the y_1-column to find that $y_1(-3) = -4$. Thus, $(y_1 \circ y_2)(-1) = -4$.

10. 6

11. Since $(y_2 \circ y_1)(1) = y_2(y_1(1))$, we first find $y_1(1)$. Locate 1 in the x column and then move across to the y_1-column to find that $y_1(1) = 8$. Now we have $y_2(y_1(1)) = y_2(8)$. However, y_2 is not defined for $x = 8$, so $(y_2 \circ y_1)(1)$ is not defined.

12. 8

13. Since $(f \circ g)(2) = f(g(2))$, we first find $g(2)$. Locate 2 in the x-column and then move across to the $g(x)$-column to find that $g(2) = 5$. Now we have $f(g(2)) = f(5)$. Locate 5 in the x-column and then move across to the $f(x)$-column to find that $f(5) = 4$. Thus, $(f \circ g)(2) = 4$.

14. Not defined

15. To find $f(g(3))$ we first find $g(3)$. Locate 3 in the x-column and then move across to the $g(x)$-column to find that $g(3) = 8$. Now we have $f(g(3)) = f(8)$. However, $f(x)$ is not defined for $x = 8$, so $f(g(3))$ is not defined.

16. 5

17. $h(x) = (7 + 5x)^2$

    This is $7 + 5x$ raised to the second power, so the two most obvious functions are $f(x) = x^2$ and $g(x) = 7 + 5x$.

18. $f(x) = x^2$, $g(x) = 3x - 1$

19. $h(x) = \sqrt{2x + 7}$

    We have $2x + 7$ and take the square root of their expression, so the two most obvious functions are $f(x) = \sqrt{x}$ and $g(x) = 2x + 7$.

20. $f(x) = \sqrt{x}$, $g(x) = 5x + 2$

21. $h(x) = \dfrac{2}{x - 3}$

This is 2 divided by $x - 3$, so two functions that can be used are $f(x) = \dfrac{2}{x}$ and $g(x) = x - 3$.

22. $f(x) = x + 4$, $g(x) = \dfrac{3}{x}$

23. $h(x) = \dfrac{1}{\sqrt{7x + 2}}$

This is the reciprocal of the square root of $7x + 2$. Two functions that can be used are $f(x) = \dfrac{1}{\sqrt{x}}$ and $g(x) = 7x + 2$.

24. $f(x) = \sqrt{x} - 3$, $g(x) = x - 7$

25. $h(x) = \dfrac{1}{\sqrt{3x}} + \sqrt{3x}$

This is the reciprocal of the square root of $3x$ plus the square root of $3x$. Two functions that can be used are $f(x) = \dfrac{1}{x} + x$ and $g(x) = \sqrt{3x}$.

26. $f(x) = \dfrac{1}{x} - x$, $g(x) = \sqrt{2x}$

27. The graph of $f(x) = x - 5$ is shown below.

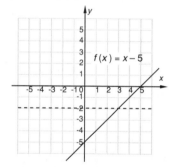

Since there is no horizontal line that crosses the graph more than once, the function is one-to-one.

28. Yes

29. $f(x) = x^2 + 1$

Observe that the graph of this function is a parabola that opens up. Thus, there are many horizontal lines that cross the graph more than once, so the function is not one-to-one. We can also draw the graph as shown below.

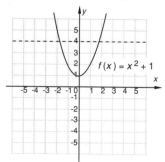

There are many horizontal lines that cross the graph more than once. In particular, the line $y = 4$ crosses the graph more than once. The function is not one-to-one.

30. No

31. The graph of $g(x) = x^3$ is shown below.

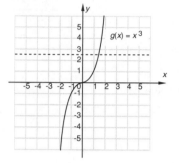

Since no horizontal line crosses the graph more than once, the function is one-to-one.

32. Yes The function is one-to-one.

33. The graph of $g(x) = |x|$ is shown below.

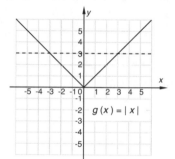

There are many horizontal lines that cross the graph more than once. In particular, the line $y = 3$ crosses the graph more than once. The function is not one-to-one.

34. No

35. a) The function $f(x) = x - 4$ is a linear function that is not constant, so it passes the horizontal-line test. Thus, f is one-to-one.

b) Replace $f(x)$ by y: $y = x - 4$

Interchange x and y: $x = y - 4$

Solve for y: $x + 4 = y$

Replace y by $f^{-1}(x)$: $f^{-1}(x) = x + 4$

36. a) Yes

b) $f^{-1}(x) = x + 2$

37. a) The function $f(x) = 3 + x$ is a linear function that is not constant, so it passes the horizontal-line test. Thus, f is one-to-one.

b) Replace $f(x)$ by y: $y = 3 + x$

Interchange x and y: $x = 3 + y$

Solve for y: $y = x - 3$

Replace y by $f^{-1}(x)$: $f^{-1}(x) = x - 3$

38. a) Yes

b) $f^{-1}(x) = x - 9$

39. a) The function $g(x) = x + 5$ is a linear function that is not constant, so it passes the horizontal-line test. Thus, g is one-to-one.

b) Replace $g(x)$ by y: $y = x + 5$

Interchange x and y: $x = y + 5$

Solve for y: $x - 5 = y$

Replace y by $g^{-1}(x)$: $g^{-1}(x) = x - 5$

40. a) Yes

b) $g^{-1}(x) = x - 8$

41. a) The function $f(x) = 4x$ is a linear function that is not constant, so it passes the horizontal-line test. Thus, f is one-to-one.

b) Replace $f(x)$ by y: $y = 4x$

Interchange x and y: $x = 4y$

Solve for y: $\dfrac{x}{4} = y$

Replace y by $f^{-1}(x)$: $f^{-1}(x) = \dfrac{x}{4}$

42. a) Yes

b) $f^{-1}(x) = \dfrac{x}{7}$

43. a) The function $g(x) = 4x - 1$ is a linear function that is not constant, so it passes the horizontal-line test. Thus, g is one-to-one.

b) Replace $g(x)$ by y: $y = 4x - 1$

Interchange variables: $x = 4y - 1$

Solve for y: $x + 1 = 4y$

$\dfrac{x+1}{4} = y$

Replace y by $g^{-1}(x)$: $g^{-1}(x) = \dfrac{x+1}{4}$

44. a) Yes

b) $g^{-1}(x) = \dfrac{x+6}{4}$

45. a) The graph of $h(x) = 5$ is shown below. The horizontal line $y = 5$ crosses the graph more than once, so the function is not one-to-one.

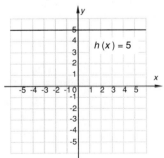

46. a) No

47. a) The graph of $f(x) = \dfrac{1}{x}$ is shown below. It passes the horizontal-line test, so the function is one-to-one.

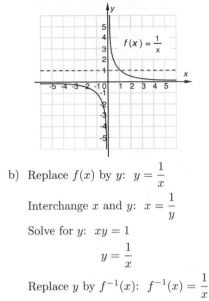

b) Replace $f(x)$ by y: $y = \dfrac{1}{x}$

Interchange x and y: $x = \dfrac{1}{y}$

Solve for y: $xy = 1$

$y = \dfrac{1}{x}$

Replace y by $f^{-1}(x)$: $f^{-1}(x) = \dfrac{1}{x}$

48. a) Yes

b) $f^{-1}(x) = \dfrac{3}{x}$

49. a) The function $f(x) = \dfrac{2x+1}{3} = \dfrac{2}{3}x + \dfrac{1}{3}$ is a linear function that is not constant, so it passes the horizontal-line test. Thus, f is one-to-one.

b) Replace $f(x)$ by y: $y = \dfrac{2x+1}{3}$

Interchange x and y: $x = \dfrac{2y+1}{3}$

Solve for y: $3x = 2y + 1$

$3x - 1 = 2y$

$\dfrac{3x-1}{2} = y$

Replace y by $f^{-1}(x)$: $f^{-1}(x) = \dfrac{3x-1}{2}$

50. a) Yes

b) $f^{-1}(x) = \dfrac{5x-2}{3}$

51. a) The graph of $f(x) = x^3 - 5$ is shown below. It passes the horizontal-line test, so the function is one-to-one.

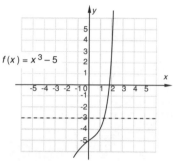

b) Replace $f(x)$ by y: $y = x^3 - 5$

Interchange x and y: $x = y^3 - 5$

Solve for y: $x + 5 = y^3$

$\sqrt[3]{x + 5} = y$

Replace y by $f^{-1}(x)$: $f^{-1}(x) = \sqrt[3]{x + 5}$

52. a) Yes

b) $f^{-1}(x) = \sqrt[3]{x - 2}$

53. a) The graph of $g(x) = (x - 2)^3$ is shown below. It passes the horizontal-line test, so the function is one-to-one.

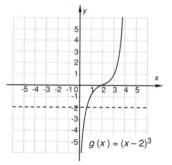

b) Replace $g(x)$ by y: $y = (x - 2)^3$

Interchange x and y: $x = (y - 2)^3$

Solve for y: $\sqrt[3]{x} = y - 2$

$\sqrt[3]{x} + 2 = y$

Replace y by $g^{-1}(x)$: $g^{-1}(x) = \sqrt[3]{x} + 2$

54. a) Yes

b) $g^{-1}(x) = \sqrt[3]{x} - 7$

55. a) The graph of $f(x) = \sqrt{x}$ is shown below. It passes the horizontal-line test, so the function is one-to-one.

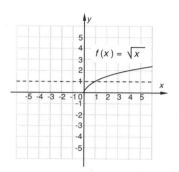

b) Replace $f(x)$ by y: $y = \sqrt{x}$ (Note that $f(x) \geq 0$.)

Interchange x and y: $x = \sqrt{y}$

Solve for y: $x^2 = y$

Replace y by $f^{-1}(x)$: $f^{-1}(x) = x^2,\ x \geq 0$

56. a) Yes

b) $f^{-1}(x) = x^2 + 1,\ x \geq 0$

57. a) The graph of $f(x) = 2x^2 + 1$, $x \geq 0$, is shown below. It passes the horizontal-line test, so the function is one-to-one.

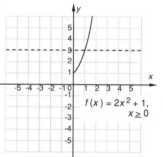

b) Replace $f(x)$ by y: $y = 2x^2 + 1$

Interchange x and y: $x = 2y^2 + 1$

Solve for y: $x - 1 = 2y^2$

$\dfrac{x - 1}{2} = y^2$

$\sqrt{\dfrac{x - 1}{2}} = y$

(We take the principal square root since $y \geq 0$.)

Replace y by $f^{-1}(x)$: $f^{-1}(x) = \sqrt{\dfrac{x - 1}{2}}$

58. a) Yes

b) $f^{-1}(x) = \sqrt{\dfrac{x + 2}{3}}$

59. First graph $f(x) = \frac{1}{3}x - 2$. Then graph the inverse function by reflecting the graph of $f(x) = \frac{1}{3}x - 2$ across the line $y = x$. The graph of the inverse function can also be found by first finding a formula for the inverse, substituting to find function values, and then plotting points.

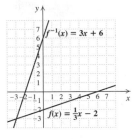

60.

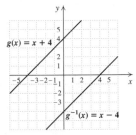

61. Follow the procedure described in Exercise 59 to graph the function and its inverse.

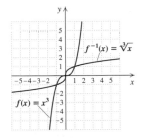

62.

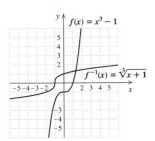

63. Use the procedure described in Exercise 59 to graph the function and its inverse.

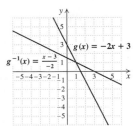

64.

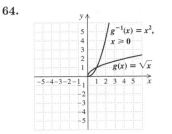

65. Use the procedure described in Exercise 59 to graph the function and its inverse.

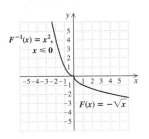

66.

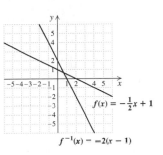

67. Use the procedure described in Exercise 59 to graph the function and its inverse.

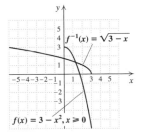

68.

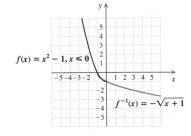

69. We check to see that $f^{-1} \circ f(x) = x$ and $f \circ f^{-1}(x) = x$.

a) $f^{-1} \circ f(x) = f^{-1}(f(x)) = f^{-1}\left(\frac{4}{5}x\right) =$

$\frac{5}{4} \cdot \frac{4}{5}x = x$

b) $f \circ f^{-1}(x) = f(f^{-1}(x)) = f\left(\dfrac{5}{4}x\right) =$

$$\dfrac{4}{5} \cdot \dfrac{5}{4}x = x$$

70. a) $f^{-1} \circ f(x) = 3\left(\dfrac{x+7}{3}\right) - 7 = x + 7 - 7 = x$

b) $f \circ f^{-1}(x) = \dfrac{(3x-7)+7}{3} = \dfrac{3x}{3} = x$

71. We check to see that $f^{-1} \circ f(x) = x$ and $f \circ f^{-1}(x) = x$.

a) $f^{-1} \circ f(x) = f^{-1}(f(x)) = f^{-1}\left(\dfrac{1-x}{x}\right) =$

$$\dfrac{1}{\dfrac{1-x}{x}+1} = \dfrac{1}{\dfrac{1-x}{x}+1} \cdot \dfrac{x}{x} = \dfrac{x}{1-x+x} =$$

$$\dfrac{x}{1} = x$$

b) $f \circ f^{-1}(x) = f(f^{-1}(x)) = f\left(\dfrac{1}{x+1}\right) =$

$$\dfrac{1-\dfrac{1}{x+1}}{\dfrac{1}{x+1}} = \dfrac{1-\dfrac{1}{x+1}}{\dfrac{1}{x+1}} \cdot \dfrac{x+1}{x+1} =$$

$$\dfrac{x+1-1}{1} = \dfrac{x}{1} = x$$

72. a) $f^{-1} \circ f(x) = \sqrt[3]{x^3-5+5} = \sqrt[3]{x^3} = x$

b) $f \circ f^{-1}(x) = (\sqrt[3]{x+5})^3 - 5 = x + 5 - 5 = x$

73. Let $y_1 = f(x)$, $y_2 = g(x)$, $y_3 = y_1(y_2)$, and $y_4 = y_2(y_1)$. A table of values shows that $y_3 \neq x$ nor is $y_4 = x$, so $f(x)$ and $g(x)$ are not inverses of each other.

74. Yes

75. Let $y_1 = f(x)$, $y_2 = g(x)$, $y_3 = y_1(y_2)$, and $y_4 = y_2(y_1)$. A table of values shows that $y_3 = x$ and $y_4 = x$ for any value of x, so $f(x)$ and $g(x)$ are inverses of each other.

76. No

77. (1) C; (2) D; (3) B; (4) A

78. (1) D; (2) C; (3) B; (4) A

79. a) $f(8) = 8 + 32 = 40$

Size 40 in France corresponds to size 8 in the U.S.

$f(10) = 10 + 32 = 42$

Size 42 in France corresponds to size 10 in the U.S.

$f(14) = 14 + 32 = 46$

Size 46 in France corresponds to size 14 in the U.S.

$f(18) = 18 + 32 = 50$

Size 50 in France corresponds to size 18 in the U.S.

b) The function $f(x) = x + 32$ is a linear function that is not constant, so it passes the horizontal-line test. Thus, f is one-to-one and, hence, has an inverse that is a function. We now find a formula for the inverse.

Replace $f(x)$ by y: $y = x + 32$

Interchange x and y: $x = y + 32$

Solve for y: $x - 32 = y$

Replace y by $f^{-1}(x)$: $f^{-1}(x) = x - 32$

c) $f^{-1}(40) = 40 - 32 = 8$

Size 8 in the U.S. corresponds to size 40 in France.

$f^{-1}(42) = 42 - 32 = 10$

Size 10 in the U.S. corresponds to size 42 in France.

$f^{-1}(46) = 46 - 32 = 14$

Size 14 in the U.S. corresponds to size 46 in France.

$f^{-1}(50) = 50 - 32 = 18$

Size 18 in the U.S. corresponds to size 50 in France.

80. a) 40; 44; 52; 60

b) $f^{-1}(x) = \dfrac{x-24}{2}$, or $\dfrac{x}{2} - 12$

c) 8; 10; 14; 18

81. *Writing Exercise*

82. *Writing Exercise*

83. $(a^5b^4)^2(a^3b^5) = (a^5)^2(b^4)^2(a^3b^5)$

$$= a^{5 \cdot 2}b^{4 \cdot 2}a^3b^5$$

$$= a^{10}b^8a^3b^5$$

$$= a^{10+3}b^{8+5}$$

$$= a^{13}b^{13}$$

84. $x^{10}y^{12}$

85. $27^{4/3} = (3^3)^{4/3} = 3^{3 \cdot \frac{4}{3}} = 3^4 = 81$

86. 125

87. $$x = \dfrac{2}{3}y - 7$$

$$x + 7 = \dfrac{2}{3}y$$

$$\dfrac{3}{2}(x+7) = y$$

88. $y = \dfrac{10-x}{3}$

89. *Writing Exercise*

90. *Writing Exercise*

91. Reflect the graph of f across the line $y = x$.

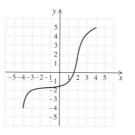

92.

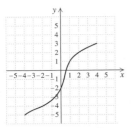

93. From Exercise 80(b), we know that a function that converts dress sizes in Italy to those in the United States is $g(x) = \dfrac{x - 24}{2}$. From Exercise 79(a), we know that a function that converts dress sizes in the United States to those in France is $f(x) = x + 32$. Then a function that converts dress sizes in Italy to those in France is

$$h(x) = (f \circ g)(x)$$
$$h(x) = f\left(\frac{x - 24}{2}\right)$$
$$h(x) = \frac{x - 24}{2} + 32$$
$$h(x) = \frac{x}{2} - 12 + 32$$
$$h(x) = \frac{x}{2} + 20.$$

94. $h(x) = 2(x - 20)$

95. *Writing Exercise*

96. $((f \circ g) \circ h)(x) = (f \circ g)(h(x))$
$$= f(g(h(x))) = f((g \circ h)(x))$$
$$= (f \circ (g \circ h))(x)$$

97. Suppose that $h(x) = (f \circ g)(x)$. First note that for $I(x) = x$, $(f \circ I)(x) = f(I(x))$ for any function f.

i) $((g^{-1} \circ f^{-1}) \circ h)(x) = ((g^{-1} \circ f^{-1}) \circ (f \circ g))(x)$
$$= ((g^{-1} \circ (f^{-1} \circ f)) \circ g)(x)$$
$$= ((g^{-1} \circ I) \circ g)(x)$$
$$= (g^{-1} \circ g)(x) = x$$

ii) $(h \circ (g^{-1} \circ f^{-1}))(x) = ((f \circ g) \circ (g^{-1} \circ f^{-1}))(x)$
$$= ((f \circ (g \circ g^{-1})) \circ f^{-1})(x)$$
$$= ((f \circ I) \circ f^{-1})(x)$$
$$= (f \circ f^{-1})(x) = x$$

Therefore, $(g^{-1} \circ f^{-1})(x) = h^{-1}(x)$.

98. (1) C; (2) A; (3) B; (4) D

99. *Writing Exercise.* Observe the following:
$$f(6) = 6 \text{ and } g(6) = 6,$$
$$f(8) = 7 \text{ and } g(7) = 8,$$
$$f(10) = 8 \text{ and } g(8) = 10,$$
$$f(12) = 9 \text{ and } g(9) = 12.$$

It appears that the functions are inverses.

100. $f(x) = \dfrac{1}{2}x + 3$, $g(x) = 2x - 6$

101. $(c \circ f)(n)$ represents the cost of mailing n copies of the book.

102. $(c \circ g)(a)$; it represents the cost of sealant required for a bamboo floor with area a.

103. $R(10) \approx 18$ and $p(18) \approx 22$, so $p(R(10)) \approx 22$ mm of mercury.

104. The pressure in the artery after 10 minutes of bicycling

105. Locate 20 on the vertical axis of the second graph, move across to the curve, and then move down to the horizontal axis to find that $p^{-1}(20) \approx 15$ liters per minute.

106. The rate of blood flow for the heart when the pressure in the artery is 20 mm of mercury

Exercise Set 11.2

1. The function values increase as x increases, so $a > 1$.

2. $0 < a < 1$

3. The function values decrease as x increases, so $0 < a < 1$.

4. $a > 1$

5. Graph: $y = 2^x$

We compute some function values, thinking of y as $f(x)$, and keep the results in a table.
$$f(0) = 2^0 = 1$$
$$f(1) = 2^1 = 2$$
$$f(2) = 2^2 = 4$$
$$f(-1) = 2^{-1} = \frac{1}{2^1} = \frac{1}{2}$$
$$f(-2) = 2^{-2} = \frac{1}{2^2} = \frac{1}{4}$$

x	y, or $f(x)$
0	1
1	2
2	4
-1	$\frac{1}{2}$
-2	$\frac{1}{4}$

Next we plot these points and connect them with a smooth curve.

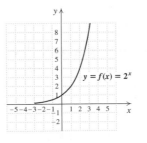

6.

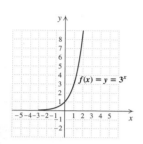

7. Graph: $y = 5^x$

We compute some function values, thinking of y as $f(x)$, and keep the results in a table.

$$f(0) = 5^0 = 1$$
$$f(1) = 5^1 = 5$$
$$f(2) = 5^2 = 25$$
$$f(-1) = 5^{-1} = \frac{1}{5^1} = \frac{1}{5}$$
$$f(-2) = 5^{-2} = \frac{1}{5^2} = \frac{1}{25}$$

x	y, or $f(x)$
0	1
1	5
2	25
-1	$\dfrac{1}{5}$
-2	$\dfrac{1}{25}$

Next we plot these points and connect them with a smooth curve.

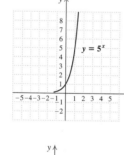

8.

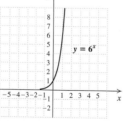

9. Graph: $y = 2^x + 3$

We compute some function values, thinking of y as $f(x)$, and keep the results in a table.

$$f(-4) = 2^{-4} + 3 = \frac{1}{2^4} + 3 = \frac{1}{16} + 3 = 3\frac{1}{16}$$
$$f(-2) = 2^{-2} + 3 = \frac{1}{2^2} + 3 = \frac{1}{4} + 3 = 3\frac{1}{4}$$

$$f(0) = 2^0 + 3 = 1 + 3 = 4$$
$$f(1) = 2^1 + 3 = 2 + 3 = 5$$
$$f(2) = 2^2 + 3 = 4 + 3 = 7$$

x	y, or $f(x)$
-4	$3\dfrac{1}{16}$
-2	$3\dfrac{1}{4}$
0	4
1	5
2	7

Next we plot these points and connect them with a smooth curve.

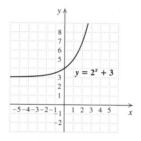

10.

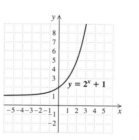

11. Graph: $y = 3^x - 1$

We compute some function values, thinking of y as $f(x)$, and keep the results in a table.

$$f(-3) = 3^{-3} - 1 = \frac{1}{3^3} - 1 = \frac{1}{27} - 1 = -\frac{26}{27}$$
$$f(-1) = 3^{-1} - 1 = \frac{1}{3} - 1 = -\frac{2}{3}$$
$$f(0) = 3^0 - 1 = 1 - 1 = 0$$
$$f(1) = 3^1 - 1 = 3 - 1 = 2$$
$$f(2) = 3^2 - 1 = 9 - 1 = 8$$

x	y, or $f(x)$
-3	$-\dfrac{26}{27}$
-1	$-\dfrac{2}{3}$
0	0
1	2
2	8

Next we plot these points and connect them with a smooth curve.

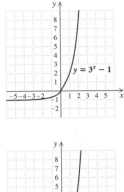

12.

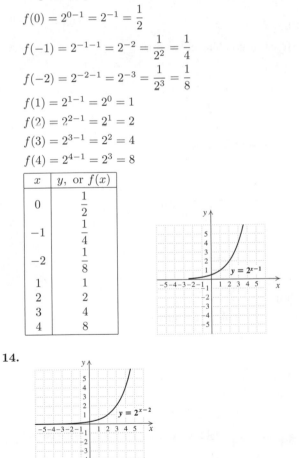

13. Graph: $y = 2^{x-1}$

We construct a table of values, thinking of y as $f(x)$. Then we plot the points and connect them with a smooth curve.

$$f(0) = 2^{0-1} = 2^{-1} = \frac{1}{2}$$

$$f(-1) = 2^{-1-1} = 2^{-2} = \frac{1}{2^2} = \frac{1}{4}$$

$$f(-2) = 2^{-2-1} = 2^{-3} = \frac{1}{2^3} = \frac{1}{8}$$

$$f(1) = 2^{1-1} = 2^0 = 1$$

$$f(2) = 2^{2-1} = 2^1 = 2$$

$$f(3) = 2^{3-1} = 2^2 = 4$$

$$f(4) = 2^{4-1} = 2^3 = 8$$

x	y, or $f(x)$
0	$\frac{1}{2}$
-1	$\frac{1}{4}$
-2	$\frac{1}{8}$
1	1
2	2
3	4
4	8

14.

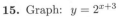

15. Graph: $y = 2^{x+3}$

We construct a table of values, thinking of y as $f(x)$. Then we plot the points and connect them with a smooth curve.

$$f(-4) = 2^{-4+3} = 2^{-1} = \frac{1}{2}$$

$$f(-2) = 2^{-2+3} = 2$$

$$f(-1) = 2^{-1+3} = 2^2 = 4$$

$$f(0) = 2^{0+3} = 2^3 = 8$$

x	y, or $f(x)$
-4	$\frac{1}{2}$
-2	2
-1	4
0	8

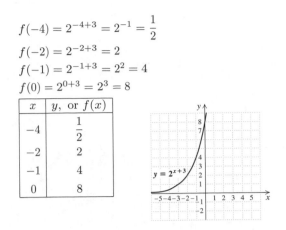

16.

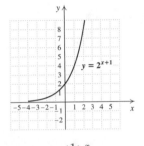

17. Graph: $y = \left(\frac{1}{5}\right)^x$

We construct a table of values, thinking of y as $f(x)$. Then we plot the points and connect them with a smooth curve.

$$f(0) = \left(\frac{1}{5}\right)^0 = 1$$

$$f(1) = \left(\frac{1}{5}\right)^1 = \frac{1}{5}$$

$$f(2) = \left(\frac{1}{5}\right)^2 = \frac{1}{25}$$

$$f(-1) = \left(\frac{1}{5}\right)^{-1} = \frac{1}{\frac{1}{5}} = 5$$

$$f(-2) = \left(\frac{1}{5}\right)^{-2} = \frac{1}{\frac{1}{25}} = 25$$

x	y, or $f(x)$
0	1
1	$\frac{1}{5}$
2	$\frac{1}{25}$
-1	5
-2	25

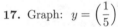

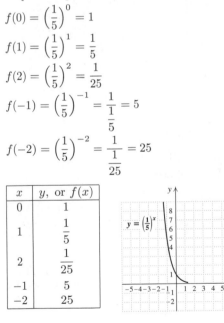

18.

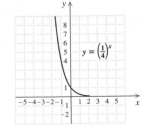

19. Graph: $y = \left(\dfrac{1}{2}\right)^x$

We construct a table of values, thinking of y as $f(x)$. Then we plot the points and connect them with a smooth curve.

$f(0) = \left(\dfrac{1}{2}\right)^0 = 1$

$f(1) = \left(\dfrac{1}{2}\right)^1 = \dfrac{1}{2}$

$f(2) = \left(\dfrac{1}{2}\right)^2 = \dfrac{1}{4}$

$f(3) = \left(\dfrac{1}{2}\right)^3 = \dfrac{1}{8}$

$f(-1) = \left(\dfrac{1}{2}\right)^{-1} = \dfrac{1}{\left(\frac{1}{2}\right)^1} = \dfrac{1}{\frac{1}{2}} = 2$

$f(-2) = \left(\dfrac{1}{2}\right)^{-2} = \dfrac{1}{\left(\frac{1}{2}\right)^2} = \dfrac{1}{\frac{1}{4}} = 4$

$f(-3) = \left(\dfrac{1}{2}\right)^{-3} = \dfrac{1}{\left(\frac{1}{2}\right)^3} = \dfrac{1}{\frac{1}{8}} = 8$

x	y, or $f(x)$
0	1
1	$\dfrac{1}{2}$
2	$\dfrac{1}{4}$
3	$\dfrac{1}{8}$
−1	2
−2	4
−3	8

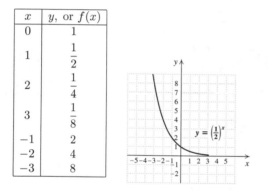

20.

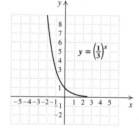

21. Graph: $y = 2^{x-3} - 1$

We construct a table of values, thinking of y as $f(x)$. Then we plot the points and connect them with a smooth curve.

$f(0) = 2^{0-3} - 1 = 2^{-3} - 1 = \dfrac{1}{8} - 1 = -\dfrac{7}{8}$

$f(1) = 2^{1-3} - 1 = 2^{-2} - 1 = \dfrac{1}{4} - 1 = -\dfrac{3}{4}$

$f(2) = 2^{2-3} - 1 = 2^{-1} - 1 = \dfrac{1}{2} - 1 = -\dfrac{1}{2}$

$f(3) = 2^{3-3} - 1 = 2^0 - 1 = 1 - 1 = 0$

$f(4) = 2^{4-3} - 1 = 2^1 - 1 = 2 - 1 = 1$

$f(5) = 2^{5-3} - 1 = 2^2 - 1 = 4 - 1 = 3$

$f(6) = 2^{6-3} - 1 = 2^3 - 1 = 8 - 1 = 7$

x	y, or $f(x)$
0	$-\dfrac{7}{8}$
1	$-\dfrac{3}{4}$
2	$-\dfrac{1}{2}$
3	0
4	1
5	3
6	7

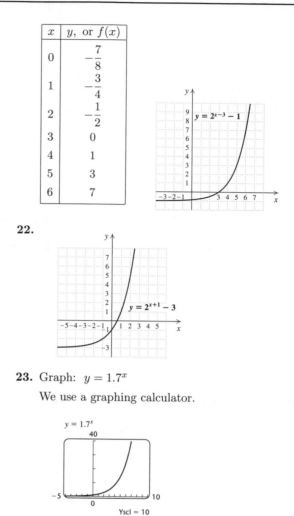

22.

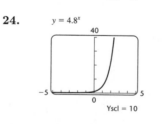

23. Graph: $y = 1.7^x$

We use a graphing calculator.

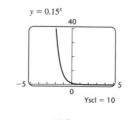

24.

25. Graph: $y = 0.15^x$

We use a graphing calculator.

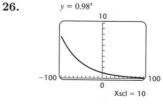

26.

27. Graph: $x = 3^y$

We can find ordered pairs by choosing values for y and then computing values for x.

For $y = 0$, $x = 3^0 = 1$.

For $y = 1$, $x = 3^1 = 3$.

For $y = 2$, $x = 3^2 = 9$.

For $y = 3$, $x = 3^3 = 27$.

For $y = -1$, $x = 3^{-1} = \dfrac{1}{3^1} = \dfrac{1}{3}$.

For $y = -2$, $x = 3^{-2} = \dfrac{1}{3^2} = \dfrac{1}{9}$.

For $y = -3$, $x = 3^{-3} = \dfrac{1}{3^3} = \dfrac{1}{27}$.

x	y
1	0
3	1
9	2
27	3
$\dfrac{1}{3}$	-1
$\dfrac{1}{9}$	-2
$\dfrac{1}{27}$	-3

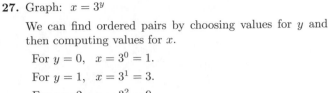
┌─ (1) Choose values for y.
└── (2) Compute values for x.

We plot the points and connect them with a smooth curve.

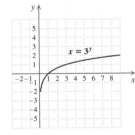

28.

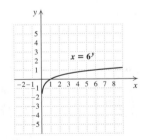

29. Graph: $x = 2^{-y} = \left(\dfrac{1}{2}\right)^y$

We can find ordered pairs by choosing values for y and then computing values for x. Then we plot these points and connect them with a smooth curve.

For $y = 0$, $x = \left(\dfrac{1}{2}\right)^0 = 1$.

For $y = 1$, $x = \left(\dfrac{1}{2}\right)^1 = \dfrac{1}{2}$.

For $y = 2$, $x = \left(\dfrac{1}{2}\right)^2 = \dfrac{1}{4}$.

For $y = 3$, $x = \left(\dfrac{1}{2}\right)^3 = \dfrac{1}{8}$.

For $y = -1$, $x = \left(\dfrac{1}{2}\right)^{-1} = \dfrac{1}{\frac{1}{2}} = 2$.

For $y = -2$, $x = \left(\dfrac{1}{2}\right)^{-2} = \dfrac{1}{\frac{1}{4}} = 4$.

For $y = -3$, $x = \left(\dfrac{1}{2}\right)^{-3} = \dfrac{1}{\frac{1}{8}} = 8$.

x	y
1	0
$\dfrac{1}{2}$	1
$\dfrac{1}{4}$	2
$\dfrac{1}{8}$	3
2	-1
4	-2
8	-3

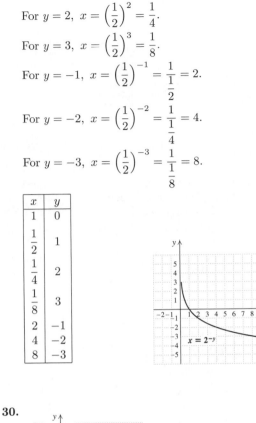

30.

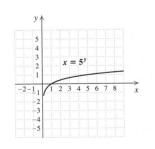

31. Graph: $x = 5^y$

We can find ordered pairs by choosing values for y and then computing values for x. Then we plot these points and connect them with a smooth curve.

For $y = 0$, $x = 5^0 = 1$.

For $y = 1$, $x = 5^1 = 5$.

For $y = 2$, $x = 5^2 = 25$.

For $y = -1$, $x = 5^{-1} = \dfrac{1}{5}$.

For $y = -2$, $x = 5^{-2} = \dfrac{1}{25}$.

x	y
1	0
5	1
25	2
$\dfrac{1}{5}$	-1
$\dfrac{1}{25}$	-2

32.

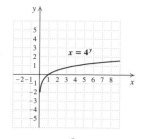

33. Graph: $x = \left(\dfrac{3}{2}\right)^y$

We can find ordered pairs by choosing values for y and then computing values for x. Then we plot these points and connect them with a smooth curve.

For $y = 0$, $x = \left(\dfrac{3}{2}\right)^0 = 1$.

For $y = 1$, $x = \left(\dfrac{3}{2}\right)^1 = \dfrac{3}{2}$.

For $y = 2$, $x = \left(\dfrac{3}{2}\right)^2 = \dfrac{9}{4}$.

For $y = 3$, $x = \left(\dfrac{3}{2}\right)^3 = \dfrac{27}{8}$.

For $y = -1$, $x = \left(\dfrac{3}{2}\right)^{-1} = \dfrac{1}{\frac{3}{2}} = \dfrac{2}{3}$.

For $y = -2$, $x = \left(\dfrac{3}{2}\right)^{-2} = \dfrac{1}{\frac{9}{4}} = \dfrac{4}{9}$.

For $y = -3$, $x = \left(\dfrac{3}{2}\right)^{-3} = \dfrac{1}{\frac{27}{8}} = \dfrac{8}{27}$.

x	y
1	0
$\dfrac{3}{2}$	1
$\dfrac{9}{4}$	2
$\dfrac{27}{8}$	3
$\dfrac{2}{3}$	-1
$\dfrac{4}{9}$	-2
$\dfrac{8}{27}$	-3

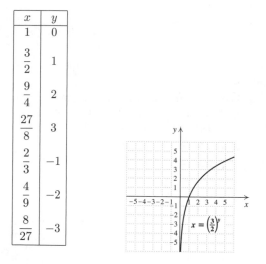

34.

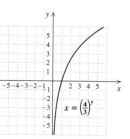

35. Graph $y = 3^x$ (see Exercise 2) and $x = 3^y$ (see Exercise 21) using the same set of axes.

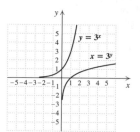

36.

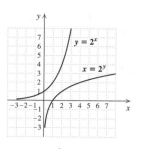

37. Graph $y = \left(\dfrac{1}{2}\right)^x$ (see Exercise 13) and $x = \left(\dfrac{1}{2}\right)^y$ (see Exercise 23) using the same set of axes.

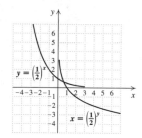

38.

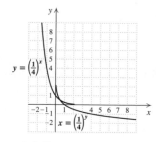

39. $y = \left(\dfrac{5}{2}\right)^x$ is an exponential function of the form $y = a^x$ with $a > 1$, so y-values will increase as x-values increase. Also, observe that when $x = 0$, $y = 1$. Thus, graph (d) corresponds to this equation.

40. (e)

41. For $x = \left(\dfrac{2}{5}\right)^y$, when $y = 0$, $x = 1$. The only graph that contains the point $(1, 0)$ is (f). This graph corresponds to the given equation.

42. (a)

43. $y = \left(\dfrac{2}{5}\right)^{x-2}$ is an exponential function of the form $y = a^x$ with $0 < a < 1$, so y-values will decrease as x-values increase. Also, observe that when $x = 2$, $y = 1$. Thus, graph (c) corresponds to the given equation.

44. (b)

45. a) In 2004, $t = 2004 - 1975 = 29$.

$$P(29) = 4(1.0164)^{29} \approx 6.4$$

The world population will be about 6.4 billion in 2004.
In 2008, $t = 2008 - 1975 = 33$.

$$P(33) = 4(1.0164)^{33} \approx 6.8$$

The world population will be about 6.8 billion in 2008.
In 2012, $t = 2012 - 1975 = 37$.

$$P(37) = 4(1.0164)^{37} \approx 7.3$$

The world population will be about 7.3 billion in 2012.

b)

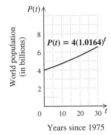

46. a) 4243; 6000; 8485; 12,000; 24,000

b)

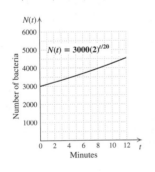

47. a) In 1930, $t = 1930 - 1900 = 30$.

$$P(t) = 150(0.960)^t$$
$$P(30) = 150(0.960)^{30}$$
$$\approx 44.079$$

In 1930, about 44.079 thousand, or 44,079, humpback whales were alive.
In 1960, $t = 1960 - 1900 = 60$.

$$P(t) = 150(0.960)^t$$
$$P(60) = 150(0.960)^{60}$$
$$\approx 12.953$$

In 1960, about 12.953 thousand, or 12,953, humpback whales were alive.

b) Plot the points found in part (a), $(30, 44,079)$ and $(60, 12,953)$ and additional points as needed and graph the function.

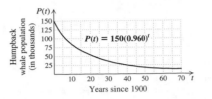

48. a) About 8706; about 13,163

b)

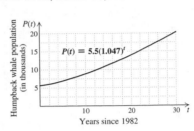

49. a) Substitute for t.

$$N(0) = 250,000\left(\frac{2}{3}\right)^0 = 250,000 \cdot 1 = 250,000;$$
$$N(1) = 250,000\left(\frac{2}{3}\right)^1 = 250,000 \cdot \frac{2}{3} = 166,667;$$
$$N(4) = 250,000\left(\frac{2}{3}\right)^4 = 250,000 \cdot \frac{16}{81} \approx 49,383;$$
$$N(10) = 250,000\left(\frac{2}{3}\right)^{10} = 250,000 \cdot \frac{1024}{59,049} \approx 4335$$

b) We use the function values computed in part (a) to draw the graph of the function. Note that the axes are scaled differently because of the large function values.

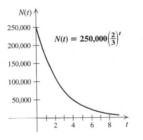

50. a) $5200; $4160; $3328; $1703.94; $558.35

b)

51. a) In 1985, $t = 1985 - 1985 = 0$.

$N(0) = 0.3(1.4477)^0 = 0.3(1) = 0.3$ million, or 300,000

In 1995, $t = 1995 - 1985 = 10$.

$N(10) = 0.3(1.4477)^{10} \approx 12.1$ million

In 2005, $t = 2005 - 1985 = 20$.

$N(20) = 0.3(1.4477)^{20} \approx 490.6$ million

In 2010, $t = 2010 - 1985 = 25$.

$N(25) = 0.3(1.4477)^{25} \approx 3119.5$ million, or 3.1195 billion

b) We use the function values computed in part (a) to draw the graph of the function. Note that the axes are scaled differently because of the large function values.

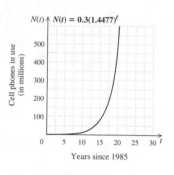

52. a) 454,354,240 cm²; 525,233,501,400 cm²

b)

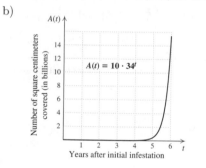

53. *Writing Exercise*

54. *Writing Exercise*

55. $5^{-2} = \dfrac{1}{5^2} = \dfrac{1}{25}$

56. $\dfrac{1}{32}$

57. $1000^{2/3} = (10^3)^{2/3} = 10^{3 \cdot \frac{2}{3}} = 10^2 = 100$

58. $\dfrac{1}{125}$

59. $\dfrac{10a^8b^7}{2a^2b^4} = \dfrac{10}{2}a^{8-2}b^{7-4} = 5a^6b^3$

60. $6x^4y$

61. *Writing Exercise*

62. *Writing Exercise*

63. Since the bases are the same, the one with the larger exponent is the larger number. Thus $\pi^{2.4}$ is larger.

64. $8^{\sqrt{3}}$

65. Graph: $y = 2^x + 2^{-x}$

Construct a table of values, thinking of y as $f(x)$. Then plot these points and connect them with a curve.

$f(0) = 2^0 + 2^{-0} = 1 + 1 = 2$

$f(1) = 2^1 + 2^{-1} = 2 + \dfrac{1}{2} = 2\dfrac{1}{2}$

$f(2) = 2^2 + 2^{-2} = 4 + \dfrac{1}{4} = 4\dfrac{1}{4}$

$f(3) = 2^3 + 2^{-3} = 8 + \dfrac{1}{8} = 8\dfrac{1}{8}$

$f(-1) = 2^{-1} + 2^{-(-1)} = \dfrac{1}{2} + 2 = 2\dfrac{1}{2}$

$f(-2) = 2^{-2} + 2^{-(-2)} = \dfrac{1}{4} + 4 = 4\dfrac{1}{4}$

$f(-3) = 2^{-3} + 2^{-(-3)} = \dfrac{1}{8} + 8 = 8\dfrac{1}{8}$

x	y, or $f(x)$
0	2
1	$2\dfrac{1}{2}$
2	$4\dfrac{1}{4}$
3	$8\dfrac{1}{8}$
-1	$2\dfrac{1}{2}$
-2	$4\dfrac{1}{4}$
-3	$8\dfrac{1}{8}$

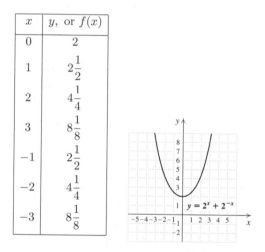

66.

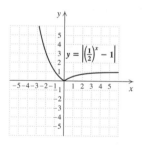

67. Graph: $y = |2^x - 2|$

We construct a table of values, thinking of y as $f(x)$. Then plot these points and connect them with a curve.

$f(0) = |2^0 - 2| = |1 - 2| = |-1| = 1$

$f(1) = |2^1 - 2| = |2 - 2| = |0| = 0$

$f(2) = |2^2 - 2| = |4 - 2| = |2| = 2$

$f(3) = |2^3 - 2| = |8 - 2| = |6| = 6$

$f(-1) = |2^{-1} - 2| = \left|\dfrac{1}{2} - 2\right| = \left|-\dfrac{3}{2}\right| = \dfrac{3}{2}$

$$f(-3) = |2^{-3} - 2| = \left|\frac{1}{8} - 2\right| = \left|-\frac{15}{8}\right| = \frac{15}{8}$$

$$f(-5) = |2^{-5} - 2| = \left|\frac{1}{32} - 2\right| = \left|-\frac{63}{32}\right| = \frac{63}{32}$$

x	y, or $f(x)$
0	1
1	0
2	2
3	6
−1	$\frac{3}{2}$
−3	$\frac{15}{8}$
−5	$\frac{63}{32}$

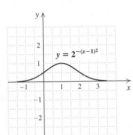

68.

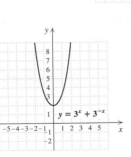

69. Graph: $y = |2x^2 - 1|$

We construct a table of values, thinking of y as $f(x)$. Then we plot these points and connect them with a curve.

$$f(0) = |2^{0^2} - 1| = |1 - 1| = 0$$
$$f(1) = |2^{1^2} - 1| = |2 - 1| = 1$$
$$f(2) = |2^{2^2} - 1| = |16 - 1| = 15$$
$$f(-1) = |2^{(-1)^2} - 1| = |2 - 1| = 1$$
$$f(-2) = |2^{(-2)^2} - 1| = |16 - 1| = 15$$

x	y, or $f(x)$
0	0
1	1
2	15
−1	1
−2	15

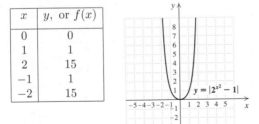

70.

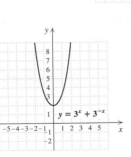

71. $y = 3^{-(x-1)}$ $x = 3^{-(y-1)}$

x	y
0	3
1	1
2	$\frac{1}{3}$
3	$\frac{1}{9}$
−1	9

x	y
3	0
1	1
$\frac{1}{3}$	2
$\frac{1}{9}$	3
9	−1

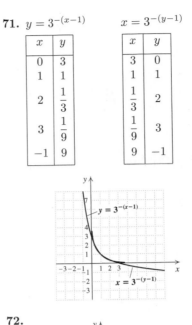

72.

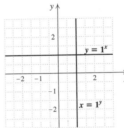

73. Enter the data points $(0, 171)$, $(1, 421)$, and $(2, 1099)$ and then use the exponential regression feature of the graphing calculator to find an exponential function that models the data.

$A(t) = 169.3393318(2.535133248)^t$, where $A(t)$ is total U.S. sales, in millions of dollars, t years after 1997.

In 2005, $t = 2005 - 1997 = 8$.

$A(8) = 169.3393318(2.535133248)^8 \approx \$288,911.0615$ million, or $\$288,911,061,500$

74. 19 words per minute; 66 words per minute; 110 words per minute

75. *Writing Exercise*

Exercise Set 11.3

1. $\log_{10} 100$ is the power to which we raise 10 to get 100. Since $10^2 = 100$, $\log_{10} 100 = 2$.

2. 3

3. $\log_2 8$ is the power to which we raise 2 to get 8. Since $2^3 = 8$, $\log_2 8 = 3$.

4. 4

5. $\log_3 81$ is the power to which we raise 3 to get 81. Since $3^4 = 81$, $\log_3 81 = 4$.

6. 3

7. $\log_4 \dfrac{1}{16}$ is the power to which we raise 4 to get $\dfrac{1}{16}$. Since $4^{-2} = \dfrac{1}{16}$, $\log_4 \dfrac{1}{16} = -2$.

8. -1

9. Since $7^{-1} = \dfrac{1}{7}$, $\log_7 \dfrac{1}{7} = -1$.

10. -2

11. Since $5^4 = 625$, $\log_5 625 = 4$.

12. 3

13. Since $6^1 = 6$, $\log_6 6 = 1$.

14. 0

15. Since $8^0 = 1$, $\log_8 1 = 0$.

16. 1

17. $\log_9 9^7$ is the power to which we raise 9 to get 9^7. Clearly, this power is 7, so $\log_9 9^7 = 7$.

18. 10

19. Since $10^{-1} = \dfrac{1}{10} = 0.1$, $\log_{10} 0.1 = -1$.

20. -2

21. Since $9^{1/2} = 3$, $\log_9 3 = \dfrac{1}{2}$.

22. $\dfrac{1}{2}$

23. Since $9 = 3^2$ and $(3^2)^{3/2} = 3^3 = 27$, $\log_9 27 = \dfrac{3}{2}$.

24. $\dfrac{3}{2}$

25. Since $1000 = 10^3$ and $(10^3)^{2/3} = 10^2 = 100$, $\log_{1000} 100 = \dfrac{2}{3}$.

26. $\dfrac{2}{3}$

27. Since $\log_5 7$ is the power to which we raise 5 to get 7, then 5 raised to this power is 7. That is, $5^{\log_5 7} = 7$.

28. 13

29. Graph: $y = \log_{10} x$

The equation $y = \log_{10} x$ is equivalent to $10^y = x$. We can find ordered pairs by choosing values for y and computing the corresponding x-values.

For $y = 0$, $x = 10^0 = 1$.

For $y = 1$, $x = 10^1 = 10$.

For $y = 2$, $x = 10^2 = 100$.

For $y = -1$, $x = 10^{-1} = \dfrac{1}{10}$.

For $y = -2$, $x = 10^{-2} = \dfrac{1}{100}$.

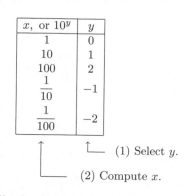

x, or 10^y	y
1	0
10	1
100	2
$\dfrac{1}{10}$	-1
$\dfrac{1}{100}$	-2

        ↑   ⌐ (1) Select y.

             ⌐ (2) Compute x.

We plot the set of ordered pairs and connect the points with a smooth curve.

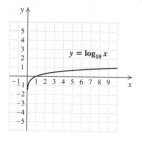

30.

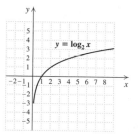

31. Graph: $y = \log_3 x$

The equation $y = \log_3 x$ is equivalent to $3^y = x$. We can find ordered pairs by choosing values for y and computing the corresponding x-values.

For $y = 0$, $x = 3^0 = 1$.

For $y = 1$, $x = 3^1 = 3$.

For $y = 2$, $x = 3^2 = 9$.

For $y = -1$, $x = 3^{-1} = \dfrac{1}{3}$.

For $y = -2$, $x = 3^{-2} = \dfrac{1}{9}$.

x, or 3^y	y
1	0
3	1
9	2
$\dfrac{1}{3}$	-1
$\dfrac{1}{9}$	-2

We plot the set of ordered pairs and connect the points with a smooth curve.

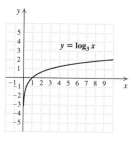

32.

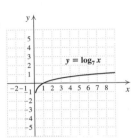

33. Graph: $f(x) = \log_6 x$

Think of $f(x)$ as y. Then $y = \log_6 x$ is equivalent to $6^y = x$. We find ordered pairs by choosing values for y and computing the corresponding x-values. Then we plot the points and connect them with a smooth curve.

For $y = 0$, $x = 6^0 = 1$.
For $y = 1$, $x = 6^1 = 6$.
For $y = 2$, $x = 6^2 = 36$.
For $y = -1$, $x = 6^{-1} = \dfrac{1}{6}$.
For $y = -2$, $x = 6^{-2} = \dfrac{1}{36}$.

x, or 6^y	y
1	0
6	1
36	2
$\dfrac{1}{6}$	-1
$\dfrac{1}{36}$	-2

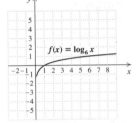

34.

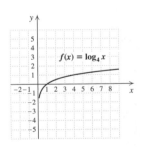

35. Graph: $f(x) = \log_{2.5} x$

Think of $f(x)$ as y. Then $y = \log_{2.5} x$ is equivalent to $2.5^y = x$. We construct a table of values, plot these points and connect them with a smooth curve.

For $y = 0, x = 2.5^0 = 1$.
For $y = 1, x = 2.5^1 = 2.5$.
For $y = 2, x = 2.5^2 = 6.25$.
For $y = 3, x = 2.5^3 = 15.625$.
For $y = -1, x = 2.5^{-1} = 0.4$.
For $y = -2, x = 2.5^{-2} = 0.16$.

x, or 2.5^y	y
1	0
2.5	1
6.25	2
15.625	3
0.4	-1
0.16	-2

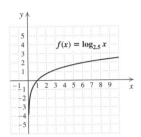

36.

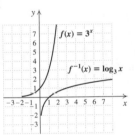

37. Graph $f(x) = 3^x$ (see Exercise Set 9.2, Exercise 6) and $f^{-1}(x) = \log_3 x$ (see Exercise 31 above) on the same set of axes.

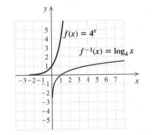

38.

39. $\log 4 \approx 0.6021$

40. 0.6990

41. $\log 13,400 \approx 4.1271$

42. 4.9689

43. $\log 0.527 \approx -0.2782$

44. -0.3072

45. $10^{2.3} \approx 199.5262$

46. 1.4894

47. $10^{-2.9523} \approx 0.0011$

48. $79,104.2833$

49. $10^{0.0012} \approx 1.0028$

50. 0.0001

51.
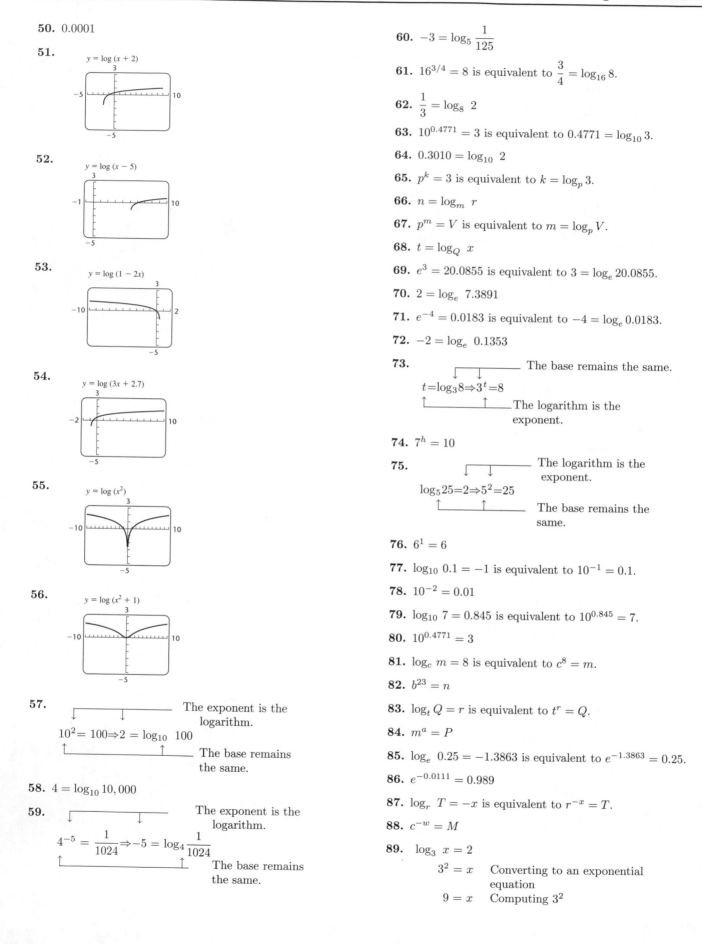

$y = \log(x + 2)$

52.

$y = \log(x - 5)$

53.

$y = \log(1 - 2x)$

54.

$y = \log(3x + 2.7)$

55.

$y = \log(x^2)$

56.

$y = \log(x^2 + 1)$

57.

The exponent is the logarithm.

$10^2 = 100 \Rightarrow 2 = \log_{10} 100$

The base remains the same.

58. $4 = \log_{10} 10{,}000$

59.

The exponent is the logarithm.

$4^{-5} = \dfrac{1}{1024} \Rightarrow -5 = \log_4 \dfrac{1}{1024}$

The base remains the same.

60. $-3 = \log_5 \dfrac{1}{125}$

61. $16^{3/4} = 8$ is equivalent to $\dfrac{3}{4} = \log_{16} 8$.

62. $\dfrac{1}{3} = \log_8 2$

63. $10^{0.4771} = 3$ is equivalent to $0.4771 = \log_{10} 3$.

64. $0.3010 = \log_{10} 2$

65. $p^k = 3$ is equivalent to $k = \log_p 3$.

66. $n = \log_m r$

67. $p^m = V$ is equivalent to $m = \log_p V$.

68. $t = \log_Q x$

69. $e^3 = 20.0855$ is equivalent to $3 = \log_e 20.0855$.

70. $2 = \log_e 7.3891$

71. $e^{-4} = 0.0183$ is equivalent to $-4 = \log_e 0.0183$.

72. $-2 = \log_e 0.1353$

73.

The base remains the same.

$t = \log_3 8 \Rightarrow 3^t = 8$

The logarithm is the exponent.

74. $7^h = 10$

75.

The logarithm is the exponent.

$\log_5 25 = 2 \Rightarrow 5^2 = 25$

The base remains the same.

76. $6^1 = 6$

77. $\log_{10} 0.1 = -1$ is equivalent to $10^{-1} = 0.1$.

78. $10^{-2} = 0.01$

79. $\log_{10} 7 = 0.845$ is equivalent to $10^{0.845} = 7$.

80. $10^{0.4771} = 3$

81. $\log_c m = 8$ is equivalent to $c^8 = m$.

82. $b^{23} = n$

83. $\log_t Q = r$ is equivalent to $t^r = Q$.

84. $m^a = P$

85. $\log_e 0.25 = -1.3863$ is equivalent to $e^{-1.3863} = 0.25$.

86. $e^{-0.0111} = 0.989$

87. $\log_r T = -x$ is equivalent to $r^{-x} = T$.

88. $c^{-w} = M$

89. $\log_3 x = 2$

$3^2 = x$ Converting to an exponential equation

$9 = x$ Computing 3^2

90. 64

91. $\log_x 64 = 3$

$x^3 = 64$ Converting to an exponential equation

$x = 4$ Taking cube roots

92. 5

93. $\log_5 25 = x$

$5^x = 25$ Converting to an exponential equation

$5^x = 5^2$

$x = 2$ The exponents must be the same.

94. 4

95. $\log_4 16 = x$

$4^x = 16$ Converting to an exponential equation

$4^x = 4^2$

$x = 2$ The exponents must be the same.

96. 3

97. $\log_x 7 = 1$

$x^1 = 7$ Converting to an exponential equation

$x = 7$ Simplifying x^1

98. 8

99. $\log_9 x = 1$

$9^1 = x$ Converting to an exponential equation

$9 = x$ Simplifying 9^1

100. 1

101. $\log_3 x = -2$

$3^{-2} = x$ Converting to an exponential equation

$\dfrac{1}{9} = x$ Simplifying

102. $\dfrac{1}{2}$

103. $\log_{32} x = \dfrac{2}{5}$

$32^{2/5} = x$ Converting to an exponential equation

$(2^5)^{2/5} = x$

$4 = x$

104. 4

105. *Writing Exercise*

106. *Writing Exercise*

107. $\dfrac{x^{12}}{x^4} = x^{12-4} = x^8$

108. a^{12}

109. $(a^4 b^6)(a^3 b^2) = a^{4+3} b^{6+2} = a^7 b^8$

110. $x^5 y^{12}$

111. $\dfrac{\dfrac{3}{x} - \dfrac{2}{xy}}{\dfrac{2}{x^2} + \dfrac{1}{xy}}$

The LCD of all the denominators is $x^2 y$. We multiply numerator and denominator by the LCD.

$$\dfrac{\dfrac{3}{x} - \dfrac{2}{xy}}{\dfrac{2}{x^2} + \dfrac{1}{xy}} \cdot \dfrac{x^2 y}{x^2 y} = \dfrac{\left(\dfrac{3}{x} - \dfrac{2}{xy}\right) x^2 y}{\left(\dfrac{2}{x^2} + \dfrac{1}{xy}\right) x^2 y}$$

$$= \dfrac{\dfrac{3}{x} \cdot x^2 y - \dfrac{2}{xy} \cdot x^2 y}{\dfrac{2}{x^2} \cdot x^2 y + \dfrac{1}{xy} \cdot x^2 y}$$

$$= \dfrac{3xy - 2x}{2y + x}, \text{ or}$$

$$\dfrac{x(3y - 2)}{2y + x}$$

112. $\dfrac{x+2}{x+1}$

113. *Writing Exercise*

114. *Writing Exercise*

115. Graph: $y = \left(\dfrac{3}{2}\right)^x$ Graph: $y = \log_{3/2} x$, or

$$x = \left(\dfrac{3}{2}\right)^y$$

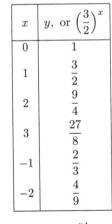

x	y, or $\left(\dfrac{3}{2}\right)^x$
0	1
1	$\dfrac{3}{2}$
2	$\dfrac{9}{4}$
3	$\dfrac{27}{8}$
-1	$\dfrac{2}{3}$
-2	$\dfrac{4}{9}$

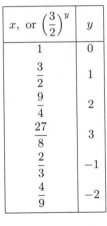

x, or $\left(\dfrac{3}{2}\right)^y$	y
1	0
$\dfrac{3}{2}$	1
$\dfrac{9}{4}$	2
$\dfrac{27}{8}$	3
$\dfrac{2}{3}$	-1
$\dfrac{4}{9}$	-2

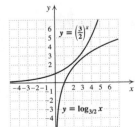

116.

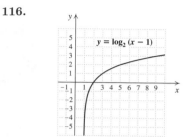

117. Graph: $y = \log_3 |x + 1|$

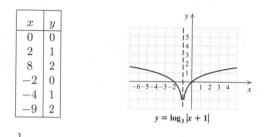

x	y
0	0
2	1
8	2
−2	0
−4	1
−9	2

$y = \log_3 |x + 1|$

118. $\dfrac{1}{9}, 9$

119. $\log_{125} x = \dfrac{2}{3}$

$$125^{2/3} = x$$
$$(5^3)^{2/3} = x$$
$$5^2 = x$$
$$25 = x$$

120. 6

121. $\log_8 (2x + 1) = -1$

$$8^{-1} = 2x + 1$$
$$\frac{1}{8} = 2x + 1$$
$$1 = 16x + 8 \qquad \text{Multiplying by 8}$$
$$-7 = 16x$$
$$-\frac{7}{16} = x$$

122. $-25, 4$

$x = -25 \;\; or \;\; x = 4$

123. Let $\log_{1/4} \dfrac{1}{64} = x.$ Then

$$\left(\frac{1}{4}\right)^x = \frac{1}{64}$$
$$\left(\frac{1}{4}\right)^x = \left(\frac{1}{4}\right)^3$$
$$x = 3.$$

Thus, $\log_{1/4} \dfrac{1}{64} = 3.$

124. -2

125. $\log_{81} 3 \cdot \log_3 81$

$$= \frac{1}{4} \cdot 4 \qquad \left(\log_{81} 3 = \frac{1}{4},\; \log_3 81 = 4\right)$$
$$= 1$$

126. 0

127. $\log_2 (\log_2 (\log_4 256))$

$$= \log_2 (\log_2 4) \qquad (\log_4 256 = 4)$$
$$= \log_2 2 \qquad\qquad (\log_2 4 = 2)$$
$$= 1$$

128. Let $b = 0$, $x = 1$, and $y = 2$. Then $0^1 = 0^2$, but $1 \neq 2$. Let $b = 1$, $x = 1$, and $y = 2$. Then $1^1 = 1^2$, but $1 \neq 2$.

129. *Writing Exercise*

Exercise Set 11.4

1. $\log_3 (81 \cdot 27) = \log_3 81 + \log_3 27$ Using the product rule

2. $\log_2 16 + \log_2 32$

3. $\log_4 (64 \cdot 16) = \log_4 64 + \log_4 16$ Using the product rule

4. $\log_5 25 + \log_5 125$

5. $\log_c rst$

$= \log_c r + \log_c s + \log_c t$ Using the product rule

6. $\log_t 3 + \log_t a + \log_t b$

7. $\log_a 5 + \log_a 14 = \log_a (5 \cdot 14)$ Using the product rule

The result can also be expressed as $\log_a 70$.

8. $\log_b (65 \cdot 2)$, or $\log_b 130$

9. $\log_c t + \log_c y = \log_c (t \cdot y)$ Using the product rule

10. $\log_t (H \cdot M)$

11. $\log_a r^8 = 8 \log_a r$ Using the power rule

12. $5 \log_b t$

13. $\log_c y^6 = 6 \log_c y$ Using the power rule

14. $7 \log_{10} y$

15. $\log_b C^{-3} = -3 \log_b C$ Using the power rule

16. $-5 \log_c M$

17. $\log_2 \dfrac{53}{17} = \log_2 53 - \log_2 17$ Using the quotient rule

18. $\log_3 23 - \log_3 9$

19. $\log_b \dfrac{m}{n} = \log_b m - \log_b n$ Using the quotient rule

20. $\log_a y - \log_a x$

21. $\log_a 15 - \log_a 3$

$= \log_a \dfrac{15}{3},$ \qquad Using the quotient rule

or $\log_a 5$

22. $\log_b \dfrac{42}{7}$, or $\log_b 6$

23.
$$\log_b 36 - \log_b 4$$
$$= \log_b \frac{36}{4}, \qquad \text{Using the quotient rule}$$
$$\text{or } \log_b 9$$

24. $\log_a \dfrac{26}{2}$, or $\log_a 13$

25. $\log_a 7 - \log_z 18 = \log_a \dfrac{7}{18}$ Using the quotient rule

26. $\log_b \dfrac{5}{13}$

27.
$$\log_a x^5 y^7 z^6$$
$$= \log_a x^5 + \log_a y^7 + \log_a z^6 \qquad \begin{array}{l}\text{Using the product}\\ \text{rule}\end{array}$$
$$= 5\log_a x + 7\log_a y + 6\log_a z \qquad \text{Using the power rule}$$

28. $\log_a x + 4\log_a y + 3\log_a z$

29.
$$\log_b \frac{xy^2}{z^3}$$
$$= \log_b xy^2 - \log_b z^3 \qquad \text{Using the quotient rule}$$
$$= \log_b x + \log_b y^2 - \log_b z^3 \qquad \begin{array}{l}\text{Using the}\\ \text{product rule}\end{array}$$
$$= \log_b x + 2\ \log_b y - 3\ \log_b z \qquad \begin{array}{l}\text{Using the}\\ \text{power rule}\end{array}$$

30. $2\ \log_b\ x + 5\ \log_b\ y - 4\ \log_b\ w - 7\ \log_b\ z$

31.
$$\log_a \frac{x^4}{y^3 z}$$
$$= \log_a x^4 - \log_a y^3 z \qquad \text{Using the quotient rule}$$
$$= \log_a x^4 - (\log_a y^3 + \log_a z) \qquad \begin{array}{l}\text{Using the}\\ \text{product rule}\end{array}$$
$$= \log_a x^4 - \log_a y^3 - \log_a z \qquad \begin{array}{l}\text{Removing}\\ \text{parentheses}\end{array}$$
$$= 4\log_a\ x - 3\log_a\ y - \log_a\ z \qquad \begin{array}{l}\text{Using the}\\ \text{power rule}\end{array}$$

32. $4\log_a\ x - \log_a\ y - 2\log_a\ z$

33.
$$\log_b \frac{xy^2}{wz^3}$$
$$= \log_b xy^2 - \log_b wz^3 \qquad \text{Using the quotient rule}$$
$$= \log_b x + \log_b y^2 - (\log_b w + \log_b z^3)$$
$$\qquad\qquad\qquad\qquad\qquad \text{Using the product rule}$$
$$= \log_b x + \log_b y^2 - \log_b w - \log_b z^3$$
$$\qquad\qquad\qquad\qquad\qquad \text{Removing parentheses}$$
$$= \log_b x + 2\log_b y - \log_b w - 3\log_b z$$
$$\qquad\qquad\qquad\qquad\qquad \text{Using the power rule}$$

34. $2\log_b\ w + \log_b\ x - 3\log_b\ y - \log_b\ z$

35.
$$\log_a \sqrt{\frac{x^7}{y^5 z^8}}$$
$$= \log_a \left(\frac{x^7}{y^5 z^8}\right)^{1/2}$$
$$= \frac{1}{2}\log_a \frac{x^7}{y^5 z^8} \qquad \text{Using the power rule}$$
$$= \frac{1}{2}(\log_a\ x^7 - \log_a\ y^5 z^8) \qquad \begin{array}{l}\text{Using the quotient}\\ \text{rule}\end{array}$$
$$= \frac{1}{2}\left[\log_a\ x^7 - (\log_a\ y^5 + \log_a\ z^8)\right]$$
$$\qquad\qquad\qquad\qquad \text{Using the product rule}$$
$$= \frac{1}{2}(\log_a\ x^7 - \log_a\ y^5 - \log_a\ z^8)$$
$$\qquad\qquad\qquad\qquad \text{Removing parentheses}$$
$$= \frac{1}{2}(7\log_a\ x - 5\log_a\ y - 8\log_a\ z)$$
$$\qquad\qquad\qquad\qquad \text{Using the power rule}$$

36. $\dfrac{1}{3}(4\ \log_c x - 3\ \log_c y - 2\ \log_c z)$

37.
$$\log_a \sqrt[3]{\frac{x^6 y^3}{a^2 z^7}}$$
$$= \log_a \left(\frac{x^6 y^3}{a^2 z^7}\right)^{1/3}$$
$$= \frac{1}{3}\log_a \frac{x^6 y^3}{a^2 z^7} \qquad \text{Using the power rule}$$
$$= \frac{1}{3}(\log_a\ x^6 y^3 - \log_a\ a^2 z^7) \qquad \begin{array}{l}\text{Using the}\\ \text{quotient rule}\end{array}$$
$$= \frac{1}{3}[\log_a\ x^6 + \log_a\ y^3 - (\log_a\ a^2 + \log_a\ z^7)]$$
$$\qquad\qquad\qquad\qquad \text{Using the product rule}$$
$$= \frac{1}{3}(\log_a\ x^6 + \log_a\ y^3 - \log_a\ a^2 - \log_a\ z^7)$$
$$\qquad\qquad\qquad\qquad \text{Removing parentheses}$$
$$= \frac{1}{3}(\log_a\ x^6 + \log_a\ y^3 - 2 - \log_a\ z^7)$$
$$\qquad\qquad\qquad \begin{array}{l}2 \text{ is the number to which}\\ \text{we raise } a \text{ to get } a^2.\end{array}$$
$$= \frac{1}{3}(6\log_a\ x + 3\log_a\ y - 2 - 7\log_a\ z)$$
$$\qquad\qquad\qquad\qquad \text{Using the power rule}$$

38. $\dfrac{1}{4}(8\ \log_a x + 12\ \log_a y - 3 - 5\ \log_a z)$

39.
$$7\log_a\ x + 3\log_a\ z$$
$$= \log_a\ x^7 + \log_a\ z^3 \qquad \text{Using the power rule}$$
$$= \log_a\ x^7 z^3 \qquad\qquad \text{Using the product rule}$$

40. $\log_b\ m^2 n^{1/2}$, or $\log_b\ m^2 \sqrt{n}$

41.
$$\log_a\ x^2 - 2\log_a\ \sqrt{x}$$
$$= \log_a\ x^2 - \log_a\ (\sqrt{x})^2 \qquad \text{Using the power rule}$$
$$= \log_a\ x^2 - \log_a\ x \qquad\qquad (\sqrt{x})^2 = x$$
$$= \log_a\ \frac{x^2}{x} \qquad\qquad\qquad \text{Using the quotient rule}$$
$$= \log_a\ x \qquad\qquad\qquad\qquad \text{Simplifying}$$

42. $\log_a \dfrac{\sqrt{a}}{x}$

43. $\dfrac{1}{2}\log_a\ x + 5\log_a\ y - 2\log_a\ x$

$= \log_a\ x^{1/2} + \log_a\ y^5 - \log_a\ x^2$ Using the power rule

$= \log_a\ x^{1/2}y^5 - \log_a\ x^2$ Using the product rule

$= \log_a \dfrac{x^{1/2}y^5}{x^2}$ Using the quotient rule

The result can also be expressed as $\log_a \dfrac{\sqrt{x}y^5}{x^2}$ or as $\log_a \dfrac{y^5}{x^{3/2}}$.

44. $\log_a \dfrac{2x^4}{y^3}$

45. $\log_a(x^2 - 4) - \log_a(x + 2)$

$= \log_a \dfrac{x^2 - 4}{x + 2}$ Using the quotient rule

$= \log_a \dfrac{(x + 2)(x - 2)}{x + 2}$

$= \log_a \dfrac{(\cancel{x+2})(x - 2)}{\cancel{x+2}}$ Simplifying

$= \log_a(x - 2)$

46. $\log_a \dfrac{2}{x - 5}$

47. $\log_b 15 = \log_b\ (3 \cdot 5)$

$= \log_b 3 + \log_b 5$ Using the product rule

$= 0.792 + 1.161$

$= 1.953$

48. 0.369

49. $\log_b \dfrac{3}{5} = \log_b 3 - \log_b 5$ Using the quotient rule

$= 0.792 - 1.161$

$= -0.369$

50. -0.792

51. $\log_b \dfrac{1}{5} = \log_b 1 - \log_b 5$ Using the quotient rule

$= 0 - 1.161$ $(\log_b 1 = 0)$

$= -1.161$

52. $\dfrac{1}{2}$

53. $\log_b\ \sqrt{b^3} = \log_b b^{3/2} = \dfrac{3}{2}$ $3/2$ is the number to which we raise b to get $b^{3/2}$.

54. 1.792

55. $\log_b 6$

Since 6 cannot be expressed using the numbers 1, 3, and 5, we cannot find $\log_b 6$ using the given information.

56. 2.745

57. $\log_b 75$

$= \log_b(3 \cdot 5^2)$

$= \log_b 3 + \log_b 5^2$ Using the product rule

$= \log_b 3 + 2\log_b 5$ Using the power rule

$= 0.792 + 2(1.161)$

$= 3.114$

58. Cannot be found

59. $\log_t\ t^9 = 9$ 9 is the power to which we raise t to get t^9.

60. 4

61. $\log_e\ e^m = m$ m is the power to which we raise e to get e^m.

62. -2

63. $\log_5\ 125 = 3$ and $\log_5\ 625 = 4$, so $\log_5\ (125 \cdot 625) = 3 + 4 = 7$.

64. 6

65. $\log_2\ 128 = 7$ and $\log_2\ 16 = 4$, so $\log_2\ \left(\dfrac{128}{16}\right) = 7 - 4 = 3$.

66. 2

67. *Writing Exercise*

68. *Writing Exercise*

69. Graph $f(x) = \sqrt{x} - 3$.

We construct a table of values, plot points, and connect them with a smooth curve. Note that we must choose nonnegative values of x in order for $\sqrt{x}$ to be a real number.

x	$f(x)$
0	-3
1	-2
4	-1
9	0

70.

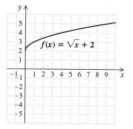

71. Graph $g(x) = \sqrt[3]{x} + 1$.

We construct a table of values, plot points, and connect them with a smooth curve.

x	$g(x)$
-8	-1
-1	0
0	1
1	2
8	3

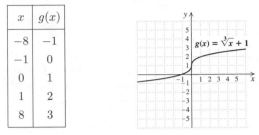

72.

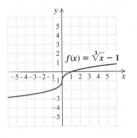

73. $(a^3 b^2)^5 (a^2 b^7) = (a^{3 \cdot 5} b^{2 \cdot 5})(a^2 b^7) =$
$a^{15} b^{10} a^2 b^7 = a^{15+2} b^{10+7} = a^{17} b^{17}$

74. $x^{11} y^6 z^8$

75. *Writing Exercise*

76. *Writing Exercise*

77. $\log_a (x^8 - y^8) - \log_a (x^2 + y^2)$

$= \log_a \dfrac{x^8 - y^8}{x^2 + y^2}$

$= \log_a \dfrac{(x^4 + y^4)(x^2 + y^2)(x + y)(x - y)}{x^2 + y^2}$

$= \log_a [(x^4 + y^4)(x^2 - y^2)]$ Simplifying

$= \log_a (x^6 - x^4 y^2 + x^2 y^4 - y^6)$

78. $\log_a (x^3 + y^3)$

79. $\log_a \sqrt{1 - s^2}$

$= \log_a (1 - s^2)^{1/2}$

$= \dfrac{1}{2} \log_a (1 - s^2)$

$= \dfrac{1}{2} \log_a [(1 - s)(1 + s)]$

$= \dfrac{1}{2} \log_a (1 - s) + \dfrac{1}{2} \log_a (1 + s)$

80. $\dfrac{1}{2} \log_a (c - d) - \dfrac{1}{2} \log_a (c + d)$

81. $\log_a \dfrac{\sqrt[3]{x^2 z}}{\sqrt[3]{y^2 z^{-2}}}$

$= \log_a \left(\dfrac{x^2 z^3}{y^2} \right)^{1/3}$

$= \dfrac{1}{3} (\log_a x^2 z^3 - \log_a y^2)$

$= \dfrac{1}{3} (2 \log_a x + 3 \log_a z - 2 \log_a y)$

$= \dfrac{1}{3} [2 \cdot 2 + 3 \cdot 4 - 2 \cdot 3]$

$= \dfrac{1}{3} (10)$

$= \dfrac{10}{3}$

82. -2

83. $\log_a x = 2$, so $a^2 = x$.

Let $\log_{1/a} x = n$ and solve for n.

$\log_{1/a} a^2 = n$ Substituting a^2 for x

$\left(\dfrac{1}{a} \right)^n = a^2$

$(a^{-1})^n = a^2$

$a^{-n} = a^2$

$-n = 2$

$n = -2$

Thus, $\log_{1/a} x = -2$ when $\log_a x = 2$.

84. False

85. True; $\log_a (Q + Q^2) = \log_a [Q(1 + Q)] = \log_a Q + \log_a (1 + Q) = \log_a Q + \log_a (Q + 1)$.

86. Graph $y_1 = \log x^2$ and $y_2 = \log x \cdot \log x$ and observe that the graphs do not coincide.

Exercise Set 11.5

---

1. 1.6094

2. 0.6931

3. 3.9512

4. 3.4012

5. -5.0832

6. -7.2225

7. 96.7583

8. 107.8516

9. 0.7850

10. -0.3939

11. 1.3877

12. 1.8199

13. 15.0293

14. 21.3276

15. 0.0305

16. 0.0714

17. 109.9472

18. 3.4212

19. We will use common logarithms for the conversion. Let $a = 10$, $b = 6$, and $M = 92$ and substitute in the change-of-base formula.

$$\log_b M = \frac{\log_a M}{\log_a b}$$

$$\log_6 92 = \frac{\log_{10} 92}{\log_{10} 6}$$

$$\approx \frac{1.963787827}{0.7781512504}$$

$$\approx 2.5237$$

20. 3.9656

21. We will use common logarithms for the conversion. Let $a = 10$, $b = 2$, and $M = 100$ and substitute in the change-of-base formula.

$$\log_2 100 = \frac{\log_{10} 100}{\log_{10} 2}$$

$$\approx \frac{2}{0.3010}$$

$$\approx 6.6439$$

22. 2.3666

23. We will use natural logarithms for the conversion. Let $a = e$, $b = 7$, and $M = 65$ and substitute in the change-of-base formula.

$$\log_7 65 = \frac{\ln 65}{\ln 7}$$

$$\approx \frac{4.1744}{1.9459}$$

$$\approx 2.1452$$

24. 2.3223

25. We will use natural logarithms for the conversion. Let $a = e$, $b = 0.5$, and $M = 5$ and substitute in the change-of-base formula.

$$\log_{0.5} 5 = \frac{\ln 5}{\ln 0.5}$$

$$\approx \frac{1.6094}{-0.6931}$$

$$\approx -2.3219$$

26. −0.4771

27. We will use common logarithms for the conversion. Let $a = 10$, $b = 2$, and $M = 0.2$ and substitute in the change-of-base formula.

$$\log_2 0.2 = \frac{\log_{10} 0.2}{\log_{10} 2}$$

$$\approx \frac{-0.6990}{0.3010}$$

$$\approx -2.3219$$

28. −3.6439

29. We will use natural logarithms for the conversion. Let $a = e$, $b = \pi$, and $M = 58$ and substitute in the change-of-base formula.

$$\log_\pi 58 = \frac{\ln 58}{\ln \pi}$$

$$\approx \frac{4.0604}{1.1447}$$

$$\approx 3.5471$$

30. 4.6284

31. Graph: $f(x) = e^x$

We find some function values with a calculator. We use these values to plot points and draw the graph.

x	e^x
0	1
1	2.7
2	7.4
3	20.1
−1	0.4
−2	0.1

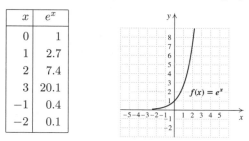

The domain is the set of real numbers and the range is $(0, \infty)$.

32.

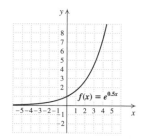

The domain is the set of real numbers and the range is $(0, \infty)$.

33. Graph: $f(x) = e^{-0.4x}$

We find some function values, plot points, and draw the graph.

x	$e^{-0.4x}$
0	1
1	0.67
2	0.45
−1	1.49
−2	2.23
−3	3.32
−4	4.95

The domain is the set of real numbers and the range is $(0, \infty)$.

34.

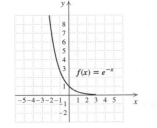

The domain is the set of real numbers and the range is $(0, \infty)$.

35. Graph: $f(x) = e^x + 1$

We find some function values, plot points, and draw the graph.

x	$e^x + 1$
0	2
1	3.72
2	8.39
-1	1.37
-2	1.14

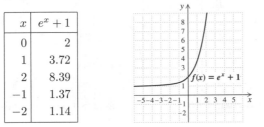

The domain is the set of real numbers and the range is $(1, \infty)$.

36.

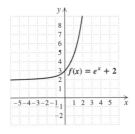

The domain is the set of real numbers and the range is $(2, \infty)$.

37. Graph: $f(x) = e^x - 2$

We find some function values, plot points, and draw the graph.

x	$e^x - 2$
0	-1
1	0.72
2	5.4
-1	-1.6
-2	-1.9

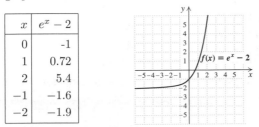

The domain is the set of real numbers and the range is $(-2, \infty)$.

38.

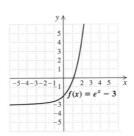

The domain is the set of real numbers and the range is $(-3, \infty)$.

39. Graph: $f(x) = 0.5e^x$

We find some function values, plot points, and draw the graph.

x	$0.5e^x$
0	0.5
1	1.36
2	3.69
-1	0.18
-2	0.07

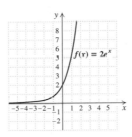

The domain is the set of real numbers and the range is $(0, \infty)$.

40.

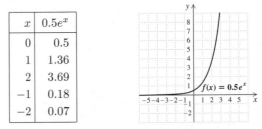

The domain is the set of real numbers and the range is $(0, \infty)$.

41. Graph: $f(x) = 2e^{-0.5x}$

We find some function values, plot points, and draw the graph.

x	$2e^{-0.5x}$
0	2
1	1.21
2	0.74
3	0.45
-1	3.30
-2	5.44
-3	8.96

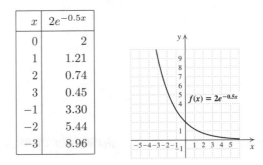

The domain is the set of real numbers and the range is $(0, \infty)$.

42.

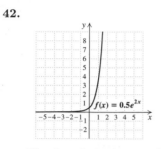

The domain is the set of real numbers and the range is $(0, \infty)$.

43. Graph: $f(x) = e^{x-2}$

We find some function values, plot points, and draw the graph.

x	e^{x-2}
0	0.14
2	1
4	7.39
-1	0.05
-2	0.02

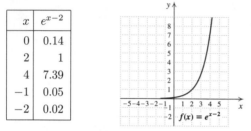

The domain is the set of real numbers and the range is $(0, \infty)$.

44.

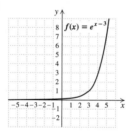

The domain is the set of real numbers and the range is $(0, \infty)$.

45. Graph: $f(x) = e^{x+3}$

We find some function values, plot points, and draw the graph.

x	e^{x+3}
0	20.09
1	54.60
-1	7.39
-3	1
-4	0.37

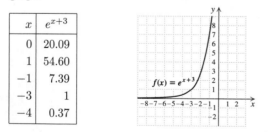

The domain is the set of real numbers and the range is $(0, \infty)$.

46.

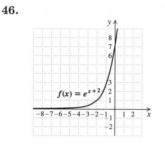

The domain is the set of real numbers and the range is $(0, \infty)$.

47. Graph: $f(x) = 2 \ln x$

x	$2 \ln x$
0.5	-1.4
1	0
2	1.4
3	2.2
4	2.8
5	3.2
6	3.6

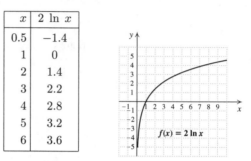

The domain is $(0, \infty)$ and the range is the set of real numbers.

48.

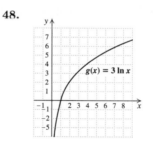

The domain is $(0, \infty)$ and the range is the set of real numbers.

49. Graph: $f(x) = 0.5 \ln x$

x	$0.5 \ln x$
0.5	-0.35
1	0
2	0.35
3	0.55
4	0.69
5	0.80

The domain is $(0, \infty)$ and the range is the set of real numbers.

50.

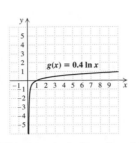

The domain is $(0, \infty)$ and the range is the set of real numbers.

51. Graph: $g(x) = \ln x + 3$

x	$\ln x + 3$
1	3
2	3.69
3	4.10
4	4.39
5	4.61

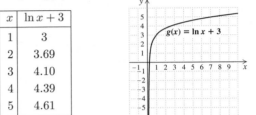

The domain is $(0, \infty)$ and the range is the set of real numbers.

52.

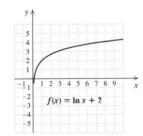

The domain is $(0, \infty)$ and the range is the set of real numbers.

53. Graph: $g(x) = \ln x - 2$

x	$\ln x - 2$
1	-2
2	-1.31
3	-0.90
4	-0.61
5	-0.39

The domain is $(0, \infty)$ and the range is the set of real numbers.

54.

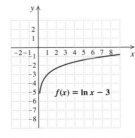

The domain is $(0, \infty)$ and the range is the set of real numbers.

55. Graph: $f(x) = \ln(x + 1)$

We find some function values, plot points, and draw the graph.

x	$\ln(x + 1)$
0	0
1	0.69
2	1.10
4	1.61
6	1.95
-1	Undefined

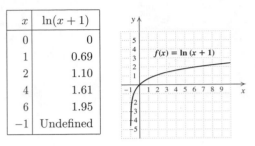

The domain is $(-1, \infty)$ and the range is the set of real numbers.

56.

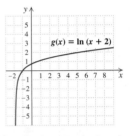

The domain is $(-2, \infty)$ and the range is the set of real numbers.

57. Graph: $g(x) = \ln(x - 3)$

We find some function values, plot points, and draw the graph.

x	$\ln(x - 3)$
3.1	-2.30
4	0
5	0.69
6	1.10
7	1.39

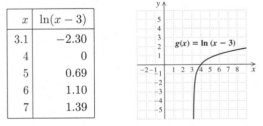

The domain is $(3, \infty)$ and the range is the set of real numbers.

58.

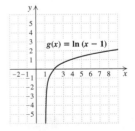

The domain is $(1, \infty)$ and the range is the set of real numbers.

59. We use the change of base formula:
$$f(x) = \frac{\log x}{\log 5} \text{ or } f(x) = \frac{\ln x}{\ln 5}$$

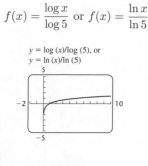

60.

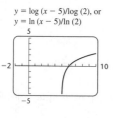

61. We use the change of base formula.
$$f(x) = \frac{\log(x-5)}{\log 2} \text{ or } f(x) = \frac{\ln(x-5)}{\ln 2}$$

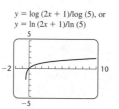

62.

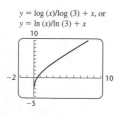

63. We use the change of base formula.
$$f(x) = \frac{\log x}{\log 3} + x \text{ or } f(x) = \frac{\ln x}{\ln 3} + x$$

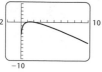

64.

65. *Writing Exercise*

66. *Writing Exercise*

67.
$$4x^2 - 25 = 0$$
$$(2x+5)(2x-5) = 0$$
$$2x+5 = 0 \quad or \quad 2x - 5 = 0$$
$$2x = -5 \quad or \qquad 2x = 5$$
$$x = -\frac{5}{2} \quad or \qquad x = \frac{5}{2}$$
The solutions are $-\dfrac{5}{2}$ and $\dfrac{5}{2}$.

68. $0, \dfrac{7}{5}$

69.
$$17x - 15 = 0$$
$$17x = 15$$
$$x = \frac{15}{17}$$
The solution is $\dfrac{15}{17}$.

70. $\dfrac{9}{13}$

71. $x^{1/2} - 6x^{1/4} + 8 = 0$
Let $u = x^{1/4}$.
$$u^2 - 6u + 8 = 0 \qquad \text{Substituting}$$
$$(u-4)(u-2) = 0$$
$$u = 4 \quad or \quad u = 2$$
$$x^{1/4} = 4 \quad or \quad x^{1/4} = 2$$
$$x = 256 \quad or \qquad x = 16 \quad \text{Raising both sides to}$$
$$\text{the fourth power}$$

Both numbers check. The solutions are 256 and 16.

72. $\dfrac{1}{4}, 9$

73. *Writing Exercise*

74. *Writing Exercise*

75. We use the change-of-base formula.
$$\log_6 81 = \frac{\log 81}{\log 6}$$
$$= \frac{\log 3^4}{\log(2 \cdot 3)}$$
$$= \frac{4 \log 3}{\log 2 + \log 3}$$
$$\approx \frac{4(0.477)}{0.301 + 0.477}$$
$$\approx 2.452$$

76. 1.262

77. We use the change-of-base formula.

$$\log_{12} 36 = \frac{\log 36}{\log 12}$$

$$= \frac{\log(2 \cdot 3)^2}{\log(2^2 \cdot 3)}$$

$$= \frac{2\log(2 \cdot 3)}{\log 2^2 + \log 3}$$

$$= \frac{2(\log 2 + \log 3)}{2\log 2 + \log 3}$$

$$\approx \frac{2(0.301 + 0.477)}{2(0.301) + 0.477}$$

$$\approx 1.442$$

78. $\ln M = \dfrac{\log M}{\log e}$

79. Use the change-of-base formula with $a = e$ and $b = 10$. We obtain

$$\log M = \frac{\ln M}{\ln 10}.$$

80. $\pm 6.0302 \times 10^{17}$

81. $\log(492x) = 5.728$

$$10^{5.728} = 492x$$

$$\frac{10^{5.728}}{492} = x$$

$$1086.5129 \approx x$$

82. 1.5893

83. $\log 692 + \log x = \log 3450$

$$\log x = \log 3450 - \log 692$$

$$\log x = \log \frac{3450}{692}$$

$$x = \frac{3450}{692}$$

$$x \approx 4.9855$$

84. (a) Domain: $\{x|x > 0\}$, or $(0, \infty)$; range: the set of real numbers;

(b) $[-3, 10, -100, 1000]$, Xscl $= 1$, Yscl $= 100$;

(c)
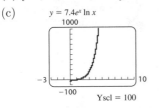
$y = 7.4e^x \ln x$
Yscl $= 100$

85. (a) Domain: $\{x|x > 0\}$, or $(0, \infty)$;
range: $\{y|y < 0.5135\}$, or $(-\infty, 0.5135)$;

(b) $[-1, 5, -10, 5]$;

(c)
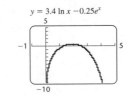
$y = 3.4 \ln x - 0.25e^x$

86. (a) Domain: $\{x|x > 2.1\}$, or $(2.1, \infty)$; range: the set of real numbers;

(b) $[-1, 10, -10, 20]$, Xscl $= 1$, Yscl $= 5$;

(c)
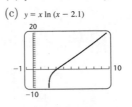
$y = x \ln(x - 2.1)$

87. (a) Domain $\{x|x > 0\}$, or $(0, \infty)$;
range: $\{y|y > -0.2453\}$, or $(-0.2453, \infty)$

(b) $[-1, 5, -1, 10]$;

(c)
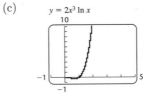
$y = 2x^3 \ln x$

Exercise Set 11.6

---

1. $2^x = 16$

$$2^x = 2^4$$

$$x = 4 \qquad \text{The exponents must be the same.}$$

The solution is 4.

2. 3

3. $3^x = 27$

$$3^x = 3^3$$

$$x = 3 \qquad \text{The exponents must be the same.}$$

The solution is 3.

4. 3

5. $2^{x+3} = 32$

$$2^{x+3} = 2^5$$

$$x + 3 = 5$$

$$x = 2$$

The solution is 2.

6. 5

7. $5^{3x} = 625$

$$5^{3x} = 5^4$$

$$3x = 4$$

$$x = \frac{4}{3}$$

The solution is $\dfrac{4}{3}$.

8. $\dfrac{3}{2}$

9. $7^{4x} = 1$

Since $a^0 = 1$ $a \neq 0$, then $4x = 0$ and thus $x = 0$. The solution is 0.

10. 0

11. $4^{2x-1} = 64$

$4^{2x-1} = 4^3$

$2x - 1 = 3$

$2x = 4$

$x = 2$

The solution is 2.

12. $\dfrac{5}{2}$

13. $3^{x^2} \cdot 3^{3x} = 81$

$3^{x^2+3x} = 3^4$

$x^2 + 3x = 4$

$x^2 + 3x - 4 = 0$

$(x + 4)(x - 1) = 0$

$x = -4 \ \ or \ \ x = 1$

The solutions are -4 and 1.

14. $-3, -1$

15. $2^x = 15$

$\log 2^x = \log 15$

$x \log 2 = \log 15$

$x = \dfrac{\log 15}{\log 2}$

$x \approx 3.907$

The solution is $\log 15 / \log 2$, or approximately 3.907.

16. $\dfrac{\log 19}{\log 2} \approx 4.248$

17. $4^{x+1} = 13$

$\log 4^{x+1} = \log 13$

$(x + 1) \log 4 = \log 13$

$x + 1 = \dfrac{\log 13}{\log 4}$

$x = \dfrac{\log 13}{\log 4} - 1$

$x \approx 0.850$

The solution is $\log 13 / \log 4 - 1$ or approximately 0.850.

18. $\dfrac{\log 17}{\log 8} + 1 \approx 2.362$

19. $e^t = 100$

$\ln e^t = \ln 100$ Taking ln on both sides

$t = \ln 100$ Finding the logarithm of the base to a power

$t \approx 4.605$ Using a calculator

20. $\ln 1000 \approx 6.908$

21. $e^{-0.07t} + 3 = 3.08$

$e^{-0.07t} = 0.08$

$\ln e^{-0.07t} = \ln 0.08$ Taking ln on both sides

$-0.07t = \ln 0.08$ Finding the logarithm of the base to a power

$t = \dfrac{\ln 0.08}{-0.07}$

$t \approx 36.082$

22. $\dfrac{\ln 5}{0.03} \approx 53.648$

23. $2^x = 3^{x-1}$

$\log 2^x = \log 3^{x-1}$

$x \ \log 2 = (x - 1) \ \log 3$

$x \ \log 2 = x \ \log 3 - \log 3$

$\log 3 = x \ \log 3 - x \ \log 2$

$\log 3 = x(\log 3 - \log 2)$

$\dfrac{\log 3}{\log 3 - \log 2} = x$

$2.710 \approx x$

24. $\dfrac{\log 3}{\log 5 - \log 3} \approx 2.151$

25. $7.2^x - 65 = 0$

$7.2^x = 65$

$\log 7.2^x = \log 65$

$x \log 7.2 = \log 65$

$x = \dfrac{\log 65}{\log 7.2}$

$x \approx 2.115$

26. $\dfrac{\log 87}{\log 4.9} \approx 2.810$

27. $e^{0.5x} - 7 = 2x + 6$

Graph $y_1 = e^{0.5x} - 7$ and $y_2 = 2x + 6$ in a window that shows the points of intersection of the graphs. One good choice is $[-10, 10, -10, 25]$, Yscl $= 5$. Use Intersect to find the first coordinates of the points of intersection. They are the solutions of the given equation. They are about -6.480 and 6.519.

28. -1.873

29. $\log_5 \ x = 3$

$x = 5^3$ Writing an equivalent exponential equation

$x = 125$

30. 81

31. $\log_4 \ x = \dfrac{1}{2}$

$x = 4^{1/2}$ Writing an equivalent exponential equation

$x = 2$

32. $\dfrac{1}{8}$

33. $\log x = 3 \qquad$ The base is 10.

$\qquad x = 10^3$

$\qquad x = 1000$

34. 10

35. $2\log x = -8$

$\qquad \log x = -4 \qquad$ The base is 10.

$\qquad x = 10^{-4}$

$\qquad x = \dfrac{1}{10,000}, \text{ or } 0.0001$

36. $\dfrac{1}{10,000}$

37. $\ln x = 1$

$\qquad x = e \approx 2.718$

38. $e^2 \approx 7.389$

39. $5\ln x = -15$

$\qquad \ln x = -3$

$\qquad x = e^{-3} \approx 0.050$

40. $e^{-1} \approx 0.368$

41. $\log_2(8 - 6x) = 5$

$\qquad 8 - 6x = 2^5$

$\qquad 8 - 6x = 32$

$\qquad -6x = 24$

$\qquad x = -4$

The answer checks. The solution is -4.

42. 66

43. $\log(x - 9) + \log x = 1 \qquad$ The base is 10.

$\qquad \log_{10}[(x - 9)(x)] = 1 \qquad$ Using the product rule

$\qquad x(x - 9) = 10^1$

$\qquad x^2 - 9x = 10$

$\qquad x^2 - 9x - 10 = 0$

$\qquad (x + 1)(x - 10) = 0$

$x = -1 \text{ or } x = 10$

Check: For -1:

$$\dfrac{\log(x - 9) + \log x = 1}{\log(-1 + 9) + \log(-1) \;?\; 1 \qquad \text{FALSE}}$$

For 10:

$$\dfrac{\log(x - 9) + \log x = 1}{\begin{array}{c} \log(10 - 9) + \log(10) \;?\; 1 \\ \log 1 + \log 10 \\ 0 + 1 \\ 1 \end{array} \Big|\; 1 \quad \text{TRUE}}$$

The number -1 does not check, because negative numbers do not have logarithms. The solution is 10.

44. 1

45. $\log x - \log(x + 3) = 1 \qquad$ The base is 10.

$\qquad \log_{10}\dfrac{x}{x + 3} = 1 \qquad$ Using the quotient rule

$\qquad \dfrac{x}{x + 3} = 10^1$

$\qquad x = 10(x + 3)$

$\qquad x = 10x + 30$

$\qquad -9x = 30$

$\qquad x = -\dfrac{10}{3}$

The number $-\dfrac{10}{3}$ does not check. The equation has no solution.

46. $\dfrac{7}{9}$

47. $\log_4(x + 3) - \log_4(x - 5) = 2$

$\qquad \log_4\dfrac{x + 3}{x - 5} = 2 \qquad$ Using the quotient rule

$\qquad \dfrac{x + 3}{x - 5} = 4^2$

$\qquad \dfrac{x + 3}{x - 5} = 16$

$\qquad x + 3 = 16(x - 5)$

$\qquad x + 3 = 16x - 80$

$\qquad 83 = 15x$

$\qquad \dfrac{83}{15} = x$

The number $\dfrac{83}{15}$ checks. It is the solution.

48. 5

49. $\log_7(x + 2) + \log_7(x + 1) = \log_7 6$

$\qquad \log_7[(x + 2)(x + 1)] = \log_7 6 \qquad$ Using the product rule

$\qquad \log_7(x^2 + 3x + 2) = \log_7 6$

$\qquad x^2 + 3x + 2 = 6 \qquad$ Using the property of logarithmic equality

$\qquad x^2 + 3x - 4 = 0$

$\qquad (x + 4)(x - 1) = 0$

$x = -4 \;\; or \;\; x = 1$

The number 1 checks, but -4 does not. The solution is 1.

50. 2

51. $\log_3(x + 4) + \log_3(x - 4) = 2$

$\qquad \log_3[(x + 4)(x - 4)] = 2$

$\qquad (x + 4)(x - 4) = 3^2$

$\qquad x^2 - 16 = 9$

$\qquad x^2 = 25$

$\qquad x = \pm 5$

The number 5 checks, but -5 does not. The solution is 5.

52. 4

53. $\log_{12}(x+5) - \log_{12}(x-4) = \log_{12} 3$

$$\log_{12} \frac{x+5}{x-4} = \log_{12} 3$$

$$\frac{x+5}{x-4} = 3 \quad \begin{array}{l}\text{Using the prop-}\\ \text{erty of logarithmic}\\ \text{equality}\end{array}$$

$$x + 5 = 3(x-4)$$

$$x + 5 = 3x - 12$$

$$17 = 2x$$

$$\frac{17}{2} = x$$

The number $\frac{17}{2}$ checks and is the solution.

54. $\frac{17}{4}$

55. $\log_2(x-2) + \log_2 x = 3$

$$\log_2[(x-2)(x)] = 3$$

$$x(x-2) = 2^3$$

$$x^2 - 2x = 8$$

$$x^2 - 2x - 8 = 0$$

$$(x-4)(x+2) = 0$$

$$x = 4 \quad or \quad x = -2$$

The number 4 checks, but -2 does not. The solution is 4.

56. $\frac{2}{5}$

57. $\ln(3x) = 3x - 8$

Graph $y_1 = \ln(3x)$ and $y_2 = 3x-8$ in a window that shows the points of intersection of the graphs. One good choice is $[-5, 5, -15, 5]$. When we use Intersect in this window we can find only the coordinates of the right-hand point of intersection. They are about $(3.445, 2.336)$, so one solution of the equation is about 3.445. To find the coordinates of the left-hand point of intersection we make the window smaller. One window that is appropriate is $[-1, 1, -15, 5]$. Using Intersect again we find that the other solution of the equation is about 0.0001. (The answer approximated to the nearest thousandth is 0.000, so we express it to the nearest ten-thousandth.)

58. -0.753, 0.753

59. Solve $\ln x = \log x$.

Graph $y_1 = \ln x$ and $y_2 = \log x$ in a window that shows the point of intersection of the graphs. One good choice is $[-5, 5, 5, 5]$. Use Intersect to find the first coordinate of the point of intersection. It is the solution of the given equation. It is 1.

60. 1, 100

61. *Writing Exercise*

62. *Writing Exercise*

63. The number of transplants performed has increased at a constant rate, so these data can be modeled better by a linear function than a quadratic function.

64. Quadratic

65. Using the data points $(0, 16)$ and $(10, 24)$, we first find the slope.

$$m - \frac{24 - 16}{10 - 0} = \frac{8}{10} = \frac{4}{5}$$

The y-intercept is $(0, 16)$, so we have $t(x) = \frac{4}{5}x + 16$, where x is the number of years after 1991 and t is in thousands.

66. $p(x) = \frac{1}{6}x^2 + \frac{23}{6}x + 25$

67.
$$\frac{1}{6}x^2 + \frac{23}{6}x + 25 = 5\left(\frac{4}{5}x + 16\right)$$

$$\frac{1}{6}x^2 + \frac{23}{6}x + 25 = 4x + 80$$

$$6\left(\frac{1}{6}x^2 + \frac{23}{6}x + 25\right) = 6(4x + 80)$$

$$x^2 + 23x + 150 = 24x + 480$$

$$x^2 - x - 330 = 0$$

We use the quadratic formula with $a = 1$, $b = -1$, and $c = -330$.

$$x = \frac{-b \pm \sqrt{b^2 - 4ac}}{2a}$$

$$= \frac{-(-1) \pm \sqrt{(-1)^2 - 4 \cdot 1 \cdot (-330)}}{2 \cdot 1}$$

$$= \frac{1 \pm \sqrt{1321}}{2} \approx \frac{1 \pm 36.35}{2}$$

$$x \approx \frac{1 + 36.35}{2} \quad or \quad x \approx \frac{1 - 36.35}{2}$$

$$x \approx 19 \qquad\quad or \quad x \approx -18$$

Only 19 has meaning in the original problem. Thus, there will be five times as many patients on the waiting list as there are transplants performed about 19 years after 1991, or in 2010.

68. $t(x) = 0.7571428571x + 15.71428571$, where x is the number of years after 1991 and t is in thousands.

69. Enter the data and then use the quadratic regression feature. We have $p(x) = 0.0892857143x^2 + 4.907142857x + 23.85714286$, where x is the number of years after 1991 and p is in thousands.

70. 2010

71. *Writing Exercise*

72. *Writing Exercise*

73.
$$100^{3x} = 1000^{2x+1}$$

$$(10^2)^{3x} = (10^3)^{2x+1}$$

$$10^{6x} = 10^{6x+1}$$

$$6x = 6x + 1$$

$$0 = 1$$

We get a false equation, so the equation has no solution.

74. $\dfrac{12}{5}$

75.
$$8^x = 16^{3x+9}$$
$$(2^3)^x = (2^4)^{3x+9}$$
$$2^{3x} = 2^{12x+36}$$
$$3x = 12x + 36$$
$$-36 = 9x$$
$$-4 = x$$
The solution is -4.

76. $\sqrt[3]{3}$

77.
$$\log_6 (\log_2 x) = 0$$
$$\log_2 x = 6^0$$
$$\log_2 x = 1$$
$$x = 2^1$$
$$x = 2$$
The solution is 2.

78. -1

79.
$$\log_5 \sqrt{x^2 - 9} = 1$$
$$\sqrt{x^2 - 9} = 5^1$$
$$(\sqrt{x^2 - 9})^2 = 5^2$$
$$x^2 - 9 = 25$$
$$x^2 = 34$$
$$x = \pm\sqrt{34}$$
The solutions are $\pm\sqrt{34}$.

80. $-3, -1$

81.
$$\log (\log x) = 5$$
$$\log x = 10^5$$
$$\log x = 100,000$$
$$x = 10^{100,000}$$
The solution is $10^{100,000}$.

82. $-625, 625$

83.
$$\log x^2 = (\log x)^2$$
$$2 \log x = (\log x)^2$$
$$0 = (\log x)^2 - 2 \log x$$
Let $u = \log x$.
$$0 = u^2 - 2u$$
$$0 = u(u - 2)$$

$$u = 0 \quad or \quad u = 2$$
$$\log x = 0 \quad or \quad \log x = 2 \quad \text{Replacing } u \text{ with } \log x$$
$$x = 10^0 \quad or \quad x = 10^2$$
$$x = 1 \quad or \quad x = 100$$
Both numbers check. The solutions are 1 and 100.

84. $\dfrac{1}{2}, 5000$

85.
$$\log x^{\log x} = 25$$
$$\log x (\log x) = 25 \quad \text{Using the power rule}$$
$$(\log x)^2 = 25$$
$$\log x = \pm 5$$
$$x = 10^5 \quad or \quad x = 10^{-5}$$
$$x = 100,000 \quad or \quad x = \frac{1}{100,000}$$
Both numbers check. The solutions are 100,000 and $\dfrac{1}{100,000}$.

86. $1, \dfrac{\log 5}{\log 3} \approx 1.465$

87.
$$(81^{x-2})(27^{x+1}) = 9^{2x-3}$$
$$[(3^4)^{x-2}][(3^3)^{x+1}] = (3^2)^{2x-3}$$
$$(3^{4x-8})(3^{3x+3}) = 3^{4x-6}$$
$$3^{7x-5} = 3^{4x-6}$$
$$7x - 5 = 4x - 6$$
$$3x = -1$$
$$x = -\frac{1}{3}$$
The solution is $-\dfrac{1}{3}$.

88. $\dfrac{3}{2}$

89.
$$2^y = 16^{x-3} \quad \text{and} \quad 3^{y+2} = 27^x$$
$$2^y = (2^4)^{x-3} \quad \text{and} \quad 3^{y+2} = (3^3)^x$$
$$y = 4x - 12 \quad \text{and} \quad y + 2 = 3x$$
$$12 = 4x - y \quad \text{and} \quad 2 = 3x - y$$
Solving this system of equations we get $x = 10$ and $y = 28$. Then $x + y = 10 + 28 = 38$.

90. -3

91. Set $S(x) = D(x)$, and solve for x.
$$e^x = 162,755\, e^{-x}$$
$$e^{2x} = 162,755 \quad \text{Multiplying by } e^x \text{ on both sides}$$
$$\ln e^{2x} = \ln 162,755$$
$$2x = \ln 162,755$$
$$x = \frac{\ln 162,755}{2}$$
$$x \approx 6$$
To find the second coordinate of the equilibrium point, find $S(6)$ or $D(6)$. We will find $S(6)$.
$$S(6) = e^6 \approx 403$$
The equilibrium point is $(6, \$403)$.

Exercise Set 11.7

1. a) Replace $N(t)$ with 200 and solve for t.

$$N(t) = 153(1.37)^t$$
$$200 = 153(1.37)^t$$
$$1.3072 \approx (1.37)^t \quad \text{Dividing by 153}$$
$$\ln 1.3072 \approx \ln(1.37)^t \quad \text{Taking the natural}$$
$$\text{logarithm on both sides}$$
$$\ln 1.3072 \approx t \ln 1.37$$
$$\frac{\ln 1.3072}{\ln 1.37} \approx t$$
$$1 \approx t$$

200 million cellular phones would be in use 1 yr after 2002, or in 2003.

b) Replace $N(t)$ with 2(153), or 306, and solve for t.

$$306 = 153(1.37)^t$$
$$2 = (1.37)^t$$
$$\ln 2 = \ln(1.37)^t$$
$$\ln 2 = t \ln(1.37)$$
$$\frac{\ln 2}{\ln 1.37} = t$$
$$2.2 \approx t$$

The doubling time is about 2.2 years.

2. a) 13.5 yr

b) 5.7 yr

3. a) Replace $A(t)$ with 40,000 and solve for t.

$$A(t) = 29,000(1.08)^t$$
$$40,000 = 29,000(1.08)^t$$
$$1.379 \approx (1.08)^t$$
$$\log 1.379 \approx \log(1.08)^t$$
$$\log 1.379 \approx t \log 1.08$$
$$\frac{\log 1.379}{\log 1.08} \approx t$$
$$4.2 \approx t$$

The amount due will reach $40,000 after about 4.2 years.

b) Replace $A(t)$ with 2(29,000), or 58,000, and solve for t.

$$58,000 = 29,000(1.08)^t$$
$$2 = (1.08)^t$$
$$\log 2 = \log(1.08)^t$$
$$\log 2 = t \log 1.08$$
$$\frac{\log 2}{\log 1.08} = t$$
$$9.0 \approx t$$

The doubling time is about 9.0 years.

4. a) 3.6 days

b) 0.6 days

5. a) Find $N(41)$.

$$N(x) = 600(0.873)^{x-16}$$
$$N(41) = 600(0.873)^{41-16}$$
$$= 600(0.873)^{25}$$
$$\approx 20.114$$

There are about 20.114 thousand, or 20,114, 41-yr-old skateboarders.

b) Substitute 2 for $N(x)$ and solve for x. (Remember that $N(x)$ is in thousands.)

$$2 = 600(0.873)^{x-16}$$
$$0.0033 \approx (0.873)^{x-16}$$
$$\log 0.0033 \approx (x-16)\log 0.873$$
$$\frac{\log 0.0033}{\log 0.873} \approx x - 16$$
$$\frac{\log 0.0033}{\log 0.873} + 16 \approx x$$
$$58 \approx x$$

There are only 2000 skateboarders at age 58.

6. a) 3.5 yr

b) 13.6 yr

7.
$$\text{pH} = -\log[H^+]$$
$$= -\log[1.3 \times 10^{-5}]$$
$$\approx -(-4.886057) \quad \text{Using a calculator}$$
$$\approx 4.9$$

The pH of fresh-brewed coffee is about 4.9.

8. 6.8

9.
$$\text{pH} = -\log[H^+]$$
$$7.0 = -\log[H^+]$$
$$-7.0 = \log[H^+]$$
$$10^{-7.0} = [H^+] \quad \text{Converting to an}$$
$$\text{exponential equation}$$

The hydrogen ion concentration is 10^{-7} moles per liter.

10. 1.58×10^{-8} moles per liter

11.
$$L = 10 \cdot \log \frac{I}{I_0}$$
$$= 10 \cdot \log \frac{3.2 \times 10^{-6}}{10^{-12}}$$
$$= 10 \cdot \log(3.2 \times 10^6)$$
$$\approx 10(6.5)$$
$$\approx 65$$

The intensity of sound in normal conversation is about 65 decibels.

12. 95 dB

13.
$$L = 10 \cdot \log \frac{I}{I_0}$$
$$105 = 10 \cdot \log \frac{I}{10^{-12}}$$
$$10.5 = \log \frac{I}{10^{-12}}$$
$$10.5 = \log I - \log 10^{-12} \quad \text{Using the quotient rule}$$
$$10.5 = \log I - (-12) \quad (\log 10^a = a)$$
$$10.5 = \log I + 12$$
$$-1.5 = \log I$$
$$10^{-1.5} = I \quad \text{Converting to an exponential equation}$$
$$3.2 \times 10^{-2} \approx I$$

The intensity of the sound is $10^{-1.5}$ W/m^2, or about 3.2×10^{-2} W/m^2.

14. $10^{-0.9}$ W/m^2

15. a) Substitute 0.06 for k:
$$P(t) = P_0\, e^{0.06t}$$

b) To find the balance after one year, replace P_0 with 5000 and t with 1. We find $P(1)$:
$$P(1) = 5000\, e^{0.06(1)} = 5000\, e^{0.06} \approx$$
$$5000(1.061836547) \approx \$5309.18$$
To find the balance after 2 years, replace P_0 with 5000 and t with 2. We find $P(2)$:
$$P(2) = 5000\, e^{0.06(2)} = 5000\, e^{0.12} \approx$$
$$5000(1.127496852) \approx \$5637.48$$

c) To find the doubling time, replace P_0 with 5000 and $P(t)$ with 10,000 and solve for t.
$$10,000 = 5000\, e^{0.06t}$$
$$2 = e^{0.06t}$$
$$\ln 2 = \ln e^{0.06t} \quad \text{Taking the natural logarithm on both sides}$$
$$\ln 2 = 0.06t \quad \text{Finding the logarithm of the base to a power}$$
$$\frac{\ln 2}{0.06} = t$$
$$11.6 \approx t$$

The investment will double in about 11.6 years.

16. a) $P(t) = P_0 e^{0.05t}$

b) \$1051.27; \$1105.17

c) 13.9 yr

17. a) $P(t) = 288.3e^{0.013t}$, where $P(t)$ is in millions and t is the number of years after 2002.

b) In 2005, $t = 2005 - 2002 = 3$. Replace t with 3 and compute $P(3)$.
$$P(3) = 288.3e^{0.013(3)}$$
$$= 288.3e^{0.039}$$
$$\approx 299.8$$

The U.S. population in 2005 will be about 299.8 million.

c) Replace $P(t)$ with 325 and solve for t.
$$325 = 288.3e^{0.013t}$$
$$1.1273 \approx e^{0.031t}$$
$$\ln 1.1273 \approx \ln e^{0.013t}$$
$$\ln 1.1273 \approx 0.013t$$
$$\frac{\ln 1.1273}{0.013} \approx t$$
$$9 \approx t$$

The U.S. population will reach 325 million about 9 years after 2002, or in 2011.

18. a) $P(t) = 6.3e^{0.014t}$, where $P(t)$ is in billions and t is the numbers of years after 2002.

b) 6.6 billion

c) 2019

19. a) Replace $N(t)$ with 60,000 and solve for t.
$$60,000 = 3000(2)^{t/20}$$
$$20 = (2)^{t/20}$$
$$\log 20 = \log(2)^{t/20}$$
$$\log 20 = \frac{t}{20} \log 2$$
$$20 \log 20 = t \log 2$$
$$\frac{20 \log 20}{\log 2} = t$$
$$86.4 \approx t$$

There will be 60,000 bacteria after about 86.4 minutes.

b) Replace $N(t)$ with 100,000,000 and solve for t.
$$100,000,000 = 3000(2)^{t/20}$$
$$33,333.333 = (2)^{t/20}$$
$$\log 33,333.333 = \log(2)^{t/20}$$
$$\log 33,333.333 = \frac{t}{20} \log 2$$
$$20 \log 33,333.333 = t \log 2$$
$$\frac{20 \log 33,333.333}{\log 2} = t$$
$$300.5 \approx t$$

About 300.5 minutes would have to pass in order for a possible infection to occur.

c) Replace $P(t)$ with 6000 and solve for t.
$$6000 = 3000(2)^{t/20}$$
$$2 = (2)^{t/20}$$
$$1 = \frac{t}{20} \quad \text{The exponents must be the same.}$$
$$t = 20$$

The doubling time is 20 minutes.

20. 19.8 years

21. a) Replace a with 1 and compute $N(1)$.

$N(a) = 2000 + 500 \log a$

$N(1) = 2000 + 500 \log 1$

$N(1) = 2000 + 500 \cdot 0$

$N(1) = 2000$

2000 units were sold after $1000 was spent.

b) Find $N(8)$.

$N(8) = 2000 + 500 \log 8$

$N(8) \approx 2451.5$

About 2452 units were sold after $8000 was spent.

c) Using the values we computed in parts (a) and (b) and any others we wish to calculate, we sketch the graph:

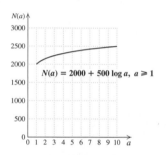

d) Replace $N(a)$ with 5000 and solve for a.

$5000 = 2000 + 500 \log a$

$3000 = 500 \log a$

$6 = \log a$

$a = 10^6 = 1,000,000$

$1,000,000 thousand, or $1,000,000,000 would have to be spent.

22. a) 68%

b) 54%; 40%

c)

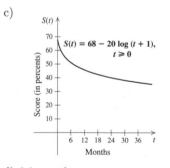

d) 6.9 months

23. a) We use the growth equation $N(t) = N_0 e^{kt}$, where t is the number of years since 1995. In 1995, at $t = 0$, 17 people were infected. We substitute 17 for N_0:

$N(t) = 17 e^{kt}$.

To find the exponential growth rate k, observe that 1 year later 29 people were infected.

$N(1) = 17 e^{k \cdot 1}$ Substituting 1 for t

$29 = 17 e^k$ Substituting 29 for $N(1)$

$1.706 \approx e^k$

$\ln 1.706 \approx \ln e^k$

$\ln 1.706 \approx k$

$0.534 \approx k$

The exponential function is $N(t) = 17 e^{0.534t}$, where t is the number of years since 1995.

b) In 2001, $t = 2001 - 1995$, or 6. Find $N(6)$.

$N(6) = 17 e^{0.534(6)}$

$= 17 e^{3.204}$

≈ 418.7

Approximately 419 people will be infected in 2001.

24. a) $N(t) = 1418 \, e^{0.036t}$, where t is the number of years after 1987

b) About 3488 heart transplants

25. We start with the exponential growth equation

$D(t) = D_0 \, e^{kt}$, where t is the number of years after 1995.

Substitute $2 D_0$ for $D(t)$ and 0.1 for k and solve for t.

$2 D_0 = D_0 \, e^{0.1t}$

$2 = e^{0.1t}$

$\ln 2 = 0.1t$

$\ln 2 = \ln e^{0.1t}$

$\dfrac{\ln 2}{0.1} = t$

$6.9 \approx t$

The demand will be double that of 1998 in $1998 + 7$, or 2005.

26. 2012

27. a) We use the exponential decay equation $W(t) = W_0 e^{-kt}$, where t is the number of years after 1996 and $W(t)$ is in millions of tons. In 1996, at $t = 0$, 17.5 million tons of yard waste were discarded. We substitute 17.5 for W_0.

$W(t) = 17.5 e^{-kt}$.

To find the exponential decay rate k, observe that 2 years after 1996, in 1998, 14.5 million tons of yard waste were discarded. We substitute 2 for t and 14.5 for $W(t)$.

$14.5 = 17.5 e^{-k \cdot 2}$

$0.8286 \approx e^{-2k}$

$\ln 0.8286 \approx \ln e^{-2k}$

$\ln 0.8286 \approx -2k$

$\dfrac{\ln 0.8286}{-2} \approx k$

$0.094 \approx k$

Then we have $W(t) = 17.5 e^{-0.094t}$, where t is the number of years after 1996 and $W(t)$ is in millions of tons.

b) In 2006, $t = 2006 - 1996 = 10$.

$$W(10) = 17.5e^{-0.094(10)}$$

$$= 17.5e^{-0.94}$$

$$\approx 6.8$$

In 2006, about 6.8 million tons of yard waste were discarded.

c) 1 ton is equivalent to 0.000001 million tons.

$$0.000001 = 17.5e^{-0.094t}$$

$$5.71 \times 10^{-8} \approx e^{-0.094t}$$

$$\ln(5.71 \times 10^{-8}) \approx \ln e^{-0.094t}$$

$$\ln(5.71 \times 10^{-8}) \approx -0.094t$$

$$\frac{\ln(5.71 \times 10^{-8})}{-0.094} \approx t$$

$$177 \approx t$$

Only one ton of yard waste will be discarded about 177 years after 1996, or in 2173.

28. a) $k \approx 0.315$; $M(t) = 5300e^{-0.315t}$, where t is the number of years after 1990

b) 64 cases

c) 2017

29. We will use the function derived in Example 7:

$$P(t) = P_0 e^{-0.00012t}$$

If the scrolls had lost 22.3% of their carbon-14 from an initial amount P_0, then $77.7\%(P_0)$ is the amount present. To find the age t of the scrolls, we substitute $77.7\%(P_0)$, or $0.777P_0$, for $P(t)$ in the function above and solve for t.

$$0.777P_0 = P_0 e^{-0.00012t}$$

$$0.777 = e^{-0.00012t}$$

$$\ln 0.777 = \ln e^{-0.00012t}$$

$$-0.2523 \approx -0.00012t$$

$$t \approx \frac{-0.2523}{-0.00012} \approx 2103$$

The scrolls are about 2103 years old.

30. 1654 yr

31. The function $P(t) = P_0 e^{-kt}$, $k > 0$, can be used to model decay. For iodine-131, $k = 9.6\%$, or 0.096. To find the half-life we substitute 0.096 for k and $\frac{1}{2}P_0$ for $P(t)$, and solve for t.

$$\frac{1}{2}P_0 = P_0 e^{-0.096t}, \text{ or } \frac{1}{2} = e^{-0.096t}$$

$$\ln \frac{1}{2} = \ln e^{-0.096t} = -0.096t$$

$$t = \frac{\ln 0.5}{-0.096} \approx \frac{-0.6931}{-0.096} \approx 7.2 \text{ days}$$

32. 11 yr

33. The function $P(t) = P_0 e^{-kt}$, $k > 0$, can be used to model decay. We substitute $\frac{1}{2}P_0$ for $P(t)$ and 1 for t and solve for the decay rate k.

$$\frac{1}{2}P_0 = P_0 e^{-k \cdot 1}$$

$$\frac{1}{2} = e^{-k}$$

$$\ln \frac{1}{2} = \ln e^{-k}$$

$$-0.693 \approx -k$$

$$0.693 \approx k$$

The decay rate is 0.693, or 69.3% per year.

34. 3.15% per year

35. a) We start with the exponential growth equation

$$V(t) = V_0 e^{kt}, \text{ where } t \text{ is the number}$$
of years after 1996.

Substituting 640,500 for V_0, we have

$$V(t) = 640,500 e^{kt}.$$

To find the exponential growth rate k, observe that the card sold for \$1.1 million, or \$1,100,000 in 2000, or 4 years after 1996. We substitute and solve for k.

$$V(5) = 640,500 e^{k \cdot 4}$$

$$1,100,000 = 640,500 e^{4k}$$

$$1.7174 \approx e^{4k}$$

$$\ln 1.7174 \approx \ln e^{4k}$$

$$\ln 1.7174 \approx 4k$$

$$\frac{\ln 1.7174}{4} \approx k$$

$$0.135 \approx k$$

Thus, the exponential growth function is $V(t) = 640,500e^{0.135t}$, where t is the number of years after 1996.

b) In 2006, $t = 2006 - 1996 = 10$

$$V(10) = 640,500e^{0.135(10)} \approx 2,470,681$$

The card's value in 2006 will be about \$2.47 million

c) Substitute $2(\$640,500)$, or \$1,281,000 for $V(t)$ and solve for t.

$$1,281,000 = 640,500 e^{0.135t}$$

$$2 = e^{0.135t}$$

$$\ln 2 = \ln e^{0.135t}$$

$$\ln 2 = 0.135t$$

$$\frac{\ln 2}{0.135} = t$$

$$5.1 \approx t$$

The doubling time is about 5.1 years.

d) Substitute $2,000,000 for $V(t)$ and solve for t.

$$2,000,000 = 640,500\,e^{0.135t}$$
$$3.1226 \approx e^{0.135t}$$
$$\ln 3.1226 \approx \ln e^{0.135t}$$
$$\ln 3.1226 \approx 0.135t$$
$$\frac{\ln 3.1226}{0.135} \approx t$$
$$8 \approx t$$

The value of the card will first exceed $2,000,000 about 8 years after 1996, or in 2004.

36. a) $k \approx 0.117$; $V(t) = 58e^{0.117t}$, where t is the number of years after 1987 and $V(t)$ is in millions of dollars

b) About $602.1 million

c) 5.9 yr

d) 24.3 yr

37. Miles per gallon first fell, then rose fairly steeply, and then rose less steeply. This does not fit an exponential model.

38. Yes

39. The ticket price increased from 1980 to 2003 at a rate that makes it appear that an exponential function might fit the data.

40. No

41. a) Enter the data and then use the exponential regression feature. We have

$$p(x) = 6.501242197(1.096109091)^x,$$

where x is the number of years after 1980.

b) $k = \ln b$

$$\approx \ln 1.096109091$$
$$\approx 0.0918, \text{ or } 9.18\%$$

c) In 2006, $t = 2006 - 1980 = 26$. We find $p(26)$ using a table of values or TRACE. If $p(x)$ was copies to the Y = screen as Y_1, we could also enter $Y_1(26)$.

$$p(26) \approx \$71$$

42. a) $p(x) = 1998.198072(1.291876847)^x$, where x is the number of years after 1995.

b) 0.256, or 25.6%

c) $33,425

43. a) Enter the data points $(0, 50)$, $(10, 100)$, $(20, 150)$, and $(3, 1500)$. (Note that 1.5 billion = 1500 million.) Then use the exponential regression feature. We have

$$P(x) = 37.29665447(1.111922582)^x,$$

where x is the number of years after 1965 and P is in millions of dollars.

b) In 2005, $t = 2005 - 1965 = 40$. We find $P(40)$ using a table of values or TRACE. If $P(x)$ was copied to the Y = screen as Y_1, then we could also enter $Y_1(40)$.

$$P(40) \approx 2600$$

We estimate that the amount spent on new stadium construction in 2005 will be about $2600 million, or about $2.6 billion.

44. a) $P(t) = 2.262404 \times 10^{-10}e^{0.0119579321t}$, where P is in billions.

b) 10.02 billion

45. a) Enter the data and use the exponential regression feature. We get

$$f(x) = 647.6297124(0.5602992676)^x.$$

b) $f(2.5) \approx 152$, so we estimate that there are 152 decayed, missing, or filled teeth per 100 patients if the fluoride count of the water is 2.5 ppm.

46. a) $P(t) = 0.5434943782e^{0.369163743t}$, where t is the number of years after 1985 and P is in millions.

b) 874 million subscribers

47. *Writing Exercise*

48. *Writing Exercise*

49. Graph $y = x^2 - 8x$.

First we find the vertex.

$$-\frac{b}{2a} = -\frac{-8}{2 \cdot 1} = 4$$

When $x = 4$, $y = 4^2 - 8 \cdot 4 = 16 - 32 = -16$.

The vertex is $(4, -16)$ and the axis of symmetry is $x = 4$. We plot a few points on either side of the vertex and graph the parabola.

x	y
4	-16
0	0
2	-12
5	-15
6	-12

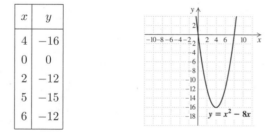

50.

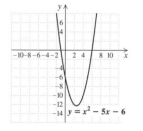

51. Graph $f(x) = 3x^2 - 5x - 1$

First we find the vertex.

$$-\frac{b}{2a} = -\frac{-5}{2 \cdot 3} = \frac{5}{6}$$

$$f\left(\frac{5}{6}\right) = 3\left(\frac{5}{6}\right)^2 - 5 \cdot \frac{5}{6} - 1 = -\frac{37}{12}$$

The vertex is $\left(\frac{5}{6}, -\frac{37}{12}\right)$ and the axis of symmetry is $x = \frac{5}{6}$. We plot a few points on either side of the vertex and graph the parabola.

x	$f(x)$
$\frac{5}{6}$	$-\frac{37}{12}$
0	-1
-1	7
2	1
3	11

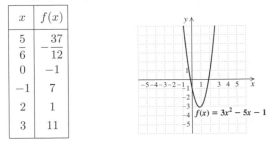

52.

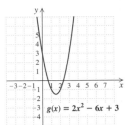

53. $x^2 - 8x = 7$

$x^2 - 8x + 16 = 7 + 16$ Adding $\left[\frac{1}{2}(-8)\right]^2$

$(x - 4)^2 = 23$

$x - 4 = \pm\sqrt{23}$

$x = 4 \pm \sqrt{23}$

The solutions are $4 \pm \sqrt{23}$.

54. $-5 \pm \sqrt{31}$

55. *Writing Exercise*

56. *Writing Exercise*

57. We will use the exponential growth equation $V(t) = V_0 e^{kt}$, where t is the number of years after 2001 and $V(t)$ is in millions of dollars. We substitute 21 for $V(t)$, 0.05 for k, and 9 for t and solve for V_0.

$21 = V_0 e^{0.05(9)}$

$21 = V_0 e^{0.45}$

$\frac{21}{e^{0.45}} = V_0$

$13.4 \approx V_0$

George Steinbrenner needs to invest \$13.4 million at 5% interest compounded continuously in order to have \$21 million to pay Derek Jeter in 2010.

58. About 80,922 yr or, with rounding of decay rate, about 80,792 yr

59. From Exercises 1 and 17 we know that in 2002 there were 153 million cellular phones in use in the U.S. and the population of the U.S. was 288.3 million. Then the percentage of U.S. residents owning a cellular phone in 2002 was

$$\frac{153}{288.3} \approx 0.5306971904 \approx 53.06971904\%.$$

In 2003, we have $N(1) \approx 209.6$ and $P(1) \approx 292.1$. Then the percentage of U.S. residents owning a cellular phone in 2003 was $\frac{209.6}{292.1} \approx 0.7175967135 \approx 71.75967135\%$.

Now we find a function that models the percentage of U.S. residents owning a cellular phone t years after 2002.

$$P(t) = P_0 e^{kt}$$

$$71.75967135 = 53.06971904 e^{k \cdot 1}$$

$$\frac{71.75967135}{53.06971904} = e^k$$

$$\ln\left(\frac{71.75967135}{53.06971904}\right) = \ln e^k$$

$$\ln\left(\frac{71.75967135}{53.06971904}\right) = k$$

$$0.302 \approx k$$

Then we have $P(t) = 53 e^{0.302t}$, rounding P_0, where t is the number of years after 2002 and P is a percent. (Note that this assumes that each resident owns no more than one cellular phone.)

60. *Writing Exercise*

61. a)

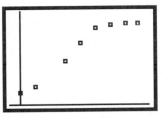

The data appear to be growing exponentially, particularly through 1980.

b) We substitute. First we use the point $(0, 35.0)$.

$35.0 = ab^0$

$35.0 = a$

Next we use the function $f(x) = 35b^x$ and the point $(50, 90.5)$.

$90.5 = 35b^{50}$

$2.5857 \approx b^{50}$

$\log 2.5857 \approx \log b^{50}$

$\log 2.5857 \approx 50 \log b$

$\frac{\log 2.5857}{50} \approx \log b$

$0.0083 \approx \log b$

$b \approx 10^{0.0083}$

$b \approx 1.0192$

We have $f(x) = 35.0(1.0192)^x$.

c) $f(90) = 35.0(1.0192)^{90} \approx 194\%$

This estimate does not make sense, since it predicts that more than 100% of U.S. households will have telephones in 2010.

d) $f(x) = \dfrac{102.4604343}{1 + 2.25595242e^{-0.0483573334x}}$

e) $f(90) \approx 99.6\%$

This estimate makes sense.

62. a) $f(x) = \dfrac{19.11252764}{1 + 4.175198683e^{-0.2798470918x}}$

b) \$18.82 billion

Chapter 12

Conic Sections

Exercise Set 12.1

1. $y = -x^2$

a) This is equivalent to $y = -(x - 0)^2 + 0$. The vertex is $(0, 0)$.

b) We choose some x-values on both sides of the vertex and compute the corresponding values of y. The graph opens down, because the coefficient of x^2, -1, is negative.

x	y
0	0
1	-1
2	-4
-1	-1
-2	-4

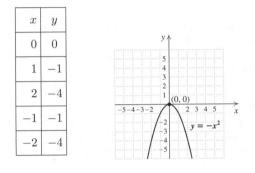

2.

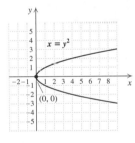

3. $y = -x^2 + 4x - 5$

a) We can find the vertex by computing the first coordinate, $x = -b/2a$, and then substituting to find the second coordinate:

$$x = -\frac{b}{2a} = -\frac{4}{2(-1)} = 2$$
$$y = -x^2 + 4x - 5 = -(2)^2 + 4(2) - 5 = -1$$

The vertex is $(2, -1)$.

b) We choose some x-values and compute the corresponding values for y. The graph opens downward because the coefficient of x^2, -1, is negative.

x	y
2	-1
3	-2
4	-5
1	-2
0	-5

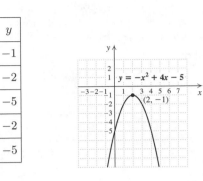

4.

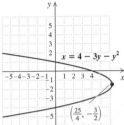

5. $x = y^2 - 4y + 1$

a) We find the vertex by completing the square.

$$x = (y^2 - 4y + 4) + 1 - 4$$
$$x = (y - 2)^2 - 3$$

The vertex is $(-3, 2)$.

b) To find ordered pairs, we choose values for y and compute the corresponding values of x. The graph opens to the right, because the coefficient of y^2, 1, is positive.

x	y
6	-1
1	0
-2	1
-3	2
-2	3

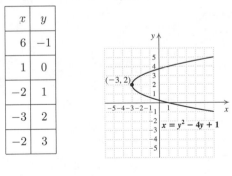

6.

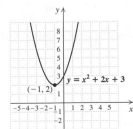

7. $x = y^2 + 1$

   a) $x = (y - 0)^2 + 1$

     The vertex is $(1, 0)$.

   b) To find the ordered pairs, we choose y-values and compute the corresponding values for x. The graph opens to the right, because the coefficient of y^2, 1, is positive.

x	y
1	0
2	1
5	2
2	-1
5	-2

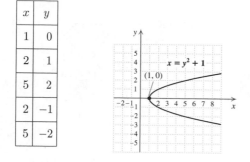

8.

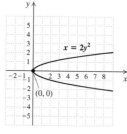

9. $x = -\dfrac{1}{2}y^2$

   a) $x = -\dfrac{1}{2}(y - 0)^2 + 0$

     The vertex is $(0, 0)$.

   b) We choose y-values and compute the corresponding values for x. The graph opens to the left, because the coefficient of y^2, $-\dfrac{1}{2}$, is negative.

x	y
0	0
-2	2
-8	4
-2	-2
-8	-4

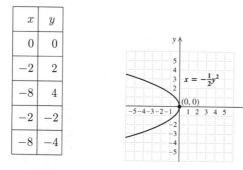

10.

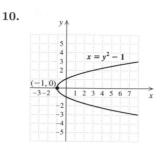

11. $x = -y^2 - 4y$

   a) We find the vertex by computing the second coordinate, $y = -b/2a$, and then substituting to find the first coordinate:

$$y = -\frac{b}{2a} = -\frac{-4}{2(-1)} = -2$$
$$x = -y^2 - 4y = (-2)^2 - 4(-2) = 4$$

     The vertex is $(4, -2)$.

   b) We choose y-values and compute the corresponding values for x. The graph opens to the left, because the coefficient of y^2, -1, is negative.

x	y
4	-2
-5	1
0	0
3	-1
3	-3

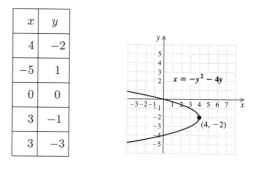

12.

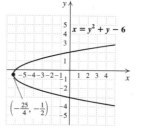

13. $x = 8 - y - y^2$

   a) We find the vertex by completing the square.

$$x = -(y^2 + y) + 8$$
$$x = -\left(y^2 + y + \frac{1}{4}\right) + 8 + \frac{1}{4}$$
$$x = -\left(y + \frac{1}{2}\right)^2 + \frac{33}{4}$$

     The vertex is $\left(\dfrac{33}{4}, -\dfrac{1}{2}\right)$.

   b) We choose y-values and compute the corresponding values for x. The graph opens to the left, because the coefficient of y^2, -1, is negative.

x	y
$\frac{33}{4}$	$-\frac{1}{2}$
8	0
6	1
2	2
8	-1
6	-2
2	-3

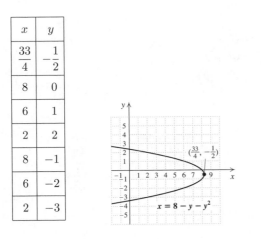

14.

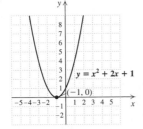

15. $y = x^2 - 2x + 1$

a) $y - (x-1)^2 + 0$

The vertex is $(1, 0)$.

b) We choose x-values and compute the corresponding values for y. The graph opens upward, because the coefficient of x^2, 1, is positive.

x	y
1	0
0	1
-1	4
2	1
3	4

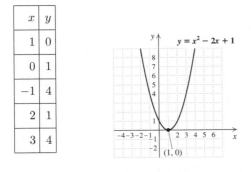

16.

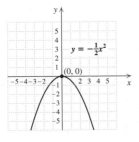

17. $x = -y^2 + 2y - 1$

a) We find the vertex by computing the second coordinate, $y = -b/2a$, and then substituting to find the first coordinate.

$$y = -\frac{b}{2a} = -\frac{2}{2(-1)} = 1$$
$$x = -y^2 + 2y - 1 = -(1)^2 + 2(1) - 1 = 0$$

The vertex is $(0, 1)$.

b) We choose y-values and compute the corresponding values for x. The graph opens to the left, because the coefficient of y^2, -1, is negative.

x	y
-4	3
-1	2
-1	0
-4	-1
-4	3

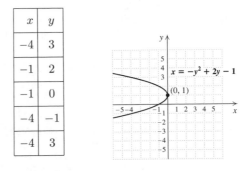

18.

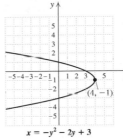

19. $x = -2y^2 - 4y + 1$

a) We find the vertex by completing the square.

$$x = -2(y^2 + 2y) + 1$$
$$x = -2(y^2 + 2y + 1) + 1 + 2$$
$$x = -2(y + 1)^2 + 3$$

The vertex is $(-3, -1)$.

b) We choose y-values and compute the corresponding values for x. The graph opens to the left, because the coefficient of y^2, -2, is negative.

x	y
3	-1
1	-2
-5	-3
1	0
-5	1

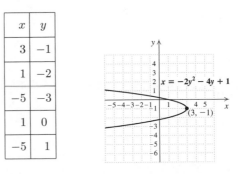

20.

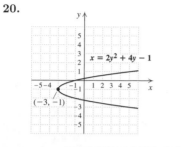

21. $d = \sqrt{(x_2 - x_1)^2 + (y_2 + y_1)^2}$ Distance formula

$\quad = \sqrt{(5 - 1)^2 + (9 - 6)^2}$ Substituting

$\quad = \sqrt{4^2 + 3^2}$

$\quad = \sqrt{25} = 5$

22. 10

23. $d = \sqrt{(x_2 - x_1)^2 + (y_2 - y_1)^2}$ Distance formula

$\quad = \sqrt{(3 - 0)^2 + [-4 - (-7)]^2}$ Substituting

$\quad = \sqrt{3^2 + 3^2}$

$\quad = \sqrt{18} \approx 4.243$ Simplifying and approximating

24. 10

25. $d = \sqrt{(x_2 - x_1)^2 + (y_2 - y_1)^2}$

$\quad = \sqrt{[6 - (-4)]^2 + (-6 - 4)^2}$

$\quad = \sqrt{200} \approx 14.142$

26. $\sqrt{464} \approx 21.541$

27. $d = \sqrt{(x_2 - x_1)^2 + (y_2 - y_1)^2}$

$\quad = \sqrt{(-9.2 - 8.6)^2 + [-3.4 - (-3.4)]^2}$

$\quad = \sqrt{(-17.8)^2 + 0^2}$

$\quad = \sqrt{316.84} = 17.8$

(Since these points are on a horizontal line, we could have found the distance between them by finding $|x_2 - x_1| = |-9.2 - 8.6| = |-17.8| = 17.8$.)

28. $\sqrt{98.93} \approx 9.946$

29. $d = \sqrt{(x_2 - x_1)^2 + (y_2 - y_1)^2}$

$d = \sqrt{\left(\dfrac{5}{7} - \dfrac{1}{7}\right)^2 + \left(\dfrac{1}{14} - \dfrac{11}{14}\right)^2}$

$\quad = \sqrt{\left(\dfrac{4}{7}\right)^2 + \left(-\dfrac{5}{7}\right)^2}$

$\quad = \sqrt{\dfrac{16}{49} + \dfrac{25}{49}}$

$\quad = \sqrt{\dfrac{41}{49}}$

$\quad = \dfrac{\sqrt{41}}{7} \approx 0.915$

30. $\sqrt{13} \approx 3.606$

31. $d = \sqrt{(x_2 - x_1)^2 + (y_2 - y_1)^2}$

$d = \sqrt{[0 - (-\sqrt{6})]^2 + (0 - \sqrt{2})^2}$

$\quad = \sqrt{6 + 2}$

$\quad = \sqrt{8} \approx 2.828$

32. $\sqrt{8} \approx 2.828$

33. $d = \sqrt{(x_2 - x_1)^2 + (y_2 - y_1)^2}$

$\quad = \sqrt{(-\sqrt{7} - \sqrt{2})^2 + [\sqrt{5} - (-\sqrt{3})]^2}$

$\quad = \sqrt{7 + 2\sqrt{14} + 2 + 5 + 2\sqrt{15} + 3}$

$\quad = \sqrt{17 + 2\sqrt{14} + 2\sqrt{15}} \approx 5.677$

34. $\sqrt{22 + 2\sqrt{40} + 2\sqrt{18}} \approx 6.568$

35. $d = \sqrt{(x_2 - x_1)^2 + (y_2 - y_1)^2}$

$d = \sqrt{(s - 0)^2 + (t - 0)^2}$

$\quad = \sqrt{s^2 + t^2}$

36. $\sqrt{p^2 + q^2}$

37. We use the midpoint formula:

$\left(\dfrac{x_1 + x_2}{2}, \dfrac{y_1 + y_2}{2}\right) = \left(\dfrac{-7 + 9}{2}, \dfrac{6 + 2}{2}\right)$, or

$\left(\dfrac{2}{2}, \dfrac{8}{2}\right)$, or $(1, 4)$

38. $\left(\dfrac{13}{2}, -1\right)$

39. We use the midpoint formula:

$\left(\dfrac{x_1 + x_2}{2}, \dfrac{y_1 + y_2}{2}\right) = \left(\dfrac{2 + 5}{2}, \dfrac{-1 + 8}{2}\right)$, or

$\left(\dfrac{7}{2}, \dfrac{7}{2}\right)$

40. $\left(0, -\dfrac{1}{2}\right)$

41. We use the midpoint formula:

$\left(\dfrac{x_1 + x_2}{2}, \dfrac{y_1 + y_2}{2}\right) = \left(\dfrac{-8 + 6}{2}, \dfrac{-5 + (-1)}{2}\right)$, or

$\left(\dfrac{-2}{2}, \dfrac{-6}{2}\right)$, or $(-1, -3)$

42. $\left(\dfrac{5}{2}, 1\right)$

43. We use the midpoint formula:

$\left(\dfrac{x_1 + x_2}{2}, \dfrac{y_1 + y_2}{2}\right) = \left(\dfrac{-3.4 + 2.9}{2}, \dfrac{8.1 + (-8.7)}{2}\right)$,

or $\left(\dfrac{-0.5}{2}, \dfrac{-0.6}{2}\right)$, or $(-0.25, -0.3)$

44. $(4.65, 0)$

45. We use the midpoint formula:

$\left(\dfrac{x_1 + x_2}{2}, \dfrac{y_1 + y_2}{2}\right) = \left(\dfrac{\dfrac{1}{6} + \left(-\dfrac{1}{3}\right)}{2}, \dfrac{-\dfrac{3}{4} + \dfrac{5}{6}}{2}\right)$,

or $\left(\dfrac{-\dfrac{1}{6}}{2}, \dfrac{\dfrac{1}{12}}{2}\right)$, or $\left(-\dfrac{1}{12}, \dfrac{1}{24}\right)$

46. $\left(-\dfrac{27}{80}, \dfrac{1}{24}\right)$

47. We use the midpoint formula:

$$\left(\frac{x_1 + x_2}{2}, \frac{y_1 + y_2}{2}\right) = \left(\frac{\sqrt{2} + \sqrt{3}}{2}, \frac{-1 + 4}{2}\right), \text{ or}$$

$$\left(\frac{\sqrt{2} + \sqrt{3}}{2}, \frac{3}{2}\right)$$

48. $\left(\dfrac{5}{2}, \dfrac{7\sqrt{3}}{2}\right)$

49. $\quad (x - h)^2 + (y - k)^2 = r^2 \quad$ Standard form

$\quad (x - 0)^2 + (y - 0)^2 = 6^2 \quad$ Substituting

$\quad\qquad\qquad x^2 + y^2 = 36 \quad$ Simplifying

50. $x^2 + y^2 = 25$

51. $\quad (x - h)^2 + (y - k)^2 = r^2 \qquad$ Standard form

$\quad (x - 7)^2 + (y - 3)^2 = (\sqrt{5})^2 \quad$ Substituting

$\quad (x - 7)^2 + (y - 3)^2 = 5$

52. $(x - 5)^2 + (y - 6)^2 = 2$

53. $\qquad (x - h)^2 + (y - k)^2 = r^2 \qquad$ Standard form

$\quad [x - (-4)]^2 + (y - 3)^2 = (4\sqrt{3})^2 \quad$ Substituting

$\qquad (x + 4)^2 + (y - 3)^2 = 48$

$\qquad\qquad\qquad [(4\sqrt{3})^2 = 16 \cdot 3 = 48]$

54. $(x + 2)^2 + (y - 7)^2 = 20$

55. $\qquad (x - h)^2 + (y - k)^2 - r^2$

$\quad [x - (-7)]^2 + [y - (-2)]^2 = (5\sqrt{2})^2$

$\qquad (x + 7)^2 + (y + 2)^2 = 50$

56. $(x + 5)^2 + (y + 8)^2 = 18$

57. Since the center is $(0, 0)$, we have

$$(x - 0)^2 + (y - 0)^2 = r^2 \text{ or } x^2 + y^2 = r^2$$

The circle passes through $(-3, 4)$. We find r^2 by substituting -3 for x and 4 for y.

$$(-3)^2 + 4^2 = r^2$$
$$9 + 16 = r^2$$
$$25 = r^2$$

Then $x^2 + y^2 = 25$ is an equation of the circle.

58. $(x - 3)^2 + (y + 2)^2 = 64$

59. Since the center is $(-4, 1)$, we have

$$[x - (-4)]^2 + (y - 1)^2 = r^2, \text{ or}$$
$$(x + 4)^2 + (y - 1)^2 = r^2.$$

The circle passes through $(-2, 5)$. We find r^2 by substituting -2 for x and 5 for y.

$$(-2 + 4)^2 + (5 - 1)^2 = r^2$$
$$4 + 16 = r^2$$
$$20 = r^2$$

Then $(x + 4)^2 + (y - 1)^2 = 20$ is an equation of the circle.

60. $(x + 1)^2 + (y + 3)^2 = 34$

61. We write standard form.

$$(x - 0)^2 + (y - 0)^2 = 7^2$$

The center is $(0, 0)$, and the radius is 7.

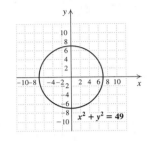

62. Center: $(0, 0)$

Radius: 6

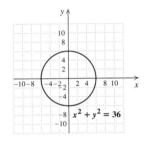

63. $\qquad (x + 1)^2 + (y + 3)^2 = 4$

$\quad [x - (-1)]^2 + [y - (-3)]^2 = 2^2 \quad$ Standard form

The center is $(-1, -3)$, and the radius is 2.

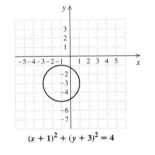

64. Center: $(2, -3)$

Radius: 1

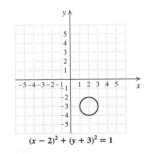

65. $(x-4)^2 + (y+3)^2 = 10$

$(x-4)^2 + [y-(-3)]^2 = (\sqrt{10})^2$

The center is $(4,-3)$, and the radius is $\sqrt{10}$.

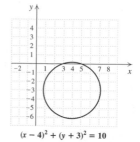

$(x-4)^2 + (y+3)^2 = 10$

66. Center: $(-5, 1)$

Radius: $\sqrt{15}$

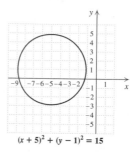

$(x+5)^2 + (y-1)^2 = 15$

67. $x^2 + y^2 = 7$

$(x-0)^2 + (y-0)^2 = (\sqrt{7})^2$ Standard form

The center is $(0,0)$, and the radius is $\sqrt{7}$.

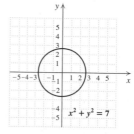

$x^2 + y^2 = 7$

68. Center: $(0,0)$

Radius: $\sqrt{8}$, or $2\sqrt{2}$

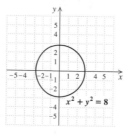

$x^2 + y^2 = 8$

69. $(x-5)^2 + y^2 = \dfrac{1}{4}$

$(x-5)^2 + (y-0)^2 = \left(\dfrac{1}{2}\right)^2$ Standard form

The center is $(5,0)$, and the radius is $\dfrac{1}{2}$.

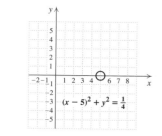

$(x-5)^2 + y^2 = \frac{1}{4}$

70. Center: $(0,1)$

Radius: $\dfrac{1}{5}$

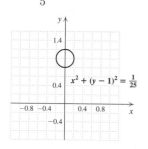

$x^2 + (y-1)^2 = \frac{1}{25}$

71. $x^2 + y^2 + 8x - 6y - 15 = 0$

$x^2 + 8x + y^2 - 6y = 15$

$(x^2 + 8x + 16) + (y^2 - 6y + 9) = 15 + 16 + 9$

Completing the square twice

$(x+4)^2 + (y-3)^2 = 40$

$[x-(-4)]^2 + (y-3)^2 = (\sqrt{40})^2$

Standard form

The center is $(-4,3)$, and the radius is $\sqrt{40}$, or $2\sqrt{10}$.

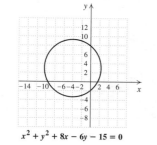

$x^2 + y^2 + 8x - 6y - 15 = 0$

72. Center: $(-3, 2)$

Radius: $\sqrt{28}$, or $2\sqrt{7}$

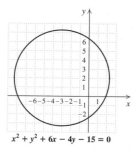

$x^2 + y^2 + 6x - 4y - 15 = 0$

73.
$$x^2 + y^2 - 8x + 2y + 13 = 0$$
$$x^2 - 8x + y^2 + 2y = -13$$
$$(x^2 - 8x + 16) + (y^2 + 2y + 1) = -13 + 16 + 1$$
Completing the square twice
$$(x - 4)^2 + (y + 1)^2 = 4$$
$$(x - 4)^2 + [y - (-1)]^2 = 2^2$$
Standard form

The center is $(4, -1)$, and the radius is 2.

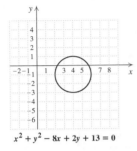

$$x^2 + y^2 - 8x + 2y + 13 = 0$$

74. Center: $(-3, -2)$

Radius: 1

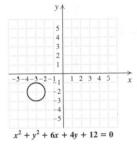

$$x^2 + y^2 + 6x + 4y + 12 = 0$$

75.
$$x^2 + y^2 + 10y - 75 = 0$$
$$x^2 + y^2 + 10y = 75$$
$$x^2 + (y^2 + 10y + 25) = 75 + 25$$
$$(x - 0)^2 + (y + 5)^2 = 100$$
$$(x - 0)^2 + [y - (-5)]^2 = 10^2$$

The center is $(0, -5)$, and the radius is 10.

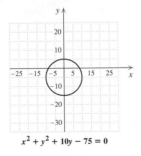

$$x^2 + y^2 + 10y - 75 = 0$$

76. Center: $(4, 0)$

Radius: 10

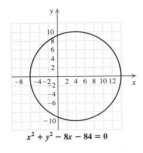

$$x^2 + y^2 - 8x - 84 = 0$$

77.
$$x^2 + y^2 + 7x - 3y - 10 = 0$$
$$x^2 + 7x + y^2 - 3y = 10$$
$$\left(x^2 + 7x + \frac{49}{4}\right) + \left(y^2 - 3y + \frac{9}{4}\right) = 10 + \frac{49}{4} + \frac{9}{4}$$
$$\left(x + \frac{7}{2}\right)^2 + \left(y - \frac{3}{2}\right)^2 = \frac{98}{4}$$
$$\left[x - \left(-\frac{7}{2}\right)\right]^2 + \left(y - \frac{3}{2}\right)^2 = \left(\sqrt{\frac{98}{4}}\right)^2$$

The center is $\left(-\frac{7}{2}, \frac{3}{2}\right)$, and the radius is $\sqrt{\frac{98}{4}}$, or $\frac{\sqrt{98}}{2}$, or $\frac{7\sqrt{2}}{2}$.

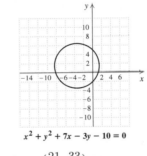

$$x^2 + y^2 + 7x - 3y - 10 = 0$$

78. Center: $\left(\frac{21}{2}, \frac{33}{2}\right)$

Radius: $\frac{\sqrt{1462}}{2}$

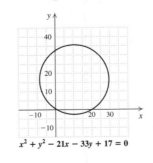

$$x^2 + y^2 - 21x - 33y + 17 = 0$$

79.
$$36x^2 + 36y^2 = 1$$
$$x^2 + y^2 = \frac{1}{36} \quad \text{Multiplying by } \frac{1}{36}$$
$$\text{on both sides}$$
$$(x-0)^2 + (y-0)^2 = \left(\frac{1}{6}\right)^2$$

The center is $(0,0)$, and the radius is $\frac{1}{6}$.

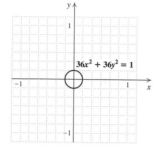

80. Center: $(0,0)$

Radius: $\frac{1}{2}$

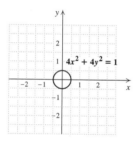

81. First we solve the equation for y.
$$x^2 + y^2 - 16 = 0$$
$$y^2 = 16 - x^2$$
$$y = \pm\sqrt{16 - x^2}$$

Then we graph $y_1 = \sqrt{16 - x^2}$ and $y_2 = -\sqrt{16 - x^2}$ on the same set of axes, choosing a squared window. We use $[-9, 9, -6, 6]$.

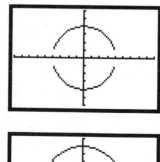

82.

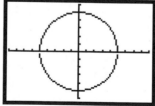

83. First we solve the equation for y. We can use the quadratic formula with $a = 1$, $b = -16$, and $c = x^2 + 14x + 54$ or we

can complete the square on the y-terms and then proceed. We will complete the square.
$$x^2 + y^2 + 14x - 16y + 54 = 0$$
$$x^2 + 14x + y^2 - 16y + 64 - 64 + 54 = 0$$
$$x^2 + 14x + (y-8)^2 - 10 = 0$$
$$(y-8)^2 = 10 - x^2 - 14x$$
$$y - 8 = \pm\sqrt{10 - x^2 - 14x}$$
$$y = 8 \pm \sqrt{10 - x^2 - 14x}$$

Then we graph $y_1 = 8 + \sqrt{10 - x^2 - 14x}$ and $y_2 = 8 - \sqrt{10 - x^2 - 14x}$ on the same set of axes, choosing a squared window. We use $[-20, 7, -1, 17]$.

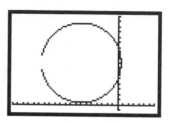

84.

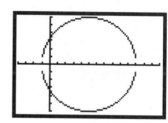

85. *Writing Exercise*

86. *Writing Exercise*

87.
$$\frac{x}{4} + \frac{5}{6} = \frac{2}{3}, \text{ LCD is } 12$$
$$12\left(\frac{x}{4} + \frac{5}{6}\right) = 12 \cdot \frac{2}{3}$$
$$12 \cdot \frac{x}{4} + 12 \cdot \frac{5}{6} = 8$$
$$3x + 10 = 8$$
$$3x = -2$$
$$x = -\frac{2}{3}$$

The solution is $-\frac{2}{3}$.

88. $\frac{25}{6}$

89. **Familiarize.** We make a drawing and label it. Let x represent the width of the border.

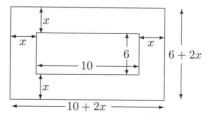

The perimeter of the larger rectangle is

$2(10 + 2x) + 2(6 + 2x)$, or $8x + 32$.

The perimeter of the smaller rectangle is

$2(10) + 2(6)$, or 32.

Translate. The perimeter of the larger rectangle is twice the perimeter of the smaller rectangle.

$$8x + 32 = 2 \cdot 32$$

Carry out. We solve the equation.

$$8x + 32 = 64$$
$$8x = 32$$
$$x = 4$$

Check. If the width of the border is 4 in., then the length and width of the larger rectangle are 18 in. and 14 in. Thus its perimeter is $2(18) + 2(14)$, or 64 in. The perimeter of the smaller rectangle is 32 in. The perimeter of the larger rectangle is twice the perimeter of the smaller rectangle.

State. The width of the border is 4 in.

90. 2640 mi

91. $3x - 8y = 5$, (1)

$2x + 6y = 5$ (2)

Multiply Equation (1) by 3, multiply Equation (2) by 4, and add.

$$9x - 24y = 15$$
$$\underline{8x + 24y = 20}$$
$$17x \quad\quad = 35$$
$$x = \frac{35}{17}$$

Now substitute $\frac{35}{17}$ for x in one of the original equations and solve for y. We use Equation (2).

$$2x + 6y = 5$$
$$2\left(\frac{35}{17}\right) + 6y = 5$$
$$\frac{70}{17} + 6y = 5$$
$$6y = \frac{15}{17}$$
$$y = \frac{5}{34}$$

The solution is $\left(\frac{35}{17}, \frac{5}{34}\right)$.

92. $\left(0, -\frac{9}{5}\right)$

93. *Writing Exercise*

94. *Writing Exercise*

95. We make a drawing of the circle with center $(3, -5)$ and tangent to the y-axis.

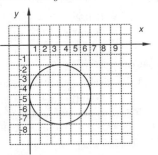

We see that the circle touches the y-axis at $(0, -5)$. Hence the radius is the distance between $(0, -5)$ and $(3, -5)$, or $\sqrt{(3-0)^2 + [-5-(-5)]^2}$, or 3. Now we write the equation of the circle.

$$(x - h)^2 + (y - k)^2 = r^2$$
$$(x - 3)^2 + [y - (-5)]^2 = 3^2$$
$$(x - 3)^2 + (y + 5)^2 = 9$$

96. $(x + 7)^2 + (y + 4)^2 = 16$

97. First we use the midpoint formula to find the center:

$$\left(\frac{7 + (-1)}{2}, \frac{3 + (-3)}{2}\right), \text{ or } \left(\frac{6}{2}, \frac{0}{2}\right), \text{ or } (3, 0)$$

The length of the radius is the distance between the center $(3, 0)$ and either endpoint of a diameter. We will use endpoint $(7, 3)$ in the distance formula:

$$r = \sqrt{(7 - 3)^2 + (3 - 0)^2} = \sqrt{25} = 5$$

Now we write the equation of the circle:

$$(x - h)^2 + (y - k)^2 = r^2$$
$$(x - 3)^2 + (y - 0)^2 = 5^2$$
$$(x - 3)^2 + y^2 = 25$$

98. $(x + 3)^2 + (y - 5)^2 = 16$

99. Let $(0, y)$ be the point on the y-axis that is equidistant from $(2, 10)$ and $(6, 2)$. Then the distance between $(2, 10)$ and $(0, y)$ is the same as the distance between $(6, 2)$ and $(0, y)$.

$$\sqrt{(0 - 2)^2 + (y - 10)^2} = \sqrt{(0 - 6)^2 + (y - 2)^2}$$
$$(-2)^2 + (y - 10)^2 = (-6)^2 + (y - 2)^2$$
$$\text{Squaring both sides}$$
$$4 + y^2 - 20y + 100 = 36 + y^2 - 4y + 4$$
$$64 = 16y$$
$$4 = y$$

This number checks. The point is $(0, 4)$.

100. $(-5, 0)$

101. a) Use the fact that the center of the circle $(0, k)$ is equidistant from the points $(-575, 0)$ and $(0, 19.5)$.

$$\sqrt{(-575-0)^2+(0-k)^2} = \sqrt{(0-0)^2+(19.5-k)^2}$$
$$\sqrt{330,625+k^2} = \sqrt{380.25-39k+k^2}$$
$$330,625+k^2 = 380.25-39k+k^2$$
$$\text{Squaring both sides}$$
$$330,244.75 = -39k$$
$$-8467.8 \approx k$$

Then the center of the circle is about $(0, -8467.8)$.

b) To find the radius we find the distance from the center, $(0, -8467.8)$ to any one of the points $(-575, 0)$, $(0, 19.5)$, or $(575, 0)$. We use $(0, 19.5)$.
$$r = \sqrt{(0-0)^2 + [19.5 - (-8467.8)]^2} \approx$$
$$8487.3 \text{ mm}$$

102. 8186.6 mm

103. a) Use the fact that the center of the circle, $(0, k)$ is equidistant from the points $(0, 2.1)$ and $(80, 0)$.
$$\sqrt{(80-0)^2+(0-k)^2} = \sqrt{(0-0)^2+(2.1-k)^2}$$
$$\sqrt{6400+k^2} = \sqrt{4.41-4.2k+k^2}$$
$$6400+k^2 = 4.41-4.2k+k^2$$
$$\text{Squaring both sides}$$
$$6395.59 = -4.2k$$
$$-1522.8 \approx k$$

Then the center of the circle is about $(0, -1522.8)$.

b) To find the radius we find the distance from the center, $(0, -1522.8)$, to either of the points $(0, 2.1)$ or $(80, 0)$. We use $(0, 2.1)$.
$$r = \sqrt{(0-0)^2 + [2.1 - (-1522.8)]^2} \approx$$
$$1524.9 \text{ cm}$$

104. a) $(0, -3)$

  b) 5 ft

105. Position a coordinate system as shown below so that the center of the top of the bowl is at the origin. Let r represent the radius of the circle.

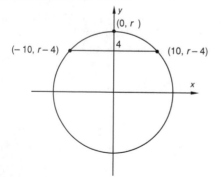

The equation of the circle is $x^2 + y^2 = r^2$, and one point on the circle is $(10, r-4)$. We substitute 10 for x and $r-4$ for y and solve for r.
$$10^2 + (r-4)^2 = r^2$$
$$100 + r^2 - 8r + 16 = r^2$$
$$r^2 - 8r + 116 = r^2$$
$$116 = 8r$$
$$14.5 = r$$

Then the original diameter of the bowl is $2r = 2(14.5)$, or 29 cm.

106. 590.49

107. First we graph $x = y^2 - y - 6$, $x = 2$, and $x = -3$ on the same set of axes.
$$x = y^2 - y - 6$$
$$x = \left(y^2 - y + \frac{1}{4}\right) - 6 - \frac{1}{4}$$
$$x = \left(y - \frac{1}{2}\right)^2 - \frac{25}{4}$$

The vertex is $\left(-\frac{25}{4}, \frac{1}{2}\right)$.

x	y
$-\frac{25}{4}$	$\frac{1}{2}$
-6	1
-4	2
0	3
-6	0
-4	-1
0	-2

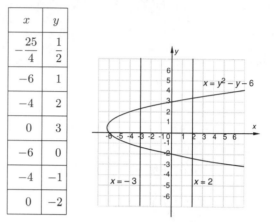

a) Graph $x = 2$ on the same set of axes as $x = y^2 - y - 6$ and approximate the y-coordinates of the points of intersection. (See the graph above.) The solutions are approximately 3.4 and -2.4.

b) Graph $x = -3$ on the same set of axes as $x = y^2 - y - 6$ and approximate the y-coordinates of the points of intersection. (See the graph above.) The solutions are approximately 2.3 and -1.3.

108.

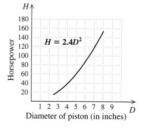

109. Let $P_1 = (x_1, y_1)$, $P_2 = (x_2, y_2)$, and $M = \left(\dfrac{x_1 + x_2}{2}, \dfrac{y_1 + y_2}{2}\right)$. Let $d(AB)$ denote the distance from point A to point B.

i) $\quad d(P_1 M)$
$$= \sqrt{\left(\frac{x_1+x_2}{2} - x_1\right)^2 + \left(\frac{y_1+y_2}{2} - y_1\right)^2}$$
$$= \frac{1}{2}\sqrt{(x_2-x_1)^2 + (y_2-y_1)^2};$$

$$d(P_2M)$$

$$= \sqrt{\left(\frac{x_1 + x_2}{2} - x_2\right)^2 + \left(\frac{y_1 + y_2}{2} - y_2\right)^2}$$

$$= \frac{1}{2}\sqrt{(x_1 - x_2)^2 + (y_1 - y_2)^2}$$

$$= \frac{1}{2}\sqrt{(x_2 - x_1)^2 + (y_2 - y_1)^2} = d(P_1M).$$

ii) $$d(P_1M) + d(P_2M)$$

$$= \frac{1}{2}\sqrt{(x_2 - x_1)^2 + (y_2 - y_1)^2} +$$

$$\frac{1}{2}\sqrt{(x_2 - x_1)^2 + (y_2 - y_1)^2}$$

$$= \sqrt{(x_2 - x_1)^2 + (y_2 - y_1)^2}$$

$$= d(P_1P_2)$$

Exercise Set 12.2

1. $\dfrac{x^2}{1} + \dfrac{y^2}{4} = 1$

$\dfrac{x^2}{1^2} + \dfrac{y^2}{2^2} = 1$

The x-intercepts are $(1, 0)$ and $(-1, 0)$, and the y-intercepts are $(0, 2)$ and $(0, -2)$. We plot these points and connect them with an oval-shaped curve.

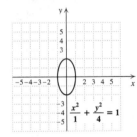

2.

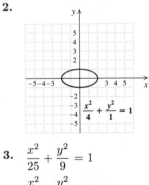

3. $\dfrac{x^2}{25} + \dfrac{y^2}{9} = 1$

$\dfrac{x^2}{5^2} + \dfrac{y^2}{3^2} = 1$

The x-intercepts are $(5, 0)$ and $(-5, 0)$, and the y-intercepts are $(0, 3)$ and $(0, -3)$. We plot these points and connect them with an oval-shaped curve.

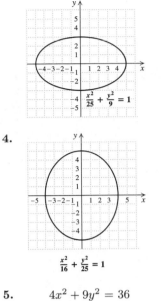

$$\frac{x^2}{16} + \frac{y^2}{25} = 1$$

4.

5. $4x^2 + 9y^2 = 36$

$\dfrac{1}{36}(4x^2 + 9y^2) = \dfrac{1}{36}(36)$ Multiplying by $\dfrac{1}{36}$

$\dfrac{x^2}{9} + \dfrac{y^2}{4} = 1$

$\dfrac{x^2}{3^2} + \dfrac{y^2}{2^2} = 1$

The x-intercepts are $(-3, 0)$ and $(3, 0)$, and the y-intercepts are $(0, -2)$ and $(0, 2)$. We plot these points and connect them with an oval-shaped curve.

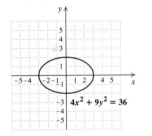

6.

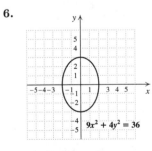

7. $16x^2 + 9y^2 = 144$

$\dfrac{x^2}{9} + \dfrac{y^2}{16} = 1$ Multiplying by $\dfrac{1}{144}$

$\dfrac{x^2}{3^2} + \dfrac{y^2}{4^2} = 1$

The x-intercepts are $(3, 0)$ and $(-3, 0)$, and the y-intercepts are $(0, 4)$ and $(0, -4)$. We plot these points and connect them with an oval-shaped curve.

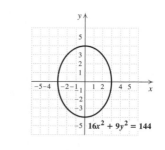

$16x^2 + 9y^2 = 144$

8.

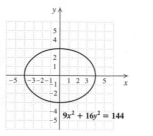

$9x^2 + 16y^2 = 144$

9. $2x^2 + 3y^2 = 6$

$$\frac{x^2}{3} + \frac{y^2}{2} = 1 \quad \text{Multiplying by } \frac{1}{6}$$

$$\frac{x^2}{(\sqrt{3})^2} + \frac{y^2}{(\sqrt{2})^2} = 1$$

The x-intercepts are $(\sqrt{3}, 0)$ and $(-\sqrt{3}, 0)$, and the y-intercepts are $(0, \sqrt{2})$ and $(0, -\sqrt{2})$. We plot these points and connect them with an oval-shaped curve.

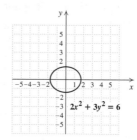

$2x^2 + 3y^2 = 6$

10.

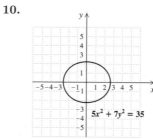

$5x^2 + 7y^2 = 35$

11. $5x^2 + 5y^2 = 125$

Observe that the x^2- and y^2-terms have the same coefficient. We divide both sides of the equation by 5 to obtain $x^2 + y^2 = 25$. This is the equation of a circle with center

$(0, 0)$ and radius 5.

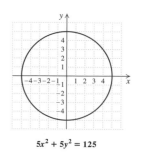

$5x^2 + 5y^2 = 125$

12.

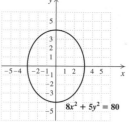

$8x^2 + 5y^2 = 80$

13. $3x^2 + 7y^2 - 63 = 0$

$$3x^2 + 7y^2 = 63$$

$$\frac{x^2}{21} + \frac{y^2}{9} = 1 \quad \text{Multiplying by } \frac{1}{63}$$

$$\frac{x^2}{(\sqrt{21})^2} + \frac{y^2}{3^2} = 1$$

The x-intercepts are $(\sqrt{21}, 0)$ and $(-\sqrt{21}, 0)$, or about $(4.583, 0)$ and $(-4.583, 0)$. The y-intercepts are $(0, 3)$ and $(0, -3)$. We plot these points and connect them with an oval-shaped curve.

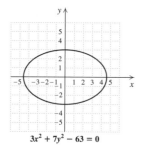

$3x^2 + 7y^2 - 63 = 0$

14.

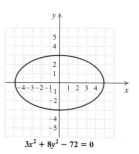

$3x^2 + 8y^2 - 72 = 0$

15.
$$8x^2 = 96 - 3y^2$$
$$8x^2 + 3y^2 = 96$$
$$\frac{x^2}{12} + \frac{y^2}{32} = 1$$
$$\frac{x^2}{(\sqrt{12})^2} + \frac{y^2}{(\sqrt{32})^2} = 1$$

The x-intercepts are $(\sqrt{12}, 0)$ and $(-\sqrt{12}, 0)$, or about $(3.464, 0)$ and $(-3.464, 0)$. The y-intercepts are $(0, \sqrt{32})$ and $(0, -\sqrt{32})$, or about $(0, 5.657)$ and $(0, -5.657)$. We plot these points and connect them with an oval-shaped curve.

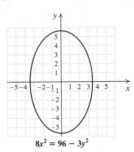

$$8x^2 = 96 - 3y^2$$

16.

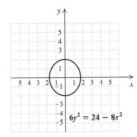

17. $16x^2 + 25y^2 = 1$

Note that $16 = \dfrac{1}{\dfrac{1}{16}}$ and $25 = \dfrac{1}{\dfrac{1}{25}}$. Thus, we can rewrite the equation:

$$\frac{x^2}{\dfrac{1}{16}} + \frac{y^2}{\dfrac{1}{25}} = 1$$

$$\frac{x^2}{\left(\dfrac{1}{4}\right)^2} + \frac{y^2}{\left(\dfrac{1}{5}\right)^2} = 1$$

The x-intercepts are $\left(\dfrac{1}{4}, 0\right)$ and $\left(-\dfrac{1}{4}, 0\right)$, and the y-intercepts are $\left(0, \dfrac{1}{5}\right)$ and $\left(0, -\dfrac{1}{5}\right)$. We plot these points and connect them with an oval-shaped curve.

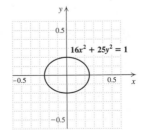

18.

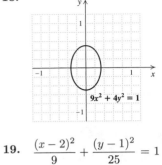

19.
$$\frac{(x-2)^2}{9} + \frac{(y-1)^2}{25} = 1$$
$$\frac{(x-2)^2}{3^2} + \frac{(y-1)^2}{5^2} = 1$$

The center of the ellipse is $(2, 1)$. Note that $a = 3$ and $b = 5$. We locate the center and then plot the points $(2+3, 1)$ $(2-3, 1)$, $(2, 1+5)$, and $(2, 1-5)$, or $(5, 1)$, $(-1, 1)$, $(2, 6)$, and $(2, -4)$. Connect these points with an oval-shaped curve.

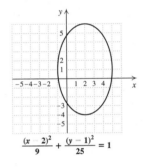

$$\frac{(x-2)^2}{9} + \frac{(y-1)^2}{25} = 1$$

20.

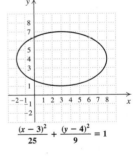

$$\frac{(x-3)^2}{25} + \frac{(y-4)^2}{9} = 1$$

21.
$$\frac{(x+4)^2}{16} + \frac{(y-3)^2}{49} = 1$$
$$\frac{(x-(-4))^2}{4^2} + \frac{(y-3)^2}{7^2} = 1$$

The center of the ellipse is $(-4, 3)$. Note that $a = 4$ and $b = 7$. We locate the center and then plot the points $(-4+4, 3)$, $(-4-4, 3)$, $(-4, 3+7)$, and $(-4, 3-7)$, or $(0, 3)$, $(-8, 3)$, $(-4, 10)$, and $(-4, -4)$. Connect these points with an oval-shaped curve.

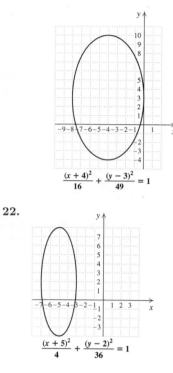

$$\frac{(x+4)^2}{16} + \frac{(y-3)^2}{49} = 1$$

22.

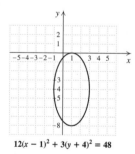

$$\frac{(x+5)^2}{4} + \frac{(y-2)^2}{36} = 1$$

23. $12(x-1)^2 + 3(y+4)^2 = 48$

$$\frac{(x-1)^2}{4} + \frac{(y+4)^2}{16} = 1$$

$$\frac{(x-1)^2}{2^2} + \frac{(y-(-4))^2}{4^2} = 1$$

The center of the ellipse is $(1,-4)$. Note that $a=2$ and $b=4$. We locate the center and then plot the points $(1+2,-4)$, $(1-2,-4)$, $(1,-4+4)$, and $(1,-4-4)$, or $(3,-4)$, $(-1,-4)$, $(1,0)$, and $(1,-8)$. Connect these points with an oval-shaped curve.

$$12(x-1)^2 + 3(y+4)^2 = 48$$

24.

$$4(x-6)^2 + 9(y+2)^2 = 36$$

25. $4(x+3)^2 + 4(y+1)^2 - 10 = 90$

$$4(x+3)^2 + 4(y+1)^2 = 100$$

Observe that the x^2- and y^2-terms have the some coefficient. Dividing both sides by 4, we have

$$(x+3)^2 + (y+1)^2 = 25.$$

This is the equation of a circle with center $(-3,-1)$ and radius 5.

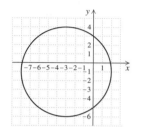

$$4(x+3)^2 + 4(y+1)^2 - 10 = 90$$

26.

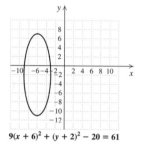

$$9(x+6)^2 + (y+2)^2 - 20 = 61$$

27. *Writing Exercise*

28. *Writing Exercise*

29. $\dfrac{3}{x-2} - \dfrac{5}{x-2} = 9$

Note that the denominators are 0 when $x=2$, so 2 cannot be a solution. We multiply by the LCD, $x-2$.

$$x-2\left(\frac{3}{x-2} - \frac{5}{x-2}\right) = (x-2)9$$

$$(x-2)\cdot\frac{3}{x-2} - (x-2)\cdot\frac{5}{x-2} = 9x-18$$

$$3-5 = 9x-18$$

$$-2 = 9x-18$$

$$16 = 9x$$

$$\frac{16}{9} = x$$

The number $\dfrac{16}{9}$ checks and is the solution.

30. $-\dfrac{19}{8}$

31. $\dfrac{x}{x-4} - \dfrac{3}{x-5} = \dfrac{2}{x-4}$

Note that $x-4$ is 0 when $x=4$ and $x-5$ is 0 when x is 5, so 4 and 5 cannot be solutions. We multiply by the LCD, $(x-4)(x-5)$.

$$(x-4)(x-5)\left(\frac{x}{x-4}-\frac{3}{x-5}\right) =$$

$$(x-4)(x-5)\cdot\frac{2}{x-4}$$

$$(x-4)(x-5)\cdot\frac{x}{x-4}-(x-4)(x-5)\frac{3}{x-5}=2(x-5)$$

$$x(x-5)-3(x-4)=2(x-5)$$

$$x^2-5x-3x+12=2x-10$$

$$x^2-8x+12=2x-10$$

$$x^2-10x+22=0$$

We use the quadratic formula with $a=1$, $b=-10$, and $c=22$.

$$x=\frac{-b\pm\sqrt{b^2-4ac}}{2a}$$

$$x=\frac{-(-10)\pm\sqrt{(-10)^2-4\cdot1\cdot22}}{2\cdot1}$$

$$x=\frac{10\pm\sqrt{12}}{2}=\frac{10\pm2\sqrt{3}}{2}$$

$$x=\frac{2(5\pm\sqrt{3})}{2\cdot1}=5\pm\sqrt{3}$$

Both numbers check. The solutions are $5\pm\sqrt{3}$.

32. $3\pm\sqrt{7}$

33.
$$9-\sqrt{2x+1}=7$$
$$-\sqrt{2x+1}=-2 \qquad \text{Isolating the radical}$$
$$(-\sqrt{2x+1})^2=(-2)^2$$
$$2x+1=4$$
$$2x=3$$
$$x=\frac{3}{2}$$

The number $\frac{3}{2}$ checks and is the solution.

34. No solution

35. *Writing Exercise*

36. *Writing Exercise*

37. Plot the given points.

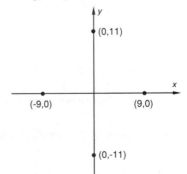

From the location of these points, we see that the ellipse that contains them is centered at the origin with $a=9$ and $b=11$. We write the equation of the ellipse:

$$\frac{x^2}{9^2}+\frac{y^2}{11^2}=1$$

$$\frac{x^2}{81}+\frac{y^2}{121}=1$$

38. $\dfrac{x^2}{49}+\dfrac{y^2}{25}=1$

39. Plot the given points.

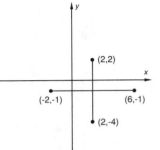

The midpoint of the segment from $(-2,-1)$ to $(6,-1)$ is $\left(\dfrac{-2+6}{2},\dfrac{-1-1}{2}\right)$, or $(2,-1)$. The midpoint of the segment from $(2,-4)$ to $(2,2)$ is $\left(\dfrac{2+2}{2},\dfrac{-4+2}{2}\right)$, or $(2,-1)$. Thus, we can conclude that $(2,-1)$ is the center of the ellipse. The distance from $(-2,-1)$ to $(2,-1)$ is $\sqrt{[2-(-2)]^2+[-1-(-1)]^2}=\sqrt{16}=4$, so $a=4$. The distance from $(2,2)$ to $(2,-1)$ is $\sqrt{(2-2)^2+(-1-2)^2}=\sqrt{9}=3$, so $b=3$. We write the equation of the ellipse.

$$\frac{(x-2)^2}{4^2}+\frac{(y-(-1))^2}{3^2}=1$$

$$\frac{(x-2)^2}{16}+\frac{(y+1)^2}{9}=1$$

40. $\dfrac{(x+1)^2}{25}+\dfrac{(y-3)^2}{16}=1$

41. We make a drawing.

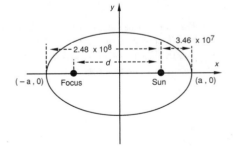

The distance between vertex $(a,0)$ and the sun is the same as the distance between vertex $(-a,0)$ and the other focus. Then

$$d=2.48\times10^8-3.46\times10^7=$$
$$2.48\times10^8-0.346\times10^8=2.134\times10^8 \text{ mi}.$$

42. a) Let $F_1 = (-c, 0)$ and $F_2 = (c, 0)$. Then the sum of the distances from the foci to P is $2a$. By the distance formula,

$$\sqrt{(x+c)^2 + y^2} + \sqrt{(x-c)^2 + y^2} = 2a, \text{ or}$$
$$\sqrt{(x+c)^2 + y^2} = 2a - \sqrt{(x-c)^2 + y^2}.$$

Squaring, we get

$$(x+c)^2 + y^2 = 4a^2 - 4a\sqrt{(x-c)^2 + y^2} + (x-c)^2 + y^2,$$

or $x^2 + 2cx + c^2 + y^2$

$$= 4a^2 - 4a\sqrt{(x-c)^2 + y^2} + x^2 - 2cx + c^2 + y^2.$$

Thus

$$-4a^2 + 4cx = -4a\sqrt{(x-c)^2 + y^2}$$
$$a^2 - cx = a\sqrt{(x-c)^2 + y^2}.$$

Squaring again, we get

$$a^4 - 2a^2cx + c^2x^2 = a^2(x^2 - 2cx + c^2 + y^2)$$
$$a^4 - 2a^2cx + c^2x^2 = a^2x^2 - 2a^2cx + a^2c^2 + a^2y^2,$$

or

$$x^2(a^2 - c^2) + a^2y^2 = a^2(a^2 - c^2)$$
$$\frac{x^2}{a^2} + \frac{y^2}{a^2 - c^2} = 1.$$

b) When P is at $(0, b)$, it follows that $b^2 = a^2 - c^2$. Substituting, we have

$$\frac{x^2}{a^2} + \frac{y^2}{b^2} = 1.$$

43. Position the ellipse on a coordinate system as shown below.

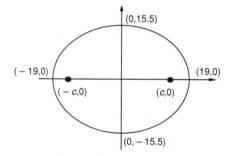

In order to best use the room's acoustics, the President and the advisor should be seated at the foci of the ellipse, or at $(-c, 0)$ and $(c, 0)$. We use the equation relating the coordinates of the foci and the intercepts to find c:

$$b^2 = a^2 - c^2$$
$$(15.5)^2 = (19)^2 - c^2$$
$$240.25 = 361 - c^2$$
$$c^2 = 120.75$$
$$c \approx 11$$

We make a sketch.

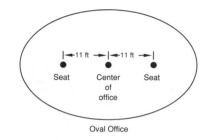

Oval Office

44. 5.66 ft

45.
$$\frac{x^2}{10,000} + \frac{y^2}{40,000} = 1, \text{ or}$$
$$\frac{x^2}{(100)^2} + \frac{y^2}{(200)^2} = 1, \text{ and}$$
$$\frac{x^2}{10,000} + \frac{y^2}{250,000} = 1, \text{ or}$$
$$\frac{x^2}{(100)^2} + \frac{y^2}{(500)^2} = 1$$

For each ellipse $a = 100$ yd and the width of the fire is twice this length, or 200 yd.

For the smaller ellipse, $b = 200$ yd, and for the larger ellipse, $b = 500$ yd. The length of the fire is the sum of these lengths, or 700 yd.

46.

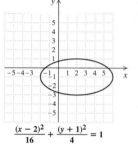

$$\frac{(x-2)^2}{16} + \frac{(y+1)^2}{4} = 1$$

47.
$$4x^2 + 24x + y^2 - 2y - 63 = 0$$
$$4(x^2 + 6x) + y^2 - 2y = 63$$
$$4(x^2 + 6x + 9 - 9) + (y^2 - 2y + 1 - 1) = 63$$
$$4(x^2 + 6x + 9) + (y^2 - 2y + 1) = 63 + 4 \cdot 9 + 1.$$
$$4(x+3)^2 + (y-1)^2 = 100$$
$$\frac{(x+3)^2}{25} + \frac{(y-1)^2}{100} = 1$$

The center of the ellipse is $(-3, 1)$. Note that $a = 5$ and $b = 10$. Locate the center and then plot the points $(-3+5, 1)$, $(-3-5, 1)$, $(-3, 1+10)$, and $(-3, 1-10)$, or $(2, 1)$, $(-8, 1)$, $(-3, 11)$, and $(-3, -9)$. Connect these points with an oval-shaped curve.

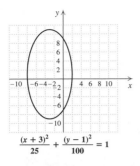

$$\frac{(x+3)^2}{25} + \frac{(y-1)^2}{100} = 1$$

Exercise Set 12.3

1. $\dfrac{y^2}{9} - \dfrac{x^2}{9} = 1$

$\dfrac{y^2}{3^2} - \dfrac{x^2}{3^2} = 1$

$a = 3$ and $b = 3$, so the asymptotes are $y = \dfrac{3}{3}x$ and $y = -\dfrac{3}{3}x$, or $y = x$ and $y = -x$. We sketch them.

Replacing x with 0 and solving for y, we get $y = \pm 3$, so the intercepts are $(0,3)$ and $(0,-3)$.

We plot the intercepts and draw smooth curves through them that approach the asymptotes.

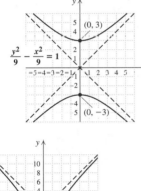

2.

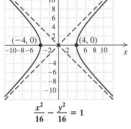

$$\frac{x^2}{16} - \frac{y^2}{16} = 1$$

3. $\dfrac{x^2}{4} - \dfrac{y^2}{25} = 1$

$\dfrac{x^2}{2^2} - \dfrac{y^2}{5^2} = 1$

$a = 2$ and $b = 5$, so the asymptotes are $y = \dfrac{5}{2}x$ and $y = -\dfrac{5}{2}x$. We sketch them.

Replacing y with 0 and solving for x, we get $x = \pm 2$, so the intercepts are $(2,0)$ and $(-2,0)$.

We plot the intercepts and draw smooth curves through them that approach the asymptotes.

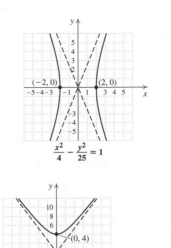

$$\frac{x^2}{4} - \frac{y^2}{25} = 1$$

4.

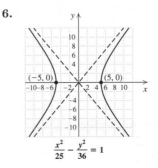

$$\frac{y^2}{16} - \frac{x^2}{9} = 1$$

5. $\dfrac{y^2}{36} - \dfrac{x^2}{9} = 1$

$\dfrac{y^2}{6^2} - \dfrac{x^2}{3^2} = 1$

$a = 3$ and $b = 6$, so the asymptotes are $y = \dfrac{6}{3}x$ and $y = -\dfrac{6}{3}x$, or $y = 2x$ and $y = -2x$. We sketch them.

Replacing x with 0 and solving for y, we get $y = \pm 6$, so the intercepts are $(0,6)$ and $(0,-6)$.

We plot the intercepts and draw smooth curves through them that approach the asymptotes.

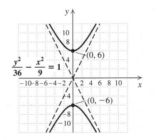

6.

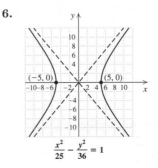

$$\frac{x^2}{25} - \frac{y^2}{36} = 1$$

7. $y^2 - x^2 = 25$

$$\frac{y^2}{25} - \frac{x^2}{25} = 1$$

$$\frac{y^2}{5^2} - \frac{x^2}{5^2} = 1$$

$a = 5$ and $b = 5$, so the asymptotes are $y = \frac{5}{5}x$ and $y = -\frac{5}{5}x$, or $y = x$ and $y = -x$. We sketch them.

Replacing x with 0 and solving for y, we get $y = \pm 5$, so the intercepts are $(0, 5)$ and $(0, -5)$.

We plot the intercepts and draw smooth curves through them that approach the asymptotes.

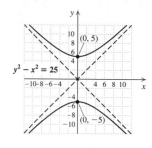

8.

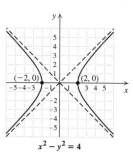

9. $25x^2 - 16y^2 = 400$

$$\frac{x^2}{16} - \frac{y^2}{25} = 1 \quad \text{Multiplying by } \frac{1}{400}$$

$$\frac{x^2}{4^2} - \frac{y^2}{5^2} = 1$$

$a = 4$ and $b = 5$, so the asymptotes are $y = \frac{5}{4}x$ and $y = -\frac{5}{4}x$. We sketch them.

Replacing y with 0 and solving for x, we get $x = \pm 4$, so the intercepts are $(4, 0)$ and $(-4, 0)$.

We plot the intercepts and draw smooth curves through them that approach the asymptotes.

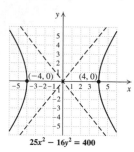

10.

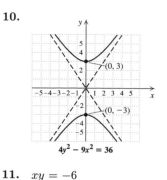

11. $xy = -6$

$$y = -\frac{6}{x} \quad \text{Solving for } y$$

We find some solutions, keeping the results in a table.

x	y
$\frac{1}{2}$	-12
1	-6
2	-3
4	$-\frac{3}{2}$
8	$-\frac{3}{4}$
$-\frac{1}{2}$	12
-1	6
-2	3
-8	$\frac{3}{4}$

Note that we cannot use 0 for x. The x-axis and the y-axis are the asymptotes.

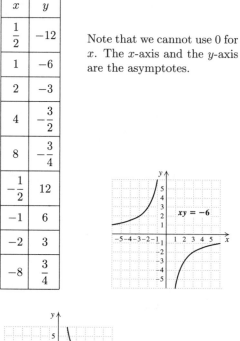

12.

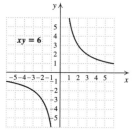

13. $xy = 4$

$$y = \frac{4}{x} \quad \text{Solving for } y$$

We find some solutions, keeping the results in a table.

x	y
$\frac{1}{2}$	8
1	4
4	1
8	$\frac{1}{2}$
$-\frac{1}{2}$	-8
-1	-4
-2	-2
-4	-1

Note that we cannot use 0 for x. The x-axis and the y-axis are the asymptotes.

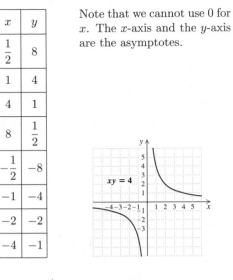

14.

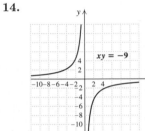

15. $xy = -2$

$$y = -\frac{2}{x} \qquad \text{Solving for } y$$

x	y
$\frac{1}{2}$	-4
1	-2
2	-1
4	$-\frac{1}{2}$
$-\frac{1}{2}$	4
-1	2
-2	1
-4	$\frac{1}{2}$

Note that we cannot use 0 for x. The x-axis and the y-axis are the asymptotes.

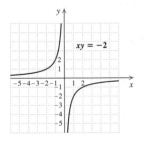

16.

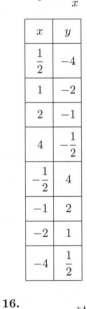

17. $xy = 1$

$$y = \frac{1}{x} \qquad \text{Solving for } y$$

x	y
$\frac{1}{4}$	4
$\frac{1}{2}$	2
1	1
2	$\frac{1}{2}$
4	$\frac{1}{4}$
$-\frac{1}{4}$	-4
$-\frac{1}{2}$	-2
-1	-1
-2	$-\frac{1}{2}$
-4	$-\frac{1}{4}$

Note that we cannot use 0 for x. The x-axis and the y-axis are the asymptotes.

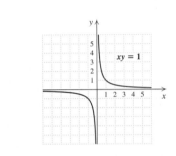

18.

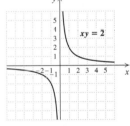

19. $x^2 + y^2 - 10x + 8y - 40 = 0$

Completing the square twice, we obtain an equivalent equation:

$$(x^2 - 10x) + (y^2 + 8y) = 40$$
$$(x^2 - 10x + 25) + (y^2 + 8y + 16) = 40 + 25 + 16$$
$$(x - 5)^2 + (y + 4)^2 = 81$$

The graph is a circle.

20. Parabola

21. $9x^2 + 4y^2 - 36 = 0$

$$9x^2 + 4y^2 = 36$$
$$\frac{x^2}{4} + \frac{y^2}{9} = 1$$

The graph is an ellipse.

22. Parabola

23. $4x^2 - 9y^2 - 72 = 0$

$$4x^2 - 9y^2 = 72$$

$$\frac{x^2}{18} - \frac{y^2}{8} = 1$$

The graph is a hyperbola.

24. Circle

25. $x^2 + y^2 = 2x + 4y + 4$

$$x^2 - 2x + y^2 - 4y = 4$$

$$(x^2 - 2x + 1) + (y^2 - 4y + 4) = 4 + 1 + 4$$

$$(x - 1)^2 + (y - 2)^2 = 9$$

The graph is a circle.

26. Circle

27. $4x^2 = 64 - y^2$

$$4x^2 + y^2 = 64$$

$$\frac{x^2}{16} + \frac{y^2}{64} = 1$$

The graph is an ellipse.

28. Hyperbola

29. $x - \dfrac{3}{y} = 0$

$$x = \frac{3}{y}$$

$$xy = 3$$

The graph is a hyperbola.

30. Parabola

31. $y + 6x = x^2 + 5$

$$y = x^2 - 6x + 5$$

The graph is a parabola.

32. Hyperbola

33. $9y^2 = 36 + 4x^2$

$$9y^2 - 4x^2 = 36$$

$$\frac{y^2}{4} - \frac{x^2}{9} = 1$$

The graph is a hyperbola.

34. Circle

35. $3x^2 + y^2 - x = 2x^2 - 9x + 10y + 40$

$$x^2 + y^2 + 8x - 10y = 40$$

Both variables are squared, so the graph is not a parabola. The plus sign between x^2 and y^2 indicates that we have either a circle or an ellipse. Since the coefficients of x^2 and y^2 are the same, the graph is a circle.

36. Ellipse

37. $16x^2 + 5y^2 - 12x^2 + 8y^2 - 3x + 4y = 568$

$$4x^2 + 13y^2 - 3x + 4y = 568$$

Both variables are squared, so the graph is not a parabola. The plus sign between x^2 and y^2 indicates that we have either a circle or an ellipse. Since the coefficients of x^2 and y^2 are different, the graph is an ellipse.

38. Ellipse

39. *Writing Exercise*

40. *Writing Exercise*

41. $5x + 6y = -12, \quad (1)$

$3x + 9y = 15 \qquad (2)$

We will use the elimination method. First multiply equation (1) by 3 and equation (2) by -2 and add.

$$\begin{array}{r} 15x + 18y = -36 \\ -6x - 18y = -30 \\ \hline 9x \qquad\quad = -66 \end{array}$$

$$x = -\frac{22}{3}$$

Now substitute $-\dfrac{22}{3}$ for x in one of the original equations and solve for y.

$$5x + 6y = -12 \quad (1)$$

$$5\left(-\frac{22}{3}\right) + 6y = -12$$

$$-\frac{110}{3} + 6y = -12$$

$$6y = \frac{74}{3}$$

$$y = \frac{37}{9}$$

The solution is $\left(-\dfrac{22}{3}, \dfrac{37}{9}\right)$.

42. $(9, -4)$

43. $y^2 - 3 = 6$

$$y^2 = 9$$

$y = 3 \;\; or \;\; y = -3$ Principle of square roots

The solutions are 3 and -3.

44. $-1, 1$

45. **Familiarize.** Let $p = $ the price of the radio before the tax was added. Then the total price is $p + 5\%p$, or $p + 0.05p$, or $1.05p$.

Translate.

$$\underbrace{\text{The total price}}_{\downarrow \atop 1.05p} \;\; \underset{=}{\overset{\downarrow}{\text{is}}} \;\; \underset{36.75}{\overset{\downarrow}{\$36.75.}}$$

Carry out. We solve the equation.

$$1.05p = 36.75$$

$$p = \frac{36.75}{1.05}$$

$$p = 35$$

Check. 5% of \$35 is \$1.75 and \$35 + \$1.75 = \$36.75. The answer checks.

State. The price before tax was \$35.

46. 69

47. *Writing Exercise*

48. *Writing Exercise*

49. Since the intercepts are $(0,6)$ and $(0,-6)$, we know that the hyperbola is of the form $\dfrac{y^2}{b^2} - \dfrac{x^2}{a^2} = 1$ and that $b = 6$. The equations of the asymptotes tell us that $b/a = 3$, so

$$\frac{6}{a} = 3$$
$$a = 2.$$

The equation is $\dfrac{y^2}{6^2} - \dfrac{x^2}{2^2} = 1$, or $\dfrac{y^2}{36} - \dfrac{x^2}{4} = 1$.

50. $\dfrac{x^2}{64} - \dfrac{y^2}{1024} = 1$

51. $\dfrac{(x-5)^2}{36} - \dfrac{(y-2)^2}{25} = 1$

$\dfrac{(x-5)^2}{6^2} - \dfrac{(y-2)^2}{5^2} = 1$

$h = 5,\ k = 2,\ a = 6,\ b = 5$

Center: $(5, 2)$

Vertices: $(5-6, 2)$ and $(5+6, 2)$, or $(-1, 2)$ and $(11, 2)$

Asymptotes: $y - 2 = \dfrac{5}{6}(x-5)$ and $y - 2 = -\dfrac{5}{6}(x-5)$

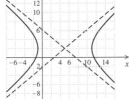

52. Center: $(2, 1)$

Vertices: $(-1, 1),\ (5, 1)$

Asymptotes: $y - 1 = \dfrac{2}{3}(x-2)$, $y - 1 = -\dfrac{2}{3}(x-2)$

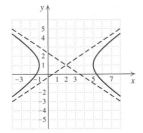

53. $8(y+3)^2 - 2(x-4)^2 = 32$

$\dfrac{(y+3)^2}{4} - \dfrac{(x-4)^2}{16} = 1$

$\dfrac{(y-(-3))^2}{2^2} - \dfrac{(x-4)^2}{4^2} = 1$

$h = 4,\ k = -3,\ a = 4,\ b = 2$

Center: $(4, -3)$

Vertices: $(4, -3+2)$ and $(4, -3-2)$, or $(4, -1)$ and $(4, -5)$

Asymptotes: $y - (-3) = \dfrac{2}{4}(x-4)$ and

$y - (-3) = -\dfrac{2}{4}(x-4)$, or $y + 3 = \dfrac{1}{2}(x-4)$ and

$y + 3 = -\dfrac{1}{2}(x-4)$

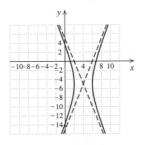

54. Center: $(4, -5)$

Vertices: $(2, -5),\ (6, -5)$

Asymptotes: $y + 5 = \dfrac{5}{2}(x-4)$, $y + 5 = -\dfrac{5}{2}(x-4)$

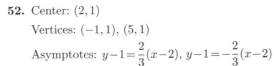

55.
$$4x^2 - y^2 + 24x + 4y + 28 = 0$$
$$4(x^2 + 6x) - (y^2 - 4y) = -28$$
$$4(x^2 + 6x + 9 - 9) - (y^2 - 4y + 4 - 4) = -28$$
$$4(x^2 + 6x + 9) - (y^2 - 4y + 4) = -28 + 4 \cdot 9 - 4$$
$$4(x+3)^2 - (y-2)^2 = 4$$
$$\frac{(x+3)^2}{1} - \frac{(y-2)^2}{4} = 1$$
$$\frac{(x-(-3))^2}{1^2} - \frac{(y-2)^2}{2^2} = 1$$

$h = -3,\ k = 2,\ a = 1,\ b = 2$

Center: $(-3, 2)$

Vertices: $(-3-1, 2)$, and $(-3+1, 2)$, or $(-4, 2)$ and $(-2, 2)$

Asymptotes: $y - 2 = \dfrac{2}{1}(x-(-3))$ and

$y - 2 = -\dfrac{2}{1}(x-(-3))$, or $y - 2 = 2(x+3)$ and

$y - 2 = -2(x+3)$

$4x^2 - y^2 + 24x + 4y + 28 = 0$

56. Center: $(-2, 1)$

Vertices: $(-2, 6)$, $(-2, -4)$

Asymptotes: $y - 1 = \dfrac{5}{2}(x + 2)$, $y - 1 = -\dfrac{5}{2}(x + 2)$

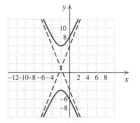

Exercise Set 12.4

1. $x^2 + y^2 = 25$,   (1)

$y - x = 1$ (2)

First solve Eq. (2) for y.

$y = x + 1$ (3)

Then substitute $x + 1$ for y in Eq. (1) and solve for x.

$$x^2 + y^2 = 25$$
$$x^2 + (x + 1)^2 = 25$$
$$x^2 + x^2 + 2x + 1 = 25$$
$$2x^2 + 2x - 24 = 0$$
$$x^2 + x - 12 = 0$$
$$(x + 4)(x - 3) = 0$$

$x + 4 = 0$ *or* $x - 3 = 0$ Principle of zero products

$x = -4$ *or* $x = 3$

Now substitute these numbers in Eq. (3) and solve for y.

$y = -4 + 1 = -3$

$y = 3 + 1 = 4$

The pairs $(-4, -3)$ and $(3, 4)$ check, so they are the solutions.

2. $(-8, -6)$, $(6, 8)$

3. $9x^2 + 4y^2 = 36$,   (1)

$3x + 2y = 6$ (2)

First solve Eq. (2) for x.

$$3x = 6 - 2y$$
$$x = 2 - \frac{2}{3}y \quad (3)$$

Then substitute $2 - \dfrac{2}{3}y$ for x in Eq. (1) and solve for y.

$$9x^2 + 4y^2 = 36$$
$$9\left(2 - \frac{2}{3}y\right)^2 + 4y^2 = 36$$
$$9\left(4 - \frac{8}{3}y + \frac{4}{9}y^2\right) + 4y^2 = 36$$
$$36 - 24y + 4y^2 + 4y^2 = 36$$
$$8y^2 - 24y = 0$$
$$y^2 - 3y = 0$$
$$y(y - 3) = 0$$

$y = 0$ *or* $y = 3$

Now substitute these numbers in Eq. (3) and solve for x.

$$x = 2 - \frac{2}{3}(0) = 2$$
$$x = 2 - \frac{2}{3}(3) = 0$$

The pairs $(2, 0)$ and $(0, 3)$ check, so they are the solutions.

4. $(0, 2)$, $(3, 0)$

5. $y = x^2$,   (1)

$3x = y + 2$ (2)

First solve Eq. (2) for y.

$y = 3x - 2$ (3)

Then substitute $3x - 2$ for y in Eq. (1) and solve for x.

$$y = x^2$$
$$3x - 2 = x^2$$
$$0 = x^2 - 3x + 2$$
$$0 = (x - 2)(x - 1)$$

$x = 2$ *or* $x = 1$

Now substitute these numbers in Eq. (3) and solve for y.

$y = 3 \cdot 2 - 2 = 4$

$y = 3 \cdot 1 - 2 = 1$

The pairs $(2, 4)$ and $(1, 1)$ check, so they are the solutions.

6. $(-2, 1)$

7. $2y^2 + xy + x^2 = 7$,   (1)

$x - 2y = 5$ (2)

First solve Eq. (2) for x.

$x = 2y + 5$ (3)

Then substitute $2y + 5$ for x in Eq. (1) and solve for y.

$$2y^2 + xy + x^2 = 7$$
$$2y^2 + (2y + 5)y + (2y + 5)^2 = 7$$
$$2y^2 + 2y^2 + 5y + 4y^2 + 20y + 25 = 7$$
$$8y^2 + 25y + 18 = 0$$
$$(8y + 9)(y + 2) = 0$$

$y = -\dfrac{9}{8}$ *or* $y = -2$

Now substitute these numbers in Eq. (3) and solve for x.

$$x = 2\left(-\frac{9}{8}\right) + 5 = \frac{11}{4}$$
$$x = 2(-2) + 5 = 1$$

The pairs $\left(\dfrac{11}{4}, -\dfrac{9}{8}\right)$ and $(1, -2)$ check, so they are the solutions.

8. $\left(\dfrac{5 + \sqrt{70}}{3}, \dfrac{-1 + \sqrt{70}}{3}\right)$, $\left(\dfrac{5 - \sqrt{70}}{3}, \dfrac{-1 - \sqrt{70}}{3}\right)$

9. $x^2 - y^2 = 16$,   (1)

$x - 2y = 1$ (2)

First solve Eq. (2) for x.

$x = 2y + 1$ (3)

Then substitute $2y + 1$ for x in Eq. (1) and solve for y.

$$x^2 - y^2 = 16$$
$$(2y + 1)^2 - y^2 = 16$$
$$4y^2 + 4y + 1 - y^2 = 16$$
$$3y^2 + 4y - 15 = 0$$
$$(3y - 5)(y + 3) = 0$$
$$y = \frac{5}{3} \ or \ y = -3$$

Now substitute these numbers in Eq. (3) and find x.

$$x = 2\left(\frac{5}{3}\right) + 1 = \frac{13}{3}$$
$$x = 2(-3) + 1 = -5$$

The pairs $\left(\frac{13}{3}, \frac{5}{3}\right)$ and $(-5, -3)$ check, so they are the solutions.

10. $\left(4, \frac{3}{2}\right)$, $(3, 2)$

11. $m^2 + 3n^2 = 10$, (1)

$m - n = 2$ (2)

First solve Eq. (2) for m.

$m = n + 2$ (3)

Then substitute $n + 2$ for m in Eq. (1) and solve for n.

$$m^2 + 3n^2 = 10$$
$$(n + 2)^2 + 3n^2 = 10$$
$$n^2 + 4n + 4 + 3n^2 = 10$$
$$4n^2 + 4n - 6 = 0$$
$$2n^2 + 2n - 3 = 0$$
$$n = \frac{-2 \pm \sqrt{2^2 - 4(2)(-3)}}{2 \cdot 2} = \frac{-1 \pm \sqrt{7}}{2}$$

Now substitute these numbers in Eq. (3) and solve for m.

$$m = \frac{-1 + \sqrt{7}}{2} + 2 = \frac{3 + \sqrt{7}}{2}$$
$$m = \frac{-1 - \sqrt{7}}{2} + 2 = \frac{3 - \sqrt{7}}{2}$$

The pairs $\left(\frac{3 + \sqrt{7}}{2}, \frac{-1 + \sqrt{7}}{2}\right)$ and $\left(\frac{3 - \sqrt{7}}{2}, \frac{-1 - \sqrt{7}}{2}\right)$ check, so they are the solutions.

12. $\left(\frac{7}{3}, \frac{1}{3}\right)$, $(1, -1)$

13. $2y^2 + xy = 5$, (1)

$4y + x = 7$ (2)

First solve Eq. (2) for x.

$x = -4y + 7$ (3)

Then substitute $-4y + 7$ for x in Eq. (3) and solve for y.

$$2y^2 + xy = 5$$
$$2y^2 + (-4y + 7)y = 5$$
$$2y^2 - 4y^2 + 7y = 5$$
$$0 = 2y^2 - 7y + 5$$
$$0 = (2y - 5)(y - 1)$$

$$y = \frac{5}{2} \ or \ y = 1$$

Now substitute these numbers in Eq. (3) and solve for x.

$$x = -4\left(\frac{5}{2}\right) + 7 = -3$$
$$x = -4(1) + 7 = 3$$

The pairs $\left(-3, \frac{5}{2}\right)$ and $(3, 1)$ check, so they are the solutions.

14. $\left(\frac{11}{4}, -\frac{5}{4}\right)$, $(1, 4)$

15. $p + q = -6$, (1)

$pq = -7$ (2)

First solve Eq. (1) for p.

$p = -q - 6$ (3)

Then substitute $-q - 6$ for p in Eq. (2) and solve for q.

$$pq = -7$$
$$(-q - 6)q = -7$$
$$-q^2 - 6q = -7$$
$$0 = q^2 + 6q - 7$$
$$0 = (q + 7)(q - 1)$$

$q = -7 \ or \ q = 1$

Now substitute these numbers in Eq. (3) and solve for p.

$$p = -(-7) - 6 = 1$$
$$p = -1 - 6 = -7$$

The pairs $(1, -7)$ and $(-7, 1)$ check, so they are the solutions.

16. $\left(\frac{7 - \sqrt{33}}{2}, \frac{7 + \sqrt{33}}{2}\right)$, $\left(\frac{7 + \sqrt{33}}{2}, \frac{7 - \sqrt{33}}{2}\right)$

17. $4x^2 + 9y^2 = 36$, (1)

$x + 3y = 3$ (2)

First solve Eq. (1) for x.

$x = -3y + 3$ (3)

Then substitute $-3y + 3$ for x in Eq. (1) and solve for y.

$$4x^2 + 9y^2 = 36$$
$$4(-3y + 3)^2 + 9y^2 = 36$$
$$4(9y^2 - 18y + 9) + 9y^2 = 36$$
$$36y^2 - 72y + 36 + 9y^2 = 36$$
$$45y^2 - 72y = 0$$
$$5y^2 - 8y = 0$$
$$y(5y - 8) = 0$$

$$y = 0 \ or \ y = \frac{8}{5}$$

Now substitute these numbers in Eq. (3) and solve for x.

$$x = -3 \cdot 0 + 3 = 3$$
$$x = -3\left(\frac{8}{5}\right) + 3 = -\frac{9}{5}$$

The pairs $(3, 0)$ and $\left(-\frac{9}{5}, \frac{8}{5}\right)$ check, so they are the solutions.

18. $(3, -5)$, $(-1, 3)$

19. $xy = 4$,   (1)

   $x + y = 5$ (2)

   First solve Eq. (2) for x.

   $x = -y + 5$ (3)

   Substitute $-y + 5$ for x in Eq. (1) and solve for y.

$$xy = 4$$
$$(-y + 5)y = 4$$
$$-y^2 + 5y = 4$$
$$0 = y^2 - 5y + 4$$
$$0 = (y - 4)(y - 1)$$

   $y = 4$ or $y = 1$

   Then substitute these numbers in Eq. (3) and solve for x.

   $x = -4 + 5 = 1$

   $x = -1 + 5 = 4$

   The pairs $(1, 4)$ and $(4, 1)$ check, so they are the solutions.

20. $(-5, -8)$, $(8, 5)$

21. $y = x^2$,   (1)

   $x = y^2$ (2)

   Eq. (1) is already solved for y. Substitute x^2 for y in Eq. (2) and solve for x.

$$x = y^2$$
$$x = (x^2)^2$$
$$x = x^4$$
$$0 = x^4 - x$$
$$0 = x(x^3 - 1)$$
$$0 = x(x - 1)(x^2 + x + 1)$$

   $x = 0$ or $x = 1$ or $x = \dfrac{-1 \pm \sqrt{1^2 - 4 \cdot 1 \cdot 1}}{2}$

   $x = 0$ or $x = 1$ or $x = -\dfrac{1}{2} \pm \dfrac{\sqrt{3}}{2}i$

   Substitute these numbers in Eq. (1) and solve for y.

   $y = 0^2 = 0$

   $y = 1^2 = 1$

   $y = \left(-\dfrac{1}{2} + \dfrac{\sqrt{3}}{2}i\right)^2 = -\dfrac{1}{2} - \dfrac{\sqrt{3}}{2}i$

   $y = \left(-\dfrac{1}{2} - \dfrac{\sqrt{3}}{2}i\right)^2 = -\dfrac{1}{2} + \dfrac{\sqrt{3}}{2}i$

   The pairs $(0, 0)$, $(1, 1)$, $\left(-\dfrac{1}{2} + \dfrac{\sqrt{3}}{2}i, -\dfrac{1}{2} - \dfrac{\sqrt{3}}{2}i\right)$,

   and $\left(-\dfrac{1}{2} - \dfrac{\sqrt{3}}{2}i, -\dfrac{1}{2} + \dfrac{\sqrt{3}}{2}i\right)$ check, so they are the solutions.

22. $(-5, 0)$, $(4, 3)$, $(4, -3)$

23. $x^2 + y^2 = 9$,   (1)

   $x^2 - y^2 = 9$ (2)

   Here we use the elimination method.

$$\begin{aligned} x^2 + y^2 &= 9 \quad (1) \\ \underline{x^2 - y^2} &= \underline{9} \quad (2) \\ 2x^2 &= 18 \quad \text{Adding} \\ x^2 &= 9 \\ x &= \pm 3 \end{aligned}$$

   If $x = 3$, $x^2 = 9$, and if $x = -3$, $x^2 = 9$, so substituting 3 or -3 in Eq. (1) gives us

$$x^2 + y^2 = 9$$
$$9 + y^2 = 9$$
$$y^2 = 0$$
$$y = 0.$$

   The pairs $(3, 0)$ and $(-3, 0)$ check. They are the solutions.

24. $(0, 2)$, $(0, -2)$

25. $x^2 + y^2 = 25$,   (1)

   $xy = 12$ (2)

   First we solve Eq. (2) for y.

$$xy = 12$$
$$y = \dfrac{12}{x}$$

   Then we substitute $\dfrac{12}{x}$ for y in Eq. (1) and solve for x.

$$x^2 + y^2 = 25$$
$$x^2 + \left(\dfrac{12}{x}\right)^2 = 25$$
$$x^2 + \dfrac{144}{x^2} = 25$$
$$x^4 + 144 = 25x^2 \quad \text{Multiplying by } x^2$$
$$x^4 - 25x^2 + 144 = 0$$
$$u^2 - 25u + 144 = 0 \qquad \text{Letting } u = x^2$$
$$(u - 9)(u - 16) = 0$$
$$u = 9 \quad \text{or} \quad u = 16$$

   We now substitute x^2 for u and solve for x.

   $x^2 = 9$ or $x^2 = 16$

   $x = \pm 3$ or $x = \pm 4$

   Since $y = 12/x$, if $x = 3$, $y = 4$; if $x = -3$, $y = -4$; if $x = 4$, $y = 3$; and if $x = -4$, $y = -3$. The pairs $(3, 4)$, $(-3, -4)$, $(4, 3)$, and $(-4, -3)$ check. They are the solutions.

26. $(-5, 3)$, $(-5, -3)$, $(4, 0)$

27. $x^2 + y^2 = 4$,   (1)

   $9x^2 + 16y^2 = 144$ (2)

$$\begin{aligned} -9x^2 - 9y^2 &= -36 \quad \text{Multiplying (1) by } -9 \\ \underline{9x^2 + 16y^2} &= \underline{144} \\ 7y^2 &= 108 \quad \text{Adding} \end{aligned}$$

$$y^2 = \frac{108}{7}$$

$$y = \pm\sqrt{\frac{108}{7}} = \pm 6\sqrt{\frac{3}{7}}$$

$$y = \pm\frac{6\sqrt{21}}{7} \qquad \text{Rationalizing the denominator}$$

Substituting $\dfrac{6\sqrt{21}}{7}$ or $-\dfrac{6\sqrt{21}}{7}$ for y in Eq. (1) gives us

$$x^2 + \frac{36 \cdot 21}{49} = 4$$

$$x^2 = 4 - \frac{108}{7}$$

$$x^2 = -\frac{80}{7}$$

$$x = \pm\sqrt{-\frac{80}{7}} = \pm 4i\sqrt{\frac{5}{7}}$$

$$x = \pm\frac{4i\sqrt{35}}{7}. \qquad \text{Rationalizing the denominator}$$

The pairs $\left(\dfrac{4i\sqrt{35}}{7}, \dfrac{6\sqrt{21}}{7}\right)$, $\left(-\dfrac{4i\sqrt{35}}{7}, \dfrac{6\sqrt{21}}{7}\right)$,

$\left(\dfrac{4i\sqrt{35}}{7}, -\dfrac{6\sqrt{21}}{7}\right)$, and $\left(-\dfrac{4i\sqrt{35}}{7}, -\dfrac{6\sqrt{21}}{7}\right)$ check.

They are the solutions.

28. $\left(\dfrac{16}{3}, \dfrac{5\sqrt{7}}{3}i\right)$, $\left(\dfrac{16}{3}, -\dfrac{5\sqrt{7}}{3}i\right)$, $\left(-\dfrac{16}{3}, \dfrac{5\sqrt{7}}{3}i\right)$,

$\left(-\dfrac{16}{3}, -\dfrac{5\sqrt{7}}{3}i\right)$

29. $x^2 + y^2 = 16,$ $x^2 + y^2 = 16,$ (1)

                   or

   $y^2 - 2x^2 = 10$ $-2x^2 + y^2 = 10$ (2)

Here we use the elimination method.

$$\begin{aligned}
2x^2 + 2y^2 &= 32 \qquad \text{Multiplying (1) by 2}\\
-2x^2 + y^2 &= 10\\
\hline
3y^2 &= 42 \qquad \text{Adding}\\
y^2 &= 14\\
y &= \pm\sqrt{14}
\end{aligned}$$

Substituting $\sqrt{14}$ or $-\sqrt{14}$ for y in Eq. (1) gives us

$$x^2 + 14 = 16$$

$$x^2 = 2$$

$$x = \pm\sqrt{2}$$

The pairs $(-\sqrt{2}, -\sqrt{14})$, $(-\sqrt{2}, \sqrt{14})$, $(\sqrt{2}, -\sqrt{14})$, and $(\sqrt{2}, \sqrt{14})$ check. They are the solutions.

30. $(-3, -\sqrt{5})$, $(-3, \sqrt{5})$, $(3, -\sqrt{5})$, $(3, \sqrt{5})$

31. $x^2 + y^2 = 5,$ (1)

     $xy = 2$ (2)

First we solve Eq. (2) for y.

$$xy = 2$$

$$y = \frac{2}{x}$$

Then we substitute $\dfrac{2}{x}$ for y in Eq. (1) and solve for x.

$$x^2 + y^2 = 5$$

$$x^2 + \left(\frac{2}{x}\right)^2 = 5$$

$$x^2 + \frac{4}{x^2} = 5$$

$$x^4 + 4 = 5x^2 \qquad \text{Multiplying by } x^2$$

$$x^4 - 5x^2 + 4 = 0$$

$$u^2 - 5u + 4 = 0 \qquad \text{Letting } u = x^2$$

$$(u - 4)(u - 1) = 0$$

$$u = 4 \; or \; u = 1$$

We now substitute x^2 for u and solve for x.

$$x^2 = 4 \quad or \quad x^2 = 1$$

$$x = \pm 2 \quad or \quad x = \pm 1$$

Since $y = 2/x$, if $x = 2$, $y = 1$; if $x = -2$, $y = -1$; if $x = 1$, $y = 2$; and if $x = -1$, $y = -2$. The pairs $(2, 1)$, $(-2, -1)$, $(1, 2)$, and $(-1, -2)$ check. They are the solutions.

32. $(4, 2)$, $(-4, -2)$, $(2, 4)$, $(-2, -4)$

33. $x^2 + y^2 = 13,$ (1)

     $xy = 6$ (2)

First we solve Eq. (2) for y.

$$xy = 6$$

$$y = \frac{6}{x}$$

Then we substitute $\dfrac{6}{x}$ for y in Eq. (1) and solve for x.

$$x^2 + y^2 = 13$$

$$x^2 + \left(\frac{6}{x}\right)^2 = 13$$

$$x^2 + \frac{36}{x^2} = 13$$

$$x^4 + 36 = 13x^2 \qquad \text{Multiplying by } x^2$$

$$x^4 - 13x^2 + 36 = 0$$

$$u^2 - 13u + 36 = 0 \qquad \text{Letting } u = x^2$$

$$(u - 9)(u - 4) = 0$$

$$u = 9 \quad or \quad u = 4$$

We now substitute x^2 for u and solve for x.

$$x^2 = 9 \quad or \quad x^2 = 4$$

$$x = \pm 3 \quad or \quad x = \pm 2$$

Since $y = 6/x$, if $x = 3$, $y = 2$; if $x = -3$, $y = -2$; if $x = 2$, $y = 3$; and if $x = -2$, $y = -3$. The pairs $(3, 2)$, $(-3, -2)$, $(2, 3)$, and $(-2, -3)$ check. They are the solutions.

34. $(4, 1)$, $(-4, -1)$, $(2, 2)$, $(-2, -2)$

35. $3xy + x^2 = 34,$ (1)
$2xy - 3x^2 = 8$ (2)

$$\begin{array}{ll} 6xy + 2x^2 = 68 & \text{Multiplying (1) by 2} \\ \underline{-6xy + 9x^2 = -24} & \text{Multiplying (2) by } -3 \\ 11x^2 = 44 & \text{Adding} \\ x^2 = 4 & \\ x = \pm 2 & \end{array}$$

Substitute for x in Eq. (1) and solve for y.

When $x = 2:$ $3 \cdot 2 \cdot y + 2^2 = 34$

$$6y + 4 = 34$$
$$6y = 30$$
$$y = 5$$

When $x = -2:$ $3(-2)(y) + (-2)^2 = 34$

$$-6y + 4 = 34$$
$$-6y = 30$$
$$y = -5$$

The pairs $(2, 5)$ and $(-2, -5)$ check. They are the solutions.

36. $(2, 1), (-2, -1)$

37. $xy - y^2 = 2,$ (1)
$2xy - 3y^2 = 0$ (2)

$$\begin{array}{ll} -2xy + 2y^2 = -4 & \text{Multiplying (1) by } -2 \\ \underline{2xy - 3y^2 = 0} & \\ -y^2 = 4 & \text{Adding} \\ y^2 = 4 & \\ y = \pm 2 & \end{array}$$

We substitute for y in Eq. (1) and solve for x.

When $y = 2:$ $x \cdot 2 - 2^2 = 2$

$$2x - 4 = 2$$
$$2x = 6$$
$$x = 3$$

When $y = -2:$ $x(-2) - (-2)^2 = 2$

$$-2x - 4 = 2$$
$$-2x = 6$$
$$x = -3$$

The pairs $(3, 2)$ and $(-3, -2)$ check. They are the solutions.

38. $\left(2, -\dfrac{4}{5}\right),$ $\left(-2, -\dfrac{4}{5}\right),$ $(5, 2), (-5, 2)$

39. $x^2 - y = 5$,   (1)
$x^2 + y^2 = 25$ (2)

We solve Eq. (1) for y.

$x^2 - 5 = y$ (3)

Substitute $x^2 - 5$ for y in Eq. (2) and solve for x.

$$x^2 + (x^2 - 5)^2 = 25$$
$$x^2 + x^4 - 10x^2 + 25 = 25$$
$$x^4 - 9x^2 = 0$$
$$u^2 - 9u = 0 \quad \text{Letting } u = x^2$$
$$u(u - 9) = 0$$

$u = 0$ or $u = 9$

$x^2 = 0$ or $x^2 = 9$

$x = 0$ or $x = \pm 3$

Substitute in Eq. (3) and solve for y.

When $x = 0:$ $y = 0^2 - 5 = -5$

When $x = 3$ or $-3:$ $y = 9 - 5 = 4$

The pairs $(0, -5)$, $(3, 4)$, and $(-3, 4)$ check. They are the solutions.

(This exercise could also be solved using the elimination method.)

40. $(-\sqrt{2}, \sqrt{2}), (\sqrt{2}, -\sqrt{2})$

41. *Familiarize.* We first make a drawing. We let l and w represent the length and width, respectively.

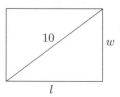

Translate. The perimeter is 28 cm.

$2l + 2w = 28,$ or $l + w = 14$

Using the Pythagorean theorem we have another equation.

$l^2 + w^2 = 10^2,$ or $l^2 + w^2 = 100$

Carry out. We solve the system:

$l + w = 14,$ (1)

$l^2 + w^2 = 100$ (2)

First solve Eq. (1) for w.

$w = 14 - l$ (3)

Then substitute $14 - l$ for w in Eq. (2) and solve for l.

$$l^2 + w^2 = 100$$
$$l^2 + (14 - l)^2 = 100$$
$$l^2 + 196 - 28l + l^2 = 100$$
$$2l^2 - 28l + 96 = 0$$
$$l^2 - 14l + 48 = 0$$
$$(l - 8)(l - 6) = 0$$

$l = 8$ or $l = 6$

If $l = 8$, then $w = 14 - 8$, or 6. If $l = 6$, then $w = 14 - 6$, or 8. Since the length is usually considered to be longer than the width, we have the solution $l = 8$ and $w = 6$, or $(8, 6)$.

Check. If $l = 8$ and $w = 6$, then the perimeter is $2 \cdot 8 + 2 \cdot 6$, or 28. The length of a diagonal is $\sqrt{8^2 + 6^2}$, or $\sqrt{100}$, or 10. The numbers check.

State. The length is 8 cm, and the width is 6 cm.

42. Length: 2 yd, width: 1 yd

43. *Familiarize*. We first make a drawing. Let l = the length and w = the width of the rectangle.

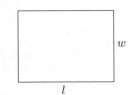

Translate.

Area: $lw = 20$

Perimeter: $2l + 2w = 18$, or $l + w = 9$

Carry out. We solve the system:

Solve the second equation for l: $l = 9 - w$

Substitute $9 - w$ for l in the first equation and solve for w.

$(9 - w)w = 20$

$9w - w^2 = 20$

$0 = w^2 - 9w + 20$

$0 = (w - 5)(w - 4)$

$w = 5 \ or \ w = 4$

If $w = 5$, then $l = 9 - w$, or 4. If $w = 4$, then $l = 9 - 4$, or 5. Since length is usually considered to be longer than width, we have the solution $l = 5$ and $w = 4$, or $(5, 4)$.

Check. If $l = 5$ and $w = 4$, the area is $5 \cdot 4$, or 20. The perimeter is $2 \cdot 5 + 2 \cdot 4$, or 18. The numbers check.

State. The length is 5 in. and the width is 4 in.

44. Length: 2 in., width: 1 in.

45. *Familiarize*. We first make a drawing. Let l = the length and w = the width of the cargo area, in feet.

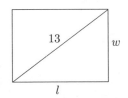

Translate. The cargo area must be 60 ft^2, so we have one equation:

$lw = 60$

The Pythagorean equation gives us another equation:

$l^2 + w^2 = 13^2$, or $l^2 + w^2 = 169$

Carry out. We solve the system of equations.

$lw = 60,$ (1)

$l^2 + w^2 = 169$ (2)

First solve Eq. (1) for w:

$lw = 60$

$w = \dfrac{60}{l}$ (3)

Then substitute $60/l$ for w in Eq. (2) and solve for l.

$$l^2 + w^2 = 169$$

$$l^2 + \left(\frac{60}{l}\right)^2 = 169$$

$$l^2 + \frac{3600}{l^2} = 169$$

$$l^4 + 3600 = 169l^2$$

$$l^4 - 169l^2 + 3600 = 0$$

Let $u = l^2$ and $u^2 = l^4$ and substitute.

$$u^2 - 169u + 3600 = 0$$

$$(u - 144)(u - 25) = 0$$

$u = 144 \quad or \quad u = 25$

$l^2 = 144 \quad or \quad l^2 = 25$ Replacing u with l^2

$l = \pm 12 \quad or \quad l = \pm 5$

Since the length cannot be negative, we consider only 12 and 5. We substitute in Eq. (3) to find w. When $l = 12$, $w = 60/12 = 5$; when $l = 5$, $w = 60/5 = 12$. Since we usually consider length to be longer than width, we check the pair (12.5).

Check. If the length is 12 ft and the width is 5 ft, then the area is $12 \cdot 5$, or 60 ft^2. Also $12^2 + 5^2 = 144 + 25 = 169 = 13^2$. The answer checks.

State. The length is 12 ft and the width is 5 ft.

46. Length: 20 ft, width: 15 ft

47. *Familiarize*. We make a drawing and label it. Let x and y represent the lengths of the legs of the triangle.

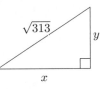

Translate. The product of the lengths of the legs is 156, so we have:

$xy = 156$

We use the Pythagorean theorem to get a second equation:

$x^2 + y^2 = (\sqrt{313})^2$, or $x^2 + y^2 = 313$

Carry out. We solve the system of equations.

$xy = 156,$ (1)

$x^2 + y^2 = 313$ (2)

First solve Equation (1) for y.

$xy = 156$

$y = \dfrac{156}{x}$

Then we substitute $\dfrac{156}{x}$ for y in Eq. (2) and solve for x.

$$x^2 + y^2 = 313 \qquad (2)$$

$$x^2 + \left(\frac{156}{x}\right)^2 = 313$$

$$x^2 + \frac{24,336}{x^2} = 313$$

$$x^4 + 24,336 = 313x^2$$

$$x^4 - 313x^2 + 24,336 = 0$$

$$u^2 - 313u + 24,336 = 0 \qquad \text{Letting } u = x^2$$

$$(u - 169)(u - 144) = 0$$

$$u - 169 = 0 \quad or \quad u - 144 = 0$$

$$u = 169 \quad or \qquad u = 144$$

We now substitute x^2 for u and solve for x.

$$x = \pm 13 \quad or \quad x = \pm 12$$

Since $y = 156/x$, if $x = 13$, $y = 12$; if $x = -13$, $y = -12$; if $x = 12$, $y = 13$; and if $x = -12$, $y = -13$. The possible solutions are $(13, 12)$, $(-13, -12)$, $(12, 13)$, and $(-12, -13)$.

Check. Since measurements cannot be negative, we consider only $(13, 12)$ and $(12, 13)$. Since both possible solutions give the same pair of legs, we only need to check $(13, 12)$. If $x = 13$ and $y = 12$, their product is 156. Also, $\sqrt{13^2 + 12^2} = \sqrt{313}$. The numbers check.

State. The lengths of the legs are 13 and 12.

48. 6 and 10; -6 and -10

49. Familiarize. Let $p = $ the principal and $r = $ the interest rate. If \$750 more had been invested, then the principle would have been $p + 750$. If the interest rate had been 1% less, it would have been $r - 0.01$. Recall that Interest = Principal $\times$ Rate.

Translate. With principal p and interest rate r, the interest is \$225, so we have

$$pr = 225. \quad (1)$$

With principal $p + 750$ and interest rate $r - 0.01$, the interest is also \$225, so we have

$$(p + 750)(r - 0.01) = 225 \quad (2)$$

Carry out. We solve the system of equations. First solve Eq. (1) for r.

$$pr = 225$$

$$r = \frac{225}{p} \quad (3)$$

Now substitute $\dfrac{225}{p}$ for r in Eq. (2) and solve for p.

$$(p + 750)\left(\frac{225}{p} - 0.01\right) = 225$$

$$225 - 0.01p + \frac{168,750}{p} - 7.5 = 225$$

$$-0.01p + \frac{168,750}{p} - 7.5 = 0$$

$$-0.01p^2 + 168,750 - 7.5p = 0 \quad \text{Multiplying by } p$$

$$p^2 + 750p + 16,875,000 = 0 \quad \text{Multiplying by}$$
$$\qquad\qquad\qquad\qquad\qquad -100 \text{ and rearranging}$$

$$(p - 3750)(p + 4500) = 0$$

$$p = 3750 \quad or \quad p = -4500$$

Since the principal cannot be negative, we consider only 3750. Substitute 3750 for p in Eq. (3) and find r.

$$r = \frac{225}{3750} = 0.06$$

Check. \$3750 $\times$ 0.06 = \$225. Also, \$3750 + \$750 = \$4500, $0.06 - 0.01 = 0.05$, and \$4500 $\times$ 0.05 = \$225. The answer checks.

State. The principal was \$3750, and the interest rate was 0.06, or 6%.

50. 24 ft, 16 ft

51. Familiarize. We first make a drawing. Let $l = $ the length and $w = $ the width.

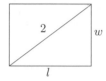

Translate.

Area: $lw = \sqrt{3}$ (1)

From the Pythagorean theorem: $l^2 + w^2 = 2^2$ (2)

Carry out. We solve the system of equations.

We first solve Eq. (1) for w.

$$lw = \sqrt{3}$$

$$w = \frac{\sqrt{3}}{l}$$

Then we substitute $\dfrac{\sqrt{3}}{l}$ for w in Eq. 2 and solve for l.

$$l^2 + \left(\frac{\sqrt{3}}{l}\right)^2 = 4$$

$$l^2 + \frac{3}{l^2} = 4$$

$$l^4 + 3 = 4l^2$$

$$l^4 - 4l^2 + 3 = 0$$

$$u^2 - 4u + 3 = 0 \quad \text{Letting } u = l^2$$

$$(u - 3)(u - 1) = 0$$

$$u = 3 \text{ or } u = 1$$

We now substitute l^2 for u and solve for l.

$$l^2 = 3 \qquad or \quad l^2 = 1$$

$$l = \pm\sqrt{3} \quad or \quad l = \pm 1$$

Measurements cannot be negative, so we only need to consider $l = \sqrt{3}$ and $l = 1$. Since $w = \sqrt{3}/l$, if $l = \sqrt{3}$, $w = 1$ and if $l = 1$, $w = \sqrt{3}$. Length is usually considered to be longer than width, so we have the solution $l = \sqrt{3}$ and $w = 1$, or $(\sqrt{3}, 1)$.

Check. If $l = \sqrt{3}$ and $w = 1$, the area is $\sqrt{3} \cdot 1 = \sqrt{3}$. Also $(\sqrt{3})^2 + 1^2 = 3 + 1 = 4 = 2^2$. The numbers check.

State. The length is $\sqrt{3}$ m, and the width is 1 m.

52. Length: $\sqrt{2}$ m, width: 1 m

53. *Writing Exercise*

54. *Writing Exercise*

55. $(-1)^9(-2)^4 = -1 \cdot 16 = -16$

56. -32

57. $\dfrac{(-1)^k}{k-5} = \dfrac{(-1)^6}{6-5} = \dfrac{1}{1} = 1$

58. $-\dfrac{1}{4}$

59. $\dfrac{n}{2}(3+n) = \dfrac{8}{2}(3+8) = 4 \cdot 11 = 44$

60. 28

61. *Writing Exercise*

62. *Writing Exercise*

63. Let (h,k) represent the point on the line $5x + 8y = -2$ which is the center of a circle that passes through the points $(-2,3)$ and $(-4,1)$. The distance between (h,k) and $(-2,3)$ is the same as the distance between (h,k) and $(-4,1)$. This gives us one equation:

$$\sqrt{[h-(-2)]^2+(k-3)^2} = \sqrt{[h-(-4)]^2+(k-1)^2}$$
$$(h+2)^2 + (k-3)^2 = (h+4)^2 + (k-1)^2$$
$$h^2+4h+4+k^2-6k+9 = h^2+8h+16+k^2-2k+1$$
$$4h - 6k + 13 = 8h - 2k + 17$$
$$-4h - 4k = 4$$
$$h + k = -1$$

We get a second equation by substituting (h,k) in $5x + 8y = -2$.

$$5h + 8k = -2$$

We now solve the following system:

$$h + k = -1,$$
$$5h + 8k = -2$$

The solution, which is the center of the circle, is $(-2,1)$.

Next we find the length of the radius. We can find the distance between either $(-2,3)$ or $(-4,1)$ and the center $(-2,1)$. We use $(-2,3)$.

$$r = \sqrt{[-2 - (-2)]^2 + (1 - 3)^2}$$
$$r = \sqrt{0^2 + (-2)^2}$$
$$r = \sqrt{4} = 2$$

We can write the equation of the circle with center $(-2,1)$ and radius 2.

$$(x - h)^2 + (y - k)^2 = r^2$$
$$[x - (-2)]^2 + (y - 1)^2 = 2^2$$
$$(x + 2)^2 + (y - 1)^2 = 4$$

64. $4x^2 + 3y^2 = 43$

65. $p^2 + q^2 = 13$,   (1)

$\dfrac{1}{pq} = -\dfrac{1}{6}$ (2)

Solve Eq. (2) for p.

$$\frac{1}{q} = -\frac{p}{6}$$
$$-\frac{6}{q} = p$$

Substitute $-6/q$ for p in Eq. (1) and solve for q.

$$\left(-\frac{6}{q}\right)^2 + q^2 = 13$$
$$\frac{36}{q^2} + q^2 = 13$$
$$36 + q^4 = 13q^2$$
$$q^4 - 13q^2 + 36 = 0$$
$$u^2 - 13u + 36 = 0 \qquad \text{Letting } u = q^2$$
$$(u - 9)(u - 4) = 0$$
$$u = 9 \quad \text{or} \quad u = 4$$
$$x^2 = 9 \quad \text{or} \quad x^2 = 4$$
$$x = \pm 3 \text{ or} \quad x = \pm 2$$

Since $p = -6/q$, if $q = 3$, $p = -2$; if $q = -3$, $p = 2$; if $q = 2$, $p = -3$; and if $q = -2$, $p = 3$. The pairs $(-2,3)$, $(2,-3)$, $(-3,2)$, and $(3,-2)$ check. They are the solutions.

66. $\left(\dfrac{1}{3},\dfrac{1}{2}\right)$, $\left(\dfrac{1}{2},\dfrac{1}{3}\right)$

67. We let x and y represent the length and width of the base of the box, respectively. Make a drawing.

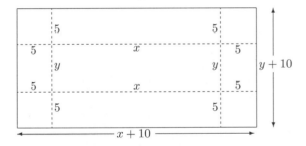

The dimensions of the metal sheet are $x + 10$ and $y + 10$.

Solve the system:

$$(x + 10)(y + 10) = 340,$$
$$x \cdot y \cdot 5 = 350$$

The solutions are $(10,7)$ and $(7,10)$. Choosing the larger number as the length, we have the solution. The dimensions of the box are 10 in. by 7 in. by 5 in.

68. 61.52 cm and 38.48 cm

69.
$$R = C$$
$$100x + x^2 = 80x + 1500$$
$$x^2 + 20x - 1500 = 0$$
$$(x - 30)(x + 50) = 0$$
$$x = 30 \text{ or } x = -50$$

Since the number of units cannot be negative, the solution of the problem is 30. Thus, 30 units must be sold in order to break even.

Chapter 13

Sequences, Series, and Probability

1. $a_n = 5n - 2$

   $a_1 = 5 \cdot 1 - 2 = 3,$

   $a_2 = 5 \cdot 2 - 2 = 8,$

   $a_3 = 5 \cdot 3 - 2 = 13,$

   $a_4 = 5 \cdot 4 - 2 = 18;$

   $a_{10} = 5 \cdot 10 - 2 = 48;$

   $a_{15} = 5 \cdot 15 - 2 = 73$

2. $5, 7, 9, 11; 23; 33$

3. $a_n = \dfrac{n}{n+1}$

   $a_1 = \dfrac{1}{1+1} = \dfrac{1}{2},$

   $a_2 = \dfrac{2}{2+1} = \dfrac{2}{3},$

   $a_3 = \dfrac{3}{3+1} = \dfrac{3}{4},$

   $u_4 = \dfrac{4}{4+1} = \dfrac{4}{5};$

   $a_{10} = \dfrac{10}{10+1} = \dfrac{10}{11};$

   $a_{15} = \dfrac{15}{15+1} = \dfrac{15}{16}$

4. $3, 6, 11, 18; 102; 227$

5. $a_n = n^2 - 2n$

   $a_1 = 1^2 - 2 \cdot 1 = -1,$

   $a_2 = 2^2 - 2 \cdot 2 = 0,$

   $a_3 = 3^2 - 2 \cdot 3 = 3,$

   $a_4 = 4^2 - 2 \cdot 4 = 8;$

   $a_{10} = 10^2 - 2 \cdot 10 = 80;$

   $a_{15} = 15^2 - 2 \cdot 15 = 195$

6. $0, \dfrac{3}{5}, \dfrac{4}{5}, \dfrac{15}{17}; \dfrac{99}{101}; \dfrac{112}{113}$

7. $a_n = n + \dfrac{1}{n}$

   $a_1 = 1 + \dfrac{1}{1} = 2,$

   $a_2 = 2 + \dfrac{1}{2} = 2\dfrac{1}{2},$

   $a_3 = 3 + \dfrac{1}{3} = 3\dfrac{1}{3},$

   $a_4 = 4 + \dfrac{1}{4} = 4\dfrac{1}{4};$

   $a_{10} = 10 + \dfrac{1}{10} = 10\dfrac{1}{10};$

   $a_{15} = 15 + \dfrac{1}{15} = 15\dfrac{1}{15}$

8. $1, -\dfrac{1}{2}, \dfrac{1}{4}, -\dfrac{1}{8}; -\dfrac{1}{512}; \dfrac{1}{16,384}$

9. $a_n = (-1)^n n^2$

   $a_1 = (-1)^1 1^2 = -1,$

   $a_2 = (-1)^2 2^2 = 4,$

   $a_3 = (-1)^3 3^2 = -9,$

   $a_4 = (-1)^4 4^2 = 16;$

   $a_{10} = (-1)^{10} 10^2 = 100;$

   $a_{15} = (-1)^{15} 15^2 = -225$

10. $-4, 5, -6, 7; 13; -18$

11. $a_n = (-1)^{n+1}(3n - 5)$

    $a_1 = (-1)^{1+1}(3 \cdot 1 - 5) = -2,$

    $a_2 = (-1)^{2+1}(3 \cdot 2 - 5) = -1,$

    $a_3 = (-1)^{3+1}(3 \cdot 3 - 5) = 4,$

    $a_4 = (-1)^{4+1}(3 \cdot 4 - 5) = -7;$

    $a_{10} = (-1)^{10+1}(3 \cdot 10 - 5) = -25;$

    $a_{15} = (-1)^{15+1}(3 \cdot 15 - 5) = 40$

12. $0, 7, -26, 63; 999; -3374$

13. $a_n = 2n - 5$

    $a_7 = 2 \cdot 7 - 5 = 14 - 5 = 9$

14. 26

15. $a_n = (3n + 1)(2n - 5)$

    $a_9 = (3 \cdot 9 + 1)(2 \cdot 9 - 5) = 28 \cdot 13 = 364$

16. 400

17. $a_n = (-1)^{n-1}(3.4n - 17.3)$

    $a_{12} = (-1)^{12-1}[3.4(12) - 17.3] = -23.5$

18. $-37,916,508.16$

19. $a_n = 3n^2(9n - 100)$

    $a_{11} = 3 \cdot 11^2(9 \cdot 11 - 100) = 3 \cdot 121(-1) = -363$

20. 9680

21. $a_n = \left(1 + \dfrac{1}{n}\right)^2$

    $a_{20} = \left(1 + \dfrac{1}{20}\right)^2 = \left(\dfrac{21}{20}\right)^2 = \dfrac{441}{400}$

22. $\dfrac{2744}{3375}$

23. $1, 3, 5, 7, 9, \ldots$

These are odd integers, so the general term could be $2n-1$.

24. $2n$

25. $1, -1, 1, -1, \ldots$

1 and -1 alternate, beginning with 1, so the general term could be $(-1)^{n+1}$.

26. $(-1)^n$

27. $-1, 2, -3, 4, \ldots$

These are the first four natural numbers, but with alternating signs, beginning with a negative number. The general term could be $(-1)^n \cdot n$.

28. $(-1)^{n+1} \cdot n$

29. $-2, 6, -18, 54, \ldots$

We can see a pattern if we write the sequence as

$-1 \cdot 2 \cdot 1, 1 \cdot 2 \cdot 3, -1 \cdot 2 \cdot 9, 1 \cdot 2 \cdot 27, \ldots$

The general term could be $(-1)^n 2(3)^{n-1}$.

30. $5n - 7$

31. $\dfrac{1}{2}, \dfrac{2}{3}, \dfrac{3}{4}, \dfrac{4}{5}, \dfrac{5}{6}, \ldots$

These are fractions in which the denominator is 1 greater than the numerator. Also, each numerator is 1 greater than the preceding numerator. The general term could be $\dfrac{n}{n+1}$.

32. $n(n+1)$

33. $5, 25, 125, 625, \ldots$

This is powers of 5, so the general term could be 5^n.

34. 4^n

35. $-1, 4, -9, 16, \ldots$

This is the squares of the first four natural numbers, but with alternating signs, beginning with a negative number. The general term could be $(-1)^n \cdot n^2$.

36. $(-1)^{n+1} \cdot n^2$

37. $1, -2, 3, -4, 5, -6, \ldots$

$S_7 = 1 - 2 + 3 - 4 + 5 - 6 + 7 = 4$

38. -8

39. $2, 4, 6, 8, \ldots$

$S_5 = 2 + 4 + 6 + 8 + 10 = 30$

40. $\dfrac{5269}{3600}$

41. $\displaystyle\sum_{k=1}^{5} \dfrac{1}{2k} = \dfrac{1}{2 \cdot 1} + \dfrac{1}{2 \cdot 2} + \dfrac{1}{2 \cdot 3} + \dfrac{1}{2 \cdot 4} + \dfrac{1}{2 \cdot 5}$

$\qquad = \dfrac{1}{2} + \dfrac{1}{4} + \dfrac{1}{6} + \dfrac{1}{8} + \dfrac{1}{10}$

$\qquad = \dfrac{60}{120} + \dfrac{30}{120} + \dfrac{20}{120} + \dfrac{15}{120} + \dfrac{12}{120}$

$\qquad = \dfrac{137}{120}$

42. $1 + \dfrac{1}{3} + \dfrac{1}{5} + \dfrac{1}{7} + \dfrac{1}{9} + \dfrac{1}{11} = \dfrac{6508}{3465}$

43. $\displaystyle\sum_{k=0}^{4} 3^k = 3^0 + 3^1 + 3^2 + 3^3 + 3^4$

$\qquad = 1 + 3 + 9 + 27 + 81$

$\qquad = 121$

44. $\sqrt{9} + \sqrt{11} + \sqrt{13} + \sqrt{15} \approx 13.7952$

45. $\displaystyle\sum_{k=1}^{8} \dfrac{k}{k+1} = \dfrac{1}{1+1} + \dfrac{2}{2+1} + \dfrac{3}{3+1} + \dfrac{4}{4+1} +$

$\qquad\qquad \dfrac{5}{5+1} + \dfrac{6}{6+1} + \dfrac{7}{7+1} + \dfrac{8}{8+1}$

$\qquad = \dfrac{1}{2} + \dfrac{2}{3} + \dfrac{3}{4} + \dfrac{4}{5} + \dfrac{5}{6} + \dfrac{6}{7} + \dfrac{7}{8} + \dfrac{8}{9}$

$\qquad = \dfrac{15,551}{2520}$

46. $-\dfrac{1}{4} + 0 + \dfrac{1}{6} + \dfrac{2}{7} = \dfrac{17}{84}$

47. $\displaystyle\sum_{k=1}^{8} (-1)^{k+1} 2^k = (-1)^2 2^1 + (-1)^3 2^2 + (-1)^4 2^3 +$

$\qquad\qquad (-1)^5 2^4 + (-1)^6 2^5 + (-1)^7 2^6 +$

$\qquad\qquad (-1)^8 2^7 + (-1)^9 2^8$

$\qquad = 2 - 4 + 8 - 16 + 32 - 64 +$

$\qquad\qquad 128 - 256$

$\qquad = -170$

48. $-4^2 + 4^3 - 4^4 + 4^5 - 4^6 + 4^7 - 4^8 = -52,432$

49. $\displaystyle\sum_{k=0}^{5} (k^2 - 2k + 3)$

$= (0^2 - 2 \cdot 0 + 3) + (1^2 - 2 \cdot 1 + 3) +$

$\quad (2^2 - 2 \cdot 2 + 3) + (3^2 - 2 \cdot 3 + 3) +$

$\quad (4^2 - 2 \cdot 4 + 3) + (5^2 - 2 \cdot 5 + 3)$

$= 3 + 2 + 3 + 6 + 11 + 18$

$= 43$

50. $4 + 2 + 2 + 4 + 8 + 14 = 34$

51. $\displaystyle\sum_{k=3}^{5} \dfrac{(-1)^k}{k(k+1)} = \dfrac{(-1)^3}{3(3+1)} + \dfrac{(-1)^4}{4(4+1)} + \dfrac{(-1)^5}{5(5+1)}$

$\qquad = \dfrac{-1}{3 \cdot 4} + \dfrac{1}{4 \cdot 5} + \dfrac{-1}{5 \cdot 6}$

$\qquad = -\dfrac{1}{12} + \dfrac{1}{20} - \dfrac{1}{30}$

$\qquad = -\dfrac{4}{60} = -\dfrac{1}{15}$

52. $\dfrac{3}{8} + \dfrac{4}{16} + \dfrac{5}{32} + \dfrac{6}{64} + \dfrac{7}{128} = \dfrac{119}{128}$

53. $\dfrac{2}{3} + \dfrac{3}{4} + \dfrac{4}{5} + \dfrac{5}{6} + \dfrac{6}{7}$

This is a sum of fractions in which the denominator is one greater than the numerator. Also, each numerator is 1 greater than the preceding numerator. Sigma notation is

$$\sum_{k=1}^{5} \frac{k+1}{k+2}.$$

54. $\displaystyle\sum_{k=1}^{5} 3k$

55. $1 + 4 + 9 + 16 + 25 + 36$

This is the sum of the squares of the first six natural numbers. Sigma notation is

$$\sum_{k=1}^{6} k^2.$$

56. $\displaystyle\sum_{k=1}^{5} \frac{1}{k^2}$

57. $4 - 9 + 16 - 25 + \ldots + (-1)^n n^2$

This is a sum of terms of the form $(-1)^k k^2$, beginning with $k = 2$ and continuing through $k = n$. Sigma notation is

$$\sum_{k=2}^{n} (-1)^k k^2.$$

58. $\displaystyle\sum_{k=3}^{n} (-1)^{k+1} k^2$

59. $5 + 10 + 15 + 20 + 25 + \ldots$

This is a sum of multiples of 5, and it is an infinite series. Sigma notation is

$$\sum_{k=1}^{\infty} 5k.$$

60. $\displaystyle\sum_{k=1}^{\infty} 7k$

61. $\dfrac{1}{1 \cdot 2} + \dfrac{1}{2 \cdot 3} + \dfrac{1}{3 \cdot 4} + \dfrac{1}{4 \cdot 5} + \ldots$

This is a sum of fractions in which the numerator is 1 and the denominator is a product of two consecutive integers. The larger integer in each product is the smaller integer in the succeeding product. It is an infinite series. Sigma notation is

$$\sum_{k=1}^{\infty} \frac{1}{k(k+1)}.$$

62. $\displaystyle\sum_{k=1}^{\infty} \frac{1}{k(k+1)^2}$

63. *Writing Exercise*

64. *Writing Exercise*

65. $\dfrac{7}{2}(a_1 + a_7) = \dfrac{7}{2}(8 + 14) = \dfrac{7}{2} \cdot 22 = 77$

66. 23

67.
$$(x + y)^3$$
$$= (x + y)(x + y)^2$$
$$= (x + y)(x^2 + 2xy + y^2)$$
$$= x(x^2 + 2xy + y^2) + y(x^2 + 2xy + y^2)$$
$$= x^3 + 2x^2y + xy^2 + x^2y + 2xy^2 + y^3$$
$$= x^3 + 3x^2y + 3xy^2 + y^3$$

68. $a^3 - 3a^2b + 3ab^2 - b^3$

69.
$$(2a - b)^3$$
$$= (2a - b)(2a - b)^2$$
$$= (2a - b)(4a^2 - 4ab + b^2)$$
$$= 2a(4a^2 - 4ab + b^2) - b(4a^2 - 4ab + b^2)$$
$$= 8a^3 - 8a^2b + 2ab^2 - 4a^2b + 4ab^2 - b^3$$
$$= 8a^3 - 12a^2b + 6ab^2 - b^3$$

70. $8x^3 + 12x^2y + 6xy^2 + y^3$

71. *Writing Exercise*

72. *Writing Exercise*

73. $a_1 = 1,\ a_{n+1} = 5a_n - 2$
$$a_1 = 1$$
$$a_2 = 5 \cdot 1 - 2 = 3$$
$$a_3 = 5 \cdot 3 - 2 = 13$$
$$a_4 = 5 \cdot 13 - 2 = 63$$
$$a_5 = 5 \cdot 63 - 2 = 313$$
$$a_6 = 5 \cdot 313 - 2 = 1563$$

74. 0, 3, 12, 147, 21,612, 467,078,547

75. Find each term by multiplying the preceding term by 2:

1, 2, 4, 8, 16, 32, 64, 128, 256, 512, 1024,

2048, 4096, 8192, 16,384, 32,768, 65,536

76. $5200, $3900, $2925, $2193.75, $1645.31, $1233.98,
$925.49, $694.12, $520.59, $390.44

77. $a_n = (-1)^n$

This sequence is of the form $-1, 1, -1, 1, \ldots$. Each pair of terms adds to 0. S_{100} has 50 such pairs, so $S_{100} = 0$. S_{101} consists of the 50 pairs in S_{100} that add to 0 as well as a_{101}, or -1, so $S_{101} = -1$.

78. $\dfrac{3}{2}, \dfrac{3}{2}, \dfrac{9}{8}, \dfrac{3}{4}, \dfrac{15}{32}, \dfrac{171}{32}$

79. $a_n = i^n$
$$a_1 = i^1 = i$$
$$a_2 = i^2 = -1$$
$$a_3 = i^3 = i^2 \cdot i = -1 \cdot i = -i$$
$$a_4 = i^4 = (i^2)^2 = (-1)^2 = 1$$
$$a_5 = i^5 = (i^2)^2 \cdot i = (-1)^2 \cdot i = 1 \cdot i = i$$
$$S_5 = i - 1 - i + 1 + i = i$$

80. $\{x | x = 4n - 1, \text{ where } n \text{ is a natural number}\}$

81. Enter $y_1 = 14x^4 + 6x^3 + 416x^2 - 655x - 1050$. Then scroll through a table of values. We see that $y_1 = 6144$ when $x = 11$, so the 11th term of the sequence is 6144.

82. 1225 handshakes

Exercise Set 13.2

1. 2, 6, 10, 14, . . .

$a_1 = 2$

$d = 4$ ($6 - 2 = 4$, $10 - 6 = 4$, $14 - 10 = 4$)

2. $a_1 = 1.06$, $d = 0.06$

3. 6, 2, −2, −6, . . .

$a_1 = 6$

$d = -4$ ($2 - 6 = -4, -2 - 2 = -4,$
                             $-6 - (-2) = -4$)

4. $a_1 = -9$, $d = 3$

5. $\dfrac{3}{2}, \dfrac{9}{4}, 3, \dfrac{15}{4}, \ldots$

$a_1 = \dfrac{3}{2}$

$d = \dfrac{3}{4}$ $\left(\dfrac{9}{4} - \dfrac{3}{2} = \dfrac{3}{4},\ 3 - \dfrac{9}{4} = \dfrac{3}{4}\right)$

6. $a_1 = \dfrac{3}{5}$, $d = -\dfrac{1}{2}$

7. \$5.12, \$5.24, \$5.36, \$5.48, . . .

$a_1 = \$5.12$

$d = \$0.12$ (\$5.24 − \$5.12 = \$0.12, \$5.36−
                   \$5.24 = \$0.12, \$5.48 − \$5.36 =
                   \$0.12)

8. $a_1 = \$214$, $d = -\$3$

9. 3, 7, 11, . . .

$a_1 = 3$, $d = 4$, and $n = 12$

$a_n = a_1 + (n - 1)d$

$a_{12} = 3 + (12 - 1)4 = 3 + 11 \cdot 4 = 3 + 44 = 47$

10. 0.57

11. 7, 4, 1, . . .

$a_1 = 7$, $d = -3$, and $n = 17$

$a_n = a_1 + (n - 1)d$

$a_{17} = 7 + (17 - 1)(-3) = 7 + 16(-3) =$
       $7 - 48 = -41$

12. $-\dfrac{17}{3}$

13. \$1200, \$964.32, \$728.64, . . .

$a_1 = \$1200$, $d = \$964.32 - \$1200 = -\$235.68,$

       and $n = 13$

$a_n = a_1 + (n - 1)d$

$a_{13} = \$1200 + (13 - 1)(-\$235.68) =$

       \$1200 + 12(−\$235.68) = \$1200 − \$2828.16 =

       −\$1628.16

14. \$7941.62

15. $a_1 = 3$, $d = 4$

$a_n = a_1 + (n - 1)d$

Let $a_n = 107$, and solve for n.

$107 = 3 + (n - 1)(4)$

$107 = 3 + 4n - 4$

$107 = 4n - 1$

$108 = 4n$

$27 = n$

The 27th term is 107.

16. 33rd

17. $a_1 = 7$, $d = -3$

$a_n = a_1 + (n - 1)d$

$-296 = 7 + (n - 1)(-3)$

$-296 = 7 - 3n + 3$

$-306 = -3n$

$102 = n$

The 102nd term is −296.

18. 46th

19. $a_n = a_1 + (n - 1)d$

$a_{17} = 2 + (17 - 1)5$ Substituting 17 for n,
                               2 for a_1, and 5 for d

     $= 2 + 16 \cdot 5$

     $= 2 + 80$

     $= 82$

20. −43

21. $a_n = a_1 + (n - 1)d$

$33 = a_1 + (8 - 1)4$ Substituting 33 for a_8,
                             8 for n, and 4 for d

$33 = a_1 + 28$

 $5 = a_1$

(Note that this procedure is equivalent to subtracting d from a_8 seven times to get a_1: $33 - 7(4) = 33 - 28 = 5$)

22. −54

23. $a_n = a_1 + (n - 1)d$

$-76 = 5 + (n - 1)(-3)$ Substituting −76 for
                                 a_n, 5 for a_1, and −3
                                 for d

$-76 = 5 - 3n + 3$

$-76 = 8 - 3n$

$-84 = -3n$

$28 = n$

24. 39

25. We know that $a_{17} = -40$ and $a_{28} = -73$. We would have to add d eleven times to get from a_{17} to a_{28}. That is,

$$-40 + 11d = -73$$
$$11d = -33$$
$$d = -3.$$

Since $a_{17} = -40$, we subtract d sixteen times to get to a_1.

$$a_1 = -40 - 16(-3) = -40 + 48 = 8$$

We write the first five terms of the sequence:

8, 5, 2, −1, −4

26. $a_1 = \dfrac{1}{3}$, $d = \dfrac{1}{2}$; $\dfrac{1}{3}, \dfrac{5}{6}, \dfrac{4}{3}, \dfrac{11}{6}, \dfrac{7}{3}$

27. $a_{13} = 13$ and $a_{54} = 54$

Observe that for this to be true, $a_1 = 1$ and $d = 1$.

28. $a_1 = 2$, $d = 2$

29. $1 + 5 + 9 + 13 + \ldots$

Note that $a_1 = 1$, $d = 4$, and $n = 20$. Before using the formula for S_n, we find a_{20}:

$$a_{20} = 1 + (20 - 1)4 \quad \text{Substituting into}$$
$$\text{the formula for } a_n$$
$$= 1 + 19 \cdot 4$$
$$= 77$$

Then

$$S_{20} = \frac{20}{2}(1 + 77) \quad \text{Using the formula for } S_n$$
$$= 10(78)$$
$$= 780.$$

30. −210

31. The sum is $1 + 2 + 3 + \ldots + 249 + 250$. This is the sum of the arithmetic sequence for which $a_1 = 1$, $a_n = 250$, and $n = 250$. We use the formula for S_n.

$$S_n = \frac{n}{2}(a_1 + a_n)$$
$$S_{300} = \frac{250}{2}(1 + 250) = 125(251) = 31,375$$

32. 80,200

33. The sum is $2 + 4 + 6 + \ldots + 98 + 100$. This is the sum of the arithmetic sequence for which $a_1 = 2$, $a_n = 100$, and $n = 50$. We use the formula for S_n.

$$S_n = \frac{n}{2}(a_1 + a_n)$$
$$S_{50} = \frac{50}{2}(2 + 100) = 25(102) = 2550$$

34. 2500

35. The sum is $6 + 12 + 18 + \ldots + 96 + 102$. This is the sum of the arithmetic sequence for which $a_1 = 6$, $a_n = 102$, and $n = 17$. We use the formula for S_n.

$$S_n = \frac{n}{2}(a_1 + a_n)$$
$$S_{17} = \frac{17}{2}(6 + 102) = \frac{17}{2}(108) = 918$$

36. 34,036

37. Before using the formula for S_n, we find a_{20}:

$$a_{20} = 4 + (20 - 1)5 \quad \text{Substituting into}$$
$$\text{the formula for } a_n$$
$$= 4 + 19 \cdot 5 = 99$$

Then

$$S_{20} = \frac{20}{2}(4 + 99) \quad \text{Using the formula}$$
$$\text{for } S_n$$
$$= 10(103) = 1030.$$

38. −1200

39. *Familiarize*. We want to find the fifteenth term and the sum of an arithmetic sequence with $a_1 = 14$, $d = 2$, and $n = 15$. We will first use the formula for a_n to find a_{15}. This result is the number of marchers in the last row. Then we will use the formula for S_n to find S_{15}. This is the total number of marchers.

Translate. Substituting into the formula for a_n, we have

$$a_{15} = 14 + (15 - 1)2.$$

Carry out. We first find a_{15}.

$$a_{15} = 14 + 14 \cdot 2 = 42$$

Then use the formula for S_n to find S_{15}.

$$S_{15} = \frac{15}{2}(14 + 42) = \frac{15}{2}(56) = 420$$

Check. We can do the calculations again. We can also do the entire addition.

$$14 + 16 + 18 + \cdots + 42.$$

State. There are 42 marchers in the last row, and there are 420 marchers altogether.

40. 3; 210

41. *Familiarize*. We go from 50 poles in a row, down to six poles in the top row, so there must be 45 rows. We want the sum $50 + 49 + 48 + \ldots + 6$. Thus we want the sum of an arithmetic sequence. We will use the formula $S_n = \frac{n}{2}(a_1 + a_n)$.

Translate. We want to find the sum of the first 45 terms of an arithmetic sequence with $a_1 = 50$ and $a_{45} = 6$.

Carry out. Substituting into the formula for S_n, we have

$$S_{45} = \frac{45}{2}(50 + 6)$$
$$= \frac{45}{2} \cdot 56 = 1260$$

Check. We can do the calculation again, or we can do the entire addition:

$$50 + 49 + 48 + \ldots + 6.$$

State. There will be 1260 poles in the pile.

42. $49.60

43. *Familiarize*. We want to find the sum of an arithmetic sequence with $a_1 = \$600$, $d = \$100$, and $n = 20$. We will use the formula for a_n to find a_{20}, and then we will use the formula for S_n to find S_{20}.

Translate. Substituting into the formula for a_n, we have
$$a_{20} = 600 + (20 - 1)(100).$$
Carry out. We first find a_{20}.
$$a_{20} = 600 + 19 \cdot 100 = 600 + 1900 = 2500$$
Then we use the formula for S_n to find S_{20}.
$$S_{20} = \frac{20}{2}(600 + 2500) = 10(3100) = 31,000$$
Check. We can do the calculation again.

State. They save $31,000 (disregarding interest).

44. $10,230

45. ***Familiarize.*** We want to find the sum of an arithmetic sequence with $a_1 = 20$, $d = 2$, and $n = 19$. We will use the formula for a_n to find a_{19}, and then we will use the formula for S_n to find S_{19}.

Translate. Substituting into the formula for a_n, we have
$$a_{19} = 20 + (19 - 1)(2).$$
Carry out. We find a_{19}.
$$a_{19} = 20 + 18 \cdot 2 = 56$$
Then we use the formula for S_n to find S_{19}.
$$S_{19} = \frac{19}{2}(20 + 56) = 722$$
Check. We can do the calculation again.

State. There are 722 seats.

46. $462,500

47. *Writing Exercise*

48. *Writing Exercise*

49. $\dfrac{3}{10x} + \dfrac{2}{15x}$, LCD is $30x$

$$= \frac{3}{10x} \cdot \frac{3}{3} + \frac{2}{15x} \cdot \frac{2}{2}$$

$$= \frac{9}{30x} + \frac{4}{30x}$$

$$= \frac{13}{30x}$$

50. $\dfrac{23}{36t}$

51.

$\log_a P = k \qquad a^k = P$ ———— The logarithm is the exponent.

———— The base does not change.

52. $e^a = t$

53.
$$4^{3x} = 8^{x+2}$$
$$(2^2)^{3x} = (2^3)^{x+2}$$
$$2^{6x} = 2^{3x+6}$$
$$6x = 3x + 6 \qquad \text{Equating exponents}$$
$$3x = 6$$
$$x = 2$$
The solution is 2.

54. 5

55. *Writing Exercise*

56. *Writing Exercise*

57. $a_1 = 1$, $d = 2$, $n = n$
$$a_n = 1 + (n-1)2 = 1 + 2n - 2 = 2n - 1$$
$$S_n = \frac{n}{2}[1 + (2n - 1)] = \frac{n}{2} \cdot 2n = n^2$$

Thus, the formula $S_n = n^2$ can be used to find the sum of the first n consecutive odd numbers starting with 1.

58. 3, 5, 7

59. $a_1 = \$8760$
$$a_2 = \$8760 + (-\$798.23) = \$7961.77$$
$$a_3 = \$8760 + 2(-\$798.23) = \$7163.54$$
$$a_4 = \$8760 + 3(-\$798.23) = \$6365.31$$
$$a_5 = \$8760 + 4(-\$798.23) = \$5567.08$$
$$a_6 = \$8760 + 5(-\$798.23) = \$4768.85$$
$$a_7 = \$8760 + 6(-\$798.23) = \$3970.62$$
$$a_8 = \$8760 + 7(-\$798.23) = \$3172.39$$
$$a_9 = \$8760 + 8(-\$798.23) = \$2374.16$$
$$a_{10} = \$8760 + 9(-\$798.23) = \$1575.93$$

60. $51,679.65

61. See the answer section in the text.

62. a) $a_t = \$5200 - \$512.50t$

b) $5200, $4687.50, $4175, $3662.50, $3150m $1612.50, $1100

c) $a_0 = \$5200$, $a_t = a_{t-1} - \$512.50$

63. Each integer from 501 through 750 is 500 more than the corresponding integer from 1 through 250. There are 250 integers from 501 through 750, so their sum is the sum of the integers from 1 to 250 plus $250 \cdot 500$. From Exercise 31, we know that the sum of the integers from 1 through 250 is 31,375. Thus, we have
$$31,375 + 250 \cdot 500, \text{ or } 156,375.$$

64. Arithmetic; $a_n = -0.75n + 165$, where $n = 1$ corresponds to age 20, $n = 2$ corresponds to age 21, and so on

65. We graph the data points, where the first coordinate 1 represents 1998, 2 represents 1999, and so on.

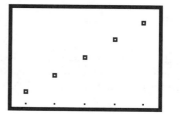

The points appear to lie on a straight line, so this could be the graph of an arithmetic sequence. The general term is

$$a_n = n + 102,$$

where $n = 1$ corresponds to 1998, $n = 2$ corresponds to 1999, and so on.

66. Not arithmetic

67. We graph the data points, where the first coordinate 1 represents 1997, 2 represents 1998, and so on.

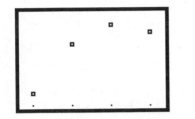

The points do not lie on a straight line, so this is not the graph of an arithmetic sequence.

Exercise Set 13.3

1. 7, 14, 28, 56, . . .

$$\frac{14}{7} = 2, \ \frac{28}{14} = 2, \ \frac{56}{28} = 2$$

$$r = 2$$

2. 3

3. 5, −5, 5, −5, . . .

$$\frac{-5}{5} = -1, \ \frac{5}{-5} = -1, \ \frac{-5}{5} = -1$$

$$r = -1$$

4. 0.1

5. $\dfrac{1}{2}, \ -\dfrac{1}{4}, \ \dfrac{1}{8}, \ -\dfrac{1}{16}, \ \ldots$

$$\frac{-\frac{1}{4}}{\frac{1}{2}} = -\frac{1}{4} \cdot \frac{2}{1} = -\frac{2}{4} = -\frac{1}{2}$$

$$\frac{\frac{1}{8}}{-\frac{1}{4}} = \frac{1}{8} \cdot \left(-\frac{4}{1}\right) = -\frac{4}{8} = -\frac{1}{2}$$

$$\frac{-\frac{1}{16}}{\frac{1}{8}} = -\frac{1}{16} \cdot \frac{8}{1} = -\frac{8}{16} = -\frac{1}{2}$$

$$r = -\frac{1}{2}$$

6. −2

7. 75, 15, 3, $\dfrac{3}{5}$, . . .

$$\frac{15}{75} = \frac{1}{5}, \ \frac{3}{15} = \frac{1}{5}, \ \frac{\frac{3}{5}}{3} = \frac{3}{5} \cdot \frac{1}{3} = \frac{1}{5}$$

$$r = \frac{1}{5}$$

8. $-\dfrac{1}{3}$

9. $\dfrac{1}{m}, \ \dfrac{3}{m^2}, \ \dfrac{9}{m^3}, \ \dfrac{27}{m^4}, \ \ldots$

$$\frac{\frac{3}{m^2}}{\frac{1}{m}} = \frac{3}{m^2} \cdot \frac{m}{1} = \frac{3}{m}$$

$$\frac{\frac{9}{m^3}}{\frac{3}{m^2}} = \frac{9}{m^3} \cdot \frac{m^2}{3} = \frac{3}{m}$$

$$\frac{\frac{27}{m^4}}{\frac{9}{m^3}} = \frac{27}{m^4} \cdot \frac{m^3}{9} = \frac{3}{m}$$

$$r = \frac{3}{m}$$

10. $\dfrac{m}{5}$

11. 3, 6, 12, . . .

$$a_1 = 3, \ n = 7, \text{ and } r = \frac{6}{3} = 2$$

We use the formula $a_n = a_1 r^{n-1}$.

$$a_7 = 3 \cdot 2^{7-1} = 3 \cdot 2^6 = 3 \cdot 64 = 192$$

12. 131,072

13. 5, $5\sqrt{2}$, 10, . . .

$$a_1 = 5, \ n = 9, \text{ and } r = \frac{5\sqrt{2}}{5} = \sqrt{2}$$

$$a_n = a_1 r^{n-1}$$

$$a_9 = 5(\sqrt{2})^{9-1} = 5(\sqrt{2})^8 = 5 \cdot 16 = 80$$

14. $108\sqrt{3}$

15. $-\dfrac{8}{243}, \ \dfrac{8}{81}, \ -\dfrac{8}{27}, \ \ldots$

$$a_1 = -\frac{8}{243}, \ n = 10, \text{ and } r = \frac{\frac{8}{81}}{-\frac{8}{243}} =$$

$$\frac{8}{81}\left(-\frac{243}{8}\right) = -3$$

$$a_n = a_1 r^{n-1}$$

$$a_{10} = -\frac{8}{243}(-3)^{10-1} = -\frac{8}{243}(-3)^9 =$$

$$-\frac{8}{243}(-19,683) = 648$$

16. 2,734,375

17. $1000, $1080, $1166.40, . . .

$$a_1 = \$1000, \ n = 12, \text{ and } r = \frac{\$1080}{\$1000} = 1.08$$

$$a_n = a_1 r^{n-1}$$

$$a_{12} = \$1000(1.08)^{12-1} \approx \$1000(2.331638997) \approx$$

$$\$2331.64$$

18. $1967.15

19. 1, 3, 9, . . .

$a_1 = 1$ and $r = \dfrac{3}{1}$, or 3

$a_n = a_1 r^{n-1}$

$a_n = 1(3)^{n-1} = 3^{n-1}$

20. $a_n = 5^{3-n}$

21. 1, −1, 1, −1, . . .

$a_1 = 1$ and $r = \dfrac{-1}{1} = -1$

$a_n = a_1 r^{n-1}$

$a_n = 1(-1)^{n-1} = (-1)^{n-1}$

22. $a_n = 2^n$

23. $\dfrac{1}{x}, \dfrac{1}{x^2}, \dfrac{1}{x^2}, \ldots$

$a_1 = \dfrac{1}{x}$ and $r = \dfrac{\frac{1}{x^2}}{\frac{1}{x}} = \dfrac{1}{x^2} \cdot \dfrac{x}{1} = \dfrac{1}{x}$

$a_n = a_1 r^{n-1}$

$a_n = \dfrac{1}{x}\left(\dfrac{1}{x}\right)^{n-1} = \dfrac{1}{x} \cdot \dfrac{1}{x^{n-1}} = \dfrac{1}{x^{1+n-1}} = \dfrac{1}{x^n}$

24. $a_n = 5\left(\dfrac{m}{2}\right)^{n-1}$

25. $6 + 12 + 24 + \ldots$

$a_1 = 6$, $n = 7$, and $r = \dfrac{12}{6} = 2$

$S_n = \dfrac{a_1(1 - r^n)}{1 - r}$

$S_7 = \dfrac{6(1 - 2^7)}{1 - 2} = \dfrac{6(1 - 128)}{-1} = \dfrac{6(-127)}{-1} = 762$

26. 10.5

27. $\dfrac{1}{18} - \dfrac{1}{6} + \dfrac{1}{2} - \ldots$

$a_1 = \dfrac{1}{18}$, $n = 7$, and $r = \dfrac{-\frac{1}{6}}{\frac{1}{18}} = -\dfrac{1}{6} \cdot \dfrac{18}{1} = -3$

$S_n = \dfrac{a_1(1 - r^n)}{1 - r}$

$S_7 = \dfrac{\frac{1}{18}\left[1 - (-3)^7\right]}{1 - (-3)} = \dfrac{\frac{1}{18}(1 + 2187)}{4} = \dfrac{\frac{1}{18}(2188)}{4} =$

$\dfrac{1}{18}(2188)\left(\dfrac{1}{4}\right) = \dfrac{547}{18}$

28. 7.7777

29. $1 + x + x^2 + x^3 + \ldots$

$a_1 = 1$, $n = 8$, and $r = \dfrac{x}{1}$, or x

$S_n = \dfrac{a_1(1 - r^n)}{1 - r}$

$S_8 = \dfrac{1(1 - x^8)}{1 - x} = \dfrac{(1 + x^4)(1 - x^4)}{1 - x} =$

$\dfrac{(1 + x^4)(1 + x^2)(1 - x^2)}{1 - x} =$

$\dfrac{(1 + x^4)(1 + x^2)(1 + x)(1 - x)}{1 - x} =$

$(1 + x^4)(1 + x^2)(1 + x)$

30. $\dfrac{1 - x^{20}}{1 - x^2}$

31. $200, $200(1.06), $200(1.06)^2$, . . .

$a_1 = \$200$, $n = 16$, and $r = \dfrac{\$200(1.06)}{\$200} = 1.06$

$S_n = \dfrac{a_1(1 - r^n)}{1 - r}$

$S_{16} = \dfrac{\$200[1 - (1.06)^{16}]}{1 - 1.06} \approx$

$\dfrac{\$200(1 - 2.540351685)}{-0.06} \approx \$5134.51$

32. $60,893.30

33. $16 + 4 + 1 + \ldots$

$|r| = \left|\dfrac{4}{16}\right| = \left|\dfrac{1}{4}\right| = \dfrac{1}{4}$, and since $|r| < 1$, the series does have a sum.

$S_\infty = \dfrac{a_1}{1 - r} = \dfrac{16}{1 - \frac{1}{4}} = \dfrac{16}{\frac{3}{4}} = 16 \cdot \dfrac{4}{3} = \dfrac{64}{3}$

34. 16

35. $7 + 3 + \dfrac{9}{7} + \ldots$

$|r| = \left|\dfrac{3}{7}\right| = \dfrac{3}{7}$, and since $|r| < 1$, the series does have a sum.

$S_\infty = \dfrac{a_1}{1 - r} = \dfrac{7}{1 - \frac{3}{7}} = \dfrac{7}{\frac{4}{7}} = 7 \cdot \dfrac{7}{4} = \dfrac{49}{4}$

36. 48

37. $3 + 15 + 75 + \ldots$

$|r| = \left|\dfrac{15}{3}\right| = |5| = 5$, and since $|r| \not< 1$ the series does not have a sum.

38. No

39. $4 - 6 + 9 - \dfrac{27}{2} + \ldots$

$|r| = \left|\dfrac{-6}{4}\right| = \left|-\dfrac{3}{2}\right| = \dfrac{3}{2}$, and since $|r| \not< 1$ the series does not have a sum.

40. −4

41. $0.43 + 0.0043 + 0.000043 + \ldots$

$|r| = \left| \dfrac{0.0043}{0.43} \right| = |0.01| = 0.01$, and since $|r| < 1$,

the series does have a sum.

$S_\infty = \dfrac{a_1}{1 - r} = \dfrac{0.43}{1 - 0.01} = \dfrac{0.43}{0.99} = \dfrac{43}{99}$

42. $\dfrac{37}{99}$

43. $\$500(1.02)^{-1} + \$500(1.02)^{-2} + \$500(1.02)^{-3} + \ldots$

$|r| = \left| \dfrac{\$500(1.02)^{-2}}{\$500(1.02)^{-1}} \right| = |(1.02)^{-1}| = (1.02)^{-1}$, or

$\dfrac{1}{1.02}$, and since $|r| < 1$, the series does have a sum.

$S_\infty = \dfrac{a_1}{1 - r} = \dfrac{\$500(1.02)^{-1}}{1 - \left(\dfrac{1}{1.02} \right)} = \dfrac{\dfrac{\$500}{1.02}}{\dfrac{0.02}{1.02}} =$

$\dfrac{\$500}{1.02} \cdot \dfrac{1.02}{0.02} = \$25,000$

44. $\$12,500$

45. $0.7777\ldots = 0.7 + 0.07 + 0.007 + 0.0007 + \ldots$

This is an infinite geometric series with $a_1 = 0.7$.

$|r| = \left| \dfrac{0.07}{0.7} \right| = |0.1| = 0.1 < 1$, so the series has a sum.

$S_\infty = \dfrac{a_1}{1 - r} = \dfrac{0.7}{1 - 0.1} = \dfrac{0.7}{0.9} = \dfrac{7}{9}$

Fractional notation for $0.7777\ldots$ is $\dfrac{7}{9}$.

46. $\dfrac{2}{9}$

47. $8.3838\ldots = 8.3 + 0.083 + 0.00083 + \ldots$

This is an infinite geometric series with $a_1 = 8.3$.

$|r| = \left| \dfrac{0.083}{8.3} \right| = |0.01| = 0.01 < 1$, so the series has a sum.

$S_\infty = \dfrac{a_1}{1 - r} = \dfrac{8.3}{1 - 0.01} = \dfrac{8.3}{0.99} = \dfrac{830}{99}$

Fractional notation for $8.3838\ldots$ is $\dfrac{830}{99}$.

48. $\dfrac{740}{99}$

49. $0.15151515\ldots = 0.15 + 0.0015 + 0.000015 + \ldots$

This is an infinite geometric series with $a_1 = 0.15$.

$|r| = \left| \dfrac{0.0015}{0.15} \right| = |0.01| = 0.01 < 1$, so the series has a sum.

$S_\infty = \dfrac{a_1}{1 - r} = \dfrac{0.15}{1 - 0.01} = \dfrac{0.15}{0.99} = \dfrac{15}{99} = \dfrac{5}{33}$

Fractional notation for $0.15151515\ldots$ is $\dfrac{5}{33}$.

50. $\dfrac{4}{33}$

51. *Familiarize.* In one year, the population will be $100,000 + 0.03(100,000)$, or $(1.03)100,000$. In two years, the population will be $(1.03)100,000 + 0.03(1.03)100,000$, or $(1.03)^2 100,000$. Thus the populations form a geometric sequence:

$100,000, \quad (1.03)100,000, \quad (1.03)^2 100,000, \ldots$

The population in 15 years will be the 16th term of the sequence.

Translate. We will use the formula $a_n = a_1 r^{n-1}$ with $a_1 = 100,000$, $r = 1.03$, and $n = 16$:

$a_{16} = 100,000(1.03)^{16-1}$

Carry out. We calculate to obtain $a_{16} \approx 155,797$.

Check. We can do the calculation again.

State. In 15 years the population will be about $155,797$.

52. About 24 years

53. *Familiarize.* The rebound distances form a geometric sequence:

$\dfrac{1}{4} \times 20, \quad \left(\dfrac{1}{4} \right)^2 \times 20, \quad \left(\dfrac{1}{4} \right)^3 \times 20, \ldots,$

or $5, \quad \dfrac{1}{4} \times 5, \quad \left(\dfrac{1}{4} \right)^2 \times 5, \ldots$

The height of the 6th rebound is the 6th term of the sequence.

Translate. We will use the formula $a_n = a_1 r^{n-1}$, with $a_1 = 5$, $r = \dfrac{1}{4}$, and $n = 6$:

$a_6 = 5 \left(\dfrac{1}{4} \right)^{6-1}$

Carry out. We calculate to obtain $a_6 = \dfrac{5}{1024}$.

Check. We can do the calculation again.

State. It rebounds $\dfrac{5}{1024}$ ft the 6th time.

54. $6\dfrac{2}{3}$ ft

55. *Familiarize.* The amounts owed at the beginning of successive years form a geometric sequence:

$\$15,000, \quad (1.085)\$15,000, \quad (1.085)^2\$15,000,$

$(1.085)^3\$15,000, \ldots$

The amount to be repaid at the end of 13 years is the amount owed at the beginning of the 14th year.

Translate. We use the formula $a_n = a_1 r^{n-1}$ with $a_1 = 15,000$, $r = 1.085$, and $n = 14$:

$a_{14} = 15,000(1.085)^{14-1}$

Carry out. We calculate to obtain $a_{14} \approx 43,318.94$.

Check. We can do the calculation again.

State. At the end of 13 years, $43,318.94 will be repaid.

56. 2710 fruit flies

57. We have a geometric sequence

$$5000, \ 5000(0.96), \ 5000(0.96)^2, \ldots$$

where the general term $5000(0.96)^n$ represents the number of fruit flies remaining alive after n minutes. We find the value of n for which the general term is 1800.

$$1800 = 5000(0.96)^n$$
$$0.36 = (0.96)^n$$
$$\log 0.36 = \log(0.96)^n$$
$$\log 0.36 = n \log 0.96$$
$$\frac{\log 0.36}{\log 0.96} = n$$
$$25 \approx n$$

It will take about 25 minutes for only 1800 fruit flies to remain alive.

58. $213,609.57

59. Familiarize. The lengths of the falls form a geometric sequence:

$$556, \ \left(\frac{3}{4}\right)556, \ \left(\frac{3}{4}\right)^2 556, \ \left(\frac{3}{4}\right)^3 556, \ \ldots$$

The total length of the first 6 falls is the sum of the first six terms of this sequence. The heights of the rebounds also form a geometric sequence:

$$\left(\frac{3}{4}\right)556, \ \left(\frac{3}{4}\right)^2 556, \ \left(\frac{3}{4}\right)^3 556, \ \ldots, \ \text{ or }$$

$$417, \ \left(\frac{3}{4}\right)417, \ \left(\frac{3}{4}\right)^2 417, \ \ldots$$

When the ball hits the ground for the 6th time, it will have rebounded 5 times. Thus the total length of the rebounds is the sum of the first five terms of this sequence.

Translate. We use the formula $S_n = \dfrac{a_1(1 - r^n)}{1 - r}$ twice, once with $a_1 = 556$, $r = \dfrac{3}{4}$, and $n = 6$ and a second time with $a_1 = 417$, $r = \dfrac{3}{4}$, and $n = 5$.

D = Length of falls + length of rebounds

$$= \frac{556\left[1 - \left(\frac{3}{4}\right)^6\right]}{1 - \frac{3}{4}} + \frac{417\left[1 - \left(\frac{3}{4}\right)^5\right]}{1 - \frac{3}{4}}.$$

Carry out. We use a calculator to obtain $D \approx 3100.35$.

Check. We can do the calculations again.

State. The ball will have traveled about 3100.35 ft.

60. 3892 ft

61. Familiarize. The heights of the stack form a geometric sequence:

$$0.02, \ 0.02(2), \ 0.02(2^2), \ldots$$

The height of the stack after it is doubled 10 times is given by the 11th term of this sequence.

Translate. We have a geometric sequence with $a_1 = 0.02$, $r = 2$, and $n = 11$. We use the formula

$$a_n = a_1 r^{n-1}.$$

Carry out. We substitute and calculate.

$$a_{11} = 0.02(2^{11-1})$$
$$a_{11} = 0.02(1024) = 20.48$$

Check. We can do the calculation again.

State. The final stack will be 20.48 in. high.

62. $2,684,354.55

63. The points lie on a straight line, so this is the graph of an arithmetic sequence.

64. Geometric

65. The points lie on the graph of an exponential function, so this is the graph of a geometric series.

66. Arithmetic

67. The points lie on the graph of an exponential function, so this is the graph of a geometric series.

68. Arithmetic

69. *Writing Exercise*

70. *Writing Exercise*

71.
$$(x + y)(x^2 + 2xy + y^2)$$
$$= x(x^2 + 2xy + y^2) + y(x^2 + 2xy + y^2)$$
$$= x^3 + 2x^2y + xy^2 + x^2y + 2xy^2 + y^3$$
$$= x^3 + 3x^2y + 3xy^2 + y^3$$

72. $a^3 - 3a^2b + 3ab^2 - b^3$

73.
$$5x - 2y = -3, \quad (1)$$
$$2x + 5y = -24 \quad (2)$$

Multiply Eq. (1) by 5 and Eq. (2) by 2 and add.

$$25x - 10y = -15$$
$$\underline{4x + 10y = -48}$$
$$29x \qquad\quad = -63$$
$$x = -\frac{63}{29}$$

Substitute $-\dfrac{63}{29}$ for x in the second equation and solve for y.

$$2\left(-\frac{63}{29}\right) + 5y = -24$$
$$-\frac{126}{29} + 5y = -24$$
$$5y = -\frac{570}{29}$$
$$y = -\frac{114}{29}$$

The solution is $\left(-\dfrac{63}{29}, -\dfrac{114}{29}\right)$.

74. $(-1, 2, 3)$

75. *Writing Exercise*

76. *Writing Exercise*

77. $x^2 - x^3 + x^4 + x^5 + \ldots$

This is a geometric series with $a_1 = x^2$ and $r = -x$.

$$S_n = \frac{a_1(1 - r^n)}{1 - r} = \frac{x^2[1 - (-x)^n]}{1 - (-x)} = \frac{x^2[1 - (-x)^n]}{1 + x}$$

78. $\dfrac{1 - x^n}{1 - x}$

79. The length of a side of the first square is 16 cm. The length of a side of the next square is the length of the hypotenuse of a right triangle with legs 8 cm and 8 cm, or $8\sqrt{2}$ cm. The length of a side of the next square is the length of the hypotenuse of a right triangle with legs $4\sqrt{2}$ cm and $4\sqrt{2}$ cm, or 8 cm. The areas of the squares form a sequence:

$$(16)^2, \quad (8\sqrt{2})^2, \quad (8)^2, \ldots, \quad \text{or}$$

$$256, \quad 128, \quad 64, \ldots$$

This is a geometric sequence with $a_1 = 256$ and $r = \dfrac{1}{2}$.

We find the sum of the infinite geometric series $256 + 128 + 64 + \ldots$.

$$S_\infty = \frac{256}{1 - \dfrac{1}{2}} = \frac{256}{\dfrac{1}{2}} = 512 \text{ cm}^2$$

80. $0.999\ldots = 0.9 + 0.09 + 0.009 + \ldots$

$$|r| = \left| \frac{0.09}{0.9} \right| = |0.1| = 0.1 < 1, \text{ so the series has a sum.}$$

$$S_\infty = \frac{0.9}{1 - 0.1} = \frac{0.9}{0.9} = 1$$

Thus, $0.999\ldots = 1$.

Exercise Set 13.4

1. $8! = 8 \cdot 7 \cdot 6 \cdot 5 \cdot 4 \cdot 3 \cdot 2 \cdot 1 = 40,320$

2. $362,880$

3. $10! = 10 \cdot 9 \cdot 8 \cdot 7 \cdot 6 \cdot 5 \cdot 4 \cdot 3 \cdot 2 \cdot 1 = 3,628,800$

4. $39,916,800$

5. $\dfrac{7!}{4!} = \dfrac{7 \cdot 6 \cdot 5 \cdot 4!}{4!} = 7 \cdot 6 \cdot 5 = 210$

6. 56

7. $\dfrac{10!}{7!} = \dfrac{10 \cdot 9 \cdot 8 \cdot 7!}{7!} = 10 \cdot 9 \cdot 8 = 720$

8. 3024

9. $\dbinom{8}{2} = \dfrac{8!}{(8-2)!2!} = \dfrac{8!}{6!2!} = \dfrac{8 \cdot 7 \cdot 6!}{6! \cdot 2 \cdot 1} = \dfrac{8 \cdot 7}{2} = 4 \cdot 7 = 28$

10. 35

11. $\dbinom{10}{6} = \dfrac{10!}{(10-6)!6!} = \dfrac{10!}{4!6!} = \dfrac{10 \cdot 9 \cdot 8 \cdot 7 \cdot 6!}{4 \cdot 3 \cdot 2 \cdot 6!} =$

$\dfrac{10 \cdot 9 \cdot 8 \cdot 7}{4 \cdot 3 \cdot 2} = 10 \cdot 3 \cdot 7 = 210$

12. 126

13. $\dbinom{20}{18} = \dfrac{20!}{(20-18)!18!} = \dfrac{20!}{2!18!} = \dfrac{20 \cdot 19 \cdot 18!}{2 \cdot 1 \cdot 18!} =$

$\dfrac{20 \cdot 19}{2} = 10 \cdot 19 = 190$

14. 4060

15. $\dbinom{35}{2} = \dfrac{35!}{(35-2)!2!} = \dfrac{35!}{33!2!} = \dfrac{35 \cdot 34 \cdot 33!}{33! \cdot 2 \cdot 1} =$

$\dfrac{35 \cdot 34}{2} = 35 \cdot 17 = 595$

16. 780

17. Expand $(m + n)^5$.

Form 1: The expansion of $(m + n)^5$ has $5 + 1$, or 6 terms. The sum of the exponents in each term is 5. The exponents of m start with 5 and decrease to 0. The last term has no factor of m. The first term has no factor of n. The exponents of n start in the second term with 1 and increase to 5. We get the coefficients from the 6th row of Pascal's triangle.

$$1$$
$$1 \qquad 1$$
$$1 \qquad 2 \qquad 1$$
$$1 \qquad 3 \qquad 3 \qquad 1$$
$$1 \qquad 4 \qquad 6 \qquad 4 \qquad 1$$
$$1 \qquad 5 \qquad 10 \qquad 10 \qquad 5 \qquad 1$$

$$(m + n)^5 = 1 \cdot m^5 + 5 \cdot m^4 n^1 + 10 \cdot m^3 \cdot n^2 +$$
$$10 \cdot m^2 \cdot n^3 + 5 \cdot m \cdot n^4 + 1 \cdot n^5$$
$$= m^5 + 5m^4 n + 10m^3 n^2 + 10m^2 n^3 +$$
$$5mn^4 + n^5$$

Form 2: We have $a = m$, $b = n$, and $n = 5$.

$$(m + n)^5 = \binom{5}{0} m^5 + \binom{5}{1} m^4 n + \binom{5}{2} m^3 n^2 +$$
$$\binom{5}{3} m^2 n^3 + \binom{5}{4} mn^4 + \binom{5}{5} n^5$$
$$= \frac{5!}{5!0!} m^5 + \frac{5!}{4!1!} m^4 n + \frac{5!}{3!2!} m^3 n^2 +$$
$$\frac{5!}{2!3!} m^2 n^3 + \frac{5!}{1!4!} mn^4 + \frac{5!}{0!5!} m^5$$
$$= m^5 + 5m^4 n + 10m^3 n^2 + 10m^2 n^3 +$$
$$5mn^4 + n^5$$

18. $a^4 - 4a^3 b + 6a^2 b^2 - 4ab^3 + b^4$

19. Expand $(x - y)^6$.

Form 1: The expansion of $(x-y)^6$ has $6+1$, or 7 terms. The sum of the exponents in each term is 6. The exponents of x start with 6 and decrease to 0. The last term has no factor of x. The first term has no factor of $-y$. The exponents of $-y$ start in the second term with 1 and increase to 6. We get the coefficients from the 7th row of Pascal's triangle.

$$
\begin{array}{ccccccccccccc}
 & & & & & & 1 & & & & & & \\
 & & & & & 1 & & 1 & & & & & \\
 & & & & 1 & & 2 & & 1 & & & & \\
 & & & 1 & & 3 & & 3 & & 1 & & & \\
 & & 1 & & 4 & & 6 & & 4 & & 1 & & \\
 & 1 & & 5 & & 10 & & 10 & & 5 & & 1 & \\
1 & & 6 & & 15 & & 20 & & 15 & & 6 & & 1
\end{array}
$$

$(x-y)^6 = 1 \cdot x^6 + 6 \cdot x^5 \cdot (-y) + 15 \cdot x^4 \cdot (-y)^2 +$
$\qquad 20 \cdot x^3 \cdot (-y)^3 + 15 \cdot x^2 \cdot (-y)^4 +$
$\qquad 6 \cdot x \cdot (-y)^5 + 1 \cdot (-y)^6$
$\quad = x^6 - 6x^5y + 15x^4y^2 - 20x^3y^3 +$
$\qquad 15x^2y^4 - 6xy^5 + y^6$

Form 2: We have $a = x$, $b = -y$, and $n = 6$.

$(x-y)^6 = \binom{6}{0}x^6 + \binom{6}{1}x^5(-y) + \binom{6}{2}x^4(-y)^2 +$
$\qquad \binom{6}{3}x^3(-y)^3 + \binom{6}{4}x^2(-y)^4 +$
$\qquad \binom{6}{5}x(-y)^5 + \binom{6}{6}(-y)^6$
$\quad = \dfrac{6!}{6!0!}x^6 + \dfrac{6!}{5!1!}x^5(-y) + \dfrac{6!}{4!2!}x^4y^2 +$
$\qquad \dfrac{6!}{3!3!}x^3(-y^3) + \dfrac{6!}{2!4!}x^2y^4 + \dfrac{6!}{1!5!}x(-y^5) +$
$\qquad \dfrac{6!}{0!6!}y^6$
$\quad = x^6 - 6x^5y + 15x^4y^2 - 20x^3y^3 +$
$\qquad 15x^2y^4 - 6xy^5 + y^6$

20. $p^7 + 7p^6q + 21p^5q^2 + 35p^4q^3 + 35p^3q^4 + 21p^2q^5 + 7pq^6 + q^7$

21. Expand $(x^2 - 3y)^5$.

We have $a = x^2$, $b = -3y$, and $n = 5$.

Form 1: We get the coefficients from the 6th row of Pascal's triangle. From Exercise 17 we know that the coefficients are

$$
\begin{array}{cccccc}
1 & 5 & 10 & 10 & 5 & 1.
\end{array}
$$
$(x^2-3y)^5 = 1 \cdot (x^2)^5 + 5 \cdot (x^2)^4 \cdot (-3y) +$
$\qquad 10 \cdot (x^2)^3 \cdot (-3y)^2 + 10 \cdot (x^2)^2 \cdot (-3y)^3 +$
$\qquad 5 \cdot (x^2) \cdot (-3y)^4 + 1 \cdot (-3y)^5$
$\quad = x^{10} - 15x^8y + 90x^6y^2 - 270x^4y^3 +$
$\qquad 405x^2y^4 - 243y^5$

Form 2:

$(x^2+3y)^5 = \binom{5}{0}(x^2)^5 + \binom{5}{1}(x^2)^4(-3y) +$
$\qquad \binom{5}{2}(x^2)^3(-3y)^2 + \binom{5}{3}(x^2)^2(-3y)^3 +$
$\qquad \binom{5}{4}x^2(-3y)^4 + \binom{5}{5}(-3y)^5$

$\quad = \dfrac{5!}{5!0!}x^{10} + \dfrac{5!}{4!1!}x^8(-3y) + \dfrac{5!}{3!2!}x^6(9y^2) +$
$\qquad \dfrac{5!}{2!3!}x^4(-27y^3) + \dfrac{5!}{1!4!}x^2(81y^4) +$
$\qquad \dfrac{5!}{0!5!}(-243y^5)$
$\quad = x^{10} - 15x^8y + 90x^6y^2 - 270x^4y^3 +$
$\qquad 405x^2y^4 - 243y^5$

22. $2187c^7 - 5103c^6d + 5103c^5d^2 - 2835c^4d^3 + 945c^3d^4 - 189c^2d^5 + 21cd^6 - d^7$

23. Expand $(3c - d)^6$.

We have $a = 3c$, $b = -d$, and $n = 6$.

Form 1: We get the coefficients from the 7th row of Pascal's triangle. From Exercise 19 we know that the coefficients are

$$
\begin{array}{ccccccc}
1 & 6 & 15 & 20 & 15 & 6 & 1.
\end{array}
$$
$(3c-d)^6 = 1 \cdot (3c)^6 + 6 \cdot (3c)^5 \cdot (-d) +$
$\qquad 15 \cdot (3c)^4 \cdot (-d)^2 + 20 \cdot (3c)^3 \cdot (-d)^3 +$
$\qquad 15 \cdot (3c)^2 \cdot (-d)^4 + 6 \cdot (3c) \cdot (-d)^5 +$
$\qquad 1 \cdot (-d)^6$
$\quad = 3^6c^6 - 6 \cdot 3^5c^5d + 15 \cdot 3^4c^4d^2 -$
$\qquad 20 \cdot 3^3c^3d^3 + 15 \cdot 3^2c^2d^4 - 6 \cdot 3cd^5 + d^6$
$\quad = 729c^6 - 6 \cdot 243c^5d + 15 \cdot 81c^4d^2 -$
$\qquad 20 \cdot 27c^3d^3 + 15 \cdot 9c^2d^4 - 6 \cdot 3cd^5 + d^6$
$\quad = 729c^6 - 1458c^5d + 1215c^4d^2 - 540c^3d^3 +$
$\qquad 135c^2d^4 - 18cd^5 + d^6$

Form 2:

$(3c-d)^6 = \binom{6}{0}(3c)^6 + \binom{6}{1}(3c)^5(-d) +$
$\qquad \binom{6}{2}(3c)^4(-d)^2 + \binom{6}{3}(3c)^3(-d)^3 +$
$\qquad \binom{6}{4}(3c)^2(-d)^4 + \binom{6}{5}(3c)(-d)^5 +$
$\qquad \binom{6}{6}(-d)^6$

$\quad = \dfrac{6!}{6!0!}(729c^6) + \dfrac{6!}{5!1!}(243c^5)(-d) +$
$\qquad \dfrac{6!}{4!2!}(81c^4)(d^2) + \dfrac{6!}{3!3!}(27c^3)(-d^3) +$
$\qquad \dfrac{6!}{2!4!}(9c^2)(d^4) + \dfrac{6!}{1!5!}(3c)(-d^5) +$
$\qquad \dfrac{6!}{0!6!}d^6$
$\quad = 729c^6 - 1458c^5d + 1215c^4d^2 - 540c^3d^3 +$
$\qquad 135c^2d^4 - 18cd^5 + d^6$

24. $t^{-12} + 12t^{-10} + 60t^{-8} + 160t^{-6} + 240t^{-4} + 192t^{-2} + 64$

25. Expand $(x - y)^3$.

We have $a = x$, $b = -y$, and $n = 3$.

Form 1: We get the coefficients from the 4th row of Pascal's triangle.

$$
\begin{array}{ccccccc}
 & & & 1 & & & \\
 & & 1 & & 1 & & \\
 & 1 & & 2 & & 1 & \\
1 & & 3 & & 3 & & 1
\end{array}
$$

$$(x - y)^3$$
$$= 1 \cdot x^3 + 3x^2(-y) + 3x(-y)^2 + 1 \cdot (-y)^3$$
$$= x^3 - 3x^2y + 3xy^2 - y^3$$

Form 2:

$$(x - y)^3$$
$$= \binom{3}{0} x^3 + \binom{3}{1} x^2(-y) + \binom{3}{2} x(-y)^2 +$$
$$\binom{3}{3} (-y)^3$$
$$= \frac{3!}{3!0!} x^3 + \frac{3!}{2!1!} x^2(-y) + \frac{3!}{1!2!} xy^2 +$$
$$\frac{3!}{0!3!} (-y^3)$$
$$= x^3 - 3x^2y + 3xy^2 - y^3$$

26. $x^5 - 5x^4y + 10x^3y^2 - 10x^2y^3 + 5xy^4 - y^5$

27. Expand $\left(x + \dfrac{2}{y}\right)^9$.

We have $a = x$, $b = \dfrac{2}{y}$, and $n = 9$.

Form 1: We get the coefficients from the 10th row of Pascal's triangle.

$$
\begin{array}{ccccccccccccccccccc}
 & & & & & & & & & 1 & & & & & & & & & \\
 & & & & & & & & 1 & & 1 & & & & & & & & \\
 & & & & & & & 1 & & 2 & & 1 & & & & & & & \\
 & & & & & & 1 & & 3 & & 3 & & 1 & & & & & & \\
 & & & & & 1 & & 4 & & 6 & & 4 & & 1 & & & & & \\
 & & & & 1 & & 5 & & 10 & & 10 & & 5 & & 1 & & & & \\
 & & & 1 & & 6 & & 15 & & 20 & & 15 & & 6 & & 1 & & & \\
 & & 1 & & 7 & & 21 & & 35 & & 35 & & 21 & & 7 & & 1 & & \\
 & 1 & & 8 & & 28 & & 56 & & 70 & & 56 & & 28 & & 8 & & 1 & \\
1 & & 9 & & 36 & & 84 & & 126 & & 126 & & 84 & & 36 & & 9 & & 1
\end{array}
$$

$$\left(x + \frac{2}{y}\right)^9 = 1 \cdot x^9 + 9x^8\left(\frac{2}{y}\right) + 36x^7\left(\frac{2}{y}\right)^2 +$$
$$84x^6\left(\frac{2}{y}\right)^3 + 126x^5\left(\frac{2}{y}\right)^4 +$$
$$126x^4\left(\frac{2}{y}\right)^5 + 84x^3\left(\frac{2}{y}\right)^6 +$$
$$36x^2\left(\frac{2}{y}\right)^7 + 9x\left(\frac{2}{y}\right)^8 + 1 \cdot \left(\frac{2}{y}\right)^9$$

$$= x^9 + \frac{18x^8}{y} + \frac{144x^7}{y^2} + \frac{672x^6}{y^3} +$$
$$\frac{2016x^5}{y^4} + \frac{4032x^4}{y^5} + \frac{5376x^3}{y^6} +$$
$$\frac{4608x^2}{y^7} + \frac{2304x}{y^8} + \frac{512}{y^9}$$

Form 2:

$$\left(x - \frac{2}{y}\right)^9$$
$$= \binom{9}{0} x^9 + \binom{9}{1} x^8\left(\frac{2}{y}\right) + \binom{9}{2} x^7\left(\frac{2}{y}\right)^2 +$$
$$\binom{9}{3} x^6\left(\frac{2}{y}\right)^3 + \binom{9}{4} x^5\left(\frac{2}{y}\right)^4 +$$
$$\binom{9}{5} x^4\left(\frac{2}{y}\right)^5 + \binom{9}{6} x^3\left(\frac{2}{y}\right)^6 +$$
$$\binom{9}{7} x^2\left(\frac{2}{y}\right)^7 + \binom{9}{8} x\left(\frac{2}{y}\right)^8 +$$
$$\binom{9}{9}\left(\frac{2}{y}\right)^9$$

$$= \frac{9!}{9!0!} x^9 + \frac{9!}{8!1!} x^8\left(\frac{2}{y}\right) + \frac{9!}{7!2!} x^7\left(\frac{4}{y^2}\right) +$$
$$\frac{9!}{6!3!} x^6\left(\frac{8}{y^3}\right) + \frac{9!}{5!4!} x^5\left(\frac{16}{y^4}\right) +$$
$$\frac{9!}{4!5!} x^4\left(\frac{32}{y^5}\right) + \frac{9!}{3!6!} x^3\left(\frac{64}{y^6}\right) +$$
$$\frac{9!}{2!7!} x^2\left(\frac{128}{y^7}\right) + \frac{9!}{1!8!} x\left(\frac{256}{y^8}\right) +$$
$$\frac{9!}{0!9!}\left(\frac{512}{y^9}\right)$$

$$= x^9 + 9x^8\left(\frac{2}{y}\right) + 36x^7\left(\frac{4}{y^2}\right) + 84x^6\left(\frac{8}{y^3}\right) +$$
$$126x^5\left(\frac{16}{y^4}\right) + 126x^4\left(\frac{32}{y^5}\right) + 84x^3\left(\frac{64}{y^6}\right) +$$
$$36x^2\left(\frac{128}{y^7}\right) + 9x\left(\frac{256}{y^8}\right) + \frac{512}{y^9}$$

$$= x^9 + \frac{18x^8}{y} + \frac{144x^7}{y^2} + \frac{672x^6}{y^3} +$$
$$\frac{2016x^5}{y^4} + \frac{4032x^4}{y^5} + \frac{5376x^3}{y^6} +$$
$$\frac{4608x^2}{y^7} + \frac{2304x}{y^8} + \frac{512}{y^9}$$

28. $19,683s^9 + \dfrac{59,049s^8}{t} + \dfrac{78,732s^7}{t^2} + \dfrac{61,236s^6}{t^3} +$
$\dfrac{30,618s^5}{t^4} + \dfrac{10,206s^4}{t^5} + \dfrac{2268s^3}{t^6} + \dfrac{324s^2}{t^7} + \dfrac{27s}{t^8} + \dfrac{1}{t^9}$

29. Expand $(a^2 - b^3)^5$.

We have $a = a^2$, $b = -b^3$, and $n = 5$.

Form 1: We get the coefficient from the 6th row of Pascal's triangle. From Exercise 17 we know that the coefficients are

$$
\begin{array}{cccccc}
1 & 5 & 10 & 10 & 5 & 1.
\end{array}
$$

$(a^2 - b^3)^5$

$= 1 \cdot (a^2)^5 + 5(a^2)^4(-b^3) + 10(a^2)^3(-b^3)^2 +$
$\quad 10(a^2)^2(-b^3)^3 + 5(a^2)(-b^3)^4 + 1 \cdot (-b^3)^5$

$= a^{10} - 5a^8b^3 + 10a^6b^6 - 10a^4b^9 +$
$\quad 5a^2b^{12} - b^{15}$

Form 2:

$(a^2 - b^3)^5$

$= \binom{5}{0}(a^2)^5 + \binom{5}{1}(a^2)^4(-b^3) +$

$\quad \binom{5}{2}(a^2)^3(-b^3)^2 + \binom{5}{3}(a^2)^2(-b^3)^3 +$

$\quad \binom{5}{4}(a^2)(-b^3)^4 + \binom{5}{5}(-b^3)^5$

$= \dfrac{5!}{5!0!}a^{10} + \dfrac{5!}{4!1!}a^8(-b^3) + \dfrac{5!}{3!2!}a^6(b^6) +$

$\quad \dfrac{5!}{2!3!}a^4(-b^9) + \dfrac{5!}{1!4!}a^2(b^{12}) + \dfrac{5!}{0!5!}(-b^{15})$

$= a^{10} - 5a^8b^3 + 10a^6b^6 - 10a^4b^9 +$
$\quad 5a^2b^{12} - b^{15}$

30. $x^{15} - 10x^{12}y + 40x^9y^2 - 80x^6y^3 + 80x^3y^4 - 32y^5$

31. Expand $(\sqrt{3} - t)^4$.

We have $a = \sqrt{3}$, $b = -t$, and $n = 4$.

Form 1: We get the coefficients from the 5th row of Pascal's triangle.

$$1$$
$$1 \quad 1$$
$$1 \quad 2 \quad 1$$
$$1 \quad 3 \quad 3 \quad 1$$
$$1 \quad 4 \quad 6 \quad 4 \quad 1$$

$(\sqrt{3} - t)^4 = 1 \cdot (\sqrt{3})^4 + 4(\sqrt{3})^3(-t) +$
$\quad 6(\sqrt{3})^2(-t)^2 + 4(\sqrt{3})(-t)^3 + 1 \cdot (-t)^4$

$\quad = 9 - 12\sqrt{3}t + 18t^2 - 4\sqrt{3}t^3 + t^4$

Form 2:

$(\sqrt{3} - t)^4 = \binom{4}{0}(\sqrt{3})^4 + \binom{4}{1}(\sqrt{3})^3(-t) +$

$\quad \binom{4}{2}(\sqrt{3})^2(-t)^2 + \binom{4}{3}(\sqrt{3})(-t)^3 +$

$\quad \binom{4}{4}(-t)^4$

$\quad = \dfrac{4!}{4!0!}(9) + \dfrac{4!}{3!1!}(3\sqrt{3})(-t) +$

$\quad \dfrac{4!}{2!2!}(3)(t^2) + \dfrac{4!}{1!3!}(\sqrt{3})(-t^3) +$

$\quad \dfrac{4!}{0!4!}(t^4)$

$\quad = 9 - 12\sqrt{3}t + 18t^2 - 4\sqrt{3}t^3 + t^4$

32. $125 + 150\sqrt{5}\,t + 375t^2 + 100\sqrt{5}\,t^3 + 75t^4 + 6\sqrt{5}\,t^5 + t^6$

33. Expand $(x^{-2} + x^2)^4$.

We have $a = x^{-2}$, $b = x^2$, and $n = 4$.

Form 1: We get the coefficients from the fifth row of Pascal's triangle. From Exercise 31 we know that the coefficients are

$$1 \quad 4 \quad 6 \quad 4 \quad 1.$$

$(x^{-2} + x^2)^4$

$= 1 \cdot (x^{-2})^4 + 4(x^{-2})^3(x^2) + 6(x^{-2})^2(x^2)^2 +$
$\quad 4(x^{-2})(x^2)^3 + 1 \cdot (x^2)^4$

$= x^{-8} + 4x^{-4} + 6 + 4x^4 + x^8$

Form 2:

$(x^{-2} + x^2)^4$

$= \binom{4}{0}(x^{-2})^4 + \binom{4}{1}(x^{-2})^3(x^2) +$

$\quad \binom{4}{2}(x^{-2})^2(x^2)^2 + \binom{4}{3}(x^{-2})(x^2)^3 +$

$\quad \binom{4}{4}(x^2)^4$

$= \dfrac{4!}{4!0!}(x^{-8}) + \dfrac{4!}{3!1!}(x^{-6})(x^2) + \dfrac{4!}{2!2!}(x^{-4})(x^4) +$

$\quad \dfrac{4!}{1!3!}(x^{-2})(x^6) + \dfrac{4!}{0!4!}(x^8)$

$= x^{-8} + 4x^{-4} + 6 + 4x^4 + x^8$

34. $x^{-3} - 6x^{-2} + 15x^{-1} - 20 + 15x - 6x^2 + x^3$

35. Find the 3rd term of $(a + b)^6$.

First, we note that $3 = 2 + 1$, $a = a$, $b = b$, and $n = 6$. Then the 3rd term of the expansion of $(a + b)^6$ is

$\binom{6}{2}a^{6-2}b^2$, or $\dfrac{6!}{4!2!}a^4b^2$, or $15a^4b^2$.

36. $21x^2y^5$

37. Find the 12th term of $(a - 3)^{14}$.

First, we note that $12 = 11 + 1$, $a = a$, $b = -3$, and $n = 14$. Then the 12th term of the expansion of $(a - 3)^{14}$ is

$\binom{14}{11}a^{14-11} \cdot (-3)^{11} = \dfrac{14!}{3!11!}a^3(-177,147)$

$\qquad = 364a^3(-177,147)$

$\qquad = -64,481,508a^3$

38. $67,584x^2$

39. Find the 5th term of $(2x^3 - \sqrt{y})^8$.

First, we note that $5 = 4 + 1$, $a = 2x^3$, $b = -\sqrt{y}$, and $n = 8$. Then the 5th term of the expansion of $(2x^3 - \sqrt{y})^8$ is

$\binom{8}{4}(2x^3)^{8-4}(-\sqrt{y})^4$

$= \dfrac{8!}{4!4!}(2x^3)^4(-\sqrt{y})^4$

$= 70(16x^{12})(y^2)$

$= 1120x^{12}y^2$

40. $\dfrac{35c^3}{b^8}$

41. The expansion of $(2u - 3v^2)^{10}$ has 11 terms so the 6th term is the middle term. Note that $6 = 5 + 1$, $a = 2u$, $b = -3v^2$, and $n = 10$. Then the 6th term of the expansion of $(2u - 3v^2)^{10}$ is

$$\binom{10}{5}(2u)^{10-5}(-3v^2)^5$$
$$= \frac{10!}{5!5!}(2u)^5(-3v^2)^5$$
$$= 252(32u^5)(-243v^{10})$$
$$= -1,959,552u^5v^{10}$$

42. $30x\sqrt{x}$, $30x\sqrt{3}$

43. The 9th term of $(x - y)^8$ is the last term, y^8.

44. $-b^9$

45. *Writing Exercise*

46. *Writing Exercise*

47. $\log_2 x + \log_2(x - 2) = 3$
$$\log_2 x(x - 2) = 3$$
$$x(x - 2) = 2^3$$
$$x^2 - 2x = 8$$
$$x^2 - 2x - 8 = 0$$
$$(x - 4)(x + 2) = 0$$
$x = 4$ *or* $x = -2$

Only 4 checks. It is the solution.

48. $\dfrac{5}{2}$

49. $e^t = 280$
$$\ln e^t = \ln 280$$
$$t = \ln 280$$
$$t \approx 5.6348$$

50. ± 5

51. *Writing Exercise*

52. *Writing Exercise*

53. Consider a set of 5 elements, $\{A, B, C, D, E\}$. List all the subsets of size 3:

$\{A, B, C\}$, $\{A, B, D\}$, $\{A, B, E\}$, $\{A, C, D\}$,
$\{A, C, E\}$, $\{A, D, E\}$, $\{B, C, D\}$, $\{B, C, E\}$,
$\{B, D, E\}$, $\{C, D, E\}$.

There are exactly 10 subsets of size 3 and $\binom{5}{3} = 10$, so there are exactly $\binom{5}{3}$ ways of forming a subset of size 3 from a set of 5 elements.

54. $\binom{5}{n}(0.325)^{5-2}(0.675)^2 \approx 0.156$

55. Find the sixth term of $(0.15 + 0.85)^8$:

$$\binom{8}{5}(0.15)^{8-5}(0.85)^5 = \frac{8!}{3!5!}(0.15)^3(0.85)^5 \approx 0.084$$

56. $\binom{5}{2}(0.325)^3(0.675)^2 + \binom{5}{3}(0.325)^2(0.675)^3 +$
$\binom{5}{4}(0.325)(0.675)^4 + \binom{5}{5}(0.675)^5 \approx 0.959$

57. Find and add the 7th through the 9th terms of $(0.15 + 0.85)^9$:

$\binom{8}{6}(0.15)^2(0.85)^6 + \binom{8}{7}(0.15)(0.85)^7 +$
$\binom{8}{8}(0.85)^8 \approx 0.89$

58. $\binom{n}{n-r} = \dfrac{n!}{[n - (n - r)!](n - r)!} = \dfrac{n!}{r!(n - r)!} =$
$\binom{n}{r}$

59. The $(r + 1)$st term of $\left(\dfrac{3x^2}{2} - \dfrac{1}{3x}\right)^{12}$ is

$\binom{12}{r}\left(\dfrac{3x^2}{2}\right)^{12-r}\left(-\dfrac{1}{3x}\right)^r$. In the term which does not contain x, the exponent of x in the numerator is equal to the exponent of x in the denominator.

$$2(12 - r) = r$$
$$24 - 2r = r$$
$$24 = 3r$$
$$8 = r$$

Find the $(8 + 1)$st, or 9th term:

$$\binom{12}{8}\left(\frac{3x^2}{2}\right)^4\left(-\frac{1}{3x}\right)^8 = \frac{12!}{4!8!}\left(\frac{3^4x^8}{2^4}\right)\left(\frac{1}{3^8x^8}\right) = \frac{55}{144}$$

60. $-4320x^6y^{9/2}$

61. $\dfrac{\binom{5}{3}(p^2)^2\left(-\frac{1}{2}p\sqrt[3]{q}\right)^3}{\binom{5}{2}(p^2)^3\left(-\frac{1}{2}p\sqrt[3]{q}\right)^2} = \dfrac{-\frac{1}{8}p^7q}{\frac{1}{4}p^8\sqrt[3]{q^2}} =$

$-\dfrac{\frac{1}{8}p^7q}{\frac{1}{4}p^8q^{2/3}} = -\dfrac{1}{8}\cdot\dfrac{4}{1}\cdot p^{7-8}\cdot q^{1-2/3} =$

$-\dfrac{1}{2}p^{-1}q^{1/3} = -\dfrac{\sqrt[3]{q}}{2p}$

62. $-\dfrac{35}{x^{1/6}}$

63. The degree of $(x^2 + 3)^4$ is the degree of $(x^2)^4 = x^8$, or 8.

64. $x^7 + 7x^6y + 21x^5y^2 + 35x^4y^3 + 35x^3y^4 + 21x^2y^5 + 7xy^6 + y^7$

Exercise Set 13.5

---

1. Since there are 52 cards and each is as likely to be selected as any other, there are 52 equally likely outcomes.

2. $\dfrac{1}{13}$

3. Since there are 52 equally likely outcomes and there are 13 ways to obtain a heart, by the Primary Principle of Probability we have

$$P(\text{drawing a heart}) = \frac{13}{52}, \text{ or } \frac{1}{4}.$$

4. $\frac{1}{2}$

5. Since there are 52 equally likely outcomes and there are 26 ways to obtain a red card (13 hearts and 13 diamonds), by the Primary Principle of Probability we have

$$P(\text{drawing a red card}) = \frac{26}{52}, \text{ or } \frac{1}{2}.$$

6. $\frac{2}{13}$

7. Since there are 52 equally likely outcomes and there are 2 ways to obtain a black ace (the ace of spades and the ace of clubs), by the Primary Principle of Probability we have

$$P(\text{drawing a black ace}) = \frac{2}{52}, \text{ or } \frac{1}{26}.$$

8. $\frac{2}{7}$

9. Since there are 14 equally likely ways of selecting a marble from a bag containing 4 red marbles and 10 green marbles, by the Primary Principle of Probability we have

$$P(\text{selecting a green marble}) = \frac{10}{14} = \frac{5}{7}.$$

10. 0

11. There are 14 equally likely ways of selecting any marble from a bag containing 4 red marbles and 10 green marbles. Since the bag does not contain any white marbles, there are 0 ways of selecting a white marble. By the Primary Principle of Probability, we have

$$P(\text{selecting a white marble}) = \frac{0}{14} = 0.$$

12. $\frac{9}{19}$

13. The roulette wheel contains 38 equally likely slots. Eighteen are red and eighteen are black, so $18 + 18$, or 36, are either red or black. Thus, by the Primary Principle of Probability,

$$P(\text{the ball falls in a red or black slot}) = \frac{36}{38} = \frac{18}{19}.$$

14. $\frac{1}{38}$

15. The roulette wheel contains 38 equally likely slots. One is the 00 slot and one is the 0 slot. Thus, by the Primary Principle of Probability,

$$P(\text{the ball falls in the 00 or 0 slot}) = \frac{2}{38} = \frac{1}{19}.$$

16. $\frac{5}{12}$

17. The yellow region occupies $\frac{1}{3}$ of one side of the dartboard or $\frac{1}{3} \cdot \frac{1}{2}$ or $\frac{1}{6}$ of the board. Thus,

$$P(\text{yellow}) = \frac{1}{6}.$$

18. $\frac{7}{12}$

19. The one red region on the left-hand side of the dartboard occupies $\frac{1}{3}$ of that side or $\frac{1}{3} \cdot \frac{1}{2}$, or $\frac{1}{6}$ of the dartboard. The two red regions on the right-hand side of the dartboard each occupy $\frac{1}{4}$ of that side, so together they occupy $2 \cdot \frac{1}{4} \cdot \frac{1}{2}$, or $\frac{1}{4}$ of the dartboard. Then all of the red regions together occupy $\frac{1}{6} + \frac{1}{4}$, or $\frac{5}{12}$ of the dartboard. The blue regions occupy the same amount of space as the red regions, or $\frac{5}{12}$ of the dartboard. Thus,

$$P(\text{red or blue}) = \frac{5}{12} + \frac{5}{12} = \frac{10}{12} = \frac{5}{6}.$$

20. 1

21. There is no green region on the dartboard. Thus, $P(\text{green}) = 0$.

22. $\frac{11}{4165}$

23. The number of ways of drawing 4 cards from a deck of 52 cards is $_{52}C_4$. Now 13 of the 52 cards are hearts, so the number of ways of drawing 4 hearts is $_{13}C_4$. Thus,

$$P(\text{getting 4 hearts}) = \frac{_{13}C_4}{_{52}C_4}, \text{ or } \frac{11}{4165}.$$

24. $\frac{30}{323}$

25. The number of ways to select 4 people from a group of $8 + 7$, or 15, is $_{15}C_4$. Two men can be chosen in $_8C_2$ ways and two women in $_7C_2$ ways. By the fundamental counting principle, the number of ways to select 2 men and 2 women is $_8C_2 \cdot _7C_2$. Thus,

$$P(\text{2 men and 2 women}) = \frac{_8C_2 \cdot _7C_2}{_{15}C_4}, \text{ or } \frac{28}{65}.$$

26. $\frac{5}{36}$

27. On each die there are 6 possible outcomes. The outcomes are paired so there are $6 \cdot 6$, or 36 possible ways in which the two can fall. Only the pair $(1, 1)$ totals 2. The probability is $\frac{1}{36}$.

28. $\frac{1}{6}$

29. On each die there are 6 possible outcomes. The outcomes are paired so there are $6 \cdot 6$, or 36 possible ways in which the two can fall. There are 6 possible doubles: (1,1), (2,2), (3,3), (4,4), (5,5), and (6,6), so the probability of rolling doubles is $\frac{6}{36}$, or $\frac{1}{6}$. Then the probability of rolling doubles three times in a row is $\frac{1}{6} \cdot \frac{1}{6} \cdot \frac{1}{6}$, or $\frac{1}{216}$.

30. $\dfrac{5}{12}$

31. The bottle contains $7 \cdot 4$, or 28 vitamins. The number of ways of selecting 4 vitamins from a group of 28 is $_{28}C_4$. The number of ways of selecting 1 vitamin A tablet from a group of 7 is $_7C_1$. The same is true for selecting 1 vitamin C, E, or B-12 tablet from a group of 7 each. Thus

P(selecting 1 each of vitamins A, C, E, and B-12) $=$

$$\dfrac{_7C_1 \cdot _7C_1 \cdot _7C_1 \cdot _7C_1}{_{28}C_4}, \text{ or } \dfrac{343}{2925}.$$

32. $\dfrac{24}{253}$

33. *Writing Exercise*

34. *Writing Exercise*

35. $2x + 5y = 7$, (1)

$3x + 2y = 16$ (2)

Multiply Equation (1) by 2, multiply Equation (2) by -5, and add.

$$\begin{array}{r} 4x + 10y = 14 \\ -15x - 10y = -80 \\ \hline -11x = -66 \\ x = 6 \end{array}$$

Substitute 6 for x in Equation (2) and solve for y.

$3 \cdot 6 + 2y = 16$

$18 + 2y = 16$

$2y = -2$

$y = -1$

The solution is $(6, -1)$.

36. -1

37.
$$\log_a \dfrac{x^2 y}{z^3}$$

$$= \log_a x^2 y - \log_a z^3 \qquad \text{Quotient rule}$$

$$= \log_a x^2 + \log_a y - \log_a z^3 \qquad \text{Product rule}$$

$$= 2\log_a x + \log_a y - 3\log_a z \qquad \text{Power rule}$$

38. $x^2 + (y+3)^2 = 12$

39. $3^4 = x$

40. $\log_4 10 = y$

41. *Writing Exercise*

42. *Writing Exercise*

43. $_{52}C_5 = \dfrac{52!}{47!5!} = \dfrac{52 \cdot 51 \cdot 50 \cdot 49 \cdot 48 \cdot 47!}{47! \cdot 5 \cdot 4 \cdot 3 \cdot 2 \cdot 1}$

$= 26 \cdot 17 \cdot 10 \cdot 49 \cdot 12$

$= 2,598,960$

44. a) 4

b) $\dfrac{4}{_{52}C_5} \approx 0.0000015$

45. Consider a suit

A K Q J 10 9 8 7 6 5 4 3 2

A straight flush can be any of the following combinations in the same suit.

K	Q	J	10	9
Q	J	10	9	8
J	10	9	8	7
10	9	8	7	6
9	8	7	6	5
8	7	6	5	4
7	6	5	4	3
6	5	4	3	2
5	4	3	2	A

Remember a straight flush does not include A K Q J 10 which is a royal flush.

a) Since there are 9 straight flushes per suit, there are $9 \cdot 4$, or 36 straight flushes in all 4 suits.

b) Since 2,598,960, or $_{52}C_5$, poker hands can be dealt from a standard 52-card deck and 36 of those hands are straight flushes, the probability of getting a straight flush is $\dfrac{36}{2,598,960}$, or 0.0000139.

46. a) $13 \cdot 48 = 624$

b) $\dfrac{624}{_{52}C_5} \approx 0.00024$

47. a) There are 13 ways to select a denomination. Then from that denomination there are $_4C_3$ ways to pick 3 of the 4 cards in that denomination. Now there are 12 ways to select any one of the remaining 12 denominations and $_4C_2$ ways to pick 2 cards from the 4 cards in that denomination. Thus the number of full houses is $(13 \cdot_4 C_3) \cdot (12 \cdot_4 C_2)$ or 3744.

b) $\dfrac{3744}{_{52}C_5} = \dfrac{3744}{2,598,960} \approx 0.00144$

48. a) $13 \cdot \dbinom{4}{2}\dbinom{12}{3}\dbinom{4}{1}\dbinom{4}{1}\dbinom{4}{1} \approx 1,098,240$

b) $\dfrac{1,098,240}{_{52}C_5} \approx 0.423$

49. a) There are 13 ways to select a denomination and then $\dbinom{4}{3}$ ways to choose 3 of the 4 cards in that denomination. Now there are $\dbinom{48}{2}$ ways to choose 2 cards from the 12 remaining denominations ($4 \cdot 12$, or 48 cards). But these combinations include the 3744 hands in a full house like Q-Q-Q-4-4 (Exercise 53), so these must be subtracted. Thus the number of three of a kind hands is $13 \cdot \dbinom{4}{3} \cdot \dbinom{48}{2} - 3744$, or 54,912.

b) $\dfrac{54,912}{_{52}C_5} = \dfrac{54,912}{2,598,960} \approx 0.0211$

50. a) $4 \cdot \dbinom{13}{5} - 4 - 36 = 5108$

   b) $\dfrac{5108}{_{52}C_5} \approx 0.00197$

51. a) There are $\dbinom{13}{2}$ ways to select 2 denominations from the 13 denominations. Then in each denomination there are $\dbinom{4}{2}$ ways to choose 2 of the 4 cards. Finally there are $\dbinom{44}{1}$ ways to choose the fifth card from the 11 remaining denominations $(4 \cdot 11$, or 44 cards). Thus the number of two pairs hands is
$$\dbinom{13}{2} \cdot \dbinom{4}{2} \cdot \dbinom{4}{2} \cdot \dbinom{44}{1}, \text{ or } 123{,}552.$$

   b) $\dfrac{123{,}552}{_{52}C_5} = \dfrac{123{,}552}{2{,}598{,}960} \approx 0.0475$

52. a) $10 \cdot 4 \cdot 4 \cdot 4 \cdot 4 \cdot 4 - 4 - 36 = 10{,}200$

   b) $\dfrac{10{,}200}{_{52}C_5} \approx 0.00392$

ELEMENTARY ALGEBRA REVIEW

Exercise Set R.1

1. False 2. True 3. True 4. False 5. True

6. True 7. 4 8. $\dfrac{11}{4}$ 9. 1.3 10. 105 11. -25

12. 5 13. $-\dfrac{11}{15}$ 14. $\dfrac{5}{8}$ 15. -6.5 16. -3.64

17. -15 18. $-\dfrac{3}{8}$ 19. 0 20. -32 21. $-\dfrac{1}{2}$

22. -1 23. 5.8 24. 0.99 25. -3 26. -90

27. 39 28. -65 29. 175 30. -12.68 31. -32

32. -7 33. 16 34. -8 35. -6 36. 720 37. 9

38. 15 39. -3 40. 8 41. -16 42. 6 43. 100

44. 56 45. 2 46. -64 47. -23 48. -55 49. 36

50. 2 51. 10 52. $-\dfrac{7}{100}$ 53. 10 54. 4 55. 7

56. 1 57. 32 58. 69 59. 28 cm^2 60. 6.2 in^2

61. $8x + 28$ 62. $15y + 3$ 63. $5x - 50$ 64. $12x - 8$

65. $-30 + 6x$ 66. $-21x + 35$ 67. $8a + 12b - 6c$

68. $40p + 5q - 25r$ 69. $2(4x + 3y)$ 70. $7(p + 2q)$

71. $3(1 + w)$ 72. $4(x + y)$ 73. $10(x + 5y + 10)$

74. $9(9p + 3q + 4)$ 75. p 76. $7x$ 77. $-m + 22$

78. $-3a - 9b$ 79. $3x + 7$ 80. $9r + 3s$ 81. $6p - 7$

82. $r - 5$ 83. $-5x + 12y$ 84. $32m - 11n$

85. $36a - 48b$ 86. $-2a + 14$ 87. $-10x + 104y + 9$

88. $96x - 77$ 89. Yes 90. No 91. No 92. Yes

93. Yes 94. Yes 95. Let n represent the number;

$3n = 348$ 96. Let n represent the number;

$256 + n = 113$ 97. Let c represent the number of

calories in a Taco Bell Beef Burrito; $c + 69 = 500$

98. Let c represent the international average per

capita consumption of Coke; $296 = 7.4c$ 99. Let l

represent the amount of water used to produce 1 lb of

lettuce; $42 = 2l$ 100. Let b represent the average

annual cost to play badminton; $470 = 458 + b$

Exercise Set R.2

1. 8 2. -10 3. 12 4. -15 5. $-\dfrac{1}{12}$ 6. $\dfrac{5}{6}$

7. -0.8 8. -2.9 9. $\dfrac{13}{3}$ 10. 9 11. $-\dfrac{5}{3}$ 12. $\dfrac{2}{5}$

13. 42 14. -12 15. -5 16. $-\dfrac{16}{3}$ 17. 2 18. -1

19. $\dfrac{25}{3}$ 20. 6 21. $-\dfrac{4}{9}$ 22. -1 23. -4 24. $\dfrac{3}{8}$

25. $\dfrac{69}{5}$ 26. $\dfrac{4}{3}$ 27. $\dfrac{9}{32}$ 28. $\dfrac{404}{185}$ 29. -2

30. $-\dfrac{20}{7}$ 31. -15 32. 12 33. $\dfrac{43}{2}$ 34. -3

35. $-\dfrac{61}{115}$ 36. $-\dfrac{1}{5}$ 37. $l = \dfrac{A}{w}$ 38. $w = \dfrac{A}{l}$

39. $q = \dfrac{p}{30}$ 40. $t = \dfrac{d}{20}$ 41. $P = IV$ 42. $A = bh$

43. $p = 2q - r$ 44. $r = p - 2q$ 45. $\pi = \dfrac{A}{r^2 + r^2h}$

46. $a = \dfrac{c - by}{x}$ 47. (a) No; (b) yes; (c) no; (d) yes

48. (a) No; (b) yes; (c) no; (d) yes

49. $\{x | x \le 12\}$, or $(-\infty, 12]$;

50. $\{y | y < -17\}$, or $(-\infty, -17)$;

51. $\{m | m > 12\}$, or $(12, \infty)$;

52. $\{x | x \ge -17\}$, or $[-17, \infty)$;

53. $\left\{x \middle| x \ge -\dfrac{3}{2}\right\}$, or $\left[-\dfrac{3}{2}, \infty\right)$;

54. $\{n | n \ge -8\}$, or $[-8, \infty)$;

55. $\{t | t < -3\}$, or $(-\infty, -3)$;

56. $\left\{ x \,\middle|\, x > \dfrac{10}{3} \right\}$, or $\left(\dfrac{10}{3}, \infty \right)$;

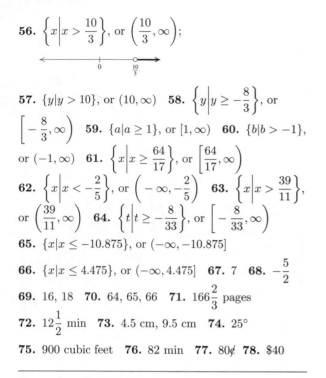

57. $\{y \,|\, y > 10\}$, or $(10, \infty)$ **58.** $\left\{ y \,\middle|\, y \geq -\dfrac{8}{3} \right\}$, or $\left[-\dfrac{8}{3}, \infty \right)$ **59.** $\{a \,|\, a \geq 1\}$, or $[1, \infty)$ **60.** $\{b \,|\, b > -1\}$, or $(-1, \infty)$ **61.** $\left\{ x \,\middle|\, x \geq \dfrac{64}{17} \right\}$, or $\left[\dfrac{64}{17}, \infty \right)$

62. $\left\{ x \,\middle|\, x < -\dfrac{2}{5} \right\}$, or $\left(-\infty, -\dfrac{2}{5} \right)$ **63.** $\left\{ x \,\middle|\, x > \dfrac{39}{11} \right\}$, or $\left(\dfrac{39}{11}, \infty \right)$ **64.** $\left\{ t \,\middle|\, t \geq -\dfrac{8}{33} \right\}$, or $\left[-\dfrac{8}{33}, \infty \right)$

65. $\{x \,|\, x \leq -10.875\}$, or $(-\infty, -10.875]$

66. $\{x \,|\, x \leq 4.475\}$, or $(-\infty, 4.475]$ **67.** 7   **68.** $-\dfrac{5}{2}$

69. 16, 18   **70.** 64, 65, 66   **71.** $166\dfrac{2}{3}$ pages

72. $12\dfrac{1}{2}$ min   **73.** 4.5 cm, 9.5 cm   **74.** 25°

75. 900 cubic feet   **76.** 82 min   **77.** 80¢   **78.** \$40

Exercise Set R.3

1.

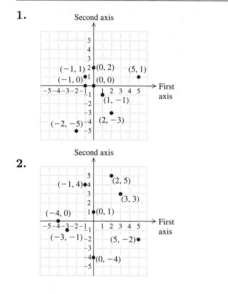

2.

3. I   **4.** II   **5.** IV   **6.** III   **7.** I, IV   **8.** III, IV

9. No   **10.** Yes   **11.** Yes   **12.** No

13.

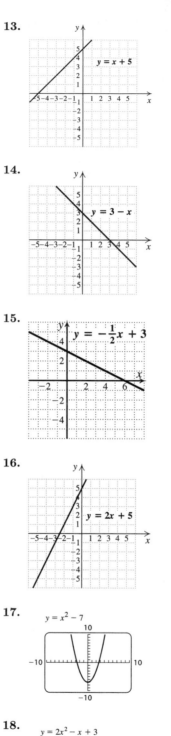

$y = x + 5$

14.

$y = 3 - x$

15.

$y = -\dfrac{1}{2}x + 3$

16.

$y = 2x + 5$

17.

$y = x^2 - 7$

18.

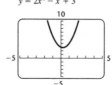

$y = 2x^2 - x + 3$

19.

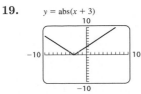

$y = \text{abs}(x + 3)$

20.

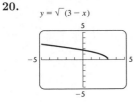

$y = \sqrt{(3 - x)}$

21.

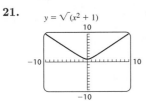

$y = \sqrt{(x^2 + 1)}$

22.

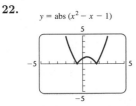

$y = \text{abs}(x^2 - x - 1)$

23. 6   **24.** 20   **25.** Approximately -2.33, or $-\dfrac{7}{3}$

26. -17.5 **27.** (a) 6; (b) $8\dfrac{1}{3}$; (c) $\dfrac{a}{3} + \dfrac{22}{3}$

28. (a) $\dfrac{1}{2}$; (b) $\dfrac{1}{4}$; (c) not defined   **29.** (a) 6; (b) 3;

(c) $20a^2 + 4a + 3$ **30.** (a) 5; (b) 5; (c) $6 - 9a^2$

31. (a) 0; (b) $\{-3, -1, 1, 2, 3\}$; (c) 3;

(d) $\{-1, 0, 2, 3, 5\}$ **32.** (a) -3;

(b) $\{x \mid -2 \le x \le 3\}$, or $[-2, 3]$; (c) 0;

(d) $\{y \mid -4 \le y \le 1\}$, or $[-4, 1]$ **33.** (a) -1;

(b) $\{x \mid -4 \le x \le 4\}$, or $[-4, 4]$; (c) $-2, 2$;

(d) $\{y \mid -5 \le y \le 3\}$, or $[-5, 3]$ **34.** (a) 2;

(b) $\{x \mid -3 < x \le 3\}$, or $(-3, 3]$;

(c) $\{x \mid -2 < x \le -1\}$, or $(-2, -1]$;

(d) $\{-2, -1, 0, 1, 2, 3\}$ **35.** No   **36.** No   **37.** Yes

38. Yes   **39.** $\{x \mid x \text{ is a real number } and \, x \ne 3\}$

40. $\{x \mid x \ge 0\}$, or $[0, \infty)$ **41.** All real numbers

42. All real numbers   **43.** $\{x \mid x \ge -6\}$, or $[-6, \infty)$

44. $\left\{ x \middle| x \text{ is a real number } and \, x \ne -\dfrac{1}{2} \right\}$

45. $x^2 + 2x - 6$ **46.** $x^2 + 4$ **47.** $-x^2 - 4$

48. $\dfrac{x^2 + x - 1}{x - 5}$ **49.** All real numbers

50. $\{x \mid x \text{ is a real number } and \, x \ne 5\}$

Exercise Set R.4

1. 1   **2.** $\dfrac{3}{2}$ **3.** -5 **4.** -3 **5.** 0   **6.** 0   **7.** $y = 5x + 3$

8. $y = -\dfrac{1}{2}x - 5$ **9.** $y = -\dfrac{3}{4}x + 8$ **10.** $y = 13x + 1$

11. Slope: $\dfrac{1}{3}$; y-intercept: $(0, -7)$ **12.** Slope: -5;

y-intercept: $(0, 8)$ **13.** Slope: -3; y-intercept: $(0, 10)$

14. Slope: $\dfrac{2}{5}$; y-intercept: $(0, -4)$ **15.** 0   **16.** 0

17. Undefined   **18.** Undefined   **19.** Parallel

20. Perpendicular   **21.** Neither   **22.** Parallel

23. $y - 3 = -1(x - (-1))$ **24.** $y - (-5) = 3(x - 2)$

25. $f(x) = -7x + 21$ **26.** $f(x) = -\dfrac{7}{6}x - \dfrac{17}{6}$

27. $f(x) = \dfrac{4}{5}x - 4$ **28.** $f(x) = x$

29.

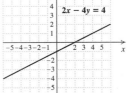

30.

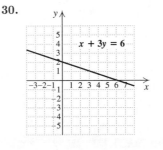

31.

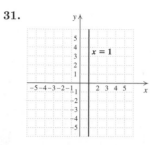

32.

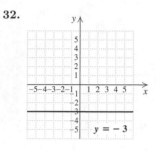

33.

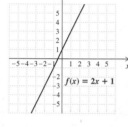

34.

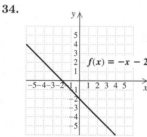

35.

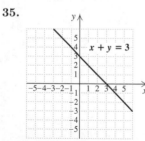

36.

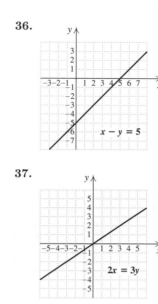

37.

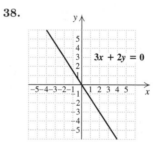

38.

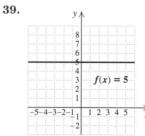

39.

40.

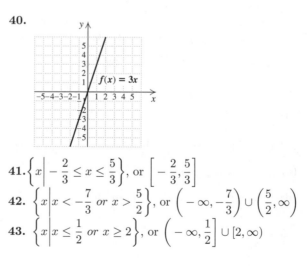

41. $\left\{ x \left| -\dfrac{2}{3} \le x \le \dfrac{5}{3} \right. \right\}$, or $\left[-\dfrac{2}{3}, \dfrac{5}{3} \right]$

42. $\left\{ x \left| x < -\dfrac{7}{3} \ or \ x > \dfrac{5}{2} \right. \right\}$, or $\left(-\infty, -\dfrac{7}{3} \right) \cup \left(\dfrac{5}{2}, \infty \right)$

43. $\left\{ x \left| x \le \dfrac{1}{2} \ or \ x \ge 2 \right. \right\}$, or $\left(-\infty, \dfrac{1}{2} \right] \cup [2, \infty)$

44. $\emptyset$ **45.** $\left\{ x \middle| x \le -\dfrac{9}{2} \text{ or } x \ge \dfrac{11}{2} \right\}$, or

$\left(-\infty, -\dfrac{9}{2} \right] \cup \left[\dfrac{11}{2}, \infty \right)$ **46.** $\left\{ -\dfrac{5}{2}, 1 \right\}$

47. $\{x | 1 < x < 4\}$, or $(1, 4)$ **48.** $\{x | x < 6 \text{ or } x > 8\}$,

or $(-\infty, 6) \cup (8, \infty)$ **49.** $\{-2, 14\}$

50. $\{x | -6 \le x \le 10\}$, or $[-6, 10]$

Exercise Set R.5

1. 1 **2.** 1 **3.** -3 **4.** 7 **5.** $\dfrac{1}{8^2} = \dfrac{1}{64}$ **6.** $\dfrac{1}{2^5} = \dfrac{1}{32}$

7. $\dfrac{1}{(-2)^3} = -\dfrac{1}{8}$ **8.** $\dfrac{1}{(-3)^2} = \dfrac{1}{9}$ **9.** $\dfrac{1}{(ab)^2}$ **10.** $\dfrac{a}{b^2}$

11. y^{10} **12.** x^t **13.** y^{-4} **14.** $a^{-2}b^{-3}$ **15.** x^{-t}

16. n^{-1} **17.** x^{13} **18.** a^2 **19.** a^6 **20.** p^5 **21.** $(4x)^8$

22. $\dfrac{b^7}{a^7}$ **23.** 7^{40} **24.** $\dfrac{1}{x^{21}}$ **25.** $x^8 y^{12}$ **26.** $-8a^6$

27. $\dfrac{y^6}{64}$ **28.** $\dfrac{a^4 b^8}{c^{12}}$ **29.** $\dfrac{9q^8}{4p^6}$ **30.** $\dfrac{x^5}{32}$ **31.** $8x^3, -6x^2,$

$x, -7$ **32.** $-a^2 b, 4a^2, -8b, 17$ **33.** 18, 36, -7, 3; 3,

9, 1, 0; 9 **34.** -8, 1, 19; 7, 1, 0; 7 **35.** -1, 4, -2; 3,

3, 3; 3 **36.** 8, -1, 1; 0, 6, 7; 7 **37.** $8p^4$; 8 **38.** $-t^3$;

-1 **39.** $x^4 + 3x^3$ **40.** $-4t^2 + 5t$ **41.** $-7t^2 + 5t + 10$

42. $8x^5 + \dfrac{3}{10}x + \dfrac{2}{3}$ **43.** 36 **44.** 78 **45.** -14

46. 12 **47.** 144 ft **48.** 64 ft **49.** $4x^3 - 3x^2 + 8x + 7$

50. $-6x^4 + 7x^2 + 4x - 23$ **51.** $-y^2 + 5y - 2$

52. $4t^2 + 5t - 12$ **53.** $-3x^2 y - y^2 + 8y$ **54.** $3ab$

55. $12x^5 - 28x^3 + 28x^2$ **56.** $a^5 b + a^2 b^3 - a^3 b^2 - 2a^2 b^2$

57. $8a^2 + 2ab + 4ay + by$ **58.** $-3x^2 - 20xy + 7y^2$

59. $x^3 + 4x^2 - 20x + 7$ **60.** $2x^3 - 5x^2 + x + 3$

61. $x^2 - 49$ **62.** $4x^2 + 4x + 1$ **63.** $x^2 + 2xy + y^2$

64. $x^2 y^2 - 1$ **65.** $6x^4 + 17x^2 - 14$ **66.** $x^4 + 4x^2 + 4$

67. $a^2 - 6ab + 9b^2$ **68.** $0.11x^4 - 1.7x^2 - 10$

69. $42a^2 - 17ay - 15y^2$ **70.** $9p^4 - 6p^2 q^3 + q^6$

71. $-t^4 - 3t^2 + 2t - 5$ **72.** $x^3 + \dfrac{5}{2}x^2 - 4$ **73.** $5x + 3$

74. $x^2 + 3x + 1 + \dfrac{6}{x - 5}$ **75.** $2x^2 - 3x + 3 + \dfrac{-2}{x + 1}$

76. $x^2 + 4x + 10$ **77.** $5x + 3 + \dfrac{3}{x^2 - 1}$

78. $2x + 3 + \dfrac{1}{x^2 + 3}$

Exercise Set R.6

1. $3x(x - 1)(x + 3)$ **2.** $xy^4(x - 2y + 3x^2 y^2)$

3. $(y - 3)^2$ **4.** $(2z + 5)(2x - 5)$ **5.** $(p + 2)(2p^3 + 1)$

6. $(3y - 1)(2y + 1)$ **7.** Prime **8.** $(y - 1)(y^2 + y + 1)$

9. $(2t + 3)(4t^2 - 6t + 9)$ **10.** $(ab + 12)^2$

11. $(m + 6)(m + 7)$ **12.** $(x - 3)(2x^2 + 1)$

13. $(x^2 + 9)(x + 3)(x - 3)$ **14.** Prime

15. $(2x + 3)(4x + 5)$ **16.** $4(x - 5)^2$

17. $(x + 2)(x + 1)(x - 1)$ **18.** $(x + 2y)(2x - 3)$

19. $(0.1t^2 - 0.2)(0.01t^4 + 0.02t^2 + 0.04)$

20. $(x - 5)(x + 4)$ **21.** $\left(x^2 + \dfrac{1}{4} \right)\left(x + \dfrac{1}{2} \right)\left(x - \dfrac{1}{2} \right)$

22. $5(x^4 + z^8)(x^2 + z^4)(x + z^2)(x - z^2)$

23. $(a + 3 + y)(a + 3 - y)$

24. $(t + p)(t - p)(t^2 + tp + p^2)(t^2 - tp + p^2)$

25. $(m + 15n)(m - 10n)$ **26.** $\left(\dfrac{1}{3} + x \right)\left(\dfrac{1}{9} - \dfrac{1}{3}x + x^2 \right)$

27. $2y(3x + 1)(4x - 3)$ **28.** $-3(y + 2)^2$ **29.** $(y - 11)^2$

30. $(p + m + n)(p - m - n)$ **31.** -7, 2 **32.** $\dfrac{5}{3}, \dfrac{7}{4}$

33. 0, 4,7 **34.** -1, 3, $\dfrac{9}{2}$ **35.** -10, 10 **36.** 0, $\dfrac{5}{8}$

37. $-\dfrac{5}{2}$, 7 **38.** -1 **39.** 0, 5 **40.** $-\dfrac{9}{10}, \dfrac{9}{10}$ **41.** -2,

6 **42.** -5, 8 **43.** -11, 5 **44.** -12, 5 **45.** -5

46. $\dfrac{1}{2}, \dfrac{3}{5}$ **47.** Base: 8 ft; height: 5 ft **48.** 12 and 13

49. 8 ft, 15 ft **50.** 300 ft